Oxford Essential Russian Dictionary

RUSSIAN–ENGLISH

ENGLISH–RUSSIAN

РУССКО-АНГЛИЙСКИЙ

АНГЛО-РУССКИЙ

OXFORD
UNIVERSITY PRESS

OXFORD
UNIVERSITY PRESS
Great Clarendon Street, Oxford OX2 6DP

Oxford University Press is a department of the University of Oxford. It furthers the University's objective of excellence in research, scholarship, and education by publishing worldwide in

Oxford New York

Auckland Cape Town Dar es Salaam Hong Kong Karachi Kuala Lumpur Madrid Melbourne Mexico City Nairobi New Delhi Shanghai Taipei Toronto

With offices in

Argentina Austria Brazil Chile Czech Republic France Greece Guatemala Hungary Italy Japan Poland Portugal Singapore South Korea Switzerland Thailand Turkey Ukraine Vietnam

Oxford is a registered trade mark of Oxford University Press in the UK and in certain other countries

Previously published as the *Oxford Russian Mini Dictionary*, 2006

First edition 2009

British Library Catalouging in Publication Data

Data available

ISBN 978-0-19-957643-2

13

Typeset by Interactive Sciences Ltd, Gloucester
Printed in Great Britain by Clays Ltd, Elcograf S.p.A

Contents/Содержание

Introduction vi

Символы фонетической транскрипции, используемые в Словаре viii

Abbreviations/Условные сокращения ix

Russian–English/русско-английский 1

English–Russian/англо-русский 287

Spelling Rules 621
Declension of Russian Adjectives 621
Declension of Russian Nouns 622
Conjugation of Russian Verbs 624

Английские неправильные глаголы 626
The Russian Alphabet 628
Английский алфавит 629

Edited by **Della Thompson**

Introduction

The *Oxford Essential Russian Dictionary* has been written for speakers of both Russian and English and contains the most useful words and expressions in use today.

The dictionary provides a handy and comprehensive reference work for tourists, students, and business people who require quick and reliable answers to their translation needs.

In order to save space, related words are often grouped together in paragraphs, as are cross-references and compound entries.

The swung dash (~) and the hyphen are also used to save space. The swung dash represents the headword preceding it in bold, or the preceding Russian word, e.g. **Georgian** *n* грузин, ~ка. The hyphen is mainly used in giving grammatical forms, to stand for part of the preceding, or (less often) following, Russian word, e.g. **приходи́ть**, (-ожу́, -о́дишь).

Russian headwords are followed by inflexional information where considered necessary. So-called regular inflexions for the purpose of this dictionary are listed in the Appendices.

Where a noun ending is given but not labelled in the singular, it is the genitive ending; other cases are named; in the plural, where cases are identifiable by their endings, they are not labelled, e.g. **сестра́** (*pl* сёстры, сестёр, сёстрам). The gender of Russian nouns can usually be deduced from their endings and it is indicated only in exceptional cases (e.g. for masculine nouns in **-а**, **-я**, and **-ь**, neuter nouns in **-мя**, and all indeclinable nouns).

Verbs are labelled *impf* or *pf* to show their aspect. Where a perfective verb is formed by the addition of a prefix to the imperfective, this is shown at the headword by a light vertical stroke, e.g. **про|лепета́ть**. When a verb requires the use of a case other than the accusative, this is indicated, e.g. **маха́ть** *impf*, **махну́ть** *pf* + *instr* wave, brandish.

Both the comma and the ampersand (&) are used to show alternatives, e.g. **хоте́ть** + *gen*, *acc* means that the Russian verb may govern either the genitive or accusative; **сирота́** *m & f* orphan means that the Russian noun is treated as masculine or feminine according to the sex of the person denoted; **Cossack** *n* каза́к, -а́чка represents the masculine and feminine translations of Cossack; **dilate** *vt & i* расширя́ть(ся) means that the Russian verb forms cover both the transitive and intransitive English verbs.

Stress

The stress of Russian words is shown by an acute accent over the vowel of the stressed syllable. The vowel **ё** has no stress mark since it is almost always stressed. The presence of two stress marks indicates that either of the marked syllables may be stressed.

Changes of stress in inflexion are shown, e.g.

i) **предложи́ть** (-жу́, -жишь)

The absence of a stress mark on the second person singular indicates that the stress is on the preceding syllable and that the rest of the conjugation is stressed in this way.

ii) **нача́ть** (.............; на́чал, -а́, -о)

The final form, на́чало, takes the stress of the first of the two preceding forms when these differ from each other. Forms that are not shown, here на́чали, are stressed like the last form given.

iii) **дождь** (-дя́)

The single form given in brackets is the genitive singular and all other forms have the same stressed syllable.

iv) **душа́** (*acc* -у; *pl* -и)

If only one case-labelled form is given in the singular, it is an exception to the regular paradigm. If only one plural form is given (the nominative), the rest follow this. In other words, in this example, the accusative singular and all the plural forms have initial stress.

v) **скоба́** (*pl* -ы, -а́м)

In the plural, forms that are not shown (here instrumental and prepositional) are stressed like the last form given.

Символы фонтетической транскрипции, используемые в Словаре

Согласные

b	*b*ut	s	*s*it
d	*d*og	t	*t*op
f	*f*ew	v	*v*oice
g	*g*et	w	*w*e
h	*h*e	z	*z*oo
j	*y*es	ʃ	*sh*e
k	*c*at	ʒ	deci*s*ion
l	*l*eg	θ	*th*in
m	*m*an	ð	*th*is
n	*n*o	ŋ	ri*ng*
p	*p*en	ʧ	*ch*ip
r	*r*ed	ʤ	*j*ar

Гласные

æ	c*a*t	aɪ	m*y*
ɑː	*ar*m	aʊ	h*ow*
e	b*e*d	eɪ	d*ay*
əː	h*er*	əʊ	n*o*
ɪ	s*i*t	eə	h*air*
iː	s*ee*	ɪə	n*ear*
ɒ	h*o*t	ɔɪ	b*oy*
ɔː	s*aw*	ʊə	p*oor*
ʌ	r*u*n	aɪə	f*ire*
ʊ	p*u*t	aʊə	s*our*
uː	t*oo*		
ə	*a*go		

(ə) обозначает безударный беглый гласный, который слышится в таких словах, как gard*e*n, carn*a*l и rhyth*m*.

(r) в конце слова обозначает согласный r, который произносится в случае, если следующее слово начинается с гласного звука, как, например, в *clutter up* и *an acre of land.*

Тильда ˜ обозначает носовой гласный звук, как в некоторых заимствованиях из французского языка, например ɑ̃ в nu*an*ce /ˈnjuːɑ̃s/.

Основное ударение в слове отмечается знаком ˈ перед ударным слогом.

Вторичное ударение в многосложном слове отмечается знаком ˌ перед соответствующим слогом.

Abbreviations
Условные сокращения

abbr	abbreviation	**сокращение**
abs	absolute	**абсолютный**
acc	accusative (case)	**винительный падеж**
adj, adjs	adjective(s)	**имя прилагательное, имена прилагательные**
adv, adv	adverb(s)	**наречие, наречия**
aeron	aeronautics	**авиация**
agric	agriculture	**сельское хозяйство**
anat	anatomy	**анатомия**
approx	approximate(ly)	**приблизительн|ый, -о**
archaeol	archaeology	**археология**
archit	architecture	**архитектура**
astron	astronomy	**астрономия**
attrib	attributive	**определительное, атрибутивное**
aux	auxiliary	**вспомогательный глагол**
bibl	biblical	**библейский термин**
biol	biology	**биология**
bot	botany	**ботаника**
chem	chemistry	**химия**
cin	cinema-(tography)	**кинематография**
coll	colloquial	**разговорное**
collect	collective	**собирательное (существительное)**
comb	combination	**сочетание**
comm	commerce	**коммерческий термин**
comp	comparative	**сравнительная степень**
comput	computing	**вычислительная техника**
conj, conjs	conjunction(s)	**союз, -ы**
cul	culinary	**кулинария**
dat	dative (case)	**дательный падеж**
def	definite	**определённый**
derog	derogatory	**пренебрежительное**
det	determinate	**определённый**
dim	diminutive	**уменьшительное**
eccl	ecclesiastical	**церковный термин**
econ	economics	**экономика**
electr	electricity	**электротехника**
electron	electronics	**электроника**
emph	emphatic	**усилительное**
esp	especially	**особенно**
etc.	etcetera	**и так далее**
f	feminine	**женский род**
fig	figurative	**в переносном смысле**
fut	future (tense)	**будущее время**
g	genitive (case)	**родительный падеж**
geog	geography	**география**
geol	geology	**геология**
geom	geometry	**геометрия**
gram	grammar	**грамматика**
hist	historical	**история**
imper	imperative	**повелительное наклонение**
impers	impersonal	**безличное**
impf	imperfective	**несовершенный вид**
indecl	indeclinable	**несклоняемое**
indef	indefinite	**неопределённый**
indet	indeterminate	**неопределённый**
inf	infinitive	**инфинитив**
instr	instrumental (case)	**творительный падеж**
int	interjection	**междометие**
interrog	interrogative	**вопросительный**
ling	linguistics	**лингвистика**
loc	locative	**местный падеж**

Abbreviations/Условные сокращения

m	masculine	**мужской род**
math	mathematics	**математика**
med	medicine	**медицин|а, -ский термин**
meteorol	meteorology	**метеорология**
mil	military	**военное дело**
mus	music(al)	**музыка, -льный термин**
n	noun	**имя существительное**
naut	nautical	**морское дело**
neg	negative	**отрицательный**
neut	neuter	**средний род**
nn	nouns	**имена существительные**
nom	nominative (case)	**именительный падеж**
o.s.	oneself	**себя**
parl	parliamentary	**парламентский термин**
part	participle	**причастие**
partl	particle	**частица**
pers	person	**лицо**
pf	perfective	**совершенный вид**
philos	philosophy	**философия**
phon	phonetics	**фонетика**
phot	photography	**фотография**
phys	physics	**физика**
pl	plural	**множественное число**
polit	political	**политический термин**
poss	possessive	**притяжательное**
predic	predicate; predicative	**сказуемое; предикативный**
pref	prefix	**префикс**
prep	preposition; prepositional (case)	**предлог предложный падеж**
pres	present (tense)	**настоящее время**
pron, prons	pronoun(s)	**местоимени|е, -я**
propr	proprietary term*	**фирменное название**
prov	proverb	**пословица**
psych	psychology	**психология**
refl	reflexive (verb)	**возвратный (глагол)**
rel	relative (pronoun)	**относительное (местоимение)**
relig	religion	**религия**
rly	railway	**железнодорожный термин**
sb	substantive	**имя существительное**
sg	singular	**единственное число**
sl	slang	**сленг**
s.o.	someone	**кто-нибудь**
sth	something	**что-нибудь**
superl	superlative	**превосходная степень**
tech	technical	**техника**
tel	telephony	**телефония**
theat	theatre	**театр, театральный термин**
theol	theology	**богословие**
trans	transitive	**переходный глагол**
univ	university	**университетский жаргон**
usu	usually	**обычно**
v	verb	**глагол**
v aux	auxiliary verb	**вспомогательный глагол**
vbl	verbal	**отглагольное**
vi	intransitive verb	**непереходный глагол**
voc	vocative (case)	**звательный падеж**
vt	transitive verb	**переходный глагол**
vulg	vulgar(ism)	**грубое**
vv	verbs	**глаголы**
zool	zoology	**зоология**

*This dictionary includes some words which are, or are asserted to be, proprietary names or trade marks. These words are labelled (*propr*). The presence or absence of this label should not be regarded as affecting the legal status of any proprietary name or trade mark.

A

а¹ *conj* and, but; **а (не) то́** or else, otherwise.
а² *int* oh, ah.
абажу́р lampshade.
абба́тство abbey.
аббревиату́ра abbreviation.
абза́ц indention; paragraph.
абонеме́нт subscription, season ticket. **абоне́нт** subscriber.
абориге́н aborigine.
або́рт abortion; **де́лать** *impf*, **с~** *pf* **~** have an abortion.
абрико́с apricot.
абсолю́тно *adv* absolutely. **абсолю́тный** absolute.
абстра́ктный abstract.
абсу́рд absurdity; the absurd. **абсу́рдный** absurd.
абсце́сс abscess.
аванга́рд advanced guard; vanguard; avant-garde. **аванга́рдный** avant-garde. **аванпо́ст** outpost; forward position.
ава́нс advance (*of money*); *pl* advances, overtures. **ава́нсом** *adv* in advance, on account.
авансце́на proscenium.
авантю́ра (*derog*) adventure; venture; escapade; shady enterprise. **авантюри́ст** (*derog*) adventurer. **авантюри́стка** (*derog*) adventuress. **авантю́рный** adventurous; adventure.
авари́йный breakdown; emergency. **ава́рия** accident, crash; breakdown.
а́вгуст August. **а́вгустовский** August.
а́виа *abbr* (*of* **авиапо́чтой**) by airmail.
авиа- *abbr in comb* (*of* **авиацио́нный**) air-, aero-; aircraft; aviation. **авиакомпа́ния** airline. **~ли́ния** air-route, airway. **~но́сец** (**-сца**) aircraft carrier. **~по́чта** airmail.
авиацио́нный aviation; flying; aircraft. **авиа́ция** aviation; aircraft; air-force.
авока́до *neut indecl* avocado (pear).
аво́сь *adv* perhaps; **на ~** at random, on the off-chance.
австрали́ец (**-и́йца**), **австрали́йка** Australian. **австрали́йский** Australian. **Австра́лия** Australia.
австри́ец (**-и́йца**), **австри́йка** Austrian. **австри́йский** Austrian. **А́встрия** Austria.
авто- *in comb* self-; auto-; automatic; motor-. **автоба́за** motor-transport depot. **~биографи́ческий** autobiographical. **~биогра́фия** autobiography; curriculum vitae. **авто́бус** bus. **~вокза́л** bus-station. **авто́граф** autograph. **~запра́вочная ста́нция** petrol station. **~кра́т** autocrat. **~крати́ческий** autocratic. **~кра́тия** autocracy. **~магистра́ль** motorway. **~маши́на** motor vehicle. **~моби́ль** *m* car. **~но́мия** autonomy. **~но́мный** autonomous; self-contained. **~пило́т** automatic pilot. **~портре́т** self-portrait. **~ру́чка** fountain-pen. **~ста́нция** bus-station. **~стра́да** motorway.
автома́т slot-machine; automatic device, weapon, etc.; sub-machine gun; robot; **(телефо́н-)~** public call-box. **автоматиза́ция** automation. **автоматизи́ровать** *impf* & *pf* automate; make automatic. **автомати́ческий** automatic.
а́втор author; composer; inventor; (*fig*) architect.
авторизо́ванный authorized.
авторите́т authority. **авторите́тный** authoritative.
а́вторск|ий author's; **~ий гонора́р**

а

royalty; **~ое прáво** copyright. **áвторство** authorship.
агá *int* aha; yes.
агéнт agent. **агéнтство** agency. **агентýра** (network of) agents.
агитáтор agitator, propagandist; canvasser. **агитациóнный** propaganda. **агитáция** propaganda, agitation; campaign. **агитúровать** *impf* (*pf* **с~**) agitate, campaign; (try to) persuade, win over. **агитпýнкт** *abbr* agitation centre.
агóния agony.
агрáрный agrarian.
агрегáт aggregate; unit.
агрессúвный aggressive. **агрéссия** aggression. **агрéссор** aggressor.
агронóм agronomist. **агронóмия** agriculture.
ад (*loc* -ý) hell.
адáптер adapter; (*mus*) pick-up.
адвокáт lawyer. **адвокатýра** legal profession; lawyers.
административный administrative. **администрáтор** administrator; manager. **администрáция** administration; management.
адмирáл admiral.
áдрес (*pl* -á) address. **адресáт** addressee. **áдресн|ый** address; **~ая кнúга** directory. **адресовáть** *impf* & *pf* address, send.
áдский infernal, hellish.
адъютáнт aide-de-camp; **стáрший ~** adjutant.
ажýрн|ый delicate, lacy; **~ая рабóта** openwork; tracery.
азáрт heat; excitement; fervour, ardour, passion. **азáртн|ый** venturesome; heated; **~ая игрá** game of chance.
áзбука alphabet; ABC.
Азербайджáн Azerbaijan. **азербайджáнец** (-нца), **азербайджáнка** Azerbaijani. **азербайджáнский** Azerbaijani.
азиáт, ~ка Asian. **азиáтский** Asian, Asiatic. **Áзия** Asia.
азóт nitrogen.
áист stork.
ай *int* oh; oo.
áйсберг iceberg.
акадéмик academician. **академúческий** academic. **акадéмия** academy.
аквалáнг aqualung.
акварéль water-colour.
аквáриум aquarium.
акведýк aqueduct.
акклиматизúровать *impf* & *pf* acclimatize; **~ся** become acclimatized.
аккомпанемéнт accompaniment; **под ~**+*gen* to the accompaniment of. **аккомпаниáтор** accompanist. **аккомпанúровать** *impf* +*dat* accompany.
аккóрд chord.
аккордеóн accordion.
аккóрдн|ый by agreement; **~ая рабóта** piece-work.
аккредитúв letter of credit. **аккредитовáть** *impf* & *pf* accredit.
аккумулятор accumulator.
аккурáтный neat, careful; punctual; exact, thorough.
акрúл acrylic. **акрúловый** acrylic.
акробáт acrobat.
аксессуáр accessory; (stage) props.
аксиóма axiom.
акт act; deed, document; **обвинúтельный ~** indictment.
актёр actor.
актúв (*comm*) asset(s).
активизáция stirring up, making (more) active. **активизúровать** *impf* & *pf* make (more) active, stir up. **актúвный** active.
актúровать *impf* & *pf* register, record.
áктовый зал assembly hall.
актрúса actress.
актуáльный topical, urgent.
акýла shark.
акýстика acoustics. **акустúческий** acoustic.
акушéр obstetrician. **акушéрка** midwife.
акцéнт accent, stress. **акцентúровать** *impf* & *pf* accent; accentuate.

акционе́р shareholder. **акционе́рный** joint-stock. **а́кция¹** share; *pl* stock. **а́кция²** action.
а́лгебра algebra.
а́либи *neut indecl* alibi.
алиме́нты (*pl*; *gen* -ов) (*law*) maintenance.
алкоголи́зм alcoholism. **алкого́лик** alcoholic. **алкого́ль** *m* alcohol. **алкого́льный** alcoholic.
аллего́рия allegory.
аллерги́я allergy.
алле́я avenue; path, walk.
аллига́тор alligator.
алло́ hello! (*on telephone*).
алма́з diamond.
алта́рь (-я́) *m* altar; chancel, sanctuary.
алфави́т alphabet. **алфави́тный** alphabetical.
а́лчный greedy, grasping.
а́лый scarlet.
альбо́м album; sketch-book.
альмана́х literary miscellany; almanac.
альпи́йский Alpine. **альпини́зм** mountaineering. **альпини́ст, альпини́стка** (mountain-) climber.
альт (-а́; *pl* -ы́) alto; viola.
альтернати́ва alternative. **альтернати́вный** alternative.
альтруисти́ческий altruistic.
алюми́ний aluminium.
амазо́нка Amazon; horsewoman; riding-habit.
амба́р barn; storehouse, warehouse.
амби́ция pride; arrogance.
амбулато́рия out-patients' department; surgery. **амбулато́рный больно́й** *sb* outpatient.
Аме́рика America. **америка́нец** (-нца), **америка́нка** American. **америка́нский** American; US.
аминокислота́ amino acid.
ами́нь *m* amen.
аммиа́к ammonia.
амни́стия amnesty.
амора́льный amoral; immoral.
амортиза́тор shock-absorber.
амортиза́ция depreciation; shock-absorption.
ампе́р (*gen pl* ампе́р) ampere.
ампута́ция amputation. **ампути́ровать** *impf* & *pf* amputate.
амфетами́н amphetamine.
амфи́бия amphibian.
амфитеа́тр amphitheatre; circle.
ана́лиз analysis; **~ кро́ви** blood test. **анализи́ровать** *impf* & *pf* analyse. **анали́тик** analyst. **аналити́ческий** analytic(al).
ана́лог analogue. **аналоги́чный** analogous. **анало́гия** analogy.
анана́с pineapple.
анархи́ст, ~ка anarchist. **анархи́ческий** anarchic. **ана́рхия** anarchy.
анатоми́ческий anatomical. **анато́мия** anatomy.
анахрони́зм anachronism. **анахрони́ческий** anachronistic.
анга́р hangar.
а́нгел angel. **а́нгельский** angelic.
анги́на sore throat.
англи́йск|ий English; **~ая була́вка** safety-pin. **англича́нин** (*pl* -ча́не, -ча́н) Englishman. **англича́нка** Englishwoman. **А́нглия** England, Britain.
анекдо́т anecdote, story; funny thing.
анеми́я anaemia.
анестезио́лог anaesthetist. **анестези́ровать** *impf* & *pf* anaesthetize. **анестези́рующее сре́дство** anaesthetic. **анестези́я** anaesthesia.
анке́та questionnaire, form.
аннекси́ровать *impf* & *pf* annex. **анне́ксия** annexation.
аннули́ровать *impf* & *pf* annul; cancel, abolish.
анома́лия anomaly. **анома́льный** anomalous.
анони́мка anonymous letter. **анони́мный** anonymous.
анонси́ровать *impf* & *pf* announce.
анoréксия anorexia.
анса́мбль *m* ensemble; company, troupe.

антагони́зм antagonism.

Анта́рктика the Antarctic.

анте́нна antenna; aerial.

антибио́тик antibiotic(s).

антидепресса́нт antidepressant.

антиква́р antiquary; antique-dealer. **антиквариа́т** antique-shop. **антиква́рный** antiquarian; antique.

антило́па antelope.

антипа́тия antipathy.

антисемити́зм anti-Semitism. **антисеми́тский** anti-Semitic.

антисе́птик antiseptic. **антисепти́ческий** antiseptic.

антите́зис (*philos*) antithesis.

антите́ло (*pl* -á) antibody.

антифри́з antifreeze.

анти́чность antiquity. **анти́чный** ancient, classical.

антоло́гия anthology.

антра́кт interval.

антраци́т anthracite.

антреко́т entrecôte, steak.

антрепренёр impresario.

антресо́ли (*pl*; *gen* -ей) mezzanine; shelf.

антропо́лог anthropologist. **антропологи́ческий** anthropological. **антрополо́гия** anthropology.

анфила́да suite (of rooms).

анчо́ус anchovy.

аншла́г 'house full' notice.

апартеид apartheid.

апати́чный apathetic. **апа́тия** apathy.

апелли́ровать *impf* & *pf* appeal. **апелляцио́нный суд** Court of Appeal. **апелля́ция** appeal.

апельси́н orange; orange-tree. **апельси́нный, апельси́новый** orange.

аплоди́ровать *impf* +*dat* applaud. **аплодисме́нты** *m pl* applause.

апло́мб aplomb.

Апока́липсис Revelation. **апокалипти́ческий** apocalyptic.

апо́стол apostle.

апостро́ф apostrophe.

аппара́т apparatus; machinery, organs. **аппарату́ра** apparatus, gear; (*comput*) hardware. **аппара́тчик** operator; apparatchik.

аппе́ндикс appendix. **аппендици́т** appendicitis.

аппети́т appetite; **прия́тного ~а!** bon appétit! **аппети́тный** appetizing.

апре́ль *m* April. **апре́льский** April.

апте́ка chemist's. **апте́карь** *m* chemist. **апте́чка** medicine chest; first-aid kit.

ара́б, ара́бка Arab. **ара́бский** Arab, Arabic.

арави́йский Arabian.

аранжи́ровать *impf* & *pf* (*mus*) arrange. **аранжиро́вка** (*mus*) arrangement.

ара́хис peanut.

арби́тр arbitrator. **арбитра́ж** arbitration.

арбу́з water-melon.

аргуме́нт argument. **аргумента́ция** reasoning; arguments. **аргументи́ровать** *impf* & *pf* argue, (try to) prove.

аре́на arena, ring.

аре́нда lease. **аренда́тор** tenant. **аре́ндная пла́та** rent. **арендова́ть** *impf* & *pf* rent.

аре́ст arrest. **арестова́ть** *pf*, **аресто́вывать** *impf* arrest; seize, sequestrate.

аристокра́т, ~ка aristocrat. **аристократи́ческий** aristocratic. **аристокра́тия** aristocracy.

арифме́тика arithmetic. **арифмети́ческий** arithmetical.

а́рия aria.

а́рка arch.

А́рктика the Arctic. **аркти́ческий** arctic.

армату́ра fittings; reinforcement; armature. **армату́рщик** fitter.

арме́йский army.

Арме́ния Armenia.

а́рмия army.

армяни́н (*pl* -я́не, -я́н), **армя́нка** Armenian. **армя́нский** Armenian.

аромáт scent, aroma. **ароматерапи́я** aromatherapy. **аромáтный** aromatic, fragrant.
арсенáл arsenal.
артéрия artery.
арти́куль *m* (*gram*) article.
артиллéрия artillery.
арти́ст, ~ка artiste, artist; expert. **артисти́ческий** artistic.
артри́т arthritis.
áрфа harp.
архаи́ческий archaic.
архáнгел archangel.
археóлог archaeologist. **археологи́ческий** archaeological. **археолóгия** archaeology.
архи́в archives. **архиви́ст** archivist. **архи́вный** archive, archival.
архиепи́скоп archbishop. **архиерéй** bishop.
архипелáг archipelago.
архитéктор architect. **архитектýра** architecture. **архитектýрный** architectural.
арши́н arshin (*71 cm.*).
асбéст asbestos.
асимметри́чный asymmetrical. **асимметри́я** asymmetry.
аскéт ascetic. **аскети́зм** asceticism. **аскети́ческий** ascetic.
асоциáльный antisocial.
аспирáнт, ~ка post-graduate student. **аспирантýра** post-graduate course.
аспири́н aspirin.
ассамблéя assembly.
ассигнáция banknote.
ассимиля́ция assimilation.
ассистéнт assistant; junior lecturer, research assistant.
ассортимéнт assortment.
ассоциáция association. **ассоции́ровать** *impf* & *pf* associate.
áстма asthma. **астмати́ческий** asthmatic.
астрóлог astrologer. **астролóгия** astrology.
астронáвт astronaut. **астронóм** astronomer. **астрономи́ческий** astronomical. **астронóмия** astronomy.
асфáльт asphalt.
атáка attack. **атаковáть** *impf* & *pf* attack.
атамáн ataman (*Cossack chieftain*); (gang-)leader.
атеи́зм atheism. **атеи́ст** atheist.
ательé *neut indecl* studio; atelier.
áтлас[1] atlas.
атлáс[2] satin. **атлáсный** satin.
атлéт athlete; strong man. **атлéтика** athletics. **атлети́ческий** athletic.
атмосфéра atmosphere. **атмосфéрный** atmospheric.
áтом atom. **áтомный** atomic.
атташé *m indecl* attaché.
аттестáт testimonial; certificate; pedigree. **аттестовáть** *impf* & *pf* attest; recommend.
аттракциóн attraction; sideshow; star turn.
аý *int* hi, cooee.
аудитóрия auditorium, lecture-room.
аукциóн auction.
аутóпсия autopsy.
афéра speculation, trickery. **афери́ст** speculator, trickster.
афи́ша placard, poster.
афори́зм aphorism.
Áфрика Africa. **африкáнец** (-нца), **африкáнка** African. **африкáнский** African.
аффéкт fit of passion; temporary insanity.
ах *int* ah, oh. **áхать** *impf* (*pf* **áхнуть**) sigh; exclaim; gasp.
аэро|вокзáл air terminal. **~динáмика** aerodynamics. **~дрóм** aerodrome, air-field. **~зóль** *m* aerosol. **~пóрт** (*loc* -ý) airport.

Б

б *partl*: *see* **бы**
бáба (*coll*) (old) woman; **снéжная ~** snowman.
бáбочка butterfly.
бáбушка grandmother; grandma.

б

багáж (-á) luggage. **багáжник** carrier; luggage-rack; boot. **багáжный вагóн** luggage-van.
багóр (-грá) boat-hook.
багрóвый crimson, purple.
бадминтóн badminton.
бáза base; depot; basis; **~ дáнных** database.
базáр market; din.
бáзис base; basis.
байдáрка canoe.
бáйка flannelette.
бак[1] tank, cistern.
бак[2] forecastle.
бакалáвр (*univ*) bachelor.
бакалéйный grocery. **бакалéя** groceries.
бáкен buoy.
бакенбáрды (*pl*; *gen* -бáрд) side-whiskers.
баклажáн (*gen pl* -ов *or* -жáн) aubergine.
бактéрия bacterium.
бал (*loc* -ý; *pl* -ы́) dance, ball.
балагáн farce.
балалáйка balalaika.
балáнс (*econ*) balance.
балансúровать *impf* (*pf* **с~**) balance; keep one's balance.
балбéс booby.
балдахúн canopy.
балерúна ballerina. **балéт** ballet.
бáлка[1] beam, girder.
бáлка[2] gully.
балкóн balcony.
балл mark (*in school*); degree; force; **вéтер в пять ~ов** wind force 5.
баллáда ballad.
баллáст ballast.
баллóн container, carboy, cylinder; balloon tyre.
баллотúровать *impf* vote; put to the vote; **~ся** stand, be a candidate (**в** *or* **на**+*acc* for).
баловáть *impf* (*pf* **из~**) spoil, pamper; **~ся** play about, get up to tricks; amuse o.s. **баловствó** spoiling; mischief.
Балтúйское мóре Baltic (Sea).
бальзáм balsam; balm.
балюстрáда balustrade.
бамбýк bamboo.
бáмпер bumper.
банáльность banality; platitude. **банáльный** banal.
банáн banana.
бáнда band, gang.
бандáж (-á) truss; belt, band.
бандерóль wrapper; printed matter, book-post.
бáнджо *neut indecl* banjo.
бандúт bandit; gangster.
банк bank.
бáнка jar; tin.
банкéт banquet.
банкúр banker. **банкнóта** banknote. **банкрóт** bankrupt. **банкрóтство** bankruptcy.
банкомáт cash machine.
бант bow.
бáня bath; bath-house.
бар bar; snack-bar.
барабáн drum. **барабáнить** *impf* drum, thump. **барабáнная перепóнка** ear-drum. **барабáнщик** drummer.
барáк wooden barrack, hut.
барáн ram; sheep. **барáнина** mutton; lamb.
барáнка ring-shaped roll; (steering-)wheel.
барахлó old clothes, jumble; odds and ends. **барахóлка** flea market.
барáшек (-шка) young ram; lamb; wing nut; catkin. **барáшковый** lambskin.
бáржá (*gen pl* барж(éй)) barge.
бáрин (*pl* -ре *or* -ры, бар) landowner; sir.
баритóн baritone.
бáрка barge.
бáрмен barman.
барóкко *neut indecl* baroque.
барóметр barometer.
барóн baron. **баронéсса** baroness.
барóчный baroque
баррикáда barricade.
барс snow-leopard.
бáрский lordly; grand.
барсýк (-á) badger.

барха́н dune.
ба́рхат (-у) velvet. **ба́рхатный** velvet.
ба́рыня landowner's wife; madam.
бары́ш (-а́) profit. **бары́шник** dealer; (ticket) speculator.
ба́рышня (*gen pl* -шень) young lady; miss.
барье́р barrier; hurdle.
бас (*pl* -ы́) bass.
баскетбо́л basket-ball.
баснословный mythical, legendary; fabulous. **ба́сня** (*gen pl* -сен) fable; fabrication.
басо́вый bass.
бассе́йн (*geog*) basin; pool; reservoir.
бастова́ть *impf* be on strike.
батальо́н battalion.
батаре́йка, батаре́я battery; radiator.
бато́н long loaf; stick, bar.
ба́тька *m*, **ба́тюшка** *m* father; priest. **ба́тюшки** *int* good gracious!
бах *int* bang!
бахва́льство bragging.
бахрома́ fringe.
бац *int* bang! crack!
баци́лла bacillus. **бациллоноси́тель** *m* carrier.
бачо́к (-чка́) cistern.
башка́ head.
башлы́к (-а́) hood.
башма́к (-а́) shoe; **под ~о́м у**+*gen* under the thumb of.
ба́шня (*gen pl* -шен) tower, turret.
баю́кать *impf* (*pf* **у~**) sing lullabies (to). **ба́юшки-баю́** *int* hushabye!
бая́н accordion.
бде́ние vigil. **бди́тельность** vigilance. **бди́тельный** vigilant.
бег (*loc* -у́; *pl* -а́) run, running; race. **бе́гать** *indet* (*det* **бежа́ть**) *impf* run.
бегемо́т hippopotamus.
бегле́ц (-а́), **бегля́нка** fugitive. **бе́глость** speed, fluency, dexterity. **бе́глый** rapid, fluent; fleeting, cursory; *sb* fugitive, runaway. **беговóй** running; race. **бего́м** *adv* running, at the double. **беготня́** running about; bustle. **бе́гство** flight; escape. **бегу́н** (-а́), **бегу́нья** (*gen pl* -ний) runner.
беда́ (*pl* -ы) misfortune; disaster; trouble; **~ в том, что** the trouble is (that). **бедне́ть** *impf* (*pf* **о~**) grow poor. **бе́дность** poverty; the poor. **бе́дный** (-ден, -дна́, -дно) poor. **бедня́га** *m*, **бедня́жка** *m* & *f* poor thing. **бедня́к** (-а́), **бедня́чка** poor peasant; poor man, poor woman.
бедро́ (*pl* бёдра, -дер) thigh; hip.
бе́дственный disastrous. **бе́дствие** disaster. **бе́дствовать** *impf* live in poverty.
бежа́ть (бегу́ *det*; *indet* бе́гать) *impf* (*pf* **по~**) run; flow; fly; boil over; *impf* & *pf* escape. **бе́женец** (-нца), **бе́женка** refugee.
без *prep*+*gen* without; **~ пяти́ (мину́т) три** five (minutes) to three; **~ че́тверти** a quarter to.
без-, безъ-, бес- *in comb* in-, un-; non-; -less. **без|алкого́льный** non-alcoholic. **~апелляцио́нный** peremptory, categorical. **~бо́жие** atheism. **~бо́жный** godless; shameless, outrageous. **~боле́зненный** painless. **~бра́чный** celibate. **~бре́жный** boundless. **~ве́стный** unknown; obscure. **~вку́сие** lack of taste, bad taste. **~вку́сный** tasteless. **~вла́стие** anarchy. **~во́дный** arid. **~возвра́тный** irrevocable; irrecoverable. **~возме́здный** free, gratis. **~во́лие** lack of will. **~во́льный** weak-willed. **~вре́дный** harmless. **~вре́менный** untimely. **~вы́ходный** hopeless, desperate; uninterrupted. **~гла́зый** one-eyed; eyeless. **~гра́мотный** illiterate. **~грани́чный** boundless, infinite. **~да́рный** untalented. **~де́йственный** inactive. **~де́йствие** inertia, idleness; negligence. **~де́йствовать** *impf* be idle, be inactive; stand idle.

б

безде́лица trifle. **безделу́шка** knick-knack. **безде́льник** idler; ne'er-do-well. **безде́льничать** *impf* idle, loaf.

бе́здна abyss, chasm; a huge number, a multitude.

без-. бездоказа́тельный unsubstantiated. **~до́мный** homeless. **~до́нный** bottomless; fathomless. **~доро́жье** lack of (good) roads; season when roads are impassable. **~ду́мный** unthinking. **~ду́шный** heartless; inanimate; lifeless. **~жа́лостный** pitiless, ruthless. **~жи́зненный** lifeless. **~забо́тный** carefree; careless. **~заве́тный** selfless, whole-hearted. **~зако́ние** lawlessness; unlawful act. **~зако́нный** illegal; lawless. **~засте́нчивый** shameless, barefaced. **~защи́тный** defenceless. **~зву́чный** silent. **~зло́бный** good-natured. **~ли́чный** characterless; impersonal. **~лю́дный** uninhabited; sparsely populated; lonely.

безме́н steelyard.

без-. безме́рный immense; excessive. **~мо́лвие** silence. **~мо́лвный** silent, mute. **~мяте́жный** serene, placid. **~надёжный** hopeless. **~надзо́рный** neglected. **~нака́занно** *adv* with impunity. **~нака́занный** unpunished. **~но́гий** legless; one-legged. **~нра́вственный** immoral.

безо *prep+gen* = **без** (*used before* **весь** *and* **вся́кий**).

безобра́зие ugliness; disgrace, scandal. **безобра́зничать** *impf* make a nuisance of o.s. **безобра́зный** ugly; disgraceful.

без-. безогово́рочный unconditional. **~опа́сность** safety; security. **~опа́сный** safe; secure. **~ору́жный** unarmed. **~основа́тельный** groundless. **~остано́вочный** unceasing; non-stop. **~отве́тный** meek, unanswering; dumb. **~отве́тственный** irresponsible. **~отка́зно** *adv* without a hitch. **~отка́зный** trouble-free, smooth-(running). **~отлага́тельный** urgent. **~относи́тельно** *adv+*к*+dat* irrespective of. **~отчётный** unaccountable. **~оши́бочный** unerring; correct. **~рабо́тица** unemployment. **~рабо́тный** unemployed. **~разли́чие** indifference. **~разли́чно** *adv* indifferently; it is all the same. **~разли́чный** indifferent. **~рассу́дный** reckless, imprudent. **~ро́дный** alone in the world; without relatives. **~ро́потный** uncomplaining; meek. **~рука́вка** sleeveless pullover. **~ру́кий** armless; one-armed. **~уда́рный** unstressed. **~у́держный** unrestrained; impetuous. **~укори́зненный** irreproachable.

безу́мец (-мца) madman. **безу́мие** madness. **безу́мный** mad. **безу́мство** madness.

без-. безупре́чный irreproachable, faultless. **~усло́вно** *adv* unconditionally; of course, undoubtedly. **~усло́вный** unconditional, absolute; indisputable, **~успе́шный** unsuccessful. **~уста́нный** tireless. **~уте́шный** inconsolable. **~уча́стие** indifference, apathy. **~уча́стный** indifferent, apathetic. **~ымя́нный** nameless, anonymous; **~ымя́нный па́лец** ring-finger. **~ыску́сный** artless, ingenuous. **~ысхо́дный** irreparable; interminable.

бейсбо́л baseball.

бека́р (*mus*) natural.

бека́с snipe.

бeко́н bacon.

Белару́сь Belarus.

беле́ть *impf* (*pf* **по~**) turn white; show white.

белизна́ whiteness. **бели́ла** (*pl*; *gen* -и́л) whitewash; Tippex (*propr*). **бели́ть** (бе́ли́шь) *impf* (*pf* **вы́~, на~, по~**) whitewash; whiten; bleach.

бе́лка squirrel.

беллетри́ст writer of fiction. **беллетри́стика** fiction.

бело- *in comb* white-, leuco-. **белогварде́ец** (-е́йца) White Guard. **~кро́вие** leukaemia. **~ку́рый** fair, blonde. **~ру́с, ~ру́ска, ~ру́сский** Belorussian. **~сне́жный** snow-white.

белови́к (-а́) fair copy. **белово́й** clean, fair.

бело́к (-лка́) white (*of egg, eye*); protein.

белошве́йка seamstress. **белошве́йный** linen.

белу́га white sturgeon. **белу́ха** white whale.

бе́л|ый (бел, -а́, бе́ло́) white; clean, blank; *sb* white person; **~ая берёза** silver birch; **~ое кале́ние** white heat; **~ый медве́дь** polar bear; **~ые но́чи** white nights, midnight sun.

бельги́ец, -ги́йка Belgian. **бельги́йский** Belgian. **Бе́льгия** Belgium.

бельё linen; bedclothes; underclothes; washing.

бельмо́ (*pl* -а) cataract.

бельэта́ж first floor; dress circle.

бемо́ль *m* (*mus*) flat.

бенефи́с benefit (performance).

бензи́н petrol.

бензо- *in comb* petrol. **бензоба́к** petrol-tank. **~во́з** petrol tanker. **~запра́вочная** *sb* filling-station. **~коло́нка** petrol pump. **~прово́д** petrol pipe, fuel line.

берёг *etc.*: *see* **бере́чь**

бе́рег (*loc* -у́; *pl* -а́) bank, shore; coast; **на ~у́ мо́ря** at the seaside. **берегово́й** coast; coastal.

бережёшь *etc.*: *see* **бере́чь. бережли́вый** thrifty. **бе́режный** careful.

берёза birch. **Берёзка** hard-currency shop.

бере́менеть *impf* (*pf* **за~**) be(come) pregnant. **бере́менная** pregnant (+*instr* with). **бере́менность** pregnancy; gestation.

бере́т beret.

бере́чь (-регу́, -режёшь; -рёг, -ла́) *impf* take care of; keep; cherish; husband; be sparing of; **~ся** take care; beware (+*gen* of).

берло́га den, lair.

беру́ *etc.*: *see* **брать**

бес devil, demon.

бес-: *see* **без-**

бесе́да talk, conversation. **бесе́дка** summer-house. **бесе́довать** *impf* talk, converse.

беси́ть (бешу́, бе́сишь) *impf* (*pf* **вз~**) enrage; **~ся** go mad; be furious.

бес-. бесконе́чность infinity; endlessness. **~коне́чный** endless. **~коры́стие** disinterestedness. **~коры́стный** disinterested. **~кра́йний** boundless.

бесо́вский devilish.

бес-. беспа́мятство unconsciousness. **~парти́йный** non-party **~перспекти́вный** without prospects; hopeless. **~пе́чность** carelessness, unconcern. **~пла́тно** *adv* free. **~пла́тный** free. **~пло́дие** sterility, barrenness. **~пло́дность** futility. **~пло́дный** sterile, barren; futile. **~поворо́тный** irrevocable. **~подо́бный** incomparable. **~позвоно́чный** invertebrate.

беспоко́ить *impf* (*pf* **о~, по~**) disturb, bother; trouble; **~ся** worry; trouble. **беспоко́йный** anxious; troubled; fidgety. **беспоко́йство** anxiety.

бес-. бесполе́зный useless. **~по́мощный** helpless; feeble. **~поро́дный** mongrel, not thoroughbred. **~поря́док** (-дка) disorder; untidy state. **~поря́дочный** disorderly; untidy. **~поса́дочный** non-stop. **~по́чвенный** groundless. **~по́шлинный** duty-free. **~поща́дный** merciless. **~пра́вный** without rights. **~преде́льный** boundless. **~предме́тный** aimless; abstract. **~препя́тственный** unhindered; unimpeded. **~преры́вный** continuous. **~преста́нный** continual.

беспризо́рник, -ница waif, homeless child. **беспризо́рный**

neglected; homeless; *sb* waif, homeless child.

б **бес-. беспримéрный** unparalleled. **~принци́пный** unscrupulous. **~пристрáстие** impartiality. **~пристрáстный** impartial. **~просвéтный** pitch-dark; hopeless; unrelieved. **~пу́тный** dissolute. **~свя́зный** incoherent. **~сердéчный** heartless. **~си́лие** impotence; feebleness. **~си́льный** impotent, powerless. **~слáвный** inglorious. **~слéдно** *adv* without trace. **~словéсный** dumb; silent, meek; (*theat*) walk-on. **~смéнный** permanent, continuous. **~смéртие** immortality. **~смéртный** immortal. **~смы́сленный** senseless; foolish; meaningless. **~смы́слица** nonsense. **~сóвестный** unscrupulous; shameless. **~сознáтельный** unconscious; involuntary. **~сóнница** insomnia. **~спóрный** indisputable. **~срóчный** indefinite; without a time limit. **~стрáстный** impassive. **~стрáшный** fearless. **~сты́дный** shameless. **~тáктный** tactless.

бестолкóвщина confusion, disorder. **бестолкóвый** muddle-headed, stupid; incoherent.

бес-. бесфóрменный shapeless. **~харáктерный** weak, spineless. **~хи́тростный** artless; unsophisticated. **~хозя́йственный** improvident. **~цвéтный** colourless. **~цéльный** aimless; pointless. **~цéнный** priceless. **~цéнок: за ~цéнок** very cheap, for a song. **~церемóнный** unceremonious. **~человéчный** inhuman. **~чéстить** (-éщу) *impf* (*pf* **о~чéстить**) dishonour. **~чéстный** dishonourable. **~чи́сленный** innumerable, countless.

бесчу́вственный insensible; insensitive. **бесчу́вствие** insensibility; insensitivity.

бешу́мный noiseless.

бетóн concrete. **бетóнный** concrete. **бетономешáлка** concrete-mixer. **бетóнщик** concrete-worker.

бечевá tow-rope; rope. **бечёвка** cord, string.

бéшенство rabies; rage. **бéшеный** rabid; furious.

бешу́ *etc*.: *see* **беси́ть**

библéйский biblical. **библиографи́ческий** bibliographical. **библиогрáфия** bibliography. **библиотéка** library. **библиотéкарь** *m*, **-тéкарша** librarian. **би́блия** bible.

бивáк bivouac, camp.

би́вень (-вня) *m* tusk.

бигуди́ *pl indecl* curlers.

бидóн can; churn.

биéние beating; beat.

бижутéрия costume jewellery.

би́знес business. **бизнесмéн** businessman.

билéт ticket; card; pass. **билéтный** ticket.

биллиóн billion.

билья́рд billiards.

бинóкль *m* binoculars.

бинт (-á) bandage. **бинтовáть** *impf* (*pf* **за~**) bandage. **бинтóвка** bandaging.

биóграф biographer. **биографи́ческий** biographical. **биогрáфия** biography. **биóлог** biologist. **биологи́ческий** biological. **биолóгия** biology. **биохи́мия** biochemistry.

би́ржа exchange.

би́рка name-plate; label.

бирюзá turquoise

бис *int* encore.

би́сер (*no pl*) beads.

бискви́т sponge cake.

битá bat.

би́тва battle.

биткóм *adv*: **~ наби́т** packed.

биту́м bitumen.

бить (бью, бьёшь) *impf* (*pf* **за~, по~, про~, удáрить**) beat; hit; defeat; sound; thump, bang; smash; **~ в цель** hit the target; **~ на**+*acc* strive for; **~ отбóй** beat a retreat; **~ по**+*dat* damage, wound; **~ся** fight; beat; struggle; break; +*instr* knock, hit, strike; +**над**+*instr* struggle with, rack one's brains over.

бифштéкс beefsteak.

бич (-á) whip, lash; scourge; homeless person. **бичевáть** (-чýю) *impf* flog; castigate.

блáго good; blessing.

блáго- *in comb* well-, good-. **Благовéщение** Annunciation. **~ви́дный** plausible. **~волéние** goodwill. **~воспи́танный** well-brought-up.

благодари́ть (-рю́) *impf* (*pf* **по~**) thank. **благодáрность** gratitude; **не стóит благодáрности** don't mention it. **благодáрный** grateful. **благодаря́** *prep*+*dat* thanks to, owing to.

благо-. благодéтель *m* benefactor. **~дéтельница** benefactress. **~дéтельный** beneficial. **~дýшный** placid; good-humoured. **~желáтель** *m* well-wisher. **~желáтельный** well-disposed; benevolent. **~звýчный** melodious, harmonious. **~надёжный** reliable. **~намéренный** well-intentioned. **~полýчие** well-being; happiness. **~полýчно** *adv* all right, well; happily; safely. **~полýчный** happy, successful; safe. **~приятный** favourable. **~приятствовать** *impf* +*dat* favour. **~разýмие** sense; prudence. **~разýмный** sensible. **~рóдие: вáше ~рóдие** Your Honour. **~рóдный** noble. **~рóдство** nobility. **~склóнность** favour, good graces. **~склóнный** favourable; gracious. **~слови́ть** *pf*, **благословля́ть** *impf* bless. **~состоя́ние** prosperity. **~твори́тель** *m*, **-ница** philanthropist. **~твори́тельный** charitable, charity. **~твóрный** salutary; beneficial; wholesome. **~устрóенный** well-equipped, well-planned; with all amenities.

блажéнный blissful; simple-minded. **блажéнство** bliss.

бланк form.

блат (*sl*) string-pulling; pull, influence. **блатнóй** criminal.

бледнéть (-éю) *impf* (*pf* **по~**) (grow) pale. **блéдность** paleness, pallor. **блéдный** (-ден, -днá, -о) pale.

блеск brightness, brilliance, lustre; magnificence.

блеснýть (-нý, -нёшь) *pf* flash, gleam; shine. **блестéть** (-ещý, -сти́шь *or* блéщешь) *impf* shine; glitter. **блёстка** sparkle; sequin. **блестя́щий** shining, bright; brilliant.

блéять (-éет) *impf* bleat.

ближáйший nearest, closest; next. **бли́же** *comp of* **бли́зкий, бли́зко. бли́жний** near, close; neighbouring; *sb* neighbour. **близ** *prep*+*gen* near, by. **бли́з|кий** (-зок, -изкá, -о) near; close; imminent; **~кие** *sb pl* one's nearest and dearest, close relatives. **бли́зко** *adv* near (**от**+*gen* to). **близнéц** (-á) twin; *pl* Gemini. **близорýкий** short-sighted. **бли́зость** closeness, proximity.

блик patch of light; highlight.

блин (-á) pancake.

блиндáж (-á) dug-out.

блистáть *impf* shine; sparkle.

блог (*comput.*) blog, weblog. **блóггер** (*comput.*) blogger, weblogger.

блок block, pulley, sheave.

блокáда blockade. **блоки́ровать** *impf* & *pf* blockade; **~ся** form a bloc. **блокнóт** writing-pad, notebook.

блонди́н, блонди́нка blond(e).

блохá (*pl* -и, -áм) flea.

блуд lechery. **блудни́ца** whore.

блуждáть *impf* roam, wander.

блýза, блýзка blouse.

блю́дечко saucer; small dish. **блю́до** dish; course. **блю́дце** saucer.

боб (-á) bean. **бобóвый** bean.

бобр (-á) beaver.

Бог (*voc* **Бóже**) God; **дай ~** God grant; **~ егó знáет** who knows? **не**

б

дай ~ God forbid; **Бо́же (мой)!** my God! good God!; **ра́ди ~а** for God's sake; **сла́ва ~у** thank God.

богате́ть *impf* (*pf* **раз~**) grow rich. **бога́тство** wealth. **бога́тый** rich, wealthy; *sb* rich man. **бога́ч** (-а́) rich man.

богаты́рь (-я́) *m* hero; strong man.

боги́ня goddess. **Богома́терь** Mother of God. **богомо́лец** (-льца), **богомо́лка** devout person; pilgrim. **богомо́лье** pilgrimage. **богомо́льный** religious, devout. **Богоро́дица** the Virgin Mary. **богосло́в** theologian. **богосло́вие** theology. **богослуже́ние** divine service. **боготвори́ть** *impf* idolize; deify. **богоху́льство** blasphemy.

бодри́ть *impf.* stimulate, invigorate; **~ся** try to keep up one's spirits. **бо́дрость** cheerfulness, courage. **бо́дрствовать** be awake; stay awake; keep vigil. **бо́дрый** (бодр, -а́, -о) cheerful, bright.

боеви́к (-а́) smash hit. **боево́й** fighting, battle. **боеголо́вка** warhead. **боеприпа́сы** (*pl*; *gen* -ов) ammunition. **боеспосо́бный** battle-worthy. **бое́ц** (бойца́) soldier; fighter, warrior.

Бо́же: *see* **Бог. бо́жеский** divine; just. **боже́ственный** divine. **божество́** deity; divinity. **бо́ж|ий** God's; **~ья коро́вка** ladybird. **божо́к** (-жка́) idol.

бой (*loc* -ю́; *pl* -и́, -ёв) battle, action, fight; fighting; slaughtering; striking; breakage(s).

бо́йкий (бо́ек, бойка́, -о) smart, sharp; glib; lively.

бойко́т boycott.

бо́йня (*gen pl* бо́ен) slaughterhouse; butchery.

бок (*loc* -у́; *pl* -а́) side; flank; **~ о́ ~** side by side; **на́ ~** to the side; **на ~у́** on one side; **по́д ~ом** near by; **с ~у** from the side, from the flank; **с ~у на́ бок** from side to side.

бока́л glass; goblet.

боково́й side; lateral. **бо́ком** *adv* sideways.

бокс boxing. **боксёр** boxer.

болва́н blockhead. **болва́нка** pig (*of iron etc.*).

болга́рин (*pl* -га́ры), **болга́рка** Bulgarian. **болга́рский** Bulgarian. **Болга́рия** Bulgaria.

бо́лее *adv* more; **~ всего́** most of all; **тем ~, что** especially as.

боле́зненный sickly; unhealthy; painful. **боле́знь** illness, disease; abnormality.

боле́льщик, -щица fan, supporter. **боле́ть**[1] (-е́ю) *impf* be ill, suffer. **боле́ть**[2] (-ли́т) *impf* ache, hurt.

боло́тистый marshy. **боло́то** marsh, bog.

болта́ть[1] *impf* stir; shake; dangle; **~ся** dangle, swing; hang about.

болта́ть[2] *impf* chat, natter. **болтли́вый** talkative; indiscreet. **болтовня́** talk; chatter; gossip. **болту́н** (-а́), **болту́нья** chatterbox.

боль pain; ache. **больни́ца** hospital. **больни́чный** hospital; **~ листо́к** medical certificate. **бо́льно**[1] *adv* painfully, badly; *predic+dat* it hurts. **бо́льно**[2] *adv* very, terribly. **больно́й** (-лен, -льна́) ill, sick; diseased; sore; *sb* patient, invalid.

бо́льше *comp of* **большо́й, мно́го**; bigger, larger; greater; more; **~ не** not any more, no longer; **~ того́** and what is more; *adv* for the most part. **большеви́к** Bolshevik. **бо́льш|ий** greater, larger; **~ей ча́стью** for the most part. **большинство́** majority. **больш|о́й** big, large; great; grown-up; **~а́я бу́ква** capital letter; **~о́й па́лец** thumb; big toe; **~и́е** *sb pl* grown-ups.

бо́мба bomb. **бомбардирова́ть** *impf* bombard; bomb. **бомбардиро́вка** bombardment, bombing. **бомбардиро́вщик** bomber. **бомбёжка** bombing. **бомби́ть**

(-блю) bomb. **бомбоубе́жище** bomb shelter.
бор (*loc* -у́; *pl* -ы) coniferous forest.
бордо́вый wine-red.
бордю́р border.
боре́ц (-рца́) fighter; wrestler.
бо́рзый swift.
бормаши́на (dentist's) drill.
бормота́ть (-очу́, -о́чешь) *impf* (*pf* **про~**) mutter, mumble.
борода́ (*acc* бо́роду; *pl* бо́роды, -ро́д, -а́м) beard. **борода́вка** wart. **борода́тый** bearded.
борозда́ (*pl* бо́розды, -о́зд, -а́м) furrow. **борозди́ть** (-зжу́) *impf* (*pf* **вз~**) furrow.
борона́ (*acc* бо́рону; *pl* бо́роны, -ро́н, -а́м) harrow. **борони́ть** *impf* (*pf* **вз~**) harrow.
боро́ться (-рю́сь, бо́решься) *impf* wrestle; struggle, fight.
борт (*loc* -у́; *pl* -а́, -о́в) side, ship's side; front; **за ~, за ~ом** overboard; **на ~, на ~у́** on board. **бортпроводни́к** (-а́) air steward. **бортпроводни́ца** air hostess.
борщ (-а́) borshch (*beetroot soup*).
борьба́ wrestling; struggle, fight.
босико́м *adv* barefoot.
босни́ец (-и́йца), **босни́йка** Bosnian. **босни́йский** Bosnian. **Бо́сния** Bosnia.
босо́й (бос, -а́, -о) barefooted. **босоно́жка** sandal.
бот, бо́тик small boat.
бота́ник botanist. **бота́ника** botany. **ботани́ческий** botanical.
боти́нок (-нка; *gen pl* -нок) (*ankle-high*) boot.
бо́цман boatswain
бо́чка barrel. **бочо́нок** (-нка) keg, small barrel.
боязли́вый timid, timorous. **боя́знь** fear, dread.
боя́рин (*pl* -я́ре, -я́р) boyar.
боя́рышник hawthorn.
боя́ться (бою́сь) *impf* +*gen* be afraid of, fear; dislike.
брак[1] marriage.
брак[2] defective goods; flaw. **бракова́ть** *impf* (*pf* **за~**) reject.
браконье́р poacher.
бракоразво́дный divorce. **бракосочета́ние** wedding.
брани́ть *impf* (*pf* **вы́~**) scold; abuse, curse; **~ся** (*pf* **по~**) swear, curse; quarrel. **бра́нн|ый** abusive; **~ое сло́во** swear-word.
брань bad language; abuse.
брасле́т bracelet.
брасс breast stroke.
брат (*pl* -тья, -тьев) brother; comrade; mate; lay brother, monk. **брата́ться** *impf* (*pf* **по~**) fraternize. **братоуби́йство** fratricide. **бра́тский** brotherly, fraternal. **бра́тство** brotherhood, fraternity.
брать (беру́, -рёшь; брал, -а́, -о) *impf* (*pf* **взять**) take; obtain; hire; seize; demand, require; surmount, clear; work; +*instr* succeed by means of; **~ся** +**за**+*acc* touch; seize; get down to; +**за**+*acc or inf* undertake; appear, come.
бра́чный marriage; mating.
бреве́нчатый log. **бревно́** (*pl* брёвна, -вен) log, beam.
бред (*loc* -у́) delirium; raving(s). **бре́дить** (-е́жу) *impf* be delirious, rave; +*instr* rave about, be infatuated with. **бредо́вый** delirious; fantastic, nonsensical.
бреду́ *etc.*: *see* **брести́. бре́жу** *etc.*: *see* **бре́дить**
бре́згать *impf* (*pf* **по~**) +*inf or instr* be squeamish about. **брезгли́вый** squeamish.
брезе́нт tarpaulin.
бре́зжить(ся *impf* dawn; gleam faintly, glimmer.
брёл *etc.*: *see* **бре́сти**
брело́к charm, pendant.
бремени́ть *impf* (*pf* **о~**) burden. **бре́мя** (-мени) *neut* burden; load.
бренча́ть (-чу́) *impf* strum; jingle.
брести́ (-еду́, -едёшь; брёл, -а́) *impf* stroll; drag o.s. along.
брете́ль, брете́лька shoulder strap.
брешь breach; gap.
бре́ю *etc.*: *see* **брить**

б

бригáда brigade; crew, team. **бригадúр** brigadier; team-leader; foreman.

бриллиáнт, брильянт diamond.

британец (-нца), **британка** Briton. **британск|ий** British; **Б~ие островá** the British Isles.

брúтва razor. **брúтвенный** shaving. **брúтый** shaved; clean-shaven. **брить** (брéю) *impf* (*pf* **по~**) shave; **~ся** shave (o.s.).

бровь (*pl* -и, -éй) (eye)brow.

брод ford.

бродúть (-ожý, -óдишь) *impf* wander, roam, stroll; ferment. **бродяга** *m* & *f* tramp, vagrant. **бродяжничество** vagrancy. **бродячий** vagrant; wandering. **брожéние** ferment, fermentation.

брóкер broker.

броне- *in comb* armoured, armour. **броневúк** (-á) armoured car. **~вóй** armoured. **~нóсец** (-сца) battleship; armadillo.

брóнза bronze; bronzes. **брóнзовый** bronze; tanned.

бронирóванный armoured.

бронúровать *impf* & *pf* (*pf also* **за~**) reserve, book.

бронхúт bronchitis.

брóня[1] reservation; commandeering.

броня[2] armour.

бросáть *impf*, **брóсить** (-óшу) *pf* throw (down); leave, desert; give up, leave off; **~ся** throw o.s., rush; *+inf* begin; *+instr* squander; pelt one another with; **~ся в глазá** be striking. **брóский** striking; garish, glaring. **бросóк** (-скá) throw; bound, spurt.

брóшка, брошь brooch.

брошюра pamphlet, brochure.

брус (*pl* -сья, -сьев) squared beam, joist; **(параллéльные) ~ья** parallel bars.

брусникá red whortleberry; red whortleberries.

брусóк (-скá) bar; ingot.

брýтто *indecl adj* gross.

брызгать (-зжу *or* -гаю) *impf*, **брызнуть** (-ну) *pf* splash; sprinkle. **брызги** (брызг) *pl* spray, splashes; fragments.

брыкáть *impf*, **брыкнýть** (-нý, -нёшь) *pf* kick.

брюзгá *m* & *f* grumbler. **брюзгливый** grumbling, peevish. **брюзжáть** (-жý) *impf* grumble.

брюква swede.

брюки (*pl*; *gen* брюк) trousers.

брюнéт dark-haired man. **брюнéтка** brunette.

брюхо (*pl* -и) belly; stomach.

брюшнóй abdominal; **~ тиф** typhoid.

бряцáть *impf* rattle; clank, clang.

бýбен (-бна) tambourine. **бубенéц** (-нцá) small bell.

бýбны (*pl*; *gen* -бён, *dat* -бнáм) (*cards*) diamonds. **бубнóвый** diamond.

бугóр (-грá) mound, hillock; bump, lump.

буддúзм Buddhism. **буддúйский** Buddhist. **буддúст** Buddhist.

бýдет that will do.

будúльник alarm-clock. **будúть** (бужý, бýдишь) *impf* (*pf* **про~, раз~**) wake; arouse.

бýдка box, booth; hut; stall.

бýдни (*pl*; *gen* **-ней**) *pl* weekdays; working days; humdrum existence. **бýдний, бýдничный** weekday; everyday; humdrum.

бýдто *conj* as if, as though; **~ (бы), (как) ~** apparently, ostensibly.

бýду *etc.*: *see* **быть. бýдучи** being. **бýдущ|ий** future; next; **~ее** *sb* future. **бýдущность** future. **бýдь(те):** *see* **быть**

бужý: *see* **будúть**

бузинá (*bot*) elder.

буй (*pl* -ú, -ёв) buoy.

бýйвол buffalo.

бýйный (бýен, буйнá, -о) violent, turbulent; luxuriant, lush. **бýйство** unruly behaviour. **бýйствовать** *impf* create an uproar, behave violently.

бук beech.
букáшка small insect.
бýква (*gen pl* букв) letter; **~ в бýкву** literally. **буквáльно** *adv* literally. **буквáльный** literal. **буквáрь** (-я́) *m* ABC. **буквоéд** pedant.
букéт bouquet; aroma.
букини́ст second-hand bookseller.
бýкля curl, ringlet.
бýковый beech.
букси́р tug-boat; tow-rope. **букси́ровать** *impf* tow.
буксовáть *impf* spin, slip.
булáвка pin.
бýлка roll; white loaf. **бýлочка** roll, bun. **бýлочная** *sb* baker's. **бýлочник** baker.
булы́жник cobble-stone, cobbles.
бульвáр avenue; boulevard.
бульдóг bulldog.
бульдóзер bulldozer.
бýлькать *impf* gurgle.
бульóн broth.
бум (*sport*) beam.
бумáга cotton; paper; document. **бумáжка** piece of paper; (bank-) note. **бумáжник** wallet; paper-maker. **бумáжный** cotton; paper.
бýнкер bunker.
бунт (*pl* -ы́) rebellion; riot; mutiny. **бунтáрь** (-я́) *m* rebel; insurgent. **бунтовáть(ся** *impf* (*pf* **вз~**) rebel; riot. **бунтовщи́к** (-á), **-щи́ца** rebel, insurgent.
бур auger.
бурáв (-á; *pl* -á) auger; gimlet. **бурáвить** (-влю) *impf* (*pf* **про~**) bore, drill.
бурáн snowstorm.
буревéстник stormy petrel.
бурéние boring, drilling.
буржуá *m indecl* bourgeois. **буржуази́я** bourgeoisie. **буржуáзный** bourgeois.
бури́льщик borer, driller. **бури́ть** *impf* (*pf* **про~**) bore, drill.
бурли́ть *impf* seethe.
бýрный (-рен, -рнá, -о) stormy; rapid; energetic.
буров|óй boring; **~áя вы́шка** derrick; **~áя (сквáжина)** borehole; **~óй станóк** drilling rig.
бýрый (бур, -á, -о) brown.
бурья́н tall weeds.
бýря storm.
бýсина bead. **бýсы** (*pl*; *gen* бус) beads.
бутафóрия (*theat*) props.
бутербрóд open sandwich.
бутóн bud.
бýтсы (*pl*; *gen* -ов) *pl* football boots.
буты́лка bottle. **буты́ль** large bottle; carboy.
буфéт snack bar; sideboard; counter. **буфéтчик** barman. **буфéтчица** barmaid.
бух *int* bang, plonk. **бýхать** *impf* (*pf* **бýхнуть**) thump, bang; bang down; thunder, thud; blurt out.
бухáнка loaf.
бухгáлтер accountant. **бухгалтéрия** accountancy; accounts department.
бýхнуть (-ну) *impf* swell.
бýхта bay.
бушевáть (-шýю) *impf* rage, storm.
буя́н rowdy. **буя́нить** *impf* create an uproar.
бы, б *partl* **I.** *+past tense or inf indicates the conditional or subjunctive.* **II.** (+**ни**) *forms indef prons and conjs.*
бывáлый experienced; former; habitual, familiar. **бывáть** *impf* be; happen; be inclined to be; **как ни в чём не бывáло** as if nothing had happened; **бывáло** *partl* used to, would; **мать бывáло чáсто пéла э́ту пéсню** my mother would often sing this song. **бы́вший** former, ex-.
бык (-á) bull, ox; pier.
были́на ancient Russian epic.
бы́ло *partl* nearly, on the point of; (only) just. **был|óй** past, bygone; **~óе** *sb* the past. **быль** true story; fact.
быстротá speed. **бы́стрый** (быстр, -á, -о) fast, quick.

б

в

быт (*loc* -у́) way of life. **бытие́** being, existence; objective reality; **книга́ Бытия́** Genesis. **бытово́й** everyday; social.

быть (*pres 3rd sg* есть, *pl* суть; *fut* бу́ду; *past* был, -а́, -о; *imper* бу́дь(те)) *impf* be; be situated; happen. **бытьё** way of life.

бычо́к (-чка́) steer.

бью *etc.*: *see* **бить**

бюдже́т budget.

бюллете́нь *m* bulletin; ballot-paper; doctor's certificate.

бюро́ *neut indecl* bureau; office; writing-desk. **бюрокра́т** bureaucrat. **бюрократи́зм** bureaucracy. **бюрократи́ческий** bureaucratic. **бюрокра́тия** bureaucracy; bureaucrats.

бюст bust. **бюстга́льтер** bra.

В

в, во *prep* **I.** +*acc* into, to; on; at; within; through; **быть в** take after; **в два ра́за бо́льше** twice as big; **в на́ши дни** in our day; **войти́ в дом** go into the house; **в понеде́льник** on Monday; **в тече́ние** +*gen* during; **в четы́ре часа́** at four o'clock **высото́й в три ме́тра** three metres high; **игра́ть в ша́хматы** play chess; **пое́хать в Москву́** go to Moscow; **сесть в ваго́н** get into the carriage; **смотре́ть в окно́** look out of the window. **II.** +*prep* in; at; **в двадца́том ве́ке** in the twentieth century; **в теа́тре** at the theatre; **в трёх киломе́трах от го́рода** three kilometres from the town; **в э́том году́** this year; **в январе́** in January.

ваго́н carriage, coach; **~-рестора́н** restaurant car. **ваго́нетка** truck, trolley. **вагоновожа́тый** *sb* tram-driver.

ва́жничать *impf* give o.s. airs; +*instr* plume o.s., pride o.s., on. **ва́жность** importance; pomposity. **ва́жный** (-жен, -жна́, -о) important; weighty; pompous.

ва́за vase, bowl.

вазели́н Vaseline (*propr*).

вака́нсия vacancy. **вака́нтный** vacant.

ва́кса (shoe-)polish.

ва́куум vacuum.

вакци́на vaccine.

вал[1] (*loc* -у́; *pl* -ы́) bank; rampart; billow, roller; barrage.

вал[2] (*loc* -у́; *pl* -ы́) shaft.

ва́ленок (-нка; *gen pl* -нок) felt boot.

вале́т knave, Jack.

ва́лик roller, cylinder.

вали́ть[1] *impf* flock, throng.

вали́ть[2] (-лю́, -лишь) *impf* (*pf* **по~**, **с~**) throw down, bring down; pile up; **~ся** fall, collapse.

валли́ец (-и́йца) Welshman. **валли́йка** Welshwoman.

валово́й gross; wholesale.

валто́рна French horn.

валу́н (-а́) boulder.

вальс waltz. **вальси́ровать** *impf* waltz.

валю́та currency; foreign currency.

валя́ть *impf* (*pf* **на~**, **с~**) drag; roll; shape; bungle; **~ дурака́** play the fool; **~ся** lie, lie about; roll, wallow.

вам, ва́ми: *see* **вы**

вампи́р vampire.

ванда́л vandal. **вандали́зм** vandalism.

вани́ль vanilla.

ва́нна bath. **ва́нная** *sb* bathroom.

ва́рвар barbarian. **ва́рварский** barbaric. **ва́рварство** barbarity; vandalism.

ва́режка mitten.

варёный boiled. **варе́нье** jam. **вари́ть** (-рю́, -ришь) *impf* (*pf* **с~**) boil; cook; **~ся** boil; cook.

вариа́нт version; option; scenario.

вас: *see* **вы**

василёк (-лька́) cornflower.

ва́та cotton wool; wadding.

ватерли́ния water-line. **ватерпа́с** (spirit-)level.

вати́н (sheet) wadding. **ва́тник** quilted jacket. **ва́тный** quilted, wadded.
ватру́шка cheese-cake.
ватт (*gen pl* ватт) watt.
ва́учер coupon (*exchangeable for government-issued share*).
ва́фля (*gen pl* -фель) wafer; waffle.
ва́хта (*naut*) watch. **вахтёр** janitor, porter.
ваш (-его) *m*, **ва́ша** (-ей) *f*, **ва́ше** (-его) *neut*, **ва́ши** (-их) *pl*, *pron* your, yours.
вбега́ть *impf*, **вбежа́ть** (вбегу́) *pf* run in.
вберу́ *etc.*: *see* **вобра́ть**
вбива́ть *impf of* **вбить**
вбира́ть *impf of* **вобра́ть**
вбить (вобью́, -бьёшь) *pf* (*impf* **вбива́ть**) drive in, hammer in.
вблизи́ *adv* (+**от**+*gen*) close (to), near by.
вбок *adv* sideways, to one side.
вброд *adv*: **переходи́ть ~** ford, wade.
вва́ливать *impf*, **ввали́ть** (-лю́, -лишь) *pf* throw heavily, heave, bundle; **~ся** fall heavily; sink, become sunken; burst in.
введе́ние introduction. **введу́** *etc.*: *see* **ввести́**
ввезти́ (-зу́, -зёшь; ввёз, -ла́) *pf* (*impf* **ввози́ть**) import; bring in.
вве́рить *pf* (*impf* **вверя́ть**) entrust, confide; **~ся** +*dat* trust in, put one's faith in.
ввернýть (-ну́, -нёшь) *pf*, **ввёртывать** *impf* screw in; insert.
вверх *adv* up, upward(s); **~дном** upside down; **~ (по ле́стнице)** upstairs. **вверху́** *adv* above, overhead.
вверя́ть(ся) *impf of* **вве́рить(ся)**
ввести́ (-еду́, -едёшь; ввёл, -а́) *pf* (*impf* **вводи́ть**) bring in; introduce.
ввиду́ *prep*+*gen* in view of.
ввинти́ть (-нчу́) *pf*, **вви́нчивать** *impf* screw in.
ввод lead-in. **вводи́ть** (-ожу́, -о́дишь) *impf of* **ввести́**. **вво́дный** introductory; parenthetic.
ввожу́ *see* **вводи́ть, ввози́ть**
ввоз importation; import(s). **ввози́ть** (-ожу́, -о́зишь) *impf of* **ввезти́**
вво́лю *adv* to one's heart's content.
ввысь *adv* up, upward(s).
ввяза́ть (-яжу́, -я́жешь) *pf*, **ввя́зывать** *impf* knit in; involve; **~ся** meddle, get or be mixed up (in).
вглубь *adv* & *prep*+*gen* deep (into), into the depths.
вгляде́ться (-яжу́сь) *pf*, **вгля́дываться** *impf* peer, look closely (**в**+*acc* at).
вгоня́ть *impf of* **вогна́ть**. **вдава́ться** (вдаю́сь, -ёшься) *impf of* **вда́ться**
вдави́ть (-авлю́, -а́вишь) *pf*, **вда́вливать** *impf* press in.
вдалеке́, вдали́ *adv* in the distance, far away. **вдаль** *adv* into the distance.
вда́ться (-а́мся, -а́шься, -а́стся, -ади́мся; -а́лся, -ла́сь) *pf* (*impf* **вдава́ться**) jut out; penetrate, go in; (*fig*) get immersed.
вдво́е *adv* twice; double; **~ бо́льше** twice as big, as much, as many. **вдвоём** *adv* (the) two together, both. **вдвойне́** *adv* twice, double; doubly.
вдева́ть *impf of* **вдеть**
вде́лать *pf*, **вде́лывать** *impf* set in, fit in.
вдёргивать *impf*, **вдёрнуть** (-ну) *pf* **в**+*acc* thread through.
вдеть (-е́ну) *pf* (*impf* **вдева́ть**) put in, thread.
вдоба́вок *adv* in addition; besides.
вдова́ widow. **вдове́ц** (-вца́) widower.
вдо́воль *adv* enough; in abundance.
вдого́нку *adv* (**за**+*instr*) after, in pursuit (of).
вдоль *adv* lengthwise; **~ и поперёк** far and wide; in detail; *prep*+*gen or* **по**+*dat* along.
вдох breath. **вдохнове́ние** inspir-

ation, **вдохновéнный** inspired. **вдохновúть** (-влю́) *pf*, **вдохновля́ть** *impf* inspire. **вдохну́ть** (-ну́, -нёшь) *pf* (*impf* **вдыхáть**) breathe in.

В

вдрéбезги *adv* to smithereens.
вдруг *adv* suddenly.
вду́маться *pf*, **вду́мываться** *impf* ponder, meditate; +**в**+*acc* think over. **вду́мчивый** thoughtful.
вдыхáние inhalation. **вдыхáть** *impf of* **вдохну́ть**
веб-сáйт (*comput*) website. **веб-странúца** (*comput*) web page.
вегетариáнец (-нца), **-нка** vegetarian. **вегетариáнский** vegetarian.
вéдать *impf* know; +*instr* manage, handle. **вéдение**[1] authority, jurisdiction.
ведéние[2] conducting, conduct; ~ **книг** book-keeping.
вéдомость (*gen pl* -éй) list, register. **вéдомственный** departmental. **вéдомство** department.
ведрó (*pl* вёдра, -дер) bucket; vedro (*approx 12 litres*).
веду́ *etc.*: *see* **вестú**. **веду́щий** leading.
ведь *partl* & *conj* you see, you know; isn't it? is it?
вéдьма witch.
вéер (*pl* -á) fan.
вéжливость politeness. **вéжливый** polite.
вездé *adv* everywhere.
везéние luck. **везу́чий** lucky. **вестú** (-зу́, -зёшь; вёз, -лá) *impf* (*pf* **по~**) convey; bring, take; *impers*+*dat* be lucky; **ему́ не везлó** he had no luck.
век (*loc* -у́; *pl* -á) century; age; life(time). **век** *adv* for ages.
вéко (*pl* -и, век) eyelid.
вековóй ancient, age-old.
вéксель (*pl* -я́, -éй) *m* promissory note, bill (of exchange).
вёл *etc.*: *see* **вестú**
велéть (-лю́) *impf* & *pf* order; **не ~** forbid.
великáн giant. **велúкий** (велúк, -а *or* -á) great; big, large; too big; ~ **пост** Lent.
велико- *in comb* great. **Великобритáния** Great Britain. **великоду́шие** magnanimity. **~ду́шный** magnanimous. **~лéпие** splendour. **~лéпный** splendid.
величáвый stately, majestic. **величáйший** greatest, supreme. **велúчественный** majestic, grand. **велúчество** Majesty. **велúчие** greatness, grandeur. **величинá** (*pl* -úны, -áм) size; quantity, magnitude; value; great figure.
велосипéд bicycle. **велосипедúст** cyclist.
вельвéт velveteen; **~ в ру́бчик** corduroy.
вельмóжа *m* grandee.
вéна vein.
венгéрец (-рца), **венгéрка** Hungarian. **венгéрский** Hungarian. **венгр** Hungarian. **Вéнгрия** Hungary.
вендéтта vendetta.
венерúческий venereal.
венéц (-нцá) crown; wreath.
вéник besom; birch twigs.
венóк (-нкá) wreath, garland.
вéнтиль *m* valve.
вентиля́тор ventilator; extractor (fan). **вентиля́ция** ventilation.
венчáние wedding; coronation. **венчáть** *impf* (*pf* **об~, по~, у~**) crown; marry; **~ся** be married, marry. **вéнчик** halo; corolla; rim; ring, bolt.
вéра faith, belief.
верáнда veranda.
вéрба willow; willow branch. **вéрбн|ый; ~ое воскресéнье** Palm Sunday.
верблю́д camel.
вербовáть *impf* (*pf* **за~**) recruit; win over. **вербóвка** recruitment.
верёвка rope; string; cord. **верёвочный** rope.
вереница row, file, line, string.
вéреск heather.
веретенó (*pl* -тёна) spindle.

верещáть (-щý) *impf* squeal; chirp.
вéрить *impf* (*pf* **по~**) believe, have faith; *+dat or* **в**+*acc* trust (in), believe in.
вермишéль vermicelli.
вернée *adv* rather. **вéрно** *partl* probably, I suppose. **вéрность** faithfulness, loyalty.
вернýть (-нý, -нёшь) *pf* (*impf* **возвращáть**) give back, return; **~ся** return.
вéрный (-рен, -рнá, -о) faithful, loyal; true; correct; reliable.
вéрование belief. **вéровать** *impf* believe. **вероисповéдание** religion; denomination. **верolóмный** treacherous, perfidious. **вероотстýпник** apostate. **веротерпи́мость** (religious) toleration. **вероя́тно** *adv* probably. **вероя́тность** probability. **вероя́тный** probable.
вéрсия version.
верстá (*pl* вёрсты) verst (*1.06 km.*).
верстáк (-á) work-bench.
вéртел (*pl* -á) spit, skewer. **вертéть** (-чý, -тишь) *impf* turn (round); twirl; **~ся** turn (round), spin. **вертля́вый** fidgety; flighty.
вертикáль vertical line. **вертикáльный** vertical.
вертолёт helicopter.
вертýшка flirt.
вéрующий *sb* believer.
верфь shipyard.
верх (*loc* -ý; *pl* -и́) top; summit; height; *pl* upper crust, top brass; high notes. **вéрхний** upper; top. **верхóвный** supreme. **верховóй** riding; *sb* rider. **верхóвье** (*gen pl* -вьев) upper reaches. **верхолáз** steeple-jack. **верхóм** *adv* on horseback; astride. **верхýшка** top, summit; apex; top brass.
верчý *etc.*: *see* **вертéть**
верши́на top, summit; peak; apex. **верши́ть** *impf* +*instr* manage, control.
вершóк vershok (*4.4 cm.*); smattering.
вес (*loc* -ý; *pl* -á) weight.
весели́ть *impf* (*pf* **раз~**) cheer, gladden; **~ся** enjoy o.s.; amuse o.s. **вéсело** *adv* merrily. **весёлый** (вéсел, -á, -о) merry; cheerful. **весéлье** merriment.
весéнний spring.
вéсить (вéшу) *impf* weigh. **вéский** weighty, solid.
веслó (*pl* вёсла, -сел) oar.
веснá (*pl* вёсны, -сен) spring. **веснóй** *adv* in (the) spring. **веснýшка** freckle.
вест (*naut*) west; west wind.
вести́ (ведý, -дёшь; вёл, -á) *impf* (*pf* **по~**) lead, take; conduct; drive; run; keep; **~ себя́** behave, conduct o.s.; **~сь** be the custom.
вестибю́ль *m* (entrance) hall, lobby.
вéстник herald; bulletin. **весть**[1] (*gen pl* -éй) news; **бéз вести** without trace. **весть**[2]: **Бог ~** God knows.
весы́ (*pl*; *gen* -óв) scales, balance; Libra.
весь (всегó *m*, **вся**, всей *f*, **всё**, всегó *neut*, **все**, всех *pl*) *pron* all, the whole of; **всегó хорóшего!** all the best!; **всё** everything; **без всегó** without anything; **все** everybody.
весьмá *adv* very, highly.
ветвь (*gen pl* -éй) branch; bough.
вéтер (-тра, *loc* -ý) wind. **ветерóк** (-ркá) breeze.
ветерáн veteran.
ветеринáр vet.
вéтка branch; twig.
вéто *neut indecl* veto.
вéтошь old clothes, rags.
вéтреный windy; frivolous. **ветров|óй** wind; **~óе стеклó** windscreen. **ветря́к** (-á) wind turbine; windmill.
вéтхий (ветх, -á, -о) old; dilapidated; **В~ завéт** Old Testament.
ветчинá ham.
ветшáть *impf* (*pf* **об~**) decay; become dilapidated.
вéха landmark.

В

ве́чер (*pl* -á) evening; party. **вечери́нка** party. **вече́рний** evening. **вече́рня** (*gen pl* -рен) vespers. **ве́чером** *adv* in the evening.

ве́чно *adv* for ever, eternally. **вечнозелёный** evergreen. **ве́чность** eternity; ages. **ве́чный** eternal.

ве́шалка peg, rack; tab, hanger. **ве́шать** *impf* (*pf* **взве́сить, пове́сить, све́шать**) hang; weigh (out); **~ся** hang o.s.; weigh o.s.

ве́шу *etc.*: *see* **ве́сить**

веща́ние broadcasting. **веща́ть** *impf* broadcast.

вещево́й clothing; **~ мешо́к** hold-all, kit-bag. **веще́ственный** substantial, material, real. **вещество́** substance; matter. **вещь** (*gen pl* -е́й) thing.

ве́ялка winnowing-machine. **ве́яние** winnowing; blowing; trend. **ве́ять** (ве́ю) *impf* (*pf* **про~**) winnow; blow; flutter.

взад *adv* backwards; **~ и вперёд** back and forth.

взаи́мность reciprocity. **взаи́мный** mutual, reciprocal.

взаимо- *in comb* inter-. **взаимоде́йствие** interaction; co-operation. **~де́йствовать** *impf* interact; cooperate. **~отноше́ние** interrelation; *pl* relations. **~по́мощь** mutual aid. **~понима́ние** mutual understanding. **~свя́зь** interdependence, correlation.

взаймы́ *adv*: **взять ~** borrow; **дать ~** lend.

взаме́н *prep+gen* instead of; in return for.

взаперти́ *adv* under lock and key; in seclusion.

взба́лмошный unbalanced, eccentric.

взбега́ть *impf*, **взбежа́ть** (-егу́) *pf* run up.

взберу́сь *etc.*: *see* **взобра́ться.**

вз|беси́ть(ся (-ешу́(сь, -е́сишь(ся) *pf.* **взбива́ть** *impf of* **взбить.** **взбира́ться** *impf of* **взобра́ться**

взби́тый whipped, beaten. **взбить** (взобью́, -бьёшь) *pf* (*impf* **взбива́ть**) beat (up), whip; shake up.

вз|борозди́ть (-зжу́) *pf.*

вз|бунтова́ться *pf.*

взбуха́ть *impf*, **взбу́хнуть** (-нет; -ух) *pf* swell (out).

вва́ливать *impf*, **взвали́ть** (-лю́, -лишь) *pf* load; +**на**+*acc* saddle with.

взве́сить (-е́шу) *pf* (*impf* **ве́шать, взве́шивать**) weigh.

взвести́ (-еду́, -едёшь; -ёл, -á) *pf* (*impf* **взводи́ть**) lead up; raise; cock; +**на**+*acc* impute to.

взве́шивать *impf of* **взве́сить**

взвива́ть(ся *impf of* **взви́ть(ся**

взвизг scream; yelp. **взви́згивать** *impf*, **взви́згнуть** (-ну) *pf* scream; yelp.

взвинти́ть (-нчу́) *pf*, **взви́нчивать** *impf* excite, work up; inflate. **взви́нченный** worked up; nervy; inflated.

взвить (взовью́, -ёшь; -ил, -á, -о) *pf* (*impf* **взвива́ть**) raise; **~ся** rise, be hoisted; soar.

взвод[1] platoon, troop.

взвод[2] notch. **взводи́ть** (-ожу́, -о́дишь) *impf of* **взвести́**

взволно́ванный agitated; worried. **вз|волнова́ть(ся** (-ну́ю(сь) *pf.*

взгляд look; glance; opinion. **взгля́дывать** *impf*, **взгляну́ть** (-яну́, -я́нешь) *pf* look, glance.

взго́рье hillock.

вздёргивать *impf*, **вздёрнуть** (-ну) *pf* hitch up; jerk up; turn up.

вздор nonsense. **вздо́рный** cantankerous; foolish.

вздорожа́ние rise in price. **вз|дорожа́ть** *pf.*

вздох sigh. **вздохну́ть** (-ну́, -нёшь) *pf* (*impf* **вздыха́ть**) sigh.

вздра́гивать *impf* (*pf* **вздро́гнуть**) shudder, quiver.

вздремну́ть *pf* have a nap, doze.

вздро́гнуть (-ну) *pf* (*impf* **вздра́гивать**) start; wince.

вздува́ть(ся *impf of* **вздуть**[1]**(ся**

вздýмать *pf* take it into one's head; **не вздýмай(те)!** don't you dare!
вздýтие swelling. **вздýтый** swollen. **вздуть**[1] *pf* (*impf* **вздувáть**) inflate; **~ся** swell.
вздуть[2] *pf* thrash.
вздыхáть *impf* (*pf* **вздохнýть**) breathe; sigh.
взимáть *impf* levy, collect.
взлáмывать *impf of* **взломáть**.
вз|лелéять *pf*.
взлёт flight; take-off. **взлетáть** *impf*, **взлетéть** (-лечý) *pf* fly (up); take off. **взлётный** take-off; **взлётно-посáдочная полосá** runway.
взлом breaking open, breaking in. **взломáть** *pf* (*impf* **взлáмывать**) break open; break up. **взлóмщик** burglar.
взлохмáченный dishevelled.
взмах stroke, wave, flap. **взмáхивать** *impf*, **взмахнýть** (-нý, -нёшь) *pf* +*instr* wave, flap.
взмóрье seaside; coastal waters.
вз|мутúть (-учý, -ýтúшь) *pf*.
взнос payment; fee, dues.
взнуздáть *pf*, **взнýздывать** *impf* bridle.
взобрáться (взберýсь, -ёшься; -áлся, -лáсь, -áлóсь) *pf* (*impf* **взбирáться**) climb (up).
взобью *etc.*: *see* **взбить**. **взовью** *etc.*: *see* **взвить**
взойтú (-йдý, -йдёшь; -ошёл, -шлá) *pf* (*impf* **вос-, всходúть**) rise, go up; **на**+*acc* mount.
взор look, glance.
взорвáть (-вý, -вёшь; -áл, -á, -о) *pf* (*impf* **взрывáть**) blow up; exasperate; **~ся** burst, explode.
взрóслый *adj & sb* adult.
взрыв explosion; outburst. **взрывáтель** *m* fuse. **взрывáть** *impf*, **взрыть** (-рóю) *pf* (*pf also* **взорвáть**) blow up; **~ся** explode. **взрывнóй** explosive; blasting. **взрывчáтка** explosive. **взрывчатый** explosive.
взъерóшенный tousled, dishevelled. **взъерóшивать** *impf*, **взъерóшить** (-шу) *pf* tousle, rumple.
взывáть *impf of* **воззвáть**
взыскáние penalty; exaction. **взыскáтельный** exacting. **взыскáть** (-ыщý, -ы́щешь) *pf*, **взы́скивать** *impf* exact, recover; call to account.
взя́тие taking, capture. **взя́тка** bribe. **взя́точничество** bribery.
взять(ся (возьмý(сь, -мёшь(ся; -я́л(ся, -á(сь, -о(сь) *pf of* **брáть(ся**
вибрáция vibration. **вибрúровать** *impf* vibrate.
вивисéкция vivisection.
вид[1] (*loc* -ý) look; appearance; shape, form; condition; view; prospect; sight; aspect; **дéлать вид** pretend; **имéть в ~ý** intend; mean; bear in mind.
вид[2] kind; species.
видáться *impf* (*pf* **по~**) meet. **вúдение**[1] sight, vision. **видéние**[2] vision, apparition.
вúдео *neut indecl* video (cassette) recorder; video film; video cassette. **видеоигрá** video game. **видеокáмера** video camera. **видеокассéта** video cassette. **видеомагнитофóн** video (cassette) recorder.
вúдеть (вúжу) *impf* (*pf* **у~**) see; **~ во сне** dream (of); **~ся** see one another; appear. **вúдимо** *adv* evidently. **вúдимость** visibility; appearance. **вúдимый** visible; apparent, evident. **вúдный** (-ден, -днá, -о) visible; distinguished.
видоизменéние modification. **видоизменúть** *pf*, **видоизменя́ть** *impf* modify.
видоискáтель *m* view-finder.
вúжу *see* **вúдеть**
вúза visa.
визг squeal; yelp. **визжáть** (-жý) *impf* squeal, yelp, squeak.
визúт visit. **визúтка** business card.
викторúна quiz.
вúлка fork; plug. **вúлы** (*pl*; *gen* вил) pitchfork.

В

В

вильну́ть (-ну́, -нёшь) *pf*, **виля́ть** *impf* twist and turn; prevaricate; +*instr* wag.
вина́ (*pl* ви́ны) fault, guilt; blame.
винегре́т Russian salad; medley.
вини́тельный accusative. **вини́ть** *impf* accuse; **~ся** (*pf* **по~**) confess.
ви́нный wine; winy. **вино́** (*pl* -а) wine.
винова́тый guilty. **вино́вник** initiator; culprit. **вино́вный** guilty.
виногра́д vine; grapes. **виногра́дина** grape. **виногра́дник** vineyard. **виногра́дный** grape; wine. **виноку́ренный заво́д** distillery.
винт (-а́) screw. **винти́ть** (-нчу́) *impf* screw up. **винто́вка** rifle. **винтово́й** screw; spiral.
виолонче́ль cello.
вира́ж (-а́) turn; bend.
виртуа́льный (*comput*) virtual.
виртуо́з virtuoso. **виртуо́зный** masterly.
ви́рус virus. **ви́русный** virus.
ви́селица gallows. **висе́ть** (вишу́) *impf* hang. **ви́снуть** (-ну; вис(нул)) *impf* hang; droop.
ви́ски *neut indecl* whisky.
висо́к (-ска́) (*anat*) temple.
високо́сный год leap-year.
вист whist.
вися́чий hanging; **~ замо́к** padlock; **~ мост** suspension bridge.
витами́н vitamin.
витиева́тый flowery, ornate. **вито́й** twisted, spiral. **вито́к** (-тка́) turn, coil.
витра́ж (-а́) stained-glass window. **витри́на** shop-window; showcase.
вить (вью, вьёшь; вил, -а́, -о) *impf* (*pf* **с~**) twist, wind, weave; **~ся** wind, twine; curl; twist; whirl.
вихо́р (-хра́) tuft. **вихра́стый** shaggy.
вихрь *m* whirlwind; vortex; **сне́жный ~** blizzard.
ви́це- *pref* vice-. **вице-адмира́л** vice-admiral. **~президе́нт** vice-president.
ВИЧ (*abbr of* **ви́рус иммунодефици́та челове́ка**) HIV.
вишнёвый cherry. **ви́шня** (*gen pl* -шен) cherry, cherries; cherry-tree.
вишу́: *see* **висе́ть**
вишь *partl* look, just look!
вка́лывать *impf* (*sl*) work hard; *impf of* **вколо́ть**
вка́пывать *impf of* **вкопа́ть**
вкати́ть (-ачу́, -а́тишь) *pf*, **вка́тывать** *impf* roll in; administer.
вклад deposit; contribution. **вкла́дка, вкладно́й лист** loose leaf, insert. **вкла́дчик** depositor.
вкла́дывать *impf of* **вложи́ть**
вкле́ивать *impf*, **вкле́ить** *pf* stick in.
вкли́ниваться *impf*, **вклини́ться** *pf* edge one's way in.
включа́тель *m* switch. **включа́ть** *impf*, **включи́ть** (-чу́) *pf* include; switch on; plug in; **~ся в**+*acc* join in, enter into. **включа́я** including. **включе́ние** inclusion, insertion; switching on. **включи́тельно** *adv* inclusive.
вкола́чивать *impf*, **вколоти́ть** (-очу́, -о́тишь) *pf* hammer in, knock in.
вколо́ть (-олю́, -о́лешь) *pf* (*impf* **вка́лывать**) stick (in).
вкопа́ть *pf* (*impf* **вка́пывать**) dig in.
вкось *adv* obliquely.
вкра́дчивый ingratiating. **вкра́дываться** *impf*, **вкра́сться** (-аду́сь, -адёшься) *pf* creep in; insinuate o.s.
вкра́тце *adv* briefly, succinctly.
вкривь *adv* aslant; wrongly, perversely.
вкруг = **вокру́г**
вкруту́ю *adv* hard(-boiled).
вкус taste. **вкуси́ть** (-ушу́, -у́сишь) *pf*, **вкуша́ть** *impf* taste; partake of. **вку́сный** (-сен, -сна́, -о) tasty, nice.
вла́га moisture.
влага́лище vagina.
владе́лец (-льца), **-лица** owner. **владе́ние** ownership; possession;

property. **владéтель** *m*, **-ница** possessor; sovereign. **владéть** (-éю) *impf* +*instr* own, possess; control.

владыка *m* master, sovereign. **владычество** dominion, sway.

влáжность humidity; moisture. **влáжный** (-жен, -жнá, -о) damp, moist, humid.

влáмываться *impf of* **вломи́ться**

влáствовать *impf* +(**над**+) *instr* rule, hold sway over. **властели́н** ruler; master. **влáстный** imperious, commanding; empowered, competent. **власть** (*gen pl* -éй) power; authority.

влéво *adv* to the left (**от**+*gen* of).

влезáть *impf*, **влезть** (-зу; влез) *pf* climb in; get in; fit in.

влёк *etc.*: *see* **влечь**

влетáть *impf*, **влетéть** (-ечу́) *pf* fly in; rush in.

влечéние attraction; inclination. **влечь** (-еку́, -ечёшь; влёк, -лá) *impf* draw; attract; ~ **за собóй** involve, entail.

вливáть *impf*, **влить** (волью́, -ёшь; влил, -á, -о) *pf* pour in; instil.

влия́ние influence. **влия́тельный** influential. **влия́ть** *impf* (*pf* **по**~) **на**+*acc* influence, affect.

вложéние enclosure; investment. **вложи́ть** (-ожу́, -óжишь) *pf* (*impf* **вклáдывать**) put in, insert; enclose; invest.

вломи́ться (-млю́сь, -мишься) *pf* (*impf* **влáмываться**) break in.

влюби́ть (-блю́, -бишь) *pf*, **влюбля́ть** *impf* make fall in love (**в**+*acc* with); **~ся** fall in love. **влюблённый** (-лён, -á) in love; *sb* lover.

вмáзать (-áжу) *pf*, **вмáзывать** *impf* cement, putty in.

вмени́ть *pf*, **вменя́ть** *impf* impute; impose. **вменя́емый** (*law*) responsible; sane.

вмéсте *adv* together; ~ **с тем** at the same time, also.

вмести́лище receptacle. **вмести́мость** capacity; tonnage. **вмести́тельный** capacious. **вмести́ть** (-ещу́) *pf* (*impf* **вмещáть**) hold, accommodate; put; **~ся** go in.

вмéсто *prep*+*gen* instead of.

вмешáтельство interference; intervention. **вмешáть** *pf*, **вмéшивать** *impf* mix in; implicate; **~ся** interfere, intervene.

вмещáть(ся *impf of* **вмести́ть(ся**

вмиг *adv* in an instant.

вминáть *impf*, **вмять** (вомну́, -нёшь) *pf* press in, dent. **вмя́тина** dent.

внаём, внаймы́ *adv* to let; for hire.

вначáле *adv* at first.

вне *prep*+*gen* outside; ~ **себя́** beside o.s.

вне- *pref* extra-; outside; -less. **внебрáчный** extra-marital; illegitimate. **~врéменный** timeless. **~клáссный** extracurricular. **~очереднóй** out of turn; extraordinary. **~штáтный** freelance, casual.

внедрéние introduction; inculcation. **внедри́ть** *pf*, **внедря́ть** *impf* inculcate; introduce; **~ся** take root.

внезáпно *adv* suddenly. **внезáпный** sudden.

внéмлю *etc.*: *see* **внимáть**

внесéние bringing in; deposit. **внести́** (-су́, -сёшь; внёс, -лá) *pf* (*impf* **вноси́ть**) bring in; introduce; deposit; insert.

внéшне *adv* outwardly. **внéшний** outer; external; outside; foreign. **внéшность** exterior; appearance.

вниз *adv* down(wards); ~ **по**+*dat* down. **внизу́** *adv* below; downstairs.

вникáть *impf*, **вни́кнуть** (-ну; вник) *pf* +**в**+*acc* go carefully into, investigate thoroughly.

внимáние attention. **внимáтельный** attentive. **внимáть** *impf* (*pf* **внять**) listen to; heed.

вничью́ *adv*: **окóнчиться** ~ end in a draw; **сыгрáть** ~ draw.

В

вновь *adv* anew, again.
вноси́ть (-ошу́, -о́сишь) *impf of* **внести́**
внук grandson; *pl* grandchildren, descendants.
вну́тренний inner; internal. **вну́тренность** interior; *pl* entrails; internal organs. **внутри́** *adv* & *prep+gen* inside. **внутрь** *adv* & *prep+gen* inside, in; inwards.
внуча́та (*pl*; *gen* -ча́т) grandchildren. **внуча́тый** second, great-; ~ **брат** second cousin; ~ **племя́нник** great-nephew. **вну́чка** grand-daughter.
внуша́ть *impf*, **внуши́ть** (-шу́) *pf* instil; +*dat* inspire with. **внуше́ние** suggestion; reproof. **внуши́тельный** inspiring; imposing.
вня́тный distinct. **внять** (*no fut*; -ял, -а́, -о) *pf of* **внима́ть**
во: *see* **в**
вобра́ть (вберу́, -рёшь; -а́л, -а́, -о) *pf* (*impf* **вбира́ть**) absorb; inhale.
вобью́ *etc.*: *see* **вбить**
вовлека́ть *impf*, **вовле́чь** (-еку́, -ечёшь; -ёк, -екла́) *pf* draw in, involve.
во́время *adv* in time; on time.
во́все *adv* quite; ~ **не** not at all.
во-вторы́х *adv* secondly.
вогна́ть (вгоню́, -о́нишь; -гна́л, -а́, -о) *pf* (*impf* **вгоня́ть**) drive in. **во́гнутый** concave. **вогну́ть** (-ну́, -нёшь) *pf* (*impf* **вгиба́ть**) bend or curve inwards.
вода́ (*acc* во́ду, *gen* -ы́; *pl* -ы) water; *pl* the waters; spa.
водвори́ть *pf*, **водворя́ть** *impf* settle, install; establish.
води́тель *m* driver. **води́ть** (вожу́, во́дишь) *impf* lead; conduct; take; drive; **~ся** be found; associate (with); be the custom.
во́дка vodka. **во́дн|ый** water; **~ые лы́жи** water-skiing; water-skis.
водо- *in comb* water, water-; hydraulic; hydro-. **водобоя́знь** hydrophobia. **~воро́т** whirlpool; maelstrom. **~ём** reservoir. **~измеще́ние** displacement. **~ка́чка** water-tower, pumping station. **~ла́з** diver. **~ле́й** Aquarius. **~непроница́емый** waterproof. **~отво́дный** drainage. **~па́д** waterfall. **~по́й** watering-place. **~прово́д** water-pipe, water-main; water supply. **~прово́дчик** plumber. **~разде́л** watershed. **~ро́д** hydrogen. **во́доросль** water-plant; seaweed. **~снабже́ние** water supply. **~сто́к** drain, gutter. **~храни́лище** reservoir.
водружа́ть *impf*, **водрузи́ть** (-ужу́) *pf* hoist; erect.
водяни́стый watery. **водяно́й** water.
воева́ть (вою́ю) *impf* wage war.
воево́да *m* voivode; commander.
воеди́но *adv* together.
военко́м military commissar.
военно- *in comb* military; war-. **вое́нно-возду́шный** air-, air-force. **вое́нно-морско́й** naval. **~пле́нный** *sb* prisoner of war. **вое́нно-полево́й суд** court-martial. **~слу́жащий** *sb* serviceman.
вое́нн|ый military; war; *sb* serviceman; **~ое положе́ние** martial law; **~ый суд** court-martial.
вожа́к (-а́) guide; leader. **вожа́тый** *sb* guide; tram-driver.
вожделе́ние desire, lust.
вождь (-я́) *m* leader, chief.
вожжа́ (*pl* -и, -е́й) rein.
вожу́ *etc.*: *see* **води́ть, вози́ть**
воз (*loc* -у́; *pl* -ы́) cart; cart-load.
возбуди́мый excitable. **возбуди́тель** *m* agent; instigator. **возбуди́ть** (-ужу́) *pf*, **возбужда́ть** *impf* excite, arouse; incite. **возбужда́ющ|ий**: **~ее сре́дство** stimulant. **возбужде́ние** excitement. **возбуждённый** excited.
возвести́ (-еду́, -дёшь; -вёл, -ла́) *pf* (*impf* **возводи́ть**) elevate; erect; level; +к+*dat* trace to.
возвести́ть (-ещу́) *pf*, **возвеща́ть** *impf* proclaim.
возводи́ть (-ожу́, -о́дишь) *impf of* **возвести́**

возвра́т return; repayment. **возврати́ть** (-ащу́) *pf*, **возвраща́ть** *impf* (*pf also* **верну́ть**) return, give back; **~ся** return; go back, come back. **возвра́тный** return; reflexive. **возвраще́ние** return.

возвы́сить *pf*, **возвыша́ть** *impf* raise; ennoble; **~ся** rise. **возвыше́ние** rise; raised place. **возвы́шенность** height; loftiness. **возвы́шенный** high; elevated.

возгла́вить (-влю) *pf*, **возглавля́ть** *impf* head.

во́зглас exclamation. **возгласи́ть** (-ашу́) *pf*, **возглаша́ть** *impf* proclaim.

возгора́емый inflammable. **возгора́ться** *impf*, **возгоре́ться** (-рю́сь) *pf* flare up; be seized (with).

воздава́ть (-даю́, -даёшь) *impf*, **возда́ть** (-а́м, -а́шь, -а́ст, -ади́м; -а́л, -а́, -о) *pf* render.

воздвига́ть *impf*, **воздви́гнуть** (-ну; -дви́г) *pf* raise.

возде́йствие influence. **возде́йствовать** *impf* & *pf* +**на**+*acc* influence.

возде́лать *pf*, **возде́лывать** *impf* cultivate, till.

воздержа́ние abstinence; abstention. **возде́ржанный** abstemious. **воздержа́ться** (-жу́сь, -жишься) *pf*, **возде́рживаться** *impf* refrain; abstain.

во́здух air. **воздухонепроница́емый** air-tight. **возду́шн|ый** air, aerial; airy; flimsy; **~ый змей** kite; **~ый шар** balloon.

воззва́ние appeal. **воззва́ть** (-зову́, -вёшь) *pf* (*impf* **взыва́ть**) appeal (**о**+*prep* for).

воззре́ние opinion, outlook.

вози́ть (вожу́, во́зишь) *impf* convey; carry; bring, take; **~ся** romp, play noisily; busy o.s.; potter about.

возлага́ть *impf of* **возложи́ть**

во́зле *adv* & *prep*+*gen* by, near; near by; past.

возложи́ть (-жу́, -жишь) *pf* (*impf* **возлага́ть**) lay; place.

возлю́бленный beloved; *sb* sweetheart.

возме́здие retribution.

возмести́ть (-ещу́) *pf*, **возмеща́ть** *impf* compensate for; refund. **возмеще́ние** compensation; refund.

возмо́жно *adv* possibly; +*comp* as ... as possible. **возмо́жность** possibility; opportunity. **возмо́жный** possible.

возмужа́лый mature; grown up. **возмужа́ть** *pf* grow up; gain strength.

возмути́тельный disgraceful. **возмути́ть** (-ущу́) *pf*, **возмуща́ть** *impf* disturb; stir up; rouse to indignation; **~ся** be indignant. **возмуще́ние** indignation. **возмущённый** (-щён, -щена́) indignant.

вознагради́ть (-ажу́) *pf*, **вознагражда́ть** *impf* reward. **вознагражде́ние** reward; fee.

возненави́деть (-и́жу) *pf* conceive a hatred for.

вознесе́ние Ascension. **вознести́** (-несу́, -несёшь; -нёс, -ла́) *pf* (*impf* **возноси́ть**) raise, lift up; **~сь** rise; ascend.

возника́ть *impf*, **возни́кнуть** (-нет; -ни́к) *pf* arise, spring up. **возникнове́ние** rise, beginning, origin.

возни́ца *m* coachman.

возноси́ть(ся (-ошу́(сь, -о́сишь(ся) *impf of* **вознести́(сь. возноше́ние** raising, elevation.

возня́ row, noise; bother.

возобнови́ть (-влю́) *pf*, **возобновля́ть** *impf* renew; restore; **~ся** begin again. **возобновле́ние** renewal; revival.

возража́ть *impf*, **возрази́ть** (-ажу́) *pf* object. **возраже́ние** objection.

во́зраст age. **возраста́ние** growth, increase. **возраста́ть** *impf*, **возрасти́** (-тёт; -ро́с, -ла́) *pf* grow, increase.

возроди́ть (-ожу́) *pf*, **возрожда́ть** *impf* revive; **~ся** revive. **возрожде́ние** revival; Renaissance.
возро́с *etc.*: *see* **возрасти́. возро́сший** increased.
во́зчик carter, carrier.
возьму́ *etc.*: *see* **взять**
во́ин warrior; soldier. **во́инск|ий** military; **~ая пови́нность** conscription. **во́инственный** warlike. **во́инствующий** militant.
вой howl(ing); wail(ing).
войду́ *etc.*: *see* **войти́**
во́йлок felt. **во́йлочный** felt.
война́ (*pl* -ы) war.
во́йско (*pl* -а́) army; *pl* troops, forces. **войсково́й** military.
войти́ (-йду́, -йдёшь; вошёл, -шла́) *pf* (*impf* **входи́ть**) go in, come in, enter; get in(to); **~ в систе́му** (*comput*) log on.
вокза́л (railway) station.
во́кмен Walkman (*propr*), personal stereo.
вокру́г *adv* & *prep*+*gen* round, around.
вол (-а́) ox, bullock.
вола́н flounce; shuttlecock.
волды́рь (-я́) *m* blister; bump.
волево́й strong-willed.
волейбо́л volleyball.
во́лей-нево́лей *adv* willy-nilly.
волк (*pl* -и, -о́в) wolf. **волкода́в** wolf-hound.
волна́ (*pl* -ы, во́лна́м) wave. **волне́ние** choppiness; agitation; emotion. **волни́стый** wavy. **волнова́ть** *impf* (*pf* **вз~**) disturb; agitate; excite; **~ся** be disturbed; worry, be nervous. **волноло́м, волноре́з** breakwater. **волну́ющий** disturbing; exciting.
волоки́та red tape; rigmarole.
волокни́стый fibrous, stringy. **волокно́** (*pl* -а) fibre.
волоку́ *etc.*: *see* **воло́чь**
во́лос (*pl* -ы, -о́с, -а́м); *pl* hair. **волоса́тый** hairy. **волосно́й** capillary.
во́лость (*pl* -и, -е́й) volost (*administrative division*).
волочи́ть (-очу́, -о́чишь) *impf* drag; **~ся** drag, trail; **+за+***instr* run after, court. **воло́чь** (-оку́, -очёшь; -о́к, -ла́) *impf* drag.
во́лчий wolf's; wolfish. **волчи́ха, волчи́ца** she-wolf.
волчо́к (-чка́) top; gyroscope.
волчо́нок (-нка; *pl* -ча́та, -ча́т) wolf cub.
волше́бник magician; wizard. **волше́бница** enchantress. **волше́бный** magic, magical; enchanting. **волшебство́** magic, enchantment.
вольнонаёмный civilian. **во́льность** liberty; license. **во́льный** (-лен, -льна́, -о, во́льны́) free; free-style.
вольт[1] (*gen pl* вольт) volt.
вольт[2] (*loc* -у́) vault.
вольфра́м tungsten.
во́ля will; liberty.
вомну́ *etc.*: *see* **вмять**
вон *adv* out; off, away.
вон *partl* there, over there.
вонза́ть *impf*, **вонзи́ть** (-нжу́) *pf* plunge, thrust.
вонь stench. **воню́чий** stinking. **воня́ть** stink.
вообража́емый imaginary. **вообража́ть** *impf*, **вообрази́ть** (-ажу́) *pf* imagine. **воображе́ние** imagination. **вообрази́мый** imaginable.
вообще́ *adv* in general; generally.
воодушеви́ть (-влю) *pf*, **воодушевля́ть** *impf* inspire. **воодушевле́ние** inspiration; fervour.
вооружа́ть *impf*, **вооружи́ть** (-жу́) *pf* arm, equip; **~ся** arm o.s.; take up arms. **вооруже́ние** arming; arms; equipment. **вооружённый** (-жён, -а́) armed; equipped.
воо́чию *adv* with one's own eyes.
во-пе́рвых *adv* first, first of all.
вопи́ть (-плю́) *impf* yell, howl. **вопию́щий** crying; scandalous.
воплоти́ть (-ощу́) *pf*, **воплоща́ть** *impf* embody. **воплоще́ние** embodiment.

вопль *m* cry, wail; howling.
вопреки́ *prep+dat* in spite of.
вопро́с question; problem. **вопроси́тельный** interrogative; questioning; ~ **знак** question-mark.
вор (*pl* -ы, -о́в) thief; criminal.
ворва́ться (-ву́сь, -вёшься; -а́лся, -ла́сь, -а́ло́сь) *pf* (*impf* **врыва́ться**) burst in.
воркотня́ grumbling.
воробе́й sparrow.
ворова́тый thievish; furtive. **ворова́ть** *impf* (*pf* **с~**) steal. **воро́вка** woman thief. **воровски́** *adv* furtively. **воровско́й** thieves'. **воровство́** stealing; theft.
во́рон raven. **воро́на** crow.
воро́нка funnel; crater.
вороно́й black.
во́рот[1] collar; neckband.
во́рот[2] winch; windlass.
воро́та (*pl*; *gen* -ро́т) gate(s); gateway; goal.
вороти́ть (-очу́, -о́тишь) *pf* bring back, get back; turn back; **~ся** return.
воротни́к (-а́) collar.
во́рох (*pl* -а́) heap, pile; heaps.
воро́чать *impf* turn; move; *+instr* have control of; **~ся** move, turn.
ворочу́(сь *etc.*: *see* **вороти́ть(ся**
вороши́ть (-шу́) *impf* stir up; turn (over).
ворс nap, pile.
ворча́ть (-чу́) *impf* grumble; growl. **ворчли́вый** peevish; grumpy.
восвоя́си *adv* home.
восемна́дцатый eighteenth. **восемна́дцать** eighteen. **во́семь** (-сьми́, *instr* -сьмью́ *or* -семью́) eight. **во́семьдесят** (-сьми́десяти, -сьмью́десятью) eighty. **восемьсо́т** (-сьмисо́т, -ста́ми) eight hundred. **во́семью** *adv* eight times.
воск wax, beeswax.
воскли́кнуть (-ну) *pf*, **восклица́ть** *impf* exclaim. **восклица́ние** exclamation. **восклица́тельный** exclamatory; ~ **знак** exclamation mark.
восково́й wax; waxy; waxed.
воскреса́ть *impf*, **воскре́снуть** (-ну; -е́с) *pf* rise from the dead; revive. **воскресе́ние** resurrection. **воскресе́нье** Sunday. **воскреси́ть** (-ешу́) *pf*, **воскреша́ть** *impf* resurrect; revive. **воскреше́ние** resurrection; revival.
воспале́ние inflammation. **воспалённый** (-лён, -а́) inflamed. **воспали́ть** *pf*, **воспаля́ть** *impf* inflame; **~ся** become inflamed.
воспита́ние upbringing, education. **воспи́танник, -ница** pupil. **воспи́танный** well-brought-up. **воспита́тель** *m* tutor; educator. **воспита́тельный** educational. **воспита́ть** *pf*, **воспи́тывать** *impf* bring up; foster; educate.
воспламени́ть *pf*, **воспламеня́ть** *impf* ignite; fire; **~ся** ignite; flare up. **воспламеня́емый** inflammable.
вос|по́льзоваться *pf*.
воспомина́ние recollection, memory; *pl* memoirs; reminiscences.
вос|препя́тствовать *pf*.
воспрети́ть (-ещу́) *pf*, **воспреща́ть** *impf* forbid. **воспреще́ние** prohibition. **воспрещённый** (-щён, -а́) prohibited.
восприи́мчивый impressionable; susceptible. **воспринима́ть** *impf*, **восприня́ть** (-иму́, -и́мешь; -и́нял, -а́, -о) *pf* perceive; grasp. **восприя́тие** perception.
воспроизведе́ние reproduction. **воспроизвести́** (-еду́, -едёшь; -вёл, -а́) *pf*, **воспроизводи́ть** (-ожу́, -о́дишь) *impf* reproduce. **воспроизводи́тельный** reproductive.
вос|проти́виться (-влюсь) *pf*.
воссоедине́ние reunification. **воссоедини́ть** *pf*, **воссоединя́ть** *impf* reunite.
восставáть (-таю́, -таёшь) *impf of* **восста́ть**.

В

восста́ние insurrection, uprising.
восстанови́ть (-влю́, -ви́шь) *pf* (*impf* **восстана́вливать**) restore; reinstate; recall; **~ про́тив**+*gen* set against. **восстановле́ние** restoration.
восста́ть (-а́ну) *pf* (*impf* **восстава́ть**) rise (up).
восто́к east.
восто́рг delight, rapture. **восторга́ться**+*instr* be delighted with, go into raptures over. **восто́рженный** enthusiastic.
восто́чный east, eastern; easterly; oriental.
востре́бование: до востре́бования to be called for, poste restante.
восхвали́ть (-лю́, -лишь) *pf*, **восхваля́ть** *impf* praise, extol.
восхити́тельный entrancing; delightful. **восхити́ть** (-хищу́) *pf*, **восхища́ть** *impf* enrapture; **~ся** +*instr* be enraptured by. **восхище́ние** delight; admiration.
восхо́д rising. **восходи́ть** (-ожу́, -о́дишь) *impf of* **взойти́; ~ к**+*dat* go back to, date from. **восхожде́ние** ascent. **восходя́щий** rising.
восше́ствие accession.
восьма́я *sb* eighth; octave. **восьмёрка** eight; figure eight; No. 8; figure of eight.
восьми- *in comb* eight-; octo-. **восьмигра́нник** octahedron. **~деся́тый** eightieth. **~ле́тний** eight-year; eight-year-old. **~со́тый** eight-hundredth. **~уго́льник** octagon. **~уго́льный** octagonal.
восьмо́й eighth.
вот *partl* here (is), there (is); this (is); **~ и всё** and that's all; **~ как!** no! really? **~ та́к!** that's right!; **~ что!** no! not really? **вот-во́т** *adv* just, on the point of; *partl* that's right!
воткну́ть (-ну́, -нёшь) *pf* (*impf* **втыка́ть**) stick in, drive in.
вотру́ *etc.*: *see* **вотре́ть**
воцари́ться *pf*, **воцаря́ться** *impf* come to the throne; set in.
вошёл *etc.*: *see* **войти́**
вошь (вши; *gen pl* вшей) louse.
вошью́ *etc.*: *see* **вшить**
во́ю *etc.*: *see* **выть**
вою́ю *etc.*: *see* **воева́ть**
впада́ть *impf*, **впасть** (-аду́) *pf* flow; lapse; fall in; +**в**+*acc* verge on, approximate to. **впаде́ние** confluence, (river-)mouth. **впа́дина** cavity, hollow; socket. **впа́лый** sunken.
впервы́е *adv* for the first time.
вперёд *adv* forward(s), ahead; in future; in advance; **идти́ ~** (*of clock*) be fast. **впереди́** *adv* in front, ahead; in (the) future; *prep*+*gen* in front of, before.
впечатле́ние impression. **впечатли́тельный** impressionable.
вписа́ть (-ишу́, -и́шешь) *pf*, **впи́сывать** *impf* enter, insert; **~ся** be enrolled, join.
впита́ть *pf*, **впи́тывать** *impf* absorb, take in; **~ся** soak.
впи́хивать *impf*, **впи́хнуть** (-ну́, -нёшь) *pf* cram in; shove.
вплавь *adv* (by) swimming.
вплести́ (-ету́, -етёшь; -ёл, -а́) *pf*, **вплета́ть** *impf* plait in, intertwine; involve.
вплотну́ю *adv* close; in earnest. **вплоть** *adv*; **~ до**+*gen* (right) up to.
вполго́лоса *adv* under one's breath.
вполне́ *adv* fully, entirely; quite.
впопыха́х *adv* hastily; in one's haste.
впо́ру *adv* at the right time; just right, exactly.
впосле́дствии *adv* subsequently.
впотьма́х *adv* in the dark.
впра́ве *adv*: **быть ~** have a right.
впра́во *adv* to the right (**от**+*gen* of).
впредь *adv* in (the) future; **~ до**+*gen* until.
впро́голодь *adv* half starving.
впро́чем *conj* however, but; though.

впры́скивание injection. **впры́скивать** *impf*, **впры́снуть** (-ну) *pf* inject.
впряга́ть *impf* **впрячь** (-ягу́, -яжёшь; -яг, -ла́) *pf* harness.
впуск admittance. **впуска́ть** *impf*, **впусти́ть** (-ущу́, -у́стишь) *pf* admit, let in.
впусту́ю *adv* to no purpose, in vain.
впущу́ *etc.*: *see* **впусти́ть**
враг (-а́) enemy. **вражда́** enmity. **вражде́бный** hostile. **враждова́ть** be at enmity. **вра́жеский** enemy.
вразбро́д *adv* separately, disunitedly.
вразре́з *adv*: **идти́ ~ с**+*instr* go against.
вразуми́тельный intelligible, clear; persuasive.
врасплóх *adv* unawares.
враста́ть *impf*, **врасти́** (-тёт; врос, -ла́) *pf* grow in; take root.
врата́рь (-я́) *m* goalkeeper.
врать (вру, врёшь; -ал, -а́, -о) *impf* (*pf* **на~, со~**) lie, tell lies; talk nonsense.
врач (-а́) doctor. **враче́бный** medical.
враща́ть *impf* rotate, revolve; **~ся** revolve, rotate. **враще́ние** rotation, revolution.
вред (-а́) harm; damage. **вреди́тель** *m* pest; wrecker; *pl* vermin. **вреди́тельство** wrecking, (act of) sabotage. **вреди́ть** (-ежу́) *impf* (*pf* **по~**) +*dat* harm; damage. **вре́дный** (-ден, -дна́, -о) harmful.
вре́зать (-е́жу) *pf*, **вреза́ть** *impf* cut in; set in; (*sl*) +*dat* hit; **~ся** cut (into); run (into); be engraved; fall in love.
времена́ми *adv* at times. **вре́менно** *adv* temporarily. **временно́й** temporal. **вре́менный** temporary; provisional. **вре́мя** (-мени; *pl* -мена́, -мён, -а́м) *neut* time; tense; **~ го́да** season; **~ от вре́мени** at times, from time to time; **на ~** for a time; **ско́лько вре́мени?** what is the time?; **тем вре́менем** meanwhile.
вро́вень *adv* level, on a level.
вро́де *prep+gen* like; *partl* such as, like; apparently.
врождённый (-дён, -а́) innate.
врозь, врозь *adv* separately, apart.
врос *etc.*: *see* **врасти́. вру** *etc.*: *see* **врать**
врун (-а́), **вру́нья** liar.
вруча́ть *impf*, **вручи́ть** (-чу́) *pf* hand, deliver; entrust.
вручну́ю *adv* by hand.
врыва́ть(ся *impf of* **ворва́ться**
вряд (ли) *adv* it's not likely; hardly, scarcely.
всади́ть (-ажу́, -а́дишь) *pf*, **вса́живать** *impf* thrust in; sink in. **вса́дник** rider, horseman. **вса́дница** rider, horsewoman.
вса́сывать *impf of* **всоса́ть**
всё, все *pron*: *see* **весь. всё** *adv* always, all the time; **~ (ещё)** still; *conj* however, nevertheless; **~ же** all the same.
все- *in comb* all-, omni-. **всевозмо́жный** of every kind; all possible. **~дозво́ленность** permissiveness. **~ме́рный** of every kind. **~ми́рный** world, worldwide; **Всеми́рная паути́на** the (world-wide) Web; **~могу́щий** omnipotent. **~наро́дно** *adv* publicly. **~наро́дный** national; nation-wide. **~объе́млющий** comprehensive, all-embracing. **~росси́йский** All-Russian. **~си́льный** omnipotent. **~сторо́нний** all-round; comprehensive.
всегда́ always.
всего́ *adv* in all, all told; only.
вселе́нная *sb* universe.
всели́ть *pf*, **вселя́ть** *impf* install, lodge; inspire; **~ся** move in, install o.s.; be implanted.
все́нощная *sb* night service.
всео́бщий general, universal.
всерьёз *adv* seriously, in earnest.
всё-таки *conj & partl* all the same,

still. **всецéло** *adv* completely.
вска́кивать *impf of* **вскочи́ть**
вскачь *adv* at a gallop.
вскипа́ть *impf*, **вс|кипéть** (-плю́) *pf* boil up; flare up.
вс|кипяти́ть(ся (-ячу́(сь) *pf*.
всколыхну́ть (-ну́, -нёшь) *pf* stir; stir up.
вскользь *adv* slightly; in passing.
вскóре *adv* soon, shortly after.
вскочи́ть (-очу́, -óчишь) *pf* (*impf* **вска́кивать**) jump up.
вскри́кивать *impf*, **вскри́кнуть** (-ну) *pf* shriek, scream. **вскрича́ть** (-чу́) *pf* exclaim.
вскрыва́ть *impf*, **вскрыть** (-рóю) *pf* open; reveal; dissect. **вскры́тие** opening; revelation; post-mortem.
вслед *adv* & *prep+dat* after; ~ **за** +*instr* after, following. **вслéдствие** *prep+gen* in consequence of.
вслепу́ю *adv* blindly; blindfold.
вслух *adv* aloud.
вслу́шаться *pf*, **вслу́шиваться** *impf* listen attentively.
всма́триваться *impf*, **всмотрéться** (-рю́сь, -ришься) *pf* look closely.
всмя́тку *adv* soft(-boiled).
всóвывать *impf of* **всу́нуть**
всоса́ть (-су́, -сёшь) *pf* (*impf* **всáсывать**) suck in; absorb; imbibe.
вс|паха́ть (-ашу́, -а́шешь) *pf*, **вспа́хивать** *impf* plough up. **вспа́шка** ploughing.
вс|пéниться *pf*.
всплеск splash. **всплёскивать** *impf*, **всплесну́ть** (-ну́, -нёшь) *pf* splash; ~ **рука́ми** throw up one's hands.
всплыва́ть *impf*, **всплыть** (-ыву́, -ывёшь; -ыл, -á, -о) *pf* rise to the surface; come to light.
вспомина́ть *impf*, **вспóмнить** *pf* remember; ~**ся** *impers +dat*: **мне вспóмнилось** I remembered.
вспомога́тельный auxiliary.
вс|потéть *pf*.
вспры́гивать *impf*, **вспры́гнуть** (-ну) *pf* jump up.
вспуха́ть *impf*, **вс|пу́хнуть** (-нет; -ух) *pf* swell up.
вспыли́ть *pf* flare up. **вспы́льчивый** hot-tempered.
вспы́хивать *impf*, **вспы́хнуть** (-ну) *pf* blaze up; flare up. **вспы́шка** flash; outburst; outbreak.
встава́ть (-таю́, -таёшь) *impf of* **встать**
вста́вить (-влю) *pf*, **вставля́ть** *impf* put in, insert. **вста́вка** insertion; framing, mounting; inset. **вставн|óй** inserted; set in; ~**ы́е зу́бы** false teeth.
встать (-а́ну) *pf* (*impf* **встава́ть**) get up; stand up.
встревóженный *adj* anxious.
вс|тревóжить (-жу) *pf*.
встрепену́ться (-ну́сь, -нёшься) *pf* rouse o.s.; start (up); beat faster.
встрéтить (-éчу) *pf*, **встреча́ть** *impf* meet (with); ~**ся** meet; be found. **встрéча** meeting. **встрéчный** coming to meet; contrary, head; counter; *sb* person met with; **пéрвый** ~ the first person you meet, anybody.
встря́ска shaking; shock. **встря́хивать** *impf*, **встряхну́ть** (-ну́, -нёшь) *pf* shake (up); rouse; ~**ся** shake o.s.; rouse o.s.
вступа́ть *impf*, **вступи́ть** (-плю́, -пишь) *pf* +**в**+*acc* enter (into); join (in); +**на**+*acc* go up, mount; ~**ся** intervene; +**за**+*acc* stand up for. **вступи́тельный** introductory; entrance. **вступлéние** entry, joining; introduction.
всу́нуть (-ну) *pf* (*impf* **всóвывать**) put in, stick in.
всхли́пнуть (-ну) *pf*, **всхли́пывать** *impf* sob.
всходи́ть (-ожу́, -óдишь) *impf of* **взойти́**. **всхóды** (*pl*; *gen* -ов) (corn-)shoots.
всю: *see* **весь**
всю́ду *adv* everywhere.
вся: *see* **весь**
вся́к|ий any; every, all kinds of; ~**ом слу́чае** in any case; **на** ~**ий**

слу́чай just in case; *pron* anyone. **вся́чески** *adv* in every possible way.
вта́йне *adv* secretly.
вта́лкивать *impf of* **втолкну́ть**. **вта́птывать** *impf of* **втопта́ть**. **вта́скивать** *impf*, **втащи́ть** (-щу́, -щишь) *pf* drag in.
втере́ть (вотру́, вотрёшь; втёр) *pf* (*impf* **втира́ть**) rub in; **~ся** insinuate o.s., worm o.s.
втира́ть(ся *impf of* **втере́ть(ся**
вти́скивать *impf*, **вти́снуть** (-ну) *pf* squeeze in; **~ся** squeeze (o.s.) in.
втихомо́лку *adv* surreptitiously.
втолкну́ть (-ну́, -нёшь) *pf* (*impf* **вта́лкивать**) push in.
втопта́ть (-пчу́, -пчешь) *pf* (*impf* **вта́птывать**) trample (in).
вторга́ться *impf*, **вто́ргнуться** (-нусь; вто́ргся, -лась) *pf* invade; intrude. **вторже́ние** invasion; intrusion.
вто́рить *impf* play or sing second part; *+dat* repeat, echo. **втори́чный** second, secondary. **вто́рник** Tuesday. **втор|о́й** second; **~о́е** *sb* second course. **второстепе́нный** secondary, minor.
второпя́х *adv* in haste.
в-тре́тьих *adv* thirdly. **втро́е** *adv* three times. **втроём** *adv* three (together). **втройне́** *adv* three times as much.
вту́лка plug.
втыка́ть *impf of* **воткну́ть**
втя́гивать *impf*, **втяну́ть** (-ну́, -нешь) *pf* draw in; **~ся** +в+*acc* enter; get used to.
вуа́ль veil.
вуз *abbr* (*of* **вы́сшее учёбное заведе́ние**) higher educational establishment; college.
вулка́н volcano.
вульга́рный vulgar.
вундерки́нд infant prodigy.
вход entrance; entry. **входи́ть** (-ожу́, -о́дишь) *impf of* **войти́**. **входно́й** entrance.
вхолосту́ю *adv* idle, free.
вцепи́ться (-плю́сь, -пишься) *pf*, **вцепля́ться** *impf* +в+*acc* clutch, catch hold of.
вчера́ *adv* yesterday. **вчера́шний** yesterday's.
вчерне́ in rough.
вчё́тверо *adv* four times. **вчетверо́м** *adv* four (together).
вши *etc*.: *see* **вошь**
вшива́ть *impf of* **вшить**
вши́вый lousy.
вширь *adv* in breadth; widely.
вшить (вошью́, -ьёшь) *pf* (*impf* **вшива́ть**) sew in.
въе́дливый corrosive; caustic.
въезд entry; entrance. **въезжа́ть** *impf*, **въе́хать** (-е́ду, -е́дешь) *pf* (+в+*acc*) ride in(to); drive in(to); crash into.
вы (вас, вам, ва́ми, вас) *pron* you.
выбега́ть *impf*, **вы́бежать** (-егу, -ежишь) *pf* run out.
вы́|белить *pf*.
вы́беру *etc*.: *see* **вы́брать. выбива́ть(ся** *impf of* **вы́бить(ся. выбира́ть(ся** *impf of* **вы́брать(ся**
вы́бить (-бью) *pf* (*impf* **выбива́ть**) knock out; dislodge; **~ся** get out; break loose; come out; **~ся из сил** exhaust o.s.
вы́бор choice; selection; *pl* election(s). **вы́борный** elective; electoral. **вы́борочный** selective.
вы́|бранить *pf*. **выбра́сывать(ся** *impf of* **вы́бросить(ся**
вы́брать (-беру) *pf* (*impf* **выбира́ть**) choose; elect; take out; **~ся** get out.
выбрива́ть *impf*, **вы́брить** (-рею) *pf* shave.
вы́бросить (-ошу) *pf* (*impf* **выбра́сывать**) throw out; throw away; **~ся** throw o.s. out, leap out.
выбыва́ть *impf*, **вы́быть** (-буду) *pf* **из**+*gen* leave, quit.
выва́ливать *impf*, **вы́валить** *pf* throw out; pour out; **~ся** tumble out.
вы́везти (-зу; -ез) *pf* (*impf* **вывози́ть**) take, bring, out; export; rescue.

вы́верить *pf* (*impf* **выверя́ть**) adjust, regulate.
вы́вернуть (-ну) *pf*, **вывёртывать** *impf* turn inside out; unscrew; wrench.
выверя́ть *impf of* **вы́верить**
вы́весить (-ешу) *pf* (*impf* **выве́шивать**) weigh; hang out. **вы́веска** sign; pretext.
вы́вести (-еду; -ел) *pf* (*impf* **выводи́ть**) lead, bring, take, out; drive out; remove; exterminate; deduce; hatch; grow, breed; erect; depict; draw; **~сь** go out of use; become extinct; come out; hatch out.
выве́тривание airing.
выве́шивать *impf of* **вы́весить**
вы́вих dislocation. **выви́хивать** *impf*, **вы́вихнуть** (-ну) *pf* dislocate.
вы́вод conclusion; withdrawal. **выводи́ть(ся** (-ожу́(сь, -о́дишь(ся) *impf of* **вы́вести(сь. вы́водок** (-дка) brood; litter.
вывожу́ *see* **выводи́ть, вывози́ть**
вы́воз export; removal. **вывози́ть** (-ожу́, -о́зишь) *impf of* **вы́везти. вывозно́й** export.
вы́гадать *pf*, **выга́дывать** *impf* gain, save.
вы́гиб curve. **выгиба́ть** *impf of* **вы́гнуть**
вы́|гладить (-ажу) *pf*.
вы́глядеть (-яжу) *impf* look, look like. **выгля́дывать** *impf*, **вы́глянуть** (-ну) *pf* look out; peep out.
вы́гнать (-гоню) *pf* (*impf* **выгоня́ть**) drive out; distil.
вы́гнутый curved, convex. **вы́гнуть** (-ну) *pf* (*impf* **выгиба́ть**) bend, arch.
выгова́ривать *impf*, **вы́говорить** *pf* pronounce, speak; *+dat* reprimand; **~ся** speak out. **вы́говор** pronunciation; reprimand.
вы́года advantage; gain. **вы́годный** advantageous; profitable.
вы́гон pasture; common. **выгоня́ть** *impf of* **вы́гнать**
выгора́ть *impf*, **вы́гореть** (-рит) *pf* burn down; fade.
вы́|гравировать *pf*.
выгружа́ть *impf*, **вы́грузить** (-ужу) *pf* unload; disembark. **вы́грузка** unloading; disembarkation.
выдава́ть (-даю́, -даёшь) *impf*, **вы́дать** (-ам, -ашь, -аст, -адим) *pf* give (out), issue; betray; extradite; +**за**+*acc* pass off as; **~ся** protrude; stand out; present itself. **вы́дача** issue; payment; extradition. **выдаю́щийся** prominent.
выдвига́ть *impf*, **вы́двинуть** (-ну) *pf* move out; pull out; put forward, nominate; **~ся** move forward, move out; come out; get on (in the world). **выдвиже́ние** nomination; promotion.
выделе́ние secretion; excretion; isolation; apportionment. **вы́делить** *pf*, **выделя́ть** *impf* pick out; detach; allot; secrete; excrete; isolate; **~ курси́вом** italicize; **~ся** stand out, be noted (*+instr* for).
выдёргивать *impf of* **вы́дернуть**
вы́держанный consistent; self-possessed; firm; matured, seasoned. **вы́держать** (-жу) *pf*, **выде́рживать** *impf* bear; endure; contain o.s.; pass (*exam*); sustain. **вы́держка**[1] endurance; self-possession; exposure.
вы́держка[2] excerpt.
вы́дернуть *pf* (*impf* **выдёргивать**) pull out.
вы́дохнуть (-ну) *pf* (*impf* **выдыха́ть**) breathe out; **~ся** have lost fragrance or smell; be past one's best.
вы́дра otter.
вы́|драть (-деру) *pf*. **вы́|дрессировать** *pf*.
выдува́ть *impf of* **вы́дуть**
вы́думанный made-up, fabricated. **вы́думать** *pf*, **выду́мывать** *impf* invent; fabricate. **вы́думка** invention; device; inventiveness.
вы́дуть *pf* (*impf* **выдува́ть**) blow; blow out.
выдыха́ние exhalation. **выды-**

ха́ть(ся *impf of* **вы́дохнуть(ся**

вы́езд departure; exit. **выездн|о́й** exit; **~ая се́ссия суда́** assizes. **вы-езжа́ть** *impf of* **вы́ехать**

вы́емка taking out; excavation; hollow.

вы́ехать (-еду) *pf* (*impf* **выезжа́ть**) go out, depart; drive out, ride out; move (house).

вы́жать (-жму, -жмешь) *pf* (*impf* **выжима́ть**) squeeze out; wring out.

вы́жечь (-жгу) *pf* (*impf* **выжига́ть**) burn out; cauterize.

выжива́ние survival. **выжива́ть** *impf of* **вы́жить**

выжига́ть *impf of* **вы́жечь**

выжида́тельный waiting; temporizing.

выжима́ть *impf of* **вы́жать**

вы́жить (-иву) *pf* (*impf* **выжива́ть**) survive; hound out; **~ из ума́** become senile.

вы́звать (-зову) *pf* (*impf* **вызыва́ть**) call (out); send for; challenge; provoke; **~ся** volunteer.

выздора́вливать *impf*, **вы́здороветь** (-ею) *pf* recover. **выздоровле́ние** recovery; convalescence.

вы́зов call; summons; challenge.

вы́золоченный gilt.

вызу́бривать *impf*, **вы́|зубрить** *pf* learn by heart.

вызыва́ть(ся *impf of* **вы́звать(ся. вызыва́ющий** defiant; provocative.

вы́играть *pf*, **выи́грывать** *impf* win; gain. **вы́игрыш** win; gain; prize. **вы́игрышный** winning; advantageous.

вы́йти (-йду; -шел, -шла) *pf* (*impf* **выходи́ть**) go out; come out; get out; appear; turn out; be used up; have expired; **~ в свет** appear; **~ за́муж (за**+*acc*) marry; **~ из себя́** lose one's temper; **~ из систе́му** (*comput*) log off.

выка́лывать *impf of* **вы́колоть. выка́пывать** *impf of* **вы́копать**

выка́рмливать *impf of* **вы́кормить**

вы́качать *pf*, **выка́чивать** *impf* pump out.

выки́дывать *impf*, **вы́кинуть** *pf* throw out, reject; put out; miscarry, abort; **~ флаг** hoist a flag. **вы́кидыш** miscarriage, abortion.

вы́кладка laying out; lay-out; facing; kit; computation, calculation. **выкла́дывать** *impf of* **вы́ложить**

выключа́тель *m* switch. **выключа́ть** *impf*, **вы́ключить** (-чу) *pf* turn off, switch off; remove, exclude.

выкола́чивать *impf*, **вы́колотить** (-лочу) *pf* knock out, beat out; beat; extort, wring out.

вы́колоть (-лю) *pf* (*impf* **выка́лывать**) put out; gouge out; tattoo.

вы́|копать *pf* (*impf also* **выка́пывать**) dig; dig up, dig out; exhume; unearth.

вы́кормить (-млю) *pf* (*impf* **выка́рмливать**) rear, bring up.

вы́корчевать (-чую) *pf*, **выкорчёвывать** *impf* uproot, root out; eradicate.

выкра́ивать *impf of* **вы́кроить**

вы́|красить (-ашу) *pf*, **выкра́шивать** *impf* paint; dye.

выкри́кивать *impf*, **вы́крикнуть** (-ну) *pf* cry out; yell.

вы́кроить *pf* (*impf* **выкра́ивать**) cut out; find (*time etc.*). **вы́кройка** pattern.

вы́крутить (-учу) *pf*, **выкру́чивать** *impf* unscrew; twist; **~ся** extricate o.s.

вы́куп ransom; redemption.

вы́|купать[1]**(ся** *pf*.

выкупа́ть[2] *impf*, **вы́купить** (-плю) *pf* ransom, redeem.

вы́лазка sally, sortie; excursion.

выла́мывать *impf of* **вы́ломать**

вылеза́ть *impf*, **вы́лезти** (-зу; -лез) *pf* climb out; come out.

вы́|лепить (-плю) *pf*.

вы́лет flight; take-off. **вылета́ть** *impf*, **вы́лететь** (-ечу) *pf* fly out; take off.

выле́чивать *impf*, **вы́лечить**

В

(-чу) *pf* cure; **~ся** recover, be cured.
вылива́ть(ся *pf of* **вы́лить(ся**
вы́|линять *pf.*
вы́лить (-лью) *pf* (*impf* **вылива́ть**) pour out; cast, found; **~ся** flow (out); be expressed.
вы́ложить (-жу) *pf* (*impf* **выкла́дывать**) lay out.
вы́ломать *pf*, **вы́ломить** (-млю) *pf* (*impf* **выла́мывать**) break open.
вы́лупиться (-плюсь) *pf*, **вылупля́ться** *impf* hatch (out).
вы́лью *etc.*: *see* **вы́лить**
вы́|мазать (-мажу) *pf*, **выма́зывать** *impf* smear, dirty.
выма́нивать *impf*, **вы́манить** *pf* entice, lure.
вы́мереть (-мрет; -мер) *pf* (*impf* **вымира́ть**) die out; become extinct. **вы́мерший** extinct.
вы́мести (-ету) *pf*, **вы́метать** *impf* sweep (out).
вымога́тельство blackmail, extortion. **вымога́ть** *impf* extort.
вымока́ть *impf*, **вы́мокнуть** (-ну; -ок) *pf* be drenched; soak; rot.
вы́молвить (-влю) *pf* say, utter.
вы́|мостить (-ощу) *pf.* **вы́мою** *etc.*: *see* **вы́мыть**
вы́мпел pennant.
вы́мрет *see* **вы́мереть. вымыва́ть(ся** *impf of* **вы́мыть(ся**
вы́мысел (-сла) invention, fabrication; fantasy.
вы́|мыть (-мою) *pf* (*impf also* **вымыва́ть**) wash; wash out, off; wash away; **~ся** wash o.s.
вы́мышленный fictitious.
вы́мя (-мени) *neut* udder.
вына́шивать *impf of* **вы́носить²**
вы́нести (-су; -нес) *pf* (*impf* **выноси́ть¹**) carry out, take out; carry away; endure.
вынима́ть *impf of* **вы́нуть**
вы́нос carrying out. **выноси́ть¹** (-ошу́, -о́сишь) *impf of* **вы́нести. вы́носить²** *pf* (*impf* **вына́шивать**) bear; nurture. **вы́носка** carrying out; removal; footnote.
выно́сливость endurance; hardiness.
вы́нудить (-ужу) *pf*, **вынужда́ть** *impf* force, compel. **вы́нужденный** forced.
вы́нуть (-ну) *pf* (*impf* **вынима́ть**) take out.
вы́пад attack; lunge. **выпада́ть** *impf of* **вы́пасть**
выпа́лывать *impf of* **вы́полоть**
выпа́ривать *impf*, **вы́парить** evaporate; steam.
выпа́рывать *impf of* **вы́пороть²**
вы́пасть (-аду; -ал) *pf* (*impf* **выпада́ть**) fall out; fall; occur, turn out; lunge.
выпека́ть *impf*, **вы́печь** (-еку; -ек) *pf* bake.
выпива́ть *impf of* **вы́пить**; enjoy a drink. **вы́пивка** drinking bout; drinks.
выпи́ливать *impf*, **вы́пилить** *pf* saw, cut out.
вы́писать (-ишу) *pf*, **выпи́сывать** *impf* copy out; write out; order; subscribe to; send for; discharge, release; **~ся** be discharged; check out. **вы́писка** writing out; extract; ordering, subscription; discharge.
вы́|пить (-пью) *pf* (*impf also* **выпива́ть**) drink; drink up.
вы́плавить (-влю) *pf*, **выплавля́ть** *impf* smelt. **вы́плавка** smelting; smelted metal.
вы́плата payment. **вы́платить** (-ачу) *pf*, **выпла́чивать** *impf* pay (out); pay off.
выплёвывать *impf of* **вы́плюнуть**
выплыва́ть *impf*, **вы́плыть** (-ыву) *pf* swim out, sail out; emerge; crop up.
вы́плюнуть (-ну) *pf* (*impf* **выплёвывать**) spit out.
выполза́ть *impf*, **вы́ползти** (-зу; -олз) *pf* crawl out.
выполне́ние execution, carrying out; fulfilment. **вы́полнить** *pf*, **выполня́ть** *impf* execute, carry out; fulfil.

вы́|полоскать (-ощу) *pf.*
вы́|полоть (-лю) *pf* (*impf also* **выпа́лывать**) weed out; weed.
вы́|пороть[1] (-рю) *pf.*
вы́пороть[2] (-рю) *pf* (*impf* **выпа́рывать**) rip out, rip up.
вы́|потрошить (-шу) *pf.*
вы́правка bearing; correction.
выпра́шивать *impf of* **вы́просить**; solicit.
выпрова́живать *impf*, **вы́проводить** (-ожу) *pf* send packing.
вы́просить (-ошу) *pf* (*impf* **выпра́шивать**) (ask for and) get.
выпряга́ть *impf of* **вы́прячь**
вы́прямить (-млю) *pf*, **выпрямля́ть** *impf* straighten (out); rectify; **~ся** become straight; draw o.s. up.
вы́прячь (-ягу; -яг) *pf* (*impf* **выпряга́ть**) unharness.
вы́пуклый protuberant; bulging; convex.
вы́пуск output; issue; discharge; part, instalment; final-year students; omission. **выпуска́ть** *impf*, **вы́пустить** (-ущу) *pf* let out; issue; produce; omit. **выпускни́к** (-а́), **-и́ца** final-year student. **выпускн|о́й** discharge; exhaust; **~о́й экза́мен** finals, final examination.
вы́путать *pf*, **выпу́тывать** *impf* disentangle; **~ся** extricate o.s.
вы́пью *etc.*: *see* **вы́пить**
выраба́тывать *impf*, **вы́работать** *pf* work out; work up; draw up; produce, make; earn. **вы́работка** manufacture; production; working out; drawing up; output; make.
выра́внивать(ся *impf of* **вы́ровнять(ся**
выража́ть *impf*, **вы́разить** (-ажу) *pf* express; **~ся** express o.s. **выраже́ние** expression. **вырази́тельный** expressive.
выраста́ть *impf*, **вы́расти** (-ту; -рос) *pf* grow, grow up. **вы́растить** (-ащу) *pf*, **выра́щивать** *impf* bring up; breed; cultivate.
вы́рвать[1] (-ву) *pf* (*impf* **вырыва́ть**[2]) pull out, tear out; extort; **~ся** break loose, break free; escape; shoot.
вы́|рвать[2] (-ву) *pf.*
вы́рез cut; décolletage. **вы́резать** (-ежу) *pf*, **выреза́ть** *impf*, **выре́зывать** *impf* cut (out); engrave. **вы́резка** cutting out, excision; cutting; fillet.
вы́ровнять *pf* (*impf* **выра́внивать**) level; straighten (out); draw up; **~ся** become level; equalize; catch up.
вы́родиться *pf*, **вырожда́ться** *impf* degenerate. **вы́родок** (-дка) degenerate; black sheep. **вырожде́ние** degeneration.
вы́ронить *pf* drop.
вы́рос *etc.*: *see* **вы́расти**
вы́рою *etc.*: *see* **вы́рыть**
выруба́ть *impf*, **вы́рубить** (-блю) *pf* cut down; cut (out); carve (out). **вы́рубка** cutting down; hewing out.
вы́|ругать(ся *pf.*
выру́ливать *impf*, **вы́|рулить** *pf* taxi.
выруча́ть *impf*, **вы́ручить** (-чу) *pf* rescue; help out; gain; make. **вы́ручка** rescue; gain; proceeds; earnings.
вырыва́ть[1] *impf*, **вы́|рыть** (-рою) *pf* dig up, unearth.
вырыва́ть[2](**ся** *impf of* **вы́рвать(ся**
вы́садить (-ажу) *pf*, **выса́живать** *impf* set down; put ashore; transplant; smash; **~ся** alight; disembark. **вы́садка** disembarkation; landing; transplanting.
выса́сывать *impf of* **вы́сосать**
вы́свободить (-божу) *pf*, **высвобожда́ть** *impf* free; release.
высека́ть *impf of* **вы́сечь**[2]
выселе́ние eviction. **вы́селить** *pf*, **выселя́ть** *impf* evict; evacuate, move; **~ся** move, remove.
вы́|сечь[1] (-еку; -сек) *pf.* **вы́сечь**[2] (-еку; -сек) (*impf* **высека́ть**) cut (out); carve.

вы́сидеть (-ижу) *pf*, **выси́живать** *impf* sit out; stay; hatch.
вы́ситься *impf* rise, tower.
выска́бливать *impf of* **вы́скоблить**
вы́сказать (-кажу) *pf*, **выска́зывать** *impf* express; state; **~ся** speak out. **выска́зывание** utterance; pronouncement.
выска́кивать *impf of* **вы́скочить**
вы́скоблить *pf* (*impf* **выска́бливать**) scrape out; erase; remove.
вы́скочить (-чу) *pf* (*impf* **выска́кивать**) jump out; spring out; **~ с**+*instr* come out with. **вы́скочка** upstart.
вы́слать (вы́шлю) *pf* (*impf* **высыла́ть**) send (out); exile; deport.
вы́следить (-ежу) *pf*, **высле́живать** *impf* trace; shadow.
выслу́живать *impf*, **вы́служить** (-жу) *pf* qualify for; serve (out); **~ся** gain promotion; curry favour.
вы́слушать *pf*, **выслу́шивать** *impf* hear out; sound; listen to.
высме́ивать *impf*, **вы́смеять** (-ею) *pf* ridicule.
вы́|сморкать(ся *pf*. **высо́вывать(ся** *impf of* **вы́сунуть(ся**
высо́кий (-о́к, -а́, -о́ко́) high; tall; lofty; elevated.
высоко- *in comb* high-, highly. **высокоблагоро́дие** (your) Honour, Worship. **~во́льтный** high-tension. **~го́рный** mountain. **~ка́чественный** high-quality. **~квалифици́рованный** highly qualified. **~ме́рие** haughtiness. **~ме́рный** haughty. **~па́рный** high-flown; bombastic. **~часто́тный** high-frequency.
вы́сосать (-осу) *pf* (*impf* **выса́сывать**) suck out.
высота́ (*pl* -ы) height, altitude. **высо́тный** high-altitude; high-rise.
вы́|сохнуть (-ну; -ох) *pf* (*impf also* **высыха́ть**) dry (out); dry up; wither (away).
вы́спаться (-плюсь, -пишься) *pf* (*impf* **высыпа́ться**²) have a good sleep.
вы́ставить (-влю) *pf*, **выставля́ть** *impf* display, exhibit; post; put forward; set down; take out; +*instr* represent as; **~ся** show off. **вы́ставка** exhibition.
выста́ивать *impf of* **вы́стоять**
вы́|стегать *pf*. **вы́|стирать** *pf*.
вы́стоять (-ою) *pf* (*impf* **выста́ивать**) stand; stand one's ground.
вы́страдать *pf* suffer; gain through suffering.
выстра́ивать(ся *impf of* **вы́строить(ся**
вы́стрел shot; report. **вы́стрелить** *pf* shoot, fire.
вы́|строгать *pf*.
вы́строить *pf* (*impf* **выстра́ивать**) build; draw up, order, arrange; form up. **~ся** form up.
вы́ступ protuberance, projection. **выступа́ть** *impf*, **вы́ступить** (-плю) *pf* come forward; come out; perform; speak; +**из**+*gen* go beyond. **выступле́ние** appearance, performance; speech; setting out.
вы́сунуть (-ну) *pf* (*impf* **высо́вывать**) put out, thrust out; **~ся** show o.s., thrust o.s. forward.
вы́|сушить(ся (-шу(сь) *pf*.
вы́сший highest; high; higher.
высыла́ть *impf of* **вы́слать**. **вы́сылка** sending, dispatch; expulsion, exile.
вы́сыпать (-плю) *pf*, **высыпа́ть** *impf* pour out; spill; **~ся**¹ pour out; spill.
высыпа́ться² *impf of* **вы́спаться**
высыха́ть *impf of* **вы́сохнуть**
высь height; summit.
выта́лкивать *impf of* **вы́толкать, вы́толкнуть**. **выта́скивать** *impf of* **вы́тащить**. **выта́чивать** *impf of* **вы́точить**
вы́|тащить (-щу) *pf* (*impf also* **выта́скивать**) drag out; pull out.
вы́|твердить (-ржу) *pf*.
вытека́ть *impf* (*pf* **вы́течь**); **~ из**+*gen* flow from, out of; result from.

вы́тереть (-тру; -тер) *pf* (*impf* **вытира́ть**) wipe (up); dry; wear out.
вы́терпеть (-плю) *pf* endure.
вы́тертый threadbare.
вы́теснить *pf*, **вытесня́ть** *impf* force out; oust; displace.
вы́течь (-чет; -ек) *pf* (*impf* **вытека́ть**) flow out, run out.
вытира́ть *impf of* **вы́тереть**
вы́толкать *pf*, **вы́толкнуть** (-ну) *pf* (*impf* **выта́лкивать**) throw out; push out.
вы́точенный turned. **вы́|точить** (-чу) *pf* (*impf also* **выта́чивать**) turn; sharpen; gnaw through.
вы́|травить (-влю) *pf*, **вытра́вливать** *impf*, **вытравля́ть** *impf* exterminate, destroy; remove; etch; trample down, damage.
вытрезви́тель *m* detoxification centre. **вы́трезвить(ся** (-влю(сь) *pf*, **вытрезвля́ть(ся** *impf* sober up.
вы́тру *etc.*: *see* **вы́тереть**
вы́|трясти (-су; -яс) *pf* shake out.
вытря́хивать *impf*, **вы́тряхнуть** (-ну) *pf* shake out.
выть (во́ю) *impf* howl; wail.
вытя́гивать *impf*, **вы́тянуть** (-ну) *pf* stretch (out); extend; extract; endure; **~ся** stretch, stretch out, stretch o.s.; shoot up; draw o.s. up. **вы́тяжка** drawing out, extraction; extract.
вы́|утюжить (-жу) *pf.*
выу́чивать *impf*, **вы́|учить** (-чу) *pf* learn; teach; **~ся** +*dat or inf* learn.
выха́живать *impf of* **вы́ходить²**
вы́хватить (-ачу) *pf*, **выхва́тывать** *impf* snatch out, up, away; pull out.
вы́хлоп exhaust. **выхлопно́й** exhaust, discharge.
вы́ход going out; departure; way out, exit; vent; appearance; yield; **~ за́муж** marriage. **вы́ходец** (-дца) emigrant; immigrant. **выходи́ть¹** (-ожу́, -о́дишь) *impf of* **вы́йти**; +**на**+*acc* look out on.
вы́ходить² (-ожу) *pf* (*impf* **выха́живать**) nurse; rear, bring up.
вы́ходка trick; prank.
выходн|о́й exit; going-out, outgoing; discharge; **~о́й день** day off; **~о́й** *sb* person off duty; day off. **выхожу́** *etc.*: *see* **выходи́ть¹**. **вы́хожу** *etc.*: *see* **вы́ходить²**
вы́цвести (-ветет) *pf*, **выцвета́ть** *impf* fade. **вы́цветший** faded.
вычёркивать *impf*, **вы́черкнуть** (-ну) *pf* cross out.
вы́черпать *pf*, **выче́рпывать** *impf* bale out.
вы́честь (-чту; -чел, -чла) *pf* (*impf* **вычита́ть**) subtract. **вы́чет** deduction.
вычисле́ние calculation. **вычисли́тель** *m* calculator. **вычисли́тельн|ый** calculating, computing; **~ая маши́на** computer; **~ая те́хника** computers; **вы́числить** *pf*, **вычисля́ть** *impf* calculate, compute.
вы́|чистить (-ищу) *pf* (*impf also* **вычища́ть**) clean, clean up.
вычита́ние subtraction. **вычита́ть** *impf of* **вы́честь**
вычища́ть *impf of* **вы́чистить**. **вы́чту** *etc.*: *see* **вы́честь**
вы́швырнуть (-ну) *pf*, **вышвы́ривать** *impf* chuck out.
вы́ше higher, taller; *prep*+*gen* beyond; over; *adv* above.
выше- *in comb* above-, afore-. **вышеизло́женный** foregoing. **~на́званный** afore-named. **~ска́занный, ~ука́занный** aforesaid. **~упомя́нутый** afore-mentioned.
вы́шел *etc.*: *see* **вы́йти**
вышиба́ла *m* chucker-out. **вышиба́ть** *impf*, **вы́шибить** (-бу; -иб) *pf* knock out; chuck out.
вышива́ние embroidery, needlework. **вышива́ть** *impf of* **вы́шить**. **вы́шивка** embroidery.
вышина́ height.
вы́шить (-шью) *pf* (*impf* **вышива́ть**) embroider. **вы́шитый** embroidered.
вы́шка tower; **(бурова́я) ~** derrick.
вы́шлю *etc.*: *see* **вы́слать**. **вы́шью** *etc.*: *see* **вы́шить**

В

вы́явить (-влю) *pf*, **выявля́ть** *impf* reveal; make known; expose; **~ся** come to light, be revealed.
выясне́ние elucidation; explanation. **вы́яснить** *pf*, **выясня́ть** *impf* elucidate; explain; **~ся** become clear; turn out.
Вьетна́м Vietnam. **вьетна́мец, -мка** Vietnamese. **вьетна́мский** Vietnamese.
вью *etc.*: *see* **вить**
вью́га snow-storm, blizzard.
вьюно́к (-нка́) bindweed.
вью́чн|ый pack; **~ое живо́тное** beast of burden.
вью́щийся climbing; curly.
вяжу́ *etc.*: **вяза́ть. вя́жущий** binding; astringent.
вяз elm.
вяза́ние knitting, crocheting; binding, tying. **вя́занка**[1] knitted garment. **вяза́нка**[2] bundle. **вя́заный** knitted, crocheted. **вяза́нье** knitting; crochet(-work). **вяза́ть** (вяжу́, вя́жешь) *impf* (*pf* **с~**) tie, bind; knit, crochet; be astringent; **~ся** accord; tally. **вя́зка** tying; knitting, crocheting; bunch.
вя́зкий (-зок, -зка́, -о) viscous; sticky; boggy. **вя́знуть** (-ну; вяз(нул), -зла) *impf* (*pf* **за~, у~**) stick, get stuck.
вя́зовый elm.
вязь ligature; arabesque.
вя́леный dried; sun-cured.
вя́лый limp; sluggish; slack. **вя́нуть** (-ну; вял) *impf* (*pf* **за~, у~**) fade, wither; flag.

Г

г. *abbr* (*of* **год**) year; (*of* **го́род**) city; (*of* **господи́н**) Mr.
г *abbr* (*of* **грамм**) gram.
га *abbr* (*of* **гекта́р**) hectare.
га́вань harbour.
гага́чий пух eiderdown.
гад reptile; repulsive person; *pl.* vermin.
гада́лка fortune-teller. **гада́ние** fortune-telling; guess-work. **гада́ть** *impf* (*pf* **по~**) tell fortunes; guess.
га́дина reptile; repulsive person; *pl* vermin. **га́дить** (га́жу) *impf* (*pf* **на~**) +**в**+*prep*, **на**+*acc*, *prep* foul, dirty, defile. **га́дкий** (-док, -дка́, -о) nasty, vile repulsive. **га́дость** filth, muck; dirty trick; *pl* filthy expressions. **гадю́ка** adder, viper; repulsive person.
га́ечный ключ spanner, wrench.
газ[1] gauze.
газ[2] gas; wind; **дать ~** step on the gas; **сба́вить ~** reduce speed.
газе́та newspaper. **газе́тчик** journalist; newspaper-seller.
газиро́ванный aerated. **га́зовый** gas.
газо́н lawn. **газонокоси́лка** lawn-mower.
газопрово́д gas pipeline; gas-main.
га́йка nut; female screw.
гала́ктика galaxy.
галантере́йный магази́н haberdasher's. **галантере́я** haberdashery.
гала́нтный gallant.
галере́я gallery. **галёрка** gallery, gods.
галифе́ *indecl pl* riding-breeches.
га́лка jackdaw.
галлюцина́ция hallucination.
гало́п gallop.
га́лочка tick.
га́лстук tie; neckerchief.
галу́шка dumpling.
га́лька pebble; pebbles, shingle.
гам din, uproar.
гама́к (-а́) hammock.
га́мма scale; gamut; range.
гангре́на gangrene.
га́нгстер gangster.
ганте́ль dumb-bell.
гара́ж (-а́) garage.
гаранти́ровать *impf* & *pf* guarantee. **гара́нтия** guarantee.
гардеро́б wardrobe; cloakroom. **гардеро́бщик, -щица** cloakroom attendant.

гарди́на curtain.
гармонизи́ровать *impf* & *pf* harmonize.
гармо́ника accordion, concertina. **гармони́ческий, гармони́чный** harmonious. **гармо́ния** harmony; concord. **гармо́нь** accordion, concertina.
гарнизо́н garrison.
гарни́р garnish; vegetables.
гарниту́р set; suite.
гарь burning; cinders.
гаси́тель *m* extinguisher; suppressor. **гаси́ть** (гашу́, га́сишь) *impf* (*pf* **за~, по~**) extinguish; suppress. **га́снуть** (-ну; гас) *impf* (*pf* **за~, по~, у~**) be extinguished, go out; grow feeble.
гастро́ли *f pl* tour; guest-appearance, performance. **гастроли́ровать** *impf* (be on) tour.
гастроно́м gourmet; provision shop. **гастрономи́ческий** gastronomic; provision. **гастроно́мия** gastronomy; provisions; delicatessen.
гауптва́хта guardroom.
гаши́ш hashish.
гварде́ец (-е́йца) guardsman. **гварде́йский** guards'. **гва́рдия** Guards.
гво́здик tack. **гвозди́ка** pink(s), carnation(s); cloves. **гво́здики** (-ов) *pl* stilettos. **гвоздь** (-я́; *pl* -и, -е́й) *m* nail; tack; crux; highlight, hit.
гг. *abbr* (*of* **го́ды**) years.
где *adv* where; **~ бы ни** wherever. **где́-либо** *adv* anywhere. **где́-нибудь** *adv* somewhere; anywhere. **где́-то** *adv* somewhere.
гекта́р hectare.
ге́лий helium.
гемоглоби́н haemoglobin.
геморро́й haemorrhoids. **гемофили́я** haemophilia.
ген gene.
ге́незис origin, genesis.
генера́л general. **генера́льн|ый** general; **~ая репети́ция** dress rehearsal.
генера́тор generator.
гене́тик geneticist. **гене́тика** genetics. **генети́ческий** genetic.
гениа́льный brilliant. **ге́ний** genius.
ге́ном genome.
гео- *in comb* geo-. **гео́граф** geographer. **~графи́ческий** geographical. **~гра́фия** geography. **гео́лог** geologist. **~логи́ческий** geological. **~ло́гия** geology. **~метри́ческий** geometric. **~ме́трия** geometry.
георги́н dahlia.
геофи́зика geophysics.
гепа́рд cheetah.
гепати́т hepatitis.
гера́нь geranium.
герб arms, coat of arms. **ге́рбов|ый** heraldic; **~ая печа́ть** official stamp.
геркуле́с Hercules; rolled oats.
герма́нец (-нца) ancient German. **Герма́ния** Germany. **герма́нский** Germanic.
гермафроди́т hermaphrodite.
германи́чный hermetic; hermetically sealed; air-tight.
герои́зм heroism. **герои́ня** heroine. **герои́ческий** heroic. **геро́й** hero. **геро́йский** heroic.
герц (*gen pl* **герц**) hertz.
ге́рцог duke. **герцоги́ня** duchess.
г-жа *abbr* (*of* **госпожа́**) Mrs.; Miss.
гиаци́нт hyacinth.
ги́бель death; destruction, ruin; loss; wreck; downfall. **ги́бельный** disastrous, fatal.
ги́бкий (-бок, -бка́, -бко) flexible, adaptable, versatile; supple. **ги́бкость** flexibility; suppleness.
ги́бнуть (-ну; ги́б(нул)) *impf* (*pf* **по~**) perish.
гибри́д hybrid.
гига́нт giant. **гига́нтский** gigantic.
гигие́на hygiene. **гигиени́ческий, -и́чный** hygienic, sanitary.
гид guide.
гидравли́ческий hydraulic.
гидро- *pref* hydro-. **~электроста́нция** hydro-electric power-station.

гиéна hyena.
гúльза cartridge-case; sleeve; (cigarette-)wrapper.
гимн hymn.
гимнáзия grammar school, high school.

гимнáст gymnast. **гимнáстика** gymnastics. **гимнастúческий** gymnastic.
гинекóлог gynaecologist. **гинекoлóгия** gynaecology.
гипéрбола hyperbole.
гипнóз hypnosis. **гипнотизёр** hypnotist. **гипнотизúровать** *impf* (*pf* **за~**) hypnotize. **гипнотúческий** hypnotic.
гипóтеза hypothesis. **гипотетúческий** hypothetical.
гиппопотáм hippopotamus.
гипс gypsum, plaster (of Paris); plaster cast. **гúпсовый** plaster.
гирлянда garland.
гúря weight.
гистерэктомúя hysterectomy.
гитáра guitar.
гл. *abbr* (*of* **главá**) chapter.
глав- *abbr in comb* head, chief, main.
главá (*pl* -ы) head; chief; chapter; cupola. **главáрь** (-я́) *m* leader, ring-leader. **главк** central directorate. **главнокомáндующий** *sb* commander-in-chief. **глáвн|ый** chief, main; **~ым óбразом** chiefly, mainly, for the most part; **~ое** *sb* the main thing; the essentials.
глагóл verb.
глáдить (-áжу) *impf* (*pf* **вы~, по~**) stroke; iron. **глáдкий** smooth; plain. **глáдко** *adv* smoothly. **гладь** smooth surface.
глаз (*loc* -ý; *pl* -á, глаз) eye; **в ~á** to one's face; **за ~á**+*gen* behind the back of; **смотрéть во все ~á** be all eyes.
глазирóванный glazed; glossy; iced; glacé.
глазнúца eye-socket. **глазнóй** eye; optic; **~ врач** oculist. **глазóк** (-зкá) peephole.
глазýнья fried eggs.
глазýрь glaze; syrup; icing.
глáнды (гланд) *pl* tonsils.
глáсность publicity; glasnost, openness. **глáсный** public; vowel; *sb* vowel.
глúна clay. **глúнистый** clayey. **глúняный** clay; clayey.
глúссер speed-boat.
глист (*intestinal*) worm.
глицерúн glycerine.
глобáльный global; extensive.
глóбус globe.
глотáть *impf* swallow. **глóтка** gullet; throat. **глотóк** (-ткá) gulp; mouthful.
глóхнуть (-ну; глох) *impf* (*pf* **за~, о~**) become deaf; die away, subside; grow wild.
глубинá (*pl* -ы) depth; heart, interior. **глубóкий** (-óк, -á, -óкó) deep; profound; late, advanced, extreme. **глубокомы́слие** profundity. **глубокоуважáемый** (*in formal letters*) dear.
глумúться (-млю́сь) *impf* mock, jeer (**над**+*instr* at). **глумлéние** mockery.
глупéть (-éю) *impf* (*pf* **по~**) grow stupid. **глупéц** (-пцá) fool. **глýпость** stupidity. **глýпый** (глуп, -á, -о) stupid.
глухáрь (-я́) *m* capercaillie. **глух|óй** (глух, -á, -о) deaf; muffled; obscure, vague; dense; wild; remote; deserted; sealed; blank; **~óй, ~áя** *sb* deaf man, woman. **глухонемóй** deaf and dumb; *sb* deaf mute. **глухотá** deafness. **глушúтель** *m* silencer. **глушúть** (-шý) *impf* (*pf* **за~, о~**) stun; muffle; dull; jam; extinguish; stifle; suppress. **глушь** backwoods.
глы́ба clod; lump, block.
глюкóза glucose.
глядéть (-яжý) *impf* (*pf* **по~, глянуть**) look, gaze, peer; **~ в óба** be on one's guard; **(тогó и) глядú** it looks as if; I'm afraid; **глядя по**+*dat* depending on.
глянец (-нца) gloss, lustre; polish.

гля́нуть (-ну) *pf* (*impf* **глядéть**) glance.
гм *int* hm!
г-н *abbr* (*of* **господи́н**) Mr.
гнать (гоню́, го́нишь; гнал, -á, -о) *impf* drive; urge (on); hunt, chase; persecute; distil; **~ся за**+*instr* pursue.
гнев anger, rage. **гнéваться** *impf* (*pf* **раз~**) be angry. **гнéвный** angry.
гнедо́й bay.
гнездо́ (*pl* гнёзда) nest.
гнёт weight; oppression. **гнету́щий** oppressive.
гни́да nit.
гниéние decay, putrefaction, rot. **гнило́й** (-ил, -á, -о) rotten; muggy. **гнить** (-ию́, -иёшь; -ил, -á, -о) *impf* (*pf* **с~**) rot. **гноéние** suppuration. **гнои́ться** *impf* (*pf* **с~**) suppurate, discharge matter. **гной** pus. **гнойни́к** abscess; ulcer. **гно́йный** purulent.
гну́сный (-сен, -снá, -о) vile.
гнуть (гну, гнёшь) *impf* (*pf* **со~**) bend; aim at; **~ся** bend; stoop.
гнушáться *impf* (*pf* **по~**) disdain; +*gen or instr* shun; abhor.
гобелéн tapestry.
гобо́й oboe.
говéть (-éю) *impf* fast.
говно́ (*vulg*) shit.
говори́ть *impf* (*pf* **по~, сказáть**) speak, talk; say; tell; **~ся: как говори́тся** as they say.
говя́дина beef. **говя́жий** beef.
го́гот cackle; loud laughter. **гоготáть** (-очу́, -о́чешь) *impf* cackle; roar with laughter.
год (*loc* -у́; *pl* -ы *or* -á, *gen* -о́в *or* лет) year. **годáми** *adv* for years (on end).
годи́ться, (-жу́сь) *impf* be fit, suitable; serve.
годи́чный a year's; annual.
го́дный (-ден, -днá, -о, -ы *or* -ы́) fit, suitable; valid.
годовáлый one-year-old. **годово́й** annual. **годовщи́на** anniversary.
гожу́сь *etc.*: *see* **годи́ться**
гол goal.
голени́ще (boot-)top. **го́лень** shin.
голлáндец (-дца) Dutchman. **Голлáндия** Holland. **голлáндка** Dutchwoman; tiled stove. **голлáндский** Dutch.
головá (*acc* го́лову; *pl* го́ловы, -о́в, -áм) head. **головáстик** tadpole. **голо́вка** head; cap, nose, tip. **головн|о́й** head; leading; **~áя боль** headache; **~о́й мозг** brain, cerebrum; **~о́й убо́р** headgear, headdress. **головокружéние** dizziness. **головоло́мка** puzzle. **головорéз** cut-throat; rascal.
го́лод hunger; famine; acute shortage. **голодáние** starvation; fasting. **голодáть** *impf* go hungry, starve; fast. **голо́дный** (го́лоден, -днá, -о, -ы *or* -ы́) hungry. **голодо́вка** hunger-strike.
гололёд, гололéдица (period of) black ice.
го́лос (*pl* -á) voice; part; vote. **голоси́ть** (-ошу́) *impf* sing loudly; cry; wail.
голосло́вный unsubstantiated, unfounded.
голосовáние voting; poll. **голосовáть** *impf* (*pf* **про~**) vote; vote on.
голосов|о́й vocal; **~ая по́чта** voice mail.
голу́бка pigeon; (my) dear, darling. **голубо́й** light blue. **голу́бчик** my dear (fellow); darling. **го́лубь** *m* pigeon, dove. **голубя́тня** (*gen pl* -тен) dovecot, pigeon-loft.
го́лый (гол, -лá, -ло) naked, bare.
гольф golf.
го́мон hubbub.
гомосексуали́ст homosexual. **гомосексуáльный** homosexual.
гондо́ла gondola.
гонéние persecution. **го́нка** race; dashing; haste.
гонорáр fee.
го́ночный racing.
гончáр (-á) potter.

Г

го́нщик racing driver *or* cyclist. **гоню́** *etc.*: *see* **гнать. гоня́ть** *impf* drive; send on errands; **~ся +за** +*instr* chase, hunt.

гора́ (*acc* го́ру; *pl* го́ры, -а́м) mountain; hill; **в го́ру** uphill; **по́д гору** downhill.

гора́здо *adv* much, far, by far.

горб (-а́, *loc* -у́) hump; bulge. **горба́тый** hunchbacked. **го́рбить** (-блю) *impf* (*pf* **с~**) arch, hunch; **~ся** stoop. **горбу́н** (-а́) *m*, **горбу́нья** (*gen pl* -ний) hunchback. **горбу́шка** (*gen pl* -шек) crust (*of loaf*).

горди́ться (-ржу́сь) *impf* put on airs; +*instr* be proud of. **го́рдость** pride. **го́рдый** (горд, -а́, -о, го́рды́) proud. **горды́ня** arrogance.

го́ре grief, sorrow; trouble. **горева́ть** (-рю́ю) *impf* grieve.

горе́лка burner. **горе́лый** burnt. **горе́ние** burning, combustion; enthusiasm.

го́рестный sad; mournful. **го́ресть** sorrow; *pl* misfortunes.

горе́ть (-рю́) *impf* burn; be on fire.

го́рец (-рца) mountain-dweller.

го́речь bitterness; bitter taste.

горизо́нт horizon. **горизонта́ль** horizontal. **горизонта́льный** horizontal.

гори́стый mountainous, hilly. **го́рка** hill; hillock; steep climb.

го́рло throat; neck. **горлово́й** throat; guttural; raucous. **го́рлышко** neck.

гормо́н hormone.

горн[1] furnace, forge.

горн[2] bugle.

го́рничная *sb* maid, chambermaid.

горнорабо́чий *sb* miner.

горноста́й ermine.

го́рный mountain; mountainous; mineral; mining. **горня́к** (-а́) miner.

го́род (*pl* -а́) town; city. **городо́к** (-дка́) small town. **городско́й** urban; city; municipal. **горожа́нин** (*pl* -а́не, -а́н) *m*, **-жа́нка** town-dweller.

гороско́п horoscope.

горо́х pea, peas. **горо́шек** (-шка) spots, spotted pattern; **души́стый ~** sweet peas; **зелёный ~** green peas. **горо́шина** pea.

горсове́т *abbr* (*of* **городско́й сове́т**) city soviet, town soviet.

горсть (*gen pl* -е́й) handful.

горта́нный guttural. **горта́нь** larynx.

горчи́ца mustard. **горчи́чник** mustard plaster.

горшо́к (-шка́) flowerpot; pot; potty; chamber-pot.

го́рький (-рек, -рька́, -о) bitter.

горю́ч|ий combustible; **~ее** *sb* fuel. **горя́чий** (-ря́ч, -а́) hot; passionate; ardent.

горячи́ться (-чу́сь) *impf* (*pf* **раз~**) get excited. **горя́чка** fever; feverish haste. **горя́чность** zeal.

гос- *abbr in comb* (*of* **госуда́рственный**) state.

го́спиталь *m* (military) hospital.

го́споди *int* good heavens! **господи́н** (*pl* -ода́, -о́д, -а́м) master; gentleman; Mr; *pl* ladies and gentlemen. **госпо́дство** supremacy. **госпо́дствовать** *impf* hold sway; prevail. **Госпо́дь** (Го́спода, *voc* Го́споди) *m* God, the Lord. **госпожа́** lady; Mrs.

гостеприи́мный hospitable. **гостеприи́мство** hospitality. **гости́ная** *sb* sitting-room, living-room, drawing-room. **гости́ница** hotel. **гости́ть** (гощу́) *impf* stay, be on a visit. **гость** (*gen pl* -е́й) *m*, **го́стья** (*gen pl* -ий) guest, visitor.

госуда́рственный State, public. **госуда́рство** State. **госуда́рыня, госуда́рь** *m* sovereign; Your Majesty.

готи́ческий Gothic.

гото́вить (-влю) *impf* (*pf* **с~**) prepare; **~ся** prepare (o.s.); be at hand. **гото́вность** readiness. **гото́вый** ready.

гофриро́ванный corrugated; waved; pleated.

грабёж robbery; pillage. **граби́тель** *m* robber. **граби́тельский** predatory; exorbitant. **гра́бить** (-блю) *impf* (*pf* **о~**) rob, pillage.

гра́бли (-бель *or* -блей) *pl* rake.

гравёр, гравиро́вщик engraver.

гра́вий gravel. **гравирова́ть** *impf* (*pf* **вы́~**) engrave; etch. **гравиро́вка** engraving.

гравитацио́нный gravitational.

гравю́ра engraving, print; etching.

град[1] city, town.

град[2] hail; volley. **гра́дина** hailstone.

гра́дус degree. **гра́дусник** thermometer.

граждани́н (*pl* гра́ждане, -дан), **гражда́нка** citizen. **гражда́нский** civil; civic; civilian. **гражда́нство** citizenship.

грамза́пись (gramophone) recording.

грамм gram.

грамма́тика grammar. **граммати́ческий** grammatical.

гра́мота reading and writing; official document; deed. **гра́мотность** literacy. **гра́мотный** literate; competent.

грампласти́нка (gramophone) record.

грана́т pomegranate; garnet. **грана́та** shell, grenade.

грандио́зный grandiose.

гранёный cut, faceted; cut-glass.

грани́т granite.

грани́ца border; boundary, limit; **за грани́цей, за грани́цу** abroad. **грани́чить** *impf* border.

грант grant.

грань border, verge; side, facet.

граф count; earl.

графа́ column. **гра́фик** graph; chart; schedule; graphic artist. **гра́фика** drawing; graphics; script.

графи́н carafe; decanter.

графи́ня countess.

графи́т graphite.

графи́ческий graphic.

графлёный ruled.

гра́фство county.

грацио́зный graceful. **гра́ция** grace.

грач (-а́) rook.

гребёнка comb. **гре́бень** (-бня) *m* comb; crest. **гребе́ц** (-бца́) rower, oarsman. **гребно́й** rowing. **гребу́** *etc.*: *see* **грести́**

грёза day-dream, dream. **гре́зить** (-е́жу) *impf* dream.

грек Greek.

гре́лка hot-water bottle.

греме́ть *impf* (*pf* **про~**) thunder, roar; rattle; resound. **грему́чая змея́** rattlesnake.

грести́ (-ебу́, -ебёшь; грёб, -бла́) *impf* row; rake.

греть (-е́ю) *impf* warm, heat; **~ся** warm o.s., bask.

грех (-а́) sin. **грехо́вный** sinful. **грехопаде́ние** the Fall; fall.

Гре́ция Greece. **гре́цкий оре́х** walnut. **греча́нка** Greek. **гре́ческий** Greek, Grecian.

греча́ха buckwheat. **гре́чневый** buckwheat.

греши́ть (-шу́) *impf* (*pf* **по~, со~**) sin. **гре́шник, -ница** sinner. **гре́шный** (-шен, -шна́, -о) sinful.

гриб (-а́) mushroom. **грибно́й** mushroom.

гри́ва mane.

гри́венник ten-copeck piece.

грим make-up; grease-paint.

гримирова́ть *impf* (*pf* **за~**) make up; *+instr* make up as.

грипп flu.

гриф neck (*of violin etc.*).

гри́фель *m* pencil lead.

гроб (*loc* -у́; *pl* -ы *or* -а́) coffin; grave. **гробни́ца** tomb. **гробово́й** coffin; deathly. **гробовщи́к** (-а́) coffin-maker; undertaker.

гроза́ (*pl* -ы) (thunder-)storm.

гроздь (*pl* -ди *or* -дья, -де́й *or* -дьев) cluster, bunch.

грози́ть(ся (-ожу́(сь) *impf* (*pf* **по~, при~**) threaten. **гро́зный** (-зен, -зна́, -о) menacing; terrible; severe.

гром (*pl* -ы, -о́в) thunder.
грома́да mass; bulk, pile. **грома́дный** huge, colossal.
громи́ть (-млю́) *impf* destroy; smash, rout.
гро́мкий (-мок, -мка́, -о) loud; famous; notorious; fine-sounding. **гро́мко** *adv* loud(ly); aloud. **громкоговори́тель** *m* loudspeaker. **громово́й** thunder; thunderous; crushing. **громогла́сный** loud; public.
громозди́ть (-зжу́) *impf* (*pf* **на~**) pile up; **~ся** tower; clamber up. **громо́здкий** cumbersome.
гро́мче *comp of* **гро́мкий, гро́мко**
гроссме́йстер grand master.
гроте́скный grotesque.
гро́хот crash, din.
грохота́ть (-очу́, -о́чешь) *impf* (*pf* **про~**) crash; rumble; roar.
грош (-а́) half-copeck piece; farthing. **гроша́вый** cheap; trifling.
грубе́ть (-е́ю) *impf* (*pf* **за~, о~, по~**) grow coarse. **груби́ть** (-блю́) *impf* (*pf* **на~**) be rude. **грубия́н** boor. **гру́бость** rudeness; coarseness; rude remark. **гру́бый** (груб, -а́, -о) coarse; rude.
гру́да heap, pile.
груди́на breastbone. **груди́нка** brisket; breast. **грудно́й** breast, chest; pectoral. **грудь** (-и́ *or* -и, *instr* -ю, *loc* -и́; *pl* -и, -е́й) breast; chest.
груз load; burden.
грузи́н (*gen pl* -и́н), **грузи́нка** Georgian. **грузи́нский** Georgian.
грузи́ть (-ужу́, -у́зишь) *impf* (*pf* **за~, на~, по~**) load; **~ся** load, take on cargo.
Гру́зия Georgia.
гру́зный (-зен, -зна́, -о) weighty; bulky. **грузови́к** (*gen* -а́) lorry, truck. **грузово́й** goods, cargo. **гру́зчик** stevedore; loader.
грунт ground, soil; priming. **грунтова́ть** *impf* (*pf* **за~**) prime. **грунтово́й** soil, earth; priming.
гру́ппа group. **группирова́ть** *impf* (*pf* **с~**) group; **~ся** group, form groups. **группиро́вка** grouping. **группово́й** group; team.
грусти́ть (-ущу́) *impf* grieve, mourn; +**по**+*dat* pine for. **гру́стный** (-тен, -тна́, -о) sad. **грусть** sadness.
гру́ша pear.
гры́жа hernia, rupture.
грызть (-зу́, -зёшь; грыз) *impf* (*pf* **раз~**) gnaw; nag; **~ся** fight; squabble. **грызу́н** (-а́) rodent.
гряда́ (*pl* -ы, -а́м) ridge; bed; row, series; bank. **гря́дка** (flower-)bed.
гряду́щий approaching; future.
гря́зный (-зен, -зна́, -о) muddy; dirty. **грязь** (*loc* -и́) mud; dirt, filth; *pl* mud-cure.
гря́нуть (-ну) *pf* ring out, crash out; strike up.
губа́ (*pl* -ы, -а́м) lip; *pl* pincers.
губерна́тор governor. **губе́рния** province. **губе́рнский** provincial.
губи́тельный ruinous; pernicious. **губи́ть** (-блю́, -бишь) *impf* (*pf* **по~**) ruin; spoil.
гу́бка sponge.
губна́я пома́да lipstick.
гу́бчатый porous, spongy.
гуверна́нтка governess. **гувернёр** tutor.
гуде́ть (гужу́) *impf* (*pf* **про~**) hum; drone; buzz; hoot. **гудо́к** (-дка́) hooter, siren, horn, whistle; hoot.
гудро́н tar. **гудро́нный** tar, tarred.
гул rumble. **гу́лкий** (-лок, -лка́, -о) resonant; booming.
гуля́нье (*gen pl* -ний) walk; fête; outdoor party. **гуля́ть** *impf* (*pf* **по~**) stroll; go for a walk; have a good time.
гуманита́рный of the humanities; humane. **гума́нный** humane.
гумно́ (*pl* -а, -мен *or* -мён, -ам) threshing-floor; barn.
гурт (-а́) herd; flock. **гуртовщи́к** (-а́) herdsman. **гурто́м** *adv* wholesale; en masse.
гуса́к (-а́) gander.

гу́сеница caterpillar; (caterpillar) track. **гу́сеничный** caterpillar.
гусёнок (-нка; *pl* -ся́та, -ся́т) gosling. **гуси́н|ый** goose; **~ая ко́жа** goose-flesh.
густе́ть (-е́ет) *impf* (*pf* **за~**) thicken. **густо́й** (густ, -а́, -о) thick, dense; rich. **густота́** thickness, density; richness.
гусы́ня goose. **гусь** (*pl* -и, -е́й) *m* goose. **гусько́м** *adv* in single file.
гутали́н shoe-polish.
гу́ща grounds, sediment; thicket; thick. **гу́ще** *comp of* **густо́й.**
ГЭС *abbr* (*of* **гидроэлектроста́нция**) hydro-electric power station.

Д

д. *abbr* (*of* **дере́вня**) village; (*of* **дом**) house.
да *conj* and; but.
да *partl* yes; really? well; *+3rd pers of v*, may, let; **да здра́вствует...!** long live ...!
дава́ть (даю́, -ёшь) *impf of* **дать; дава́й(те)** let us, let's; come on; **~ся** yield; come easy.
дави́ть (-влю́, -вишь) *impf* (*pf* **за~, по~, раз~, у~**) press; squeeze; crush; oppress; **~ся** choke; hang o.s. **да́вка** crushing; crush. **давле́ние** pressure.
да́вний ancient; of long standing. **давно́** *adv* long ago; for a long time. **да́вность** antiquity; remoteness; long standing. **давны́м-давно́** *adv* long long ago.
дади́м *etc.*: *see* **дать. даю́** *etc.*: *see* **дава́ть**
да́же *adv* even.
да́лее *adv* further; **и так ~** and so on, etc. **далёкий** (-ёк, -а́, -ёко́) distant, remote; far (-away). **далеко́** *adv* far; far off; by a long way; **~ за** long after; **~ не** far from. **даль** (*loc* -и́) distance. **дальне́йший** further. **да́льний** distant, remote; long; **~ Восто́к** the Far East. **дальнозо́ркий** long-sighted. **да́льность** distance; range. **да́льше** *adv* further; then, next; longer.
дам *etc.*: *see* **дать**
да́ма lady; partner; queen.
да́мба dike; dam.
да́мский ladies'.
Да́ния Denmark.
да́нные *sb pl* data; facts. **да́нный** given, present. **дань** tribute; debt.
данти́ст dentist.
дар (*pl* -ы́) gift. **дари́ть** (-рю́, -ришь) *impf* (*pf* **по~**) *+dat* give, make a present.
дарова́ние talent. **дарова́ть** *impf & pf* grant, confer. **дарови́тый** gifted. **дарово́й** free (of charge). **да́ром** *adv* free, gratis; in vain.
да́та date.
да́тельный dative.
дати́ровать *impf & pf* date.
да́тский Danish. **датча́нин** (*pl* -а́не, -а́н), **датча́нка** Dane.
дать (дам, дашь, даст, дади́м; дал, -а́, да́ло́) *pf* (*impf* **дава́ть**) give; grant; let; **~ взаймы́** lend; **~ся** *pf of* **дава́ться**
да́ча dacha; **на да́че** in the country. **да́чник** (holiday) visitor.
два *m & neut*, **две** *f* (двух, -ум, -умя́, -ух) two. **двадцатиле́тний** twenty-year; twenty-year-old. **двадца́т|ый** twentieth; **~ые го́ды** the twenties. **два́дцать** (-и́, *instr* -ью́) twenty. **два́жды** *adv* twice; double. **двена́дцатый** twelfth. **двена́дцать** twelve.
дверь (*loc* -и́; *pl* -и, -е́й, *instr* -я́ми *or* -ьми́) door.
две́сти (двухсо́т, -умста́м, -умяста́ми, -ухста́х) two hundred.
дви́гатель *m* engine, motor; motive force. **дви́гать** (-аю *or* -и́жу) *impf*, **дви́нуть** (-ну) *pf* move; set in motion; advance; **~ся** move; advance; get started. **движе́ние** movement; motion; exercise; traffic. **дви́жимость** chattels; personal property. **дви́жимый** movable; moved. **дви́жущий** motive.

дво́е (-и́х) two; two pairs.
двое- *in comb* two-; double(-). **двоебо́рье** biathlon. **~же́нец** (-нца) bigamist. **~жёнство** bigamy. **~то́чие** colon.
двои́ться *impf* divide in two; appear double; **у него́ двои́лось в глаза́х** he saw double. **двои́чный** binary. **дво́йка** two; figure 2; No. 2. **двойни́к** (-а́) double. **двойно́й** double, twofold; binary. **дво́йня** (*gen pl* -о́ен) twins. **дво́йственный** two-faced; dual.
двор (-а́) yard; courtyard; homestead; court. **дворе́ц** (-рца́) palace. **дво́рник** yard caretaker; windscreen-wiper. **дво́рня** servants. **дворо́вый** yard, courtyard; *sb* house-serf. **дворяни́н** (*pl* -я́не, -я́н), **дворя́нка** member of the nobility or gentry. **дворя́нство** nobility, gentry.
двоюродн|ый; ~ый брат, ~ая сестра́ (first) cousin; **~ый дя́дя, ~ая тётка** first cousin once removed. **двоя́кий** double; twofold.
дву-, двух- *in comb* two-; bi-; double. **двубо́ртный** double-breasted. **~ли́чный** two-faced. **~но́гий** two-legged. **~ру́чный** two-handed; two-handled. **~ру́шник** double-dealer. **~смы́сленный** ambiguous. **~(х)спа́льный** double. **~сторо́нний** double-sided; two-way; bilateral. **~хгоди́чный** two-year. **~хле́тний** two-year; two-year-old; biennial. **~хме́стный** two-seater; two-berth. **~хмото́рный** twin-engined. **~хсотле́тие** bicentenary. **~хсо́тый** two-hundredth. **~хта́ктный** two-stroke. **~хэта́жный** two-storey. **~язы́чный** bilingual.
деба́ты (-ов) *pl* debate.
де́бет debit. **дебетова́ть** *impf* & *pf* debit.
деби́т yield, output.
де́бри (-ей) *pl* jungle; thickets; the wilds.
дебю́т début.
де́ва maid, maiden; Virgo.
девальва́ция devaluation.
дева́ться *impf of* **де́ться**
деви́з motto; device.
деви́ца spinster; girl. **де́вич|ий** girlish, maidenly; **~ья фами́лия** maiden name. **де́вка** wench, lass; tart. **де́вочка** (little) girl. **де́вственник, -ица** virgin. **де́вственный** virgin; innocent. **де́вушка** girl. **девчо́нка** girl.
девяно́сто ninety. **девяно́стый** ninetieth. **девя́тка** nine; figure 9; No. 9. **девятна́дцатый** nineteenth. **девятна́дцать** nineteen. **девя́тый** ninth. **де́вять** (-и́, *instr* -ью) nine. **девятьсо́т** (-тисо́т, -тиста́м, -тьюста́ми, -тиста́х) nine hundred.
дегенери́ровать *impf* & *pf* degenerate.
дёготь (-гтя) tar.
дегуста́ция tasting.
дед grandfather; grandad. **де́душка** grandfather; grandad.
дееприча́стие adverbial participle.
дежу́рить *impf* be on duty. **дежу́рный** duty; on duty; *sb* person on duty. **дежу́рство** (being on) duty.
дезерти́р deserter. **дезерти́ровать** *impf* & *pf* desert.
дезинфе́кция disinfection. **дезинфици́ровать** *impf* & *pf* disinfect.
дезодора́нт deodorant; air-freshener.
дезориента́ция disorientation. **дезориенти́ровать** *impf* & *pf* disorient; **~ся** lose one's bearings.
де́йственный efficacious; effective. **де́йствие** action; operation; effect; act. **действи́тельно** *adv* really; indeed. **действи́тельность** reality; validity; efficacy. **действи́тельный** actual; valid; efficacious; active. **де́йствовать** *impf* (*pf* **по~**) affect, have an effect; act; work. **де́йствующ|ий**

Д

active; in force; working; **~ее лицо́** character; **~ие ли́ца** cast.
декабри́ст Decembrist. **дека́брь** (-я́) *m* December. **дека́брьский** December.
дека́да ten-day period *or* festival.
дека́н dean. **декана́т** office of dean.
деклама́ция recitation, declamation. **деклами́ровать** *impf* (*pf* **про~**) recite, declaim.
деклара́ция declaration.
декорати́вный decorative. **декора́тор** scene-painter. **декора́ция** scenery.
декре́т decree; maternity leave. **декре́тный о́тпуск** maternity leave.
де́ланный artificial, affected. **де́лать** *impf* (*pf* **с~**) make; do; **~ вид** pretend; **~ся** become; happen.
делега́т delegate. **делега́ция** delegation; group.
делёж (-а́), **делёжка** sharing; partition. **деле́ние** division; point (*on a scale*).
деле́ц (-льца́) smart operator.
делика́тный delicate.
дели́мое *sb* dividend. **дели́мость** divisibility. **дели́тель** *m* divisor. **дели́ть** (-лю́, -лишь) *impf* (*pf* **по~, раз~**) divide; share; **~ шесть на́ три** divide six by three; **~ся** divide; be divisible; +*instr* share.
де́ло (*pl* -а́) business; affair; matter; deed; thing; case; **в са́мом де́ле** really, indeed; **~ в том** the point is; **как (ва́ши) дела́?** how are things?; **на са́мом де́ле** in actual fact; **по де́лу, по дела́м** on business. **делови́тый** business-like, efficient. **делово́й** business; business-like. **де́льный** efficient; sensible.
де́льта delta.
дельфи́н dolphin.
демаго́г demagogue.
демобилиза́ция demobilization. **демобилизова́ть** *impf* & *pf* demobilize.
демокра́т democrat. **демократиза́ция** democratization. **демократизи́ровать** *impf* & *pf* democratize. **демократи́ческий** democratic. **демокра́тия** democracy.
де́мон demon.
демонстра́ция demonstration. **демонстри́ровать** *impf* & *pf* demonstrate.
де́нежный monetary; money; **~ перево́д** money order.
де́нусь *etc.*: *see* **де́ться**
день (дня) *m* day; afternoon; **днём** in the afternoon; **на днях** the other day; one of these days; **че́рез ~** every other day.
де́ньги (-нег, -ьга́м) *pl* money.
департа́мент department.
депо́ *neut indecl* depot.
депорта́ция deportation. **депорти́ровать** *impf* & *pf* deport.
депута́т (*parl*) deputy; delegate.
дёргать *impf* (*pf* **дёрнуть**) pull, tug; pester; **~ся** twitch; jerk.
деревéнский village; rural. **дере́вня** (*pl* -и, -ве́нь, -вня́м) village; the country. **де́рево** (*pl* -е́вья, -ьев) tree; wood. **деревя́нный** wood; wooden.
держа́ва power. **держа́ть** (-жу́, -жишь) *impf* hold; support; keep; **~ пари́** bet; **~ себя́** behave; **~ся +за**+*acc* hold on to; be held up; hold o.s.; hold out; +*gen* keep to.
дерза́ние daring. **дерза́ть** *impf*, **дерзну́ть** (-ну́, -нёшь) *pf* dare. **де́рзкий** impudent; daring. **де́рзость** impertinence; daring.
дёрн turf.
дёрнуть(ся (-ну(сь) *pf of* **дёргать(ся**
деру́ *etc.*: *see* **драть**
деса́нт landing; landing force.
десе́рт dessert.
де́скать *partl indicating reported speech.*
десна́ (*pl* дёсны, -сен) gum.
де́спот despot.
десятиле́тие decade; tenth anniversary. **десятиле́тка** ten-year

(*secondary*) school. **десятиле́тний** ten-year; ten-year-old. **десяти́чный** decimal. **деся́тка** ten; figure 10; No. 10; tenner (*10-rouble note*). **деся́ток** (-тка) ten; decade. **деся́тый** tenth. **де́сять** (-и́, *instr* -ью́) ten.

Д

дета́ль detail; part, component. **дета́льный** detailed; minute.

детдо́м (*pl* -а́) children's home.

детекти́в detective story.

детёныш young animal; *pl* young. **де́ти** (-те́й, -тям, -тьми́, -тях) *pl* children. **детса́д** (*pl* -ы́) kindergarten.

де́тская *sb* nursery. **де́тский** children's; childish. **де́тство** childhood.

де́ться (де́нусь) *pf* (*impf* **дева́ться**) get to, disappear to.

дефе́кт defect.

дефи́с hyphen.

дефици́т deficit; shortage. **дефици́тный** scarce.

дешеве́ть (-е́ет) *impf* (*pf* **по~**) fall in price. **деше́вле** *comp of* **дёшево, дешёвый. дёшево** *adv* cheap, cheaply. **дешёвый** (дёшев, -а́, -о) cheap.

де́ятель *m*: **госуда́рственный ~** statesman; **обще́ственный ~** public figure. **де́ятельность** activity; work. **де́ятельный** active, energetic.

джаз jazz.

дже́мпер pullover.

джентльме́н gentleman.

джинсо́вый denim. **джи́нсы** (-ов) *pl* jeans.

джо́йстик joystick.

джу́нгли (-ей) *pl* jungle.

диабе́т diabetes. **диабе́тик** diabetic.

диа́гноз diagnosis.

диагона́ль diagonal.

диагра́мма diagram.

диале́кт dialect. **диале́ктика** dialectics.

диало́г dialogue.

диа́метр diameter.

диапазо́н range; band.

диапозити́в slide.

диафра́гма diaphragm.

дива́н sofa; divan.

диверса́нт saboteur. **диве́рсия** sabotage.

диви́зия division.

ди́вный marvellous. **ди́во** wonder, marvel.

дида́ктика didactics.

дие́з (*mus*) sharp.

дие́та diet. **диети́ческий** dietetic.

диза́йн design. **диза́йнер** designer.

ди́зель *m* diesel; diesel engine. **ди́зельный** diesel.

дизентери́я dysentery.

дика́рь (-я́) *m*, **дика́рка** savage. **ди́кий** wild; savage; queer; preposterous. **дикобра́з** porcupine. **дикорасту́щий** wild. **ди́кость** wildness, savagery; absurdity.

дикта́нт dictation. **дикта́тор** dictator. **диктату́ра** dictatorship.

диктова́ть *impf* (*pf* **про~**) dictate. **ди́ктор** announcer. **ди́кция** diction.

диле́мма dilemma.

дилета́нт dilettante.

дина́мика dynamics.

динами́т dynamite.

динами́ческий dynamic.

дина́стия dynasty.

диноза́вр dinosaur.

дипло́м diploma; degree; degree work. **диплома́т** diplomat. **дипломати́ческий** diplomatic.

директи́ва instructions; directives. **дире́ктор** (*pl* **~а́**) director; principal. **дире́кция** management.

дирижа́бль *m* airship, dirigible.

дирижёр conductor. **дирижи́ровать** *impf* +*instr* conduct.

диск disc, disk; dial; discus.

ди́скант treble.

дисково́д disk drive.

дискоте́ка discotheque.

дискре́тный discrete.

дискримина́ция discrimination.

диску́ссия discussion, debate.

диспансе́р clinic.

диспе́тчер controller.

ди́спут public debate.
диссерта́ция dissertation, thesis.
дистанцио́нный distance, distant, remote; remote-control. **диста́нция** distance; range; region.
дисципли́на discipline.
дитя́ (дитя́ти; *pl* де́ти, -е́й) *neut* child; baby.
дифтери́я diphtheria.
дифто́нг diphthong.
диффама́ция libel.
дичь game.
длина́ length. **дли́нный** (-нен, -нна́, -о) long. **дли́тельность** duration. **дли́тельный** long, protracted. **дли́ться** *impf* (*pf* про~) last.
для *prep+gen* for; for the sake of; ~ **того́, что́бы...** in order to.
днева́льный *sb* (*mil*) orderly. **дневни́к** (-а́) diary, journal. **дневно́й** day; daily. **днём** *adv* in the day time; in the afternoon. **дни** *etc.*: *see* **день**
дни́ще bottom.
ДНК *abbr* (*of* **дезоксирибонуклеи́новая кислота́**) DNA.
дно (дна; *pl* до́нья, -ьев) bottom.
до *prep+gen* (up) to; as far as; until; before; to the point of; **до на́шей э́ры** BC; **до сих пор** till now; **до тех пор** till then, before; **до того́, как** before; **до того́, что** to such an extent that, until; **мне не до** I'm not in the mood for.
доба́вить (-влю) *pf*, **добавля́ть** *impf* (+*acc or gen*) add. **доба́вка** addition; second helping. **добавле́ние** addition; supplement; extra. **доба́вочный** additional.
добега́ть *impf*, **добежа́ть** (-егу́) *pf* +**до**+*gen* run to, as far as; reach.
добива́ть *impf*, **доби́ть** (-бью́, -бьёшь) *pf* finish (off); **~ся** +*gen* get, obtain; **~ся своего́** get one's way.
добира́ться *impf of* **добра́ться**
до́блесть valour.
добра́ться (-беру́сь, -ёшься; -а́лся, -ла́сь, -а́ло́сь) *pf* (*impf* **добира́ться**) +**до**+*gen* get to, reach.
добро́ good; ~ **пожа́ловать!** welcome!; **э́то не к добру́** it is a bad sign.
добро- *in comb* good-, well-. **доброво́лец** (-льца) volunteer. **~во́льно** *adv* voluntarily. **~во́льный** voluntary. **~де́тель** virtue. **~де́тельный** virtuous. **~ду́шие** good nature. **~ду́шный** good-natured. **~жела́тельный** benevolent. **~ка́чественный** of good quality; benign. **~со́вестный** conscientious.
доброта́ goodness, kindness. **добро́тный** of good quality. **до́брый** (добр, -а́, -о, до́бры́) good; kind; **бу́дьте добры́** +*imper* please; would you be kind enough to.
добыва́ть *impf*, **добы́ть** (-бу́ду; до́был, -а́, -о) *pf* get, obtain, procure; mine. **добы́ча** output; mining; booty.
добью́ *etc.*: *see* **доби́ть. доведу́** *etc.*: *see* **довести́**
довезти́ (-езу́, -езёшь; -вёз, -ла́) *pf* (*impf* **довози́ть**) take (to), carry (to), drive (to).
дове́ренность warrant; power of attorney. **дове́ренный** trusted; *sb* agent, proxy. **дове́рие** trust, confidence. **дове́рить** *pf* (*impf* **доверя́ть**) entrust; **~ся** +*dat* trust in; confide in.
до́верху *adv* to the top.
дове́рчивый trustful, credulous. **доверя́ть** *impf of* **дове́рить**; (+*dat*) to trust.
дове́сок (-ска) makeweight.
довести́ (-еду́, -едёшь; -вёл, -а́) *pf*, **доводи́ть** (-ожу́, -о́дишь) *impf* lead, take (to); bring, drive (to). **до́вод** argument, reason.
довое́нный pre-war.
довози́ть (-ожу́, -о́зишь) *impf of* **довезти́**
дово́льно *adv* enough; quite, fairly. **дово́льный** satisfied; pleased. **дово́льство** contentment. **дово́льствоваться** *impf* (*pf* у~) be content.
догада́ться *pf*, **дога́дываться**

impf guess; suspect. **дога́дка** surmise, conjecture. **дога́дливый** quick-witted.
до́гма dogma.
догна́ть (-гоню́, -го́нишь; -гна́л, -а́, -о) *pf* (*impf* **догоня́ть**) catch up (with).
Д **догова́риваться** *impf*, **договори́ться** *pf* come to an agreement; arrange. **до́гово́р** (*pl* -ы *or* -а́, -о́в) agreement; contract; treaty. **догово́рный** contractual; agreed.
догоня́ть *impf of* **догна́ть**
догора́ть *impf*, **догоре́ть** (-ри́т) *pf* burn out, burn down.
дое́ду *etc.*: *see* **дое́хать. доезжа́ть** *impf of* **дое́хать**
дое́хать (-е́ду) *pf* (*impf* **доезжа́ть**) +**до**+*gen* reach, arrive at.
дожда́ться (-ду́сь, -дёшься; -а́лся, -ла́сь, -а́ло́сь) *pf* +*gen* wait for, wait until.
дождеви́к (-а́) raincoat. **дождево́й** rain(y). **дождли́вый** rainy. **дождь** (-я́) *m* rain; ~ **идёт** it is raining.
дожива́ть *impf*, **дожи́ть** (-иву́, -ивёшь; до́жи́л, -а́, -о) *pf* live out; spend.
дожида́ться *impf* +*gen* wait for.
до́за dose.
дозво́лить *pf*, **дозволя́ть** *impf* permit.
дозвони́ться *pf* get through, reach by telephone.
дозо́р patrol.
дозрева́ть *impf*, **дозре́ть** (-е́ет) *pf* ripen.
доистори́ческий prehistoric.
дои́ть *impf* (*pf* **по**~) milk.
дойти́ (дойду́, -дёшь; дошёл, -шла́) *pf* (*impf* **доходи́ть**) +**до**+*gen* reach; get through to.
док dock.
доказа́тельный conclusive. **доказа́тельство** proof, evidence. **доказа́ть** (-ажу́, -а́жешь) *pf*, **дока́зывать** *impf* demonstrate, prove.
докати́ться (-ачу́сь, -а́тишься) *pf*, **дока́тываться** *impf* roll; boom; +**до**+*gen* sink into.
докла́д report; lecture. **докладна́я (запи́ска)** report; memo. **докла́дчик** speaker, lecturer. **докла́дывать** *impf of* **доложи́ть**
до́красна́ *adv* to red heat; to redness.
до́ктор (*pl* -а́) doctor. **до́кторский** doctoral. **до́кторша** woman doctor; doctor's wife.
доктри́на doctrine.
докуме́нт document; deed. **документа́льный** documentary. **документа́ция** documentation; documents.
долби́ть (-блю́) *impf* hollow; chisel; repeat; swot up.
долг (*loc* -у́; *pl* -и́) duty; debt; **взять в** ~ borrow; **дать в** ~ lend.
до́лгий (до́лог, -лга́, -о) long. **до́лго** *adv* long, (for) a long time. **долгове́чный** lasting; durable. **долгожда́нный** long-awaited. **долгоигра́ющая пласти́нка** LP.
долголе́тие longevity. **долголе́тний** of many years; long-standing. **долгосро́чный** long-term.
долгота́ (*pl* -ы) length; longitude.
долево́й lengthwise. **до́лее** *adv* longer.
должа́ть *impf* (*pf* **за**~) borrow.
до́лжен (-жна́) *predic*+*dat* in debt to; +*inf* obliged, bound; likely; must, have to, ought to; **должно́ быть** probably. **должни́к** (-а́), **-ни́ца** debtor. **до́лжное** *sb* due. **должностно́й** official. **до́лжность** (*gen pl* -е́й) post, office; duties. **до́лжный** due, fitting.
доли́на valley.
до́ллар dollar.
доложи́ть[1] (-ожу́, -о́жишь) *pf* (*impf* **докла́дывать**) add.
доложи́ть[2] (-ожу́, -о́жишь) *pf* (*impf* **докла́дывать**) +*acc or* **о**+*prep* report; announce.
доло́й *adv* away, off; +*acc* down with!
долото́ (*pl* -а) chisel.
до́лька segment; clove.
до́льше *adv* longer.

до́ля (*gen pl* **-е́й**) portion; share; lot, fate.
дом (*pl* -а́) house; home. **до́ма** *adv* at home. **дома́шн|ий** house; home; domestic; home-made; **~яя хозя́йка** housewife.
до́менн|ый blast-furnace; **~ая печь** blast-furnace.
домини́ровать *impf* dominate, predominate.
домкра́т jack.
до́мна blast-furnace.
домовладе́лец (-льца), **-лица** house-owner; landlord. **домово́дство** housekeeping; domestic science. **домо́вый** house; household; housing.
домога́тельство solicitation; bid. **домога́ться** *impf* +*gen* solicit, bid for.
домо́й *adv* home, homewards. **домохозя́йка** housewife. **домрабо́тница** domestic servant, maid.
домофо́н entryphone (*propr*).
доне́льзя *adv* in the extreme.
донесе́ние dispatch, report. **донести́** (-су́, -сёшь; -нёс, -сла́) *pf* (*impf* **доноси́ть**) report, announce; +*dat* inform; +**на**+*acc* inform against; **~сь** be heard; +**до**+*gen* reach.
до́низу *adv* to the bottom; **све́рху ~** from top to bottom.
до́нор donor.
доно́с denunciation, information. **доноси́ть(ся** (-ношу́(сь, -но́сишь(ся) *impf of* **донести́(сь**
доно́счик informer.
донско́й Don.
доны́не *adv* hitherto.
до́нья *etc.*: *see* **дно**
до н.э. *abbr* (*of* **до на́шей э́ры**) BC.
допла́та additional payment, excess fare. **доплати́ть** (-ачу́, -а́тишь) *pf*, **допла́чивать** *impf* pay in addition; pay the rest.
допо́длинно *adv* for certain. **допо́длинный** authentic, genuine.
дополне́ние supplement, addition; (*gram*) object. **дополни́тельно** *adv* in addition. **дополни́тельный** supplementary, additional. **допо́лнить** *pf*, **дополня́ть** *impf* supplement.
допра́шивать *impf*, **допроси́ть** (-ошу́, -о́сишь) *pf* interrogate. **допро́с** interrogation.
до́пуск right of entry, admittance. **допуска́ть** *impf*, **допусти́ть** (-ущу́, -у́стишь) *pf* admit; permit; tolerate; suppose. **допусти́мый** permissible, acceptable. **допуще́ние** assumption.
дореволюцио́нный pre-revolutionary.
доро́га road; way; journey; route; **по доро́ге** on the way.
до́рого *adv* dear, dearly. **дорогови́зна** high prices. **дорого́й** (до́рог, -а́, -о) dear.
доро́дный portly.
дорожа́ть *impf* (*pf* **вз~, по~**) rise in price, go up. **доро́же** *comp of* **до́рого, дорого́й**. **дорожи́ть** (-жу́) *impf* +*instr* value.
доро́жка path; track; lane; runway; strip, runner, stair-carpet. **доро́жный** road; highway; travelling.
доса́да annoyance. **досади́ть** (-ажу́) *pf*, **досажда́ть** *impf* +*dat* annoy. **доса́дный** annoying. **доса́довать** be annoyed (**на**+*acc* with).
доска́ (*acc* до́ску; *pl* -и, -со́к, -ска́м) board; slab; plaque.
досло́вный literal; word-for-word.
досмо́тр inspection.
доспе́хи *pl* armour.
досро́чный ahead of time, early.
достава́ть(ся (-таю́(сь, -ёшь(ся) *impf of* **доста́ть(ся**
доста́вить (-влю) *pf*, **доставля́ть** *impf* deliver; supply; cause, give. **доста́вка** delivery.
доста́ну *etc.*: *see* **доста́ть**
доста́ток (-тка) sufficiency; prosperity. **доста́точно** *adv* enough, sufficiently. **доста́точный** sufficient; adequate.
доста́ть (-а́ну) *pf* (*impf* **достава́ть**)

take (out); get, obtain; +*gen or* **до**+*gen* touch; reach; *impers* suffice; **~ся** +*dat* be inherited by; fall to the lot of; **емý достáнется** he'll catch it.

достигáть *impf*, **достúгнуть, достúчь** (-úгну; -стúг) *pf* +*gen* reach, achieve; +*gen or* **до**+*gen* reach. **достижéние** achievement.

достовéрный reliable, trustworthy; authentic.

достóинство dignity; merit; value. **достóйный** deserved; suitable; worthy; +*gen* worthy of.

достопримечáтельность sight, notable place.

достоя́ние property.

дóступ access. **достýпный** accessible; approachable; reasonable; available.

досýг leisure, (spare) time. **досýжий** leisure; idle.

дóсыта *adv* to satiety.

досьé *neut indecl* dossier.

досягáемый attainable.

дотáция grant, subsidy.

дотлá utterly; to the ground.

дотрáгиваться *impf*, **дотрóнуться** (-нусь) *pf* +**до**+*gen* touch.

дотя́гивать *impf*, **дотянýть** (-янý, -я́нешь) *pf* draw, drag, stretch out; hold out; live; put off; **~ся** stretch, reach; drag on.

дóхлый dead; sickly. **дóхнуть**[1] (-нет; дох) (*pf* **из~, по~, с~**) die; kick the bucket.

дохнýть[2] (-нý, -нёшь) *pf* draw a breath.

дохóд income; revenue. **доходúть** (-ожý, -óдишь) *impf of* **дойтú. дохóдный** profitable. **дохóдчивый** intelligible.

доцéнт reader, senior lecturer.

дóчиста *adv* clean; completely.

дóчка daughter. **дочь** (-чери, *instr* -черью; *pl* -чери, -черéй, *instr* -черьмú) daughter.

дошёл *etc.*: *see* **дойтú**

дошкóльник, -ница child under school age. **дошкóльный** pre-school.

дощáтый plank, board. **дощéчка** small plank, board; plaque.

доя́рка milkmaid.

драгоцéнность jewel; treasure; *pl* jewellery; valuables. **драгоцéнный** precious.

дразнúть (-ню́, -нишь) *impf* tease.

дрáка fight.

дракóн dragon.

дрáма drama. **драматúческий** dramatic. **драматýрг** playwright. **драматургúя** dramatic art; plays.

драп thick woollen cloth.

драпирóвка draping; curtain; hangings. **драпирóвщик** upholsterer.

драть (дерý, -рёшь; драл, -á, -о) *impf* (*pf* **вы́~, за~, со~**) tear (up); irritate; make off; flog; **~ся** fight.

дрéбезги *pl*; **в ~** to smithereens. **дребезжáть** (-жúт) *impf* jingle, tinkle.

древесúна wood; timber. **древéсный** wood; **~ ýголь** charcoal.

дрéвко (*pl* -и, -ов) pole, staff; shaft.

древнегрéческий ancient Greek. **древнееврéйский** Hebrew. **древнерýсский** Old Russian. **дрéвний** ancient; aged. **дрéвность** antiquity.

дрейф drift; leeway. **дрейфовáть** *impf* drift.

дремáть (-млю́, -млешь) *impf* doze; slumber. **дремóта** drowsiness.

дремýчий dense.

дрессирóванный trained; performing. **дрессировáть** *impf* (*pf* **вы́~**) train; school. **дрессирóвка** training. **дрессирóвщик** trainer.

дробúть (-блю́) *impf* (*pf* **раз~**) break up, smash; crush; **~ся** break to pieces, smash. **дробовúк** (-á) shot-gun. **дробь** (small) shot; drumming; fraction. **дрóбный** fractional.

дровá (дров) *pl* firewood.

дрóгнуть (-ну) *pf*, **дрожáть** (-жý) *impf* tremble; shiver; quiver.

дро́жжи (-е́й) *pl* yeast.
дрожь shivering, trembling.
дрозд (-а́) thrush; **чёрный ~** blackbird.
дро́ссель *m* throttle, choke.
дро́тик javelin, dart.
друг[1] (*pl* -узья́, -зе́й) friend; boyfriend. **друг**[2]: **~ дру́га (дру́гу)** each other, one another. **друго́й** other, another; different; **на ~ день** (the) next day. **дру́жба** friendship. **дружелю́бный, дру́жеский, дружественный** friendly. **дружи́ть** (-жу́, -у́жишь) *impf* be friends. **дру́жный** (-жен, -жна́, -о) friendly; harmonious; simultaneous, general; concerted.
дря́блый (дрябл, -а́, -о) flabby.
дря́зги (-зг) *pl* squabbles.
дрянно́й worthless; good-for-nothing. **дрянь** rubbish.
дряхле́ть (-е́ю) *impf* (*pf* **о~**) become decrepit. **дря́хлый** (-хл, -ла́, -о) decrepit, senile.
дуб (*pl* -ы) oak; blockhead. **дуби́на** club, cudgel; blockhead. **дуби́нка** truncheon, baton.
дублёнка sheepskin coat.
дублёр understudy. **дублика́т** duplicate. **дубли́ровать** duplicate; understudy; dub.
дубо́вый oak; coarse; clumsy.
дуга́ (*pl* -и) arc; arch.
ду́дка pipe, fife.
ду́ло muzzle; barrel.
ду́ма thought; Duma (*lower house of Russian parliament*). **ду́мать** *impf* (*pf* **по~**) think; *+inf* think of, intend. **ду́маться** *impf* (*impers +dat*) seem.
дунове́ние puff, breath.
дупло́ (*pl* -а, -пел) hollow; hole; cavity.
ду́ра, дура́к (-а́) fool. **дура́чить** (-чу) *impf* (*pf* **о~**) fool, dupe; **~ся** play the fool.
дуре́ть (-е́ю) *impf* (*pf* **о~**) grow stupid.
дурма́н narcotic; intoxicant. **дурма́нить** *impf* (*pf* **о~**) stupefy.
дурно́й (-рен, -рна́, -о) bad, evil; ugly; **мне ду́рно** I feel faint, sick. **дурнота́** faintness; nausea.
ду́тый hollow; inflated. **дуть** (ду́ю) *impf* (*pf* **по~**) blow; **ду́ет** there is a draught. **ду́ться** (ду́юсь) *impf* pout; sulk.
дух spirit; spirits; heart; mind; breath; ghost; smell; **в ~е** in a good mood; **не в моём ~е** not to my taste; **ни слу́ху ни ~у** no news, not a word. **духи́** (-о́в) *pl* scent, perfume. **Ду́хов день** Whit Monday. **духове́нство** clergy. **духови́дец** (-дца) clairvoyant; medium. **духо́вка** oven. **духо́вный** spiritual; ecclesiastical. **духово́й** wind. **духота́** stuffiness, closeness.
душ shower(-bath).
душа́ (*acc* -у; *pl* -и) soul; heart; feeling; spirit; inspiration; **в душе́** inwardly; at heart; **от всей души́** with all one's heart.
душева́я *sb* shower-room.
душевнобольно́й mentally ill, insane; *sb* mental patient; lunatic. **душе́вный** mental; sincere, cordial.
души́стый fragrant; **~ горо́шек** sweet pea(s).
души́ть (-шу́, -шишь) *impf* (*pf* **за~**) strangle; stifle, smother.
души́ться (-шу́сь, -шишься) *impf* (*pf* **на~**) use, put on, perfume.
ду́шный (-шен, -шна́, -о) stuffy, close.
дуэ́ль duel.
дуэ́т duet.
ды́бом *adv* on end; **у меня́ во́лосы вста́ли ~** my hair stood on end. **дыбы́: станови́ться на ~** rear; resist.
дым (*loc* -у́; *pl* -ы) smoke. **дыми́ть** (-млю) *impf* (*pf* **на~**) smoke; **~ся** smoke; billow. **ды́мка** haze. **ды́мный** smoky. **дымов|о́й**: **~а́я труба́** flue, chimney. **дымо́к** (-мка́) puff of smoke. **дымохо́д** flue.
ды́ня melon.
дыра́ (*pl* -ы), **ды́рка** (*gen pl* -рок) hole; gap.

Д

дыха́ние breathing; breath. **дыха́тельн|ый** respiratory; breathing; **~ое го́рло** windpipe. **дыша́ть** (-шу́, -шишь) *impf* breathe.
дья́вол devil. **дья́вольский** devilish, diabolical.
дья́кон (*pl* -а́) deacon.
дю́жина dozen.
дюйм inch.
дю́на dune.
дя́дя (*gen pl* -ей) *m* uncle.
дя́тел (-тла) woodpecker.

Е

ева́нгелие gospel; the Gospels. **евангели́ческий** evangelical.
евре́й, евре́йка Jew; Hebrew. **евре́йский** Jewish.
е́вро *neut indecl* euro
Евро́па Europe. **европе́ец** (-е́йца) European. **европе́йский** European.
Еги́пет Egypt. **еги́петский** Egyptian. **египтя́нин** (*pl* -я́не, -я́н), **египтя́нка** Egyptian.
его́ *see* **он, оно́**; *pron* his; its.
еда́ food; meal.
едва́ *adv* & *conj* hardly; just; scarcely; **~ ли** hardly; **~ (ли) не** almost, all but.
еди́м *etc.*: *see* **есть**[1]
едине́ние unity. **едини́ца** (figure) one; unity; unit; individual. **едини́чный** single; individual.
едино- *in comb* mono-, uni-; one; co-. **единобра́чие** monogamy. **~вла́стие** autocracy. **~вре́менно** *adv* only once; simultaneously. **~гла́сие, ~ду́шие** unanimity. **~гла́сный, ~ду́шный** unanimous. **~кро́вный брат** half-brother. **~мы́слие** like-mindedness; agreement. **~мы́шленник** like-minded person. **~утро́бный брат** half-brother.
еди́нственно *adv* only, solely. **еди́нственный** only, sole. **еди́нство** unity. **еди́ный** one; single; united.
е́дкий (е́док, едка́, -о) caustic; pungent.
едо́к (-а́) mouth, head; eater.
е́ду *etc.*: *see* **е́хать**
её *see* **она́**; *pron* her, hers; its.
ёж (ежа́) hedgehog.
еже- *in comb* every; -ly. **ежего́дник** annual, year-book. **~го́дный** annual. **~дне́вный** daily. **~ме́сячник, ~ме́сячный** monthly. **~неде́льник, ~неде́льный** weekly.
ежеви́ка (*no pl*; *usu collect*) blackberry; blackberries; blackberry bush.
е́жели *conj* if.
ёжиться (ёжусь) *impf* (*pf* **съ~**) huddle up; shrink away.
езда́ ride, riding; drive, driving; journey. **е́здить** (е́зжу) *impf* go; ride, drive; **~ верхо́м** ride. **ездо́к** (-а́) rider.
ей *see* **она́**
ей-бо́гу *int* really! truly!
ел *etc.*: *see* **есть**[1]
е́ле *adv* scarcely; only just. **е́ле-е́ле** *emphatic variant of* **е́ле**
ёлка fir-tree, spruce; Christmas tree. **ёлочка** herring-bone pattern. **ёлочный** Christmas-tree. **ель** fir-tree; spruce.
ем *etc.*: *see* **есть**[1]
ёмкий capacious. **ёмкость** capacity.
ему́ *see* **он, оно́**
епи́скоп bishop.
е́ресь heresy. **ерети́к** (-а́) heretic. **ерети́ческий** heretical.
ёрзать *impf* fidget.
еро́шить (-шу) *impf* (*pf* **взъ~**) ruffle, rumple.
ерунда́ nonsense.
е́сли *conj* if; **~ бы** if only; **~ бы не** but for, if it were not for; **~ не** unless.
ест *see* **есть**[1]
есте́ственно *adv* naturally. **есте́ственный** natural. **естество́** nature; essence. **естествозна́ние** (natural) science.
есть[1] (ем, ешь, ест, еди́м; ел) *impf* (*pf* **съ~**) eat; corrode, eat away.

есть[2] *see* **быть**; is, are; there is, there are; **у меня́ ~** I have.
ефре́йтор lance-corporal.
е́хать (**е́ду**) *impf* (*pf* **по~**) go; ride, drive; travel; **~ верхо́м** ride.
ехи́дный malicious, spiteful.
ешь *see* **есть**[1]
ещё *adv* still; yet; (some) more; any more; yet, further; again; +*comp* still, even; **всё ~** still; **~ бы!** of course! and how!; **~ не, нет ~** not yet; **~ раз** once more; **кто ~?** who else? **пока́ ~** for the time being. **что ~?** what else?
е́ю *see* **она́**

Ж

ж *conj*: *see* **же**
жа́ба toad.
жа́бра (*gen pl* **-бр**) gill.
жа́воронок (**-нка**) lark.
жа́дничать *impf* be greedy; be mean. **жа́дность** greed; meanness. **жа́дный** (**-ден, -дна́, -о**) greedy; avid; mean.
жа́жда thirst; +*gen* thirst, craving for. **жа́ждать** (**-ду**) *impf* thirst, yearn.
жаке́т, жаке́тка jacket.
жале́ть (**-е́ю**) *impf* (*pf* **по~**) pity, feel sorry for; regret; +*acc or gen* grudge.
жа́лить *impf* (*pf* **у~**) sting, bite.
жа́лкий (**-лок, -лка́, -о**) pitiful. **жа́лко** *predic*: *see* **жаль**
жа́ло sting.
жа́лоба complaint. **жа́лобный** plaintive.
жа́лованье salary. **жа́ловать** *impf* (*pf* **по~**) +*acc or dat of person, instr or acc of thing* grant, bestow on; **~ся** complain (**на**+*acc* of, about).
жа́лостливый compassionate. **жа́лостный** piteous; compassionate. **жа́лость** pity. **жаль, жа́лко** *predic, impers* (it is) a pity; +*dat* it grieves; +*gen* grudge; **как ~** what a pity; **мне ~ его́** I'm sorry for him.
жалюзи́ *neut indecl* Venetian blind.
жанр genre.
жар (*loc* **-у́**) heat; heat of the day; fever; (high) temperature; ardour. **жара́** heat; hot weather.
жарго́н slang.
жа́реный roast; grilled; fried. **жа́рить** *impf* (*pf* **за~, из~**) roast; grill; fry; scorch, burn; **~ся** roast, fry. **жа́рк|ий** (**-рок, -рка́, -о**) hot; passionate; **-ое** *sb* roast (meat). **жаро́вня** (*gen pl* **-вен**) brazier. **жар-пти́ца** Firebird. **жа́рче** *comp of* **жа́ркий**
жа́тва harvest. **жать**[1] (**жну, жнёшь**) *impf* (*pf* **с~**) reap, cut.
жать[2] (**жму, жмёшь**) *impf* press, squeeze; pinch; oppress.
жва́чка chewing, rumination; cud; chewing-gum. **жва́чн|ый** ruminant; **~ое** *sb* ruminant.
жгу *etc.*: *see* **жечь**
жгут (**-а́**) plait; tourniquet.
жгу́чий burning. **жёг** *etc.*: *see* **жечь**
ждать (**жду, ждёшь; -ал, -а́, -о**) *impf* +*gen* wait (for); expect.
же, ж *conj* but; and; however; also; *partl* giving emphasis or expressing identity; **мне же ка́жется** it seems to me, however; **сего́дня же** this very day; **что же ты де́лаешь?** what on earth are you doing?
жева́тельная рези́нка chewing-gum. **жева́ть** (**жую́, жуёшь**) *impf* chew; ruminate.
жезл (**-а́**) rod; staff.
жела́ние wish, desire. **жела́нный** longed-for; beloved. **жела́тельный** desirable; advisable. **жела́ть** *impf* (*pf* **по~**) +*gen* wish for, desire; want.
желе́ *neut indecl* jelly.
железа́ (*pl* **же́лезы, -лёз, -за́м**) gland; *pl* tonsils.
железнодоро́жник railwayman. **железнодоро́жный** railway. **желе́зн|ый** iron; **~ая доро́га** railway. **желе́зо** iron.

е ж

железобето́н reinforced concrete. **жёлоб** (*pl* -á) gutter. **желобо́к** (-бка́) groove, channel, flute.
желте́ть (-е́ю) *impf* (*pf* **по~**) turn yellow; be yellow. **желто́к** (-тка́) yolk. **желту́ха** jaundice. **жёлтый** (жёлт, -а́, жёлто́) yellow.
желу́док (-дка) stomach. **желу́дочный** stomach; gastric.
жёлудь (*gen pl* -е́й) *m* acorn.
жёлчный bilious; gall; irritable. **жёлчь** bile, gall.
жема́ниться *impf* mince, put on airs. **жема́нный** mincing, affected. **жема́нство** affectedness.
же́мчуг (*pl* -á) pearl(s). **жемчу́жина** pearl. **жемчу́жный** pear(ly).
жена́ (*pl* жёны) wife. **жена́тый** married.
жени́ть (-ню́, -нишь) *impf* & *pf* (*pf also* **по~**) marry. **жени́тьба** marriage. **жени́ться** (-ню́сь, -нишься) *impf* & *pf* (+**на**+*prep*) marry, get married (to). **жени́х** (-á) fiancé; bridegroom. **же́нский** woman's; feminine; female. **же́нственный** womanly, feminine. **же́нщина** woman.
жердь (*gen pl* -е́й) pole; stake.
жеребёнок (-нка; *pl* -бя́та, -бя́т) foal. **жеребе́ц** (-бца́) stallion.
жеребьёвка casting of lots.
жерло́ (*pl* -а) muzzle; crater.
жёрнов (*pl* -á, -о́в) millstone.
же́ртва sacrifice; victim. **же́ртвенный** sacrificial. **же́ртвовать** *impf* (*pf* **по~**) present, make a donation (of); +*instr* sacrifice.
жест gesture. **жестикули́ровать** *impf* gesticulate.
жёсткий (-ток, -тка́, -о) hard, tough; rigid, strict; **~ диск** (*comput*) hard disk.
жесто́кий (-то́к, -á, -о) cruel; severe. **жесто́кость** cruelty.
жесть tin(-plate). **жестяно́й** tin.
жето́н medal; counter; token.
жечь (жгу, жжёшь; жёг, жгла) *impf* (*pf* **с~**) burn; **~ся** burn, sting; burn o.s.

живи́тельный invigorating. **жи́вность** poultry, fowl. **жив|о́й** (жив, -á, -о) living, alive; lively; vivid; brisk; animated; bright; **на ~у́ю ни́тку** hastily, anyhow; **шить на ~у́ю ни́тку** tack. **живопи́сец** (-сца) painter. **живопи́сный** picturesque. **жи́вопись** painting. **жи́вость** liveliness.
живо́т (-á) abdomen; stomach. **животново́дство** animal husbandry. **живо́тное** *sb* animal. **живо́тный** animal.
живу́ *etc.*: *see* **жить. живу́чий** hardy. **живьём** *adv* alive.
жи́дк|ий (-док, -дка́, -о) liquid; watery; weak; sparse; **~ий криста́лл** liquid crystal. **жи́дкость** liquid, fluid; wateriness, weakness. **жи́жа** sludge; slush; liquid. **жи́же** *comp of* **жи́дкий**
жи́зненный life, of life; vital; living; **~ у́ровень** standard of living. **жизнеописа́ние** biography. **жизнера́достный** cheerful. **жизнеспосо́бный** capable of living; viable. **жизнь** life.
жи́ла vein; tendon, sinew.
жиле́т, жиле́тка waistcoat.
жиле́ц (-льца́), **жили́ца** lodger; tenant; inhabitant.
жили́ще dwelling, abode. **жили́щный** housing; living.
жи́лка vein; fibre; streak.
жил|о́й dwelling; habitable; **~о́й дом** dwelling house; block of flats; **~а́я пло́щадь, жилпло́щадь** floor-space; housing, accommodation. **жильё** habitation; dwelling.
жир (*loc* -у́; *pl* -ы) fat; grease. **жире́ть** (-ре́ю) *impf* (*pf* **о~, раз~**) grow fat. **жи́рный** (-рен, -рна́, -о) fatty; greasy; rich. **жирово́й** fatty; fat.
жира́ф giraffe.
жите́йский worldly; everyday. **жи́тель** *m* inhabitant; dweller. **жи́тельство** residence. **жи́тница** granary. **жи́то** corn, cereal. **жить** (живу́, -вёшь; жил, -á, -о) *impf* live. **житьё** life; existence; habitation.

жму *etc.*: *see* **жать²**
жму́риться *impf* (*pf* **за~**) screw up one's eyes, frown.
жнивьё (*pl* -ья, -ьев) stubble (-field). **жну** *etc.*: *see* **жать¹**
жоке́й jockey.
жонглёр juggler.
жрать (жру, жрёшь; -ал, -а́, -о) guzzle.
жре́бий lot; fate, destiny; **~ бро́шен** the die is cast.
жрец priest. **жри́ца** priestess.
жужжа́ть (-жжу́) hum, buzz, drone; whiz(z).
жук (-а́) beetle.
жу́лик petty thief; cheat. **жу́льничать** *impf* (*pf* **с~**) cheat.
жура́вль (-я́) *m* crane.
жури́ть *impf* reprove.
журна́л magazine, periodical. **журнали́ст** journalist. **журнали́стика** journalism.
журча́ние babble; murmur. **журча́ть** (-чи́т) *impf* babble, murmur.
жу́ткий (-ток, -тка́, -о) uncanny; terrible, terrifying. **жу́тко** *adv* terrifyingly; terribly, awfully.
жую́ *etc.*: *see* **жева́ть**
жюри́ *neut indecl* judges.

З

за *prep* **I.** +*acc* (*indicating motion or action*) *or instr* (*indicating rest or state*) behind; beyond; across, the other side of; at; to; **за́ го́род, за́ городом** out of town; **за рубежо́м** abroad; **сесть за роя́ль** sit down at the piano; **сиде́ть за роя́лем** be at the piano; **за́ угол, за угло́м** round the corner. **II.** +*acc* after; over; during, in the space of; by; for; to; **за ва́ше здоро́вье!** your health!; **вести́ за́ руку** lead by the hand; **далеко́ за́ полночь** long after midnight; **за два дня до**+*gen* two days before; **за́ три киломе́тра от дере́вни** three kilometres from the village; **плати́ть за биле́т** pay for a ticket; **за после́днее вре́мя** lately. **III.** +*instr* after; for; because of; at, during; **год за го́дом** year after year; **идти́ за молоко́м** go for milk; **за обе́дом** at dinner.
заба́ва amusement; game; fun. **забавля́ть** *impf* amuse; **~ся** amuse o.s. **заба́вный** amusing, funny.
забастова́ть *pf* strike; go on strike. **забасто́вка** strike. **забасто́вщик** striker.
забве́ние oblivion.
забе́г heat, race. **забега́ть** *impf*, **забежа́ть** (-егу́) *pf* run up; +к+*dat* drop in on; **~ вперёд** run ahead; anticipate.
за|бере́менеть (-ею) *pf* become pregnant.
заберу́ *etc.*: *see* **забра́ть**
забива́ние jamming. **забива́ть(ся** *impf of* **заби́ть(ся¹**
забинтова́ть *pf*, **забинто́вывать** *impf* bandage.
забира́ть(ся *impf of* **забра́ть(ся**
заби́тый downtrodden. **заби́ть¹** (-бью́, -бьёшь) *pf* (*impf* **забива́ть**) drive in, hammer in; score; seal, block up; obstruct; choke; jam; cram; beat up; beat; **~ся** hide, take refuge; become cluttered *or* clogged; +**в**+*acc* get into, penetrate. **за|би́ть(ся²** *pf* begin to beat. **забия́ка** *m* & *f* squabbler; bully.
заблаговре́менно *adv* in good time; well in advance. **заблаговре́менный** timely.
заблесте́ть (-ещу́, -ести́шь *or* -е́щешь) *pf* begin to shine, glitter, glow.
заблуди́ться (-ужу́сь, -у́дишься) *pf* get lost. **заблу́дший** lost, stray. **заблужда́ться** *impf* be mistaken. **заблужде́ние** error; delusion.
забо́й (pit-)face.
заболева́емость sickness rate. **заболева́ние** sickness, illness; falling ill. **заболева́ть¹** *impf*, **заболе́ть¹** (-е́ю) *pf* fall ill; +*instr* go down with. **заболева́ть²**

impf, **заболе́ть²** (-ли́т) *pf* (begin to) ache, hurt.
забо́р¹ fence.
забо́р² taking away; obtaining on credit.
забо́та concern; care; trouble(s). **забо́тить** (-о́чу) *impf* (*pf* **о~**) trouble, worry; **~ся** *impf* (*pf* **по~**) worry; take care (**о**+*prep* of); take trouble; care. **забо́тливый** solicitous, thoughtful.
за|бракова́ть *pf*.
забра́сывать *impf of* **заброса́ть, забро́сить**
забра́ть (-беру́, -берёшь; -а́л, -а́, -о) *pf* (*impf* **забира́ть**) take; take away; seize; appropriate; **~ся** climb; get to, into.
забреда́ть *impf*, **забрести́** (-еду́, -едёшь; -ёл, -а́) *pf* stray, wander; drop in.
за|брони́ровать *pf*.
заброса́ть *pf* (*impf* **забра́сывать**) fill up; bespatter, deluge. **забро́сить** (-о́шу) *pf* (*impf* **забра́сывать**) throw; abandon; neglect. **забро́шенный** neglected; deserted.
забры́згать *pf*, **забры́згивать** *impf* splash, bespatter.
забыва́ть *impf*, **забы́ть** (-бу́ду) *pf* forget; **~ся** doze off; lose consciousness; forget o.s. **забы́вчивый** forgetful. **забытьё** oblivion; drowsiness.
забью́ *etc.*: *see* **заби́ть**
зава́ливать *impf*, **завали́ть** (-лю́, -лишь) *pf* block up; pile; cram; overload; knock down; make a mess of; **~ся** fall; collapse; tip up.
зава́ривать *impf*, **завари́ть** (-арю́, -а́ришь) *pf* make; brew; weld. **зава́рка** brewing; brew; welding.
заведе́ние establishment. **заве́довать** *impf* +*instr* manage.
заве́домо *adv* wittingly. **заве́домый** notorious, undoubted.
заведу́ *etc.*: *see* **завести́**
заве́дующий *sb* (+*instr*) manager; head.
завезти́ (-зу́, -зёшь; -ёз, -ла́) *pf* (*impf* **завози́ть**) convey, deliver.
за|вербова́ть *pf*.
завери́тель *m* witness. **заве́рить** *pf* (*impf* **заверя́ть**) assure; certify; witness.
заверну́ть (-ну́, -нёшь) *pf* (*impf* **завёртывать, завора́чивать**) wrap, wrap up; roll up; screw tight, screw up; turn (off); drop in, call in.
заверте́ться (-рчу́сь, -ртишься) *pf* begin to turn *or* spin; lose one's head.
завёртывать *impf of* **заверну́ть**
заверша́ть *impf*, **заверши́ть** (-шу́) *pf* complete, conclude. **заверше́ние** completion; end.
заверя́ть *impf of* **заве́рить**
заве́са veil, screen. **заве́сить** (-е́шу) *pf* (*impf* **заве́шивать**) curtain (off).
завести́ (-еду́, -ёшь; -вёл, -а́) *pf* (*impf* **заводи́ть**) take, bring; drop off; start up; acquire; introduce; wind (up), crank; **~сь** be; appear; be established; start.
заве́т behest, bidding, ordinance; Testament. **заве́тный** cherished; secret.
заве́шивать *impf of* **заве́сить**
завеща́ние will, testament. **завеща́ть** bequeath.
завзя́тый inveterate.
завива́ть(ся *impf of* **зави́ть(ся.** **зави́вка** waving; wave.
зави́дно *impers*+*dat*: **мне ~** I feel envious. **зави́дный** enviable. **зави́довать** *impf* (*pf* **по~**) +*dat* envy.
завинти́ть (-нчу́) *pf*, **зави́нчивать** *impf* screw up.
зависа́ть *impf*, **зави́снуть** (-нет, -ви́с(нул)) *pf* (*comput*) crash.
зави́сеть (-йшу) *impf* +**от**+*gen* depend on. **зави́симость** dependence; **в зави́симости от** depending on, subject to. **зави́симый** dependent.
зави́стливый envious. **за́висть** envy.

завито́й (за́вит, -а́, -о) curled, waved. **завито́к** (-тка́) curl, lock; flourish. **зави́ть** (-вью́, -вьёшь; -и́л, -а́, -о) *pf* (*impf* **завива́ть**) curl, wave; **~ся** curl, wave, twine; have one's hair curled.

завладева́ть *impf*, **завладе́ть** (-е́ю) *pf* +*instr* take possession of; seize.

завлека́тельный alluring; fascinating. **завлека́ть** *impf*, **завле́чь** (-еку́, -ечёшь; -лёк, -ла́) *pf* lure; fascinate.

заво́д[1] factory; works; studfarm.

заво́д[2] winding mechanism. **заводи́ть(ся** (-ожу́(сь, -о́дишь(ся) *impf of* **завести́(сь. заводно́й** clockwork; winding, cranking.

заводско́й factory; *sb* factory worker. **заво́дчик** factory owner.

за́водь backwater.

завоева́ние winning; conquest; achievement. **завоева́тель** *m* conqueror. **завоева́ть** (-ою́ю) *pf*, **завоёвывать** *impf* conquer; win, gain; try to get.

завожу́ *etc.*: *see* **заводи́ть, завози́ть**

заво́з delivery; carriage. **завози́ть** (-ожу́, -о́зишь) *impf of* **завезти́**

завора́чивать *impf of* **заверну́ть. заворо́т** turn, turning; sharp bend.

заво́ю *etc.*: *see* **завы́ть**

завсегда́ *adv* always. **завсегда́тай** habitué, frequenter.

за́втра tomorrow. **за́втрак** breakfast; lunch. **за́втракать** *impf* (*pf* **по~**) have breakfast; have lunch. **за́втрашний** tomorrow's; **~ день** tomorrow.

завыва́ть *impf*, **завы́ть** (-во́ю) *pf* (begin to) howl.

завяза́ть (-яжу́, -я́жешь) *pf* (*impf* **завя́зывать**) tie, tie up; start; **~ся** start; arise; (*of fruit*) set. **завя́зка** string, lace; start; opening.

за|вя́знуть (-ну; -я́з) *pf.* **завя́зывать(ся** *impf of* **завяза́ть(ся**

за|вя́нуть (-ну; -я́л) *pf.*

загада́ть *pf*, **зага́дывать** *impf* think of; plan ahead; guess at the future; **~ зага́дку** ask a riddle. **зага́дка** riddle; enigma. **зага́дочный** enigmatic, mysterious.

зага́р sunburn, tan.

за|гаси́ть (-ашу́, -а́сишь) *pf.* **за|га́снуть** (-ну) *pf.*

загво́здка snag; difficulty.

заги́б fold; exaggeration. **загиба́ть** *impf of* **загну́ть**

за|гипнотизи́ровать *pf.*

загла́вие title; heading. **загла́вн|ый** title; **~ая бу́ква** capital letter.

загла́дить (-а́жу) *pf*, **загла́живать** *impf* iron, iron out; make up for; expiate; **~ся** iron out, become smooth; fade.

за|гло́хнуть (-ну; -гло́х) *pf.*

заглуша́ть *impf*, **за|глуши́ть** (-шу́) *pf* drown, muffle; jam; suppress, stifle; alleviate.

загляде́нье lovely sight. **загляде́ться** (-яжу́сь) *pf*, **загля́дываться** *impf* **на**+*acc* stare at; be lost in admiration of. **загля́дывать** *impf*, **загляну́ть** (-ну́, -нешь) *pf* peep; drop in.

загна́ть (-гоню́, -го́нишь; -а́л, -а́, -о) *pf* (*impf* **загоня́ть**) drive in, drive home; drive; exhaust.

загнива́ние decay; suppuration. **загнива́ть** *impf*, **загни́ть** (-ию́, -иёшь; -и́л, -а́, -о) *pf* rot; decay; fester.

загну́ть (-ну́, -нёшь) *pf* (*impf* **загиба́ть**) turn up, turn down; bend.

загова́ривать *impf*, **заговори́ть** *pf* begin to speak; tire out with talk; cast a spell over; protect with a charm (**от**+*gen* against). **за́говор** plot; spell. **загово́рщик** conspirator.

заголо́вок (-вка) title; heading; headline.

заго́н enclosure, pen; driving in. **загоня́ть**[1] *impf of* **загна́ть. загоня́ть**[2] *pf* tire out; work to death.

загора́живать *impf of* **загороди́ть**

загора́ть *impf*, **загоре́ть** (-рю́) *pf* become sunburnt; **~ся** catch fire;

3

blaze; *impers+dat* want very much. **загоре́лый** sunburnt.

загороди́ть (-рожу́, -ро́дишь) *pf* (*impf* **загора́живать**) enclose, fence in; obstruct. **загоро́дка** fence, enclosure.

за́городный suburban; country.

загота́вливать *impf*, **заготовля́ть** *impf*, **загото́вить** (-влю) *pf* lay in (a stock of); store; prepare. **загото́вка** (State) procurement.

загради́ть (-ажу́) *pf*, **огражда́ть** *impf* block, obstruct; bar. **загражде́ние** obstruction; barrier.

З

грани́ца abroad, foreign parts. **заграни́чный** foreign.

загреба́ть *impf*, **загрести́** (-ебу́, -ебёшь; -ёб, -ла́) *pf* rake up, gather; rake in.

загри́вок (-вка) withers; nape (of the neck).

за|гримирова́ть *pf*.

загроможда́ть *impf*, **загромозди́ть** (-зжу́) *pf* block up, encumber; cram.

загружа́ть *impf*, **за|грузи́ть** (-ужу́, -у́зишь) *pf* load; feed; (*comput*) boot; load; download; **~ся** *+instr* load up with, take on. **загру́зка** loading, feeding; charge, load, capacity.

за|грунтова́ть *pf*.

загрусти́ть (-ущу́) *pf* grow sad.

загрязне́ние pollution. **за|грязни́ть** *pf*, **загрязня́ть** *impf* soil; pollute; **~ся** become dirty.

загс *abbr* (*of* **(отде́л) за́писи а́ктов гражда́нского состоя́ния**) registry office.

загуби́ть (-блю́, -бишь) *pf* ruin; squander, waste.

загуля́ть *pf*, **загу́ливать** *impf* take to drink.

за|густе́ть *pf*.

зад (*loc* -у́; *pl* -ы́) back; hindquarters; buttocks; **~ом напере́д** back to front.

задава́ть(ся (-даю́(сь) *impf of* **зада́ть(ся**

задави́ть (-влю́, -вишь) *pf* crush; run over.

задади́м *etc.*, **зада́м** *etc.*: *see* **зада́ть**

зада́ние task, job.

зада́тки (-тков) *pl* abilities, promise.

зада́ток (-тка) deposit, advance.

зада́ть (-а́м, -а́шь, -а́ст, -ади́м; за́дал, -а́, -о) *pf* (*impf* **задава́ть**) set; give; **~ вопро́с** ask a question; **~ся** turn out well; succeed; **~ся мы́слью, це́лью** make up one's mind. **зада́ча** problem; task.

задвига́ть *impf*, **задви́нуть** (-ну) *pf* bolt; bar; push; **~ся** shut; slide. **задви́жка** bolt; catch.

задво́рки (-рок) *pl* back yard; backwoods.

задева́ть *impf of* **заде́ть**

заде́лать *pf*, **заде́лывать** *impf* do up; block up, close up.

заде́ну *etc.*: *see* **заде́ть. задёргивать** *impf of* **задёрнуть**

задержа́ние detention. **задержа́ть** (-жу́, -жишь) *pf*, **заде́рживать** *impf* delay; withhold; arrest; **~ся** stay too long; be delayed. **заде́ржка** delay.

задёрнуть (-ну) *pf* (*impf* **задёргивать**) pull; draw.

задеру́ *etc.*: *see* **задра́ть**

заде́ть (-е́ну) *pf* (*impf* **задева́ть**) brush (against), graze; offend; catch (against).

зади́ра *m* & *f* bully; troublemaker. **задира́ть** *impf of* **задра́ть**

за́дн|ий back, rear; **дать ~ий ход** reverse; **~яя мысль** ulterior motive; **~ий план** background; **~ий прохо́д** anus. **за́дник** back; backdrop.

задо́лго *adv* **+до**+*gen* long before.

за|должа́ть *pf*. **задо́лженность** debts.

задо́р fervour. **задо́рный** provocative; fervent.

задохну́ться (-ну́сь, -нёшься; -о́хся *or* -у́лся) *pf* (*impf* **задыха́ться**) suffocate; choke; pant.

за|дра́ть (-деру́, -дерёшь; -а́л, -а́, -о) *pf* (*impf also* **задира́ть**) tear to pieces, kill; lift up; break; provoke, insult.

задрема́ть (-млю́, -млешь) *pf* doze off.

задрожа́ть (-жу́) *pf* begin to tremble.

задува́ть *impf of* **заду́ть**

заду́мать *pf*, **заду́мывать** *impf* plan; intend; think of; **~ся** become thoughtful; meditate. **заду́мчивость** reverie. **заду́мчивый** pensive.

заду́ть (-у́ю) *pf* (*impf* **задува́ть**) blow out; begin to blow.

задуше́вный sincere; intimate.

за|души́ть (-ушу́, -у́шишь) *pf*.

задыха́ться *impf of* **задохну́ться**

заеда́ть *impf of* **зае́сть**

зае́зд calling in; lap, heat. **зае́здить** (-зжу) *pf* override; wear out. **заезжа́ть** *impf of* **зае́хать. зае́зженный** hackneyed; worn out. **зае́зжий** visiting.

заём (за́йма) loan.

зае́сть (-е́м, -е́шь, -е́ст, -еди́м) *pf* (*impf* **заеда́ть**) torment; jam; entangle.

зае́хать (-е́ду) *pf* (*impf* **заезжа́ть**) call in; enter, ride in, drive in; reach; **+за**+*acc* go past; **+за**+*instr* call for, fetch.

за|жа́рить(ся *pf*.

зажа́ть (-жму́, -жмёшь) *pf* (*impf* **зажима́ть**) squeeze; grip; suppress.

заже́чь (-жгу́, -жжёшь; -жёг, -жгла́) *pf* (*impf* **зажига́ть**) set fire to; kindle; light; **~ся** catch fire.

зажива́ть *impf of* **зажи́ть. заживи́ть** (-влю́) *pf*, **заживля́ть** *impf* heal. **за́живо** *adv* alive.

зажига́лка lighter. **зажига́ние** ignition. **зажига́тельный** inflammatory; incendiary. **зажига́ть(ся** *impf of* **заже́чь(ся**

зажи́м clamp; terminal; suppression. **зажима́ть** *impf of* **зажа́ть. зажимно́й** tight-fisted.

зажи́точный prosperous. **зажи́ть** (-иву́, -ивёшь; -ил, -а́, -о) *pf* (*impf* **зажива́ть**) heal; begin to live.

зажму́ *etc.*: *see* **зажа́ть. за|жму́риться** *pf*.

зазвене́ть (-и́т) *pf* begin to ring.

зазелене́ть (-е́ет) *pf* turn green.

заземле́ние earthing; earth. **заземли́ть** *pf*, **заземля́ть** *impf* earth.

зазнава́ться (-наю́сь, -наёшься) *impf*, **зазна́ться** *pf* give o.s. airs.

зазу́брина notch.

за|зубри́ть (-рю́, -у́бри́шь) *pf*.

заи́грывать *impf* flirt.

зáика *m* & *f* stammerer. **заика́ние** stammer. **заика́ться** *impf*, **заикну́ться** (-ну́сь, -нёшься) *pf* stammer, stutter; **+о**+*prep* mention.

заи́мствование borrowing. **заи́мствовать** *impf* & *pf* (*pf also* **по~**) borrow.

заинтересо́ванный interested. **заинтересова́ть** *pf*, **заинтересо́вывать** *impf* interest; **~ся** +*instr* become interested in.

заи́скивать *impf* ingratiate o.s.

зайду́ *etc.*: *see* **зайти́. займу́** *etc.*: *see* **заня́ть**

зайти́ (-йду́, -йдёшь; зашёл, -шла́) *pf* (*impf* **заходи́ть**) call; drop in; set; **+в**+*acc* reach; **+за**+*acc* go behind, turn; **+за** +*instr* call for, fetch.

за́йчик little hare (*esp. as endearment*); reflection of sunlight. **зайчи́ха** doe hare.

закабали́ть *pf*, **закабаля́ть** *impf* enslave.

закады́чный intimate, bosom.

зака́з order; **на ~** to order. **заказа́ть** (-ажу́, -а́жешь) *pf*, **зака́зывать** *impf* order; book. **заказн|о́й** made to order; **~о́е (письмо́)** registered letter. **зака́зчик** customer, client.

зака́л temper; cast. **зака́ливать** *impf*, **закали́ть** (-лю́) *pf* (*impf also* **закаля́ть**) temper; harden. **зака́лка** tempering, hardening.

зака́лывать *impf of* **заколо́ть. закаля́ть** *impf of* **закали́ть. зака́нчивать(ся** *impf of* **зако́нчить(ся**

зака́пать *pf*, **зака́пывать**[1] *impf* begin to drip; rain; spot.

зака́пывать[2] *impf of* **закопа́ть**
зака́т sunset. **заката́ть** *pf*, **зака́тывать**[1] *impf* begin to roll; roll up; roll out. **закати́ть** (-ачу́, -а́тишь) *pf*, **зака́тывать**[2] *impf* roll; **~ся** roll; set.
заква́ска ferment; leaven.
закида́ть *pf*, **заки́дывать**[1] *impf* shower; bespatter.
заки́дывать[2] *impf*, **заки́нуть** (-ну) *pf* throw (out, away).
закипа́ть *impf*, **закипе́ть** (-пи́т) *pf* begin to boil.

закиса́ть *impf*, **заки́снуть** (-ну; -и́с, -ла) *pf* turn sour; become apathetic. **за́кись** oxide.
закла́д pawn; pledge; bet; **би́ться об ~** bet; **в ~е** in pawn. **закла́дка** laying; bookmark. **закладно́й** pawn. **закла́дывать** *impf of* **заложи́ть**
закле́ивать *impf*, **закле́ить** *pf* glue up.
за|клейми́ть (-млю́) *pf*.
заклепа́ть *pf*, **заклёпывать** *impf* rivet. **заклёпка** rivet; riveting.
заклина́ние incantation; spell. **заклина́ть** *impf* invoke; entreat.
заключа́ть *impf*, **заключи́ть** (-чу́) *pf* conclude; enter into; contain; confine. **заключа́ться** consist; lie, be. **заключе́ние** conclusion; decision; confinement. **заключённый** *sb* prisoner. **заключи́тельный** final, concluding.
закля́тие pledge. **закля́тый** sworn.
закова́ть (-кую́, -куёшь) *pf*, **зако́вывать** *impf* chain; shackle.
закола́чивать *impf of* **заколоти́ть**
заколдо́ванный bewitched; **~ круг** vicious circle. **заколдова́ть** *pf* bewitch; lay a spell on.
зако́лка hair-grip; hair-slide.
заколоти́ть (-лочу́, -ло́тишь) *pf* (*impf* **закола́чивать**) board up; knock in; knock insensible.
за|коло́ть (-олю́, -о́лешь) *pf* (*impf also* **зака́лывать**) stab; pin up; (*impers*) **у меня́ заколо́ло в боку́** I have a stitch.
зако́н law. **законнорождённый** legitimate. **зако́нность** legality. **зако́нный** legal; legitimate.
законо- *in comb* law, legal. **законове́дение** law, jurisprudence. **~да́тельный** legislative. **~да́тельство** legislation. **~ме́рность** regularity, normality. **~ме́рный** regular, natural. **~прое́кт** bill.
за|консерви́ровать *pf*. **за|конспекти́ровать** *pf*.
зако́нченность completeness. **зако́нченный** finished; accomplished. **зако́нчить** (-чу) *pf* (*impf* **зака́нчивать**) end, finish; **~ся** end, finish.
закопа́ть *pf* (*impf* **зака́пывать**[2]) begin to dig; bury.
закопте́лый sooty, smutty. **за|копте́ть** (-ти́т) *pf*. **за|копти́ть** (-пчу́) *pf*.
закорене́лый deep-rooted; inveterate.
закосне́лый incorrigible.
закоу́лок (-лка) alley; nook.
закочене́лый numb with cold. **за|кочене́ть** (-е́ю) *pf*.
закра́дываться *impf of* **закра́сться**
закра́сить (-а́шу) *pf* (*impf* **закра́шивать**) paint over.
закра́сться (-аду́сь, -адёшься) *pf* (*impf* **закра́дываться**) steal in, creep in.
закра́шивать *impf of* **закра́сить**
закрепи́тель *m* fixative. **закрепи́ть** (-плю́) *pf*, **закрепля́ть** *impf* fasten; fix; consolidate; **+за**+*instr* assign to; **~ за собо́й** secure.
закрепости́ть (-ощу́) *pf*, **закрепоща́ть** *impf* enslave. **закрепоще́ние** enslavement; slavery, serfdom.
закрича́ть (-чу́) *pf* cry out; begin to shout.
закро́йщик cutter.
закро́ю *etc.*: *see* **закры́ть**
закругле́ние rounding; curve. **закругли́ть** (-лю́) *pf*, **закругля́ть** *impf* make round; round off; **~ся**

become round; round off.

закружи́ться (-ужу́сь, -у́жишься) *pf* begin to whirl *or* go round.

за|крути́ть (-учу́, -у́тишь) *pf*, **закру́чивать** *impf* twist, twirl; wind round; turn; screw in; turn the head of; **~ся** twist, twirl, whirl; wind round.

закрыва́ть *impf*, **закры́ть** (-ро́ю) *pf* close, shut; turn off; close down; cover; **~ся** close, shut; end; close down; cover o.s.; shelter. **закры́тие** closing; shutting; closing down; shelter. **закры́тый** closed, shut; private.

закули́сный behind the scenes; backstage.

закупа́ть *impf*, **закупи́ть** (-плю́, -пишь) *pf* buy up; stock up with. **заку́пка** purchase.

заку́поривать *impf*, **заку́порить** *pf* cork; stop up; coop up. **заку́порка** corking; thrombosis.

заку́почный purchase. **заку́пщик** buyer.

заку́ривать *impf*, **закури́ть** (-рю́, -ришь) *pf* light up; begin to smoke.

закуси́ть (-ушу́, -у́сишь) *pf*, **заку́сывать** *impf* have a snack; bite. **заку́ска** hors-d'oeuvre; snack. **заку́сочная** *sb* snack-bar.

за|ку́тать *pf*, **заку́тывать** *impf* wrap up; **~ся** wrap o.s. up.

зал hall; **~ ожида́ния** waiting-room.

залега́ть *impf of* **зале́чь**

за|ледене́ть (-е́ю) *pf*.

залежа́лый stale, long unused. **залежа́ться** (-жу́сь) *pf*, **залёживаться** *impf* lie too long; find no market; become stale. **за́лежь** deposit, seam; stale goods.

залеза́ть *impf*, **зале́зть** (-зу; -е́з) *pf* climb, climb up; get in; creep in.

за|лепи́ть (-плю́, -пишь) *pf*, **залепля́ть** *impf* paste over; glue up.

залета́ть *impf*, **залете́ть** (-ечу́) *pf* fly; **+в**+*acc* fly into.

зале́чивать *impf*, **залечи́ть** (-чу́, -чишь) *pf* heal, cure; **~ся** heal (up).

зале́чь (-ля́гу, -ля́жешь; залёг, -ла́) *pf* (*impf* **залега́ть**) lie down; lie low; lie, be deposited.

зали́в bay; gulf. **залива́ть** *impf*, **зали́ть** (-лью́, -льёшь; за́лил, -а́, -о) *pf* flood, inundate; spill on; extinguish; spread; **~ся** be flooded; pour, spill; +*instr* break into.

зало́г deposit; pledge; security, mortgage; token; voice. **заложи́ть** (-жу́, -жишь) *pf* (*impf* **закла́дывать**) lay; put; mislay; pile up; pawn, mortgage; harness; lay in. **зало́жник** hostage.

залп volley, salvo; **~ом** without pausing for breath.

залью́ *etc.*: *see* **зали́ть. заля́гу** *etc.*: *see* **зале́чь**

зам *abbr* (*of* **замести́тель**) assistant, deputy. **зам-** *abbr in comb* (*of* **замести́тель**) assistant, deputy, vice-.

за|ма́зать (-а́жу) *pf*, **зама́зывать** *impf* paint over; putty; smear; soil; **~ся** get dirty. **зама́зка** putty; puttying.

зама́лчивать *impf of* **замолча́ть**

зама́нивать *impf*, **замани́ть** (-ню́, -нишь) *pf* entice; decoy. **зама́нчивый** tempting.

за|марино́вать *pf*.

за|маскирова́ть *pf*, **замаскиро́вывать** *impf* mask; disguise; **~ся** disguise o.s.

зама́хиваться *impf*, **замахну́ться** (-ну́сь, -нёшься) *pf* +*instr* raise threateningly.

зама́чивать *impf of* **замочи́ть**

замедле́ние slowing down, deceleration; delay. **заме́длить** *pf*, **замедля́ть** *impf* slow down; slacken; delay; **~ся** slow down.

замёл *etc.*: *see* **замести́**

заме́на substitution; substitute. **замени́мый** replaceable. **замени́тель** *m* (+*gen*) substitute (for). **замени́ть** (-ню́, -нишь) *pf*, **заменя́ть** *impf* replace; be a substitute for.

З

замере́ть (-мру́, -мрёшь; за́мер, -ла́, -о) *pf* (*impf* **замира́ть**) stand still; freeze; die away.

замерза́ние freezing. **замерза́ть** *impf*, **за|мёрзнуть** (-ну; замёрз) *pf* freeze (up); freeze to death.

заме́рить *pf* (*impf* **замеря́ть**) measure, gauge.

замеси́ть (-ешу́, -е́сишь) *pf* (*impf* **заме́шивать²**) knead.

замести́ (-ету́, -етёшь; -мёл, -а́) *pf* (*impf* **замета́ть**) sweep up; cover.

замести́тель *m* substitute; assistant, deputy, vice-. **замести́ть** (-ещу́) *pf* (*impf* **замеща́ть**) replace; deputize for.

З

замета́ть *impf of* **замести́**

заме́тить (-е́чу) *pf* (*impf* **замеча́ть**) notice; note; remark. **заме́тка** mark; note. **заме́тный** noticeable; outstanding.

замеча́ние remark; reprimand. **замеча́тельный** remarkable; splendid. **замеча́ть** *impf of* **заме́тить**

замеша́тельство confusion; embarrassment. **замеша́ть** *pf*, **заме́шивать¹** *impf* mix up, entangle. **заме́шивать²** *impf of* **замеси́ть**

замеща́ть *impf of* **замести́ть**. **замеще́ние** substitution; filling.

зами́нка hitch; hesitation.

замира́ть *impf of* **замере́ть**

за́мкнутый reserved; closed, exclusive. **замкну́ть** (-ну́, -нёшь) *pf* (*impf* **замыка́ть**) lock; close; **~ся** close; shut o.s. up; become reserved.

за́мок¹ (-мка) castle.

замо́к² (-мка́) lock; padlock; clasp.

замолка́ть *impf*, **замо́лкнуть** (-ну; -мо́лк) *pf* fall silent; stop.

замолча́ть (-чу́) *pf* (*impf* **зама́лчивать**) fall silent; cease corresponding; hush up.

замора́живать *impf*, **заморо́зить** (-ро́жу) *pf* freeze. **заморо́женный** frozen; iced. **за́морозки** (-ов) *pl* (slight) frosts.

замо́рский overseas.

за|мочи́ть (-чу́, -чишь) *pf* (*impf* also **зама́чивать**) wet; soak; ret.

замо́чная сква́жина keyhole.

замру́ *etc.*: *see* **замере́ть**

за́муж *adv*: **вы́йти ~** (**за**+*acc*) marry. **за́мужем** *adv* married (**за** +*instr* to).

за|му́чить (-чу) *pf* torment; wear out; bore to tears. **за|му́читься** (-чусь) *pf*.

за́мша suede.

замыка́ние locking; short circuit. **замыка́ть(ся** *impf of* **замкну́ть(ся**

за́мысел (-сла) project, plan. **замы́слить** *pf*, **замышля́ть** *impf* plan; contemplate.

за́навес, занаве́ска curtain.

занести́ (-су́, -сёшь; -ёс, -ла́) *pf* (*impf* **заноси́ть**) bring; note down; (*impers*) cover with snow etc.; (*impers*) skid.

занима́ть *impf* (*pf* **заня́ть**) occupy; interest; engage; borrow; **~ся** +*instr* be occupied with; work at; study.

зано́за splinter. **занози́ть** (-ожу́) *pf* get a splinter in.

зано́с snow-drift; skid. **заноси́ть** (-ошу́, -о́сишь) *impf of* **занести́**. **зано́счивый** arrogant.

заня́тие occupation; *pl* studies. **занято́й** busy. **за́нятый** (-нят, -а́, -о) occupied; taken; engaged. **заня́ть(ся** (займу́(сь, -мёшь(ся; за́нял(ся, -а́(сь, -о(сь) *pf of* **занима́ть(ся**

заодно́ *adv* in concert; at one; at the same time.

заостри́ть *pf*, **заостря́ть** *impf* sharpen; emphasize.

зао́чник, -ница student taking correspondence course; external student. **зао́чно** *adv* in one's absence; by correspondence course. **зао́чный курс** correspondence course.

за́пад west. **за́падный** west, western; westerly.

западня́ (*gen pl* -не́й) trap; pitfall, snare.

за|пакова́ть *pf*, **запако́вывать**

impf pack; wrap up.

запáл ignition; fuse. **запáльная свечá** (spark-)plug.

запáс reserve; supply; hem. **запасáть** *impf*, **запастú** (-сý, -сёшь; -áс, -лá) *pf* lay in a stock of; **~ся** +*instr* stock up with. **запаснóй, запáсный** spare; reserve; **~ вы́ход** emergency exit.

зáпах smell.

запáхивать *impf*, **запахнýть²** (-нý, -нёшь) *pf* wrap up.

запáхнуть¹ (-ну; -áх) *pf* begin to smell.

за|пáчкать *pf*.

запевáть *impf of* **запéть**; lead the singing.

запекáть(ся *impf of* **запéчь(ся. запекý** *etc.*: *see* **запéчь**

за|пеленáть *pf*.

заперéть (-прý, -прёшь; зáпер, -лá, -ло) *pf* (*impf* **запирáть**) lock; lock in; bar; **~ся** lock o.s. in.

запéть (-пою, -поёшь) *pf* (*impf* **запевáть**) begin to sing.

запечáтать *pf*, **запечáтывать** *impf* seal. **запечатлевáть** *impf*, **запечатлéть** (-éю) *pf* imprint, engrave.

запéчь (-екý, -ечёшь; -пёк, -лá) *pf* (*impf* **запекáть**) bake; **~ся** bake; become parched; clot, coagulate.

запивáть *impf of* **запúть**

запинáться *impf of* **запнýться. запúнка** hesitation.

запирáть(ся *impf of* **заперéть(ся**

записáть (-ишý, -úшешь) *pf*, **запúсывать** *impf* note; take down; record; enter; enrol; **~ся** register, enrol (**в**+*acc* at, in). **запúска** note. **записн|óй** note; inveterate; **~áя кнúжка** notebook. **зáпись** recording; registration; record.

запúть (-пью, -пьёшь; зáпил, -á, -о) *pf* (*impf* **запивáть**) begin drinking; wash down (with).

запихáть *pf*, **запúхивать** *impf*, **запихнýть** (-нý, -нёшь) *pf* push in, cram in.

запишý *etc.*: *see* **записáть**

заплáкать (-áчу) *pf* begin to cry.

за|планúровать *pf*.

заплáта patch.

за|платúть (-ачý, -áтишь) *pf* pay (**за**+*acc* for).

заплáчу *etc.*: *see* **заплáкать. заплачý** *see* **заплатúть**

заплестú (-етý, -етёшь; -ёл, -á) *pf*, **заплетáть** *impf* plait.

за|пломбировáть *pf*.

заплы́в heat, round. **заплывáть** *impf*, **заплы́ть** (-ывý, -ывёшь; -ы́л, -á, -о) *pf* swim in, sail in; swim out, sail out; be bloated.

запнýться (-нýсь, -нёшься) *pf* (*impf* **запинáться**) hesitate; stumble.

заповéдник reserve; preserve; **госудáрственный ~** national park. **заповéдный** prohibited. **зáповедь** precept; commandment.

заподáзривать *impf*, **заподóзрить** *pf* suspect (**в**+*prep* of).

запоздáлый belated; delayed. **запоздáть** *pf* (*impf* **запáздывать**) be late.

запóй hard drinking.

заползáть *impf*, **заползтú** *pf* (-зý, -зёшь; -óлз, -злá) creep, crawl.

запóлнить *pf*, **заполнять** *impf* fill (in, up).

запоминáть *impf*, **запóмнить** *pf* remember; memorize; **~ся** stay in one's mind.

зáпонка cuff-link; stud.

запóр bolt; lock; constipation.

за|потéть (-éет) *pf* mist over.

запою *etc.*: *see* **запéть**

запрáвить (-влю) *pf*, **заправля́ть** *impf* tuck in; prepare; refuel; season, dress; mix in; **~ся** refuel. **заправка** refuelling; seasoning, dressing.

запрáшивать *impf of* **запросúть**

запрéт prohibition, ban. **запретúть** (-ещý) *pf*, **запрещáть** *impf* prohibit, ban. **запрéтный** forbidden. **запрещéние** prohibition.

за|программúровать *pf*.

запрóс inquiry; overcharging; *pl* needs. **запросúть** (-ошý, -óсишь) *pf* (*impf* **запрáшивать**) inquire.

З

зáпросто *adv* without ceremony.
запрошý *etc.*: *see* **запросить.** **запрý** *etc.*: *see* **заперéть**
запрýда dam, weir; mill-pond.
запрягáть *impf*, **запрячь** (-ягý, -яжёшь; -яг, -лá) *pf* harness; yoke.
запугáть *pf*, **запýгивать** *impf* cow, intimidate.
зáпуск launching. **запускáть** *impf*, **запустить** (-ущý, -ýстишь) *pf* thrust (in); start; launch; (+*acc or instr*) fling; neglect. **запустéлый** neglected; desolate. **запустéние** neglect; desolation.

за|пýтать *pf*, **запýтывать** *impf* tangle; confuse; **~ся** get tangled; get involved.
запущý *etc.*: *see* **запустить**
запчáсть (*gen pl* -éй) *abbr* (*of* **запаснáя часть**) spare part.
запыхáться *pf* be out of breath.
запью *etc.*: *see* **запить**
запя́стье wrist.
запятáя *sb* comma.
за|пятнáть *pf*.
зарабáтывать *impf*, **заработать** *pf* earn; start (up). **зáработн|ый**: **~ая плáта** wages; pay. **зáработок** (-тка) earnings.
заражáть *impf*, **заразить** (-ажý) *pf* infect; **~ся** +*instr* be infected with, catch. **зарáза** infection. **заразительный** infectious. **зарáзный** infectious.
зарáнее *adv* in good time; in advance.
зарастáть *impf*, **зарасти** (-тý, -тёшь; -рóс, -лá) *pf* be overgrown; heal.
зáрево glow.
за|регистрировать(ся *pf*.
за|рéзать (-éжу) *pf* kill, knife; slaughter.
зарекáться *impf of* **зарéчься**
зарекомендовáть *pf*: **~ себя́** +*instr* show o.s. to be.
зарéчься (-екýсь, -ечёшься; -ёкся, -еклáсь) *pf* (*impf* **зарекáться**) +*inf* renounce.
за|ржавéть (-éет) *pf*.
зарисóвка sketching; sketch.
зародить (-ожý) *pf*, **зарождáть** *impf* generate; **~ся** be born; arise. **зарóдыш** foetus; embryo. **зарождéние** conception; origin.
зарóк vow, pledge.
зарóс *etc.*: *see* **зарасти**
зарóю *etc.*: *see* **зарыть**
зарплáта *abbr* (*of* **зáработная плáта**) wages; pay.
зарубáть *impf of* **зарубить**
зарубéжный foreign.
зарубéжье foreign countries.
зарубить (-блю, -бишь) *pf* (*impf* **зарубáть**) kill, cut down; notch. **зарýбка** notch.
заручáться *impf*, **заручиться** (-учýсь) *pf* +*instr* secure.
зарывáть *impf*, **зарыть** (-рóю) *pf* bury.
заря́ (*pl* **зóри, зорь**) dawn.
заря́д charge; supply. **зарядить** (-яжý, -я́дишь) *pf*, **заряжáть** *impf* load; charge; stoke; **~ся** be loaded; be charged. **заря́дка** loading; charging; exercises.
засáда ambush. **засадить** (-ажý, -áдишь) *pf*, **засáживать** *impf* plant; drive; set (**за**+*acc* to); **~ (в тюрьмý)** put in prison. **засáживаться** *impf of* **засéсть**
засáливать *impf of* **засолить**
засветить (-ечý, -éтишь) *pf* light; **~ся** light up.
за|свидéтельствовать *pf*.
засéв sowing; seed; sown area. **засевáть** *impf of* **засéять**
заседáние meeting; session. **заседáть** *impf* sit, be in session.
засéивать *impf of* **засéять.** **засéк** *etc.*: *see* **засéчь.** **засекáть** *impf of* **засéчь**
засекрéтить (-рéчу) *pf*, **засекрéчивать** *impf* classify as secret; clear, give access to secret material.
засекý *etc.*: *see* **засéчь.** **засéл** *etc.*: *see* **засéсть**
заселéние settlement. **заселить** *pf*, **заселя́ть** *impf* settle; colonize; populate.
засéсть (-ся́ду; -сéл) *pf* (*impf* **засá-**

живаться) sit down; sit tight; settle; lodge in.

засе́чь (-еку́, -ечёшь; -ёк, -ла́) *pf* (*impf* **засека́ть**) flog to death; notch.

засе́ять (-е́ю) *pf* (*impf* **засева́ть, засе́ивать**) sow.

заси́лье dominance, sway.

заслони́ть *pf*, **заслоня́ть** *impf* cover, screen; push into the background. **засло́нка** (*furnace, oven*) door.

заслу́га merit, desert; service. **заслу́женный** deserved, merited; Honoured; time-honoured. **заслу́живать** *impf*, **заслужи́ть** (-ужу́, -у́жишь) *pf* deserve; earn; +*gen* be worthy of.

засмея́ться (-ею́сь, -еёшься) begin to laugh.

заснима́ть *impf of* **засня́ть**

засну́ть (-ну́, -нёшь) *pf* (*impf* **засыпа́ть**) fall asleep.

засня́ть (-ниму́, -и́мешь; -я́л, -а́, -о) *pf* (*impf* **заснима́ть**) photograph.

засо́в bolt, bar.

засо́вывать *impf of* **засу́нуть**

засо́л salting, pickling. **засоли́ть** (-олю́, -о́ли́шь) *pf* (*impf* **заса́ливать**) salt, pickle.

засоре́ние littering; contamination; obstruction. **засори́ть** *pf*, **засоря́ть** *impf* litter; get dirt into; clog.

за|со́хнуть (-ну; -со́х) *pf* (*impf also* **засыха́ть**) dry (up); wither.

заста́ва gate; outpost.

застава́ть (-таю́, -таёшь) *impf of* **заста́ть**

заста́вить (-влю) *pf*, **заставля́ть** *impf* make; compel.

заста́иваться *impf of* **застоя́ться**. **заста́ну** *etc.*: *see* **заста́ть**

заста́ть (-а́ну) *pf* (*impf* **застава́ть**) find; catch.

застёгивать *impf*, **застегну́ть** (-ну́, -нёшь) *pf* fasten, do up. **застёжка** fastening; clasp, buckle; **~-мо́лния** zip.

застекли́ть *pf*, **застекля́ть** *impf* glaze.

засте́нок (-нка) torture chamber.

засте́нчивый shy.

застига́ть *impf*, **засти́гнуть, засти́чь** (-и́гну; -сти́г) *pf* catch; take unawares.

засти́чь *see* **засти́гнуть**

засто́й stagnation. **засто́йный** stagnant.

за|сто́пориться *pf*.

застоя́ться (-и́тся) *pf* (*impf* **заста́иваться**) stagnate; stand too long.

застра́ивать *impf of* **застро́ить**

застрахо́ванный insured. **за|страхова́ть** *pf*, **застрахо́вывать** *impf* insure.

застрева́ть *impf of* **застря́ть**

застрели́ть (-елю́, -е́лишь) *pf* shoot (dead); **~ся** shoot o.s.

застро́ить (-о́ю) *pf* (*impf* **застра́ивать**) build over, on, up. **застро́йка** building.

застря́ть (-я́ну) *pf* (*impf* **застрева́ть**) stick; get stuck.

за́ступ spade.

заступа́ться *impf*, **заступи́ться** (-плю́сь, -пишься) *pf* +**за**+*acc* stand up for. **засту́пник** defender. **засту́пничество** protection; intercession.

застыва́ть *impf*, **засты́ть** (-ы́ну) *pf* harden, set; become stiff; freeze; be petrified.

засу́нуть (-ну) *pf* (*impf* **засо́вывать**) thrust in, push in.

за́суха drought.

засы́пать[1] (-плю) *pf*, **засыпа́ть** *impf* fill up; strew.

засыпа́ть[2] *impf of* **засну́ть**

засыха́ть *impf of* **засо́хнуть**. **廷за́сяду**

затаённый (-ён, -ена́) secret; repressed. **зата́ивать** *impf*, **затаи́ть** *pf* suppress; conceal; harbour; **~ дыха́ние** hold one's breath.

зата́пливать *impf of* **затопи́ть**. **зата́птывать** *impf of* **затопта́ть**

зата́скивать *impf*, **затащи́ть** (-щу́, -щишь) *pf* drag in; drag off; drag away.

затвердева́ть *impf*, **за|тверде́ть** (-е́ет) *pf* become hard; set. **затверде́ние** hardening; callus.

затво́р bolt; lock; shutter; flood-gate. **затвори́ть** (-рю́, -ришь) *pf*, **затворя́ть** *impf* shut, close; **~ся** shut o.s. up, lock o.s. in. **затво́рник** hermit, recluse.

затева́ть *impf of* **зате́ять**

затёк *etc.*: *see* **зате́чь. затека́ть** *impf of* **зате́чь**

зате́м *adv* then, next; **~ что** because.

затемне́ние darkening, obscuring; blacking out; black-out. **затемни́ть** *pf*, **затемня́ть** *impf* darken, obscure; black out.

зате́ривать *impf*, **затеря́ть** *pf* lose, mislay; **~ся** be lost; be mislaid; be forgotten.

зате́чь (-ечёт, -еку́т; -тёк, -кла́) *pf* (*impf* **затека́ть**) pour, flow; swell up; become numb.

зате́я undertaking, venture; escapade; joke. **зате́ять** *pf* (*impf* **затева́ть**) undertake, venture.

затиха́ть *impf*, **зати́хнуть** (-ну; -ти́х) *pf* die down, abate; fade. **зати́шье** calm; lull.

заткну́ть (-ну́, -нёшь) *pf* (*impf* **затыка́ть**) stop up; stick, thrust.

затмева́ть *impf*, **затми́ть** (-ми́шь) *pf* darken; eclipse; overshadow. **затме́ние** eclipse.

зато́ *conj* but then, but on the other hand.

затону́ть (-о́нет) *pf* sink, be submerged.

затопи́ть[1] (-плю́, -пишь) *pf* (*impf* **зата́пливать**) light; turn on the heating.

затопи́ть[2] (-плю́, -пишь) *pf*, **затопля́ть** *impf* flood, submerge; sink.

затопта́ть (-пчу́, -пчешь) *pf* (*impf* **зата́птывать**) trample (down).

зато́р obstruction, jam; congestion.

за|тормози́ть (-ожу́) *pf*.

заточа́ть *impf*, **заточи́ть** (-чу́) *pf* incarcerate. **заточе́ние** incarceration.

затра́гивать *impf of* **затро́нуть**

затра́та expense; outlay. **затра́тить** (-а́чу) *pf*, **затра́чивать** *impf* spend.

затре́бовать *pf* request, require; ask for.

затро́нуть (-ну) *pf* (*impf* **затра́гивать**) affect; touch (on).

затрудне́ние difficulty. **затрудни́тельный** difficult. **затрудни́ть** *pf*, **затрудня́ть** *impf* trouble; make difficult; hamper; **~ся** +*inf or instr* find difficulty in.

за|тупи́ться (-пится) *pf*.

за|туши́ть (-шу́, -шишь) *pf* extinguish; suppress.

за́тхлый musty, mouldy; stuffy.

затыка́ть *impf of* **заткну́ть**

заты́лок (-лка) back of the head; scrag-end.

затя́гивать *impf*, **затяну́ть** (-ну́, -нешь) *pf* tighten; cover; close, heal; spin out; **~ся** be covered; close; be delayed; drag on; inhale. **затя́жка** inhaling; prolongation; delaying, putting off; lagging. **затяжно́й** long-drawn-out.

зауря́дный ordinary; mediocre.

зау́треня morning service.

зау́чивать *impf*, **заучи́ть** (-чу́, -чишь) *pf* learn by heart.

за|фарширова́ть *pf*. **за|фикси́ровать** *pf*. **за|фрахтова́ть** *pf*.

захва́т seizure, capture. **захвати́ть** (-ачу́, -а́тишь) *pf*, **захва́тывать** *impf* take; seize; thrill. **захва́тнический** aggressive. **захва́тчик** aggressor. **захва́тывающий** gripping.

захлебну́ться (-ну́сь, -нёшься) *pf*, **захлёбываться** *impf* choke (**от**+*gen* with).

захлестну́ть (-ну́, -нёшь) *pf*, **захлёстывать** *impf* flow over, swamp, overwhelm.

захло́пнуть (-ну) *pf*, **захло́пывать** *impf* slam, bang; **~ся** slam (to).

захо́д sunset; calling in. **заходи́ть** (-ожу́, -о́дишь) *impf of* **зайти**

захолу́стный remote, provincial. **захолу́стье** backwoods.
за|хорони́ть (-ню́, -нишь) *pf*. **за|хоте́ть(ся** (-очу́(сь, -о́чешь(ся, -оти́м(ся) *pf*.
зацвести́ (-етёт; -вёл, -а́) *pf*, **зацвета́ть** *impf* come into bloom.
зацепи́ть (-плю́, -пишь) *pf*, **зацепля́ть** *impf* hook; engage; sting; catch (**за**+*acc* on); **~ся за**+*acc* catch on; catch hold of.
зачасту́ю *adv* often.
зача́тие conception. **зача́ток** (-тка) embryo; rudiment; germ. **зача́точный** rudimentary. **зача́ть** (-чну́, -чнёшь; -ча́л, -а́, -о) *pf* (*impf* **зачина́ть**) conceive.
зачёл *etc*.: *see* **заче́сть**
заче́м *adv* why; what for. **заче́м-то** *adv* for some reason.
зачёркивать *impf*, **зачеркну́ть** (-ну́, -нёшь) *pf* cross out.
зачерпну́ть (-ну́, -нёшь) *pf*, **заче́рпывать** *impf* scoop up; draw up.
за|черстве́ть (-е́ет) *pf*.
заче́сть (-чту́, -чтёшь; -чёл, -чла́) *pf* (*impf* **зачи́тывать**) take into account, reckon as credit. **зачёт** test; **получи́ть, сдать ~ по**+*dat* pass a test in; **поста́вить ~ по**+*dat* pass in. **зачётная кни́жка** (student's) record book.
зачина́ть *impf of* **зача́ть. зачи́нщик** instigator.
зачи́слить *pf*, **зачисля́ть** *impf* include; enter; enlist; **~ся** join, enter.
зачи́тывать *impf of* **заче́сть.**
зачту́ *etc*.: *see* **заче́сть. зашёл** *etc*.: *see* **зайти́**
зашива́ть *impf*, **заши́ть** (-шью́, -шьёшь) *pf* sew up.
за|шифрова́ть *pf*, **зашифро́вывать** *impf* encipher, encode.
за|шнурова́ть *pf*, **зашнуро́вывать** *impf* lace up.
за|шпаклева́ть (-лю́ю) *pf*. **за|што́пать** *pf*. **за|штрихова́ть** *pf*.
зашью́ *etc*.: *see* **заши́ть**
защи́та defence; protection. **защити́ть** (-ищу́) *pf*, **защища́ть** *impf* defend, protect. **защи́тник** defender. **защи́тный** protective.
заяви́ть (-влю́, -вишь) *pf*, **заявля́ть** *impf* announce, declare; **~ся** turn up. **зая́вка** claim; demand. **заявле́ние** statement; application.
за́яц (за́йца) hare; stowaway; **е́хать за́йцем** travel without a ticket.
зва́ние rank; title. **зва́ный** invited; **~ обе́д** banquet, dinner. **зва́тельный** vocative. **звать** (зову́, -вёшь; звал, -а́, -о) *impf* (*pf* **по~**) call; ask, invite; **как вас зову́т?** what is your name?; **~ся** be called.
звезда́ (*pl* звёзды) star. **звёздный** star; starry; starlit; stellar. **звёздочка** little star; asterisk.
звене́ть (-ню́) *impf* ring; +*instr* jingle, clink.
звено́ (*pl* зве́нья, -ьев) link; team, section; unit; component. **звеньево́й** *sb* section leader.
звери́нец (-нца) menagerie. **звероводство** fur farming. **зве́рский** brutal; terrific. **зве́рство** atrocity. **зве́рствовать** *impf* commit atrocities. **зверь** (*pl* -и, -е́й) *m* wild animal.
звон ringing (sound); peal, chink, clink. **звони́ть** *impf* (*pf* **по~**) ring; ring up; **~ кому́-нибу́дь (по телефо́ну)** ring s.o. up. **зво́нкий** (-нок, -нка́, -о) ringing, clear. **звоно́к** (-нка́) bell; (*telephone*) call.
звук sound.
звуко- *in comb* sound. **звукоза́пись** (sound) recording. **~изоля́ция** sound-proofing. **~непроница́емый** sound-proof. **~снима́тель** *m* pick-up.
звуково́й sound; audio; acoustic. **звуча́ние** sound(ing); vibration. **звуча́ть** (-чи́т) *impf* (*pf* **про~**) be heard; sound. **зву́чный** (-чен, -чна́, -о) sonorous.
зда́ние building.
здесь *adv* here. **зде́шний** local; **не ~** a stranger here.
здоро́ваться *impf* (*pf* **по~**) exchange greetings. **здо́рово** *adv*

З

splendidly; very (much); well done!; great! **здоро́вый** healthy, strong; well; wholesome, sound. **здоро́вье** health; **за ва́ше ~!** your health! **как ва́ше ~?** how are you? **здра́вница** sanatorium.

здравомы́слящий sensible, judicious. **здравоохране́ние** public health.

здра́вствовать *impf* be healthy; prosper. **здра́вствуй(те)** how do you do?; hello! **да здра́вствует!** long live! **здра́вый** sensible; **~ смысл** common sense.

З

зе́бра zebra.

зева́ть *impf*, **зевну́ть** (-ну́, -нёшь) *pf* yawn; gape; (*pf also* **про~**) miss, let slip, lose. **зево́к** (-вка́), **зево́та** yawn.

зелене́ть (-е́ет) *impf* (*pf* **по~**) turn green; show green. **зелёный** (зе́лен, -а́, -о) green; **~ лук** spring onions. **зе́лень** green; greenery; greens.

земе́льный land.

земле- *in comb* land; earth. **землевладе́лец** (-льца) landowner. **~де́лец** (-льца) farmer. **~де́лие** farming, agriculture. **~де́льческий** agricultural. **~ко́п** navvy. **~ро́йный** excavating. **~трясе́ние** earthquake.

земля́ (*acc* -ю; *pl* -и, земе́ль, -ям) earth; ground; land; soil. **земля́к** (-а́) fellow-countryman. **земляни́ка** (*no pl*; *usu collect*) wild strawberry; wild strawberries. **земля́нка** dug-out; mud hut. **земляно́й** earthen; earth. **земля́чка** country-woman. **земно́й** earthly; terrestrial; ground; mundane; **~ шар** the globe.

зени́т zenith. **зени́тный** zenith; anti-aircraft.

зе́ркало (*pl* -а́) mirror. **зерка́льный** mirror; smooth; plate-glass.

зерни́стый grainy. **зерно́** (*pl* зёрна, зёрен) grain; seed; kernel, core; **ко́фе в зёрнах** coffee beans. **зерново́й** grain. **зерновы́е** *sb pl* cereals. **зернохрани́лище** granary.

зигза́г zigzag.

зима́ (*acc* -у; *pl* -ы) winter. **зи́мний** winter, wintry. **зимова́ть** *impf* (*pf* **пере~, про~**) spend the winter; hibernate. **зимо́вка** wintering; hibernation. **зимо́вье** winter quarters. **зимо́й** *adv* in winter.

зия́ть *impf* gape, yawn.

злак grass; cereal.

злить (злю) *impf* (*pf* **обо~, о~, разо~**) anger; irritate; **~ся** be angry, be in a bad temper; rage. **зло** (*gen pl* зол) evil; harm; misfortune; malice.

зло- *in comb* evil, harm, malice. **злове́щий** ominous. **~во́ние** stink. **~во́нный** stinking. **~ка́чественный** malignant; pernicious. **~па́мятный** rancorous, unforgiving. **~ра́дный** malevolent, gloating. **~сло́вие** malicious gossip. **~умы́шленник** malefactor; plotter. **~язы́чный** slanderous.

зло́ба spite; anger; **~ дня** topic of the day, latest news. **зло́бный** malicious. **злободне́вный** topical. **злоде́й** villain. **злоде́йский** villainous. **злоде́йство** villainy; crime, evil deed. **злодея́ние** crime, evil deed. **злой** (зол, зла) evil; wicked; malicious; vicious; bad-tempered; severe. **зло́стный** malicious; intentional. **злость** malice; fury.

злоупотреби́ть (-блю́) *pf*, **злоупотребля́ть** *impf* +*instr* abuse. **злоупотребле́ние** +*instr* abuse of.

зме́йный snake; cunning. **змей** snake; dragon; kite. **змея́** (*pl* -и) snake.

знак sign; mark; symbol.

знако́мить (-млю) *impf* (*pf* **о~, по~**) acquaint; introduce; **~ся** become acquainted; get to know; +**с**+*instr* meet, make the acquaintance of. **знако́мство** acquaintance; (circle of) acquaintances. **знако́м|ый** familiar; **быть ~ым с**+*instr* be acquainted with, know; **~ый, ~ая** *sb* acquaintance.

знамена́тель *m* denominator. **знамена́тельный** significant. **зна́мение** sign. **знамени́тость** celebrity. **знамени́тый** celebrated, famous. **зна́мя** (-мени; *pl* -мёна) *neut* banner; flag.

зна́ние knowledge.

зна́тный (-тен, -тна́, -о) distinguished; aristocratic; splendid.

знато́к (-а́) expert; connoisseur. **знать** *impf* know; **дать ~** inform, let know.

значе́ние meaning; significance; importance. **зна́чит** so then; that means. **значи́тельный** considerable; important; significant. **зна́чить** (-чу) *impf* mean; signify; be of importance; **~ся** be; be mentioned, appear. **значо́к** (-чка́) badge; mark.

зна́ющий expert; learned.

знobи́ть *impf, impers+acc*: **меня́**, *etc.*, **знобит** I, *etc.*, feel shivery.

зной intense heat. **зно́йный** hot; burning.

зов call, summons. **зову́** *etc.*: *see* **звать**

зо́дчество architecture. **зо́дчий** *sb* architect.

зол *see* **зло, злой**

зола́ ashes, cinders.

золо́вка sister-in-law (*husband's sister*).

золоти́стый golden. **зо́лото** gold. **золото́й** gold; golden.

золочёный gilt, gilded.

зо́на zone; region.

зонд probe. **зонди́ровать** *impf* sound, probe.

зонт (-а́), **зо́нтик** umbrella.

зоо́лог zoologist. **зоологи́ческий** zoological. **зооло́гия** zoology. **зоопа́рк** zoo. **зооте́хник** livestock specialist.

зо́ри *etc.*: *see* **заря́**

зо́ркий (-рок, -рка́, -о) sharp-sighted; perspicacious.

зрачо́к (-чка́) pupil (*of the eye*).

зре́лище sight; spectacle.

зре́лость ripeness; maturity; **аттеста́т зре́лости** school-leaving certificate. **зре́лый** (зрел, -а́, -о) ripe, mature.

зре́ние (eye)sight, vision; **то́чка зре́ния** point of view.

зреть (-е́ю) *impf* (*pf* **со~**) ripen; mature.

зри́мый visible.

зри́тель *m* spectator, observer; *pl* audience. **зри́тельный** visual; optic; **~ зал** hall, auditorium.

зря *adv* in vain.

зуб (*pl* -ы *or* -бья, -о́в *or* -бьев) tooth; cog. **зуби́ло** chisel. **зубно́й** dental; tooth; **~ врач** dentist. **зубоврачéбный** dentists', dental; **~ кабине́т** dental surgery. **зубочи́стка** toothpick.

зубр (European) bison; die-hard.

зубри́ть (-рю́, зу́бришь) *impf* (*pf* **вы́~, за~**) cram.

зубча́тый toothed; serrated.

зуд itch. **зуде́ть** (-и́т) itch.

зы́бкий (-бок, -бка́, -о) unsteady, shaky; vacillating. **зыбь** (*gen pl* -е́й) ripple, rippling.

зюйд (*naut*) south; south wind.

зя́блик chaffinch.

зя́бнуть (-ну; зяб) *impf* suffer from cold, feel the cold.

зябь land ploughed in autumn for spring sowing.

зять (*pl* -тья́, -тьёв) son-in-law; brother-in-law (*sister's husband or husband's sister's husband*).

И, Й

и *conj* and; even; too; (*with neg*) either; **и... и** both … and.

и́бо *conj* for.

и́ва willow.

игла́ (*pl* -ы) needle; thorn; spine; quill. **иглоука́лывание** acupuncture.

игнори́ровать *impf & pf* ignore.

и́го yoke.

иго́лка needle.

игóрный gaming, gambling. **игрá** (*pl* -ы) play, playing; game; hand; turn; **~ слов** pun. **игрáльн|ый** playing; **~ые кóсти** dice. **игрáть** *impf* (*pf* **сыгрáть**) play; act; **~ в**+*acc* play (*game*); **~ на**+*prep* play (*an instrument*). **игри́вый** playful. **игрóк** (-á) player; gambler. **игрýшка** toy.

идеáл ideal. **идеали́зм** idealism. **идеáльный** ideal.

идéйный high-principled; acting on principle; ideological.

идеологи́ческий ideological. **идеолóгия** ideology.

И

идёт *etc.*: *see* **идти́**

идéя idea; concept.

иди́ллия idyll.

идиóт idiot.

и́дол idol.

идти́ (идý, идёшь; шёл, шла) *impf* (*pf* **пойти́**) go; come; run, work; pass; go on, be in progress; be on; fall; +(к+)*dat* suit.

иерéй priest.

иждивéнец (-нца), **-вéнка** dependant. **иждивéние** maintenance; **на иждивéнии** at the expense of.

из, изо *prep*+*gen* from, out of, of.

избá (*pl* -ы) izba (*hut*).

избáвить (-влю) *pf*, **избавля́ть** *impf* save, deliver; **~ся** be saved, escape; **~ся от** get rid of; get out of.

избалóванный spoilt. **из|баловáть**

избегáть *impf*, **избéгнуть** (-ну; -бéг(нул)) *pf*, **избежáть** (-егý) *pf* +*gen or inf* avoid; escape.

изберý *etc.*: *see* **избрáть**

избивáть *impf of* **изби́ть. избиéние** slaughter, massacre; beating, beating-up.

избирáтель *m*, **~ница** elector, voter. **избирáтельный** electoral; election. **избирáть** *impf of* **избрáть**

изби́тый trite, hackneyed. **изби́ть** (изобью́, -бьёшь) *pf* (*impf* **избивáть**) beat unmercifully, beat up; massacre.

и́збранн|ый selected; select; **~ые** *sb pl* the élite. **избрáть** (-берý, -берёшь; -áл, -á, -о) *pf* (*impf* **избирáть**) elect; choose.

избы́ток (-тка) surplus; abundance. **избы́точный** surplus; abundant.

и́зверг monster. **извержéние** eruption; expulsion; excretion.

извернýться (-нýсь, -нёшься) *pf* (*impf* **изворáчиваться**) dodge, be evasive.

извéстие news; information; *pl* proceedings. **извести́ть** (-ещý) *pf* (*impf* **извещáть**) inform, notify.

извёстка lime.

извéстно it is (well) known; of course, certainly. **извéстность** fame, reputation. **извéстный** known; well-known, famous; notorious; certain.

известня́к (-á) limestone. **и́звесть** lime.

извещáть *impf of* **извести́ть. извещéние** notification; advice.

извивáться *impf* coil; writhe; twist, wind; meander. **изви́лина** bend, twist. **изви́листый** winding; meandering.

извинéние excuse; apology. **извини́ть** *pf*, **извиня́ть** *impf* excuse; **извини́те (меня́)** excuse me, (I'm) sorry; **~ся** apologize; excuse o.s.

изви́ться (изовью́сь, -вьёшься; -и́лся, -áсь, -ось) *pf* coil; writhe.

извлекáть *impf*, **извлéчь** (-екý, -ечёшь; -ёк, -лá) *pf* extract; derive, elicit.

извнé *adv* from outside.

извóзчик cabman; carrier.

изворáчиваться *impf of* **извернýться. изворóт** bend, twist; *pl* tricks, wiles. **изворóтливый** resourceful; shrewd.

извратúть (-ащý) *pf*, **извращáть** *impf* distort; pervert. **извращéние** perversion; distortion. **извращённый** perverted, unnatural.

изги́б bend, twist. **изгибáть(ся** *impf of* **изогнýть(ся**

изгна́ние banishment; exile. **изгна́нник** exile. **изгна́ть** (-гоню́, -го́нишь; -а́л, -а́, -о) *pf* (*impf* **изгоня́ть**) banish; exile.
изголо́вье bed-head.
изголода́ться be famished, starve; +**по**+*dat* yearn for.
изгоню́ *etc.*: *see* **изгна́ть. изгоня́ть** *impf of* **изгна́ть**
и́згородь fence, hedge.
изгота́вливать *impf*, **изгото́вить** (-влю) *pf*, **изготовля́ть** *impf* make, manufacture; **~ся** get ready. **изготовле́ние** making, manufacture.
издава́ть (-даю́, -даёшь) *impf of* **изда́ть**
и́здавна *adv* from time immemorial; for a very long time.
издади́м *etc.*: *see* **изда́ть**
издалека́, и́здали *advs* from afar.
изда́ние publication; edition; promulgation. **изда́тель** *m* publisher. **изда́тельство** publishing house. **изда́ть** (-а́м, -а́шь, -а́ст, -ади́м; -а́л, -а́, -о) *pf* (*impf* **издава́ть**) publish; promulgate; produce; emit; **~ся** be published.
издева́тельство mockery; taunt. **издева́ться** *impf* (+**над** +*instr*) mock (at).
изде́лие work; make; article; *pl* wares.
изде́ржки (-жек) *pl* expenses; costs; cost.
из|до́хнуть *pf.*
из|жа́рить(ся *pf.*
изжо́га heartburn.
из-за *prep*+*gen* from behind; because of.
излага́ть *impf of* **изложи́ть**
излече́ние treatment; recovery; cure. **излечи́ть** (-чу́, -чишь) cure; **~ся** be cured; +**от**+*gen* rid o.s. of.
изли́шек (-шка) surplus; excess. **изли́шество** excess; over-indulgence. **изли́шний** (-шен, -шня) superfluous.
изложе́ние exposition; account. **изложи́ть** (-жу́, -жишь) *pf* (*impf* **излага́ть**) expound; set forth; word.
изло́м break, fracture; sharp bend. **излома́ть** *pf* break; smash; wear out; warp.
излуча́ть *impf* radiate, emit. **излуче́ние** radiation; emanation.
из|ма́зать (-а́жу) *pf* dirty, smear all over; use up; **~ся** get dirty, smear o.s. all over.
изме́на betrayal; treason; infidelity.
измене́ние change, alteration; inflection. **измени́ть**[1] (-ню́, -нишь) *pf* (*impf* **изменя́ть**[1]) change, alter; **~ся** change.
измени́ть[2] (-ню́, -нишь) *pf* (*impf* **изменя́ть**[2]) +*dat* betray; be unfaithful to. **изме́нник, -ица** traitor.
изменя́емый variable. **изменя́ть**[1,2](**ся** *impf of* **измени́ть**[1,2](**ся**
измере́ние measurement, measuring. **изме́рить** *pf*, **измеря́ть** *impf* measure, gauge.
измождённый (-ён, -а́) worn out.
из|му́чить (-чу) *pf* torment; tire out, exhaust; **~ся** be exhausted. **изму́ченный** worn out.
измышле́ние fabrication, invention.
измя́тый crumpled, creased; haggard, jaded. **из|мя́ть(ся** (изомну́(сь, -нёшь(ся) *pf.*
изна́нка wrong side; seamy side.
из|наси́ловать *pf* rape, assault.
изна́шивание wear (and tear). **изна́шивать(ся** *impf of* **износи́ть(ся**
изне́женный pampered; delicate; effeminate.
изнемога́ть *impf*, **изнемо́чь** (-огу́, -о́жешь; -о́г, -ла́) *pf* be exhausted. **изнеможе́ние** exhaustion.
изно́с wear; wear and tear; deterioration. **износи́ть** (-ошу́, -о́сишь) *pf* (*impf* **изна́шивать**) wear out; **~ся** wear out; be used up. **изно́шенный** worn out; threadbare.
изнуре́ние exhaustion. **из-**

нурённый (-ён, -ена́) exhausted, worn out; jaded. **изнури́тельный** exhausting.
изнутри́ *adv* from inside, from within.
изо *see* **из**
изоби́лие abundance, plenty. **изоби́ловать** *impf* +*instr* abound in, be rich in. **изоби́льный** abundant.
изоблича́ть *impf*, **изобличи́ть** (-чу́) *pf* expose; show. **изобличе́ние** exposure; conviction.
изобража́ть *impf*, **изобрази́ть** (-ажу́) *pf* represent, depict, portray (+*instr* as); **~ из себя́**+*acc* make o.s. out to be. **изображе́ние** image; representation; portrayal. **изобрази́тельн|ый** graphic; decorative; **~ые иску́сства** fine arts.
изобрести́ (-ету́, -етёшь; -ёл, -а́) *pf*, **изобрета́ть** *impf* invent; devise. **изобрета́тель** *m* inventor. **изобрета́тельный** inventive. **изобрете́ние** invention.
изобью́ *etc*.: *see* **изби́ть. изовью́сь** *etc*.: *see* **изви́ться**
изо́гнутый bent, curved; winding. **изогну́ть(ся** (-ну́(сь, -нёшь(ся) *pf* (*impf* **изгиба́ть(ся**) bend, curve.
изоли́ровать *impf* & *pf* isolate; insulate. **изоля́тор** insulator; isolation ward; solitary confinement cell. **изоля́ция** isolation; quarantine; insulation.
изомну́(сь *etc*.: *see* **измя́ть**
изо́рванный tattered, torn. **изорва́ть** (-ву́, -вёшь; -а́л, -а́, -о) *pf* tear, tear to pieces; **~ся** be in tatters.
изощрённый (-рён, -а́) refined; keen. **изощри́ться** *pf*, **изощря́ться** *impf* acquire refinement; excel.
из-под *prep*+*gen* from under.
Изра́иль *m* Israel. **изра́ильский** Israeli.
из|расхо́довать(ся *pf*.
и́зредка *adv* now and then.
изре́зать (-е́жу) *pf* cut up.
изрече́ние dictum, saying.
изры́ть (-ро́ю) *pf* dig up, plough up. **изры́тый** pitted.
изря́дно *adv* fairly, pretty. **изря́дный** fair, handsome; fairly large.
изуве́чить (-чу) *pf* maim, mutilate.
изуми́тельный amazing. **изуми́ть** (-млю́) *pf*, **изумля́ть** *impf* amaze; **~ся** be amazed. **изумле́ние** amazement.
изумру́д emerald.
изуро́дованный maimed; disfigured. **из|уро́довать** *pf*.
изуча́ть *impf*, **изучи́ть** (-чу́, -чишь) *pf* learn, study. **изуче́ние** study.
изъе́здить (-зжу) *pf* travel all over; wear out.
изъяви́ть (-влю́, -вишь) *pf*, **изъявля́ть** *impf* express.
изъя́н defect, flaw.
изъя́тие withdrawal; removal; exception. **изъя́ть** (изыму́, -мешь) *pf*. **изыма́ть** *impf* withdraw.
изыска́ние investigation, research; prospecting; survey. **изы́сканный** refined. **изыска́ть** (-ыщу́, -ы́щешь) *pf*, **изы́скивать** *impf* search out; (try to) find.
изю́м raisins.
изя́щество elegance, grace. **изя́щный** elegant, graceful.
ика́ть *impf*, **икну́ть** (-ну́, -нёшь) *pf* hiccup.
ико́на icon.
ико́та hiccup, hiccups.
икра́[1] (hard) roe; caviare.
икра́[2] (*pl* -ы) calf (*of leg*).
ил silt; sludge.
и́ли *conj* or; **~... ~** either ... or.
и́листый muddy, silty.
иллюзиони́ст conjurer. **иллю́зия** illusion.
иллюмина́тор porthole. **иллюмина́ция** illumination.
иллюстра́ция illustration. **иллюстри́ровать** *impf* & *pf* illustrate.
им *see* **он, они́, оно́**
им. *abbr* (*of* **и́мени**) named after.
и́мени *etc*.: *see* **и́мя**
име́ние estate.

имени́ны (-и́н) *pl* name-day (party). **имени́тельный** nominative. **и́менно** *adv* namely; exactly, precisely; **вот ~!** exactly!

име́ть (-е́ю) *impf* have; **~ де́ло с**+*instr* have dealings with; **~ ме́сто** take place; **~ся** be; be available.

и́ми *see* **они́**

имита́ция imitation. **имити́ровать** *impf* imitate.

иммигра́нт, ~ка immigrant. **иммигра́ция** immigration.

импера́тор emperor. **импера́торский** imperial. **императри́ца** empress. **империали́зм** imperialism. **империали́ст** imperialist. **империалисти́ческий** imperialist(ic). **импе́рия** empire.

и́мпорт import. **импорти́ровать** *impf & pf* import. **и́мпортный** import(ed).

импровиза́ция improvisation. **импровизи́ровать** *impf & pf* improvise.

и́мпульс impulse.

иму́щество property.

и́мя (и́мени; *pl* имена́, -ён) *neut* name; first name; noun; **~ прилага́тельное** adjective; **~ существи́тельное** noun; **~ числи́тельное** numeral.

и́на́че *adv* differently, otherwise; **так и́ли ~** in any event; *conj* otherwise, or else.

инвали́д disabled person; invalid. **инвали́дность** disablement, disability.

инвента́рь (-я́) *m* stock; equipment; inventory.

инде́ец (-е́йца) (American) Indian. **инде́йка** (*gen pl* -е́ек) turkey(-hen). **инде́йский** (American) Indian.

и́ндекс index; code.

индиа́нка Indian; American Indian. **инди́ец** (-и́йца) Indian.

индивидуали́зм individualism. **индивидуа́льность** individuality. **индивидуа́льный** individual. **индиви́дуум** individual.

инди́йский Indian. **И́ндия** India.

инду́с, инду́ска Hindu.

индустриализа́ция industrialization. **индустриализи́ровать** *impf & pf* industrialize. **индустриа́льный** industrial. **инду́стрия** industry.

индю́к, индю́шка turkey.

и́ней hoar-frost.

ине́ртность inertia; sluggishness. **ине́рция** inertia.

инжене́р engineer; **~-меха́ник** mechanical engineer; **~-строи́тель** *m* civil engineer.

инжи́р fig.

инициа́л initial.

инициати́ва initiative. **инициа́тор** initiator.

инквизи́ция inquisition.

инкруста́ция inlaid work, inlay.

инкуба́тор incubator.

ино- *in comb* other, different; hetero-. **иногоро́дний** of, from, another town. **~ро́дный** foreign. **~сказа́тельный** allegorical. **~стра́нец** (-нца), **~стра́нка** (*gen pl* -нок) foreigner. **~стра́нный** foreign. **~язы́чный** foreign.

иногда́ *adv* sometimes.

ино́й different; other; some; **~ раз** sometimes.

и́нок monk. **и́нокиня** nun.

инотде́л foreign department.

инсектици́д insecticide.

инспе́ктор inspector. **инспе́кция** inspection; inspectorate.

инста́нция instance.

инсти́нкт instinct. **инстинкти́вный** instinctive.

институ́т institute.

инстру́ктор instructor. **инстру́кция** instructions.

инструме́нт instrument; tool.

инсули́н insulin.

инсцениро́вка dramatization, adaptation; pretence.

интегра́ция integration.

интелле́кт intellect. **интеллектуа́льный** intellectual.

интеллиге́нт intellectual. **интеллиге́нтный** cultured, educated.

интеллигéнция intelligentsia.
интенси́вность intensity. **интенси́вный** intensive.
интеракти́вный interactive.
интервáл interval.
интервéнция intervention.
интервью́ *neut indecl* interview.
интерéс interest. **интерéсный** interesting. **интересовáть** *impf* interest; **~ся** be interested (*+instr* in).
интернáт boarding-school.
интернационáльный international.
Интернéт the Internet; **в ~е** on the Internet.

И

интерни́ровать *impf & pf* intern.
интерпретáция interpretation. **интерпрети́ровать** *impf & pf* interpret.
интерьéр interior.
инти́мный intimate.
интонáция intonation.
интри́га intrigue; plot. **интриговáть** *impf*, (*pf* **за~**) intrigue.
интуи́ция intuition.
инфáркт infarct; coronary (thrombosis), heart attack.
инфекциóнный infectious. **инфéкция** infection.
инфля́ция inflation.
информáтика IT.
информáция information.
инфракрáсный infra-red.
иóд *etc.*: *see* **йод**
ио́н ion.
ипохóндрик hypochondriac. **ипохóндрия** hypochondria.
ипподрóм racecourse.
Ирáк Iraq. **ирáкец** (-кца) Iraqi. **ирáкский** Iraqi.
Ирáн Iran. **ирáнец** (-нца), **ирáнка** Iranian. **ирáнский** Iranian.
ирлáндец (-дца) Irishman. **Ирлáндия** Ireland. **ирлáндка** Irishwoman. **ирлáндский** Irish.
ирони́ческий ironic. **ирóния** irony.
ирригáция irrigation.
иск suit, action.
искажáть *impf*, **искази́ть** (-ажу́) *pf* distort, pervert; misrepresent. **искажéние** distortion, perversion.
искалéченный crippled, maimed. **искалéчить** (-чу́) *pf* cripple, maim; break.
искáть (ищу́, и́щешь) *impf* (*+acc or gen*) seek, look for.
исключáть *impf*, **исключи́ть** (-чу́) *pf* exclude; eliminate; expel. **исключáя** *prep+gen* except. **исключéние** exception; exclusion; expulsion; elimination; **за исключéнием** *+gen* with the exception of. **исключи́тельно** *adv* exceptionally; exclusively. **исключи́тельный** exceptional; exclusive.
искóнный primordial.
ископáемое *sb* mineral; fossil. **ископáемый** fossilized, fossil.
искорени́ть *pf*, **искореня́ть** *impf* eradicate.
и́скоса *adv* askance; sidelong.
и́скра spark.
и́скренний sincere. **и́скренность** sincerity.
искривлéние bend; distortion, warping.
ис|купáть[1]**(ся** *pf.*
искупáть[2] *impf*, **искупи́ть** (-плю́, -пишь) *pf* atone for; make up for. **искуплéние** redemption, atonement.
искуси́ть (-ушу́) *pf of* **искушáть**
искýсный skilful; expert. **искýсственный** artificial; feigned. **искýсство** art; skill. **искусствовéд** art historian.
искушáть *impf* (*pf* **искуси́ть**) tempt; seduce. **искушéние** temptation, seduction.
испáнец (-нца) Spaniard. **Испáния** Spain. **испáнка** Spanish woman. **испáнский** Spanish.
испарéние evaporation; *pl* fumes. **испари́ться** *pf*, **испаря́ться** *impf* evaporate.
ис|пáчкать *pf.* **ис|пéчь** (-еку́, -ечёшь) *pf.*
исповéдовать *impf & pf* confess; profess; **~ся** confess; make one's confession; **+в+***prep* unburden

o.s. of. **йсповедь** confession.
испoдтишкá *adv* in an underhand way; on the quiet.
исполи́н giant. **исполи́нский** gigantic.
исполкóм *abbr* (*of* **исполни́тельный комитéт**) executive committee.
исполнéние fulfilment, execution. **исполни́тель** *m*, **~ница** executor; performer. **исполни́тельный** executive. **испóлнить** *pf*, **исполня́ть** *impf* carry out, execute; fulfil; perform; **~ся** be fulfilled.
испóльзование utilization. **испóльзовать** *impf* & *pf* make (good) use of, utilize.
ис|пóртить(ся (-рчу(сь) *pf*. **испóрченный** depraved; spoiled; rotten.
исправи́тельный correctional; corrective. **испрáвить** (-влю) *pf*, **исправля́ть** *impf* rectify, correct; mend; reform; **~ся** improve, reform. **исправлéние** repairing; improvement; correction. **испрáвленный** improved, corrected; revised; reformed. **испрáвный** in good order; punctual; meticulous.
ис|прóбовать *pf*.
испу́г fright. **ис|пугáть(ся** *pf*.
испускáть *impf*, **испусти́ть** (-ущу́, -у́стишь) *pf* emit, let out.
испытáние test, trial; ordeal. **испытáть** *pf*, **испы́тывать** *impf* test; try; experience.
исслéдование investigation; research. **исслéдователь** *m* researcher; investigator. **исслéдовательский** research. **исслéдовать** *impf* & *pf* investigate, examine; research into.
истаскáться *pf*, **истáскиваться** *impf* wear out; be worn out.
истекáть *impf of* **истéчь. истéкший** past.
истéрика hysterics. **истери́ческий** hysterical. **истери́я** hysteria.
истечéние outflow; expiry. **истéчь** (-ечёт; -тёк, -лá) *pf* (*impf* **истекáть**) elapse; expire.
и́стина truth. **и́стинный** true.
истлевáть *impf*, **истлéть** (-éю) *pf* rot, decay; be reduced to ashes.
истóк source.
истолковáть *pf*, **истолкóвывать** *impf* interpret; comment on.
ис|толóчь (-лку́, -лчёшь; -лóк, -лклá) *pf*.
истóма languor.
исторгáть *impf*, **истóргнуть** (-ну; -óрг) *pf* throw out.
истóрик historian. **истори́ческий** historical; historic. **истóрия** history; story; incident.
истóчник spring; source.
истощáть *impf*, **истощи́ть** (-щу́) *pf* exhaust; emaciate. **истощéние** emaciation; exhaustion.
ис|трáтить (-áчу) *pf*.
истреби́тель *m* destroyer; fighter. **истреби́ть** (-блю) *pf*, **истребля́ть** *impf* destroy; exterminate.
ис|тупи́ться (-пится) *pf*.
истязáние torture. **истязáть** *impf* torture.
исхóд outcome; end; Exodus. **исходи́ть** (-ожу́, -óдишь) *impf* (+**из** *or* **от**+*gen*) issue (from), come (from); proceed (from). **исхóдный** initial; departure.
исхудáлый undernourished, emaciated.
исцелéние healing; recovery. **исцели́ть** *pf*, **исцеля́ть** *impf* heal, cure.
исчезáть *impf*, **исчéзнуть** (-ну; -éз) *pf* disappear, vanish. **исчезновéние** disappearance.
исчéрпать *pf*, **исчéрпывать** *impf* exhaust; conclude. **исчéрпывающий** exhaustive.
исчислéние calculation; calculus.
итáк *conj* thus; so then.
Итáлия Italy. **итальня́нец** (-нца), **итальня́нка** Italian. **итальня́нский** Italian.
ИТАР-ТÁСС *abbr* (*of* **Информациóнное телеграфное агéнтство**

И

России; *see* **ТАСС)** ITAR-Tass.
и т.д. *abbr* (*of* **и так да́лее**) etc., and so on.
ито́г sum; total; result. **итого́** *adv* in all, altogether.
и т.п. *abbr* (*of* **и тому́ подо́бное**) etc., and so on.
иуде́й, иуде́йка Jew. **иуде́йский** Judaic.
их their, theirs; *see* **они́**.
ища́к (-а́) donkey.
ище́йка bloodhound; police dog.
ищу́ *etc.*: *see* **иска́ть**
ию́ль *m* July. **ию́льский** July.
ию́нь *m* June. **ию́ньский** June.
йо́га yoga.
йод iodine.
йо́та iota.

К

к, ко *prep+dat* to, towards; by; for; on; on the occasion of; **к пе́рвому января́** by the first of January; **к тому́ вре́мени** by then; **к тому́ же** besides, moreover; **к чему́?** what for?
-ка *partl modifying force of imper or expressing decision or intention*; **да́йте-ка пройти́** let me pass, please; **скажи́-ка мне** do tell me.
каба́к (-а́) tavern.
кабала́ servitude.
каба́н (-а́) wild boar.
кабаре́ *neut indecl* cabaret.
кабачо́к (-чка́) marrow.
ка́бель *m* cable. **ка́бельтов** cable, hawser.
каби́на cabin; booth; cockpit; cubicle; cab. **кабине́т** study; surgery; room; office; Cabinet.
каблу́к (-а́) heel.
каботáж coastal shipping. **кабота́жный** coastal.
кабы́ if.
кавале́р knight; partner, gentleman. **кавалери́йский** cavalry. **кавалери́ст** cavalryman. **кавале́рия** cavalry.
ка́верзный tricky.
Кавка́з the Caucasus. **кавка́зец** (-зца́), **кавка́зка** Caucasian. **кавка́зский** Caucasian.
кавы́чки (-чек) *pl* inverted commas, quotation marks.
каде́т cadet. **каде́тский ко́рпус** military school.
ка́дка tub, vat.
кадр frame, still; close-up; cadre; *pl* establishment; staff; personnel; specialists. **ка́дровый** (*mil*) regular; skilled, trained.
кады́к (-а́) Adam's apple.
каждодне́вный daily, everyday. **ка́ждый** each, every; *sb* everybody.
ка́жется *etc.*: *see* **каза́ться**
каза́к (-а́; *pl* -аки́, -ако́в), **каза́чка** Cossack.
каза́рма barracks.
каза́ться (кажу́сь, ка́жешься) *impf* (*pf* **по~**) seem, appear; *impers* **ка́жется, каза́лось** apparently; **каза́лось бы** it would seem; *+dat*: **мне ка́жется** it seems to me; I think.
Казахста́н Kazakhstan. **каза́чий** Cossack.
казема́т casemate.
казённый State; government; fiscal; public; formal; banal, conventional. **казна́** Exchequer, Treasury; public purse; the State. **казначе́й** treasurer, bursar; paymaster.
казино́ *neut indecl* casino.
казни́ть *impf & pf* execute; punish; castigate. **казнь** execution.
кайма́ (*gen pl* каём) border, edging.
как *adv* how; what; **вот ~!** you don't say!; **~ вы ду́маете?** what do you think?; **~ его зову́т?** what is his name?; **~ же** naturally, of course; **~ же так?** how is that?; **~ ни** however. **как** *conj* as; like; when; since; *+neg* but, except, than; **в то вре́мя ~** while, whereas; **~ мо́жно, ~ нельзя́**+*comp* as … as possible; ~

мо́жно скоре́е as soon as possible; **~ нельзя́ лу́чше** as well as possible; **~ то́лько** as soon as, when; **ме́жду тем, ~** while, whereas. **как бу́дто** *conj* as if; *partl* apparently. **как бы** how; as if; **как бы... не** what if, supposing; **как бы... ни** however. **ка́к-либо** *adv* somehow. **ка́к-нибудь** *adv* somehow; anyhow. **как раз** *adv* just, exactly. **как-то** *adv* somehow; once.
кака́о *neut indecl* cocoa.
како́в (-á, -ó, -ы́) *pron* what, what sort (of); **~ он?** what is he like?; **~ он собо́й?** what does he look like?; **пого́да-то какова́!** what weather! **каково́** *adv* how. **како́й** *pron* what; (such) as; which; **~... ни** whatever, whichever. **како́й-либо, како́й-нибудь** *prons* some; any; only. **како́й-то** *pron* some; a; a kind of.
как раз, ка́к-то *see* **как**
ка́ктус cactus.
кал faeces, excrement.
каламбу́р pun.
кале́ка *m* & *f* cripple.
календа́рь (-я́) *m* calendar.
кале́ние incandescence.
кале́чить (-чу) *impf* (*pf* **ис~, по~**) cripple, maim; **~ся** become a cripple.
кали́бр calibre; bore; gauge.
ка́лий potassium.
кали́тка (wicket-)gate.
каллигра́фия calligraphy.
кало́рия calorie.
кало́ша galosh.
ка́лька tracing-paper; tracing.
калькуля́ция calculation.
кальсо́ны (-н) *pl* long johns.
ка́льций calcium.
ка́мбала flat-fish; plaice; flounder.
камени́стый stony, rocky. **каменноуго́льный** coal; **~ бассе́йн** coal-field. **ка́менный** stone; rock; stony; hard, immovable; **~ век** Stone Age; **~ у́голь** coal. **каменоло́мня** (*gen pl* -мен) quarry. **ка́менщик** (stone)mason; bricklayer. **ка́мень** (-мня; *pl* -мни, -мне́й) *m* stone.
ка́мера chamber; cell; camera; inner tube, (football) bladder; **~ хране́ния** cloak-room, left-luggage office. **ка́мерный** chamber. **камерто́н** tuning-fork.
ками́н fireplace; fire.
камко́рдер camcorder.
камо́рка closet, very small room.
кампа́ния campaign; cruise.
камы́ш (-á) reed, rush; cane.
кана́ва ditch; gutter.
Кана́да Canada. **кана́дец** (-дца), **кана́дка** Canadian. **кана́дский** Canadian.
кана́л canal; channel. **канализа́ция** sewerage (system).
канаре́йка canary.
кана́т rope; cable.
канва́ canvas; groundwork; outline, design.
кандалы́ (-о́в) *pl* shackles.
кандида́т candidate; **~ нау́к** person with higher degree. **кандидату́ра** candidature.
кани́кулы (-ул) *pl* vacation; holidays.
кани́стра can, canister.
канони́ческий canon(ical).
кано́э *neut indecl* canoe.
кант edging; mount. **кантова́ть** *impf*; **«не ~»** 'this way up'.
кану́н eve.
ка́нуть (-ну) *pf* drop, sink; **как в во́ду ~** vanish into thin air.
канцеля́рия office. **канцеля́рский** office; clerical. **канцеля́рщина** red-tape.
ка́нцлер chancellor.
ка́пать (-аю *or* -плю) *impf* (*pf* **ка́пнуть, на~**) drip, drop; trickle; +*instr* spill.
капе́лла choir; chapel.
ка́пелька small drop; a little; **~ росы́** dew-drop.
капельме́йстер conductor; bandmaster.
капилля́р capillary.
капита́л capital. **капитали́зм** capitalism. **капитали́ст** capitalist. **капиталисти́ческий** capitalist. **капита́льный** capital; main, fundamental; major.

К

капита́н captain; skipper.
капитули́ровать *impf* & *pf* capitulate. **капитуля́ция** capitulation.
капка́н trap.
ка́пля (*gen pl* -пель) drop; bit, scrap. **ка́пнуть** (-ну) *pf of* **ка́пать**
капо́т hood, cowl, cowling; bonnet; house-coat.
капри́з caprice. **капри́зничать** *impf* play up. **капри́зный** capricious.
капу́ста cabbage.
капюшо́н hood.
ка́ра punishment.
кара́бкаться *impf* (*pf* **вс~**) clamber.

К

карава́н caravan; convoy.
кара́кули *f pl* scribble.
караме́ль caramel; caramels.
каранда́ш (-á) pencil.
каранти́н quarantine.
кара́т carat.
кара́тельный punitive. **кара́ть** *impf* (*pf* **по~**) punish.
карау́л guard; watch; **~!** help! **карау́лить** *impf* guard; lie in wait for. **карау́льный** guard; *sb* sentry, sentinel, guard.
карбюра́тор carburettor.
каре́та carriage, coach.
ка́рий brown; hazel.
карикату́ра caricature; cartoon.
карка́с frame; framework.
ка́ркать *impf*, **ка́ркнуть** (-ну) *pf* caw, croak.
ка́рлик, ка́рлица dwarf; pygmy. **ка́рликовый** dwarf; pygmy.
карма́н pocket. **карма́нник** pickpocket. **карма́нный** *adj* pocket.
карни́з cornice; ledge.
карп carp.
ка́рта map; (playing-)card.
карта́вить (-влю) *impf* burr.
картёжник gambler.
карте́чь case-shot, grape-shot.
карти́на picture; scene. **карти́нка** picture; illustration. **карти́нный** picturesque; picture.
карто́н cardboard. **карто́нка** cardboard box.
картоте́ка card-index.
карто́фель *m* potatoes; potato(-plant). **карто́фельн|ый** potato; **~ое пюре́** mashed potatoes.
ка́рточка card; season ticket; photo. **ка́рточный** card.
карто́шка potatoes; potato.
ка́ртридж cartridge.
карусе́ль merry-go-round.
ка́рцер cell, lock-up.
карье́р[1] full gallop.
карье́р[2] quarry; sand-pit.
карье́ра career. **карьери́ст** careerist.
каса́ние contact. **каса́тельная** *sb* tangent. **каса́ться** *impf* (*pf* **косну́ться**) *+gen or* **до**+*gen* touch; touch on; concern; **что каса́ется** as regards.
ка́ска helmet.
каска́д cascade.
каспи́йский Caspian.
ка́сса till; cash-box; booking-office; box-office; cash-desk; cash.
кассе́та cassette. **кассе́тный магнитофо́н** cassette recorder.
касси́р, касси́рша cashier.
кастра́т eunuch. **кастра́ция** castration. **кастри́ровать** *impf* & *pf* castrate, geld.
кастрю́ля saucepan.
катало́г catalogue.
ката́ние rolling; driving; **~ верхо́м** riding; **~ на конька́х** skating.
катапу́льта catapult. **катапульти́ровать(ся** *impf* & *pf* catapult.
ката́р catarrh.
катара́кта cataract.
катастро́фа catastrophe. **катастрофи́ческий** catastrophic.
ката́ть *impf* roll; (take for a) drive; **~ся** (*pf* **по~**) roll, roll about; go for a drive; **~ся верхо́м** ride, go riding; **~ся на конька́х** skate, go skating.
категори́ческий categorical. **катего́рия** category.
ка́тер (*pl* -á) cutter; launch.
кати́ть (-ачу́, -а́тишь) *impf* bowl along, rip, tear; **~ся** rush, tear; flow, stream, roll; **кати́сь, кати́-**

тесь get out! clear off! **като́к** (-тка́) skating-rink; roller.
като́лик, католи́чка Catholic. **католи́ческий** Catholic.
ка́торга penal servitude, hard labour. **ка́торжник** convict. **ка́торжн|ый** penal; **~ые рабо́ты** hard labour; drudgery.
кату́шка reel, bobbin; spool; coil.
каучу́к rubber.
кафе́ *neut indecl* café.
ка́федра pulpit; rostrum; chair; department.
ка́фель *m* Dutch tile.
кача́лка rocking-chair. **кача́ние** rocking, swinging; pumping. **кача́ть** *impf* (*pf* **качну́ть**) *+acc or instr* rock, swing; shake; **~ся** rock, swing; roll; reel. **каче́ли** (-ей) *pl* swing.
ка́чественный qualitative; high-quality. **ка́чество** quality; **в ка́честве**+*gen* as, in the capacity of.
ка́чка rocking; tossing.
качну́ть(ся (-ну́(сь, -нёшь(ся) *pf of* **кача́ть(ся. качу́** *etc.*: *see* **кати́ть**
ка́ша gruel, porridge; **завари́ть ка́шу** stir up trouble.
ка́шель (-шля) cough. **ка́шлянуть** (-ну) *pf*, **ка́шлять** *impf* (have a) cough.
кашта́н chestnut. **кашта́новый** chestnut.
каю́та cabin, stateroom.
ка́ющийся penitent. **ка́яться** (ка́юсь) *impf* (*pf* **по~, рас~**) repent; confess; **ка́юсь** I (must) confess.
кв. *abbr* (*of* **квадра́тный**) square; (*of* **кварти́ра**) flat.
квадра́т square; quad; **в квадра́те** squared; **возвести́ в ~** square. **квадра́тный** square; quadratic.
ква́кать *impf*, **ква́кнуть** (-ну) *pf* croak.
квалифика́ция qualification. **квалифици́рованный** qualified, skilled.
квант, ква́нта quantum. **ква́нтовый** quantum.
кварта́л block; quarter. **кварта́льный** quarterly.
кварте́т quartet.
кварти́ра flat; apartment(s); quarters. **квартира́нт, -ра́нтка** lodger; tenant. **кварти́рная пла́та, квартпла́та** rent.
кварц quartz.
квас (*pl* **~ы́**) kvass. **ква́сить** (-а́шу) *impf* sour; pickle. **ква́шеная капу́ста** sauerkraut.
кве́рху *adv* up, upwards.
квит, кви́ты quits.
квита́нция receipt. **квито́к** (-тка́) ticket, check.
КГБ *abbr* (*of* **Комите́т госуда́рственной безопа́сности**) KGB.
ке́гля skittle.
кедр cedar.
ке́ды (-ов) *pl* trainers.
кекс (fruit-)cake.
ке́лья (*gen pl* -лий) cell.
кем *see* **кто**
ке́мпинг campsite.
кенгуру́ *m indecl* kangaroo.
ке́пка cloth cap.
кера́мика ceramics.
керога́з stove. **кероси́н** paraffin. **кероси́нка** paraffin stove.
ке́та Siberian salmon. **ке́тов|ый**: **~ая икра́** red caviare.
кефи́р kefir, yoghurt.
киберне́тика cybernetics.
кива́ть *impf*, **кивну́ть** (-ну́, -нёшь) *pf* (**голово́й**) nod (one's head); (+**на**+*acc*) motion (to). **киво́к** (-вка́) nod.
кида́ть *impf* (*pf* **ки́нуть**) throw, fling; **~ся** fling o.s.; rush; +*instr* throw.
кий (-я́; *pl* -и́, -ёв) (*billiard*) cue.
килев|о́й keel; **~а́я ка́чка** pitching.
кило́ *neut indecl* kilo. **килова́тт** kilowatt. **килогра́мм** kilogram. **киломе́тр** kilometre.
киль *m* keel; fin. **кильва́тер** wake.
ки́лька sprat.
кинжа́л dagger.
кино́ *neut indecl* cinema.
кино- *in comb* film-, cine-. **киноаппара́т** cinecamera. **~арти́ст, ~арти́стка** film actor, actress.

К

~журна́л news-reel. **~за́л** cinema; auditorium. **~звезда́** film-star. **~зри́тель** *m* film-goer. **~карти́на** film. **~опера́тор** camera-man. **~плёнка** film. **~режиссёр** film director. **~теа́тр** cinema. **~хро́ника** news-reel.
ки́нуть(ся (-ну(сь) *pf of* **кида́ть(ся**
кио́ск kiosk, stall.
ки́па pile, stack; bale.
кипари́с cypress.
кипе́ние boiling. **кипе́ть** (-плю́) *impf* (*pf* **вс~**) boil, seethe.
кипу́чий boiling, seething; ebullient. **кипяти́льник** kettle, boiler. **кипяти́ть** (-ячу́) *impf* (*pf* **вс~**) boil; **~ся** boil; get excited. **кипято́к** (-тка́) boiling water. **кипячёный** boiled.
Кирги́зия Kirghizia.
кирка́ pick(axe).
кирпи́ч (-а́) brick; bricks. **кирпи́чный** brick; brick-red.
кисе́ль *m* kissel, blancmange.
кисе́т tobacco-pouch.
кисе́я muslin.
кислоро́д oxygen. **кислота́** (*pl* -ы) acid; acidity. **кисло́тный** acid. **ки́слый** sour; acid. **ки́снуть** (-ну; кис) *impf* (*pf* **про~**) turn sour.
ки́сточка brush; tassel. **кисть** (*gen pl* -е́й) cluster, bunch; brush; tassel; hand.
кит (-а́) whale.
кита́ец (-а́йца; *pl* -цы, -цев) Chinese. **Кита́й** China. **кита́йский** Chinese. **китая́нка** Chinese (woman).
китобо́й whaler. **кито́вый** whale.
кичи́ться (-чу́сь) *impf* plume o.s.; strut. **кичли́вость** conceit. **кичли́вый** conceited.
кише́ть (-ши́т) *impf* swarm, teem.
кише́чник bowels, intestines. **кише́чный** intestinal. **кишка́** gut, intestine; hose.
клавеси́н harpsichord. **клавиату́ра** keyboard. **кла́виша** key. **кла́вишный: ~ инструме́нт** keyboard instrument.
клад treasure.
кла́дбище cemetery, graveyard.
кла́дка laying; masonry. **кладова́я** *sb* pantry; store-room. **кладовщи́к** (-а́) storeman. **кладу́** *etc.*: *see* **класть**
кла́няться *impf* (*pf* **поклони́ться**) +*dat* bow to; greet.
кла́пан valve; vent.
кларне́т clarinet.
класс class; class-room. **кла́ссик** classic. **кла́ссика** the classics. **классифици́ровать** *impf* & *pf* classify. **класси́ческий** classical. **кла́ссный** class; first-class. **кла́ссовый** class.
класть (-аду́, -адёшь; -ал) *impf* (*pf* **положи́ть, сложи́ть**) lay; put.
клева́ть (клюю́, клюёшь) *impf* (*pf* **клю́нуть**) peck; bite.
кле́вер (*pl* -а́) clover.
клевета́ slander; libel. **клевета́ть** (-ещу́, -е́щешь) *impf* (*pf* **на~**) +**на**+*acc* slander; libel. **клеветни́к** (-а́), **-ни́ца** slanderer. **клеветни́ческий** slanderous; libellous.
клеёнка oilcloth. **кле́ить** *impf* (*pf* **с~**) glue; stick; **~ся** stick; become sticky. **клей** (*loc* -ю́; *pl* -и́) glue, adhesive. **кле́йкий** sticky.
клейми́ть (-млю́) *impf* (*pf* **за~**) brand; stamp; stigmatize. **клеймо́** (*pl* -а) brand; stamp; mark.
кле́йстер paste.
клён maple.
клепа́ть *impf* rivet.
кле́тка cage; check; cell. **кле́точка** cellule. **кле́точный** cellular. **клетча́тка** cellulose. **кле́тчатый** checked.
клёш flare.
клешня́ (*gen pl* -е́й) claw.
кле́щи (-е́й) *pl* pincers, tongs.
клие́нт client. **клиенту́ра** clientèle.
кли́зма enema.
клик cry, call. **кли́кать** (-и́чу) *impf*, **кли́кнуть** (-ну) *pf* call.
кли́макс menopause.

кли́мат climate. **климати́ческий** climatic.
клин (*pl* -нья, -ньев) wedge. **клино́к** (-нка́) blade.
кли́ника clinic. **клини́ческий** clinical.
клипс clip-on ear-ring.
клич call. **кли́чка** name; nickname. **кли́чу** *etc.*: *see* **кли́кать**
клок (-а́; *pl* -о́чья, -ьев *or* -и́, -о́в) rag, shred; tuft.
кло́кот bubbling; gurgling. **клокота́ть** (-о́чет) *impf* bubble; gurgle; boil up.
клони́ть (-ню́, -нишь) *impf* bend; incline; +к+*dat* drive at; **~ся** bow, bend; +к+*dat* near, approach.
клон clone.
клоп (-а́) bug.
кло́ун clown.
клочо́к (-чка́) scrap, shred. **кло́чья** *etc.*: *see* **клок**
клуб[1] club.
клуб[2] (*pl* -ы́) puff; cloud.
клу́бень (-бня) *m* tuber.
клуби́ться *impf* swirl; curl.
клубни́ка (*no pl*; *usu collect*) strawberry; strawberries.
клубо́к (-бка́) ball; tangle.
клу́мба (flower-)bed.
клык (-а́) fang; tusk; canine (*tooth*).
клюв beak.
клю́ква cranberry; cranberries.
клю́нуть (-ну) *pf of* **клева́ть**
ключ[1] (-а́) key; clue; keystone; clef; wrench, spanner.
ключ[2] (-а́) spring; source.
ключево́й key. **ключи́ца** collarbone.
клю́шка (hockey) stick; (golf-) club.
клюю́ *etc.*: *see* **клева́ть**
кля́кса blot, smudge.
кляну́ *etc.*: *see* **клясть**
кля́нчить (-чу́) *impf* (*pf* **вы́~**) beg.
кляп gag.
клясть (-яну́, -янёшь; -ял, -а́, -о) *impf* curse; **~ся** (*pf* **по~ся**) swear, vow. **кля́тва** oath, vow. **кля́твенный** on oath.
кни́га book.
книго- *in comb* book, biblio-. **книгове́дение**[1] bibliography. **~веде́ние**[2] book-keeping. **~изда́тель** *m* publisher. **~лю́б** bibliophile. **~храни́лище** library; book-stack.
кни́жечка booklet. **кни́жка** book; note-book; bank-book. **кни́жный** book; bookish.
кни́зу *adv* downwards.
кно́пка drawing-pin; press-stud; (push-)button, knob.
кнут (-а́) whip.
княги́ня princess. **кня́жество** principality. **княжна́** (*gen pl* -жо́н) princess. **князь** (*pl* -зья́, -зе́й) *m* prince.
ко *see* **к** *prep.*
коали́ция coalition.
кобура́ holster.
кобы́ла mare; (vaulting-)horse.
ко́ваный forged; wrought; terse.
кова́рный insidious, crafty; perfidious. **кова́рство** insidiousness, craftiness; perfidy.
кова́ть (кую́, -ёшь) *impf* (*pf* **под~**) forge; hammer; shoe.
ковёр (-вра́) carpet; rug; mat.
кове́ркать *impf* (*pf* **ис~**) distort, mangle, ruin.
ко́вка forging; shoeing.
коври́жка honeycake, gingerbread.
ко́врик rug; mat.
ковче́г ark.
ковш (-а́) scoop, ladle.
ковы́ль *m* feather-grass.
ковыля́ть *impf* hobble.
ковырну́ть (-ну́, -нёшь) *pf*, **ковыря́ть** *impf* dig into; tinker; +в+*prep* pick (at); **~ся** rummage; tinker.
когда́ *adv* when; **~ (бы) ни** whenever; *conj* when; while, as; if. **когда́-либо, когда́-нибудь** *advs* some time; ever. **когда́-то** *adv* once; formerly; some time.
кого́ *see* **кто**
ко́готь (-гтя; *pl* -гти, -гте́й) *m* claw; talon.

К

код code.
кодеин codeine.
кóдекс code.
кóе-где́ *adv* here and there. **кóе-кáк** *adv* anyhow; somehow (or other). **кóе-какóй** *pron* some. **кóе-ктó** *pron* somebody; some people. **кóе-чтó** (-чегó) *pron* something; a little.
кóжа skin; leather; peel. **кóжанка** leather jacket. **кóжаный** leather. **кожéвенный** leather; tanning. **кóжный** skin. **кожурá** rind, peel, skin.
козá (*pl* -ы) goat, nanny-goat. **козёл** (-злá) billy-goat. **козерóг** ibex; Capricorn. **кóзий** goat; ~ **пух** angora. **козлёнок** (-нка; *pl* -ля́та, -ля́т) kid.
кóзлы (-зел) *pl* coach driver's seat; trestle(s); saw-horse.
кóзни (-ей) *pl* machinations.
козырёк (-рькá) peak.
козырнóй trump. **козырнýть** (-нý, -нёшь) *pf*, **козыря́ть** *impf* lead trumps; trump; play one's trump card; salute. **кóзырь** (*pl* -и, -éй) *m* trump.
кóйка (*gen pl* кóек) berth, bunk; bed.
кокаин cocaine.
кóка-кóла Coca-Cola (*propr*).
кокéтка coquette. **кокéтство** coquetry.
коклю́ш whooping-cough.
кóкон cocoon.
кокóс coconut.
кокс coke.
коктéйль *m* cocktail.
кол (-á; *pl* -лья, -ьев) stake, picket.
кóлба retort.
колбасá (*pl* -ы) sausage.
колгóтки (-ток) *pl* tights.
колдовáть *impf* practise witchcraft. **колдовствó** sorcery. **колдýн** (-á) sorcerer, wizard. **колдýнья** (*gen pl* -ний) witch, sorceress.
колебáние oscillation; variation; hesitation. **колебáть** (-éблю) *impf* (*pf* **по~**) shake; **~ся** oscillate; fluctuate; hesitate.
колéно (*pl* -и, -ей, -ям) knee; (*in pl*) lap. **колéнчатый** crank, cranked; bent; ~ **вал** crankshaft.
колесни́ца chariot. **колесó** (*pl* -ёса) wheel.
колея́ rut; track, gauge.
кóлика (*usu pl*) colic; stitch.
коли́чественн|ый quantitative; **~ое числи́тельное** cardinal number. **коли́чество** quantity; number.
коллéга *m* & *f* colleague. **коллéгия** board; college.
коллекти́в collective. **коллективизáция** collectivization. **коллекти́вный** collective. **коллекционéр** collector. **коллéкция** collection.
колли́зия clash, conflict.
колóда block; pack (*of cards*).
колóдец (-дца) well.
кóлокол (*pl* -á, -óв) bell. **колокóльный** bell. **колокóльня** bell-tower. **колокóльчик** small bell; bluebell.
колониали́зм colonialism. **колониáльный** colonial. **колонизáтор** colonizer. **колонизáция** colonization. **колонизовáть** *impf* & *pf* colonize. **колóния** colony.
колóнка geyser; (*street*) water fountain; stand-pipe; column; **бензи́новая ~** petrol pump. **колóнна** column.
колори́т colouring, colour. **колори́тный** colourful, graphic.
кóлос (-óсья, -ьев) ear. **колоси́ться** *impf* form ears.
колоссáльный huge; terrific.
колоти́ть (-очý, -óтишь) *impf* (*pf* **по~**) beat; pound; thrash; smash; **~ся** pound, thump; shake.
колóть[1] (-лю́, -лешь) *impf* (*pf* **рас~**) break, chop.
колóть[2] (-лю́, -лешь) *impf* (*pf* **за~**, **кольнýть**) prick; stab; sting; slaughter; **~ся** prick.
колпáк (-á) cap; hood, cowl.
колхóз *abbr* (*of* **коллекти́вное хозя́йство**) kolkhoz, collective farm.

колхо́зник, ~ица kolkhoz member. **колхо́зный** kolkhoz.
колыбе́ль cradle.
колыха́ть (-ы́шу) *impf*, **колыхну́ть** (-ну́, -нёшь) *pf* sway, rock; **~ся** sway; flutter.
кольну́ть (-ну́, -нёшь) *pf of* **коло́ть**
кольцо́ (*pl* -а, -ле́ц, -льцам) ring.
колю́ч|ий prickly; sharp; **~ая про́волока** barbed wire. **колю́чка** prickle; thorn.
коля́ска carriage; pram; side-car.
ком (*pl* -мья, -мьев) lump; ball.
ком *see* **кто**
кома́нда command; order; detachment; crew; team. **команди́р** commander. **командирова́ть** *impf* & *pf* post, send on a mission. **командиро́вка** posting; mission, business trip. **командиро́вочные** *sb pl* travelling expenses. **кома́ндование** command. **кома́ндовать** *impf* (*pf* **с~**) give orders; be in command; +*instr* command. **кома́ндующий** *sb* commander.
кома́р (-а́) mosquito.
комба́йн combine harvester.
комбина́т industrial complex. **комбина́ция** combination; manoeuvre; slip. **комбинезо́н** overalls, boiler suit; dungarees. **комбини́ровать** *impf* (*pf* **с~**) combine.
коме́дия comedy.
коменда́нт commandant; manager; warden. **комендату́ра** commandant's office.
коме́та comet.
ко́мик comic actor; comedian. **ко́микс** comic, comic strip.
комисса́р commissar.
комиссионе́р (commission-) agent, broker. **комиссио́нн|ый** commission; **~ый магази́н** second-hand shop; **~ые** *sb pl* commission. **коми́ссия** commission; committee.
комите́т committee.
коми́ческий comic; comical. **коми́чный** comical, funny.
ко́мкать *impf* (*pf* **с~**) crumple.
коммента́рий commentary; *pl* comment. **коммента́тор** commentator. **комменти́ровать** *impf* & *pf* comment (on).
коммерса́нт merchant; businessman **комме́рция** commerce. **комме́рческий** commercial.
коммивояжёр commercial traveller.
комму́на commune. **коммуна́льный** communal; municipal. **коммуни́зм** communism.
коммуника́ция communication.
коммуни́ст, ~ка communist. **коммунисти́ческий** communist.
коммута́тор switchboard.
коммюнике́ *neut indecl* communiqué.
ко́мната room. **ко́мнатный** room; indoor.
комо́д chest of drawers.
комо́к (-мка́) lump.
компа́кт-ди́ск compact disc. **компа́ктный** compact.
компа́ния company. **компаньо́н, ~ка** companion; partner.
компа́ртия Communist Party.
ко́мпас compass.
компенса́ция compensation. **компенси́ровать** *impf* & *pf* compensate.
ко́мплекс complex. **ко́мплексный** complex, compound, composite; combined. **компле́кт** (complete) set; complement; kit. **комплектова́ть** *impf* (*pf* **с~, у~**) complete; bring up to strength. **компле́кция** build; constitution.
комплиме́нт compliment.
компози́тор composer. **компози́ция** composition.
компоне́нт component.
компо́ст compost.
компо́стер punch. **компости́ровать** *impf* (*pf* **про~**) punch.
компо́т stewed fruit.
компре́ссор compressor.
компромети́ровать *impf* (*pf* **с~**) compromise. **компроми́сс** compromise.

К

компью́тер computer.
комсомо́л Komsomol. **комсомо́лец** (-льца), **-лка** Komsomol member. **комсомо́льский** Komsomol.
кому́ *see* **кто**
комфо́рт comfort.
конве́йер conveyor.
конве́рт envelope; sleeve.
конвои́р escort. **конвои́ровать** *impf* escort. **конво́й** escort, convoy.
конгре́сс congress.
конденса́тор condenser.
конди́терская *sb* confectioner's, cake shop.
кондиционе́р air-conditioner. **кондицио́нный** air-conditioning.
конду́ктор (*pl* -á), **-торша** conductor; guard.
конево́дство horse-breeding. **конёк** (-нька́) *dim of* **конь**; hobby(-horse).
коне́ц (-нца́) end; **в конце́ концо́в** in the end, after all. **коне́чно** *adv* of course. **коне́чность** extremity. **коне́чный** final, last; ultimate; finite.
кони́ческий conic, conical.
конкре́тный concrete.
конкуре́нт competitor. **конкуре́нция** competition. **конкури́ровать** *impf* compete. **ко́нкурс** competition; contest.
ко́нница cavalry. **ко́нный** horse; mounted; equestrian; **~ заво́д** stud.
конопля́ hemp.
консервати́вный conservative. **консерва́тор** Conservative.
консервато́рия conservatoire.
консерви́ровать *impf* & *pf* (*pf also* **за~**) preserve; can, bottle. **консе́рвн|ый** preserving; **~ая ба́нка** tin; **~ый нож** tin-opener. **консе́рвооткрыва́тель** *m* tin-opener. **консе́рвы** (-ов) *pl* tinned goods.
конси́лиум consultation.
конспе́кт synopsis, summary. **конспекти́ровать** *impf* (*pf* **за~**, **про~**) make an abstract of.
конспирати́вный secret, clandestine. **конспира́ция** security.
констата́ция ascertaining; establishment. **констати́ровать** *impf* & *pf* ascertain; establish.
конституцио́нный constitutional. **конститу́ция** constitution.
конструи́ровать *impf* & *pf* (*pf also* **с~**) construct; design. **конструкти́вный** structural; constructional; constructive. **констру́ктор** designer, constructor. **констру́кция** construction; design.
ко́нсул consul. **ко́нсульство** consulate.
консульта́ция consultation; advice; clinic; tutorial. **консульти́ровать** *impf* (*pf* **про~**) advise; **+с+***instr* consult; **~ся** obtain advice; **+с+***instr* consult.
конта́кт contact. **конта́ктные ли́нзы** *f pl* contact lenses.
конте́йнер container.
конте́кст context.
контине́нт continent.
конто́ра office. **конто́рский** office.
контраба́нда contraband. **контрабанди́ст** smuggler.
контраба́с double-bass.
контра́кт contract.
контра́льто *neut*/*fem indecl* contralto (*voice*/*person*).
контрама́рка complimentary ticket.
контрапу́нкт counterpoint.
контра́ст contrast.
контрибу́ция indemnity.
контрнаступле́ние counter-offensive.
контролёр inspector; ticket-collector. **контроли́ровать** *impf* (*pf* **про~**) check; inspect. **контро́ль** *m* control; check; inspection. **контро́льн|ый** control; **~ая рабо́та** test.
контрразве́дка counter-intelligence; security service.
контрреволю́ция counter-revolution.

контýзия bruising; shell-shock.
кóнтур contour, outline; circuit.
конурá kennel.
кóнус cone.
конфедерáция confederation.
конферéнция conference.
конфéта sweet.
конфисковáть *impf & pf* confiscate.
конфлúкт conflict.
конфóрка ring (*on stove*).
конфýз discomforture, embarrassment. **конфýзить** (-ýжу) *impf* (*pf* **с~**) confuse, embarrass; **~ся** feel embarrassed.
концентрáт concentrate. **концентрациóнный** concentration. **концентрáция** concentration. **концентрúровать(ся** *impf* (*pf* **с~**) concentrate.
концéпция conception.
концéрт concert; concerto. **концертмéйстер** leader. **концéртный** concert.
концлáгерь *abbr* (*of* **концентрациóнный лáгерь**) concentration camp.
кончáть *impf*, **кóнчить** *pf* finish; end; +*inf* stop; **~ся** end, finish; expire. **кóнчик** tip. **кончúна** decease.
конь (-я́; *pl* -и, -éй) *m* horse; knight. **конькú** (-óв) *pl* skates; **~ на рóликах** roller skates. **конькобéжец** (-жца) skater.
конья́к (-á) cognac.
кóнюх groom, stable-boy. **конюшня** (*gen pl* -шен) stable.
кооператúв cooperative. **кооператúвный** cooperative. **кооперáция** cooperation.
координáта coordinate. **координáция** coordination.
копáть *impf* (*pf* **копнýть, вы́~**) dig; dig up, dig out; **~ся** rummage.
копéйка copeck.
кóпи (-ей) *pl* mines.
копúлка money-box.
копúрка carbon paper. **копировáльный** copying. **копúровать** *impf* (*pf* **с~**) copy; imitate.
копúть (-плю́, -пишь) *impf* (*pf* **на~**) save (up); accumulate; **~ся** accumulate.
кóпия copy.
копнá (*pl* -ы, -пён) shock, stook.
копнýть (-нý, -нёшь) *pf of* **копáть**
кóпоть soot.
коптéть (-пчý) *impf* swot; vegetate. **коптúть** (-пчý) *impf* (*pf* **за~, на~**) smoke, cure; blacken with smoke. **копчéние** smoking; smoked foods. **копчёный** smoked.
копы́то hoof.
копьё (*pl* -я, -пий) spear, lance.
корá bark; cortex; crust.
корабéльный ship; naval. **кораблевождéние** navigation. **кораблекрушéние** shipwreck. **кораблестроéние** shipbuilding. **корáбль** (-я́) *m* ship, vessel; nave.
корáлл coral.
корéйский Korean. **Корéя** Korea.
коренáстый thickset. **корени́ться** *impf* be rooted. **коренóй** radical, fundamental; native. **кóрень** (-рня; *pl* -и, -éй) *m* root. **корешóк** (-шкá) root(let); spine; counterfoil.
корзúна, корзúнка basket.
коридóр corridor.
корúца cinnamon.
корúчневый brown.
кóрка crust; rind, peel.
корм (*loc* -ý; *pl* -á) fodder.
кормá stern.
кормúлец (-льца) bread-winner. **кормúть** (-млю́, -мишь) *impf* (*pf* **на~, по~, про~**) feed; **~ся** feed; +*instr* live on, make a living by. **кормлéние** feeding. **кормовóй**[1] fodder.
кормовóй[2] stern.
корневóй root; radical. **корнеплóды** (-ов) root-crops.
корóбить (-блю) *impf* (*pf* **по~**) warp; jar upon; **~ся** (*pf also* **с~ся**) warp.
корóбка box.
корóва cow.

К

королéва queen. **королéвский** royal. **королéвство** kingdom. **корóль** (-я́) *m* king.

коромы́сло yoke; beam; rocking shaft.

корóна crown.

коронаротромбóз coronary (thrombosis).

корóнка crown. **короновáть** *impf* & *pf* crown.

корóткий (кóрóток, -ткá, кóрóткó, кóрóтки́) short; intimate. **кóротко** *adv* briefly; intimately. **коротковóлновый** short-wave. **корóче** *comp of* **корóткий, кóротко**

корпорáция corporation.

кóрпус (*pl* -ы, -ов *or* -á, -óв) corps; services; building; hull; housing, case; body.

корректи́ровать *impf* (*pf* **про~, с~**) correct, edit. **коррéктный** correct, proper. **коррéктор** (*pl* -á) proof-reader. **корректу́ра** proof-reading; proof.

корреспондéнт correspondent. **корреспондéнция** correspondence.

коррóзия corrosion.

коррýпция corruption.

корт (tennis-)court.

кортéж cortège; motorcade.

кóртик dirk.

кóрточки (-чек) *pl*; **сидéть на кóрточках** squat.

корчевáть (-чýю) *impf* root out.

кóрчить (-чу) *impf* (*pf* **с~**) contort; *impers* convulse; **~ из себя́** pose as; **~ся** writhe.

кóршун kite.

коры́стный mercenary. **коры́сть** avarice; profit.

коры́то trough; wash-tub.

корь measles.

косá[1] (*acc* -у; *pl* -ы) plait, tress.

косá[2] (*acc* кóсý; *pl* -ы) spit.

косá[3] (*acc* кóсý; *pl* -ы) scythe.

кóсвенный indirect.

коси́лка mowing-machine, mower. **коси́ть**[1] (кошý, кóсишь) *impf* (*pf* **с~**) cut; mow (down).

коси́ть[2] (кошý) *impf* (*pf* **по~, с~**) squint; be crooked; **~ся** slant; look sideways; look askance.

космéтика cosmetics, make-up.

косми́ческий cosmic; space. **космодрóм** spacecraft launching-site. **космонáвт, -нáвтка** cosmonaut, astronaut. **кóсмос** cosmos; (outer) space.

косноязы́чный tongue-tied.

коснýться (-нýсь, -нёшься) *pf of* **касáться**

косоглáзие squint. **косóй** (кос, -á, -о) slanting; oblique; sidelong; squinting, cross-eyed.

костёр (-трá) bonfire; camp-fire.

костля́вый bony. **кóстный** bone. **кóсточка** (small) bone; stone.

косты́ль (-я́) *m* crutch.

кость (*loc* и́; *pl* -и, -éй) bone; die.

костю́м clothes; suit. **костюмирóванный** fancy-dress.

костянóй bone; ivory.

косы́нка (*triangular*) head-scarf, shawl.

кот (-á) tom-cat.

котёл (-тлá) boiler; copper, cauldron. **котелóк** (-лкá) pot; mess-tin; bowler (hat). **котéльная** *sb* boiler-room, -house.

котёнок (-нка; *pl* -тя́та, -тя́т) kitten.

кóтик fur-seal; sealskin.

котлéта rissole; burger; **отбивнáя ~** chop.

котловáн foundation pit, trench.

котóмка knapsack.

котóрый *pron* which, what; who; that; **~ час?** what time is it?

котя́та *etc.*: *see* **котёнок**

кóфе *m indecl* coffee. **кофевáрка** percolator. **кофеи́н** caffeine.

кóфта, кóфточка blouse, top.

кочáн (-á *or* -чнá) (cabbage-) head.

кочевáть (-чýю) *impf* be a nomad; wander; migrate. **кочéвник** nomad. **кочевóй** nomadic.

кочегáр stoker, fireman. **кочегáрка** stokehold, stokehole.

коченéть *impf* (*pf* **за~, о~**) grow numb.

кочергá (*gen pl* -рёг) poker.

кóчка hummock.

кошелёк (-лька́) purse.
ко́шка cat.
кошма́р nightmare. **кошма́рный** nightmarish.
кошу́ *etc.*: *see* **коси́ть**
кощу́нство blasphemy.
коэффицие́нт coefficient.
КП *abbr* (*of* **Коммунисти́ческая па́ртия**) Communist Party. **КПСС** *abbr* (*of* **Коммунисти́ческая па́ртия Сове́тского Сою́за**) Communist Party of the Soviet Union, CPSU.
краб crab.
кра́деный stolen. **краду́** *etc.*: *see* **красть**
кра́жа theft; ~ **со взло́мом** burglary.
край (*loc* -ю́; *pl* -я́, -ёв) edge; brink; land; region. **кра́йне** *adv* extremely. **кра́йний** extreme; last; outside, wing; **по кра́йней ме́ре** at least. **кра́йность** extreme; extremity.
крал *etc.*: *see* **красть**
кран tap; crane.
крапи́ва nettle.
краса́вец (-вца) handsome man. **краса́вица** beauty. **краси́вый** beautiful; handsome.
краси́тель *m* dye. **кра́сить** (-а́шу) *impf* (*pf* **вы**~, **о**~, **по**~) paint; colour; dye; stain; ~**ся** (*pf* **на**~) make-up. **кра́ска** paint, dye; colour.
красне́ть (-е́ю) *impf* (*pf* **по**~) blush; redden; show red.
красноарме́ец (-е́йца) Red Army man. **красноарме́йский** Red Army. **красноречи́вый** eloquent.
краснота́ redness. **красну́ха** German measles. **кра́сн|ый** (-сен, -сна́, -о) red; beautiful; fine; ~**ое де́рево** mahogany; ~**ая сморо́дина** (*no pl*; *usu collect*) redcurrant; redcurrants; ~**ая строка́** (first line of) new paragraph.
красова́ться *impf* impress by one's beauty; show off. **красота́** (*pl* -ы) beauty. **кра́сочный** paint; ink; colourful.
красть (-аду́, -адёшь; крал) *impf* (*pf* **у**~) steal; ~**ся** creep.
кра́тер crater.
кра́ткий (-ток, -тка́, -о) short; brief. **кратковре́менный** brief; transitory. **краткосро́чный** short-term.
кра́тное *sb* multiple.
кратча́йший *superl of* **кра́ткий**. **кра́тче** *comp of* **кра́ткий, кра́тко**
крах crash; failure.
крахма́л starch. **крахма́лить** *impf* (*pf* **на**~) starch.
кра́ше *comp of* **краси́вый, краси́во**
кра́шеный painted; coloured; dyed; made up. **кра́шу** *etc.*: *see* **кра́сить**
креве́тка shrimp; prawn.
креди́т credit. **креди́тный** credit. **кредито́р** creditor. **кредитоспосо́бный** solvent.
кре́йсер (*pl* -а́, -о́в) cruiser.
крем cream.
кремато́рий crematorium.
креме́нь (-мня́) *m* flint.
кремль (-я́) *m* citadel; Kremlin.
кре́мний silicon.
кре́мовый cream.
крен list, heel; bank. **крени́ться** *impf* (*pf* **на**~) heel over, list; bank.
крепи́ть (-плю́) *impf* strengthen; support; make fast; constipate; ~**ся** hold out. **кре́пк|ий** (-пок, -пка́, -о) strong; firm; ~**ие напи́тки** spirits. **крепле́ние** strengthening; fastening.
кре́пнуть (-ну; -еп) *impf* (*pf* **о**~) get stronger.
крепостни́чество serfdom. **крепостн|о́й** serf; ~**о́е пра́во** serfdom; ~**о́й** *sb* serf.
кре́пость fortress; strength.
кре́пче *comp of* **кре́пкий, кре́пко**
кре́сло (*gen pl* -сел) arm-chair; stall.
крест (-а́) cross. **крести́ны** (-и́н) *pl* christening. **крести́ть** (крещу́, -е́стишь) *impf* & *pf* (*pf also* **о**~, **пере**~) christen; make sign of the cross over; ~**ся** cross o.s.; be

К

christened. **крест-на́крест** *adv* crosswise. **кре́стник, кре́стница** god-child. **крёстн|ый; ~ая (мать)** godmother; **~ый оте́ц** godfather. **кресто́вый похо́д** crusade. **крестоно́сец** (-сца) crusader.

крестья́нин (*pl* -я́не, -я́н), **крестья́нка** peasant. **крестья́нский** peasant. **крестья́нство** peasantry.

креще́ние christening; Epiphany. **крещён|ый** (-ён, -ена́) baptized; *sb* Christian. **крещу́** *etc.*: *see* **крести́ть**

крива́я *sb* curve. **кривизна́** crookedness; curvature. **криви́ть** (-влю́) *impf* (*pf* **по~, с~**) bend, distort; **~ душо́й** go against one's conscience; **~ся** become crooked or bent; make a wry face. **кривля́ться** *impf* give o.s. airs.

криво́й (крив, -á, -о) crooked; curved; one-eyed.

кри́зис crisis.

крик cry, shout.

кри́кет cricket.

кри́кнуть (-ну) *pf of* **крича́ть**

кримина́льный criminal.

криста́лл crystal. **кристалли́ческий** crystal.

крите́рий criterion.

кри́тик critic. **кри́тика** criticism; critique. **критикова́ть** *impf* criticize. **крити́ческий** critical.

крича́ть (-чу́) *impf* (*pf* **кри́кнуть**) cry, shout.

кров roof; shelter.

крова́вый bloody.

крова́тка, крова́ть bed.

кровено́сный blood-; circulatory.

кро́вля (*gen pl* -вель) roof.

кро́вный blood; thoroughbred; vital, intimate.

крово- *in comb* blood. **кровожа́дный** bloodthirsty. **~излия́ние** haemorrhage. **~обраще́ние** circulation. **~проли́тие** bloodshed. **~проли́тный** bloody. **~смеше́ние** incest. **~тече́ние** bleeding; haemorrhage. **~точи́ть** (-чи́т) *impf* bleed.

кровь (*loc* -и́) blood. **кровяно́й** blood.

крои́ть (крою́) *impf* (*pf* **с~**) cut (out). **кро́йка** cutting out.

крокоди́л crocodile.

кро́лик rabbit.

кроль *m* crawl(-stroke).

крольчи́ха she-rabbit, doe.

кро́ме *prep+gen* except; besides; **~ того́** besides, moreover.

кро́мка edge.

кро́на crown; top.

кронште́йн bracket; corbel.

кропотли́вый painstaking; laborious.

кросс cross-country race.

кроссво́рд crossword (puzzle).

крот (-á) mole.

кро́ткий (-ток, -тка́, -тко) meek, gentle. **кро́тость** gentleness; mildness.

кро́хотный, кро́шечный tiny. **кро́шка** crumb; a bit.

круг (*loc* -у́; *pl* -и́) circle; circuit; sphere. **круглосу́точный** round-the-clock. **кру́глый** (кругл, -á, -о) round; complete; **~ год** all the year round. **кругово́й** circular; all-round. **кругозо́р** prospect; outlook. **круго́м** *adv* around; *prep+gen* round. **кругосве́тный** round-the-world.

кружевно́й lace; lacy. **кру́жево** (*pl* -á, -ев, -áм) lace.

кружи́ть (-ужу́, -у́жишь) *impf* whirl, spin round; **~ся** whirl, spin round.

кру́жка mug.

кружо́к (-жка́) circle, group.

круи́з cruise.

крупа́ (*pl* -ы) groats; sleet. **крупи́ца** grain.

кру́пный large, big; great; coarse; **~ый план** close-up.

крутизна́ steepness.

крути́ть (-учу́, -у́тишь) *impf* (*pf* **за~, с~**) twist, twirl; roll; turn, wind; **~ся** turn, spin; whirl.

круто́й (крут, -á, -о) steep; sudden; sharp; severe; drastic. **кру́ча** steep slope. **кру́че** *comp of* **круто́й, кру́то**

кручу́ *etc.*: *see* **крути́ть**
круше́ние crash; ruin; collapse.
крыжо́вник gooseberries; gooseberry bush.
крыла́тый winged. **крыло́** (*pl* -лья, -льев) wing; vane; mudguard.
крыльцо́ (*pl* -а, -ле́ц, -ца́м) porch; (front, back) steps.
Кры́м the Crimea. **кры́мский** Crimean.
кры́са rat.
крыть (кро́ю) *impf* cover; roof; trump; **~ся** be, lie; be concealed. **кры́ша** roof. **кры́шка** lid.
крюк (-а́; *pl* -ки́, -ко́в *or* -ючья, -чьев) hook; detour. **крючо́к** (-чка́) hook.
кря́ду *adv* in succession.
кряж ridge.
кря́кать *impf*, **кря́кнуть** (-ну) *pf* quack.
кряхте́ть (-хчу́) *impf* groan.
кста́ти *adv* to the point; opportunely; at the same time; by the way.
кто (кого́, кому́, кем, ком) *pron* who; anyone; **~ (бы) ни** whoever. **кто́-либо, кто́-нибудь** *prons* anyone; someone. **кто́-то** *pron* someone.
куб (*pl* -ы́) cube; boiler; **в ~е** cubed.
ку́бик brick, block.
куби́нский Cuban.
куби́ческий cubic; cube.
ку́бок (-бка) goblet; cup.
кубоме́тр cubic metre.
кувши́н jug; pitcher. **кувши́нка** water-lily.
кувырка́ться *impf*, **кувыркну́ться** (-ну́сь) *pf* turn somersaults. **кувырко́м** *adv* head over heels; topsy-turvy.
куда́ *adv* where (to); what for; +*comp* much, far; **~ (бы) ни** wherever. **куда́-либо, куда́-нибудь** *adv* anywhere, somewhere. **куда́-то** *adv* somewhere.
ку́дри (-е́й) *pl* curls. **кудря́вый** curly; florid.
кузне́ц (-а́) blacksmith. **кузне́чик** grasshopper. **ку́зница** forge, smithy.
ку́зов (*pl* -а́) basket; body.
ку́кла doll; puppet. **ку́колка** dolly; chrysalis. **ку́кольный** doll's; puppet.
кукуру́за maize.
куку́шка cuckoo.
кула́к (-а́) fist; kulak. **кула́цкий** kulak. **кула́чный** fist.
кулёк (-лька́) bag.
кули́к (-а́) sandpiper.
кулина́рия cookery. **кулина́рный** culinary.
кули́сы (-и́с) wings; **за кули́сами** behind the scenes.
кули́ч (-а́) Easter cake.
кулуа́ры (-ов) *pl* lobby.
кульмина́ция culmination.
культ cult. **культиви́ровать** *impf* cultivate.
культу́ра culture; standard; cultivation. **культури́зм** body-building. **культу́рно** *adv* in a civilized manner. **культу́рный** cultured; cultivated; cultural.
куми́р idol.
кумы́с koumiss (*fermented mare's milk*).
куни́ца marten.
купа́льный bathing. **купа́льня** bathing-place. **купа́ть** *impf* (*pf* вы́~, ис~) bathe; bath; **~ся** bathe; take a bath.
купе́ *neut indecl* compartment.
купе́ц (-пца́) merchant. **купе́ческий** merchant. **купи́ть** (-плю́, -пишь) *pf* (*impf* **покупа́ть**) buy.
ку́пол (*pl* -а́) cupola, dome.
купо́н coupon.
купчи́ха merchant's wife; female merchant.
кура́нты (-ов) *pl* chiming clock; chimes.
курга́н barrow; tumulus.
куре́ние smoking. **кури́льщик, -щица** smoker.
кури́ный hen's; chicken's.
кури́ть (-рю́, -ришь) *impf* (*pf* **по~**) smoke; **~ся** burn; smoke.
ку́рица (*pl* ку́ры, кур) hen, chicken.
куро́к (-рка́) cocking-piece; **взве-**

К

сти́ ~ cock a gun; **спусти́ть ~** pull the trigger.
куропа́тка partridge.
куро́рт health-resort; spa.
курс course; policy; year; exchange rate. **курса́нт** student.
курси́в italics.
курси́ровать *impf* ply.
курсо́р (*comput*) cursor.
ку́ртка jacket.
курча́вый curly(-headed).
ку́ры *etc.*: *see* **ку́рица**
курьёз a funny thing. **курьёзный** curious.
курье́р messenger; courier. **курье́рский** express.
куря́тник hen-house.
куря́щий *sb* smoker.
куса́ть *impf* bite; sting; **~ся** bite.
кусо́к (-ска́) piece; lump. **кусо́чек** (-чка) piece.
куст (-а́) bush, shrub. **куста́рник** bush(es), shrub(s).
куста́рн|ый hand-made; handicrafts; primitive; **~ая промы́шленность** cottage industry. **куста́рь** (-я́) *m* craftsman.
ку́тать *impf* (*pf* **за~**) wrap up; **~ся** muffle o.s. up.
кути́ть (кучу́, ку́тишь) *impf*, **кутну́ть** (-ну́, -нёшь) *pf* carouse; go on a binge.
куха́рка cook. **ку́хня** (*gen pl* -хонь) kitchen; cuisine. **ку́хонный** kitchen.
ку́ча heap; heaps.
ку́чер (*pl* -а́) coachman.
ку́чка small heap *or* group.
кучу́ *see* **кути́ть**
куша́к (-а́) sash; girdle.
ку́шанье food; dish. **ку́шать** *impf* (*pf* **по~, с~**) eat.
куше́тка couch.
кую́ *etc.*: *see* **кова́ть**

Л

лабора́нт, -а́нтка laboratory assistant. **лаборато́рия** laboratory.
ла́ва lava.
лави́на avalanche.
ла́вка bench; shop. **ла́вочка** small shop.
лавр bay tree, laurel.
ла́герный camp. **ла́герь** (*pl* -я́ *or* -и, -е́й *or* -ей) *m* camp; campsite.
лад (*loc* -у́; *pl* -ы́, -о́в) harmony; manner, way; stop, fret.
ла́дан incense.
ла́дить (ла́жу) *impf* get on, be on good terms. **ла́дно** *adv* all right; very well! **ла́дный** fine, excellent; harmonious.
ладо́нь palm.
ладья́ rook, castle; boat.
ла́жу *etc.*: *see* **ла́дить, ла́зить**
лазаре́т field hospital; sick-bay.
ла́зать *see* **ла́зить. лазе́йка** hole; loop-hole.
ла́зер laser.
ла́зить (ла́жу), **ла́зать** *impf* climb, clamber.
лазу́рный sky-blue, azure. **лазу́рь** azure.
лазу́тчик scout; spy.
лай bark, barking. **ла́йка**[1] (Siberian) husky, laika.
ла́йка[2] kid. **ла́йковый** kid; kidskin.
ла́йнер liner; airliner.
лак varnish, lacquer.
лака́ть *impf* (*pf* **вы~**) lap.
лаке́й footman, man-servant; lackey.
лакирова́ть *impf* (*pf* **от~**) varnish; lacquer.
ла́кмус litmus.
ла́ковый varnished, lacquered.
ла́комиться (-млюсь) *impf* (*pf* **по~**) +*instr* treat o.s. to. **ла́комка** *m* & *f* gourmand. **ла́комство** delicacy. **ла́комый** dainty, tasty; **+до** fond of.
лакони́чный laconic.
ла́мпа lamp; valve, tube. **лампа́да** icon-lamp. **ла́мпочка** lamp; bulb.
ландша́фт landscape.
ла́ндыш lily of the valley.
лань fallow deer; doe.
ла́па paw; tenon.
ла́поть (-птя; *pl* -и, -е́й) *m* bast shoe.

ла́почка pet, sweetie.
лапша́ noodles; noodle soup.
ларёк (-рька́) stall. **ларь** (-я́) *m* chest; bin.
ла́ска[1] caress.
ла́ска[2] weasel.
ласка́ть *impf* caress, fondle; **~ся** +к+*dat* make up to; fawn upon. **ла́сковый** affectionate, tender.
ла́сточка swallow.
латви́ец (-и́йца), **-и́йка** Latvian. **латви́йский** Latvian. **Ла́твия** Latvia.
лати́нский Latin.
лату́нь brass.
ла́ты (лат) *pl* armour.
латы́нь Latin.
латы́ш, латы́шка Latvian, Lett. **латы́шский** Latvian, Lettish.
лауреа́т prize-winner.
ла́цкан lapel.
лачу́га hovel, shack.
ла́ять (ла́ю) *impf* bark.
лба *etc.*: *see* **лоб**
лгать (лгу, лжёшь; лгал, -á, -о) *impf* (*pf* **на~, со~**) lie; tell lies; +**на**+*acc* slander. **лгун** (-á), **лгу́нья** liar.
лебеди́ный swan. **лебёдка** swan, pen; winch. **ле́бедь** (*pl* -и, -е́й) *m* swan, cob.
лев (льва) lion.
левобере́жный left-bank. **левша́** (*gen pl* -е́й) *m* & *f* left-hander. **ле́вый** *adj* left; left-hand; left-wing.
лёг *etc.*: *see* **лечь**
лега́льный legal.
леге́нда legend. **легенда́рный** legendary.
лёгк|ий (-гок, -гка́, лёгки́) light; easy; slight, mild; **~ая атле́тика** field and track events. **легко́** *adv* easily, lightly, slightly.
легко- *in comb* light; easy, easily. **легкове́рный** credulous. **~ве́с** light-weight. **~мы́сленный** thoughtless; flippant, frivolous, superficial. **~мы́слие** flippancy, frivolity.
легков|о́й: **~а́я маши́на** (private) car. **лёгкое** *sb* lung. **лёгкость** lightness; easiness. **ле́гче** *comp of* **лёгкий, легко́**
лёд (льда, *loc* -у) ice. **ледене́ть** (-е́ю) *impf* (*pf* **за~, о~**) freeze; grow numb with cold. **ледене́ц** (-нца́) fruit-drop. **леденя́щий** chilling, icy.
ле́ди *f indecl* lady.
ле́дник[1] ice-box; refrigerator van. **ледни́к**[2] (-á) glacier. **леднико́вый** glacial; **~ пери́од** Ice Age. **ледо́вый** ice. **ледоко́л** ice-breaker. **ледяно́й** ice; icy.
лежа́ть (-жу́) *impf* lie; be, be situated. **лежа́чий** lying (down).
ле́звие (cutting) edge; razor-blade.
лезть (-зу; лез) *impf* (*pf* **по~**) climb; clamber, crawl; get, go; fall out.
лейбори́ст Labourite.
ле́йка watering-can.
лейтена́нт lieutenant.
лека́рство medicine.
ле́ксика vocabulary. **лексико́н** lexicon; vocabulary.
ле́ктор lecturer. **ле́кция** lecture.
леле́ять (-е́ю) *impf* (*pf* **вз~**) cherish, foster.
лён (льна) flax.
лени́вый lazy.
ленингра́дский (of) Leningrad. **ле́нинский** (of) Lenin; Leninist.
лени́ться (-ню́сь, -нишься) *impf* (*pf* **по~**) be lazy; +*inf* be too lazy to.
ле́нта ribbon; band; tape.
лентя́й, -я́йка lazy-bones. **лень** laziness.
лепесто́к (-тка́) petal.
ле́пет babble; prattle. **лепета́ть** (-ечу́, -е́чешь) *impf* (*pf* **про~**) babble, prattle.
лепёшка scone; tablet, pastille.
лепи́ть (-плю́, -пишь) *impf* (*pf* **вы́~, за~, с~**) model, fashion; mould; **~ся** cling; crawl. **ле́пка** modelling. **лепно́й** modelled, moulded.
лес (*loc* -у́; *pl* -á) forest, wood; *pl* scaffolding.

ле́са́ (*pl* ле́сы) fishing-line.
лесни́к (-а́) forester. **лесни́чий** *sb* forestry officer; forest warden. **лесно́й** forest.
лесо- *in comb* forest, forestry; timber, wood. **лесово́дство** forestry. **~загото́вка** logging. **~пи́лка, ~пи́льня** (*gen pl* -лен) sawmill. **~ру́б** woodcutter.
ле́стница stairs, staircase; ladder.
ле́стный flattering. **лесть** flattery.
лёт (*loc* -у́) flight, flying.
лета́ (лет) *pl* years; age; **ско́лько вам лет?** how old are you?
лета́тельный flying. **лета́ть** *impf*, **лете́ть** (лечу́) *impf* (*pf* **полете́ть**) fly; rush; fall.
ле́тний summer.
лётный flying, flight.
Л **ле́то** (*pl* -а́) summer; *pl* years. **ле́том** *adv* in summer.
ле́топись chronicle.
летосчисле́ние chronology.
лету́ч|ий flying; passing; brief; volatile; **~ая мышь** bat. **лётчик, -чица** pilot.
лече́бница clinic. **лече́бный** medical; medicinal. **лече́ние** (medical) treatment. **лечи́ть** (-чу́, -чишь) *impf* treat (**от** for); **~ся** be given, have treatment (**от** for).
лечу́ *etc.*: *see* **лете́ть, лечи́ть**
лечь (ля́гу, ля́жешь; лёг, -ла́) *pf* (*impf* **ложи́ться**) lie, lie down; go to bed.
лещ (-а́) bream.
лжесвиде́тельство false witness.
лжец (-а́) liar. **лжи́вый** lying; deceitful.
ли, ль *interrog partl & conj* whether, if; **ли,... ли** whether … or; **ра́но ли, по́здно ли** sooner or later.
либера́л liberal. **либера́льный** liberal.
ли́бо *conj* or; **~... ~** either … or.
ли́вень (-вня) *m* heavy shower, downpour.
ливре́я livery.
ли́га league.
ли́дер leader. **лиди́ровать** *impf & pf* be in the lead.
лиза́ть (лижу́, -ешь) *impf*, **лизну́ть** (-ну́, -нёшь) *pf* lick.
ликвида́ция liquidation; abolition. **ликвиди́ровать** *impf & pf* liquidate; abolish.
ликёр liqueur.
ликова́ние rejoicing. **ликова́ть** *impf* rejoice.
ли́лия lily.
лило́вый lilac, violet.
лима́н estuary.
лими́т limit.
лимо́н lemon. **лимона́д** lemonade; squash. **лимо́нный** lemon.
ли́мфа lymph.
лингви́ст linguist. **лингви́стика** linguistics. **лингвисти́ческий** linguistic.
лине́йка ruler; line. **лине́йный** linear; **~ кора́бль** battleship.
ли́нза lens.
ли́ния line.
лино́леум lino(leum).
линя́ть *impf* (*pf* **вы~, по~, с~**) fade; moult.
ли́па lime tree.
ли́пкий (-пок, -пка́, -о) sticky. **ли́пнуть** (-ну; лип) *impf* stick.
ли́повый lime.
ли́ра lyre. **ли́рик** lyric poet. **ли́рика** lyric poetry. **лири́ческий** lyric; lyrical.
лиса́ (*pl* -ы), **-си́ца** fox.
лист (-а́; *pl* -ы́ *or* -ья, -о́в *or* -ьев) leaf; sheet; page; form; **игра́ть с ~а́** play at sight. **листа́ть** *impf* leaf through. **листва́** foliage. **ли́ственница** larch **ли́ственный** deciduous. **листо́вка** leaflet. **листово́й** sheet, plate; leaf. **листо́к** (-тка́) *dim of* **лист**; leaflet; form, pro-forma.
Литва́ Lithuania.
лите́йный founding, casting.
литера́тор man of letters. **литерату́ра** literature. **литерату́рный** literary.
лито́вец (-вца), **лито́вка** Lithuanian. **лито́вский** Lithuanian.
лито́й cast.
литр litre.

лить (лью, льёшь; лил, -á, -o) *impf* (*pf* **с~**) pour; shed; cast, mould. **литьё** founding, casting, moulding; castings, mouldings. **ли́ться** (льётся; ли́лся, -áсь, ли́лóсь) *impf* flow; pour.
лиф bodice. **ли́фчик** bra.
лифт lift.
лихóй[1] (лих, -á, -o) dashing, spirited.
лихóй[2] (лих, -á, -o, ли́хи́) evil.
лихорáдка fever. **лихорáдочный** feverish.
лицевóй facial; exterior; front.
лицемéр hypocrite. **лицемéрие** hypocrisy. **лицемéрный** hypocritical.
лицó (*pl* -a) face; exterior; right side; person; **быть к лицý** +*dat* suit, befit. **личи́нка** larva, grub; maggot. **ли́чно** *adv* personally, in person. **ли́чность** personality; person. **ли́чный** personal; private; **~ состáв** staff, personnel.
лишáй lichen; herpes; shingles. **лишáйник** lichen.
лишáть(ся *impf of* **лиши́ть(ся**
лишéние deprivation; privation. **лишённый** (-ён, -енá) +*gen* lacking in, devoid of. **лиши́ть** (-шý) *pf* (*impf* **лишáть**) +*gen* deprive of; **~ся** +*gen* lose, be deprived of. **ли́шн|ий** superfluous; unnecessary; spare; **~ раз** once more; **с ~им** odd, and more.
лишь *adv* only; *conj* as soon as; **~ бы** if only, provided that.
лоб (лба, *loc* лбу) forehead.
лóбзик fret-saw.
лови́ть (-влю́, -вишь) *impf* (*pf* **поймáть**) catch, try to catch.
лóвкий (-вок, -вкá, -o) adroit; cunning. **лóвкость** adroitness; cunning.
лóвля (*gen pl* -вель) catching, hunting; fishing-ground. **ловýшка** trap.
лóвче *comp of* **лóвкий**
логари́фм logarithm.
лóгика logic. **логи́ческий, логи́чный** logical.
лóговище, лóгово den, lair.
лóдка boat.
лóдырничать *impf* loaf, idle about. **лóдырь** *m* loafer, idler.
лóжа box; (masonic) lodge.
ложби́на hollow.
лóже couch; bed.
ложи́ться (-жýсь) *impf of* **лечь**
лóжка spoon.
лóжный false. **ложь** (лжи) lie, falsehood.
лозá (*pl* -ы) vine.
лóзунг slogan, catchword.
локáтор radar *or* sonar apparatus.
локомоти́в locomotive.
лóкон lock, curl.
лóкоть (-ктя; *pl* -и, -éй) *m* elbow.
лом (*pl* -ы, -óв) crowbar; scrap, waste. **лóманый** broken. **ломáть** *impf* (*pf* **по~, с~**) break; cause to ache; **~ся** break; crack; put on airs; be obstinate.
ломбáрд pawnshop.
лóмберный стол card-table.
ломи́ть (лóмит) *impf* break; break through, rush; *impers* cause to ache; **~ся** be (near to) breaking. **лóмка** breaking; *pl* quarry. **лóмкий** (-мок, -мкá, -o) fragile, brittle.
ломóть (-мтя́; *pl* -мти́) *m* large slice; hunk; chunk. **лóмтик** slice.
лóно bosom, lap.
лóпасть (*pl* -и, -éй) blade; fan, vane; paddle.
лопáта spade; shovel. **лопáтка** shoulder-blade; shovel; trowel.
лóпаться *impf*, **лóпнуть** (-ну) *pf* burst; split; break; fail; crash.
лопýх (-á) burdock.
лорд lord.
лоси́на elk-skin, chamois leather; elk-meat.
лоск lustre, shine.
лоскýт (-á; *pl* -ы *or* -ья, -óв *or* -ьев) rag, shred, scrap.
лосни́ться *impf* be glossy, shine.
лóсóсь *m* salmon.
лось (*pl* -и, -éй) *m* elk.
лосьóн lotion; aftershave; cream.
лот lead, plummet.
лотерéя lottery, raffle.

Л

лото́к (-тка́) hawker's stand *or* tray; chute; gutter; trough.
лохма́тый shaggy; dishevelled.
лохмо́тья (-ьев) *pl* rags.
ло́цман pilot.
лошади́ный horse; equine. **ло́шадь** (*pl* -и, -е́й, *instr* -дьми́ *or* -дя́ми) horse.
лощёный glossy, polished.
лощи́на hollow, depression.
лоя́льный fair, honest; loyal.
лубо́к (-бка́) splint; popular print.
луг (*loc* -у́; *pl* -а́) meadow.
лу́жа puddle.
лужа́йка lawn, glade.
лужёный tin-plated.
лук[1] onions.
лук[2] bow.
Л
лука́вить (-влю) *impf* (*pf* **с~**) be cunning. **лука́вство** craftiness. **лука́вый** crafty, cunning.
лу́ковица onion; bulb
луна́ (*pl* -ы) moon. **луна́тик** sleep-walker.
лу́нка hole; socket.
лу́нный moon; lunar.
лу́па magnifying-glass.
лупи́ть (-плю́, -пишь) *impf* (*pf* **от~**) flog.
луч (-а́) ray; beam. **лучево́й** ray, beam; radial; radiation. **лучеза́рный** radiant.
лучи́на splinter.
лу́чше better; **~ всего́, ~ всех** best of all. **лу́чш|ий** better; best; **в ~ем слу́чае** at best; **всего́ ~его!** all the best!
лы́жа ski. **лы́жник** skier. **лы́жный спорт** skiing. **лыжня́** ski-track.
лы́ко bast.
лысе́ть (-е́ю) *impf* (*pf* **об~, по~**) grow bald. **лы́сина** bald spot; blaze. **лы́сый** (лыс, -а́, -о) bald.
ль *see* **ли**
льва *etc.*: *see* **лев. льви́ный** lion, lion's. **льви́ца** lioness.
льго́та privilege; advantage. **льго́тный** privileged; favourable.
льда *etc.*: *see* **лёд. льди́на** block of ice; ice-floe.
льна *etc.*: *see* **лён. льново́дство** flax-growing.
льнуть (-ну, -нёшь) *impf* (*pf* **при~**) **+к+***dat* cling to; have a weakness for; make up to.
льняно́й flax, flaxen; linen; linseed.
льсте́ц (-а́) flatterer. **льсти́вый** flattering; smooth-tongued. **льстить** (льщу) *impf* (*pf* **по~**) *+dat* flatter.
лью *etc.*: *see* **лить**
любе́зность courtesy; kindness; compliment. **любе́зн|ый** courteous; obliging; kind; **бу́дьте ~ы** be so kind (as to).
люби́мец (-мца), **-мица** pet, favourite. **люби́мый** beloved; favourite. **люби́тель** *m*, **-ница** lover; amateur. **люби́тельский** amateur. **люби́ть** (-блю́, -бишь) *impf* love; like.
любова́ться *impf* (*pf* **по~**) *+instr or* **на+***acc* admire.
любо́вник lover. **любо́вница** mistress. **любо́вный** love-; loving. **любо́вь** (-бви́, *instr* -бо́вью) love.
любозна́тельный inquisitive.
любо́й any; either; *sb* anyone.
любопы́тный curious; inquisitive. **любопы́тство** curiosity.
лю́бящий loving.
лю́ди (-е́й, -ям, -дьми́, -ях) *pl* people. **лю́дный** populous; crowded. **людое́д** cannibal; ogre. **людско́й** human.
люк hatch(way); trap; manhole.
лю́лька cradle.
люминесце́нтный luminescent. **люминесце́нция** luminescence.
лю́стра chandelier.
лю́тня (*gen pl* -тен) lute.
лю́тый (лют, -а́, -о) ferocious.
ляга́ть *impf*, **лягну́ть** (-ну́, -нёшь) *pf* kick; **~ся** kick.
ля́гу *etc.*: *see* **лечь**
лягу́шка frog.
ля́жка thigh, haunch.
ля́згать *impf* clank; *+instr* rattle.
ля́мка strap; **тяну́ть ля́мку** toil.

M

мавзоле́й mausoleum.

мавр, маврита́нка Moor. **маврита́нский** Moorish.

магази́н shop.

маги́стр (holder of) master's degree.

магистра́ль main; main line, main road.

маги́ческий magic(al). **ма́гия** magic.

магнети́зм magnetism.

ма́гний magnesium.

магни́т magnet. **магни́тный** magnetic. **магнитофо́н** tape-recorder.

мада́м *f indecl* madam, madame.

мажо́р major (key); cheerful mood. **мажо́рный** major; cheerful.

ма́зать (ма́жу) *impf* (*pf* **вы~, за~, из~, на~, по~, про~**) oil, grease; smear, spread; soil; **~ся** get dirty; make up. **мазо́к** (-зка́) touch, dab; smear. **мазу́т** fuel oil. **мазь** ointment; grease.

маис maize.

май May. **ма́йский** May.

ма́йка T-shirt.

майо́р major.

мак poppy, poppy-seeds.

макаро́ны (-н) *pl* macaroni.

мака́ть *impf* (*pf* **макну́ть**) dip.

маке́т model; dummy.

макну́ть (-ну́, -нёшь) *pf of* **мака́ть**

макре́ль mackerel.

максима́льный maximum. **ма́ксимум** maximum; at most.

макулату́ра waste paper; pulp literature.

маку́шка top; crown.

мал *etc.*: *see* **ма́лый**

малахи́т malachite.

мале́йший least, slightest. **ма́ленький** little; small.

мали́на (*no pl*; *usu collect*) raspberry; raspberries; raspberry-bush. **мали́новый** raspberry.

ма́ло *adv* little, few; not enough; **~ того́** moreover; **~ того́ что...** not only ....

мало- *in comb* (too) little. **малова́жный** of little importance. **~вероя́тный** unlikely. **~гра́мотный** semi-literate; crude. **~ду́шный** faint-hearted. **~иму́щий** needy. **~кро́вие** anaemia. **~ле́тний** young; juvenile; minor. **~о́пытный** inexperienced. **~чи́сленный** small (in number), few.

мало-ма́льски *adv* in the slightest degree; at all. **мало-пома́лу** *adv* little by little.

ма́л|ый (мал, -а́) little, (too) small; **са́мое ~ое** at the least; *sb* fellow; lad. **малы́ш** (-а́) kiddy; little boy. **ма́льчик** boy. **мальчи́шка** *m* urchin, boy. **мальчуга́н** little boy. **малю́тка** *m* & *f* baby.

маля́р (-а́) painter, decorator.

малярия malaria.

ма́ма mother, mummy. **мама́ша** mummy. **ма́мин** mother's.

ма́монт mammoth.

мандари́н mandarin, tangerine.

манда́т warrant; mandate.

манёвр manoeuvre; shunting. **маневри́ровать** *impf* (*pf* **с~**) manoeuvre; shunt; +*instr* make good use of.

мане́ж riding-school.

манеке́н dummy; mannequin. **манеке́нщик, -щица** model.

мане́ра manner; style. **мане́рный** affected.

манже́та cuff.

маникю́р manicure.

манипули́ровать *impf* manipulate. **манипуля́ция** manipulation; machination.

мани́ть (-ню́, -нишь) *impf* (*pf* **по~**) beckon; attract; lure.

манифе́ст manifesto. **манифеста́ция** demonstration.

мани́шка (false) shirt-front.

ма́ния mania; **~ вели́чия** megalomania.

ма́нная ка́ша semolina.

мано́метр pressure-gauge.
ма́нтия cloak; robe, gown.
мануфакту́ра manufacture; textiles.
манья́к maniac.
марафо́нский бег marathon.
ма́рганец (-нца) manganese.
маргари́н margarine.
маргари́тка daisy.
марино́ванный pickled. **маринова́ть** *impf* (*pf* **за~**) pickle; put off.
марионе́тка puppet.
ма́рка stamp; counter; brand; trade-mark; grade; reputation.
ма́ркетинг marketing.
ма́ркий easily soiled.
маркси́зм Marxism. **маркси́ст** Marxist. **маркси́стский** Marxist.
ма́рлевый gauze. **ма́рля** gauze; cheesecloth.
мармела́д fruit jellies.
ма́рочный high-quality.
Марс Mars.
март March. **ма́ртовский** March.
марты́шка marmoset; monkey.
марш march.
ма́ршал marshal.
маршировáть *impf* march.
маршру́т route, itinerary.
ма́ска mask. **маскара́д** masked ball; masquerade. **маскирова́ть** *impf* (*pf* **за~**) disguise; camouflage. **маскиро́вка** disguise; camouflage.
Ма́сленица Shrovetide. **маслёнка** butter-dish; oil-can. **масли́на** olive. **ма́сло** (*pl* -á, ма́сел, -сла́м) butter; oil; oil paints. **маслобо́йка** churn. **маслобо́йня** (*gen pl* -óен), **маслозаво́д** dairy. **масляни́стый** oily. **ма́сляный** oil.
ма́сса mass; a lot, lots.
масса́ж massage. **масси́ровать** *impf* & *pf* massage.
масси́в massif; expanse, tract. **масси́вный** massive.
ма́ссовый mass.
ма́стер (*pl* -á), **мастери́ца** foreman, forewoman; (master) craftsman; expert. **мастери́ть** *impf* (*pf* **с~**) make, build. **мастерска́я** *sb* workshop. **мастерско́й** masterly. **мастерство́** craft; skill.
масти́ка mastic; putty; floor-polish.
масти́тый venerable.
масть (*pl* -и, -е́й) colour; suit.
масшта́б scale.
мат[1] checkmate.
мат[2] mat.
мат[3] foul language.
матема́тик mathematician. **матема́тика** mathematics. **математи́ческий** mathematical.
материа́л material. **материали́зм** materialism. **материалисти́ческий** materialist. **материа́льный** material.
матери́к (-á) continent; mainland. **материко́вый** continental.
матери́нский maternal, motherly. **матери́нство** maternity.
мате́рия material; pus; topic.
ма́тка womb; female.
ма́товый matt; frosted.
матра́с, матра́ц mattress.
матрёшка Russian doll.
ма́трица matrix; die, mould.
матро́с sailor, seaman.
матч match.
мать (ма́тери, *instr* -рью; *pl* -тери, -ре́й) mother.
ма́фия Mafia.
мах swing, stroke. **маха́ть** (машу́, ма́шешь) *impf*, **махну́ть** (-ну́, -нёшь) *pf* +*instr* wave; brandish; wag; flap; go; rush.
махина́ция machinations.
махови́к (-á) fly-wheel.
махро́вый dyed-in-the-wool; terry.
ма́чеха stepmother.
ма́чта mast.
маши́на machine; car. **машина́льный** mechanical. **машини́ст** operator; engine-driver; scene-shifter. **машини́стка** typist; **~-стенографи́стка** shorthand-typist. **маши́нка** machine; typewriter; sewing-machine. **машинопи́сный** typewritten. **маши́-**

нопись typing; typescript. **машинострое́ние** mechanical engineering.
мая́к (-á) lighthouse; beacon.
ма́ятник pendulum. **ма́яться** *impf* toil; suffer; languish.
мгла haze; gloom.
мгнове́ние instant, moment. **мгнове́нный** instantaneous, momentary.
ме́бель furniture. **меблиро́ванный** furnished. **меблиро́вка** furnishing; furniture.
мегава́тт (*gen pl* -áтт) megawatt. **мего́м** megohm. **мегато́нна** megaton.
мёд (*loc* -ý; *pl* -ы́) honey.
меда́ль medal. **медальо́н** medallion.
медве́дица she-bear. **медве́дь** *m* bear. **медве́жий** bear('s). **медвежо́нок** (-нка; *pl* -жáта, -жáт) bear cub.
ме́дик medical student; doctor. **медикаме́нты** (-ов) *pl* medicines.
медици́на medicine. **медици́нский** medical.
ме́дленный slow. **медли́тельный** sluggish; slow. **ме́длить** *impf* linger; be slow.
ме́дный copper; brass.
медо́вый honey; **~ ме́сяц** honeymoon.
медосмо́тр medical examination, check-up. **медпу́нкт** first aid post. **медсестра́** (*pl* -сёстры, -сестёр, -сёстрам) nurse.
меду́за jellyfish.
медь copper.
меж *prep+instr* between.
меж- *in comb* inter-.
межа́ (*pl* -и, меж, -áм) boundary.
междоме́тие interjection.
ме́жду *prep+instr* between; among; **~ про́чим** incidentally, by the way; **~ тем** meanwhile; **~ тем, как** while.
между- *in comb* inter-. **междугоро́дный** inter-city. **~наро́дный** international.
межконтинента́льный intercontinental. **межплане́тный** interplanetary.
мезони́н attic (storey); mezzanine (floor).
Ме́ксика Mexico.
мел (*loc* -ý) chalk.
мёл *etc.*: *see* **мести́**
меланхо́лия melancholy.
меле́ть (-éет) *impf* (*pf* **об~**) grow shallow.
мелиора́ция land improvement.
ме́лкий (-лок, -лкá, -о) small; shallow; fine; petty. **ме́лко** *adv* fine, small. **мелкобуржуа́зный** petty bourgeois. **мелково́дный** shallow.
мелоди́чный melodious, melodic. **мело́дия** melody.
ме́лочный petty. **ме́лочь** (*pl* -и, -éй) small items; (small) change; *pl* trifles, trivialities.
мель (*loc* -и́) shoal; bank; **на мели́** aground.
мелька́ть *impf*, **мелькну́ть** (-нý, -нёшь) *pf* be glimpsed fleetingly. **ме́льком** *adv* in passing; fleetingly.
ме́льник miller. **ме́льница** mill.
мельча́йший *superl of* **ме́лкий**. **ме́льче** *comp of* **ме́лкий, ме́лко.**
мелюзга́ small fry.
мелю́ *etc.*: *see* **моло́ть**
мембра́на membrane; diaphragm.
мемора́ндум memorandum.
мемуа́ры (-ов) *pl* memoirs.
ме́на exchange, barter.
ме́неджер manager.
ме́нее *adv* less; **тем не ~** none the less.
мензу́рка measuring-glass.
менов́ой exchange; barter.
менуэ́т minuet.
ме́ньше smaller; less. **меньшеви́к** (-á) Menshevik. **ме́ньший** lesser, smaller; younger. **меньшинство́** minority.
меню́ *neut indecl* menu.
меня́ *see* **я** *pron*
меня́ть *impf* (*pf* **об~, по~**) change; exchange; **~ся** change; *+instr* exchange.

ме́ра measure.
мере́щиться (-щусь) *impf* (*pf* **по~**) seem, appear.
мерза́вец (-вца) swine, bastard.
ме́рзкий (-зок, -зка́, -о) disgusting.
мерзлота́: ве́чная ~ permafrost.
мёрзнуть (-ну; мёрз) *impf* (*pf* **за~**) freeze.
ме́рзость vileness; abomination.
меридиа́н meridian.
мери́ло standard, criterion.
ме́рин gelding.
ме́рить *impf* (*pf* **по~, с~**) measure; try on. **ме́рка** measure.
ме́рный measured; rhythmical.
мероприя́тие measure.
мертве́ть (-е́ю) *impf* (*pf* **о~, по~**) grow numb; be benumbed. **мертве́ц** (-а́) corpse, dead man.
мёртвый (мёртв, -а́, мёртво́) dead.

М

мерца́ть *impf* twinkle; flicker.
меси́ть (мешу́, ме́сишь) *impf* (*pf* **с~**) knead.
ме́сса Mass.
места́ми *adv* here and there, in places. **месте́чко** (*pl* -и, -чек) small town.
мести́ (мету́, -тёшь; мёл, -а́) *impf* sweep; whirl.
ме́стность terrain; locality; area.
ме́стный local; locative.
-ме́стный *in comb* -berth, -seater.
ме́сто (*pl* -а́) place; site; seat; room; job. **местожи́тельство** (place of) residence. **местоиме́ние** pronoun. **местонахожде́ние** location, whereabouts. **месторожде́ние** deposit; layer.
месть vengeance, revenge.
ме́сяц month; moon. **ме́сячный** monthly; *sb pl* period.
мета́лл metal. **металли́ческий** metal, metallic. **металлу́ргия** metallurgy.
мета́н methane.
мета́ние throwing, flinging. **мета́ть**[1] (мечу́, ме́чешь) *impf* (*pf* **метну́ть**) throw, fling; **~ся** rush about; toss (and turn).
мета́ть[2] *impf* (*pf* **на~, с~**) tack.
метафи́зика metaphysics.
мета́фора metaphor.
метёлка panicle.
мете́ль snow-storm.
мете́ор meteor. **метеори́т** meteorite. **метеоро́лог** meteorologist. **метеорологи́ческий** meteorological. **метеороло́гия** meteorology.
метеосво́дка weather report. **метеоста́нция** weather-station.
ме́тить[1] (ме́чу) *impf* (*pf* **на~, по~**) mark.
ме́тить[2] (ме́чу) *impf* (*pf* **на~**) aim; mean.
ме́тка marking, mark.
ме́ткий (-ток, -тка́, -о) well-aimed, accurate.
метла́ (*pl* мётлы, -тел) broom.
метну́ть (-ну́, -нёшь) *pf of* **мета́ть**[1]
ме́тод method. **мето́дика** method(s); methodology. **методи́чный** methodical. **методоло́гия** methodology.
метр metre.
ме́трика birth certificate. **метри́ческ|ий**[1]: **~ое свиде́тельство** birth certificate.
метри́ческий[2] metric; metrical.
метро́ *neut indecl*, **метрополите́н** Metro; underground.
мету́ *etc.*: *see* **мести́**
мех[1] (*loc* -у́; *pl* -а́) fur.
мех[2] (*pl* -и́) wine-skin, water-skin; *pl* bellows.
механиза́ция mechanization. **механи́зм** mechanism; gear(ing).
меха́ник mechanic. **меха́ника** mechanics; trick; knack. **механи́ческий** mechanical; mechanistic.
мехово́й fur.
меч (-а́) sword.
ме́ченый marked.
мече́ть mosque.
мечта́ (day-)dream. **мечта́тельный** dreamy. **мечта́ть** *impf* dream.
ме́чу *etc.*: *see* **ме́тить.** **мечу́** *etc.*: *see* **мета́ть**
меша́лка mixer.
меша́ть[1] *impf* (*pf* **по~**) *+dat* hin-

der; prevent; disturb.
меша́ть² *impf* (*pf* **по~, с~**) stir; mix; mix up; **~ся** (**в**+*acc*) interfere (in), meddle (with).
мешо́к (-шка́) bag; sack. **мешкови́на** sacking, hessian.
мещани́н (*pl* -а́не, -а́н) petty bourgeois; Philistine. **меща́нский** bourgeois, narrow-minded; Philistine. **меща́нство** petty bourgeoisie; philistinism, narrow-mindedness.
миг moment, instant.
мига́ть *impf*, **мигну́ть** (-ну́, -нёшь) *pf* blink; wink, twinkle.
ми́гом *adv* in a flash.
мигра́ция migration.
мигре́нь migraine.
мизантро́п misanthrope.
мизи́нец (-нца) little finger; little toe.
микро́б microbe.
микроволно́вая печь microwave oven.
микро́н micron.
микроорганизм micro-organism.
микроско́п microscope. **микроскопи́ческий** microscopic.
микросхе́ма microchip.
микрофо́н (*gen pl* -н) microphone.
ми́ксер (*cul*) mixer, blender.
миксту́ра medicine, mixture.
ми́ленький pretty; sweet; dear.
милитари́зм militarism.
милиционе́р militiaman, policeman. **мили́ция** militia, police force.
миллиа́рд billion, a thousand million. **миллиме́тр** millimetre. **миллио́н** million. **миллионе́р** millionaire.
милосе́рдие mercy, charity. **милосе́рдный** merciful, charitable.
ми́лостивый gracious, kind. **ми́лостыня** alms. **ми́лость** favour, grace. **ми́лый** (мил, -а́, -о) nice; kind; sweet; dear.
ми́ля mile.
ми́мика (facial) expression; mimicry.
ми́мо *adv* & *prep* +*gen* by, past. **мимолётный** fleeting. **мимохо́дом** *adv* in passing.
ми́на¹ mine; bomb.
ми́на² expression, mien.
минда́ль (-я́) *m* almond(-tree); almonds.
минера́л mineral. **минерало́гия** mineralogy. **минера́льный** mineral.
миниатю́ра miniature. **миниатю́рный** miniature; tiny.
минима́льный minimum. **ми́нимум** minimum.
министе́рство ministry. **мини́стр** minister.
минова́ть *impf* & *pf* pass; *impers*+*dat* escape.
миномёт mortar. **миноно́сец** (-сца) torpedo-boat.
мино́р minor (key); melancholy.
мину́вш|ий past; **~ее** *sb* the past.
ми́нус minus.
мину́та minute. **мину́тный** minute; momentary.
мину́ть (-нешь; ми́нул) *pf* pass.
мир¹ (*pl* -ы́) world.
мир² peace.
мира́ж mirage.
мири́ть *impf* (*pf* **по~, при~**) reconcile; **~ся** be reconciled. **ми́рный** peace; peaceful.
мировоззре́ние (world-)outlook; philosophy. **мирово́й** world. **мирозда́ние** universe.
миролюби́вый peace-loving.
ми́ска basin, bowl.
мисс *f indecl* Miss.
миссионе́р missionary.
ми́ссис *f indecl* Mrs.
ми́ссия mission.
ми́стер Mr.
ми́стика mysticism.
мистифика́ция hoax.
ми́тинг mass meeting; rally.
митрополи́т metropolitan.
миф myth. **мифи́ческий** mythical. **мифологи́ческий** mythological. **мифоло́гия** mythology.
ми́чман warrant officer.
мише́нь target.

М

ми́шка (Teddy) bear.
младе́нец (-нца) baby; infant. **мла́дший** younger; youngest; junior.
млекопита́ющие *sb pl* mammals. **Мле́чный Путь** Milky Way.
мне *see* **я** *pron*
мне́ние opinion.
мни́мый imaginary; sham. **мни́тельный** hypochondriac; mistrustful. **мнить** (мню) *impf* think.
мно́гие *sb pl* many (people); **~ое** *sb* much, a great deal. **мно́го** *adv+gen* much; many; **на ~** by far.
много- *in comb* many-, poly-, multi-, multiple-. **многобо́рье** combined event. **~гра́нный** polyhedral; many-sided. **~де́тный** having many children. **~же́нство** polygamy. **~значи́тельный** significant. **~кра́тный** repeated; frequentative. **~ле́тний** lasting, living, many years; of many years' standing; perennial. **~лю́дный** crowded. **~национа́льный** multi-national. **~обеща́ющий** promising. **~обра́зие** diversity. **~сло́вный** verbose. **~сторо́нний** multi-lateral; many-sided, versatile. **~то́чие** dots, omission points. **~уважа́емый** respected; Dear. **~уго́льный** polygonal. **~цве́тный** multi-coloured; multiflorous. **~чи́сленный** numerous. **~эта́жный** many-storeyed. **~язы́чный** polyglot.
мно́жественный plural. **мно́жество** great number. **мно́жить** (-жу) *impf* (*pf* **у~**) multiply; increase.
мной *etc.*: *see* **я** *pron.* **мну** *etc.*: *see* **мять**
мобилиза́ция mobilization. **мобилизова́ть** *impf* & *pf* mobilize.
мог *etc.*: *see* **мочь**
моги́ла grave. **моги́льный** (of the) grave; sepulchral.
могу́ *etc.*: *see* **мочь. могу́чий** mighty. **могу́щественный** powerful. **могу́щество** power, might.
мо́да fashion.
модели́ровать *impf* & *pf* design. **моде́ль** model; pattern. **моделье́р** fashion designer. **моде́льный** model; fashionable.
модернизи́ровать *impf* & *pf* modernize.
моде́м (*comput*) modem.
моди́стка milliner.
модифика́ция modification. **модифици́ровать** *impf* & *pf* modify.
мо́дный (-ден, -дна́, -о) fashionable; fashion.
мо́жет *see* **мочь**
можжеве́льник juniper.
мо́жно one may, one can; it is permissible; it is possible; **как ~**+*comp* as … as possible; **как ~ скоре́е** as soon as possible.
моза́ика mosaic; jigsaw.
мозг (*loc* -у́; *pl* -и́) brain; marrow. **мозгово́й** cerebral.
мозо́ль corn; callus.
мой (моего́) *m*, **моя́** (мое́й) *f*, **моё** (моего́) *neut*, **мои́** (-и́х) *pl pron* my; mine; **по-мо́ему** in my opinion; in my way.
мо́йка washing.
мо́кнуть (-ну; мок) *impf* get wet; soak. **мокро́та** phlegm. **мо́крый** wet, damp.
мол (*loc* -у́) mole, pier.
молва́ rumour, talk.
моле́бен (-бна) church service.
моле́кула molecule. **молекуля́рный** molecular.
моли́тва prayer. **моли́ть** (-лю́, -лишь) *impf* pray; beg; **~ся** (*pf* **по~ся**) pray.
моллю́ск mollusc.
молниено́сный lightning. **мо́лния** lightning; zip(-fastener).
молодёжь youth, young people. **молоде́ть** (-е́ю) *impf* (*pf* **по~**) get younger, look younger. **молоде́ц** (-дца́) fine fellow *or* girl; **~!** well done! **молодожёны** (-ов) *pl* newly-weds. **молодо́й** (мо́лод, -а́,

-о) young. **мо́лодость** youth. **моло́же** *comp of* **молодо́й**

молоко́ milk.

мо́лот hammer. **молоти́ть** (-очу́, -о́тишь) *impf* (*pf* **с~**) thresh; hammer. **молото́к** (-тка́) hammer. **мо́лотый** ground. **моло́ть** (мелю́, ме́лешь) *impf* (*pf* **с~**) grind, mill.

моло́чная *sb* dairy. **моло́чный** milk; dairy; milky.

мо́лча *adv* silently, in silence. **молчали́вый** silent, taciturn; tacit. **молча́ние** silence. **молча́ть** (-чу́) *impf* be *or* keep silent.

моль moth.

мольба́ entreaty.

мольбе́рт easel.

моме́нт moment; feature. **момента́льно** *adv* instantly. **момента́льный** instantaneous.

мона́рх monarch. **монархи́ст** monarchist.

монасты́рь (-я́) *m* monastery; convent. **мона́х** monk. **мона́хиня** nun.

монго́л, ~ка Mongol.

моне́та coin.

моногра́фия monograph.

моноли́тный monolithic.

моноло́г monologue.

монопо́лия monopoly.

моното́нный monotonous.

монта́ж (-а́) assembling, mounting; editing. **монта́жник** rigger, fitter. **монтёр** fitter, mechanic. **монти́ровать** *impf* (*pf* **с~**) mount; install, fit; edit.

монуме́нт monument. **монумента́льный** monumental.

мора́ль moral; morals, ethics. **мора́льный** moral; ethical.

морг morgue.

морга́ть *impf*, **моргну́ть** (-ну́, -нёшь) *pf* blink; wink.

мо́рда snout, muzzle; (ugly) mug.

мо́ре (*pl* -я́, -е́й) sea.

морепла́вание navigation. **морепла́ватель** *m* seafarer. **мореходный** nautical.

морж (-а́), **моржи́ха** walrus.

Мо́рзе *indecl* Morse; **а́збука ~** Morse code.

мори́ть *impf* (*pf* **у~**) exhaust; **~ го́лодом** starve.

морко́вка carrot. **морко́вь** carrots.

моро́женое *sb* ice-cream. **моро́женый** frozen, chilled. **моро́з** frost; *pl* intensely cold weather. **морози́лка** freezer compartment; freezer. **морози́льник** deep-freeze. **моро́зить** (-о́жу) freeze. **моро́зный** frosty.

мороси́ть *impf* drizzle.

морск|о́й sea; maritime; marine, nautical; **~а́я сви́нка** guinea-pig; **~о́й флот** navy, fleet.

мо́рфий morphine.

морщи́на wrinkle; crease. **мо́рщить** (-щу) *impf* (*pf* **на~, по~, с~**) wrinkle; pucker; **~ся** knit one's brow; wince; crease, wrinkle.

моря́к (-а́) sailor, seaman.

москви́ч (-а́), **~ка** Muscovite. **моско́вский** (of) Moscow.

мост (мо́ста́, *loc* -у́; *pl* -ы́) bridge. **мо́стик** bridge. **мости́ть** (-ощу́) *impf* (*pf* **вы́~**) pave. **мостки́** (-о́в) *pl* planked footway. **мостова́я** *sb* roadway; pavement. **мостово́й** bridge.

мота́ть[1] *impf* (*pf* **мотну́ть, на~**) wind, reel.

мота́ть[2] *impf* (*pf* **про~**) squander.

мота́ться *impf* dangle; wander; rush about.

моти́в motive; reason; tune; motif. **мотиви́ровать** *impf* & *pf* give reasons for, justify. **мотиviро́вка** reason(s); justification.

мотну́ть (-ну́, -нёшь) *pf of* **мота́ть**

мото- *in comb* motor-, engine-. **мотого́нки** (-нок) *pl* motor-cycle races. **~пе́д** moped. **~пехо́та** motorized infantry. **~ро́ллер** (motor-)scooter. **~ци́кл** motor cycle.

мото́к (-тка́) skein, hank.

мото́р motor, engine. **моτори́ст** motor-mechanic. **мото́рный** motor; engine.

моты́га hoe, mattock.

М

мотылёк (-лька́) butterfly, moth.
мох (мха *or* мо́ха, *loc* мху; *pl* мхи, мхов) moss. **мохна́тый** hairy, shaggy.
моча́ urine.
моча́лка loofah.
мочево́й пузы́рь bladder. **мочи́ть** (-чу́, -чишь) *impf* (*pf* **за~**, **на~**) wet, moisten; soak; **~ся** (*pf* **по~ся**) urinate.
мо́чка ear lobe.
мочь (могу́, мо́жешь; мог, -ла́) *impf* (*pf* **с~**) be able; **мо́жет (быть)** perhaps.
моше́нник rogue. **моше́нничать** *impf* (*pf* **с~**) cheat, swindle. **моше́ннический** rascally.
мо́шка midge. **мошкара́** (swarm of) midges.
мо́щность power; capacity. **мо́щный** (-щен, -щна́, -о) powerful.
мощу́ *etc.*: *see* **мости́ть**
мощь power.
мо́ю *etc.*: *see* **мыть. мо́ющий** washing; detergent.
мрак darkness, gloom. **мракобе́с** obscurantist.
мра́мор marble. **мра́морный** marble.
мра́чный dark; gloomy.
мсти́тельный vindictive. **мстить** (мщу) *impf* (*pf* **ото~**) take vengeance on; **+за+***acc* avenge.
мудре́ц (-а́) sage, wise man. **му́дрость** wisdom. **му́дрый** (-др, -а́, -о) wise, sage.
муж (*pl* -жья́ *or* -и́) husband. **мужа́ть** *impf* grow up; mature; **~ся** take courage. **мужеподо́бный** mannish; masculine. **му́жественный** manly, steadfast. **му́жество** courage.
мужи́к (-а́) peasant; fellow.
мужско́й masculine; male. **мужчи́на** *m* man.
му́за muse.
музе́й museum.
му́зыка music. **музыка́льный** musical. **музыка́нт** musician.
му́ка[1] torment.
мука́[2] flour.
мультиплика́ция, мультфи́льм cartoon film.
му́мия mummy.
мунди́р (full-dress) uniform.
мундшту́к (-а́) mouthpiece; cigarette-holder.
муниципа́льный municipal.
мураве́й (-вья́) ant. **мураве́йник** ant-hill.
мурлы́кать (-ы́чу *or* -каю) *impf* purr.
муска́т nutmeg.
му́скул muscle. **му́скульный** muscular.
му́сор refuse; rubbish. **му́сорный я́щик** dustbin.
мусульма́нин (*pl* -ма́не, -ма́н), **-а́нка** Muslim.
мути́ть (мучу́, му́ти́шь) *impf* (*pf* **вз~**) make muddy; stir up, upset. **му́тный** (-тен, -тна́, -о) turbid, troubled; dull. **муть** sediment; murk.
му́ха fly.
муче́ние torment, torture. **му́ченик, му́ченица** martyr. **мучи́тельный** agonizing. **му́чить** (-чу) *impf* (*pf* **за~, из~**) torment; harass; **~ся** torment o.s.; suffer agonies.
мучно́й flour, meal; starchy.
мха *etc.*: *see* **мох**
мчать (мчу) *impf* rush along, whirl along; **~ся** rush.
мщу *etc.*: *see* **мстить**
мы (нас, нам, на́ми, нас) *pron* we; **мы с ва́ми** you and I.
мы́лить *impf* (*pf* **на~**) soap; **~ся** wash o.s. **мы́ло** (*pl* -а́) soap. **мы́льница** soap-dish. **мы́льный** soap, soapy.
мыс cape, promontory.
мы́сленный mental. **мысли́мый** conceivable. **мысли́тель** *m* thinker. **мы́слить** *impf* think; conceive. **мысль** thought; idea. **мы́слящий** thinking.
мыть (мо́ю) *impf* (*pf* **вы~, по~**) wash; **~ся** wash (o.s.).
мыча́ть (-чу́) *impf* (*pf* **про~**) low, moo; bellow; mumble.

мышело́вка mousetrap.
мы́шечный muscular.
мы́шле́ние thinking, thought.
мы́шца muscle.
мышь (*gen pl* -е́й) mouse.
мэр mayor. **мэ́рия** town hall.
мя́гкий (-гок, -гка́, -о) soft; mild; ~ **знак** soft sign, the letter **ь**. **мя́гче** *comp of* **мя́гкий, мя́гко. мя́коть** fleshy part, flesh; pulp.
мяси́стый fleshy; meaty. **мясни́к** (-а́) butcher. **мясно́й** meat. **мя́со** meat; flesh. **мясору́бка** mincer.
мя́та mint; peppermint.
мяте́ж (-а́) mutiny, revolt. **мяте́жник** mutineer, rebel. **мяте́жный** rebellious; restless.
мя́тный mint, peppermint.
мять (мну, мнёшь) *impf* (*pf* **из~, раз~, с~**) work up; knead; crumple; **~ся** become crumpled; crush (easily).
мяу́кать *impf* miaow.
мяч (-а́), **мя́чик** ball.

Н

на¹ *prep* **I.** +*acc* on; on to, to, into; at; till, until; for; by. **II.** +*prep* on, upon; in; at.
на² *partl* here; here you are.
наба́вить (-влю) *pf*, **набавля́ть** *impf* add (to), increase.
наба́т alarm-bell.
набе́г raid, foray.
набекре́нь *adv* aslant.
на|бели́ть (-е́ли́шь) *pf*. **на́бело** *adv* without corrections.
на́бережная *sb* embankment, quay.
наберу́ *etc.*: *see* **набра́ть**
набива́ть(ся *impf of* **наби́ть(ся. наби́вка** stuffing, padding; (textile) printing.
набира́ть(ся *impf of* **набра́ть(ся**
наби́тый packed, stuffed; crowded. **наби́ть** (-бью, -бьёшь) *pf* (*impf* **набива́ть**) stuff, pack, fill; smash; print; hammer, drive; **~ся** crowd in.
наблюда́тель *m* observer. **наблюда́тельный** observant; observation. **наблюда́ть** *impf* observe, watch; +**за**+*instr* look after; supervise. **наблюде́ние** observation; supervision.
на́божный devout, pious.
на́бок *adv* on one side, crooked.
наболе́вший sore, painful.
набо́р recruiting; collection, set; type-setting.
набра́сывать(ся *impf of* **наброса́ть, набро́сить(ся**
набра́ть (-беру́, -берёшь; -а́л, -а́, -о) *pf* (*impf* **набира́ть**) gather; enlist; compose, set up; ~ **но́мер** dial a number; **~ся** assemble, collect; +*gen* find, acquire, pick up; **~ся сме́лости** pluck up courage.
набрести́ (-еду́, -дёшь; -ёл, -ела́) *pf* +**на**+*acc* come across.
наброса́ть *pf* (*impf* **набра́сывать**) throw (down); sketch; jot down. **набро́сить** (-о́шу) *pf* (*impf* **набра́сывать**) throw; **~ся** throw o.s.; **~ся на** attack. **набро́сок** (-ска) sketch, draft.
набуха́ть *impf*, **набу́хнуть** (-нет; -у́х) *pf* swell.
набью́ *etc.*: *see* **наби́ть**
наважде́ние delusion.
нава́ливать *impf*, **навали́ть** (-лю́, -лишь) *pf* heap, pile up; load; **~ся** lean; +**на**+*acc* fall (up)on.
наведе́ние laying (on); placing.
наведу́ *etc.*: *see* **навести́**
наве́к, наве́ки *adv* for ever.
навёл *etc.*: *see* **навести́**
наве́рно, наве́рное *adv* probably. **наверняка́** *adv* certainly, for sure.
наверста́ть *pf*, **навёрстывать** *impf* make up for.
наве́рх *adv* up(wards); upstairs. **наверху́** *adv* above; upstairs.
наве́с awning.
наве́сить (-е́шу) *pf* (*impf* **наве́шивать**) hang (up). **навесно́й** hanging.
навести́ (-еду́, -едёшь; -вёл, -а́) *pf* (*impf* **наводи́ть**) direct; aim; cover

(with), spread; introduce, bring; make.
навестúть (-ещý) *pf* (*impf* **навещáть**) visit.
навéшать *pf*, **навéшивать**[1] *impf* hang (out); weigh out.
навéшивать[2] *impf of* **навéсить**. **навещáть** *impf of* **навестúть**
нáвзничь *adv* backwards, on one's back.
навзры́д *adv*: **плáкать ~** sob.
навигáция navigation.
нависáть *impf*, **навúснуть** (-нет; -вúс) *pf* overhang, hang (over); threaten. **навúсший** beetling.
навлекáть *impf*, **навлéчь** (-екý, -ечёшь; -ёк, -лá) *pf* bring, draw; incur.
наводúть (-ожý, -óдишь) *impf of* **навестú; наводя́щий вопрóс** leading question. **навóдка** aiming; applying.
наводнéние flood. **наводнúть** *pf*, **наводня́ть** *impf* flood; inundate.
навóз dung, manure.
нáволочка pillowcase.
на|врáть (-рý, -рёшь; -áл, -á, -о) *pf* tell lies, romance; talk nonsense; **+в+***prep* make mistake(s) in.
навредúть (-ежý) *pf +dat* harm.
навсегдá *adv* for ever.
навстрéчу *adv* to meet; **идтú ~** go to meet; meet halfway.
навы́ворот *adv* inside out; back to front.
нáвык experience, skill.
навы́нос *adv* to take away.
навы́пуск *adv* worn outside.
навьючивать *impf*, **на|вьючить** (-чу) *pf* load.
навязáть (-яжý, -я́жешь) *pf*, **навя́зывать** *impf* tie, fasten; thrust, foist; **~ся** thrust o.s. **навя́зчивый** importunate; obsessive.
на|гáдить (-áжу) *pf*.
нагáн revolver.
нагибáть(ся *impf of* **нагнýть(ся**
нагишóм *adv* stark naked.
наглéц (-á) impudent fellow. **нáглость** impudence. **нáглый** (нагл, -á, -о) impudent.
нагля́дный clear, graphic; visual.
нагнáть (-гоню́, -гóнишь; -áл, -á, -о) *pf* (*impf* **нагоня́ть**) overtake, catch up (with); inspire, arouse.
нагнестú (-етý, -етёшь) *pf*, **нагнетáть** *impf* compress; supercharge.
нагноéние suppuration. **нагнóиться** *pf* suppurate.
нагнýть (-нý, -нёшь) *pf* (*impf* **нагибáть**) bend; **~ся** bend, stoop.
наговáривать *impf*, **наговорúть** *pf* slander; talk a lot (of); record.
нагóй (наг, -á, -о) naked, bare.
нáголо́ *adv* naked, bare.
нагоня́ть *impf of* **нагнáть**
нагорáть *impf*, **нагорéть** (-рúт) *pf* be consumed; *impers+dat* be scolded.
нагóрный upland, mountain; mountainous.
наготá nakedness, nudity.
награ́бить (-блю) *pf* amass by dishonest means.
нагрáда reward; decoration; prize. **наградúть** (-ажý) *pf*, **награждáть** *impf* reward; decorate; award prize to.
нагревáтельный heating. **нагревáть** *impf*, **нагрéть** (-éю) *pf* warm, heat; **~ся** get hot, warm up.
нагромождáть *impf*, **на|громоздúть** (-зжý) *pf* heap up, pile up. **нагромождéние** heaping up; conglomeration.
на|грубúть (-блю́) *pf*.
нагружáть *impf*, **на|грузúть** (-ужý, -ýзишь) *pf* load; **~ся** load o.s. **нагрýзка** loading; load; work; commitments.
нагря́нуть (-ну) *pf* appear unexpectedly.
над, надо *prep+instr* over, above; on, at.
надавúть (-влю́, -вишь) *pf*, **надáвливать** *impf* press; squeeze out; crush.
надбáвка addition, increase.
надвигáть *impf*, **надвúнуть** (-ну) *pf* move, pull, push; **~ся** approach.

на́двое *adv* in two.
надгро́бие epitaph. **надгро́бный** (*on or over a*) grave.
надева́ть *impf of* **наде́ть**
наде́жда hope. **надёжность** reliability. **надёжный** reliable.
наде́л allotment.
наде́лать *pf* make; cause; do.
надели́ть (-лю́, -ли́шь) *pf*, **наделя́ть** *impf* endow, provide.
наде́ть (-е́ну) *pf* (*impf* **надева́ть**) put on.
наде́яться (-е́юсь) *impf* (*pf* **по~**) hope; rely.
надзира́тель *m* overseer, supervisor. **надзира́ть** *impf* +**за**+*instr* supervise, oversee. **надзо́р** supervision; surveillance.
надла́мывать(ся *impf of* **надломи́ть(ся**
надлежа́щий fitting, proper, appropriate. **надлежи́т** (-жа́ло) *impers* (+*dat*) it is necessary, required.
надло́м break; crack; breakdown. **надломи́ть** (-млю́, -мишь) *pf* (*impf* **надла́мывать**) break; crack; breakdown; **~ся** break, crack, breakdown. **надло́мленный** broken.
надме́нный haughty, arrogant.
на́до[1] (+*dat*) it is necessary; I (*etc.*) must, ought to; I (*etc.*) need. **на́добность** necessity, need.
надо[2]: *see* **над**.
надоеда́ть *impf*, **надое́сть** (-е́м, -е́шь, -е́ст, -еди́м) *pf* +*dat* bore, pester. **надое́дливый** boring, tiresome.
надо́лго *adv* for a long time.
надорва́ть (-ву́, -вёшь; -а́л, -а́, -о) *pf* (*impf* **надрыва́ть**) tear; strain; **~ся** tear; overstrain o.s.
на́дпись inscription.
надре́з cut, incision. **надре́зать** (-е́жу) *pf*, **надреза́ть** *impf*, **надре́зывать** *impf* make an incision in.
надруга́тельство outrage. **надруга́ться** *pf* +**над**+*instr* outrage, insult.
надры́в tear; strain; breakdown; outburst. **надрыва́ть(ся** *impf of* **надорва́ть(ся**. **надры́вный** hysterical; heartrending.
надста́вить (-влю) *pf*, **надставля́ть** *impf* lengthen.
надстра́ивать *impf*, **надстро́ить** (-о́ю) *pf* build on top; extend upwards. **надстро́йка** building upwards; superstructure.
надува́тельство swindle. **надува́ть(ся** *impf. of* **наду́ть(ся**. **надувно́й** pneumatic, inflatable.
наду́манный far-fetched.
наду́тый swollen; haughty; sulky. **наду́ть** (-у́ю) *pf* (*impf* **надува́ть**) inflate; swindle; **~ся** swell out; sulk.
на|души́ть(ся (-шу́(сь, -шишь(ся) *pf*.
наеда́ться *impf of* **нае́сться**
наедине́ *adv* privately, alone.
нае́зд flying visit; raid. **нае́здник, -ица** rider. **наезжа́ть** *impf of* **нае́здить, нае́хать**; pay occasional visits.
наём (на́йма) hire; renting; **взять в ~** rent; **сдать в ~** let. **наёмник** hireling; mercenary. **наёмный** hired, rented.
нае́сться (-е́мся, -е́шься, -е́стся, -еди́мся) *pf* (*impf* **наеда́ться**) eat one's fill; stuff o.s.
нае́хать (-е́ду) *pf* (*impf* **наезжа́ть**) arrive unexpectedly; +**на**+*acc* run into, collide with.
нажа́ть (-жму́, -жмёшь) *pf* (*impf* **нажима́ть**) press; put pressure (on).
нажда́к (-а́) emery. **нажда́чная бума́га** emery paper.
нажи́ва profit, gain.
нажива́ть(ся *impf of* **нажи́ть(ся**
нажи́м pressure; clamp. **нажима́ть** *impf of* **нажа́ть**.
нажи́ть (-иву́, -ивёшь; на́жил, -а́, -о) *pf* (*impf* **нажива́ть**) acquire; contract, incur; **~ся** (-жи́лся, -а́сь) get rich.
нажму́ *etc.*: *see* **нажа́ть**
наза́втра *adv* (the) next day.
наза́д *adv* back(wards); **(тому́) ~** ago.

Н

назва́ние name; title. **назва́ть** (-зову́, -зовёшь; -а́л, -а́, -о) *pf* (*impf* **называ́ть**) call, name; **~ся** be called.
назе́мный ground, surface.
на́зло́ *adv* out of spite; to spite.
назнача́ть *impf*, **назна́чить** (-чу) *pf* appoint; fix, set; prescribe. **назначе́ние** appointment; fixing, setting; prescription.
назову́ *etc.*: *see* **назва́ть**
назо́йливый importunate.
назрева́ть *impf*, **назре́ть** (-е́ет) *pf* ripen, mature; become imminent.
называ́емый: так ~ so-called.
называ́ть(ся *impf of* **назва́ть(ся.**
наибо́лее *adv* (the) most.
наибо́льший greatest, biggest.
наи́вный naive.
наивы́сший highest.
наигра́ть *pf*, **наи́грывать** *impf* win; play, pick out.
н **наизна́нку** *adv* inside out.
наизу́сть *adv* by heart.
наилу́чший best.
наименова́ние name; title.
на́искось *adv* obliquely.
найму́ *etc.*: *see* **наня́ть**
найти́ (-йду́, -йдёшь; нашёл, -шла́, -шло́) *pf* (*impf* **находи́ть**) find; **~сь** be found; be, be situated.
наказа́ние punishment. **наказа́ть** (-ажу́, -а́жешь) *pf*, **нака́зывать** *impf* punish.
нака́л incandescence. **нака́ливать** *impf*, **накали́ть** *pf*, **накаля́ть** *impf* heat; make red-hot; strain, make tense; **~ся** glow, become incandescent; become strained.
нака́лывать(ся *impf of* **наколо́ть(ся**
накану́не *adv* the day before.
нака́пливать(ся *impf of* **накопи́ть(ся**
накача́ть *pf*, **нака́чивать** *impf* pump (up).
наки́дка cloak, cape; extra charge. **наки́нуть** (-ну) *pf*, **наки́дывать** *impf* throw; throw on; **~ся** throw o.s.; **~ся на** attack.
на́кипь scum; scale.
накладна́я *sb* invoice. **наклад|но́й** laid on; false; **~ы́е расхо́ды** overheads. **накла́дывать** *impf of* **наложи́ть**
на|клевета́ть (-ещу́, -е́щешь) *pf.*
накле́ивать *impf*, **накле́ить** *pf* stick on. **накле́йка** sticking (on, up); label.
накло́н slope, incline. **наклоне́ние** inclination; mood. **наклони́ть** (-ню́, -нишь) *pf*, **наклоня́ть** *impf* incline, bend; **~ся** stoop, bend. **накло́нный** inclined, sloping.
нако́лка pinning; (*pinned-on*) ornament for hair; tattoo. **наколо́ть**[1] (-лю́, -лешь) *pf* (*impf* **нака́лывать**) prick; pin; **~ся** prick o.s.
наколо́ть[2] (-лю́, -лешь) *pf* (*impf* **нака́лывать**) chop.
наконе́ц *adv* at last. **наконе́чник** tip, point.
на|копи́ть (-плю́, -пишь) *pf*, **накопля́ть** *impf* (*impf also* **нака́пливать**) accumulate; **~ся** accumulate. **накопле́ние** accumulation.
на|копти́ть (-пчу́) *pf.* **на|корми́ть** (-млю́, -мишь) *pf.*
накра́сить (-а́шу) *pf* paint; make up. **на|кра́ситься** (-а́шусь) *pf.*
на|крахма́лить *pf.*
на|крени́ть *pf.* **накрени́ться** (-ни́тся) *pf*, **накреня́ться** *impf* tilt; list.
накрича́ть (-чу́) *pf* (+**на**+*acc*) shout (at).
накро́ю *etc.*: *see* **накры́ть**
накрыва́ть *impf*, **накры́ть** (-ро́ю) *pf* cover; catch; **~ (на) стол** lay the table; **~ся** cover o.s.
накури́ть (-рю́, -ришь) *pf* fill with smoke.
налага́ть *impf of* **наложи́ть**
нала́дить (-а́жу) *pf*, **нала́живать** *impf* regulate, adjust; repair; organize; **~ся** come right; get going.
на|лга́ть (-лгу́, -лжёшь; -а́л, -а́, -о) *pf.*
нале́во *adv* to the left.
налёг *etc.*: *see* **нале́чь. налега́ть** *impf of* **нале́чь**

накладна́я *sb* invoice. **накладн|о́й** laid on; false; **~ы́е расхо́ды** overheads. **накла́дывать** *impf of* **наложи́ть**
на|клевета́ть (-ещу́, -е́щешь) *pf.*
накле́ивать *impf*, **накле́ить** *pf* stick on. **накле́йка** sticking (on, up); label.
накло́н slope, incline. **наклоне́ние** inclination; mood. **наклони́ть** (-ню́, -нишь) *pf*, **наклоня́ть** *impf* incline, bend; **~ся** stoop, bend. **накло́нный** inclined, sloping.
нако́лка pinning; (*pinned-on*) ornament for hair; tattoo. **наколо́ть**[1] (-лю́, -лешь) *pf* (*impf* **нака́лывать**) prick; pin; **~ся** prick o.s.
наколо́ть[2] (-лю́, -лешь) *pf* (*impf* **нака́лывать**) chop.
наконе́ц *adv* at last. **наконе́чник** tip, point.
на|копи́ть (-плю́, -пишь) *pf*, **накопля́ть** *impf* (*impf also* **нака́пливать**) accumulate; **~ся** accumulate. **накопле́ние** accumulation.
на|копти́ть (-пчу́) *pf.* **на|корми́ть** (-млю́, -мишь) *pf.*
накра́сить (-а́шу) *pf* paint; make up. **на|кра́ситься** (-а́шусь) *pf.*
на|крахма́лить *pf.*
на|крени́ть *pf.* **накрени́ться** (-ни́тся) *pf*, **накреня́ться** *impf* tilt; list.
накрича́ть (-чу́) *pf* (+**на**+*acc*) shout (at).
накро́ю *etc.*: *see* **накры́ть**
накрыва́ть *impf*, **накры́ть** (-ро́ю) *pf* cover; catch; **~ (на) стол** lay the table; **~ся** cover o.s.
накури́ть (-рю́, -ришь) *pf* fill with smoke.
налага́ть *impf of* **наложи́ть**
нала́дить (-а́жу) *pf*, **нала́живать** *impf* regulate, adjust; repair; organize; **~ся** come right; get going.
на|лга́ть (-лгу́, -лжёшь; -а́л, -а́, -о) *pf.*
нале́во *adv* to the left.
налёг *etc.*: *see* **нале́чь. налега́ть** *impf of* **нале́чь**

налегке́ *adv* lightly dressed; without luggage.
налёт raid; flight; thin coating. **налета́ть**[1] *pf* have flown. **налета́ть**[2] *impf*, **налете́ть** (-лечу́) *pf* swoop down; come flying; spring up.
нале́чь (-ля́гу, -ля́жешь; -лёг, -ла́) *pf* (*impf* **налега́ть**) lean, apply one's weight, lie; apply o.s.
налжёшь *etc.*: *see* **налга́ть**
налива́ть(ся *impf of* **нали́ть(ся**. **нали́вка** fruit liqueur.
нали́ть (-лью́, -льёшь; на́ли́л, -а́, -о) *pf* (*impf* **налива́ть**) pour (out), fill; **~ся** (-и́лся́, -а́сь, -и́ло́сь) pour in; ripen.
налицо́ *adv* present; available.
нали́чие presence. **нали́чн|ый** on hand; cash; **~ые (де́ньги)** ready money.
нало́г tax. **налогоплате́льщик** taxpayer. **нало́женн|ый: ~ым платежо́м** C.O.D. **наложи́ть** (-жу́, -жишь) *pf* (*impf* **накла́дывать, налага́ть**) lay (in, on), put (in, on); apply; impose.
налью́ *etc.*: *see* **нали́ть**
наля́гу *etc.*: *see* **нале́чь**
нам *etc.*: *see* **мы**
на|ма́зать (-а́жу) *pf*, **нама́зывать** *impf* oil, grease; smear, spread.
нама́тывать *impf of* **намота́ть**. **нама́чивать** *impf of* **намочи́ть**
намёк hint. **намека́ть** *impf*, **намекну́ть** (-ну́, -нёшь) *pf* hint.
намерева́ться *impf*+*inf* intend to. **наме́рен** *predic*: **я ~(а)**+*inf* I intend to. **наме́рение** intention. **наме́ренный** intentional.
на|мета́ть *pf*. **на|ме́тить**[1] (-е́чу) *pf*.
наме́тить[2] (-е́чу) *pf* (*impf* **намеча́ть**) plan; outline; nominate; **~ся** be outlined, take shape.
намно́го *adv* much, far.
намока́ть *impf*, **намо́кнуть** (-ну) *pf* get wet.
намо́рдник muzzle.
на|мо́рщить(ся (-щу(сь) *pf*.
на|мота́ть *pf* (*impf also* **нама́тывать**) wind, reel.
на|мочи́ть (-очу́, -о́чишь) *pf* (*impf also* **нама́чивать**) wet; soak; splash, spill.
намы́ливать *impf*, **на|мы́лить** *pf* soap.
нанести́ (-су́, -сёшь; -ёс, -ла́) *pf* (*impf* **наноси́ть**) carry, bring; draw, plot; inflict.
на|низа́ть (-ижу́, -и́жешь) *pf*, **нани́зывать** *impf* string, thread.
нанима́тель *m* tenant; employer. **нанима́ть(ся** *impf of* **наня́ть(ся**
наноси́ть (-ошу́, -о́сишь) *impf of* **нанести́**
наня́ть (найму́, -мёшь; на́нял, -а́, -о) *pf* (*impf* **нанима́ть**) hire; rent; **~ся** get a job.
наоборо́т *adv* on the contrary; back to front; the other, the wrong, way (round); vice versa.
нао́тмашь *adv* violently.
наотре́з *adv* flatly, point-blank.
напада́ть *impf of* **напа́сть**. **напада́ющий** *sb* forward. **нападе́ние** attack; forwards.
напа́рник co-driver, (work)mate.
напа́сть (-аду́, -адёшь; -а́л) *pf* (*impf* **напада́ть**) **на**+*acc* attack; descend on; seize; come upon. **напа́сть** misfortune.
напе́в tune. **напева́ть** *impf of* **напе́ть**
напербо́й *adv* interrupting, vying with, one another.
наперёд *adv* in advance.
наперекор *adv*+*dat* in defiance of, counter to.
напёрсток (-тка) thimble.
напе́ть (-пою́, -поёшь) *pf* (*impf* **напева́ть**) sing; hum, croon.
на|печа́тать(ся *pf*. **напива́ться** *impf of* **напи́ться**
напи́льник file.
на|писа́ть (-ишу́, -и́шешь) *pf*.
напи́ток (-тка) drink. **напи́ться** (-пью́сь, -пьёшься; -и́лся, -а́сь, -и́ло́сь) *pf* (*impf* **напива́ться**) quench one's thirst, drink; get drunk.
напиха́ть *pf*, **напи́хивать** *impf* cram, stuff.

Н

на|плева́ть (-люю, -люёшь) *pf*; **~!** to hell with it! who cares?
наплы́в influx; accumulation; canker.
наплюю́ *etc.*: *see* **наплева́ть**
напова́л outright.
наподо́бие *prep+gen* like, not unlike.
на|пои́ть (-ою́, -о́ишь) *pf.*
напока́з *adv* for show.
наполни́тель *m* filler. **напо́лнить(ся** *pf*, **наполня́ть(ся** *impf* fill.
наполови́ну *adv* half.
напомина́ние reminder. **напомина́ть** *impf*, **напо́мнить** *pf* (+*dat*) remind.
напо́р pressure. **напо́ристый** energetic, pushing.
напосле́док *adv* in the end; after all.
напою́ *etc.*: *see* **напе́ть, напои́ть**
Н **напр.** *abbr* (*of* **наприме́р**) e.g., for example.
напра́вить (-влю) *pf*, **направля́ть** *impf* direct; send; sharpen; **~ся** make (for), go (towards). **направле́ние** direction; trend; warrant; order. **напра́вленный** purposeful.
напра́во *adv* to the right.
напра́сно *adv* in vain, for nothing; unjustly, mistakenly.
напра́шиваться *impf of* **напроси́ться**
наприме́р for example.
на|прока́зничать *pf.*
напрока́т *adv* for, on, hire.
напролёт *adv* through, without a break.
напроло́м *adv* straight, regardless of obstacles.
напроси́ться (-ошу́сь, -о́сишься) *pf* (*impf* **напра́шиваться**) thrust o.s.; suggest itself; **~ на** ask for, invite.
напро́тив *adv* opposite; on the contrary. **напро́тив** *prep+gen* opposite.
напряга́ть(ся *impf of* **напря́чь(ся. напряже́ние** tension; exertion; voltage. **напряжённый** tense; intense; intensive.
напрями́к *adv* straight (out).
напря́чь (-ягу́, -яжёшь; -я́г, -ла́) *pf* (*impf* **напряга́ть**) strain; **~ся** strain o.s.
на|пуга́ть(ся *pf.* **на|пу́дриться** *pf.*
напуска́ть *impf*, **напусти́ть** (-ущу́, -у́стишь) *pf* let in; let loose; **~ся +на+***acc* fly at, go for.
напу́тать *pf* **+в+***prep* make a mess of.
на|пыли́ть *pf.*
напью́сь *etc.*: *see* **напи́ться**
наравне́ *adv* level; equally.
наспа́шку *adv* unbuttoned.
нараста́ние growth, accumulation. **нараста́ть** *impf*, **нарасти́** (-тёт; -ро́с, -ла́) *pf* grow; increase.
нарасхва́т *adv* very quickly, like hot cakes.
нарва́ть[1] (-рву́, -рвёшь; -а́л, -а́, -о) *pf* (*impf* **нарыва́ть**) pick; tear up.
нарва́ть[2] (-вёт; -а́л, -а́, -о) *pf* (*impf* **нарыва́ть**) gather.
нарва́ться (-ву́сь, -вёшься; -а́лся, -ала́сь, -а́ло́сь) *pf* (*impf* **нарыва́ться**) **+на+***acc* run into, run up against.
наре́зать (-е́жу) *pf*, **нареза́ть** *impf* cut (up), slice, carve; thread, rifle.
наре́чие[1] dialect.
наре́чие[2] adverb.
на|рисова́ть *pf.*
нарко́з narcosis. **наркома́н, -ма́нка** drug addict. **наркома́ния** drug addiction. **нарко́тик** narcotic.
наро́д people. **наро́дность** nationality; national character. **наро́дный** national; folk; popular; people's.
наро́с *etc.*: *see* **нарасти́**
наро́чно *adv* on purpose, deliberately. **на́рочный** *sb* courier.
нару́жность exterior. **нару́жный** external, outward. **нару́жу** *adv* outside.
нару́чник handcuff. **нару́чный** wrist.

нарушéние breach; infringement. **нарушитель** *m* transgressor. **на-рýшить** (-шу) *pf*, **нарушáть** *impf* break; disturb, infringe, violate.

нарци́сс narcissus; daffodil.

нáры (нар) *pl* plank-bed.

нары́в abscess, boil. **нарывáть(ся** *impf of* **нарвáть(ся**

наря́д[1] order, warrant.

наря́д[2] attire; dress. **наряди́ть** (-яжý) *pf* (*impf* **наряжáть**) dress (up); **~ся** dress up. **наря́дный** well-dressed.

нарядý *adv* alike, equally; side by side.

наряжáть(ся *impf of* **наря-ди́ть(ся. нас** *see* **мы**

насади́ть (-ажý, -áдишь) *pf*, **наса-ждáть** *impf* (*impf also* **насáжи-вать**) plant; propagate; implant. **насáдка** setting, fixing. **наса-ждéние** planting; plantation; propagation. **насáживать** *impf of* **насади́ть**

насекóмое *sb* insect.

населéние population. **на-селённость** density of popula-tion. **населённый** populated; **~ пункт** settlement; built-up area. **насели́ть** *pf*, **населя́ть** *impf* set-tle, people.

наси́лие violence, force. **наси́ло-вать** *impf* (*pf* **из~**) coerce; rape. **наси́лу** *adv* with difficulty. **на-си́льник** aggressor; rapist; viola-tor. **наси́льно** *adv* by force. **на-си́льственный** violent, forcible.

наскáкивать *impf of* **наскочи́ть**

насквóзь *adv* through, throughout.

наскóлько *adv* how much?, how far?; as far as.

нáскоро *adv* hastily.

наскочи́ть (-очý, -óчишь) *pf* (*impf* **наскáкивать**) +**на**+*acc* run into, collide with; fly at.

наскýчить (-чу) *pf* bore.

наслади́ться (-ажýсь) *pf*, **насла-ждáться** *impf* (+*instr*) enjoy, take pleasure. **наслаждéние** pleasure, enjoyment.

наслéдие legacy; heritage. **на-|следи́ть** (-ежý) *pf*. **наслéдник** heir; successor. **наслéдница** heir-ess. **наслéдный** next in succes-sion. **наслéдовать** *impf* & *pf* (*pf also* **у~**) inherit, succeed to. **на-слéдственность** heredity. **на-слéдственный** hereditary, in-herited. **наслéдство** inheritance; heritage.

нáсмерть *adv* to (the) death.

на|смеши́ть (-шý) *pf* **насмéшка** mockery; gibe. **насмéшливый** mocking.

нáсморк runny nose; cold.

на|сори́ть *pf*.

насóс pump.

нáспех *adv* hastily.

на|сплéтничать *pf*. **наставáть** (-таёт) *impf of* **настáть**

наставлéние exhortation; direc-tions, manual.

настáвник tutor, mentor.

настáивать[1] *impf of* **настоя́ть**[1]. **настáивать**[2]**(ся** *impf of* **на-стоя́ть**[2]**(ся**

настáть (-áнет) *pf* (*impf* **наста-вáть**) come, begin, set in.

нáстежь *adv* wide (open).

настелю́ *etc.*: *see* **настлáть**

настигáть *impf*, **насти́гнуть, на-сти́чь** (-и́гну; -и́г) *pf* catch up with, overtake.

насти́л flooring, planking. **насти-лáть** *impf of* **настлáть**

насти́чь *see* **настигáть**

настлáть (-телю́, -тéлешь) *pf* (*impf* **настилáть**) lay, spread.

настóйка liqueur, cordial.

настóйчивый persistent; urgent.

настóлько *adv* so, so much.

настóльный table, desk; refer-ence.

насторáживать *impf*, **настoро-жи́ть** (-жý) *pf* set; prick up; **~ся** prick up one's ears. **насторóжен-ный** (-ен, -енна) guarded; alert.

настоя́тельный insistent; urgent. **настоя́ть**[1] (-ою́) *pf* (*impf* **настáи-вать**[1]) insist.

настоя́ть[2] (-ою́) *pf* (*impf* **настáи-**

Н

вать²) brew; **~ся** draw, stand.

настоящее *sb* the present. **настоящий** (the) present, this; real, genuine.

настраивать(ся *impf of* **настроить(ся**

настричь (-игу, -ижёшь; -иг) *pf* shear, clip.

настроение mood. **настроить** (-ою) *pf* (*impf* **настраивать**) tune (in); dispose; **~ся** dispose o.s. **настройка** tuning. **настройщик** tuner.

на|строчить (-чу) *pf.*

наступательный offensive. **наступать¹** *impf of* **наступить¹**

наступать² *impf of* **наступить²**. **наступающий¹** coming.

наступающий² *sb* attacker.

наступить¹ (-плю, -пишь) *pf* (*impf* **наступать¹**) tread; attack; advance.

Н **наступить²** (-упит) *pf* (*impf* **наступать²**) come, set in. **наступление¹** coming.

наступление² offensive, attack.

насупиться (-плюсь) *pf*, **насупливаться** *impf* frown.

насухо *adv* dry. **насушить** (-шу, -шишь) *pf* dry.

насущный urgent, vital; **хлеб ~** daily bread.

насчёт *prep+gen* about, concerning; as regards. **насчитать** *pf*, **насчитывать** *impf* count; hold; **~ся** *+gen* number.

насыпать (-плю) *pf*, **насыпать** *impf* pour in, on; fill; spread; heap up. **насыпь** embankment.

насытить (-ыщу) *pf*, **насыщать** *impf* satiate; saturate; **~ся** be full; be saturated.

наталкивать(ся *impf of* **натолкнуть(ся**. **натапливать** *impf of* **натопить**

натаскать *pf*, **натаскивать** *impf* train; coach, cram; bring in, lay in.

натворить *pf* do, get up to.

натереть (-тру, -трёшь; -тёр) *pf* (*impf* **натирать**) rub on, in; polish; chafe; grate; **~ся** rub o.s.

натиск onslaught.

наткнуться (-нусь, -нёшься) *pf* (*impf* **натыкаться**) *+на+acc* run into; strike, stumble on.

натолкнуть (-ну, -нёшь) *pf* (*impf* **наталкивать**) push; lead; **~ся** run against, across.

натопить (-плю, -пишь) *pf* (*impf* **натапливать**) heat (up); stoke up; melt.

на|точить (-чу, -чишь) *pf.*

натощак *adv* on an empty stomach.

натравить (-влю, -вишь) *pf*, **натравливать** *impf*, **натравлять** *impf* set (on); stir up.

на|тренировать(ся *pf.*

натрий sodium.

натура nature. **натуральный** natural; genuine. **натурщик, -щица** artist's model.

натыкать(ся *impf of* **наткнуть(ся**

натюрморт still life.

натягивать *impf*, **натянуть** (-ну, -нешь) *pf* stretch; draw; pull (on); **~ся** stretch. **натянутость** tension. **натянутый** tight; strained.

наугад *adv* at random.

наука science; learning.

наутро *adv* (the) next morning.

на|учить(ся (-чу(сь, -чишь(ся) *pf.*

научн|ый scientific; **~ая фантастика** science fiction.

наушник ear-flap; ear-phone.

нафталин naphthalene.

нахал, -халка impudent creature. **нахальный** impudent. **нахальство** impudence.

нахватать *pf*, **нахватывать** *impf* pick up, get hold of; **~ся** *+gen* pick up.

нахлебник hanger-on.

нахлынуть (-нет) *pf* well up; surge; gush.

на|хмурить(ся *pf.*

находить(ся (-ожу(сь, -одишь(ся) *impf of* **найти(сь**. **находка** find. **находчивый** resourceful, quick-witted.

нацеливать *impf*, **на|целить** *pf*

aim; **~ся** (take) aim.
наце́нка surcharge, mark-up.
наци́зм Nazism. **национализа́ция** nationalization. **национализи́ровать** *impf* & *pf* nationalize. **национали́зм** nationalism. **националисти́ческий** nationalist(ic). **национа́льность** nationality; ethnic group. **национа́льный** national. **наци́ст, -и́стка** Nazi. **наци́стский** Nazi. **на́ция** nation. **нацме́н, -ме́нка** *abbr* member of national minority.
нача́ло beginning; origin; principle, basis. **нача́льник** head, chief; boss. **нача́льный** initial; primary. **нача́льство** the authorities; command. **нача́ть** (-чну́, -чнёшь; на́чал, -а́, -о) *pf* (*impf* **начина́ть**) begin; **~ся** begin.
начерта́ть *pf* trace, inscribe. **на|черти́ть** (-рчу́, -ртишь) *pf*.
начина́ние undertaking. **начина́ть(ся** *impf of* **нача́ть(ся. начина́ющий** *sb* beginner.
начини́ть *pf*, **начиня́ть** *impf* stuff, fill. **начи́нка** stuffing, filling.
начи́стить (-и́щу) *pf* (*impf* **начища́ть**) clean. **на́чисто** *adv* clean; flatly, decidedly; openly, frankly. **начистоту́** *adv* openly, frankly.
начи́танность learning; wide reading. **начи́танный** well-read.
начища́ть *impf of* **начи́стить**
наш (-его) *m*, **на́ша** (-ей) *f*, **на́ше** (-его) *neut*, **на́ши** (-их) *pl*, *pron* our, ours.
нашаты́рный спирт ammonia. **нашаты́рь** (-я́) *m* sal-ammoniac; ammonia.
нашёл *etc.*: *see* **найти́**
наше́ствие invasion.
нашива́ть *impf*, **наши́ть** (-шью́, -шьёшь) *pf* sew on. **наши́вка** stripe, chevron; tab.
нашлёпать *impf* slap.
нашуме́ть (-млю́) *pf* make a din; cause a sensation.
нашью́ *etc.*: *see* **наши́ть**
нащу́пать *pf*, **нащу́пывать** *impf* grope for.
на|электризова́ть *pf*.
наяву́ *adv* awake; in reality.
не *partl* not.
не- *pref* un-, in-, non-, mis-, dis-; -less; not. **неаккура́тный** careless; untidy; unpunctual. **небезразли́чный** not indifferent. **небезызве́стный** not unknown; notorious; well-known.
небеса́ *etc.*: *see* **не́бо²**. **небе́сный** heavenly; celestial.
не-. неблагода́рный ungrateful; thankless. **неблагонадёжный** unreliable. **неблагополу́чный** unsuccessful, bad, unfavourable. **неблагоприя́тный** unfavourable. **неблагоразу́мный** imprudent. **неблагоро́дный** ignoble, base.
нёбо¹ palate.
не́бо² (*pl* -беса́, -бе́с) sky; heaven.
не-. небога́тый of modest means, modest. **небольшо́й** small, not great; **с небольши́м** a little over.
небосво́д firmament. **небоскло́н** horizon. **небоскрёб** skyscraper.
небо́сь *adv* I dare say; probably.
не-. небре́жный careless. **небыва́лый** unprecedented; fantastic. **небыли́ца** fable, cock-and-bull story. **небытие́** non-existence. **небью́щийся** unbreakable. **нева́жно** *adv* not too well, indifferently. **нева́жный** unimportant; indifferent. **невдалеке́** *adv* not far away. **неве́дение** ignorance. **неве́домый** unknown; mysterious. **неве́жа** *m* & *f* boor, lout. **неве́жда** *m* & *f* ignoramus. **неве́жественный** ignorant. **неве́жество** ignorance. **неве́жливый** rude. **невели́кий** (-и́к, -а́, -и́ко́) small. **неве́рие** unbelief, atheism; scepticism. **неве́рный** (-рен, -рна́, -о) incorrect, wrong; inaccurate, unsteady; unfaithful. **невероя́тный** improbable; incredible. **неве́рующий** unbelieving; *sb* atheist. **невесёлый** joyless, sad. **невесо́мый** weightless; imponderable.
неве́ста fiancée; bride. **неве́стка**

Н

daughter-in-law; brother's wife, sister-in-law.

не-. невзгóда adversity. **невзирáя на** *prep+acc* regardless of. **невзначáй** *adv* by chance. **невзрáчный** unattractive, plain. **невúданный** unprecedented, unheard-of. **невúдимый** invisible. **невúнность** innocence. **невúнный, невинóвный** innocent. **невменя́емый** irresponsible. **невмешáтельство** non-intervention; non-interference. **невмоготý, невмóчь** *advs* unbearable, too much (for). **невнимáтельный** inattentive, thoughtless.

нéвод seine(-net).

не-. невозвратúмый, невозврáтный irrevocable, irrecoverable. **невозмóжный** impossible. **невозмутúмый** imperturbable.

Н

невóльник, -ница slave. **невóльный** involuntary; unintentional; forced. **невóля** captivity; necessity.

не-. невообразúмый unimaginable, inconceivable. **невооружённ|ый** unarmed; **~ным глáзом** with the naked eye. **невоспúтанный** ill-bred, bad-mannered. **невоспламеня́ющийся** non-flammable. **невосприúмчивый** unreceptive; immune.

невралгúя neuralgia.

невредúмый safe, unharmed.

неврóз neurosis. **неврологúческий** neurological. **невротúческий** neurotic.

не-. невы́годный disadvantageous; unprofitable. **невы́держанный** lacking self-control; unmatured. **невыносúмый** unbearable. **невыполнúмый** impracticable. **невысóкий** (-сóк, -á, -óкó) low; short.

нéга luxury; bliss.

негатúвный negative.

нéгде *adv* (there is) nowhere.

не-. негúбкий (-бок, -бкá, -о) inflexible, stiff. **неглáсный** secret. **неглубóкий** (-óк, -á, -о) shallow. **неглýпый** (-ýп, -á, -о) sensible, quite intelligent. **негóдный** (-ден, -днá, -о) unfit, unsuitable; worthless. **негодовáние** indignation. **негодовáть** *impf* be indignant. **негодя́й** scoundrel. **негостеприúмный** inhospitable.

негр Negro, black man.

негрáмотность illiteracy. **негрáмотный** illiterate.

негритя́нка Negress, black woman. **негритя́нский** Negro.

не-. негрóмкий (-мок, -мкá, -о) quiet. **недáвний** recent. **недáвно** *adv* recently. **недалёкий** (-ёк, -á, -ёкó) near; short; not bright, dull-witted. **недалёкó** *adv* not far, near. **недáром** *adv* not for nothing, not without reason. **недвúжимость** real estate. **недвúжимый** immovable. **недвусмы́сленный** unequivocal. **недействúтельный** ineffective; invalid. **неделúмый** indivisible.

недéльный of a week, week's. **недéля** week.

не-. недёшево *adv* dear(ly). **недоброжелáтель** *m* ill-wisher. **недоброжелáтельность** hostility. **недоброкáчественный** of poor quality. **недобросóвестный** unscrupulous; careless. **недóбрый** (-óбр, -брá, -о) unkind; bad. **недовéрие** distrust. **недовéрчивый** distrustful **недовóльный** dissatisfied. **недовóльство** dissatisfaction. **недоедáние** malnutrition. **недоедáть** *impf* be undernourished.

не-. недóлгий (-лог, -лгá, -о) short, brief. **недóлго** *adv* not long. **недолговéчный** short-lived. **недомогáние** indisposition. **недомогáть** *impf* be unwell. **недомы́слие** thoughtlessness. **недонóшенный** premature. **недооцéнивать** *impf*, **недооценúть** (-ню́, -нишь) *pf* underestimate; underrate. **недооцéнка** underestimation. **недопустúмый** inadmissible, intolerable. **недора-**

зумéние misunderstanding. **недорогóй** (-дóрог, -á, -о) inexpensive. **недосмотрéть** (-рю́,-ришь) *pf* overlook. **недоспáть** (-плю́; -áл, -á, -о) *pf* (*impf* **недосыпáть**) not have enough sleep.

недоставáть (-таёт) *impf*, **недостáть** (-áнет) *pf impers* be missing, be lacking. **недостáток** (-тка) shortage, deficiency. **недостáточный** insufficient, inadequate. **недостáча** lack, shortage.

не-. недостижи́мый unattainable. **недостóйный** unworthy, **недосту́пный** inaccessible. **недосчитáться** *pf*, **недосчи́тываться** *impf* miss, find missing, be short (of). **недосыпáть** *impf of* **недоспáть. недосягáемый** unattainable.

недоумевáть *impf* be at a loss, be bewildered. **недоумéние** bewilderment.

не-. недоу́чка *m* & *f* half-educated person. **недочёт** deficit; defect.

нéдра (недр) *pl* depths, heart, bowels.

не-. нéдруг enemy. **недружелю́бный** unfriendly.

неду́г illness, disease.

недурнóй not bad; not bad-looking.

не-. неестéственный unnatural. **нежда́нный** unexpected. **нежелáние** unwillingness. **нежелáтельный** undesirable.

нéжели than.

неженáтый unmarried.

нéженка *m* & *f* big baby.

нежилóй uninhabited; uninhabitable.

нéжиться (-жусь) *impf* luxuriate, bask. **нéжность** tenderness; *pl* endearments. **нéжный** tender; affectionate.

не-. незабвéнный unforgettable. **незабу́дка** forget-me-not. **незабывáемый** unforgettable. **незави́симость** independence. **незави́симый** independent. **недóлго** *adv* not long. **незаконнорождённый** illegitimate. **незакóнный** illegal, illicit; illegitimate. **незакóнченный** unfinished. **незамени́мый** irreplaceable. **незамерзáющий** ice-free; anti-freeze. **незамéтный** imperceptible. **незаму́жняя** unmarried. **незапáмятный** immemorial. **незаслу́женный** unmerited. **незаурядный** uncommon, outstanding.

нéзачем *adv* there is no need.

не-. незащищённый unprotected. **незвáный** uninvited. **нездорóвиться** *impf*, *impers* +*dat*: **мне нездорóвится** I don't feel well. **нездорóвый** unhealthy. **нездорóвье** ill health. **незнакóмец** (-мца), **незнакóмка** stranger. **незнакóмый** unknown, unfamiliar. **незнáние** ignorance. **незначи́тельный** insignificant. **незрéлый** unripe, immature. **незри́мый** invisible. **незы́блемый** unshakable, firm. **неизбéжность** inevitability. **неизбéжный** inevitable. **неизвéданный** unknown.

неизвéстность uncertainty; ignorance; obscurity. **неизвéстный** unknown; *sb* stranger.

не-. неизлечи́мый incurable. **неизмéнный** unchanged, unchanging; devoted. **неизменя́емый** unalterable. **неизмери́мый** immeasurable, immense. **неизу́ченный** unstudied; unexplored. **неиму́щий** poor. **неинтерéсный** uninteresting. **нейскренний** insincere. **неискушённый** inexperienced, unsophisticated. **неисполни́мый** impracticable. **неисправи́мый** incorrigible; irreparable. **неисправный** out of order, defective; careless. **неисслéдованный** unexplored. **неиссякáемый** inexhaustible. **нейстовство** fury, frenzy; atrocity. **нейстовый** furious, frenzied, uncontrolled. **неистощи́мый, неисчерпáемый** inexhaustible. **неисчи-**

Н

сли́мый innumerable.
нейло́н, нейло́новый nylon.
нейро́н neuron.
нейтрализа́ция neutralization. **нейтрализова́ть** *impf* & *pf* neutralize. **нейтралите́т** neutrality. **нейтра́льный** neutral. **нейтро́н** neutron.
неквалифици́рованный unskilled.
не́кий *pron* a certain, some.
не́когда[1] *adv* once, formerly.
не́когда[2] *adv* there is no time; **мне** ~ I have no time.
не́кого (не́кому, не́кем, не́ о ком) *pron* there is nobody.
некомпете́нтный not competent, unqualified.
не́котор|ый *pron* some; **~ые** *sb pl* some (people).
некраси́вый plain, ugly; not nice.
некроло́г obituary.
некста́ти *adv* at the wrong time, out of place.
не́кто *pron* somebody; a certain.
не́куда *adv* there is nowhere.
не-. некульту́рный uncivilized, uncultured. **некуря́щий** *sb* non-smoker. **нела́дный** wrong. **нелега́льный** illegal. **нелёгкий** not easy; heavy. **неле́пость** absurdity, nonsense. **неле́пый** absurd. **нело́вкий** awkward. **нело́вкость** awkwardness.
нельзя́ *adv* it is impossible; it is not allowed.
не-. нелюби́мый unloved. **нелюди́мый** unsociable. **нема́ло** *adv* quite a lot (of). **нема́лый** considerable. **неме́дленно** *adv* immediately. **неме́дленный** immediate.
неме́ть (-е́ю) *impf* (*pf* **о~**) become dumb. **не́мец** (-мца) German. **неме́цкий** German.
немину́емый inevitable.
не́мка German woman.
немно́гие *sb pl* (a) few. **немно́го** *adv* a little; some; a few. **немно́жко** *adv* a little.
немо́й (нем, -á, -о) dumb, mute, silent. **немота́** dumbness.
не́мощный feeble.
немы́слимый unthinkable.
ненави́деть (-и́жу) *impf* hate. **ненави́стный** hated; hateful. **не́нависть** hatred.
не-. ненагля́дный beloved. **ненадёжный** unreliable. **ненадо́лго** *adv* for a short time. **нена́стье** bad weather. **ненасы́тный** insatiable. **ненорма́льный** abnormal. **нену́жный** unnecessary, unneeded. **необду́манный** thoughtless, hasty. **необеспе́ченный** without means, unprovided for. **необита́емый** uninhabited. **необозри́мый** boundless, immense. **необосно́ванный** unfounded, groundless. **необрабо́танный** uncultivated; crude; unpolished. **необразо́ванный** uneducated.
необходи́мость necessity. **необходи́мый** necessary.
не-. необъясни́мый inexplicable. **необъя́тный** immense. **необыкнове́нный** unusual. **необыча́йный** extraordinary. **необы́чный** unusual. **необяза́тельный** optional. **неограни́ченный** unlimited. **неоднокра́тный** repeated. **неодобри́тельный** disapproving. **неодушевлённый** inanimate.
неожи́данность unexpectedness. **неожи́данный** unexpected, sudden.
неоклассици́зм neoclassicism.
не-. неоко́нченный unfinished. **неопла́ченный** unpaid. **неопра́вданный** unjustified. **неопределённый** indefinite; infinitive; vague. **неопровержи́мый** irrefutable. **неопублико́ванный** unpublished. **нео́пытный** inexperienced. **неоргани́ческий** inorganic. **неоспори́мый** incontestable. **неосторо́жный** careless. **неосуществи́мый** impracticable. **неотврати́мый** inevitable.
не́откуда *adv* there is nowhere.
не-. неотло́жный urgent. **неотрази́мый** irresistible. **неотсту́п-**

ный persistent. **неотъéмлемый** inalienable. **неофициáльный** unofficial. **неохóта** reluctance. **неохóтно** *adv* reluctantly. **неоценúмый** inestimable, invaluable. **непартúйный** non-party; unbefitting a member of the (Communist) Party. **непереводúмый** untranslatable. **непереxóдный** intransitive. **неплатёжеспосóбный** insolvent.

не-. неплóхо *adv* not badly, quite well. **неплохóй** not bad, quite good. **непобедúмый** invincible. **неповиновéние** insubordination. **неповорóтливый** clumsy. **неповторúмый** inimitable, unique. **непогóда** bad weather. **непогрешúмый** infallible. **неподалёку** *adv* not far (away). **неподвúжный** motionless, immovable; fixed. **неподдéльный** genuine; sincere. **неподкýпный** incorruptible. **неподражáемый** inimitable. **неподходя́щий** unsuitable, inappropriate. **непоколебúмый** unshakable, steadfast. **непокóрный** recalcitrant, unruly.

не-. неполáдки (-док) *pl* defects. **неполноцéнность; кóмплекс неполноцéнности** inferiority complex. **неполноцéнный** defective; inadequate. **непóлный** incomplete; not (a) full. **непомéрный** excessive. **непонимáние** incomprehension, lack of understanding. **непоня́тный** incomprehensible. **непоправúмый** irreparable. **непоря́док** (-дка) disorder. **непоря́дочный** dishonourable. **непосéда** *m & f* fidget. **непосúльный** beyond one's strength. **непослéдовательный** inconsistent. **непослушáние** disobedience. **непослýшный** disobedient. **непосрéдственный** immediate; spontaneous. **непостижúмый** incomprehensible. **непостоя́нный** inconstant, changeable. **непохóжий** unlike; different.

не-. неправда untruth. **неправдоподóбный** improbable. **непрáвильно** *adv* wrong. **непрáвильный** irregular; wrong. **непрáвый** wrong. **непрактúчный** unpractical. **непревзойдённый** unsurpassed. **непредвúденный** unforeseen. **непредубеждённый** unprejudiced. **непредусмóтренный** unforeseen. **непредусмотрúтельный** short-sighted. **непреклóнный** inflexible; adamant. **непрелóжный** immutable.

не-. непремéнно *adv* without fail. **непремéнный** indispensable. **непреодолúмый** insuperable. **непререкáемый** unquestionable. **непреры́вно** *adv* continuously. **непреры́вный** continuous. **непрестáнный** incessant. **непривéтливый** unfriendly; bleak. **непривлекáтельный** unattractive. **непривы́чный** unaccustomed. **непригля́дный** unattractive. **непригóдный** unfit, useless. **неприéмлемый** unacceptable. **неприкосновéнность** inviolability, immunity. **неприкосновéнный** inviolable; reserve. **неприлúчный** indecent. **непримирúмый** irreconcilable. **непринуждённый** unconstrained; relaxed. **неприспосóбленный** unadapted; maladjusted. **непристóйный** obscene. **неприступный** inaccessible. **непритязáтельный, неприхотлúвый** unpretentious, simple. **неприя́зненный** hostile, inimical. **неприя́знь** hostility. **неприя́тель** *m* enemy. **неприя́тельский** enemy. **неприя́тность** unpleasantness; trouble. **неприя́тный** unpleasant.

не-. непровéренный unverified. **непрогля́дный** pitch-dark. **непроéзжий** impassable. **непрозрáчный** opaque. **непроизводúтельный** unproductive. **непроизвóльный** involuntary. **непромокáемый** waterproof. **непроницáемый** impenetrable.

непрости́тельный unforgivable. **непроходи́мый** impassable. **непро́чный** (-чен, -чна́, -о) fragile, flimsy.

не прочь *predic* not averse.

не-. непро́шеный uninvited, unsolicited. **неработоспосо́бный** disabled. **нерабо́чий: ~ день** day off. **нера́венство** inequality. **неравноме́рный** uneven. **нера́вный** unequal. **ненради́вый** lackadaisical. **неразбери́ха** muddle. **неразбо́рчивый** not fastidious; illegible. **неразвито́й** (-ра́звит, -а́, -о) undeveloped; backward. **неразгово́рчивый** taciturn. **неразделённый: ~ая любо́вь** unrequited love. **неразличи́мый** indistinguishable. **неразлу́чный** inseparable. **неразрешённый** unsolved; forbidden. **неразреши́мый** insoluble. **неразры́вный** indissoluble. **неразу́мный** unwise; unreasonable. **нераствори́мый** insoluble.

нерв nerve. **не́рвничать** *impf* fret, be nervous. **нервнобольно́й** *sb* neurotic. **не́рвный** (-вен, -вна́, -о) nervous; nerve; irritable. **нерво́зный** nervy, irritable.

не-. нереа́льный unreal; unrealistic. **нере́дкий** (-док, -дка́, -о) not infrequent, not uncommon. **нереши́тельность** indecision. **нереши́тельный** indecisive, irresolute. **нержаве́ющая сталь** stainless steel. **неро́вный** (-вен, -вна́, -о) uneven, rough; irregular. **неруши́мый** inviolable.

неря́ха *m & f* sloven. **неря́шливый** slovenly.

не-. несбы́точный unrealizable. **несваре́ние желу́дка** indigestion. **несве́жий** (-е́ж, -а́) not fresh; tainted; weary. **несвоевре́менный** ill-timed; overdue. **несво́йственный** not characteristic. **несгора́емый** fireproof. **несерьёзный** not serious.

несессе́р case.

несимметри́чный asymmetrical.

нескла́дный incoherent; awkward.

несклоня́емый indeclinable.

не́сколько (-их) *pron* some, several; *adv* somewhat.

не-. несконча́емый interminable. **нескро́мный** (-мен, -мна́, -о) immodest; indiscreet. **несло́жный** simple. **несл́ыханный** unprecedented. **несл́ышный** inaudible. **несме́тный** countless, incalculable. **несмолка́емый** ceaseless.

несмотря́ на *prep+acc* in spite of.

не-. несно́сный intolerable. **несоблюде́ние** non-observance. **несовершенноле́тний** underage; *sb* minor. **несоверше́нный** imperfect, incomplete; imperfective. **несоверше́нство** imperfection. **несовмести́мый** incompatible. **несогла́сие** disagreement. **несогласо́ванный** uncoordinated. **несозна́тельный** irresponsible. **несоизмери́мый** incommensurable. **несокруши́мый** indestructible. **несомне́нный** undoubted, unquestionable. **несообра́зный** incongruous. **несоотве́тствие** disparity. **несостоя́тельный** insolvent; of modest means; untenable. **неспе́лый** unripe. **неспоко́йный** restless; uneasy. **неспосо́бный** not bright; incapable. **несправедли́вость** injustice. **несправедли́вый** unjust, unfair; incorrect. **несравне́нный** (-е́нен, -е́нна) incomparable. **несравни́мый** incomparable. **нестерпи́мый** unbearable.

нести́ (-су́, -сёшь; нёс, -ла́) *impf* (*pf* **по~, с~**) carry; bear; bring, take; suffer; incur; lay; **~сь** rush, fly; float, be carried.

не-. несто́йкий unstable. **несуще́ственный** immaterial, inessential.

несу́ *etc.*: *see* **нести́**

несхо́дный unlike, dissimilar.

несчастли́вый unfortunate, unlucky; unhappy. **несча́стный** unhappy, unfortunate; **~ слу́чай** accident. **несча́стье** misfortune; **к несча́стью** unfortunately.

несчётный innumerable.

нет *partl* no, not; nothing. **нет, не́ту** there is not, there are not.

не-. нетакти́чный tactless. **нетвёрдый** (-ёрд, -а́, -о) unsteady, shaky. **нетерпели́вый** impatient. **нетерпе́ние** impatience. **нетерпи́мый** intolerable, intolerant. **нетороплй́вый** leisurely. **нето́чный** (-чен, -чна́, -о) inaccurate, inexact. **нетре́звый** drunk. **нетро́нутый** untouched; chaste, virginal. **нетрудово́й дохо́д** unearned income. **нетрудоспосо́бность** disability.

не́тто *indecl adj & adv* net(t).

не́ту *see* **нет**

не-. неубеди́тельный unconvincing. **неуваже́ние** disrespect. **неуве́ренность** uncertainty. **неуве́ренный** uncertain. **неувяда́емый, неувяда́ющий** unfading. **неугомо́нный** indefatigable. **неуда́ча** failure. **неуда́чливый** unlucky. **неуда́чник, -ница** unlucky person, failure. **неуда́чный** unsuccessful, unfortunate. **неудержи́мый** irrepressible. **неудо́бный** uncomfortable; inconvenient; embarrassing. **неудо́бство** discomfort; inconvenience; embarrassment. **неудовлетворе́ние** dissatisfaction. **неудовлетворённый** dissatisfied. **неудовлетвори́тельный** unsatisfactory. **неудово́льствие** displeasure.

неуже́ли? *partl* really?

не-. неузнава́емый unrecognizable. **неукло́нный** steady; undeviating. **неуклю́жий** clumsy. **неуловй́мый** elusive; subtle. **неуме́лый** inept; clumsy. **неуме́ренный** immoderate. **неуме́стный** inappropriate; irrelevant. **неумоли́мый** implacable, inexorable. **неумы́шленный** unintentional.

не-. неупла́та non-payment. **неуравнове́шенный** unbalanced. **неурожа́й** bad harvest. **неуро́чный** untimely, inopportune. **неуря́дица** disorder, mess. **неуспева́емость** poor progress. **неусто́йка** forfeit. **неусто́йчивый** unstable; unsteady. **неусту́пчивый** unyielding. **неуте́шный** inconsolable. **неутоли́мый** unquenchable. **неутоми́мый** tireless. **не́уч** ignoramus. **неучти́вый** discourteous. **неуязви́мый** invulnerable.

нефри́т jade.

нефте- *in comb* oil, petroleum. **нефтено́сный** oil-bearing. **~перего́нный заво́д** oil refinery. **~прово́д** (oil) pipeline. **~проду́кты** (-ов) *pl* petroleum products.

нефть oil, petroleum. **нефтяно́й** oil, petroleum.

не-. нехва́тка shortage. **нехорошо́** *adv* badly. **нехоро́ш|ий** (-о́ш, -а́) bad; **~о** it is bad, it is wrong. **не́хотя** *adv* unwillingly; unintentionally. **нецелесообра́зный** inexpedient; pointless. **нецензу́рный** unprintable. **нечая́нный** unexpected; accidental.

не́чего (**не́чему, -чем, не́ о чем**) *pron* (*with separable pref*) (there is) nothing.

нечелове́ческий inhuman, superhuman.

нече́стный dishonest, unfair.

нечётный odd.

нечистопло́тный dirty; slovenly; unscrupulous. **нечистота́** (*pl* **-о́ты, -о́т**) dirtiness, filth; *pl* sewage. **нечи́стый** (-и́ст, -а́, -о) dirty, unclean; impure; unclear. **не́чисть** evil spirits; scum.

нечленоразде́льный inarticulate.

не́что *pron* something.

не-. неэконо́мный uneconomical. **неэффекти́вный** ineffective; inefficient. **нея́вка** failure to appear. **нея́ркий** dim, faint; dull, subdued. **нея́сный** (-сен, -сна́, -о) not clear; vague.

ни *partl* not a; **ни оди́н (одна́, одно́)**

not a single; (*with prons and pronominal advs*) -ever; **кто... ни** whoever. **ни** *conj*: **ни... ни** neither … nor; **ни то ни сё** neither one thing nor the other.
ни́ва cornfield, field.
нивели́р level.
нигде́ *adv* nowhere.
нидерла́ндец (-дца; *gen pl* -дцев) Dutchman. **нидерла́ндка** Dutchwoman. **нидерла́ндский** Dutch. **Нидерла́нды** (-ов) *pl* the Netherlands.
ни́же *adj* lower, humbler; *adv* below; *prep+gen* below, beneath. **нижесле́дующий** following. **ни́жн|ий** lower, under-; **~ее бельё** underclothes; **~ий эта́ж** ground floor. **низ** (*loc* -у́; *pl* -ы́) bottom; *pl* lower classes; low notes.

Н

низа́ть (нижу́, ни́жешь) *impf* (*pf* **на~**) string, thread.
низверга́ть *impf*, **низве́ргнуть** (-ну; -е́рг) *pf* throw down, overthrow; **~ся** crash down; be overthrown. **низверже́ние** overthrow.
низи́на low-lying place. **ни́зкий** (-зок, -зка́, -о) low; base. **низкопоклóнство** servility. **низкопрóбный** low-grade. **низкорóслый** undersized. **низкосóртный** low-grade.
ни́зменность lowland; baseness. **ни́зменный** low-lying; base.
низóвье (*gen pl* -ьев) the lower reaches. **ни́зость** baseness, meanness. **ни́зш|ий** lower, lowest; **~ее образова́ние** primary education.
ника́к *adv* in no way. **никакóй** *pron* no; no … whatever
ни́кель *m* nickel.
нике́м *see* **никтó**. **никогда́** *adv* never. **никтó** (-когó, -комý, -ке́м, ни о кóм) *pron* (*with separable pref*) nobody, no one. **никуда́** nowhere. **никчёмный** useless. **нима́ло** *adv* not in the least.
нимб halo, nimbus.
ни́мфа nymph; pupa.
ниоткýда *adv* from nowhere.
нипочём *adv* it is nothing; dirt cheap; in no circumstances.
нискóлько *adv* not at all.
ниспроверга́ть *impf*, **ниспрове́ргнуть** (-ну; -е́рг) *pf* overthrow. **ниспроверже́ние** overthrow.
нисходя́щий descending.
ни́тка thread; string; **до ни́тки** to the skin; **на живýю ни́тку** hastily, anyhow. **ни́точка** thread. **нить** thread; filament.
ничегó *etc.*: *see* **ничтó**. **ничегó** *adv* all right; it doesn't matter, never mind; *as indecl adj* not bad, pretty good. **ниче́й** (-чья́, -чьё) *pron* nobody's; **ничья́ земля́** no man's land. **ничья́** *sb* draw; tie.
ничкóм *adv* face down, prone.
ничтó (-чегó, -чемý, -че́м, ни о чём) *pron* (*with separable pref*) nothing. **ничтóжество** nonentity, nobody. **ничтóжный** insignificant; worthless.
ничýть *adv* not a bit.
ничьё, ничья́: *see* **ниче́й**
ни́ша niche, recess.
ни́щенка beggar-woman. **ни́щенский** beggarly. **нищета́** poverty. **ни́щий** (нищ, -а́, -е) destitute, poor; *sb* beggar.
но *conj* but; still.
нова́тор innovator. **нова́торский** innovative. **нова́торство** innovation.
Нóвая Зела́ндия New Zealand.
нове́йший newest, latest.
нове́лла short story.
нóвенький brand-new.
новизна́ novelty; newness. **нови́нка** novelty. **новичóк** (-чка́) novice.
ново- *in comb* new(ly). **новобра́нец** (-нца) new recruit. **~бра́чный** *sb* newly-wed. **~введе́ние** innovation. **~гóдний** new year's. **~зела́ндец** (-дца; *gen pl* -дцев), **~зела́ндка** New-Zealander. **~зела́ндский** New Zealand. **~лýние** new moon. **~прибы́вший** newly-arrived; *sb* new-

comer. **~рождённый** newborn. **~сёл** new settler. **~се́лье** new home; house-warming. **новостро́йка** new building.

но́вость (*gen pl* -е́й) news; novelty. **но́вшество** innovation, novelty. **но́вый** (нов, -а́, -о) new; modern; ~ **год** New Year.

нога́ (*acc* но́гу; *pl* но́ги, ног, нога́м) foot, leg.

но́готь (-гтя; *gen pl* -те́й) *m* finger-nail, toe-nail.

нож (-а́) knife.

но́жка small foot or leg; leg; stem, stalk.

но́жницы (-иц) *pl* scissors, shears.

но́жны (-жен) *pl* sheath, scabbard.

ножо́вка saw, hacksaw.

ноздря́ (*pl* -и, -е́й) nostril.

нока́ут knock-out. **нокаути́ровать** *impf* & *pf* knock out.

нолево́й, нулево́й zero. **ноль** (-я́), **нуль** (-я́) *m* nought, zero, nil.

номенклату́ра nomenclature; top positions in government.

но́мер (*pl* -а́) number; size; (hotel-)room; item; trick. **номеро́к** (-рка́) tag; label, ticket.

номина́л face value. **номина́льный** nominal.

нора́ (*pl* -ы) burrow, hole.

Норве́гия Norway. **норве́жец** (-жца), **норве́жка** Norwegian. **норве́жский** Norwegian.

норд (*naut*) north; north wind.

но́рка mink.

но́рма standard, norm; rate. **нормализа́ция** standardization. **норма́льно** all right, OK. **норма́льный** normal; standard. **нормирова́ние, нормиро́вка** regulation; rate-fixing; rationing. **нормирова́ть** *impf* & *pf* regulate, standardize; ration.

нос (*loc* -у́; *pl* -ы́) nose; beak; bow, prow. **но́сик** (*small*) nose; spout.

носи́лки (-лок) *pl* stretcher; litter. **носи́льщик** porter. **носи́тель** *m*, **~ница** (*fig*) bearer; (*med*) carrier. **носи́ть** (-ошу́, -о́сишь) *impf* carry, bear; wear; **~ся** rush, tear along, fly; float, be carried; wear. **но́ска** carrying, wearing. **но́ский** hard-wearing.

носово́й nose; nasal; ~ **плато́к** (pocket) handkerchief. **носо́к** (-ска́) little nose; toe; sock. **носоро́г** rhinoceros.

но́та note; *pl* music. **нота́ция** notation; lecture, reprimand.

нота́риус notary.

ночева́ть (-чу́ю) *impf* (*pf* **пере~**) spend the night. **ночёвка** spending the night. **ночле́г** place to spend the night; passing the night. **ночле́жка** doss-house. **ночни́к** (-а́) night-light. **ночн|о́й** night, nocturnal; **~а́я руба́шка** nightdress; **~о́й горшо́к** potty; chamber-pot. **ночь** (*loc* -и́; *gen pl* -е́й) night. **но́чью** *adv* at night.

но́ша burden. **но́шеный** worn; second-hand.

но́ю *etc.*: *see* **ныть**

ноя́брь (-я́) *m* November. **ноя́брьский** November.

нрав disposition, temper; *pl* customs, ways. **нра́виться** (-влюсь) *impf* (*pf* **по~**) +*dat* please; **мне нра́вится** I like. **нра́вственность** morality, morals. **нра́вственный** moral.

ну *int* & *partl* well, well then.

ну́дный tedious.

нужда́ (*pl* -ы) need. **нужда́ться** *impf* be in need; +**в**+*prep* need, require. **ну́жн|ый** (-жен, -жна́, -о, ну́жны́) necessary; **~о** it is necessary; +*dat* I, *etc.*, must, ought to, need.

нулево́й, нуль *see* **нолево́й, ноль**

нумера́ция numeration; numbering. **нумерова́ть** *impf* (*pf* **про~**) number.

нутро́ inside, interior; instinct(s).

ны́не *adv* now; today. **ны́нешний** present; today's. **ны́нче** *adv* today; now.

нырну́ть (-ну́, -нёшь) *pf*, **ныря́ть** *impf* dive.

ныть (но́ю) *impf* ache; whine. **нытьё** whining.

н.э. *abbr* (*of* **на́шей э́ры**) AD.
нюх scent; flair. **ню́хать** *impf* (*pf* **по~**) smell, sniff.
ня́нчить (-чу) *impf* nurse, look after; **~ся с**+*instr* nurse; fuss over. **ня́нька** nanny. **ня́ня** (*children's*) nurse, nanny.

O

о, об, обо *prep* **I.** +*prep* of, about, concerning. **II.** +*acc* against; on, upon.
о *int* oh!
оа́зис oasis.
об *see* **о** *prep*.
о́ба (обо́их) *m & neut*, **о́бе** (обе́их) *f* both.
обалдева́ть *impf*, **обалде́ть** (-е́ю) *pf* go crazy; become dulled; be stunned.
обанкро́титься (-о́чусь) *pf* go bankrupt.
обая́ние fascination, charm. **обая́тельный** fascinating, charming.
обва́л fall(ing); crumbling; collapse; caving-in; landslide; **(сне́жный) ~** avalanche. **обвали́ть** (-лю́, -лишь) *pf* (*impf* **обва́ливать**) cause to fall *or* collapse; crumble; heap round; **~ся** collapse, cave in; crumble.
обваля́ть *pf* (*impf* **обва́ливать**) roll.
обва́ривать *impf*, **обвари́ть** (-рю́, -ришь) *pf* pour boiling water over; scald; **~ся** scald o.s.
обведу́ *etc.*: *see* **обвести́. обвёл** *etc.*: *see* **обвести́. об|венча́ть(ся** *pf*.
оберну́ть (-ну́, -нёшь) *pf*, **обвёртывать** *impf* wrap, wrap up.
обве́с short weight. **обве́сить** (-е́шу) *pf* (*impf* **обве́шивать**) cheat in weighing.
обвести́ (-еду́, -едёшь; -ёл, -ела́) *pf* (*impf* **обводи́ть**) lead round, take round; encircle; surround; outline; dodge.
обве́тренный weather-beaten.
обветша́лый decrepit. **об|ветша́ть** *pf*.
обве́шивать *impf of* **обве́сить.**
обвива́ть(ся *impf of* **обви́ть(ся**
обвине́ние charge, accusation; prosecution. **обвини́тель** *m* accuser; prosecutor. **обвини́тельный** accusatory; **~ акт** indictment; **~ пригово́р** verdict of guilty. **обвини́ть** *pf*, **обвиня́ть** *impf* prosecute, indict; +**в**+*prep* accuse of, charge with. **обвиня́емый** *sb* the accused; defendant.
обви́ть (обовью́, обовьёшь; обви́л, -á, -о) *pf* (*impf* **обвива́ть**) wind round; **~ся** wind round.
обводи́ть (-ожу́, -о́дишь) *impf of* **обвести́**
обвора́живать *impf*, **обворожи́ть** (-жу́) *pf* charm, enchant. **обворожи́тельный** charming, enchanting.
обвяза́ть (-яжу́, -я́жешь) *pf*, **обвя́зывать** *impf* tie round; **~ся** +*instr* tie round o.s.
обго́н passing. **обгоня́ть** *impf of* **обогна́ть**
обгора́ть *impf*, **обгоре́ть** (-рю́) *pf* be burnt, be scorched. **обгоре́лый** burnt, charred, scorched.
обде́лать *pf* (*impf* **обде́лывать**) finish; polish, set; manage, arrange.
обдели́ть (-лю́, -лишь) *pf* (*impf* **обделя́ть**) +*instr* do out of one's (fair) share of.
обде́лывать *impf of* **обде́лать.**
обделя́ть *impf of* **обдели́ть**
обдеру́ *etc.*: *see* **ободра́ть. обдира́ть** *impf of* **ободра́ть**
обду́манный deliberate, well-considered. **обду́мать** *pf*, **обду́мывать** *impf* consider, think over.
о́бе: *see* **о́ба. обега́ть** *impf of* **обежа́ть. обегу́** *etc.*: *see* **обежа́ть**
обе́д dinner, lunch. **обе́дать** *impf* (*pf* **по~**) have dinner, have lunch,

dine. **обе́денный** dinner.
обедне́вший impoverished. **обедне́ние** impoverishment. **о|беднéть** (-е́ю) *pf*.
обе́дня (*gen pl* -ден) Mass.
обежа́ть (-егу́) *pf* (*impf* **обега́ть**) run round; run past.
обезбо́ливание anaesthetization. **обезбо́ливать** *impf*, **обезбо́лить** *pf* anaesthetize.
обезвре́дить (-е́жу) *pf*, **обезвре́живать** *impf* render harmless.
обездо́ленный unfortunate, hapless.
обеззара́живающий disinfectant.
обезли́ченный depersonalized; robbed of individuality.
обезобра́живать *impf*, **о|безобра́зить** (-а́жу) *pf* disfigure.
обезопа́сить (-а́шу) *pf* secure.
обезору́живать *impf*, **обезору́жить** (-жу) *pf* disarm.
обезу́меть (-ею) *pf* lose one's senses, lose one's head.
обезья́на monkey; ape.
обели́ть *pf*, **обеля́ть** *impf* vindicate; clear of blame.
оберега́ть *impf*, **обере́чь** (-егу́, -ежёшь; -рёг, -ла́) *pf* guard; protect.
оберну́ть (-ну́, -нёшь) *pf*, **обёртывать** *impf* (*impf also* **обора́чивать**) twist; wrap up; turn; **~ся** turn (round); turn out; *+instr or* **в**+*acc* turn into. **обёртка** wrapper; (dust-) jacket, cover. **обёрточный** wrapping.
оберу́ *etc.*: *see* **обобра́ть**
обескура́живать *impf*, **обескура́жить** (-жу) *pf* discourage; dishearten.
обескро́вить (-влю) *pf*, **обескро́вливать** *impf* drain of blood, bleed white; render lifeless.
обеспе́чение securing, guaranteeing; ensuring; provision; guarantee; security. **обеспе́ченность** security; *+instr* provision of. **обеспе́ченный** well-to-do; well provided for. **обеспе́чивать** *impf*, **обеспе́чить** (-чу) *pf* provide for; secure; ensure; protect; *+instr* provide with.
о|беспоко́ить(ся *pf*.
обесси́леть (-ею) *pf* grow weak, lose one's strength. **обесси́ливать** *impf*, **обесси́лить** *pf* weaken.
о|бессла́вить (-влю) *pf*.
обессме́ртить (-рчу) *pf* immortalize.
обесцене́ние depreciation. **обесце́нивать** *impf*, **обесце́нить** *pf* depreciate; cheapen; **~ся** depreciate.
о|бесче́стить (-е́щу) *pf*.
обе́т vow, promise. **обетова́нный** promised. **обеща́ние** promise. **обеща́ть** *impf* & *pf* (*pf also* **по~**) promise.
обжа́лование appeal. **обжа́ловать** *pf* appeal against.
обже́чь (обожгу́, обожжёшь; обжёг, обожгла́) *pf*, **обжига́ть** *impf* burn; scorch; bake; **~ся** burn o.s.; burn one's fingers.
обжо́ра *m* & *f* glutton. **обжо́рство** gluttony.
обзавести́сь (-еду́сь, -едёшься; -вёлся, -ла́сь) *pf*, **обзаводи́ться** (-ожу́сь, -о́дишься) *impf +instr* provide o.s. with; acquire.
обзову́ *etc.*: *see* **обозва́ть**
обзо́р survey, review.
обзыва́ть *impf of* **обозва́ть**
обива́ть *impf of* **оби́ть. оби́вка** upholstering; upholstery.
оби́да offence, insult; nuisance. **оби́деть** (-и́жу) *pf*, **обижа́ть** *impf* offend; hurt, wound; **~ся** take offence; feel hurt. **оби́дный** offensive; annoying. **оби́дчивый** touchy. **оби́женный** offended.
оби́лие abundance. **оби́льный** abundant.
обира́ть *impf of* **обобра́ть**
обита́емый inhabited. **обита́тель** *m* inhabitant. **обита́ть** *impf* live.
оби́ть (обобью́, -ьёшь) *pf* (*impf* **обива́ть**) upholster; knock off.

О

обихо́д custom, (general) use, practice. **обихо́дный** everyday.
обкла́дывать(ся *impf of* **обложи́ть(ся**
обкра́дывать *impf of* **обокра́сть**
обла́ва raid; cordon, cordoning off.
облага́емый taxable. **облага́ть(ся** *impf of* **обложи́ть(ся**: **~ся нало́гом** be liable to tax.
облада́ние possession. **облада́тель** *m* possessor. **облада́ть** *impf+instr* possess.
о́блако (*pl* -а́, -о́в) cloud.
обла́мывать(ся *impf of* **облома́ть(ся, обломи́ться**
областно́й regional. **о́бласть** (*gen pl* -е́й) region; field, sphere.
о́блачность cloudiness. **о́блачный** cloudy.
облёг *etc.*: *see* **обле́чь. облега́ть** *impf of* **обле́чь**
облегча́ть *impf*, **облегчи́ть** (-чу́) *pf* lighten; relieve; alleviate; facilitate. **облегче́ние** relief.
обледене́лый ice-covered. **обледене́ние** icing over. **обледене́ть** (-е́ет) *pf* become covered with ice.
обле́злый shabby; mangy.
облека́ть(ся *impf of* **обле́чь**[2]**(ся.**
облеку́ *etc.*: *see* **обле́чь**[2]
облепи́ть (-плю́, -пишь) *pf*, **облепля́ть** *impf* stick to, cling to; throng round; plaster.
облета́ть *impf*, **облете́ть** (-лечу́) fly (round); spread (all over); fall.
обле́чь[1] (-ля́жет; -лёг, -ла́) *pf* (*impf* **облега́ть**) cover, envelop; fit tightly.
обле́чь[2] (-еку́, -ечёшь; -ёк, -кла́) *pf* (*impf* **облека́ть**) clothe, invest; **~ся** clothe o.s.; *+gen* take the form of.
облива́ть(ся *impf of* **обли́ть(ся**
облига́ция bond.
облиза́ть (-ижу́, -и́жешь) *pf*, **обли́зывать** *impf* lick (all over); **~ся** smack one's lips.
о́блик look, appearance.
о́бли́тый (о́бли́т, -а́, -о) covered, enveloped. **обли́ть** (оболью́, -льёшь; о́бли́л, -ила́, -о) *pf* (*impf* **облива́ть**) pour, sluice, spill; **~ся** sponge down, take a shower; pour over o.s.
облицева́ть (-цу́ю) *pf*, **облицо́вывать** *impf* face. **облицо́вка** facing; lining.
облича́ть *impf*, **обличи́ть** (-чу́) *pf* expose; reveal; point to. **обличе́ние** exposure, denunciation. **обличи́тельный** denunciatory.
обложе́ние taxation; assessment. **обложи́ть** (-жу́, -жишь) *pf* (*impf* **обкла́дывать, облага́ть**) edge; face; cover; surround; assess; **круго́м обложи́ло (не́бо)** the sky is completely overcast; **~ нало́гом** tax; **~ся** *+instr* surround o.s. with. **обло́жка** (dust-)cover; folder.
облока́чиваться *impf*, **облокоти́ться** (-очу́сь, -о́ти́шься) *pf* **на**+*acc* lean one's elbows on.
облома́ть *pf* (*impf* **обла́мывать**) break off; **~ся** break off. **обломи́ться** (-ло́мится) *pf* (*impf* **обла́мываться**) break off. **обло́мок** (-мка) fragment.
облу́пленный chipped.
облучи́ть (-чу́) *pf*, **облуча́ть** *impf* irradiate. **облуче́ние** irradiation.
об|лысе́ть (-е́ю) *pf*.
обля́жет *etc.*: *see* **обле́чь**[1]
обма́зать (-а́жу) *pf*, **обма́зывать** *impf* coat; putty; besmear; **~ся** *+instr* get covered with.
обма́кивать *impf*, **обмакну́ть** (-ну́, -нёшь) *pf* dip.
обма́н deceit; illusion; **~ зре́ния** optical illusion. **обма́нный** deceitful. **обману́ть** (-ну́, -нешь) *pf*, **обма́нывать** *impf* deceive; cheat; **~ся** be deceived. **обма́нчивый** deceptive. **обма́нщик** deceiver; fraud.
обма́тывать(ся *impf of* **обмота́ть(ся**
обма́хивать *impf*, **обмахну́ть** (-ну́, -нёшь) *pf* brush off; fan; **~ся** fan o.s.
обмёл *etc.*: *see* **обмести́**

обмеле́ние shallowing. **об|меле́ть** (-е́ет) *pf* become shallow.

обме́н exchange; barter; **в ~ за**+*acc* in exchange for; **~ веще́ств** metabolism. **обме́нивать** *impf*, **обмени́ть** (-ню́, -нишь) *pf*, **об|меня́ть** *pf* exchange; **~ся** +*instr* exchange. **обме́нный** exchange.

обме́р measurement; false measure.

обмере́ть (обомру́, -рёшь; о́бмер, -ла́, -ло) *pf* (*impf* **обмира́ть**) faint; **~ от у́жаса** be horror-struck.

обме́ривать *impf*, **обме́рить** *pf* measure; cheat in measuring.

обмести́ (-ету́, -етёшь; -мёл, -а́) *pf*, **обмета́ть**[1] *impf* sweep off, dust.

обмета́ть[2] (-ечу́ *or* -а́ю, -е́чешь *or* -а́ешь) *pf* (*impf* **обмётывать**) oversew.

обмету́ *etc.*: *see* **обмести́**.

обмётывать *impf of* **обмета́ть**.

обмира́ть *impf of* **обмере́ть**.

обмо́лвиться (-влюсь) *pf* make a slip of the tongue; +*instr* say, utter. **обмо́лвка** slip of the tongue.

обморо́женный frost-bitten.

о́бморок fainting-fit, swoon.

обмота́ть *pf* (*impf* **обма́тывать**) wind round; **~ся** +*instr* wrap o.s. in. **обмо́тка** winding; *pl* puttees.

обмо́ю *etc.*: *see* **обмы́ть**

обмундирова́ние fitting out (with uniform); uniform. **обмундирова́ть** *pf*, **обмундиро́вывать** *impf* fit out (with uniform).

обмыва́ть *impf*, **обмы́ть** (-мо́ю) *pf* bathe, wash; **~ся** wash, bathe.

обмяка́ть *impf*, **обмя́кнуть** (-ну; -мя́к) *pf* become soft *or* flabby.

обнадёживать *impf*, **обнадёжить** (-жу) *pf* reassure.

обнажа́ть *impf*, **обнажи́ть** (-жу́) *pf* bare, uncover; reveal. **обнажённый** (-ён, -ена́) naked, bare; nude.

обнаро́довать *impf* & *pf* promulgate.

обнару́же́ние revealing; discovery; detection. **обнару́живать** *impf*, **обнару́жить** (-жу) *pf* display; reveal; discover; **~ся** come to light.

обнести́ (-су́, -сёшь; -нёс, -ла́) *pf* (*impf* **обноси́ть**) enclose; +*instr* serve round; pass over, leave out.

обнима́ть(ся *impf of* **обня́ть(ся**.

обниму́ *etc.*: *see* **обня́ть**

обнища́ние impoverishment.

обнови́ть (-влю́) *pf*, **обновля́ть** *impf* renovate; renew. **обно́вка** new acquisition; new garment. **обновле́ние** renovation, renewal.

обноси́ть (-ошу́, -о́сишь) *impf of* **обнести́**; **~ся** *pf* have worn out one's clothes.

обня́ть (-ниму́, -ни́мешь; о́бнял, -а́, -о) *pf* (*impf* **обнима́ть**) embrace; clasp; **~ся** embrace; hug one another.

обо *see* **о** *prep*.

обобра́ть (оберу́, -рёшь; обобра́л, -а́, -о) *pf* (*impf* **обира́ть**) rob; pick.

обобща́ть *impf*, **обобщи́ть** (-щу́) *pf* generalize. **обобще́ние** generalization. **обобществи́ть** (-влю́) *pf*, **обобществля́ть** *impf* socialize; collectivize. **обобществле́ние** socialization; collectivization.

обобью́ *etc.*: *see* **оби́ть**. **обовью́** *etc.*: *see* **обви́ть**

обогати́ть (-ащу́) *pf*, **обогаща́ть** *impf* enrich; **~ся** become rich; enrich o.s. **обогаще́ние** enrichment.

обогна́ть (обгоню́, -о́нишь; обогна́л, -а́, -о) *pf* (*impf* **обгоня́ть**) pass; outstrip.

обогну́ть (-ну́, -нёшь) *pf* (*impf* **огиба́ть**) round, skirt; bend round.

обогрева́тель *m* heater. **обогрева́ть** *impf*, **обогре́ть** (-е́ю) *pf* heat, warm; **~ся** warm up.

о́бод (*pl* -о́дья, -ьев) rim. **ободо́к** (-дка́) thin rim, narrow border.

обо́дранный ragged. **ободра́ть** (обдеру́, -рёшь; -а́л, -а́, -о) *pf* (*impf* **обдира́ть**) skin, flay; peel; fleece.

ободре́ние encouragement, reassurance. **ободри́тельный** encouraging, reassuring. **ободри́ть** *pf*, **ободря́ть** *impf* encourage, reassure; **~ся** cheer up, take heart.

обожа́ть *impf* adore.

обожгу́ *etc.*: *see* **обже́чь**

обожестви́ть (-влю) *pf*, **обожествля́ть** *impf* deify.

обожжённый (-ён, -ена́) burnt, scorched.

обо́з string of vehicles; transport.

обозва́ть (обзову́, -вёшь; -а́л, -а́, -о) *pf* (*impf* **обзыва́ть**) call; call names.

обозлённый (-ён, -а́) angered; embittered. **обо|зли́ть** *pf*, **о|зли́ть** *pf* anger; embitter; **~ся** get angry.

обозна́ться *pf* mistake s.o. for s.o. else.

обознача́ть *impf*, **обозна́чить** (-чу) *pf* mean; mark; **~ся** appear, reveal o.s. **обозначе́ние** sign, symbol.

О **обозрева́тель** *m* reviewer; columnist. **обозрева́ть** *impf*, **обозре́ть** (-рю) *pf* survey. **обозре́ние** survey; review; revue. **обозри́мый** visible.

обо́и (-ев) *pl* wallpaper.

обо́йма (*gen pl* **-о́йм**) cartridge clip.

обойти́ (-йду́, -йдёшь; -ошёл, -ошла́) *pf* (*impf* **обходи́ть**) go round; pass; avoid; pass over; **~сь** manage, make do; **+с+***instr* treat.

обокра́сть (обкраду́, -дёшь) *pf* (*impf* **обкра́дывать**) rob.

оболо́чка casing; membrane; cover, envelope, jacket; shell.

обольсти́тель *m* seducer. **обольсти́тельный** seductive. **обольсти́ть** (-льщу́) *pf*, **обольща́ть** *impf* seduce. **обольще́ние** seduction; delusion.

оболью́ *etc.*: *see* **обли́ть**

обомру́ *etc.*: *see* **обмере́ть**

обоня́ние (sense of) smell. **обоня́тельный** olfactory.

обопру́ *etc.*: *see* **опере́ть**

обора́чивать(ся *impf of* **оберну́ть(ся, обороти́ть(ся**

обо́рванный torn, ragged. **оборва́ть** (-ву́, -вёшь; -а́л, -а́, -о) *pf* (*impf* **обрыва́ть**) tear off; break; snap; cut short; **~ся** break; snap; fall; stop suddenly.

обо́рка frill, flounce.

оборо́на defence. **оборони́тельный** defensive. **оборони́ть** *pf*, **обороня́ть** *impf* defend; **~ся** defend o.s. **оборо́нный** defence, defensive.

оборо́т turn; revolution; circulation; turnover; back; **~ ре́чи** (turn of) phrase; **смотри́ на ~е** P.T.O. **обороти́ть** (-рочу́, -ро́тишь) *pf* (*impf* **обора́чивать**) turn; **~ся** turn (round); *+instr or* **в**+*acc* turn into. **оборо́тный** circulating; reverse; **~ капита́л** working capital.

обору́дование equipping; equipment. **обору́довать** *impf* & *pf* equip.

обоснова́ние basing; basis, ground. **обосно́ванный** well-founded. **обоснова́ть** *pf*, **обосно́вывать** *impf* ground, base; substantiate; **~ся** settle down.

обосо́бленный isolated, solitary.

обостре́ние aggravation. **обострённый** keen; strained; sharp, pointed. **обостри́ть** *pf*, **обостря́ть** *impf* sharpen; strain; aggravate; **~ся** become strained; be aggravated; become acute.

оботру́ *etc.*: *see* **обтере́ть**

обо́чина verge; shoulder, edge.

обошёл *etc.*: *see* **обойти́**. **обошью́** *etc.*: *see* **обши́ть**

обою́дный mutual, reciprocal.

обраба́тывать *impf*, **обрабо́тать** *pf* till, cultivate; work, work up; treat, process. **обрабо́тка** working (up); processing; cultivation.

об|ра́довать(ся *pf*.

о́браз shape, form; image; manner; way; icon; **гла́вным ~ом** mainly; **таки́м ~ом** thus. **образе́ц** (-зца́) model; pattern; sample. **о́б-**

разный graphic; figurative. **образова́ние** formation; education. **образо́ванный** educated. **образова́тельный** educational. **образова́ть** *impf* & *pf*, **образо́вывать** *impf* form; **~ся** form; arise; turn out well.

образу́мить (-млю) *pf* bring to reason; **~ся** see reason.

образцо́вый model. **обра́зчик** specimen, sample.

обра́мить (-млю) *pf*, **обрамля́ть** *impf* frame.

обраста́ть *impf*, **обрасти́** (-ту́, -тёшь; -ро́с, -ла́) *pf* be overgrown.

обрати́мый reversible, convertible. **обрати́ть** (-ащу́) *pf*, **обраща́ть** *impf* turn; convert; **~ внима́ние на**+*acc* pay *or* draw attention to; **~ся** turn; appeal; apply; address; **+в**+*acc* turn into; **+с**+*instr* treat; handle. **обра́тно** *adv* back; backwards; conversely; **~ пропорциона́льный** inversely proportional. **обра́тный** reverse; return; opposite; inverse. **обраще́ние** appeal, address; conversion; (**+с**+*instr*) treatment (of); handling (of); use (of).

обре́з edge; sawn-off gun; **в ~**+*gen* only just enough. **обре́зать** (-е́жу) *pf*, **обреза́ть** *impf* cut (off); clip, trim; pare; prune; circumcise; **~ся** cut o.s. **обре́зок** (-зка) scrap; *pl* ends; clippings.

обрека́ть *impf of* **обре́чь. обреку́** *etc.*: *see* **обре́чь. обрёл** *etc.*: *see* **обрести́**

обремени́тельный onerous. **о|бремени́ть** *pf*, **обременя́ть** *impf* burden.

обрести́ (-ету́, -етёшь; -рёл, -а́) *pf*, **обрета́ть** *impf* find.

обрече́ние doom. **обречённый** doomed. **обре́чь** (-еку́, -ечёшь; -ёк, -ла́) *pf* (*impf* **обрека́ть**) doom.

обрисова́ть *pf*, **обрисо́вывать** *impf* outline, depict; **~ся** appear (in outline).

оброни́ть (-ню́, -нишь) *pf* drop; let drop.

обро́с *etc.*: *see* **обрасти́.**

обруба́ть *impf*, **обруби́ть** (-блю́, -бишь) *pf* chop off; cut off. **обру́бок** (-бка) stump.

об|руга́ть *pf*.

о́бруч (*pl* -и, -е́й) hoop. **обруча́льн|ый** engagement; **~ое кольцо́** betrothal ring, wedding ring. **обруча́ть** *impf*, **обручи́ть** (-чу́) betroth; **~ся +с**+*instr* become engaged to. **обруче́ние** engagement.

обру́шивать *impf*, **об|ру́шить** (-шу) *pf* bring down; **~ся** come down, collapse.

обры́в precipice. **обрыва́ть(ся** *impf of* **оборва́ть(ся. обры́вок** (-вка) scrap; snatch.

обры́згать *pf*, **обры́згивать** *impf* splash; sprinkle.

обрю́зглый flabby.

обря́д rite, ceremony.

обсервато́рия observatory.

обслу́живание service; maintenance. **обслу́живать** *impf*, **обслужи́ть** (-жу́, -жишь) *pf* serve; operate.

обсле́дование inspection. **обсле́дователь** *m* inspector. **обсле́довать** *impf* & *pf* inspect.

обсо́хнуть (-ну; -о́х) *pf* (*impf* **обсыха́ть**) dry (off).

обста́вить (-влю) *pf*, **обставля́ть** *impf* surround; furnish; arrange. **обстано́вка** furniture; situation, conditions; set.

обстоя́тельный thorough, reliable; detailed. **обстоя́тельство** circumstance. **обстоя́ть** (-ои́т) *impf* be; go; **как обстои́т де́ло?** how is it going?

обстре́л firing, fire; **под ~ом** under fire. **обстре́ливать** *impf*, **обстреля́ть** *pf* fire at; bombard.

обступа́ть *impf*, **обступи́ть** (-у́пит) *pf* surround.

обсуди́ть (-ужу́, -у́дишь) *pf*, **обсужда́ть** *impf* discuss. **обсужде́ние** discussion.

обсчита́ть *pf*, **обсчи́тывать** *impf* shortchange; **~ся** miscount, miscalculate.

О

обсы́пать (-плю) *pf*, **обсыпа́ть** *impf* strew; sprinkle.
обсыха́ть *impf of* **обсо́хнуть. об-та́чивать** *impf of* **обточи́ть**
обтека́емый streamlined.
обтере́ть (оботру́, -трёшь; обтёр) *pf* (*impf* **обтира́ть**) wipe; rub; **~ся** dry o.s.; sponge down.
о(б)теса́ть (-ешу́, -е́шешь) *pf*, **о(б)тёсывать** *impf* rough-hew; teach good manners to; trim.
обтира́ние sponge-down. **обти-ра́ть(ся** *pf of* **обтере́ть(ся**
обточи́ть (-чу́, -чишь) *pf* (*impf* **об-та́чивать**) grind; machine.
обтрёпанный frayed; shabby.
обтя́гивать *impf*, **обтяну́ть** (-ну́, -нешь) *pf* cover; fit close. **обтя́жка** cover; skin; **в обтя́жку** close-fitting.
обува́ть(ся *impf of* **обу́ть(ся. о́бувь** footwear; boots, shoes.
обу́гливать *impf*, **обу́глить** *pf* char; carbonize; **~ся** char, become charred.

О

обу́за burden.
обузда́ть *pf*, **обу́здывать** *impf* bridle, curb.
обурева́ть *impf* grip; possess.
обусло́вить (-влю) *pf*, **обусло́-вливать** *impf* cause; +*instr* make conditional on; **~ся** +*instr* be conditional on; depend on.
обу́тый shod. **обу́ть** (-у́ю) *pf* (*impf* **обува́ть**) put shoes on; **~ся** put on one's shoes.
о́бу́х butt, back.
обуча́ть *impf*, **об|учи́ть** (-чу́, -чишь) *pf* teach; train; **~ся** +*dat or inf* learn. **обуче́ние** teaching; training.
обхва́т girth; **в ~е** in circumference. **обхвати́ть** (-ачу́, -а́тишь) *pf*, **обхва́тывать** *impf* embrace; clasp.
обхо́д round(s); roundabout way; bypass. **обходи́тельный** courteous; pleasant. **обходи́ть(ся** (-ожу́(сь, -о́дишь(ся) *impf of* **обой-ти́(сь. обхо́дный** roundabout.
обша́ривать *impf*, **обша́рить** *pf* rummage through, ransack.
обшива́ть *impf of* **обши́ть. об-ши́вка** edging; trimming; boarding, panelling; plating.
обши́рный extensive; vast.
обши́ть (обошью́, -шьёшь) *pf* (*impf* **обшива́ть**) edge; trim; make outfit(s) for; plank.
обшла́г (-а́; *pl* -а́, -о́в) cuff.
обща́ться *impf* associate.
обще- *in comb* common(ly), general(ly). **общедосту́пный** moderate in price; popular. **~жи́тие** hostel. **~изве́стный** generally known. **~наро́дный** national, public. **~образова́тельный** of general education. **~при́нятый** generally accepted. **~сою́зный** *hist* All-Union. **~челове́ческий** common to all mankind; universal.
обще́ние contact; social intercourse. **обще́ственность** (the) public; public opinion; community. **обще́ственный** social, public; voluntary. **о́бщество** society; company.
о́бщ|ий general; common; **в ~ем** on the whole, in general. **общи́на** community; commune.
об|щипа́ть (-плю́, -плешь) *pf*.
общи́тельный sociable. **о́б-щность** community.
объеда́ть(ся *impf of* **объе́сть(ся**
объедине́ние unification; merger; union, association. **объе-динённый** (-ён, -а́) united. **объе-дини́тельный** unifying. **объедини́ть** *pf*, **объединя́ть** *impf* unite; join; combine; **~ся** unite.
объе́дки (-ов) *pl* leftovers, scraps.
объе́зд riding round; detour.
объе́здить (-зжу, -здишь) *pf* (*impf* **объезжа́ть**) travel over; break in.
объезжа́ть *impf of* **объе́здить, объе́хать**
объе́кт object; objective; establishment, works. **объекти́в** lens. **объекти́вность** objectivity. **объ-екти́вный** objective.

объём volume; scope. **объёмный** by volume, volumetric.
объе́сть (-е́м, -е́шь, -е́ст, -еди́м) *pf* (*impf* **объеда́ть**) gnaw (round), nibble; **~ся** overeat.
объе́хать (-е́ду) *pf* (*impf* **объезжа́ть**) drive *or* go round; go past; travel over.
объяви́ть (-влю́, -вишь) *pf*, **объявля́ть** *impf* declare, announce; **~ся** turn up; +*instr* declare o.s. **объявле́ние** declaration, announcement; advertisement.
объясне́ние explanation. **объясни́мый** explainable. **объясни́ть** *pf*, **объясня́ть** *impf* explain; **~ся** be explained; make o.s. understood; **+с**+*instr* have it out with.
объя́тие embrace.
обыва́тель *m* Philistine. **обыва́тельский** narrow-minded.
обыгра́ть *pf*, **обы́грывать** *impf* beat (*in a game*).
обы́денный ordinary; everyday.
обыкнове́ние habit. **обыкнове́нно** *adv* usually. **обыкнове́нный** usual; ordinary.
о́быск search. **обыска́ть** (-ыщу́, -ы́щешь) *pf*, **обы́скивать** *impf* search.
обы́чай custom; usage. **обы́чно** *adv* usually. **обы́чный** usual.
обя́занность duty; responsibility. **обя́занный** (+*inf*) obliged; +*dat* indebted to (+*instr* for). **обяза́тельно** *adv* without fail. **обяза́тельный** obligatory. **обяза́тельство** obligation; commitment. **обяза́ть** (-яжу́, -я́жешь) *pf*, **обя́зывать** *impf* bind; commit; oblige; **~ся** pledge o.s., undertake.
ова́л oval. **ова́льный** oval.
ова́ция ovation.
овдове́ть (-е́ю) *pf* become a widow, widower.
овёс (овса́) oats.
ове́чка *dim of* **овца́**; harmless person.
овладева́ть *impf*, **овладе́ть** (-е́ю) *pf* +*instr* seize; capture; master.
о́вод (*pl* -ы *or* -а́) gadfly.
о́вощ (*pl* -и, -е́й) vegetable. **овощно́й** vegetable.
овра́г ravine, gully.
овся́нка oatmeal; porridge. **овся́ный** oat, oatmeal.
овца́ (*pl* -ы, ове́ц, о́вцам) sheep; ewe. **овча́рка** sheep-dog. **овчи́на** sheepskin.
ога́рок (-рка) candle-end.
огиба́ть *impf of* **обогну́ть**
оглавле́ние table of contents.
огласи́ть (-ашу́) *pf*, **оглаша́ть** *impf* announce; fill (with sound); **~ся** resound. **огла́ска** publicity. **оглаше́ние** publication.
огло́бля (*gen pl* -бель) shaft.
о|гло́хнуть (-ну; -о́х) *pf*.
оглуша́ть *impf*, **о|глуши́ть** (-шу́) *pf* deafen; stun. **оглуши́тельный** deafening.
огляде́ть (-яжу́) *pf*, **огля́дывать** *impf*, **огляну́ть** (-ну́, -нешь) *pf* look round; look over; **~ся** look round; look back. **огля́дка** looking back.
огнево́й fire; fiery. **о́гненный** fiery. **огнеопа́сный** inflammable. **огнеприпа́сы** (-ов) *pl* ammunition. **огнесто́йкий** fire-proof. **огнестре́льн|ый: ~ое ору́жие** firearm(s). **огнетуши́тель** *m* fire-extinguisher. **огнеупо́рный** fire-resistant.
ого́ *int* oho!
огова́ривать *impf*, **оговори́ть** *pf* slander; stipulate (for); **~ся** make a proviso; make a slip (of the tongue). **огово́р** slander. **огово́рка** reservation, proviso; slip of the tongue.
оголённый bare, nude. **оголи́ть** *pf* (*impf* **оголя́ть**) bare; strip; **~ся** strip o.s.; become exposed.
оголя́ть(ся *impf of* **оголи́ть(ся**
огонёк (-нька́) (*small*) light; zest. **ого́нь** (огня́) *m* fire; light.
огора́живать *impf*, **огороди́ть** (-рожу́, -ро́дишь) *pf* fence in, enclose; **~ся** fence o.s. in. **огоро́д** kitchen-garden. **огоро́дный** kitchen-garden.

огорча́ть *impf*, **огорчи́ть** (-чу́) *pf* grieve, pain; **~ся** grieve, be distressed. **огорче́ние** grief; chagrin.

о|гра́бить (-блю) *pf*. **ограбле́ние** robbery; burglary.

огра́да fence. **огради́ть** (-ажу́) *pf*, **огражда́ть** *impf* guard, protect.

ограниче́ние limitation, restriction. **ограни́ченный** limited. **ограни́чивать** *impf*, **ограни́чить** (-чу) *pf* limit, restrict; **~ся** +*instr* limit *or* confine o.s. to; be limited to.

огро́мный huge; enormous.

о|грубе́ть (-е́ю) *pf*.

огры́зок (-зка) bit, end; stub.

огуре́ц (-рца́) cucumber.

ода́лживать *impf of* **одолжи́ть**

одарённый gifted. **ода́ривать** *impf*, **одари́ть** *pf*, **одаря́ть** *impf* give presents (to); +*instr* endow with.

одева́ть(ся *impf of* **оде́ть(ся**

О

оде́жда clothes; clothing.

одеколо́н eau-de-Cologne.

одели́ть *pf*, **оделя́ть** *impf* (+*instr*) present (with); endow (with).

оде́ну *etc.*: *see* **оде́ть**. **одёргивать** *impf of* **одёрнуть**

о|деревене́ть (-е́ю) *pf*.

одержа́ть (-жу́, -жишь) *pf*, **оде́рживать** *impf* gain. **одержи́мый** possessed.

одёрнуть (-ну) *pf* (*impf* **одёргивать**) pull down, straighten.

оде́тый dressed; clothed. **оде́ть** (-е́ну) *pf* (*impf* **одева́ть**) dress; clothe; **~ся** dress (o.s.). **одея́ло** blanket. **одея́ние** garb, attire.

оди́н (одного́), **одна́** (одно́й), **одно́** (одного́); *pl* **одни́** (одни́х) one; a, an; a certain; alone; only; nothing but; same; **одно́ и то же** the same thing; **оди́н на оди́н** in private; **оди́н раз** once; **одни́м сло́вом** in a word; **по одному́** one by one.

одина́ковый identical, the same, equal.

оди́ннадцатый eleventh. **оди́ннадцать** eleven.

одино́кий solitary; lonely; single. **одино́чество** solitude; loneliness. **одино́чка** *m* & *f* (one) person alone. **одино́чн|ый** individual; one-man; single; **~ое заключе́ние** solitary confinement.

одича́лый wild.

одна́жды *adv* once; one day; once upon a time.

одна́ко *conj* however.

одно- *in comb* single, one; uni-, mono-, homo-. **однобо́кий** one-sided. **~вре́ме́нно** *adv* simultaneously, at the same time. **~вре́ме́нный** simultaneous. **~зву́чный** monotonous. **~зна́чащий** synonymous. **~зна́чный** synonymous; one-digit. **~имённый** of the same name. **~кла́ссник** classmate. **~клё́точный** unicellular. **~кра́тный** single. **~ле́тний** one-year; annual. **~ме́стный** single-seater. **~обра́зие, ~обра́зность** monotony. **~обра́зный** monotonous. **~ро́дность** homogeneity, uniformity. **~ро́дный** homogeneous; similar. **~сторо́нний** one-sided; unilateral; one-way. **~фами́лец** (-льца) person of the same surname. **~цве́тный** one-colour; monochrome. **~эта́жный** one-storeyed.

одобре́ние approval. **одобри́тельный** approving. **одо́брить** *pf*, **одобря́ть** *impf* approve (of).

одолева́ть *impf*, **одоле́ть** (-е́ю) *pf* overcome.

одолжа́ть *impf*, **одолжи́ть** (-жу́) *pf* lend; **+у+***gen* borrow from. **одолже́ние** favour.

о|дряхле́ть (-е́ю) *pf*.

одува́нчик dandelion.

оду́маться *pf*, **оду́мываться** *impf* change one's mind.

одуре́лый stupid. **о|дуре́ть** (-е́ю) *pf*.

одурма́нивать *impf*, **о|дурма́нить** *pf* stupefy. **одуря́ть** *impf* stupefy.

одухотворённый inspired; spiritual. **одухотвори́ть** *pf*, **одухо-**

творя́ть *impf* inspire.
одушеви́ть (-влю) *pf*, **одушевля́ть** *impf* animate. **одушевле́ние** animation.
оды́шка shortness of breath.
ожере́лье necklace.
ожесточа́ть *impf*, **ожесточи́ть** (-чу́) *pf* embitter, harden. **ожесточе́ние** bitterness. **ожесточённый** bitter; hard.
оживá́ть *impf of* **ожи́ть**
оживи́ть (-влю́) *pf*, **оживля́ть** *impf* revive; enliven; **~ся** become animated. **оживле́ние** animation; reviving; enlivening. **оживлённый** animated, lively.
ожида́ние expectation; waiting. **ожида́ть** *impf +gen or acc* wait for; expect.
ожире́ние obesity. **о|жире́ть** (-е́ю) *pf*.
ожи́ть (-иву́, -ивёшь; о́жил, -а́, -о) *pf* (*impf* **ожива́ть**) come to life, revive.
ожо́г burn, scald.
озабо́ченность preoccupation; anxiety. **озабо́ченный** preoccupied; anxious.
озагла́вить (-лю) *pf*, **озагла́вливать** *impf* entitle; head. **озада́чивать** *impf*, **озада́чить** (-чу) *pf* perplex, puzzle.
озари́ть *pf*, **озаря́ть** *impf* light up, illuminate; **~ся** light up.
оздорови́тельный бег jogging. **оздоровле́ние** sanitation.
озелени́ть *pf*, **озеленя́ть** *impf* plant (*with trees etc.*).
о́зеро (*pl* озёра) lake.
ози́мые *sb* winter crops. **ози́мый** winter. **о́зимь** winter crop.
озира́ться *impf* look round; look back.
о|зли́ть(ся: *see* **обозли́ть(ся**
озло́бить (-блю) *pf*, **озлобля́ть** *impf* embitter; **~ся** grow bitter. **озлобле́ние** bitterness, animosity. **озло́бленный** embittered.
о|знако́мить (-млю) *pf*, **ознакомля́ть** *impf* **с**+*instr* acquaint with; **~ся с**+*instr* familiarize o.s. with.
ознаменова́ть *pf*, **ознамено́вывать** *impf* mark; celebrate.
означа́ть *impf* mean, signify.
озно́б shivering, chill.
озо́н ozone.
озорни́к (-а́) mischief-maker. **озорно́й** naughty, mischievous. **озорство́** mischief.
озя́бнуть (-ну; озя́б) *pf* be cold, be freezing.
ой *int* oh.
оказа́ть (-ажу́, -а́жешь) *pf* (*impf* **ока́зывать**) render, provide, show; **~ся** turn out, prove; find o.s., be found.
ока́зия unexpected event, funny thing.
ока́зывать(ся *impf of* **оказа́ть(ся**
окамене́лость fossil. **окамене́лый** fossilized; petrified. **о|камене́ть** (-е́ю) *pf*.
окантовка mount.
ока́нчивать(ся *impf of* **око́нчить(ся**. **ока́пывать(ся** *impf of* **окопа́ть(ся**
ока́янный damned, cursed.
океа́н ocean. **океа́нский** ocean; oceanic.
оки́дывать *impf*, **оки́нуть** (-ну) *pf*; **~ взгля́дом** take in at a glance, glance over.
о́кисел (-сла) oxide. **окисле́ние** oxidation. **о́кись** oxide.
оккупа́нт invader. **оккупа́ция** occupation. **оккупи́ровать** *impf* & *pf* occupy.
окла́д salary scale; (basic) pay.
оклевета́ть (-ещу́, -е́щешь) *pf* slander.
окле́ивать *impf*, **окле́ить** *pf* cover; paste over; **~ обо́ями** paper.
окно́ (*pl* о́кна) window.
о́ко (*pl* о́чи, оче́й) eye.
око́вы (око́в) *pl* fetters.
околдова́ть *pf*, **околдо́вывать** *impf* bewitch.
о́коло *adv* & *prep+gen* by; close (to), near; around; about.
око́льный roundabout.
око́нный window.

окончáние end; conclusion, termination; ending. **окончáтельный** final. **окóнчить** (-чу) *pf* (*impf* **окáнчивать**) finish, end; **~ся** finish, end.

окóп trench. **окопáть** *pf* (*impf* **окáпывать**) dig round; **~ся** entrench o.s., dig in. **окóпный** trench.

óкорок (*pl* -á, -óв) ham, gammon.

окоченéлый stiff with cold. **о|коченéть** (-éю) *pf*.

окóшечко, окóшко (*small*) window.

окрáина outskirts, outlying districts.

о|крáсить (-áшу) *pf*, **окрáшивать** *impf* paint, colour; dye. **окрáска** painting; colouring; dyeing; coloration.

о|крéпнуть (-ну) *pf*. **о|крестúть(ся** (-ещý(сь, -éстишь(ся) *pf*.

окрéстность environs. **окрéстный** neighbouring.

óкрик hail; shout. **окрúкивать** *impf*, **окрúкнуть** (-ну) *pf* hail, call, shout to.

окровáвленный blood-stained.

óкруг (*pl* ~á) district. **окрýга** neighbourhood. **округлúть** *pf*, **округлять** *impf* round; round off. **окрýглый** rounded. **окружáть** *impf*, **окружúть** (-жý) *pf* surround; encircle. **окружáющ|ий** surrounding; **~ее** *sb* environment; **~ие** *sb pl* associates. **окружéние** encirclement; environment. **окружнóй** district. **окрýжность** circumference.

окрылúть *pf*, **окрылять** *impf* inspire, encourage.

октáва octave.

октáн octane.

октябрь (-я) *m* October. **октябрьский** October.

окулúст oculist.

окунáть *impf*, **окунýть** (-нý, -нёшь) *pf* dip; **~ся** dip; plunge; become absorbed.

óкунь (*pl* -и, -éй) *m* perch.

окупáть *impf*, **окупúть** (-плю, -пишь) *pf* compensate, repay; **~ся** be repaid, pay for itself.

окýрок (-рка) cigarette-end.

окýтать *pf*, **окýтывать** *impf* wrap up; shroud, cloak.

окýчивать *impf*, **окýчить** (-чу) *pf* earth up.

олáдья (*gen pl* -ий) fritter; drop-scone.

оледенéлый frozen. **о|леденéть** (-éю) *pf*.

олéний deer, deer's; reindeer. **олéнина** venison. **олéнь** *m* deer; reindeer.

олúва olive. **олúвковый** olive; olive-coloured.

олигáрхия oligarchy.

олимпиáда olympiad; Olympics. **олимпúйск|ий** Olympic; Olympian; **~ие úгры** Olympic games.

олúфа drying oil (*e.g. linseed oil*).

олицетворéние personification; embodiment. **олицетворúть** *pf*, **олицетворять** *impf* personify, embody.

óлово tin. **оловянный** tin.

ом ohm.

омáр lobster.

омерзéние loathing. **омерзúтельный** loathsome.

омертвéлый stiff, numb; necrotic. **о|мертвéть** (-éю) *pf*.

омлéт omelette.

омоложéние rejuvenation.

омóним homonym.

омóю *etc.*: *see* **омыть**

омрачáть *impf*, **омрачúть** (-чý) *pf* darken, cloud.

óмут whirlpool; maelstrom.

омывáть *impf*, **омыть** (омóю) *pf* wash; **~ся** be washed.

он (егó, емý, им, о нём) *pron* he. **онá** (её, ей, ей (éю), о ней) *pron* she.

ондáтра musk-rat.

онемéлый numb. **о|немéть** (-éю) *pf*.

онú (их, им, úми, о них) *pron* they. **онó** (егó, емý, им, о нём) *pron* it; this, that.

опадáть *impf of* **опáсть**.

опáздывать *impf of* **опоздáть**

опáла disgrace.

о|пали́ть *pf.*
опа́ловый opal.
опа́лубка casing.
опаса́ться *impf +gen* fear; avoid, keep off. **опасе́ние** fear; apprehension.
опа́сность danger; peril. **опа́сный** dangerous.
опа́сть (-адёт) *pf* (*impf* **опада́ть**) fall, fall off; subside.
опе́ка guardianship; trusteeship. **опека́емый** *sb* ward. **опека́ть** *impf* be guardian of; take care of. **опеку́н** (-á), **-у́нша** guardian; tutor; trustee.
о́пера opera.
операти́вный efficient; operative, surgical; operation(s), operational. **опера́тор** operator; cameraman. **операцио́нн|ый** operating; **~ая** *sb* operating theatre. **опера́ция** operation.
опереди́ть (-режу́) *pf*, **опережа́ть** *impf* outstrip, leave behind.
опере́ние plumage.
опере́тта, -е́тка operetta.
опере́ть (обопру́, -прёшь; опёр, -ла́) *pf* (*impf* **опира́ть**) **+о+***acc* lean against; **~ся на** *or* **о+***acc* lean on, lean against.
опери́ровать *impf & pf* operate on; operate, act; *+instr* use.
о́перный opera; operatic.
о|печа́лить(ся *pf.*
опеча́тать *pf* (*impf* **опеча́тывать**) seal up.
опеча́тка misprint.
опеча́тывать *impf of* **опеча́тать**
опе́шить (-шу) *pf* be taken aback.
опи́лки (-лок) *pl* sawdust; filings.
опира́ть(ся *impf of* **опере́ть(ся**
описа́ние description. **описа́тельный** descriptive. **описа́ть** (-ишу́, -и́шешь) *pf*, **опи́сывать** *impf* describe; **~ся** make a slip of the pen. **опи́ска** slip of the pen. **о́пись** inventory.
о́пиум opium.
опла́кать (-а́чу) *pf*, **опла́кивать** *impf* mourn for; bewail.
опла́та payment. **оплати́ть** (-ачу́, -а́тишь) *pf*, **опла́чивать** *impf* pay (for).
опла́чу *etc.*: *see* **опла́кать. оплачу́** *etc.*: *see* **оплати́ть**
оплеу́ха slap in the face.
оплодотвори́ть *pf*, **оплодотворя́ть** *impf* impregnate; fertilize.
о|пломбирова́ть *pf.*
опло́т stronghold, bulwark.
опло́шность blunder, mistake.
оповести́ть (-ещу́) *pf*, **оповеща́ть** *impf* notify. **оповеще́ние** notification.
опозда́вший *sb* late-comer. **опозда́ние** lateness; delay. **опозда́ть** *pf* (*impf* **опа́здывать**) be late; **+на+***acc* miss.
опознава́тельный distinguishing; **~ знак** landmark. **опознава́ть** (-наю́, -наёшь) *impf*, **опозна́ть** *pf* identify. **опозна́ние** identification.
о|позо́рить(ся *pf.*
опольза́ть *impf*, **оползти́** (-зёт; -о́лз, -ла́) *pf* slip, slide. **о́ползень** (-зня) *m* landslide.
ополче́ние militia.
опо́мниться *pf* come to one's senses.
опо́р: **во весь ~** at full speed.
опо́ра support; pier; **то́чка опо́ры** fulcrum, foothold.
опора́жнивать *impf of* **опорожни́ть**
опо́рный support, supporting, supported; bearing.
опоро́жни́ть *pf*, **опорожня́ть** *impf* (*impf also* **опора́жнивать**) empty.
о|поро́чить (-чу) *pf.*
опохмели́ться *pf*, **опохмеля́ться** *impf* take a hair of the dog that bit you.
опо́шлить *pf*, **опошля́ть** *impf* vulgarize, debase.
опоя́сать (-я́шу) *pf*, **опоя́сывать** *impf* gird; girdle.
оппозицио́нный opposition. **оппози́ция** opposition.
оппортуни́зм opportunism.
опра́ва setting, mounting; spectacle frames.

оправда́ние justification; excuse; acquittal. **оправда́тельный пригово́р** verdict of not guilty. **оправда́ть** *pf*, **опра́вдывать** *impf* justify; excuse; acquit; **~ся** justify o.s.; be justified.

опра́вить (-влю) *pf*, **оправля́ть** *impf* set right, adjust; mount; **~ся** put one's dress in order; recover; +**от**+*gen* get over.

опра́шивать *impf of* **опроси́ть**

определе́ние definition; determination; decision. **определённый** definite; certain. **определи́мый** definable. **определи́ть** *pf*, **определя́ть** *impf* define; determine; appoint; **~ся** be formed; be determined; find one's position.

опроверга́ть *impf*, **опрове́ргнуть** (-ну; -ве́рг) *pf* refute, disprove. **опроверже́ние** refutation; denial.

опроки́дывать *impf*, **опроки́нуть** (-ну) *pf* overturn; topple; **~ся** overturn; capsize.

опроме́тчивый rash, hasty.

опро́с (cross-)examination; (opinion) poll. **опроси́ть** (-ошу́, -о́сишь) *pf* (*impf* **опра́шивать**) question; (cross-)examine. **опро́сный лист** questionnaire.

опры́скать *pf*, **опры́скивать** *impf* sprinkle; spray.

опря́тный neat, tidy.

о́птик optician. **о́птика** optics. **опти́ческий** optic, optical.

оптима́льный optimal. **оптими́зм** optimism. **оптими́ст** optimist. **оптимисти́ческий** optimistic.

опто́вый wholesale. **о́птом** *adv* wholesale.

опубликова́ние publication; promulgation. **о|публикова́ть** *pf*, **опублико́вывать** *impf* publish; promulgate.

опуска́ть(ся *impf of* **опусти́ть(ся**

опусте́лый deserted. **о|пусте́ть** (-е́ет) *pf*.

опусти́ть (-ущу́, -у́стишь) *pf* (*impf* **опуска́ть**) lower; let down; turn down; omit; post; **~ся** lower o.s.; sink; fall; go down; go to pieces.

опустоша́ть *impf*, **опустоши́ть** (-шу́) *pf* devastate. **опустоше́ние** devastation. **опустоши́тельный** devastating.

опу́тать *pf*, **опу́тывать** *impf* entangle; ensnare.

опуха́ть *impf*, **о|пу́хнуть** (-ну; опу́х) *pf* swell, swell up. **о́пухоль** swelling; tumour.

опу́шка edge of a forest; trimming.

опущу́ *etc.*: *see* **опусти́ть**

опыле́ние pollination. **опыли́ть** *pf*, **опыля́ть** *impf* pollinate.

о́пыт experience; experiment. **о́пытный** experienced; experimental.

опьяне́ние intoxication. **о|пьяне́ть** (-е́ю) *pf*, **о|пьяни́ть** *pf*, **опьяня́ть** *impf* intoxicate, make drunk.

опя́ть *adv* again.

ора́ва crowd, horde.

ора́кул oracle.

орангута́нг orangutan.

ора́нжевый orange. **оранжере́я** greenhouse, conservatory.

ора́тор orator. **орато́рия** oratorio.

ора́ть (ору́, орёшь) *impf* yell.

орби́та orbit; (eye-)socket.

о́рган[1] organ; body. **орга́н**[2] (*mus*) organ. **организа́тор** organizer. **организацио́нный** organization(al). **организа́ция** organization. **органи́зм** organism. **организо́ванный** organized. **организова́ть** *impf* & *pf* (*pf also* **с~**) organize; **~ся** be organized; organize. **органи́ческий** organic.

о́ргия orgy.

орда́ (*pl* -ы) horde.

о́рден (*pl* -а́) order.

о́рдер (*pl* -а́) order; warrant; writ.

орди́ната ordinate.

ордина́тор house-surgeon.

орёл (орла́) eagle; **~ или ре́шка?** heads or tails?

О

орео́л halo.
оре́х nut, nuts; walnut. **оре́ховый** nut; walnut. **оре́шник** hazel; hazel-thicket.
оригина́л original; eccentric. **оригина́льный** original.
ориента́ция orientation. **ориенти́р** landmark; reference point. **ориенти́роваться** *impf* & *pf* orient o.s.; +**на**+*acc* head for; aim at. **ориентиро́вка** orientation. **ориентиро́вочный** reference; tentative; approximate.
орке́стр orchestra.
орли́ный eagle; aquiline.
орна́мент ornament; ornamental design.
о|робе́ть (-е́ю) *pf*.
ороси́тельный irrigation. **ороси́ть** (-ошу́) *pf*, **ороша́ть** *impf* irrigate. **ороше́ние** irrigation; **поля́ ороше́ния** sewage farm.
ору́ *etc.*: *see* **ора́ть**
ору́дие instrument; tool; gun. **оруди́йный** gun. **ору́довать** *impf* +*instr* handle; run. **оруже́йный** arms; gun. **ору́жие** arm, arms; weapons.
орфографи́ческий orthographic(al). **орфогра́фия** orthography, spelling.
оса́ (*pl* -ы) wasp.
оса́да siege. **осади́ть**[1] (-ажу́) *pf* (*impf* **осажда́ть**) besiege.
осади́ть[2] (-ажу́, -а́дишь) *pf* (*impf* **оса́живать**) check; force back; rein in; take down a peg.
оса́дный siege.
оса́док (-дка) sediment; fall-out; after-taste; *pl* precipitation, fall-out. **оса́дочный** sedimentary.
осажда́ть *impf of* **осади́ть**[1]
оса́живать *impf of* **осади́ть**[2]. **осажу́** *see* **осади́ть**[1,2]
оса́нка carriage, bearing.
осва́ивать(ся *impf of* **осво́ить(ся**
осведоми́тельный informative; information. **осве́домить** (-млю) *pf*, **осведомля́ть** *impf* inform; **~ся о**+*prep* inquire about, ask after. **осведомле́ние** notification. **осведомлённый** well-informed, knowledgeable.
освежа́ть *impf*, **освежи́ть** (-жу́) *pf* refresh; air. **освежи́тельный** refreshing.
освети́тельный illuminating. **освети́ть** (-ещу́) *pf*, **освеща́ть** *pf* light up; illuminate; throw light on; **~ся** light up. **освеще́ние** lighting, illumination. **освещённый** (-ён, -а́) lit.
о|свиде́тельствовать *pf*.
освиста́ть (-ищу́, -и́щешь) *pf*, **осви́стывать** *impf* hiss (off); boo.
освободи́тель *m* liberator. **освободи́тельный** liberation, emancipation. **освободи́ть** (-ожу́) *pf*, **освобожда́ть** *impf* liberate; emancipate; dismiss; vacate; empty; **~ся** free o.s.; become free. **освобожде́ние** liberation; release; emancipation; vacation. **освобождённый** (-ён, -а́) freed, free; exempt.
освое́ние mastery; opening up. **осво́ить** *pf* (*impf* **осва́ивать**) master; become familiar with; **~ся** familiarize o.s.
освящённый (-ён, -ена́) consecrated; sanctified; **~ века́ми** time-honoured.
оседа́ть *impf of* **осе́сть**
о|седла́ть *pf*, **осёдлывать** *impf* saddle.
осе́длый settled.
осека́ться *impf of* **осе́чься**
осёл (-сла́) donkey; ass.
осело́к (-лка́) touchstone; whetstone.
осени́ть *pf* (*impf* **осеня́ть**) overshadow; dawn upon.
осе́нний autumn(al). **о́сень** autumn. **о́сенью** *adv* in autumn.
осеня́ть *impf of* **осени́ть**
осе́сть (ося́ду; осе́л) *pf* (*impf* **оседа́ть**) settle; subside.
осётр (-а́) sturgeon. **осетри́на** sturgeon.
осе́чка misfire. **осе́чься** (-еку́сь, -ечёшься; -ёкся, -екла́сь) *pf* (*impf* **осека́ться**) stop short.

О

оси́ливать *impf*, **оси́лить** *pf* overpower; master.
оси́на aspen.
о|си́пнуть (-ну; оси́п) get hoarse.
осироте́лый orphaned. **осироте́ть** (-е́ю) *pf* be orphaned.
оска́ливать *impf*, **о|ска́лить** *pf*; ~ **зу́бы**, ~**ся** bare one's teeth.
о|сканда́лить(ся *pf*.
оскверни́ть *pf*, **осквернять** *impf* profane; defile.
оско́лок (-лка) splinter; fragment.
оско́мина bitter taste (in the mouth); **наби́ть оско́мину** set the teeth on edge.
оскорби́тельный insulting, abusive. **оскорби́ть** (-блю) *pf*, **оскорбля́ть** *impf* insult; offend; ~**ся** take offence. **оскорбле́ние** insult. **оскорблённый** (-ён, -á) insulted.
ослабева́ть *impf*, **о|слабе́ть** (-е́ю) *pf* weaken; slacken. **осла́бить** (-блю) *pf*, **ослабля́ть** *impf* weaken; slacken. **ослабле́ние** weakening; slackening, relaxation.
ослепи́тельный blinding, dazzling. **ослепи́ть** (-плю) *pf*, **ослепля́ть** *impf* blind, dazzle. **ослепле́ние** blinding, dazzling; blindness. **о|сле́пнуть** (-ну; -е́п) *pf*.
осли́ный donkey; asinine. **осли́ца** she-ass.
осложне́ние complication. **осложни́ть** *pf*, **осложня́ть** *impf* complicate; ~**ся** become complicated.
ослы́шаться (-шусь) *pf* mishear.
осма́тривать(ся *impf of* **осмотре́ть(ся**. **осме́ивать** *impf of* **осмея́ть**
о|смеле́ть (-е́ю) *pf*. **осме́ливаться** *impf*, **осме́литься** *pf* dare; venture.
осмея́ть (-ею́, -еёшь) *pf* (*impf* **осме́ивать**) ridicule.
осмо́тр examination, inspection. **осмотре́ть** (-рю́, -ришь) *pf* (*impf* **осма́тривать**) examine, inspect; look round; ~**ся** look round. **осмотри́тельный** circumspect.
осмы́сленный sensible, intelligent. **осмы́сливать** *impf*, **осмы́слить** *pf*, **осмысля́ть** *impf* interpret; comprehend.
оснасти́ть (-ащу́) *pf*, **оснаща́ть** *impf* fit out, equip. **осна́стка** rigging. **оснаще́ние** fitting out; equipment.
осно́ва base, basis, foundation; *pl* fundamentals; stem (*of a word*). **основа́ние** founding, foundation; base; basis; reason; **на како́м основа́нии?** on what grounds? **основа́тель** *m* founder. **основа́тельный** well-founded; solid; thorough. **основа́ть** (-ну́ю, -нуёшь) *pf*, **осно́вывать** *impf* found; base; ~**ся** settle; be founded, be based. **основно́й** fundamental, basic; main; **в основно́м** in the main, on the whole. **основополо́жник** founder.
осо́ба person. **осо́бенно** *adv* especially. **осо́бенность** peculiarity; **в осо́бенности** in particular. **осо́бенный** special, particular, peculiar. **особня́к** (-á) private residence; detached house. **особняко́м** *adv* by o.s. **осо́бо** *adv* apart; especially. **осо́бый** special; particular.
осознава́ть (-наю́, -наёшь) *impf*, **осозна́ть** *pf* realize.
осо́ка sedge.
о́спа smallpox; pock-marks.
оспа́ривать *impf*, **оспо́рить** *pf* dispute; contest.
о|срами́ть(ся (-млю́(сь) *pf*. **остава́ться** (-таю́сь, -таёшься) *impf of* **оста́ться**
ост (*naut*) east; east wind.
оста́вить (-влю) *pf*, **оставля́ть** *impf* leave; abandon; reserve.
остальн|о́й the rest of; ~**о́е** *sb* the rest; ~**ы́е** *sb pl* the others.
остана́вливать(ся *impf of* **останови́ть(ся**
оста́нки (-ов) *pl* remains.

останови́ть (-влю́, -ви́шь) *pf* (*impf* **остана́вливать**) stop; restrain; **~ся** stop, halt; stay; **+на**+*prep* dwell on; settle on. **остано́вка** stop.

оста́ток (-тка) remainder; rest; residue; *pl* remains; leftovers. **оста́ться** (-а́нусь) *pf* (*impf* **остава́ться**) remain; stay; *impers* it remains, it is necessary; **нам не остаётся ничего́ друго́го, как** we have no choice but.

остекли́ть *pf*, **остекля́ть** *impf* glaze.

остервене́ть *pf* become enraged.

остерега́ть *impf*, **остере́чь** (-регу́, -режёшь; -рёг, -ла́) *pf* warn; **~ся** (+*gen*) beware (of).

о́стов frame, framework; skeleton.

о|столбене́ть (-е́ю) *pf*.

осторо́жно *adv* carefully; **~!** look out! **осторо́жность** care, caution. **осторо́жный** careful, cautious.

остригáть(ся *impf of* **остри́чь(ся**

остриё point; spike; (cutting) edge. **остри́ть**[1] *impf* sharpen. **остри́ть**[2] *impf* (*pf* **с~**) be witty.

о|стри́чь (-игу́, -ижёшь; -и́г) *pf* (*impf also* **остригáть**) cut, clip; **~ся** have one's hair cut.

о́стров (*pl* -а́) island. **острово́к** (-вка́) islet; **~ безопа́сности** (traffic) island.

остро́та[1] witticism, joke. **острота́**[2] sharpness; keenness; pungency.

остроу́мие wit. **остроу́мный** witty.

о́стрый (остр, -а́, -о) sharp; pointed; acute; keen. **остря́к** (-а́) wit.

о|студи́ть (-ужу́, -у́дишь) *pf*, **остужа́ть** *impf* cool.

оступа́ться *impf*, **оступи́ться** (-плю́сь, -пишься) *pf* stumble.

остыва́ть *impf*, **осты́ть** (-ы́ну) *pf* get cold; cool down.

осуди́ть (-ужу́, -у́дишь) *pf*, **осужда́ть** *impf* condemn; convict. **осужде́ние** condemnation; conviction. **осуждённый** (-ён, -а́) condemned, convicted; *sb* convict.

осу́нуться (-нусь) *pf* grow thin, become drawn.

осуша́ть *impf*, **осуши́ть** (-шу́, -шишь) *pf* drain; dry. **осуше́ние** drainage.

осуществи́мый feasible. **осуществи́ть** (-влю́) *pf*, **осуществля́ть** *impf* realize, bring about; accomplish; **~ся** be fulfilled, come true. **осуществле́ние** realization; accomplishment.

осчастли́вить (-влю) *pf*, **осчастли́вливать** *impf* make happy.

осы́пать (-плю) *pf*, **осыпа́ть** *impf* strew; shower; **~ся** crumble; fall. **о́сыпь** scree.

ось (*gen pl* -е́й) axis; axle.

осьмино́г octopus.

ося́ду *etc.*: *see* **осе́сть**

осяза́емый tangible. **осяза́ние** touch. **осяза́тельный** tactile; tangible. **осяза́ть** *impf* feel.

от, ото *prep*+*gen* from; of; against.

ота́пливать *impf of* **отопи́ть**

ота́ра flock (*of sheep*).

отба́вить (-влю) *pf*, **отбавля́ть** *impf* pour off; **хоть отбавля́й** more than enough.

отбега́ть *impf*, **отбежа́ть** (-егу́) *pf* run off.

отберу́ *etc.*: *see* **отобра́ть**

отбива́ть(ся *impf of* **отби́ть(ся**

отбивна́я котле́та cutlet, chop.

отбира́ть *impf of* **отобра́ть**

отби́ть (отобью́, -ёшь) *pf* (*impf* **отбива́ть**) beat (off), repel; win over; break off; **~ся** break off; drop behind; **+от**+*gen* defend o.s. against.

о́тблеск reflection.

отбо́й repelling; retreat; ringing off; **бить ~** beat a retreat; **дать ~** ring off.

отбо́йный молото́к (-тка́) pneumatic drill.

отбо́р selection. **отбо́рный** choice, select(ed).

отбра́сывать *impf*, **отбро́сить**

О

(-óшу) *pf* throw off *or* away; hurl back; reject; ~ **тень** cast a shadow. **отбрóсы** (-ов) *pl* garbage.

отбывáть *impf*, **отбы́ть** (-бу́ду; óтбыл, -á, -о) *pf* depart; serve (*a sentence*).

отвáга courage, bravery.

отвáживаться *impf*, **отвáжиться** (-жусь) *pf* dare. **отвáжный** courageous.

отвáл dump, slag-heap; casting off; **до ~а** to satiety. **отвáливать** *impf*, **отвали́ть** (-лю́, -лишь) *pf* push aside; cast off; fork out.

отвáр broth; decoction. **отвáривать** *impf*, **отвари́ть** (-рю́, -ришь) *pf* boil. **отварнóй** boiled.

отвéдать *pf* (*impf* **отвéдывать**) taste, try.

отведу́ *etc.*: *see* **отвести́**

отвéдывать *impf of* **отвéдать**

отвезти́ (-зу́, -зёшь; -вёз, -лá) *pf* (*impf* **отвози́ть**) take *or* cart away.

О

отвёл *etc.*: *see* **отвести́**

отвергáть *impf*, **отвéргнуть** (-ну; -вéрг) *pf* reject; repudiate.

отвéрженный outcast.

отверну́ть (-ну́, -нёшь) *pf* (*impf* **отвёртывать, отворáчивать**) turn aside; turn down; turn on; unscrew; screw off; **~ся** turn away; come unscrewed.

отвéрстие opening; hole.

отвертéть (-рчу́, -ртишь) *pf* (*impf* **отвёртывать**) unscrew; twist off; **~ся** come unscrewed; get off. **отвёртка** screwdriver.

отвёртывать(ся *impf of* **отверну́ть(ся, отвертéть(ся**

отвéс plumb; vertical slope. **отвéсить** (-éшу) *pf* (*impf* **отвéшивать**) weigh out. **отвéсный** perpendicular, sheer.

отвести́ (-еду́, -едёшь; -вёл, -á) *pf* (*impf* **отводи́ть**) lead, take; draw *or* take aside; deflect; draw off; reject; allot.

отвéт answer.

ответви́ться *pf*, **ответвля́ться** *impf* branch off. **ответвлéние** branch, offshoot.

отвéтить (-éчу) *pf*, **отвечáть** *impf* answer; +**на**+*acc* reply to; +**за**+*acc* answer for. **отвéтный** in reply, return. **отвéтственность** responsibility. **отвéтственный** responsible. **отвéтчик** defendant.

отвéшивать *impf of* **отвéсить**.

отвéшу *etc.*: *see* **отвéсить**

отвинти́ть (-нчу́) *pf*, **отви́нчивать** *impf* unscrew.

отвисáть *impf*, **отви́снуть** (-нет; -и́с) *pf* hang down, sag. **отви́слый** hanging, baggy.

отвлекáть *impf*, **отвлéчь** (-еку́, -ечёшь; -влёк, -лá) *pf* distract, divert; **~ся** be distracted. **отвлечённый** abstract.

отвóд taking aside; diversion; leading, taking; rejection; allotment. **отводи́ть** (-ожу́, -óдишь) *impf of* **отвести́**.

отвоевáть (-ою́ю) *pf*, **отвоёвывать** *impf* win back; spend in fighting.

отвози́ть (-ожу́, -óзишь) *impf of* **отвезти́**. **отворáчивать(ся** *impf of* **отверну́ть(ся**

отвори́ть (-рю́, -ришь) *pf* (*impf* **отворя́ть**) open; **~ся** open.

отворя́ть(ся *impf of* **отвори́ть(ся**.

отвою́ю *etc.*: *see* **отвоевáть**

отврати́тельный disgusting. **отвращéние** disgust, repugnance.

отвыкáть *impf*, **отвы́кнуть** (-ну; -вы́к) *pf* +**от** *or inf* lose the habit of; grow out of.

отвязáть (-яжу́, -я́жешь) *pf*, **отвя́зывать** *impf* untie, unfasten; **~ся** come untied, come loose; +**от**+*gen* get rid of; leave alone.

отгадáть *pf*, **отгáдывать** *impf* guess. **отгáдка** answer.

отгибáть(ся *impf of* **отогну́ть(ся**

отглáдить (-áжу) *pf*, **отглáживать** *impf* iron (out).

отговáривать *impf*, **отговори́ть** *pf* dissuade; **~ся** +*instr* plead. **отговóрка** excuse, pretext.

отголóсок (-ска) echo.

отгоня́ть *impf of* **отогнáть**

отгора́живать *impf*, **отгороди́ть** (-ожу́, -о́дишь) *pf* fence off; partition off; **~ся** shut o.s. off.

отдава́ть¹(ся (-даю́(сь) *impf of* **отда́ть(ся. отдава́ть²** (-аёт) *impf impers+instr* taste of; smell of; smack of; **от него́ отдаёт во́дкой** he reeks of vodka.

отдале́ние removal; distance. **отдалённый** remote. **отдали́ть** *pf*, **отдаля́ть** *impf* remove; estrange; postpone; **~ся** move away; digress.

отда́ть (-а́м, -а́шь, -а́ст, -ади́м; о́тдал, -а́, -о) *pf* (*impf* **отдава́ть¹**) give back, return; give; give up; give away; recoil; cast off; **~ся** give o.s. (up); resound. **отда́ча** return; payment; casting off; efficiency; output; recoil.

отде́л department; section.

отде́лать *pf* (*impf* **отде́лывать**) finish, put the finishing touches to; trim; **~ся** +**от**+*gen* get rid of; +*instr* get off with.

отделе́ние separation; department; compartment; section. **отдели́ть** (-елю́, -е́лишь) *pf* (*impf* **отделя́ть**) separate; detach; **~ся** separate; detach o.s.; get detached.

отде́лка finishing; finish, decoration. **отде́лывать(ся** *impf of* **отде́лать(ся**

отде́льно separately; apart. **отде́льный** separate. **отделя́ть(ся** *impf of* **отдели́ть(ся**

отдёргивать *impf*, **отдёрнуть** (-ну) *pf* draw *or* pull aside *or* back.

отдеру́ *etc.*: *see* **отодра́ть. отдира́ть** *impf of* **отодра́ть**

отдохну́ть (-ну́, -нёшь) *pf* (*impf* **отдыха́ть**) rest.

отду́шина air-hole, vent.

о́тдых rest. **отдыха́ть** *impf* (*pf* **отдохну́ть**) rest; be on holiday.

отдыша́ться (-шу́сь, -шишься) *pf* recover one's breath.

отека́ть *impf of* **оте́чь. о|тели́ться** (-е́лится) *pf*.

оте́ль *m* hotel.

отеса́ть *etc.*: *see* **обтеса́ть**

оте́ц (отца́) father. **оте́ческий** fatherly, paternal. **оте́чественный** home, native. **оте́чество** native land, fatherland.

оте́чь (-еку́, -ечёшь; отёк, -ла́) *pf* (*impf* **отека́ть**) swell (up).

отжива́ть *impf*, **отжи́ть** (-иву́, -ивёшь; о́тжил, -а́, -о) *pf* become obsolete *or* outmoded. **отжи́вший** obsolete; outmoded.

о́тзвук echo.

о́тзыв¹ opinion; reference; review; response. **отзы́в²** recall. **отзыва́ть(ся** *impf of* **отозва́ть(ся. отзы́вчивый** responsive.

отка́з refusal; repudiation; failure; natural. **отказа́ть** (-ажу́, -а́жешь) *pf*, **отка́зывать** *impf* break down; (+*dat* **в**+*prep*) refuse, deny (*s.o. sth*); **~ся** (+**от**+*gen or* +*inf*) refuse; turn down; renounce, give up.

отка́лывать(ся *impf of* **отколо́ть(ся. отка́пывать** *impf of* **откопа́ть. отка́рмливать** *impf of* **откорми́ть**

откати́ть (-ачу́, -а́тишь) *pf*, **отка́тывать** *impf* roll away; **~ся** roll away *or* back; be forced back.

откача́ть *pf*, **отка́чивать** *impf* pump out; give artificial respiration to.

отка́шливаться *impf*, **отка́шляться** *pf* clear one's throat.

откидно́й folding, collapsible. **отки́дывать** *impf*, **отки́нуть** (-ну) *pf* fold back; throw aside.

откла́дывать *impf of* **отложи́ть**

откле́ивать *impf*, **откле́ить** (-е́ю) *pf* unstick; **~ся** come unstuck.

о́тклик response; comment; echo. **отклика́ться** *impf*, **откли́кнуться** (-нусь) *pf* answer, respond.

отклоне́ние deviation; declining, refusal; deflection. **отклони́ть** (-ню́, -нишь) *pf*, **отклоня́ть** *impf* deflect; decline; **~ся** deviate; diverge.

О

отключа́ть *impf*, **отключи́ть** (-чу́) *pf* cut off, disconnect.
отколоти́ть (-очу́, -о́тишь) *pf* knock off; beat up.
отколо́ть (-лю́, -лешь) *pf* (*impf* **отка́лывать**) break off; chop off; unpin; **~ся** break off; come unpinned; break away.
откопа́ть *pf* (*impf* **отка́пывать**) dig up; exhume.
откорми́ть (-млю́, -мишь) *pf* (*impf* **отка́рмливать**) fatten.
отко́с slope.
открепи́ть (-плю́) *pf*, **открепля́ть** *impf* unfasten; **~ся** become unfastened.
открове́ние revelation. **открове́нный** frank; outspoken; unconcealed. **откро́ю** *etc.*: *see* **откры́ть**
открути́ть (-учу́, -у́тишь) *pf*, **откру́чивать** *impf* untwist, unscrew.
открыва́ть *impf*, **откры́ть** (-ро́ю) *pf* open; reveal; discover; turn on; **~ся** open; come to light, be revealed. **откры́тие** discovery; revelation; opening. **откры́тка** postcard, card. **откры́то** openly. **откры́тый** open.
отку́да *adv* from where; from which; how; **~ ни возьми́сь** from out of nowhere. **отку́да-либо, -нибудь** from somewhere or other. **отку́да-то** from somewhere.
отку́поривать *impf*, **отку́порить** *pf* uncork.
откуси́ть (-ушу́, -у́сишь) *pf*, **отку́сывать** *impf* bite off.
отлага́тельство delay. **отлага́ть** *impf of* **отложи́ть**
от|лакирова́ть *pf*. **отла́мывать** *impf of* **отлома́ть, отломи́ть**
отлепи́ть (-плю́, -пишь) *pf* unstick, take off; **~ся** come unstuck, come off.
отлёт flying away; departure. **отлета́ть** *impf*, **отлете́ть** (-лечу́) *pf*, fly, fly away, fly off; rebound.
отли́в ebb, ebb-tide; tint; play of colours. **отлива́ть** *impf*, **отли́ть** (отолью́; о́тлил, -а́, -о) *pf* pour off; pump out; cast, found; (*no pf*) +*instr* be shot with. **отли́вка** casting; moulding.
отлича́ть *impf*, **отличи́ть** (-чу́) *pf* distinguish; **~ся** distinguish o.s.; differ; +*instr* be notable for. **отли́чие** difference; distinction; **знак отли́чия** order, decoration; **с отли́чием** with honours. **отли́чник** outstanding student, worker, etc. **отличи́тельный** distinctive; distinguishing. **отли́чный** different; excellent.
отло́гий sloping.
отложе́ние sediment; deposit. **отложи́ть** (-ожу́, -о́жишь) *pf* (*impf* **откла́дывать, отлага́ть**) put aside; postpone; deposit.
отлома́ть, отломи́ть (-млю́, -мишь) *pf* (*impf* **отла́мывать**) break off.
от|лупи́ть *pf*.
отлуча́ть *impf*, **отлучи́ть** (-чу́) *pf* (**от це́ркви**) excommunicate; **~ся** absent o.s. **отлу́чка** absence.
отлы́нивать *impf* +**от**+*gen* shirk.
отма́хиваться *impf*, **отмахну́ться** (-ну́сь, -нёшься) *pf* **от**+*gen* brush off; brush aside.
отмежева́ться (-жу́юсь) *pf*, **отмежёвываться** *impf* **от**+*gen* dissociate o.s. from.
о́тмель (sand-)bank.
отме́на abolition; cancellation. **отмени́ть** (-ню́, -нишь) *pf*, **отменя́ть** *impf* repeal; abolish; cancel.
отмере́ть (отомрёт; о́тмер, -ла́, -ло) *pf* (*impf* **отмира́ть**) die off; die out.
отме́ривать *impf*, **отме́рить** *pf*, **отмеря́ть** *impf* measure off.
отмести́ (-ету́, -етёшь; -ёл, -а́) *pf* (*impf* **отмета́ть**) sweep aside.
отмета́ть *impf of* **отмести́**
отме́тить (-е́чу) *pf*, **отмеча́ть** *impf* mark, note; celebrate; **~ся** sign one's name; sign out. **отме́тка** note; mark.
отмира́ть *impf of* **отмере́ть**
отмора́живать *impf*, **отморо́-**

О

зить (-о́жу) *pf* injure by frost-bite. **отморо́жение** frost-bite. **отморо́женный** frost-bitten.

отмо́ю *etc.*: *see* **отмы́ть**

отмыва́ть *impf*, **отмы́ть** (-мо́ю) *pf* wash clean; wash off; **~ся** wash o.s. clean; come out.

отмыка́ть *impf of* **отомкну́ть**

отмы́чка master key.

отнести́ (-су́, -сёшь; -нёс, -ла́) *pf* (*impf* **относи́ть**) take; carry away; ascribe, attribute; **~сь к**+*dat* treat; regard; apply to; concern, have to do with.

отнима́ть(ся *impf of* **отня́ть(ся**

относи́тельно *adv* relatively; *prep*+*gen* concerning. **относи́тельность** relativity. **относи́тельный** relative. **относи́ть(ся** (-ошу́(сь, -о́сишь(ся) *impf of* **отнести́(сь. отноше́ние** attitude; relation; respect; ratio; **в отноше́нии** +*gen*, **по отноше́нию к**+*dat* with regard to; **в прямо́м (обра́тном) отноше́нии** in direct (inverse) ratio.

отны́не *adv* henceforth.

отню́дь not at all.

отня́тие taking away; amputation. **отня́ть** (-ниму́, -ни́мешь; о́тнял, -а́, -о) *pf* (*impf* **отнима́ть**) take (away); amputate; **~ от груди́** wean; **~ся** be paralysed.

ото: *see* **от**

отобража́ть *impf*, **отобрази́ть** (-ажу́) *pf* reflect; represent. **отображе́ние** reflection; representation.

отобра́ть (отберу́, -рёшь; отобра́л, -а́, -о) *pf* (*impf* **отбира́ть**) take (away); select.

отобью́ *etc.*: *see* **отби́ть**

отовсю́ду *adv* from everywhere.

отогна́ть (отгоню́, -о́нишь; отогна́л, -а́, -о) *pf* (*impf* **отгоня́ть**) drive away, off.

отогну́ть (-ну́, -нёшь) *pf* (*impf* **отгиба́ть**) bend back; **~ся** bend.

отогрева́ть *impf*, **отогре́ть** (-е́ю) *pf* warm.

отодвига́ть *impf*, **отодви́нуть** (-ну) *pf* move aside; put off.

отодра́ть (отдеру́, -рёшь; отодра́л, -а́, -о) *pf* (*impf* **отдира́ть**) tear off, rip off.

отож(д)естви́ть (-влю́) *pf*, **отож(д)ествля́ть** *impf* identify.

отозва́ть (отзову́, -вёшь; отозва́л, -а́, -о)*pf* (*impf* **отзыва́ть**) take aside; recall; **~ся на**+*acc* answer; **на**+*acc or prep* tell on; have an effect on.

отойти́ (-йду́, -йдёшь; отошёл, -шла́) *pf* (*impf* **отходи́ть**) move away; depart; withdraw; digress; come out; recover.

отолью́ *etc.*: *see* **отли́ть. отомрёт** *etc.*: *see* **отмере́ть. ото|мсти́ть** (-мщу́) *pf.*

отомкну́ть (-ну́, -нёшь) *pf* (*impf* **отмыка́ть**) unlock, unbolt.

отопи́тельный heating. **отопи́ть** (-плю́, -пишь) *pf* (*impf* **ота́пливать**) heat. **отопле́ние** heating.

отопру́ *etc.*: *see* **отпере́ть. отопью́** *etc.*: *see* **отпи́ть**

ото́рванный cut off, isolated. **оторва́ть** (-ву́, -вёшь) *pf* (*impf* **отрыва́ть**) tear off; tear away; **~ся** come off, be torn off; be cut off, lose touch; break away; tear o.s. away; **~ся от земли́** take off.

оторопе́ть (-е́ю) *pf* be struck dumb.

отосла́ть (-ошлю́, -ошлёшь) *pf* (*impf* **отсыла́ть**) send (off); send back; +**к**+*dat* refer to.

отоспа́ться (-сплю́сь; -а́лся, -ала́сь, -ось) *pf* (*impf* **отсыпа́ться**) catch up on one's sleep.

отошёл *etc.*: *see* **отойти́. отошлю́** *etc.*: *see* **отосла́ть**

отпада́ть *impf of* **отпа́сть.**

от|пари́ровать *pf.* **отпа́рывать** *impf of* **отпоро́ть**

отпа́сть (-адёт) *pf* (*impf* **отпада́ть**) fall off; fall away; pass.

отпева́ние funeral service.

отпере́ть (отопру́, -прёшь; о́тпер, -ла́, -ло) *pf* (*impf* **отпира́ть**) unlock; **~ся** open; +**от**+*gen* deny; disown.

от|печа́тать *pf*, **отпеча́тывать** *impf* print (off); type (out); imprint. **отпеча́ток** (-тка) imprint, print.

отпива́ть *impf of* **отпи́ть**

отпи́ливать *impf*, **отпили́ть** (-лю́, -лишь) *pf* saw off.

от|пира́тельство denial. **отпира́ть(ся** *impf of* **отпере́ть(ся**

отпи́ть (отопью́, -пьёшь; о́тпи́л, -а́, -о) *pf* (*impf* **отпива́ть**) take a sip of.

отпи́хивать *impf*, **отпихну́ть** (-ну́, -нёшь) *pf* push off; shove aside.

отплати́ть (-ачу́, -а́тишь) *pf*, **отпла́чивать** *impf* +*dat* pay back.

отплыва́ть *impf*, **отплы́ть** (-ыву́, -ывёшь; -ы́л, -а́, -о) *pf* (set) sail; swim off. **отплы́тие** sailing, departure.

о́тповедь rebuke.

отполза́ть *impf*, **отползти́** (-зу́, -зёшь; -о́лз, -ла́) *pf* crawl away.

О **от|полирова́ть** *pf*. **от|полоска́ть** (-ощу́) *pf*.

отпо́р repulse; rebuff.

отноро́ть (-рю́, -решь) *pf* (*impf* **отпа́рывать**) rip off.

отправи́тель *m* sender. **отпра́вить** (-влю) *pf*, **отправля́ть** *impf* send, dispatch; **~ся** set off, start. **отпра́вка** dispatch. **отправле́ние** sending; departure; performance. **отправн|о́й**: **~о́й пункт**, **~а́я то́чка** starting-point.

от|пра́здновать *pf*.

отпра́шиваться *impf*, **отпроси́ться** (-ошу́сь, -о́сишься) *pf* ask for leave, get leave.

отпры́гивать *impf*, **отпры́гнуть** (-ну) *pf* jump *or* spring back *or* aside.

о́тпрыск offshoot, scion.

отпряга́ть *impf of* **отпря́чь**

отпря́нуть (-ну) *pf* recoil, start back.

отпря́чь (-ягу́, -яжёшь; -я́г, -ла́) *pf* (*impf* **отпряга́ть**) unharness.

отпу́гивать *impf*, **отпугну́ть** (-ну́, -нёшь) *pf* frighten off.

о́тпуск (*pl* -а́) leave, holiday(s). **отпуска́ть** *impf*, **отпусти́ть** (-ущу́, -у́стишь) *pf* let go, let off; set free; release; slacken; (let) grow; allot; remit. **отпускни́к** (-а́) person on leave. **отпускно́й** holiday; leave. **отпуще́ние** remission; **козёл отпуще́ния** scapegoat.

отраба́тывать *impf*, **отрабо́тать** *pf* work off; master. **отрабо́танный** worked out; waste, spent, exhaust.

отра́ва poison. **отрави́ть** (-влю́, -вишь) *pf*, **отравля́ть** *impf* poison.

отра́да joy, delight. **отра́дный** gratifying, pleasing.

отража́тель *m* reflector; scanner. **отража́ть** *impf*, **отрази́ть** (-ажу́) *pf* reflect; repulse; **~ся** be reflected; +**на**+*prep* affect. **отраже́ние** reflection; repulse.

о́трасль branch.

отраста́ть *impf*, **отрасти́** (-тёт; отро́с, -ла́) *pf* grow. **отрасти́ть** (-ащу́) *pf*, **отра́щивать** *impf* (let) grow.

от|реаги́ровать *pf*. **от|регули́ровать** *pf*. **от|редакти́ровать** *pf*.

отре́з cut; length. **отре́зать** (-е́жу) *pf*, **отреза́ть** *impf* cut off; snap.

о|трезве́ть (-е́ю) *pf*. **отрезви́ть** (-влю́, -ви́шь) *pf*, **отрезвля́ть** *impf* sober; **~ся** sober up.

отре́зок (-зка) piece; section; segment.

отрека́ться *impf of* **отре́чься**

от|рекомендова́ть(ся *pf*.

отрёкся *etc*.: *see* **отре́чься**. **от|ремонти́ровать** *pf*. **от|репети́ровать** *pf*.

отре́пье, отре́пья (-ьев) *pl* rags.

от|реставри́ровать *pf*.

отрече́ние renunciation; **~ от престо́ла** abdication. **отре́чься** (-еку́сь, -ечёшься) *pf* (*impf* **отрека́ться**) renounce.

отреша́ться *impf*, **отреши́ться** (-шу́сь) *pf* renounce; get rid of.

отрица́ние denial; negation. **отрица́тельный** negative. **отрица́ть** *impf* deny.

отро́с *etc.*: *see* **отрасти́. отро́сток** (-тка) shoot, sprout; appendix.
о́трочество adolescence.
отруба́ть *impf of* **отруби́ть**
о́труби (-ей) *pl* bran.
отруби́ть (-блю́, -бишь) *pf* (*impf* **отруба́ть**) chop off; snap back.
от|руга́ть *pf.*
отры́в tearing off; alienation, isolation; **в ~е от**+*gen* out of touch with; **~ (от земли́)** take-off. **отрыва́ть(ся** *impf of* **оторва́ть(ся. отры́вистый** staccato; disjointed. **отрывно́й** tear-off. **отры́вок** (-вка) fragment, excerpt. **отры́вочный** fragmentary, scrappy.
отры́жка belch; throw-back.
от|ры́ть (-ро́ю) *pf.*
отря́д detachment; order.
отря́хивать *impf*, **отряхну́ть** (-ну́, -нёшь) *pf* shake down *or* off.
от|салютова́ть *pf.*
отса́сывание suction. **отса́сывать** *impf of* **отсоса́ть**
отсве́чивать *impf* be reflected; +*instr* shine with.
отсе́в sifting, selection; dropping out. **отсева́ть(ся, отсе́ивать(ся** *impf of* **отсе́ять(ся**
отсе́к compartment. **отсека́ть** *impf*, **отсе́чь** (-еку́, -ечёшь; -сёк, -ла́) *pf* chop off.
отсе́ять (-е́ю) *pf* (*impf* **отсева́ть, отсе́ивать**) sift, screen; eliminate; **~ся** drop out.
отсиде́ть (-ижу́) *pf*, **отси́живать** *impf* make numb by sitting; sit through; serve out.
отска́кивать *impf*, **отскочи́ть** (-чу́, -чишь) *pf* jump aside *or* away; rebound; come off.
отслу́живать *impf*, **отслужи́ть** (-жу́, -жишь) *pf* serve one's time; be worn out.
отсоса́ть (-осу́, -осёшь) *pf* (*impf* **отса́сывать**) suck off, draw off.
отсо́хнуть (-ну́) *pf* (*impf* **отсыха́ть**) wither.
отсро́чивать *impf*, **отсро́чить** *pf* postpone, defer. **отсро́чка** postponement, deferment.
отстава́ние lag; lagging behind. **отстава́ть** (-таю́, -аёшь) *impf of* **отста́ть**
отста́вить (-влю) *pf*, **отставля́ть** *impf* set *or* put aside. **отста́вка** resignation; retirement; **в отста́вке** retired; **вы́йти в отста́вку** resign, retire. **отставно́й** retired.
отста́ивать(ся *impf of* **отстоя́ть(ся**
отста́лость backwardness. **отста́лый** backward. **отста́ть** (-а́ну) *pf* (*impf* **отстава́ть**) fall behind; lag behind; become detached; lose touch; break (off); be slow. **отстаю́щий** *sb* backward pupil.
от|стега́ть *pf.*
отстёгивать *impf*, **отстегну́ть** (-ну́, -нёшь) *pf* unfasten, undo; **~ся** come unfastened *or* undone.
отстоя́ть[1] (-ою́) *pf* (*impf* **отста́ивать**) defend; stand up for. **отстоя́ть**[2] (-ои́т) *impf* **на**+*acc* be … distant (**от**+*gen* from). **отстоя́ться** *pf* (*impf* **отста́иваться**) settle; become stabilized.
отстра́ивать(ся *impf of* **отстро́ить(ся**
отстране́ние pushing aside; dismissal. **отстрани́ть** *pf*, **отстраня́ть** *impf* push aside; remove; suspend; **~ся** move away; keep aloof; **~ся от** dodge.
отстре́ливаться *impf*, **отстреля́ться** *pf* fire back.
отстрига́ть *impf*, **отстри́чь** (-игу́, -ижёшь; -ри́г) *pf* cut off.
отстро́ить *pf* (*impf* **отстра́ивать**) finish building; build up.
отступа́ть *impf*, **отступи́ть** (-плю́, -пишь) *pf* step back; recede; retreat; back down; **~ от**+*gen* give up; deviate from; **~ся от**+*gen* give up; go back on. **отступле́ние** retreat; deviation; digression. **отступн|о́й: ~ы́е де́ньги, ~о́е** *sb* indemnity, compensation. **отступя́** *adv* (farther) off, away (**от**+*gen* from).
отсу́тствие absence; lack. **отсу́тствовать** *impf* be absent. **отсу́т-**

О

ствующий absent; *sb* absentee.
отсчита́ть *pf*, **отсчи́тывать** *impf* count off.
отсыла́ть *impf of* **отосла́ть**
отсы́пать (-плю) *pf*, **отсыпа́ть** *impf* pour out; measure off.
отсыпа́ться *impf of* **отоспа́ться**
отсыре́лый damp. **от|сыре́ть** (-е́ет) *pf*.
отсыха́ть *impf of* **отсо́хнуть**
отсю́да *adv* from here; hence.
отта́ивать *impf of* **оттая́ть**
отта́лкивать *impf of* **оттолкну́ть. отта́лкивающий** repulsive, repellent.
отта́чивать *impf of* **отточи́ть**
отта́ять (-а́ю) *pf* (*impf* **отта́ивать**) thaw out.
отте́нок (-нка) shade, nuance; tint.
о́ттепель thaw.
оттесни́ть *pf*, **оттесня́ть** *impf* drive back; push aside.
о́ттиск impression; off-print, reprint.
О **оттого́** *adv* that is why; **~, что** because.
оттолкну́ть (-ну́, -нёшь) *pf* (*impf* **отта́лкивать**) push away; antagonize; **~ся** push off.
оттопы́ренный protruding. **оттопы́ривать** *impf*, **оттопы́рить** *pf* stick out; **~ся** protrude; bulge.
отточи́ть (-чу́, -чишь) *pf* (*impf* **отта́чивать**) sharpen.
отту́да *adv* from there.
оття́гивать *impf*, **оттяну́ть** (-ну́, -нешь) *pf* draw out; draw off; delay. **оття́жка** delay.
отупе́ние stupefaction. **о|тупе́ть** (-е́ю) *pf* sink into torpor.
от|утю́жить (-жу) *pf*.
отуча́ть *impf*, **отучи́ть** (-чу́, -чишь) *pf* break (of); **~ся** break o.s. (of).
отха́ркать *pf*, **отха́ркивать** *impf* expectorate.
отхвати́ть (-чу́, -тишь) *pf*, **отхва́тывать** *impf* snip *or* chop off.
отхлебну́ть (-ну́, -нёшь) *pf*, **отхлёбывать** *impf* sip, take a sip of.
отхлы́нуть (-нет) *pf* flood *or* rush back.
отхо́д departure; withdrawal. **отходи́ть** (-ожу́, -о́дишь) *impf of* **отойти́. отхо́ды** (-ов) *pl* waste.
отцвести́ (-ету́, -етёшь; -ёл, -а́) *pf*, **отцвета́ть** *impf* finish blossoming, fade.
отцепи́ть (-плю́, -пишь) *pf*, **отцепля́ть** *impf* unhook; uncouple.
отцо́вский father's; paternal.
отча́иваться *impf of* **отча́яться**
отча́ливать *impf*, **отча́лить** *pf* cast off.
отча́сти *adv* partly.
отча́яние despair. **отча́янный** desperate. **отча́яться** (-а́юсь) *pf* (*impf* **отча́иваться**) despair.
отчего́ *adv* why. **отчего́-либо, -нибудь** *adv* for some reason or other. **отчего́-то** *adv* for some reason.
от|чека́нить *pf*.
о́тчество patronymic.
отчёт account; **отда́ть себе́ ~ в**+*prep* be aware of, realize. **отчётливый** distinct; clear. **отчётность** book-keeping; accounts. **отчётный** *adj*: **~ год** financial year, current year; **~ докла́д** report.
отчи́зна native land. **о́тчий** paternal. **о́тчим** step-father.
отчисле́ние deduction; dismissal. **отчи́слить** *pf*, **отчисля́ть** *impf* deduct; dismiss.
отчита́ть *pf*, **отчи́тывать** *impf* tell off; **~ся** report back.
отчужде́ние alienation; estrangement.
отшатну́ться (-ну́сь, -нёшься) *pf*, **отша́тываться** *impf* start back, recoil; **+от**+*gen* give up, forsake.
отшвы́ривать *impf*, **отшвырну́ть** (-ну́, -нёшь) *pf* fling away; throw off.
отше́льник hermit; recluse.
отшлёпать *pf* spank.
от|шлифова́ть *pf*. **от|штукату́рить** *pf*.
отщепе́нец (-нца) renegade.
отъе́зд departure. **отъезжа́ть** *impf*, **отъе́хать** (-е́ду) *pf* drive off, go off.

отъя́вленный inveterate.
отыгра́ть *pf*, **оты́грывать** *impf* win back; **~ся** win back what one has lost.
отыска́ть (-ыщу́, -ы́щешь) *pf*, **оты́скивать** *impf* find; look for; **~ся** turn up, appear.
отяготи́ть (-ощу́) *pf*, **отягоща́ть** *impf* burden.
офице́р officer. **офице́рский** officer's, officers'.
официа́льный official.
официа́нт waiter. **официа́нтка** waitress.
официо́з semi-official organ. **официо́зный** semi-official.
оформи́тель *m* designer; stage-painter. **офо́рмить** (-млю) *pf*, **оформля́ть** *impf* design; put into shape; make official; process; **~ся** take shape; go through the formalities. **оформле́ние** design; mounting, staging; processing.
ох *int* oh! ah!
оха́пка armful.
о|характеризова́ть *pf*.
о́хать *impf* (*pf* **о́хнуть**) moan; sigh.
охва́т scope; inclusion; outflanking. **охвати́ть** (-ачу́, -а́тишь) *pf*, **охва́тывать** *impf* envelop; seize; comprehend.
охладева́ть *impf*, **охладе́ть** (-е́ю) *pf* grow cold. **охлади́ть** (-ажу́) *pf*, **охлажда́ть** *impf* cool; **~ся** become cool, cool down. **охлажде́ние** cooling; coolness.
о|хмеле́ть (-е́ю) *pf*. **о́хнуть** (-ну) *pf of* **о́хать**
охо́та[1] hunt, hunting; chase.
охо́та[2] wish, desire.
охо́титься (-о́чусь) *impf* hunt. **охо́тник**[1] hunter.
охо́тник[2] volunteer; enthusiast.
охо́тничий hunting.
охо́тно *adv* willingly, gladly.
о́хра ochre.
охра́на guarding; protection; guard. **охрани́ть** *pf*, **охраня́ть** *impf* guard, protect.
охри́плый, охри́пший hoarse.
о|хри́пнуть (-ну; охри́п) *pf* become hoarse.
о|цара́пать(ся *pf*.
оце́нивать *impf*, **оцени́ть** (-ню́, -нишь) *pf* estimate; appraise. **оце́нка** estimation; appraisal; estimate. **оце́нщик** valuer.
о|цепене́ть (-е́ю) *pf*.
оцепи́ть (-плю́, -пишь) *pf*, **оцепля́ть** *impf* surround; cordon off.
оча́г (-а́) hearth; centre; breeding ground; hotbed.
очарова́ние charm, fascination. **очарова́тельный** charming. **очарова́ть** *pf*, **очаро́вывать** *impf* charm, fascinate.
очеви́дец (-дца) eye-witness. **очеви́дно** *adv* obviously, evidently. **очеви́дный** obvious.
о́чень *adv* very; very much.
очередно́й next in turn; usual, regular; routine. **о́чередь** (*gen pl* -е́й) turn; queue.
о́черк essay, sketch.
о|черни́ть *pf*.
о|черстве́ть (-е́ю) *pf*.
очерта́ние outline(s), contour(s). **очерти́ть** (-рчу́, -ртишь) *pf*, **оче́рчивать** *impf* outline.
о́чи *etc.*: *see* **о́ко**
очисти́тельный cleansing. **о|чи́стить** (-и́щу) *pf*, **очища́ть** *impf* clean; refine; clear; peel; **~ся** clear o.s.; become clear (**от**+*gen* of). **очи́стка** cleaning; purification; clearance. **очи́стки** (-ов) *pl* peelings. **очище́ние** cleansing; purification.
очки́ (-о́в) *pl* spectacles. **очко́** (*gen pl* -о́в) pip; point. **очко́вая змея́** cobra.
очну́ться (-ну́сь, -нёшься) *pf* wake up; regain consciousness.
о́чн|ый: ~ое обуче́ние classroom instruction; **~ая ста́вка** confrontation.
очути́ться (-у́тишься) *pf* find o.s.
оше́йник collar.
ошеломи́тельный stunning. **ошеломи́ть** (-млю́) *pf*, **ошеломля́ть** *impf* stun.

ошиба́ться *impf*, **ошиби́ться** (-бу́сь, -бёшься; -и́бся) *pf* be mistaken, make a mistake; be wrong. **оши́бка** mistake; error. **оши́бочный** erroneous.
ошпа́ривать *impf*, **о|шпа́рить** *pf* scald.
о|штрафова́ть *pf*. **о|штукату́рить** *pf*.
ощети́ниваться *impf*, **о|щети́ниться** *pf* bristle (up).
о|щипа́ть (-плю́, -плешь) *pf*, **ощи́пывать** *impf* pluck.
ощу́пать *pf*, **ощу́пывать** *impf* feel; grope about. **о́щупь: на ~** to the touch; by touch. **о́щупью** *adv* gropingly; by touch.
ощути́мый, ощути́тельный perceptible; appreciable. **ощути́ть** (-ущу́) *pf*, **ощуща́ть** *impf* feel, sense. **ощуще́ние** sensation; feeling.

О

П

П

па *neut indecl* dance step.
павильо́н pavilion; film studio.
павли́н peacock.
па́водок (-дка) (sudden) flood.
па́вший fallen.
па́губный pernicious, ruinous.
па́даль carrion.
па́дать *impf* (*pf* **пасть, упа́сть**) fall; **~ ду́хом** lose heart. **паде́ж** (-а́) case. **паде́ние** fall; degradation; incidence. **па́дкий на**+*acc* *or* **до**+*gen* having a weakness for.
па́дчерица step-daughter.
паёк (пайка́) ration.
па́зуха bosom; sinus; axil.
пай (*pl* -и́, -ёв) share. **па́йщик** shareholder.
паке́т package; packet; paper bag.
Пакиста́н Pakistan. **пакиста́нец** (-нца), **-а́нка** Pakistani. **пакиста́нский** Pakistani.
па́кля tow; oakum.
пакова́ть *impf* (*pf* **за~, у~**) pack.
па́костный dirty, mean. **па́кость** dirty trick; obscenity.
пакт pact.
пала́та chamber, house. **пала́тка** tent; stall, booth.
пала́ч (-а́) executioner.
па́лец (-льца) finger; toe.
палиса́дник (*small*) front garden.
палиса́ндр rosewood.
пали́тра palette.
пали́ть¹ *impf* (*pf* **о~, с~**) burn; scorch.
пали́ть² *impf* (*pf* **вы~, пальну́ть**) fire, shoot.
па́лка stick; walking-stick.
пало́мник pilgrim. **пало́мничество** pilgrimage.
па́лочка stick; bacillus; wand; baton.
па́луба deck.
пальба́ fire.
па́льма palm(-tree). **па́льмовый** palm.
пальну́ть (-ну́, -нёшь) *pf of* **пали́ть**
пальто́ *neut indecl* (over)coat.
паля́щий burning, scorching.
па́мятник monument; memorial. **па́мятный** memorable; memorial. **па́мять** memory; consciousness; **на ~** as a keepsake.
панаце́я panacea.
пане́ль footpath; panel(ling), wainscot(ing). **пане́льный** panelling.
па́ника panic. **паникёр** alarmist.
панихи́да requiem.
пани́ческий panic; panicky.
панно́ *neut indecl* panel.
панора́ма panorama.
пансио́н boarding-house; board and lodging. **пансиона́т** holiday hotel. **пансионе́р** boarder; guest.
панталo´ны (-о́н) *pl* knickers.
панте́ра panther.
пантоми́ма mime.
па́нцирь *m* armour, coat of mail.
па́па¹ *m* pope.
па́па² *m*, **папа́ша** *m* daddy.
папа́ха tall fur cap.
папиро́са (*Russian*) cigarette.
па́пка file; folder.
па́поротник fern.

пар¹ (*loc* -ý; *pl* -ы́) steam.
пар² (*loc* -ý; *pl* -ы́) fallow.
па́ра pair; couple; (two-piece) suit.
пара́граф paragraph.
пара́д parade; review. **пара́дн|ый** parade; gala; main, front; **~ая фо́рма** full dress (uniform).
парадо́кс paradox. **парадокса́льный** paradoxical.
парази́т parasite.
парализова́ть *impf* & *pf* paralyse. **парали́ч** (-á) paralysis.
паралле́ль parallel. **паралле́льный** parallel.
пара́метр parameter.
парано́йя paranoia.
парашю́т parachute.
паре́ние soaring.
па́рень (-рня; *gen pl* -рне́й) *m* lad; fellow.
пари́ *neut indecl* bet; **держа́ть ~** bet, lay a bet.
пари́к (-á) wig. **парикма́хер** hairdresser. **парикма́херская** *sb* hairdresser's.
пари́ровать *impf* & *pf* (*pf also* **от~**) parry, counter.
парите́т parity.
пари́ть¹ *impf* soar, hover.
па́рить² *impf* steam; stew; *impers* **па́рит** it is sultry; **~ся** (*pf* **по~ся**) steam, sweat; stew.
парк park; depot; stock.
парке́т parquet.
парла́мент parliament. **парламента́рный** parliamentarian. **парламентёр** envoy; bearer of flag of truce. **парла́ментский** parliamentary; **~ зако́н** Act of Parliament.
парни́к (-á) hotbed; seed-bed. **парнико́в|ый** *adj*: **~ые расте́ния** hothouse plants.
парни́шка *m* boy, lad.
парно́й fresh; steamy.
па́рный (forming a) pair; twin.
паро- *in comb* steam-. **парово́з** (steam-)engine, locomotive. **~обра́зный** vaporous. **~хо́д** steamer; steamship. **~хо́дство** steamship-line.
парово́й steam; steamed.
паро́дия parody.
паро́ль *m* password.
паро́м ferry(-boat).
парт- *abbr in comb* Party. **партбиле́т** Party (membership) card. **~ко́м** Party committee. **~организа́ция** Party organization.
па́рта (*school*) desk.
парте́р stalls; pit.
партиза́н (*gen pl* -а́н) partisan; guerilla. **партиза́нский** partisan, guerilla; unplanned.
парти́йный party; Party; *sb* Party member.
партиту́ра (*mus*) score.
па́ртия party; group; batch; game, set; part.
партнёр partner.
па́рус (*pl* -á, -о́в) sail. **паруси́на** canvas. **па́русник** sailing vessel. **па́русный** sail; **~ спорт** sailing.
парфюме́рия perfumes.
парча́ (*gen pl* -е́й) brocade.
па́сека apiary, beehive.
пасётся *see* **пасти́сь**
па́сквиль *m* lampoon; libel.
па́смурный overcast; gloomy.
па́спорт (*pl* -á) passport.
пасса́ж passage; arcade.
пассажи́р passenger.
пасси́вный passive.
па́ста paste.
па́стбище pasture.
па́ства flock.
пасте́ль pastel.
пастерна́к parsnip.
пасти́ (-сý, -сёшь; пас, -ла́) *impf* graze; tend.
пасти́сь (-сётся; па́сся, -ла́сь) *impf* graze. **пасту́х** (-á) shepherd. **па́стырь** *m* pastor.
пасть¹ mouth; jaws.
пасть² (падý, -дёшь; пал) *pf of* **па́дать**
Па́сха Easter; Passover.
па́сынок (-нка) stepson, stepchild.
пат stalemate.
пате́нт patent.
патети́ческий passionate.
па́тока treacle; syrup.

П

патоло́гия pathology.
патриа́рх patriarch.
патрио́т, ~ка patriot. **патрио-ти́зм** patriotism. **патриоти́че-ский** patriotic.
патро́н cartridge; chuck; lamp-socket.
патру́ль (-я́) *m* patrol.
па́уза pause; (*also mus*) rest.
пау́к (-а́) spider. **паути́на** cobweb; gossamer; web.
па́фос zeal, enthusiasm.
пах (*loc* -у́) groin.
па́харь *m* ploughman. **паха́ть** (пашу́, па́шешь) *impf* (*pf* **вс~**) plough.
па́хнуть[1] (-ну; пах) *impf* smell (+*instr* of).
пахну́ть[2] (-нёт) *pf* puff, blow.
па́хота ploughing. **па́хотный** arable.
паху́чий odorous, strong-smelling.
пацие́нт, ~ка patient.
пацифи́зм pacificism. **пацифи́ст** pacifist.
па́чка bundle; packet, pack; tutu.
па́чкать *impf* (*pf* **за~, ис~**) dirty, soil, stain.
пашу́ *etc.*: *see* **паха́ть. па́шня** (*gen pl* -шен) ploughed field.
паште́т pâté.
пая́льная ла́мпа blow-lamp. **пая́льник** soldering iron. **пая́ть** (-я́ю) *impf* solder.
пая́ц clown, buffoon.
пев́ец (-вца́), **певи́ца** singer. **пе-ву́чий** melodious. **пе́вчий** singing; *sb* chorister.
пе́гий piebald.
педаго́г teacher; pedagogue. **пе-даго́гика** pedagogy. **педагоги́че-ский** pedagogical; educational; **~ институ́т** (teachers') training college.
педа́ль pedal.
педиа́тр paediatrician. **педиатри́-ческий** paediatric.
педикю́р chiropody.
пейза́ж landscape; scenery.
пёк *see* **печь. пека́рный** baking. **пека́рня** (*gen pl* -рен) bakery. **пе́-карь** (*pl* -я́, -е́й) *m* baker. **пе́кло** scorching heat; hell-fire. **пеку́** *etc.*: *see* **печь**
пелена́ (*gen pl* -лён) shroud. **пе-лена́ть** *impf* (*pf* **за~**) swaddle; put a nappy on.
пе́ленг bearing. **пеленгова́ть** *impf* & *pf* take the bearings of.
пелёнка nappy.
пельме́нь *m* meat dumpling.
пе́на foam; scum; froth.
пена́л pencil-case.
пе́ние singing.
пе́нистый foamy; frothy. **пе́-ниться** *impf* (*pf* **вс~**) foam.
пе́нка skin. **пенопла́ст** plastic foam.
пеницилли́н penicillin.
пенсионе́р, пенсионе́рка pensioner. **пенсио́нный** pensionable. **пе́нсия** pension.
пень (пня) *m* stump, stub.
пенька́ hemp.
пе́пел (-пла) ash, ashes. **пе́пель-ница** ashtray.
перве́йший the first; first-class. **пе́рвенец** (-нца) first-born. **пе́р-венство** first place; championship. **пе́рвенствовать** *impf* take first place; take priority. **перви́ч-ный** primary.
перво- *in comb* first; prime. **пер-вобы́тный** primitive; primeval. **~исто́чник** source; origin. **~кла́ссный** first-class. **~ку́рс-ник** first-year student. **~нача́ль-ный** original; primary. **~со́рт-ный** best-quality; first-class. **~степе́нный** paramount.
пе́рвое *sb* first course. **пе́рвый** first; former.
перга́мент parchment.
перебега́ть *impf*, **перебежа́ть** (-бегу́) *pf* cross, run across; desert. **перебе́жчик** deserter; turncoat.
переберу́ *etc.*: *see* **перебра́ть**
перебива́ть(ся *impf of* **пере-би́ть(ся**
перебира́ть(ся *impf of* **пере-бра́ть(ся**
переби́ть (-бью́, -бьёшь) *pf* (*impf*

П

перебива́ть) interrupt; slaughter; beat; break; re-upholster; **~ся** break; make ends meet. **перебо́й** interruption; stoppage; irregularity.

перебо́рка sorting out; partition; bulkhead.

переборо́ть (-рю́, -решь) *pf* overcome.

переборщи́ть (-щу́) *pf* go too far; overdo it.

перебра́сывать(ся *impf of* **перебро́сить(ся**

перебра́ть (-беру́, -берёшь; -а́л, -а́, -о) *pf* (*impf* **перебира́ть**) sort out; look through; turn over in one's mind; finger; **~ся** get over, cross; move.

перебро́сить (-о́шу) *pf* (*impf* **перебра́сывать**) throw over; transfer; **~ся** fling o.s.; spread. **перебро́ска** transfer.

перебью́ *etc.*: *see* **перебить**

перева́л crossing; pass. **перева́ливать** *impf*, **перевали́ть** (-лю́, -лишь) *pf* transfer, shift; cross, pass.

перева́ривать *impf*, **перевари́ть** (-рю́, -ришь) *pf* reheat; overcook; digest; tolerate.

переведу́ *etc.*: *see* **перевести**

перевезти́ (-зу́, -зёшь; -вёз, -ла́) *pf* (*impf* **перевози́ть**) take across; transport; (re)move.

переверну́ть (-ну́, -нёшь) *pf*, **перевёртывать** *impf* (*impf also* **перевора́чивать**) turn (over); upset; turn inside out; **~ся** turn (over).

переве́с preponderance; advantage. **переве́сить** (-е́шу) *pf* (*impf* **переве́шивать**) re-weigh; outweigh; tip the scales; hang elsewhere.

перевести́ (-веду́, -ведёшь; -вёл, -а́) *pf* (*impf* **переводи́ть**) take across; transfer, move, shift; translate; convert; **~сь** be transferred; run out; become extinct.

переве́шивать *impf of* **переве́сить**. **перевира́ть** *impf of* **переврать**

перево́д transfer, move, shift; translation; conversion; waste. **переводи́ть(ся** (-ожу́(сь, -о́дишь(ся) *impf of* **перевести́(сь**. **переводн|о́й**: **~а́я бума́га** carbon paper; **~а́я карти́нка** transfer. **перево́дный** transfer; translated. **перево́дчик, ~ица** translator; interpreter.

перево́з transporting; ferry. **перевози́ть** (-ожу́, -о́зишь) *impf of* **перевезти́**. **перево́зка** conveyance. **перево́зчик** ferryman; removal man.

перевооружа́ть *impf*, **перевооружи́ть** (-жу́) *pf* rearm; **~ся** rearm. **перевооруже́ние** rearmament.

перевоплоти́ть (-лощу́) *pf*, **перевоплоща́ть** *impf* reincarnate; **~ся** be reincarnated. **перевоплоще́ние** reincarnation.

перевора́чивать(ся *impf of* **переверну́ть(ся**. **переворо́т** revolution; overturn; cataclysm; **госуда́рственный ~** coup d'état.

перевоспита́ние re-education. **перевоспита́ть** *pf*, **перевоспи́тывать** *impf* re-educate.

перевра́ть (-ру́, -рёшь; -а́л, -а́, -о) *pf* (*impf* **перевира́ть**) garble; misquote.

перевыполне́ние overfulfilment. **перевы́полнить** *pf*, **перевыполня́ть** *impf* over-fulfil.

перевяза́ть (-яжу́, -я́жешь) *pf*, **перевя́зывать** *impf* bandage; tie up; re-tie. **перевя́зка** dressing, bandage.

переги́б bend; excess, extreme. **перегиба́ть(ся** *impf of* **перегну́ть(ся**

перегля́дываться *impf*, **перегляну́ться** (-ну́сь, -нешься) *pf* exchange glances.

перегна́ть (-гоню́, -го́нишь; -а́л, -а́, -о) *pf* (*impf* **перегоня́ть**) outdistance; surpass; drive; distil.

перегно́й humus.

перегну́ть (-ну́, -нёшь) *pf* (*impf* **перегиба́ть**) bend; **~ па́лку** go too far; **~ся** bend; lean over.

П

переговáривать *impf*, **переговорúть** *pf* talk; out-talk; **~ся** (**с**+*instr*) exchange remarks (with). **перегово́ры** (-ов) *pl* negotiations, parley. **переговóрный** *adj*: **~ пункт** public call-boxes; trunk-call office.

перегóн driving; stage. **перегóнка** distillation. **перегóнный** distilling, distillation. **перегоню́** *etc.*: *see* **перегнáть. перегоня́ть** *impf of* **перегнáть**

перегорáживать *impf of* **перегородúть**

перегорáть *impf*, **перегорéть** (-рúт) *pf* burn out, fuse.

перегородúть (-рожу́, -рóдишь) *pf* (*impf* **перегорáживать**) partition off; block. **перегорóдка** partition.

перегрéв overheating. **перегревáть** *impf*, **перегрéть** (-éю) *pf* overheat; **~ся** overheat.

перегружáть *impf*, **перегрузúть** (-ужу́, -у́зишь) *pf* overload; transfer. **перегру́зка** overload; transfer.

перегрызáть *impf*, **перегры́зть** (-зу́, -зёшь; -гры́з) *pf* gnaw through.

пéред, пéредо, пред, прéдо *prep*+*instr* before; in front of; compared to. **перёд** (пéреда; *pl* -á) front, forepart.

передавáть (-даю́, -даёшь) *impf*, **передáть** (-áм, -áшь, -áст, -адúм; пéредал, -á, -о) *pf* pass, hand, hand over; transfer; hand down; make over; tell; communicate; convey; give too much; **~ся** pass; be transmitted; be communicated; be inherited. **передáтчик** transmitter. **передáча** passing; transmission; communication; transfer; broadcast; drive; gear, gearing.

передвигáть *impf*, **передвúнуть** (-ну) *pf* move, shift; **~ся** move, shift. **передвижéние** movement; transportation. **передвúжка** movement; *in comb* travelling; itinerant. **передвижнóй** movable, mobile.

переделáть *pf*, **передéлывать** *impf* alter; refashion. **передéлка** alteration.

передёргивать(ся *impf of* **передёрнуть(ся**

передержáть (-жу́, -жишь) *pf*, **передéрживать** *impf* overdo; overcook; overexpose.

передёрнуть (-ну) *pf* (*impf* **передёргивать**) pull aside *or* across; cheat; distort; **~ся** wince.

перéдний front; **~ план** foreground. **перéдник** apron. **перéдняя** *sb* (entrance) hall, lobby. **пéредо:** *see* **пéред. передовúк** (-á) exemplary worker. **передовúца** leading article. **передовóй** advanced; foremost; leading.

передохну́ть (-ну́, -нёшь) *pf* pause for breath.

передрáзнивать *impf*, **передразнúть** (-ню́, -нишь) *pf* mimic.

переду́мать *pf*, **переду́мывать** *impf* change one's mind.

переды́шка respite.

переéзд crossing; move. **переезжáть** *impf*, **переéхать** (-éду) *pf* cross; run over, knock down; move (house).

пережáривать *impf*, **пережáрить** *pf* overdo, overcook.

переждáть (-жду́, -ждёшь; -áл, -á, -о) *pf* (*impf* **пережидáть**) wait for the end of.

пережёвывать *impf* chew; repeat over and over again.

переживáние experience. **переживáть** *impf of* **пережúть**

пережидáть *impf of* **переждáть**

пережитóе *sb* the past. **пережúток** (-тка) survival; vestige. **пережúть** (-иву́, -ивёшь; пéрежил, -á, -о) *pf* (*impf* **переживáть**) experience; go through; endure; outlive.

перезарядúть (-яжу́, -я́дишь) *pf*, **перезаряжáть** *impf* recharge, reload.

перезвáнивать *impf*, **перезвонúть** *pf* +*dat* ring back.

пере|зимова́ть *pf.*
перезре́лый overripe.
переигра́ть *pf*, **переи́грывать** *impf* play again; overact.
переизбира́ть *impf*, **переизбра́ть** (-беру́, -берёшь; -бра́л, -а́, -о) *pf* re-elect. **переизбра́ние** re-election.
переиздава́ть (-даю́, -даёшь) *impf*, **переизда́ть** (-а́м, -а́шь, -а́ст, -адим; -а́л, -а́, -о) *pf* republish, reprint. **переизда́ние** republication; new edition.
переименова́ть *pf*, **переимено́вывать** *impf* rename.
перейму́ *etc.*: *see* **переня́ть**
перейти́ (-йду́, -йдёшь; перешёл, -шла́) *pf* (*impf* **переходи́ть**) cross; go, walk, pass; move, change, switch; turn (**в**+*acc* to, into).
перека́пывать *impf of* **перекопа́ть**
перекати́ть (-чу́, -тишь) *pf*, **перека́тывать** *impf* roll; **~ся** roll.
перекача́ть *pf*, **перека́чивать** *impf* pump (across).
переквалифици́роваться *impf* & *pf* retrain.
переки́дывать *impf*, **переки́нуть** (-ну) *pf* throw over; **~ся** leap.
пе́рекись peroxide.
перекла́дина cross-beam; joist; horizontal bar.
перекла́дывать *impf of* **переложи́ть**
перекли́чка roll-call.
переключа́тель *m* switch. **переключа́ть** *impf*, **переключи́ть** (-чу́) *pf* switch (over); **~ся** switch (over) (**на**+*acc* to).
перекова́ть (-кую́, -куёшь) *pf*, **переко́вывать** *impf* re-shoe; re-forge.
перекопа́ть *pf* (*impf* **перека́пывать**) dig (all of); dig again.
перекоси́ть (-ошу́, -о́сишь) *pf* warp; distort; **~ся** warp; become distorted.
перекочева́ть (-чу́ю) *pf*, **перекочёвывать** *impf* migrate.
переко́шенный distorted, twisted.
перекра́ивать *impf of* **перекрои́ть**
перекра́сить (-а́шу) *pf*, **перекра́шивать** *impf* (re-)paint; (re-)dye; **~ся** change colour; turn one's coat.
пере|крести́ть (-ещу́, -е́стишь) *pf*, **перекре́щивать** *impf* cross; **~ся** cross, intersect; cross o.s. **перекрёстн|ый** cross; **~ый допро́с** cross-examination; **~ый ого́нь** cross-fire; **~ая ссы́лка** cross-reference. **перекрёсток** (-тка) cross-roads, crossing.
перекри́кивать *impf*, **перекрича́ть** (-чу́) *pf* shout down.
перекрои́ть (-ою́) *pf* (*impf* **перекра́ивать**) cut out again; reshape.
перекрыва́ть *impf*, **перекры́ть** (-ро́ю) *pf* re-cover; exceed. **перекры́тие** ceiling.
перекую́ *etc.*: *see* **перекова́ть**
перекупа́ть *impf*, **перекупи́ть** (-плю́, -пишь) *pf* buy up; buy by outbidding s.o. **переку́пщик** second-hand dealer.
перекуси́ть (-ушу́, -у́сишь) *pf*, **переку́сывать** *impf* bite through; have a snack.
перелага́ть *impf of* **переложи́ть**
перела́мывать *impf of* **переломи́ть**
перелеза́ть *impf*, **переле́зть** (-зу; -е́з) *pf* climb over.
переле́сок (-ска) copse.
перелёт migration; flight. **перелета́ть** *impf*, **перелете́ть** (-лечу́) *pf* fly over. **перелётный** migratory.
перелива́ние decanting; transfusion. **перелива́ть** *impf of* **перели́ть. перелива́ться** *impf of* **перели́ться**; gleam; modulate.
перелиста́ть *pf*, **перели́стывать** *impf* leaf through.
перели́ть (-лью́, -льёшь; -и́л, -а́, -о) *pf* (*impf* **перелива́ть**) pour; decant; let overflow; transfuse. **перели́ться** (-льётся; -ли́лся, -лила́сь, -ли́ло́сь) *pf* (*impf* **перелива́ться**) flow; overflow.

П

перелицева́ть (-цу́ю) *pf*, **перелицо́вывать** *impf* turn; have turned.

переложе́ние arrangement. **переложи́ть** (-жу́, -жишь) *pf* (*impf* **перекла́дывать, перелага́ть**) put elsewhere; shift; transfer; interlay; put in too much; set; arrange; transpose.

перело́м breaking; fracture; turning-point, crisis; sudden change. **перелома́ть** *pf* break; **~ся** break, be broken. **переломи́ть** (-млю́, -мишь) *pf* (*impf* **перела́мывать**) break in two; master. **перело́мный** critical.

перелью́ *etc.*: *see* **перели́ть**

перема́нивать *impf*, **перемани́ть** (-ню́, -нишь) *pf* win over; entice.

перемежа́ться *impf* alternate.

переме́на change; break. **перемени́ть** (-ню́, -нишь) *pf*, **переменя́ть** *impf* change; **~ся** change. **переме́нный** variable; **~ ток** alternating current. **переме́нчивый** changeable.

П

перемести́ть (-мещу́) *pf* (*impf* **перемеща́ть**) move; transfer; **~ся** move.

перемеша́ть *pf*, **переме́шивать** *impf* mix; mix up; shuffle; **~ся** get mixed (up).

перемеща́ть(ся *impf of* **перемести́ть(ся. перемеще́ние** transference; displacement. **перемещённ|ый** displaced; **~ые ли́ца** displaced persons.

переми́рие armistice, truce.

перемыва́ть *impf*, **перемы́ть** (-мо́ю) *pf* wash (up) again.

перенапряга́ть *impf*, **перенапря́чь** (-ягу́, -яжёшь: -я́г, -ла́) *pf* overstrain.

перенаселе́ние overpopulation. **перенаселённый** (-лён, -а́) overpopulated; overcrowded.

перенести́ (-су́, -сёшь; -нёс, -ла́) *pf* (*impf* **переноси́ть**) carry, move, take; transfer; take over; postpone; endure, bear; **~сь** be carried; be carried away.

перенима́ть *impf of* **переня́ть**

перено́с transfer; word division; **знак ~а** end-of-line hyphen. **переноси́мый** endurable. **переноси́ть(ся** (-ошу́(сь, -о́сишь(ся) *impf of* **перенести́(сь**

перено́сица bridge (*of the nose*).

перено́ска carrying over; transporting; carriage. **перено́сный** portable; figurative. **перено́счик** carrier.

пере|ночева́ть (-чу́ю) *pf.* **переношу́** *etc.*: *see* **переноси́ть**

переня́ть (-ейму́, -еймёшь; пе́ренял, -а́, -о) *pf* (*impf* **перенима́ть**) imitate; adopt.

переоборудовать *impf* & *pf* re-equip.

переобува́ться *impf*, **переобу́ться** (-у́юсь, -у́ешься) *pf* change one's shoes.

переодева́ться *impf*, **переоде́ться** (-е́нусь) *pf* change (one's clothes).

переосвиде́тельствовать *impf* & *pf* re-examine.

переоце́нивать *impf*, **переоцени́ть** (-ню́, -нишь) *pf* overestimate; revalue. **переоце́нка** overestimation; revaluation.

перепа́чкать *pf* make dirty; **~ся** get dirty.

пе́репел (*pl* -а́) quail.

перепелена́ть *pf* change (*a baby*).

перепеча́тать *pf*, **перепеча́тывать** *impf* reprint. **перепеча́тка** reprint.

перепи́ливать *impf*, **перепили́ть** (-лю́, -лишь) *pf* saw in two.

переписа́ть (-ишу́, -и́шешь) *pf*, **перепи́сывать** *impf* copy; re-write; make a list of. **перепи́ска** copying; correspondence. **перепи́сываться** *impf* correspond. **пе́репись** census.

перепла́вить (-влю) *pf*, **переплавля́ть** *impf* smelt.

переплати́ть (-ачу́, -а́тишь) *pf*, **перепла́чивать** *impf* overpay.

переплести́ (-лету́, -летёшь; -лёл,

-á) *pf*, **переплетáть** *impf* bind; interlace, intertwine; re-plait; **~ся** interlace, interweave; get mixed up. **переплёт** binding. **переплётчик** bookbinder.

переплывáть *impf*, **переплы́ть** (-ывý, -ывёшь; -ы́л, -á, -о) *pf* swim *or* sail across.

переподготóвка further training; refresher course.

переползáть *impf*, **переползти́** (-зý, -зёшь; -óлз, -лá) *pf* crawl *or* creep across.

переполнéние overfilling; overcrowding. **переполненный** overcrowded; too full. **перепóлнить** *pf*, **переполня́ть** *impf* overfill; overcrowd.

переполóх commotion.

перепóнка membrane; web.

перепрáва crossing; ford.

перепрáвить (-влю) *pf*, **переправля́ть** *impf* convey; take across; forward; **~ся** cross, get across.

перепродавáть (-даю, -даёшь) *impf*, **перепродáть** (-áм, -áшь, -áст, -ади́м; -прóдáл, -á, -о) *pf* re-sell. **перепродáжа** re-sale.

перепроизвóдство overproduction.

перепры́гивать *impf*, **перепры́гнуть** (-ну) *pf* jump (over).

перепугáть *pf* frighten, scare; **~ся** get a fright.

пере|пýтать *pf*, **перепýтывать** *impf* tangle; confuse, mix up.

перепýтье cross-roads.

перерабáтывать *impf*, **перерабóтать** *pf* convert; treat; re-make; re-cast; process; work overtime; overwork; **~ся** overwork. **перерабóтка** processing; reworking; overtime work.

перераспределéние redistribution. **перераспредели́ть** *pf*, **перераспределя́ть** *impf* redistribute.

перерастáние outgrowing; escalation; development (into). **перерастáть** *impf*, **перерасти́** (-тý, -тёшь; -рóс, -лá) *pf* outgrow; develop.

перерасхóд over-expenditure; overdraft. **перерасхóдовать** *impf* & *pf* expend too much of.

перерасчёт recalculation.

перервáть (-вý, -вёшь; -áл, -á, -о) *pf* (*impf* **перерывáть**) break, tear asunder; **~ся** break, come apart.

перерéзать (-éжу) *pf*, **перерезáть** *impf*, **перерéзывать** *impf* cut; cut off; kill.

перероди́ть (-ожý) *pf*, **перерождáть** *impf* regenerate; **~ся** be reborn; be regenerated; degenerate. **перерождéние** regeneration; degeneration.

перерóс *etc.*: *see* **перерасти́. перерóю** *etc.*: *see* **переры́ть**

перерубáть *impf*, **перерубить** (-блю, -бишь) *pf* chop in two.

переры́в break; interruption; interval.

перерывáть[1]**(ся** *impf of* **перервáть(ся**

перерывáть[2] *impf*, **переры́ть** (-рóю) *pf* dig up; rummage through.

пересади́ть (-ажý, -áдишь) *pf*, **пересáживать** *impf* transplant; graft; seat somewhere else. **пересáдка** transplantation; grafting; change.

пересáживаться *impf of* **пересéсть. пересáливать** *impf of* **пересоли́ть**

пересдавáть (-даю́сь) *impf*, **пересдáть** (-áм, -áшь, -áст, -ади́м; -дáл, -á, -о) *pf* sublet; re-sit.

пересекáть(ся *impf of* **пересéчь(ся**

переселéнец (-нца) settler; immigrant. **переселéние** migration; immigration, resettlement; moving. **пересели́ть** *pf*, **переселя́ть** *impf* move; **~ся** move; migrate.

пересéсть (-ся́ду) *pf* (*impf* **пересáживаться**) change one's seat; change (*trains etc.*).

пересечéние crossing, intersection. **пересéчь** (-секý, -сечёшь; -сёк, -лá) *pf* (*impf* **пересекáть**) cross; intersect; **~ся** cross, intersect.

П

пересиливать *impf*, **пересилить** *pf* overpower.

пересказ (re)telling; exposition. **пересказать** (-ажу, -ажешь) *pf*, **пересказывать** *impf* retell.

перескакивать *impf*, **перескочить** (-чу, -чишь) *pf* jump *or* skip (over).

переслать (-ешлю, -шлёшь) *pf* (*impf* **пересылать**) send; forward.

пересматривать *impf*, **пересмотреть** (-трю, -тришь) *pf* look over; reconsider. **пересмотр** revision; reconsideration; review.

пересолить (-олю, -олишь) *pf* (*impf* **пересаливать**) over-salt; overdo it.

пересохнуть (-нет; -ох) *pf* (*impf* **пересыхать**) dry up, become parched.

переспать (-плю; -ал, -а, -о) *pf* oversleep; spend the night.

переспелый overripe.

переспрашивать *impf*, **переспросить** (-ошу, -осишь) *pf* ask again.

П

переставать (-таю, -таёшь) *impf of* **перестать**

переставить (-влю) *pf*, **переставлять** *impf* move; re-arrange; transpose. **перестановка** rearrangement; transposition.

перестать (-ану) *pf* (*impf* **переставать**) stop, cease.

перестрадать *pf* have suffered.

перестраивать(ся *impf of* **перестроить(ся**

перестраховка re-insurance; overcautiousness.

перестрелка exchange of fire. **перестрелять** *pf* shoot (down).

перестроить *pf* (*impf* **перестраивать**) rebuild; reorganize; retune; **~ся** re-form; reorganize o.s.; switch over (**на**+*acc* to). **перестройка** reconstruction; reorganization; retuning; perestroika.

переступать *impf*, **переступить** (-плю, -пишь) *pf* step over; cross; overstep.

пересчитать *pf*, **пересчитывать** *impf* (*pf also* **перечесть**) re-count; count.

пересылать *impf of* **переслать**. **пересылка** sending, forwarding.

пересыпать *impf*, **пересыпать** (-плю, -плешь) *pf* pour; sprinkle; pour too much.

пересыхать *impf of* **пересохнуть**.

пересяду *etc.*: *see* **пересесть**. **перетапливать** *impf of* **перетопить**

перетаскивать *impf*, **перетащить** (-щу, -щишь) *pf* drag (over, through); move.

перетереть (-тру, -трёшь; -тёр) *pf*, **перетирать** *impf* wear out, wear down; grind; wipe; **~ся** wear out *or* through.

перетопить (-плю, -пишь) *pf* (*impf* **перетапливать**) melt.

перетру *etc.*: *see* **перетереть**

переть (пру, прёшь; пёр, -ла) *impf* go; make *or* force one's way; haul; come out.

перетягивать *impf*, **перетянуть** (-ну, -нешь) *pf* pull, draw; win over; outweigh.

переубедить *pf*, **переубеждать** *impf* make change one's mind.

переулок (-лка) side street, alley, lane.

переустройство reconstruction, reorganization.

переутомить (-млю) *pf*, **переутомлять** *impf* overtire; **~ся** overtire o.s. **переутомление** overwork.

переучёт stock-taking.

переучивать *impf*, **переучить** (-чу, -чишь) *pf* teach again.

перефразировать *impf* & *pf* paraphrase.

перехватить (-ачу, -атишь) *pf*, **перехватывать** *impf* intercept; snatch a bite (of); borrow.

перехитрить *pf* outwit.

переход transition; crossing; conversion. **переходить** (-ожу, -одишь) *impf of* **перейти**. **переходный** transitional; transitive. **переходящий** transient; intermittent; brought forward.

перец (-рца) pepper.

перечёл *etc.*: *see* **перечéсть**
пéречень (-чня) *m* list, enumeration.
перечёркивать *impf*, **перечеркнýть** (-нý, -нёшь) *pf* cross out, cancel.
перечéсть (-чтý, -чтёшь; -чёл, -члá) *pf*: *see* **пересчитáть, перечитáть**
перечислéние enumeration; transfer. **перечúслить** *pf*, **перечислять** *impf* enumerate; transfer.
перечитáть *pf*, **перечúтывать** *impf* (*pf also* **перечéсть**) re-read.
перéчить (-чу) *impf* contradict; cross, go against.
пéречница pepper-pot.
перечтý *etc.*: *see* **перечéсть. перéчу** *etc.*: *see* **перéчить**
перешáгивать *impf*, **перешагнýть** (-нý, -нёшь) *pf* step over.
перешéек (-éйка) isthmus, neck.
перешёл *etc.*: *see* **перейтú**
перешивáть *impf*, **перешúть** (-шью, -шьёшь) *pf* alter; have altered.
перешлю *etc.*: *see* **переслáть**
переэкзаменовáть *pf.*, **переэкзаменóвывать** *impf* re-examine; **~ся** retake an exam.
перúла (-úл) *pl* railing(s); banisters.
перúна feather-bed.
перúод period. **периóдика** periodicals. **периодúческий** periodical; recurring.
пéристый feathery; cirrus.
периферúя periphery.
перламýтр mother-of-pearl. **перламýтровый** mother-of-pearl.
перлóв|ый: ~ая крупá pearl barley.
перманéнт perm. **перманéнтный** permanent.
пернáтый feathered. **пернáтые** *sb pl* birds. **перó** (*pl* **пéрья, -ьев**) feather; nib. **перочúнный нож, нóжик** penknife.
перпендикулярный perpendicular.
перрóн platform.
перс Persian. **персúдский** Persian.
пéрсик peach.
персиянка Persian woman.
персóна person; **сóбственной персóной** in person. **персонáж** character; personage. **персонáл** personnel, staff. **персонáльный** personal.
перспектúва perspective; vista; prospect. **перспектúвный** perspective; long-term; promising.
пéрстень (-тня) *m* ring.
перфокáрта punched card.
пéрхоть dandruff.
перчáтка glove.
пéрчить (-чу) *impf* (*pf* **по~**) pepper.
пёс (пса) dog.
пéсенник song-book; (choral) singer; song-writer. **пéсенный** song; of songs.
песéц (-цá) (polar) fox.
песнь (*gen pl* -ей) song; canto. **пéсня** (*gen pl* -сен) song.
песóк (-скá) sand. **песóчный** sand; sandy.
пессимúзм pessimism. **пессимúст** pessimist. **пессимистúческий** pessimistic.
пестротá diversity of colours; diversity. **пёстрый** variegated; diverse; colourful.
песчáник sandstone. **песчáный** sandy. **песчúнка** grain of sand.
петербýргский (of) St Petersburg.
петúция petition.
петлúца buttonhole; tab. **пéтля** (*gen pl* -тель) loop; noose; buttonhole; stitch; hinge.
петрýшка[1] parsley.
петрýшка[2] *m* Punch; *f* Punch-and-Judy show.
петýх (-á) cock. **петушóк** (-шкá) cockerel.
петь (пою, поёшь) *impf* (*pf* **про~, с~**) sing.
пехóта infantry, foot. **пехотúнец** (-нца) infantryman. **пехóтный** infantry.

П

печáлить *impf* (*pf* **о~**) sadden; **~ся** grieve, be sad. **печáль** sorrow. **печáльный** sad.
печáтать *impf* (*pf* **на~, от~**) print; **~ся** write, be published; be at the printer's. **печáтн|ый** printing; printer's; printed; **~ые бýквы** block capitals; **~ый станóк** printing-press. **печáть** seal, stamp; print; printing; press.
печéние baking.
печёнка liver.
печёный baked.
пéчень liver.
печéнье pastry; biscuit. **пéчка** stove. **печнóй** stove; oven; kiln. **печь** (*loc* -и́; *gen pl* -éй) stove; oven; kiln. **печь** (пекý, -чёшь; пёк, -лá) *impf* (*pf* **ис~**) bake; **~ся** bake.
пешехóд pedestrian. **пешехóдный** pedestrian; foot-. **пéший** pedestrian; foot. **пéшка** pawn. **пешкóм** *adv* on foot.
пещéра cave. **пещéрный** cave; **~ человéк** cave-dweller.
П **пиани́но** *neut indecl* (upright) piano. **пиани́ст, ~ка** pianist.
пивнáя *sb* pub. **пивнóй** beer. **пи́во** beer. **пивовáр** brewer.
пигмéй pygmy.
пиджáк (-á) jacket.
пижáма pyjamas.
пижóн dandy.
пик peak; **часы́ пик** rush-hour.
пи́ка lance.
пикáнтный piquant; spicy.
пикáп pick-up (van).
пикé *neut indecl* dive.
пикéт picket. **пикéтчик** picket.
пи́ки (пик) *pl* (*cards*) spades.
пики́ровать *impf* & *pf* (*pf also* **с~**) dive.
пикирóвщик, пики́рующий бомбардирóвщик dive-bomber.
пикни́к (-á) picnic.
пи́кнуть (-ну) *pf* squeak; make a sound.
пи́ковый of spades.
пилá (*pl* -ы) saw; nagger. **пилёный** sawed, sawn. **пили́ть** (-лю́, -лишь) *impf* saw; nag (at). **пи́лка** sawing; fret-saw; nail-file.
пилóт pilot.
пилóтка forage-cap.
пилоти́ровать *impf* pilot.
пилю́ля pill.
пинáть *impf* (*pf* пнуть) kick. **пинóк** (-нкá) kick.
пингви́н penguin.
пинцéт tweezers.
пиóн peony.
пионéр pioneer. **пионéрский** pioneer.
пипéтка pipette.
пир (*loc* -ý; *pl* -ы) feast, banquet. **пировáть** *impf* feast.
пирами́да pyramid.
пирáт pirate.
пирóг (-á) pie. **пирóжное** *sb* cake, pastry. **пирожóк** (-жкá) pasty.
пирс pier.
пируэ́т pirouette.
пи́ршество feast; celebration.
пи́саный handwritten. **пи́сарь** (*pl* -я́) *m* clerk. **писáтель** *m*, **писáтельница** writer, author. **писáть** (пишý, пи́шешь) *impf* (*pf* **на~**) write; paint; **~ мáслом** paint in oils; **~ся** be spelt.
писк squeak, chirp. **пискли́вый** squeaky. **пи́скнуть** (-ну) *pf of* **пищáть**
пистолéт pistol; gun; **~-пулемёт** sub-machine gun.
пистóн (percussion-)cap; piston.
писчебумáжный stationery. **пи́счая бумáга** writing paper. **пи́сьменно** *adv* in writing. **пи́сьменность** literature. **пи́сьменный** writing, written. **письмó** (*pl* -а, -сем) letter.
питáние nourishment; feeding. **питáтельный** nutritious; alimentary; feed. **питáть** *impf* feed; nourish; supply; **~ся** feed; eat; live; +*instr* feed on.
питóмец (-мца) charge; pupil; alumnus. **питóмник** nursery.
пить (пью, пьёшь; пил, -á, -о) *impf* (*pf* **вы~**) drink. **питьевóй** drinkable; drinking.

пиха́ть *impf*, **пихну́ть** (-ну́, -нёшь) *pf* push, shove.
пи́хта (silver) fir.
пи́чкать *impf* (*pf* **на~**) stuff.
пи́шущ|ий writing; **~ая маши́нка** typewriter.
пи́ща food.
пища́ть (-щу́) *impf* (*pf* **пи́скнуть**) squeak; cheep.
пищеваре́ние digestion. **пищево́д** oesophagus, gullet. **пищево́й** food.
пия́вка leech.
ПК *abbr* (*of* **персона́льный компью́тер**) PC (*personal computer*).
пла́вание swimming; sailing; voyage. **пла́вательный** swimming; **~ бассе́йн** swimming-pool. **пла́вать** *impf* swim; float; sail. **плавба́за** depot ship, factory ship.
плави́льный melting, smelting. **плави́льня** foundry. **пла́вить** (-влю) *impf* (*pf* **рас~**) melt, smelt; **~ся** melt. **пла́вка** fusing; melting.
пла́вки (-вок) *pl* bathing trunks.
пла́вкий fusible; fuse. **плавле́ние** melting.
плавни́к (-а́) fin; flipper. **пла́вный** smooth, flowing; liquid. **плаву́чий** floating.
плагиа́т plagiarism. **плагиа́тор** plagiarist.
пла́зма plasma.
плака́т poster; placard.
пла́кать (-а́чу) *impf* cry, weep; **~ся** complain, lament; +**на**+*acc* complain of; bemoan.
пла́кса cry-baby. **плакси́вый** whining. **плаку́чий** weeping.
пла́менный flaming; ardent. **пла́мя** (-мени) *neut* flame; blaze.
план plan
планёр glider. **планери́зм** gliding. **планери́ст** glider-pilot.
плане́та planet. **плане́тный** planetary.
плани́рование[1] planning.
плани́рование[2] gliding; glide.
плани́ровать[1] *impf* (*pf* **за~**) plan.
плани́ровать[2] *impf* (*pf* **с~**) glide (down).
пла́нка lath, slat.
пла́новый planned, systematic; planning. **планоме́рный** systematic, planned.
планта́ция plantation.
пласт (-а́) layer; stratum. **пласти́на** plate. **пласти́нка** plate; (*gramophone*) record.
пласти́ческий, пласти́чный plastic. **пластма́сса** plastic. **пластма́ссовый** plastic.
пла́стырь *m* plaster.
пла́та pay; charge; fee. **платёж** (-а́) payment. **платёжеспосо́бный** solvent. **платёжный** pay.
пла́тина platinum.
плати́ть (-ачу́, -а́тишь) *impf* (*pf* **за~, у~**) pay; **~ся** (*pf* **по~ся**) **за**+*acc* pay for. **пла́тный** paid; requiring payment.
плато́к (-тка́) shawl; head-scarf; handkerchief.
платони́ческий platonic.
платфо́рма platform; truck.
пла́тье (*gen pl* -ьев) clothes, clothing; dress; gown. **платяно́й** clothes.
плафо́н ceiling; lamp shade.
плацда́рм bridgehead, beachhead; base; springboard.
плацка́рта reserved-seat ticket.
плач weeping. **плаче́вный** lamentable. **пла́чу** *etc.*: *see* **пла́кать**
плачу́ *etc.*: *see* **плати́ть**
плашмя́ *adv* flat, prone.
плащ (-а́) cloak; raincoat.
плебе́й plebeian.
плева́тельница spittoon. **плева́ть** (плюю́, плюёшь) *impf* (*pf* **на~, плю́нуть**) spit; *inf*+*dat*: **мне ~** I don't give a damn (**на**+*acc* about); **~ся** spit. **плево́к** (-вка́) spit, spittle.
плеври́т pleurisy.
плед rug; plaid.
плёл *etc.*: *see* **плести́**
племенно́й tribal; pedigree. **пле́мя** (-мени; *pl* -мена́, -мён) *neut* tribe. **племя́нник** nephew. **племя́нница** niece.

П

плен (*loc* -ý) captivity.
плена́рный plenary.
плени́тельный captivating. **плени́ть** *pf* (*impf* **пленя́ть**) captivate; **~ся** be captivated.
плёнка film; tape; pellicle.
пле́нник prisoner. **пле́нный** captive.
пле́нум plenary session.
пленя́ть(ся *impf of* **плени́ть(ся**
пле́сень mould.
плеск splash, lapping. **плеска́ть** (-ещý, -е́щешь) *impf* (*pf* **плесну́ть**) splash; lap; **~ся** splash; lap.
пле́сневеть (-еет) *impf* (*pf* **за~**) go mouldy, grow musty.
плесну́ть (-нý, -нёшь) *pf of* **плеска́ть**
плести́ (-етý, -етёшь; плёл, -á) *impf* (*pf* **с~**) plait; weave; **~сь** trudge along. **плете́ние** plaiting; wickerwork. **плетёный** wattled; wicker. **плете́нь** (-тня́) *m* wattle fencing. **плётка, плеть** (*gen pl* -е́й) lash.
пле́чико (*pl* -и, -ов) shoulder-strap; *pl* coat-hanger. **плечи́стый** broad-shouldered. **плечо́** (*pl* -и, -áм) shoulder.
плеши́вый bald. **плеши́на, плешь** bald patch.
плещу́ *etc.*: *see* **плеска́ть**
пли́нтус plinth; skirting-board.
плис velveteen.
плиссирова́ть *impf* pleat.
плита́ (*pl* -ы) slab; flag-(stone); stove, cooker; **моги́льная ~** gravestone. **пли́тка** tile; (thin) slab; stove, cooker; **~ шокола́да** bar of chocolate. **пли́точный** tiled.
плове́ц (-вцá), **пловчи́ха** swimmer. **плову́чий** floating; buoyant.
плод (-á) fruit. **плоди́ть** (-ожý) *impf* (*pf* **рас~**) produce, procreate; **~ся** propagate.
плодо- *in comb* fruit-. **плодови́тый** fruitful, prolific; fertile. **~во́дство** fruit-growing. **~но́сный** fruit-bearing, fruitful. **~овощно́й** fruit and vegetable. **~ро́дный** fertile. **~тво́рный** fruitful.
пло́мба seal; filling. **пломбирова́ть** *impf* (*pf* **за~, о~**) fill; seal.
пло́ский (-сок, -скá, -о) flat; trivial.
плоско- *in comb* flat. **плоского́рье** plateau. **~гу́бцы** (-ев) *pl* pliers. **~до́нный** flat-bottomed.
пло́скость (*gen pl* -е́й) flatness; plane; platitude.
плот (-á) raft.
плоти́на dam; weir; dyke.
пло́тник carpenter.
пло́тность solidity; density. **пло́тный** (-тен, -тнá, -о) thick; compact; dense; solid, strong; hearty.
плотоя́дный carnivorous. **плоть** flesh.
плохо́й bad; poor.
площа́дка area, (sports) ground, court, playground; site; landing; platform. **пло́щадь** (*gen pl* -е́й) area; space; square.
плуг (*pl* -и́) plough.
плут (-á) cheat, swindler; rogue. **плутова́тый** cunning. **плутовско́й** roguish; picaresque.
плуто́ний plutonium.
плыть (-ывý, -ывёшь; плыл, -á, -о) *impf* swim; float; sail.
плю́нуть (-ну) *pf of* **плева́ть**
плюс plus; advantage.
плюш plush.
плющ (-á) ivy.
плюю́ *etc.*: *see* **плева́ть**
пляж beach.
пляса́ть (-яшý, -я́шешь) *impf* (*pf* **с~**) dance. **пля́ска** dance; dancing.
пневмати́ческий pneumatic.
пневмони́я pneumonia.
пнуть (пну, пнёшь) *pf of* **пина́ть**
пня *etc.*: *see* **пень**
по *prep* **I.** *+dat* on; along; round, about; by; over; according to; in accordance with; for; in; at; by (reason of); on account of; from; **по понеде́льникам** on Mondays; **по профе́ссии** by profession; **по ра́дио** over the radio. **II.** *+dat or acc of cardinal number, forms distributive number*: **по́ два, по́ двое** in twos, two by two; **по пять руб-**

ле́й шту́ка at five roubles each. **III.** +*acc* to, up to; for, to get; **идти́ по во́ду** go to get water; **по пе́рвое сентября́** up to (and including) 1st September. **IV.** +*prep* on, (immediately) after; **по прибы́тии** on arrival.

по- *pref* **I.** *in comb +dat of adjs, or with advs in* **-и**, *indicates manner, use of a named language, or accordance with the opinion or wish of*: **говори́ть по-ру́сски** speak Russian; **жить по-ста́рому** live in the old style; **по-мо́ему** in my opinion. **II.** *in comb with adjs and nn, indicates situation along or near a thing*: **помо́рье** seaboard, coastal region. **III.** *in comb with comp of adjs indicates a smaller degree of comparison*: **поме́ньше** a little less.

поба́иваться *impf* be rather afraid.

побе́г[1] flight; escape.

побе́г[2] shoot; sucker.

побегу́шки: **быть на побегу́шках** run errands.

побе́да victory. **победи́тель** *m* victor; winner. **победи́ть** *pf* (*impf* **побежда́ть**) conquer; win. **побе́дный, победоно́сный** victorious, triumphant.

по|бежа́ть *pf.*

побежда́ть *impf of* **победи́ть**

по|беле́ть (-е́ю) *pf.* **по|бели́ть** *pf.* **побе́лка** whitewashing.

побере́жный coastal. **побере́жье** (sea-)coast.

по|беспоко́ить(ся *pf.*

побира́ться *impf* beg; live by begging.

по|би́ть(ся (-бью́(сь, -бьёшь(ся) *pf.* **по|благодари́ть** *pf.*

побла́жка indulgence.

по|бледне́ть (-е́ю) *pf.*

поблёскивать *impf* gleam.

побли́зости *adv* nearby.

побо́и (-ев) *pl* beating. **побо́ище** slaughter; bloody battle.

побо́рник champion, advocate. **поборо́ть** (-рю́, -решь) *pf* overcome.

побо́чный secondary; done on the side; ~ **проду́кт** by-product.

по|брани́ться *pf.*

по|брата́ться *pf.* **побрати́м** twin town.

по|бре́згать *pf.* **по|бри́ть(ся** (-бре́ю(сь) *pf.*

побуди́тельный stimulating. **побуди́ть** (-ужу́) *pf*, **побужда́ть** *impf* induce, prompt. **побужде́ние** motive; inducement.

побыва́ть *pf* have been, have visited; look in, visit. **побы́вка** leave. **побы́ть** (-бу́ду, -дешь; по́был, -а́, -о) *pf* stay (for a short time).

побью́(сь *etc.*: *see* **поби́ть(ся**

пова́диться (-а́жусь) get into the habit (of). **пова́дка** habit.

по|вали́ть(ся (-лю́(сь, -лишь(ся) *pf.*

пова́льно *adv* without exception. **пова́льный** general, mass.

по́вар (*pl* -а́) cook, chef. **пова́ренный** culinary; cookery, cooking.

по-ва́шему *adv* in your opinion.

пове́дать *pf* disclose; relate.

поведе́ние behaviour.

поведу́ *etc.*: *see* **повести́. по|везти́** (-зу́, -зёшь; -вёз, -ла́) *pf.* **повёл** *etc.*: *see* **повести́**

повелева́ть *impf* +*instr* rule (over); +*dat* command. **повеле́ние** command. **повели́тельный** imperious; imperative.

по|венча́ть(ся *pf.*

поверга́ть *impf*, **пове́ргнуть** (-ну; -ве́рг) *pf* throw down; plunge.

пове́ренная *sb* confidante. **пове́ренный** *sb* attorney; confidant; ~ **в дела́х** chargé d'affaires. **по|ве́рить**[1]. **пове́рить**[2] *pf* (*impf* **поверя́ть**) check; confide. **пове́рка** check; roll-call.

поверну́ть (-ну́, -нёшь) *pf*, **повёртывать** *impf* (*impf also* **повора́чивать**) turn; **~ся** turn.

пове́рх *prep*+*gen* over. **пове́рхностный** surface, superficial. **пове́рхность** surface.

пове́рье (*gen pl* -ий) popular be-

П

lief, superstition. **поверя́ть** *impf of* **пове́рить²**
пове́са playboy.
по|веселе́ть (-е́ю) *pf.*
повесели́ть *pf* cheer (up), amuse; **~ся** have fun.
пове́сить(ся (-ве́шу(сь) *pf of* **ве́шать(ся**
повествова́ние narrative, narration. **повествова́тельный** narrative. **повествова́ть** *impf* **+о+***prep* narrate, relate.
по|вести́ (-еду́, -едёшь; -вёл, -а́) *pf* (*impf* **поводи́ть**) *+instr* move.
пове́стка notice; summons; **~ (дня)** agenda.
по́весть (*gen pl* -е́й) story, tale.
пове́трие epidemic; craze.
пове́шу *etc.*: *see* **пове́сить. по|вздо́рить** *pf.*
повзросле́ть (-е́ю) *pf* grow up.
по|вида́ть(ся *pf.*
по-ви́димому apparently.
пови́дло jam.
по|вини́ться *pf.*
пови́нность duty, obligation; **во́инская ~** conscription. **пови́нный** guilty.
повинова́ться *impf* & *pf* obey. **повинове́ние** obedience.
повиса́ть *impf*, **по|ви́снуть** (-ну; -ви́с) *pf* hang (on); hang down, droop.
повле́чь (-еку́, -ечёшь; -ёк, -ла́) *pf* **(за собо́й)** entail, bring in its train.
по|влия́ть *pf.*
по́вод¹ occasion, cause; **по ~у**+*gen* as regards, concerning.
по́вод² (*loc* -у́; *pl* -о́дья, -ьев) rein; **быть на ~у́ у**+*gen* be under the thumb of. **поводи́ть** (-ожу́, -о́дишь) *impf of* **повести́. поводо́к** (-дка́) leash. **поводы́рь** (-я́) *m* guide.
пово́зка cart; vehicle.
повора́чивать(ся *impf of* **поверну́ть(ся, повороти́ть(ся; повора́чивайся, -айтесь!** get a move on!
поворо́т turn, turning; bend; turning-point. **повороти́ть(ся** (-рочу́(сь, -ро́тишь(ся) *pf* (*impf* **повора́чивать(ся**) turn. **поворо́тливый** agile, nimble; manoeuvrable. **поворо́тный** turning; rotary; revolving.
по|вреди́ть (-ежу́) *pf*, **повреждА́ть** *impf* damage; injure; **~ся** be damaged; be injured. **поврежде́ние** damage, injury.
повремени́ть *pf* wait a little; **+с+***instr* delay over.
повседне́вный daily; everyday.
повсеме́стно *adv* everywhere. **повсеме́стный** universal, general.
повста́нец (-нца) rebel, insurgent. **повста́нческий** rebel; insurgent.
повсю́ду *adv* everywhere.
повторе́ние repetition. **повтори́ть** *pf*, **повторя́ть** *impf* repeat; **~ся** repeat o.s.; be repeated; recur. **повто́рный** repeated.
повы́сить (-ы́шу) *pf*, **повыша́ть** *impf* raise, heighten; **~ся** rise. **повыше́ние** rise; promotion. **повы́шенный** heightened, high.
повяза́ть (-яжу́, -я́жешь) *pf*, **повя́зывать** *impf* tie. **повя́зка** band; bandage.
по|гада́ть *pf.*
пога́нка toadstool. **пога́ный** foul; unclean.
погаса́ть *impf*, **по|га́снуть** (-ну) *pf* go out, be extinguished. **по|гаси́ть** (-ашу́, -а́сишь) *pf.* **погаша́ть** *impf* liquidate, cancel. **пога́шенный** used, cancelled, cashed.
погиба́ть *impf*, **по|ги́бнуть** (-ну; -ги́б) *pf* perish; be lost. **поги́бель** ruin. **поги́бший** lost; ruined; killed.
по|гла́дить (-а́жу) *pf.*
поглоти́ть (-ощу́, -о́тишь) *pf*, **поглоща́ть** *impf* swallow up; absorb. **поглоще́ние** absorption.
по|глупе́ть (-е́ю) *pf.*
по|гляде́ть (-яжу́) *pf.* **погля́дывать** *impf* glance (from time to time); **+за+***instr* keep an eye on.
погна́ть (-гоню́, -го́нишь; -гна́л, -а́, -о) *pf* drive; **~ся за+***instr* run after; start in pursuit of.

по|гну́ть(ся (-ну́(сь, -нёшь(ся) *pf.* **по|гнуша́ться** *pf.*
поговори́ть *pf* have a talk.
погово́рка saying, proverb.
пого́да weather.
погоди́ть (-ожу́) *pf* wait a little; **немно́го погодя́** a little later.
поголо́вно *adv* one and all. **поголо́вный** general; capitation. **поголо́вье** number.
пого́н (*gen pl* -о́н) shoulder-strap.
пого́нщик driver. **погоню́** *etc.*: *see* **погна́ть. пого́ня** pursuit, chase. **погоня́ть** *impf* urge on, drive.
погорячи́ться (-чу́сь) *pf* get worked up.
пого́ст graveyard.
погранíчник frontier guard. **пограни́чный** frontier.
по́греб (*pl* -а́) cellar. **погреба́льный** funeral. **погреба́ть** *impf of* **погрести́. погребе́ние** burial.
погрему́шка rattle.
погрести́¹ (-ебу́, -ебёшь; -рёб, -ла́) *pf* (*impf* **погреба́ть**) bury.
погрести́² (-ебу́, -ебёшь; -рёб, -ла́) *pf* row for a while.
погре́ть (-е́ю) *pf* warm; **~ся** warm o.s.
по|греши́ть (-шу́) *pf* sin; err. **погре́шность** error, mistake.
по|грози́ть(ся (-ожу́(сь) *pf.* **по|грубе́ть** (-е́ю) *pf.*
погружа́ть *impf*, **по|грузи́ть** (-ужу́, -у́зишь) *pf* load; ship; dip, plunge, immerse; **~ся** sink, plunge; dive; be plunged, absorbed. **погруже́ние** submergence; immersion; dive. **погру́зка** loading; shipment.
погряза́ть *impf*, **по|гря́знуть** (-ну; -я́з) *pf* be bogged down; wallow.
по|губи́ть (-блю́, -бишь) *pf.* **по|гуля́ть** *pf.*
под, подо *prep* **I.** +*acc or instr* under; near, close to; **взять по́д руку**+*acc* take the arm of; **~ ви́дом**+*gen* under the guise of; **по́д гору** downhill; **~ Москво́й** in the environs of Moscow. **II.** +*instr* occupied by, used as; (meant, implied) by; in, with; **говя́дина ~ хре́ном** beef with horse-radish. **III.** +*acc* towards; to (the accompaniment of); in imitation of; on; for, to serve as; **ему́ ~ пятьдеся́т (лет)** he is getting on for fifty.
подава́ть(ся (-даю́(сь, -даёшь(ся) *impf of* **пода́ть(ся**
подави́ть (-влю́, -вишь) *pf*, **подавля́ть** *impf* suppress; depress; overwhelm. **по|дави́ться** (-влю́сь, -вишься) *pf.* **подавле́ние** suppression; repression. **пода́вленность** depression. **пода́вленный** suppressed; depressed. **подавля́ющий** overwhelming.
пода́вно *adv* all the more.
пода́гра gout.
пода́льше *adv* a little further.
по|дари́ть (-рю́, -ришь) *pf.* **пода́рок** (-рка) present.
пода́тливый pliant, pliable. **по́дать** (*gen pl* -е́й) tax. **пода́ть** (-а́м, -а́шь, -а́ст, -ади́м; по́дал, -а́, -о) *pf* (*impf* **подава́ть**) serve; give; put, move, turn; put forward, present, hand in; **~ся** move; give way; yield; **+на**+*acc* set out for. **пода́ча** giving, presenting; serve; feed, supply. **пода́чка** handout, crumb. **подаю́** *etc.*: *see* **подава́ть.** **подая́ние** alms.
подбега́ть *impf*, **подбежа́ть** (-егу́) *pf* come running (up).
подбива́ть *impf of* **подби́ть**
подберу́ *etc.*: *see* **подобра́ть. подбира́ть(ся** *impf of* **подобра́ть(ся**
подби́ть (-добью́, -добьёшь) *pf* (*impf* **подбива́ть**) line; re-sole; bruise; put out of action; incite.
подбодри́ть *pf*, **подбодря́ть** *impf* cheer up, encourage; **~ся** cheer up, take heart.
подбо́р selection, assortment.
подборо́док (-дка) chin.
подбоче́нившись *adv* with hands on hips.
подбра́сывать *impf*, **подбро́сить** (-ро́шу) *pf* throw up.
подва́л cellar; basement. **подва́льный** basement, cellar.

П

подведу́ *etc.*: *see* **подвести́**
подвезти́ (-зу́, -зёшь; -вёз, -ла́) *pf* (*impf* **подвози́ть**) bring, take; give a lift.
подвене́чный wedding.
подверга́ть *impf*, **подве́ргнуть** (-ну; -ве́рг) *pf* subject; expose; **~ся** +*dat* undergo. **подве́рженный** subject, liable.
подверну́ть (-ну́, -нёшь) *pf*, **подвёртывать** *impf* turn up; tuck under; sprain; tighten; **~ся** be sprained; be turned up; be tucked under.
подве́сить (-е́шу) *pf* (*impf* **подве́шивать**) hang up, suspend. **подвесно́й** hanging, suspended.
подвести́ (-еду́, -едёшь; -вёл, -а́) *pf* (*impf* **подводи́ть**) lead up, bring up; place (under); bring under, subsume; let down; **~ итоги** reckon up; sum up.
подве́шивать *impf of* **подве́сить**
по́двиг exploit, feat.
подвига́ть(ся *impf of* **подви́нуть(ся**
подви́жник religious ascetic; champion.
подвижно́й mobile; **~ соста́в** rolling-stock. **подви́жность** mobility. **подви́жный** mobile; lively; agile.
подвиза́ться *impf* (**в** *or* **на** +*prep*) work (in).
подви́нуть (-ну) *pf* (*impf* **подвига́ть**) move; push; advance; **~ся** move; advance.
подвла́стный +*dat* subject to; under the control of.
подво́да cart. **подводи́ть** (-ожу́, -о́дишь) *impf of* **подвести́**
подво́дн|ый submarine; underwater; **~ая скала́** reef.
подво́з transport; supply. **подвози́ть** (-ожу́, -о́зишь) *impf of* **подвезти́**
подворо́тня (*gen pl* -тен) gateway.
подво́х trick.
подвы́пивший tipsy.
подвяза́ть (-яжу́, -я́жешь) *pf*, **подвя́зывать** *impf* tie up. **подвя́зка** garter; suspender.
подгиба́ть *impf of* **подогну́ть**
подгляде́ть (-яжу́) *pf*, **подгля́дывать** *impf* peep; spy.
подгова́ривать *impf*, **подговори́ть** *pf* incite.
подгоню́ *etc.*: *see* **подогна́ть**. **подгоня́ть** *impf of* **подогна́ть**
подгора́ть *impf*, **подгоре́ть** (-ри́т) *pf* get a bit burnt. **подгоре́лый** slightly burnt.
подготови́тельный preparatory. **подгото́вить** (-влю) *pf*, **подгота́вливать** *impf* prepare; **~ся** prepare, get ready. **подгото́вка** preparation, training.
поддава́ться (-даю́сь, -даёшься) *impf of* **подда́ться**
подда́кивать *impf* agree, assent.
по́дданный *sb* subject; citizen. **по́дданство** citizenship. **подда́ться** (-а́мся, -а́шься, -а́стся, -адимся; -а́лся, -ла́сь) *pf* (*impf* **поддава́ться**) yield, give way.
подде́лать *pf*, **подде́лывать** *impf* counterfeit; forge. **подде́лка** falsification; forgery; imitation. **подде́льный** false, counterfeit.
поддержа́ть (-жу́, -жишь) *pf*, **подде́рживать** *impf* support; maintain. **подде́ржка** support.
по|де́йствовать *pf*.
поде́лать *pf* do; **ничего́ не поде́лаешь** it can't be helped.
по|дели́ть(ся (-лю́(сь, -лишь(ся) *pf*.
поде́лка *pl* small (hand-made) articles.
подело́м *adv*: **~ ему́** (*etc.*) it serves him (*etc.*) right.
подённый by the day. **подёнщик, -ица** day-labourer.
подёргиваться *impf* twitch.
подёржанный second-hand.
подёрнуть (-нет) *pf* cover.
подеру́ *etc.*: *see* **подра́ть**. **по|дешеве́ть** (-е́ет) *pf*.
поджа́ривать(ся *impf*, **поджа́рить(ся** *pf* fry, roast, grill; toast. **поджа́ристый** brown(ed).
поджа́рый lean, wiry.

П

поджа́ть (-дожму́, -дожмёшь) *pf* (*impf* **поджима́ть**) draw in, draw under; **~ губы** purse one's lips.

подже́чь (-дожгу́, -ожжёшь; -жёг, -дожгла́) *pf*, **поджига́ть** *impf* set fire to; burn. **поджига́тель** *m* arsonist; instigator.

поджида́ть *impf* (+*gen*) wait (for).

поджима́ть *impf of* **поджа́ть**

поджо́г arson.

подзаголо́вок (-вка) subtitle, subheading.

подзащи́тный *sb* client.

подземе́лье (*gen pl* -лий) cave; dungeon. **подзе́мный** underground.

подзову́ *etc.*: *see* **подозва́ть**

подзо́рная труба́ telescope.

подзыва́ть *impf of* **подозва́ть**

по|диви́ться (-влю́сь) *pf.*

подка́пывать(ся *impf of* **подкопа́ть(ся**

подкарау́ливать *impf*, **подкарау́лить** *pf* be on the watch (for).

подкати́ть (-ачу́, -а́тишь) *pf*, **подка́тывать** *impf* roll up, drive up; roll.

подка́шивать(ся *impf of* **подкоси́ть(ся**

подки́дывать *impf*, **подки́нуть** (-ну) *pf* throw up. **подки́дыш** foundling.

подкла́дка lining. **подкла́дывать** *impf of* **подложи́ть**

подкле́ивать *impf*, **подкле́ить** *pf* glue (up); mend.

подко́ва (horse-)shoe. **под|кова́ть** (-кую́, -ёшь) *pf*, **подко́вывать** *impf* shoe.

подко́жный hypodermic.

подкоми́ссия, подкомите́т subcommittee.

подко́п undermining; underground passage. **подкопа́ть** *pf* (*impf* **подка́пывать**) undermine; **~ся под**+*acc* undermine; burrow under.

подкоси́ть (-ошу́, -о́сишь) *pf* (*impf* **подка́шивать**) cut down; **~ся** give way.

подкра́дываться *impf of* **подкра́сться**

подкра́сить (-а́шу) *pf* (*impf* **подкра́шивать**) touch up; **~ся** make up lightly.

подкра́сться (-аду́сь, -адёшься) *pf* (*impf* **подкра́дываться**) sneak up.

подкра́шивать(ся *impf of* **подкра́сить(ся. подкра́шу** *etc.*: *see* **подкра́сить**

подкрепи́ть (-плю́) *pf*, **подкрепля́ть** *impf* reinforce; support; corroborate; fortify; **~ся** fortify o.s. **подкрепле́ние** confirmation; sustenance; reinforcement.

подкрути́ть (-учу́, -у́тишь) *pf* (*impf* **подкру́чивать**) tighten up.

по́дкуп bribery. **подкупа́ть** *impf*, **подкупи́ть** (-плю́, -пишь) *pf* bribe; win over.

подла́диться (-а́жусь) *pf*, **подла́живаться** *impf* +**к**+*dat* adapt o.s. to; make up to.

подла́мываться *impf of* **подломи́ться**

по́дле *prep*+*gen* by the side of, beside.

подлежа́ть (-жу́) *impf* +*dat* be subject to; **не подлежи́т сомне́нию** it is beyond doubt. **подлежа́щее** *sb* subject. **подлежа́щий**+*dat* subject to.

подлеза́ть *impf*, **подле́зть** (-зу; -ез) *pf* crawl (under).

подле́сок (-ска) undergrowth.

подле́ц (-а́) scoundrel.

подлива́ть *impf of* **подли́ть. подли́вка** sauce, dressing; gravy.

подли́за *m* & *f* toady. **подлиза́ться** (-ижу́сь, -и́жешься) *pf*, **подли́зываться** *impf* +**к**+*dat* suck up to.

по́длинник original. **по́длинно** *adv* really. **по́длинный** genuine; authentic; original; real.

подли́ть (-долью́, -дольёшь; по́дли́л, -а́, -о) *pf* (*impf* **подлива́ть**) pour; add.

подло́г forgery.

подло́дка submarine.

подложи́ть (-жу́, -жишь) *pf* (*impf* **подкла́дывать**) add; +**под**+*acc* lay under; line.

П

подло́жный false, spurious; counterfeit, forged.
подлоко́тник arm (*of chair*).
подломи́ться (-о́мится) *pf* (*impf* **подла́мываться**) break; give way.
по́длость meanness, baseness; mean trick. **по́длый** (подл, -á, -o) mean, base.
подма́зать (-а́жу) *pf*, **подма́зывать** *impf* grease; bribe.
подмасте́рье (*gen pl* -ьев) *m* apprentice.
подме́н, подме́на replacement. **подме́нивать** *impf*, **подмени́ть** (-ню́, -нишь) *pf*, **подменя́ть** *impf* replace.
подмести́ (-ету́, -етёшь; -мёл, -á) *pf*, **подмета́ть**[1] *impf* sweep.
подмета́ть[2] *pf* (*impf* **подмётывать**) tack.
подме́тить (-е́чу) *pf* (*impf* **подмеча́ть**) notice.
подмётка sole.
подмётывать *impf of* **подмета́ть**[2]. **подмеча́ть** *impf of* **подме́тить**

П

подмеша́ть *pf*, **подме́шивать** *impf* mix in, stir in.
подми́гивать *impf*, **подмигну́ть** (-ну́, -нёшь) *pf* +*dat* wink at.
подмо́га help.
подмока́ть *impf*, **подмо́кнуть** (-нет; -мо́к) *pf* get damp, get wet.
подмора́живать *impf*, **подморо́зить** *pf* freeze.
подмоско́вный (situated) near Moscow.
подмо́стки (-ов) *pl* scaffolding; stage.
подмо́ченный damp; tarnished.
подмыва́ть *impf*, **подмы́ть** (-о́ю) *pf* wash; wash away; **его́ так и подмыва́ет** he feels an urge (to).
подмы́шка armpit.
поднево́льный dependent; forced.
поднести́ (-су́, -сёшь; -ёс, -ла́) *pf* (*impf* **подноси́ть**) present; take, bring.
поднима́ть(ся *impf of* **подня́ть(ся**
поднови́ть (-влю́) *pf*, **подновля́ть** *impf* renew, renovate.
подного́тная *sb* ins and outs.
подно́жие foot; pedestal. **подно́жка** running-board. **подно́жный корм** pasture.
подно́с tray. **подноси́ть** (-ошу́, -о́сишь) *impf of* **поднести́**. **подноше́ние** giving; present.
подня́тие raising. **подня́ть** (-ниму́, -ни́мешь; по́днял, -á, -o) *pf* (*impf* **поднима́ть, подыма́ть**) raise; lift (up); rouse; **~ся** rise; go up.
подо *see* **под**
подоба́ть *impf* befit, become. **подоба́ющий** proper.
подо́бие likeness; similarity. **подо́бн|ый** like, similar; **и тому́ ~ое** and so on, and such like; **ничего́ ~ого!** nothing of the sort!
подобостра́стие servility. **подобостра́стный** servile.
подобра́ть (-дберу́, -дберёшь; -бра́л, -á, -o) *pf* (*impf* **подбира́ть**) pick up; tuck up, put up; pick; **~ся** steal up.
подобью́ *etc.*: *see* **подби́ть**
подогна́ть (-дгоню́, -дго́нишь; -а́л, -á, -o) *pf* (*impf* **подгоня́ть**) drive; urge on; adjust.
подогну́ть (-ну́, -нёшь) *pf* (*impf* **подгиба́ть**) tuck in; bend under.
подогрева́ть *impf*, **подогре́ть** (-е́ю) *pf* warm up.
пододвига́ть *impf*, **пододви́нуть** (-ну) *pf* move up.
пододея́льник blanket cover; top sheet.
подожгу́ *etc.*: *see* **подже́чь**
подожда́ть (-ду́, -дёшь; -а́л, -á, -o) *pf* wait (+*gen or acc* for).
подожму́ *etc.*: *see* **поджа́ть**
подозва́ть (-дзову́, -дзовёшь; -а́л, -á, -o) *pf* (*impf* **подзыва́ть**) call to; beckon.
подозрева́емый suspected; suspect. **подозрева́ть** *impf* suspect. **подозре́ние** suspicion. **подозри́тельный** suspicious.
по|дои́ть (-ою́, -о́ишь) *pf*.

подойти́ (-йду́, -йдёшь; -ошёл, -шла́) *pf* (*impf* **подходи́ть**) approach; come up; +*dat* suit, fit.
подоко́нник window-sill.
подо́л hem.
подо́лгу *adv* for ages; for hours (*etc.*) on end.
подолью́ *etc.*: *see* **подли́ть**
подо́нки (-ов) *pl* dregs; scum.
подоплёка underlying cause.
подопру́ *etc.*: *see* **подпере́ть**
подо́пытный experimental.
подорва́ть (-рву́, -рвёшь; -а́л, -а́, -о) *pf* (*impf* **подрыва́ть**) undermine; blow up.
по|дорожа́ть *pf.*
подоро́жник plantain. **подоро́жный** roadside.
подосла́ть (-ошлю́, -ошлёшь) *pf* (*impf* **подсыла́ть**) send (secretly).
подоспева́ть *impf*, **подоспе́ть** (-е́ю) *pf* arrive, appear (in time).
подостла́ть (-дстелю́, -дсте́лешь) *pf* (*impf* **подстила́ть**) lay under.
подотде́л section, subdivision.
подотру́ *etc.*: *see* **подтере́ть**
подотчётный accountable.
по|до́хнуть (-ну) *pf* (*impf also* **подыха́ть**).
подохо́дный нало́г income-tax.
подо́шва sole; foot.
подошёл *etc.*: *see* **подойти́. подошлю́** *etc.*: *see* **подосла́ть подошью́** *etc.*: *see* **подши́ть.**
подпада́ть *impf*, **подпа́сть** (-аду́, -адёшь; -а́л) *pf* **под**+*acc* fall under.
подпева́ть *impf* (+*dat*) sing along (with).
подпере́ть (-допру́; -пёр) *pf* (*impf* **подпира́ть**) prop up.
подпи́ливать *impf*, **подпили́ть** (-лю́, -лишь) *pf* saw; saw a little off.
подпира́ть *impf of* **подпере́ть**
подписа́ние signing. **подписа́ть** (-ишу́, -и́шешь) *pf*, **подпи́сывать** *impf* sign; **~ся** sign; subscribe. **подпи́ска** subscription. **подписно́й** subscription. **подпи́счик** subscriber. **по́дпись** signature.
подплыва́ть *impf*, **подплы́ть** (-ыву́, -ывёшь; -плы́л, -а́, -о) *pf* **к**+*dat* swim *or* sail up to.
подполза́ть *impf*, **подползти́** (-зу́, -зёшь; -по́лз, -ла́) *pf* creep up (**к**+*dat* to); +**под**+*acc* crawl under.
подполко́вник lieutenant-colonel.
подпо́лье cellar; underground. **подпо́льный** underfloor; underground.
подпо́ра, подпо́рка prop, support.
подпо́чва subsoil.
подпра́вить (-влю) *pf*, **подправля́ть** *impf* touch up, adjust.
подпры́гивать *impf*, **подпры́гнуть** (-ну) *pf* jump up (and down).
подпуска́ть *impf*, **подпусти́ть** (-ущу́, -у́стишь) *pf* allow to approach.
подраба́тывать *impf*, **подрабо́тать** *pf* earn on the side; work up.
подра́внивать *impf of* **подровня́ть**
подража́ние imitation. **подража́ть** *impf* imitate.
подразделе́ние subdivision. **подраздели́ть** *pf*, **подразделя́ть** *impf* subdivide.
подразумева́ть *impf* imply, mean; **~ся** be meant, be understood.
подраста́ть *impf*, **подрасти́** (-ту́, -тёшь; -ро́с, -ла́) *pf* grow.
по|дра́ть(ся (-деру́(сь, -дерёшь(ся, -а́л(ся, -ла́(сь, -о́(сь *or* -о(сь) *pf.*
подре́зать (-е́жу) *pf*, **подреза́ть** *impf* cut; clip, trim.
подро́бно *adv* in detail. **подро́бность** detail. **подро́бный** detailed.
подровня́ть *pf* (*impf* **подра́внивать**) level, even; trim.
подро́с *etc.*: *see* **подрасти́. подро́сток** (-тка) adolescent; youth.
подро́ю *etc.*: *see* **подры́ть**
подруба́ть[1] *impf*, **подруби́ть** (-блю́, -бишь) *pf* chop down; cut short(er).

П

подруба́ть[2] *impf*, **подруби́ть** (-блю́, -бишь) *pf* hem.

подру́га friend; girlfriend. **по-дру́жески** *adv* in a friendly way. **подружи́ться** (-жу́сь) *pf* make friends.

по-друго́му *adv* differently.

подру́чный at hand; improvised; *sb* assistant.

подры́в undermining; injury.

подрыва́ть[1] *impf of* **подорва́ть**

подрыва́ть[2] *impf*, **подры́ть** (-ро́ю) *pf* undermine, sap. **подрывно́й** blasting, demolition; subversive.

подря́д[1] *adv* in succession.

подря́д[2] contract. **подря́дчик** contractor.

подса́живаться *impf of* **подсе́сть**

подса́ливать *impf of* **подсоли́ть**

подсве́чник candlestick.

подсе́сть (-ся́ду; -се́л) *pf* (*impf* **подса́живаться**) sit down (**к**+*dat* near).

подсказа́ть (-ажу́, -а́жешь) *pf*, **подска́зывать** *impf* prompt; suggest. **подска́зка** prompting.

подска́кивать *impf*, **подскочи́ть** (-чу́, -чишь) *pf* jump (up); soar; come running.

подсласти́ть (-ащу́) *pf*, **подсла́щивать** *impf* sweeten.

подсле́дственный under investigation.

подслу́шать *pf*, **подслу́шивать** *impf* overhear; eavesdrop, listen.

подсма́тривать *impf*, **подсмотре́ть** (-рю́, -ришь) *pf* spy (on).

подсне́жник snowdrop.

подсо́бный subsidiary; auxiliary.

подсо́вывать *impf of* **подсу́нуть**

подсозна́ние subconscious (mind). **подсозна́тельный** subconscious.

подсоли́ть (-со́ли́шь) *pf* (*impf* **подса́ливать**) add salt to.

подсо́лнечник sunflower. **подсо́лнечный** sunflower.

подсо́хнуть (-ну) *pf* (*impf* **подсыха́ть**) dry out a little.

подспо́рье help.

подста́вить (-влю) *pf*, **подставля́ть** *impf* put (under); bring up; expose; ~ **но́жку** +*dat* trip up. **подста́вка** stand; support. **подставно́й** false.

подстака́нник glass-holder.

подстелю́ *etc.*: *see* **подостла́ть**

подстерега́ть *impf*, **подстере́чь** (-егу́, -ежёшь; -рёг, -ла́) *pf* lie in wait for.

подстила́ть *impf of* **подостла́ть**. **подсти́лка** litter.

подстра́ивать *impf of* **подстро́ить**

подстрека́тель *m* instigator. **подстрека́тельство** instigation. **подстрека́ть** *impf*, **подстрекну́ть** (-ну́, -нёшь) *pf* instigate, incite.

подстре́ливать *impf*, **подстрели́ть** (-лю́, -лишь) *pf* wound.

подстрига́ть *impf*, **подстри́чь** (-игу́, -ижёшь; -и́г) *pf* cut; clip, trim; **~ся** have a hair-cut.

подстро́ить *pf* (*impf* **подстра́ивать**) build on; cook up.

подстро́чн|ый literal; **~ое приме́чание** footnote.

по́дступ approach. **подступа́ть** *impf*, **подступи́ть** (-плю́, -пишь) *pf* approach; **~ся к**+*dat* approach.

подсуди́мый *sb* defendant; the accused. **подсу́дный**+*dat* under the jurisdiction of.

подсу́нуть (-ну) *pf* (*impf* **подсо́вывать**) put, shove; palm off.

подсчёт calculation; count. **подсчита́ть** *pf*, **подсчи́тывать** count (up); calculate.

подсыла́ть *impf of* **подосла́ть**. **подсыха́ть** *impf of* **подсо́хнуть**. **подся́ду** *etc.*: *see* **подсе́сть**. **подта́лкивать** *impf of* **подтолкну́ть**

подта́скивать *impf of* **подтащи́ть**

подтасова́ть *pf*, **подтасо́вывать** *impf* shuffle unfairly; juggle with.

подта́чивать *impf of* **подточи́ть**

подтащи́ть (-щу́, -щишь) *pf* (*impf* **подта́скивать**) drag up.

подтверди́ть (-ржу́) *pf*, **подтвержда́ть** *impf* confirm; corroborate. **подтвержде́ние** confirmation, corroboration.

подтёк bruise. **подтека́ть** *impf of* **подте́чь**; leak.

подтере́ть (-дотру́, -дотрёшь; подтёр) *pf* (*impf* **подтира́ть**) wipe (up).

подте́чь (-ечёт; -тёк, -ла́) *pf* (*impf* **подтека́ть**) **под**+*acc* flow under.

подтира́ть *impf of* **подтере́ть**

подтолкну́ть (-ну́, -нёшь) *pf* (*impf* **подта́лкивать**) push; urge on.

подточи́ть (-чу́, -чишь) *pf* (*impf* **подта́чивать**) sharpen; eat away; undermine.

подтру́нивать *impf*, **подтрун́ить** *pf* **над**+*instr* tease.

подтя́гивать *impf*, **подтяну́ть** (-ну́, -нешь) *pf* tighten; pull up; move up; **~ся** tighten one's belt *etc.*; move up; pull o.s. together. **подтя́жки** (-жек) *pl* braces, suspenders. **подтя́нутый** smart.

по|ду́мать *pf* think (for a while). **поду́мывать** *impf*+*inf or* **о**+*prep* think about.

по|ду́ть (-у́ю) *pf*.

поду́шка pillow; cushion.

подхали́м *m* toady. **подхали́мство** grovelling.

подхвати́ть (-ачу́, -а́тишь) *pf*, **подхва́тывать** *impf* catch (up), pick up, take up.

подхлестну́ть (-ну́, -нёшь) *pf*, **подхлёстывать** *impf* whip up.

подхо́д approach. **подходи́ть** (-ожу́, -о́дишь) *impf of* **подойти́**. **подходя́щий** suitable.

подцепи́ть (-плю́, -пишь) *pf*, **подцепля́ть** *impf* hook on; pick up.

подча́с *adv* sometimes.

подчёркивать *impf*, **подчеркну́ть** (-ну́, -нёшь) *pf* underline; emphasize.

подчине́ние subordination; submission. **подчинённый** subordinate. **подчини́ть** *pf*, **подчиня́ть** *impf* subordinate, subject; **~ся** +*dat* submit to.

подшива́ть *impf of* **подши́ть**. **подши́вка** hemming; lining; soling.

подши́пник bearing.

подши́ть (-дошью́, -дошьёшь) *pf* (*impf* **подшива́ть**) hem, line; sole.

подшути́ть (-учу́, -у́тишь) *pf*, **подшу́чивать** *impf* **над**+*instr* mock; play a trick on.

подъе́ду *etc.*: *see* **подъе́хать**

подъе́зд entrance, doorway; approach. **подъезжа́ть** *impf of* **подъе́хать**

подъём lifting; raising; ascent; climb; enthusiasm; instep; reveille. **подъёмник** lift, elevator, hoist. **подъёмный** lifting; **~ кран** crane; **~ мост** drawbridge.

подъе́хать (-е́ду) *pf* (*impf* **подъезжа́ть**) drive up.

подыма́ть(ся *impf of* **подня́ть(ся**

подыска́ть (-ыщу́, -ы́щешь) *pf*, **поды́скивать** *impf* seek (out).

подыто́живать *impf*, **подыто́жить** (-жу) *pf* sum up.

подыха́ть *impf of* **подо́хнуть**

подыша́ть (-шу́, -шишь) *pf* breathe.

поеда́ть *impf of* **пое́сть**

поеди́нок (-нка) duel.

по́езд (*pl* -а́) train. **пое́здка** trip.

пое́сть (-е́м, -е́шь, -е́ст, -еди́м; -е́л) *pf* (*impf* **поеда́ть**) eat, eat up; have a bite to eat.

по|е́хать (-е́ду) *pf* go; set off.

по|жале́ть (-е́ю) *pf*.

по|жа́ловать(ся *pf*. **пожа́луй** *adv* perhaps. **пожа́луйста** *partl* please; you're welcome.

пожа́р fire. **пожа́рище** scene of a fire. **пожа́рник, пожа́рный** *sb* fireman. **пожа́рн|ый** fire; **~ая кома́нда** fire-brigade; **~ая ле́стница** fire-escape; **~ая маши́на** fire-engine.

пожа́тие handshake. **пожа́ть**[1] (-жму́, -жмёшь) *pf* (*impf* **пожима́ть**) press; **~ ру́ку**+*dat* shake hands with; **~ плеча́ми** shrug one's shoulders.

пожа́ть[2] (-жну́, -жнёшь) *pf* (*impf* **пожина́ть**) reap.

П

пожела́ние wish, desire. **по|поже-ла́ть** *pf.*
по|желте́ть (-е́ю) *pf.*
по|жени́ть (-ню́, -нишь) *pf.* **пожени́ться** (-же́нимся) *pf* get married.
поже́ртвование donation. **по|же́ртвовать** *pf.*
пожива́ть *impf* live; **как (вы) пожива́ете?** how are you (getting on)? **пожи́зненный** life(long). **пожило́й** elderly.
пожима́ть *impf of* **пожа́ть**. **пожина́ть** *impf of* **пожа́ть²**. **пожира́ть** *impf of* **пожра́ть**
пожи́тки (-ов) *pl* belongings.
пожи́ть (-иву́, -ивёшь; по́жил, -а́, -о) *pf.* live for a while; stay.
пожму́ *etc.*: *see* **пожа́ть¹**. **пожну́** *etc.*: *see* **пожа́ть²**
пожра́ть (-ру́, -рёшь; -а́л, -а́, -о) *pf* (*impf* **пожира́ть**) devour.
по́за pose.
по|забо́титься (-о́чусь) *pf.*
позабыва́ть *impf*, **позабы́ть** (-у́ду) *pf* forget all about.
по|зави́довать *pf.* **по|за́втракать** *pf.*
позавчера́ *adv* the day before yesterday.
позади́ *adv* & *prep+gen* behind.
по|заи́мствовать *pf.*
позапро́шлый before last.
по|зва́ть (-зову́, -зовёшь; -а́л, -а́, -о) *pf.*
позволе́ние permission. **позволи́тельный** permissible. **позво́лить** *pf*, **позволя́ть** *impf +dat* allow, permit; **позво́ль(те)** allow me; excuse me.
по|звони́ть *pf.*
позвоно́к (-нка́) vertebra. **позвоно́чник** spine. **позвоно́чн|ый** spinal; vertebrate; **~ые** *sb pl* vertebrates.
поздне́е *adv* later. **по́здний** late; **по́здно** it is late.
по|здоро́ваться *pf.* **поздра́вить** (-влю) *pf*, **поздравля́ть** *impf* **с**+*instr* congratulate on. **поздравле́ние** congratulation.
по|зелене́ть (-е́ет) *pf.*
по́зже *adv* later (on).
пози́ровать *impf* pose.
позити́в positive. **позити́вный** positive.
пози́ция position.
познава́тельный cognitive. **познава́ть** (-наю́, -наёшь) *impf of* **позна́ть**
по|знако́мить(ся (-млю(сь) *pf.*
позна́ние cognition. **позна́ть** *pf* (*impf* **познава́ть**) get to know.
позоло́та gilding. **по|золоти́ть** (-лочу́) *pf.*
позо́р shame, disgrace. **позо́рить** *impf* (*pf* **о~**) disgrace; **~ся** disgrace o.s. **позо́рный** shameful.
поигра́ть *pf* play (for a while).
поимённо *adv* by name.
по́имка capture.
поинтересова́ться *pf* be curious.
поиска́ть (-ищу́, -и́щешь) *pf* look for. **по́иски** (-ов) *pl* search.
пои́стине *adv* indeed.
пои́ть (пою́, по́ишь) *impf* (*pf* **на~**) give something to drink; water.
пойду́ *etc.*: *see* **пойти́**
по́йло swill.
пойма́ть *pf of* **лови́ть**. **пойму́** *etc.*: *see* **поня́ть**
пойти́ (-йду́, -йдёшь; пошёл, -шла́) *pf of* **идти́, ходи́ть**; go, walk; begin to walk; +*inf* begin; **пошёл!** off you go! I'm off; **пошёл вон!** be off!
пока́ *adv* for the present; cheerio; **~ что** in the meanwhile. **пока́** *conj* while; **~ не** until.
пока́з showing, demonstration. **показа́ние** testimony, evidence; reading. **показа́тель** *m* index. **показа́тельный** significant; model; demonstration. **показа́ть** (-ажу́, -а́жешь) *pf*, **пока́зывать** *impf* show. **по|каза́ться** (-ажу́сь, -а́жешься) *pf*, **пока́зываться** *impf* show o.s.; appear. **показно́й** for show; ostentatious. **показу́ха** show.
по|кале́чить(ся (-чу(сь) *pf.*
пока́мест *adv* & *conj* for the present; while; meanwhile.

по|кара́ть *pf.*
по|ката́ться *pf.*
покати́ть (-чу́, -тишь) *pf* start (rolling); **~ся** start rolling.
пока́тый sloping; slanting.
покача́ть *pf* rock, swing; **~ голово́й** shake one's head. **пока́чивать** rock slightly; **~ся** rock; stagger. **покачну́ть** (-ну́, -нёшь) shake; rock; **~ся** sway, totter, lurch.
пока́шливать *impf* have a slight cough.
покая́ние confession; repentance. **по|ка́яться** *pf.*
поквита́ться *pf* be quits; get even.
покида́ть *impf*, **поки́нуть** (-ну) *pf* leave; abandon. **поки́нутый** deserted.
поклада́я: не ~ рук untiringly.
покла́дистый complaisant, obliging.
покло́н bow; greeting; regards. **поклоне́ние** worship. **поклони́ться** (-ню́сь, -нишься) *pf of* **кла́няться. покло́нник** admirer; worshipper. **поклоня́ться** *impf* +*dat* worship.
по|кля́сться (-яну́сь, -нёшься; -я́лся, -ла́сь) *pf.*
поко́иться *impf* rest, repose. **поко́й** rest, peace; room. **поко́йник, -ица** the deceased. **поко́йный** calm, quiet; deceased.
по|колеба́ть(ся (-е́блю(сь) *pf.*
поколе́ние generation.
по|колоти́ть(ся (-очу́(сь, -о́тишь(ся) *pf.*
поко́нчить (-чу) *pf* **с**+*instr* finish; put an end to; **~ с собо́й** commit suicide.
покоре́ние conquest. **покори́ть** *pf* (*impf* **покоря́ть**) subdue; conquer; **~ся** submit.
по|корми́ть(ся (-млю́(сь, -мишь(ся) *pf.*
поко́рный humble; submissive, obedient.
по|коро́бить(ся (-блю(сь) *pf.*
покоря́ть(ся *impf of* **покори́ть(ся**
поко́с mowing; meadow(-land).
покоси́вшийся rickety, ramshackle. **по|коси́ть(ся** (-ошу́(сь) *pf.*
по|кра́сить (-а́шу) *pf.* **покра́ска** painting, colouring.
по|красне́ть (-е́ю) *pf.* **по|криви́ть(ся** (-влю́(сь) *pf.*
покро́в cover. **покрови́тель** *m*, **покрови́тельница** patron; sponsor. **покрови́тельственный** protective; patronizing. **покрови́тельство** protection, patronage. **покрови́тельствовать** *impf* +*dat* protect, patronize.
покро́й cut.
покроши́ть (-шу́, -шишь) *pf* crumble; chop.
покрути́ть (-учу́, -у́тишь) *pf* twist.
покрыва́ло cover; bedspread; veil. **покрыва́ть** *impf*, **по|кры́ть** (-ро́ю) *pf* cover; **~ся** cover o.s.; get covered. **покры́тие** covering; surfacing; payment. **покры́шка** cover; tyre.
покупа́тель *m* buyer; customer. **покупа́ть** *impf of* **купи́ть. поку́пка** purchase. **покупно́й** bought, purchased; purchase.
по|кури́ть (-рю́, -ришь) *pf* have a smoke.
по|ку́шать *pf.*
покуше́ние +**на**+*acc* attempted assassination of.
пол[1] (*loc* -у́; *pl* -ы́) floor.
пол[2] sex.
пол- *in comb with n in gen, in oblique cases usu* **полу-**, half.
пола́ (*pl* -ы) flap; **из-под полы́** on the sly.
полага́ть *impf* suppose, think. **полага́ться** *impf of* **положи́ться; полага́ется** *impers* one is supposed to; +*dat* it is due to.
по|ла́комить(ся (-млю(сь) *pf.*
полго́да (полуго́да) *m* half a year.
по́лдень (-дня *or* -лу́дня) *m* noon. **полдне́вный** *adj.*
по́ле (*pl* -я́, -е́й) field; ground; margin; brim. **полев|о́й** field; **~ы́е цветы́** wild flowers.
полежа́ть (-жу́) *pf* lie down for a while.

П

поле́зн|ый useful; helpful; good, wholesome; **~ая нагру́зка** payload.
по|ле́зть (-зу; -ле́з) *pf.*
полемизи́ровать *impf* debate, engage in controversy. **поле́мика** controversy; polemics. **полеми́ческий** polemical.
по|лени́ться (-ню́сь, -ни́шься) *pf.*
поле́но (*pl* -е́нья, -ьев) log.
полёт flight. **по|лете́ть** (-лечу́) *pf.*
по́лзать *indet impf*, **ползти́** (-зу́, -зёшь; полз, -ла́) *det impf* crawl, creep; ooze; fray. **ползу́чий** creeping.
поли- *in comb* poly-.
полива́ть(ся *impf of* **поли́ть(ся**. **поли́вка** watering.
полига́мия polygamy.
полигло́т polyglot.
полиграфи́ческий printing. **полиграфи́я** printing.
полиго́н range.
поликли́ника polyclinic.
полиме́р polymer.
полиня́лый faded. **по|линя́ть** *pf.*
полиомиели́т poliomyelitis
полирова́ть *impf* (*pf* **от~**) polish. **поліро́вка** polishing; polish.
полит- *abbr in comb* (*of* **полити́ческий**) political. **политзаключённый** *sb* political prisoner.
политехни́ческий polytechnic.
поли́тик politician. **поли́тика** policy; politics. **полити́ческий** political; **полити́чески корре́ктный** politically correct.
поли́ть (-лью́, -льёшь; по́лил, -а́, -о) *pf* (*impf* **полива́ть**) pour over; water; **~ся** *+instr* pour over o.s.
полице́йский police; *sb* policeman. **поли́ция** police.
пол́ичн|ое *sb*: **с ~ым** red-handed.
полк (-а́, *loc* -у́) regiment.
по́лка shelf; berth.
полко́вник colonel. **полково́дец** (-дца) commander; general. **полково́й** regimental.
пол-ли́тра half a litre.
полне́ть (-е́ю) *impf* (*pf* **по~**) put on weight.

П

по́лно *adv* that's enough! stop it!
полно- *in comb* full; completely. **полнолу́ние** full moon. **~метра́жный** full-length. **~пра́вный** enjoying full rights; competent. **~це́нный** of full value.
полномо́чие (*usu pl*) authority, power. **полномо́чный** plenipotentiary.
по́лностью *adv* in full; completely. **полнота́** completeness; corpulence.
по́лночь (-л(у́)ночи) midnight.
по́лный (-лон, -лна́, по́лно́) full; complete; plump.
полови́к (-а́) mat, matting.
полови́на half; **два с полови́ной** two and a half; **~ шесто́го** half-past five. **полови́нка** half.
полови́ца floor-board.
полово́дье high water.
полово́й[1] floor.
полово́й[2] sexual.
поло́гий gently sloping.
положе́ние position; situation; status; regulations; thesis; provisions. **поло́женный** agreed; determined. **поло́жим** let us assume; suppose. **положи́тельный** positive. **положи́ть** (-жу́, -жишь) *pf* (*impf* **класть**) put; lay (down); **~ся** (*impf* **полага́ться**) rely.
по́лоз (*pl* -о́зья, -ьев) runner.
по|лома́ть(ся *pf.* **поло́мка** breakage.
полоса́ (*acc* по́лосу́; *pl* по́лосы, -ло́с, -а́м) stripe; strip; band; region; belt; period. **полоса́тый** striped.
полоска́ть (-ощу́, -о́щешь) *impf* (*pf* **вы~, от~, про~**) rinse; **~ го́рло** gargle; **~ся** paddle; flap.
по́лость[1] (*gen pl* -е́й) cavity.
по́лость[2] (*gen pl* -е́й) travelling rug.
полоте́нце (*gen pl* -нец) towel.
полотёр floor-polisher.
поло́тнище width; panel. **полотно́** (*pl* -а, -тен) linen; canvas. **полотня́ный** linen.
поло́ть (-лю́, -лешь) *impf* (*pf* **вы~**) weed.

полощу́ *etc.*: *see* **полоска́ть**
полти́нник fifty copecks.
полтора́ (-лу́тора) *m* & *neut*, **полторы́** (-лу́тора) *f* one and a half. **полтора́ста** (полу́т-) a hundred and fifty.
полу-[1] *see* **пол-**
полу-[2] *in comb* half-, semi-, demi-. **полуботи́нок** (-нка; *gen pl* -нок) shoe. **~го́дие** half a year. **~годи́чный** six months', lasting six months. **~годова́лый** six-month-old. **~годово́й** half-yearly, six-monthly. **~гра́мотный** semi-literate. **~защи́тник** half-back. **~кру́г** semicircle. **~кру́глый** semicircular. **~ме́сяц** crescent (moon). **~мра́к** semi-darkness. **~но́чный** midnight. **~о́стров** peninsula. **~откры́тый** ajar. **~проводни́к** (-а́) semi-conductor, transistor. **~ста́нок** (-нка) halt. **~тьма́** semi-darkness. **~фабрика́т** semi-finished product, convenience food. **~фина́л** semi-final. **~часово́й** half-hourly. **~ша́рие** hemisphere. **~шу́бок** (-бка) sheepskin coat.
полу́денный midday.
получа́тель *m* recipient. **получа́ть** *impf*, **получи́ть** (-чу́, -чишь) *pf* get, receive, obtain; **~ся** come, turn up; turn out; **из э́того ничего́ не получи́лось** nothing came of it. **получе́ние** receipt. **полу́чка** receipt; pay(-packet).
полу́чше *adv* a little better.
полчаса́ (получа́са) *m* half an hour.
по́лчище horde.
по́лый hollow; flood.
по|лысе́ть (-е́ю) *pf*.
по́льза use; benefit, profit; **в по́льзу**+*gen* in favour of, on behalf of. **по́льзование** use. **по́льзоваться** *impf* (*pf* **вос~**) +*instr* make use of, utilize; profit by; enjoy.
по́лька Pole; polka. **по́льский** Polish; *sb* polonaise.
по|льсти́ть(ся (-льщу́(сь)
полью́ *etc. see* **поли́ть**
По́льша Poland.
полюби́ть (-блю́, -бишь) *pf* come to like; fall in love with.
по|любова́ться (-бу́юсь) *pf*.
полюбо́вный amicable.
по|любопы́тствовать *pf*.
по́люс pole.
поля́к Pole.
поля́на glade, clearing.
поляриза́ция polarization. **поля́рник** polar explorer. **поля́рн|ый** polar; **~ая звезда́** pole-star.
пом- *abbr in comb* (*of* **помо́щник**) assistant. **~на́ч** assistant chief, assistant head.
пома́да pomade; lipstick.
помаза́ние anointment. **по|ма́зать(ся** (-а́жу(сь) *pf*. **помазо́к** (-зка́) small brush.
помале́ньку *adv* gradually; gently; modestly; so-so.
пома́лкивать *impf* hold one's tongue.
по|мани́ть (-ню́, -нишь) *pf*.
пома́рка blot; pencil mark; correction.
по|ма́слить *pf*.
помаха́ть (-машу́, -ма́шешь) *pf*, **пома́хивать** *impf* +*instr* wave; wag.
поме́длить *pf* +**с**+*instr* delay.
поме́ньше a little smaller; a little less.
по|меня́ть(ся *pf*.
помере́ть (-мру́, -мрёшь; -мер, -ла́, -ло) *pf* (*impf* **помира́ть**) die.
по|мере́щиться (-щусь) *pf*. **по|ме́рить** *pf*.
помертве́лый deathly pale. **по|мертве́ть** (-е́ю) *pf*.
помести́ть (-ещу́) *pf* (*impf* **помеща́ть**) accommodate; place, locate; invest; **~ся** lodge; find room. **поме́стье** (*gen pl* -тий, -тьям) estate.
по́месь cross(-breed), hybrid.
помёт dung; droppings; litter, brood.
поме́та, поме́тка mark, note. **по|ме́тить** (-е́чу) *pf* (*impf also* **поме-**

П

ча́ть) mark; date; **~ га́лочкой** tick.

поме́ха hindrance; obstacle; *pl* interference.

помеча́ть *impf of* **поме́тить**

поме́шанный mad; *sb* lunatic. **помеша́тельство** madness; craze. **по|меша́ть** *pf.* **помеша́ться** *pf* go mad.

помеща́ть *impf of* **помести́ть. помеща́ться** *impf of* **помести́ться**; be (situated); be accommodated, find room. **помеще́ние** premises; apartment, room, lodging; location; investment. **поме́щик** landowner.

помидо́р tomato.

поми́лование forgiveness. **поми́ловать** *pf* forgive.

поми́мо *prep+gen* apart from; besides; without the knowledge of.

помина́ть *impf of* **помяну́ть; не ~ ли́хом** remember kindly. **поми́нки** (-нок) *pl* funeral repast.

помира́ть *impf of* **помере́ть**

по|мири́ть(ся *pf.*

П

по́мнить *impf* remember.

помога́ть *impf of* **помо́чь**

по-мо́ему *adv* in my opinion.

помо́и (-ев) *pl* slops. **помо́йка** (*gen pl* -о́ек) rubbish dump. **помо́йный** slop.

помо́л grinding.

помо́лвка betrothal.

по|моли́ться (-лю́сь, -лишься) *pf.* **по|молоде́ть** (-е́ю) *pf.*

помолча́ть (-чу́) *pf* be silent for a time.

помо́рье: *see* **по-** II.

по|мо́рщиться (-щу́сь) *pf.*

помо́ст dais; rostrum.

по|мочи́ться (-чу́сь, -чишься) *pf.*

помо́чь (-огу́, -о́жешь; -о́г, -ла́) *pf* (*impf* **помога́ть**) (*+dat*) help. **помо́щник, помо́щница** assistant. **по́мощь** help; **на ~!** help!

помо́ю *etc.*: *see* **помы́ть**

по́мпа pump.

помутне́ние dimness, clouding.

помча́ться (-чу́сь) *pf* rush; dart off.

помыка́ть *impf +instr* order about.

по́мысел (-сла) intention; thought.

по|мы́ть(ся (-мо́ю(сь) *pf.*

помяну́ть (-ну́, -нешь) *pf* (*impf* **помина́ть**) mention; pray for.

помя́тый crumpled. **по|мя́ться** (-мнётся) *pf.*

по|наде́яться (-е́юсь) *pf* count, rely.

пона́добиться (-блюсь) *pf* be *or* become necessary; **е́сли пона́добится** if necessary.

понапра́сну *adv* in vain.

понаслы́шке *adv* by hearsay.

по-настоя́щему *adv* properly, truly.

понача́лу *adv* at first.

понево́ле *adv* willynilly; against one's will.

понеде́льник Monday.

понемно́гу, понемно́жку *adv* little by little.

по|нести́(сь (-су́(сь, -сёшь(ся; -нёс(ся, -ла́(сь) *pf.*

понижа́ть *impf*, **пони́зить** (-ни́жу) *pf* lower; reduce; **~ся** fall, drop, go down. **пониже́ние** fall; lowering; reduction.

поника́ть *impf*, **по|ни́кнуть** (-ну; -ни́к) *pf* droop, wilt.

понима́ние understanding. **понима́ть** *impf of* **поня́ть**

по-но́вому *adv* in a new fashion.

поно́с diarrhoea.

поноси́ть[1] (-ошу́, -о́сишь) *pf* carry; wear.

поноси́ть[2] (-ошу́, -о́сишь) *impf* abuse (*verbally*).

поно́шенный worn; threadbare.

по|нра́виться (-влюсь) *pf.*

понто́н pontoon.

пону́дить (-у́жу) *pf*, **понужда́ть** *impf* compel.

понука́ть *impf* urge on.

пону́рить *pf*: **~ го́лову** hang one's head. **пону́рый** downcast.

по|ню́хать *pf.* **поню́шка: ~ табаку́** pinch of snuff.

поня́тие concept; notion, idea.

поня́тливый bright, quick. **поня́тн|ый** understandable, comprehensible; clear; **~о** naturally; **~о?** (do you) see? **поня́ть** (пойму́, -мёшь; по́нял, -а́, -о) *pf* (*impf* **понима́ть**) understand; realize.
по|обе́дать *pf.* **по|обеща́ть** *pf.*
по́одаль *adv* at some distance.
поодино́чке *adv* one by one.
поочерёдно *adv* in turn.
поощре́ние encouragement. **поощри́ть** *pf*, **поощря́ть** *impf* encourage.
поп (-а́) priest.
попада́ние hit. **попада́ть(ся** *impf of* **попа́сть(ся**
попадья́ priest's wife.
попа́ло: *see* **попа́сть. по|па́риться** *pf.*
попа́рно *adv* in pairs, two by two.
попа́сть (-аду́, -адёшь; -а́л) *pf* (*impf* **попада́ть**) **+в+***acc* hit; get (in)to, find o.s. in; **+на+***acc* hit upon, come on; **не туда́ ~** get the wrong number; **~ся** be caught; find o.s.; turn up; **что попадётся** anything. **попа́ло** *with prons & advs*: **где ~** anywhere; **как ~** anyhow; **что ~** the first thing to hand.
поперёк *adv & prep+gen* across.
попереме́нно *adv* in turns.
попере́чник diameter. **попере́чн|ый** transverse, diametrical, cross; **~ый разре́з, ~ое сече́ние** cross-section.
поперхну́ться (-ну́сь, -нёшься) *pf* choke.
по|пе́рчить (-чу́) *pf.*
попече́ние care; charge; **на попече́нии+***gen* in the care of. **попечи́тель** *m* guardian, trustee.
попира́ть *impf* (*pf* **попра́ть**) trample on; flout.
попи́ть (-пью, -пьёшь; по́пи́л, -ла, по́пи́ло) *pf* have a drink.
поплаво́к (-вка́) float.
попла́кать (-а́чу) *pf* cry a little.
по|плати́ться (-чу́сь, -тишься) *pf.*
поплы́ть (-ыву́, -ывёшь; -ы́л, -ыла́, -о) *pf.* start swimming.
попо́йка drinking-bout.
попола́м *adv* in two, in half; half-and-half.
поползнове́ние half a mind; pretension(s).
пополне́ние replenishment; reinforcement. **по|полне́ть** (-е́ю) *pf.* **попо́лнить** *pf*, **пополня́ть** *impf* replenish; re-stock; reinforce.
пополу́дни *adv* in the afternoon; p.m.
попо́на horse-cloth.
по|по́тчевать (-чую) *pf.*
поправи́мый rectifiable. **попра́вить** (-влю) *pf*, **поправля́ть** *impf* repair; correct, put right; set straight; **~ся** correct o.s.; get better, recover; improve. **попра́вка** correction; repair; adjustment; recovery.
попра́ть *pf of* **попира́ть**
по-пре́жнему *adv* as before.
попрёк reproach. **попрека́ть** *impf*, **попрекну́ть** (-ну́, -нёшь) *pf* reproach.
по́прище field; walk of life.
по|про́бовать *pf.* **по|проси́ть(ся** (-ошу́(сь, -о́сишь(ся) *pf.*
по́просту *adv* simply; without ceremony.
попроша́йка *m & f* cadger. **попроша́йничать** *impf* cadge.
попроща́ться *pf* (**+с+***instr*) say goodbye (to).
попры́гать *pf* jump, hop.
попуга́й parrot.
популя́рность popularity. **популя́рный** popular.
попусти́тельство connivance.
по-пусто́му, по́пусту *adv* in vain.
попу́тно *adv* at the same time; in passing. **попу́тный** passing. **попу́тчик** fellow-traveller.
по|пыта́ться *pf.* **попы́тка** attempt.
по|пя́титься (-я́чусь) *pf.* **попя́тный** backward; **идти́ на ~** go back on one's word.
по́ра[1] pore.
пора́[2] (*acc* -у; *pl* -ы, пор, -а́м) time; it is time; **до каки́х пор?** till

П

when?; **до сих пор** till now; **с каких пор?** since when?
поработать *pf* do some work.
поработить (-ощу́) *pf*, **порабощать** *impf* enslave. **порабощение** enslavement.
поравняться *pf* come alongside.
по|радовать(ся *pf.*
поражать *impf*, **по|разить** (-ажу́) *pf* hit; strike; defeat; affect; astonish; **~ся** be astounded. **поражение** defeat. **поразительный** striking; astonishing.
по-разному *adv* differently.
поранить *pf* wound; injure.
порвать (-ву́, -вёшь; -ва́л, -а́, -о) *pf* (*impf* **порывать**) tear (up); break, break off; **~ся** tear; break (off).
по|редеть (-е́ет) *pf.*
порез cut. **порезать** (-е́жу) *pf* cut; **~ся** cut o.s.
порей leek.
по|рекомендовать *pf.* **по|ржаветь** (-е́ет) *pf.*
пористый porous.
порицание reprimand. **порицать** *impf* reprimand.
порка flogging.
поровну *adv* equally.
порог threshold; rapids.
порода breed, race, species; (*also* **горная порода**) rock. **породистый** thoroughbred. **породить** (-ожу́) *pf* (*impf* **порождать**) give birth to; give rise to.
по|роднить(ся *pf.* **породный** pedigree.
порождать *impf of* **породить**
порознь *adv* separately, apart.
порой, порою *adv* at times.
порок vice; defect.
поросёнок (-нка; *pl* -ся́та, -ся́т) piglet.
поросль shoots; young wood.
пороть[1] (-рю́, -решь) *impf* (*pf* **вы~**) thrash; whip.
пороть[2] (-рю́, -решь) *impf* (*pf* **рас~**) undo, unpick; **~ся** come unstitched.
порох (*pl* ~а́) gunpowder, powder. **пороховой** powder.
порочить (-чу) *impf* (*pf* **о~**) discredit; smear. **порочный** vicious, depraved; faulty.
порошить (-ши́т) *impf* snow slightly.
порошок (-шка́) powder.
порт (*loc* -у́; *pl* -ы, -о́в) port.
портативный portable; **~ компьютер** laptop; **~ телефон** mobile phone.
портвейн port (wine).
портить (-чу) *impf* (*pf* **ис~**) spoil; corrupt; **~ся** deteriorate; go bad.
портниха dressmaker. **портновский** tailor's. **портной** *sb* tailor.
портовый port.
портрет portrait.
портсигар cigarette-case.
португалец (-льца), **-лка** Portuguese. **Португалия** Portugal. **португальский** Portuguese.
портфель *m* brief-case; portfolio.
портьера curtain(s), portière.
портянка foot-binding; puttee
поругание desecration.
поруганный desecrated; outraged. **поругать** *pf* scold, swear at; **~ся** swear; fall out.
порука bail; guarantee; surety; **на поруки** on bail.
по-русски *adv* (in) Russian.
поручать *impf of* **поручить. поручение** assignment; errand; message.
поручень (-чня) *m* handrail.
поручительство guarantee; bail.
поручить (-чу́, -чишь) *pf* (*impf* **поручать**) entrust; instruct.
поручиться (-чу́сь, -чишься) *pf of* **ручаться**
порхать *impf*, **порхнуть** (-ну́, -нёшь) *pf* flutter, flit.
порция portion; helping.
порча spoiling; damage; curse.
поршень (-шня) *m* piston.
порыв[1] gust; rush; fit
порыв[2] breaking. **порывать(ся**[1] *impf of* **порвать(ся**
порываться[2] *impf* make jerky movements; endeavour. **порывистый** gusty; jerky; impetuous; fitful.

поря́дковый ordinal. **поря́док** (-дка) order; sequence; manner, way; procedure; **всё в поря́дке** everything is alright; **~ дня** agenda, order of the day. **поря́дочный** decent; honest; respectable; fair, considerable.

посади́ть (-ажу́, -а́дишь) *pf of* **сади́ть, сажа́ть. поса́дка** planting; embarkation; boarding; landing. **поса́дочный** planting; landing.

посажу́ *etc.*: *see* **посади́ть. по|сва́тать(ся** *pf.* **по|свеже́ть** (-е́ет) *pf.* **по|свети́ть** (-ечу́, -е́тишь) *pf.* **по|светле́ть** (-е́ет) *pf.*

посви́стывать *impf* whistle.

по-сво́ему *adv* (in) one's own way.

посвяти́ть (-ящу́) *pf*, **посвяща́ть** *impf* devote; dedicate; let in; ordain. **посвяще́ние** dedication; initiation; ordination.

посе́в sowing; crops. **посевн|о́й** sowing; **~а́я пло́щадь** area under crops.

по|седе́ть (-е́ю) *pf.*

поселе́нец (-нца) settler; exile. **поселе́ние** settlement; exile. **по|сели́ть** *pf*, **поселя́ть** *impf* settle; lodge; arouse; **~ся** settle, take up residence. **посёлок** (-лка) settlement; housing estate.

посеребрённый (-рён, -а́) silver-plated. **по|серебри́ть** *pf.*

посереди́не *adv* & *prep+gen* in the middle (of).

посети́тель *m* visitor. **посети́ть** (-ещу́) *pf* (*impf* **посеща́ть**) visit; attend.

по|се́товать *pf.*

посеща́емость attendance. **посеща́ть** *impf of* **посети́ть. посеще́ние** visit.

по|се́ять (-е́ю) *pf.*

посиде́ть (-ижу́) *pf* sit (for a while).

поси́льный within one's powers; feasible.

посине́лый gone blue. **по|сине́ть** (-е́ю) *pf.*

по|скака́ть (-ачу́, -а́чешь) *pf.*

поскользну́ться (-ну́сь, -нёшься) *pf* slip.

поско́льку *conj* as far as, (in) so far as.

по|скро́мничать *pf.* **по|скупи́ться** (-плю́сь) *pf.*

посла́нец (-нца) messenger, envoy. **посла́ние** message; epistle. **посла́нник** envoy, minister. **посла́ть** (-шлю́, -шлёшь) *pf* (*impf* **посыла́ть**) send.

по́сле *adv* & *prep+gen* after; afterwards.

после- *in comb* post-; after-. **послевое́нный** post-war. **~за́втра** *adv* the day after tomorrow. **~родово́й** post-natal. **~сло́вие** epilogue; concluding remarks.

после́дний last; recent; latest; latter. **после́дователь** *m* follower. **после́довательность** sequence; consistency. **после́довательный** consecutive; consistent. **по|сле́довать** *pf.* **после́дствие** consequence. **после́дующий** subsequent; consequent.

посло́вица proverb, saying.

по|служи́ть (-жу́, -жишь) *pf.* **послужно́й** service.

послуша́ние obedience. **по|слу́шать(ся** *pf.* **послу́шный** obedient.

по|слы́шаться (-шится) *pf.*

посма́тривать *impf* look from time to time.

посме́иваться *impf* chuckle.

посме́ртный posthumous.

по|сме́ть (-е́ю) *pf.*

посмея́ние ridicule. **посмея́ться** (-ею́сь, -еёшься) *pf* laugh; **+над** +*instr* laugh at.

по|смотре́ть(ся (-рю́(сь, -ришь(ся) *pf.*

посо́бие aid; allowance, benefit; textbook. **посо́бник** accomplice.

по|сове́товать(ся *pf.* **по|соде́йствовать** *pf.*

посо́л (-сла́) ambassador.

по|соли́ть (-олю́, -о́ли́шь) *pf.*

посо́льство embassy.

поспа́ть (-сплю; -а́л, -а́, -о) *pf* sleep; have a nap.

поспева́ть[1] *impf*, **по|спе́ть**[1] (-е́ет) *pf* ripen.

П

поспева́ть² *impf*, **поспе́ть²** (-е́ю) *pf* have time; be in time (**к**+*dat*, **на**+*acc* for); +**за**+*instr* keep up with.
по|спеши́ть (-шу́) *pf*. **поспе́шный** hasty, hurried.
по|спо́рить *pf*. **по|спосо́бствовать** *pf*.
посрами́ть (-млю́) *pf*, **посрамля́ть** *impf* disgrace.
посреди́, посреди́не *adv* & *prep*+*gen* in the middle (of). **посре́дник** mediator. **посре́дничество** mediation. **посре́дственный** mediocre. **посре́дством** *prep*+*gen* by means of.
по|ссо́рить(ся *pf*.
пост¹ (-а́, *loc* -у́) post.
пост² (-а́, *loc* -у́) fast(ing).
по|ста́вить¹ (-влю) *pf*.
поста́вить² (-влю) *pf*, **поставля́ть** *impf* supply. **поста́вка** delivery. **поставщи́к** (-а́) supplier.
постаме́нт pedestal.
постанови́ть (-влю́, -вишь) *pf* (*impf* **постановля́ть**) decree; decide.
постано́вка production; arrangement; putting, placing.
постановле́ние decree; decision. **постановля́ть** *impf of* **постанови́ть**
постано́вщик producer; (film) director.
по|стара́ться *pf*.
по|старе́ть (-е́ю) *pf*. **по-ста́рому** *adv* as before.
посте́ль bed. **постелю́** *etc*.: *see* **постла́ть**
постепе́нный gradual.
по|стесня́ться *pf*.
постига́ть *impf of* **пости́чь. пости́гнуть:** *see* **пости́чь. постиже́ние** comprehension, grasp. **постижи́мый** comprehensible.
постила́ть *impf of* **постла́ть**
постира́ть *pf* do some washing.
пости́ться (-щу́сь) *impf* fast.
пости́чь, пости́гнуть (-и́гну; -и́г(нул)) *pf* (*impf* **постига́ть**) comprehend, grasp; befall.
по|стла́ть (-стелю́, -сте́лешь) *pf* (*impf also* **постила́ть**) spread; make (*bed*).
по́стн|ый lenten; lean; glum; **~ое ма́сло** vegetable oil.
постово́й on point duty.
посто́й billeting.
посто́льку: ~, поско́льку *conj* to that extent, insofar as.
по|сторони́ться (-ню́сь, -нишься) *pf*. **посторо́нний** strange; foreign; extraneous, outside; *sb* stranger, outsider.
постоя́нный permanent; constant; continual; **~ый ток** direct current. **постоя́нство** constancy.
по|стоя́ть (-ою́) *pf* stand (for a while); +**за**+*acc* stand up for.
пострада́вший *sb* victim. **по|страда́ть** *pf*.
постriга́ться *impf*, **постри́чься** (-игу́сь, -ижёшься; -и́гся) *pf* take monastic vows; get one's hair cut.
построе́ние construction; building; formation. **по|стро́ить(ся** (-ро́ю(сь) *pf*. **постро́йка** building.
постскри́птум postscript.
постули́ровать *impf* & *pf* postulate.
поступа́тельный forward. **поступа́ть** *impf*, **поступи́ть** (-плю́, -пишь) *pf* act; do; be received; +**в** *or* **на**+*acc* enter, join; +**с**+*instr* treat; **~ся** +*instr* waive, forgo. **поступле́ние** entering, joining; receipt. **посту́пок** (-пка) act, deed. **по́ступь** gait; step.
по|стуча́ть(ся (-чу́(сь) *pf*.
по|стыди́ться (-ыжу́сь) *pf*. **посты́дный** shameful.
посу́да crockery; dishes. **посу́дный** china; dish.
по|сули́ть *pf*.
посчастли́виться *pf impers* (+*dat*) be lucky; **ей посчастли́вилось** +*inf* she had the luck to.
посчита́ть *pf* count (up). **по|счита́ться** *pf*.
посыла́ть *impf of* **посла́ть. посы́лка** sending; parcel; errand;

premise. **посыльный** *sb* messenger.

посыпать (-плю, -плешь) *pf*, **посыпать** *impf* strew. **посыпаться** (-плется) *pf* begin to fall; rain down.

посягательство encroachment; infringement. **посягать** *impf*, **посягнуть** (-ну, -нёшь) *pf* encroach, infringe.

пот (*loc* -у; *pl* -ы) sweat.

потайной secret.

потакать *impf* +*dat* indulge.

потасовка brawl.

поташ (-а) potash.

по-твоему *adv* in your opinion.

потворствовать *impf* (+*dat*) be indulgent (towards), pander (to).

потёк damp patch.

потёмки (-мок) *pl* darkness. **по|темнеть** (-еет) *pf*.

потенциал potential. **потенциальный** potential.

по|теплеть (-еет) *pf*.

потерпевший *sb* victim. **по|терпеть** (-плю, -пишь) *pf*.

потеря loss; waste; *pl* casualties. **по|терять(ся** *pf*.

по|теснить *pf*. **по|тесниться** *pf* sit closer, squeeze up.

потеть (-ею) *impf* (*pf* **вс~, за~**) sweat; mist over.

потеха fun. **по|тешить(ся** (-шу(сь) *pf*. **потешный** amusing.

потечь (-чёт, -тёк, -ла) *pf* begin to flow.

потирать *impf* rub.

потихоньку *adv* softly; secretly; slowly.

потный (-тен, -тна, -тно) sweaty.

поток stream; torrent; flood.

потолок (-лка) ceiling.

по|толстеть (-ею) *pf*.

потом *adv* later (on); then. **потомок** (-мка) descendant. **потомство** posterity.

потому *adv* that is why; ~ **что** *conj* because.

по|тонуть (-ну, -нешь) *pf*. **потоп** flood, deluge. **по|топить** (-плю, -пишь) *pf*, **потоплять** *impf* sink.

по|топтать (-пчу, -пчешь) *pf*. **по|торопить(ся** (-плю(сь, -пишь(ся) *pf*.

поточный continuous; production-line.

по|тратить (-ачу) *pf*.

потребитель *m* consumer, user. **потребительский** consumer; consumers'. **потребить** (-блю) *pf*, **потреблять** *impf* consume. **потребление** consumption. **потребность** need, requirement. **по|требовать(ся** *pf*.

по|тревожить(ся (-жу(сь) *pf*.

потрёпанный shabby; tattered. **по|трепать(ся** (-плю(сь, -плешь(ся) *pf*.

по|трескаться *pf*. **потрескивать** *impf* crackle.

потрогать *pf* touch, feel, finger.

потроха (-ов) *pl* giblets. **потрошить** (-шу) *impf* (*pf* **вы~**) disembowel, clean.

потрудиться (-ужусь, -удишься) *pf* do some work; take the trouble.

потрясать *impf*, **потрясти** (-су, -сёшь; -яс, -ла) *pf* shake; rock; stagger; +*acc or instr* brandish, shake. **потрясающий** staggering, tremendous. **потрясение** shock.

потуги *f pl* vain attempts; **родовые ~** labour.

потупить (-плю) *pf*, **потуплять** *impf* lower; **~ся** look down.

по|тускнеть (-еет) *pf*.

потустороний мир the next world.

потухать *impf*, **по|тухнуть** (-нет, -ух) *pf* go out; die out. **потухший** extinct; lifeless.

по|тушить (-шу, -шишь) *pf*.

потчевать (-чую) *impf* (*pf* **по~**) +*instr* treat to.

потягиваться *impf*, **по|тянуться** (-нусь, -нешься) *pf* stretch o.s. **по|тянуть** (-ну, -нешь) *pf*.

по|ужинать *pf*. **по|умнеть** (-ею) *pf*.

поучать *impf* preach at.

поучительный instructive.

похабный obscene.

П

похвала́ praise. **по|хвали́ть(ся** (-лю́(сь, -лишь(ся) *pf*. **похва́льный** laudable; laudatory.

по|хва́стать(ся *pf*.

похити́тель *m* kidnapper; abductor; thief. **похи́тить** (-хи́щу) *pf*, **похища́ть** *impf* kidnap; abduct; steal. **похище́ние** theft; kidnapping; abduction.

похлёбка broth, soup.

похло́пать *pf* slap; clap.

по|хлопота́ть (-очу́, -о́чешь) *pf*.

похме́лье hangover.

похо́д campaign; march; hike; excursion.

по|хода́тайствовать *pf*.

походи́ть (-ожу́, -о́дишь) *impf* **на**+*acc* resemble.

похо́дка gait, walk. **похо́дный** mobile, field; marching. **похожде́ние** adventure.

похо́жий alike; ~ **на** like.

похолода́ние drop in temperature.

по|хорони́ть (-ню́, -нишь) *pf*. **похоро́нный** funeral. **по́хороны** (-ро́н, -рона́м) *pl* funeral.

по|хороше́ть (-е́ю) *pf*.

по́хоть lust.

по|худе́ть (-е́ю) *pf*.

по|целова́ть(ся *pf*. **поцелу́й** kiss.

поча́ток (-тка) ear; (corn) cob.

по́чва soil; ground; basis. **по́чвенный** soil; ~ **покро́в** top-soil.

почём *adv* how much; how; ~ **знать?** who can tell?; ~ **я зна́ю?** how should I know?

почему́ *adv* why. **почему́-либо, -нибудь** *advs* for some reason or other. **почему́-то** *adv* for some reason.

по́черк hand(writing).

почерне́лый blackened, darkened. **по|черне́ть** (-е́ю) *pf*.

почерпну́ть (-ну́, -нёшь) *pf* draw, scoop up; glean.

по|черстве́ть (-е́ю) *pf*. **по|чеса́ть(ся** (-ешу́(сь, -е́шешь(ся) *pf*.

по́честь honour. **почёт** honour; respect. **почётный** of honour; honourable; honorary.

по́чечный renal; kidney.

почива́ть *impf of* **почи́ть**

почи́н initiative.

по|чини́ть (-ню́, -нишь) *pf*, **починя́ть** *impf* repair, mend. **почи́нка** repair.

по|чи́стить(ся (-и́щу(сь) *pf*.

почита́ть[1] *impf* honour; revere.

почита́ть[2] *pf* read for a while.

почи́ть (-и́ю, -и́ешь) *pf* (*impf* **почива́ть**) rest; pass away; ~ **на ла́врах** rest on one's laurels.

по́чка[1] bud.

по́чка[2] kidney.

по́чта post, mail; post-office. **почтальо́н** postman. **почта́мт** (*main*) post-office.

почте́ние respect. **почте́нный** venerable; considerable.

почти́ *adv* almost.

почти́тельный respectful. **почти́ть** (-чту́) *pf* honour.

почто́в|ый postal; **~ая ка́рточка** postcard; **~ый перево́д** postal order; **~ый я́щик** letter-box.

по|чу́вствовать *pf*.

по|чу́диться (-ишься) *pf*.

пошатну́ть (-ну́, -нёшь) *pf* shake; **~ся** shake; stagger.

по|шевели́ть(ся (-елю́(сь, -е́ли́шь(ся) *pf*. **пошёл** *etc*.: *see* **пойти́**

поши́вочный sewing.

по́шлина duty.

по́шлость vulgarity; banality. **по́шлый** vulgar; banal.

пошту́чный by the piece.

по|шути́ть (-учу́, -у́тишь) *pf*.

поща́да mercy. **по|щади́ть** (-ажу́) *pf*.

по|щекота́ть (-очу́, -о́чешь) *pf*.

пощёчина slap in the face.

по|щу́пать *pf*.

поэ́зия poetry. **поэ́ма** poem. **поэ́т** poet. **поэти́ческий** poetic.

поэ́тому *adv* therefore.

пою́ *etc*.: *see* **петь, пои́ть**

появи́ться (-влю́сь, -вишься) *pf*, **появля́ться** *impf* appear. **появле́ние** appearance.

по́яс (*pl* -а́) belt; girdle; waistband; waist; zone.

поясне́ние explanation. **поясни́тельный** explanatory. **поясни́ть** *pf* (*impf* **поясня́ть**) explain, elucidate.

поясни́ца small of the back. **поясно́й** waist; to the waist; zonal.

поясня́ть *impf of* **поясни́ть**

пра- *pref* first; great-. **праба́бушка** great-grandmother.

пра́вда (the) truth. **правди́вый** true; truthful. **правдоподо́бный** likely; plausible. **пра́ведный** righteous; just.

пра́вило rule; principle.

пра́вильн|ый right, correct; regular; **~о!** that's right!

прави́тель *m* ruler. **прави́тельственный** government(al). **прави́тельство** government. **пра́вить**[1] (-влю) *+instr* rule, govern; drive.

пра́вить[2] (-влю) *impf* correct. **пра́вка** correcting.

правле́ние board; administration; government.

пра́|внук, ~внучка great-grandson, -granddaughter.

пра́во[1] (*pl* -á) law; right; **(води́тельские) права́** driving licence; **на права́х**+*gen* in the capacity of, as.

пра́во[2] *adv* really.

право-[1] *in comb* law; right. **правове́рный** orthodox. **~ме́рный** lawful, rightful. **~мо́чный** competent. **~наруше́ние** infringement of the law, offence. **~нару-ши́тель** *m* offender, delinquent. **~писа́ние** spelling, orthography. **~сла́вный** orthodox; *sb* member of the Orthodox Church. **~су́дие** justice.

право-[2] *in comb* right, right-hand. **правосторо́нний** right; right-hand.

правово́й legal.

правота́ rightness; innocence.

пра́вый[1] right; right-hand; right-wing.

пра́вый[2] (прав, -á, -о) right, correct; just.

пра́вящий ruling.

пра́дед great-grandfather; *pl* ancestors. **праде́душка** *m* great-grandfather.

пра́здник (public) holiday. **пра́здничный** festive. **пра́зднование** celebration. **пра́здновать** *impf* (*pf* **от~**) celebrate. **пра́здность** idleness. **пра́здный** idle; useless.

пра́ктика practice; practical work. **практикова́ть** *impf* practise; **~ся** (*pf* **на~ся**) be practised; +в+*prep* practise. **практи́ческий, практи́чный** practical.

пра́отец (-тца) forefather.

пра́порщик ensign.

прапра́дед great-great-grandfather. **прароди́тель** *m* forefather.

прах dust; remains.

пра́чечная *sb* laundry. **пра́чка** laundress.

пребыва́ние stay. **пребыва́ть** *impf* be; reside.

превзойти́ (-йду́, -йдёшь; -ошёл, -шла́) *pf* (*impf* **превосходи́ть**) surpass; excel.

превозмога́ть *impf*, **превозмо́чь** (-огу́, -о́жешь; -о́г, -ла́) *pf* overcome.

превознести́ (-су́, -сёшь; -ёс, -ла́) *pf*, **превозноси́ть** (-ошу́, -о́сишь) *impf* extol, praise.

превосходи́тельство Excellency. **превосходи́ть** (-ожу́, -о́дишь) *impf of* **превзойти́. превосхо́дный** superlative; superb, excellent. **превосхо́дство** superiority. **превосходя́щий** superior.

преврати́ть (-ащу́) *pf*, **превраща́ть** *impf* convert, turn, reduce; **~ся** turn, change. **превра́тный** wrong; changeful. **превраще́ние** transformation.

превы́сить (-ы́шу) *pf*, **превыша́ть** *impf* exceed. **превыше́ние** exceeding, excess.

прегра́да obstacle; barrier. **прегради́ть** (-ажу́) *pf*, **прегражда́ть** *impf* bar, block.

пред *prep+instr*: *see* **пе́ред**

П

предава́ть(ся (-даю́(сь, -даёшь(ся) *impf of* **преда́ть(ся**
преда́ние legend; tradition; handing over, committal. **пре́данность** devotion. **пре́данный** devoted. **преда́тель** *m*, **~ница** betrayer, traitor. **преда́тельский** treacherous. **преда́тельство** treachery. **преда́ть** (-а́м, -а́шь, -а́ст, -ади́м; пре́дал, -а́, -о) *pf* (*impf* **предава́ть**) hand over, commit; betray; **~ся** abandon o.s.; give way, indulge.
предаю́ *etc.*: *see* **предава́ть**
предвари́тельный preliminary; prior. **предвари́ть** *pf*, **предваря́ть** *impf* forestall, anticipate.
предве́стник forerunner; harbinger. **предвеща́ть** *impf* portend; augur.
предвзя́тый preconceived; biased.
предви́деть (-и́жу) *impf* foresee.
предвкуси́ть (-ушу́, -у́сишь) *pf*, **предвкуша́ть** *impf* look forward to.
П **предводи́тель** *m* leader. **предводи́тельствовать** *impf* +*instr* lead.
предвое́нный pre-war.
предвосхи́тить (-и́щу) *pf*, **предвосхища́ть** *impf* anticipate.
предвы́борный (pre-)election.
предго́рье foothills.
преддве́рие threshold.
преде́л limit; bound. **преде́льный** boundary; maximum; utmost.
предзнаменова́ние omen, augury.
предисло́вие preface.
предлага́ть *impf of* **предложи́ть**.
предло́г[1] pretext.
предло́г[2] preposition.
предложе́ние[1] sentence; clause.
предложе́ние[2] offer; proposition; proposal; motion; suggestion; supply. **предложи́ть** (-жу́, -жишь) *pf* (*impf* **предлага́ть**) offer; propose; suggest; order.
предло́жный prepositional.
предме́стье suburb.
предме́т object; subject.
предназнача́ть *impf*, **предназна́чить** (-чу) *pf* destine, intend; earmark.
преднаме́ренный premeditated.
пре́до: *see* **пе́ред**
пре́док (-дка) ancestor.
предопределе́ние predetermination. **предопредели́ть** *pf*, **предопределя́ть** *impf* predetermine, predestine.
предоста́вить (-влю) *pf*, **предоставля́ть** *impf* grant; leave; give.
предостерега́ть *impf*, **предостере́чь** (-егу́, -ежёшь; -ёг, -ла́) *pf* warn. **предостереже́ние** warning. **предосторо́жность** precaution.
предосуди́тельный reprehensible.
предотврати́ть (-ащу́) *pf*, **предотвраща́ть** *impf* avert, prevent.
предохране́ние protection; preservation. **предохрани́тель** *m* guard; safety device, safety-catch; fuse. **предохрани́тельный** preservative; preventive; safety. **предохрани́ть** *pf*, **предохраня́ть** *impf* preserve, protect.
предписа́ние order; *pl* directions, instructions. **предписа́ть** (-ишу́, -и́шешь) *pf*, **предпи́сывать** *impf* order, direct; prescribe.
предпле́чье forearm.
предполага́емый supposed. **предполага́ется** *impers* it is proposed. **предполага́ть** *impf*, **предположи́ть** (-жу́, -о́жишь) *pf* suppose, assume. **предположе́ние** supposition, assumption. **предположи́тельный** conjectural; hypothetical.
предпосле́дний penultimate, last-but-one.
предпосы́лка precondition; premise.
предпоче́сть (-чту́, -чтёшь; -чёл, -чла́) *pf*, **предпочита́ть** *impf* prefer. **предпочте́ние** preference.

предпочти́тельный preferable.
предприи́мчивый enterprising.
предпринима́тель *m* owner; entrepreneur; employer. **предпринима́тельство: свобо́дное ~** free enterprise. **предпринима́ть** *impf*, **предприня́ть** (-иму́, -и́мешь; -и́нял, -а́, -о) *pf* undertake. **предприя́тие** undertaking, enterprise.
предрасположе́ние predisposition.
предрассу́док (-дка) prejudice.
предрека́ть *impf*, **предре́чь** (-еку́, -ечёшь; -рёк, -ла́) *pf* foretell.
предреша́ть *impf*, **предреши́ть** (-шу́) *pf* decide beforehand; predetermine.
председа́тель *m* chairman.
предсказа́ние prediction. **предсказа́ть** (-ажу́, -а́жешь) *pf*, **предска́зывать** *impf* predict; prophesy.
предсме́ртный dying.
представа́ть (-таю́, -таёшь) *impf of* **предста́ть**
представи́тель *m* representative. **представи́тельный** representative; imposing. **представи́тельство** representation; representatives.
предста́вить (-влю) *pf*, **представля́ть** *impf* present; submit; introduce; represent; **~ себе́** imagine; **представля́ть собо́й** represent, be; **~ся** present itself, occur; seem; introduce o.s.; *+instr* pretend to be. **представле́ние** presentation; performance; idea, notion.
предста́ть (-а́ну) *pf* (*impf* **представа́ть**) appear.
предстоя́ть (-ои́т) *impf* be in prospect, lie ahead. **предстоя́щий** forthcoming; imminent.
предте́ча *m* & *f* forerunner, precursor.
предубежде́ние prejudice.
предугада́ть *pf*, **предуга́дывать** *impf* guess; foresee.
предупреди́тельный preventive; warning; courteous, obliging.
предупреди́ть (-ежу́) *pf*, **предупрежда́ть** *impf* warn; give notice; prevent; anticipate. **предупрежде́ние** notice; warning; prevention.
предусма́тривать *impf*, **предусмотре́ть** (-рю́, -ришь) *pf* envisage, foresee; provide for. **предусмотри́тельный** prudent; far-sighted.
предчу́вствие presentiment; foreboding. **предчу́вствовать** *impf* have a presentiment (about).
предше́ственник predecessor. **предше́ствовать** *impf +dat* precede.
предъяви́тель *m* bearer. **предъяви́ть** (-влю́, -вишь) *pf*, **предъявля́ть** *impf* show, produce; bring (*lawsuit*); **~ пра́во на**+*acc* lay claim to.
предыду́щий previous.
прее́мник successor. **прее́мственность** succession; continuity.
пре́жде *adv* first; formerly; *prep+gen* before; **~ всего́** first of all; first and foremost; **~ чем** *conj* before. **преждевре́менный** premature. **пре́жний** previous, former.
презервати́в condom.
президе́нт president. **президе́нтский** presidential. **прези́диум** presidium.
презира́ть *impf* despise. **презре́ние** contempt. **презре́нный** contemptible. **презри́тельный** scornful.
преиму́щественно *adv* mainly, chiefly, principally. **преиму́щественный** main, primary; preferential. **преиму́щество** advantage; preference; **по преиму́ществу** for the most part.
преиспо́дняя *sb* the underworld.
прейскура́нт price list, catalogue.
преклоне́ние admiration. **преклони́ть** *pf*, **преклоня́ть** *impf* bow, bend; **~ся** bow down; *+dat or* **перед**+*instr* admire, worship. **преклóнный: ~ во́зраст** old age.

П

прекра́сный beautiful; fine; excellent.

прекрати́ть (-ащу́) *pf*, **прекраща́ть** *impf* stop, discontinue; **~ся** cease, end. **прекраще́ние** halt; cessation.

преле́стный delightful. **пре́лесть** charm, delight.

преломи́ть (-млю, -мишь) *pf*, **преломля́ть** *impf* refract. **преломле́ние** refraction.

прельсти́ть (-льщу́) *pf*, **прельща́ть** *impf* attract; entice; **~ся** be attracted; fall (+*instr* for).

прелюбоде́яние adultery.

прелю́дия prelude.

преми́нуть (-ну) *pf with neg* not fail.

премирова́ть *impf* & *pf* award a prize to; give a bonus. **пре́мия** prize; bonus; premium.

премье́р prime minister; lead(ing actor). **премье́ра** première. **премье́р-мини́стр** prime minister. **премье́рша** leading lady.

П

пренебрега́ть *impf*, **пренебре́чь** (-егу́, -ежёшь; -ёг, -ла́) *pf* +*instr* scorn; neglect. **пренебреже́ние** scorn; neglect. **пренебрежи́тельный** scornful.

пре́ния (-ий) *pl* debate.

преоблада́ние predominance. **преоблада́ть** *impf* predominate; prevail.

преобража́ть *impf*, **преобрази́ть** (-ажу́) *pf* transform. **преображе́ние** transformation; Transfiguration. **преобразова́ние** transformation; reform. **преобразова́ть** *pf*, **преобразо́вывать** *impf* transform; reform, reorganize.

преодолева́ть *impf*, **преодоле́ть** (-е́ю) *pf* overcome.

препара́т preparation.

препина́ние: зна́ки препина́ния punctuation marks.

препира́тельство altercation, wrangling.

преподава́ние teaching. **преподава́тель** *m*, **~ница** teacher.

преподава́тельский teaching. **преподава́ть** (-даю́, -даёшь) *impf* teach.

преподнести́ (-су́, -сёшь; -ёс, -ла́) *pf*, **преподноси́ть** (-ошу́, -о́сишь) present with, give.

препроводи́ть (-вожу́, -во́дишь) *pf*, **препровожда́ть** *impf* send, forward.

препя́тствие obstacle; hurdle. **препя́тствовать** *impf* (*pf* **вос~**) +*dat* hinder.

прерва́ть (-ву́, -вёшь; -а́л, -а́, -о) *pf* (*impf* **прерыва́ть**) interrupt; break off; **~ся** be interrupted; break.

пререка́ние argument. **пререка́ться** *impf* argue.

прерыва́ть(ся *impf of* **прерва́ть(ся**

пресека́ть *impf*, **пресе́чь** (-еку́, -ечёшь; -ёк, -екла́) *pf* stop; put an end to; **~ся** stop; break.

пресле́дование pursuit; persecution; prosecution. **пресле́довать** *impf* pursue; haunt; persecute; prosecute.

пресловутый notorious.

пресмыка́ться *impf* grovel. **пресмыка́ющееся** *sb* reptile.

пресново́дный freshwater. **пре́сный** fresh; unleavened; insipid; bland.

пресс press. **пре́сса** the press. **пресс-конфере́нция** press-conference.

престаре́лый aged.

прести́ж prestige.

престо́л throne.

преступле́ние crime. **престу́пник** criminal. **престу́пность** criminality; crime, delinquency. **престу́пный** criminal.

пресы́титься (-ы́щусь) *pf*, **пресыща́ться** *impf* be satiated. **пресыще́ние** surfeit, satiety.

претвори́ть *pf*, **претворя́ть** *impf* (**в**+*acc*) turn, change, convert; **~ в жизнь** realize, carry out.

претенде́нт claimant; candidate; pretender. **претендова́ть** *impf*

на+*acc* lay claim to; have pretensions to. **прете́нзия** claim; pretension; **быть в прете́нзии на**+*acc* have a grudge, a grievance, against.

претерпева́ть *impf*, **претерпе́ть** (-плю́, -пишь) *pf* undergo; suffer.

пре́ть (пре́ет) *impf* (*pf* **со~**) rot.

преувеличе́ние exaggeration. **преувели́чивать** *impf*, **преувели́чить** (-чу) *pf* exaggerate.

преуменьша́ть *impf*, **преуме́ньшить** (-е́ньшу́) *pf* underestimate; understate.

преуспева́ть *impf*, **преуспе́ть** (-е́ю) *pf* be successful; thrive.

преходя́щий transient.

прецеде́нт precedent.

при *prep* +*prep* by, at; in the presence of; attached to, affiliated to; with; about; on; in the time of; under; during; when, in case of; **~ всём том** for all that.

приба́вить (-влю) *pf*, **прибавля́ть** add; increase; **~ся** increase; rise; wax; **день приба́вился** the days are getting longer. **приба́вка** addition; increase. **прибавле́ние** addition; supplement, appendix. **приба́вочный** additional; surplus.

Приба́лтика the Baltic States.

прибау́тка humorous saying.

прибега́ть[1] *impf of* **прибежа́ть**

прибега́ть[2] *impf*, **прибе́гнуть** (-ну; -бе́г) *pf* +**к**+*dat* resort to.

прибежа́ть (-егу́) *pf* (*impf* **прибега́ть**) come running.

прибе́жище refuge.

приберега́ть *impf*, **прибере́чь** (-егу́, -ежёшь; -ёг, -ла́) *pf* save (up), reserve.

приберу́ *etc.*: *see* **прибра́ть. прибива́ть** *impf of* **приби́ть. прибира́ть** *impf of* **прибра́ть**

приби́ть (-бью́, -бьёшь) *pf* (*impf* **прибива́ть**) nail; flatten; drive.

приближа́ть *impf*, **прибли́зить** (-и́жу) *pf* bring *or* move nearer; **~ся** approach; draw nearer. **приближе́ние** approach. **приблизи́тельный** approximate.

прибо́й surf, breakers.

прибо́р instrument, device, apparatus; set. **прибо́рная доска́** instrument panel; dashboard.

прибра́ть (-беру́, -берёшь; -а́л, -а́, -о) *pf* (*impf* **прибира́ть**) tidy (up); put away.

прибре́жный coastal; offshore.

прибыва́ть *impf*, **прибы́ть** (-бу́ду; при́был, -а́, -о) *pf* arrive; increase, grow; rise; wax. **при́быль** profit, gain; increase, rise. **при́быльный** profitable. **прибы́тие** arrival.

прибью́ *etc.*: *see* **приби́ть**

прива́л halt.

прива́ривать *impf*, **привари́ть** (-рю́, -ришь) *pf* weld on.

приватиза́ция privatization. **приватизи́ровать** *impf* & *pf* privatize.

приведу́ *etc.*: *see* **привести́**

привезти́ (-зу́, -зёшь; -ёз, -ла́) (*impf* **привози́ть**) bring.

привере́дливый pernickety.

приве́рженец (-нца) adherent. **приве́рженный** devoted.

приве́сить (-е́шу) *pf* (*impf* **приве́шивать**) hang up, suspend.

привести́ (-еду́, -едёшь; -ёл, -а́) *pf* (*impf* **приводи́ть**) bring; lead; take; reduce; cite; put in(to), set.

приве́т greeting(s); regards; hi! **приве́тливый** friendly; affable. **приве́тствие** greeting; speech of welcome. **приве́тствовать** *impf* & *pf* greet, salute; welcome.

приве́шивать *impf of* **приве́сить**

привива́ть(ся *impf of* **приви́ть(ся. приви́вка** inoculation.

привиде́ние ghost; apparition. **при|ви́деться** (-дится) *pf*.

привилегиро́ванный privileged. **привиле́гия** privilege.

привинти́ть (-нчу́) *pf*, **приви́нчивать** *impf* screw on.

приви́ть (-вью́, -вьёшь; -и́л, -а́, -о) *pf* (*impf* **привива́ть**) inoculate; graft; inculcate; foster; **~ся** take; become established.

П

при́вкус after-taste; smack.

привлека́тельный attractive. **привлека́ть** *impf*, **привле́чь** (-еку́, -ечёшь; -ёк, -ла́) *pf* attract; draw; draw in, win over; (*law*) have up; ~ **к суду́** sue. **привлече́ние** attraction.

приво́д drive, gear. **приводи́ть** (-ожу́, -о́дишь) *impf of* **привести́**. **приводно́й** driving.

привожу́ *etc.*: *see* **приводи́ть, привози́ть**

приво́з bringing; importation; load. **привози́ть** (-ожу́, -о́зишь) *impf of* **привезти́**. **привозно́й, приво́зный** imported.

приво́льный free.

привстава́ть (-таю́, -таёшь) *impf*, **привста́ть** (-а́ну) *pf* half-rise; rise.

привыка́ть *impf*, **привы́кнуть** (-ну; -ы́к) *pf* get accustomed. **привы́чка** habit. **привы́чный** habitual, usual.

привью́ *etc.*: *see* **приви́ть**

привя́занность attachment; affection. **привяза́ть** (-яжу́, -я́жешь) *pf*, **привя́зывать** *impf* attach; tie, bind; ~**ся** become attached; attach o.s.; +**к**+*dat* pester. **привя́зчивый** annoying; affectionate. **при́вязь** tie; lead, leash; tether.

пригиба́ть *impf of* **пригну́ть**

пригласи́ть (-ашу́) *pf*, **приглаша́ть** *impf* invite. **приглаше́ние** invitation.

пригляде́ться (-яжу́сь) *pf*, **пригля́дываться** *impf* look closely; +**к**+*dat* scrutinize; get used to.

пригна́ть (-гоню́, -го́нишь; -а́л, -а́, -о) *pf* (*impf* **пригоня́ть**) bring in; fit, adjust.

пригну́ть (-ну́, -нёшь) *pf* (*impf* **пригиба́ть**) bend down.

пригова́ривать[1] *impf* keep saying.

пригова́ривать[2] *impf*, **приговори́ть** *pf* sentence, condemn. **пригово́р** verdict, sentence.

пригоди́ться (-ожу́сь) *pf* prove useful. **приго́дный** fit, suitable.

пригоня́ть *impf of* **пригна́ть**

пригора́ть *impf*, **пригоре́ть** (-ри́т) *pf* be burnt.

при́город suburb. **при́городный** suburban.

приго́рок (-рка) hillock.

при́горшня (*gen pl* -ей) handful.

приготови́тельный preparatory. **пригото́вить** (-влю) *pf*, **приготовля́ть** *impf* prepare; ~**ся** prepare. **приготовле́ние** preparation.

пригрева́ть *impf*, **пригре́ть** (-е́ю) *pf* warm; cherish.

при|грози́ть (-ожу́) *pf.*

придава́ть (-даю́, -даёшь) *impf*, **прида́ть** (-а́м, -а́шь, -а́ст, -ади́м; при́дал, -а́, -о) *pf* add; give; attach. **прида́ча** adding; addition; **в прида́чу** into the bargain.

придави́ть (-влю́, -вишь) *pf*, **прида́вливать** *impf* press (down).

прида́ное *sb* dowry. **прида́ток** (-тка) appendage.

придвига́ть *impf*, **придви́нуть** (-ну) *pf* move up, draw up; ~**ся** move up, draw near.

придво́рный court.

приде́лать *pf*, **приде́лывать** *impf* attach.

приде́рживаться *impf* hold on, hold; +*gen* keep to.

придеру́сь *etc.*: *see* **придра́ться**. **придира́ться** *impf of* **придра́ться**. **приди́рка** quibble; fault-finding. **приди́рчивый** fault-finding.

придоро́жный roadside.

придра́ться (-деру́сь, -дерёшься; -а́лся, -а́сь, -а́ло́сь) *pf* (*impf* **придира́ться**) find fault.

приду́ *etc.*: *see* **прийти́**

приду́мать *pf*, **приду́мывать** *impf* think up, invent.

прие́ду *etc.*: *see* **прие́хать**. **прие́зд** arrival. **приезжа́ть** *impf of* **прие́хать**. **прие́зжий** newly arrived; *sb* newcomer.

приём receiving; reception; surgery; welcome; admittance; dose; go; movement; method, way;

trick. **приéмлемый** acceptable. **приёмная** *sb* waiting-room; reception room. **приёмник** (radio) receiver. **приёмный** receiving; reception; entrance; foster, adopted.

приéхать (-éду) *pf* (*impf* **приезжáть**) arrive, come.

прижáть (-жмý, -жмёшь) *pf* (*impf* **прижимáть**) press; clasp; **~ся** nestle up.

прижéчь (-жгý, -жжёшь; -жёг, -жглá) *pf* (*impf* **прижигáть**) cauterize.

приживáться *impf of* **прижúться**

прижигáние cauterization. **прижигáть** *impf of* **прижéчь**

прижимáть(ся *impf of* **прижáть(ся**

прижúться (-ивýсь, -ивёшься; -жúлся, -áсь) *pf* (*impf* **приживáться**) become acclimatized.

прижмý *etc.*: *see* **прижáть**

приз (*pl* -ы́) prize.

призвáние vocation. **призвáть** (-зовý, -зовёшь; -áл, -á, -о) *pf* (*impf* **призывáть**) call; call upon; call up.

призéмистый stocky, squat.

приземлéние landing. **приземлúться** *pf*, **приземлять́ся** *impf* land.

призёр prizewinner.

прúзма prism.

признавáть (-наю́, -наёшь) *impf*, **признáть** *pf* recognize; admit; **~ся** confess. **прúзнак** sign, symptom; indication. **признáние** confession, declaration; acknowledgement; recognition. **прúзнанный** acknowledged, recognized. **признáтельный** grateful.

призовý *etc.*: *see* **призвáть**

прúзрак spectre, ghost. **прúзрачный** ghostly; illusory, imagined.

призы́в call, appeal; slogan; call-up. **призывáть** *impf of* **призвáть. призывнóй** conscription.

прúиск mine.

прийтú (придý, -дёшь; пришёл, -шлá) *pf* (*impf* **приходúть**) come; arrive; **~ в себя́** regain consciousness; **~сь** +**по**+*dat* fit; suit; +**на**+*acc* fall on; *impers*+*dat* have to; happen (to), fall to the lot (of).

прикáз order, command. **прикáзание** order, command. **приказáть** (-ажý, -áжешь) *pf*, **прикáзывать** *impf* order, command.

прикáлывать *impf of* **приколóть.**

прикасáться *impf of* **прикоснýться**

прикáнчивать *impf of* **прикóнчить**

прикатúть (-ачý, -áтишь) *pf*, **прикáтывать** *impf* roll up.

прикúдывать *impf*, **прикúнуть** (-ну) *pf* throw in, add; weigh; estimate; **~ся** +*instr* pretend (to be).

приклáд[1] butt.

приклáд[2] trimmings. **прикладнóй** applied. **приклáдывать(ся** *impf of* **приложúть(ся**

приклéивать *impf*, **приклéить** *pf* stick; glue.

приключáться *impf*, **приключúться** *pf* happen, occur. **приключéние** adventure. **приключéнческий** adventure.

приковáть (-кую́, -куёшь) *pf*, **прикóвывать** *impf* chain; rivet.

приколáчивать *impf*, **приколотúть** (-очý, -óтишь) *pf* nail.

приколóть (-лю́, -лешь) *pf* (*impf* **прикáлывать**) pin; stab.

прикомандировáть *pf*, **прикомандирóвывать** *impf* attach.

прикóнчить (-чу) *pf* (*impf* **прикáнчивать**) use up; finish off.

прикосновéние touch; concern. **прикоснýться** (-нýсь, -нёшься) *pf* (*impf* **прикасáться**) **к**+*dat* touch.

прикрепúть (-плю́) *pf*, **прикреплять́** *impf* fasten, attach. **прикреплéние** fastening; registration.

прикрывáть *impf*, **прикры́ть** (-рóю) *pf* cover; screen; shelter. **прикры́тие** cover; escort.

прикýривать *impf*, **прикурúть** (-рю́, -ришь) *pf* get a light.

прикусúть (-ушý, -ýсишь) *pf*, **прикýсывать** *impf* bite.

П

прила́вок (-вка) counter.
прилага́тельное *sb* adjective.
прилага́ть *impf of* **приложи́ть**
прила́дить (-а́жу) *pf*, **прила́живать** *impf* fit, adjust.
приласка́ть *pf* caress, pet; **~ся** snuggle up.
прилега́ть *impf* (*pf* **приле́чь**) к+*dat* fit; adjoin. **прилега́ющий** close-fitting; adjoining, adjacent.
приле́жный diligent.
прилепи́ть(ся (-плю́(сь, -пишь(ся) *pf*, **прилепля́ть(ся** *impf* stick.
прилёт arrival. **прилета́ть** *impf*, **прилете́ть** (-ечу́) *pf* arrive, fly in; come flying.
приле́чь (-ля́гу, -ля́жешь; -ёг, -гла́) *pf* (*impf* **прилега́ть**) lie down.
прили́в flow, flood; rising tide; surge. **прилива́ть** *impf of* **прили́ть. прили́вный** tidal.
прилипа́ть *impf*, **прили́пнуть** (-нет; -ли́п) *pf* stick.
прили́ть (-льёт; -и́л, -а́, -о) *pf* (*impf* **прилива́ть**) flow; rush.

П

прили́чие decency. **прили́чный** decent.
приложе́ние application; enclosure; supplement; appendix. **приложи́ть** (-жу́, -жишь) *pf* (*impf* **прикла́дывать, прилага́ть**) put; apply; affix; add; enclose; **~ся** take aim; +*instr* put, apply; +к+*dat* kiss.
прильёт *etc*.: *see* **прили́ть. при|льну́ть** (-ну́, -нёшь) *pf*. **прися́гу** *etc*.: *see* **приле́чь**
прима́нивать *impf*, **примани́ть** (-ню́, -нишь) *pf* lure; entice. **прима́нка** bait, lure.
примене́ние application; use. **примени́ть** (-ню́, -нишь) *pf*, **применя́ть** *impf* apply; use; **~ся** adapt o.s., conform.
приме́р example.
при|ме́рить *pf* (*impf also* **примеря́ть**) try on. **приме́рка** fitting.
приме́рно *adv* approximately. **приме́рный** exemplary; approximate.
примеря́ть *impf of* **приме́рить**
при́месь admixture.
приме́та sign, token. **приме́тный** perceptible; conspicuous.
примеча́ние note, footnote; *pl* comments. **примеча́тельный** notable.
примеша́ть *pf*, **приме́шивать** *impf* add, mix in.
примина́ть *impf of* **примя́ть**
примире́ние reconciliation. **примири́тельный** conciliatory. **при|мири́ть** *pf*, **примиря́ть** *impf* reconcile; conciliate; **~ся** be reconciled.
примити́вный primitive.
примкну́ть (-ну́, -нёшь) *pf* (*impf* **примыка́ть**) join; fix, attach.
примну́ *etc*.: *see* **примя́ть**
примо́рский seaside; maritime. **примо́рье** seaside.
примо́чка wash, lotion.
приму́ *etc*.: *see* **приня́ть**
примча́ться (-чу́сь) *pf* come tearing along.
примыка́ть *impf of* **примкну́ть;** +к+*dat* adjoin. **примыка́ющий** affiliated.
примя́ть (-мну́, -мнёшь) *pf* (*impf* **примина́ть**) crush; trample down.
принадлежа́ть (-жу́) *impf* belong. **принадле́жность** belonging; membership; *pl* accessories; equipment.
принести́ (-су́, -сёшь; -нёс, -ла́) *pf* (*impf* **приноси́ть**) bring; fetch.
принижа́ть *impf*, **прини́зить** (-и́жу) *pf* humiliate; belittle.
принима́ть(ся *impf of* **приня́ть(ся**
приноси́ть (-ошу́, -о́сишь) *impf of* **принести́. приноше́ние** gift, offering.
при́нтер (*comput*) printer.
принуди́тельный compulsory. **прину́дить** (-у́жу) *pf*, **принужда́ть** *impf* compel. **принужде́ние** compulsion, coercion. **принуждённый** constrained, forced.
принц prince. **принце́сса** princess.
при́нцип principle. **принци-**

пиа́льно *adv* on principle; in principle. **принципиа́льный** of principle; general.

приня́тие taking; acceptance; admission. **при́нято** it is accepted, it is usual; **не ~** it is not done. **приня́ть** (-иму́, -и́мешь; при́нял, -а́, -о) *pf* (*impf* **принима́ть**) take; accept; take over; receive; **+за+***acc* take for; **~ уча́стие** take part; **~ся** begin; take; take root; **~ за рабо́ту** set to work.

приободри́ть *pf*, **приободря́ть** *impf* cheer up; **~ся** cheer up.

приобрести́ (-ету́, -етёшь; -рёл, -а́) *pf*, **приобрета́ть** *impf* acquire. **приобрете́ние** acquisition.

приобща́ть *impf*, **приобщи́ть** (-щу́) *pf* join, attach, unite; **~ся к+***dat* join in.

приорите́т priority.

приостана́вливать *impf*, **приостанови́ть** (-влю́, -вишь) *pf* stop, suspend; **~ся** stop. **приостано́вка** halt, suspension.

приоткрыва́ть *impf*, **приоткры́ть** (-ро́ю) *pf* open slightly.

припа́док (-дка) fit; attack.

припа́сы (-ов) *pl* supplies.

припе́в refrain.

приписа́ть (-ишу́, -и́шешь) *pf*, **припи́сывать** *impf* add; attribute. **припи́ска** postscript; codicil.

припло́д offspring; increase.

приплыва́ть *impf*, **приплы́ть** (-ыву́, -ывёшь; -ы́л, -а́, -о) *pf* swim up; sail up.

приплю́снуть (-ну) *pf*, **приплю́щивать** *impf* flatten.

приподнима́ть *impf*, **приподня́ть** (-ниму́, -ни́мешь; -о́днял, -а́, -о) *pf* raise (a little); **~ся** raise o.s. (a little).

припо́й solder.

приполза́ть *impf*, **приползти́** (-зу́, -зёшь; -полз, -ла́) *pf* creep up, crawl up.

припомина́ть *impf*, **припо́мнить** *pf* recollect.

припра́ва seasoning, flavouring. **припра́вить** (-влю) *pf*, **приправля́ть** *impf* season, flavour.

припря́тать (-я́чу) *pf*, **припря́тывать** *impf* secrete, put by.

припу́гивать *impf*, **припугну́ть** (-ну́, -нёшь) *pf* scare.

прирабо́тывать *impf*, **прирабо́тать** *pf* earn ... extra. **при́работок** (-тка) additional earnings.

прира́внивать *impf*, **приравня́ть** *pf* equate (with **к+***dat*).

прираста́ть *impf*, **прирасти́** (-тёт; -ро́с, -ла́) *pf* adhere; take; increase; accrue.

приро́да nature. **приро́дный** natural; by birth; innate. **прирождённый** innate; born.

приро́с *etc.*: *see* **прирасти́**. **приро́ст** increase.

прируча́ть *impf*, **приручи́ть** (-чу́) *pf* tame; domesticate.

приса́живаться *impf of* **присе́сть**

присва́ивать *impf*, **присво́ить** *pf* appropriate; award.

приседа́ть *impf*, **присе́сть** (-ся́ду) *pf* (*impf also* **приса́живаться**) sit down, take a seat.

прискака́ть (-ачу́, -а́чешь) *pf* come galloping.

приско́рбный sorrowful.

присла́ть (-ишлю́, -ишлёшь) *pf* (*impf* **присыла́ть**) send.

прислони́ть(ся (-оню́(сь, -о́нишь(ся) *pf*, **прислоня́ть(ся** *impf* lean, rest.

прислу́га servant; crew. **прислу́живать** *impf* (**к+***dat*) wait (on), attend.

прислу́шаться *pf*, **прислу́шиваться** *impf* listen; **+к+***dat* listen to; heed.

присма́тривать *impf*, **присмотре́ть** (-рю́, -ришь) *pf* **+за +***instr* look after, keep an eye on; **~ся** (**к+***dat*) look closely (at). **присмо́тр** supervision.

при|сни́ться *pf*.

присоедине́ние joining; addition; annexation. **присоедини́ть** *pf*, **присоединя́ть** *impf* join; add; annex; **~ся к+***dat* join; subscribe to (*an opinion*).

П

приспосо́бить (-блю) *pf*, **приспособля́ть** *impf* fit, adjust, adapt; **~ся** adapt o.s. **приспособле́ние** adaptation; device; appliance. **приспособля́емость** adaptability.

пристава́ть (-таю, -таёшь) *impf of* **приста́ть**

приста́вить (-влю) *pf* (*impf* **приставля́ть**) **к**+*dat* place, set, *or* lean against; add; appoint to look after.

приста́вка prefix.

приставля́ть *impf of* **приста́вить**

при́стальный intent.

приста́нище refuge, shelter.

при́стань (*gen pl* -е́й) landing-stage; pier; wharf.

приста́ть (-а́ну) *pf* (*impf* **пристава́ть**) stick, adhere (**к**+*dat* to); pester.

пристёгивать *impf*, **пристегну́ть** (-ну́, -нёшь) *pf* fasten.

присто́йный decent, proper.

пристра́ивать(ся *impf of* **пристро́ить(ся**

П

пристра́стие predilection, passion; bias. **пристра́стный** biased.

пристре́ливать *impf*, **пристрели́ть** *pf* shoot (down).

пристро́ить (-о́ю) *pf* (*impf* **пристра́ивать**) add, build on; fix up; **~ся** be fixed up, get a place. **пристро́йка** annexe, extension.

при́ступ assault; fit, attack. **приступа́ть** *impf*, **приступи́ть** (-плю́, -пишь) *pf* **к**+*dat* set about, start.

при|стыди́ть (-ыжу́) *pf*.

при|стыкова́ться *pf*.

присуди́ть (-ужу́, -у́дишь) *pf*, **присужда́ть** *impf* sentence, condemn; award; confer. **присужде́ние** awarding; conferment.

прису́тствие presence. **прису́тствовать** *impf* be present, attend. **прису́тствующие** *sb pl* those present.

прису́щий inherent; characteristic.

присыла́ть *impf of* **присла́ть**

прися́га oath. **присяга́ть** *impf*, **присягну́ть** (-ну́, -нёшь) *pf* swear.

прися́ду *etc.*: *see* **присе́сть**

прися́жный *sb* juror.

прита́йться *pf* hide.

прита́птывать *impf of* **притопта́ть**

прита́скивать *impf*, **притащи́ть** (-ащу́, -а́щишь) *pf* bring, drag, haul; **~ся** drag o.s.

притвори́ться *pf*, **притворя́ться** *impf* +*instr* pretend to be. **притво́рный** pretended, feigned. **притво́рство** pretence, sham. **притво́рщик** sham; hypocrite.

притека́ть *impf of* **прите́чь**

притесне́ние oppression. **притесни́ть** *pf*, **притесня́ть** *impf* oppress.

прите́чь (-ечёт, -еку́т; -ёк, -ла́) *pf* (*impf* **притека́ть**) pour in.

притиха́ть *impf*, **прити́хнуть** (-ну; -и́х) *pf* quiet down.

прито́к tributary; influx.

при́толока lintel.

прито́м *conj* (and) besides.

прито́н den, haunt.

притопта́ть (-пчу́, -пчешь) *pf* (*impf* **прита́птывать**) trample down.

при́торный sickly-sweet, luscious, cloying.

притра́гиваться *impf*, **притро́нуться** (-нусь) *pf* touch.

притупи́ть (-плю́, -пишь) *pf*, **притупля́ть** *impf* blunt, dull; deaden; **~ся** become blunt *or* dull.

при́тча parable.

притяга́тельный attractive, magnetic. **притя́гивать** *impf of* **притяну́ть**

притяжа́тельный possessive.

притяже́ние attraction.

притяза́ние claim, pretension. **притяза́тельный** demanding.

притя́нутый far-fetched. **притяну́ть** (-ну́, -нешь) *pf* (*impf* **притя́гивать**) attract; drag (up).

приуро́чивать *impf*, **приуро́чить** (-чу) *pf* **к**+*dat* time for.

приуса́дебный: **~ уча́сток** individual plot (*in kolkhoz*).

приуча́ть *impf*, **приучи́ть** (-чу́,

-чишь) *pf* train, school.
прихлеба́тель *m* sponger.
прихо́д coming, arrival; receipts; parish. **приходи́ть(ся** (-ожу́(сь, -о́дишь(ся) *impf of* **прийти́(сь. прихо́дный** receipt. **приходя́щий** non-resident; ~ **больно́й** outpatient. **прихожа́нин** (*pl* -а́не, -а́н), **-а́нка** parishioner.
прихо́жая *sb* hall, lobby.
прихотли́вый capricious; fanciful, intricate. **при́хоть** whim, caprice.
прихра́мывать limp (slightly).
прице́л sight; aiming. **прице́ливаться** *impf*, **прице́литься** *pf* take aim.
прице́ниваться *impf*, **прицени́ться** (-ню́сь, -нишься) *pf* (**к**+*dat*) ask the price (of).
прице́п trailer. **прицепи́ть** (-плю́, -пишь) *pf*, **прицепля́ть** *impf* hitch, hook on; **~ся к**+*dat* stick to, cling to. **прице́пка** hitching, hooking on; quibble. **прицепно́й**: ~ **ваго́н** trailer.
прича́л mooring; mooring line. **прича́ливать** *impf*, **прича́лить** *pf* moor.
прича́стие[1] participle. **прича́стие**[2] communion. **причасти́ть** (-ащу́) *pf* (*impf* **причаща́ть**) give communion to; **~ся** receive communion.
прича́стный[1] participial. **прича́стный**[2] concerned; privy.
причаща́ть *impf of* **причасти́ть**
причём *conj* moreover, and.
причеса́ть (-ешу́, -е́шешь) *pf*, **причёсывать** *impf* comb; do the hair (of); **~ся** do one's hair, have one's hair done. **причёска** hair-do; haircut.
причи́на cause; reason. **причини́ть** *pf*, **причиня́ть** *impf* cause.
причи́слить *pf*, **причисля́ть** *impf* number, rank (**к**+*dat* among); add on.
причита́ние lamentation. **причита́ть** *impf* lament.
причита́ться *impf* be due.
причмо́кивать *impf*, **причмо́кнуть** (-ну) *pf* smack one's lips.
причу́да caprice, whim.
при|чу́диться *pf*.
причу́дливый odd; fantastic; whimsical.
при|швартова́ть *pf*. **пришёл** *etc.*: *see* **прийти́**
прише́лец (-льца) newcomer.
прише́ствие coming; advent.
пришива́ть *impf*, **приши́ть** (-шью́, -шьёшь) *pf* sew on.
пришлю́ *etc.*: *see* **присла́ть**
пришпи́ливать *impf*, **пришпи́лить** *pf* pin on.
пришпо́ривать *impf*, **пришпо́рить** *pf* spur (on).
прищеми́ть (-млю́) *pf*, **прищемля́ть** *impf* pinch.
прище́пка clothes-peg.
прищу́риваться *impf*, **прищу́риться** *pf* screw up one's eyes.
прию́т shelter, refuge. **приюти́ть** (-ючу́) *pf* shelter; **~ся** take shelter.
прия́тель *m*, **прия́тельница** friend. **прия́тельский** friendly. **прия́тный** nice, pleasant.
про *prep+acc* about; for; ~ **себя́** to o.s.
про|анализи́ровать *pf*.
про́ба test; hallmark; sample.
пробе́г run; race. **пробега́ть** *impf*, **пробежа́ть** (-егу́) *pf* run; cover; run past. **пробе́жка** run.
пробе́л blank, gap; flaw.
проберу́ *etc.*: *see* **пробра́ть. пробива́ть(ся** *impf of* **проби́ть(ся. пробира́ть(ся** *impf of* **пробра́ть(ся**
проби́рка test-tube. **пробирова́ть** *impf* test, assay.
про|би́ть (-бью́, -бьёшь) *pf* (*impf also* **пробива́ть**) make a hole in; pierce; punch; **~ся** force, make, one's way.
про́бка cork; stopper; fuse; (traffic) jam, congestion. **про́бковый** cork.
пробле́ма problem.
про́блеск flash; gleam, ray.
про́бный trial, test; ~ **ка́мень**

П

touchstone. **прóбовать** *impf* (*pf* **ис~, по~**) try; attempt.
пробóина hole.
пробóр parting.
про|бормотáть (-очý, -óчешь) *pf.*
пробрáть (-берý, -берёшь; -áл, -á, -о) *pf* (*impf* **пробирáть**) penetrate; scold; **~ся** make *or* force one's way.
пробýду *etc.*: *see* **пробы́ть**
про|будúть (-ужý, -ýдишь) *pf*, **пробуждáть** *impf* wake (up); arouse; **~ся** wake up. **пробуждéние** awakening.
про|бурáвить (-влю) *pf*, **пробурáвливать** *impf* bore (through), drill.
про|бурúть *pf.*
пробы́ть (-бýду; прóбыл, -á, -о) *pf* stay; be.
пробью́ *etc.*: *see* **пробúть**
провáл failure; downfall; gap. **провáливать** *impf*, **провалúть** (-лю́, -лишь) *pf* bring down; ruin; reject, fail; **~ся** collapse; fall in; fail; disappear.
провéдать *pf*, **провéдывать** *impf* call on; learn.
проведéние conducting; construction; installation.
провезтú (-зý, -зёшь; -ёз, -лá) *pf* (*impf* **провозúть**) convey, transport.
провéрить *pf*, **проверя́ть** *impf* check; test. **провéрка** checking, check; testing.
про|вестú (-едý, -едёшь; -ёл, -á) *pf* (*impf also* **проводúть**) lead, take; build; install; carry out; conduct; pass; draw; spend; +*instr* pass over.
провéтривать *impf*, **провéтрить** *pf* air.
про|вéять (-éю) *pf.*
провидéние Providence.
провúзия provisions.
провинúться *pf* be guilty; do wrong.
провинциáльный provincial. **провúнция** province; the provinces.
прóвод (*pl* -á) wire, lead, line. **проводúмость** conductivity. **проводúть**[1] (-ожý, -óдишь) *impf of* **провестú**; conduct.
проводúть[2] (-ожý, -óдишь) *pf* (*impf* **провожáть**) accompany; see off.
провóдка leading, taking; building; installation; wiring, wires.
проводнúк[1] (-á) guide; conductor.
проводнúк[2] (-á) conductor; bearer; transmitter.
прóводы (-ов) *pl* send-off. **провожáтый** *sb* guide, escort. **провожáть** *impf of* **проводúть**
провóз conveyance, transport.
провозгласúть (-ашý) *pf*, **провозглашáть** *impf* proclaim; propose. **провозглашéние** proclamation.
провозúть (-ожý, -óзишь) *impf of* **провезтú**
провокáтор agent provocateur. **провокáция** provocation.
прóволока wire. **прóволочный** wire.
провóрный quick; agile. **провóрство** quickness; agility.
провоцúровать *impf* & *pf* (*pf* **с~**) provoke.
прогадáть *pf*, **прогáдывать** *impf* miscalculate.
прогáлина glade; space.
прогибáть(ся *impf of* **прогнýть(ся**
проглáтывать *impf*, **проглотúть** (-очý, -óтишь) *pf* swallow.
проглядéть (-яжý) *pf*, **прогля́дывать**[1] *impf* overlook; look through. **проглянýть** (-я́нет) *pf*, **прогля́дывать**[2] *impf* show, peep through, appear.
прогнáть (-гоню́, -гóнишь; -áл, -á, -о) *pf* (*impf* **прогоня́ть**) drive away; banish; drive; sack.
прогнивáть *impf*, **прогнúть** (-ниёт; -úл, -á, -о) *pf* rot through.
прогнóз prognosis; (weather) forecast.
прогнýть (-нý, -нёшь) *pf* (*impf* **прогибáть**) cause to sag; **~ся** sag, bend.

проговáривать *impf*, **проговорúть** *pf* say, utter; talk; **~ся** let the cat out of the bag.
проголодáться *pf* get hungry.
про|голосовáть *pf.*
прогóн purlin; girder; stairwell.
прогонять *impf of* **прогнáть**
прогорáть *impf*, **прогорéть** (-рю́) *pf* burn (through); burn out; go bankrupt.
прогóрклый rancid, rank.
прогрáмма programme; syllabus. **программúровать** *impf* (*pf* **за~**) programme. **программúст** (computer) programmer.
прогревáть *impf*, **прогрéть** (-éю) *pf* heat; warm up; **~ся** warm up.
про|гремéть (-млю́) *pf.* **про|грохотáть** (-очу́, -óчешь) *pf.*
прогрéсс progress. **прогрессúвный** progressive. **прогрессúровать** *impf* progress.
прогрызáть *impf*, **прогры́зть** (-зу́, -зёшь; -ы́з) *pf* gnaw through.
про|гудéть (-гужу́) *pf.*
прогу́л truancy; absenteeism. **прогу́ливать** *impf*, **прогулять** *pf* play truant, be absent, (from); miss; take for a walk; **~ся** take a walk. **прогу́лка** walk, stroll; outing. **прогу́льщик** absentee, truant.
продавáть (-даю́, -даёшь) *impf*, **продáть** (-áм, -áшь, -áст, -адúм; прóдал, -á, -о) *pf* sell. **продавáться** (-даётся) *impf* be for sale; sell. **продавéц** (-вцá) seller, vendor; salesman. **продавщúца** seller, vendor; saleswoman. **продáжа** sale. **продáжный** for sale; corrupt.
продвигáть *impf*, **продвúнуть** (-ну) *pf* move on, push forward; advance; **~ся** advance; move forward; push on. **продвижéние** advancement.
продевáть *impf of* **продéть**
про|декламúровать *pf.*
продéлать *pf*, **продéлывать** *impf* do, perform, make. **продéлка** trick; prank.
продемонстрúровать *pf* demonstrate, show.
продёргивать *impf of* **продёрнуть**
продержáть (-жу́, -жишь) *pf* hold; keep; **~ся** hold out.
продёрнуть (-ну, -нешь) *pf* (*impf* **продёргивать**) pass, run; criticize severely.
продéть (-éну) *pf* (*impf* **продевáть**) pass; **~ нúтку в иróлку** thread a needle.
продешевúть (-влю́) *pf* sell too cheap.
про|диктовáть *pf.*
продлевáть *impf*, **продлúть** *pf* prolong. **продлéние** extension. **про|длúться** *pf.*
продмáг grocery. **продовóльственный** food. **продовóльствие** food; provisions.
продолговáтый oblong.
продолжáтель *m* continuer. **продолжáть** *impf*, **продóлжить** (-жу) *pf* continue; prolong; **~ся** continue, last, go on. **продолжéние** continuation; sequel; **в ~**+*gen* in the course of. **продолжúтельность** duration. **продолжúтельный** long; prolonged.
продóльный longitudinal.
продрóгнуть (-ну; -óг) *pf* be chilled to the bone.
продтовáры (-ов) *pl* food products.
продувáть *impf* **проду́ть**
продýкт product; *pl* food-stuffs. **продуктúвность** productivity. **продуктúвный** productive. **продуктóвый** food. **продýкция** production.
продýманный well thought-out. **продýмать** *pf*, **продýмывать** *impf* think over; think out.
продýть (-у́ю, -у́ешь) *pf* (*impf* **продувáть**) blow through.
продырявить (-влю) *pf* make a hole in.
проедáть *impf of* **проéсть. проéду** *etc.*: *see* **проéхать**
проéзд passage, thoroughfare;

П

trip. **проéздить** (-зжу) *pf* (*impf* **проезжáть**) spend travelling. **проездн|óй** travelling; **~óй билéт** ticket; **~áя плáта** fare; **~ы́е** *sb pl* travelling expenses. **проезжáть** *impf of* **проéздить, проéхать. проéзжий** passing (by); *sb* passer-by.

проéкт project, plan, design; draft. **проектúровать** *impf* (*pf* **с~**) project; plan. **проéктный** planning; planned. **проéктор** projector.

проекциóнный фонáрь projector. **проéкция** projection.

проéсть (-éм, -éшь, -éст, -едúм; -éл) *pf* (*impf* **проедáть**) eat through, corrode; spend on food.

проéхать (-éду) *pf* (*impf* **проезжáть**) pass, ride, drive (by, through); cover.

прожáренный (*cul*) well-done.

прожевáть (-жую́, -жуёшь) *pf*, **прожёвывать** *impf* chew well.

прожéктор (*pl* -ы *or* -á) searchlight.

П **прожéчь** (-жгу́, -жжёшь; -жёг, -жглá) *pf* (*impf* **прожигáть**) burn (through).

проживáть *impf of* **прожúть. прожигáть** *impf of* **прожéчь**

прожúточный мúнимум living wage. **прожúть** (-иву́, -ивёшь; -óжил, -á, -о) *pf* (*impf* **проживáть**) live; spend.

прожóрливый gluttonous.

прóза prose. **прозаúческий** prose; prosaic.

прозвáние, прóзвище nickname. **прозвáть** (-зову́, -зовёшь; -áл, -á, -о) *pf* (*impf* **прозывáть**) nickname, name.

про|звучáть *pf*.

про|зевáть *pf*. **про|зимовáть** *pf*.

прозову́ *etc.*: *see* **прозвáть**

прозорлúвый perspicacious.

прозрáчный transparent.

прозревáть *impf*, **прозрéть** *pf* regain one's sight; see clearly. **прозрéние** recovery of sight; insight.

прозывáть *impf of* **прозвáть**

прозябáние vegetation. **прозябáть** *impf* vegetate.

проигрáть *pf*, **проúгрывать** *impf* lose; play; **~ся** gamble away all one's money. **проúгрыватель** *m* record-player. **прóигрыш** loss.

произведéние work; production; product. **произвестú** (-еду́, -едёшь; -ёл, -á) *pf*, **производúть** (-ожу́, -óдишь) *impf* make; carry out; produce; +**в**+*acc*/*nom pl* promote to (the rank of). **производúтель** *m* producer. **производúтельность** productivity. **производúтельный** productive. **произвóдный** derivative. **произвóдственный** industrial; production. **произвóдство** production.

произвóл arbitrariness; arbitrary rule. **произвóльный** arbitrary.

произнестú (-су́, -сёшь; -ёс, -лá) *pf*, **произносúть** (-ошу́, -óсишь) *impf* pronounce; utter. **произношéние** pronunciation.

произойтú (-ойдёт; -ошёл, -шлá) *pf* (*impf* **происходúть**) happen, occur; result; be descended.

произрастáть *impf*, **произрастú** (-ту́; -тёшь; -рос, -лá) *pf* sprout; grow.

прóиски (-ов) *pl* intrigues.

проистекáть *impf*, **проистéчь** (-ечёт; -ёк, -лá) *pf* spring, result.

происходúть (-ожу́, -óдишь) *impf of* **произойтú. происхождéние** origin; birth.

происшéствие event, incident.

пройдóха *m* & *f* sly person.

пройтú (-йду́, -йдёшь; -ошёл, -шлá) *pf* (*impf* **проходúть**) pass; go; go past; cover; study; get through; **~сь** (*impf* **прохáживаться**) take a stroll.

прок use, benefit.

прокажённый *sb* leper. **прокáза**[1] leprosy.

прокáза[2] mischief, prank. **прокáзничать** *impf* (*pf* **на~**) be up to mischief. **прокáзник** prankster.

прока́лывать *impf of* **проколо́ть**
прока́пывать *impf of* **прокопа́ть**
прока́т hire.
прокати́ться (-ачу́сь, -а́тишься) *pf* roll; go for a drive.
прока́тный rolling; rolled.
прокипяти́ть (-ячу́) *pf* boil (thoroughly).
прокиса́ть *impf*, **про|ки́снуть** (-нет) *pf* turn (sour).
прокла́дка laying; construction; washer; packing. **прокла́дывать** *impf of* **проложи́ть**
проклама́ция leaflet.
проклина́ть *impf*, **прокля́сть** (-яну́, -янёшь; -о́клял, -а́, -о) *pf* curse, damn. **прокля́тие** curse; damnation. **прокля́тый** (-я́т, -а́, -о) damned.
проко́л puncture.
проколо́ть (-лю́, -лешь) *pf* (*impf* **прока́лывать**) prick, pierce.
прокомменти́ровать *pf* comment (upon).
про|компости́ровать *pf.* **про|конспекти́ровать** *pf.* **про|консульти́ровать(ся** *pf.* **про|контроли́ровать** *pf.*
прокопа́ть *pf* (*impf* **прока́пывать**) dig, dig through.
проко́рм nourishment, sustenance. **про|корми́ть(ся** (-млю́(сь, -мишь(ся) *pf.*
про|корректи́ровать *pf.*
прокра́дываться *impf*, **прокра́сться** (-аду́сь, -адёшься) *pf* steal in.
прокурату́ра office of public prosecutor. **прокуро́р** public prosecutor.
прокуси́ть (-ушу́, -у́сишь) *pf*, **проку́сывать** *impf* bite through.
прокути́ть (-учу́, -у́тишь) *pf*, **проку́чивать** *impf* squander; go on a binge.
пролага́ть *impf of* **проложи́ть**
прола́мывать *impf of* **пролома́ть**
пролега́ть *impf* lie, run.
пролеза́ть *impf*, **проле́зть** (-зу; -ле́з) *pf* get through, climb through.
про|лепета́ть (-ечу́, -е́чешь) *pf.*
пролёт span; stairwell; bay.
пролетариа́т proletariat. **пролета́рий** proletarian. **пролета́рский** proletarian.
пролета́ть *impf*, **пролете́ть** (-ечу́) *pf* fly; cover; fly by, past, through.
проли́в strait. **пролива́ть** *impf*, **проли́ть** (-лью́, -льёшь; -о́ли́л, -а́, -о) *pf* spill, shed; **~ся** be spilt.
проло́г prologue.
проложи́ть (-жу́, -жишь) *pf* (*impf* **прокла́дывать, пролага́ть**) lay; build; interlay.
проло́м breach, break. **пролома́ть, проломи́ть** (-млю́, -мишь) *pf* (*impf* **прола́мывать**) break (through).
пролью́ *etc.*: *see* **проли́ть**
про|ма́зать (-а́жу) *pf.* **прома́тывать(ся** *impf of* **промота́ть(ся**
про́мах miss; slip, blunder. **прома́хиваться** *impf*, **промахну́ться** (-ну́сь, -нёшься) *pf* miss; make a blunder.
прома́чивать *impf of* **промочи́ть**
промедле́ние delay. **проме́длить** *pf* delay; procrastinate.
промежу́ток (-тка) interval; space. **промежу́точный** intermediate
промелькну́ть (-ну́, -нёшь) *pf* flash (past, by).
проме́нивать *impf*, **променя́ть** *pf* exchange.
промерза́ть *impf*, **промёрзнуть** (-ну; -ёрз) *pf* freeze through. **промёрзлый** frozen.
промока́ть *impf*, **промо́кнуть** (-ну; -мо́к) *pf* get soaked; let water in.
промо́лвить (-влю) *pf* say, utter.
промолча́ть (-чу́) *pf* keep silent.
про|мота́ть *pf* (*impf also* **прома́тывать**) squander.
промочи́ть (-чу́, -чишь) *pf* (*impf* **прома́чивать**) soak, drench.
промо́ю *etc.*: *see* **промы́ть**
промтова́ры (-ов) *pl* manufactured goods.
промча́ться (-чу́сь) *pf* rush by.
промыва́ть *impf of* **промы́ть**

П

про́мысел (-сла) trade, business; *pl* works. **промысло́вый** producers'; business; game.

промы́ть (-мо́ю) *pf* (*impf* **промыва́ть**) wash (thoroughly); bathe; ~ **мозги́**+*dat* brain-wash.

про|мыча́ть (-чу́) *pf*.

промы́шленник industrialist. **промы́шленность** industry. **промы́шленный** industrial.

пронести́ (-су́, -сёшь; -ёс, -ла́) *pf* (*impf* **проноси́ть**) carry (past, through); pass (over); **~сь** rush past, through; scud (past); fly; spread.

пронза́ть *impf*, **пронзи́ть** (-нжу́) *pf* pierce, transfix. **пронзи́тельный** piercing.

пронза́ть (-ижу́, -и́жешь) *pf*, **прони́зывать** *impf* pierce; permeate.

проника́ть *impf*, **прони́кнуть** (-ну; -и́к) *pf* penetrate; percolate; **~ся** be imbued. **проникнове́ние** penetration; feeling. **проникнове́нный** heartfelt.

проница́емый permeable. **проница́тельный** perspicacious.

проноси́ть(ся (-ошу́(сь, -о́сишь(ся) *impf of* **пронести́(сь. про|нумерова́ть** *pf*.

проню́хать *pf*, **проню́хивать** *impf* smell out, get wind of.

прообраз prototype.

пропага́нда propaganda. **пропаганди́ст** propagandist.

пропада́ть *impf of* **пропа́сть. пропа́жа** loss.

пропа́лывать *impf of* **прополо́ть**

про́пасть precipice; abyss; lots of.

пропа́сть (-аду́, -адёшь) *pf* (*impf* **пропада́ть**) be missing; be lost; disappear; be done for, die; be wasted. **пропа́щий** lost; hopeless.

пропека́ть(ся *impf of* **пропе́чь(ся. про|пе́ть** (-пою́, -поёшь) *pf*.

пропе́чь (-еку́, -ечёшь; -ёк, -ла́) *pf* (*impf* **пропека́ть**) bake thoroughly; **~ся** get baked through.

пропива́ть *impf of* **пропи́ть**

прописа́ть (-ишу́, -и́шешь) *pf*, **пропи́сывать** *impf* prescribe; register; **~ся** register. **пропи́ска** registration; residence permit. **прописн|о́й: ~а́я бу́ква** capital letter; **~а́я и́стина** truism. **про́писью** *adv* in words.

пропита́ние subsistence, sustenance. **пропита́ть** *pf*, **пропи́тывать** *impf* impregnate, saturate.

пропи́ть (-пью́, -пьёшь; -о́пи́л, -á, -o) *pf* (*impf* **пропива́ть**) spend on drink.

проплыва́ть *impf*, **проплы́ть** (-ыву́, -ывёшь; -ы́л, -á, -o) *pf* swim, sail, *or* float past *or* through.

пропове́дник preacher; advocate. **пропове́довать** *impf* preach; advocate. **про́поведь** sermon; advocacy.

прополза́ть *impf*, **проползти́** (-зу́, -зёшь; -по́лз, -ла́) *pf* crawl, creep.

пропо́лка weeding. **прополо́ть** (-лю́, -лешь) *pf* (*impf* **пропа́лывать**) weed.

про|полоска́ть (-ощу́, -о́щешь) *pf*.

пропорциона́льный proportional, proportionate. **пропо́рция** proportion.

про́пуск (*pl* -á *or* -и, -о́в *or* -ов) pass, permit; password; admission; omission; non-attendance; blank, gap. **пропуска́ть** *impf*, **пропусти́ть** (-ущу́, -у́стишь) *pf* let pass; let in; pass; leave out; miss. **пропускно́й** admission.

про|пылесо́сить *pf*.

пропью́ *etc.*: *see* **пропи́ть**

пpopа́б works superintendent.

прораба́тывать *impf*, **прорабо́тать** *pf* work (through, at); study; pick holes in.

прораста́ние germination; sprouting. **прораста́ть** *impf*, **прорасти́** (-тёт; -ро́с, -ла́) *pf* germinate, sprout.

прорва́ть (-ву́, -вёшь; -а́л, -á, -o) *pf* (*impf* **прорыва́ть**) break through; **~ся** burst open; break through.

про|реаги́ровать *pf*.

прореди́ть (-ежу́) *pf*, **проре́живать** *impf* thin out.

проре́з cut; slit, notch. **про|ре́зать** (-е́жу) *pf*, **прореза́ть** *impf* (*impf also* **проре́зывать**) cut through; **~ся** be cut, come through.
проре́зывать(ся *impf of* **проре́зать(ся**. **про|репети́ровать** *pf*.
проре́ха tear, slit; flies; deficiency.
про|рецензи́ровать *pf*.
проро́к prophet.
пророни́ть *pf* utter.
проро́с *etc.*: *see* **прорасти́**
проро́ческий prophetic. **проро́чество** prophecy.
проро́ю *etc.*: *see* **проры́ть**
прорuба́ть *impf*, **прорубить** (-блю́, -бишь) *pf* cut *or* hack through. **про́рубь** ice-hole.
проры́в break; break-through; hitch. **прорыва́ть**[1]**(ся** *impf of* **прорва́ть(ся**
прорыва́ть[2] *impf*, **проры́ть** (-ро́ю) *pf* dig through; **~ся** dig one's way through.
проса́чиваться *impf of* **просочи́ться**
просве́рливать *impf*, **просверли́ть** *pf* drill, bore; perforate.
просве́т (clear) space; shaft of light; ray of hope; opening. **просвети́тельный** educational. **просвети́ть**[1] (-ещу́) *pf* (*impf* **просвеща́ть**) enlighten.
просвети́ть[2] (-ечу́, -е́тишь) *pf* (*impf* **просве́чивать**) X-ray.
просветле́ние brightening (up); lucidity. **про|светле́ть** (-е́ет) *pf*.
просве́чивание radioscopy. **просве́чивать** *impf of* **просвети́ть**; be translucent; be visible.
просвеща́ть *impf of* **просвети́ть**. **просвеще́ние** enlightenment.
просви́ра communion bread.
про́седь streak(s) of grey.
просе́ивать *impf of* **просе́ять**
про́сека cutting, ride.
просёлок (-лка) country road.
просе́ять (-е́ю) *pf* (*impf* **просе́ивать**) sift.
про|сигнализи́ровать *pf*.
просиде́ть (-ижу́) *pf*, **проси́живать** *impf* sit.
проси́тельный pleading. **проси́ть** (-ошу́, -о́сишь) *impf* (*pf* **по~**) ask; beg; invite; **~ся** ask; apply.
проска́кивать *impf of* **проскочи́ть**
проска́льзывать *impf*, **проскользну́ть** (-ну́, -нёшь) *pf* slip, creep.
проскочи́ть (-чу́, -чишь) *pf* (*impf* **проска́кивать**) rush by; slip through; creep in.
просла́вить (-влю) *pf*, **прославля́ть** *impf* glorify; make famous; **~ся** become famous. **просла́вленный** renowned.
проследи́ть (-ежу́) *pf*, **просле́живать** *impf* track (down); trace.
прослези́ться (-ежу́сь) *pf* shed a few tears.
просло́йка layer, stratum.
прослужи́ть (-жу́, -жишь) *pf* serve (for a certain time).
про|слу́шать *pf*, **прослу́шивать** *impf* hear; listen to; miss, not catch.
про|слы́ть (-ыву́, -ывёшь; -ы́л, -а́, -о) *pf*.
просма́тривать *impf*, **просмотре́ть** (-рю́, -ришь) *pf* look over; overlook. **просмо́тр** survey; view, viewing; examination.
просну́ться (-ну́сь, -нёшься) *pf* (*impf* **просыпа́ться**) wake up.
про́со millet.
просо́вывать(ся *impf of* **просу́нуть(ся**
про|со́хнуть (-ну; -о́х) *pf* (*impf also* **просыха́ть**) dry out.
просочи́ться (-и́тся) *pf* (*impf* **проса́чиваться**) percolate; seep (out); leak (out).
проспа́ть (-плю́; -а́л, -а́, -о) *pf* (*impf* **просыпа́ть**) sleep (through); oversleep.
проспе́кт avenue.
про|спряга́ть *pf*.
просро́ченный overdue; expired. **просро́чить** (-чу) *pf* allow to run out; be behind with; overstay. **просро́чка** delay; expiry of time limit.

П

простáивать *impf of* **простоя́ть**
простáк (-á) simpleton.
простéнок (-нка) pier (*between windows*).
простерéться (-трётся; -тёрся) *pf*, **простирáться** *impf* extend.
простúтельный pardonable, excusable. **простúть** (-ощу́) *pf* (*impf* **прощáть**) forgive; excuse; **~ся** (с+*instr*) say goodbye (to).
проститу́тка prostitute. **проститу́ция** prostitution.
прóсто *adv* simply.
простоволóсый bare-headed. **простоду́шный** simple-hearted; ingenuous.
простóй[1] downtime.
прост|óй[2] simple; plain; mere; **~ы́м глáзом** with the naked eye; **~óе числó** prime number.
простоквáша thick sour milk.
прóсто-нáпросто *adv* simply.
простонарóдный of the common people.
простóр spaciousness; space. **простóрный** spacious.
просторéчие popular speech. **простосердéчный** simple-hearted.
простотá simplicity.
простоя́ть (-ою́) *pf* (*impf* **простáивать**) stand (idle).
прострáнный extensive, vast. **прострáнственный** spatial. **прострáнство** space.
прострéл lumbago. **прострéливать** *impf*, **прострелúть** (-лю́, -лишь) *pf* shoot through.
про|строчúть (-очу́, -óчишь) *pf*.
просту́да cold. **простудúться** (-ужу́сь, -у́дишься) *pf*, **простужáться** *impf* catch (a) cold.
проступáть *impf*, **проступúть** (-ит) *pf* appear.
просту́пок (-пка) misdemeanour.
простыня́ (*pl* прóстыни, -ы́нь, -ня́м) sheet.
просты́ть (-ы́ну) *pf* get cold.
просу́нуть (-ну) *pf* (*impf* **просóвывать**) push, thrust.
просу́шивать *impf*, **просушúть** (-шу́, -шишь) *pf* dry out; **~ся** (get) dry.
просуществовáть *pf* exist; endure.
просчёт error. **просчитáться** *pf*, **просчúтываться** *impf* miscalculate.
просы́пать (-плю) *pf*, **просыпáть**[1] *impf* spill; **~ся** get spilt.
просыпáть[2] *impf of* **проспáть**. **просыпáться** *impf of* **проснýться**. **просыхáть** *impf of* **просóхнуть**
прóсьба request.
протáлкивать(ся *impf of* **протолкнýть(ся**. **протáпливать** *impf of* **протопúть**
протáптывать *impf of* **протоптáть**
протáскивать *impf*, **протащúть** (-щу́, -щишь) *pf* drag, push (through).
протéз artificial limb, prosthesis; **зубнóй ~** denture.
протеúн protein.
протекáть *impf of* **протéчь**
протéкция patronage.
протерéть (-тру́, -трёшь; -тёр) *pf* (*impf* **протирáть**) wipe (over); wear (through).
протéст protest. **протестáнт, ~ка** Protestant. **протестовáть** *impf* protest.
протéчь (-ечёт; -тёк, -лá) *pf* (*impf* **протекáть**) flow; leak; seep; pass; take its course.
прóтив *prep+gen* against; opposite; contrary to, as against.
прóтивень (-вня) *m* baking-tray; meat-pan.
протúвиться (-влюсь) *impf* (*pf* **вос~**) +*dat* oppose; resist. **протúвник** opponent; the enemy. **протúвный**[1] opposite; contrary. **протúвный**[2] nasty, disgusting.
противо- *in comb* anti-, contra-, counter-. **противовéс** counterbalance. **~возду́шный** anti-aircraft. **~гáз** gas-mask. **~дéйствие** opposition. **~дéйствовать** *impf* +*dat* op-

pose, counteract. **~естéственный** unnatural. **~закóнный** illegal. **~зачáточный** contraceptive. **~полóжность** opposite; opposition, contrast. **~полóжный** opposite; contrary. **~постáвить** (-влю) *pf*, **~поставля́ть** *impf* oppose; contrast. **~речи́вый** contradictory; conflicting. **~рéчие** contradiction. **~рéчить** (-чу) *impf* +*dat* contradict. **~стоя́ть** (-ою́) *impf* +*dat* resist, withstand. **~тáнковый** anti-tank. **~я́дие** antidote.

протирáть *impf of* **протерéть**

проти́скивать *impf*, **проти́снуть** (-ну) *pf* force, squeeze (through, into).

проткнýть (-нý, -нёшь) *pf* (*impf* **протыкáть**) pierce.

протокóл minutes; report; protocol.

протолкнýть (-нý, -нёшь) *pf* (*impf* **протáлкивать**) push through; **~ся** push one's way through.

протóн proton.

протопи́ть (-плю́, -пишь) *pf* (*impf* **протáпливать**) heat (thoroughly).

протоптáть (-пчý, -пчешь) *pf* (*impf* **протáптывать**) tread; wear out.

проторённый beaten, well-trodden.

прототи́п prototype.

протóчный flowing, running.

про|трáлить *pf*. **протрý** *etc*.: *see* **протерéть**. **про|труби́ть** (-блю́) *pf*.

протрезви́ться (-влю́сь) *pf*, **протрезвля́ться** *impf* sober up.

протухáть *impf*, **протýхнуть** (-нет; -ýх) *pf* become rotten; go bad.

протыкáть *impf of* **проткнýть**

протя́гивать *impf*, **протянýть** (-нý, -нешь) *pf* stretch; extend; hold out; **~ся** stretch out; extend; last. **протяжéние** extent, stretch; period. **протя́жный** long-drawn-out; drawling.

проýчивать *impf*, **проучи́ть** (-чý, -чишь) *pf* study; teach a lesson.

профáн ignoramus.

профанáция profanation.

профессионáл professional. **профессионáльный** professional; occupational. **профéссия** profession. **профéссор** (*pl* -á) professor.

профилáктика prophylaxis; preventive measures.

прóфиль *m* profile; type.

про|фильтровáть *pf*.

профсою́з trade-union.

прохáживаться *impf of* **пройти́сь**

прохвóст scoundrel.

прохлáда coolness. **прохлади́тельный** refreshing, cooling. **прохлáдный** cool, chilly.

прохóд passage; gangway, aisle; duct. **проходи́мец** (-мца) rogue. **проходи́мый** passable. **проходи́ть** (-ожý, -óдишь) *impf of* **пройти́**. **проходнóй** entrance; communicating. **проходя́щий** passing. **прохóжий** passing, in transit; *sb* passer-by.

процветáние prosperity. **процветáть** *impf* prosper, flourish.

процеди́ть (-ежý, -éдишь) *pf* (*impf* **процéживать**) filter, strain.

процедýра procedure; (*usu in pl*) treatment.

процéживать *pf of* **процеди́ть**

процéнт percentage; per cent; interest.

процéсс process; trial; legal proceedings. **процéссия** procession.

про|цити́ровать *pf*.

прочёска screening; combing.

прочéсть (-чтý, -чтёшь; -чёл, -члá) *pf of* **читáть**

прóчий other.

прочи́стить (-и́щу) *pf* (*impf* **прочищáть**) clean; clear.

про|читáть *pf*, **прочи́тывать** *impf* read (through).

прочищáть *impf of* **прочи́стить**

прóчность firmness, stability, durability. **прóчный** (-чен, -чнá, -о) firm, sound, solid; durable.

прочтéние reading. **прочтý** *etc*.: *see* **прочéсть**

П

прочу́вствовать *pf* feel deeply; experience, go through.
прочь *adv* away, off; averse to.
проше́дший past; last. **прошёл** *etc.*: *see* **пройти́**
проше́ние application, petition.
прошепта́ть (-пчу́, -пчешь) *pf* whisper.
проше́ствие: по проше́ствии +*gen* after.
прошива́ть *impf*, **проши́ть** (-шью́, -шьёшь) *pf* sew, stitch.
прошлого́дний last year's. **про́шл|ый** past; last; **~ое** *sb* the past.
про|шнурова́ть *pf.* **про|штуди́ровать** *pf.* **прошью́** *etc.*: *see* **проши́ть**
проща́й(те) goodbye. **проща́льный** parting; farewell. **проща́ние** farewell; parting. **проща́ть(ся** *impf of* **прости́ть(ся**
про́ще simpler, plainer.
проще́ние forgiveness, pardon.
прощу́пать *pf*, **прощу́пывать** *impf* feel.
П **про|экзаменова́ть** *pf.*
прояви́тель *m* developer. **прояви́ть** (-влю́, -вишь) *pf*, **проявля́ть** *impf* show, display; develop; **~ся** reveal itself. **проявле́ние** display; manifestation; developing.
проясни́ться *pf*, **проясня́ться** *impf* clear, clear up.
пруд (-а́, *loc* -у́) pond. **пруди́ть** (-ужу́, -у́дишь) *impf* (*pf* **за~**) dam.
пружи́на spring. **пружи́нистый** springy. **пружи́нный** spring.
пру́сский Prussian.
прут (-а *or* -а́; *pl* -тья) twig.
пры́гать *impf*, **пры́гнуть** (-ну) *pf* jump, leap; bounce; **~ с шесто́м** pole-vault. **прыгу́н** (-а́), **прыгу́нья** (*gen pl* -ний) jumper. **прыжо́к** (-жка́) jump; leap; **прыжки́** jumping; **прыжки́ в во́ду** diving; **~ в высоту́** high jump; **~ в длину́** long jump.
пры́скать *impf*, **пры́снуть** (-ну) *pf* spurt; sprinkle; burst out laughing.
прыть speed; energy.
прыщ (-а́), **пры́щик** pimple.
пряди́льный spinning. **пряди́льня** (*gen pl* -лен) (spinning-)mill. **пряди́льщик** spinner. **пряду́** *etc.*: *see* **прясть.** **прядь** lock; strand. **пря́жа** yarn, thread.
пря́жка buckle, clasp.
пря́лка distaff; spinning-wheel.
пряма́я *sb* straight line. **пря́мо** *adv* straight; straight on; frankly; really.
прямоду́шие directness, straightforwardness. **~ду́шный** direct, straightforward.
прямо́й (-ям, -а́, -о) straight; upright, erect; through; direct; straightforward; real.
прямолине́йный rectilinear; straightforward. **прямоуго́льник** rectangle. **прямоуго́льный** rectangular.
пря́ник spice cake. **пря́ность** spice. **пря́ный** spicy; heady.
прясть (-яду́, -ядёшь; -ял, -яла́, -о) *impf* (*pf* **с~**) spin.
пря́тать (-я́чу) *impf* (*pf* **с~**) hide; **~ся** hide. **пря́тки** (-ток) *pl* hide-and-seek.
пса *etc.*: *see* **пёс**
псало́м (-лма́) psalm. **псалты́рь** Psalter.
псевдони́м pseudonym.
псих madman, lunatic. **психиатри́я** psychiatry. **пси́хика** psyche; psychology. **психи́ческий** mental, psychical.
психоана́лиз psychoanalysis. **психо́з** psychosis. **психо́лог** psychologist. **психологи́ческий** psychological. **психоло́гия** psychology. **психопа́т** psychopath. **психопати́ческий** psychopathic. **психосомати́ческий** psychosomatic. **психотерапе́вт** psychotherapist. **психотерапи́я** psychotherapy. **психоти́ческий** psychotic.
птене́ц (-нца́) nestling; fledgeling. **пти́ца** bird. **птицефе́рма**

poultry-farm. **пти́чий** bird, bird's, poultry. **пти́чка** bird; tick.
пу́блика public; audience. **публика́ция** publication; notice, advertisement. **публикова́ть** *impf* (*pf* **о~**) publish. **публици́стика** writing on current affairs. **публи́чность** publicity. **публи́чный** public; **~ дом** brothel.
пу́гало scarecrow. **пуга́ть** *impf* (*pf* **ис~, на~**) frighten, scare; **~ся** (+*gen*) be frightened (of). **пуга́ч** (-а́) toy pistol. **пугли́вый** fearful.
пу́говица button.
пуд (*pl* -ы́) pood (= *16.38 kg*). **пудово́й, пудо́вый** one pood in weight.
пу́дель *m* poodle.
пу́динг blancmange.
пу́дра powder. **пу́дреница** powder compact. **пу́дреный** powdered. **пу́дриться** *impf* (*pf* **на~**) powder one's face.
пуза́тый pot-bellied.
пузырёк (-рька́) vial; bubble. **пузы́рь** (-я́) *m* bubble; blister; bladder.
пук (*pl* -и́) bunch, bundle; tuft.
пу́кать *impf*, **пу́кнуть** *pf* fart.
пулемёт machine-gun. **пулемётчик** machine-gunner. **пуленепробива́емый** bullet-proof.
пульвериза́тор atomizer; spray.
пульс pulse. **пульса́р** pulsar. **пульси́ровать** *impf* pulsate.
пульт desk, stand; control panel.
пу́ля bullet.
пункт point; spot; post; item. **пункти́р** dotted line. **пункти́рный** dotted, broken.
пунктуа́льный punctual.
пунктуа́ция punctuation.
пунцо́вый crimson.
пуп (-а́) navel. **пупови́на** umbilical cord. **пупо́к** (-пка́) navel; gizzard.
пурга́ blizzard.
пурита́нин (*pl* -та́не, -та́н), **-а́нка** Puritan.
пу́рпур purple, crimson. **пурпу́р|ный, ~овый** purple.
пуск starting (up). **пуска́й** *see* **пусть. пуска́ть(ся** *impf of* **пусти́ть(ся. пусково́й** starting.
пусте́ть (-е́ет) *impf* (*pf* **о~**) empty; become deserted.
пусти́ть (пущу́, пу́стишь) *pf* (*impf* **пуска́ть**) let go; let in; let; start; send; set in motion; throw; put forth; **~ся** set out; start.
пустова́ть *impf* be *or* stand empty. **пусто́й** (-ст, -а́, -о) empty; uninhabited; idle; shallow. **пустота́** (*pl* -ы) emptiness; void; vacuum; futility. **пустоте́лый** hollow.
пусты́нный uninhabited; deserted; desert. **пусты́ня** desert. **пусты́рь** (-я́) *m* waste land; vacant plot.
пусты́шка blank; hollow object; dummy.
пусть, пуска́й *partl* let; all right; though, even if.
пустя́к (-а́) trifle. **пустяко́вый** trivial.
пу́таница muddle, confusion. **пу́таный** muddled, confused. **пу́тать** *impf* (*pf* **за~, пере~, с~**) tangle; confuse; mix up; **~ся** get confused *or* mixed up.
путёвка pass; place on a group tour. **путеводи́тель** *m* guide, guide-book. **путево́й** travelling; road. **путём** *prep*+*gen* by means of. **путеше́ственник** traveller. **путеше́ствие** journey; voyage. **путеше́ствовать** *impf* travel; voyage.
пу́ты (пут) *pl* shackles.
путь (-и́, *instr* -ём, *prep* -и́) way; track; path; course; journey; voyage; means; **в пути́** en route, on one's way.
пух (*loc* -у́) down; fluff.
пу́хлый (-хл, -а́, -о) plump. **пу́хнуть** (-ну; пух) *impf* (*pf* **вс~, о~**) swell.
пухови́к (-а́) feather-bed. **пухо́вка** powder-puff. **пухо́вый** downy.
пучи́на abyss; the deep.
пучо́к (-чка́) bunch, bundle.
пу́шечный gun, cannon.

пушúнка bit of fluff. **пушúстый** fluffy.

пу́шка gun, cannon.

пушнúна furs, pelts. **пушнóй** fur; fur-bearing.

пу́ще *adv* more; **~ всегó** most of all.

пущу́ *etc.*: *see* **пустúть**

пчелá (*pl* -ёлы) bee. **пчелúный** bee, bees'. **пчеловóд** bee-keeper. **пчéльник** apiary.

пшенúца wheat. **пшенúчный** wheat(en).

пшённый millet. **пшенó** millet.

пыл (*loc* -у́) heat, ardour. **пылáть** *impf* blaze; burn.

пылесóс vacuum cleaner. **пылесóсить** *impf* (*pf* **про~**) vacuum(-clean). **пылúнка** speck of dust. **пылúть** *impf* (*pf* **за~, на~**) raise a dust; cover with dust; **~ся** get dusty.

пы́лкий ardent; fervent.

пыль (*loc* -и́) dust. **пы́льный** (-лен, -льнá, -о) dusty. **пыльцá** pollen.

П **пырéй** couch grass.

Р **пырну́ть** (-ну́, -нёшь) *pf* jab.

пытáть *impf* torture. **пытáться** *impf* (*pf* **по~**) try. **пы́тка** torture, torment. **пытлúвый** inquisitive.

пыхтéть (-хчу́) *impf* puff, pant.

пы́шка bun.

пы́шность splendour. **пы́шный** (-шен, -шнá, -шно) splendid; lush.

пьедестáл pedestal.

пьéса play; piece.

пью *etc.*: *see* **пить**

пьянéть (-éю) *impf* (*pf* **о~**) get drunk. **пьянúть** *impf* (*pf* **о~**) intoxicate, make drunk. **пья́ница** *m* & *f* drunkard. **пья́нство** drunkenness. **пья́нствовать** *impf* drink heavily. **пья́ный** drunk.

пюпúтр lectern; stand.

пюрé *neut indecl* purée.

пядь (*gen pl* -éй) span; **ни пя́ди** not an inch.

пя́льцы (-лец) *pl* embroidery frame.

пятá (*pl* -ы, -áм) heel.

пятáк (-á), **пятачóк** (-чкá) five-copeck piece. **пятёрка** five; figure 5; No. 5; fiver (5-*rouble note*).

пяти- *in comb* five; penta-. **пятибóрье** pentathlon. **~десятилéтие** fifty years; fiftieth anniversary, birthday. **П~деся́тница** Pentecost. **~деся́тый** fiftieth; **~деся́тые гóды** the fifties. **~конéчный** five-pointed. **~лéтие** five years; fifth anniversary. **~лéтка** five-year plan. **~сóтый** five-hundredth. **~угóльник** pentagon. **~угóльный** pentagonal.

пя́титься (пя́чусь) *impf* (*pf* **по~**) move backwards; back.

пя́тка heel.

пятнáдцатый fifteenth. **пятнáдцать** fifteen.

пятнáть *impf* (*pf* **за~**) spot, stain. **пятнáшки** (-шек) *pl* tag. **пятнúстый** spotted.

пя́тница Friday.

пятнó (*pl* -а, -тен) stain; spot; blot; **родúмое ~** birth-mark.

пя́тый fifth. **пять** (-и́, *instr* -ью) five. **пятьдеся́т** (-úдесяти, *instr* -ью́десятью) fifty. **пятьсóт** (-тисóт, -тистáм) five hundred. **пя́тью** *adv* five times.

Р

раб (-á), **рабá** slave. **рабовладéлец** (-льца) slave-owner. **раболéпие** servility. **раболéпный** servile. **раболéпствовать** cringe, fawn.

рабóта work; job; functioning. **рабóтать** *impf* work; function; be open; **~ над**+*instr* work on. **рабóтник, -ица** worker. **работоспосóбность** capacity for work, efficiency. **работоспосóбный** able-bodied, hardworking. **работя́щий** hardworking. **рабóчий** *sb* worker. **рабóч|ий** worker's; working; **~ая сúла** manpower.

рáбский slave; servile. **рáбство**

slavery. **рабы́ня** female slave.
равви́н rabbi.
ра́венство equality. **равне́ние** alignment. **равни́на** plain.
равно́ *adv* alike; equally; **~ как** as well as. **равно́** *predic*: *see* **ра́вный**
равно- *in comb* equi-, iso-. **равнобе́дренный** isosceles. **~ве́сие** equilibrium; balance. **~де́нствие** equinox. **~ду́шие** indifference. **~ду́шный** indifferent. **~ме́рный** even; uniform. **~пра́вие** equality of rights. **~пра́вный** having equal rights. **~си́льный** of equal strength; equal, equivalent, tantamount. **~сторо́нний** equilateral. **~це́нный** of equal value; equivalent.
ра́вный (-вен, -вна́) equal. **равно́** *predic* make(s), equals; **всё ~о́** (it is) all the same. **равня́ть** *impf* (*pf* **с~**) make even; treat equally; +**с**+*instr* compare with, treat as equal to; **~ся** compete, compare; be equal; be tantamount.
рад (-а, -о) *predic* glad.
рада́р radar.
ра́ди *prep+gen* for the sake of.
радиа́тор radiator. **радиа́ция** radiation.
ра́дий radium.
радика́льный radical.
ра́дио *neut indecl* radio.
радио- *in comb* radio-; radioactive. **радиоакти́вный** radioactive. **~веща́ние** broadcasting. **~волна́** radio-wave. **~гра́мма** radio-telegram. **радио́лог** radiologist. **~ло́гия** radiology. **~лока́тор** radar (set). **~люби́тель** *m* radio amateur, ham. **~ма́як** (-а́) radio beacon. **~переда́тчик** transmitter. **~переда́ча** broadcast. **~приёмник** radio (set). **~свя́зь** radio communication. **~слу́шатель** *m* listener. **~ста́нция** radio station. **~электро́ника** radioelectronics.
радио́ла radiogram.
ради́ровать *impf* & *pf* radio. **ради́ст** radio operator.
ра́диус radius.
ра́довать *impf* (*pf* **об~, по~**) gladden, make happy; **~ся** be glad, rejoice. **ра́достный** joyful. **ра́дость** gladness, joy.
ра́дуга rainbow. **ра́дужн|ый** iridescent; cheerful; **~ая оболо́чка** iris.
раду́шие cordiality. **раду́шный** cordial.
ражу́ *etc.*: *see* **рази́ть**
раз (*pl* -ы́, раз) time, occasion; one; **ещё ~** (once) again; **как ~** just, exactly; **не ~** more than once; **ни ~у** not once. **раз** *adv* once, one day. **раз** *conj* if; since.
разба́вить (-влю) *pf*, **разбавля́ть** *impf* dilute.
разбаза́ривать *impf*, **разбаза́рить** *pf* squander.
разба́лтывать(ся *impf of* **разболта́ть(ся**
разбе́г running start. **разбега́ться** *impf*, **разбежа́ться** (-е́гусь) *pf* take a run, run up; scatter.
разберу́ *etc.*: *see* **разобра́ть**
разбива́ть(ся *impf of* **разби́ть(ся. разби́вка** laying out; spacing (out).
разбинтова́ть *pf*, **разбинто́вывать** *impf* unbandage.
разбира́тельство investigation. **разбира́ть** *impf of* **разобра́ть**; **~ся** *impf of* **разобра́ться**
разби́ть (-зобью́, -зобьёшь) *pf* (*impf* **разбива́ть**) break; smash; divide (up); damage; defeat; mark out; space (out); **~ся** break, get broken; hurt o.s. **разби́тый** broken; jaded.
раз|богате́ть (-е́ю) *pf*.
разбо́й robbery. **разбо́йник** robber. **разбо́йничий** robber.
разболе́ться[1] (-ли́тся) *pf* begin to ache badly.
разболе́ться[2] (-е́юсь) *pf* become ill.
разболта́ть[1] *pf* (*impf* **разба́лтывать**) divulge, give away.
разболта́ть[2] *pf* (*impf* **разба́лты-**

Р

вать) shake up; loosen; **~ся** work loose; get out of hand.

разбомби́ть (-блю́) *pf* bomb, destroy by bombing.

разбо́р analysis; critique; discrimination; investigation. **разбо́рка** sorting out; dismantling. **разбо́рный** collapsible. **разбо́рчивый** legible; discriminating.

разбра́сывать *impf of* **разброса́ть**

разбреда́ться *impf*, **разбрести́сь** (-едётся; -ёлся, -ла́сь) *pf* disperse; straggle. **разбро́д** disorder.

разбро́санный scattered; disconnected, incoherent. **разброса́ть** *pf* (*impf* **разбра́сывать**) throw about; scatter.

раз|буди́ть (-ужу́, -у́дишь) *pf*.

разбуха́ть *impf*, **разбу́хнуть** (-нет; -бу́х) *pf* swell.

разбушева́ться (-шу́юсь) *pf* fly into a rage; blow up; rage.

разва́л breakdown, collapse. **разва́ливать** *impf*, **развали́ть** (-лю́, -лишь) *pf* pull down; mess up; **~ся** collapse; go to pieces; tumble down; sprawl. **разва́лина** ruin; wreck.

Р

ра́зве *partl* really?; **~ (то́лько), ~ (что)** except that, only.

развева́ться *impf* fly, flutter.

разве́дать *pf* (*impf* **разве́дывать**) find out; reconnoitre.

разведе́ние breeding; cultivation.

разведённ|ый divorced; **~ый, ~ая** *sb* divorcee.

разве́дка intelligence (service); reconnaissance; prospecting. **разве́дочный** prospecting, exploratory.

разведу́ *etc.*: *see* **развести́**

разве́дчик intelligence officer; scout; prospector. **разве́дывать** *impf of* **разве́дать**

развезти́ (-зу́, -зёшь; -ёз, -ла́) *pf* (*impf* **развози́ть**) convey, transport; deliver.

разве́ивать(ся *impf of* **разве́ять(ся**. **развёл** *etc.*: *see* **развести́**

развенча́ть *pf*, **разве́нчивать** *impf* dethrone; debunk.

развёрнутый extensive, all-out; detailed. **разверну́ть** (-ну́, -нёшь) *pf* (*impf* **развёртывать, развора́чивать**) unfold, unwrap; unroll; unfurl; deploy; expand; develop; turn; scan; display; **~ся** unfold, unroll, come unwrapped; deploy; develop; spread; turn.

развёрстка allotment, apportionment.

развёртывать(ся *impf of* **разверну́ть(ся**

раз|весели́ть *pf* cheer up, amuse; **~ся** cheer up.

разве́сить[1] (-е́шу) *pf* (*impf* **разве́шивать**) spread; hang (out).

разве́сить[2] (-е́шу) *pf* (*impf* **разве́шивать**) weigh out. **разве́ска** weighing. **развесно́й** sold by weight.

развести́ (-еду́, -едёшь; -ёл, -а́) *pf* (*impf* **разводи́ть**) take; separate; divorce; dilute; dissolve; start; breed; cultivate; **~сь** get divorced; breed, multiply.

разветви́ться (-ви́тся) *pf*, **разветвля́ться** *impf* branch; fork. **разветвле́ние** branching, forking; branch; fork.

разве́шать *pf*, **разве́шивать** *impf* hang.

разве́шивать *impf of* **разве́сить, разве́шать. разве́шу** *etc.*: *see* **разве́сить**

разве́ять (-е́ю) *pf* (*impf* **разве́ивать**) scatter, disperse; dispel; **~ся** disperse; be dispelled.

развива́ть(ся *impf of* **разви́ть(ся**

разви́лка fork.

развинти́ть (-нчу́) *pf*, **разви́нчивать** *impf* unscrew.

разви́тие development. **развито́й** (ра́звит, -а́, -о) developed; mature. **разви́ть** (-зовью́; -зовьёшь; -и́л, -а́, -о) *pf* (*impf* **развива́ть**) develop; unwind; **~ся** develop.

развлека́ть *impf*, **развле́чь** (-еку́, -ечёшь; -ёк, -ла́) *pf* entertain, amuse; **~ся** have a good time;

amuse o.s. **развлече́ние** entertainment, amusement.

разво́д divorce. **разводи́ть(ся** (-ожу́(сь, -о́дишь(ся) *impf of* **развести́(сь. разво́дка** separation. **разводно́й: ~ ключ** adjustable spanner; **~ мост** drawbridge.

развози́ть (-ожу́, -о́зишь) *impf of* **развезти́**

разволнова́ть(ся *pf* get excited, be agitated.

развора́чивать(ся *impf of* **разверну́ть(ся**

разворова́ть *pf*, **разворо́вывать** *impf* loot; steal.

разворо́т U-turn; turn; development.

развра́т depravity, corruption. **развратить** (-ащу́) *pf*. **развраща́ть** *impf* corrupt; deprave. **развра́тничать** *impf* lead a depraved life. **развра́тный** debauched, corrupt. **развращённый** (-ён, -а́) corrupt.

развяза́ть (-яжу́, -я́жешь) *pf*, **развя́зывать** *impf* untie; unleash; **~ся** come untied; **~ся с**+*instr* rid o.s. of. **развя́зка** dénouement; outcome. **развя́зный** overfamiliar.

разгада́ть *pf*, **разга́дывать** *impf* solve, guess, interpret. **разга́дка** solution.

разга́р height, climax.

разгиба́ть(ся *impf of* **разогну́ть(ся**

разглаго́льствовать *impf* hold forth.

разгла́дить (-а́жу) *pf*, **разгла́живать** *impf* smooth out; iron (out).

разгласи́ть (-ашу́) *pf*, **разглаша́ть** *impf* divulge; +**о**+*prep* trumpet. **разглаше́ние** disclosure.

разгляде́ть (-яжу́) *pf*, **разгля́дывать** *impf* make out, discern.

разгне́вать *pf* anger. **раз|гне́ваться** *pf*.

разгова́ривать *impf* talk, converse. **разгово́р** conversation. **разгово́рник** phrase-book. **разгово́рный** colloquial. **разгово́рчивый** talkative.

разго́н dispersal; running start; distance. **разгоня́ть(ся** *impf of* **разогна́ть(ся**

разгора́живать *impf of* **разгороди́ть**

разгора́ться *impf*, **разгоре́ться** (-рю́сь) *pf* flare up.

разгороди́ть (-ожу́, -о́ди́шь) *pf* (*impf* **разгора́живать**) partition off.

раз|горячи́ть(ся (-чу́(сь) *pf*.

разгра́бить (-блю) *pf* plunder, loot. **разграбле́ние** plunder, looting.

разграниче́ние demarcation; differentiation. **разграни́чивать** *impf*, **разграни́чить** (-чу) *pf* delimit; differentiate.

разгреба́ть *impf*, **разгрести́** (-ебу́, -ебёшь; -ёб, -ла́) *pf* rake *or* shovel (away).

разгро́м crushing defeat; devastation; havoc. **разгроми́ть** (-млю́) *pf* rout, defeat.

разгружа́ть *impf*, **разгрузи́ть** (-ужу́, -у́зи́шь) *pf* unload; relieve; **~ся** unload; be relieved. **разгру́зка** unloading; relief.

разгрыза́ть *impf*, **раз|гры́зть** (-зу́, -зёшь; -ы́з) *pf* crack.

разгу́л revelry; outburst. **разгу́ливать** *impf* stroll about. **разгу́ливаться** *impf*, **разгуля́ться** *pf* spread o.s.; become wide awake; clear up. **разгу́льный** wild, rakish.

раздава́ть(ся (-даю́(сь, -даёшь(ся) *impf of* **разда́ть(ся**

раз|дави́ть (-влю́, -вишь) *pf*. **разда́вливать** *impf* crush; run over.

разда́ть (-а́м, -а́шь, -а́ст, -ади́м; ро́зо *or* разда́л, -а́, -о) *pf* (*impf* **раздава́ть**) distribute, give out; **~ся** be heard; resound; ring out; make way; expand; put on weight. **разда́ча** distribution. **раздаю́** *etc.*: *see* **раздава́ть**

раздва́ивать(ся *impf of* **раздво́ить(ся**

Р

раздвига́ть *impf*, **раздви́нуть** (-ну) *pf* move apart; **~ся** move apart. **раздвижно́й** expanding; sliding.

раздвое́ние division; split; **~ ли́чности** split personality. **раз-дво́енный** forked; cloven; split. **раздвои́ть** *pf* (*impf* **раздва́ивать**) divide into two; bisect; **~ся** fork; split.

раздева́лка cloakroom. **разде-ва́ть(ся** *impf of* **разде́ть(ся**

разде́л division; section.

разде́латься *pf* +**c**+*instr* finish with; settle accounts with.

разделе́ние division. **раздели́-мый** divisible. **раз|дели́ть** (-лю́, -лишь) *pf*, **разделя́ть** *impf* divide; separate; share; **~ся** divide; be divided; be divisible; separate. **разде́льный** separate.

разде́ну *etc.*: *see* **разде́ть. раз-деру́** *etc.*: *see* **разодра́ть**

разде́ть (-де́ну) *pf* (*impf* **разде-ва́ть**) undress; **~ся** undress; take off one's coat.

раздира́ть *impf of* **разодра́ть**

раздобыва́ть *impf*, **раздобы́ть** (-бу́ду) *pf* get, get hold of.

раздо́лье expanse; liberty. **раз-до́льный** free.

раздо́р discord.

раздоса́довать *pf* vex.

раздража́ть *impf*, **раздражи́ть** (-жу́) *pf* irritate; annoy; **~ся** get annoyed. **раздраже́ние** irritation. **раздражи́тельный** irritable.

раз|дроби́ть (-блю́) *pf*, **раздро-бля́ть** *impf* break; smash to pieces.

раздува́ть(ся *impf of* **разду́ть(ся**

разду́мать *pf*, **разду́мывать** *impf* change one's mind; ponder. **разду́мье** meditation; thought.

разду́ть (-у́ю) *pf* (*impf* **раздува́ть**) blow; fan; exaggerate; whip up; swell; **~ся** swell.

разева́ть *impf of* **рази́нуть**

разжа́лобить (-блю) *pf* move (to pity).

разжа́ловать *pf* demote.

разжа́ть (-зожму́, -мёшь) *pf* (*impf* **разжима́ть**) unclasp, open; release.

разжева́ть (-жую́, -жуёшь) *pf*, **разжёвывать** *impf* chew.

разже́чь (-зожгу́, -зожжёшь; -жёг, -зожгла́) *pf*, **разжига́ть** *impf* kindle; rouse.

разжима́ть *impf of* **разжа́ть. раз-|жире́ть** (-е́ю) *pf*.

рази́нуть (-ну) *pf* (*impf* **разева́ть**) open; **~ рот** gape. **рази́ня** *m* & *f* scatter-brain.

рази́тельный striking. **рази́ть** (ражу́) *impf* (*pf* **по~**) strike.

разлага́ть(ся *impf of* **разло-жи́ть(ся**

разла́д discord; disorder.

разла́мывать(ся *impf of* **разло-ма́ть(ся, разломи́ть(ся. разлёгся** *etc.*: *see* **разле́чься**

разлеза́ться *impf*, **разле́зться** (-зется; -ле́зся) *pf* come to pieces; fall apart.

разлета́ться *impf*, **разлете́ться** (-лечу́сь) *pf* fly away; scatter; shatter; rush.

разле́чься (-ля́гусь; -лёгся, -гла́сь) *pf* stretch out.

разли́в bottling; flood; overflow. **разлива́ть** *impf*, **разли́ть** (-золью́, -зольёшь; -и́л, -а́, -о) *pf* pour out; spill; flood (with); **~ся** spill; overflow; spread. **разлив-но́й** draught.

различа́ть *impf*, **различи́ть** (-чу́) *pf* distinguish; discern; **~ся** differ. **разли́чие** distinction; difference. **различи́тельный** distinctive, distinguishing. **разли́чный** different.

разложе́ние decomposition; decay; disintegration. **разложи́ть** (-жу́, -жишь) *pf* (*impf* **разлага́ть, раскла́дывать**) put away; spread (out); distribute; break down; decompose; resolve; corrupt; **~ся** decompose; become demoralized; be corrupted; disintegrate, go to pieces.

разло́м breaking; break. **разлома́ть, разломи́ть** (-млю́, -мишь) *pf* (*impf* **разла́мывать**) break to pieces; pull down; **~ся** break to pieces.

разлу́ка separation. **разлуча́ть** *impf*, **разлучи́ть** (-чу́) *pf* separate, part; **~ся** separate, part.

разлюби́ть (-блю́, -бишь) *pf* stop loving *or* liking.

разля́гусь *etc.*: *see* **разле́чься**

разма́зать (-а́жу) *pf*, **разма́зывать** *impf* spread, smear.

разма́лывать *impf of* **размоло́ть**

разма́тывать *impf of* **размота́ть**

разма́х sweep; swing; span; scope. **разма́хивать** *impf* +*instr* swing; brandish. **разма́хиваться** *impf*, **размахну́ться** (-ну́сь, -нёшься) *pf* swing one's arm. **разма́шистый** sweeping.

размежева́ние demarcation, delimitation. **размежева́ть** (-жу́ю) *pf*, **размежёвывать** *impf* delimit.

размёл *etc.*: *see* **размести́**

размельча́ть *impf*, **раз|мельчи́ть** (-чу́) *pf* crush, pulverize.

размелю́ *etc.*: *see* **размоло́ть**

разме́н exchange. **разме́нивать** *impf*, **разменя́ть** *pf* change; **~ся** +*instr* exchange; dissipate. **разме́нная моне́та** (small) change.

разме́р size; measurement; amount; scale, extent; *pl* proportions. **разме́ренный** measured. **разме́рить** *pf*, **размеря́ть** *impf* measure.

размести́ (-ету́, -етёшь; -мёл, -а́) *pf* (*impf* **размета́ть**) sweep clear; sweep away.

размести́ть (-ещу́) *pf* (*impf* **размеща́ть**) place, accommodate; distribute; **~ся** take one's seat.

размета́ть *impf of* **размести́**

разме́тить (-е́чу) *pf*, **размеча́ть** *impf* mark.

размеша́ть *pf*, **разме́шивать** *impf* stir (in).

размеща́ть(ся *impf of* **размести́ть(ся**. **размеще́ние** placing; accommodation; distribution.

размещу́ *etc.*: *see* **размести́ть**

размина́ть(ся *impf of* **размя́ть(ся**

рамзи́нка limbering up.

размину́ться (-ну́сь, -нёшься) *pf* pass; +**с**+*instr* pass; miss.

размножа́ть *impf*, **размно́жить** (-жу) *pf* multiply, duplicate; breed; **~ся** multiply; breed.

размозжи́ть (-жу́) *pf* smash.

размо́лвка tiff.

размоло́ть (-мелю́, -ме́лешь) *pf* (*impf* **разма́лывать**) grind.

размора́живать *impf*, **разморо́зить** (-о́жу) *pf* unfreeze, defrost; **~ся** unfreeze; defrost.

размота́ть *pf* (*impf* **разма́тывать**) unwind.

размыва́ть *impf*, **размы́ть** (-о́ет) *pf* wash away; erode.

размыка́ть *impf of* **разомкну́ть**

размышле́ние reflection; meditation. **размышля́ть** *impf* reflect, ponder.

размягча́ть *impf*, **размягчи́ть** (-чу́) *pf* soften; **~ся** soften.

размяка́ть *impf*, **размя́кнуть** (-ну; -мя́к) *pf* soften.

раз|мя́ть (-зомну́, -зомнёшь) *pf* (*impf also* **размина́ть**) knead; mash; **~ся** stretch one's legs; limber up.

разна́шивать *impf of* **разноси́ть**

разнести́ (-су́, -сёшь; -ёс, -ла́) *pf* (*impf* **разноси́ть**) carry; deliver; spread; note down; smash; scold; scatter; *impers* make puffy, swell.

разнима́ть *impf of* **разня́ть**

ра́зниться *impf* differ. **ра́зница** difference.

разно- *in comb* different, vari-, hetero-. **разнобо́й** lack of co-ordination; difference. **~ви́дность** variety. **~гла́сие** disagreement; discrepancy. **~обра́зие** variety, diversity. **~обра́зный** various, diverse. **~речи́вый** contradictory. **~ро́дный** heterogeneous. **~сторо́нний** many-sided; versatile. **~цве́тный** variegated. **~ше́рстный** of different colours; ill-assorted.

Р

разноси́ть[1] (-ошу́, -о́сишь) *pf* (*impf* **разна́шивать**) wear in.
разноси́ть[2] (-ошу́, -о́сишь) *impf of* **разнести́**. **разно́ска** delivery.
ра́зность difference.
разно́счик pedlar.
разношу́ *etc.*: *see* **разноси́ть**
разну́зданный unbridled.
ра́зн|ый different; various; **~ое** *sb* various things.
разню́хать *pf*, **разню́хивать** *impf* smell out.
разня́ть (-ниму́, -ни́мешь; ро́з- *or* разня́л, -а́, -о) *pf* (*impf* **разнима́ть**) take to pieces; separate.
разоблача́ть *impf*, **разоблачи́ть** (-чу́) *pf* expose. **разоблаче́ние** exposure.
разобра́ть (-зберу́, -рёшь; -а́л, -а́, -о) *pf* (*impf* **разбира́ть**) take to pieces; buy up; sort out; investigate; analyse; understand; **~ся** sort things out; **+в**+*prep* investigate, look into; understand.
разобща́ть *impf*, **разобщи́ть** (-щу́) *pf* separate; estrange, alienate.
Р **разобью́** *etc.*: *see* **разби́ть**. **разовью́** *etc.*: *see* **разви́ть**
ра́зовый single.
разогна́ть (-згоню́, -о́нишь; -гна́л, -а́, -о) *pf* (*impf* **разгоня́ть**) scatter; disperse; dispel; drive fast; **~ся** gather speed.
разогну́ть (-ну́, -нёшь) *pf* (*impf* **разгиба́ть**) unbend, straighten; **~ся** straighten up.
разогрева́ть *impf*, **разогре́ть** (-е́ю) *pf* warm up.
разоде́ть(ся (-е́ну(сь) *pf* dress up.
разодра́ть (-здеру́, -рёшь; -а́л, -а́, -о) *pf* (*impf* **раздира́ть**) tear (up); lacerate.
разожгу́ *etc.*: *see* **разже́чь**. **разожму́** *etc.*: *see* **разжа́ть**
разо|зли́ть *pf*.
разойти́сь (-йду́сь, -йдёшься; -ошёлся, -ошла́сь) *pf* (*impf* **расходи́ться**) disperse; diverge; radiate; differ; conflict; part; be spent; be sold out.
разолью́ *etc.*: *see* **разли́ть**
ра́зом *adv* at once, at one go.
разомкну́ть (-ну, -нёшь) *pf* (*impf* **размыка́ть**) open; break.
разомну́ *etc.*: *see* **размя́ть**
разорва́ть (-ву́, -вёшь; -а́л, -а́, -о) *pf* (*impf* **разрыва́ть**) tear; break (off); blow up; **~ся** tear; break; explode.
разоре́ние ruin; destruction. **разори́тельный** ruinous; wasteful. **разори́ть** *pf* (*impf* **разоря́ть**) ruin; destroy; **~ся** ruin o.s.
разоружа́ть *impf*, **разоружи́ть** (-жу́) *pf* disarm; **~ся** disarm. **разоруже́ние** disarmament.
разоря́ть(ся *impf of* **разори́ть(ся**
разосла́ть (-ошлю́, -ошлёшь) *pf* (*impf* **рассыла́ть**) distribute, circulate.
разостла́ть, расстели́ть (-сстелю́, -те́лешь) *pf* (*impf* **расстила́ть**) spread (out); lay; **~ся** spread.
разотру́ *etc.*: *see* **растере́ть**
разочарова́ние disappointment.
разочарова́ть *pf*, **разочаро́вывать** *impf* disappoint; **~ся** be disappointed.
разочту́ *etc.*: *see* **расче́сть**. **разошёлся** *etc.*: *see* **разойти́сь**. **разошлю́** *etc.*: *see* **разосла́ть**. **разошью́** *etc.*: *see* **расши́ть**
разраба́тывать *impf*, **разрабо́тать** *pf* cultivate; work, exploit; work out; develop. **разрабо́тка** cultivation; exploitation; working out; mining; quarry.
разража́ться *impf*, **разрази́ться** (-ажу́сь) *pf* break out; burst out.
разраста́ться *impf*, **разрасти́сь** (-тётся; -ро́сся, -ла́сь) *pf* grow; spread.
разрежённый (-ён, -а́) rarefied.
разре́з cut; section; point of view. **разре́зать** (-е́жу) *pf*, **разреза́ть** *impf* cut; slit.
разреша́ть *impf*, **разреши́ть** (-шу́) *pf* (+*dat*) allow; solve; settle; **~ся** be allowed; be solved; be settled. **разреше́ние** permission;

permit; solution; settlement. **разреши́мый** solvable.
разро́зненный uncoordinated; odd; incomplete.
разро́сся *etc.*: *see* **разрасти́сь.**
разро́ю *etc.*: *see* **разры́ть**
разруба́ть *impf*, **разруби́ть** (-блю́, -бишь) *pf* cut; chop up.
разру́ха ruin, collapse. **разруша́ть** *impf*, **разру́шить** (-шу) *pf* destroy; demolish; ruin; **~ся** go to ruin, collapse. **разруше́ние** destruction. **разруши́тельный** destructive.
разры́в break; gap; rupture; burst. **разрыва́ть**[1]**(ся** *impf of* **разорва́ть(ся**
разрыва́ть[2] *impf of* **разры́ть**
разрывно́й explosive.
разрыда́ться *pf* burst into tears.
разры́ть (-ро́ю) *pf* (*impf* **разрыва́ть**) dig (up).
раз|рыхли́ть *pf*, **разрыхля́ть** *impf* loosen; hoe.
разря́д[1] category; class.
разря́д[2] discharge. **разряди́ть** (-яжу́, -я́дишь) *pf* (*impf* **разряжа́ть**) unload; discharge; space out; **~ся** run down; clear, ease. **разря́дка** spacing (out); discharging; unloading; relieving.
разряжа́ть(ся *impf of* **разряди́ть(ся**
разубеди́ть (-ежу́) *pf*, **разубежда́ть** *impf* dissuade; **~ся** change one's mind.
разува́ться *impf of* **разу́ться**
разуве́рить *pf*, **разуверя́ть** *impf* dissuade, undeceive; **~ся** (**в**+*prep*) lose faith (in).
разузнава́ть (-наю́, -наёшь) *impf*, **разузна́ть** *pf* (try to) find out.
разукра́сить (-а́шу) *pf*, **разукра́шивать** *impf* adorn, embellish.
ра́зум reason; intellect. **разуме́ться** (-е́ется) *impf* be understood, be meant; **(само́ собо́й) разуме́ется** of course; it goes without saying. **разу́мный** rational, intelligent; sensible; reasonable; wise.
разу́ться (-у́юсь) *pf* (*impf* **разува́ться**) take off one's shoes.
разу́чивать *impf*, **разучи́ть** (-чу́, -чишь) *pf* learn (up). **разу́чиваться** *impf*, **разучи́ться** (-чу́сь, -чишься) *pf* forget (how to).
разъеда́ть *impf of* **разъе́сть**
разъедини́ть *pf*, **разъединя́ть** *impf* separate; disconnect.
разъе́дусь *etc.*: *see* **разъе́хаться**
разъе́зд departure; siding (track); mounted patrol; *pl* travel; journeys. **разъездно́й** travelling. **разъезжа́ть** *impf* drive *or* ride about; travel; **~ся** *impf of* **разъе́хаться**
разъе́сть (-е́ст, -едя́т; -е́л) *pf* (*impf* **разъеда́ть**) eat away; corrode.
разъе́хаться (-е́дусь) *pf* (*impf* **разъезжа́ться**) depart; separate; pass (one another); miss one another.
разъярённый (-ён, -а́) furious. **разъяри́ть** *pf*, **разъяря́ть** *impf* infuriate; **~ся** get furious.
разъясне́ние explanation; interpretation. **разъясни́тельный** explanatory.
разъясни́ть *pf*, **разъясня́ть** *impf* explain; interpret; **~ся** become clear, be cleared up.
разыгра́ть *pf*, **разы́грывать** *impf* perform; draw; raffle; play a trick on; **~ся** get up; run high.
разыска́ть (-ыщу́, -ы́щешь) *pf* find. **разы́скивать** *impf* search for.
рай (*loc* -ю́) paradise; garden of Eden.
райко́м district committee.
райо́н region. **райо́нный** district.
ра́йский heavenly.
рак crayfish; cancer; Cancer.
раке́та[1], **раке́тка** racket.
раке́та[2] rocket; missile; flare.
ра́ковина shell; sink.
ра́ковый cancer; cancerous.
раку́шка cockle-shell, mussel.
ра́ма frame. **ра́мка** frame; *pl* framework.
ра́мпа footlights.
ра́на wound. **ране́ние** wounding;

wound. **рáненый** wounded; injured.
ранг rank.
рáнец (-нца) knapsack; satchel.
рáнить *impf* & *pf* wound; injure.
рáнний early. **рáно** *adv* early. **рáньше** *adv* earlier; before; formerly.
рапи́ра foil.
рáпорт report. **рапортовáть** *impf* & *pf* report.
рáса race. **раси́зм,** racism. **раси́стский** racist.
раскáиваться *impf of* **раскáяться**
раскалённый (-ён, -á) scorching; incandescent. **раскали́ть** *pf* (*impf* **раскаля́ть**) make red-hot; **~ся** become red-hot. **раскáлывать(ся** *impf of* **расколóть(ся. раскаля́ть(ся** *impf of* **раскали́ть(ся. раскáпывать** *impf of* **раскопáть**
раскáт roll, peal. **раскатáть** *pf*, **раскáтывать** *impf* roll (out), smooth out, level; drive *or* ride (about). **раскáтистый** rolling, booming. **раскати́ться** (-ачýсь, -áтишься) *pf*, **раскáтываться** *impf* gather speed; roll away; peal, boom.
раскачáть *pf*, **раскáчивать** *impf* swing; rock; **~ся** swing, rock.
раскáяние repentance. **рас|кáяться** *pf* (*impf also* **раскáиваться**) repent.
расквитáться *pf* settle accounts.
раски́дывать *impf*, **раски́нуть** (-ну) *pf* stretch (out); spread; pitch; **~ся** spread out; sprawl.
раскладнóй folding. **раскладýшка** camp-bed. **раскля́дывать** *impf of* **разложи́ть**
раскля́няться *pf* bow; take leave.
расклéивать *impf*, **расклéить** *pf* unstick; stick (up); **~ся** come unstuck.
раскóл split; schism. **рас|колóть** (-лю́, -лешь) *pf* (*impf also* **раскáлывать**) split; break; disrupt; **~ся** split. **раскóльник** dissenter.
раскопáть *pf* (*impf* **раскáпывать**) dig up, unearth, excavate. **раскóпки** (-пок) *pl* excavations.
раскóсый slanting.
раскрáивать *impf of* **раскрои́ть**
раскрáсить (-áшу) *pf*, *impf* **раскрáшивать** paint, colour.
раскрепости́ть (-ощý) *pf*, **раскрепощáть** *impf* liberate. **раскрепощéние** emancipation.
раскритиковáть *pf* criticize harshly.
раскрои́ть *pf* (*impf* **раскрáивать**) cut out.
раскрóю *etc.*: *see* **раскры́ть**
раскрути́ть (-учý, -ýтишь) *pf*, **раскрýчивать** *impf* untwist; **~ся** come untwisted.
раскрывáть *impf*, **раскры́ть** (-óю) *pf* open; expose; reveal; discover; **~ся** open; uncover o.s.; come to light.
раскупáть *impf*, **раскупи́ть** (-ýпит) *pf* buy up.
раскýпоривать *impf*, **раскýпорить** *pf* uncork, open.
раскуси́ть (-ушý, -ýсишь) *pf*, **раскýсывать** *impf* bite through; see through.
рáсовый racial.
распáд disintegration; collapse. **распадáться** *impf of* **распáсться**
распаковáть *pf*, **распакóвывать** *impf* unpack.
распáрывать(ся *impf of* **распорóть(ся**
распáсться (-адётся) *pf* (*impf* **распадáться**) disintegrate, fall to pieces.
распахáть (-ашý, -áшешь) *pf*, **распáхивать**[1] *impf* plough up.
распáхивать[2] *impf*, **распахнýть** (-нý, -нёшь) *pf* throw open; **~ся** fly open, swing open.
распашóнка baby's vest.
распевáть *impf* sing.
распечáтать *pf*, **распечáтывать** *impf* open; unseal.
распи́ливать *impf*, **распили́ть** (-лю́, -лишь) *pf* saw up.
распинáть *impf of* **распя́ть**
расписáние time-table. **распи-**

са́ть (-ишу́, -и́шешь) *pf*, **распи́сывать** *impf* enter; assign; paint; **~ся** sign; register one's marriage; +в+*prep* sign for; acknowledge. **распи́ска** receipt. **расписно́й** painted, decorated.

распиха́ть *pf*, **распи́хивать** *impf* push, shove, stuff.

рас|пла́вить (-влю) *pf*, **расплавля́ть** *impf* melt, fuse. **распла́вленный** molten.

распла́каться (-а́чусь) *pf* burst into tears.

распласта́ть *pf*, **распла́стывать** *impf* spread; flatten; split; **~ся** sprawl.

распла́та payment; retribution. **расплати́ться** (-ачу́сь, -а́тишься) *pf*, **распла́чиваться** *impf* (+с+*instr*) pay off; get even; +за+*acc* pay for.

расплеска́ть(ся (-ещу́(сь, -е́щешь(ся) *pf*, **расплёскивать(ся** *impf* spill.

расплести́ (-ету́, -етёшь; -ёл, -а́) *pf*, **расплета́ть** *impf* unplait; untwist.

рас|плоди́ть(ся (-ожу́(сь) *pf*.

расплыва́ться *impf*, **расплы́ться** (-ывётся; -ы́лся, -а́сь) *pf* run. **расплы́вчатый** indistinct; vague.

расплю́щивать *impf*, **расплю́щить** (-щу) *pf* flatten out, hammer out.

распну́ *etc.*: *see* **распя́ть**

распознава́ть (-наю́, -наёшь) *impf*, **распозна́ть** *pf* recognize, identify; diagnose.

располага́ть *impf* +*instr* have at one's disposal. **располага́ться** *impf of* **расположи́ться**

располза́ться *impf*, **расползти́сь** (-зётся; -о́лзся, -зла́сь) *pf* crawl (away); give at the seams.

расположе́ние disposition; arrangement; situation; tendency; liking; mood. **располо́женный** disposed, inclined. **расположи́ть** (-жу́, -жишь) *pf* (*impf* **располага́ть**) dispose; set out; win over; **~ся** settle down.

распо́рка cross-bar, strut.

рас|поро́ть (-рю́, -решь) *pf* (*impf also* **распа́рывать**) unpick, rip; **~ся** rip, come undone.

распоряди́тель *m* manager. **распоряди́тельный** capable; efficient. **распоряди́ться** (-яжу́сь) *pf*, **распоряжа́ться** *impf* order, give orders; see; +*instr* manage, deal with. **распоря́док** (-дка) order; routine. **распоряже́ние** order; instruction; disposal, command.

распра́ва violence; reprisal.

распра́вить (-влю) *pf*, **расправля́ть** *impf* straighten; smooth out; spread.

распра́виться (-влюсь) *pf*, **расправля́ться** *impf* с+*instr* deal with severely; make short work of.

распределе́ние distribution; allocation. **распредели́тель** *m* distributor. **распредели́тельный** distributive, distributing; ~ щит switchboard. **распредели́ть** *pf*, **распределя́ть** *impf* distribute; allocate.

распродава́ть (-даю́, -даёшь) *impf*, **распрода́ть** (-а́м, -а́шь, -а́ст, -ади́м; -о́дал, -а́, -о) *pf* sell off; sell out of. **распрода́жа** (clearance) sale.

распростёртый outstretched; prostrate.

распростране́ние spreading; dissemination. **распространённый** (-ён, -а́) widespread, prevalent. **распространи́ть** *pf*, **распространя́ть** *impf* spread; **~ся** spread.

ра́спря (*gen pl* -ей) quarrel.

распряга́ть *impf*, **распря́чь** (-ягу́, -яжёшь; -я́г, -ла́) *pf* unharness.

распрями́ться *pf*, **распрямля́ться** *impf* straighten up.

распуска́ть *impf*, **распусти́ть** (-ущу́, -у́стишь) *pf* dismiss; dissolve; let out; relax; let get out of hand; melt; spread; **~ся** open; come loose; dissolve; melt; get out of hand; let o.s. go.

распу́тать *pf* (*impf* **распу́тывать**) untangle; unravel.
распу́тица season of bad roads.
распу́тный dissolute. **распу́тство** debauchery.
распу́тывать *impf of* **распу́тать**
распу́тье crossroads.
распуха́ть *impf*, **распу́хнуть** (-ну; -у́х) *pf* swell (up).
распу́щенный undisciplined; spoilt; dissolute.
распыли́тель *m* spray, atomizer. **распыли́ть** *pf*, **распыля́ть** *impf* spray; pulverize; disperse.
распя́тие crucifixion; crucifix. **распя́ть** (-пну́, -пнёшь) *pf* (*impf* **распина́ть**) crucify.
расса́да seedlings. **рассади́ть** (-ажу́, -а́дишь) *pf*, **расса́живать** *impf* plant out; seat; separate, seat separately.
расса́живаться *impf of* **рассе́сться. расса́сываться** *impf of* **рассоса́ться**
рассвести́ (-етёт; -ело́) *pf*, **рассвета́ть** *impf* dawn. **рассве́т** dawn.
Р
рас|свирепе́ть (-е́ю) *pf*.
расседла́ть *pf* unsaddle.
рассе́ивание dispersal, scattering. **рассе́ивать(ся** *impf of* **рассе́ять(ся**
рассека́ть *impf of* **рассе́чь**
расселе́ние settling, resettlement; separation.
рассе́лина cleft, fissure.
рассели́ть *pf*, **расселя́ть** *impf* settle, resettle; separate.
рас|серди́ть(ся (-жу́(сь, -рдишь(ся) *pf*.
рассе́сться (-ся́дусь) *pf* (*impf* **расса́живаться**) take seats.
рассе́чь (-еку́, -ечёшь; -ёк, -ла́) *pf* (*impf* **рассека́ть**) cut (through); cleave.
рассе́янность absent-mindedness; dispersion. **рассе́янный** absent-minded; diffused; scattered. **рассе́ять** (-е́ю) *pf* (*impf* **рассе́ивать**) disperse, scatter; dispel; **~ся** disperse, scatter; clear; divert o.s.
расска́з story; account. **рассказа́ть** (-ажу́, -а́жешь) *pf*, **расска́зывать** *impf* tell, recount. **расска́зчик** story-teller, narrator.
рассла́бить (-блю) *pf*, **расслабля́ть** *impf* weaken; **~ся** relax.
рассла́ивать(ся *impf of* **расслои́ть(ся**
рассле́дование investigation, examination; inquiry; **произвести́ ~**+*gen* hold an inquiry into. **рассле́довать** *impf* & *pf* investigate, look into, hold an inquiry into.
расслои́ть *pf* (*impf* **рассла́ивать**) divide into layers; **~ся** become stratified; flake off.
рассл́ышать (-шу) *pf* catch.
рассма́тривать *impf of* **рассмотре́ть**; examine; consider.
рас|смеши́ть (-шу́) *pf*.
рассмея́ться (-ею́сь, -еёшься) *pf* burst out laughing.
рассмотре́ние examination; consideration. **рассмотре́ть** (-рю́, -ришь) *pf* (*impf* **рассма́тривать**) examine, consider; discern, make out.
рассова́ть (-сую́, -суёшь) *pf*, **рассо́вывать** *impf* **по**+*dat* shove into.
рассо́л brine; pickle.
рассо́риться *pf* **с**+*instr* fall out with.
рас|сортирова́ть *pf*, **рассортиро́вывать** *impf* sort out.
рассоса́ться (-сётся) *pf* (*impf* **расса́сываться**) resolve.
рассо́хнуться (-нется; -о́хся) *pf* (*impf* **рассыха́ться**) crack.
расспра́шивать *impf*, **расспроси́ть** (-ошу́, -о́сишь) *pf* question; make inquiries of.
рассро́чить (-чу) *pf* spread (over a period). **рассро́чка** instalment.
расстава́ние parting. **расстава́ться** (-таю́сь, -таёшься) *impf of* **расста́ться**
расста́вить (-влю) *pf*, **расставля́ть** *impf* place, arrange; move apart. **расстано́вка** arrangement; pause.

расста́ться (-а́нусь) *pf* (*impf* **расстава́ться**) part, separate.

расстёгивать *impf*, **расстегну́ть** (-ну́, -нёшь) *pf* undo, unfasten; **~ся** come undone; undo one's coat.

расстели́ть(ся, *etc.*: *see* **разостла́ть(ся. расстила́ть(ся, -а́ю(сь** *impf of* **разостла́ть(ся**

расстоя́ние distance.

расстра́ивать(ся *impf of* **расстро́ить(ся**

расстре́л execution by firing squad. **расстре́ливать** *impf*, **расстреля́ть** *pf* shoot.

расстро́енный disordered; upset; out of tune. **расстро́ить** *pf* (*impf* **расстра́ивать**) upset; thwart; disturb; throw into confusion; put out of tune; **~ся** be upset; get out of tune; fall into confusion; fall through. **расстро́йство** upset; disarray; confusion; frustration.

расступа́ться *impf*, **расступи́ться** (-у́пится) *pf* part, make way.

рассуди́тельный reasonable; sensible. **рассуди́ть** (-ужу́, -у́дишь) *pf* judge; think; decide. **рассу́док** (-дка) reason; intellect. **рассужда́ть** *impf* reason; +о+*prep* discuss. **рассужде́ние** reasoning; discussion; argument.

рассую́ *etc.*: *see* **рассова́ть**

рассчи́танный deliberate; intended. **рассчита́ть** *pf*, **рассчи́тывать** *impf*, **расче́сть** (разочту́, -тёшь; расчёл, разочла́) *pf* calculate; count; depend; **~ся** settle accounts.

рассыла́ть *impf of* **разосла́ть. рассы́лка** distribution. **рассы́льный** *sb* delivery man.

рассы́пать (-плю) *pf*, **рассыпа́ть** *impf* spill; scatter; **~ся** spill, scatter; spread out; crumble. **рассы́пчатый** friable; crumbly.

рассыха́ться *impf of* **рассо́хнуться. расся́дусь** *etc.*: *see* **рассе́сться. раста́лкивать** *impf of* **растолка́ть. раста́пливать(ся** *impf of* **растопи́ть(ся**

растаска́ть *pf*, **раста́скивать** *impf*, **растащи́ть** (-щу́, -щишь) *pf* pilfer, filch.

растащи́ть *see* **растаска́ть. рас|та́ять** (-а́ю) *pf.*

раство́р[1] solution; mortar. **раство́р**[2] opening, span. **раствори́мый** soluble. **раствори́тель** *m* solvent. **раствори́ть**[1] *pf* (*impf* **растворя́ть**) dissolve; **~ся** dissolve.

раствори́ть[2] (-рю́, -ришь) *pf* (*impf* **растворя́ть**) open; **~ся** open.

растворя́ть(ся *impf of* **раствори́ть(ся. растека́ться** *impf of* **расте́чься**

расте́ние plant.

растере́ть (разотру́, -трёшь; растёр) *pf* (*impf* **растира́ть**) grind; spread; rub; massage.

растерза́ть *pf*, **расте́рзывать** *impf* tear to pieces.

расте́рянность confusion, dismay. **расте́рянный** confused, dismayed. **растеря́ть** *pf* lose; **~ся** get lost; lose one's head.

расте́чься (-ечётся, -еку́тся; -тёкся, -ла́сь) *pf* (*impf* **растека́ться**) run; spread.

расти́ (-ту́, -тёшь; рос, -ла́) *impf* grow; grow up.

растира́ние grinding; rubbing, massage. **растира́ть(ся** *impf of* **растере́ть(ся**

расти́тельность vegetation; hair. **расти́тельный** vegetable. **расти́ть** (ращу́) *impf* bring up; train; grow.

растлева́ть *impf*, **растли́ть** *pf* seduce; corrupt.

растолка́ть *pf* (*impf* **раста́лкивать**) push apart; shake.

растолкова́ть *pf*, **растолко́вывать** *impf* explain.

рас|толо́чь (-лку́, -лчёшь; -ло́к, -лкла́) *pf.*

растолсте́ть (-е́ю) *pf* put on weight.

растопи́ть[1] (-плю́, -пишь) *pf* (*impf* **раста́пливать**) melt; thaw; **~ся** melt.

растопи́ть² (-плю́, -пишь) *pf* (*impf* **раста́пливать**) light, kindle; **~ся** begin to burn.
растопта́ть (-пчу́, -пчешь) *pf* trample, stamp on.
расторга́ть *impf*, **расто́ргнуть** (-ну; -о́рг) *pf* annul, dissolve. **расторже́ние** annulment, dissolution.
расторо́пный quick; efficient.
расточа́ть *impf*, **расточи́ть** (-чу́) *pf* squander, dissipate. **расточи́тельный** extravagant, wasteful.
растрави́ть (-влю́, -вишь) *pf*, **растравля́ть** *impf* irritate.
растра́та spending; waste; embezzlement. **растра́тить** (-а́чу) *pf*, **растра́чивать** *impf* spend; waste; embezzle.
растрёпанный dishevelled; tattered. **рас|трепа́ть** (-плю́, -плешь) *pf* disarrange; tatter.
растре́скаться *pf*, **растре́скиваться** *impf* crack, chap.
растро́гать *pf* move, touch; **~ся** be moved.
расту́щий growing.
Р
растя́гивать *impf*, **растяну́ть** (-ну́, -нешь) *pf* stretch (out); strain, sprain; drag out; **~ся** stretch; drag on; sprawl. **растяже́ние** tension; strain, sprain. **растяжи́мый** tensile; stretchable. **растя́нутый** stretched; long-winded.
рас|фасова́ть *pf*.
расформирова́ть *pf*, **расформиро́вывать** *impf* break up; disband.
расха́живать *impf* walk about; pace up and down.
расхва́ливать *impf*, **расхвали́ть** (-лю́, -лишь) *pf* lavish praises on.
расхвата́ть *pf*, **расхва́тывать** *impf* seize on, buy up.
расхити́тель *m* embezzler. **расхи́тить** (-и́щу) *pf*, **расхища́ть** *impf* steal, misappropriate. **расхище́ние** misappropriation.
расхля́банный loose; lax.
расхо́д expenditure; consumption; *pl* expenses, outlay. **расходи́ться** (-ожу́сь, -о́дишься) *impf of* **разойти́сь**. **расхо́дование** expense, expenditure. **расхо́довать** *impf* (*pf* **из~**) spend; consume. **расхожде́ние** divergence.
расхола́живать *impf*, **расхолоди́ть** (-ожу́) *pf* damp the ardour of.
расхоте́ть (-очу́, -о́чешь, -оти́м) *pf* no longer want.
расхохота́ться (-очу́сь, -о́чешься) *pf* burst out laughing.
расцара́пать *pf* scratch (all over).
расцвести́ (-ету́, -етёшь; -ёл, -а́) *pf*, **расцвета́ть** *impf* blossom; flourish. **расцве́т** blossoming (out); flowering, heyday.
расцве́тка colours; colouring.
расце́нивать *impf*, **расцени́ть** (-ню́, -нишь) *pf* estimate, value; consider. **расце́нка** valuation; price; (wage-)rate.
расцепи́ть (-плю́, -пишь) *pf*, **расцепля́ть** *impf* uncouple, unhook.
расчеса́ть (-ешу́, -е́шешь) *pf* (*impf* **расчёсывать**) comb; scratch. **расчёска** comb.
расче́сть *etc.*: *see* **рассчита́ть**.
расчёсывать *impf of* **расчеса́ть**
расчёт¹ calculation; estimate; gain; settlement. **расчётливый** thrifty; careful. **расчётный** calculation; pay; accounts; calculated.
расчи́стить (-и́щу) *pf*, **расчища́ть** *impf* clear; **~ся** clear. **расчи́стка** clearing.
рас|члени́ть *pf*, **расчленя́ть** *impf* dismember; divide.
расшата́ть *pf*, **расша́тывать** *impf* shake loose, make rickety; impair.
расшевели́ть (-лю́, -е́ли́шь) *pf* stir; rouse.
расшиба́ть *impf*, **расшиби́ть** (-бу́, -бёшь; -и́б) *pf* smash to pieces; hurt; stub; **~ся** hurt o.s.
расшива́ть *impf of* **расши́ть**
расшире́ние widening; expansion; dilation, dilatation. **расши́-**

рить *pf*, **расширя́ть** *impf* widen; enlarge; expand; **~ся** broaden, widen; expand, dilate.
расши́ть (разошью́, -шьёшь) *pf* (*impf* **расшива́ть**) embroider; unpick.
расшифрова́ть *pf*, **расшифро́вывать** *impf* decipher.
расшнурова́ть *pf*, **расшнуро́вывать** *impf* unlace.
расще́лина crevice.
расщепи́ть (-плю́) *pf*, **расщепля́ть** *impf* split; **~ся** split. **расщепле́ние** splitting; fission.
ратифици́ровать *impf* & *pf* ratify.
рать army, battle.
ра́унд round.
рафини́рованный refined.
рацио́н ration.
рационализа́ция rationalization. **рационализи́ровать** *impf* & *pf* rationalize. **рациона́льный** rational; efficient.
ра́ция walkie-talkie.
рвану́ться (-ну́сь, -нёшься) *pf* dart, dash.
рва́ный torn; lacerated. **рвать**[1] (рву, рвёшь; рвал, -а́, -о) *impf* tear (out); pull out; pick; blow up; break off; **~ся** break; tear; burst, explode; be bursting.
рвать[2] (рвёт; рва́ло) *impf* (*pf* **вы́~**) *impers+acc* vomit.
рвач (-а́) self-seeker.
рве́ние zeal.
рво́та vomiting.
реабилита́ция rehabilitation. **реабилити́ровать** *impf* & *pf* rehabilitate.
реаги́ровать *impf* (*pf* **от~**, **про~**) react.
реакти́в reagent. **реакти́вный** reactive; jet-propelled. **реа́ктор** reactor.
реакционе́р reactionary. **реакцио́нный** reactionary. **реа́кция** reaction.
реализа́ция realization. **реали́зм** realism. **реализова́ть** *impf* & *pf* realize. **реали́ст** realist. **реалисти́ческий** realistic.
реа́льность reality; practicability. **реа́льный** real; practicable.
ребёнок (-нка; *pl* ребя́та, -я́т *and* де́ти, -е́й) child; infant.
ребро́ (*pl* рёбра, -бер) rib; edge.
ребя́та (-я́т) *pl* children; guys; lads. **ребя́ческий** child's; childish. **ребя́чество** childishness. **ребя́читься** (-чусь) *impf* be childish.
рёв roar; howl.
рева́нш revenge; return match.
ревера́нс curtsey.
реве́ть (-ву́, -вёшь) *impf* roar; bellow; howl.
ревизио́нный inspection; auditing. **реви́зия** inspection; audit; revision. **ревизо́р** inspector.
ревмати́зм rheumatism.
ревни́вый jealous. **ревнова́ть** *impf* (*pf* **при~**) be jealous. **ре́вностный** zealous. **ре́вность** jealousy.
револьве́р revolver.
революционе́р revolutionary. **революцио́нный** revolutionary. **револю́ция** revolution.
рега́та regatta.
ре́гби *neut indecl* rugby.
ре́гент regent.
регио́н region. **региона́льный** regional.
регистра́тор registrar. **регистрату́ра** registry. **регистра́ция** registration. **регистри́ровать** *impf* & *pf* (*pf also* **за~**) register, record; **~ся** register; register one's marriage.
регла́мент standing orders; time-limit. **регламента́ция** regulation. **регламенти́ровать** *impf* & *pf* regulate.
регресси́ровать *impf* regress.
регули́ровать *impf* (*pf* **от~**, **у~**) regulate; adjust. **регулиро́вщик** traffic controller. **регуля́рный** regular. **регуля́тор** regulator.
редакти́ровать *impf* (*pf* **от~**) edit. **реда́ктор** editor. **реда́кторский** editorial. **редакцио́нный** editorial, editing. **реда́кция** edi-

Р

torial staff; editorial office; editing.
реде́ть (-е́ет) *impf* (*pf* **по~**) thin (out).
реди́с radishes. **реди́ска** radish.
ре́дкий (-док, -дка́, -о) thin; sparse; rare. **ре́дко** *adv* sparsely; rarely, seldom. **ре́дкость** rarity.
редколле́гия editorial board.
рее́стр register.
режи́м régime; routine; procedure; regimen; conditions.
режиссёр-(постано́вщик) producer; director.
ре́жущий cutting, sharp. **ре́зать** (ре́жу) *impf* (*pf* **за~, про~, с~**) cut; engrave; kill, slaughter.
резви́ться (-влю́сь) *impf* gambol, play. **ре́звый** frisky, playful.
резе́рв reserve. **резе́рвный** reserve; back-up.
резервуа́р reservoir.
резе́ц (-зца́) cutter; chisel; incisor.
резиде́нция residence.
рези́на rubber. **рези́нка** rubber; elastic band. **рези́новый** rubber.
ре́зкий sharp; harsh; abrupt; shrill. **резно́й** carved. **резня́** carnage.
резолю́ция resolution.
резона́нс resonance; response.
результа́т result.
резьба́ carving, fretwork.
резюме́ *neut indecl* résumé.
рейд[1] roads, roadstead.
рейд[2] raid.
ре́йка lath, rod.
рейс trip; voyage; flight.
рейту́зы (-у́з) *pl* leggings; riding breeches.
река́ (*acc* ре́ку́; *pl* -и, ре́ка́м) river.
ре́квием requiem.
реквизи́т props.
рекла́ма advertising, advertisement. **реклами́ровать** *impf* & *pf* advertise. **рекла́мный** publicity.
рекоменда́тельный of recommendation. **рекоменда́ция** recommendation; reference. **рекомендова́ть** *impf* & *pf* (*pf also* **от~, по~**) recommend; **~ся** introduce o.s.; be advisable.
реконструи́ровать *impf* & *pf* reconstruct. **реконстру́кция** reconstruction.
реко́рд record. **реко́рдный** record, record-breaking. **рекордсме́н, -е́нка** record-holder.
ре́ктор principal (*of university*).
реле́ (*electr*) *neut indecl* relay.
религио́зный religious. **рели́гия** religion.
рели́квия relic.
релье́ф relief. **релье́фный** relief; raised, bold.
рельс rail.
рема́рка stage direction.
реме́нь (-мня́) *m* strap; belt.
реме́сленник artisan, craftsman. **реме́сленный** handicraft; mechanical. **ремесло́** (*pl* -ёсла, -ёсел) craft; trade.
ремо́нт repair(s); maintenance. **ремонти́ровать** *impf* & *pf* (*pf also* **от~**) repair; recondition. **ремо́нтный** repair.
ре́нта rent; income. **рента́бельный** paying, profitable.
рентге́н X-rays. **рентге́новский** X-ray. **рентгено́лог** radiologist. **рентгеноло́гия** radiology.
реорганиза́ция reorganization. **реорганизова́ть** *impf* & *pf* reorganize.
ре́па turnip.
репатрии́ровать *impf* & *pf* repatriate.
репертуа́р repertoire.
репети́ровать *impf* (*pf* **от~, про~, с~**) rehearse; coach. **репети́тор** coach. **репети́ция** rehearsal.
ре́плика retort; cue.
репорта́ж report; reporting. **репортёр** reporter.
репре́ссия repression.
репроду́ктор loud-speaker. **репроду́кция** reproduction.
репута́ция reputation.
ресни́ца eyelash.
респу́блика republic. **республика́нский** republican.

рессо́ра spring.
реставра́ция restoration. **реставри́ровать** *impf* & *pf* (*pf also* **от~**) restore.
рестора́н restaurant.
ресу́рс resort; *pl* resources.
ретрансля́тор (radio-)relay.
рефера́т synopsis, abstract; paper, essay.
рефере́ндум referendum.
рефле́кс reflex. **рефле́ктор** reflector.
рефо́рма reform. **реформи́ровать** *impf* & *pf* reform.
рефрижера́тор refrigerator.
рецензи́ровать *impf* (*pf* **про~**) review. **реце́нзия** review.
реце́пт prescription; recipe.
рециди́в relapse. **рецидиви́ст** recidivist.
речево́й speech; vocal.
ре́чка river. **речно́й** river.
речь (*gen pl* -е́й) speech.
реша́ть(ся *impf of* **реши́ть(ся. реша́ющий** decisive, deciding. **реше́ние** decision; solution.
решётка grating; grille, railing; lattice; trellis; fender, (fire)guard; (fire-)grate; tail. **решето́** (*pl* -ёта) sieve. **решётчатый** lattice, latticed.
реши́мость resoluteness; resolve. **реши́тельно** *adv* resolutely; definitely; absolutely. **реши́тельность** determination. **реши́тельный** definite; decisive. **реши́ть** (-шу́) *pf* (*impf* **реша́ть**) decide; solve; **~ся** make up one's mind.
ржаве́ть (-е́ет) *impf* (*pf* **за~, по~**) rust. **ржа́вчина** rust. **ржа́вый** rusty.
ржано́й rye.
ржать (ржу, ржёшь) *impf* neigh.
ри́млянин (*pl* -яне, -ян), **ри́млянка** Roman. **ри́мский** Roman.
ринг boxing ring.
ри́нуться (-нусь) *pf* rush, dart.
рис rice.
риск risk. **риско́ванный** risky; risqué. **рискова́ть** *impf*, **рискну́ть** *pf* run risks; *+instr or inf* risk.
рисова́ние drawing. **рисова́ть** *impf* (*pf* **на~**) draw; paint, depict; **~ся** be silhouetted; appear; pose.
ри́совый rice.
рису́нок (-нка) drawing; figure; pattern, design.
ритм rhythm. **ритми́ческий, ритми́чный** rhythmic.
ритуа́л ritual.
риф reef.
ри́фма rhyme. **рифмова́ть** *impf* rhyme; **~ся** rhyme.
робе́ть (-е́ю) *impf* (*pf* **о~**) be timid. **ро́бкий** (-бок, -бка́, -о) timid, shy. **ро́бость** shyness.
ро́бот robot.
ров (рва, *loc* -у) ditch.
рове́сник coeval. **ро́вно** *adv* evenly; exactly; absolutely. **ро́вный** flat; even; level; equable; exact; equal. **ровня́ть** *impf* (*pf* **с~**) even, level.
рог (*pl* -а́, -о́в) horn; antler. **рога́тка** catapult. **рога́тый** horned. **рогови́ца** cornea. **рогово́й** horn; horny; horn-rimmed.
род (*loc* -у́; *pl* -ы́) family, kin, clan; birth, origin, stock; generation; genus; sort, kind. **роди́льный** maternity. **ро́дина** native land; homeland. **ро́динка** birth-mark. **роди́тели** (-ей) *pl* parents. **роди́тельный** genitive. **роди́тельский** parental. **роди́ть** (рожу́, -и́л, -ила́, -о) *impf* & *pf* (*impf also* **рожа́ть, рожда́ть**) give birth to; **~ся** be born.
родни́к (-а́) spring.
родни́ть *impf* (*pf* **по~**) make related, link; **~ся** become related. **родн|о́й** own; native; home; **~о́й брат** brother; **~ы́е** *sb pl* relatives. **родня́** relative(s); kinsfolk. **родово́й** tribal; ancestral; generic; gender. **родонача́льник** ancestor; father. **родосло́вн|ый** genealogical; **~ая** *sb* genealogy, pedigree. **ро́дственник** relative. **ро́дственный** related. **родство́**

р

relationship, kinship. **ро́ды** (-ов) *pl* childbirth; labour.
ро́жа (ugly) mug.
рожа́ть, рожда́ть(ся *impf of* **роди́ть(ся. рожда́емость** birth-rate. **рожде́ние** birth. **рожде́ственский** Christmas. **Рождество́** Christmas.
рожь (ржи) rye.
ро́за rose.
ро́зга (*gen pl* -зог) birch.
ро́здал *etc.*: *see* **разда́ть**
розе́тка electric socket, power point; rosette.
ро́зница retail; **в ~у** retail. **ро́зничный** retail. **рознь** difference; dissension.
ро́знял *etc.*: *see* **разня́ть**
ро́зовый pink.
ро́зыгрыш draw; drawn game.
ро́зыск search; inquiry.
рои́ться swarm. **рой** (*loc* -ю́; *pl* -и́, -ёв) swarm.
рок fate.
рокиро́вка castling.
рок-му́зыка rock music.
рокова́й fateful; fatal.
ро́кот roar, rumble. **рокота́ть** (-о́чет) *impf* roar, rumble.
ро́лик roller; castor; *pl* roller skates.
роль (*gen pl* -е́й) role.
ром rum.
рома́н novel; romance. **романи́ст** novelist.
рома́нс (*mus*) romance.
рома́нтик romantic. **рома́нтика** romance. **романти́ческий, романти́чный** romantic.
рома́шка camomile.
ромб rhombus.
роня́ть *impf* (*pf* **урони́ть**) drop.
ро́пот murmur, grumble. **ропта́ть** (-пщу́, -пщешь) *impf* murmur, grumble.
рос *etc.*: *see* **расти́**
роса́ (*pl* -ы) dew. **роси́стый** dewy.
роско́шный luxurious; luxuriant. **ро́скошь** luxury; luxuriance.
ро́слый strapping.
ро́спись painting(s), mural(s).
ро́спуск dismissal; disbandment.
росси́йский Russian. **Росси́я** Russia.
ро́ссыпи *f pl* deposit.
рост growth; increase; height, stature.
ро́стбиф roast beef.
ростовщи́к (-а́) usurer, money-lender.
росто́к (-тка́) sprout, shoot.
ро́счерк flourish.
рот (рта, *loc* рту) mouth.
ро́та company.
рота́тор duplicator.
ро́тный company; *sb* company commander.
ротозе́й, -зе́йка gaper, rubber-neck; scatter-brain.
ро́ща grove.
ро́ю *etc.*: *see* **рыть**
роя́ль *m* (grand) piano.
ртуть mercury.
руба́нок (-нка) plane.
руба́ха, руба́шка shirt.
рубе́ж (-а́) boundary, border(line); line; **за ~о́м** abroad.
рубе́ц (-бца́) scar; weal; hem; tripe.
руби́н ruby. **руби́новый** ruby; ruby-coloured.
руби́ть (-блю́, -бишь) *impf* (*pf* **с~**) fell; hew, chop; mince; build (of logs).
ру́бище rags.
ру́бка[1] felling; chopping; mincing.
ру́бка[2] deck house; **боева́я ~** conning-tower; **рулева́я ~** wheel-house.
рублёвка one-rouble note. **рублёвый** (one-)rouble.
ру́бленый minced, chopped; of logs.
рубль (-я́) *m* rouble.
ру́брика rubric, heading.
ру́бчатый ribbed. **ру́бчик** scar; rib.
ру́гань abuse, swearing. **руга́тельный** abusive. **руга́тельство** oath, swear-word. **руга́ть** *impf* (*pf* **вы́~, об~, от~**) curse, swear at; abuse; **~ся** curse, swear; swear at one another.

рудá (*pl* -ы) ore. **рудни́к** (-á) mine, pit. **рудни́чный** mine, pit; **~ газ** fire-damp. **рудокóп** miner.
ружéйный rifle, gun. **ружьё** (*pl* -ья, -жей, -ьям) gun, rifle.
руи́на *usu pl* ruin.
рукá (*acc* -у; *pl* -и, рук, -áм) hand; arm; **идти́ пóд руку с**+*instr* walk arm in arm with; **под рукóй** at hand; **рукóй подáть** a stone's throw away; **э́то мне нá руку** that suits me.
рукáв (-á; *pl* -á, -óв) sleeve. **рукави́ца** mitten; gauntlet.
руководи́тель *m* leader; manager; instructor; guide. **руководи́ть** (-ожу́) *impf* +*instr* lead; guide; direct, manage. **руковóдство** leadership; guidance; direction; guide; handbook, manual; leaders. **руковóдствоваться** +*instr* follow; be guided by. **руководя́щий** leading; guiding.
рукодéлие needlework.
рукомóйник washstand.
рукопáшный hand-to-hand.
рукопи́сный manuscript. **ру́копись** manuscript.
рукоплескáние applause. **рукоплескáть** (-ещу́, -éщешь) *impf* +*dat* applaud.
рукопожáтие handshake.
рукоя́тка handle.
рулевóй steering; *sb* helmsman.
рулéтка tape-measure; roulette.
рули́ть *impf* (*pf* **вы́~**) taxi.
руль (-я́) *m* rudder; helm; (steering-)wheel; handlebar.
румы́н (*gen pl* -ы́н), **~ка** Romanian. **Румы́ния** Romania. **румы́нский** Romanian.
румя́на (-я́н) *pl* rouge. **румя́нец** (-нца) (high) colour; flush; blush. **румя́ный** rosy, ruddy.
ру́пор megaphone; mouthpiece.
русáк (-á) hare.
русáлка mermaid.
ру́сло river-bed; course.
ру́сский Russian; *sb* Russian.
ру́сый light brown.
Русь (*hist*) Russia.
рути́на routine.
ру́хлядь junk.
ру́хнуть (-ну) *pf* crash down.
ручáтельство guarantee. **ручáться** *impf* (*pf* **поручи́ться**) +**за**+*acc* vouch for, guarantee.
ручéй (-чья́) brook.
ру́чка handle; (door-)knob; (chair-)arm; pen; **ручн|óй** hand; arm; manual; tame; **~ы́е часы́** wrist-watch.
ру́шить (-у) *impf* (*pf* **об~**) pull down; **~ся** collapse.
РФ *abbr* (*of* **Росси́йская Федерáция**) Russian Federation.
ры́ба fish. **рыбáк** (-á) fisherman. **рыбáлка** fishing. **рыбáцкий, рыбáчий** fishing. **ры́бий** fish; fishy; **~ жир** cod-liver oil. **ры́бный** fish. **рыболóв** fisherman. **рыболóвный** fishing.
рывóк (-вкá) jerk.
рыдáние sobbing. **рыдáть** *impf* sob.
ры́жий (рыж, -á, -е) red, red-haired; chestnut.
ры́ло snout; mug.
ры́нок (-нка) market; market-place. **ры́ночный** market.
рысáк (-á) trotter.
рысь[1] (*loc* -и́) trot; **~ю, на рыся́х** at a trot.
рысь[2] lynx.
ры́твина rut, groove. **ры́ть(ся** (рóю(сь) *impf* (*pf* **вы́~, от~**) dig; rummage.
рыхли́ть *impf* (*pf* **вз~, раз~**) loosen. **ры́хлый** (-л, -á, -о) friable; loose.
ры́царский chivalrous. **ры́царь** *m* knight.
рычáг (-á) lever.
рычáть (-чу́) *impf* growl, snarl.
рья́ный zealous.
рюкзáк (*gen* -á) rucksack.
рю́мка wineglass.
ряби́на[1] rowan, mountain ash.
ряби́на[2] pit, pock. **ряби́ть** (-и́т) *impf* ripple; *impers*: **у меня́ ряби́т в глазáх** I am dazzled. **рябóй** pock-marked. **ря́бчик** hazel hen,

hazel grouse. **рябь** ripples; dazzle.
ря́вкать *impf*, **ря́вкнуть** (-ну) *pf* bellow, roar.
ряд (*loc* -у́; *pl* -ы́) row; line; file, rank; series; number. **рядово́й** ordinary; common; **~ соста́в** rank and file; *sb* private. **ря́дом** *adv* alongside; close by; **+с+***instr* next to.
ря́са cassock.

С

с, со *prep* **I.** +*gen* from; since; off; for, with; on; by; **с ра́дости** for joy; **с утра́** since morning. **II.** +*acc* about; the size of; **с неде́лю** for about a week. **III.** +*instr* with; and; **мы с ва́ми** you and I; **что с ва́ми?** what is the matter?
са́бля (*gen pl* -бель) sabre.
сабота́ж sabotage. **саботи́ровать** *impf* & *pf* sabotage.
са́ван shroud; blanket.
с|агити́ровать *pf*.
сад (*loc* -у́; *pl* -ы́) garden. **сади́ть** (сажу́, са́дишь) *impf* (*pf* **по~**) plant. **сади́ться** (сажу́сь) *impf of* **сесть. садо́вник, -ница** gardener. **садово́дство** gardening; horticulture. **садо́вый** garden; cultivated.
сади́зм sadism. **сади́ст** sadist. **сади́стский** sadistic.
са́жа soot.
сажа́ть *impf* (*pf* **посади́ть**) plant; seat; set, put. **са́женец** (-нца) seedling; sapling.
са́же́нь (*pl* -и, -жен *or* -же́не́й) sazhen (*2.13 metres*).
сажу́ *etc.*: *see* **сади́ть**
са́йка roll.
сайт (*comput*) (web)site.
саксофо́н saxophone.
сала́зки (-зок) *pl* toboggan.
сала́т lettuce; salad.
са́ло fat, lard; suet; tallow.
сало́н salon; saloon.
салфе́тка napkin.
са́льный greasy; tallow; obscene.
салю́т salute. **салютова́ть** *impf* & *pf* (*pf also* **от~**) +*dat* salute.
сам (-ого́) *m*, **сама́** (-о́й, *acc* -оё) *f*, **само́** (-ого́) *neut*, **са́ми** (-и́х) *pl*, *pron* -self, -selves; myself, *etc.*, ourselves, *etc.*; **~ по себе́** in itself; by o.s.; **~ собо́й** of itself, of its own accord; **~о́ собо́й (разуме́ется)** of course; it goes without saying.
са́мбо *neut indecl abbr* (*of* **самозащи́та без ору́жия**) unarmed combat.
саме́ц (-мца́) male. **са́мка** female.
само- *in comb* self-, auto-. **самобы́тный** original, distinctive. **~возгора́ние** spontaneous combustion. **~во́льный** wilful; unauthorized. **~де́льный** home-made. **~держа́вие** autocracy. **~держа́вный** autocratic. **~де́ятельность** amateur work, amateur performance; initiative. **~дово́льный** self-satisfied. **~ду́р** petty tyrant. **~ду́рство** high-handedness. **~забве́ние** selflessness. **~забве́нный** selfless. **~защи́та** self-defence. **~зва́нец** (-нца) impostor, pretender. **~ка́т** scooter. **~кри́тика** self-criticism. **~люби́вый** proud; touchy. **~лю́бие** pride, self-esteem. **~мне́ние** conceit, self-importance. **~наде́янный** presumptuous. **~облада́ние** self-control. **~обма́н** self-deception. **~оборо́на** self-defence. **~образова́ние** self-education. **~обслу́живание** self-service. **~определе́ние** self-determination. **~отве́рженность** selflessness. **~отве́рженный** selfless. **~поже́ртвование** self-sacrifice. **~ро́док** (-дка) nugget; person with natural talent. **~сва́л** tip-up lorry. **~созна́ние** (self-) consciousness. **~сохране́ние** self-preservation. **~стоя́тельность** independence. **~стоя́тельный** independent. **~су́д**

lynch law, mob law. **~тёк** drift. **~тёком** *adv* by gravity; of its own accord. **~убийственный** suicidal. **~убийство** suicide. **~убийца** *m* & *f* suicide. **~уваже́ние** self-respect. **~уве́ренность** self-confidence. **~уве́ренный** self-confident. **~униже́ние** self-abasement. **~управле́ние** self-government. **~управля́ющийся** self-governing. **~упра́вный** arbitrary. **~учи́тель** *m* self-instructor, manual. **~у́чка** *m* & *f* self-taught person. **~хо́дный** self-propelled. **~чу́вствие** general state; **как ва́ше ~чу́вствие?** how do you feel?

самова́р samovar.

самого́н home-made vodka.

самолёт aeroplane.

самоцве́т semi-precious stone.

са́мый *pron* (the) very, (the) right; (the) same; (the) most.

сан dignity, office.

санато́рий sanatorium.

санда́лия sandal.

са́ни (-е́й) *pl* sledge, sleigh.

санита́р medical orderly; stretcher-bearer. **санитари́я** sanitation. **санита́рка** nurse. **санита́рн|ый** medical; health; sanitary; **~ая маши́на** ambulance; **~ый у́зел = сану́зел.**

са́нки (-нок) *pl* sledge; toboggan.

санкциони́ровать *impf* & *pf* sanction. **са́нкция** sanction.

сано́вник dignitary.

санпу́нкт medical centre.

санскри́т Sanskrit.

санте́хник plumber.

сантиме́тр centimetre; tape-measure.

сану́зел (-зла́) sanitary arrangements; WC.

санча́сть (*gen pl* -е́й) medical unit.

сапёр sapper.

сапо́г(-а́; *gen pl* -о́г) boot. **сапо́жник** shoemaker; cobbler. **сапо́жный** shoe.

сапфи́р sapphire.

сара́й shed; barn.

саранча́ locust(s).

сарафа́н sarafan; pinafore dress.

сарде́лька small fat sausage.

сарди́на sardine.

сарка́зм sarcasm. **саркасти́ческий** sarcastic.

сатана́ *m* Satan. **сатани́нский** satanic.

сателли́т satellite.

сати́н sateen.

сати́ра satire. **сати́рик** satirist. **сатири́ческий** satirical.

Сау́довская Ара́вия Saudi Arabia.

сафья́н morocco. **сафья́новый** morocco.

са́хар sugar. **сахари́н** saccharine. **са́харистый** sugary. **са́харница** sugar-basin. **са́харн|ый** sugar; sugary; **~ый заво́д** sugar-refinery; **~ый песо́к** granulated sugar; **~ая пу́дра** castor sugar; **~ая свёкла** sugar-beet.

сачо́к (-чка́) net.

сба́вить (-влю) *pf*, **сбавля́ть** *impf* take off; reduce.

с|баланси́ровать *pf*.

сбе́гать[1] *pf* run; **+за+***instr* run for. **сбега́ть**[2] *impf*, **сбежа́ть** (-егу́) *pf* run down (from); run away; disappear; **~ся** come running.

сберега́тельная ка́сса savings bank. **сберега́ть** *impf*, **сбере́чь** (-егу́, -ежёшь; -ёг, -ла́) *pf* save; save up; preserve. **сбереже́ние** economy; saving; savings. **сберка́сса** savings bank.

сбива́ть *impf*, **с|бить** (собью́, -бьёшь) *pf* bring down, knock down; knock off; distract; wear down; knock together; churn; whip, whisk; **~ся** be dislodged; slip; go wrong; be confused; **~ся с пути́** lose one's way; **~ся с ног** be run off one's feet. **сби́вчивый** confused; inconsistent.

сближа́ть *impf*, **сбли́зить** (-и́жу) *pf* bring (closer) together, draw together; **~ся** draw together; become good friends. **сближе́ние**

С

rapprochement; closing in.
сбо́ку *adv* from one side; on one side.
сбор collection; duty; fee, toll; takings; gathering. **сбо́рище** crowd, mob. **сбо́рка** assembling, assembly; gather. **сбо́рник** collection. **сбо́рный** assembly; mixed, combined; prefabricated; detachable. **сбо́рочный** assembly. **сбо́рщик** collector; assembler.
сбра́сывать(ся *impf of* **сбро́сить(ся**
сбрива́ть *impf*, **сбрить** (сбре́ю) *pf* shave off.
сброд riff-raff.
сброс fault, break. **сбро́сить** (-о́шу) *pf* (*impf* **сбра́сывать**) throw down, drop; throw off; shed; discard.
сбру́я (*collect*) (riding) tack.
сбыва́ть *impf*, **сбыть** (сбу́ду; сбыл, -а́, -о) *pf* sell, market; get rid of; **~ся** come true, be realized. **сбыт** (*no pl*) sale; market.
св. *abbr* (*of* **свято́й**) Saint.
сва́дебный wedding. **сва́дьба** (*gen pl* -деб) wedding.
сва́ливать *impf*, **с|вали́ть** (-лю́, -лишь) *pf* throw down; overthrow; pile up; **~ся** fall (down), collapse. **сва́лка** dump; scuffle.
с|валя́ть *pf*.
сва́ривать *impf*, **с|вари́ть** (-рю́, -ришь) *pf* boil; cook; weld. **сва́рка** welding.
сварли́вый cantankerous.
сварно́й welded. **сва́рочный** welding. **сва́рщик** welder.
сва́стика swastika.
сва́тать *impf* (*pf* **по~, со~**) propose as a husband or wife; propose to; **~ся к**+*dat or* **за**+*acc* propose to.
сва́я pile.
све́дение piece of information; knowledge; *pl* information, intelligence; knowledge. **све́дущий** knowledgeable; versed.
сведу́ *etc.*: *see* **свести́**
свежезаморо́женный fresh-frozen; chilled. **све́жесть** freshness. **свеже́ть** (-е́ет) *impf* (*pf* **по~**) become cooler; freshen. **све́жий** (-еж, -а́, -о́, -и) fresh; new.
свезти́ (-зу́, -зёшь; свёз, -ла́) *pf* (*impf* **свози́ть**) take; bring *or* take down *or* away.
свёкла beet, beetroot.
свёкор (-кра) father-in-law. **свекро́вь** mother-in-law.
свёл *etc.*: *see* **свести́**
сверга́ть *impf*, **све́ргнуть** (-ну; сверг) *pf* throw down, overthrow. **сверже́ние** overthrow.
све́рить *pf* (*impf* **сверя́ть**) collate.
сверка́ть *impf* sparkle, twinkle; glitter; gleam. **сверкну́ть** (-ну́, -нёшь) *pf* flash.
сверли́льный drill, drilling; boring. **сверли́ть** *impf* (*pf* **про~**) drill; bore (through); nag. **сверло́** drill. **сверля́щий** gnawing, piercing.
сверну́ть (-ну́, -нёшь) *pf* (*impf* **свёртывать, свора́чивать**) roll (up); turn; curtail, cut down; **~ ше́ю**+*dat* wring the neck of; **~ся** roll up, curl up; curdle, coagulate; contract.
све́рстник contemporary.
свёрток (-тка) package, bundle. **свёртывание** rolling (up); curdling; coagulation; curtailment, cuts. **свёртывать(ся** *impf of* **сверну́ть(ся**
сверх *prep*+*gen* over, above, on top of; beyond; in addition to; **~ того́** moreover.
сверх- *in comb* super-, over-, hyper-. **сверхзвуково́й** supersonic. **~пла́новый** over and above the plan. **~при́быль** excess profit. **~проводни́к** (-а́) superconductor. **~секре́тный** top secret. **~уро́чный** overtime. **~уро́чные** *sb pl* overtime. **~челове́к** superman. **~челове́ческий** superhuman. **~есте́ственный** supernatural.
све́рху *adv* from above; **~ до́низу** from top to bottom.

С

сверчо́к (-чка́) cricket.
сверше́ние achievement.
сверя́ть *impf of* **све́рить**
све́сить (-е́шу) *pf* (*impf* **све́шивать**) let down, lower; **~ся** hang over, lean over.
свести́ (-еду́, -едёшь; -ёл, -а́) *pf* (*impf* **своди́ть**) take; take down; take away; remove; bring together; reduce, bring; cramp.
свет[1] light; daybreak.
свет[2] world; society.
света́ть *impf impers* dawn. **свети́ло** luminary. **свети́ть** (-ечу́, -е́тишь) *impf* (*pf* **по~**) shine; +*dat* light; light the way for; **~ся** shine, gleam. **светле́ть** (-е́ет) *impf* (*pf* **по~, про~**) brighten (up); grow lighter. **све́тлость** brightness; Grace. **све́тлый** light; bright; joyous. **светлячо́к** (-чка́) glow-worm.
свето- *in comb* light, photo-. **светонепроница́емый** light-proof. **~фи́льтр** light filter. **~фо́р** traffic light(s).
светово́й light; luminous; **~ день** daylight hours.
светопреставле́ние end of the world.
све́тский fashionable; refined; secular.
светя́щийся luminous, fluorescent. **свеча́** (*pl* -и, -е́й) candle; (spark-)plug. **свече́ние** luminescence, fluorescence. **све́чка** candle. **свечу́** *etc.*: *see* **свети́ть**
с|ве́шать *pf.* **све́шивать(ся** *impf of* **све́сить(ся. свива́ть** *impf of* **свить**
свида́ние meeting; appointment; **до свида́ния!** goodbye!
свиде́тель *m*, **-ница** witness. **свиде́тельство** evidence; testimony; certificate. **свиде́тельствовать** *impf* (*pf* **за~, о~**) give evidence, testify; be evidence (of); witness.
свина́рник pigsty.
свине́ц (-нца́) lead.
свини́на pork. **сви́нка** mumps. **свино́й** pig; pork. **сви́нство** despicable act; outrage; squalor.
свинцо́вый lead; leaden.
свинья́ (*pl* -ньи, -не́й, -ньям) pig, swine.
свире́ль (reed-)pipe.
свирепе́ть (-е́ю) *impf* (*pf* **рас~**) grow savage; become violent. **свире́пствовать** *impf* rage; be rife. **свире́пый** fierce, ferocious.
свиса́ть *impf*, **сви́снуть** (-ну; -ис) *pf* hang down, dangle; trail.
свист whistle; whistling. **свиста́ть** (-ищу́, -и́щешь) *impf* whistle. **свисте́ть** (-ищу́) *impf*, **сви́стнуть** (-ну) *pf* whistle; hiss. **свисто́к** (-тка́) whistle.
сви́та suite; retinue.
сви́тер sweater.
сви́ток (-тка) roll, scroll. **с|вить** (совью́, совьёшь; -ил, -а́, -о) *pf* (*impf also* **свива́ть**) twist, wind; **~ся** roll up.
свихну́ться (-ну́сь, -нёшься) *impf* go mad; go astray.
свищ (-а́) flaw; (knot-)hole; fistula.
свищу́ *etc.*: *see* **свиста́ть, свисте́ть**
свобо́да freedom. **свобо́дно** *adv* freely; easily; fluently; loose(ly). **свобо́дный** free; easy; vacant; spare; loose; flowing. **свободолюби́вый** freedom-loving. **свободомы́слие** free-thinking.
свод code; collection; arch, vault.
своди́ть (-ожу́, -о́дишь) *impf of* **свести́**
сво́дка summary; report. **сво́дный** composite; step-.
сво́дчатый arched, vaulted.
своево́лие self-will, wilfulness. **своево́льный** wilful.
своевре́менно *adv* in good time; opportunely. **своевре́менный** timely, opportune.
своенра́вие capriciousness. **своенра́вный** wilful, capricious.
своеобра́зие originality; peculiarity. **своеобра́зный** original; peculiar.
свожу́ *etc.*: *see* **своди́ть, свози́ть. свози́ть** (-ожу́, -о́зишь) *impf of* **свезти́**

С

свой (своегó) *m*, **своя́** (своéй) *f*, **своё** (своегó) *neut*, **свои́** (свои́х) *pl, pron* one's (own); my, his, her, its; our, your, their. **свóйственный** peculiar, characteristic. **свóйство** property, attribute, characteristic.

свóлочь swine; riff-raff.

свóра leash; pack.

сворáчивать *impf of* **свернýть, своротить. с|воровáть** *pf.*

своротить (-очý, -óтишь) *pf* (*impf* **сворáчивать**) dislodge, shift; turn; twist.

свояк brother-in-law (*husband of wife's sister*). **свояченица** sister-in-law (*wife's sister*).

свыкáться *impf*, **свы́кнуться** (-нусь; -ы́кся) *pf* get used.

свысокá *adv* haughtily. **свы́ше** *adv* from above. **свы́ше** *prep+gen* over; beyond.

свя́занный constrained; combined; bound; coupled. **с|вязáть** (-яжý, -я́жешь) *pf*, **свя́зывать** *impf* tie, bind; connect; **~ся** get in touch; get involved. **связи́ст, -и́стка** signaller; worker in communication services. **свя́зка** sheaf, bundle; ligament. **свя́зный** connected, coherent. **связь** (*loc* -и́) connection; link, bond; liaison; communication(s).

святи́лище sanctuary. **свя́тки** (-ток) *pl* Christmas-tide. **свя́то** *adv* piously; religiously. **свят|óй** (-ят, -á, -о) holy; **~óй, ~áя** *sb* saint. **святы́ня** sacred object *or* place. **свящéнник** priest. **свящéнный** sacred.

сгиб bend. **сгибáть** *impf of* **согнýть**

сглáдить (-áжу) *pf*, **сглáживать** *impf* smooth out; smooth over, soften.

сглáзить (-áжу) *pf* put the evil eye on.

сгнивáть *impf*, **с|гнить** (-ию́, -иёшь; -ил, -á, -о) *pf* rot.

с|гнои́ться *pf.*

сговáриваться *impf*, **сговори́ться** *pf* come to an arrangement; arrange. **сгóвор** agreement. **сговóрчивый** compliant.

сгоня́ть *impf of* **согнáть**

сгорáние combustion; **дви́гатель внýтреннего сгорáния** internal-combustion engine. **сгорáть** *impf of* **сгорéть**

с|гóрбить(ся (-блю(сь) *pf.*

с|горéть (-рю́) *pf* (*impf also* **сгорáть**) burn down; be burnt down; be used up; burn; burn o.s. out. **сгорячá** *adv* in the heat of the moment.

с|готóвить(ся (-влю(сь) *pf.*

сгребáть *impf*, **сгрести́** (-ебý, -ебёшь; -ёб, -лá) *pf* rake up, rake together.

сгружáть *impf*, **сгрузи́ть** (-ужý, -ýзишь) *pf* unload.

с|группировáть(ся *pf.*

сгусти́ть (-ущý) *pf*, **сгущáть** *impf* thicken; condense; **~ся** thicken; condense; clot. **сгýсток** (-тка) clot. **сгущéние** thickening, condensation; clotting.

сдавáть (сдаю́, сдаёшь) *impf of* **сдать; ~ экзáмен** take an examination; **~ся** *impf of* **сдáться**

сдави́ть (-влю́, -вишь) *pf*, **сдáвливать** *impf* squeeze.

сдать (-ам, -ашь, -аст, -ади́м; -ал, -á, -о) *pf* (*impf* **сдавáть**) hand in, hand over; pass; let, hire out; surrender, give up; deal; **~ся** surrender, yield. **сдáча** handing over; hiring out; surrender; change; deal.

сдвиг displacement; fault; change, improvement. **сдвигáть** *impf*, **сдви́нуть** (-ну) *pf* shift, move; move together; **~ся** move, budge; come together.

с|дéлать(ся *pf.* **сдéлка** transaction; deal, bargain. **сдéльн|ый** piece-work; **~ая рабóта** piece-work. **сдéльщина** piece-work.

сдёргивать *impf of* **сдёрнуть**

сдéржанный restrained, reserved. **сдержáть** (-жý, -жишь) *pf*, **сдéрживать** *impf* hold back; restrain; keep.

сдёрнуть (-ну) *pf* (*impf* **сдёргивать**) pull off.

сдеру́ *etc.*: *see* **содра́ть. сдира́ть** *impf of* **содра́ть**

сдо́ба shortening; fancy bread, bun(s). **сдо́бный** (-бен, -бна́, -о) rich, short.

с|до́хнуть (-нет; сдох) *pf* die; kick the bucket.

сдружи́ться (-жу́сь) *pf* become friends.

сдува́ть *impf*, **сду́нуть** (-ну) *pf*, **сдуть** (-у́ю) *pf* blow away *or* off.

сеа́нс performance; showing; sitting.

себесто́имость prime cost; cost (price).

себя́ (*dat & prep* себе́, *instr* собо́й *or* собо́ю) *refl pron* oneself; myself, yourself, himself, *etc.*; **ничего́ себе́** not bad; **собо́й** -looking, in appearance.

себялю́бие selfishness.

сев sowing.

се́вер north. **се́верный** north, northern; northerly. **се́веро-восто́к** north-east **се́веро-восто́чный** north-east(ern). **се́веро-за́пад** north-west. **се́веро-за́падный** north-west(ern). **северя́нин** (*pl* -я́не, -я́н) northerner.

севооборо́т crop rotation.

сего́ *see* **сей. сего́дня** *adv* today. **сего́дняшний** of today, today's.

седе́ть (-е́ю) *impf* (*pf* **по~**) turn grey. **седина́** (*pl* -ы) grey hair(s).

седла́ть *impf* (*pf* **о~**) saddle. **седло́** (*pl* сёдла, -дел) saddle.

седоборо́дый grey-bearded. **седоволо́сый** grey-haired. **седо́й** (сед, -á, -о) grey(-haired).

седо́к (-á) passenger; rider.

седьмо́й seventh.

сезо́н season. **сезо́нный** seasonal.

сей (сего́) *m*, **сия́** (сей) *f*, **сие́** (сего́) *neut*, **сии́** (сих) *pl*, *pron* this; these; **сию́ мину́ту** at once, instantly.

сейсми́ческий seismic.

сейф safe.

сейча́с *adv* (just) now; soon; immediately.

сёк *etc.*: *see* **сечь**

секре́т secret.

секретариа́т secretariat.

секрета́рский secretarial. **секрета́рша, секрета́рь** (-я́) *m* secretary.

секре́тный secret.

секс sex. **сексуа́льный** sexual; sexy.

сексте́т sextet.

се́кта sect. **секта́нт** sectarian.

се́ктор sector.

секу́ *etc.*: *see* **сечь**

секуляриза́ция secularization.

секу́нда second. **секунда́нт** second. **секу́ндный** second. **секундоме́р** stop-watch.

секцио́нный sectional. **се́кция** section.

селёдка herring.

селезёнка spleen.

се́лезень (-зня) *m* drake.

селе́кция breeding.

селе́ние settlement, village.

сели́тра saltpetre, nitre.

сели́ть(ся *impf* (*pf* **по~**) settle. **село́** (*pl* сёла) village.

сельдере́й celery.

сельдь (*pl* -и, -е́й) herring.

се́льск|ий rural; village; **~ое хозя́йство** agriculture. **сельскохозя́йственный** agricultural.

сельсове́т village soviet.

сема́нтика semantics. **семанти́ческий** semantic.

семафо́р semaphore; signal.

сёмга (smoked) salmon.

семе́йный family; domestic. **семе́йство** family.

се́мени *etc.*: *see* **се́мя**

семени́ть *impf* mince.

семени́ться *impf* seed. **семенни́к** (-á) testicle; seed-vessel. **семенно́й** seed; seminal.

семёрка seven; figure 7; No. 7. **се́меро** (-ы́х) seven.

семе́стр term, semester.

се́мечко (*pl* -и) seed; *pl* sunflower seeds.

С

семидесятиле́тие seventy years; seventieth anniversary, birthday. **семидеся́т|ый** seventieth; **~ые го́ды** the seventies. **семиле́тка** seven-year school. **семиле́тний** seven-year; seven-year-old.

семина́р seminar. **семина́рия** seminary.

семисо́тый seven-hundredth. **семна́дцатый** seventeenth. **семна́дцать** seventeen. **семь** (-ми́, -мью) seven. **се́мьдесят** (-ми́десяти, -мью́десятью) seventy. **семьсо́т** (-мисо́т, *instr* -мьюста́ми) seven hundred. **се́мью** *adv* seven times.

семья́ (*pl* -мьи, -ме́й, -мьям) family. **семьяни́н** family man.

се́мя (-мени; *pl* -мена́, -мя́н, -мена́м) seed; semen, sperm.

сена́т senate. **сена́тор** senator.

се́ни (-е́й) *pl* (entrance-)hall.

се́но hay. **сенова́л** hayloft. **сеноко́с** haymaking; hayfield.

сенсацио́нный sensational. **сенса́ция** sensation.

сенте́нция maxim.

сентимента́льный sentimental.

сентя́брь (-я́) *m* September. **сентя́брьский** September.

С

се́псис sepsis.

се́ра sulphur; ear-wax.

серб, ~ка Serb. **Се́рбия** Serbia. **се́рбский** Serb(ian). **сербскохорва́тский** Serbo-Croat(ian).

серва́нт sideboard.

се́рвер (*comput*) server.

серви́з service, set. **сервирова́ть** *impf* & *pf* serve; lay (a table). **сервиро́вка** laying; table lay-out.

серде́чник core. **серде́чность** cordiality; warmth. **серде́чный** heart; cardiac; cordial; warm(-hearted). **серди́тый** angry. **серди́ть** (-ржу́, -рдишь) *impf* (*pf* **рас~**) anger; **~ся** be angry. **сердобо́льный** tender-hearted. **се́рдце** (*pl* -а́, -де́ц) heart; **в сердца́х** in anger; **от всего́ се́рдца** from the bottom of one's heart. **сердцебие́ние** palpitation. **сердцеви́дный** heart-shaped. **сердцеви́на** core, pith, heart.

серебрёный silver-plated. **серебри́стый** silvery. **серебри́ть** *impf* (*pf* **по~**) silver, silver-plate; **~ся** become silvery. **серебро́** silver. **сере́бряный** silver.

середи́на middle.

серёжка earring; catkin.

серена́да serenade.

се́ренький grey; dull.

сержа́нт sergeant.

сери́йный serial; mass. **се́рия** series; part.

се́рный sulphur; sulphuric.

серогла́зый grey-eyed.

се́рость uncouthness; ignorance.

серп (-а́) sickle; **~ луны́** crescent moon.

серпанти́н streamer.

сертифика́т certificate.

се́рый (сер, -а́, -о) grey; dull; uneducated.

серьга́ (*pl* -и, -рёг) earring.

серьёзность seriousness. **серьёзный** serious.

се́ссия session.

сестра́ (*pl* сёстры, сестёр, сёстрам) sister.

сесть (ся́ду) *pf* (*impf* **сади́ться**) sit down; land; set; shrink; **+на+***acc* board, get on.

се́тка net, netting; (luggage-) rack; string bag; grid.

се́товать *impf* (*pf* **по~**) complain.

сетча́тка retina. **сеть** (*loc* -и́; *pl* -и, -е́й) net; network.

сече́ние section. **сечь** (секу́, сечёшь; сёк) *impf* (*pf* **вы~**) cut to pieces; flog; **~ся** split.

се́ялка seed drill. **се́ять** (се́ю) *impf* (*pf* **по~**) sow.

сжа́литься *pf* take pity (**над** +*instr*) on.

сжа́тие pressure; grasp, grip; compression. **сжа́тый** compressed; compact; concise.

с|жать[1] (сожну́, -нёшь) *pf*.

сжать[2] (сожму́, -мёшь) *pf* (*impf* **сжима́ть**) squeeze; compress; grip; clench; **~ся** tighten, clench; shrink, contract.

с|жечь (сожгу́, сожжёшь; сжёг, сожгла́) *pf* (*impf* **сжига́ть**) burn (down); cremate.

сжива́ться *impf of* **сжи́ться**

сжига́ть *impf of* **сжечь**

сжима́ть(ся *impf of* **сжа́ть²(ся**

сжи́ться (-иву́сь, -ивёшься; -и́лся, -а́сь) *pf* (*impf* **сжива́ться**) **с**+*instr* get used to.

с|жу́льничать *pf.*

сза́ди *adv* from behind; behind. **сза́ди** *prep*+*gen* behind.

сзыва́ть *impf of* **созва́ть**

сиби́рский Siberian. **Сиби́рь** Siberia. **сибиря́к** (-а́), **сибиря́чка** Siberian.

сига́ра cigar. **сигаре́та** cigarette.

сигна́л signal. **сигнализа́ция** signalling. **сигнализи́ровать** *impf* & *pf* (*pf also* **про~**) signal. **сигна́льный** signal. **сигна́льщик** signal-man.

сиде́лка sick-nurse. **сиде́ние** sitting. **сиде́нье** seat. **сиде́ть** (-ижу́) *impf* sit; be; fit. **сидя́чий** sitting; sedentary.

сие́ *etc.*: *see* **сей**

си́зый (сиз, -а́, -о) (blue-)grey.

сий *see* **сей**

си́ла strength; force; power; **в си́лу** +*gen* on the strength of, because of; **не по ~ам** beyond one's powers; **си́лой** by force. **сила́ч** (-а́) strong man. **си́литься** *impf* try, make efforts. **силово́й** power; of force.

сило́к (-лка́) noose, snare.

си́лос silo; silage.

силуэ́т silhouette.

си́льно *adv* strongly, violently; very much, greatly. **си́льный** (-лен *or* -лён, -льна́, -о) strong; powerful; intense, hard.

симбио́з symbiosis.

си́мвол symbol. **символизи́ровать** *impf* symbolize. **символи́зм** symbolism. **символи́ческий** symbolic.

сим-ка́рта SIM (card).

симметри́я symmetry.

симпатизи́ровать *impf* +*dat* like, sympathize with. **симпати́чный** likeable, nice. **симпа́тия** liking; sympathy.

симпо́зиум symposium.

симпто́м symptom.

симули́ровать *impf* & *pf* simulate, feign. **симуля́нт** malingerer, sham. **симуля́ция** simulation, pretence.

симфо́ния symphony.

синаго́га synagogue.

синева́ blue. **синева́тый** bluish. **синегла́зый** blue-eyed. **сине́ть** (-е́ю) *impf* (*pf* **по~**) turn blue; show blue. **си́ний** (синь, -ня́, -не) (dark) blue.

сини́ца titmouse.

сино́д synod. **сино́ним** synonym. **си́нтаксис** syntax.

си́нтез synthesis. **синтези́ровать** *impf* & *pf* synthesize. **синтети́ческий** synthetic.

си́нус sine; sinus.

синхронизи́ровать *impf* & *pf* synchronize.

синь¹ blue. **синь²** *see* **си́ний. си́нька** blueing; blue-print. **синя́к** (-а́) bruise.

сиони́зм Zionism.

си́плый hoarse, husky. **си́пнуть** (-ну; сип) *impf* (*pf* **о~**) become hoarse, husky.

сире́на siren; hooter.

сире́невый lilac(-coloured). **сире́нь** lilac.

Си́рия Syria.

сиро́п syrup.

сирота́ (*pl* -ы) *m* & *f* orphan. **сиротли́вый** lonely.

систе́ма system. **систематизи́ровать** *impf* & *pf* systematize. **системати́ческий, системати́чный** systematic.

си́тец (-тца) (printed) cotton; chintz.

си́то sieve.

ситуа́ция situation.

си́тцевый print, chintz.

си́филис syphilis.

сифо́н siphon.

сия́ *see* **сей**

С

сия́ние radiance. **сия́ть** *impf* shine, beam.

сказ tale. **сказа́ние** story, legend. **сказа́ть** (-ажу́, -а́жешь) *pf* (*impf* **говори́ть**) say; speak; tell. **сказа́ться** (-ажу́сь, -а́жешься) *pf*, **ска́зываться** *impf* tell (on); declare o.s. **сказа́тель** *m* story-teller. **ска́зка** (fairy-)tale; fib. **ска́зочный** fairy-tale; fantastic. **сказу́емое** *sb* predicate.

скака́лка skipping-rope. **скака́ть** (-ачу́, -а́чешь) *impf* (*pf* **по~**) skip, jump; gallop. **скаково́й** race, racing.

скала́ (*pl* -ы) rock; cliff. **скали́стый** rocky.

ска́лить *impf* (*pf* **о~**); **~ зу́бы** bare one's teeth; grin; **~ся** bare one's teeth.

ска́лка rolling-pin.

скалола́з rock-climber.

ска́лывать *impf of* **сколо́ть**

скальп scalp.

ска́льпель *m* scalpel.

скаме́ечка footstool; small bench. **скаме́йка** bench. **скамья́** (*pl* ска́мьи, -е́й) bench; **~ подсуди́мых** dock.

сканда́л scandal; brawl, rowdy scene. **скандали́ст** trouble-maker. **сканда́литься** *impf* (*pf* **о~**) disgrace o.s. **сканда́льный** scandalous.

скандина́вский Scandinavian.

сканди́ровать *impf & pf* declaim.

ска́нер (*comput, med*) scanner.

ска́пливать(ся *impf of* **скопи́ть(ся**

скарб goods and chattels.

ска́редный stingy.

скарлати́на scarlet fever.

скат slope; pitch.

ската́ть *pf* (*impf* **ска́тывать**) roll (up).

ска́терть (*pl* -и, -е́й) table-cloth.

скати́ть (-ачу́, -а́тишь) *pf*, **ска́тывать¹** *impf* roll down; **~ся** roll down; slip, slide. **ска́тывать²** *impf of* **ската́ть**

скафа́ндр diving-suit; space-suit.

ска́чка gallop, galloping. **ска́чки** (-чек) *pl* horse-race; races. **скачо́к** (-чка́) jump, leap.

ска́шивать *impf of* **скоси́ть**

сква́жина slit, chink; well.

сквер public garden.

скве́рно badly; bad. **сквернослови́ть** (-влю) *impf* use foul language. **скве́рный** foul; bad.

сквози́ть *impf* be transparent; show through; **сквози́т** *impers* there is a draught. **сквозно́й** through; transparent. **сквозня́к** (-а́) draught. **сквозь** *prep+acc* through.

скворе́ц (-рца́) starling.

скеле́т skeleton.

ске́птик sceptic. **скептици́зм** scepticism. **скепти́ческий** sceptical.

скетч sketch.

ски́дка reduction. **ски́дывать** *impf*, **ски́нуть** (-ну) *pf* throw off *or* down; knock off.

ски́петр sceptre.

скипида́р turpentine.

скирд (-а́; *pl* -ы́), **скирда́** (*pl* -ы, -а́м) stack, rick.

скиса́ть *impf*, **ски́снуть** (-ну; скис) *pf* go sour.

скита́лец (-льца) wanderer. **скита́ться** *impf* wander.

скиф Scythian.

склад¹ depot; store.

склад² mould; turn; logical connection; **~ ума́** mentality.

скла́дка fold; pleat; crease; wrinkle.

скла́дно *adv* smoothly.

складно́й folding, collapsible.

скла́дный (-ден, -дна, -о) well-knit, well-built; smooth, coherent.

скла́дчина: в скла́дчину by clubbing together. **скла́дывать(ся** *impf of* **сложи́ть(ся**

скле́ивать *impf*, **с|кле́ить** *pf* stick together; **~ся** stick together.

склеп (burial) vault, crypt.

склепа́ть *pf*, **склёпывать** *impf* rivet. **склёпка** riveting.

склеро́з sclerosis.

С

скло́ка squabble.

склон slope; **на ~е лет** in one's declining years. **склоне́ние** inclination; declension. **склони́ть** (-ню́, -ни́шь) *pf*, **склоня́ть** *impf* incline; bow; win over; decline; **~ся** bend, bow; yield; be declined. **скло́нность** inclination; tendency. **скло́нный** (-нен, -нна́, -нно) inclined, disposed. **склоня́емый** declinable.

скля́нка phial; bottle; (*naut*) bell.

скоба́ (*pl* -ы, -а́м) cramp, clamp; staple.

ско́бка *dim of* **скоба́**; bracket; *pl* parenthesis, parentheses.

скобли́ть (-облю́, -о́бли́шь) *impf* scrape, plane.

ско́ванность constraint. **ско́ванный** constrained; bound. **скова́ть** (скую́, скуёшь) *pf* (*impf* **ско́вывать**) forge; chain; fetter; pin down, hold, contain.

сковорода́ (*pl* ско́вороды, -ро́д, -а́м), **сковоро́дка** frying-pan.

ско́вывать *impf of* **скова́ть**

скола́чивать *impf*, **сколоти́ть** (-очу́, -о́тишь) *pf* knock together.

сколо́ть (-лю́, -лешь) *pf* (*impf* **ска́лывать**) chop off; pin together.

скольже́ние sliding, slipping; glide. **скользи́ть** (-льжу́) *impf*, **скользну́ть** (-ну́, -нёшь) *pf* slide; slip; glide. **ско́льзкий** (-зок, -зка́, -о) slippery. **скользя́щий** sliding.

ско́лько *adv* how much; how many; as far as.

с|кома́ндовать *pf.* **с|комбини́ровать** *pf.* **с|ко́мкать** *pf.* **с|комплектова́ть** *pf.* **с|компромети́ровать** *pf.* **с|конструи́ровать** *pf.*

сконфу́женный embarrassed, confused, disconcerted. **с|конфу́зить(ся** (-у́жу(сь) *pf.*

с|концентри́ровать *pf.*

сконча́ться *pf* pass away, die.

с|копи́ровать *pf.*

скопи́ть (-плю́, -пишь) *pf* (*impf* **ска́пливать**) save (up); amass; **~ся** accumulate. **скопле́ние** accumulation; crowd.

ско́пом *adv* in a crowd, en masse.

скорбе́ть (-блю́) *impf* grieve. **ско́рбный** sorrowful. **скорбь** (*pl* -и, -е́й) sorrow.

скоре́е, скоре́й *comp of* **ско́ро, ско́рый**; *adv* rather, sooner; **как мо́жно ~** as soon as possible; **~ всего́** most likely.

скорлупа́ (*pl* -ы) shell.

скорня́к (-а́) furrier.

ско́ро *adv* quickly; soon.

скоро- *in comb* quick-, fast-. **скорова́рка** pressure-cooker. **~гово́рка** patter; tongue-twister. **ско́ропись** cursive; shorthand. **~по́ртящийся** perishable. **~пости́жный** sudden. **~спе́лый** early; fast-ripening; premature; hasty. **~сшива́тель** *m* binder, file. **~те́чный** transient, short-lived.

скоростно́й high-speed. **ско́рость** (*gen pl* -е́й) speed; gear.

скорпио́н scorpion; Scorpio.

с|корректи́ровать *pf.* **с|ко́рчить(ся** (-чу(сь) *pf.*

ско́р|ый (скор, -а́, -о) quick, fast; near; forthcoming; **~ая по́мощь** first-aid; ambulance.

с|коси́ть[1] (-ошу́, -о́сишь) *pf* (*impf also* **ска́шивать**) mow.

с|коси́ть[2] (-ошу́) *pf* (*impf also* **ска́шивать**) squint; cut on the cross.

скот (-а́), **скоти́на** cattle; livestock; beast. **ско́тный** cattle.

ското- *in comb* cattle. **скотобо́йня** (*gen pl* -о́ен) slaughter-house. **~во́д** cattle-breeder. **~во́дство** cattle-raising.

ско́тский cattle; brutish. **ско́тство** brutish condition; brutality.

скра́сить (-а́шу) *pf*, **скра́шивать** *impf* smooth over; relieve.

скребо́к (-бка́) scraper. **скребу́** *etc.*: *see* **скрести́**

скре́жет grating; gnashing. **скрежета́ть** (-ещу́, -е́щешь) *impf* grate; *+instr* gnash.

скре́па clamp, brace; countersignature.

скрепи́ть (-плю́) *pf*, **скрепля́ть**

С

impf fasten (together), make fast; clamp; countersign, ratify; **скрепя́ се́рдце** reluctantly. **скре́пка** paper-clip. **скрепле́ние** fastening; clamping; tie, clamp.

скрести́ (-ебу́, -ебёшь; -ёб, -ла́) *impf* scrape; scratch; **~сь** scratch.

скрести́ть (-ещу́) *pf*, **скре́щивать** *impf* cross; interbreed. **скреще́ние** crossing. **скре́щивание** crossing; interbreeding.

с|криви́ть(ся (-влю(сь) *pf*.

скрип squeak, creak. **скрипа́ч** (-а́) violinist. **скрипе́ть** (-плю́) *impf*, **скри́пнуть** (-ну) *pf* squeak, creak; scratch. **скрипи́чный** violin; **~ ключ** treble clef. **скри́пка** violin. **скрипу́чий** squeaky, creaking.

с|кро́йть *pf*.

скро́мничать *impf* (*pf* **по~**) be (too) modest. **скро́мность** modesty. **скро́мный** (-мен, -мна́, -о) modest.

скро́ю *etc.*: *see* **скрыть. скрою́** *etc.*: *see* **скро́йть**

скрупулёзный scrupulous.

с|крути́ть (-учу́, -у́тишь) *pf*, **скру́чивать** *impf* twist; roll; tie up.

скрыва́ть *impf*, **скрыть** (-о́ю) *pf* hide, conceal; **~ся** hide, go into hiding, be hidden; steal away; disappear. **скры́тничать** *impf* be secretive. **скры́тный** secretive. **скры́тый** secret, hidden; latent.

скря́га *m & f* miser.

ску́дный (-ден, -дна́, -о) scanty; meagre. **ску́дость** scarcity, paucity.

ску́ка boredom.

скула́ (*pl* -ы) cheek-bone. **скула́стый** with high cheek-bones.

скули́ть *impf* whine, whimper.

ску́льптор sculptor. **скульпту́ра** sculpture.

ску́мбрия mackerel.

скунс skunk.

скупа́ть *impf of* **скупи́ть**

скупе́ц (-пца́) miser.

скупи́ть (-плю́, -пишь) *pf* (*impf* **скупа́ть**) buy (up).

скупи́ться (-плю́сь) *impf* (*pf* **по~**) be stingy; skimp; be sparing (of +**на**+*acc*).

ску́пка buying (up).

ску́по *adv* sparingly. **скупо́й** (-п, -а́, -о) stingy, meagre. **ску́пость** stinginess.

ску́пщик buyer(-up).

ску́тер (*pl* -а́) outboard speed-boat.

скуча́ть *impf* be bored; +**по** +*dat* miss, yearn for.

ску́ченность density, overcrowding. **ску́ченный** dense, overcrowded. **ску́чить** (-чу) *pf* crowd (together); **~ся** cluster; crowd together.

ску́чный (-чен, -чна́, -о) boring; **мне ску́чно** I'm bored.

с|ку́шать *pf*. **скую́** *etc.*: *see* **скова́ть**

слабе́ть (-е́ю) *impf* (*pf* **о~**) weaken, grow weak. **слаби́тельн|ый** laxative; **~ое** *sb* laxative. **сла́бить** *impf impers*: **его́ сла́бит** he has diarrhoea.

слабо- *in comb* weak, feeble, slight. **слабово́лие** weakness of will. **~во́льный** weak-willed. **~не́рвный** nervy, nervous. **~ра́звитый** under-developed. **~у́мие** feeble-mindedness. **~у́мный** feeble-minded.

сла́бость weakness. **сла́бый** (-б, -а́, -о) weak.

сла́ва glory; fame; **на сла́ву** wonderfully well. **сла́вить** (-влю) *impf* celebrate, sing the praises of; **~ся** (+*instr*) be famous (for). **сла́вный** glorious, renowned; nice.

славяни́н (*pl* -я́не, -я́н), **славя́нка** Slav. **славянофи́л** Slavophil(e). **славя́нский** Slav, Slavonic.

слага́емое *sb* component, term, member. **слага́ть** *impf of* **сложи́ть**

сла́дить (-а́жу) *pf* **с**+*instr* cope with, handle; arrange.

сла́дк|ий (-док, -дка́, -о) sweet; **~ое** *sb* sweet course. **сладостра́стник** voluptuary. **сладостра́стный**

С

voluptuous. **сла́дость** joy; sweetness; *pl* sweets.
сла́женность harmony. **сла́женный** co-ordinated, harmonious.
сла́мывать *impf of* **сломи́ть**
сла́нец (-нца) shale, slate.
сластёна *m* & *f* person with a sweet tooth. **сласть** (*pl* -и, -е́й) delight; *pl* sweets, sweet things.
слать (шлю, шлёшь) *impf* send.
слаща́вый sugary, sickly-sweet. **сла́ще** *comp of* **сла́дкий**
сле́ва *adv* to *or* on the left; ~ **напра́во** from left to right.
слёг *etc.*: *see* **слечь**
слегка́ *adv* slightly; lightly.
след (следа́, *dat* -у, *loc* -у́; *pl* -ы) track; footprint; trace. **следи́ть**[1] (-ежу́) *impf* +**за**+*instr* watch; follow; keep up with; look after; keep an eye on. **следи́ть**[2] (-ежу́) *impf* (*pf* **на**~) leave footprints. **сле́дование** movement. **сле́дователь** *m* investigator. **сле́довательно** *adv* consequently. **сле́довать** *impf* (*pf* **по**~) **I.** +*dat or* **за**+*instr* follow; go, be bound; **II.** *impers* (+*dat*) ought; be owing, be owed; **вам сле́дует** +*inf* you ought to; **как сле́дует** properly; as it should be; **ско́лько с меня́ сле́дует?** how much do I owe (you)? **сле́дом** *adv* (**за**+*instr*) immediately after, close behind. **сле́дственный** investigation, inquiry. **сле́дствие**[1] consequence. **сле́дствие**[2] investigation. **сле́дующий** following, next. **сле́жка** shadowing.
слеза́ (*pl* -ёзы, -а́м) tear.
слеза́ть *impf of* **слезть**
слези́ться (-и́тся) *impf* water. **слезли́вый** tearful. **слёзный** tear; tearful. **слезоточи́вый** watering; ~ **газ** tear-gas.
слезть (-зу; слез) *pf* (*impf* **слеза́ть**) climb *or* get down; dismount; get off; come off.
слепе́нь (-пня́) *m* horse-fly.
слепе́ц (-пца́) blind man. **слепи́ть**[1] *impf* blind; dazzle.
с|лепи́ть[2] (-плю́, -пишь) *pf* stick together.
сле́пнуть (-ну; слеп) *impf* (*pf* **о**~) go blind. **сле́по** *adv* blindly. **слеп|о́й** (-п, -а́, -о) blind; ~**ые** *sb pl* the blind.
сле́пок (-пка) cast.
слепота́ blindness.
сле́сарь (*pl* -я́ *or* -и) *m* metalworker; locksmith.
слёт gathering; rally. **слета́ть** *impf*, **слете́ть** (-ечу́) *pf* fly down *or* away; fall down *or* off; ~**ся** fly together; congregate.
слечь (сля́гу, -я́жешь; слёг, -ла́) *pf* take to one's bed.
сли́ва plum; plum-tree.
слива́ть(ся *impf of* **сли́ть(ся.** **сли́вки** (-вок) *pl* cream. **сли́вочн|ый** cream; creamy; ~**ое ма́сло** butter; ~**ое моро́женое** dairy ice-cream.
сли́зистый slimy. **слизня́к** (-а́) slug. **слизь** mucus; slime.
с|линя́ть *pf.*
слипа́ться *impf*, **сли́пнуться** (-нется; -и́пся) *pf* stick together.
сли́тно together, as one word. **сли́ток** (-тка) ingot, bar. **с|лить** (солью́, -ьёшь; -ил, -а́, -о) *pf* (*impf also* **слива́ть**) pour, pour out *or* off; fuse, amalgamate; ~**ся** flow together; blend; merge.
слича́ть *impf*, **сличи́ть** (-чу́) *pf* collate; check. **сличе́ние** collation, checking.
сли́шком *adv* too; too much.
слия́ние confluence; merging; merger.
слова́к, -а́чка Slovak. **слова́цкий** Slovak.
слова́рный lexical; dictionary. **слова́рь** (-я́) *m* dictionary; vocabulary. **слове́сность** literature; philology. **слове́сный** verbal, oral. **сло́вно** *conj* as if; like, as. **сло́во** (*pl* -а́) word; **одни́м** ~**м** in a word. **сло́вом** *adv* in a word. **словообразова́ние** word-formation. **словоохо́тливый** talkative. **словосочета́ние** word

С

combination, phrase. **слово-употреблéние** usage.

слог[1] style.

слог[2] (*pl* -и, -óв) syllable.

слоёный flaky.

сложéние composition; addition; build, constitution. **сложи́ть** (-жý, -жишь) *pf* (*impf* **класть, склáдывать, слагáть**) put *or* lay (together); pile, stack; add, add up; fold (up); compose; take off, put down; lay down; **~ся** turn out; take shape; arise; club together. **слóжность** complication; complexity. **слóжный** (-жен, -жнá, -о) complicated; complex; compound.

слои́стый stratified; flaky. **слой** (*pl* -и́, -ёв) layer; stratum.

слом demolition, pulling down.

с|ломáть(ся *pf.* **сломи́ть** (-млю, -мишь) *pf* (*impf* **слáмывать**) break (off); overcome; **сломя́ гóлову** at breakneck speed; **~ся** break.

слон (-á) elephant; bishop. **слони́ха** she-elephant. **слонóв|ый** elephant; **~ая кость** ivory.

слоня́ться *impf* loiter, mooch (about).

слугá (*pl* -и) *m* (man) servant. **служáнка** servant, maid. **слýжащий** *sb* employee. **слýжба** service; work. **служéбный** office; official; auxiliary; secondary. **служéние** service, serving. **служи́ть** (-жý, -жишь) *impf* (*pf* **по~**) serve; work.

с|лукáвить (-влю) *pf.*

слух hearing; ear; rumour; **по ~у** by ear. **слухов|óй** acoustic, auditory, aural; **~óй аппарáт** hearing aid; **~óе окнó** dormer (window).

слýчай incident, event; case; opportunity; chance; **ни в кóем слýчае** in no circumstances. **случáйно** *adv* by chance, accidentally; by any chance. **случáйность** chance. **случáйный** accidental; chance; incidental. **случáться** *impf*, **случи́ться** *pf* happen.

слýшание listening; hearing. **слýшатель** *m* listener; student; *pl* audience. **слýшать** *impf* (*pf* **по~, про~**) listen (to); hear; attend lectures on; **(я) слýшаю!** hello!; very well; **~ся** *+acc* obey, *+gen* heed.

слыть (-ывý, -ывёшь; -ыл, -á, -о) *impf* (*pf* **про~**) have the reputation (*+instr or* **за**+*acc* for).

слыхáть *impf*, **слы́шать** (-шу) *impf* (*pf* **у~**) hear; sense. **слы́шаться** (-шится) *impf* (*pf* **по~**) be heard. **слы́шимость** audibility. **слы́шимый** audible. **слы́шный** (-шен, -шнá, -шно) audible.

слюдá mica.

слюнá (*pl* -и, -éй) saliva; spit; *pl* spittle. **слюня́вый** dribbling.

сля́гу *etc.*: *see* **слечь**

сля́коть slush.

см. *abbr* (*of* **смотри́**) see, *vide.*

смáзать (-áжу) *pf*, **смáзывать** *impf* lubricate; grease; slur over. **смáзка** lubrication; greasing; grease. **смáзочный** lubricating.

смак relish. **смаковáть** *impf* relish; savour.

с|маневри́ровать *pf.*

смáнивать *impf*, **смани́ть** (-ню́, -нишь) *pf* entice.

с|мастери́ть *pf.* **смáтывать** *impf of* **смотáть**

смáхивать *impf*, **смахнýть** (-нý, -нёшь) *pf* brush away *or* off.

смáчивать *impf of* **смочи́ть**

смéжный adjacent.

смекáлка native wit.

смёл *etc.*: *see* **смести́**

смелéть (-éю) *impf* (*pf* **о~**) grow bolder. **смéлость** boldness, courage. **смéлый** (-л, -лá, -ло) bold, courageous. **смельчáк** (-á) daredevil.

смелю́ *etc.*: *see* **смолóть**

смéна changing; change; replacement(s); relief; shift. **смени́ть** (-ню́, -нишь) *pf*, **сменя́ть**[1] *impf* change; replace; relieve; **~ся** hand over; be relieved; take turns; *+instr* give place to. **смéнный** shift; changeable. **смéнщик** relief; *pl* new shift. **сменя́ть**[2] *pf* exchange.

с|мéрить *pf.*
смеркáться *impf,* **смéркнуться** (-нется) *pf* get dark.
смертéльный mortal, fatal, death; extreme. **смéртность** mortality. **смéртный** mortal; death; deadly, extreme. **смерть** (*gen pl* -éй) death.
смерч whirlwind; waterspout.
смеси́тельный mixing. **с|меси́ть** (-ешý, -éсишь) *pf.*
смести́ (-етý, -етёшь; -ёл, -á) *pf* (*impf* **сметáть**) sweep off, away.
смести́ть (-ещý) *pf* (*impf* **смещáть**) displace; remove.
смесь mixture; medley.
смéта estimate.
сметáна sour cream.
с|метáть[1] *pf* (*impf also* **смётывать**) tack (together).
сметáть[2] *impf of* **смести́**
смéтливый quick, sharp.
сметý *etc.*: *see* **смести́. смётывать** *impf of* **сметáть**
сметь (-éю) *impf* (*pf* **по~**) dare.
смех laughter; laugh. **смехотвóрный** laughable.
смéшанный mixed; combined. **с|мешáть** *pf,* **смéшивать** *impf* mix, blend; confuse; **~ся** mix, (inter)blend; get mixed up. **смешéние** mixture; mixing up.
смеши́ть (-шý) *impf* (*pf* **на~, рас~**) make laugh. **смешли́вый** given to laughing. **смешнóй** (-шóн, -шнá) funny; ridiculous.
смешý *etc.*: *see* **смеси́ть, смеши́ть**
смещáть(ся *impf of* **смести́ть(ся. смещéние** displacement, removal. **смещý** *etc.*: *see* **смести́ть**
смея́ться (-еюсь, -еёшься) *impf* laugh (at +**над**+*instr*).
смирéние humility, meekness. **смирéнный** humble, meek. **смири́тельн|ый: ~ая рубáшка** strait-jacket. **смири́ть** *pf,* **смиря́ть** *impf* restrain, subdue; **~ся** submit; resign o.s. **сми́рно** *adv* quietly; **~!** attention! **сми́рный** quiet; submissive.
смогý *etc.*: *see* **смочь**
смолá (*pl* -ы) resin; pitch, tar; rosin. **смоли́стый** resinous.
смолкáть *impf,* **смóлкнуть** (-ну; -олк) *pf* fall silent.
смóлоду *adv* from one's youth.
с|молоти́ть (-очý, -óтишь) *pf.*
с|молóть (смелю́, смéлешь) *pf.*
смоляннóй pitch, tar, resin.
с|монти́ровать *pf.*
сморкáть *impf* (*pf* **вы́~**) blow; **~ся** blow one's nose.
сморóдина (*no pl*; *usu collect*) currant; currants; currant-bush.
смóрщенный wrinkled. **с|мóрщить(ся** (-щу(сь) *pf.*
смотáть *pf* (*impf* **смáтывать**) wind, reel.
смотр (*loc* -ý; *pl* -óтры) review, inspection. **смотрéть** (-рю́, -ришь) *impf* (*pf* **по~**) look (at **на**+*acc*); see; watch; look through; examine; +**за**+*instr* look after; +**в**+*acc*, **на**+*acc* look on to; +*instr* look (like); **смотри́(те)!** take care!; **смотря́** it depends; **смотря́ по**+*dat* depending on; **~ся** look at o.s. **смотровóй** observation, inspection.
смочи́ть (-чý, -чишь) *pf* (*impf* **смáчивать**) moisten.
с|мочь (-огý, -óжешь; смог, -лá) *pf.*
с|мошéнничать *pf.* **смóю** *etc.*: *see* **смы́ть**
смрад stench. **смрáдный** stinking.
СМС-сообщéние text message.
смýглый (-гл, -á, -о) dark-complexioned, swarthy.
смути́ть (-ущý) *pf,* **смущáть** *impf* embarrass, confuse; **~ся** be embarrassed, be confused. **смýтный** vague; dim; troubled. **смущéние** embarrassment, confusion. **смущённый** (-ён, -á) embarrassed, confused.
смывáть *impf of* **смыть**
смыкáть(ся *impf of* **сомкнýть(ся**
смысл sense; meaning. **смы́слить** *impf* understand. **смыслов́ой** semantic.
смыть (смóю) *pf* (*impf* **смывáть**) wash off, away.

смычо́к (-чка́) bow.
смышлёный clever.
смягча́ть *impf*, **смягчи́ть** (-чу́) *pf* soften; alleviate; **~ся** soften; relent; grow mild.
смяте́ние confusion; commotion.
с|мять(ся (сомну́(сь, -нёшь(ся) *pf*.
снабди́ть (-бжу́) *pf*, **снабжа́ть** *impf* +*instr* supply with. **снабже́ние** supply, supplying.
сна́йпер sniper.
снару́жи *adv* on *or* from (the) outside.
снаря́д projectile, missile; shell; contrivance; tackle, gear. **снаряди́ть** (-яжу́) *pf*, **снаряжа́ть** *impf* equip, fit out. **снаряже́ние** equipment, outfit.
снасть (*gen pl* -е́й) tackle; *pl* rigging.
снача́ла *adv* at first; all over again.
сна́шивать *impf of* **сноси́ть**
СНГ *abbr* (*of* **Содру́жество незави́симых госуда́рств**) CIS.
снег (*loc* -у́; *pl* -а́) snow.
снеги́рь (-я́) bullfinch.
снегово́й snow. **снегопа́д** snowfall. **Снегу́рочка** Snow Maiden. **снежи́нка** snow-flake. **сне́жн|ый** snow(y); **~ая ба́ба** snowman. **снежо́к** (-жка́) light snow; snowball.
снести́[1] (-су́, -сёшь; -ёс, -ла́) *pf* (*impf* **сноси́ть**) take; bring together; bring *or* fetch down; carry away; blow off; demolish; endure; **~сь** communicate (**с**+*instr* with).
с|нести́[2]**(сь** (-су́(сь, -сёшь(ся; снёс(ся, -сла́(сь) *pf*.
снижа́ть *impf*, **сни́зить** (-и́жу) *pf* lower; bring down; reduce; **~ся** come down; fall. **сниже́ние** lowering; loss of height.
снизойти́ (-йду́, -йдёшь; -ошёл, -шла́) *pf* (*impf* **снисходи́ть**) condescend.
сни́зу *adv* from below.
снима́ть(ся *impf of* **сня́ть(ся**. **сни́мок** (-мка) photograph.
сниму́ *etc*.: *see* **снять**
сниска́ть (-ищу́, -и́щешь) *pf*, **сни́скивать** *impf* gain, win.
снисходи́тельность condescension; leniency. **снисходи́тельный** condescending; lenient. **снисходи́ть** (-ожу́, -о́дишь) *impf of* **снизойти́**. **снисхожде́ние** indulgence, leniency.
сни́ться *impf* (*pf* **при~**) *impers*+*dat* dream.
снobи́зм snobbery.
сно́ва *adv* again, anew.
снова́ть (сную́, снуёшь) *impf* rush about.
сновиде́ние dream.
сноп (-а́) sheaf.
сноро́вка knack, skill.
снос demolition; drift; wear. **сноси́ть**[1] (-ошу́, -о́сишь) *pf* (*impf* **сна́шивать**) wear out. **сноси́ть**[2]**(ся** (-ошу́(сь, -о́сишь(ся) *impf of* **снести́(сь**. **сно́ска** footnote. **сно́сно** *adv* tolerably, so-so. **сно́сный** tolerable; fair.
снотво́рный soporific.
сноха́ (*pl* -и) daughter-in-law.
сноше́ние intercourse; relations, dealings.
сношу́ *etc*.: *see* **сноси́ть**
сня́тие taking down; removal; making. **снять** (сниму́, -и́мешь; -ял, -а́, -о) *pf* (*impf* **снима́ть**) take off; take down; gather in; remove; rent; take; make; photograph; **~ся** come off; move off; be photographed.
со *see* **с** *prep*.
со- *pref* co-, joint. **соа́втор** co-author.
соба́ка dog. **соба́чий** dog's; canine. **соба́чка** little dog; trigger.
соберу́ *etc*.: *see* **собра́ть**
собе́с *abbr* (*of* **социа́льное обеспе́чение**) social security (department).
собесе́дник interlocutor, companion. **собесе́дование** conversation.
собира́тель *m* collector. **собира́ть(ся** *impf of* **собра́ть(ся**

собла́зн temptation. **соблазни́тель** *m*, **~ница** tempter; seducer. **соблазни́тельный** tempting; seductive. **соблазни́ть** *pf*, **соблазня́ть** *impf* tempt; seduce.

соблюда́ть *impf*, **со|блюсти́** (-юду́, -дёшь; -ю́л, -á) *pf* observe; keep (to). **соблюде́ние** observance; maintenance.

собо́й, собо́ю *see* **себя́**

соболе́знование sympathy, condolence(s). **соболе́зновать** *impf* +*dat* sympathize *or* commiserate with.

со́боль (*pl* -и *or* -я́) *m* sable.

собо́р cathedral; council, synod. **собо́рный** cathedral.

собра́ние meeting; assembly; collection. **со́бранный** collected; concentrated.

собра́т (*pl* -ья, -ьев) colleague.

собра́ть (-беру́, -берёшь; -áл, -á, -о) *pf* (*impf* **собира́ть**) gather; collect; **~ся** gather; prepare; intend, be going; +**с**+*instr* collect.

со́бственник owner, proprietor. **со́бственнический** proprietary; proprietorial. **со́бственно** *adv*: **~ (говоря́)** strictly speaking, as a matter of fact. **собственнору́чно** *adv* personally, with one's own hand. **со́бственность** property; ownership. **со́бственн|ый** (one's) own; proper; true; **имя ~ое** proper name; **~ой персо́ной** in person.

собы́тие event.

собью́ *etc.*: *see* **сбить**

сова́ (*pl* -ы) owl.

сова́ть (сую́, -ёшь) *impf* (*pf* **су́нуть**) thrust, shove; **~ся** push, push in; butt in.

соверша́ть *impf*, **соверши́ть** (-шу́) *pf* accomplish; carry out; commit; complete; **~ся** happen; be accomplished. **соверше́ние** accomplishment; perpetration. **соверше́нно** *adv* perfectly; absolutely, completely. **совершенноле́тие** majority. **совершенноле́тний** of age. **соверше́нный**[1] perfect; absolute, complete. **соверше́нный**[2] perfective. **соверше́нство** perfection. **соверше́нствование** perfecting; improvement. **соверше́нствовать** *impf* (*pf* **у~**) perfect; improve; **~ся в**+*instr* perfect o.s. in; improve.

со́вестливый conscientious. **со́вестно** *impers*+*dat* be ashamed. **со́весть** conscience.

сове́т advice, counsel; opinion; council; soviet, Soviet. **сове́тник** adviser. **сове́товать** *impf* (*pf* **по~**) advise; **~ся с**+*instr* consult, ask advice of. **советóлог** Kremlinologist. **сове́тск|ий** Soviet; **~ая власть** the Soviet regime; **~ий Сою́з** the Soviet Union. **сове́тчик** adviser.

совеща́ние conference. **совеща́тельный** consultative, deliberative. **совеща́ться** *impf* deliberate; consult.

совлада́ть *pf* **с**+*instr* control, cope with.

совмести́мый compatible. **совмести́тель** *m* person holding more than one office. **совмести́ть** (-ещу́) *pf*, **совмеща́ть** *impf* combine; **~ся** coincide; be combined, combine. **совме́стно** jointly. **совме́стный** joint, combined.

сово́к (-вка́) shovel; scoop; dustpan.

совокупи́ться (-плю́сь) *pf*, **совокупля́ться** *impf* copulate. **совокупле́ние** copulation. **совоку́пно** *adv* jointly. **совоку́пность** aggregate, sum total.

совпада́ть *impf*, **совпа́сть** (-адёт) *pf* coincide; agree, tally. **совпаде́ние** coincidence.

совратить (-ащу́) *pf* (*impf* **совраща́ть**) pervert, seduce.

со|вра́ть (-вру́, -врёшь; -áл, -á, -о) *pf*.

совраща́ть(ся *impf of* **соврати́ть(ся**. **совраще́ние** perverting, seduction.

совреме́нник contemporary. **совреме́нность** the present (time);

С

contemporaneity. **совреме́нный** contemporary; modern.

совру́ *etc.*: *see* **совра́ть**

совсе́м *adv* quite; entirely.

совхо́з State farm.

совью́ *etc.*: *see* **свить**

согла́сие consent; assent; agreement; harmony. **согласи́ться** (-ашу́сь) *pf* (*impf* **соглаша́ться**) consent; agree. **согла́сно** *adv* in accord, in harmony; *prep+dat* in accordance with. **согла́сн|ый**[1] agreeable (to); in agreement; harmonious. **согла́сный**[2] consonant(al); *sb* consonant.

согласова́ние co-ordination; agreement. **согласо́ванность** co-ordination. **согласова́ть** *pf*, **согласо́вывать** *impf* co-ordinate; make agree; **~ся** conform; agree.

соглаша́ться *impf of* **согласи́ться. соглаше́ние** agreement. **соглашу́** *etc.*: *see* **согласи́ть**

согна́ть (сгоню́, сго́нишь; -а́л, -а́, -о) *pf* (*impf* **сгоня́ть**) drive away; drive together.

со|гну́ть (-ну́, -нёшь) *pf* (*impf also* **сгиба́ть**) bend, curve; **~ся** bend (down).

согрева́ть *impf*, **согре́ть** (-е́ю) *pf* warm, heat; **~ся** get warm; warm o.s.

со|греши́ть (-шу́) *pf*.

со́да soda.

соде́йствие assistance. **соде́йствовать** *impf* & *pf* (*pf also* **по~**) +*dat* assist; promote; contribute to.

содержа́ние maintenance, upkeep; content(s); pay. **содержа́тельный** rich in content; pithy. **содержа́ть** (-жу́, -жишь) *impf* keep; maintain; contain; **~ся** be kept; be maintained; be; be contained. **содержи́мое** *sb* contents.

со|дра́ть (сдеру́, -рёшь; -а́л, -а́, -о) *pf* (*impf also* **сдира́ть**) tear off, strip off; fleece.

содрога́ние shudder. **содрога́ться** *impf*, **содрогну́ться** (-ну́сь, -нёшься) *pf* shudder.

содру́жество concord; commonwealth.

соедине́ние joining, combination; joint; compound; formation. **Соединённое Короле́вство** United Kingdom. **Соединённые Шта́ты (Аме́рики)** *m pl* United States (of America). **соединённый** (-ён, -а́) united, joint. **соедини́тельный** connective, connecting. **соедини́ть** *pf*, **соединя́ть** *impf* join, unite; connect; combine; **~ся** join, unite; combine.

сожале́ние regret; pity; **к сожале́нию** unfortunately. **сожале́ть** (-е́ю) *impf* regret, deplore.

сожгу́ *etc.*: *see* **сжечь. сожже́ние** burning; cremation.

сожи́тель *m*, **~ница** room-mate, flat-mate; lover. **сожи́тельство** co-habitation.

сожму́ *etc.*: *see* **сжать**[2]. **сожну́** *etc.*: *see* **сжать**[1]. **созва́ниваться** *impf of* **созвони́ться**

созва́ть (-зову́, -зовёшь; -а́л, -а́, -о) *pf* (*impf* **сзыва́ть, созыва́ть**) call together; call; invite.

созве́здие constellation.

созвони́ться *pf* (*impf* **созва́ниваться**) ring up; speak on the telephone.

созву́чие accord; assonance. **созву́чный** harmonious; +*dat* in keeping with.

создава́ть (-даю́, -даёшь) *impf*, **созда́ть** (-а́м, -а́шь, -а́ст, -ади́м; со́зда́л, -а́, -о) *pf* create; establish; **~ся** be created; arise, spring up. **созда́ние** creation; work; creature. **созда́тель** *m* creator; originator.

созерца́ние contemplation. **созерца́тельный** contemplative. **созерца́ть** *impf* contemplate.

созида́ние creation. **созида́тельный** creative.

сознава́ть (-наю́, -наёшь) *impf*, **созна́ть** *pf* be conscious of, realize; acknowledge; **~ся** confess. **созна́ние** consciousness; ac-

knowledgement; confession. **созна́тельность** awareness, consciousness. **созна́тельный** conscious; deliberate.
созову́ *etc.*: *see* **созва́ть**
созрева́ть *impf*, **со|зре́ть** (-е́ю) *pf* ripen, mature.
созы́в summoning, calling. **созыва́ть** *impf of* **созва́ть**
соизмери́мый commensurable.
соиска́ние competition. **соиска́тель** *m*, **~ница** competitor, candidate.
сойти́ (-йду́, -йдёшь; сошёл, -шла́) *pf* (*impf* **сходи́ть**) go *or* come down; get off; leave; come off; pass, go off; **~ с ума́** go mad, go out of one's mind; **~сь** meet; gather; become friends; become intimate; agree.
сок (*loc* -у́) juice.
со́кол falcon.
сократи́ть (-ащу́) *pf*, **сокраща́ть** *impf* shorten; abbreviate; reduce; **~ся** grow shorter; decrease; contract. **сокраще́ние** shortening; abridgement; abbreviation; reduction.
сокрове́нный secret; innermost. **сокро́вище** treasure. **сокро́вищница** treasure-house.
сокруша́ть *impf*, **сокруши́ть** (-шу́) *pf* shatter; smash; distress; **~ся** grieve, be distressed. **сокруше́ние** smashing; grief. **сокрушённый** (-ён, -а́) grief-stricken. **сокруши́тельный** shattering.
сокры́тие concealment.
со|лга́ть (-лгу́, -лжёшь; -а́л, -а́, -о) *pf.*
солда́т (*gen pl* -а́т) soldier. **солда́тский** soldier's.
соле́ние salting; pickling. **солёный** (со́лон, -а́, -о) salt(y); salted; pickled. **соле́нье** salted food(s); pickles.
солида́рность solidarity. **соли́дный** solid; strong; reliable; respectable; sizeable.
соли́ст, соли́стка soloist.
соли́ть (-лю́, со́ли́шь) *impf* (*pf* **по~**) salt; pickle.
со́лнечный sun; solar; sunny; **~ свет** sunlight; sunshine; **~ уда́р** sunstroke. **со́лнце** sun. **солнцепёк: на ~е** in the sun. **солнцестоя́ние** solstice.
со́ло *neut indecl* solo; *adv* solo.
солове́й (-вья́) nightingale.
со́лод malt.
солодко́вый liquorice.
соло́ма straw; thatch. **соло́менный** straw; thatch. **соло́минка** straw.
со́лон *etc.*: *see* **солёный. солони́на** corned beef. **соло́нка** salt-cellar. **солонча́к** (-а́) saline soil; *pl* salt marshes. **соль** (*pl* -и, -е́й) salt.
со́льный solo.
солью́ *etc.*: *see* **слить**
соляно́й, соля́ный salt, saline; **соля́ная кислота́** hydrochloric acid.
со́мкнутый close. **сомкну́ть** (-ну́, -нёшь) *pf* (*impf* **смыка́ть**) close; **~ся** close.
сомнева́ться *impf* doubt, have doubts. **сомне́ние** doubt. **сомни́тельный** doubtful.
сомну́ *etc.*: *see* **смять**
сон (сна) sleep; dream. **сонли́вость** sleepiness; somnolence. **сонли́вый** sleepy. **со́нный** sleepy; sleeping.
сона́та sonata.
соне́т sonnet.
сообража́ть *impf*, **сообрази́ть** (-ажу́) *pf* consider, think out; weigh; understand. **соображе́ние** consideration; understanding; notion. **сообрази́тельный** quick-witted.
сообра́зный с+*instr* conforming to, in keeping with.
сообща́ *adv* together. **сообща́ть** *impf*, **сообщи́ть** (-щу́) *pf* communicate, report, announce; impart; +*dat* inform. **сообще́ние** communication, report; announcement. **соо́бщество** association.

сообщник accomplice.

соорудить (-ужу) *pf*, **сооружать** *impf* build, erect. **сооружение** building; structure.

соответственно *adv* accordingly, correspondingly; *prep* +*dat* according to, in accordance with. **соответственный** corresponding. **соответствие** accordance, correspondence. **соответствовать** *impf* correspond, conform. **соответствующий** corresponding; suitable.

соотечественник fellow-countryman.

соотношение correlation.

соперник rival. **соперничать** *impf* compete, vie. **соперничество** rivalry.

сопеть (-плю) *impf* wheeze; snuffle.

сопка hill, mound.

сопливый snotty.

сопоставить (-влю) *pf*, **сопоставлять** *impf* compare. **сопоставление** comparison.

сопредельный contiguous.

со|преть *pf*.

соприкасаться *impf*, **соприкоснуться** (-нусь, -нёшься) *pf* adjoin; come into contact. **соприкосновение** contact.

сопроводительный accompanying. **сопроводить** (-ожу) *pf*, **сопровождать** *impf* accompany; escort. **сопровождение** accompaniment; escort.

сопротивление resistance. **сопротивляться** *impf* +*dat* resist, oppose.

сопутствовать *impf* +*dat* accompany.

сопьюсь *etc.*: *see* **спиться**

сор litter, rubbish.

соразмерить *pf*, **соразмерять** *impf* balance, match. **соразмерный** proportionate, commensurate.

соратник comrade-in-arms.

сорвать (-ву, -вёшь; -ал, -а, -о) *pf* (*impf* **срывать**) tear off, away, down; break off; pick; get; break; ruin, spoil; vent; **~ся** break away, break loose; fall, come down; fall through.

с|организовать *pf*.

соревнование competition; contest. **соревноваться** *impf* compete.

сорить *impf* (*pf* **на~**) +*acc or instr* litter; throw about. **сорн|ый** rubbish, refuse; **~ая трава** weed(s). **сорняк** (-а) weed.

сорок (-а) forty.

сорока magpie.

сороков|ой fortieth; **~ые годы** the forties.

сорочка shirt; blouse; shift.

сорт (*pl* -а) grade, quality; sort. **сортировать** *impf* (*pf* **рас~**) sort, grade. **сортировка** sorting. **сортировочн|ый** sorting; **~ая** *sb* marshalling-yard. **сортировщик** sorter. **сортный** high quality.

сосать (-су, -сёшь) *impf* suck.

со|сватать *pf*.

сосед (*pl* -и, -ей, -ям), **соседка** neighbour. **соседний** neighbouring; adjacent, next. **соседский** neighbours'. **соседство** neighbourhood. **сосиска** frankfurter, sausage.

соска (*baby's*) dummy.

соскакивать *impf of* **соскочить**

соскальзывать *impf*, **соскользнуть** (-ну, -нёшь) *pf* slide down, slide off.

соскочить (-чу, -чишь) *pf* (*impf* **соскакивать**) jump off *or* down; come off.

соскучиться (-чусь) *pf* get bored; **~ по**+*dat* miss.

сослагательный subjunctive.

сослать (сошлю, -лёшь) *pf* (*impf* **ссылать**) exile, deport; **~ся на**+*acc* refer to; cite; plead, allege.

сословие estate; class.

сослуживец (-вца) colleague.

сосна (*pl* -ы, -сен) pine(-tree). **сосновый** pine; deal.

сосок (-ска) nipple, teat.

сосредото́ченный concentrated. **сосредото́чивать** *impf*, **сосредото́чить** (-чу) *pf* concentrate; focus; **~ся** concentrate.

соста́в composition; structure; compound; staff; strength; train; **в ~е** *+gen* consisting of. **состави́тель** *m* compiler. **соста́вить** (-влю) *pf*, **составля́ть** *impf* put together; make (up); draw up; compile; be, constitute; total; **~ся** form, be formed. **составно́й** compound; component, constituent.

со|ста́рить(ся *pf*.

состоя́ние state, condition; fortune. **состоя́тельный** well-to-do; well-grounded. **состоя́ть** (-ою́) *impf* be; *+***из***+gen* consist of; *+***в***+prep* consist in, be. **состоя́ться** (-ои́тся) *pf* take place.

сострада́ние compassion. **сострада́тельный** compassionate.

с|остри́ть *pf*. **со|стря́пать** *pf*.

со|стыкова́ться *pf*, **состыко́вываться** *impf* dock.

состяза́ние competition, contest. **состяза́ться** *impf* compete.

сосу́д vessel.

сосу́лька icicle.

сосуществова́ние co-existence.

со|счита́ть *pf*. **сот** *see* **сто.**

сотворе́ние creation. **со|твори́ть** *pf*.

со|тка́ть (-ку́, -кёшь; -а́л, -ала́, -о) *pf*.

со́тня (*gen pl* -тен) a hundred.

со́товый cellular; **~ телефо́н** mobile phone, cell phone.

сотру́ *etc.*: *see* **стере́ть**

сотру́дник collaborator; colleague; employee. **сотру́дничать** *impf* collaborate; *+***в***+prep* contribute to. **сотру́дничество** collaboration.

сотряса́ть *impf*, **сотрясти́** (-су́, -сёшь; -я́с, -ла́) *pf* shake; **~ся** tremble. **сотрясе́ние** shaking; concussion.

со́ты (-ов) *pl* honeycomb.

со́тый hundredth.

со́ус sauce; gravy; dressing.

соуча́стие participation; complicity. **соуча́стник** participant; accomplice.

софа́ (*pl* -ы) sofa.

соха́ (*pl* -и) (*wooden*) plough.

со́хнуть (-ну; сох) *impf* (*pf* **вы́~, за~, про~**) (get) dry; wither.

сохране́ние preservation; conservation; (safe)keeping; retention. **сохрани́ть** *pf*, **сохраня́ть** *impf* preserve, keep; **~ся** remain (intact); last out; be well preserved. **сохра́нный** safe.

социа́л-демокра́т Social Democrat. **социа́л-демократи́ческий** Social Democratic. **социали́зм** socialism. **социали́ст** socialist. **социалисти́ческий** socialist. **социа́льн|ый** social; **~ое обеспече́ние** social security. **социо́лог** sociologist. **социоло́гия** sociology.

соцреали́зм socialist realism.

сочета́ние combination. **сочета́ть** *impf* & *pf* combine; **~ся** combine; harmonize; match.

сочине́ние composition; work. **сочини́ть** *pf*, **сочиня́ть** *impf* compose; write; make up.

сочи́ться (-и́тся) *impf* ooze (out), trickle; **~ кро́вью** bleed.

со́чный (-чен, -чна́, -о) juicy; rich.

сочту́ *etc.*: *see* **счесть**

сочу́вствие sympathy. **сочу́вствовать** *impf +dat* sympathize with.

сошёл *etc.*: *see* **сойти́. сошлю́** *etc.*: *see* **сосла́ть. сошью́** *etc.*: *see* **сшить**

сощу́ривать *impf*, **со|щу́рить** *pf* screw up, narrow; **~ся** screw up one's eyes; narrow.

сою́з[1] union; alliance; league. **сою́з**[2] conjunction. **сою́зник** ally. **сою́зный** allied; Union.

спад recession; abatement. **спада́ть** *impf of* **спасть**

спазм spasm.

спа́ивать *impf of* **спая́ть, спои́ть**

спа́йка soldered joint; solidarity, unity.

с|пали́ть *pf.*
спа́льн|ый sleeping; **~ый ваго́н** sleeping car; **~ое ме́сто** berth. **спа́льня** (*gen pl* -лен) bedroom.
спа́ржа asparagus.
спартакиа́да sports meeting.
спаса́тельный rescue; **~ жиле́т** life jacket; **~ круг** lifebuoy; **~ по́яс** lifebelt. **спаса́ть(ся** *impf of* **спасти́(сь. спасе́ние** rescue, escape; salvation. **спаси́бо** thank you. **спаси́тель** *m* rescuer; saviour. **спаси́тельный** saving; salutary.
спасти́ (-су́, -сёшь; спас, -ла́) *pf* (*impf* **спаса́ть**) save; rescue; **~сь** escape; be saved.
спасть (-адёт) *pf* (*impf* **спада́ть**) fall (down); abate.
спать (сплю; -ал, -а́, -о) *impf* sleep; **лечь ~** go to bed.
спа́янность cohesion, unity. **спа́янный** united. **спая́ть** *pf* (*impf* **спа́ивать**) solder, weld; unite.
спекта́кль *m* performance; show.
спектр spectrum.
спекули́ровать *impf* speculate. **спекуля́нт** speculator, profiteer. **спекуля́ция** speculation; profiteering.
спе́лый ripe.
сперва́ *adv* at first; first.
спе́реди *adv* in front, from the front; *prep+gen* (from) in front of.
спёртый close, stuffy.
спеси́вый arrogant, haughty. **спесь** arrogance, haughtiness.
спеть[1] (-е́ет) *impf* (*pf* **по~**) ripen.
с|петь[2] (спою́, споёшь) *pf.*
спец- *abbr in comb* (*of* **специа́льный**) special. **спецко́р** special correspondent. **~оде́жда** protective clothing; overalls.
специализа́ция specialization. **специализи́роваться** *impf & pf* specialize. **специали́ст, ~ка** specialist, expert. **специа́льность** speciality; profession. **специа́льный** special; specialist.
специ́фика specific character.
специфи́ческий specific.
спе́ция spice.
спецо́вка protective clothing; overall(s).
спеши́ть (-шу́) *impf* (*pf* **по~**) hurry, be in a hurry; be fast.
спе́шка hurry, haste. **спе́шный** urgent.
спива́ться *impf of* **спи́ться**
СПИД *abbr* (*of* **синдро́м приобретённого иммуу́нного дефици́та**) Aids.
с|пики́ровать *pf.*
спи́ливать *impf*, **спили́ть** (-лю́, -лишь) *pf* saw down, off.
спина́ (*acc* -у; *pl* -ы) back. **спи́нка** back. **спинно́й** spinal; **~ мозг** spinal cord.
спира́ль spiral.
спирт alcohol, spirit(s). **спиртн|о́й** alcoholic; **~о́е** *sb* alcohol. **спирто́вка** spirit-stove. **спиртово́й** spirit, alcoholic.
списа́ть (-ишу́, -и́шешь) *pf*, **спи́сывать** *impf* copy; **~ся** exchange letters. **спи́сок** (-ска) list; record.
спи́ться (сопью́сь, -ьёшься; -и́лся, -а́сь) *pf* (*impf* **спива́ться**) take to drink.
спи́хивать *impf*, **спихну́ть** (-ну́, -нёшь) *pf* push aside, down.
спи́ца knitting-needle; spoke.
спи́чечн|ый match; **~ая коро́бка** match-box. **спи́чка** match.
спишу́ *etc.*: *see* **списа́ть**
сплав[1] floating. **сплав**[2] alloy. **спла́вить**[1] (-влю) *pf*, **сплавля́ть**[1] *impf* float; raft; get rid of. **спла́вить**[2] (-влю) *pf*, **сплавля́ть**[2] *impf* alloy; **~ся** fuse.
с|плани́ровать *pf.* **спла́чивать(ся** *impf of* **сплоти́ть(ся. сплёвывать** *impf of* **сплю́нуть**
с|плести́ (-ету́, -етёшь; -ёл, -а́) *pf*, **сплета́ть** *impf* weave; plait; interlace. **сплете́ние** interlacing; plexus.
сплё́тник, -ница gossip, scandalmonger. **сплётничать** *impf* (*pf* **на~**) gossip. **сплё́тня** (*gen pl* -тен) gossip, scandal.

С

сплоти́ть (-очу́) *pf* (*impf* **спла́чивать**) join; unite, rally; **~ся** unite, rally; close ranks. **сплоче́ние** uniting. **сплочённость** cohesion, unity. **сплочённый** (-ён, -á) united; firm; unbroken.

сплошно́й solid; complete; continuous; utter. **сплошь** *adv* all over; completely; **~ да ря́дом** pretty often.

сплю *see* **спать**

сплю́нуть (-ну) *pf* (*impf* **сплёвывать**) spit; spit out.

сплю́щивать *impf*, **сплю́щить** (-щу) *pf* flatten; **~ся** become flat.

с|пляса́ть (-яшу́, -я́шешь) *pf*.

сподви́жник comrade-in-arms.

спои́ть (-ою́, -о́ишь) *pf* (*impf* **спа́ивать**) make a drunkard of.

споко́йн|ый quiet; calm; **~ой но́чи** good night! **споко́йствие** quiet; calm, serenity.

спола́скивать *impf of* **сполосну́ть**

сполза́ть *impf*, **сползти́** (-зу́, -зёшь; -олз, -ла́) *pf* climb down; slip (down); fall away.

сполна́ *adv* in full.

сполосну́ть (-ну́, -нёшь) *pf* (*impf* **спола́скивать**) rinse.

спо́нсор sponsor, backer.

спор argument; controversy; dispute. **спо́рить** *impf* (*pf* **по~**) argue; dispute; debate. **спо́рный** debatable, questionable; disputed; moot.

спо́ра spore.

спорт sport. **спорти́вный** sports; **~ зал** gymnasium. **спортсме́н, ~ка** athlete, player.

спо́соб way, method; **таки́м ~ом** in this way. **спосо́бность** ability, aptitude; capacity. **спосо́бный** able; clever; capable. **спосо́бствовать** *impf* (*pf* **по~**) +*dat* assist; further.

споткну́ться (-ну́сь, -нёшься) *pf*, **спотыка́ться** *impf* stumble.

спохвати́ться (-ачу́сь, -а́тишься) *pf*, **спохва́тываться** *impf* remember suddenly.

спою́ *etc.*: *see* **спеть, спои́ть**

спра́ва *adv* to *or* on the right.

справедли́вость justice; fairness; truth. **справедли́вый** just; fair; justified.

спра́вить (-влю) *pf*, **справля́ть** *impf* celebrate. **спра́виться**[1] (-влюсь) *pf*, **справля́ться** *impf* **с**+*instr* cope with, manage. **спра́виться**[2] (-влюсь) *pf*, **справля́ться** *impf* inquire; +**в**+*prep* consult. **спра́вка** information; reference; certificate; **наводи́ть спра́вку** make inquiries. **спра́вочник** reference-book, directory. **спра́вочный** inquiry, information, reference.

спра́шивать(ся *impf of* **спроси́ть(ся**

спринт sprint. **спри́нтер** sprinter.

с|провоци́ровать *pf*. **с|проекти́ровать** *pf*.

спрос demand; asking; **без ~у** without permission. **спроси́ть** (-ошу́, -о́сишь) *pf* (*impf* **спра́шивать**) ask (for); inquire; **~ся** ask permission.

спрут octopus.

спры́гивать *impf*, **спры́гнуть** (-ну) *pf* jump off, jump down.

спры́скивать *impf*, **спры́снуть** (-ну) *pf* sprinkle.

спряга́ть *impf* (*pf* **про~**) conjugate. **спряже́ние** conjugation.

с|прясть (-яду́, -ядёшь; -ял, -я́ла́, -о) *pf*. **с|пря́тать(ся** (-я́чу(сь) *pf*.

спу́гивать *impf*, **спугну́ть** (-ну́, -нёшь) *pf* frighten off.

спуск lowering; descent; slope. **спуска́ть** *impf*, **спусти́ть** (-ущу́, -у́стишь) *pf* let down, lower; release; let out; send out; go down; forgive; squander; **~ кора́бль** launch a ship; **~ куро́к** pull the trigger; **~ пе́тлю** drop a stitch; **~ся** go down, descend. **спускно́й** drain. **спусково́й** trigger. **спустя́** *prep*+*acc* after; *adv* later.

с|пу́тать(ся *pf*.

спу́тник satellite, sputnik; (travelling) companion.

С

спущу́ *etc.*: *see* **спусти́ть**
спя́чка hibernation; sleepiness.
ср. *abbr* (*of* **сравни́**) cf.
сраба́тывать *impf*, **срабо́тать** *pf* make; work, operate.
сравне́ние comparison; simile. **сра́внивать** *impf of* **сравни́ть, сравня́ть. сравни́мый** comparable. **сравни́тельно** *adv* comparatively. **сравни́тельный** comparative. **сравни́ть** *pf* (*impf* **сра́внивать**) compare; **~ся с**+*instr* compare with. **с|равня́ть** *pf* (*impf also* **сра́внивать**) make even, equal; level.
сража́ть *impf*, **срази́ть** (-ажу́) *pf* strike down; overwhelm, crush; **~ся** fight. **сраже́ние** battle.
сра́зу *adv* at once.
срам shame. **срами́ть** (-млю́) *impf* (*pf* **о~**) shame; **~ся** cover o.s. with shame. **срамота́** shame.
сраста́ние growing together. **сраста́ться** *impf*, **срасти́сь** (-тётся; сро́сся, -ла́сь) *pf* grow together; knit.
среда́[1] (*pl* -ы) environment, surroundings; medium. **среда́**[2] (*acc* -у; *pl* -ы, -а́м *or* -ам) Wednesday. **среди́** *prep*+*gen* among; in the middle of; **~ бе́ла дня** in broad daylight. **средиземномо́рский** Mediterranean. **сре́дне** *adv* so-so. **средневеко́вый** medieval. **средневеко́вье** the Middle Ages. **сре́дний** middle; medium; mean; average; middling; secondary; neuter; **~ее** *sb* mean, average. **средото́чие** focus. **сре́дство** means; remedy.
срез cut; section; slice. **с|ре́зать** (-е́жу) *pf*. **среза́ть** *impf* cut off; slice; fail; **~ся** fail.
с|репети́ровать *pf*.
срисова́ть *pf*, **срисо́вывать** *impf* copy.
с|ровня́ть *pf*.
сродство́ affinity.
срок date; term; time, period; **в ~, к ~у** in time, to time.
сро́сся *etc.*: *see* **срасти́сь**
сро́чно *adv* urgently. **сро́чность** urgency. **сро́чный** urgent; for a fixed period.
сро́ю *etc.*: *see* **срыть**
сруб felling; framework. **сруба́ть** *impf*, **с|руби́ть** (-блю́, -бишь) *pf* cut down; build (*of logs*).
срыв disruption; breakdown; ruining. **срыва́ть**[1]**(ся** *impf of* **сорва́ть(ся**
срыва́ть[2] *impf*, **срыть** (сро́ю) *pf* raze to the ground.
с́ряду *adv* running.
сса́дина scratch. **ссади́ть** (-ажу́, -а́дишь) *pf*, **сса́живать** *impf* set down; help down; turn off.
ссо́ра quarrel. **ссо́рить** *impf* (*pf* **по~**) cause to quarrel; **~ся** quarrel.
СССР *abbr* (*of* **Сою́з Сове́тских Социалисти́ческих Респу́блик**) USSR.
ссу́да loan. **ссуди́ть** (-ужу́, -у́дишь) *pf*, **ссужа́ть** *impf* lend, loan.
ссыла́ть(ся *impf of* **сосла́ть(ся. ссы́лка**[1] exile. **ссы́лка**[2] reference. **ссы́льный, ссы́льная** *sb* exile.
ссы́пать (-плю) *pf*, **ссыпа́ть** *impf* pour.
стабилиза́тор stabilizer; tailplane. **стабилизи́ровать(ся** *impf* & *pf* stabilize. **стаби́льность** stability. **стаби́льный** stable, firm.
ста́вень (-вня; *gen pl* -вней) *m*, **ста́вня** (*gen pl* -вен) shutter.
ста́вить (-влю) *impf* (*pf* **по~**) put, place, set; stand; station; erect; install; apply; present, stage. **ста́вка**[1] rate; stake. **ста́вка**[2] headquarters.
ста́вня *see* **ста́вень**
стадио́н stadium.
ста́дия stage.
ста́дность herd instinct. **ста́дный** gregarious. **ста́до** (*pl* -а́) herd, flock.
стаж length of service; probation. **стажёр** probationer; student on a special non-degree course. **стажи-**

С

ро́вка period of training.
стака́н glass.
сталелите́йный steel-founding; **~ заво́д** steel foundry. **сталепла́вильный** steel-making; **~ заво́д** steel works. **сталепрока́тный** (steel-)rolling; **~ стан** rolling-mill.
ста́лкивать(ся *impf of* **столкну́ть(ся**
ста́ло быть *conj* consequently.
сталь steel. **стально́й** steel.
стаме́ска chisel.
стан[1] figure, torso.
стан[2] camp.
стан[3] mill.
станда́рт standard. **станда́ртный** standard.
стани́ца Cossack village.
станкострое́ние machine-tool engineering.
станови́ться (-влю́сь, -ви́шься) *impf of* **стать**[1]
стано́к (-нка́) machine tool, machine.
ста́ну *etc.*: *see* **стать**[2]
станцио́нный station. **ста́нция** station.
ста́пель (*pl* -я́) *m* stocks.
ста́птывать(ся *impf of* **стопта́ть(ся**
стара́ние effort. **стара́тельность** diligence. **стара́тельный** diligent. **стара́ться** *impf* (*pf* **по~**) try.
старе́ть *impf* (*pf* **по~, у~**) grow old. **ста́рец** (-рца) elder, (*venerable*) old man. **стари́к** (-а́) old man. **старина́** antiquity, olden times; antique(s); old fellow. **стари́нный** ancient; old; antique. **ста́рить** *impf* (*pf* **со~**) age, make old; **~ся** age, grow old.
старо- *in comb* old. **старове́р** Old Believer. **~жи́л** old resident. **~мо́дный** old-fashioned. **~славя́нский** Old Slavonic.
ста́роста head; monitor; churchwarden. **ста́рость** old age.
старт start; **на ~!** on your marks! **ста́ртёр** starter. **стартова́ть** *impf* & *pf* start. **ста́ртовый** starting.
стару́ха, стару́шка old woman. **ста́рческий** old man's; senile. **ста́рше** *comp of* **ста́рый. ста́рш|ий** oldest, eldest; older, elder; senior; head; **~ие** *sb pl* (one's) elders; **~ий** *sb* chief; man in charge. **старшина́** *m* sergeant-major; petty officer; leader. **ста́рый** (-ар, -а́, -о) old. **старьё** old things, junk.
ста́скивать *impf of* **стащи́ть**
с|тасова́ть *pf.*
стати́ст extra.
стати́стика statistics. **статисти́ческий** statistical.
ста́тный stately.
ста́тский civil, civilian.
ста́тус status. **ста́тус-кво́** *neut indecl* status quo.
статуэ́тка statuette.
ста́туя statue.
стать[1] (-а́ну) *pf* (*impf* **станови́ться**) stand; take up position; stop; cost; begin; +*instr* become; +**с**+*instr* become of; **не ~** *impers*+*gen* cease to be; disappear; **его́ не ста́ло** he is no more; **~ на коле́ни** kneel.
стать[2] physique, build.
ста́ться (-а́нется) *pf* happen.
статья́ (*gen pl* -е́й) article; clause; item; matter.
стациона́р permanent establishment; hospital. **стациона́рный** stationary; permanent; **~ больно́й** in-patient.
ста́чечник striker. **ста́чка** strike.
с|тащи́ть (-щу́, -щишь) *pf* (*impf also* **ста́скивать**) drag off, pull off.
ста́я flock; school, shoal; pack.
ствол (-а́) trunk; barrel.
ство́рка leaf, fold.
сте́бель (-бля; *gen pl* -бле́й) *m* stem, stalk.
стёган|ый quilted; **~ое одея́ло** quilt, duvet. **стега́ть**[1] *impf* (*pf* **вы́~**) quilt.
стега́ть[2] *impf*, **стегну́ть** (-ну́) *pf* (*pf also* **от~**) whip, lash.
стежо́к (-жка́) stitch.
стезя́ path, way.

стёк *etc.*: *see* **стечь. стека́ть(ся** *impf of* **сте́чь(ся**

стекло́ (*pl* -ёкла, -кол) glass; lens; (window-)pane.

стекло- *in comb* glass. **стекловолокно́** glass fibre. **~очисти́тель** *m* windscreen-wiper. **~ре́з** glass-cutter. **~тка́нь** fibreglass.

стекля́нный glass; glassy. **стеко́льщик** glazier.

стели́ть *see* **стлать**

стелла́ж (-а́) shelves, shelving.

сте́лька insole.

стелю́ *etc.*: *see* **стлать**

с|темне́ть (-е́ет) *pf*.

стена́ (*acc* -у; *pl* -ы, -а́м) wall. **стенгазе́та** wall newspaper.

стенд stand.

сте́нка wall; side. **стенно́й** wall.

стеногра́мма shorthand record. **стено́граф, стенографи́ст, ~ка** stenographer. **стенографи́ровать** *impf & pf* take down in shorthand. **стенографи́ческий** shorthand. **стеногра́фия** shorthand.

стенокарди́я angina.

степе́нный staid; middle-aged.

сте́пень (*gen pl* -е́й) degree; extent; power.

степно́й steppe. **степь** (*loc* -и́; *gen pl* -е́й) steppe.

стервя́тник vulture.

стерегу́ *etc.*: *see* **стере́чь**

сте́рео *indecl adj* stereo. **сте́рео-** *in comb* stereo. **стереоти́п** stereotype. **стереоти́пный** stereotype(d). **стереофони́ческий** stereo(phonic). **~фо́ния** stereo(phony).

стере́ть (сотру́, сотрёшь; стёр) *pf* (*impf* **стира́ть**¹) wipe off; rub out, rub sore; **~ся** rub off; wear down; be effaced.

стере́чь (-регу́, -режёшь; -ёг, -ла́) *impf* guard; watch for.

сте́ржень (-жня) *m* pivot; rod; core.

стерилизова́ть *impf & pf* sterilize. **стери́льный** sterile.

сте́рлинг sterling.

сте́рлядь (*gen pl* -е́й) sterlet.

стерпе́ть (-плю́, -пишь) *pf* bear, endure.

стёртый worn, effaced.

стесне́ние constraint. **стесни́тельный** shy; inconvenient. **с|тесни́ть** *pf*, **стесня́ть** *impf* constrain; hamper; inhibit. **с|тесни́ться** *pf*, **стесня́ться** *impf* (*pf also* **по~**) +*inf* feel too shy (to), be ashamed to.

стече́ние confluence; gathering; combination. **стечь** (-чёт; -ёк, -ла́) *pf* (*impf* **стека́ть**) flow down; **~ся** flow together; gather.

стилисти́ческий stylistic. **стиль** *m* style. **сти́льный** stylish; period.

сти́мул stimulus, incentive. **стимули́ровать** *impf & pf* stimulate.

стипе́ндия grant.

стира́льный washing.

стира́ть¹**(ся** *impf of* **стере́ть(ся**

стира́ть² *impf* (*pf* **вы́~**) wash, launder; **~ся** wash. **сти́рка** washing, wash, laundering.

сти́скивать *impf*, **сти́снуть** (-ну) *pf* squeeze; clench; hug.

стих (-а́) verse; line; *pl* poetry.

стиха́ть *impf of* **сти́хнуть**

стихи́йный elemental; spontaneous. **стихи́я** element.

сти́хнуть (-ну; стих) *pf* (*impf* **стиха́ть**) subside; calm down.

стихотворе́ние poem. **стихотво́рный** in verse form.

стлать, стели́ть (стелю́, сте́лешь) *impf* (*pf* **по~**) spread; **~ посте́ль** make a bed; **~ся** spread; creep.

сто (ста; *gen pl* сот) a hundred.

стог (*loc* -е & -у́; *pl* -а́) stack, rick.

сто́имость cost; value. **сто́ить** *impf* cost; be worth(while); deserve.

стой *see* **стоя́ть**

сто́йка counter, bar; prop; upright; strut. **сто́йкий** firm; stable; steadfast. **сто́йкость** firmness, stability; steadfastness. **сто́йло** stall. **стоймя́** *adv* upright.

сток flow; drainage; drain, gutter; sewer.

стол (-á) table; desk; cuisine.
столб (-á) post, pole, pillar, column. **столбене́ть** (-е́ю) *impf* (*pf* **о~**) be rooted to the ground. **столбня́к** (-á) stupor; tetanus.
столе́тие century; centenary. **столе́тний** hundred-year-old; of a hundred years.
столи́ца capital; metropolis. **столи́чный** (of the) capital.
столкнове́ние collision; clash. **столкну́ть** (-ну́, -нёшь) *pf* (*impf* **ста́лкивать**) push off, away; cause to collide; bring together; **~ся** collide, clash; +**с**+*instr* run into.
столо́вая *sb* dining-room; canteen. **столо́вый** table.
столп (-á) pillar.
столпи́ться *pf* crowd.
столь *adv* so. **сто́лько** *adv* so much, so many.
столя́р (-á) joiner, carpenter. **столя́рный** joiner's.
стомато́лог dentist.
стометро́вка (the) hundred metres.
стон groan. **стона́ть** (-ну́, -нешь) *impf* groan.
стоп! *int* stop!
стопа́[1] foot.
стопа́[2] (*pl* -ы) ream; pile.
сто́пка[1] pile.
сто́пка[2] small glass.
сто́пор stop, catch. **сто́пориться** *impf* (*pf* **за~**) come to a stop.
стопроце́нтный hundred-percent.
стоп-сигна́л brake-light.
стопта́ть (-пчу́, -пчешь) *pf* (*impf* **ста́птывать**) wear down; **~ся** wear down.
с|торгова́ть(ся *pf.*
сто́рож (*pl* -á) watchman, guard. **сторожево́й** watch; patrol-. **сторожи́ть** (-жу́) *impf* guard, watch (over).
сторона́ (*acc* сто́рону; *pl* сто́роны, -ро́н, -áм) side; direction; hand; feature; part; land; **в сто́рону** aside; **с моéй стороны́** for my part; **с одно́й стороны́** on the one hand. **сторони́ться** (-ню́сь, -ни́шься) *impf* (*pf* **по~**) stand aside; +*gen* avoid. **сторо́нник** supporter, advocate.
сто́чный sewage, drainage.
стоя́нка stop; parking; stopping place, parking space; stand; rank. **стоя́ть** (-ою́) *impf* (*pf* **по~**) stand; be; stay; stop; have stopped; +**за**+*acc* stand up for; **~ на колéнях** kneel. **стоя́чий** standing; upright; stagnant.
сто́ящий deserving; worthwhile.
стр. *abbr* (*of* **страни́ца**) page.
страда́ (*pl* -ды) (hard work at) harvest time.
страда́лец (-льца) sufferer. **страда́ние** suffering. **страда́тельный** passive. **страда́ть** (-а́ю *or* -ра́жду) *impf* (*pf* **по~**) suffer; **~ за** +*gen* feel for.
стра́жа guard, watch; **под стра́жей** under arrest, in custody; **стоя́ть на стра́же** +*gen* guard.
страна́ (*pl* -ы) country; land; **~ све́та** cardinal point.
страни́ца page.
стра́нник, стра́нница wanderer.
стра́нно *adv* strangely. **стра́нность** strangeness; eccentricity. **стра́нн|ый** (-а́нен, -анна́, -о) strange.
стра́нствие wandering. **стра́нствовать** *impf* wander.
Страстн|о́й of Holy Week; **~а́я пя́тница** Good Friday.
стра́стный (-тен, -тна́, -о) passionate. **страсть**[1] (*gen pl* -е́й) passion. **страсть**[2] *adv* awfully, frightfully.
стратеги́ческий strategic(al). **страте́гия** strategy.
стратосфе́ра stratosphere.
стра́ус ostrich.
страх fear.
страхова́ние insurance; **~ жи́зни** life insurance. **страхова́ть** *impf* (*pf* **за~**) insure (**от**+*gen* against); **~ся** insure o.s. **страхо́вка** insurance.
страши́ться (-шу́сь) *impf* +*gen* be afraid of. **стра́шно** *adv* awfully.

С

стра́шный (-шен, -шна́, -о) terrible, awful.

стрекоза́ (*pl* -ы) dragonfly.

стрекота́ть (-очу́, -о́чешь) *impf* chirr.

стрела́ (*pl* -ы) arrow; boom. **стреле́ц** (-льца́) Sagittarius. **стре́лка** pointer; hand; needle; arrow; spit; points. **стрелко́вый** rifle; shooting; infantry. **стрело́к** (-лка́) shot; rifleman, gunner. **стре́лочник** pointsman. **стрельба́** (*pl* -ы) shooting, firing. **стре́льчатый** lancet; arched. **стреля́ть** *impf* shoot; fire; **~ся** shoot o.s.; fight a duel.

стремгла́в *adv* headlong.

стреми́тельный swift; impetuous. **стреми́ться** (-млю́сь) *impf* strive. **стремле́ние** striving, aspiration. **стремни́на** rapid(s).

стре́мя (-мени; *pl* -мена́, -мя́н, -а́м) *neut* stirrup. **стремя́нка** stepladder.

стресс stress. **стре́ссовый** stressful, stressed.

стри́женый short; short-haired, cropped; shorn. **стри́жка** haircut; shearing. **стричь** (-игу́, -ижёшь; -иг) *impf* (*pf* **о~**) cut, clip; cut the hair of; shear; **~ся** have one's hair cut.

строга́ть *impf* (*pf* **вы́~**) plane, shave.

стро́гий strict; severe. **стро́гость** strictness.

строево́й combatant; line; drill. **строе́ние** building; structure; composition.

строжа́йший, стро́же *superl* & *comp of* **стро́гий**

строи́тель *m* builder. **строи́тельный** building, construction. **строи́тельство** building, construction; building site. **стро́ить** *impf* (*pf* **по~**) build; construct; make; base; draw up; **~ся** be built, be under construction; draw up; **стро́йся!** fall in! **строй** (*loc* -ю́; *pl* -и *or* -и́, -ев *or* -ёв) system; régime; structure; pitch; formation. **стро́йка** building; building-site. **стро́йность** proportion; harmony; balance, order. **стро́йный** (-о́ен, -ойна́, -о) harmonious, orderly, well-proportioned, shapely.

строка́ (*acc* -о́ку́; *pl* -и, -а́м) line; **кра́сная ~** new paragraph.

строп, стро́па sling; shroud line.

стропи́ло rafter, beam.

строптИ́вый refractory.

строфа́ (*pl* -ы, -а́м) stanza.

строчи́ть (-чу́, -о́чи́шь) *impf* (*pf* **на~, про~**) stitch; scribble, dash off. **стро́чка** stitch; line.

стро́ю *etc.*: *see* **стро́ить**

струга́ть *impf* (*pf* **вы́~**) plane. **стру́жка** shaving.

струи́ться *impf* stream.

структу́ра structure.

струна́ (*pl* -ы) string. **стру́нный** stringed.

струп (*pl* -пья, -пьев) scab.

с|тру́сить (-у́шу) *pf.*

стручо́к (-чка́) pod.

струя́ (*pl* -и, -уй) jet, spurt, stream.

стря́пать *impf* (*pf* **со~**) cook; concoct. **стряпня́** cooking.

стря́хивать *impf*, **стряхну́ть** (-ну́, -нёшь) *pf* shake off.

студени́стый jelly-like.

студе́нт, студе́нтка student. **студе́нческий** student.

сту́день (-дня) *m* jelly; aspic.

студи́ть (-ужу́, -у́дишь) *impf* (*pf* **о~**) cool.

сту́дия studio.

сту́жа severe cold, hard frost.

стук knock; clatter. **сту́кать** *impf*, **сту́кнуть** (-ну) *pf* knock; bang; strike; **~ся** knock (o.s.), bang. **стука́ч** (-а́) informer.

стул (*pl* -лья, -льев) chair. **стульча́к** (-а́) (*lavatory*) seat. **сту́льчик** stool.

сту́па mortar.

ступа́ть *impf*, **ступи́ть** (-плю́, -пишь) *pf* step; tread. **ступе́нчатый** stepped, graded. **ступе́нь** (*gen pl* -е́не́й) step, rung; stage, grade. **ступе́нька** step. **ступня́** foot; sole.

С

стуча́ть (-чу́) *impf* (*pf* **по~**) knock; chatter; pound; **~ся в**+*acc* knock at.
стушева́ться (-шу́юсь) *pf*, **стушёвываться** *impf* efface o.s.
с|туши́ть (-шу́, -шишь) *pf*.
стыд (-а́) shame. **стыди́ть** (-ыжу́) *impf* (*pf* **при~**) put to shame; **~ся** (*pf* **по~ся**) be ashamed. **стыдли́вый** bashful. **сты́дн|ый** shameful; **~о!** shame! **~о** *impers*+*dat* **ему́ ~о** he is ashamed; **как тебе́ не ~о!** you ought to be ashamed of yourself!
стык joint; junction. **стыкова́ть** *impf* (*pf* **со~**) join end to end; **~ся** (*pf* **при~ся**) dock. **сты-ко́вка** docking.
сты́нуть, стыть (-ы́ну; стыл) *impf* cool; get cold.
сты́чка skirmish; squabble.
стюарде́сса stewardess.
стя́гивать *impf*, **стяну́ть** (-ну́, -нешь) *pf* tighten; pull together; assemble; pull off; steal; **~ся** tighten; assemble.
стяжа́тель (-я) *m* money-grubber. **стяжа́ть** *impf* & *pf* gain, win.
суббо́та Saturday.
субсиди́ровать *impf* & *pf* subsidize. **субси́дия** subsidy.
субъе́кт subject; ego; person; character, type. **субъекти́вный** subjective.
сувени́р souvenir.
суверените́т sovereignty. **суве-ре́нный** sovereign.
сугли́нок (-нка) loam.
сугро́б snowdrift.
сугу́бо *adv* especially.
суд (-а́) court; trial; verdict.
суда́ *etc.*: *see* **суд, су́дно**[1]
суда́к (-а́) pike-perch.
суде́бный judicial; legal; forensic. **суде́йский** judge's; referee's, umpire's. **суди́мость** previous convictions. **суди́ть** (сужу́, су́дишь) *impf* judge; try; referee, umpire; foreordain; **~ся** go to law.
су́дно[1] (*pl* -да́, -о́в) vessel, craft.
су́дно[2] (*gen pl* -ден) bed-pan.
судово́й ship's; marine.
судомо́йка kitchen-maid; scullery.
судопроизво́дство legal proceedings.
су́дорога cramp, convulsion. **су́-дорожный** convulsive.
судострое́ние shipbuilding. **су-додстро́ительный** shipbuilding. **судохо́дный** navigable; shipping.
судьба́ (*pl* -ы, -деб) fate, destiny.
судья́ (*pl* -дьи, -де́й, -дьям) *m* judge; referee; umpire.
суеве́рие superstition. **суеве́р-ный** superstitious.
суета́ bustle, fuss. **суети́ться** (-ечу́сь) *impf* bustle, fuss. **суетли́-вый** fussy, bustling.
сужде́ние opinion; judgement.
суже́ние narrowing; constriction. **су́живать** *impf*, **су́зить** (-у́жу) *pf* narrow, contract; **~ся** narrow; taper.
сук (-а́, *loc* -у́; *pl* су́чья, -ьев *or* -и́, -о́в) bough.
су́ка bitch. **су́кин** *adj*: **~ сын** son of a bitch.
сукно́ (*pl* -а, -кон) cloth; **положи́ть под ~** shelve. **суко́нный** cloth; clumsy, crude.
сули́ть *impf* (*pf* **по~**) promise.
султа́н plume.
сумасбро́д, сумасбро́дка nutcase. **сумасбро́дный** wild, mad. **сумасбро́дство** wild behaviour. **сумасше́дш|ий** mad; **~ий** *sb*, **~ая** *sb* lunatic. **сумасше́ствие** madness.
сумато́ха turmoil; bustle.
сумбу́р confusion. **сумбу́рный** confused.
су́меречный twilight. **су́мерки** (-рек) *pl* twilight, dusk.
суме́ть (-е́ю) *pf* +*inf* be able to, manage to.
су́мка bag.
су́мма sum. **сумма́рный** summary; total. **сумми́ровать** *impf* & *pf* add up; summarize.
су́мрак twilight; murk. **су́мрач-ный** gloomy.

су́мчатый marsupial.
сунду́к (-а́) trunk, chest.
су́нуть(ся (-ну(сь) *pf of* **сова́ть(ся**
суп (*pl* -ы́) soup.
суперма́ркет supermarket.
суперобло́жка dust-jacket.
супру́г husband, spouse; *pl* husband and wife, (*married*) couple. **супру́га** wife, spouse. **супру́жеский** conjugal. **супру́жество** matrimony.
сургу́ч (-а́) sealing-wax.
сурди́нка mute; **под сурди́нку** on the sly.
суро́вость severity, sternness. **суро́вый** severe, stern; bleak; unbleached.
суро́к (-рка́) marmot.
суррога́т substitute.
су́слик ground-squirrel.
суста́в joint, articulation.
су́тки (-ток) *pl* twenty-four hours; a day.
су́толока commotion.
су́точн|ый daily; round-the-clock; **~ые** *sb pl* per diem allowance.
суту́литься *impf* stoop. **суту́лый** round-shouldered.
суть essence, main point.
С **суфлёр** prompter. **суфли́ровать** *impf +dat* prompt.
су́ффикс suffix.
суха́рь (-я́) *m* rusk; *pl* bread-crumbs. **су́хо** *adv* drily; coldly.
сухожи́лие tendon.
сухо́й (сух, -а́, -о) dry; cold. **сухопу́тный** land. **су́хость** dryness; coldness. **сухоща́вый** lean, skinny.
сучкова́тый knotty; gnarled. **сучо́к** (-чка́) twig; knot.
су́ша (dry) land. **су́ше** *comp of* **сухо́й. сушёный** dried. **суши́лка** dryer; drying-room. **суши́ть** (-шу́, -шишь) *impf* (*pf* **вы~**) dry, dry out, up; **~ся** (get) dry.
суще́ственный essential, vital. **существи́тельное** *sb* noun. **существо́** being, creature; essence. **существова́ние** existence. **существова́ть** *impf* exist. **су́щий** absolute, downright. **су́щность** essence.
сую́ *etc.*: *see* **сова́ть. с|фабрикова́ть** *pf.* **с|фальши́вить** (-влю) *pf.*
с|фантази́ровать *pf.*
сфе́ра sphere. **сфери́ческий** spherical.
сфинкс sphinx.
с|формирова́ть(ся *pf.* **с|формова́ть** *pf.* **с|формули́ровать** *pf.* **с|фотографи́ровать(ся** *pf.*
схвати́ть (-ачу́, -а́тишь) *pf,* **схва́тывать** *impf* (*impf also* **хвата́ть**) seize; catch; grasp; **~ся** snatch, catch; grapple. **схва́тка** skirmish; *pl* contractions.
схе́ма diagram; outline, plan; circuit. **схемати́ческий** schematic; sketchy. **схемати́чный** sketchy.
с|хитри́ть *pf.*
схлы́нуть (-нет) *pf* (break and) flow back; subside.
сход coming off; descent; gathering. **сходи́ть**[1]**(ся** (-ожу́(сь, -о́дишь(ся) *impf of* **сойти́(сь. сходи́ть**[2] (-ожу́, -о́дишь) *pf* go; **+за** *+instr* go to fetch. **схо́дка** gathering, meeting. **схо́дный** (-ден, -дна́, -о) similar; reasonable. **схо́дня** (*gen pl* -ей) (*usu pl*) gangplank. **схо́дство** similarity.
с|хорони́ть(ся (-ню́(сь, -нишь(ся) *pf.*
сцеди́ть (-ежу́, -е́дишь) *pf,* **сце́живать** *impf* strain off, decant.
сце́на stage; scene. **сцена́рий** scenario; script. **сценари́ст** script-writer. **сцени́ческий** stage.
сцепи́ть (-плю́, -пишь) *pf,* **сцепля́ть** *impf* couple; **~ся** be coupled; grapple. **сце́пка** coupling. **сцепле́ние** coupling; clutch.
счастли́вец (**-вца**), **счастли́вчик** lucky man. **счастли́вица** lucky woman. **счастли́в|ый** (сча́стлив) happy; lucky; **~о!** all the best!; **~ого пути́** bon voyage. **сча́стье** happiness; good fortune.
сче́сть(ся (сочту́(сь, -тёшь(ся;

счёл(ся, сочла́(сь) *pf of* **считáть(ся. счёт** (*loc* -ý; *pl* -á) bill; account; counting, calculation; score; expense. **счётный** calculating; accounts. **счетовóд** book-keeper, accountant. **счётчик** counter; meter. **счёты** (-ов) *pl* abacus.

счи́стить (-йщу) *pf* (*impf* **счищáть**) clean off; clear away.

считáть *impf* (*pf* **со~, счесть**) count; reckon; consider; **~ся** (*pf also* **по~ся**) settle accounts; be considered; +**с**+*instr* take into consideration; reckon with.

счищáть *impf of* **счи́стить**

США *pl indecl abbr* (*of* **Соединённые Штáты Амéрики**) USA.

сшибáть *impf*, **сшиби́ть** (-бý, -бёшь; сшиб) *pf* strike, hit, knock (off); **~ с ног** knock down; **~ся** collide; come to blows.

сшивáть *impf*, **с|шить** (сошью́, -ьёшь) *pf* sew (together).

съедáть *impf of* **съесть. съедóбный** edible; nice.

съéду *etc.*: *see* **съéхать**

съёживаться *impf*, **съ|ёжиться** (-жусь) *pf* shrivel, shrink.

съезд congress; conference; arrival. **съéздить** (-зжу) *pf* go, drive, travel.

съезжáть(ся *impf of* **съéхать(ся.**

съел *etc.*: *see* **съесть**

съёмка removal; survey, surveying; shooting. **съёмный** detachable, removable. **съёмщик, съёмщица** tenant; surveyor.

съестнóй food; **~óе** *sb* food (supplies). **съ|есть** (-ем, -ешь, -ест, -еди́м; съел) *pf* (*impf also* **съедáть**)

съéхать (-éду) *pf* (*impf* **съезжáть**) go down; come down; move; **~ся** meet; assemble.

съ|язви́ть (-влю́) *pf*.

сы́воротка whey; serum.

сыгрáть *pf of* **игрáть; ~ся** play (well) together.

сын (*pl* сыновья́, -вéй, -вья́м *or* -ы́, -óв) son. **сынóвний** filial. **сынóк** (-нкá) little son; sonny.

сы́пать (-плю) *impf* pour; pour forth; **~ся** fall; pour out; rain down; fray. **сыпнóй тиф** typhus. **сыпýчий** friable; free-flowing; shifting. **сыпь** rash, eruption.

сыр (*loc* -ý; *pl* -ы́) cheese.

сырéть (-éю) *impf* (*pf* **от~**) become damp.

сырéц (-рцá) raw product.

сыр|óй (сыр, -á, -о) damp; raw; uncooked; unboiled; unfinished; unripe. **сы́рость** dampness. **сырьё** raw material(s).

сыскáть (сыщý, сы́щешь) *pf* find.

сы́тный (-тен, -тнá, -о) filling. **сы́тость** satiety. **сы́тый** (сыт, -á, -о) full.

сыч (-á) little owl.

сы́щик detective.

с|эконóмить (-млю) *pf*.

сэр sir.

сюдá *adv* here, hither.

сюжéт subject; plot; topic. **сюжéтный** subject; having a theme.

сюи́та suite.

сюрпри́з surprise.

сюрреали́зм surrealism. **сюрреалисти́ческий** surrealist.

сюртýк (-á) frock-coat.

сяк *adv*: *see* **так. сям** *adv*: *see* **там**

С
Т

Т

та *see* **тот**

табáк (-á) tobacco. **табакéрка** snuff-box. **табáчный** tobacco.

тáбель (-я; *pl* -и, -ей *or* -я́, -éй) *m* table, list. **тáбельный** table; time.

таблéтка tablet.

табли́ца table; **~ умножéния** multiplication table.

тáбор (gipsy) camp.

табýн (-á) herd.

табурéт, табурéтка stool.

таврó (*pl* -а, -áм) brand.

тавтолóгия tautology.

таджик, -и́чка Tadzhik.

Таджикистáн Tadzhikistan.
таёжный taiga.
таз (*loc* -ý; *pl* -ы́) basin; pelvis. **тазобéдренный** hip. **тáзовый** pelvic.
таи́нственный mysterious; secret. **таи́ть** *impf* hide, harbour; **~ся** hide; lurk.
Тайвáнь *m* Taiwan.
тайгá taiga.
тайкóм *adv* secretly, surreptitiously; **~ от**+*gen* behind the back of.
тайм half; period of play.
тáйна secret; mystery. **тайни́к** (-á) hiding-place; *pl* recesses. **тáйный** secret; privy.
тайфу́н typhoon.
так *adv* so; like this; as it should be; just like that; **и ~** even so; as it is; **и ~ дáлее** and so on; **~ и сяк** this way and that; **не ~** wrong; **~ же** in the same way; **~ же... как** as … as; **~ и есть** I thought so!; **~ емý и нáдо** serves him right; **~ и́ли инáче** one way or another; **~ себé** so-so. **так** *conj* then; so; **~ как** as, since; **~ что** so.
такелáж rigging.
тáкже *adv* also, too, as well.
такóв *m* (-á *f*, -ó *neut*, -ы́ *pl*) *pron* such.
Т **так|óй** *pron* such (a); **в ~óм слу́чае** in that case; **кто он ~óй?** who is he?; **~óй же** the same; **~и́м óбразом** in this way; **что э́то ~óе?** what is this? **такóй-то** *pron* so-and-so; such-and-such.
тáкса fixed rate; tariff.
таксёр taxi-driver. **такси́** *neut indecl* taxi. **таксист** taxi-driver. **таксопáрк** taxi depot.
такт time; bar; beat; tact.
тáк-таки after all, really.
тáктика tactics. **такти́ческий** tactical.
такти́чность tact. **такти́чный** tactful.
тáктов|ый time, timing; **~ая чертá** bar-line.
талáнт talent. **талáнтливый** talented.
талисмáн talisman.
тáлия waist.
талóн, талóнчик coupon.
тáлый thawed, melted.
тальк talc; talcum powder.
там *adv* there; **~ и сям** here and there; **~ же** in the same place; ibid.
тамадá *m* toast-master.
тáмбур[1] tambour; lobby; platform. **тáмбур**[2] chain-stitch.
тамóженник customs official. **тамóженный** customs. **тамóжня** custom-house.
тáмошний of that place, local.
тампóн tampon.
тáнгенс tangent.
тáнго *neut indecl* tango.
тáнец (-нца) dance; dancing.
тани́н tannin.
танк tank. **тáнкер** tanker. **танки́ст** member of a tank crew. **тáнковый** tank, armoured.
танцевáльный dancing; **~ вéчер** dance. **танцевáть** (-цýю) *impf* dance. **танцóвщик, танцóвщица** (ballet) dancer. **танцóр, танцóрка** dancer.
тáпка, тáпочка slipper.
тáра packing; tare.
таракáн cockroach.
тарáн battering-ram.
тарáнтул tarantula.
тарéлка plate; cymbal; satellite dish.
тари́ф tariff.
таскáть *impf* drag, lug; carry; pull; take; pull out; swipe; wear; **~ся** drag; hang about.
тасовáть *impf* (*pf* **с~**) shuffle.
ТАСС *abbr* (*of* **Телеграфное агéнтство Совéтского Сою́за**) Tass (Telegraph Agency of the Soviet Union).
татáрин, татáрка Tatar.
татуирóвка tattooing, tattoo.
тафтá taffeta.
тахтá ottoman.
тáчка wheelbarrow.
тащи́ть (-щý, -щишь) *impf* (*pf* **вы́~, с~**) pull; drag, lug; carry;

take; pull out; swipe; **~ся** drag o.s. along; drag.

та́ять (та́ю) *impf* (*pf* **рас~**) melt; thaw; dwindle.

ТВ *abbr* (*of* **телеви́дение**) TV, television.

тварь creature(s); wretch.

тверде́ть (-е́ет) *impf* (*pf* **за~**) harden, become hard. **тверди́ть** (-ржу́) *impf* (*pf* **вы́~**) repeat, say again and again; memorize. **твёрдо** *adv* hard; firmly, firm. **твердоло́бый** thick-skulled; die-hard. **твёрдый** hard; firm; solid; steadfast; **~ знак** hard sign, ъ; **~ое те́ло** solid. **тверды́ня** stronghold.

твой (-его́) *m*, **твоя́** (-е́й) *f*, **твоё** (-его́) *neut*, **твои́** (-и́х) *pl* your, yours.

творе́ние creation, work; creature. **творе́ц** (-рца́) creator. **твори́тельный** instrumental. **твори́ть** *impf* (*pf* **со~**) create; do; make; **~ся** happen.

творо́г (-а́) curds; cottage cheese.

тво́рческий creative. **тво́рчество** creation; creative work; works.

те *see* **тот**

т.е. *abbr* (*of* **то есть**) that is, i.e.

теа́тр theatre. **театра́льный** theatre; theatrical.

тебя́ *etc.*: *see* **ты**

те́зис thesis.

тёзка *m* & *f* namesake.

тёк *see* **течь**

текст text; libretto, lyrics.

тексти́ль *m* textiles. **тексти́льный** textile.

тексту́ра texture.

теку́чий fluid; unstable. **теку́щий** current; routine.

теле- *in comb* tele-; television. **телеви́дение** television. **~визио́нный** television. **~ви́зор** television (set). **~гра́мма** telegram. **~гра́ф** telegraph (office). **~графи́ровать** *impf* & *pf* telegraph. **~гра́фный** telegraph(ic). **~зри́тель** *m* (television) viewer. **~объекти́в** telephoto lens. **~пати́ческий** telepathic. **~па́тия** telepathy. **~ско́п** telescope. **~ста́нция** television station. **~сту́дия** television studio. **~фо́н** telephone; (telephone) number; **(по)звони́ть по ~фо́ну** +*dat* ring up. **~фон-автома́т** public telephone, call-box. **~фони́ст, -и́стка** (telephone) operator. **~фо́нный** telephone; **~фо́нная кни́га** telephone directory; **~фо́нная ста́нция** telephone exchange; **~фо́нная тру́бка** receiver. **~фон-отве́тчик** answering machine. **~це́нтр** television centre.

теле́га cart, wagon. **теле́жка** small cart; trolley.

те́лекс telex.

телёнок (-нка; *pl* -я́та, -я́т) calf.

теле́сн|ый bodily; corporal; **~ого цве́та** flesh-coloured.

Теле́ц (-льца́) Taurus.

тели́ться *impf* (*pf* **о~**) calve. **тёлка** heifer.

те́ло (*pl* -а́) body. **телогре́йка** padded jacket. **телосложе́ние** build. **телохрани́тель** *m* bodyguard.

теля́та *etc.*: *see* **телёнок. теля́тина** veal. **теля́чий** calf; veal.

тем *conj* (so much) the; **~ лу́чше** so much the better; **~ не ме́нее** nevertheless.

тем *see* **тот, тьма**

те́ма subject; theme. **тема́тика** subject-matter; themes. **темати́ческий** subject; thematic.

тембр timbre.

темне́ть (-е́ет) *impf* (*pf* **по~, с~**) become dark. **темни́ца** dungeon. **темно́** *predic* it is dark. **темноко́жий** dark-skinned, swarthy. **тёмно-си́ний** dark blue. **темнота́** darkness. **тёмный** dark.

темп tempo; rate.

темпера́мент temperament. **темпера́ментный** temperamental.

температу́ра temperature.

те́мя (-мени) *neut* crown, top of the head.

Т

тенде́нция tendency; bias.
тенево́й, тени́стый shady.
те́ннис tennis. **теннеси́ст, -и́стка** tennis-player. **те́ннисн|ый** tennis; **~ая площа́дка** tennis-court.
те́нор (*pl* -а́) tenor.
тент awning.
тень (*loc* -и́; *pl* -и, -е́й) shade; shadow; phantom; ghost; particle, vestige, atom; suspicion; **те́ни для век** *pl* eyeshadow.
тео́лог theologian. **теологи́ческий** theological. **теоло́гия** theology.
теоре́ма theorem. **теоре́тик** theoretician. **теорети́ческий** theoretical. **тео́рия** theory.
тепе́решн|ий present. **тепе́рь** *adv* now; today.
тепле́ть (-е́ет) *impf* (*pf* **по~**) get warm. **те́плиться** (-ится) *impf* flicker; glimmer. **тепли́ца** greenhouse, conservatory. **тепли́чный** hothouse. **тепло́** heat; warmth. **тепло́** *adv* warmly; *predic* it is warm.
тепло- *in comb* heat; thermal; thermo-. **теплово́з** diesel locomotive. **~кро́вный** warm-blooded. **~обме́н** heat exchange. **~прово́дный** heat-conducting. **~сто́йкий** heat-resistant. **~хо́д** motor ship. **~центра́ль** heat and power station.

Т

теплово́й heat; thermal. **теплота́** heat; warmth. **тёплый** (-пел, -пла́, тёпло́) warm.
тера́кт terrorist act.
терапе́вт therapeutist. **терапи́я** therapy.
тереби́ть (-блю́) *impf* pull (at); pester.
тере́ть (тру, трёшь; тёр) *impf* rub; grate; **~ся** rub o.s.; **~ся о́коло** +*gen* hang about, hang around; **~ся среди́** +*gen* mix with.
терза́ть *impf* tear to pieces; torment; **~ся** +*instr* suffer; be a prey to.
тёрка grater.
те́рмин term. **терминоло́гия** terminology.
терми́ческий thermic, thermal. **термо́метр** thermometer. **те́рмос** thermos (flask). **термоста́т** thermostat. **термоя́дерный** thermonuclear.
терно́вник sloe, blackthorn. **терни́стый** thorny.
терпели́вый patient. **терпе́ние** patience. **терпе́ть** (-плю́, -пишь) *impf* (*pf* **по~**) suffer; bear, endure. **терпе́ться** (-пится) *impf impers*+*dat*: **ему́ не те́рпится** +*inf* he is impatient to. **терпи́мость** tolerance. **терпи́мый** tolerant; tolerable.
те́рпкий (-пок, -пка́, -о) astringent; tart.
терра́са terrace.
территориа́льный territorial. **террито́рия** territory.
терро́р terror. **терроризи́ровать** *impf* & *pf* terrorize. **террори́ст** terrorist.
тёртый grated; experienced.
терье́р terrier.
теря́ть *impf* (*pf* **по~, у~**) lose; shed; **~ся** get lost; disappear; fail, decline; become flustered.
тёс boards, planks. **теса́ть** (тешу́, те́шешь) *impf* cut, hew.
тесёмка ribbon, braid.
тесни́ть *impf* (*pf* **по~, с~**) crowd; squeeze, constrict; be too tight; **~ся** press through; move up; crowd, jostle. **теснота́** crowded state; crush. **те́сн|ый** crowded; (too) tight; close; compact; **~о** it is crowded.
тесо́вый board, plank.
тест test.
те́сто dough; pastry.
тесть *m* father-in-law.
тесьма́ ribbon, braid.
те́терев (*pl* -а́) black grouse. **тетёрка** grey hen.
тётка aunt.
тетра́дка, тетра́дь exercise book.
тётя (*gen pl* -ей) aunt.
тех- *abbr in comb* (*of* **техни́ческий**) technical.
те́хник technician. **те́хника** tech-

nical equipment; technology; technique. **тéхникум** technical college. **техни́ческ|ий** technical; **~ие услóвия** specifications. **технóлог** technologist. **технологи́ческий** technological. **техноло́гия** technology. **техперсонáл** technical personnel.

течéние flow; course; current, stream; trend.

течь[1] (-чёт; тёк, -лá) *impf* flow; stream; leak. **течь**[2] leak.

тéшить (-шу) *impf* (*pf* **по~**) amuse; gratify; **~ся** (+*instr*) amuse o.s. (with).

тешу́ *etc.*: *see* **тесáть**

тёща mother-in-law.

тигр tiger. **тигри́ца** tigress.

тик[1] tic.

тик[2] teak.

ти́на slime, mud.

тип type. **типи́чный** typical. **типовóй** standard; model. **типогрáфия** printing-house, press. **типогрáфский** typographical.

тир shooting-range, -gallery.

ти́раж (-á) draw; circulation; edition.

тирáн tyrant. **тирáнить** *impf* tyrannize. **тирани́ческий** tyrannical. **тирани́я** tyranny.

тирé *neut indecl* dash.

ти́скать *impf*, **ти́снуть (-ну)** *pf* press, squeeze. **тиски́** (-óв) *pl* vice; **в тискáх** +*gen* in the grip of. **тиснéние** stamping; imprint; design. **тиснёный** stamped.

титáн[1] titanian.

титáн[2] boiler.

титáн[3] titan.

титр title, sub-title.

ти́тул title; title-page. **ти́тульный** title.

тиф (*loc* -ý) typhus.

ти́хий (тих, -á, -о) quiet; silent; calm; slow. **тихоокеáнский** Pacific. **ти́ше** *comp of* **ти́хий, ти́хо; ти́ше!** quiet! **тишинá** quiet, silence.

т. к. *abbr* (*of* **так как**) as, since.

ткáный woven. **ткань** fabric, cloth; tissue. **ткать** (тку, ткёшь; -ал, -áлá, -о) *impf* (*pf* **со~**) weave. **ткáцкий** weaving; **~ станóк** loom. **ткач, ткачи́ха** weaver.

ткну́ть(ся (-у(сь, -ёшь(ся) *pf of* **ты́кать(ся**

тлéние decay; smouldering. **тлеть** (-éет) *impf* rot, decay; smoulder; **~ся** smoulder.

тля aphis.

тмин caraway(-seeds).

то *pron* that; **а не тó** or else, otherwise; **(да) и тó** and even then, and that; **тó есть** that is (to say); **то и дéло** every now and then. **то** *conj* then; **не то..., не то** either … or; half …, half; **то..., то** now …, now; **то ли..., то ли** whether … or.

-то *partl* just, exactly; **в тóм-то и дéло** that's just it.

тобóй *see* **ты**

товáр goods; commodity.

товáрищ comrade; friend; colleague. **товáрищеский** comradely; friendly.

товáрищество comradeship; company; association.

товáрный goods; commodity.

товаро- *in comb* commodity; goods. **товарообмéн** barter. **~оборóт** (sales) turnover. **~отправи́тель** *m* consignor. **~получáтель** *m* consignee.

тогдá *adv* then; **~ как** whereas. **тогдáшний** of that time.

тогó *see* **тот**

тождéственный identical. **тóждество** identity.

тóже *adv* also, too.

ток (*pl* -и) current.

токáрный turning; **~ станóк** lathe. **тóкарь** (*pl* -я́, -éй *or* -и, -ей) *m* turner, lathe operator.

токси́ческий toxic.

толк sense; use; **бéз ~у** senselessly; **знать ~ в**+*prep* know well; **сбить с ~у** confuse; **с ~ом** intelligently.

толкáть *impf* (*pf* **толкну́ть**) push, shove; jog; **~ся** jostle.

тóлки (-ов) *pl* rumours, gossip.

толкну́ть(ся (-ну́(сь, -нёшь(ся) *pf of* **толкáть(ся**

Т

толкова́ние interpretation; *pl* commentary. **толкова́ть** *impf* interpret; explain; talk. **толко́вый** intelligent; clear; **~ слова́рь** defining dictionary. **то́лком** *adv* plainly; seriously.

толкотня́ crush, squash.

толку́ *etc.*: *see* **толо́чь**

толку́чка crush, squash; second-hand market.

толокно́ oatmeal.

толо́чь (-лку́, -лчёшь; -ло́к, -лкла́) *impf* (*pf* **ис~, рас~**) pound, crush.

толпа́ (*pl* -ы) crowd. **толпи́ться** *impf* crowd; throng.

толсте́ть (-е́ю) *impf* (*pf* **по~**) grow fat; put on weight. **толстоко́жий** thick-skinned; pachydermatous. **то́лстый** (-а́, -о) fat; thick. **толстя́к** (-а́) fat man *or* boy.

толчёный crushed; ground. **толчёт** *etc.*: *see* **толо́чь**

толчея́ crush, squash.

толчо́к (-чка́) push, shove; (*sport*) put; jolt; shock, tremor.

то́лща thickness; thick. **то́лще** *comp of* **то́лстый. толщина́** thickness; fatness.

толь *m* roofing felt.

Т **то́лько** *adv* only, merely; **~ что** (only) just; *conj* only, but; **(как) ~, (лишь) ~** as soon as; **~ бы** if only.

том (*pl* **~а́**) volume. **то́мик** small volume.

тома́т tomato. **тома́тный** tomato.

томи́тельный tedious, wearing; agonizing. **томи́ть (-млю́)** *impf* (*pf* **ис~**) tire; torment; **~ся** languish; be tormented. **томле́ние** languor. **то́мный** (-мен, -мна́, -о) languid, languorous.

тон (*pl* -а́ *or* -ы, -о́в) tone; note; shade; form. **тона́льность** key.

то́ненький thin; slim. **то́нкий** (-нок, -нка́, -о) thin; slim; fine; refined; subtle; keen. **то́нкость** thinness; slimness; fineness; subtlety.

то́нна ton.

тонне́ль *see* **тунне́ль**

то́нус tone.

тону́ть (-ну́, -нешь) *impf* (*pf* **по~, у~**) sink; drown.

то́ньше *comp of* **то́нкий**

то́пать *impf* (*pf* **то́пнуть**) stamp.

топи́ть[1] (-плю́, -пишь) *impf* (*pf* **по~, у~**) sink; drown; ruin; **~ся** drown o.s.

топи́ть[2] (-плю́, -пишь) *impf* stoke; heat; melt (down); **~ся** burn; melt. **то́пка** stoking; heating; melting (down); furnace.

то́пкий boggy, marshy.

то́пливный fuel. **то́пливо** fuel.

то́пнуть (-ну) *pf of* **то́пать**

топографи́ческий topographical. **топогра́фия** topography.

то́поль (*pl* -я́ *or* -и) *m* poplar.

топо́р (-а́) axe. **топо́рик** hatchet. **топори́ще** axe-handle. **топо́рный** axe; clumsy, crude.

то́пот tramp; clatter. **топта́ть** (-пчу́, -пчешь) *impf* (*pf* **по~**) trample (down); **~ся** stamp; **~ся на ме́сте** mark time.

топча́н (-а́) trestle-bed.

топь bog, marsh.

торг (*loc* -у́; *pl* -и́) trading; bargaining; *pl* auction. **торгова́ть** *impf* (*pf* **с~**) trade; **~ся** bargain, haggle. **торго́вец** (-вца) merchant; tradesman. **торго́вка** market-woman; stall-holder. **торго́вля** trade. **торго́вый** trade, commercial; merchant. **торгпре́д** *abbr* trade representative.

торе́ц (-рца́) butt-end; wooden paving-block.

торже́ственный solemn; ceremonial. **торжество́** celebration; triumph. **торжествова́ть** *impf* celebrate; triumph.

торможе́ние braking. **то́рмоз** (*pl* -а́ *or* -ы) brake. **тормози́ть** (-ожу́) *impf* (*pf* **за~**) brake; hamper.

тормоши́ть (-шу́) *impf* pester; bother.

торопи́ть (-плю́, -пишь) *impf* (*pf* **по~**) hurry; hasten; **~ся** hurry.

торопли́вый hasty.
торпе́да torpedo.
торс torso.
торт cake.
торф peat. **торфяно́й** peat.
торча́ть (-чу́) *impf* stick out; protrude; hang about.
торше́р standard lamp.
тоска́ melancholy; boredom; nostalgia; **~ по**+*dat* longing for. **тоскли́вый** melancholy; depressed; dreary. **тоскова́ть** *impf* be melancholy, depressed; long; **~ по**+*dat* miss.
тост toast.
тот *m* (та *f*, то *neut*, те *pl*) *pron* that; the former; the other; the one; the same; the right; **и ~ и друго́й** both; **к тому́ же** moreover; **не ~** the wrong; **ни ~ ни друго́й** neither; **тот, кто** the one who, the person who. **то́тчас** *adv* immediately.
тоталитари́зм totalitarianism. **тоталита́рный** totalitarian.
тота́льный total.
точи́лка sharpener; pencil-sharpener. **точи́ло** whetstone, grindstone. **точи́льный** grinding, sharpening; **~ ка́мень** whetstone, grindstone. **точи́льщик** (knife-)grinder. **точи́ть** (-чу́, -чишь) *impf* (*pf* **вы́~, на~**) sharpen; hone; turn; eat away; gnaw at.
то́чка spot; dot; full stop; point; **~ зре́ния** point of view; **~ с запято́й** semicolon. **то́чно**[1] *adv* exactly, precisely; punctually. **то́чно**[2] *conj* as though, as if. **то́чность** punctuality; precision; accuracy; **в то́чности** exactly, precisely. **то́чный** (-чен, -чна́, -о) exact, precise; accurate; punctual. **то́чь-в-то́чь** *adv* exactly; word for word.
тошни́ть *impf impers*: **меня́ тошни́т** I feel sick. **тошнота́** nausea. **тошнотво́рный** sickening, nauseating.
то́щий (тощ, -á, -e) gaunt, emaciated; skinny; empty; poor.
трава́ (*pl* -ы) grass; herb. **трави́нка** blade of grass.
трави́ть (-влю, -вишь) *impf* (*pf* **вы́~, за~**) poison; exterminate, destroy; etch; hunt; torment; badger. **травле́ние** extermination; etching. **тра́вля** hunting; persecution; badgering.
тра́вма trauma, injury.
травоя́дный herbivorous. **травяни́стый, травяно́й** grass; herbaceous; grassy.
траге́дия tragedy. **тра́гик** tragedian. **траги́ческий, траги́чный** tragic.
традицио́нный traditional. **тради́ция** tradition.
траекто́рия trajectory.
тракта́т treatise; treaty.
тракти́р inn, tavern.
трактова́ть *impf* interpret; treat, discuss. **тракто́вка** treatment; interpretation.
тра́ктор tractor. **трактори́ст** tractor driver.
трал trawl. **тра́лить** *impf* (*pf* **про~**) trawl; sweep. **тра́льщик** trawler; mine-sweeper.
трамбова́ть *impf* (*pf* **у~**) ram, tamp.
трамва́й tram. **трамва́йный** tram.
трампли́н spring-board; ski-jump.
транзи́стор transistor; transistor radio.
транзи́тный transit.
транс trance.
трансатланти́ческий transatlantic.
трансли́ровать *impf* & *pf* broadcast, transmit. **трансляцио́нный** transmission; broadcasting. **трансля́ция** broadcast, transmission.
тра́нспорт transport; consignment. **транспортёр** conveyor. **транспорти́р** protractor. **транспорти́ровать** *impf* & *pf* transport. **тра́нспортный** transport.
трансформа́тор transformer.

траншéя trench.
трап ladder.
трáпеза meal.
трапéция trapezium; trapeze.
трáсса line, course, direction; route, road.
трáта expenditure; waste. **трáтить** (-áчу) *impf* (*pf* **ис~, по~**) spend, expend; waste.
трáулер trawler.
трáур mourning. **трáурный** mourning; funeral; mournful.
трафарéт stencil; stereotype; cliché. **трафарéтный** stencilled; conventional, stereotyped.
трáчу *etc.*: *see* **трáтить**
трéбование demand; request; requirement; requisition, order; *pl* needs. **трéбовательный** demanding. **трéбовать** *impf* (*pf* **по~**) summon; +*gen* demand, require; need; **~ся** be needed, be required.
тревóга alarm; anxiety. **тревóжить** (-жу) *impf* (*pf* **вс~, по~**) alarm; disturb; worry; **~ся** worry, be anxious; trouble o.s. **тревóжный** worried, anxious; alarming; alarm.
трéзвенник teetotaller. **трезвéть** (-éю) *impf* (*pf* **о~**) sober up.
трезвóн peal (*of bells*); rumours; row.
трéзвость sobriety. **трéзвый** (-зв, -á, -о) sober; teetotal.
трéйлер trailer.
трель trill; warble.
трéнер trainer, coach.
трéние friction.
тренировáть *impf* (*pf* **на~**) train, coach; **~ся** be in training. **тренирóвка** training, coaching. **тренирóвочный** training.
трепáть (-плю, -плешь) *impf* (*pf* **ис~, по~, рас~**) blow about; dishevel; wear out; pat; **~ся** fray; wear out; flutter. **трéпет** trembling; trepidation. **трепетáть** (-ещý, -éщешь) *impf* tremble; flicker; palpitate. **трéпетный** trembling; flickering; palpitating; timid.
треск crack; crackle; fuss.
трескá cod.
трéскаться[1] *impf* (*pf* **по~**) crack; chap.
трéскаться[2] *impf of* **трéснуться**
трéснуть (-нет) *pf* snap, crackle; crack; chap; bang; **~ся** (*impf* **трéскаться**) +*instr* bang.
трест trust.
трéт|ий (-ья, -ье) third; **~ье** *sb* sweet (course).
третировать *impf* slight.
треть (*gen pl* -éй) third. **трéтье** *etc.*: *see* **трéтий**. **треугóльник** triangle. **треугóльный** triangular.
трéфы (треф) *pl* clubs.
трёх- *in comb* three-, tri-. **трёхгодичный** three-year. **~голóсный** three-part. **~грáнный** three-edged; trihedral. **~колёсный** three-wheeled. **~лéтний** three-year; three-year old. **~мéрный** three-dimensional. **~мéсячный** three-month; quarterly; three-month-old. **~пóлье** three-field system. **~сóтый** three-hundredth. **~сторóнний** three-sided; trilateral; tripartite. **~этáжный** three-storeyed.
трещáть (-щý) *impf* crack; crackle; creak; chirr; crack up; chatter. **трéщина** crack, split; fissure; chap.
три (трёх, -ём, -емя́, -ёх) three.
трибýна platform, rostrum; stand. **трибунáл** tribunal.
тригономéтрия trigonometry.
тридцатилéтний thirty-year; thirty-year old. **тридцáтый** thirtieth. **три́дцать** (-и́, *instr* -ью) thirty. **три́жды** *adv* three times; thrice.
трикó *neut indecl* tricot; tights; knickers. **трикотáж** knitted fabric; knitwear. **трикотáжный** jersey, tricot; knitted.
тринáдцатый thirteenth. **тринáдцать** thirteen. **триóль** triplet.
три́ппер gonorrhoea.
три́ста (трёхсóт, -ёмстáм, -емястáми, -ёхстáх) three hundred.

трито́н *zool* triton.
триу́мф triumph.
тро́гательный touching, moving. **тро́гать(ся** *impf of* **тро́нуть(ся**
тро́е (-и́х) *pl* three. **троебо́рье** triathlon. **троекра́тный** thrice-repeated. **Тро́ица** Trinity; **тро́ица** trio. **Тро́ицын день** Whit Sunday. **тро́йка** three; figure 3; troika; No. 3; three-piece suit. **тройно́й** triple, treble; three-ply. **тро́йственный** triple; tripartite.
тролле́йбус trolley-bus.
тромб blood clot.
тромбо́н trombone.
трон throne.
тро́нуть (-ну) *pf* (*impf* **тро́гать**) touch; disturb; affect; **~ся** start, set out; be touched; be affected.
тропа́ path.
тро́пик tropic.
тропи́нка path.
тропи́ческий tropical.
трос rope, cable.
тростни́к (-а́) reed, rush. **тро́сточка, трость** (*gen pl* **~е́й**) cane, walking-stick.
тротуа́р pavement.
трофе́й trophy; *pl* spoils (*of war*), booty.
трою́родн|ый: ~ый брат, ~ая сестра́ second cousin.
тру *etc.*: *see* **тере́ть**
труба́ (*pl* -ы) pipe; chimney; funnel; trumpet; tube. **труба́ч** (-а́) trumpeter; trumpet-player. **труби́ть** (-блю́) *impf* (*pf* **про~**) blow, sound; blare. **тру́бка** tube; pipe; (*telephone*) receiver. **трубопрово́д** pipe-line; piping; manifold. **трубочи́ст** chimney-sweep. **тру́бочный** pipe. **тру́бчатый** tubular.
труд (-а́) labour; work; effort; **с ~о́м** with difficulty. **труди́ться** (-ужу́сь, -у́дишься) *impf* toil, labour, work; trouble. **тру́дно** *predic* it is difficult. **тру́дность** difficulty. **тру́дный** (-ден, -дна́, -о) difficult; hard.
трудо- *in comb* labour, work. **трудоде́нь** (-дня́) *m* work-day (*unit*). **~ёмкий** labour-intensive. **~люби́вый** industrious. **~лю́бие** industry. **~спосо́бность** ability to work. **~спосо́бный** able-bodied; capable of working.
трудово́й work; working; earned; hard-earned. **трудя́щ|ийся** working; **~иеся** *sb pl* the workers. **тру́женик, тру́женица** toiler.
труп corpse; carcass.
тру́ппа troupe, company.
трус coward.
тру́сики (-ов) *pl* shorts; trunks; pants.
труси́ть[1] (-ушу́) *impf* trot, jog along.
тру́сить[2] (-у́шу) *impf* (*pf* **с~**) be a coward; lose one's nerve; be afraid. **труси́ха** coward. **трусли́вый** cowardly. **тру́сость** cowardice.
трусы́ (-о́в) *pl* shorts; trunks; pants.
труха́ dust; trash.
тру́шу́ *etc.*: *see* **труси́ть**[1], **тру́сить**[2]
трущо́ба slum; godforsaken hole.
трюк stunt; trick.
трюм hold.
трюмо́ *neut indecl* pier-glass.
трю́фель (*gen pl* -ле́й) *m* truffle.
тря́пка rag; spineless creature; *pl* clothes. **тряпьё** rags; clothes.
тряси́на quagmire. **тря́ска** shaking, jolting. **трясти́** (-су́, -сёшь; -яс, -ла́) *impf*, **тряхну́ть** (-ну́, -нёшь) *pf* (*pf also* **вы~**) shake; shake out; jolt; **~сь** shake; tremble, shiver; jolt.
тсс *int* sh! hush!
туале́т dress; toilet. **туале́тный** toilet.
туберкулёз tuberculosis.
ту́го *adv* tight(ly), taut; with difficulty. **туго́й** (туг, -а́, -о) tight; taut; tightly filled; difficult.
туда́ *adv* there, thither; that way; to the right place; **ни ~ ни сюда́** neither one way nor the other; **~ и обра́тно** there and back.

ту́же *comp of* **ту́го, туго́й**
тужу́рка (double-breasted) jacket.
туз (-а́, *acc* -а́) ace; bigwig.
тузе́мец (-мца), **-мка** native.
ту́ловище trunk; torso.
тулу́п sheepskin coat.
тума́н fog; mist; haze. **тума́нить** *impf* (*pf* **за~**) dim, cloud, obscure; **~ся** grow misty; be befogged. **тума́нность** fog, mist; nebula; obscurity. **тума́нный** foggy; misty; hazy; obscure, vague.
ту́мба post; bollard; pedestal. **ту́мбочка** bedside table.
ту́ндра tundra.
тунея́дец (-дца) sponger.
туни́ка tunic.
тунне́ль *m*, **тонне́ль** *m* tunnel.
тупе́ть (-е́ю) *impf* (*pf* **о~**) become blunt; grow dull. **тупи́к** (-а́) cul-de-sac, dead end; impasse; **поста́вить в ~** stump, nonplus. **тупи́ться** (-пится) *impf* (*pf* **за~, ис~**) become blunt. **тупи́ца** *m* & *f* blockhead, dimwit. **тупо́й** (туп, -а́, -о) blunt; obtuse; dull; vacant, stupid. **ту́пость** bluntness; vacancy; dullness, slowness.
тур turn; round.
тура́ rook, castle.
турба́за holiday village, campsite.
турби́на turbine.
туре́цкий Turkish; **~ бараба́н** bass drum.
тури́зм tourism. **тури́ст, -и́стка** tourist. **тури́ст(и́че)ский** tourist.
туркме́н (*gen pl* **-ме́н**), **~ка** Turkmen. **Туркмениста́н** Turkmenistan.
турне́ *neut indecl* tour.
турне́пс swede.
турни́р tournament.
ту́рок (-рка) Turk. **турча́нка** Turkish woman. **Ту́рция** Turkey.
ту́склый dim, dull; lacklustre. **тускне́ть** (-е́ет) *impf* (*pf* **по~**) grow dim.
тут *adv* here; now; **~ же** there and then.
ту́фля shoe.
ту́хлый (-хл, -а́, -о) rotten, bad. **ту́хнуть**[1] (-нет; тух) go bad.
ту́хнуть[2] (-нет; тух) *impf* (*pf* **по~**) go out.
ту́ча cloud; storm-cloud.
ту́чный (-чен, -чна́, -чно) fat; rich, fertile.
туш flourish.
ту́ша carcass.
тушева́ть (-шу́ю) *impf* (*pf* **за~**) shade.
тушёный stewed. **туши́ть**[1] (-шу́, -шишь) *impf* (*pf* **с~**) stew.
туши́ть[2] (-шу́, -шишь) *impf* (*pf* **за~, по~**) extinguish.
тушу́ю *etc.*: *see* **тушева́ть. тушь** Indian ink; **~ (для ресни́ц)** mascara.
тща́тельность care. **тща́телный** careful; painstaking.
тщеду́шный feeble, frail.
тщесла́вие vanity, vainglory. **тщесла́вный** vain. **тщета́** vanity. **тще́тный** vain, futile.
ты (тебя́, тебе́, тобо́й, тебе́) you; thou; **быть на ты с**+*instr* be on intimate terms with.
ты́кать (ты́чу) *impf* (*pf* **ткнуть**) poke; prod; stick.
ты́ква pumpkin; gourd.
тыл (*loc* -у́; *pl* -ы́) back; rear. **ты́льный** back; rear.
тын paling; palisade.
ты́сяча (*instr* -ей *or* -ью) thousand. **тысячеле́тие** millennium; thousandth anniversary. **ты́сячный** thousandth; of (many) thousands.
тычи́нка stamen.
тьма[1] dark, darkness.
тьма[2] host, multitude.
тюбете́йка skull-cap.
тю́бик tube.
тюк (-а́) bale, package.
тюле́нь *m* seal.
тюльпа́н tulip.
тюре́мный prison. **тюре́мщик** gaoler. **тюрьма́** (*pl* -ы, -рем) prison, gaol.
тюфя́к (-а́) mattress.
тя́га traction; thrust; draught; at-

traction; craving. **тяга́ться** *impf* vie, contend. **тяга́ч** (-а́) tractor.

тя́гостный burdensome; painful. **тя́гость** burden. **тяготе́ние** gravity, gravitation; bent, inclination. **тяготе́ть** (-е́ю) *impf* gravitate; be attracted; **~ над** hang over. **тяготи́ть** (-ощу́) *impf* be a burden on; oppress.

тягу́чий malleable, ductile; viscous; slow.

тя́жба lawsuit; competition.

тяжело́ *adv* heavily; seriously. **тяжело́** *predic* it is hard; it is painful. **тяжелоатле́т** weight-lifter. **тяжелове́с** heavyweight. **тяжелове́сный** heavy; ponderous. **тяжёлый** (-ёл, -а́) heavy; hard; serious; painful. **тя́жесть** gravity; weight; heaviness; severity. **тя́жкий** heavy; severe; grave.

тяну́ть (-ну́, -нешь) *impf* (*pf* **по~**) pull; draw; drag; drag out; weigh; *impers* attract; be tight; **~ся** stretch; extend; stretch out; stretch o.s.; drag on; crawl; drift; move along one after another; last out; reach.

тяну́чка toffee.

У

у *prep+gen* by; at; with; from, of; belonging to; **у меня́ (есть)** I have; **у нас** at our place; in our country.

уба́вить (-влю) *pf*, **убавля́ть** *impf* reduce, diminish.

у|баю́кать *pf*, **убаю́кивать** *impf* lull (to sleep).

убега́ть *impf of* **убежа́ть**

убеди́тельный convincing; earnest. **убеди́ть** (-и́шь) *pf* (*impf* **убежда́ть**) convince; persuade; **~ся** be convinced; make certain.

убежа́ть (-егу́) *pf* (*impf* **убега́ть**) run away; escape; boil over.

убежда́ть(ся *impf of* **убеди́ть(ся. убежде́ние** persuasion; conviction, belief. **убеждённость** conviction. **убеждённый** (-ён, -а́) convinced; staunch.

убе́жище refuge, asylum; shelter.

уберега́ть *impf*, **убере́чь** (-регу́, -режёшь; -рёг, -гла́) *pf* protect, preserve; **~ся от**+*gen* protect o.s. against.

уберу́ *etc.*: *see* **убра́ть**

убива́ть(ся *impf of* **уби́ть(ся. уби́йственный** deadly; murderous; killing. **уби́йство** murder. **уби́йца** *m* & *f* murderer.

убира́ть(ся *impf of* **убра́ть(ся; убира́йся!** clear off!

уби́тый killed; crushed; *sb* dead man. **уби́ть** (убью́, -ьёшь) *pf* (*impf* **убива́ть**) kill; murder; **~ся** hurt o.s.

убо́гий wretched. **убо́жество** poverty; squalor.

убо́й slaughter.

убо́р dress, attire.

убо́рка harvesting; clearing up. **убо́рная** *sb* lavatory; dressing-room. **убо́рочн|ый** harvesting; **~ая маши́на** harvester. **убо́рщик, убо́рщица** cleaner. **убра́нство** furniture. **убра́ть** (уберу́, -рёшь; -а́л, -а́, -о) *pf* (*impf* **убира́ть**) remove; take away; put away; harvest; clear up; decorate; **~ посте́ль** make a bed; **~ со стола́** clear the table; **~ся** tidy up, clean up; clear off.

убыва́ть *impf*, **убы́ть** (убу́ду; у́был, -а́, -о) *pf* diminish; subside; wane; leave. **у́быль** diminution; casualties. **убы́ток** (-тка) loss; *pl* damages. **убы́точный** unprofitable.

убью́ *etc.*: *see* **уби́ть**

уважа́емый respected; dear. **уважа́ть** *impf* respect. **уваже́ние** respect; **с ~м** yours sincerely. **уважи́тельный** valid; respectful.

уве́домить (-млю) *pf*, **уведомля́ть** *impf* inform. **уведомле́ние** notification.

уведу́ *etc.*: *see* **увести́**

увезти́ (-зу́, -зёшь; увёз, -ла́) *pf* (*impf* **увози́ть**) take (away); steal; abduct.

Т
У

увекове́чивать *impf*, **увекове́чить** (-чу) *pf* immortalize; perpetuate.

увёл *etc.*: *see* **увести́**

увеличе́ние increase; magnification; enlargement. **увели́чивать** *impf*, **увели́чить** (-чу) *pf* increase; magnify; enlarge; **~ся** increase, grow. **увеличи́тель** *m* enlarger. **увеличи́тельн|ый** magnifying; enlarging; **~ое стекло́** magnifying glass.

у|венча́ть *pf*, **уве́нчивать** *impf* crown; **~ся** be crowned.

уве́ренность confidence; certainty. **уве́ренный** confident; sure; certain. **уве́рить** *pf* (*impf* **уверя́ть**) assure; convince; **~ся** satisfy o.s.; be convinced.

уверну́ться (-ну́сь, -нёшься) *pf*, **увёртываться** *impf* **от**+*gen* evade. **увёртка** dodge, evasion; subterfuge; *pl* wiles. **увёртливый** evasive, shifty.

увертю́ра overture.

уверя́ть(ся *impf of* **уве́рить(ся**

увеселе́ние amusement, entertainment. **увесели́тельный** entertainment; pleasure. **увеселя́ть** *impf* amuse, entertain.

уве́систый weighty.

увести́ (-еду́, -едёшь; -ёл, -а́) *pf* (*impf* **уводи́ть**) take (away); walk off with.

У

уве́чить (-чу) *impf* maim, cripple. **уве́чный** maimed, crippled; *sb* cripple. **уве́чье** maiming; injury.

уве́шать *pf*, **уве́шивать** *impf* hang (+*instr* with).

увеща́ть *impf*, **увещева́ть** *impf* exhort, admonish.

у|вида́ть *pf* see. **у|ви́деть(ся** (-и́жу(сь) *pf*.

уви́ливать *impf*, **увильну́ть** (-ну́, -нёшь) *pf* **от**+*gen* dodge; evade.

увлажни́ть *pf*, **увлажня́ть** *impf* moisten.

увлека́тельный fascinating. **увлека́ть** *impf*, **увле́чь** (-еку́, -ечёшь; -ёк, -ла́) *pf* carry away; fascinate; **~ся** be carried away; become mad (+*instr* about). **увлече́ние** animation; passion; crush.

уво́д withdrawal; stealing. **уводи́ть** (-ожу́, -о́дишь) *impf of* **увести́**

увози́ть (-ожу́, -о́дишь) *impf of* **увезти́**

уво́лить *pf*, **увольня́ть** *impf* discharge, dismiss; retire; **~ся** be discharged, retire. **увольне́ние** discharge, dismissal.

увы́ *int* alas!

увяда́ть *impf of* **увя́нуть**. **увя́дший** withered.

увяза́ть[1] *impf of* **увя́знуть**

увяза́ть[2] (-яжу́, -я́жешь) *pf* (*impf* **увя́зывать**) tie up; pack up; co-ordinate; **~ся** pack; tag along. **увя́зка** tying up; co-ordination.

у|вя́знуть (-ну; -я́з) *pf* (*impf also* **увяза́ть**) get bogged down.

увя́зывать(ся *impf of* **увяза́ть(ся**

у|вя́нуть (-ну) *pf* (*impf also* **увяда́ть**) fade, wither.

угада́ть *pf*, **уга́дывать** *impf* guess.

уга́р carbon monoxide (poisoning); ecstasy. **уга́рный газ** carbon monoxide.

угаса́ть *impf*, **у|га́снуть** (-нет; -а́с) *pf* go out; die down.

угле- *in comb* coal; charcoal; carbon. **углево́д** carbohydrate. **~водоро́д** hydrocarbon. **~добы́ча** coal extraction. **~кислота́** carbonic acid; carbon dioxide. **~ки́слый** carbonate (of). **~ро́д** carbon.

углово́й corner; angular.

углуби́ть (-блю́) *pf*, **углубля́ть** *impf* deepen; **~ся** deepen; delve deeply; become absorbed. **углубле́ние** depression, dip; deepening. **углублённый** deepened; profound; absorbed.

угна́ть (угоню́, -о́нишь; -а́л, -а́, -о) *pf* (*impf* **угоня́ть**) drive away; despatch; steal; **~ся за**+*instr* keep pace with.

угнета́тель *m* oppressor. **угнета́ть** *impf* oppress; depress. **угне-**

тéние oppression; depression. **угнетённый** oppressed; depressed.

уговáривать *impf*, **уговорúть** *pf* persuade; **~ся** arrange, agree. **уговóр** persuasion; agreement.

угóда: **в угóду** +*dat* to please. **угодúть** (-ожý) *pf*, **угождáть** *impf* fall, get; bang; (+*dat*) hit; +*dat or* **на**+*acc* please. **угóдливый** obsequious. **угóдно** *predic*+*dat*: **как вам ~** as you wish; **что вам ~?** what would you like?; *partl* **кто ~** anyone (you like); **что ~** anything (you like).

угóдье (*gen pl* -ий) land.

ýгол (углá, *loc* -ý) corner; angle.

уголóвник criminal. **уголóвный** criminal.

уголóк (-лкá, *loc* -ý) corner.

ýголь (ýгля́; *pl* ýгли, -ей *or* -éй) *m* coal; charcoal.

угóльник set square.

ýгольный coal; carbon(ic).

угомонúть *pf* calm down; **~ся** calm down.

угóн driving away; stealing. **угоня́ть** *impf of* **угнáть**

угорáть *impf*, **угорéть** (-рю́) *pf* get carbon monoxide poisoning; be mad. **угорéлый** mad; possessed.

ýгорь[1] (угря́) *m* eel.

ýгорь[2] (угря́) *m* blackhead.

угостúть (-ощý) *pf*, **угощáть** *impf* entertain; treat. **угощéние** entertaining, treating; refreshments.

угрожáть *impf* threaten. **угрóза** threat, menace.

угрóзыск *abbr* criminal investigation department.

угрызéние pangs.

угрю́мый sullen, morose.

удавáться (удаётся) *impf of* **удáться**

у|давúть(ся (-влю́(сь, -вишь(ся) *pf*. **удáвка** running-knot, half hitch.

удалéние removal; sending away; moving off. **удалúть** *pf* (*impf* **удаля́ть**) remove; send away; move away; **~ся** move off, away; retire.

удалóй, удáлый (-áл, -á, -о) daring, bold. **ýдаль, удальствó** daring, boldness.

удаля́ть(ся *impf of* **удалúть(ся**

удáр blow; stroke; attack; kick; thrust; seizure; bolt. **ударéние** accent; stress; emphasis. **удáрить** *pf*, **ударя́ть** *impf* (*impf also* **бить**) strike; hit; beat; **~ся** strike, hit; +**в**+*acc* break into; burst into. **удáрник, -ница** shock-worker. **удáрный** percussion; shock; stressed; urgent.

удáться (-áстся, -аду́тся; -áлся, -лáсь) *pf* (*impf* **удавáться**) succeed, be a success; *impers* +*dat* +*inf* succeed, manage; **мне удалóсь найтú рабóту** I managed to find a job. **удáча** good luck; success. **удáчный** successful; felicitous.

удвáивать *impf*, **удвóить** (-óю) *pf* double, redouble. **удвоéние** (re)doubling.

удéл lot, destiny.

уделúть *pf* (*impf* **уделя́ть**) spare, give.

уделя́ть *impf of* **уделúть**

удержáние deduction; retention, keeping. **удержáть** (-жý, -жишь) *pf*, **удéрживать** *impf* hold (on to); retain; restrain; suppress; deduct; **~ся** hold out; stand firm; refrain (from).

удерý *etc.*: *see* **удрáть**

удешевúть (-влю́) *pf*, **удешевля́ть** *impf* reduce the price of.

удивúтельный surprising, amazing; wonderful. **удивúть** (-влю́) *pf*, **удивля́ть** *impf* surprise, amaze; **~ся** be surprised, be amazed. **удивлéние** surprise, amazement.

удилá (-úл) *pl* bit.

удúлище fishing-rod.

удирáть *impf of* **удрáть**

удúть (ужý, ýдишь) *impf* fish for; **~ рыбу** fish; **~ся** bite.

удлинéние lengthening; extension. **удлинúть** *pf*, **удлиня́ть** *impf* lengthen; extend; **~ся** become longer; be extended.

У

удо́бно *adv* comfortably; conveniently. **удо́бный** comfortable; convenient.
удобовари́мый digestible.
удобре́ние fertilization; fertilizer. **удо́брить** *pf*, **удобря́ть** *impf* fertilize.
удо́бство comfort; convenience.
удовлетворе́ние satisfaction; gratification. **удовлетворённый** (-рён, -á) satisfied. **удовлетвори́тельный** satisfactory. **удовлетвори́ть** *pf*, **удовлетворя́ть** *impf* satisfy; +*dat* meet; +*instr* supply with; **~ся** be satisfied.
удово́льствие pleasure. **у|дово́льствоваться** *pf*.
удо́й milk-yield; milking.
удоста́ивать(ся *impf of* **удосто́ить(ся**
удостовере́ние certification; certificate; **~ ли́чности** identity card. **удостове́рить** *pf*, **удостоверя́ть** *impf* certify, witness; **~ся** make sure (**в**+*prep* of), assure o.s.
удосто́ить *pf* (*impf* **удоста́ивать**) make an award to; +*gen* award; +*instr* favour with; **~ся** +*gen* be awarded; be favoured with.
у́дочка (fishing-)rod.
удра́ть (удеру́, -ёшь; удра́л, -á, -о) *pf* (*impf* **удира́ть**) make off.
удруча́ть *impf*, **удручи́ть** (-чу́) *pf* depress. **удручённый** (-чён, -á) depressed.
удуша́ть *impf*, **удуши́ть** (-шу́, -шишь) *pf* stifle, suffocate. **удуше́ние** suffocation. **уду́шливый** stifling. **уду́шье** asthma; asphyxia.
уедине́ние solitude; seclusion. **уединённый** secluded; lonely. **уедини́ться** *pf*, **уединя́ться** *impf* seclude o.s.
уе́зд uyezd, District.
уезжа́ть *impf*, **уе́хать** (уе́ду) *pf* go away, depart.
уж[1] (-á) grass-snake.
уж[2]: *see* **уже́**[2]. **уж**[3], **уже́**[3] *partl* indeed; really.
у|жа́лить *pf*.

У

у́жас horror, terror; *predic* it is awful. **ужаса́ть** *impf*, **ужасну́ть** (-ну́, -нёшь) *pf* horrify; **~ся** be horrified, be terrified. **ужа́сно** *adv* terribly; awfully. **ужа́сный** awful, terrible.
у́же[1] *comp of* **у́зкий**
уже́[2], **уж**[2] *adv* already; **~ не** no longer. **уже́**[3]: *see* **уж**[3]
уже́ние fishing.
ужива́ться *impf of* **ужи́ться.** **ужи́вчивый** easy to get on with.
ужи́мка grimace.
у́жин supper. **у́жинать** *impf* (*pf* **по~**) have supper.
ужи́ться (-иву́сь, -ивёшься; -и́лся, -ла́сь) *pf* (*impf* **ужива́ться**) get on.
ужу́ *see* **уди́ть**
узако́нивать *impf*, **узако́нить** *pf* legalize.
узбе́к, -е́чка Uzbek. **Узбекиста́н** Uzbekistan.
узда́ (*pl* -ы) bridle.
у́зел (узла́) knot; junction; centre; node; bundle.
у́зкий (у́зок, узка́, -о) narrow; tight; narrow-minded. **узколе́йка** narrow-gauge railway.
узлова́тый knotty. **узлов|о́й** junction; main, key; **~а́я ста́нция** junction.
узнава́ть (-наю́, -наёшь) *impf*, **узна́ть** *pf* recognize; get to know; find out.
у́зник, у́зница prisoner.
узо́р pattern, design. **узо́рчатый** patterned.
у́зость narrowness; tightness.
узурпа́тор usurper. **узурпи́ровать** *impf* & *pf* usurp.
у́зы (уз) *pl* bonds, ties.
уйду́ *etc.*: *see* **уйти́.**
у́йма lots (of).
уйму́ *etc.*: *see* **уня́ть**
уйти́ (уйду́, -дёшь; ушёл, ушла́) *pf* (*impf* **уходи́ть**) go away, leave, depart; escape; retire; bury o.s.; be used up; pass away.
ука́з decree; edict. **указа́ние** indication; instruction. **ука́занный** appointed, stated. **указа́тель** *m*

indicator; gauge; index; directory. **указа́тельный** indicating; demonstrative; ~ **па́лец** index finger. **указа́ть** (-ажу́, -а́жешь) *pf*, **ука́зывать** *impf* show; indicate; point; point out. **ука́зка** pointer; orders.

ука́лывать *impf of* **уколо́ть**

уката́ть *pf*, **ука́тывать**[1] *impf* roll; flatten; wear out. **укати́ть** (-ачу́, -а́тишь) *pf*, **ука́тывать**[2] *impf* roll away; drive off; **~ся** roll away.

укача́ть *pf*, **ука́чивать** *impf* rock to sleep; make sick.

укла́д structure; style; organization. **укла́дка** packing; stacking; laying; setting. **укла́дчик** packer; layer. **укла́дывать(ся**[1] *impf of* **уложи́ть(ся**

укла́дываться[2] *impf of* **уле́чься**

укло́н slope; incline; gradient; bias; deviation. **уклоне́ние** deviation; digression. **уклони́ться** *pf*, **уклоня́ться** *impf* deviate; **+от**+*gen* turn (off, aside); avoid; evade. **укло́нчивый** evasive.

уклю́чина rowlock.

уко́л prick; injection; thrust. **уколо́ть** (-лю́, -лешь) *pf* (*impf* **ука́лывать**) prick; wound.

у|комплектова́ть *pf*, **укомплекто́вывать** *impf* complete; bring up to (full) strength; man; *+instr* equip with.

уко́р reproach.

укора́чивать *impf of* **укороти́ть**

укорени́ть *pf*, **укореня́ть** *impf* implant, inculcate; **~ся** take root.

укори́зна reproach. **укори́зненный** reproachful. **укори́ть** *pf* (*impf* **укоря́ть**) reproach (**в**+*prep* with).

укороти́ть (-очу́) *pf* (*impf* **укора́чивать**) shorten.

укоря́ть *impf of* **укори́ть**

уко́с (hay-)crop.

укра́дкой *adv* stealthily. **украду́** *etc.*: *see* **укра́сть**

Украи́на Ukraine. **украи́нец** (**-нца**), **украи́нка** Ukrainian. **украи́нский** Ukrainian.

укра́сить (-а́шу) *pf* (*impf* **украша́ть**) adorn, decorate; **~ся** be decorated; adorn o.s.

у|кра́сть (-аду́, -дёшь) *pf*.

украша́ть(ся *impf of* **укра́сить(ся**. **украше́ние** decoration; adornment.

укрепи́ть (-плю́) *pf*, **укрепля́ть** *impf* strengthen; fix; fortify; **~ся** become stronger; fortify one's position. **укрепле́ние** strengthening; reinforcement; fortification.

укро́мный secluded, cosy.

укро́п dill.

укроти́тель *m* (animal-)tamer. **укроти́ть** (-ощу́) *pf*, **укроща́ть** *impf* tame; curb; **~ся** become tame; calm down. **укроще́ние** taming.

укро́ю *etc.*: *see* **укры́ть**

укрупне́ние enlargement; amalgamation. **укрупни́ть** *pf*, **укрупня́ть** *impf* enlarge; amalgamate.

укрыва́тель *m* harbourer. **укрыва́тельство** harbouring; receiving. **укрыва́ть** *impf*, **укры́ть** (-ро́ю) *pf* cover; conceal, harbour; shelter; receive; **~ся** cover o.s.; take cover. **укры́тие** cover; shelter.

у́ксус vinegar.

уку́с bite; sting. **укуси́ть** (-ушу́, -у́сишь) *pf* bite; sting.

уку́тать *pf*, **уку́тывать** *impf* wrap up; **~ся** wrap o.s. up.

укушу́ *etc.*: *see* **укуси́ть**

ул. *abbr* (*of* **у́лица**) street, road.

ула́вливать *impf of* **улови́ть**

ула́дить (-а́жу) *pf*, **ула́живать** *impf* settle, arrange.

у́лей (у́лья) (bee)hive.

улета́ть *impf*, **улете́ть** (улечу́) *pf* fly (away). **улету́чиваться**, *impf*, **улету́читься** (-чусь) *pf* evaporate; vanish.

уле́чься (уля́гусь, -я́жешься; улёгся, -гла́сь) *pf* (*impf* **укла́дываться**) lie down; settle; subside.

ули́ка clue; evidence.

ули́тка snail.

у́лица street; **на у́лице** in the street; outside.
улича́ть *impf*, **уличи́ть** (-чу́) *pf* establish the guilt of.
у́личный street.
уло́в catch. **улови́мый** perceptible; audible. **улови́ть** (-влю́, -вишь) *pf* (*impf* **ула́вливать**) catch; seize. **уло́вка** trick, ruse.
уложе́ние code. **уложи́ть** (-жу́, -жишь) *pf* (*impf* **укла́дывать**) lay; pack; pile; **~ спать** put to bed; **~ся** pack (up); fit in.
улуча́ть *impf*, **улучи́ть** (-чу́) *pf* find, seize.
улучша́ть *impf*, **улу́чшить** (-шу) *pf* improve; better; **~ся** improve; get better. **улучше́ние** improvement.
улыба́ться *impf*, **улыбну́ться** (-ну́сь, -нёшься) *pf* smile. **улы́бка** smile.
ультима́тум ultimatum.
ультра- *in comb* ultra-. **ультразвуково́й** supersonic. **~фиоле́товый** ultra-violet.
уля́гусь *etc.*: *see* **уле́чься**
ум (-а́) mind, intellect; head; **сойти́ с ~а́** go mad.
умали́ть *pf* (*impf* **умаля́ть**) belittle.
умалишённый mad; *sb* lunatic.
ума́лчивать *impf of* **умолча́ть**
умаля́ть *impf of* **умали́ть**
уме́лец (-льца) skilled craftsman. **уме́лый** able, skilful. **уме́ние** ability, skill.
уменьша́ть *impf*, **уме́ньшить** (-шу) *pf* reduce, diminish, decrease; **~ся** diminish, decrease; abate. **уменьше́ние** decrease, reduction; abatement. **уменьши́тельный** diminutive.
уме́ренность moderation. **уме́ренный** moderate; temperate.
умере́ть (умру́, -рёшь; у́мер, -ла́, -о) *pf* (*impf* **умира́ть**) die.
уме́рить *pf* (*impf* **умеря́ть**) moderate; restrain.
умертви́ть (-рщвлю́, -ртви́шь) *pf*, **умерщвля́ть** *impf* kill, destroy; mortify. **у́мерший** dead; *sb* the deceased. **умерщвле́ние** killing, destruction; mortification.
умеря́ть *impf of* **уме́рить**
умести́ть (-ещу́) *pf* (*impf* **умеща́ть**) fit in, find room for; **~ся** fit in. **уме́стный** appropriate; pertinent; timely.
уме́ть (-е́ю) *impf* be able, know how.
умеща́ть(ся *impf of* **умести́ть(ся**
умиле́ние tenderness; emotion. **умили́ть** *pf*, **умиля́ть** *impf* move, touch; **~ся** be moved.
умира́ние dying. **умира́ть** *impf of* **умере́ть. умира́ющий** dying; *sb* dying person.
умиротворе́ние pacification; appeasement. **умиротвори́ть** *pf*, **умиротворя́ть** *impf* pacify; appease.
умне́ть (-е́ю) *impf* (*pf* **по~**) grow wiser. **у́мница** good girl; *m & f* clever person.
умножа́ть *impf*, **у|мно́жить** (-жу) *pf* multiply; increase; **~ся** increase, multiply. **умноже́ние** multiplication; increase. **умножи́тель** *m* multiplier.
у́мный (умён, умна́, у́мно́) clever, wise, intelligent. **умозаключе́ние** deduction; conclusion.
умоли́ть *pf* (*impf* **умоля́ть**) move by entreaties.
умолка́ть *impf*, **умо́лкнуть** (-ну; -о́лк) *pf* fall silent; stop. **умолча́ть** (-чу́) *pf* (*impf* **ума́лчивать**) fail to mention; hush up.
умоля́ть *impf of* **умоли́ть**; beg, entreat.
умопомеша́тельство derangement.
умори́тельный incredibly funny, killing. **у|мори́ть** *pf* kill; exhaust.
умо́ю *etc.*: *see* **умы́ть. умру́** *etc.*: *see* **умере́ть**
у́мственный mental, intellectual.
умудри́ть *pf*, **умудря́ть** *impf* make wiser; **~ся** contrive.
умыва́льная *sb* wash-room. **умыва́льник** wash-stand, wash-

basin. **умыва́ть(ся** *impf of* **умы́ть(ся**

у́мысел (-сла) design, intention.

умы́ть (умо́ю) *pf* (*impf* **умыва́ть**) wash; **~ся** wash (o.s.).

умы́шленный intentional.

у|насле́довать *pf.*

унести́ (-су́, -сёшь; -ёс, -ла́) *pf* (*impf* **уноси́ть**) take away; carry off, make off with; **~сь** speed away; fly by; be carried (away).

универма́г *abbr* department store. **универса́льн|ый** universal; all-round; versatile; all-purpose; **~ магази́н** department store; **~ое сре́дство** panacea. **универса́м** *abbr* supermarket.

университе́т university. **университе́тский** university.

унижа́ть *impf*, **уни́зить** (-и́жу) *pf* humiliate; **~ся** humble o.s.; stoop. **униже́ние** humiliation. **уни́женный** humble. **унизи́тельный** humiliating.

уника́льный unique.

унима́ть(ся *impf of* **уня́ть(ся**

унисо́н unison.

унита́з lavatory pan.

унифици́ровать *impf & pf* standardize.

уничижи́тельный pejorative.

уничтожа́ть *impf*, **уничто́жить** (-жу) *pf* destroy, annihilate; abolish; do away with. **уничтоже́ние** destruction, annihilation; abolition.

уноси́ть(ся (-ошу́(сь, -о́сишь(ся) *impf of* **унести́(сь**

у́нция ounce.

унова́ть *impf* be dejected. **уны́лый** dejected; doleful, cheerless. **уны́ние** dejection, despondency.

уня́ть (уйму́, -мёшь; -я́л, -а́, -о) *pf* (*impf* **унима́ть**) calm, soothe; **~ся** calm down.

упа́док (-дка) decline; decay; **~ ду́ха** depression. **упа́дочнический** decadent. **упа́дочный** depressive; decadent. **упаду́** *etc.*: *see* **упа́сть**

у|пакова́ть *pf*, **упако́вывать** *impf* pack (up). **упако́вка** packing; wrapping. **упако́вщик** packer.

упа́сть (-аду́, -адёшь) *pf of* **па́дать**

упере́ть (упру́, -рёшь; -ёр) *pf*, **упира́ть** *impf* rest, lean; **~ на**+*acc* stress; **~ся** rest, lean; resist; +**в**+*acc* come up against.

упи́танный well-fed; fattened.

упла́та payment. **у|плати́ть** (-ачу́, -а́тишь) *pf*, **упла́чивать** *impf* pay.

уплотне́ние compression; condensation; consolidation; sealing. **уплотни́ть** *pf*, **уплотня́ть** *impf* condense; compress; pack more into.

уплыва́ть *impf*, **уплы́ть** (-ыву́, -ывёшь; -ы́л, -а́, -о) *pf* swim *or* sail away; pass.

упова́ть *impf* +**на**+*acc* put one's trust in.

уподо́биться (-блюсь) *pf*, **уподобля́ться** *impf* +*dat* become like.

упое́ние ecstasy, rapture. **упои́тельный** intoxicating, ravishing.

уполза́ть *impf*, **уползти́** (-зу́, -зёшь; -о́лз, -зла́) *pf* creep away, crawl away.

уполномо́ченный *sb* (authorized) agent, representative; proxy. **уполнома́чивать, уполномо́чивать** *impf*, **уполномо́чить** (-чу) *pf* authorize, empower.

упомина́ние mention. **упомина́ть** *impf*, **упомяну́ть** (-ну́, -нешь) *pf* mention, refer to.

упо́р prop, support; **в ~** point-blank; **сде́лать ~ на**+*acc or prep* lay stress on. **упо́рный** stubborn; persistent. **упо́рство** stubbornness; persistence. **упо́рствовать** *impf* be stubborn; persist (**в**+*prep* in).

упоря́дочивать *impf*, **упоря́дочить** (-чу) *pf* regulate, put in order.

употреби́тельный (widely-) used; common. **употреби́ть** (-блю́) *pf*, **употребля́ть** *impf* use. **употребле́ние** use; usage.

упра́ва justice.

У

управдóм *abbr* manager (*of block of flats*). **упрáвиться** (-влюсь) *pf*, **управля́ться** *impf* cope, manage; +**с**+*instr* deal with. **управлéние** management; administration; direction; control; driving, steering; government. **управля́емый снаря́д** guided missile. **управля́ть** *impf* +*instr* manage, direct, run; govern; be in charge of; operate; drive. **управля́ющий** *sb* manager.

упражнéние exercise. **упражня́ть** *impf* exercise, train; **~ся** practise, train.

упраздни́ть *pf*, **упраздня́ть** *impf* abolish.

упрáшивать *impf of* **упроси́ть**

упрёк reproach. **упрекáть** *impf*, **упрекнýть** (-нý, -нёшь) *pf* reproach.

упроси́ть (-ошý, -óсишь) *pf* (*impf* **упрáшивать**) entreat; prevail upon.

упрости́ть (-ощý) *pf* (*impf* **упрощáть**) (over-)simplify.

упрóчивать *impf*, **упрóчить** (-чу) *pf* strengthen, consolidate; **~ся** be firmly established.

упрошý *etc.*: *see* **упроси́ть**

упрощáть *impf of* **упрости́ть. упрощённый** (-щён, -á) (over-)simplified.

У

упрý *etc.*: *see* **уперéть**

упрýгий elastic; springy. **упрýгость** elasticity; spring. **упрýже** *comp of* **упрýгий**

упря́жка harness; team. **упряжнóй** draught. **ýпряжь** harness.

упря́миться (-млюсь) *impf* be obstinate; persist. **упря́мство** obstinacy. **упря́мый** obstinate; persistent.

упускáть *impf*, **упусти́ть** (-ущý, -ýстишь) *pf* let go, let slip; miss. **упущéние** omission; slip; negligence.

урá *int* hurrah!

уравнéние equalization; equation. **урáвнивать** *impf*, **уравня́ть** *pf* equalize. **уравни́тельный** equalizing, levelling. **уравновéсить** (-éшу) *pf*, **уравновéшивать** *impf* balance; counterbalance. **уравновéшенность** composure. **уравновéшенный** balanced, composed.

ураґáн hurricane; storm.

урáльский Ural.

урáн uranium; Uranus. **урáновый** uranium.

урвáть (-вý, -вёшь; -áл, -á, -о) *pf* (*impf* **урывáть**) snatch.

урегули́рование regulation; settlement. **у|регули́ровать** *pf*.

урéзать (-éжу) *pf*, **урезáть, урéзывать** *impf* cut off; shorten; reduce.

ýрка *m & f* (*sl*) lag, convict.

ýрна urn; litter-bin.

ýровень (-вня) *m* level; standard.

урóд freak, monster.

уроди́ться (-ожýсь) *pf* ripen; grow.

урóдливость deformity; ugliness. **урóдливый** deformed; ugly; bad. **урóдовать** *impf* (*pf* **из~**) disfigure; distort. **урóдство** disfigurement; ugliness.

урожáй harvest; crop; abundance. **урожáйность** yield; productivity. **урожáйный** productive, high-yield.

урождённый née. **урожéнец** (-нца), **урожéнка** native. **урожýсь** *see* **уроди́ться**

урóк lesson.

урóн losses; damage. **урони́ть** (-ню́, -нишь) *pf of* **роня́ть**

урчáть (-чý) *impf* rumble.

урывáть *impf of* **урвáть. урывкáми** *adv* in snatches, by fits and starts.

ус (*pl* -ы́) whisker; tendril; *pl* moustache.

усади́ть (-ажý, -áдишь) *pf*, **усáживать** *impf* seat, offer a seat; plant. **усáдьба** (*gen pl* -деб *or* -дьб) country estate; farmstead. **усáживаться** *impf of* **усéсться**

усáтый moustached; whiskered.

усвáивать *impf*, **усвóить** *pf* master; assimilate; adopt. **усвоéние**

mastering; assimilation; adoption.

усе́рдие zeal; diligence. **усе́рдный** zealous; diligent.

усе́сться (уся́дусь; -е́лся) *pf* (*impf* **уса́живаться**) take a seat; settle down (to).

усиде́ть (-ижу́) *pf* remain seated; hold down a job. **уси́дчивый** assiduous.

у́сик tendril; runner; antenna; *pl* small moustache.

усиле́ние strengthening; reinforcement; intensification; amplification. **уси́ленный** intensified, increased; earnest. **уси́ливать** *impf*, **уси́лить** *pf* intensify, increase; amplify; strengthen, reinforce; **~ся** increase, intensify; become stronger. **уси́лие** effort. **усили́тель** *m* amplifier; booster.

ускака́ть (-ачу́, -а́чешь) *pf* skip off; gallop off.

ускольза́ть *impf*, **ускользну́ть** (-ну́, -нёшь) *pf* slip off; steal away; escape.

ускоре́ние acceleration. **уско́ренный** accelerated; rapid; crash. **ускори́тель** accelerator. **уско́рить** *pf*, **ускоря́ть** *impf* quicken; accelerate; hasten; **~ся** accelerate, be accelerated; quicken.

усло́вие condition. **усло́виться** (-влюсь) *pf*, **усло́вливаться, усла́вливаться** *impf* agree; arrange. **усло́вленный** agreed, fixed. **усло́вность** convention. **усло́вный** conditional; conditioned; conventional; agreed; relative.

усложне́ние complication. **усложни́ть** *pf*, **усложня́ть** *impf* complicate; **~ся** become complicated.

услу́га service; good turn. **услу́жливый** obliging.

услыха́ть (-ы́шу) *pf*, **у|слы́шать** (-ы́шу) *pf* hear; sense; scent.

усма́тривать *impf of* **усмотре́ть**

усмеха́ться *impf*, **усмехну́ться** (-ну́сь, -нёшься) *pf* smile; grin; smirk. **усме́шка** smile; grin; sneer.

усмире́ние pacification; suppression. **усмири́ть** *pf*, **усмиря́ть** *impf* pacify; calm; suppress.

усмотре́ние discretion, judgement. **усмотре́ть** (-рю́, -ришь) *pf* (*impf* **усма́тривать**) perceive; see; regard; **+за+***instr* keep an eye on.

усну́ть (-ну́, -нёшь) *pf* go to sleep.

усоверше́нствование advanced studies; improvement, refinement. **у|соверше́нствовать(ся** *pf*.

усомни́ться *pf* doubt.

успева́емость progress. **успева́ть** *impf*, **успе́ть** (-е́ю) *pf* have time; manage; succeed. **успе́х** success; progress. **успе́шный** successful.

успока́ивать *impf*, **успоко́ить** *pf* calm, quiet, soothe; **~ся** calm down; abate. **успока́ивающий** calming, sedative. **успокое́ние** calming, soothing; calm; peace. **успокои́тельн|ый** calming; reassuring; **~ое** *sb* sedative, tranquillizer.

уста́ (-т, -та́м) *pl* mouth.

уста́в regulations, statutes; charter.

устава́ть (-таю́, -ёшь) *impf of* **уста́ть; не устава́я** incessantly.

уста́вить (-влю) *pf*, **уставля́ть** *impf* set, arrange; cover, fill; direct; **~ся** find room, go in; stare.

уста́лость tiredness. **уста́лый** tired.

устана́вливать *impf*, **установи́ть** (-влю́, -вишь) *pf* put, set up; install; set; establish; fix; **~ся** dispose o.s.; be established; set in. **устано́вка** putting, setting up; installation; setting; plant, unit; directions. **установле́ние** establishment. **устано́вленный** established, prescribed.

уста́ну *etc.*: *see* **уста́ть**

устарева́ть *impf*, **у|старе́ть** (-е́ю) *pf* become obsolete; become antiquated. **устаре́лый** obsolete; antiquated, out-of-date.

устáть (-áну) *pf* (*impf* **уставáть**) get tired.
устилáть *impf*, **устлáть** (-телю́, -тéлешь) *pf* cover; pave.
у́стный oral, verbal.
усто́й abutment; foundation, support. **усто́йчивость** stability, steadiness. **усто́йчивый** stable, steady. **устоя́ть** (-ою́) *pf* keep one's balance; stand firm; **~ся** settle; become fixed.
устрáивать(ся *impf of* **устро́ить(ся**
устранéние removal, elimination. **устранúть** *pf*, **устраня́ть** *impf* remove; eliminate; **~ся** resign, retire.
устрашáть *impf*, **устрашúть** (-шу́) *pf* frighten; **~ся** be frightened.
устремúть (-млю́) *pf*, **устремля́ть** *impf* direct, fix; **~ся** rush; be directed; concentrate. **устремлéние** rush; aspiration.
у́стрица oyster.
устро́итель *m*, **~ница** organizer. **устро́ить** *pf* (*impf* **устрáивать**) arrange, organize; make; cause; settle, put in order; place, fix up; get; suit; **~ся** work out; manage; settle down; be found, get fixed up. **устро́йство** arrangement; construction; mechanism, device; system.
У **усту́п** shelf, ledge. **уступáть** *impf*, **уступúть** (-плю́, -пишь) *pf* yield; give up; **~ доро́гу** make way. **усту́пка** concession. **усту́пчивый** pliable; compliant.
устыдúться (-ыжу́сь) *pf* (+*gen*) be ashamed (of).
у́стье (*gen pl* -ьев) mouth; estuary.
усугу́бить (-у́блю) *pf*, **усугубля́ть** *impf* increase; aggravate.
усы́ *see* **ус**
усыновúть (-влю́) *pf*, **усыновля́ть** *impf* adopt. **усыновлéние** adoption.
усы́пать (-плю) *pf*, **усыпáть** *impf* strew, scatter.
усыпúтельный soporific. **усыпúть** (-плю́) *pf*, **усыпля́ть** *impf* put to sleep; lull; weaken.
уся́дусь *etc.*: *see* **усéсться**
утáивать *impf*, **утаúть** *pf* conceal; keep secret.
утáптывать *impf of* **утоптáть**
утáскивать *impf*, **утащúть** (-щу́, -щишь) *pf* drag off.
у́тварь utensils.
утвердúтельный affirmative. **утвердúть** (-ржу́) *pf*, **утверждáть** *impf* confirm; approve; ratify; establish; assert; **~ся** gain a foothold; become established; be confirmed. **утверждéние** approval; confirmation; ratification; assertion; establishment.
утекáть *impf of* **утéчь**
утёнок (-нка; *pl* утя́та, -я́т) duckling.
утеплúть *pf*, **утепля́ть** *impf* warm.
утерéть (утру́, -рёшь; утёр) *pf* (*impf* **утирáть**) wipe (off, dry).
утерпéть (-плю́, -пишь) *pf* restrain o.s.
утёс cliff, crag.
утéчка leak, leakage; escape; loss. **утéчь** (-еку́, -ечёшь; утёк, -лá) *pf* (*impf* **утекáть**) leak, escape; pass.
утешáть *impf*, **утéшить** (-шу) *pf* console; **~ся** console o.s. **утешéние** consolation. **утешúтельный** comforting.
утилизúровать *impf* & *pf* utilize.
утúль *m*, **утильсырьё** scrap.
утúный duck, duck's.
утирáть(ся *impf of* **утерéть(ся**
утихáть *impf*, **утúхнуть** (-ну; -их) *pf* abate, subside; calm down.
у́тка duck; canard.
уткну́ть (-ну́, -нёшь) *pf* bury; fix; **~ся** bury o.s.
утолúть *pf* (*impf* **утоля́ть**) quench; satisfy; relieve.
утолщéние thickening; bulge.
утоля́ть *impf of* **утолúть**
утомúтельный tedious; tiring. **утомúть** (-млю́) *pf*, **утомля́ть** *impf* tire, fatigue; **~ся** get tired. **утомлéние** weariness. **утомлённый** weary.

у|тону́ть (-ну́, -нешь) *pf* drown, be drowned; sink.
утончённый refined.
у|топи́ть(ся (-плю́(сь, -пишь(ся) *pf*. **уто́пленник** drowned man.
утопи́ческий utopian. **уто́пия** Utopia.
утопта́ть (-пчу́, -пчешь) *pf* (*impf* **ута́птывать**) trample down.
уточне́ние more precise definition; amplification. **уточни́ть** *pf*, **уточня́ть** *impf* define more precisely; amplify.
утра́ивать *impf of* **утро́ить**
у|трамбова́ть *pf*, **утрамбо́вывать** *impf* ram, tamp; **~ся** become flat.
утра́та loss. **утра́тить** (-а́чу) *pf*, **утра́чивать** *impf* lose.
у́тренний morning. **у́тренник** morning performance; early-morning frost.
утри́ровать *impf* & *pf* exaggerate.
у́тро (-а *or* -а́, -у *or* -у́; *pl* -а, -ам *or* -а́м) morning.
утро́ба womb; belly.
утро́ить *pf* (*impf* **утра́ивать**) triple, treble.
утру́ *etc.*: *see* **утере́ть, у́тро**
утружда́ть *impf* trouble, tire.
утю́г (-а́) iron. **утю́жить** (-жу) *impf* (*pf* **вы́~, от~**) iron.
ух *int* oh, ooh, ah.
уха́ fish soup.
уха́б pot-hole. **уха́бистый** bumpy.
уха́живать *impf* **за**+*instr* tend; look after; court.
ухвати́ть (-ачу́, -а́тишь) *pf*, **ухва́тывать** *impf* seize; grasp; **~ся за**+*acc* grasp, lay hold of; set to; seize; jump at. **ухва́тка** grip; skill; trick; manner.
ухитри́ться *pf*, **ухитря́ться** *impf* manage, contrive. **ухищре́ние** device, trick.
ухмы́лка smirk. **ухмыльну́ться** (-ну́сь, -нёшься) *pf*, **ухмыля́ться** *impf* smirk.
у́хо (*pl* у́ши, уше́й) ear; ear-flap.
ухо́д[1] **+за**+*instr* care of; tending, looking after.
ухо́д[2] leaving, departure. **уходи́ть** (-ожу́, -о́дишь) *impf of* **уйти́**
ухудша́ть *impf*, **уху́дшить** (-шу) *pf* make worse; **~ся** get worse. **ухудше́ние** deterioration.
уцеле́ть (-е́ю) *pf* remain intact; survive.
уце́нивать *impf*, **уцени́ть** (-ню́, -нишь) *pf* reduce the price of.
уцепи́ть (-плю́, -пишь) *pf* catch hold of, seize; **~ся за**+*acc* catch hold of, seize; jump at.
уча́ствовать *impf* take part; hold shares. **уча́ствующий** *sb* participant. **уча́стие** participation; share; sympathy.
участи́ть (-ащу́) *pf* (*impf* **учаща́ть**) make more frequent; **~ся** become more frequent, quicken.
уча́стливый sympathetic. **уча́стник** participant. **уча́сток** (-тка) plot; part, section; sector; district; field, sphere. **у́часть** lot, fate.
учаща́ть(ся *impf of* **участи́ть(ся**
уча́щийся *sb* student; pupil. **учёба** studies; course; training. **уче́бник** text-book. **уче́бный** educational; school; training. **уче́ние** learning; studies; apprenticeship; teaching; doctrine; exercise.
учени́к (-а́), **учени́ца** pupil; apprentice; disciple. **учени́ческий** pupil'(s); apprentice('s); unskilled; crude. **учёность** learning, erudition. **учён|ый** learned; scholarly; academic; scientific; **~ая сте́пень** (*university*) degree; **~ый** *sb* scholar; scientist.
уче́сть (учту́, -тёшь; учёл, учла́) *pf* (*impf* **учи́тывать**) take stock of; take into account; discount. **учёт** stock-taking; calculation; taking into account; registration; discount; **без ~а** +*gen* disregarding; **взять на ~** register. **учётный** registration; discount.
учи́лище (*specialist*) school.
у|чини́ть *pf*, **учиня́ть** *impf* make; carry out; commit.
учи́тель (*pl* -я́) *m*, **учи́тельница** teacher. **учи́тельск|ий** teacher's,

teachers'; **~ая** *sb* staff-room.
учи́тывать *impf of* **уче́сть**
учи́ть (учу́, у́чишь) *impf* (*pf* **вы́~, на~, об~**) teach; be a teacher; learn; **~ся** be a student; +*dat or inf* learn, study.
учреди́тельный constituent.
учреди́ть (-ежу́) *pf*, **учрежда́ть** *impf* found, establish. **учрежде́ние** founding; establishment; institution.
учти́вый civil, courteous.
учту́ *etc.*: *see* **уче́сть**
уша́нка hat with ear-flaps.
ушёл *etc.*: *see* **уйти́. у́ши** *etc.*: *see* **у́хо**
уши́б injury; bruise. **ушиба́ть** *impf*, **ушиби́ть** (-бу́, -бёшь; уши́б) *pf* injure; bruise; hurt; **~ся** hurt o.s.
ушко́ (*pl* -и́, -о́в) eye; tab.
ушно́й ear, aural.
уще́лье ravine, gorge, canyon.
ущеми́ть (-млю́) *pf*, **ущемля́ть** *impf* pinch, jam; limit; encroach on; hurt. **ущемле́ние** pinching, jamming; limitation; hurting.
уще́рб detriment; loss; damage; prejudice. **уще́рбный** waning.
ущипну́ть (-ну́, -нёшь) *pf of* **щипа́ть**
Уэ́льс Wales. **уэ́льский** Welsh.
ую́т cosiness, comfort. **ую́тный** cosy, comfortable.
уязви́мый vulnerable. **уязви́ть** (-влю́) *pf*, **уязвля́ть** *impf* wound, hurt.
уясни́ть *pf*, **уясня́ть** *impf* understand, make out.

Ф

фа́брика factory. **фабрика́нт** manufacturer. **фабрика́т** finished product, manufactured product. **фабрикова́ть** *impf* (*pf* **с~**) fabricate, forge. **фабри́чн|ый** factory; manufacturing; factory-made; **~ая ма́рка, ~ое клеймо́** trade-mark.
фа́була plot, story.
фаго́т bassoon.
фа́за phase; stage.
фаза́н pheasant.
фа́зис phase.
файл (*comput*) file.
фа́кел torch, flare.
факс fax.
факси́миле *neut indecl* facsimile.
факт fact; **соверши́вшийся ~** fait accompli. **факти́чески** *adv* in fact; virtually. **факти́ческий** actual; real; virtual.
фа́ктор factor.
факту́ра texture; style, execution.
факультати́вный optional. **факульте́т** faculty, department.
фа́лда tail (*of coat*).
фальсифика́тор falsifier, forger. **фальсифика́ция** falsification; adulteration; forgery. **фальсифици́ровать** *impf* & *pf* falsify; forge; adulterate. **фальши́вить** (-влю) *impf* (*pf* **с~**) be a hypocrite; sing *or* play out of tune. **фальши́вка** forged document. **фальши́вый** false; spurious; forged; artificial; out of tune. **фальшь** deception; falseness.
фами́лия surname. **фамилья́рничать** be over-familiar. **фамилья́рность** (over-)familiarity. **фамилья́рный** (over-)familiar; unceremonious.
фанати́зм fanaticism. **фана́тик** fanatic.
фане́ра veneer; plywood.
фантазёр dreamer, visionary. **фантази́ровать** *impf* (*pf* **с~**) dream; make up, dream up; improvise. **фанта́зия** fantasy; fancy; imagination; whim. **фанта́стика** fiction, fantasy. **фантасти́ческий, фантасти́чный** fantastic.
фа́ра headlight.
фарао́н pharaoh; faro.
фарва́тер fairway, channel.
фармазо́н freemason.
фармаце́вт pharmacist.
фарс farce.

фа́ртук apron.

фарфо́р china; porcelain. **фарфо́ровый** china.

фарцо́вщик currency speculator.

фарш stuffing; minced meat. **фаршировáть** *impf* (*pf* **за~**) stuff.

фаса́д façade.

фасовáть *impf* (*pf* **рас~**) package.

фасо́ль kidney bean(s), French bean(s); haricot beans.

фасо́н cut; fashion; style; manner. **фасо́нный** shaped.

фата́ veil.

фатали́зм fatalism. **фата́льный** fatal.

фаши́зм Fascism. **фаши́ст** Fascist. **фаши́стский** Fascist.

фая́нс faience, pottery.

февра́ль (-я́) *m* February. **февра́льский** February.

федера́льный federal. **федера́ция** federation.

феери́ческий fairy-tale.

фейерве́рк firework(s).

фе́льдшер (*pl* -а́), **-шери́ца** (*partly-qualified*) medical assistant.

фельето́н feuilleton, feature.

фемини́зм feminism. **феминисти́ческий, фемини́стский** feminist.

фен (hair-)dryer.

фено́мен phenomenon. **феномена́льный** phenomenal.

феода́л feudal lord. **феодали́зм** feudalism. **феода́льный** feudal.

ферзь (-я́) *m* queen.

фе́рма[1] farm.

фе́рма[2] girder, truss.

ферма́та (*mus*) pause.

ферме́нт ferment.

фе́рмер farmer.

фестива́ль *m* festival.

фетр felt. **фе́тровый** felt.

фехтова́льщик, -щица fencer. **фехтова́ние** fencing. **фехтова́ть** *impf* fence.

фе́я fairy.

фиа́лка violet.

фиа́ско *neut indecl* fiasco.

фи́бра fibre.

фигля́р buffoon.

фигу́ра figure; court-card; (chess-)piece. **фигура́льный** figurative, metaphorical. **фигури́ровать** *impf* figure, appear. **фигури́ст, -и́стка** figure-skater. **фигу́рка** figurine, statuette; figure. **фигу́рн|ый** figured; **~ое ката́ние** figure-skating.

фи́зик physicist. **фи́зика** physics. **физио́лог** physiologist. **физиологи́ческий** physiological. **физиоло́гия** physiology. **физионо́мия** physiognomy; face, expression. **физиотерапе́вт** physiotherapist. **физи́ческий** physical; physics. **физкульту́ра** *abbr* P.E., gymnastics. **физкульту́рный** *abbr* gymnastic; athletic; **~ зал** gymnasium.

фикса́ж fixer. **фикса́ция** fixing. **фикси́ровать** *impf* & *pf* (*pf also* **за~**) fix; record.

фикти́вный fictitious. **~ брак** marriage of convenience. **фи́кция** fiction.

филантро́п philanthropist. **филантро́пия** philanthropy.

филармо́ния philharmonic society; concert hall.

филатели́ст philatelist.

филе́ *neut indecl* sirloin; fillet.

филиа́л branch.

фили́стер philistine.

фило́лог philologist. **филологи́ческий** philological. **филоло́гия** philology.

фило́соф philosopher. **филосо́фия** philosophy. **филосо́фский** philosophical.

фильм film. **фильмоско́п** projector.

фильтр filter. **фильтрова́ть** *impf* (*pf* **про~**) filter.

фина́л finale; final. **фина́льный** final.

финанси́ровать *impf* & *pf* finance. **фина́нсовый** financial. **фина́нсы** (-ов) *pl* finance, finances.

фи́ник date.
фи́ниш finish; finishing post.
фи́нка Finn. **Финля́ндия** Finland. **финля́ндский** Finnish. **финн** Finn. **фи́нский** Finnish.
фиоле́товый violet.
фи́рма firm; company. **фи́рменное блю́до** speciality of the house.
фисгармо́ния harmonium.
фити́ль (-я́) *m* wick; fuse.
флаг flag. **фла́гман** flagship.
флако́н bottle, flask.
фланг flank; wing.
флане́ль flannel.
флегмати́чный phlegmatic.
флейта flute.
фле́ксия inflexion. **флекти́вный** inflected.
фли́гель (*pl* -я́) *m* wing; annexe.
флирт flirtation. **флиртова́ть** *impf* flirt.
флома́стер felt-tip pen.
фло́ра flora.
флот fleet. **фло́тский** naval.
флю́гер (*pl* -а́) weather-vane.
флюоресце́нтный fluorescent.
флюс[1] gumboil, abscess.
флюс[2] (*pl* -ы́) flux.
фля́га flask; churn. **фля́жка** flask.
фойе́ *neut indecl* foyer.
фо́кус[1] trick.
фо́кус[2] focus. **фокуси́ровать** *impf* focus.
фо́кусник conjurer, juggler.
ф **фолиа́нт** folio.
фольга́ foil.
фолькло́р folklore.
фон background.
фона́рик small lamp; torch. **фона́рный** lamp; ~ **столб** lamp-post. **фона́рь** (-я́) *m* lantern; lamp; light.
фонд fund; stock; reserves.
фоне́тика phonetics. **фонети́ческий** phonetic.
фонта́н fountain.
форе́ль trout.
фо́рма form; shape; mould, cast; uniform. **форма́льность** formality. **форма́льный** formal.
форма́т format. **форма́ция** structure; stage; formation; mentality. **фо́рменный** uniform; proper, regular. **формирова́ние** forming; unit, formation. **формирова́ть** *impf* (*pf* **с~**) form; organize; **~ся** form, develop. **формова́ть** *impf* (*pf* **с~**) form, shape; mould, cast.
фо́рмула formula. **формули́ровать** *impf* & *pf* (*pf also* **с~**) formulate. **формулиро́вка** formulation; wording; formula. **формуля́р** log-book; library card.
форси́ровать *impf* & *pf* force; speed up.
форсу́нка sprayer; injector.
фортепья́но *neut indecl* piano.
фо́рточка small hinged (window-)pane.
форту́на fortune.
фо́рум forum
фо́сфор phosphorus.
фо́то *neut indecl* photo(graph).
фото- *in comb* photo-, photoelectric. **фотоаппара́т** camera. **~бума́га** photographic paper. **~гени́чный** photogenic. **фото́граф** photographer. **~графи́ровать** *impf* (*pf* **с~**) photograph. **~графи́роваться** be photographed, have one's photograph taken. **~графи́ческий** photographic. **~гра́фия** photography; photograph; photographer's studio. **~ко́пия** photocopy. **~люби́тель** *m* amateur photographer. **~объекти́в** (camera) lens. **~репортёр** press photographer. **~хро́ника** news in pictures. **~элеме́нт** photoelectric cell.
фрагме́нт fragment.
фра́за sentence; phrase. **фразеоло́гия** phraseology.
фрак tail-coat, tails.
фракцио́нный fractional; factional. **фра́кция** fraction; faction.
франк franc.
франкмасо́н Freemason.
франт dandy.

Фра́нция France. **францу́женка** Frenchwoman. **францу́з** Frenchman. **францу́зский** French.

фрахт freight. **фрахтова́ть** *impf* (*pf* **за~**) charter.

фрега́т frigate.

фре́ска fresco.

фронт (*pl* -ы, -о́в) front. **фронтови́к** (-а́) front-line soldier. **фронтово́й** front(-line).

фронто́н pediment.

фрукт fruit. **фрукто́вый** fruit; **~ сад** orchard.

ФСБ *abbr* (*of* **Федера́льная слу́жба безопа́сности**) Federal Security Service.

фтор fluorine. **фто́ристый** fluorine; fluoride. **~ ка́льций** calcium fluoride.

фу *int* ugh! oh!

фуга́нок (-нка) smoothing-plane.

фуга́с landmine. **фуга́сный** high-explosive.

фунда́мент foundation. **фундамента́льный** solid, sound; main; basic.

функциона́льный functional. **функциони́ровать** *impf* function. **фу́нкция** function.

фунт pound.

фура́ж (-а́) forage, fodder. **фура́жка** peaked cap, forage-cap.

фурго́н van; caravan.

фут foot; foot-rule. **футбо́л** football. **футболи́ст** footballer. **футбо́лка** T-shirt, sports shirt. **футбо́льный** football; **~ мяч** football.

футля́р case, container.

футури́зм futurism.

фуфа́йка jersey; sweater.

фы́ркать *impf*, **фы́ркнуть** (-ну) *pf* snort.

фюзеля́ж fuselage.

Х

хала́т dressing-gown. **хала́тный** careless, negligent.

халту́ра pot-boiler; hackwork; money made on the side. **халту́рщик** hack.

хам boor, lout. **ха́мский** boorish, loutish. **ха́мство** boorishness, loutishness.

хамелео́н chameleon.

хан khan.

хандра́ depression. **хандри́ть** *impf* be depressed.

ханжа́ hypocrite. **ха́нжеский** sanctimonious, hypocritical.

хао́с chaos. **хаоти́чный** chaotic.

хара́ктер character. **характеризова́ть** *impf* & *pf* (*pf also* **о~**) describe; characterize; **~ся** be characterized. **характери́стика** reference; description. **характе́рный** characteristic; distinctive; character.

ха́ркать *impf*, **ха́ркнуть** (-ну) *pf* spit.

ха́ртия charter.

ха́та peasant hut.

хвала́ praise. **хвале́бный** laudatory. **хвалёный** highly-praised. **хвали́ть** (-лю́, -лишь) *impf* (*pf* **по~**) praise; **~ся** boast.

хва́стать(ся *impf* (*pf* **по~**) boast. **хвастли́вый** boastful. **хвастовство́** boasting. **хвасту́н** (-а́) boaster.

хвата́ть[1] *impf*, **хвати́ть** (-ачу́, -а́тишь) *pf* (*pf also* **схвати́ть**) snatch, seize; grab; **~ся** remember; *+gen* realize the absence of; +**за**+*acc* snatch at, clutch at; take up.

хвата́ть[2] *impf*, **хвати́ть** (-а́тит) *pf*, *impers* (*+gen*) suffice, be enough; last out; **вре́мени не хвата́ло** there was not enough time; **у нас не хвата́ет де́нег** we haven't enough money; **хва́тит!** that will do!; **э́того ещё не хвата́ло!** that's all we needed! **хва́тка** grasp, grip; method; skill.

хво́йн|ый coniferous; **~ые** *sb pl* conifers.

хвора́ть *impf* be ill.

хво́рост brushwood; (*pastry*) straws. **хворости́на** stick, switch.

хвост (-á) tail; tail-end. **хво́стик** tail. **хвостово́й** tail.
хво́я needle(s); (*coniferous*) branch(es).
херуви́м cherub.
хиба́р(к)а shack, hovel.
хи́жина shack, hut.
хи́лый (-л, -á, -о) sickly.
химе́ра chimera.
хи́мик chemist. **химика́т** chemical. **хими́ческий** chemical. **хи́мия** chemistry.
химчи́стка dry-cleaning; dry-cleaner's.
хи́на, хини́н quinine.
хиру́рг surgeon. **хирурги́ческий** surgical. **хирурги́я** surgery.
хитре́ц (-á) cunning person. **хитри́ть** *impf* (*pf* **с~**) use cunning, be crafty. **хи́трость** cunning; ruse; skill; intricacy. **хи́трый** cunning; skilful; intricate.
хихи́кать *impf*, **хихи́кнуть** (-ну) *pf* giggle, snigger.
хище́ние theft; embezzlement. **хи́щник** predator, bird *or* beast of prey. **хи́щнический** predatory. **хи́щн|ый** predatory; rapacious; **~ые пти́цы** birds of prey.
хладнокро́вие coolness, composure. **хладнокро́вный** cool, composed.
хлам rubbish.
хлеб (*pl* -ы, -ов *or* -á, -óв) bread; loaf; grain. **хлеба́ть** *impf*, **хлебну́ть** (-ну́, -нёшь) *pf* gulp down. **хле́бный** bread; baker's; grain. **хлебозаво́д** bakery. **хлебопека́рня** (*gen pl* -рен) bakery.
хлев (*loc* -ý; *pl* -á) cow-shed.
хлеста́ть (-ещу́, -е́щешь) *impf*, **хлестну́ть** (-ну́, -нёшь) *pf* lash; whip.
хлоп *int* bang! **хло́пать** *impf* (*pf* **хло́пнуть**) bang; slap; **~ (в ладо́ши)** clap.
хлопково́дство cotton-growing. **хло́пковый** cotton.
хло́пнуть (-ну) *pf of* **хло́пать**
хлопо́к[1] (-пка́) clap.
хло́пок[2] (-пка) cotton.
хлопота́ть (-очу́, -о́чешь) *impf* (*pf* **по~**) busy o.s.; bustle about; take trouble; **+о**+*prep or* **за**+*acc* petition for. **хлопотли́вый** troublesome; exacting; busy, bustling. **хло́поты** (-óт) *pl* trouble; efforts.
хлопчатобума́жный cotton.
хло́пья (-ьев) *pl* flakes.
хлор chlorine. **хло́ристый, хло́рный** chlorine; chloride. **хло́рка** bleach. **хлорофи́лл** chlorophyll. **хлорофо́рм** chloroform.
хлы́нуть (-нет) *pf* gush, pour.
хлыст (-á) whip, switch.
хмеле́ть (-е́ю) *impf* (*pf* **за~, о~**) get tipsy. **хмель** (*loc* -ю́) *m* hop, hops; drunkenness; **во хмелю́** tipsy. **хмельно́й** (-лён, -льна́) drunk; intoxicating.
хму́рить *impf* (*pf* **на~**): **~ бро́ви** knit one's brows; **~ся** frown; become gloomy; be overcast. **хму́рый** gloomy; overcast.
хны́кать (-ы́чу *or* -аю) *impf* whimper, snivel.
хо́бби *neut indecl* hobby.
хо́бот trunk. **хобото́к** (-тка́) proboscis.
ход (*loc* -ý; *pl* -ы, -ов *or* -ы́ *or* -á, -óв) motion; going; speed; course; operation; stroke; move; manoeuvre; entrance; passage; **в ~ý** in demand; **дать за́дний ~** reverse; **дать ~** set in motion; **на ~ý** in transit, on the move; in motion; in operation; **по́лным ~ом** at full speed; **пусти́ть в ~** start, set in motion; **три часа́ ~у** three hours' journey.
хода́тайство petitioning; application. **хода́тайствовать** *impf* (*pf* **по~**) petition, apply.
ходи́ть (хожу́, хо́дишь) *impf* walk; go; run; pass, go round; lead, play; move; **+в**+*prep* wear; **+за** +*instr* look after. **хо́дкий** (-док, -дка́, -о) fast; marketable; popular. **ходьба́** walking; walk. **ходя́чий** walking; able to walk; popular; current.
хозрасчёт *abbr* (*of* **хозя́йствен-**

ный расчёт) self-financing system.

хозя́ин (*pl* -я́ева, -я́ев) owner, proprietor; master; boss; landlord; host; **хозя́ева по́ля** home team. **хозя́йка** owner; mistress; hostess; landlady. **хозя́йничать** *impf* keep house; be in charge; lord it. **хозя́йственник** financial manager. **хозя́йственный** economic; household; economical. **хозя́йство** economy; housekeeping; equipment; farm; **дома́шнее ~** housekeeping; **се́льское ~** agriculture.

хоккеи́ст (ice-)hockey-player. **хокке́й** hockey, ice-hockey.

холе́ра cholera.

холестери́н cholesterol.

холл hall, vestibule.

холм (-а́) hill. **холми́стый** hilly.

хо́лод (*pl* -а́, -о́в) cold; coldness; cold weather. **холоди́льник** refrigerator. **хо́лодно** *adv* coldly. **холо́дн|ый** (хо́лоден, -дна́, -о) cold; inadequate, thin; **~ое ору́жие** cold steel.

холо́п serf.

холосто́й (хо́лост, -а́) unmarried, single; bachelor; idle; blank. **холостя́к** (-а́) bachelor.

холст (-а́) canvas; linen.

холу́й (-луя́) *m* lackey.

хому́т (-а́) (horse-)collar; burden.

хомя́к (-а́) hamster.

хор (*pl* хо́ры) choir; chorus.

хорва́т, ~ка Croat. **Хорва́тия** Croatia. **хорва́тский** Croatian.

хорёк (-рька́) polecat.

хореографи́ческий choreographic. **хореогра́фия** choreography.

хори́ст member of a choir or chorus.

хорони́ть (-ню́, -нишь) *impf* (*pf* **за~, по~, с~**) bury.

хоро́шенький pretty; nice. **хороше́нько** *adv* properly, thoroughly. **хороше́ть** (-е́ю) *impf* (*pf* **по~**) grow prettier. **хоро́ший** (-о́ш, -а́, -о́) good; nice; pretty, nice-looking; **хорошо́** *predic* it is good; it is nice. **хорошо́** *adv* well; nicely; all right! good.

хо́ры (хор *or* -ов) *pl* gallery.

хоте́ть (хочу́, хо́чешь, хоти́м) *impf* (*pf* **за~**) wish; +*gen*, *acc* want; **~ пить** be thirsty; **~ сказа́ть** mean; **~ся** *impers* +*dat* want; **мне хоте́лось бы** I should like; **мне хо́чется** I want.

хоть *conj* although; even if; *partl* at least, if only; for example; **~ бы** if only. **хотя́** *conj* although; **~ бы** even if; if only.

хо́хот loud laugh(ter). **хохота́ть** (-очу́, -о́чешь) *impf* laugh loudly.

хочу́ *etc.*: *see* **хоте́ть**

храбре́ц (-а́) brave man. **храбри́ться** make a show of bravery; pluck up courage. **хра́брость** bravery. **хра́брый** brave.

храм temple, church.

хране́ние keeping; storage; **ка́мера хране́ния** cloakroom, left-luggage office. **храни́лище** storehouse, depository. **храни́тель** *m* keeper, custodian; curator. **храни́ть** *impf* keep; preserve; **~ся** be, be kept.

храпе́ть (-плю́) *impf* snore; snort.

хребе́т (-бта́) spine; (mountain) range; ridge.

хрен horseradish.

хрестома́тия reader.

хрип wheeze. **хрипе́ть** (-плю́) *impf* wheeze. **хри́плый** (-пл, -а́, -о) hoarse. **хри́пнуть** (-ну; хрип) *impf* (*pf* **о~**) become hoarse. **хрипота́** hoarseness.

христиани́н (*pl* -а́не, -а́н), **христиа́нка** Christian. **христиа́нский** Christian. **христиа́нство** Christianity. **Христо́с** (-иста́) Christ.

хром chromium; chrome.

хромати́ческий chromatic.

хрома́ть *impf* limp; be poor. **хромо́й** (хром, -а́, -о) lame; *sb* lame person.

хромосо́ма chromosome.

хромота́ lameness.

хро́ник chronic invalid. **хро́ника** chronicle; news items; newsreel. **хрони́ческий** chronic.
хронологи́ческий chronological. **хроноло́гия** chronology.
хру́пкий (-пок, -пка́, -о) fragile; frail. **хру́пкость** fragility; frailness.
хруст crunch; crackle.
хруста́ль (-я́) *m* cut glass; crystal. **хруста́льный** cut-glass; crystal; crystal-clear.
хрусте́ть (-ущу́) *impf*, **хру́стнуть** (-ну) *pf* crunch; crackle.
хрю́кать *impf*, **хрю́кнуть** (-ну) *pf* grunt.
хрящ (-а́) cartilage, gristle. **хряще-во́й** cartilaginous, gristly.
худе́ть (-е́ю) *impf* (*pf* **по~**) grow thin.
ху́до harm; evil. **ху́до** *adv* ill, badly.
худоба́ thinness.
худо́жественный art, arts; artistic; **~ фильм** feature film. **худо́жник** artist.
худо́й[1] (худ, -а́, -о) thin, lean.
худо́й[2] (худ, -а́, -о) bad; full of holes; worn; **ему́ ху́до** he feels bad.
худоща́вый thin, lean.
ху́дший *superl of* **худо́й, плохо́й** (the) worst. **ху́же** *comp of* **худо́й, ху́до, плохо́й, пло́хо** worse.
хула́ abuse, criticism.
хулига́н hooligan. **хулига́нить** *impf* behave like a hooligan. **хулига́нство** hooliganism.
ху́нта junta.
ху́тор (*pl* -а́) farm; small village.

Ц

ца́пля (*gen pl* -пель) heron.
цара́пать *impf*, **цара́пнуть** (-ну) *pf* (*pf also* **на~, о~**) scratch; scribble; **~ся** scratch; scratch one another. **цара́пина** scratch.
цари́зм tsarism. **цари́ть** *impf* reign, prevail. **цари́ца** tsarina; queen. **ца́рский** tsar's; royal; tsarist; regal. **ца́рство** kingdom, realm; reign. **ца́рствование** reign. **ца́рствовать** *impf* reign. **царь** (-я́) *m* tsar; king.
цвести́ (-ету́, -етёшь; -ёл, -а́) *impf* flower, blossom; flourish.
цвет[1] (*pl* -а́) colour; **~ лица́** complexion.
цвет[2] (*loc* -у́; *pl* -ы́) flower; prime; **в цвету́** in blossom. **цветни́к** (-а́) flower-bed, flower-garden.
цветн|о́й coloured; colour; non-ferrous; **~а́я капу́ста** cauliflower; **~о́е стекло́** stained glass.
цветов|о́й colour; **~а́я слепота́** colour-blindness.
цвето́к (-тка́; *pl* цветы́ *or* цветки́, -о́в) flower. **цвето́чный** flower. **цвету́щий** flowering; prosperous.
цеди́ть (цежу́, це́дишь) *impf* strain, filter.
целе́бный curative, healing.
целево́й earmarked for a specific purpose. **целенапра́вленный** purposeful. **целесообра́зный** expedient. **целеустремлённый** (-ён, -ённа *or* -ена́) purposeful.
целико́м *adv* whole; entirely.
целина́ virgin lands, virgin soil. **цели́нн|ый** virgin; **~ые зе́мли** virgin lands.
цели́тельный healing, medicinal.
це́лить(ся *impf* (*pf* **на~**) aim, take aim.
целлофа́н cellophane.
целова́ть *impf* (*pf* **по~**) kiss; **~ся** kiss.
це́лое *sb* whole; integer. **целому́дренный** chaste. **целому́дрие** chastity. **це́лостность** integrity. **це́лый** (цел, -а́, -о) whole; safe, intact.
цель target; aim, object, goal.
це́льный (-лен, -льна́, -о) of one piece, solid; whole; integral; single. **це́льность** wholeness.
цеме́нт cement. **цементи́ровать** *impf & pf* cement. **цеме́нтный** cement.

цена́ (*acc* -у; *pl* -ы) price, cost; worth.

ценз qualification. **це́нзор** censor. **цензу́ра** censorship.

цени́тель *m* judge, connoisseur. **цени́ть** (-ню́, -нишь) *impf* value; appreciate. **це́нность** value; price; *pl* valuables; values. **це́нный** valuable.

цент cent. **це́нтнер** centner (*100kg*).

центр centre. **централиза́ция** centralization. **централизова́ть** *impf* & *pf* centralize. **центра́льный** central. **центробе́жный** centrifugal.

цепене́ть (-е́ю) *impf* (*pf* **о~**) freeze; become rigid. **це́пкий** tenacious; prehensile; sticky; obstinate. **це́пкость** tenacity. **цепля́ться** *impf* **за**+*acc* clutch at; cling to.

цепно́й chain. **цепо́чка** chain; file. **цепь** (*loc* -и́; *gen pl* -е́й) chain; series; circuit.

церемо́ниться *impf* (*pf* **по~**) stand on ceremony. **церемо́ния** ceremony.

церковнославя́нский Church Slavonic. **церко́вный** church; ecclesiastical. **це́рковь** (-кви; *pl* -и, -е́й, -а́м) church.

цех (*loc* -у́; *pl* -и *or* -а́) shop; section; guild.

цивилиза́ция civilization. **цивилизо́ванный** civilized. **цивилизова́ть** *impf* & *pf* civilize.

циге́йка beaver lamb.

цикл cycle.

цико́рий chicory.

цили́ндр cylinder; top hat. **цилиндри́ческий** cylindrical.

цимба́лы (-а́л) *pl* cymbals.

цинга́ scurvy.

цини́зм cynicism. **ци́ник** cynic. **цини́чный** cynical.

цинк zinc. **ци́нковый** zinc.

цино́вка mat.

цирк circus.

циркули́ровать *impf* circulate. **ци́ркуль** *m* (pair of) compasses; dividers. **циркуля́р** circular. **циркуля́ция** circulation.

цисте́рна cistern, tank.

цитаде́ль citadel.

цита́та quotation. **цити́ровать** *impf* (*pf* **про~**) quote.

ци́трус citrus. **ци́трусов|ый** citrous; **~ые** *sb pl* citrus plants.

циферблА́т dial, face.

ци́фра figure; number, numeral. **цифрово́й** numerical, digital.

цо́коль *m* socle, plinth.

цыга́н (*pl* -е, -а́н *or* -ы, -ов), **цыга́нка** gipsy. **цыга́нский** gipsy.

цыплёнок (-нка *pl* -ля́та, -ля́т) chicken; chick.

цы́почки: на ~, на цы́почках on tip-toe.

Ч

чаба́н (-а́) shepherd.

чад (*loc* -у́) fumes, smoke.

чадра́ yashmak.

чай (*pl* -и́, -ёв) tea. **чаевы́е** (-ы́х) *sb pl* tip.

ча́йка (*gen pl* ча́ек) (sea-)gull.

ча́йная *sb* tea-shop. **ча́йник** teapot; kettle. **ча́йный** tea. **чайхана́** tea-house.

чалма́ turban.

чан (*loc* -у́; *pl* -ы́) vat, tub.

чарова́ть *impf* bewitch; charm.

час (*with numerals* -а́, *loc* -у́; *pl* -ы́) hour; *pl* guard-duty; **кото́рый час?** what's the time?; **~** one o'clock; **в два ~а́** at two o'clock; **стоя́ть на ~а́х** stand guard; **~ы́ пик** rush-hour. **часо́вня** (*gen pl* -вен) chapel. **часово́й** *sb* sentry. **часово́й** clock, watch; of one hour, hour-long. **часовщи́к** (-а́) watchmaker.

части́ца small part; particle. **части́чно** *adv* partly, partially. **части́чный** partial.

ча́стник private trader.

ча́стность detail; **в ча́стности** in particular. **ча́стный** private; per-

sonal; particular, individual.
ча́сто *adv* often; close, thickly. **частоко́л** paling, palisade. **частота́** (*pl* -ы) frequency. **часто́тный** frequency. **часту́шка** ditty. **ча́стый** (част, -а́, -о) frequent; close (together); dense; close-woven; rapid.
часть (*gen pl* -е́й) part; department; field; unit.
часы́ (-о́в) *pl* clock, watch.
чат (*comput*) IRC (Internet Relay Chat).
ча́хлый stunted; sickly, puny. **чахо́тка** consumption.
ча́ша bowl; chalice; ~ **весо́в** scale, pan. **ча́шка** cup; scale, pan.
ча́ща thicket.
ча́ще *comp of* **ча́сто, ча́стый;** ~ **всего́** most often, mostly.
ча́яние expectation; hope. **ча́ять** (ча́ю) *impf* hope, expect.
чва́нство conceit, arrogance.
чего́ *see* **что**
чей *m*, **чья** *f*, **чьё** *neut*, **чьи** *pl pron* whose. **че́й-либо, че́й-нибудь** anyone's. **че́й-то** someone's.
чек cheque; bill; receipt.
чека́нить *impf* (*pf* **вы́~, от~**) mint, coin; stamp. **чека́нка** coinage, minting. **чека́нный** stamped, engraved.
чёлка fringe; forelock.
чёлн (-а́; *pl* чёлны́) dug-out (canoe); boat. **челно́к** (-а́) dug-out (canoe); shuttle.
челове́к (*pl* люди; with numerals, *gen* -ве́к, -ам) man, person.
человеко- *in comb* man-, anthropo-. **человеколюби́вый** philanthropic. **~лю́бие** philanthropy. **~ненави́стнический** misanthropic. **челове́ко-ча́с** (*pl* -ы́) man-hour.
челове́чек (-чка) little man. **челове́ческий** human; humane. **челове́чество** mankind. **челове́чность** humaneness. **челове́чный** humane.
че́люсть jaw(-bone); dentures, false teeth.
чем, чём *see* **что. чем** *conj* than; **~..., тем...**+*comp* the more ..., the more.
чемода́н suitcase.
чемпио́н, ~ка champion, titleholder. **чемпиона́т** championship.
чему́ *see* **что**
чепуха́ nonsense; trifle.
че́пчик cap; bonnet.
че́рви (-е́й), **че́рвы** (черв) *pl* hearts. **черво́нн|ый** of hearts; **~ое зо́лото** pure gold.
червь (-я́; *pl* -и, -е́й) *m* worm; bug. **червя́к** (-а́) worm.
черда́к (-а́) attic, loft.
черёд (-а́, *loc* -у́) turn; **идти́ свои́м ~о́м** take its course. **чередова́ние** alternation. **чередова́ть** *impf* alternate; **~ся** alternate, take turns.
че́рез, чрез *prep*+*acc* across; over; through; via; in; after; every other.
черёмуха bird cherry.
черено́к (-нка́) handle; graft, cutting.
че́реп (*pl* -а́) skull.
черепа́ха tortoise; turtle; tortoiseshell. **черепа́ховый** tortoise; turtle; tortoiseshell. **черепа́ший** tortoise, turtle; very slow.
черепи́ца tile. **черепи́чный** tile; tiled.
черепо́к (-пка́) potsherd, fragment of pottery.
чересчу́р *adv* too; too much.
чере́шневый cherry. **чере́шня** (*gen pl* -шен) cherry(-tree).
черке́с, черке́шенка Circassian.
черкну́ть (-ну́, -нёшь) *pf* scrape; leave a mark on; scribble.
черне́ть (-е́ю) *impf* (*pf* **по~**) turn black; show black. **черни́ка** (*no pl*; *usu collect*) bilberry; bilberries. **черни́ла** (-и́л) *pl* ink. **черни́льный** ink. **черни́ть** *impf* (*pf* **о~**) blacken; slander.
черно- *in comb* black; unskilled; rough. **чёрно-бе́лый** black-and-white. **~бу́рый** dark-brown;

Ч

~бу́рая лиса́ silver fox. **~воло́сый** black-haired. **~гла́зый** black-eyed. **~зём** chernozem, black earth. **~ко́жий** black; *sb* black. **~мо́рский** Black-Sea. **~рабо́чий** *sb* unskilled worker, labourer. **~сли́в** prunes. **~сморо́динный** blackcurrant.

черновик (-а́) rough copy, draft. **чернов́ой** rough; draft. **чернота́** blackness; darkness. **чёрн|ый** (-рен, -рна́) black; back; unskilled; ferrous; gloomy; *sb* (*derog*) black person; **~ая сморо́дина** (*no pl*; *usu collect*) blackcurrant(s).

черпа́к (-а́) scoop. **че́рпать** *impf*, **черпну́ть** (-ну́, -нёшь) *pf* draw; scoop; extract.

черстве́ть (-е́ю) *impf* (*pf* **за~, о~, по~**) get stale; become hardened. **чёрствый** (чёрств, -а́, -о) stale; hard.

чёрт (*pl* че́рти, -е́й) devil.

черта́ line; boundary; trait, characteristic. **чертёж** (-а́) drawing; blueprint, plan. **чертёжник** draughtsman. **чертёжный** drawing. **черти́ть** (-рчу́, -ртишь) *impf* (*pf* **на~**) draw.

чёртов *adj* devil's; devilish. **черто́вский** devilish.

чертополо́х thistle.

чёрточка line; hyphen. **черче́ние** drawing. **черчу́** *etc.*: *see* **черти́ть**

чеса́ть (чешу́, -шешь) *impf* (*pf* **по~**) scratch; comb; card; **~ся** scratch o.s.; itch; comb one's hair.

чесно́к (-а́) garlic.

че́ствование celebration. **че́ствовать** *impf* celebrate; honour. **че́стность** honesty. **че́стный** (-тен, -тна́, -о) honest. **честолюби́вый** ambitious. **честолю́бие** ambition. **честь** (*loc* -и́) honour; **отда́ть ~** +*dat* salute.

чета́ pair, couple.

четве́рг (-а́) Thursday. **четвере́ньки: на ~, на четвере́ньках** on hands and knees. **четвёрка** four; figure 4; No. 4. **че́тверо** (-ых) four. **четвероно́г|ий** four-legged; **~ое** *sb* quadruped. **четверости́шие** quatrain. **четвёртый** fourth. **че́тверть** (*gen pl* -е́й) quarter; quarter of an hour; **без че́тверти час** a quarter to one. **четверть-фина́л** quarter-final.

чёткий (-ток, -тка́, -о) precise; clear-cut; clear; distinct. **чёткость** precision; clarity.

чётный even.

четы́ре (-рёх, -рьмя́, -рёх) four. **четы́реста** (-рёхсо́т, -ьмяста́ми, -ёхста́х) four hundred.

четырёх- *in comb* four-, tetra-. **четырёхкра́тный** fourfold. **~ме́стный** four-seater. **~со́тый** four-hundredth. **~уго́льник** quadrangle. **~уго́льный** quadrangular.

четы́рнадцатый fourteenth. **четы́рнадцать** fourteen.

чех Czech.

чехо́л (-хла́) cover, case.

чечеви́ца lentil; lens.

че́шка Czech. **че́шский** Czech.

чешу́ *etc.*: *see* **чеса́ть**

чешу́йка scale. **чешуя́** scales.

чи́бис lapwing.

чиж (-а́) siskin.

чин (*pl* -ы́) rank.

чини́ть[1] (-ню́, -нишь) *impf* (*pf* **по~**) repair, mend.

чини́ть[2] *impf* (*pf* **у~**) carry out; cause; **~ препя́тствия** +*dat* put obstacles in the way of.

чино́вник civil servant; official.

чип (micro)chip.

чи́псы (-ов) *pl* (potato) crisps.

чири́кать *impf*, **чири́кнуть** (-ну) *pf* chirp.

чи́ркать *impf*, **чи́ркнуть** (-ну) *pf* +*instr* strike.

чи́сленность numbers; strength. **чи́сленный** numerical. **числи́тель** *m* numerator. **числи́тельное** *sb* numeral. **чи́слить** *impf* count, reckon; **~ся** be; +*instr* be reckoned. **число́** (*pl* -а, -сел) number; date, day; **в числе́** +*gen* among; **в том числе́** including; **еди́нственное ~** singular; **мно́же-**

Ч

ственное ~ plural. **числово́й** numerical.

чисти́лище purgatory.

чи́стильщик cleaner. **чи́стить** (чи́щу) *impf* (*pf* **вы́~, о~, по~**) clean; peel; clear. **чи́стка** cleaning; purge. **чи́сто** *adv* cleanly, clean; purely; completely. **чистово́й** fair, clean. **чистокро́вный** thoroughbred. **чистописа́ние** calligraphy. **чистоплóтный** clean; neat; decent. **чистосерде́чный** frank, sincere. **чистота́** cleanness; neatness; purity. **чи́стый** clean; neat; pure; complete.

чита́емый widely-read, popular. **чита́льный** reading. **чита́тель** *m* reader. **чита́ть** *impf* (*pf* **про~, проче́сть**) read; recite; **~ ле́кции** lecture; **~ся** be legible; be discernible. **чи́тка** reading.

чиха́ть *impf*, **чихну́ть** (-ну́, -нёшь) *pf* sneeze.

чи́ще *comp of* **чи́сто, чи́стый**

чи́щу *etc.*: *see* **чи́стить**

член member; limb; term; part; article. **члени́ть** *impf* (*pf* **рас~**) divide; articulate. **член-корреспонде́нт** corresponding member, associate. **членоразде́льный** articulate. **чле́нский** membership. **чле́нство** membership.

чмо́кать *impf*, **чмо́кнуть** (-ну) *pf* smack; squelch; kiss noisily; **~ губа́ми** smack one's lips.

чо́каться *impf*, **чо́кнуться** (-нусь) *pf* clink glasses.

чо́порный prim; stand-offish.

чрева́тый +*instr* fraught with. **чре́во** belly, womb. **чревовеща́тель** *m* ventriloquist.

чрез *see* **че́рез. чрезвыча́йн|ый** extraordinary; extreme; **~ое положе́ние** state of emergency. **чрезме́рный** excessive.

чте́ние reading. **чтец** (-а́) reader; reciter.

чтить (чту) *impf* honour.

что, чего́, чему́, чем, о чём *pron* what?; how?; why?; how much?; which, what, who; anything; **в чём де́ло?** what is the matter? **для чего́?** what ... for? why?; **~ ему́ до э́того?** what does it matter to him?; **~ с тобо́й?** what's the matter (with you)?; **~ за** what? what sort of?; what (a) ...!; **что** *conj* that. **что (бы) ни** *pron* whatever, no matter what.

чтоб, что́бы *conj* in order (to), so as; that; to. **что́-либо, что́-нибудь** *prons* anything. **что́-то¹** *pron* something. **что́-то²** *adv* somewhat, slightly; somehow, for some reason.

чу́вственность sensuality. **чувстви́тельность** sensitivity; perceptibility; sentimentality. **чувстви́тельный** sensitive; perceptible; sentimental. **чу́вство** feeling; sense; senses; **прийти́ в ~** come round. **чу́вствовать** *impf* (*pf* **по~**) feel; realize; appreciate; **~ себя́** +*adv or instr* feel a certain way; **~ся** be perceptible; make itself felt.

чугу́н (-а́) cast iron. **чугу́нный** cast-iron.

чуда́к (-а́), **чуда́чка** eccentric, crank. **чуда́чество** eccentricity.

чудеса́ *etc.*: *see* **чу́до. чуде́сный** miraculous; wonderful.

чу́диться (-ишься) *impf* (*pf* **по~, при~**) seem.

чу́дно *adv* wonderfully; wonderful! **чудно́й** (-дён, -дна́) odd, strange. **чу́дный** wonderful; magical. **чу́до** (*pl* -деса́) miracle; wonder. **чудо́вище** monster. **чудо́вищный** monstrous. **чудоде́йственный** miracle-working; miraculous. **чу́дом** *adv* miraculously. **чудотво́рный** miraculous, miracle-working.

чужби́на foreign land. **чужда́ться** *impf* +*gen* avoid; stand aloof from. **чу́ждый** (-жд, -а́, -о) alien (to); +*gen* free from, devoid of. **чужезе́мец** (-мца), **-зе́мка** foreigner. **чужезе́мный** foreign. **чужо́й** someone else's, others'; strange, alien; foreign.

ч

чула́н store-room; larder.
чуло́к (-лка́; *gen pl* -ло́к) stocking.
чума́ plague.
чума́зый dirty.
чурба́н block. **чу́рка** block, lump.
чу́ткий (-ток, -тка́, -о) keen; sensitive; sympathetic; delicate. **чу́ткость** keenness; delicacy.
чу́точка: ни чу́точки not in the least; **чу́точку** a little (bit).
чу́тче *comp of* **чу́ткий**
чуть *adv* hardly; just; very slightly; **~ не** almost; **~-чуть** a tiny bit.
чутьё scent; flair.
чу́чело stuffed animal, stuffed bird; scarecrow.
чушь nonsense.
чу́ять (чу́ю) *impf* scent; sense.
чьё *etc.*: *see* **чей**

Ш

ша́баш sabbath.
шабло́н template; mould, stencil; cliché. **шабло́нный** stencil; trite; stereotyped.
шаг (with numerals -а́, *loc* -у́; *pl* -и́) step; footstep; pace. **шага́ть** *impf*, **шагну́ть** (-ну́, -нёшь) *pf* step; stride; pace; make progress. **ша́гом** *adv* at walking pace.
ша́йба washer; puck.
ша́йка[1] tub.
ша́йка[2] gang, band.
шака́л jackal.
шала́ш (-а́) cabin, hut.
шали́ть *impf* be naughty; play up. **шаловли́вый** mischievous, playful. **ша́лость** prank; *pl* mischief. **шалу́н** (-а́), **шалу́нья** (*gen pl* -ний) naughty child.
шаль shawl.
шально́й mad, crazy.
ша́мкать *impf* mumble.
шампа́нское *sb* champagne.
шампиньо́н field mushroom.
шампу́нь *m* shampoo.
шанс chance.
шанта́ж (-а́) blackmail. **шантажи́ровать** *impf* blackmail.
ша́пка hat; banner headline. **ша́почка** hat.
шар (with numerals -а́; *pl* -ы́) sphere; ball; balloon.
шара́хать *impf*, **шара́хнуть** (-ну) hit; **~ся** dash; shy.
шарж caricature.
ша́рик ball; corpuscle. **ша́рикова|ый: ~ая (авто)ру́чка** ball-point pen; **~ый подши́пник** ball-bearing. **шарикоподши́пник** ball-bearing.
ша́рить *impf* grope; sweep.
ша́ркать *impf*, **ша́ркнуть** (-ну) *pf* shuffle; scrape.
шарлата́н charlatan.
шарма́нка barrel-organ. **шарма́нщик** organ-grinder.
шарни́р hinge, joint.
шарова́ры (-а́р) *pl* (*wide*) trousers.
шарови́дный spherical. **шарово́й** ball; globular. **шарообра́зный** spherical.
шарф scarf.
шасси́ *neut indecl* chassis.
шата́ть *impf* rock, shake; *impers* +*acc* **его́ шата́ет** he is reeling; **~ся** sway; reel, stagger; come loose, be loose; be unsteady; loaf about.
шатёр (-тра́) tent; marquee.
ша́ткий unsteady; shaky.
шату́н (-а́) connecting-rod.
ша́фер (*pl* -а́) best man.
шах check; **~ и мат** checkmate. **шахмати́ст** chess-player. **ша́хматы** (-ат) *pl* chess; chessmen.
ша́хта mine, pit; shaft. **шахтёр** miner. **шахтёрский** miner's; mining.
ша́шка[1] draught; *pl* draughts.
ша́шка[2] sabre.
шашлы́к (-а́) kebab; barbecue.
шва *etc.*: *see* **шов**
шва́бра mop.
шваль rubbish; riff-raff.
шварто́в mooring-line; *pl* moorings. **швартова́ть** *impf* (*pf* **при~**) moor; **~ся** moor.
швед, ~ка Swede. **шве́дский** Swedish.

шве́йн|ый sewing; **~ая маши́на** sewing-machine.
швейца́р porter, doorman.
швейца́рец (-рца), **-ца́рка** Swiss. **Швейца́рия** Switzerland. **швейца́рский** Swiss.
Шве́ция Sweden.
швея́ seamstress.
швырну́ть (-ну́, -нёшь) *pf*, **швыря́ть** *impf* throw, fling; **~ся** +*instr* throw (about); treat carelessly.
шевели́ть (-елю́, -е́ли́шь) *impf*, **шевельну́ть** (-ну́, -нёшь) *pf* (*pf also* **по~**) (+*instr*) move, stir; **~ся** move, stir.
шеде́вр masterpiece.
ше́йка (*gen pl* ше́ек) neck.
шёл *see* **идти́**
ше́лест rustle. **шелесте́ть** (-сти́шь) *impf* rustle.
шёлк (*loc* -у́; *pl* -а́) silk. **шелкови́стый** silky. **шелкови́ца** mulberry(-tree). **шелкови́чный** mulberry; **~ червь** silkworm. **шёлковый** silk.
шелохну́ть (-ну́, -нёшь) *pf* stir, agitate; **~ся** stir, move.
шелуха́ skin; peelings; pod. **шелуши́ть** (-шу́) peel; shell; **~ся** peel (off), flake off.
шепеля́вить (-влю) *impf* lisp. **шепеля́вый** lisping.
шепну́ть (-ну́, -нёшь) *pf*, **шепта́ть** (-пчу́, -пчешь) *impf* whisper; **~ся** whisper (together). **шёпот** whisper. **шёпотом** *adv* in a whisper.
шере́нга rank; file.
шерохова́тый rough; uneven.
шерсть wool; hair, coat. **шерстяно́й** wool(len).
герша́вый rough.
шест (-а́) pole; staff.
ше́ствие procession. **ше́ствовать** process; march.
шестёрка six; figure 6; No. 6.
шестерня́ (*gen pl* -рён) gearwheel, cogwheel.
ше́стеро (-ы́х) six.
шести- *in comb* six-, hexa-, sex(i)-. **шестигра́нник** hexahedron. **~дне́вка** six-day (*working*) week. **~деся́тый** sixtieth. **~ме́сячный** six-month; six-month-old. **~со́тый** six-hundredth. **~уго́льник** hexagon.
шестнадцатиле́тний sixteen-year; sixteen-year-old. **шестна́дцатый** sixteenth. **шестна́дцать** sixteen. **шесто́й** sixth. **шесть** (-и́, *instr* -ью) six. **шестьдеся́т** (-и́десяти, *instr* -ью́десятью) sixty. **шестьсо́т** (-исо́т, -иста́м, -ьюста́ми, -иста́х) six hundred. **ше́стью** *adv* six times.
шеф boss, chief; patron, sponsor. **шеф-по́вар** chef. **ше́фство** patronage, adoption. **ше́фствовать** *impf* +**над**+ *instr* adopt; sponsor.
ше́я neck.
ши́ворот collar.
шика́рный chic, smart; splendid.
ши́ло (*pl* -ья, -ьев) awl.
шимпанзе́ *m indecl* chimpanzee.
ши́на tyre; splint.
шине́ль overcoat.
шинкова́ть *impf* shred, chop.
ши́нный tyre.
шип (-а́) thorn, spike, crampon; pin; tenon.
шипе́ние hissing; sizzling. **шипе́ть** (-плю́) *impf* hiss; sizzle; fizz.
шипо́вник dog-rose.
шипу́чий sparkling; fizzy. **шипу́чка** fizzy drink. **шипя́щий** sibilant.
ши́ре *comp of* **широ́кий, широ́ко́.** **ширина́** width; gauge. **ши́рить** *impf* extend, expand; **~ся** spread, extend.
ши́рма screen.
широ́к|ий (-о́к, -а́, -о́ко́) wide, broad; **това́ры ~ого потребле́ния** consumer goods. **широ́ко́** *adv* wide, widely, broadly.
широко- *in comb* wide-, broad-. **широковеща́ние** broadcasting. **~веща́тельный** broadcasting. **~экра́нный** wide-screen.
широта́ (*pl* -ы) width, breadth; latitude. **широ́тный** of latitude; latitudinal. **широча́йший** *superl*

of **широ́кий. ширпотре́б** *abbr* consumption; consumer goods. **ширь** (wide) expanse.

шить (шью, шьёшь) *impf* (*pf* **с~**) sew; make; embroider. **шитьё** sewing; embroidery.

ши́фер slate.

шифр cipher, code; shelf mark. **шифро́ванный** coded. **шифрова́ть** *impf* (*pf* **за~**) encipher. **шифро́вка** enciphering; coded communication.

ши́шка cone; bump; lump; (*sl*) big shot.

шкала́ (*pl* -ы) scale; dial.

шкату́лка box, casket, case.

шкаф (*loc* -у́; *pl* -ы́) cupboard; wardrobe. **шка́фчик** cupboard, locker.

шквал squall.

шкив (*pl* -ы́) pulley.

шко́ла school. **шко́льник** schoolboy. **шко́льница** schoolgirl. **шко́льный** school.

шку́ра skin, hide, pelt. **шку́рка** skin; rind; sandpaper.

шла *see* **идти́**

шлагба́ум barrier.

шлак slag; dross; clinker. **шлакобло́к** breeze-block.

шланг hose.

шлейф train.

шлем helmet.

шлёпать *impf*, **шлёпнуть** (-ну) *pf* smack, spank; shuffle; tramp; **~ся** fall flat, plop down.

шли *see* **идти́**

шлифова́льный polishing; grinding. **шлифова́ть** *impf* (*pf* **от~**) polish; grind. **шлифо́вка** polishing.

шло *see* **идти́. шлю** *etc.*: *see* **слать**

шлюз lock, sluice.

шлю́пка boat.

шля́па hat. **шля́пка** hat; head.

шмель (-я́) *m* bumble-bee.

шмон *sl* search, frisking.

шмы́гать *impf*, **шмыгну́ть** (-ыгну́, -ыгнёшь) *pf* dart, rush; +*instr* rub, brush; **~ но́сом** sniff.

шни́цель *m* schnitzel.

шнур (-а́) cord; lace; flex, cable.

шнурова́ть *impf* (*pf* **за~, про~**) lace up; tie. **шнуро́к** (-рка́) lace.

шов (шва) seam; stitch; joint.

шовини́зм chauvinism. **шовини́ст** chauvinist. **шовинисти́ческий** chauvinistic.

шок shock. **шоки́ровать** *impf* shock.

шокола́д chocolate. **шокола́дка** chocolate, bar of chocolate. **шокола́дный** chocolate.

шо́рох rustle.

шо́рты (шорт) *pl* shorts.

шо́ры (шор) *pl* blinkers.

шоссе́ *neut indecl* highway.

шотла́ндец (-дца) Scotsman, Scot. **Шотла́ндия** Scotland. **шотла́ндка**[1] Scotswoman. **шотла́ндка**[2] tartan. **шотла́ндский** Scottish, Scots.

шо́у *neut indecl* show; **~ -би́знес** show business.

шофёр driver; chauffeur. **шофёрский** driver's; driving.

шпа́га sword.

шпага́т cord; twine; string; splits.

шпаклева́ть (-лю́ю) *impf* (*pf* **за~**) caulk; fill, putty. **шпаклёвка** filling, puttying; putty.

шпа́ла sleeper.

шпана́ (*sl*) hooligan(s); riff-raff.

шпарга́лка crib.

шпа́рить *impf* (*pf* **о~**) scald.

шпат spar.

шпиль *m* spire; capstan. **шпи́лька** hairpin; hat-pin; tack; stiletto heel.

шпина́т spinach.

шпингале́т (vertical) bolt; catch, latch.

шпио́н spy. **шпиона́ж** espionage. **шпио́нить** *impf* spy (**за** +*instr* on). **шпио́нский** spy's; espionage.

шпо́ра spur.

шприц syringe.

шпро́та sprat.

шпу́лька spool, bobbin.

шрам scar.

шрапне́ль shrapnel.

шрифт (*pl* -ы́) type, print.

шт. *abbr* (*of* **шту́ка**) item, piece.

штаб (*pl* -ы́) staff; headquarters.

шта́бель (*pl* -я́) *m* stack.
штабно́й staff; headquarters.
штамп die, punch; stamp; cliché. **штампо́ванный** punched, stamped, pressed; trite; stock.
шта́нга bar, rod, beam; weight. **штанги́ст** weight-lifter.
штани́шки (-шек) *pl* (*child's*) shorts. **штаны́** (-о́в) trousers.
штат[1] State.
штат[2], **шта́ты** (-ов) *pl* staff, establishment.
штати́в tripod, base, stand.
шта́тный staff; established.
шта́тск|ий civilian; **~ое (пла́тье)** civilian clothes; **~ий** *sb* civilian.
ште́мпель (*pl* -я́) *m* stamp; **почто́вый ~** postmark.
ште́псель (*pl* -я́) *m* plug, socket.
штиль *m* calm.
штифт (-а́) pin, dowel.
што́льня (*gen pl* -лен) gallery.
што́пать *impf* (*pf* **за~**) darn. **што́пка** darning; darning wool.
што́пор corkscrew; spin.
што́ра blind.
шторм gale.
штраф fine. **штрафно́й** penal; penalty. **штрафова́ть** *impf* (*pf* **о~**) fine.
штрих (-а́) stroke; feature. **штрихова́ть** *impf* (*pf* **за~**) shade, hatch.
штуди́ровать *impf* (*pf* **про~**) study.
шту́ка item, one; piece; trick.
штукату́р plasterer. **штукату́рить** *impf* (*pf* **от~, о~**) plaster. **штукату́рка** plastering; plaster.
штурва́л (steering-)wheel, helm.
штурм storm, assault.
шту́рман (*pl* -ы *or* -а́) navigator.
штурмова́ть *impf* storm, assault. **штурмов|о́й** assault; storming; **~а́я авиа́ция** ground-attack aircraft. **штурмовщи́на** rushed work.
шту́чный piece, by the piece.
штык (-а́) bayonet.
штырь (-я́) *m* pintle, pin.
шу́ба fur coat.
шу́лер (*pl* -а́) card-sharper.
шум noise; uproar, racket; stir. **шуме́ть** (-млю́) *impf* make a noise; row; make a fuss. **шу́мный** (-мен, -мна́, -о) noisy; loud; sensational.
шумов|о́й sound; **~ы́е эффе́кты** sound effects. **шумо́к** (-мка́) noise; **под ~** on the quiet.
шу́рин brother-in-law (*wife's brother*).
шурф prospecting shaft.
шурша́ть (-шу́) *impf* rustle.
шу́стрый (-тёр, -тра́, -о) smart, bright, sharp.
шут (-а́) fool; jester. **шути́ть** (-чу́, -тишь) *impf* (*pf* **по~**) joke; play, trifle; **+над+***instr* make fun of. **шу́тка** joke, jest. **шутли́вый** humorous; joking, light-hearted. **шу́точный** comic; joking. **шутя́** *adv* for fun, in jest; easily.
шушу́каться *impf* whisper together.
шху́на schooner.
шью *etc.*: *see* **шить**

Щ

щаве́ль (-я́) *m* sorrel.
щади́ть (щажу́) *impf* (*pf* **по~**) spare.
щебёнка, ще́бень (-бня) *m* crushed stone, ballast; road-metal.
ще́бет twitter, chirp. **щебета́ть** (-ечу́, -е́чешь) *impf* twitter, chirp.
щего́л (-гла́) goldfinch.
щёголь *m* dandy, fop. **щегольну́ть** (-ну́, -нёшь) *pf*, **щеголя́ть** *impf* dress fashionably; strut about; *+instr* show off, flaunt. **щегольско́й** foppish.
ще́дрость generosity. **ще́дрый** (-др, -а́, -о) generous; liberal.
щека́ (*acc* щёку; *pl* щёки, -а́м) cheek.
щеко́лда latch, catch.
щекота́ть (-очу́, -о́чешь) *impf* (*pf* **по~**) tickle. **щеко́тка** tickling, tickle. **щекотли́вый** ticklish, delicate.

щёлкать *impf*, **щёлкнуть** (-ну) *pf* crack; flick; trill; +*instr* click, snap, pop.
щёлок bleach. **щелочно́й** alkaline. **щёлочь** (*gen pl* -е́й) alkali.
щелчо́к (-чка́) flick; slight; blow.
щель (*gen pl* -е́й) crack; chink; slit; crevice; slit trench.
щеми́ть (-млю́) *impf* constrict; ache; oppress.
щено́к (-нка́; *pl* -нки́, -о́в *or* -ня́та, -я́т) pup; cub.
щепа́ (*pl* -ы, -а́м), **ще́пка** splinter, chip; kindling.
щепети́льный punctilious.
ще́пка *see* **щепа́**
щепо́тка, ще́по́ть pinch.
щети́на bristle; stubble. **щети́нистый** bristly. **щети́ниться** *impf* (*pf* **о~**) bristle. **щётка** brush; fetlock.
щи (щей *or* щец, щам, ща́ми) *pl* shchi, cabbage soup.
щи́колотка ankle.
щипа́ть (-плю́, -плешь) *impf*, **щипну́ть** (-ну́, -нёшь) *pf* (*pf also* **об~, о~, ущипну́ть**) pinch, nip; sting, bite; burn; pluck; nibble; **~ся** pinch. **щипко́м** *adv* pizzicato. **щипо́к** (-пка́) pinch, nip. **щипцы́** (-о́в) *pl* tongs, pincers, pliers; forceps.
щит (-а́) shield; screen; sluice-gate; (tortoise-)shell; board; panel. **щитови́дный** thyroid. **щито́к** (-тка́) dashboard.
щу́ка pike.
щуп probe. **щу́пальце** (*gen pl* -лец) tentacle; antenna. **щу́пать** *impf* (*pf* **по~**) feel, touch.
щу́плый (-пл, -а́, -о) weak, puny.
щу́рить *impf* (*pf* **со~**) screw up, narrow; **~ся** screw up one's eyes; narrow.

Э

эбе́новый ebony.
эвакуа́ция evacuation. **эвакуи́рованный** *sb* evacuee. **эвакуи́ровать** *impf* & *pf* evacuate.
эвкали́пт eucalyptus.
эволюциони́ровать *impf* & *pf* evolve. **эволюцио́нный** evolutionary. **эволю́ция** evolution.
эги́да aegis.
эгои́зм egoism, selfishness. **эгои́ст, ~ка** egoist. **эгоисти́ческий, эгоисти́чный** egoistic, selfish.
эй *int* hi! hey!
эйфори́я euphoria.
эква́тор equator.
эквивале́нт equivalent.
экзальта́ция exaltation.
экза́мен examination; **вы́держать, сдать ~** pass an examination. **экзамена́тор** examiner. **экзаменова́ть** *impf* (*pf* **про~**) examine; **~ся** take an examination.
экзеку́ция (corporal) punishment.
экзе́ма eczema.
экземпля́р specimen; copy.
экзистенциали́зм existentialism.
экзоти́ческий exotic.
э́кий what (a).
экипа́ж[1] carriage.
экипа́ж[2] crew. **экипирова́ть** *impf* & *pf* equip. **экипиро́вка** equipping; equipment.
эклекти́зм eclecticism.
экле́р éclair.
экологи́ческий ecological. **эколо́гия** ecology.
эконо́мика economics; economy. **экономи́ст** economist. **эконо́мить** (-млю) *impf* (*pf* **с~**) use sparingly; save; economize. **экономи́ческий** economic; economical. **экономи́чный** economical. **эконо́мия** economy; saving. **эконо́мка** housekeeper. **эконо́мный** economical; thrifty.
экра́н screen. **экраниза́ция** filming; film version.
экскава́тор excavator.
эксклюзи́вный exclusive.
экскурса́нт tourist. **экскурсио́нный** excursion. **экску́рсия** (conducted) tour; excursion. **экскурсово́д** guide.

экспанси́вный effusive.
экспатриа́нт expatriate.
экспеди́тор shipping agent. **экспеди́ция** expedition; dispatch; forwarding office.
экспериме́нт experiment. **эксперимента́льный** experimental. **эксперименти́ровать** *impf* experiment.
экспе́рт expert. **эксперти́за** (expert) examination; commission of experts.
эксплуата́тор exploiter. **эксплуатацио́нный** operating. **эксплуата́ция** exploitation; operation. **эксплуати́ровать** *impf* exploit; operate, run.
экспози́ция lay-out; exposition; exposure. **экспона́т** exhibit. **экспоно́метр** exposure meter.
э́кспорт export. **экспорти́ровать** *impf* & *pf* export. **э́кспортный** export.
экспре́сс express (*train etc.*).
экспро́мт impromptu. **экспро́мтом** *adv* impromptu.
экспроприа́ция expropriation. **экспроприи́ровать** *impf* & *pf* expropriate.
экста́з ectasy.
экстравага́нтный eccentric, bizarre.
экстра́кт extract.
экстреми́ст extremist. **экстреми́стский** extremist.
э́кстренный urgent; emergency; special.
эксцентри́чный eccentric.
эксце́сс excess.
эласти́чный elastic; supple.
элева́тор grain elevator; hoist.
элега́нтный elegant, smart.
эле́гия elegy.
электризова́ть *impf* (*pf* **на~**) electrify. **эле́ктрик** electrician. **электрифика́ция** electrification. **электрифици́ровать** *impf* & *pf* electrify. **электри́ческий** electric(al). **электри́чество** electricity. **электри́чка** electric train.
электро- *in comb* electro-, electric, electrical. **электробытово́й** electrical. **~во́з** electric locomotive. **электро́лиз** electrolysis. **~магни́тный** electromagnetic. **~монтёр** electrician. **~одея́ло** electric blanket. **~по́езд** electric train. **~прибо́р** electrical appliance. **~про́вод** (*pl* -á) electric cable. **~прово́дка** electric wiring. **~ста́нция** power-station. **~те́хник** electrical engineer. **~те́хника** electrical engineering. **~шо́к** electric shock, electric-shock treatment. **~эне́ргия** electrical energy.
электро́д electrode.
электро́н electron. **электро́ника** electronics.
электро́нн|ый electron; electronic; **~ая по́чта** email; **~ое письмо́** email (letter); **~ый а́дрес** email address.
элеме́нт element; cell; character. **элемента́рный** elementary.
эли́та élite.
э́ллипс elipse.
эма́левый enamel. **эмалирова́ть** *impf* enamel. **эма́ль** enamel.
эмансипа́ция emancipation.
эмба́рго *neut indecl* embargo.
эмбле́ма emblem.
эмбрио́н embryo.
эмигра́нт emigrant, émigré. **эмигра́ция** emigration. **эмигри́ровать** *impf* & *pf* emigrate.
эмоциона́льный emotional. **эмо́ция** emotion.
эмпири́ческий empirical.
эму́льсия emulsion.
э́ндшпиль *m* end-game.
энерге́тика power engineering. **энергети́ческий** energy. **энерги́чный** energetic. **эне́ргия** energy.
энтомоло́гия entomology.
энтузиа́зм enthusiasm. **энтузиа́ст** enthusiast.
энциклопеди́ческий encyclopaedic. **энциклопе́дия** encyclopaedia.
эпигра́мма epigram. **эпи́граф** epigraph.
эпиде́мия epidemic.

эпизо́д episode. **эпизоди́ческий** episodic; sporadic.
эпиле́псия epilepsy. **эпиле́птик** epileptic.
эпило́г epilogue. **эпита́фия** epitaph. **эпи́тет** epithet. **эпице́нтр** epicentre.
эпопе́я epic.
эпо́ха epoch, era.
э́ра era; **до на́шей э́ры** BC; **на́шей э́ры** AD.
эре́кция erection.
эро́зия erosion.
эроти́зм eroticism. **эро́тика** sensuality. **эроти́ческий, эроти́чный** erotic, sensual.
эруди́ция erudition.
эска́дра (*naut*) squadron. **эскадри́лья** (*gen pl* -лий) (*aeron*) squadron. **эскадро́н** (*mil*) squadron.
эскала́тор escalator. **эскала́ция** escalation.
эски́з sketch; draft. **эски́зный** sketch; draft.
эскимо́с, эскимо́ска Eskimo.
эско́рт escort.
эсми́нец (-нца) *abbr* (*of* **эска́дренный миноно́сец**) destroyer.
эссе́нция essence.
эстака́да trestle bridge; overpass; pier, boom.
эста́мп print, engraving, plate.
эстафе́та relay race; baton.
эсте́тика aesthetics. **эстети́ческий** aesthetic.
эсто́нец (-нца), **эсто́нка** Estonian. **Эсто́ния** Estonia. **эсто́нский** Estonian.
эстра́да stage, platform; variety. **эстра́дный** stage; variety; ~ **конце́рт** variety show.
эта́ж (-а́) storey, floor. **этаже́рка** shelves.
э́так *adv* so, thus; about. **э́такий** such (a), what (a).
этало́н standard.
эта́п stage; halting-place.
э́тика ethics.
этике́т etiquette.
этике́тка label.
эти́л ethyl.
этимоло́гия etymology.
эти́ческий, эти́чный ethical.
этни́ческий ethnic. **этногра́фия** ethnography.
э́то *partl* this (is), that (is), it (is).
э́тот *m*, **э́та** *f*, **э́то** *neut*, **э́ти** *pl* *pron* this, these.
этю́д study, sketch; étude.
эфеме́рный ephemeral.
эфио́п, ~ка Ethiopian. **эфио́пский** Ethiopian.
эфи́р ether; air. **эфи́рный** ethereal; ether, ester.
эффе́кт effect. **эффекти́вность** effectiveness. **эффекти́вный** effective. **эффе́ктный** effective; striking.
эх *int* eh! oh!
э́хо echo.
эшафо́т scaffold.
эшело́н echelon; special train.

Ю

юбиле́й anniversary; jubilee. **юбиле́йный** jubilee.
ю́бка skirt. **ю́бочка** short skirt.
ювели́р jeweller. **ювели́рный** jeweller's, jewellery; fine, intricate.
юг south; **на ~е** in the south. **ю́го-восто́к** south-east. **ю́го-за́пад** south-west. **югосла́в, ~ка** Yugoslav. **Югосла́вия** Yugoslavia. **югосла́вский** Yugoslav.
юдофо́б anti-Semite. **юдофо́бство** anti-Semitism.
южа́нин (*pl* -а́не, -а́н), **южа́нка** southerner. **ю́жный** south, southern; southerly.
юла́ top; fidget. **юли́ть** *impf* fidget.
ю́мор humour. **юмори́ст** humourist. **юмористи́ческий** humorous.
ю́ность youth. **ю́ноша** (*gen pl* -шей) *m* youth. **ю́ношеский** youthful. **ю́ношество** youth; young people. **ю́ный** (юн, -а́, -о) young; youthful.
юпи́тер floodlight.

юриди́ческий legal, juridical. **юриско́нсульт** legal adviser. **юри́ст** lawyer.
ю́ркий (-рок, -рка́, -рко) quick-moving, brisk; smart.
юро́дивый crazy.
ю́рта yurt, nomad's tent.
юсти́ция justice.
юти́ться (ючу́сь) *impf* huddle (together).

Я

я (меня́, мне, мной (-о́ю), (обо) мне) *pron* I.
я́беда *m* & *f*, tell-tale; informer.
я́блоко (*pl* -и, -ок) apple; **глазно́е** ~ eyeball. **я́блоневый, я́блочный** apple. **я́блоня** apple-tree.
яви́ться (явлю́сь, я́вишься) *pf*, **явля́ться** *impf* appear; arise; +*instr* be, serve as. **я́вка** appearance, attendance; secret rendezvous. **явле́ние** phenomenon; appearance; occurrence; scene. **я́вный** obvious; overt. **я́вственный** clear. **я́вствовать** be clear, be obvious.
ягнёнок (-нка; *pl* -ня́та, -я́т) lamb.
я́года berry; berries.
я́годица buttock(s).
ягуа́р jaguar.
яд poison; venom.
я́дерный nuclear.
ядови́тый poisonous; venomous.
ядрёный healthy; bracing; juicy. **ядро́** (*pl* -а, я́дер) kernel, core; nucleus; (cannon-) ball; shot.
я́зва ulcer, sore. **я́звенн|ый** ulcerous; **~ая боле́знь** ulcers. **язви́тельный** caustic, sarcastic. **язви́ть** (-влю́) *impf* (*pf* **съ~**) be sarcastic.
язы́к (-а́) tongue; clapper; language. **языкове́д** linguist. **языкове́дение, языкозна́ние** linguistics. **языково́й** linguistic. **языко́вый** tongue; lingual. **язычко́вый** reed. **язы́чник** heathen, pagan. **язычо́к** (-чка́) tongue; reed; catch.
яи́чко (*pl* -и, -чек) egg; testicle. **яи́чник** ovary. **яи́чница** fried eggs. **яйцо́** (*pl* я́йца, яи́ц) egg; ovum.
я́кобы *conj* as if; *partl* supposedly.
я́корн|ый anchor; **~ая стоя́нка** anchorage. **я́корь** (*pl* -я́) *m* anchor.
я́лик skiff.
я́ма pit, hole.
ямщи́к (-а́) coachman.
янва́рский January. **янва́рь** (-я́) *m* January.
янта́рный amber. **янта́рь** (-я́) *m* amber.
япо́нец (-нца), **япо́нка** Japanese. **Япо́ния** Japan. **япо́нский** Japanese.
ярд yard.
я́ркий (я́рок, ярка́, -о) bright; colourful, striking.
ярлы́к (-а́) label; tag.
я́рмарка fair.
ярмо́ (*pl* -а) yoke.
яро́вой spring.
я́ростный furious, fierce. **я́рость** fury.
я́рус circle; tier; layer.
я́рче *comp of* **я́ркий**
я́рый fervent; furious; violent.
я́сень *m* ash(-tree).
я́сли (-ей) *pl* manger; crèche, day nursery.
ясне́ть (-е́ет) *impf* become clear, clear. **я́сно** *adv* clearly. **ясновиде́ние** clairvoyance. **ясновидец** (-дца), **ясновидица** clairvoyant. **я́сность** clarity; clearness. **я́сный** (я́сен, ясна́, -о) clear; bright; fine.
я́ства (яств) *pl* victuals.
я́стреб (*pl* -а́) hawk.
я́хта yacht.
яче́йка cell.
ячме́нь[1] (-я́) *m* barley.
ячме́нь[2] (-я́) *m* stye.
я́щерица lizard.
я́щик box; drawer.
ящу́р foot-and-mouth (disease).

A

a /ə, eɪ/, **an** /æn, ən/ *indef article, not usu translated*; **twice a week** два ра́за в неде́лю.

aback /ə'bæk/ *adv*: **take ~** озада́чивать *impf*, озада́чить *pf*.

abacus /'æbəkəs/ *n* счёты *m pl*.

abandon /ə'bænd(ə)n/ *vt* покида́ть *impf*, поки́нуть *pf*; (*give up*) отка́зываться *impf*, отказа́ться *pf* от+*gen*; **~ o.s. to** предава́ться *impf*, преда́ться *pf* +*dat*. **abandoned** /ə'bænd(ə)nd/ *adj* поки́нутый; (*profligate*) распу́тный.

abase /ə'beɪs/ *vt* унижа́ть *impf*, уни́зить *pf*. **abasement** /-mənt/ *n* униже́ние.

abate /ə'beɪt/ *vi* затиха́ть *impf*, зати́хнуть *pf*.

abattoir /'æbə,twɑː(r)/ *n* скотобо́йня.

abbey /'æbɪ/ *n* абба́тство.

abbreviate /ə'briːvɪ,eɪt/ *vt* сокраща́ть *impf*, сократи́ть *pf*. **abbreviation** /-'eɪʃ(ə)n/ *n* сокраще́ние.

abdicate /'æbdɪ,keɪt/ *vi* отрека́ться *impf*, отре́чься *pf* от престо́ла. **abdication** /-'keɪʃ(ə)n/ *n* отрече́ние (от престо́ла).

abdomen /'æbdəmən/ *n* брюшна́я по́лость. **abdominal** /-'dɒmɪn(ə)l/ *adj* брюшно́й.

abduct /əb'dʌkt/ *vt* похища́ть *impf*, похи́тить *pf*. **abduction** /-'dʌkʃ(ə)n/ *n* похище́ние.

aberration /,æbə'reɪʃ(ə)n/ *n* (*mental*) помутне́ние рассу́дка.

abet /ə'bet/ *vt* подстрека́ть *impf*, подстрекну́ть *pf* (к соверше́нию преступле́ния *etc.*).

abhor /əb'hɔː(r)/ *vt* ненави́деть *impf*. **abhorrence** /-'hɒrəns/ *n* отвраще́ние. **abhorrent** /-'hɒrənt/ *adj* отврати́тельный.

abide /ə'baɪd/ *vt* (*tolerate*) выноси́ть *impf*, вы́нести *pf*; **~ by** (*rules etc.*) сле́довать *impf*, по~ *pf*.

ability /ə'bɪlɪtɪ/ *n* спосо́бность.

abject /'æbdʒekt/ *adj* (*wretched*) жа́лкий; (*humble*) уни́женный; **~ poverty** кра́йняя нищета́.

ablaze /ə'bleɪz/ *predic* охва́ченный огнём.

able /'eɪb(ə)l/ *adj* спосо́бный, уме́лый; **be ~ to** мочь *impf*, с~ *pf*; (*know how to*) уме́ть *impf*, с~ *pf*.

abnormal /æb'nɔːm(ə)l/ *adj* ненорма́льный. **abnormality** /-'mælɪtɪ/ *n* ненорма́льность.

aboard /ə'bɔːd/ *adv* на борт(у́); (*train*) в по́езд(е).

abode /ə'bəʊd/ *n* жили́ще; **of no fixed ~** без постоя́нного местожи́тельства.

abolish /ə'bɒlɪʃ/ *vt* отменя́ть *impf*, отмени́ть *pf*. **abolition** /,æbə'lɪʃ(ə)n/ *n* отме́на.

abominable /ə'bɒmɪnəb(ə)l/ *adj* отврати́тельный. **abomination** /-'neɪʃ(ə)n/ *n* ме́рзость.

aboriginal /,æbə'rɪdʒɪn(ə)l/ *adj* коренно́й; *n* абориге́н, коренно́й жи́тель *m*. **aborigine** /-nɪ/ *n* абориге́н, коренно́й жи́тель *m*.

abort /ə'bɔːt/ *vi* (*med*) выки́дывать *impf*, вы́кинуть *pf*; *vt* (*terminate*) прекраща́ть *impf*, прекрати́ть *pf*. **abortion** /ə'bɔːʃ(ə)n/ *n* або́рт; **have an ~** де́лать *impf*, с~ *pf* або́рт. **abortive** /-tɪv/ *adj* безуспе́шный.

abound /ə'baʊnd/ *vi* быть в изоби́лии; **~ in** изоби́ловать *impf* +*instr*.

about /ə'baʊt/ *adv* & *prep* (*approximately*) о́коло+*gen*; (*concerning*) о+*prep*, насчёт+*gen*; (*up and down*) по+*dat*; (*in the vicinity*) круго́м; **be ~ to** собира́ться *impf*, собра́ться *pf* +*inf*.

above /ə'bʌv/ *adv* наверху́; (*higher*

a

up) вы́ше; **from ~** све́рху; свы́ше; *prep* над+*instr*; (*more than*) свы́ше+*gen*. **above-board** *adj* че́стный. **above-mentioned** *adj* вышеупомя́нутый.

abrasion /ə'breɪʒ(ə)n/ *n* истира́ние; (*wound*) ссáдина. **abrasive** /-sɪv/ *adj* абрази́вный; (*manner*) колю́чий; *n* абрази́вный материа́л.

abreast /ə'brest/ *adv* в ряд; **keep ~ of** идти́ в но́гу с+*instr*.

abridge /ə'brɪdʒ/ *vt* сокраща́ть *impf*, сократи́ть *pf*. **abridgement** /-mənt/ *n* сокраще́ние.

abroad /ə'brɔːd/ *adv* за грани́цей, за грани́цу; **from ~** из-за грани́цы.

abrupt /ə'brʌpt/ *adj* (*steep*) круто́й; (*sudden*) внеза́пный; (*curt*) ре́зкий.

abscess /'æbsɪs/ *n* абсце́сс.

abscond /əb'skɒnd/ *vi* скрыва́ться *impf*, скры́ться *pf*.

absence /'æbs(ə)ns/ *n* отсу́тствие. **absent** /-s(ə)nt/ *adj* отсу́тствующий; **be ~** отсу́тствовать *impf*; *vt*: **~ o.s.** отлуча́ться *impf*, отлучи́ться *pf*. **absentee** /ˌæbs(ə)n'tiː/ *n* отсу́тствующий *sb*. **absenteeism** *n* /-'tiːɪz(ə)m/ прогу́л. **absent-minded** *adj* рассе́янный.

absolute /'æbsəˌluːt/ *adj* абсолю́тный; (*complete*) по́лный, соверше́нный.

absolution /ˌæbsə'luːʃ(ə)n/ *n* отпуще́ние грехо́в. **absolve** /əb'zɒlv/ *vt* проща́ть *impf*, прости́ть *pf*.

absorb /əb'zɔːb/ *vt* впи́тывать *impf*, впита́ть *pf*. **absorbed** /əb'zɔːbd/ *adj* поглощённый. **absorbent** /əb'zɔːbənt/ *adj* всасы́вающий. **absorption** /əb'zɔːpʃ(ə)n/ *n* впи́тывание; (*mental*) погружённость.

abstain /əb'steɪn/ *vi* возде́рживаться *impf*, воздержа́ться *pf* (**from** от+*gen*). **abstemious** /əb'stiːmɪəs/ *adj* возде́ржанный. **abstention** /əb'stenʃ(ə)n/ *n* воздержа́ние; (*person*) воздержа́вшийся *sb*. **abstinence** /'æbstɪnəns/ *n* воздержа́ние.

abstract /'æbstrækt/ *adj* абстра́ктный, отвлечённый; *n* рефера́т.

absurd /əb'sɜːd/ *adj* абсу́рдный. **absurdity** /-dɪtɪ/ *n* абсу́рд.

abundance /ə'bʌnd(ə)ns/ *n* оби́лие. **abundant** /-d(ə)nt/ *adj* оби́льный.

abuse *vt* /ə'bjuːz/(*insult*) руга́ть *impf*, вы́~, об~, от~ *pf*; (*misuse*) злоупотребля́ть *impf*, злоупотреби́ть *pf*; *n* /ə'bjuːs/ (*curses*) ру́гань, руга́тельства *neut pl*; (*misuse*) злоупотребле́ние. **abusive** /-sɪv/ *adj* оскорби́тельный, руга́тельный.

abut /ə'bʌt/ *vi* примыка́ть *impf* (**on** к+*dat*).

abysmal /ə'bɪzm(ə)l/ *adj* (*extreme*) безграни́чный; (*bad*) ужа́сный. **abyss** /ə'bɪs/ *n* бе́здна.

academic /ˌækə'demɪk/ *adj* академи́ческий. **academician** /əˌkædə'mɪʃ(ə)n/ *n* акаде́мик. **academy** /ə'kædəmɪ/ *n* акаде́мия.

accede /æk'siːd/ *vi* вступа́ть *impf*, вступи́ть *pf* (**to** в, на+*acc*); (*assent*) соглаша́ться *impf*, согласи́ться *pf*.

accelerate /ək'seləˌreɪt/ *vt* & *i* ускоря́ть(ся) *impf*, уско́рить(ся) *pf*; (*motoring*) дава́ть *impf*, дать *pf* газ. **acceleration** /-'reɪʃ(ə)n/ *n* ускоре́ние. **accelerator** /-ˌreɪtə(r)/ *n* ускори́тель *m*; (*pedal*) акселера́тор.

accent *n* /'æksent/ акце́нт; (*stress*) ударе́ние; *vt* /æk'sent/ де́лать *impf*, с~ *pf* ударе́ние на+*acc*. **accentuate** /æk'sentjʊˌeɪt/ *vt* акценти́ровать *impf* & *pf*.

accept /ək'sept/ *vt* принима́ть *impf*, приня́ть *pf*. **acceptable** /-təb(ə)l/ *adj* прие́млемый. **acceptance** /-t(ə)ns/ *n* приня́тие.

access /'ækses/ *n* до́ступ. **accessible** /ək'sesɪb(ə)l/ *adj* досту́пный. **accession** /ək'seʃ(ə)n/ *n* вступле́ние (на престо́л). **accessories** /ək'sesərɪz/ *n* принадле́жности *f pl*. **accessory** /ək'sesərɪ/ *n* (*accomplice*) соуча́стник, -ица.

accident /ˈæksɪd(ə)nt/ *n* (*chance*) случа́йность; (*mishap*) несча́стный слу́чай; (*crash*) ава́рия; **by ~** случа́йно. **accidental** /-ˈdent(ə)l/ *adj* случа́йный.

acclaim /əˈkleɪm/ *vt* (*praise*) восхваля́ть *impf*, восхвали́ть *pf*; *n* восхвале́ние.

acclimatization /əˌklaɪmətaɪˈzeɪʃ(ə)n/ *n* акклиматиза́ция. **acclimatize** /əˈklaɪməˌtaɪz/ *vt* акклиматизи́ровать *impf* & *pf*.

accommodate /əˈkɒməˌdeɪt/ *vt* помеща́ть *impf*, помести́ть *pf*; (*hold*) вмеща́ть *impf*, вмести́ть *pf*. **accommodating** /-ˌdeɪtɪŋ/ *adj* услу́жливый. **accommodation** /-ˈdeɪʃ(ə)n/ *n* (*hotel*) но́мер; (*home*) жильё.

accompaniment /əˈkʌmpənɪmənt/ *n* сопровожде́ние; (*mus*) аккомпанеме́нт. **accompanist** /-nɪst/ *n* аккомпаниа́тор. **accompany** /-nɪ/ *vt* сопровожда́ть *impf*, сопроводи́ть *pf*; (*escort*) провожа́ть *impf*, проводи́ть *pf*; (*mus*) аккомпани́ровать *impf* +*dat*.

accomplice /əˈkʌmplɪs/ *n* соуча́стник, -ица.

accomplish /əˈkʌmplɪʃ/ *vt* соверша́ть *impf*, соверши́ть *pf*. **accomplished** /-plɪʃt/ *adj* зако́нченный. **accomplishment** /-plɪʃmənt/ *n* выполне́ние; (*skill*) соверше́нство.

accord /əˈkɔːd/ *n* согла́сие; **of one's own ~** доброво́льно; **of its own ~** сам собо́й, сам по себе́. **accordance** /-dəns/ *n*: **in ~ with** в соотве́тствии с+*instr*, согла́сно+*dat*. **according** /-dɪŋ/ *adv*: **~ to** по+*dat*, **~ to him** по его́ слова́м. **accordingly** /-dɪŋlɪ/ *adv* соотве́тственно.

accordion /əˈkɔːdɪən/ *n* аккордео́н.

accost /əˈkɒst/ *vt* пристава́ть *impf*, приста́ть *pf* к+*dat*.

account /əˈkaʊnt/ *n* (*comm*) счёт; (*report*) отчёт; (*description*) описа́ние; **on no ~** ни в ко́ем слу́чае; **on ~** в счёт причита́ющейся су́ммы; **on ~ of** из-за+*gen*, по причи́не+*gen*; **take into ~** принима́ть *impf*, приня́ть *pf* в расчёт; *vi*: **~ for** объясня́ть *impf*, объясни́ть *pf*. **accountable** /-təb(ə)l/ *adj* отве́тственный.

accountancy /əˈkaʊntənsɪ/ *n* бухгалте́рия. **accountant** /-tənt/ *n* бухга́лтер.

accrue /əˈkruː/ *vi* нараста́ть *impf*, нарасти́ *pf*.

accumulate /əˈkjuːmjʊˌleɪt/ *vt* & *i* нака́пливать(ся) *impf*, копи́ть(ся) *impf*, на~ *pf*. **accumulation** /-ˈleɪʃ(ə)n/ *n* накопле́ние. **accumulator** /-ˌleɪtə(r)/ *n* аккумуля́тор.

accuracy /ˈækjʊrəsɪ/ *n* то́чность. **accurate** /-rət/ *adj* то́чный.

accusation /ˌækjuːˈzeɪʃ(ə)n/ *n* обвине́ние. **accusative** /əˈkjuːzətɪv/ *adj* (*n*) вини́тельный (паде́ж). **accuse** /əˈkjuːz/ *vt* обвиня́ть *impf*, обвини́ть *pf* (**of** в+*prep*); **the ~d** обвиня́емый *sb*.

accustom /əˈkʌstəm/ *vt* приуча́ть *impf*, приучи́ть *pf* (**to** к+*dat*). **accustomed** /-təmd/ *adj* привы́чный; **be, get ~** привыка́ть *impf*, привы́кнуть *pf* (**to** к+*dat*).

ace /eɪs/ *n* туз; (*pilot*) ас.

ache /eɪk/ *n* боль; *vi* боле́ть *impf*.

achieve /əˈtʃiːv/ *vt* достига́ть *impf*, дости́чь & дости́гнуть *pf* +*gen*. **achievement** /-mənt/ *n* достиже́ние.

acid /ˈæsɪd/ *n* кислота́; *adj* ки́слый; **~ rain** кисло́тный дождь. **acidity** /əˈsɪdɪtɪ/ *n* кислота́.

acknowledge /əkˈnɒlɪdʒ/ *vt* признава́ть *impf*, призна́ть *pf*; (**~** *receipt of*) подтвержда́ть *impf*, подтверди́ть *pf* получе́ние +*gen*. **acknowledgement** /-mənt/ *n* призна́ние; подтвержде́ние.

acne /ˈæknɪ/ *n* прыщи́ *m pl*.

acorn /ˈeɪkɔːn/ *n* жёлудь *m*.

acoustic /əˈkuːstɪk/ *adj* акусти́ческий. **acoustics** /-stɪks/ *n pl* аку́стика.

acquaint /əˈkweɪnt/ *vt* знако́мить

impf, по~ *pf.* **acquaintance** /-t(ə)ns/ *n* знако́мство; (*person*) знако́мый *sb.* **acquainted** /-tɪd/ *adj* знако́мый.

acquiesce /ˌækwɪ'es/ *vi* соглаша́ться *impf*, согласи́ться *pf.* **acquiescence** /-s(ə)ns/ *n* согла́сие.

acquire /ə'kwaɪə(r)/ *vt* приобрета́ть *impf*, приобрести́ *pf.* **acquisition** /ˌækwɪ'zɪʃ(ə)n/ *n* приобрете́ние. **acquisitive** /ə'kwɪzɪtɪv/ *adj* стяжа́тельский.

acquit /ə'kwɪt/ *vt* опра́вдывать *impf*, оправда́ть *pf*; ~ **o.s.** вести́ *impf* себя́. **acquittal** /-t(ə)l/ *n* оправда́ние.

acre /'eɪkə(r)/ *n* акр.

acrid /'ækrɪd/ *adj* е́дкий.

acrimonious /ˌækrɪ'məʊnɪəs/ *adj* язви́тельный.

acrobat /'ækrəˌbæt/ *n* акроба́т. **acrobatic** /-'bætɪk/ *adj* акробати́ческий.

across /ə'krɒs/ *adv* & *prep* че́рез+*acc*; (*athwart*) попере́к (+*gen*); (*to, on, other side*) на ту сто́рону (+*gen*), на той стороне́ (+*gen*); (*crosswise*) кре́ст-на́крест.

acrylic /ə'krɪlɪk/ *n* акри́л; *adj* акри́ловый.

act /ækt/ *n* (*deed*) акт, посту́пок; (*law*) акт, зако́н; (*of play*) де́йствие; (*item*) но́мер; *vi* поступа́ть *impf*, поступи́ть *pf*; де́йствовать *impf*, по~ *pf*; *vt* игра́ть *impf*, сыгра́ть *pf.* **acting** /'æktɪŋ/ *n* игра́; (*profession*) актёрство; *adj* исполня́ющий обя́занности +*gen.* **action** /'ækʃ(ə)n/ *n* де́йствие, посту́пок; (*law*) иск, проце́сс; (*battle*) бой; ~ **replay** повто́р; **be out of** ~ не рабо́тать *impf.* **activate** /'æktɪˌveɪt/ *vt* приводи́ть *impf*, привести́ *pf* в де́йствие. **active** /'æktɪv/ *adj* акти́вный; ~ **service** действи́тельная слу́жба; ~ **voice** действи́тельный зало́г. **activity** /æk'tɪvɪtɪ/ *n* де́ятельность. **actor** /'æktə(r)/ *n* актёр. **actress** /'æktrɪs/ *n* актри́са.

actual /'æktʃʊəl/ *adj* действи́тельный. **actuality** /-'ælɪtɪ/ *n* действи́тельность. **actually** /'æktʃʊəlɪ/ *adv* на са́мом де́ле, факти́чески.

acumen /'ækjʊmən/ *n* проница́тельность.

acupuncture /'ækjuːˌpʌŋktʃə(r)/ *n* иглоука́лывание.

acute /ə'kjuːt/ *adj* о́стрый.

AD *abbr* н.э. (на́шей э́ры).

adamant /'ædəmənt/ *adj* непрекло́нный.

adapt /ə'dæpt/ *vt* приспособля́ть *impf*, приспосо́бить *pf*; (*theat*) инсцени́ровать *impf* & *pf*; ~ **o.s.** приспособля́ться *impf*, приспосо́биться *pf.* **adaptable** /-təb(ə)l/ *adj* приспособля́ющийся. **adaptation** /ˌædæp'teɪʃ(ə)n/ *n* приспособле́ние; (*theat*) инсцениро́вка. **adapter** /-tə(r)/ *n* ада́птер.

add /æd/ *vt* прибавля́ть *impf*, приба́вить *pf*; (*say*) добавля́ть *impf*, доба́вить *pf*; ~ **together** скла́дывать *impf*, сложи́ть *pf*; ~ **up** сумми́ровать *impf* & *pf*; ~ **up to** составля́ть *impf*, соста́вить *pf*; (*fig*) своди́ться *impf*, свести́сь *pf* к+*dat.* **addenda** /ə'dendə/ *n* приложе́ния *pl.*

adder /'ædə(r)/ *n* гадю́ка.

addict /'ædɪkt/ *n* наркома́н, ~ка. **addicted** /ə'dɪktɪd/ *adj*: **be** ~ **to** быть рабо́м+*gen*; **become** ~ **to** пристрасти́ться *pf* к+*dat.* **addiction** /ə'dɪkʃ(ə)n/ *n* (*passion*) пристра́стие; (*to drugs*) наркома́ния.

addition /ə'dɪʃ(ə)n/ *n* прибавле́ние; дополне́ние; (*math*) сложе́ние; **in** ~ вдоба́вок, кро́ме того́. **additional** /-n(ə)l/ *adj* доба́вочный. **additive** /'ædɪtɪv/ *n* доба́вка.

address /ə'dres/ *n* а́дрес; (*speech*) речь; ~ **book** записна́я кни́жка; *vt* адресова́ть *impf* & *pf*; (*speak to*) обраща́ться *impf*, обрати́ться *pf* к+*dat*; ~ **a meeting** выступа́ть *impf*, вы́ступить *pf* на собра́нии. **addressee** /ˌædre'siː/ *n* адреса́т.

adept /ˈædept/ *adj* свéдущий; *n* мáстер.

adequate /ˈædɪkwət/ *adj* достáточный.

adhere /ədˈhɪə(r)/ *vi* прилипáть *impf*, прилипнуть *pf* (**to** к+*dat*); (*fig*) придéрживаться *impf* +*gen*. **adherence** /-rəns/ *n* привéрженность. **adherent** /-rənt/ *n* привéрженец. **adhesive** /ədˈhiːsɪv/ *adj* ли́пкий; *n* клéйкое веществó.

ad hoc /æd ˈhɒk/ *adj* специáльный.

ad infinitum /æd ˌɪnfɪˈnaɪtəm/ *adv* до бесконéчности.

adjacent /əˈdʒeɪs(ə)nt/ *adj* смéжный.

adjective /ˈædʒɪktɪv/ *n* (и́мя) прилагáтельное.

adjoin /əˈdʒɔɪn/ *vt* прилегáть *impf* к+*dat*.

adjourn /əˈdʒɜːn/ *vt* отклáдывать *impf*, отложи́ть *pf*; *vi* объявля́ть *impf*, объяви́ть *pf* переры́в; (*move*) переходи́ть *impf*, перейти́ *pf*.

adjudicate /əˈdʒuːdɪˌkeɪt/ *vi* выноси́ть *impf*, вы́нести *pf* решéние (**in** по+*dat*); суди́ть *impf*.

adjust /əˈdʒʌst/ *vt* & *i* приспосабля́ть(ся) *impf*, приспосóбить(ся) *pf*; *vt* пригоня́ть *impf*, пригнáть *pf*; (*regulate*) регули́ровать *impf*, от~ *pf*. **adjustable** /-təb(ə)l/ *adj* регули́руемый. **adjustment** /-mənt/ *n* регули́рование, подгóнка.

ad lib /æd ˈlɪb/ *vt* & *i* импровизи́ровать *impf*, сымпровизи́ровать *pf*.

administer /ədˈmɪnɪstə(r)/ *vt* (*manage*) управля́ть *impf* +*instr*; (*give*) давáть *impf*, дать *pf*. **administration** /-ˈstreɪʃ(ə)n/ *n* управлéние; (*government*) прави́тельство. **administrative** /-strətɪv/ *adj* администрати́вный. **administrator** /-ˌstreɪtə(r)/ *n* администрáтор.

admirable /ˈædmərəb(ə)l/ *adj* похвáльный.

admiral /ˈædmər(ə)l/ *n* адмирáл.

admiration /ˌædmɪˈreɪʃ(ə)n/ *n* восхищéние. **admire** /ədˈmaɪə(r)/ *vt* (*look at*) любовáться *impf*, по~ *pf* +*instr*, на+*acc*; (*respect*) восхищáться *impf*, восхити́ться *pf* +*instr*. **admirer** /ədˈmaɪərə(r)/ *n* поклóнник.

admissible /ədˈmɪsɪb(ə)l/ *adj* допусти́мый. **admission** /ədˈmɪʃ(ə)n/ *n* (*access*) дóступ; (*entry*) вход; (*confession*) признáние. **admit** /ədˈmɪt/ *vt* (*allow in*) впускáть *impf*, впусти́ть *pf*; (*confess*) признавáть *impf*, признáть *pf*. **admittance** /ədˈmɪt(ə)ns/ *n* дóступ. **admittedly** /ədˈmɪtɪdlɪ/ *adv* признáться.

admixture /ædˈmɪkstʃə(r)/ *n* при́месь.

adolescence /ˌædəˈles(ə)ns/ *n* óтрочество. **adolescent** /-s(ə)nt/ *adj* подрóстковый; *n* подрóсток.

adopt /əˈdɒpt/ *vt* (*child*) усыновля́ть *impf*, усынови́ть *pf*; (*thing*) усвáивать *impf*, усвóить *pf*; (*accept*) принимáть *impf*, приня́ть *pf*. **adoptive** /-tɪv/ *adj* приёмный. **adoption** /əˈdɒpʃ(ə)n/ *n* усыновлéние; приня́тие.

adorable /əˈdɔːrəb(ə)l/ *adj* прелéстный. **adoration** /ˌædəˈreɪʃ(ə)n/ *n* обожáние. **adore** /əˈdɔː(r)/ *vt* обожáть *impf*.

adorn /əˈdɔːn/ *vt* украшáть *impf*, укрáсить *pf*. **adornment** /-mənt/ *n* украшéние.

adrenalin /əˈdrenəlɪn/ *n* адренали́н.

adroit /əˈdrɔɪt/ *adj* лóвкий.

adulation /ˌædjʊˈleɪʃ(ə)n/ *n* преклонéние.

adult /ˈædʌlt/ *adj* & *n* взрóслый (*sb*).

adulterate /əˈdʌltəˌreɪt/ *vt* фальсифици́ровать *impf* & *pf*.

adultery /əˈdʌltərɪ/ *n* супрýжеская измéна.

advance /ədˈvɑːns/ *n* (*going forward*) продвижéние (вперёд); (*progress*) прогрéсс; (*mil*) наступлéние; (*of pay etc.*) авáнс; **in ~** зарáнее; *pl* (*overtures*) авáнсы *m pl*; *vi* (*go forward*) продвигáться *impf*, продви́нуться *pf* вперёд; идти́ *impf* вперёд; (*mil*) наступáть *impf*; *vt* продвигáть *impf*, продви́нуть *pf*; (*put forward*) выдвигáть *impf*, вы́двинуть *pf*. **advanced** /əd'vɑːnst/ *adj* (*modern*) передовóй. **advancement** /-mənt/ *n* продвижéние.

advantage /əd'vɑːntɪdʒ/ *n* преимýщество; (*profit*) вы́года, пóльза; **take ~ of** пóльзоваться *impf*, вос~ *pf* +*instr*. **advantageous** /ˌædvən'teɪdʒəs/ *adj* вы́годный.

adventure /əd'ventʃə(r)/ *n* приключéние. **adventurer** /-rə(r)/ *n* искáтель *m* приключéний. **adventurous** /-rəs/ *adj* предприи́мчивый.

adverb /'ædvɜːb/ *n* нарéчие.

adversary /'ædvəsərɪ/ *n* проти́вник. **adverse** /'ædvɜːs/ *adj* неблагоприя́тный. **adversity** /əd'vɜːsɪtɪ/ *n* несчáстье.

advertise /'ædvəˌtaɪz/ *vt* (*publicize*) реклами́ровать *impf* & *pf*; *vt* & *i* (~ *for*) давáть *impf*, дать *pf* объявлéние о+*prep*. **advertisement** /əd'vɜːtɪsmənt/ *n* объявлéние, реклáма.

advice /əd'vaɪs/ *n* совéт. **advisable** /əd'vaɪzəb(ə)l/ *adj* желáтельный. **advise** /əd'vaɪz/ *vt* совéтовать *impf*, по~ *pf* +*dat* & *inf*; (*notify*) уведомля́ть *impf*, увéдомить *pf*. **advisedly** /əd'vaɪzɪdlɪ/ *adv* намéренно. **adviser** /əd'vaɪzə(r)/ *n* совéтник. **advisory** /əd'vaɪzərɪ/ *adj* совещáтельный.

advocate *n* /'ædvəkət/ (*supporter*) сторóнник; *vt* /'ædvəˌkeɪt/ выступáть *impf*, вы́ступить *pf* за+*acc*; (*advise*) совéтовать *impf*, по~ *pf*.

aegis /'iːdʒɪs/ *n* эги́да.

aerial /'eərɪəl/ *n* антéнна; *adj* воздýшный.

aerobics /eə'rəʊbɪks/ *n* аэрóбика.

aerodrome /'eərəˌdrəʊm/ *n* аэродрóм. **aerodynamics** /-daɪ'næmɪks/ *n* аэродинáмика. **aeroplane** /-ˌpleɪn/ *n* самолёт. **aerosol** /-ˌsɒl/ *n* аэрозóль *m*.

aesthetic /iːs'θetɪk/ *adj* эстети́ческий. **aesthetics** /-tɪks/ *n pl* эстéтика.

afar /ə'fɑː(r)/ *adv*: **from ~** издалекá.

affable /'æfəb(ə)l/ *adj* привéтливый.

affair /ə'feə(r)/ *n* (*business*) дéло; (*love*) ромáн.

affect /ə'fekt/ *vt* влия́ть *impf*, по~ *pf* на+*acc*; (*touch*) трóгать *impf*, трóнуть *pf*; (*concern*) затрáгивать *impf*, затрóнуть *pf*; **affectation** /ˌæfek'teɪʃ(ə)n/ *n* жемáнство. **affected** /-tɪd/ *adj* жемáнный. **affection** /ə'fekʃ(ə)n/ *n* привя́занность. **affectionate** /ə'fekʃənət/ *adj* нéжный.

affiliated /ə'fɪlɪˌeɪtɪd/ *adj* свя́занный (**to** с+*instr*).

affinity /ə'fɪnɪtɪ/ *n* (*relationship*) родствó; (*resemblance*) схóдство; (*attraction*) влечéние.

affirm /ə'fɜːm/ *vt* утверждáть *impf*. **affirmation** /ˌæfə'meɪʃ(ə)n/ *n* утверждéние. **affirmative** /ə'fɜːmətɪv/ *adj* утверди́тельный.

affix /ə'fɪks/ *vt* прикрепля́ть *impf*, прикрепи́ть *pf*.

afflict /ə'flɪkt/ *vt* постигáть *impf*, пости́чь *pf*; **be afflicted with** страдáть *impf* +*instr*. **affliction** /ə'flɪkʃ(ə)n/ *n* болéзнь.

affluence /'æflʊəns/ *n* богáтство. **affluent** /-ənt/ *adj* богáтый.

afford /ə'fɔːd/ *vt* позволя́ть *impf*, позвóлить *pf* себé; (*supply*) предоставля́ть *impf*, предостáвить *pf*.

affront /ə'frʌnt/ *n* оскорблéние; *vt* оскорбля́ть *impf*, оскорби́ть *pf*.

afield /ə'fiːld/ *adv*: **far ~** далекó; **farther ~** дáльше.

afloat /ə'fləʊt/ *adv* & *predic* на водé.

afoot /ə'fʊt/ *predic*: **be ~** готóвиться *impf*.

aforesaid /ə'fɔːsed/ *adj* вышеупомя́нутый.

afraid /ə'freɪd/ *predic*: **be ~** боя́ться *impf*.

afresh /ə'freʃ/ *adv* снóва.

Africa /ˈæfrɪkə/ *n* А́фрика. **African** /-kən/ *n* африка́нец, -ка́нка; *adj* африка́нский.

after /ˈɑːftə(r)/ *adv* пото́м; *prep* по́сле +*gen*; (*time*) че́рез+*acc*; (*behind*) за+*acc*, *instr*; **~ all** в конце́ концо́в; *conj* по́сле того́, как.

aftermath /ˈɑːftəmæθ/ *n* после́дствия *neut pl.* **afternoon** /-ˈnuːn/ *n* втора́я полови́на дня; **in the ~** днём. **aftershave** /-ʃeɪv/ *n* лосьо́н по́сле бритья́. **afterthought** /-θɔːt/ *n* запозда́лая мысль.

afterwards /ˈɑːftəwədz/ *adv* пото́м.

again /əˈgen/ *adv* опя́ть; (*once more*) ещё раз; (*anew*) сно́ва.

against /əˈgenst/ *prep* (*opposing*) про́тив+*gen*; (*touching*) к+*dat*; (*hitting*) о+*acc*.

age /eɪdʒ/ *n* во́зраст; (*era*) век, эпо́ха; *vt* ста́рить *impf*, со~ *pf*; *vi* старе́ть *impf*, по~ *pf*. **aged** /ˈeɪdʒɪd/ *adj* престаре́лый.

agency /ˈeɪdʒənsɪ/ *n* аге́нтство.

agenda /əˈdʒendə/ *n* пове́стка дня. **agent** /ˈeɪdʒ(ə)nt/ *n* аге́нт.

aggravate /ˈægrəˌveɪt/ *vt* ухудша́ть *impf*, уху́дшить *pf*; (*annoy*) раздража́ть *impf*, раздражи́ть *pf*.

aggregate /ˈægrɪgət/ *adj* совоку́пный; *n* совоку́пность.

aggression /əˈgreʃ(ə)n/ *n* агре́ссия. **aggressive** /-sɪv/ *adj* агресси́вный. **aggressor** /-sə(r)/ *n* агре́ссор.

aggrieved /əˈgriːvd/ *adj* оби́женный.

aghast /əˈgɑːst/ *predic* в у́жасе (**at** от +*gen*).

agile /ˈædʒaɪl/ *adj* прово́рный. **agility** /-ˈdʒɪlɪtɪ/ *n* прово́рство.

agitate /ˈædʒɪˌteɪt/ *vt* волнова́ть *impf*, вз~ *pf*; *vi* агити́ровать *impf*. **agitation** /-ˈteɪʃ(ə)n/ *n* волне́ние; агита́ция.

agnostic /ægˈnɒstɪk/ *n* агно́стик. **agnosticism** /-tɪˌsɪz(ə)m/ *n* агностици́зм.

ago /əˈgəʊ/ *adv* (тому́) наза́д; **long ~** давно́.

agonize /ˈægəˌnaɪz/ *vi* мучи́ться *impf*. **agonizing** /-zɪŋ/ *adj* мучи́тельный. **agony** /ˈægənɪ/ *n* аго́ния.

agrarian /əˈgreərɪən/ *adj* агра́рный.

agree /əˈgriː/ *vi* соглаша́ться *impf*, согласи́ться *pf*; (*arrange*) догова́риваться *impf*, договори́ться *pf*. **agreeable** /-əb(ə)l/ *adj* (*pleasant*) прия́тный. **agreement** /-mənt/ *n* согла́сие; (*treaty*) соглаше́ние; **in ~** согла́сен (-сна).

agricultural /ˌægrɪˈkʌltʃər(ə)l/ *adj* сельскохозя́йственный. **agriculture** /ˈægrɪkʌltʃə(r)/ *n* се́льское хозя́йство.

aground /əˈgraʊnd/ *predic* на мели́; *adv*: **run ~** сади́ться *impf*, сесть *pf* на мель.

ahead /əˈhed/ *adv* (*forward*) вперёд; (*in front*) впереди́; **~ of time** досро́чно.

aid /eɪd/ *vt* помога́ть *impf*, помо́чь *pf* +*dat*; *n* по́мощь; (*teaching*) посо́бие; **in ~ of** в по́льзу +*gen*.

Aids /eɪdz/ *n* СПИД.

ailing /ˈeɪlɪŋ/ *adj* (*ill*) больно́й.

ailment /ˈeɪlmənt/ *n* неду́г.

aim /eɪm/ *n* цель, намере́ние; **take ~** прице́ливаться *impf*, прице́литься *pf* (**at** в+*acc*); *vi* цели́ться *impf*, на~ *pf* (**at** в+*acc*); (*also fig*) ме́тить *impf*, на~ *pf* (**at** в+*acc*); *vt* наце́ливать *impf*, наце́лить *pf*; (*also fig*) наводи́ть *impf*, навести́ *pf*. **aimless** /ˈeɪmlɪs/ *adj* бесце́льный.

air /eə(r)/ *n* во́здух; (*look*) вид; **by ~** самолётом; **on the ~** в эфи́ре; *attrib* возду́шный; *vt* (*ventilate*) прове́тривать *impf*, прове́трить *pf*; (*make known*) выставля́ть *impf*, вы́ставить *pf* напока́з. **air-conditioning** *n* кондициони́рование во́здуха. **aircraft** *n* самолёт. **aircraft-carrier** *n* авиано́сец. **airfield** *n* аэродро́м. **air force** *n* ВВС (вое́нно-возду́шные си́лы) *f pl.* **air hostess** *n* стюарде́сса. **airless** /-l(ə)s/ *adj* ду́шный. **airlift** *n* возду́шные перево́зки *f pl*; *vt* перевози́ть *impf*, перевезти́ *pf* по во́здуху. **airline** *n* авиакомпа́ния. **airlock** *n* возду́шная про́бка. **airmail** *n* а́виа(по́чта). **airman** *n* лётчик. **airport** *n* аэропо́рт. **air raid** *n* возду́шный налёт. **airship** *n* дирижа́бль *m*. **airstrip** *n* взлётно-поса́дочная полоса́. **airtight** *adj* гермети́чный. **air traffic controller** *n* диспе́тчер. **airwaves** *n pl* радиово́лны *f pl*.

aisle /aɪl/ *n* боково́й неф; (*passage*) прохо́д.

ajar /ə'dʒɑː(r)/ *predic* приоткры́тый.

akin /ə'kɪn/ *predic* (*similar*) похо́жий; **be ~ to** быть сродни́ к+*dat*.

alabaster /'ælə,bæstə(r)/ *n* алеба́стр.

alacrity /ə'lækrɪtɪ/ *n* быстрота́.

alarm /ə'lɑːm/ *n* трево́га; *vt* трево́жить *impf*, вс~ *pf*; **~ clock** буди́льник. **alarming** /-mɪŋ/ *adj* трево́жный. **alarmist** /-mɪst/ *n* паникёр; *adj* паникёрский.

alas /ə'læs/ *int* увы́!

album /'ælbəm/ *n* альбо́м.

alcohol /'ælkə,hɒl/ *n* алкого́ль *m*, спирт; спиртны́е напи́тки *m pl*. **alcoholic** /,ælkə'hɒlɪk/ *adj* алкого́льный; *n* алкого́лик, -и́чка.

alcove /'ælkəʊv/ *n* алько́в.

alert /ə'lɜːt/ *adj* бди́тельный; *n* трево́га; *vt* предупрежда́ть *impf*, предупреди́ть *pf*.

algebra /'ældʒɪbrə/ *n* а́лгебра.

alias /'eɪlɪəs/ *adv* ина́че (называ́емый); *n* кли́чка, вы́мышленное и́мя *neut*.

alibi /'ælɪ,baɪ/ *n* а́либи *neut indecl*.

alien /'eɪlɪən/ *n* иностра́нец, -нка; *adj* иностра́нный; **~ to** чу́ждый +*dat*. **alienate** /-,neɪt/ *vt* отчужда́ть *impf*. **alienation** /-'neɪʃ(ə)n/ *n* отчужде́ние.

alight[1] /ə'laɪt/ *vi* сходи́ть *impf*, сойти́ *pf*; (*bird*) сади́ться *impf*, сесть *pf*.

alight[2] /ə'laɪt/ *predic*: **be ~** горе́ть *impf*; (*shine*) сия́ть *impf*.

align /ə'laɪn/ *vt* выра́внивать *impf*, вы́ровнять *pf*. **alignment** /-mənt/ *n* выра́внивание.

alike /ə'laɪk/ *predic* похо́ж; *adv* одина́ково.

alimentary /,ælɪ'mentərɪ/ *adj*: **~ canal** пищевари́тельный кана́л.

alimony /'ælɪmənɪ/ *n* алиме́нты *m pl*.

alive /ə'laɪv/ *predic* жив, в живы́х.

alkali /'ælkə,laɪ/ *n* щёлочь. **alkaline** /-,laɪn/ *adj* щелочно́й.

all /ɔːl/ *adj* весь; *n* всё, *pl* все; *adv* совсе́м, соверше́нно; **~ along** всё вре́мя; **~ right** хорошо́, ла́дно; (*not bad*) та́к себе; непло́хо; **~ the same** всё равно́; **in ~** всего́; **two ~** по́ два; **not at ~** нисколько.

allay /ə'leɪ/ *vt* успока́ивать *impf*, успоко́ить *pf*.

allegation /,ælɪ'geɪʃ(ə)n/ *n* утвержде́ние. **allege** /ə'ledʒ/ *vt* утвержда́ть *impf*. **allegedly** /ə'ledʒɪdlɪ/ *adv* я́кобы.

allegiance /ə'liːdʒ(ə)ns/ *adv* ве́рность.

allegorical /,ælɪ'gɒrɪk(ə)l/ *adj* аллегори́ческий. **allegory** /'ælɪgərɪ/ *n* аллего́рия.

allergic /ə'lɜːdʒɪk/ *adj* аллерги́ческий; **be ~ to** име́ть аллерги́ю к+*dat*. **allergy** /'ælədʒɪ/ *n* аллерги́я.

alleviate /ə'liːvɪ,eɪt/ *vt* облегча́ть *impf*, облегчи́ть *pf*. **alleviation** /-'eɪʃ(ə)n/ *n* облегче́ние.

alley /'ælɪ/ *n* переу́лок.

alliance /ə'laɪəns/ *n* сою́з. **allied** /'ælaɪd/ *adj* сою́зный.

alligator /'ælɪ,geɪtə(r)/ *n* аллига́тор.

allocate /'ælə,keɪt/ *vt* (*distribute*) распределя́ть *impf*, распредели́ть *pf*; (*allot*) выделя́ть *impf*, вы́делить *pf*. **allocation** /-'keɪʃ(ə)n/ *n* распределе́ние; выделе́ние.

allot /ə'lɒt/ *vt* выделя́ть *impf*, вы́делить *pf*; (*distribute*) распределя́ть *impf*, распредели́ть *pf*. **allotment** /-mənt/ *n* выделе́ние; (*land*) уча́сток.

allow /ə'laʊ/ *vt* разреша́ть *impf*,

разреши́ть *pf*; (*let happen*; *concede*) допуска́ть *impf*, допусти́ть *pf*; ~ **for** учи́тывать *impf*, уче́сть *pf*. **allowance** /-əns/ *n* (*financial*) посо́бие; (*deduction*, *also fig*) ски́дка; **make ~(s) for** учи́тывать *impf*, уче́сть *pf*.

alloy /'ælɔɪ/ *n* сплав.

all-round /'ɔːlraʊnd/ *adj* разносторо́нний.

allude /ə'luːd/ *vi* ссыла́ться *impf*, сосла́ться *pf* (**to** на+*acc*).

allure /ə'ljʊə(r)/ *vt* зама́нивать *impf*, замани́ть *pf*. **allure(ment)** (/-mənt/) *n* прима́нка. **alluring** /-rɪŋ/ *adj* зама́нчивый.

allusion /ə'luːʒ(ə)n/ *n* ссы́лка.

ally *n* /'ælaɪ/ сою́зник; *vt* /ə'laɪ/ соединя́ть *impf*, соедини́ть *pf*; ~ **oneself with** вступа́ть *impf*, вступи́ть *pf* в сою́з с+*instr*.

almighty /ɔːl'maɪtɪ/ *adj* всемогу́щий.

almond /'ɑːmənd/ *n* (*tree*; *pl collect*) минда́ль *m*; (*nut*) минда́льный оре́х.

almost /'ɔːlməʊst/ *adv* почти́, едва́ не.

alms /ɑːmz/ *n pl* ми́лостыня.

aloft /ə'lɒft/ *adv* наве́рх(-у́).

alone /ə'ləʊn/ *predic* оди́н; (*lonely*) одино́к; *adv* то́лько; **leave** ~ оставля́ть *impf*, оста́вить *pf* в поко́е; **let** ~ не говоря́ уже́ о+*prep*.

along /ə'lɒŋ/ *prep* по+*dat*, (*position*) вдоль+*gen*; *adv* (*onward*) да́льше; **all** ~ всё вре́мя; ~ **with** вме́сте с+*instr*. **alongside** /ə,lɒŋ'saɪd/ *adv* & *prep* ря́дом (с +*instr*).

aloof /ə'luːf/ *predic* & *adv* (*distant*) сде́ржанный; (*apart*) в стороне́.

aloud /ə'laʊd/ *adv* вслух.

alphabet /'ælfə,bet/ *n* алфави́т. **alphabetical** /,ælfə'betɪk(ə)l/ *adj* алфави́тный.

alpine /'ælpaɪn/ *adj* альпи́йский.

already /ɔːl'redɪ/ *adv* уже́.

also /'ɔːlsəʊ/ *adv* та́кже, то́же.

altar /'ɔːltə(r)/ *n* алта́рь *m*.

alter /'ɔːltə(r)/ *vt* (*modify*) переде́лывать *impf*, переде́лать *pf*; *vt* & *i* (*change*) изменя́ть(ся) *impf*, измени́ть(ся) *pf*. **alteration** /-'reɪʃ(ə)n/ *n* переде́лка; измене́ние.

alternate *adj* /ɔːl'tɜːnət/ череду́ющийся; *vt* & *i* /'ɔːltə,neɪt/ чередова́ть(ся) *impf*; **alternating current** переме́нный ток; **on ~ days** че́рез день. **alternation** /,ɔːltə'neɪʃ(ə)n/ *n* чередова́ние. **alternative** /ɔːl'tɜːnətɪv/ *n* альтернати́ва; *adj* альтернати́вный.

although /ɔːl'ðəʊ/ *conj* хотя́.

altitude /'æltɪ,tjuːd/ *n* высота́.

alto /'æltəʊ/ *n* альт.

altogether /,ɔːltə'geðə(r)/ *adv* (*fully*) совсе́м; (*in total*) всего́.

altruistic /,æltruː'ɪstɪk/ *adj* альтруисти́ческий.

aluminium /,æljʊ'mɪnɪəm/ *n* алюми́ний.

always /'ɔːlweɪz/ *adv* всегда́; (*constantly*) постоя́нно.

Alzheimer's disease /'æltsˌhaɪməz/ *n* боле́знь Альцге́ймера.

a.m. *abbr* (*morning*) утра́; (*night*) но́чи.

amalgamate /ə'mælgə,meɪt/ *vt* & *i* слива́ть(ся) *impf*, сли́ть(ся) *pf*; (*chem*) амальгами́ровать(ся) *impf* & *pf*. **amalgamation** /-'meɪʃ(ə)n/ *n* слия́ние; (*chem*) амальгами́рование.

amass /ə'mæs/ *vt* копи́ть *impf*, на~ *pf*.

amateur /'æmətə(r)/ *n* люби́тель *m*, ~ница; *adj* люби́тельский. **amateurish** /-rɪʃ/ *adj* дилета́нтский.

amaze /ə'meɪz/ *vt* изумля́ть *impf*, изуми́ть *pf*. **amazement** /-mənt/ *n* изумле́ние. **amazing** /-zɪŋ/ *adj* изуми́тельный.

ambassador /æm'bæsədə(r)/ *n* посо́л.

amber /'æmbə(r)/ *n* янта́рь *m*.

ambience /'æmbɪəns/ *n* среда́; атмосфе́ра.

ambiguity /,æmbɪ'gjuːɪtɪ/ *n* двусмы́сленность. **ambiguous**

a

/æm'bɪgjuːəs/ *adj* двусмы́сленный.

ambition /æm'bɪʃ(ə)n/ *n* (*quality*) честолю́бие; (*aim*) мечта́. **ambitious** /-'bɪʃəs/ *adj* честолюби́вый.

amble /'æmb(ə)l/ *vi* ходи́ть *indet*, идти́ *det* неторопли́вым ша́гом.

ambulance /'æmbjʊləns/ *n* маши́на ско́рой по́мощи.

ambush /'æmbʊʃ/ *n* заса́да; *vt* напада́ть *impf*, напа́сть *pf* из заса́ды на+*acc*.

ameliorate /ə'miːlɪəˌreɪt/ *vt* & *i* улучша́ть(ся) *impf*, улу́чшить(ся) *pf*. **amelioration** /-'reɪʃ(ə)n/ *n* улучше́ние.

amen /eɪ'men/ *int* ами́нь!

amenable /ə'miːnəb(ə)l/ *adj* сгово́рчивый (**to** +*dat*)

amend /ə'mend/ *vt* (*correct*) исправля́ть *impf*, испра́вить *pf*; (*change*) вноси́ть *impf*, внести́ *pf* попра́вки в+*acc*. **amendment** /-mənt/ *n* попра́вка, исправле́ние. **amends** /ə'mendz/ *n pl*: **make ~ for** загла́живать *impf*, загла́дить *pf*.

amenities /ə'miːnɪtɪz/ *n pl* удо́бства *neut pl*.

America /ə'merɪkə/ *n* Аме́рика. **American** /-kən/ *adj* америка́нский; *n* америка́нец, -нка. **Americanism** /-kəˌnɪz(ə)m/ *n* американи́зм.

amiable /'eɪmɪəb(ə)l/ *adj* любе́зный. **amicable** /'æmɪkəb(ə)l/ *adj* дружелю́бный.

amid(st) /ə'mɪdst/ *prep* среди́+*gen*.

amino acid /əˌmiːnəʊ 'æsɪd/ *n* аминокислота́.

amiss /ə'mɪs/ *adv* нела́дный; **take ~** обижа́ться *impf*, оби́деться *pf* на+*acc*.

ammonia /ə'məʊnɪə/ *n* аммиа́к; (*liquid* ~) нашаты́рный спирт.

ammunition /ˌæmjʊ'nɪʃ(ə)n/ *n* боеприпа́сы *m pl*.

amnesia /æm'niːzɪə/ *n* амнези́я.

amnesty /'æmnɪstɪ/ *n* амни́стия.

among(st) /ə'mʌŋ(st)/ *prep* (*amidst*) среди́+*gen*, (*between*) ме́жду+*instr*.

amoral /eɪ'mɒr(ə)l/ *adj* амора́льный.

amorous /'æmərəs/ *adj* влю́бчивый.

amorphous /ə'mɔːfəs/ *adj* бесфо́рменный.

amortization /əˌmɔːtaɪ'zeɪʃ(ə)n/ *n* амортиза́ция.

amount /ə'maʊnt/ *n* коли́чество; *vi*: **~ to** составля́ть *impf*, соста́вить *pf*; (*be equivalent to*) быть равноси́льным+*dat*.

ampere /'æmpeə(r)/ *n* ампе́р.

amphetamine /æm'fetəmɪn/ *n* амфетами́н.

amphibian /æm'fɪbɪən/ *n* амфи́бия. **amphibious** /-'fɪbɪəs/ *adj* земново́дный; (*mil*) пла́вающий.

amphitheatre /'æmfɪˌθɪətə(r)/ *n* амфитеа́тр.

ample /'æmp(ə)l/ *adj* доста́точный. **amplification** /ˌæmplɪfɪ'keɪʃ(ə)n/ *n* усиле́ние. **amplifier** /'æmplɪˌfaɪə(r)/ *n* усили́тель *m*. **amplify** /'æmplɪˌfaɪ/ *vt* уси́ливать *impf*, уси́лить *pf*. **amply** /'æmplɪ/ *adv* доста́точно.

amputate /'æmpjʊˌteɪt/ *vt* ампути́ровать *impf* & *pf*. **amputation** /-'teɪʃ(ə)n/ *n* ампута́ция.

amuse /ə'mjuːz/ *vt* забавля́ть *impf*; развлека́ть *impf*, развле́чь *pf*. **amusement** /-mənt/ *n* заба́ва, развлече́ние; *pl* аттракцио́ны *m pl*. **amusing** /-zɪŋ/ *adj* заба́вный; (*funny*) смешно́й.

anachronism /ə'nækrəˌnɪz(ə)m/ *n* анахрони́зм. **anachronistic** /-'nɪstɪk/ *adj* анахрони́ческий.

anaemia /ə'niːmɪə/ *n* анеми́я. **anaemic** /-mɪk/ *adj* анеми́чный.

anaesthesia /ˌænɪs'θiːzɪə/ *n* анестези́я. **anaesthetic** /-'θetɪk/ *n* обезбо́ливающее сре́дство. **anaesthetist** /ə'niːsθətɪst/ *n* анестезио́лог. **anaesthetize** /ə'niːsθəˌtaɪz/ *vt* анестези́ровать *impf* & *pf*.

anagram /'ænəˌgræm/ *n* анагра́мма.

analogous /ə'næləgəs/ *adj* аналоги́чный. **analogue** /ˈænəˌlɒg/ *n* ана́лог. **analogy** /əˈnælədʒɪ/ *n* анало́гия.

analyse /ˈænəˌlaɪz/ *vt* анализи́ровать *impf* & *pf*. **analysis** /əˈnælɪsɪs/ *n* ана́лиз. **analyst** /ˈænəlɪst/ *n* анали́тик; психоанали́тик. **analytical** /ˌænəˈlɪtɪk(ə)l/ *adj* аналити́ческий.

anarchic /əˈnɑːkɪk/ *adj* анархи́ческий. **anarchist** /ˈænəkɪst/ *n* анархи́ст, ~ка; *adj* анархи́стский. **anarchy** /ˈænəkɪ/ *n* ана́рхия.

anathema /əˈnæθəmə/ *n* ана́фема.

anatomical /ˌænəˈtɒmɪk(ə)l/ *adj* анатоми́ческий. **anatomy** /əˈnætəmɪ/ *n* анато́мия.

ancestor /ˈænsestə(r)/ *n* пре́док. **ancestry** /-strɪ/ *n* происхожде́ние.

anchor /ˈæŋkə(r)/ *n* я́корь *m*; *vt* ста́вить *impf*, по~ *pf* на я́корь; *vi* станови́ться *impf*, стать *pf* на я́корь. **anchorage** /ˈæŋkərɪdʒ/ *n* я́корная стоя́нка.

anchovy /ˈæntʃəvɪ/ *n* анчо́ус.

ancient /ˈeɪnʃ(ə)nt/ *adj* дре́вний, стари́нный.

and /ænd, ənd/ *conj* и, (*but*) а; с+*instr*; **you ~ I** мы с ва́ми; **my wife ~ I** мы с жено́й.

anecdote /ˈænɪkˌdəʊt/ *n* анекдо́т.

anew /əˈnjuː/ *adv* сно́ва.

angel /ˈeɪndʒ(ə)l/ *n* а́нгел. **angelic** /ænˈdʒelɪk/ *adj* а́нгельский.

anger /ˈæŋgə(r)/ *n* гнев; *vt* серди́ть *impf*, рас~ *pf*.

angina /ænˈdʒaɪnə/ *n* стенокарди́я.

angle[1] /ˈæŋg(ə)l/ *n* у́гол; (*fig*) то́чка зре́ния.

angle[2] /ˈæŋg(ə)l/ *vi* уди́ть *impf* ры́бу. **angler** /-glə(r)/ *n* рыболо́в.

angry /ˈæŋgrɪ/ *adj* серди́тый.

anguish /ˈæŋgwɪʃ/ *n* страда́ние, му́ка. **anguished** /-gwɪʃt/ *adj* отча́янный.

angular /ˈæŋgjʊlə(r)/ *adj* углово́й; (*sharp*) углова́тый.

animal /ˈænɪm(ə)l/ *n* живо́тное *sb*; *adj* живо́тный. **animate** /-mət/ *adj* живо́й. **animated** /-meɪtɪd/ *adj* оживлённый; **~ cartoon** мультфи́льм. **animation** /-ˈmeɪʃ(ə)n/ *n* оживле́ние.

animosity /ˌænɪˈmɒsɪtɪ/ *n* вражде́бность.

ankle /ˈæŋk(ə)l/ *n* лоды́жка.

annals /ˈæn(ə)lz/ *n pl* ле́топись.

annex /əˈneks/ *vt* аннекси́ровать *impf* & *pf*. **annexation** /-ˈseɪʃ(ə)n/ *n* анне́ксия. **annexe** /ˈæneks/ *n* пристро́йка.

annihilate /əˈnaɪəˌleɪt/ *vt* уничтожа́ть *impf*, уничто́жить *pf*. **annihilation** /-ˈleɪʃ(ə)n/ *n* уничтоже́ние.

anniversary /ˌænɪˈvɜːsərɪ/ *n* годовщи́на.

annotate /ˈænəˌteɪt/ *vt* комменти́ровать *impf* & *pf*. **annotated** /-tɪd/ *adj* снабжённый коммента́риями. **annotation** /ˌænəˈteɪʃ(ə)n/ *n* аннота́ция.

announce /əˈnaʊns/ *vt* объявля́ть *impf*, объяви́ть *pf*; заявля́ть *impf*, заяви́ть *pf*; (*radio*) сообща́ть *impf*, сообщи́ть *pf*. **announcement** /-mənt/ *n* объявле́ние; сообще́ние. **announcer** /-sə(r)/ *n* ди́ктор.

annoy /əˈnɔɪ/ *vt* досажда́ть *impf*, досади́ть *pf*; раздража́ть *impf*, раздражи́ть *pf*. **annoyance** /-əns/ *n* доса́да. **annoying** /-ɪŋ/ *adj* доса́дный.

annual /ˈænjʊəl/ *adj* ежего́дный, (*of a given year*) годово́й; *n* (*book*) ежего́дник; (*bot*) одноле́тник. **annually** /-lɪ/ *adv* ежего́дно. **annuity** /əˈnjuːɪtɪ/ *n* (ежего́дная) ре́нта.

annul /əˈnʌl/ *vt* аннули́ровать *impf* & *pf*. **annulment** /-mənt/ *n* аннули́рование.

anoint /əˈnɔɪnt/ *vt* пома́зывать *impf*, пома́зать *pf*.

anomalous /əˈnɒmələs/ *adj* анома́льный. **anomaly** /-lɪ/ *n* анома́лия.

anonymous /əˈnɒnɪməs/ *adj* анони́мный. **anonymity** /ˌænəˈnɪmɪtɪ/ *n* анони́мность.

anorak /ˈænəˌræk/ *n* ку́ртка.

anorexia /ˌænəˈreksɪə/ *n* анорéксия.

another /əˈnʌðə(r)/ *adj, pron* другóй; ~ **one** ещё (оди́н); **in ~ ten years** ещё чéрез дéсять лет.

answer /ˈɑːnsə(r)/ *n* отвéт; *vt* отвечáть *impf*, отвéтить *pf* (*person*) +*dat*, (*question*) на+*acc*; ~ **the door** отворя́ть *impf*, отвори́ть *pf* дверь; ~ **the phone** подходи́ть *impf*, подойти́ *pf* к телефóну. **answerable** /-rəb(ə)l/ *adj* отвéтственный. **answering machine** *n* телефóн-отвéтчик.

ant /ænt/ *n* муравéй.

antagonism /ænˈtægəˌnɪz(ə)m/ *n* антагони́зм. **antagonistic** /ænˌtægəˈnɪstɪk/ *adj* антагонисти́ческий. **antagonize** /ænˈtægəˌnaɪz/ *vt* настрáивать *impf*, настрóить *pf* прóтив себя́.

Antarctic /ænˈtɑːktɪk/ *n* Антáрктика.

antelope /ˈæntɪˌləʊp/ *n* антилóпа.

antenna /ænˈtenə/ *n* ýсик; (*also radio*) антéнна.

anthem /ˈænθəm/ *n* гимн.

anthology /ænˈθɒlədʒɪ/ *n* антолóгия.

anthracite /ˈænθrəˌsaɪt/ *n* антраци́т.

anthropological /ˌænθrəpəˈlɒdʒɪk(ə)l/ *adj* антропологи́ческий. **anthropologist** /ˌænθrəˈpɒlədʒɪst/ *n* антропóлог. **anthropology** /ˌænθrəˈpɒlədʒɪ/ антропológия.

anti-aircraft /ˌæntɪˈeəkrɑːft/ *adj* зени́тный. **antibiotic** /ˌæntɪbaɪˈɒtɪk/ *n* антибиóтик. **antibody** /ˈæntɪˌbɒdɪ/*n* антитéло. **anticlimax** /-ˈklaɪmæks/*n* разочаровáние. **anticlockwise** /-ˈklɒkwaɪz/ *adj* & *adv* прóтив часовóй стрéлки. **antidepressant** /-dɪˈpres(ə)nt/ *n* антидепрессáнт. **antidote** /ˈæntɪˌdəʊt/ *n* противоя́дие. **antifreeze** /ˈæntɪˌfriːz/ *n* антифри́з.

antipathy /ænˈtɪpəθɪ/ *n* антипáтия. **anti-Semitic** /ˌæntɪsɪˈmɪtɪk/ *adj* антисеми́тский. **anti-Semitism** /ˌæntɪˈsemɪˌtɪz(ə)m/ *n* антисеми́тизм. **antiseptic** /ˌæntɪˈseptɪk/ *adj* антисепти́ческий; *n* антисéптик. **antisocial** /ˌæntɪˈsəʊʃ(ə)l/*adj* асоциáльный. **anti-tank** /ˌæntɪˈtæŋk/*adj* противотáнковый. **antithesis** /ænˈtɪθɪsɪs/ *n* противополóжность; (*philos*) антитéзис.

anticipate /ænˈtɪsɪˌpeɪt/ *vt* ожидáть *impf* +*gen*; (*with pleasure*) предвкушáть *impf*, предвкуси́ть *pf*; (*forestall*) предупреждáть *impf*, предупреди́ть *pf*. **anticipation** /-ˈpeɪʃ(ə)n/ *n* ожидáние; предвкушéние; предупреждéние.

antics /ˈæntɪks/ *n* вы́ходки *f pl*.

antiquarian /ˌæntɪˈkweərɪən/ *adj* антиквáрный. **antiquated** /ˈæntɪˌkweɪtɪd/ *adj* устарéлый. **antique** /ænˈtiːk/ *adj* стари́нный; *n* антиквáрная вещь; ~ **shop** антиквáрный магази́н. **antiquity** /ænˈtɪkwɪtɪ/ *n* дрéвность.

antler /ˈæntlə(r)/ *n* олéний рог.

anus /ˈeɪnəs/ *n* зáдний прохóд.

anvil /ˈænvɪl/ *n* наковáльня.

anxiety /æŋˈzaɪətɪ/ *n* беспокóйство. **anxious** /ˈæŋkʃ(ə)s/ *adj* беспокóйный; **be** ~ беспокóиться *impf*; тревóжиться *impf*.

any /ˈenɪ/ *adj, pron* (*some*) какóй-нибудь; скóлько-нибудь; (*every*) вся́кий, любóй; (*anybody*) ктó-нибудь, (*anything*) чтó-нибудь; (*with neg*) никакóй, ни оди́н; нискóлько; никтó, ничтó; *adv* скóлько-нибудь; (*with neg*) нискóлько, ничýть. **anybody, anyone** *pron* ктó-нибудь; (*everybody*) вся́кий, любóй; (*with neg*) никтó. **anyhow** *adv* кáк-нибудь; кóе-как; (*with neg*) никáк; *conj* во вся́ком слýчае; всё равнó. **anyone** *see* **anybody**. **anything** *pron* чтó-нибудь; всё (что угóдно); (*with neg*) ничегó. **anyway** *adv* во вся́ком слýчае; как бы то ни́ было. **anywhere** *adv* где/кудá угóдно; (*with neg, interrog*) гдé-нибудь, кудá-нибудь.

apart /əˈpɑːt/ *adv* (*aside*) в стороне́, в сто́рону; (*separately*) врозь; (*distant*) друг от дру́га; (*into pieces*) на ча́сти; ~ **from** кро́ме+*gen*.

apartheid /ə'pɑːteɪt/ *n* апартеи́д.

apartment /ə'pɑːtmənt/ *n* (*flat*) кварти́ра.

apathetic /ˌæpə'θetɪk/ *adj* апати́чный. **apathy** /'æpəθɪ/ *n* апа́тия.

ape /eɪp/ *n* обезья́на; *vt* обезья́нничать *impf*, с~ *pf* с+*gen*.

aperture /'æpəˌtjʊə(r)/ *n* отве́рстие.

apex /'eɪpeks/ *n* верши́на.

aphorism /'æfəˌrɪz(ə)m/ *n* афори́зм.

apiece /ə'piːs/ *adv* (*per person*) на ка́ждого; (*per thing*) за шту́ку; (*amount*) по+*dat or acc with numbers*.

aplomb /ə'plɒm/ *n* апло́мб.

Apocalypse /ə'pɒkəlɪps/ *n* Апока́липсис. **apocalyptic** /-'lɪptɪk/ *adj* апокалипти́ческий.

apologetic /əˌpɒlə'dʒetɪk/ *adj* извиня́ющийся; **be** ~ извиня́ться *impf*. **apologize** /ə'pɒləˌdʒaɪz/ *vi* извиня́ться *impf*, извини́ться *pf* (**to** пе́ред +*instr*; **for** за+*acc*). **apology** /ə'pɒlədʒɪ/ *n* извине́ние.

apostle /ə'pɒs(ə)l/ *n* апо́стол.

apostrophe /ə'pɒstrəfɪ/ *n* апостро́ф.

appal /ə'pɔːl/ *vi* ужаса́ть *impf*, ужасну́ть *pf*. **appalling** /-lɪŋ/ *adj* ужа́сный.

apparatus /ˌæpə'reɪtəs/ *n* аппара́т; прибо́р; (*gymnastic*) гимнасти́ческие снаря́ды *m pl*.

apparel /ə'pær(ə)l/ *n* одея́ние.

apparent /ə'pærənt/ *adj* (*seeming*) ви́димый; (*manifest*) очеви́дный. **apparently** /-lɪ/ *adv* ка́жется, по-ви́димому.

apparition /ˌæpə'rɪʃ(ə)n/ *n* виде́ние.

appeal /ə'piːl/ *n* (*request*) призы́в, обраще́ние; (*law*) апелля́ция, обжа́лование; (*attraction*) привлека́тельность; ~ **court** апелляцио́нный суд; *vi* (*request*) взыва́ть *impf*, воззва́ть *pf* (**to** к+*dat*; **for** о+*prep*); обраща́ться *impf*, обрати́ться *pf* (с призы́вом); (*law*) апелли́ровать *impf* & *pf*; ~ **to** (*attract*) привлека́ть *impf*, привле́чь *pf*.

appear /ə'pɪə(r)/ *vi* появля́ться *impf*, появи́ться *pf*; (*in public*) выступа́ть *impf*, вы́ступить *pf*; (*seem*) каза́ться *impf*, по~ *pf*. **appearance** /-rəns/ *n* появле́ние; выступле́ние; (*aspect*) вид.

appease /ə'piːz/ *vt* умиротворя́ть *impf*, умиротвори́ть *pf*.

append /ə'pend/ *vt* прилага́ть *impf*, приложи́ть *pf*. **appendicitis** /əˌpendɪ'saɪtɪs/ *n* аппендици́т. **appendix** /ə'pendɪks/ *n* приложе́ние; (*anat*) аппенди́кс.

appertain /ˌæpə'teɪn/ *vi*: ~ **to** относи́ться *impf* +*dat*.

appetite /'æpɪˌtaɪt/ *n* аппети́т. **appetizing** /-ˌtaɪzɪŋ/ *adj* аппети́тный.

applaud /ə'plɔːd/ *vt* аплоди́ровать *impf* +*dat*. **applause** /-'plɔːz/ *n* аплодисме́нты *m pl*.

apple /'æp(ə)l/ *n* я́блоко; *adj* я́блочный; ~ **tree** я́блоня.

appliance /ə'plaɪəns/ *n* прибо́р. **applicable** /ə'plɪkəb(ə)l/ *adj* примени́мый. **applicant** /'æplɪkənt/ *n* кандида́т. **application** /ˌæplɪ'keɪʃ(ə)n/ *n* (*use*) примене́ние; (*putting on*) наложе́ние; (*request*) заявле́ние. **applied** /ə'plaɪd/ *adj* прикладно́й. **apply** /ə'plaɪ/ *vt* (*use*) применя́ть *impf*, примени́ть *pf*; (*put on*) накла́дывать *impf*, наложи́ть *pf*; *vi* (*request*) обраща́ться *impf*, обрати́ться *pf* (**to** к+*dat*; **for** за +*acc*); ~ **for** (*job*) подава́ть *impf*, пода́ть *pf* заявле́ние на+*acc*; ~ **to** относи́ться *impf* к+*dat*.

appoint /ə'pɔɪnt/ *vt* назнача́ть *impf*, назна́чить *pf*. **appointment** /-mənt/ *n* назначе́ние; (*job*) до́лжность; (*meeting*) свида́ние.

apposite /'æpəzɪt/ *adj* уме́стный.

appraise /ə'preɪz/ *vt* оце́нивать *impf*, оцени́ть *pf*.

appreciable /ə'priːʃəb(ə)l/ *adj* за-

a

ме́тный; (*considerable*) значи́тельный. **appreciate** /ə'priːʃɪˌeɪt/ *vt* цени́ть *impf*; (*understand*) понима́ть *impf*, поня́ть *pf*; *vi* повыша́ться *impf*, повы́ситься *pf* в цене́. **appreciation** /əˌpriːʃɪ'eɪʃ(ə)n/ *n* (*estimation*) оце́нка; (*gratitude*) призна́тельность; (*rise in value*) повыше́ние цены́. **appreciative** /ə'priːʃətɪv/ *adj* призна́тельный (**of** за+*acc*).

apprehension /ˌæprɪ'henʃ(ə)n/ *n* (*fear*) опасе́ние. **apprehensive** /-'hensɪv/ *adj* опаса́ющийся.

apprentice /ə'prentɪs/ *n* учени́к; *vt* отдава́ть *impf*, отда́ть *pf* в уче́ние. **apprenticeship** /-ʃɪp/ *n* учени́чество.

approach /ə'prəʊtʃ/ *vt & i* подходи́ть *impf*, подойти́ *pf* (к+*dat*); приближа́ться *impf*, прибли́зиться *pf* (к+*dat*); *vt* (*apply to*) обраща́ться *impf*, обрати́ться *pf* к+*dat*; *n* приближе́ние; подхо́д; подъе́зд; (*access*) по́дступ.

approbation /ˌæprə'beɪʃ(ə)n/ *n* одобре́ние.

appropriate *adj* /ə'prəʊprɪət/ подходя́щий; *vt* /ə'prəʊprɪˌeɪt/ присва́ивать *impf*, присво́ить *pf*. **appropriation** /-'eɪʃ(ə)n/ *n* присвое́ние.

approval /ə'pruːv(ə)l/ *n* одобре́ние; **on** ~ на про́бу. **approve** /ə'pruːv/ *vt* утвержда́ть *impf*, утверди́ть *pf*; *vt & i* (~ **of**) одобря́ть *impf*, одо́брить *pf*.

approximate *adj* /ə'prɒksɪmət/ приблизи́тельный; *vi* /ə'prɒksɪˌmeɪt/ приближа́ться *impf* (**to** к+*dat*). **approximation** /əˌprɒksɪ'meɪʃ(ə)n/ *n* приближе́ние.

apricot /'eɪprɪˌkɒt/ *n* абрико́с.

April /'eɪpr(ə)l/ *n* апре́ль *m*; *adj* апре́льский.

apron /'eɪprən/ *n* пере́дник.

apropos /'æprəˌpəʊ/ *adv*: ~ **of** по по́воду+*gen*.

apt /æpt/ *adj* (*suitable*) уда́чный; (*inclined*) скло́нный. **aptitude** /'æptɪˌtjuːd/ *n* спосо́бность.

aqualung /'ækwəˌlʌŋ/ *n* аквала́нг. **aquarium** /ə'kweərɪəm/ *n* аква́риум. **Aquarius** /ə'kweərɪəs/ *n* Водоле́й. **aquatic** /ə'kwætɪk/ *adj* водяно́й; (*of sport*) во́дный. **aqueduct** /'ækwɪˌdʌkt/ *n* акведу́к.

aquiline /'ækwɪˌlaɪn/ *adj* орли́ный.

Arab /'ærəb/ *n* ара́б, ~ка; *adj* ара́бский. **Arabian** /ə'reɪbɪən/ *adj* арави́йский. **Arabic** /'ærəbɪk/ *adj* ара́бский.

arable /'ærəb(ə)l/ *adj* па́хотный.

arbitrary /'ɑːbɪtrərɪ/ *adj* произво́льный. **arbitrate** /-ˌtreɪt/ *vi* де́йствовать *impf* в ка́честве трете́йского судьи́. **arbitration** /-'treɪʃ(ə)n/ *n* арбитра́ж, трете́йское реше́ние. **arbitrator** /-ˌtreɪtə(r)/ *n* арби́тр, трете́йский судья́ *m*.

arc /ɑːk/ *n* дуга́. **arcade** /ɑː'keɪd/ *n* арка́да, (*shops*) пасса́ж.

arch[1] /ɑːtʃ/ *n* а́рка, свод; (*of foot*) свод стопы́; *vt & i* выгиба́ть(ся) *impf*, вы́гнуть(ся) *pf*.

arch[2] /ɑːtʃ/ *adj* игри́вый.

archaeological /ˌɑːkɪə'lɒdʒɪk(ə)l/ *adj* археологи́ческий. **archaeologist** /ˌɑːkɪ'ɒlədʒɪst/ *n* архео́лог. **archaeology** /ˌɑːkɪ'ɒlədʒɪ/ *n* археоло́гия.

archaic /ɑː'keɪɪk/ *adj* архаи́ческий.

archangel /'ɑːkˌeɪndʒ(ə)l/ *n* арха́нгел.

archbishop /ɑːtʃ'bɪʃəp/ *n* архиепи́скоп.

arched /ɑːtʃt/ *adj* сво́дчатый.

arch-enemy /ɑːtʃ'enəmɪ/ *n* закля́тый враг.

archer /'ɑːtʃə(r)/ *n* стрело́к из лу́ка. **archery** /-rɪ/ *n* стрельба́ из лу́ка.

archipelago /ˌɑːkɪ'peləˌgəʊ/ *n* архипела́г.

architect /'ɑːkɪˌtekt/ *n* архите́ктор. **architectural** /-'tektʃər(ə)l/ *adj* архитекту́рный. **architecture** /'ɑːkɪˌtektʃə(r)/ *n* архитекту́ра.

archive(s) /'ɑːkaɪv(z)/ *n* архи́в.

archway /'ɑːtʃweɪ/*n* сво́дчатый прохо́д.

Arctic /ˈɑːktɪk/ *adj* аркти́ческий; *n* А́рктика.

ardent /ˈɑːd(ə)nt/ *adj* горя́чий. **ardour** /ˈɑːdə(r)/ *n* пыл.

arduous /ˈɑːdjʊəs/ *adj* тру́дный.

area /ˈeərɪə/ *n* (*extent*) пло́щадь; (*region*) райо́н; (*sphere*) о́бласть.

arena /əˈriːnə/ *n* аре́на.

argue /ˈɑːgjuː/ *vt* (*maintain*) утвержда́ть *impf*; дока́зывать *impf*; *vi* спо́рить *impf*, по~ *pf*. **argument** /-mənt/ *n* (*dispute*) спор; (*reason*) до́вод. **argumentative** /ˌɑːgjuːˈmentətɪv/ *adj* лю́бящий спо́рить.

aria /ˈɑːrɪə/ *n* а́рия.

arid /ˈærɪd/ *adj* сухо́й.

Aries /ˈeəriːz/ *n* Ове́н.

arise /əˈraɪz/ *vi* возника́ть *impf*, возни́кнуть *pf*.

aristocracy /ˌærɪˈstɒkrəsɪ/ *n* аристокра́тия. **aristocrat** /ˈærɪstəˌkræt/ *n* аристокра́т, ~ка. **aristocratic** /ˌærɪstəˈkrætɪk/ *adj* аристократи́ческий.

arithmetic /əˈrɪθmətɪk/ *n* арифме́тика. **arithmetical** /ˌærɪθˈmetɪk(ə)l/ *adj* арифмети́ческий.

ark /ɑːk/ *n* (Но́ев) ковче́г.

arm[1] /ɑːm/ *n* (*of body*) рука́; (*of chair*) ру́чка; **~ in ~** по́д руку; **at ~'s length** (*fig*) на почти́тельном расстоя́нии; **with open ~s** с распростёртыми объя́тиями.

arm[2] /ɑːm/ *n pl* (*weapons*) ору́жие; *vt* вооружа́ть *impf*, вооружи́ть *pf*. **armaments** /ˈɑːməmənts/ *n pl* вооруже́ние.

armchair /ˈɑːmtʃeə(r)/ *n* кре́сло.

Armenia /ɑːˈmiːnɪə/ *n* Арме́ния. **Armenian** /-ən/ *n* армяни́н, армя́нка; *adj* армя́нский.

armistice /ˈɑːmɪstɪs/ *n* переми́рие.

armour /ˈɑːmə(r)/ *n* (*for body*) доспе́хи *m pl*; (*for vehicles*; *fig*) броня́. **armoured** /ˈɑːməd/ *adj* брониро́ванный; (*vehicles etc.*) бронета́нковый, броне-; **~ car** броневи́к. **armoury** /ˈɑːmərɪ/ *n* арсена́л.

armpit /ˈɑːmpɪt/ *n* подмы́шка.

army /ˈɑːmɪ/ *n* а́рмия; *adj* арме́йский.

aroma /əˈrəʊmə/ *n* арома́т. **aromatherapy** /əˌrəʊməˈθerəpɪ/ *n* ароматерапи́я **aromatic** /ˌærəˈmætɪk/ *adj* ароматичный.

around /əˈraʊnd/ *adv* круго́м; *prep* вокру́г+*gen*; **all ~** повсю́ду.

arouse /əˈraʊz/ *vt* (*wake up*) буди́ть *impf*, раз~ *pf*; (*stimulate*) возбужда́ть *impf*, возбуди́ть *pf*.

arrange /əˈreɪndʒ/ *vt* расставля́ть *impf*, расста́вить *pf*; (*plan*) устра́ивать *impf*, устро́ить *pf*; (*mus*) аранжи́ровать *impf* & *pf*; *vi*: **~ to** догова́риваться *impf*, договори́ться *pf* +*inf*. **arrangement** /-mənt/ *n* расположе́ние; устро́йство; (*agreement*) соглаше́ние; (*mus*) аранжиро́вка; *pl* приготовле́ния *neut pl*.

array /əˈreɪ/ *vt* выставля́ть *impf*, вы́ставить *pf*; *n* (*dress*) наря́д; (*display*) колле́кция.

arrears /əˈrɪəz/ *n pl* задо́лженность.

arrest /əˈrest/ *vt* арестőвывать *impf*, арестова́ть *pf*; *n* аре́ст.

arrival /əˈraɪv(ə)l/ *n* прибы́тие, прие́зд; (*new ~*) вновь прибы́вший *sb*. **arrive** /əˈraɪv/ *vi* прибыва́ть *impf*, прибы́ть *pf*; приезжа́ть *impf*, прие́хать *pf*.

arrogance /ˈærəgəns/ *n* высокоме́рие. **arrogant** /-gənt/ *adj* высокоме́рный.

arrow /ˈærəʊ/ *n* стрела́; (*pointer*) стре́лка.

arsenal /ˈɑːsən(ə)l/ *n* арсена́л.

arsenic /ˈɑːsənɪk/ *n* мышья́к.

arson /ˈɑːs(ə)n/ *n* поджо́г.

art /ɑːt/ *n* иску́сство; *pl* гумани-та́рные нау́ки *f pl*; *adj* худо́жественный.

arterial /ɑːˈtɪərɪəl/ *adj*: **~ road** магистра́ль. **artery** /ˈɑːtərɪ/ *n* арте́рия.

artful /ˈɑːtfʊl/ *adj* хи́трый.

arthritis /ɑːˈθraɪtɪs/ *n* артри́т.

article /ˈɑːtɪk(ə)l/ *n* (*literary*) статья́; (*clause*) пункт; (*thing*) предме́т; (*gram*) арти́кль *m*.

a

articulate *vt* /ɑː'tɪkjʊˌleɪt/ произноси́ть *impf*, произнести́ *pf*; (*express*) выража́ть *impf*, вы́разить *pf*; *adj* /ɑː'tɪkjʊlət/ (*of speech*) членоразде́льный; **be ~** чётко выража́ть *impf* свои́ мы́сли. **articulated lorry** /ɑː'tɪkjʊˌleɪtɪd 'lɒrɪ/ *n* грузово́й автомоби́ль с прице́пом.
artifice /'ɑːtɪfɪs/ *n* хи́трость. **artificial** /ˌɑːtɪ'fɪʃ(ə)l/ *adj* иску́сственный.
artillery /ɑː'tɪlərɪ/ *n* артилле́рия.
artisan /ˌɑːtɪ'zæn/ *n* реме́сленник.
artist /'ɑːtɪst/ *n* худо́жник. **artiste** /ɑː'tiːst/ *n* арти́ст, **~**ка. **artistic** /ɑː'tɪstɪk/ *adj* худо́жественный.
artless /'ɑːtlɪs/ *adj* простоду́шный.
as /æz, əz/ *adv* как; *conj* (*when*) когда́; в то вре́мя как; (*because*) так как; (*manner*) как; (*though, however*) как ни; *rel pron* како́й; кото́рый; что; **as ... as** так (же)... как; **as for, to** относи́тельно+*gen*; что каса́ется +*gen*; **as if** как бу́дто; **as it were** ка́к бы; так сказа́ть; **as soon as** как то́лько; **as well** та́кже; то́же.
asbestos /æs'bestɒs/ *n* асбе́ст.
ascend /ə'send/ *vt* (*go up*) поднима́ться *impf*, подня́ться *pf* по+*dat*; (*throne*) всходи́ть *impf*, взойти́ *pf* на+*acc*; *vi* возноси́ться *impf*, вознести́сь *pf*. **ascendancy** /ə'send(ə)nsɪ/ *n* власть. **Ascension** /ə'senʃ(ə)n/ *n* (*eccl*) Вознесе́ние. **ascent** /ə'sent/ *n* восхожде́ние (**of** на+*acc*).
ascertain /ˌæsə'teɪn/ *vt* устана́вливать *impf*, установи́ть *pf*.
ascetic /ə'setɪk/ *adj* аскети́ческий; *n* аске́т. **asceticism** /ə'setɪˌsɪz(ə)m/ *n* аскети́зм.
ascribe /ə'skraɪb/ *vt* припи́сывать *impf*, приписа́ть *pf* (**to** +*dat*).
ash[1] /æʃ/ *n* (*tree*) я́сень *m*.
ash[2] /æʃ/, **ashes** /'æʃɪz/ *n* зола́, пе́пел; (*human remains*) прах. **ashtray** *n* пе́пельница.
ashamed /ə'ʃeɪmd/ *predic*: **he is ~** ему́ сты́дно; **be, feel, ~ of** стыди́ться *impf*, по**~** *pf* +*gen*.
ashen /'æʃ(ə)n/ *adj* (*pale*) ме́ртвенно-бле́дный.
ashore /ə'ʃɔː(r)/ *adv* на бе́рег(у́).
Asia /'eɪʃə/ *n* А́зия. **Asian, Asiatic** /'eɪʃ(ə)n, ˌeɪʃɪ'ætɪk/ *adj* азиа́тский; *n* азиа́т, **~**ка.
aside /ə'saɪd/ *adv* в сто́рону.
ask /ɑːsk/ *vt* & *i* (*enquire of*) спра́шивать *impf*, спроси́ть *pf*; (*request*) проси́ть *impf*, по**~** *pf* (**for** *acc*, *gen*, о+*prep*); (*invite*) приглаша́ть *impf*, пригласи́ть *pf*; (*demand*) тре́бовать *impf* +*gen* (**of** от+*gen*); **~ after** осведомля́ться *impf*, осве́домиться *pf* о+*prep*; **~ a question** задава́ть *impf*, зада́ть *pf* вопро́с.
askance /ə'skɑːns/ *adv* ко́со.
askew /ə'skjuː/ *adv* кри́во.
asleep /ə'sliːp/ *predic* & *adv*: **be ~** спать *impf*; **fall ~** засыпа́ть *impf*, засну́ть *pf*.
asparagus /ə'spærəgəs/ *n* спа́ржа.
aspect /'æspekt/ *n* вид; (*side*) сторона́.
aspersion /ə'spɜːʃ(ə)n/ *n* клевета́.
asphalt /'æsfælt/ *n* асфа́льт.
asphyxiate /æs'fɪksɪˌeɪt/ *vt* удуша́ть *impf*, удуши́ть.
aspiration /ˌæspɪ'reɪʃ(ə)n/ *n* стремле́ние. **aspire** /ə'spaɪə(r)/ *vi* стреми́ться *impf* (**to** к+*dat*).
aspirin /'æsprɪn/ *n* аспири́н; (*tablet*) табле́тка аспири́на.
ass /æs/ *n* осёл.
assail /ə'seɪl/ *vt* напада́ть *impf*, напа́сть *pf* на+*acc*; (*with questions*) забра́сывать *impf*, заброса́ть *pf* вопро́сами. **assailant** /-lənt/ *n* напада́ющий *sb*.
assassin /ə'sæsɪn/ *n* уби́йца *m* & *f*. **assassinate** /-ˌneɪt/ *vt* убива́ть *impf*, уби́ть *pf*. **assassination** /-'neɪʃ(ə)n/ *n* уби́йство.
assault /ə'sɔːlt/ *n* нападе́ние; (*mil*) штурм; **~ and battery** оскорбле́ние де́йствием; *vt* напада́ть *impf*, напа́сть *pf* на+*acc*.
assemblage /ə'semblɪdʒ/ *n* сбо́рка. **assemble** /ə'semb(ə)l/ *vt* & *i* собира́ть(ся) *impf*, со-

бра́ть(ся) *pf.* **assembly** /əˈsemblɪ/ *n* собра́ние; (*of machine*) сбо́рка.

assent /əˈsent/ *vi* соглаша́ться *impf*, согласи́ться *pf* (**to** на+*acc*); *n* согла́сие.

assert /əˈsɜːt/ *vt* утвержда́ть *impf*; ~ **o.s.** отста́ивать *impf*, отстоя́ть *pf* свои́ права́. **assertion** /əˈsɜːʃ(ə)n/ *n* утвержде́ние. **assertive** /əˈsɜːtɪv/ *adj* насто́йчивый.

assess /əˈses/ *vt* (*amount*) определя́ть *impf*, определи́ть *pf*; (*value*) оце́нивать *impf*, оцени́ть *pf.* **assessment** /-mənt/ *n* определе́ние; оце́нка.

asset /ˈæset/ *n* це́нное ка́чество; (*comm*; *also pl*) акти́в.

assiduous /əˈsɪdjʊəs/ *adj* приле́жный.

assign /əˈsaɪn/ *vt* (*appoint*) назнача́ть *impf*, назна́чить *pf*; (*allot*) отводи́ть *impf*, отвести́ *pf.* **assignation** /ˌæsɪgˈneɪʃ(ə)n/ *n* свида́ние. **assignment** /əˈsaɪnmənt/ *n* (*task*) зада́ние; (*mission*) командиро́вка.

assimilate /əˈsɪmɪˌleɪt/ *vt* усва́ивать *impf*, усво́ить *pf.* **assimilation** /-ˈleɪʃ(ə)n/ *n* усвое́ние.

assist /əˈsɪst/ *vt* помога́ть *impf*, помо́чь *pf* +*dat.* **assistance** /-təns/ *n* по́мощь. **assistant** /-tənt/ *n* помо́щник, ассисте́нт.

associate *vt* /əˈsəʊsɪˌeɪt/ ассоции́ровать *impf* & *pf*; *vi* обща́ться *impf* (**with** с+*instr*); *n* /əˈsəʊʃɪət/ колле́га *m* & *f.* **association** /əˌsəʊsɪˈeɪʃ(ə)n/ *n* о́бщество, ассоциа́ция.

assorted /əˈsɔːtɪd/ *adj* ра́зный. **assortment** /əˈsɔːtmənt/ *n* ассортиме́нт.

assuage /əˈsweɪdʒ/ *vt* (*calm*) успока́ивать *impf*, успоко́ить *pf*; (*alleviate*) смягча́ть *impf*, смягчи́ть *pf.*

assume /əˈsjuːm/ *vt* (*take on*) принима́ть *impf*, приня́ть *pf*; (*suppose*) предполага́ть *impf*, предположи́ть *pf*; ~**d name** вы́мышленное и́мя *neut*; **let us** ~ допу́стим. **assumption** /əˈsʌmpʃ(ə)n/ *n* (*taking on*) приня́тие на себе́; (*supposition*) предположе́ние.

assurance /əˈʃʊərəns/ *n* завере́ние; (*self-*~) самоуве́ренность. **assure** /əˈʃʊə(r)/ *vt* уверя́ть *impf*, уве́рить *pf.*

asterisk /ˈæstərɪsk/ *n* звёздочка.

asthma /ˈæsmə/ *n* а́стма. **asthmatic** /æsˈmætɪk/ *adj* астмати́ческий.

astonish /əˈstɒnɪʃ/ *vt* удивля́ть *impf*, удиви́ть *pf.* **astonishing** /-ʃɪŋ/ *adj* удиви́тельный. **astonishment** /-mənt/ *n* удивле́ние.

astound /əˈstaʊnd/ *vt* изумля́ть *impf*, изуми́ть *pf.* **astounding** /-dɪŋ/ *adj* изуми́тельный.

astray /əˈstreɪ/ *adv*: **go** ~ сбива́ться *impf*, сби́ться *pf* с пути́; **lead** ~ сбива́ть *impf*, сбить *pf* с пути́.

astride /əˈstraɪd/ *prep* верхо́м на +*prep.*

astringent /əˈstrɪndʒ(ə)nt/ *adj* вя́жущий; те́рпкий.

astrologer /əˈstrɒlədʒə(r)/ *n* астро́лог. **astrology** /-dʒɪ/ *n* астроло́гия. **astronaut** /ˈæstrəˌnɔːt/ *n* астрона́вт. **astronomer** /əˈstrɒnəmə(r)/ *n* астроно́м. **astronomical** /ˌæstrəˈnɒmɪk(ə)l/ *adj* астрономи́ческий. **astronomy** /əˈstrɒnəmɪ/ *n* астроно́мия.

astute /əˈstjuːt/ *adj* проница́тельный.

asunder /əˈsʌndə(r)/ *adv* (*apart*) врозь; (*in pieces*) на ча́сти.

asylum /əˈsaɪləm/ *n* сумасше́дший дом; (*refuge*) убе́жище; ~ **seeker** претенде́нт, ~ка на получе́ние (политѝческого) убе́жища.

asymmetrical /ˌeɪsɪˈmetrɪk(ə)l/ *adj* асимметри́чный.

at /æt, *unstressed* ət/ *prep* (*position*) на+*prep*, в+*prep*, у+*gen*: **at a concert** на конце́рте; **at the cinema** в кино́; **at the window** у окна́; (*time*) в+*acc*: **at two o'clock** в два часа́; на+*acc*: **at Easter** на Па́сху; (*price*) по+*dat*: **at 5p a pound** по

a

пяти́ пе́нсов за фунт; (*speed*): **at 60 mph** со ско́ростью шестьдеся́т миль в час; **~ first** снача́ла, сперва́; **~ home** до́ма; **~ last** наконе́ц; **~ least** по кра́йней ме́ре; **~ that** на том; (*moreover*) к тому́ же.

atheism /ˈeɪθɪˌɪz(ə)m/ *n* атеи́зм. **atheist** /-ɪst/ *n* атеи́ст, ~ка.

athlete /ˈæθliːt/ *n* спортсме́н, ~ка. **athletic** /æθˈletɪk/ *adj* атлети́ческий. **athletics** /æθˈletɪks/ *n* (лёгкая) атле́тика.

atlas /ˈætləs/ *n* а́тлас.

atmosphere /ˈætməsˌfɪə(r)/ *n* атмосфе́ра. **atmospheric** /ˌætməsˈferɪk/ *adj* атмосфе́рный.

atom /ˈætəm/ *n* а́том; **~ bomb** а́томная бо́мба. **atomic** /əˈtɒmɪk/ *adj* а́томный.

atone /əˈtəʊn/ *vi* искупа́ть *impf*, искупи́ть *pf* (**for** +*acc*). **atonement** /-mənt/ *n* искупле́ние.

atrocious /əˈtrəʊʃəs/ *adj* ужа́сный. **atrocity** /əˈtrɒsɪtɪ/ *n* зве́рство.

attach /əˈtætʃ/ *vt* (*fasten*) прикрепля́ть *impf*, прикрепи́ть *pf*; (*append*) прилага́ть *impf*, приложи́ть *pf*; (*attribute*) придава́ть *impf*, прида́ть *pf*; **attached to** (*devoted*) привя́занный к+*dat*. **attaché** /əˈtæʃeɪ/ *n* атташе́ *m indecl*. **attachment** /əˈtætʃmənt/ *n* прикрепле́ние; привя́занность; (*tech*) принадле́жность.

attack /əˈtæk/ *vt* напада́ть *impf*, напа́сть *pf* на+*acc*; *n* нападе́ние; (*of illness*) припа́док.

attain /əˈteɪn/ *vt* достига́ть *impf*, дости́чь & дости́гнуть *pf* +*gen*. **attainment** /-mənt/ *n* достиже́ние.

attempt /əˈtempt/ *vt* пыта́ться *impf*, по~ *pf* +*inf*; *n* попы́тка.

attend /əˈtend/ *vt* & *i* (*be present at*) прису́тствовать *impf* (на +*prep*); *vt* (*accompany*) сопровожда́ть *impf*, сопроводи́ть *pf*; (*go to regularly*) посеща́ть *impf*, посети́ть *pf*; **~ to** занима́ться *impf*, заня́ться *pf*. **attendance** /-dəns/ *n* (*presence*) прису́тствие; (*number*) посеща́емость. **attendant** /-dənt/ *adj* сопровожда́ющий; *n* дежу́рный *sb*; (*escort*) провожа́тый *sb*.

attention /əˈtenʃ(ə)n/ *n* внима́ние; **pay ~** обраща́ть *impf*, обрати́ть *pf* внима́ние (**to** на+*acc*); *int* (*mil*) сми́рно! **attentive** /əˈtentɪv/ *adj* внима́тельный; (*solicitous*) забо́тливый.

attest /əˈtest/ *vt* & *i* (*also* **~ to**) заверя́ть *impf*, заве́рить *pf*; свиде́тельствовать *impf*, за~ *pf* (о+*prep*).

attic /ˈætɪk/ *n* черда́к.

attire /əˈtaɪə(r)/ *vt* наряжа́ть *impf*, наряди́ть *pf*; *n* наря́д.

attitude /ˈætɪˌtjuːd/ *n* (*posture*) по́за; (*opinion*) отноше́ние (**towards** к+*dat*).

attorney /əˈtɜːnɪ/ *n* пове́ренный *sb*; **power of ~** дове́ренность.

attract /əˈtrækt/ *vt* привлека́ть *impf*, привле́чь *pf*. **attraction** /əˈtrækʃ(ə)n/ *n* привлека́тельность; (*entertainment*) аттракцио́н. **attractive** /-tɪv/ *adj* привлека́тельный.

attribute *vt* /əˈtrɪbjuːt/ припи́сывать *impf*, приписа́ть *pf*; *n* /ˈætrɪˌbjuːt/ (*quality*) сво́йство. **attribution** /ˌætrɪˈbjuːʃ(ə)n/ *n* /ˈætrɪˌbjuːt/ припи́сывание. **attributive** /əˈtrɪbjuːtɪv/ *adj* атрибути́вный.

attrition /əˈtrɪʃ(ə)n/ *n*: **war of ~** война́ на истоще́ние.

aubergine /ˈəʊbəˌʒiːn/ *n* баклажа́н.

auburn /ˈɔːbən/ *adj* тёмно-ры́жий.

auction /ˈɔːkʃ(ə)n/ *n* аукцио́н; *vt* продава́ть *impf*, прода́ть *pf* с аукцио́на. **auctioneer** /ˌɔːkʃəˈnɪə(r)/ *n* аукциони́ст.

audacious /ɔːˈdeɪʃəs/ *adj* (*bold*) сме́лый; (*impudent*) де́рзкий. **audacity** /ɔːˈdæsɪtɪ/ *n* сме́лость; де́рзость.

audible /ˈɔːdɪb(ə)l/ *adj* слы́шный. **audience** /ˈɔːdɪəns/ *n* пу́блика, аудито́рия; (*listeners*) слу́шатели *m pl*, (*viewers, spectators*) зри́тели *m pl*; (*interview*) аудие́нция.

audit /'ɔ:dɪt/ *n* прове́рка счето́в, реви́зия; *vt* проверя́ть *impf*, прове́рить *pf* (счета́+*gen*). **audition** /ɔ:'dɪʃ(ə)n/ *n* про́ба; *vt* устра́ивать *impf*, устро́ить *pf* про́бу +*gen*. **auditor** /'ɔ:dɪtə(r)/ *n* ревизо́р. **auditorium** /ˌɔ:dɪ'tɔ:rɪəm/ *n* зри́тельный зал.

augment /ɔ:g'ment/ *n* увели́чивать *impf*, увели́чить *pf*.

augur /'ɔ:gə(r)/ *vt & i* предвеща́ть *impf*.

August /'ɔ:gəst/ *n* а́вгуст; *adj* а́вгустовский. **august** /ɔ:'gʌst/ *adj* вели́чественный.

aunt /ɑ:nt/ *n* тётя, тётка.

au pair /əʊ 'peə(r)/ *n* домрабо́тница иностра́нного происхожде́ния.

aura /'ɔ:rə/ *n* орео́л.

auspices /'ɔ:spɪsɪz/ *n pl* покрови́тельство. **auspicious** /ɔ:'spɪʃ(ə)s/ *adj* благоприя́тный.

austere /ɒ'stɪə(r)/ *adj* стро́гий. **austerity** /ɒ'sterɪtɪ/ *n* стро́гость.

Australia /ɒ'streɪlɪə/ *n* Австра́лия. **Australian** /-ən/ *n* австрали́ец, -и́йка; *adj* австрали́йский.

Austria /'ɒstrɪə/ *n* А́встрия. **Austrian** /-ən/ *n* австри́ец, -и́йка; *adj* австри́йский.

authentic /ɔ:'θentɪk/ *adj* по́длинный. **authenticate** /-ˌkeɪt/ *vt* устана́вливать *impf*, установи́ть *pf* по́длинность+*gen*. **authenticity** /-'tɪsɪtɪ/ *n* по́длинность.

author /'ɔ:θə(r)/ *n* а́втор.

authoritarian /ɔ:ˌθɒrɪ'teərɪən/ *adj* авторита́рный. **authoritative** /ɔ:'θɒrɪtətɪv/ *adj* авторите́тный. **authority** /ɔ:'θɒrɪtɪ/ *n* (*power*) власть, полномо́чие; (*weight; expert*) авторите́т; (*source*) авторите́тный исто́чник. **authorization** /ˌɔ:θəraɪ'zeɪʃ(ə)n/ *n* уполномо́чивание; (*permission*) разреше́ние. **authorize** /'ɔ:θəˌraɪz/ *vt* (*action*) разреша́ть *impf*, разреши́ть *pf*; (*person*) уполномо́чивать *impf*, уполномо́чить *pf*.

authorship /'ɔ:θəʃɪp/ *n* а́вторство.

autobiographical /ˌɔ:təʊˌbaɪə'græfɪk(ə)l/ *adj* автобиографи́ческий. **autobiography** /ˌɔ:təʊbaɪ'ɒgrəfɪ/ *n* автобиогра́фия. **autocracy** /ɔ:'tɒkrəsɪ/ *n* автокра́тия. **autocrat** /'ɔ:təˌkræt/ *n* автокра́т. **autocratic** /ˌɔ:tə'krætɪk/ *adj* автократи́ческий. **autograph** /'ɔ:təˌgrɑ:f/ *n* авто́граф. **automatic** /ˌɔ:tə'mætɪk/ *adj* автомати́ческий. **automation** /ˌɔ:tə'meɪʃ(ə)n/ *n* автоматиза́ция. **automaton** /ɔ:'tɒmət(ə)n/ *n* автома́т. **automobile** /'ɔ:təməˌbi:l/ *n* автомоби́ль *m*. **autonomous** /ɔ:'tɒnəməs/ *adj* автоно́мный. **autonomy** /ɔ:'tɒnəmɪ/ *n* автоно́мия. **autopilot** /'ɔ:təʊˌpaɪlət/ *n* автопило́т. **autopsy** /'ɔ:tɒpsɪ/ *n* вскры́тие; ауто́псия.

autumn /'ɔ:təm/ *n* о́сень. **autumn(al)** /ɔ:'tʌmn(ə)l/ *adj* осе́нний.

auxiliary /ɔ:g'zɪljərɪ/ *adj* вспомога́тельный; *n* помо́щник, -ица.

avail /ə'veɪl/ *n*: **to no ~** напра́сно; *vt*: **~ o.s. of** по́льзоваться *impf*, вос~ *pf* +*instr*. **available** /-ləb(ə)l/ *adj* досту́пный, нали́чный.

avalanche /'ævəˌlɑ:ntʃ/ *n* лави́на.

avant-garde /ˌævɑ̃'gɑ:d/ *n* аванга́рд; *adj* аванга́рдный.

avarice /'ævərɪs/ *n* жа́дность. **avaricious** /-'rɪʃ(ə)s/ *adj* жа́дный.

avenge /ə'vendʒ/ *vt* мстить *impf*, ото~ *pf* за+*acc*. **avenger** /-dʒə(r)/ *n* мсти́тель *m*.

avenue /'ævəˌnju:/ *n* (*of trees*) алле́я; (*wide street*) проспе́кт; (*means*) путь *m*.

average /'ævərɪdʒ/ *n* сре́днее число́, сре́днее *sb*; **on ~** в сре́днем; *adj* сре́дний; *vt* де́лать *impf* в сре́днем; *vt & i*: **~ (out at)** составля́ть *impf*, соста́вить *pf* в сре́днем.

averse /ə'vɜ:s/ *adj*: **not ~ to** не прочь +*inf*, не про́тив+*gen*. **aversion** /ə'vɜ:ʃ(ə)n/ *n* отвраще́ние. **avert** /ə'vɜ:t/ *vt* (*ward off*) предотвраща́ть *impf*, предотврати́ть *pf*; (*turn away*) отводи́ть *impf*, отвести́ *pf*.

aviary /ˈeɪvɪərɪ/ *n* пти́чник.
aviation /ˌeɪvɪˈeɪʃ(ə)n/ *n* авиа́ция.
avid /ˈævɪd/ *adj* жа́дный; (*keen*) стра́стный.
avocado /ˌævəˈkɑːdəʊ/ *n* авока́до *neut indecl.*
avoid /əˈvɔɪd/ *vt* избега́ть *impf*, избежа́ть *pf* +*gen*; (*evade*) уклоня́ться *impf*, уклони́ться *pf* от+*gen*. **avoidance** /-dəns/ *n* избежа́ние, уклоне́ние.
avowal /əˈvaʊ(ə)l/ *n* призна́ние. **avowed** /əˈvaʊd/ *adj* при́знанный.
await /əˈweɪt/ *vt* ждать *impf* +*gen*.
awake /əˈweɪk/ *predic*: **be ~** не спать *impf*. **awake(n)** /-kən/ *vt* пробужда́ть *impf*, пробуди́ть *pf*; *vi* просыпа́ться *impf*, просну́ться *pf*.
award /əˈwɔːd/ *vt* присужда́ть *impf*, присуди́ть *pf* (*person dat*, *thing acc*); награжда́ть *impf*, награди́ть *pf* (*person acc*, *thing instr*); *n* награ́да.
aware /əˈweə(r)/ *predic*: **be ~ of** сознава́ть *impf*; знать *impf*. **awareness** /-n(ə)s/ *n* созна́ние.
away /əˈweɪ/ *adv* прочь; **be ~** отсу́тствовать *impf*; **far ~** (*from*) далеко́ (от+*gen*); **5 miles ~** в пяти́ ми́лях отсю́да; **~ game** игра́ на чужо́м по́ле.
awe /ɔː/ *n* благогове́йный страх. **awful** /ˈɔːfʊl/ *adj* ужа́сный. **awfully** /ˈɔːfʊlɪ/ *adv* ужа́сно.
awhile /əˈwaɪl/ *adv* не́которое вре́мя.
awkward /ˈɔːkwəd/ *adj* нело́вкий. **awkwardness** /-nɪs/ *n* нело́вкость.
awning /ˈɔːnɪŋ/ *n* наве́с, тент.
awry /əˈraɪ/ *adv* ко́со.
axe /æks/ *n* топо́р; *vt* уре́зывать, уреза́ть *impf*, уре́зать *pf*.
axiom /ˈæksɪəm/ *n* аксио́ма. **axiomatic** /-ˈmætɪk/ *adj* аксиомати́ческий.
axis /ˈæksɪs/ *n* ось.
axle /ˈæks(ə)l/ *n* ось.
ay /aɪ/ *int* да!; *n* (*in vote*) го́лос «за».
Azerbaijan /ˌæzəbaɪˈdʒɑːn/ *n* Азербайджа́н. **Azerbaijani** /-nɪ/ *n* азербайджа́нец (-нца), -а́нка; *adj* азербайджа́нский.
azure /ˈæʒə(r)/ *n* лазу́рь; *adj* лазу́рный.

B

BA *abbr* (*univ*) бакала́вр.
babble /ˈbæb(ə)l/ *n* (*voices*) болтовня́; (*water*) журча́ние; *vi* болта́ть *impf*; (*water*) журча́ть *impf*.
baboon /bəˈbuːn/ *n* павиа́н.
baby /ˈbeɪbɪ/ *n* ребёнок; **~-sit** присма́тривать за детьми́ в отсу́тствие роди́телей; **~-sitter** приходя́щая ня́ня. **babyish** /ˈbeɪbɪɪʃ/ *adj* ребя́ческий.
bachelor /ˈbætʃələ(r)/ *n* холостя́к; (*univ*) бакала́вр.
bacillus /bəˈsɪləs/ *n* баци́лла.
back /bæk/ *n* (*of body*) спина́; (*rear*) за́дняя часть; (*reverse*) оборо́т; (*of seat*) спи́нка; (*sport*) защи́тник; *adj* за́дний; *vt* (*support*) подде́рживать *impf*, поддержа́ть *pf*; (*car*) отодвига́ть *impf*, отодви́нуть *pf*; (*horse*) ста́вить *impf*, по~ *pf* на+*acc*; (*finance*) финанси́ровать *impf* & *pf*; *vi* отодвига́ться *impf*, отодви́нуться *pf* наза́д; **backed out of the garage** вы́ехал за́дом из гара́жа; **~ down** уступа́ть *impf*, уступи́ть *pf*; **~ out** уклоня́ться *impf*, уклони́ться *pf* (**of** от+*gen*); **~ up** (*support*) подде́рживать *impf*, поддержа́ть *pf*; (*confirm*) подкрепля́ть *impf*, подкрепи́ть *pf*. **backbiting** *n* спле́тня. **backbone** *n* позвоно́чник; (*support*) гла́вная опо́ра; (*firmness*) твёрдость хара́ктера. **backcloth, backdrop** *n* за́дник; (*fig*) фон. **backer** /ˈbækə(r)/ *n* спо́нсор; (*supporter*) сторо́нник. **backfire** *vi* дава́ть *impf*, дать *pf* отсе́чку. **background** *n* фон, за́дний план; (*person's*) происхо-

жде́ние. **backhand(er)** *n* уда́р сле́ва. **backhanded** *adj* (*fig*) сомни́тельный. **backhander** *n* (*bribe*) взя́тка. **backing** /ˈbækɪŋ/ *n* подде́ржка. **backlash** *n* реа́кция. **backlog** *n* задо́лженность. **backside** *n* зад. **backstage** *adv* за кули́сами; *adj* закули́сный. **backstroke** *n* пла́вание на спине́. **backup** *n* подде́ржка; (*copy*) резе́рвная ко́пия; *adj* вспомога́тельный. **backward** /ˈbækwəd/ *adj* отста́лый. **backward(s)** /ˈbækwəd(z)/ *adv* наза́д. **backwater** *n* за́водь. **back yard** *n* за́дний двор.

bacon /ˈbeɪkən/ *n* беко́н.

bacterium /bækˈtɪərɪəm/ *n* бакте́рия.

bad /bæd/ *adj* плохо́й; (*food etc.*) испо́рченный; (*language*) гру́бый; **~-mannered** невоспи́танный; **~ taste** безвку́сица; **~-tempered** раздражи́тельный.

badge /bædʒ/ *n* значо́к.

badger /ˈbædʒə(r)/ *n* барсу́к; *vt* трави́ть *impf*, за~ *pf*.

badly /ˈbædlɪ/ *adv* пло́хо; (*very much*) о́чень.

badminton /ˈbædmɪnt(ə)n/ *n* бадминто́н.

baffle /ˈbæf(ə)l/ *vt* озада́чивать *impf*, озада́чить *pf*.

bag /bæg/ *n* (*handbag*) су́мка; (*plastic* ~, *sack*, *under eyes*) мешо́к; (*paper* ~) бума́жный паке́т; *pl* (*luggage*) бага́ж.

baggage /ˈbægɪdʒ/ *n* бага́ж.

baggy /ˈbægɪ/ *adj* мешкова́тый.

bagpipe /ˈbægpaɪp/ *n* волы́нка.

bail[1] /beɪl/ *n* (*security*) поручи́тельство; **release on ~** отпуска́ть *impf*, отпусти́ть *pf* на пору́ки; *vt* (~ *out*) брать *impf*, взять *pf* на пору́ки; (*help*) выруча́ть *impf*, вы́ручить *pf*.

bail[2] /beɪl/, **bale**[2] /beɪl/ *vt* выче́рпывать *impf*, вы́черпнуть *pf* (во́ду из+*gen*); **~ out** *vi* выбра́сываться *impf*, вы́броситься *pf* с парашю́том.

bailiff /ˈbeɪlɪf/ *n* суде́бный исполни́тель.

bait /beɪt/ *n* нажи́вка; прима́нка (*also fig*); *vt* (*torment*) трави́ть *impf*, за~ *pf*.

bake /beɪk/ *vt & i* пе́чь(ся) *impf*, ис~ *pf*. **baker** /ˈbeɪkə(r)/ *n* пе́карь *m*, бу́лочник. **bakery** /ˈbeɪkərɪ/ *n* пека́рня; (*shop*) бу́лочная *sb*.

balalaika /ˌbæləˈlaɪkə/ *n* балала́йка.

balance /ˈbæləns/ *n* (*scales*) весы́ *m pl*; (*equilibrium*) равнове́сие; (*econ*) бала́нс; (*remainder*) оста́ток; **~ sheet** бала́нс; *vt* (*make equal*) уравнове́шивать *impf*, уравнове́сить *pf*; *vt & i* (*econ*; *hold steady*) баланси́ровать *impf*, с~ *pf*.

balcony /ˈbælkənɪ/ *n* балко́н.

bald /bɔːld/ *adj* лы́сый; **~ patch** лы́сина. **balding** /ˈbɔːldɪŋ/ *adj* лысе́ющий. **baldness** /ˈbɔːldnɪs/ *n* плеши́вость.

bale[1] /beɪl/ *n* (*bundle*) ки́па.

bale[2] /beɪl/ *see* **bail**[2]

balk /bɔːlk/ *vi* арта́читься *impf*, за~ *pf*; **she balked at the price** цена́ её испуга́ла.

ball[1] /bɔːl/ *n* (*in games*) мяч; (*sphere*; *billiards*) шар; (*wool*) клубо́к; **~-bearing** шарикоподши́пник; **~-point (pen)** ша́риковая ру́чка.

ball[2] /bɔːl/ *n* (*dance*) бал.

ballad /ˈbæləd/ *n* балла́да.

ballast /ˈbæləst/ *n* балла́ст.

ballerina /ˌbæləˈriːnə/ *n* балери́на.

ballet /ˈbæleɪ/ *n* бале́т. **ballet-dancer** *n* арти́ст, ~ка, бале́та.

balloon /bəˈluːn/ *n* возду́шный шар.

ballot /ˈbælət/ *n* голосова́ние. **ballot-paper** *n* избира́тельный бюллете́нь *m*; *vt* держа́ть *impf* голосова́ние между́+*instr*.

balm /bɑːm/ *n* бальза́м. **balmy** /ˈbɑːmɪ/ *adj* (*soft*) мя́гкий.

Baltic /ˈbɔːltɪk/ *n* Балти́йское мо́ре; **~ States** прибалти́йские госуда́рства, Приба́лтика.

b

balustrade /ˌbæləˈstreɪd/ *n* балюстра́да.
bamboo /bæmˈbuː/ *n* бамбу́к.
bamboozle /bæmˈbuːz(ə)l/ *vt* надува́ть *impf*, наду́ть *pf*.
ban /bæn/ *n* запре́т; *vt* запреща́ть *impf*, запрети́ть *pf*.
banal /bəˈnɑːl/ *adj* бана́льный. **banality** /bəˈnælɪtɪ/ *n* бана́льность.
banana /bəˈnɑːnə/ *n* бана́н.
band /bænd/ *n* (*stripe, strip*) полоса́; (*braid, tape*) тесьма́; (*category*) катего́рия; (*of people*) гру́ппа; (*gang*) ба́нда; (*mus*) орке́стр; (*radio*) диапазо́н; *vi*: **~ together** объединя́ться *impf*, объедини́ться *pf*.
bandage /ˈbændɪdʒ/ *n* бинт; *vt* бинтова́ть *impf*, за~ *pf*.
bandit /ˈbændɪt/ *n* банди́т.
bandstand /ˈbændstænd/ *n* эстра́да для орке́стра.
bandwagon /ˈbændwægən/ *n*: **jump on the ~** по́лзоваться *impf*, вос~ *pf* благоприя́тными обстоя́тельствами.
bandy-legged /ˈbændɪˌlegd/ *adj* кривоно́гий.
bane /beɪn/ *n* отра́ва.
bang /bæŋ/ *n* (*blow*) уда́р; (*noise*) стук; (*of gun*) вы́стрел; *vt* (*strike*) ударя́ть *impf*, уда́рить *pf*; *vi* хло́пать *impf*, хло́пнуть *pf*; (*slam shut*) захло́пываться *impf*, захло́пнуться *pf*; **~ one's head** ударя́ться *impf*, уда́риться *pf* голово́й; **~ the door** хло́пать *impf*, хло́пнуть *pf* две́рью.
bangle /ˈbæŋg(ə)l/ *n* брасле́т.
banish /ˈbænɪʃ/ *vt* изгоня́ть *impf*, изгна́ть *pf*.
banister /ˈbænɪstə(r)/ *n* пери́ла *neut pl*.
banjo /ˈbændʒəʊ/ *n* ба́нджо *neut indecl*.
bank[1] /bæŋk/ *n* (*of river*) бе́рег; (*of earth*) вал; *vt* сгреба́ть *impf*, сгрести́ *pf* в ку́чу; *vi* (*aeron*) накреня́ться *impf*, накрени́ться *pf*.
bank[2] /bæŋk/ *n* (*econ*) банк; **~ account** счёт в ба́нке; **~ holiday** установленный пра́здник; *vi* (*keep money*) держа́ть *impf* де́ньги (в ба́нке); *vt* (*put in ~*) класть *impf*, положи́ть *pf* в банк; **~ on** полага́ться *impf*, положи́ться *pf* на+*acc*. **banker** /ˈbæŋkə(r)/ *n* банки́р. **banknote** *n* банкно́та.
bankrupt /ˈbæŋkrʌpt/ *n* банкро́т; *adj* обанкро́тившийся; *vt* доводи́ть *impf*, довести́ *pf* до банкро́тства. **bankruptcy** /-sɪ/ *n* банкро́тство.
banner /ˈbænə(r)/ *n* зна́мя *neut*.
banquet /ˈbæŋkwɪt/ *n* банке́т, пир.
banter /ˈbæntə(r)/ *n* подшу́чивание.
baptism /ˈbæptɪz(ə)m/ *n* креще́ние. **baptize** /bæpˈtaɪz/ *vt* крести́ть *impf*, о~ *pf*.
bar /bɑː(r)/ *n* (*beam*) брус; (*of cage*) решётка; (*of chocolate*) пли́тка; (*of soap*) кусо́к; (*barrier*) прегра́да; (*law*) адвокату́ра; (*counter*) сто́йка; (*room*) бар; (*mus*) такт; *vt* (*obstruct*) прегражда́ть *impf*, прегради́ть *pf*; (*prohibit*) запреща́ть *impf*, запрети́ть *pf*.
barbarian /bɑːˈbeərɪən/ *n* ва́рвар. **barbaric** /bɑːˈbærɪk/, **barbarous** /ˈbɑːbərəs/ *adj* ва́рварский.
barbecue /ˈbɑːbɪˌkjuː/ *n* (*party*) шашлы́к; *vt* жа́рить *impf*, за~ *pf* на ве́ртеле.
barbed wire /ˌbɑːbd ˈwaɪə(r)/ *n* колю́чая про́волока.
barber /ˈbɑːbə(r)/ *n* парикма́хер; **~'s shop** парикма́херская *sb*.
bar code /ˈbɑː kəʊd/ *n* маркиро́вка.
bard /bɑːd/ *n* бард.
bare /beə(r)/ *adj* (*naked*) го́лый; (*empty*) пусто́й; (*small*) минима́льный; *vt* обнажа́ть *impf*, обнажи́ть *pf*; **~ one's teeth** ска́лить *impf*, о~ *pf* зу́бы. **barefaced** *adj* на́глый. **barefoot** *adj* босо́й. **barely** /ˈbeəlɪ/ *adv* едва́.
bargain /ˈbɑːgɪn/ *n* (*deal*) сде́лка; (*good buy*) вы́годная сде́лка; *vi* торгова́ться *impf*, с~ *pf*; **~ for, on** (*expect*) ожида́ть *impf* +*gen*.

barge /bɑːdʒ/ *n* ба́ржа́; *vi*: ~ **into** (*room etc.*) врыва́ться *impf*, ворва́ться *pf* в+*acc*.
baritone /ˈbærɪˌtəʊn/ *n* барито́н.
bark[1] /bɑːk/ *n* (*of dog*) лай; *vi* ла́ять *impf*.
bark[2] /bɑːk/ *n* (*of tree*) кора́.
barley /ˈbɑːlɪ/ *n* ячме́нь *m*.
barmaid /ˈbɑːmeɪd/ *n* буфе́тчица. **barman** /ˈbɑːmən/ *n* буфе́тчик.
barmy /ˈbɑːmɪ/ *adj* тро́нутый.
barn /bɑːn/ *n* амба́р.
barometer /bəˈrɒmɪtə(r)/ *n* баро́метр.
baron /ˈbærən/ *n* баро́н. **baroness** /-nɪs/ *n* барone´сса.
baroque /bəˈrɒk/ *n* баро́кко *neut indecl*; *adj* баро́чный.
barrack[1] /ˈbærək/ *n* каза́рма.
barrack[2] /ˈbærək/ *vt* осви́стывать *impf*, освиста́ть *pf*.
barrage /ˈbærɑːʒ/ *n* (*in river*) запру́да; (*gunfire*) огнево́й вал; (*fig*) град.
barrel /ˈbær(ə)l/ *n* бо́чка; (*of gun*) ду́ло.
barren /ˈbærən/ *adj* беспло́дный.
barricade *n* /ˈbærɪˌkeɪd/ баррика́да; *vt* /ˌbærɪˈkeɪd/ баррикади́ровать *impf*, за~ *pf*.
barrier /ˈbærɪə(r)/ *n* барье́р.
barring /ˈbɑːrɪŋ/ *prep* исключа́я.
barrister /ˈbærɪstə(r)/ *n* адвока́т.
barrow /ˈbærəʊ/ *n* теле́жка.
barter /ˈbɑːtə(r)/ *n* ба́ртер, товарообме́н; *vi* обме́ниваться *impf*, обменя́ться *pf* това́рами.
base[1] /beɪs/ *adj* ни́зкий; (*metal*) неблагоро́дный.
base[2] /beɪs/ *n* осно́ва; (*also mil*) ба́за; *vt* осно́вывать *impf*, основа́ть *pf*. **baseball** *n* бейсбо́л. **baseless** /ˈbeɪslɪs/ *adj* необосно́ванный. **basement** /ˈbeɪsmənt/ *n* подва́л.
bash /bæʃ/ *vt* тре́снуть *pf*; *n*: **have a** ~! попро́буй(те)!
bashful /ˈbæʃfʊl/ *adj* засте́нчивый.
basic /ˈbeɪsɪk/ *adj* основно́й. **basically** /-kəlɪ/ *adv* в основно́м.
basin /ˈbeɪs(ə)n/ *n* таз; (*geog*) бассе́йн.
basis /ˈbeɪsɪs/ *n* осно́ва, ба́зис.
bask /bɑːsk/ *vi* гре́ться *impf*; (*fig*) наслажда́ться *impf*, наслади́ться *pf* (**in** +*instr*).
basket /ˈbɑːskɪt/ *n* корзи́на. **basketball** *n* баскетбо́л.
bass /beɪs/ *n* бас; *adj* басо́вый.
bassoon /bəˈsuːn/ *n* фаго́т.
bastard /ˈbɑːstəd/ *n* (*sl*) негодя́й.
baste /beɪst/ *vt* (*cul*) полива́ть *impf*, поли́ть *pf* жи́ром.
bastion /ˈbæstɪən/ *n* бастио́н.
bat[1] /bæt/ *n* (*zool*) лету́чая мышь.
bat[2] /bæt/ *n* (*sport*) бита́; *vi* бить *impf*, по~ *pf* по мячу́.
bat[3] /bæt/ *vt*: **he didn't ~ an eyelid** он и гла́зом не моргну́л.
batch /bætʃ/ *n* па́чка; (*of loaves*) вы́печка.
bated /ˈbeɪtɪd/ *adj*: **with ~ breath** затаи́в дыха́ние.
bath /bɑːθ/ *n* (*vessel*) ва́нна; *pl* пла́вательный бассе́йн; **have a bath** принима́ть *impf*, приня́ть *pf* ва́нну; *vt* купа́ть *impf*, вы́~, ис~ *pf*. **bathe** /beɪð/ *vi* купа́ться *impf*, вы́~, ис~ *pf*; *vt* омыва́ть *impf*, омы́ть *pf*. **bather** /ˈbeɪðə(r)/ *n* купа́льщик, -ица. **bath-house** *n* ба́ня. **bathing** /ˈbeɪðɪŋ/ *n*: ~ **cap** купа́льная ша́почка; ~ **costume** купа́льный костю́м. **bathroom** *n* ва́нная *sb*.
baton /ˈbæt(ə)n/ *n* (*staff of office*) жезл; (*sport*) эстафе́та; (*mus*) (дирижёрская) па́лочка.
battalion /bəˈtælɪən/ *n* батальо́н.
batten /ˈbæt(ə)n/ *n* ре́йка.
batter /ˈbætə(r)/ *n* взби́тое те́сто; *vt* колоти́ть *impf*, по~ *pf*.
battery /ˈbætərɪ/ *n* батаре́я.
battle /ˈbæt(ə)l/ *n* би́тва; (*fig*) борьба́; *vi* боро́ться *impf*. **battlefield** *n* по́ле бо́я. **battlement** /-mənt/ *n* зубча́тая стена́. **battleship** *n* лине́йный кора́бль *m*.
bawdy /ˈbɔːdɪ/ *adj* непристо́йный.
bawl /bɔːl/ *vi* ора́ть *impf*.
bay[1] /beɪ/ *n* (*bot*) ла́вр; *adj* лавро́вый.
bay[2] /beɪ/ *n* (*geog*) зали́в.

b

bay[3] /beɪ/ *n* (*recess*) пролёт; **~ window** фона́рь *m*.
bay[4] /beɪ/ *vi* (*bark*) ла́ять *impf*; (*howl*) выть *impf*.
bay[5] /beɪ/ *adj* (*colour*) гнедо́й.
bayonet /ˈbeɪəˌnet/ *n* штык.
bazaar /bəˈzɑː(r)/ *n* база́р.
BC *abbr* до н.э. (до на́шей э́ры).
be[1] /biː/ *v* **1.** быть: *usually omitted in pres*: **he is a teacher** он учи́тель. **2.** (*exist*) существова́ть *impf*. **3.** (*frequentative*) быва́ть *impf*. **4.** (**~** *situated*) находи́ться *impf*; (*stand*) стоя́ть *impf*; (*lie*) лежа́ть *impf*. **5.** (*in general definitions*) явля́ться *impf +instr*: **Moscow is the capital of Russia** столи́цей Росси́и явля́ется го́род Москва́. **6.: there is, are** име́ется, име́ются; (*emph*) есть.
be[2] /biː/ *v aux* **1.** *be+inf, expressing duty, plan*: до́лжен*+inf*. **2.** *be +past participle passive, expressing passive*: быть*+past participle passive in short form*: **it was done** бы́ло сде́лано; *impers construction of 3 pl+acc*: **I was beaten** меня́ би́ли; *reflexive construction*: **music was heard** слы́шалась му́зыка. **3.** *be+pres participle active, expressing continuous tenses*: *imperfective aspect*: **I am reading** я чита́ю.
beach /biːtʃ/ *n* пляж.
beacon /ˈbiːkən/ *n* мая́к, сигна́льный ого́нь *m*.
bead /biːd/ *n* бу́сина; (*drop*) ка́пля; *pl* бу́сы *f pl*.
beak /biːk/ *n* клюв.
beaker /ˈbiːkə(r)/ *n* (*child's*) ча́шка с но́сиком; (*chem*) мензу́рка.
beam /biːm/ *n* ба́лка; (*ray*) луч; *vi* (*shine*) сия́ть *impf*.
bean /biːn/ *n* фасо́ль, боб.
bear[2] /beə(r)/ *n* медве́дь *m*.
bear[2] /beə(r)/ *vt* (*carry*) носи́ть *indet*, нести́ *det*, по**~** *pf*; (*endure*) терпе́ть *impf*; (*child*) роди́ть *impf* & *pf*; **~ out** подтвержда́ть *impf*, подтверди́ть *pf*; **~ up** держа́ться *impf*. **bearable** /ˈbeərəb(ə)l/ *adj* терпи́мый.
beard /ˈbɪəd/ *n* борода́. **bearded** /-dɪd/ *adj* борода́тый.
bearer /ˈbeərə(r)/ *n* носи́тель *m*; (*of cheque*) предъяви́тель *m*; (*of letter*) пода́тель *m*.
bearing /ˈbeərɪŋ/ *n* (*deportment*) оса́нка; (*relation*) отноше́ние; (*position*) пе́ленг; (*tech*) подши́пник; **get one's ~s** ориенти́роваться *impf* & *pf*; **lose one's ~s** потеря́ть *pf* ориентиро́вку.
beast /biːst/ *n* живо́тное *sb*; (*fig*) скоти́на *m* & *f*. **beastly** /ˈbiːstlɪ/ *adj* (*coll*) проти́вный.
beat /biːt/ *n* бой; (*round*) обхо́д; (*mus*) такт; *vt* бить *impf*, по**~** *pf*; (*sport*) выи́грывать *impf*, вы́играть *pf* у*+gen*; (*cul*) взбива́ть *impf*, взбить *pf*; *vi* би́ться *impf*, **~ off** отбива́ть *impf*, отби́ть *pf*; **~ up** избива́ть *impf*, изби́ть *pf*. **beating** /ˈbiːtɪŋ/ *n* битьё; (*defeat*) пораже́ние; (*of heart*) бие́ние.
beautiful /ˈbjuːtɪfʊl/ *adj* краси́вый. **beautify** /-ˌfaɪ/ *vt* украша́ть *impf* укра́сить *pf*. **beauty** /ˈbjuːtɪ/ *n* красота́; (*person*) краса́вица.
beaver /ˈbiːvə(r)/ *n* бобр.
because /bɪˈkɒz/ *conj* потому́, что; так как; *adv*: **~ of** из-за*+gen*.
beckon /ˈbekən/ *vt* мани́ть *impf*, по**~** *pf* к себе́.
become /bɪˈkʌm/ *vi* станови́ться *impf*, стать *pf +instr*; **~ of** ста́ться *pf* с*+instr*. **becoming** /-mɪŋ/ *adj* (*dress*) иду́щий к лицу́*+dat*.
bed /bed/ *n* крова́ть, посте́ль; (*garden*) гря́дка; (*sea*) дно; (*river*) ру́сло; (*geol*) пласт; **go to ~** ложи́ться *impf*, лечь *pf* спать; **make the ~** стели́ть *impf*, по**~** *pf* посте́ль. **bed and breakfast** *n* (*hotel*) ма́ленькая гости́ница. **bedclothes** *n pl*, **bedding** /ˈbedɪŋ/ *n* посте́льное бельё. **bedridden** /ˈbedrɪd(ə)n/ *adj* прико́ванный к посте́ли. **bedroom** *n* спа́льня. **bedside table** *n* ту́мбочка. **bedsitter** /ˈbedsɪtə(r)/ *n* одноко́мнатная кварти́ра. **bedspread** *n* по-

крыва́ло. **bedtime** *n* вре́мя *neut* ложи́ться спать.
bedlam /ˈbedləm/ *n* бедла́м.
bedraggled /bɪˈdræg(ə)ld/ *adj* растрёпанный.
bee /biː/ *n* пчела́. **beehive** *n* у́лей.
beech /biːtʃ/ *n* бук.
beef /biːf/ *n* говя́дина. **beefburger** *n* котле́та.
beer /bɪə(r)/ *n* пи́во.
beetle /ˈbiːt(ə)l/ *n* жук.
beetroot /ˈbiːtruːt/ *n* свёкла.
befall /bɪˈfɔːl/ *vt* & *i* случа́ться *impf*, случи́ться *pf* (+*dat*).
befit /bɪˈfɪt/ *vt* подходи́ть *impf*, подойти́ *pf* +*dat*.
before /bɪˈfɔː(r)/ *adv* ра́ньше; *prep* пе́ред+*instr*, до+*gen*; *conj* до того́ как; пре́жде чем; (*rather than*) скоре́е чем; **the day ~ yesterday** позавчера́. **beforehand** *adv* зара́нее.
befriend /bɪˈfrend/ *vt* дружи́ться *impf*, по~ *pf* с+*instr*.
beg /beg/ *vt* (*ask*) о́чень проси́ть *impf*, по~ *pf* (*person*+*acc*; *thing* +*acc or gen*); *vi* ни́щенствовать *impf*; (*of dog*) служи́ть *impf*; **~ for** проси́ть *impf*, по~ *pf* +*acc or gen*; **~ pardon** проси́ть *impf* проще́ние.
beggar /ˈbegə(r)/ *n* ни́щий *sb*.
begin /bɪˈgɪn/ *vt* (& *i*) начина́ть(ся) *impf*, нача́ть(ся) *pf*. **beginner** /-ˈgɪnə(r)/ *n* начина́ющий *sb*. **beginning** /-ˈgɪnɪŋ/ *n* нача́ло.
begrudge /bɪˈgrʌdʒ/ *vt* (*give reluctantly*) жале́ть *impf*, со~ *pf* о+*prep*.
beguile /bɪˈgaɪl/ *vt* (*charm*) очаро́вывать *impf*, очарова́ть *pf*; (*seduce, delude*) обольща́ть *impf*, обольсти́ть *pf*.
behalf /bɪˈhɑːf/ *n*: **on ~ of** от и́мени +*gen*; (*in interest of*) в по́льзу +*gen*.
behave /bɪˈheɪv/ *vi* вести́ *impf* себя́. **behaviour** /-ˈheɪvjə(r)/ *n* поведе́ние.
behest /bɪˈhest/ *n* заве́т.
behind /bɪˈhaɪnd/ *adv*, *prep* сза́ди (+*gen*), позади́ (+*gen*), за (+*acc*, *instr*); *n* зад; **be, fall, ~** отстава́ть *impf*, отста́ть *pf*.
behold /bɪˈhəʊld/ *vt* смотре́ть *impf*, по~ *pf*. **beholden** /-d(ə)n/ *predic*: **~ to** обя́зан+*dat*.
beige /beɪʒ/ *adj* бе́жевый.
being /ˈbiːɪŋ/ *n* (*existence*) бытие́; (*creature*) существо́.
Belarus /ˌbeləˈrʌs/ *n* Белару́сь.
belated /bɪˈleɪtɪd/ *adj* запозда́лый.
belch /beltʃ/ *vi* рыга́ть *impf*, рыгну́ть *pf*; *vt* изверга́ть *impf*, изве́ргнуть *pf*.
beleaguer /bɪˈliːgə(r)/ *vt* осажда́ть *impf*, осади́ть *pf*.
belfry /ˈbelfrɪ/ *n* колоко́льня.
Belgian /ˈbeldʒ(ə)n/ *n* бельги́ец, -ги́йка; *adj* бельги́йский. **Belgium** /-dʒəm/ *n* Бе́льгия.
belie /bɪˈlaɪ/ *vt* противоре́чить *impf* +*dat*.
belief /bɪˈliːf/ *n* (*faith*) ве́ра; (*confidence*) убежде́ние. **believable** /-ˈliːvəb(ə)l/ *adj* правдоподо́бный. **believe** /-ˈliːv/ *vt* ве́рить *impf*, по~ *pf* +*dat*; **~ in** ве́рить *impf* в+*acc*. **believer** /-ˈliːvə(r)/ *n* ве́рующий *sb*.
belittle /bɪˈlɪt(ə)l/ *vt* умаля́ть *impf*, умали́ть *pf*.
bell /bel/ *n* ко́локол; (*doorbell*) звоно́к; **~ tower** колоко́льня.
bellicose /ˈbelɪˌkəʊz/ *adj* вои́нственный. **belligerence** /bɪˈlɪdʒər(ə)ns/ *n* вои́нственность. **belligerent** /bɪˈlɪdʒərənt/ *adj* вою́ющий; (*aggressive*) вои́нственный.
bellow /ˈbeləʊ/ *vt* & *i* реве́ть *impf*.
bellows /ˈbeləʊz/ *n pl* мехи́ *m pl*.
belly /ˈbelɪ/ *n* живо́т.
belong /bɪˈlɒŋ/ *vi* принадлежа́ть *impf* (**to** (к)+*dat*). **belongings** /-ɪŋz/ *n pl* пожи́тки (-ков) *pl*.
Belorussian /ˌbeləʊˈrʌʃ(ə)n/ *n* белору́с, ~ка; *adj* белору́сский.
beloved /bɪˈlʌvɪd/ *adj* & *sb* возлю́бленный.
below /bɪˈləʊ/ *adv* (*position*) внизу́; *prep* (*position*) под +*instr*; (*less than*) ни́же+*gen*.
belt /belt/ *n* (*strap*) по́яс, (*also tech*)

b

ремéнь; (*zone*) зóна, полосá.

bench /bentʃ/ *n* скамéйка; (*for work*) станóк.

bend /bend/ *n* изгѝб; *vt* (& *i*, *also* ~ **down**) сгибáть(ся) *impf*, согнýть(ся) *pf*; ~ **over** склоняться *impf*, склонѝться *pf* над+*instr*.

beneath /bɪˈniːθ/ *prep* под+*instr*.

benediction /ˌbenɪˈdɪkʃ(ə)n/ *n* благословéние.

benefactor /ˈbenɪˌfæktə(r)/ *n* благодéтель *m*. **benefactress** /-ˌfæktrɪs/ *n* благодéтельница

beneficial /ˌbenɪˈfɪʃ(ə)l/ *adj* полéзный. **beneficiary** /-ˈfɪʃərɪ/ *n* получáтель *m*; (*law*) наслéдник. **benefit** /ˈbenɪfɪt/ *n* пóльза; (*allowance*) посóбие; (*theat*) бенефѝс; *vt* приносѝть *impf*, принестѝ *pf* пóльзу +*dat*; *vi* извлекáть *impf*, извлéчь *pf* вы́году.

benevolence /bɪˈnevəl(ə)ns/ *n* благожелáтельность. **benevolent** /-l(ə)nt/ *adj* благожелáтельный.

benign /bɪˈnaɪn/ *adj* дóбрый, мя́гкий; (*tumour*) доброкáчественный.

bent /bent/ *n* склóнность.

bequeath /bɪˈkwiːð/ *vt* завещáть *impf* & *pf* (**to**+*dat*). **bequest** /bɪˈkwest/ *n* посмéртный дар.

berate /bɪˈreɪt/ *vt* ругáть *impf*, вы́~ *pf*.

bereave /bɪˈriːv/ *vt* лишáть *impf*, лишѝть *pf* (**of** +*gen*). **bereavement** /-mənt/ *n* тяжёлая утрáта.

berry /ˈberɪ/ *n* я́года.

berserk /bəˈsɜːk/ *adj*: **go** ~ взбесѝться *pf*.

berth /bɜːθ/ *n* (*bunk*) кóйка; (*naut*) стоя́нка; *vi* причáливать *impf*, причáлить *pf*.

beseech /bɪˈsiːtʃ/ *vt* умоля́ть *impf*, умолѝть *pf*.

beset /bɪˈset/ *vt* осаждáть *impf*, осадѝть *pf*.

beside /bɪˈsaɪd/ *prep* óколо+*gen*, ря́дом с+*instr*; ~ **the point** некстáти; ~ **o.s.** вне себя́. **besides** /bɪˈsaɪdz/ *adv* крóме тогó; *prep* крóме+*gen*.

besiege /bɪˈsiːdʒ/ *vt* осаждáть *impf*, осадѝть *pf*.

besotted /bɪˈsɒtɪd/ *adj* одурмáненный.

bespoke /bɪˈspəʊk/ *adj* сдéланный на закáз.

best /best/ *adj* лýчший, сáмый лýчший; *adv* лýчше всегó, бóльше всегó; **all the** ~! всегó наилýчшего! **at** ~ в лýчшем слýчае; **do one's** ~ дéлать *impf*, с~ *pf* всё возмóжное; ~ **man** шáфер.

bestial /ˈbestɪəl/ *adj* звéрский. **bestiality** /ˌbestɪˈælɪtɪ/ *n* звéрство.

bestow /bɪˈstəʊ/ *vt* даровáть *impf* & *pf*.

bestseller /ˌbestˈselə(r)/ *n* бестсéллер.

bet /bet/ *n* парѝ *neut indecl*; (*stake*) стáвка; *vi* держáть *impf* парѝ (**on** на+*acc*); *vt* (*stake*) стáвить *impf*, по~ *pf*; **he bet me £5** он поспóрил со мной на 5 фýнтов.

betray /bɪˈtreɪ/ *vt* изменя́ть *impf*, изменѝть *pf*+*dat*. **betrayal** /-ˈtreɪəl/ *n* измéна.

better /ˈbetə(r)/ *adj* лýчший; *adv* лýчше; (*more*) бóльше; *vt* улучшáть *impf*, улýчшить *pf*; **all the** ~ тем лýчше; ~ **off** бóлее состоя́тельный; ~ **o.s.** выдвигáться *impf*, вы́двинуться *pf*; **get** ~ (*health*) поправля́ться *impf*, попрáвиться *pf*; **get the** ~ **of** брать *impf*, взять *pf* верх над+*instr*; **had** ~: **you had** ~ **go** вам (*dat*) лýчше бы пойтѝ; **think** ~ **of** передýмывать *impf*, передýмать *pf*. **betterment** /-mənt/ *n* улучшéние.

between /bɪˈtwiːn/ *prep* мéжду +*instr*.

bevel /ˈbev(ə)l/ *vt* скáшивать *impf*, скосѝть *pf*.

beverage /ˈbevərɪdʒ/ *n* напѝток.

bevy /ˈbevɪ/ *n* стáйка.

beware /bɪˈweə(r)/ *vi* остерегáться *impf*, остерéчься *pf* (**of** +*gen*).

bewilder /bɪˈwɪldə(r)/ *vt* сбивáть *impf*, сбить *pf* с тóлку. **bewildered** /-dəd/ *adj* озадáченный.

bewilderment /-mənt/ *n* замеша́тельство.
bewitch /bɪˈwɪtʃ/ *vt* заколдо́вывать *impf*, заколдова́ть *pf*; (*fig*) очаро́вывать *impf*, очарова́ть *pf*. **bewitching** /-tʃɪŋ/ *adj* очарова́тельный.
beyond /bɪˈjɒnd/ *prep* за+*acc* & *instr*; по ту сто́рону+*gen*; (*above*) сверх+*gen*; (*outside*) вне+*gen*; **the back of ~** край све́та.
bias /ˈbaɪəs/ *n* (*inclination*) укло́н; (*prejudice*) предупрежде́ние. **biased** /ˈbaɪəst/ *adj* предупреждённый.
bib /bɪb/ *n* нагру́дник.
Bible /ˈbaɪb(ə)l/ *n* Би́блия. **biblical** /ˈbɪblɪk(ə)l/ *adj* библе́йский.
bibliographical /ˌbɪblɪəˈgræfɪk(ə)l/ *n* библиографи́ческий. **bibliography** /ˌbɪblɪˈɒgrəfɪ/ *n* библиогра́фия.
bicarbonate (of soda) /baɪˈkɑːbənɪt/ *n* питьева́я со́да.
biceps /ˈbaɪseps/ *n* би́цепс.
bicker /ˈbɪkə(r)/ *vi* препира́ться *impf*.
bicycle /ˈbaɪsɪk(ə)l/ *n* велосипе́д.
bid /bɪd/ *n* предложе́ние цены́; (*attempt*) попы́тка; *vt* & *i* предлага́ть *impf*, предложи́ть *pf* (це́ну) (**for** за+*acc*); *vt* (*command*) прика́зывать *impf*, приказа́ть *pf* +*dat*. **bidding** /ˈbɪdɪŋ/ *n* предложе́ние цены́; (*command*) приказа́ние.
bide /baɪd/ *vt*: **~ one's time** ожида́ть *impf* благоприя́тного слу́чая.
biennial /baɪˈenɪəl/ *adj* двухле́тний; *n* двухле́тник.
bier /bɪə(r)/ *n* катафа́лк.
bifocals /baɪˈfəʊk(ə)lz/ *n pl* бифока́льные очки́ *pl*.
big /bɪg/ *adj* большо́й; (*also important*) кру́пный.
bigamist /ˈbɪgəmɪst/ *n* (*man*) двоеже́нец; (*woman*) двуму́жница. **bigamy** /-mɪ/ *n* двубра́чие.
bigwig /ˈbɪgwɪg/ *n* ши́шка.
bike /baɪk/ *n* велосипе́д. **biker** /ˈbaɪkə(r)/ *n* мотоцикли́ст.
bikini /bɪˈkiːnɪ/ *n* бики́ни *neut indecl*.
bilateral /baɪˈlætər(ə)l/ *adj* двусторо́нний.
bilberry /ˈbɪlbərɪ/ *n* черни́ка (*no pl*; *usu collect*).
bile /baɪl/ *n* жёлчь. **bilious** /ˈbɪljəs/ *adj* жёлчный.
bilingual /baɪˈlɪŋgw(ə)l/ *adj* двуязы́чный.
bill[1] /bɪl/ *n* счёт; (*parl*) законопрое́кт; (*~ of exchange*) ве́ксель; (*poster*) афи́ша; *vt* (*announce*) объявля́ть *impf*, объяви́ть *pf* в афи́шах; (*charge*) присыла́ть *impf*, присла́ть *pf* счёт+*dat*.
bill[2] /bɪl/ *n* (*beak*) клюв.
billet /ˈbɪlɪt/ *vt* расквартиро́вывать *impf*, расквартирова́ть *pf*.
billiards /ˈbɪljədz/ *n* билья́рд.
billion /ˈbɪljən/ *n* биллио́н.
billow /ˈbɪləʊ/ *n* вал; *vi* вздыма́ться *impf*.
bin /bɪn/ *n* му́сорное ведро́.
bind /baɪnd/ *vt* (*tie*) свя́зывать *impf*, связа́ть *pf*; (*oblige*) обя́зывать *impf*, обяза́ть *pf*; (*book*) переплета́ть *impf*, переплести́ *pf*. **binder** /ˈbaɪndə(r)/ *n* (*person*) переплётчик; (*for papers*) па́пка. **binding** /ˈbaɪndɪŋ/ *n* переплёт.
binge /bɪndʒ/ *n* кутёж; **~ drinking** попо́йка.
binoculars /bɪˈnɒkjʊləz/ *n pl* бино́кль *m*.
biochemistry /ˌbaɪəʊˈkemɪstrɪ/ *n* биохи́мия. **biographer** /baɪˈɒgrəfə(r)/ *n* био́граф. **biographical** /ˌbaɪəˈgræfɪk(ə)l/ *adj* биографи́ческий. **biography** /baɪˈɒgrəfɪ/ *n* биогра́фия. **biological** /ˌbaɪəˈlɒdʒɪk(ə)l/ *adj* биологи́ческий. **biologist** /baɪˈɒlədʒɪst/ *n* био́лог. **biology** /baɪˈɒlədʒɪ/ *n* биоло́гия.
bipartisan /ˌbaɪpɑːtɪˈzæn/ *adj* двухпарти́йный.
birch /bɜːtʃ/ *n* берёза; (*rod*) ро́зга.
bird /bɜːd/ *n* пти́ца; **~ flu** пти́чий грипп; **~ of prey** хи́щная пти́ца.
birth /bɜːθ/ *n* рожде́ние; (*descent*) происхожде́ние; **~ certificate**

b

ме́трика; ~ **control** противозача́точные ме́ры *f pl*. **birthday** *n* день *m* рожде́ния; **fourth** ~ четырёхле́тие. **birthplace** *n* ме́сто рожде́ния. **birthright** *n* пра́во по рожде́нию.

biscuit /ˈbɪskɪt/ *n* пече́нье.

bisect /baɪˈsekt/ *vt* разреза́ть *impf*, разре́зать *pf* попола́м.

bisexual /baɪˈseksjʊəl/ *adj* бисексуа́льный.

bishop /ˈbɪʃəp/ *n* епи́скоп; (*chess*) слон.

bit[1] /bɪt/ *n* (*piece*) кусо́чек; **a** ~ немно́го; **not a** ~ ничу́ть.

bit[2] /bɪt/ *n* (*tech*) сверло́; (*bridle*) удила́ (-л) *pl*.

bitch /bɪtʃ/ *n* (*coll*) сте́рва. **bitchy** /ˈbɪtʃɪ/ *adj* стерво́зный.

bite /baɪt/ *n* уку́с; (*snack*) заку́ска; (*fishing*) клёв; *vt* куса́ть *impf*, укуси́ть *pf*; *vi* (*fish*) клева́ть *impf*, клю́нуть *pf*. **biting** /ˈbaɪtɪŋ/ *adj* е́дкий.

bitter /ˈbɪtə(r)/ *adj* го́рький. **bitterness** /-nɪs/ *n* го́речь.

bitumen /ˈbɪtjʊmɪn/ *n* биту́м.

bivouac /ˈbɪvʊˌæk/ *n* бива́к.

bizarre /bɪˈzɑː(r)/ *adj* стра́нный.

black /blæk/ *adj* чёрный; ~ **eye** подби́тый глаз; ~ **market** чёрный ры́нок; *v*: ~ **out** (*vt*) затемня́ть *impf*, затемни́ть *pf*; (*vi*) теря́ть *impf*, по~ *pf* созна́ние; *n* (*colour*) чёрный цвет; (~ *person*) негр, ~итя́нка; (*mourning*) тра́ур. **blackberry** *n* ежеви́ка (*no pl*; *usu collect*). **blackbird** *n* чёрный дрозд. **blackboard** *n* доска́. **blackcurrant** *n* чёрная сморо́дина (*no pl*; *usu collect*). **blacken** /ˈblækən/ *vt* (*fig*) черни́ть *impf*, о~ *pf*. **blackleg** *n* штрейкбре́хер. **blacklist** *n* вноси́ть *impf*, внести́ *pf* в чёрный спи́сок. **blackmail** *n* шанта́ж; *vt* шантажи́ровать *impf*. **blackout** *n* затемне́ние; (*faint*) поте́ря созна́ния. **blacksmith** *n* кузне́ц.

bladder /ˈblædə(r)/ *n* пузы́рь *m*.

blade /bleɪd/ *n* (*knife*) ле́звие; (*oar*) ло́пасть; (*grass*) были́нка.

blame /bleɪm/ *n* вина́, порица́ние; *vt* вини́ть *impf* (**for** в+*prep*); **be to** ~ быть винова́тым. **blameless** /ˈbleɪmlɪs/ *adj* безупре́чный.

blanch /blɑːntʃ/ *vt* (*vegetables*) ошпа́ривать *impf*, ошпа́рить *pf*; *vi* бледне́ть *impf*, по~ *pf*.

bland /blænd/ *adj* мя́гкий; (*dull*) пре́сный.

blandishments /ˈblændɪʃmənts/ *n pl* лесть.

blank /blæŋk/ *adj* (*look*) отсу́тствующий; (*paper*) чи́стый; *n* (*space*) про́пуск; (*form*) бланк; (*cartridge*) холосто́й патро́н; ~ **cheque** незапо́лненный чек.

blanket /ˈblæŋkɪt/ *n* одея́ло.

blare /bleə(r)/ *vi* труби́ть *impf*, про~ *pf*.

blasé /ˈblɑːzeɪ/ *adj* пресы́щенный.

blasphemous /ˈblæsfəməs/ *adj* богоху́льный. **blasphemy** /-fəmɪ/ *n* богоху́льство.

blast /blɑːst/ *n* (*wind*) поры́в ве́тра; (*explosion*) взрыв; *vt* взрыва́ть *impf*, взорва́ть *pf*; ~ **off** стартова́ть *impf* & *pf*. **blast-furnace** *n* до́мна.

blatant /ˈbleɪt(ə)nt/ *adj* я́вный.

blaze /bleɪz/ *n* (*flame*) пла́мя *neut*; (*fire*) пожа́р; *vi* пыла́ть *impf*.

blazer /ˈbleɪzə(r)/ *n* лёгкий пиджа́к.

bleach /bliːtʃ/ *n* хло́рка, отбе́ливатель *m*; *vt* отбе́ливать *impf*, отбели́ть *pf*.

bleak /bliːk/ *adj* пусты́нный; (*dreary*) уны́лый.

bleary-eyed /ˈblɪərɪˌaɪd/ *adj* с затума́ненными глаза́ми.

bleat /bliːt/ *vi* бле́ять *impf*.

bleed /bliːd/ *vi* кровоточи́ть *impf*.

bleeper /ˈbliːpə(r)/ *n* персона́льный сигнализа́тор.

blemish /ˈblemɪʃ/ *n* пятно́.

blend /blend/ *n* смесь; *vt* сме́шивать *impf*, смеша́ть *pf*; *vi* гармони́ровать *impf*. **blender** /ˈblendə(r)/ *n* ми́ксер.

bless /bles/ *vt* благословля́ть *impf*, благослови́ть *pf*. **blessed** /ˈblesɪd, blest/ *adj* благослове́н-

ный. **blessing** /ˈblesɪŋ/ *n* (*action*) благословéние; (*object*) блáго.
blight /blaɪt/ *vt* губи́ть *impf*, по~ *pf*.
blind /blaɪnd/ *adj* слепóй; **~ alley** тупи́к; *n* штóра; *vt* ослепля́ть *impf*, ослепи́ть *pf*. **blindfold** *vt* завя́зывать *impf*, завязáть *pf* глазá+*dat*. **blindness** /ˈblaɪndnɪs/ *n* слепотá.
blink /blɪŋk/ *vi* мигáть *impf*, мигнýть *pf*. **blinkers** /ˈblɪŋkəz/ *n pl* шóры (-р) *pl*.
bliss /blɪs/ *n* блажéнство. **blissful** /ˈblɪsfʊl/ *adj* блажéнный.
blister /ˈblɪstə(r)/ *n* пузы́рь *m*, волды́рь *m*.
blithe /blaɪð/ *adj* весёлый; (*carefree*) беспéчный.
blitz /blɪts/ *n* бомбёжка.
blizzard /ˈblɪzəd/ *n* метéль.
bloated /ˈbləʊtɪd/ *adj* вздýтый.
blob /blɒb/ *n* (*liquid*) кáпля; (*colour*) кля́кса.
bloc /blɒk/ *n* блок.
block /blɒk/ *n* (*wood*) чурбáн; (*stone*) глы́ба; (*flats*) жилóй дом; *vt* преграждáть *impf*, прегради́ть *pf*; **~ up** забивáть *impf*, заби́ть *pf*.
blockade /blɒˈkeɪd/ *n* блокáда; *vt* блоки́ровать *impf* & *pf*.
blockage /ˈblɒkɪdʒ/ *n* затóр.
bloke /bləʊk/ *n* пáрень *m*.
blond /blɒnd/ *n* блонди́н, ~ка; *adj* белокýрый.
blood /blʌd/ *n* кровь; **~ donor** дóнор; **~-poisoning** *n* заражéние крóви; **~ pressure** кровянóе давлéние; **~ relation** бли́зкий рóдственник, -ая рóдственница; **~ transfusion** переливáние крóви. **bloodhound** *n* ищéйка. **bloodshed** *n* кровопроли́тие. **bloodshot** *adj* нали́тый крóвью. **bloodthirsty** *adj* кровожáдный. **bloody** /ˈblʌdɪ/ *adj* кровáвый.
bloom /bluːm/ *n* расцвéт; *vi* цвести́ *pf*.
blossom /ˈblɒsəm/ *n* цвет; **in ~** в цветý.
blot /blɒt/ *n* кля́кса; пятнó; *vt* (*dry*) промокáть *impf*, промокнýть *pf*; (*smudge*) пáчкать *impf*, за~ *pf*.
blotch /blɒtʃ/ *n* пятнó.
blotting-paper /ˈblɒtɪŋˌpeɪpə(r)/ *n* промокáтельная бумáга.
blouse /blaʊz/ *n* кóфточка, блýзка.
blow[1] /bləʊ/ *n* удáр.
blow[2] /bləʊ/ *vt* & *i* дуть *impf*, по~ *pf*; **~ away** сноси́ть *impf*, снести́ *pf*; **~ down** вали́ть *impf*, по~ *pf*; **~ one's nose** сморкáться *impf*, сморкнýться *pf*; **~ out** задувáть *impf*, задýть *pf*; **~ over** (*fig*) проходи́ть *impf*, пройти́ *pf*; **~ up** взрывáть *impf*, взорвáть *pf*; (*inflate*) надувáть *impf*, надýть *pf*. **blow-lamp** *n* паяльная лáмпа.
blubber[1] /ˈblʌbə(r)/ *n* вóрвань.
blubber[2] /ˈblʌbə(r)/ *vi* ревéть *impf*.
bludgeon /ˈblʌdʒ(ə)n/ *vt* (*compel*) вынуждáть *impf*, вы́нудить *pf*.
blue /bluː/ *adj* (*dark*) си́ний; (*light*) голубóй; *n* си́ний, голубóй, цвет. **bluebell** *n* колокóльчик. **bluebottle** *n* си́няя мýха. **blueprint** *n* си́нька, светокóпия; (*fig*) проéкт.
bluff /blʌf/ *n* блеф; *vi* блефовáть *impf*.
blunder /ˈblʌndə(r)/ *n* оплóшность; *vi* оплошáть *pf*.
blunt /blʌnt/ *adj* тупóй; (*person*) прямóй; *vt* тупи́ть *impf*, за~, ис~ *pf*.
blur /blɜː(r)/ *vt* затумáнивать *impf*, затумáнить *pf*. **blurred** /blɜːd/ *adj* расплы́вчатый.
blurt /blɜːt/ *vt*: **~ out** выбáлтывать *impf*, вы́болтать *pf*.
blush /blʌʃ/ *vi* краснéть *impf*, по~ *pf*.
bluster /ˈblʌstə(r)/ *vi* бушевáть *impf*; *n* пусты́е словá *neut pl*.
boar /bɔː(r)/ *n* бóров; (*wild*) кабáн.
board /bɔːd/ *n* доскá; (*committee*) правлéние, совéт; **on ~** на борт(ý); *vt* сади́ться *impf*, сесть *pf* (на корáбль, в пóезд и т.д.); **~ up** забивáть *impf*, заби́ть *pf*. **boarder** /ˈbɔːdə(r)/ *n* пансионéр.

b

boarding-house /ˈbɔːdɪŋˌhaʊs/ *n* пансио́н. **boarding-school** *n* интерна́т.

boast /bəʊst/ *vi* хва́статься *impf*, по~ *pf*; *vt* горди́ться *impf* +*instr*. **boaster** /ˈbəʊstə(r)/ *n* хвасту́н. **boastful** /ˈbəʊstfʊl/ *adj* хвастли́вый.

boat /bəʊt/ *n* (*small*) ло́дка; (*large*) кора́бль *m*.

bob /bɒb/ *vi* подпры́гивать *impf*, подпры́гнуть *pf*.

bobbin /ˈbɒbɪn/ *n* кату́шка.

bobsleigh /ˈbɒbsleɪ/ *n* бо́бсле́й.

bode /bəʊd/ *vt*: **~well/ill** предвеща́ть *impf* хоро́шее/недо́брое.

bodice /ˈbɒdɪs/ *n* лиф, корса́ж.

bodily /ˈbɒdɪlɪ/ *adv* целико́м; *adj* теле́сный.

body /ˈbɒdɪ/ *n* те́ло, ту́ловище; (*corpse*) труп; (*group*) о́рган; (*main part*) основна́я часть. **bodyguard** *n* телохрани́тель *m*. **bodywork** *n* ку́зов.

bog /bɒg/ *n* боло́та; **get ~ged down** увяза́ть *impf*, увя́знуть *pf*. **boggy** /ˈbɒgɪ/ *adj* боло́тистый.

bogus /ˈbəʊgəs/ *adj* подде́льный.

boil[1] /bɔɪl/ *n* (*med*) фуру́нкул.

boil[2] /bɔɪl/ *vi* кипе́ть *impf*, вс~ *pf*; *vt* кипяти́ть *impf*, вс~ *pf*; (*cook*) вари́ть *impf*, с~ *pf*; **~ down to** сходи́ться *impf*, сойти́сь *pf* к тому́, что; **~ over** выкипа́ть *impf*, вы́кипеть *pf*; *n* кипе́ние; **bring to the ~** доводи́ть *impf*, довести́ *pf* до кипе́ния. **boiled** /bɔɪld/ *adj* варёный. **boiler** /ˈbɔɪlə(r)/ *n* котёл; **~ suit** комбинезо́н. **boiling** /ˈbɔɪlɪŋ/ *adj* кипя́щий; **~ point** то́чка кипе́ния; **~ water** кипято́к.

boisterous /ˈbɔɪstərəs/ *adj* шумли́вый.

bold /bəʊld/ *adj* сме́лый; (*type*) жи́рный.

bollard /ˈbɒlɑːd/ *n* (*in road*) столб; (*on quay*) пал.

bolster /ˈbəʊlstə(r)/ *n* ва́лик; *vt*: **~ up** подпира́ть *impf*, подпере́ть *pf*.

bolt /bəʊlt/ *n* засо́в; (*tech*) болт; *vt* запира́ть *impf*, запере́ть *pf* на засо́в; скрепля́ть *impf*, скрепи́ть *pf* болта́ми; *vi* (*flee*) удира́ть *impf*, удра́ть *pf*; (*horse*) понести́ *pf*.

bomb /bɒm/ *n* бо́мба; *vt* бомби́ть *impf*. **bombard** /bɒmˈbɑːd/ *vt* бомбарди́ровать *impf*. **bombardment** /bɒmˈbɑːdmənt/ *n* бомбардиро́вка. **bomber** /ˈbɒmə(r)/ *n* бомбардиро́вщик.

bombastic /bɒmˈbæstɪk/ *adj* напы́щенный.

bond /bɒnd/ *n* (*econ*) облига́ция; (*link*) связь; *pl* око́вы (-в) *pl*, (*fig*) у́зы (уз) *pl*.

bone /bəʊn/ *n* кость.

bonfire /ˈbɒnˌfaɪə(r)/ *n* костёр.

bonnet /ˈbɒnɪt/ *n* ка́пор; (*car*) капо́т.

bonus /ˈbəʊnəs/ *n* пре́мия.

bony /ˈbəʊnɪ/ *adj* кости́стый.

boo /buː/ *vt* осви́стывать *impf*, освиста́ть *pf*; *vi* улюлю́кать *impf*.

booby trap /ˈbuːbɪ ˌtræp/ *n* лову́шка.

book /bʊk/ *n* кни́га; *vt* (*order*) зака́зывать *impf*, заказа́ть *pf*; (*reserve*) брони́ровать *impf*, за~ *pf*. **bookbinder** *n* переплётчик. **bookcase** *n* кни́жный шкаф. **booking** /ˈbʊkɪŋ/ *n* зака́з; **~ office** ка́сса. **bookkeeper** /ˈbʊkˌkiːpə(r)/ *n* бухга́лтер. **bookmaker** /ˈbʊkˌmeɪkə(r)/ *n* букме́кер. **bookshop** *n* кни́жный магази́н.

boom[1] /buːm/ *n* (*barrier*) бон.

boom[2] /buːm/ *n* (*sound*) гул; (*econ*) бум; *vi* гуде́ть *impf*; (*fig*) процвета́ть *impf*.

boorish /ˈbʊərɪʃ/ *adj* ха́мский.

boost /buːst/ *n* соде́йствие; *vt* увели́чивать *impf*, увели́чить *pf*.

boot /buːt/ *n* боти́нок; (*high*) сапо́г; (*football*) бу́тса; (*car*) бага́жник.

booth /buːð/ *n* кио́ск, бу́дка; (*polling*) каби́на.

booty /ˈbuːtɪ/ *n* добы́ча.

booze /buːz/ *n* вы́пивка; *vi* выпива́ть *impf*.

border /ˈbɔːdə(r)/ *n* (*frontier*) грани́ца; (*trim*) кайма́; (*gardening*) бордю́р; *vi* грани́чить *impf* (**on** с +*instr*). **borderline** *n* грани́ца.

bore[1] /bɔː(r)/ *n* (*calibre*) кана́л (ствола́); *vt* сверли́ть *impf*, про~ *pf*.

bore[2] /bɔː(r)/ *n* (*thing*) ску́ка; (*person*) ску́чный челове́к; *vt* надоеда́ть *impf*, надое́сть *pf* +*dat*. **bored** /bɔːd/ *impers*+*dat* +ску́чно: **I'm ~** мне ску́чно; **we were ~** нам бы́ло ску́чно. **boredom** /ˈbɔːdəm/ *n* ску́ка. **boring** /ˈbɔːrɪŋ/ *adj* ску́чный.

born /bɔːn/ *adj* прирождённый; **be ~** роди́ться *impf* & *pf*.

borough /ˈbʌrə/ *n* райо́н.

borrow /ˈbɒrəʊ/ *vt* одолжа́ть *impf*, одолжи́ть *pf* (**from** у+*gen*).

Bosnia /ˈbɒznɪə/ *n* Бо́сния. **Bosnian** /-ən/ *n* босни́ец, -и́йка; *adj* босни́йский.

bosom /ˈbʊz(ə)m/ *n* грудь.

boss /bɒs/ *n* нача́льник; *vt* кома́ндовать *impf*, с~ *pf* +*instr*. **bossy** /ˈbɒsɪ/ *adj* команди́рский.

botanical /bəˈtænɪk(ə)l/ *adj* ботани́ческий. **botanist** /ˈbɒtənɪst/ *n* бота́ник. **botany** /ˈbɒtənɪ/ *n* бота́ника.

botch /bɒtʃ/ *vt* зала́тывать *impf*, зала́тать *pf*.

both /bəʊθ/ *adj* & *pron* о́ба *m* & *neut*, о́бе *f*; **~ ... and** и... и.

bother /ˈbɒðə(r)/ *n* доса́да; *vt* беспоко́ить *impf*.

bottle /ˈbɒt(ə)l/ *n* буты́лка; *vt* разлива́ть *impf*, разли́ть *pf* по буты́лкам; **~ up** сде́рживать *impf*, сдержа́ть *pf*.

bottom /ˈbɒtəm/ *n* (*of river, container, etc.*) дно; (*of mountain*) подно́жие; (*buttocks*) зад; **at the ~ of** (*stairs, page*) внизу́ +*gen*; **get to the ~ of** добира́ться *impf*, добра́ться *pf* до су́ти +*gen*; *adj* ни́жний. **bottomless** /-lɪs/ *adj* бездо́нный.

bough /baʊ/ *n* сук.

boulder /ˈbəʊldə(r)/ *n* валу́н.

bounce /baʊns/ *vi* подпры́гивать *impf*, подпры́гнуть *pf*; (*cheque*) верну́ться *pf*.

bound[1] /baʊnd/ *n* (*limit*) преде́л; *vt* ограни́чивать *impf*, ограни́чить *pf*.

bound[2] /baʊnd/ *n* (*spring*) прыжо́к; *vi* пры́гать *impf*, пры́гнуть *pf*.

bound[3] /baʊnd/ *adj*: **he is ~ to be there** он обяза́тельно там бу́дет.

bound[4] /baʊnd/ *adj*: **to be ~ for** направля́ться *impf* в+*acc*.

boundary /ˈbaʊndərɪ/ *n* грани́ца.

boundless /ˈbaʊndlɪs/ *adj* безграни́чный.

bountiful /ˈbaʊntɪfʊl/ *adj* (*generous*) ще́дрый; (*ample*) оби́льный. **bounty** /ˈbaʊntɪ/ *n* ще́дрость; (*reward*) пре́мия.

bouquet /buːˈkeɪ/ *n* буке́т.

bourgeois /ˈbʊəʒwɑː/ *adj* буржуа́зный. **bourgeoisie** /ˌbʊəʒwɑːˈziː/ *n* буржуази́я.

bout /baʊt/ *n* (*med*) при́ступ; (*sport*) схва́тка.

bow[1] /bəʊ/ *n* (*weapon*) лук; (*knot*) бант; (*mus*) смычо́к.

bow[2] /baʊ/ *n* (*obeisance*) покло́н; *vi* кла́няться *impf*, поклони́ться *pf*; *vt* склоня́ть *impf*, склони́ть *pf*.

bow[3] /baʊ/ *n* (*naut*) нос.

bowel /ˈbaʊəl/ *n* кишка́; (*depths*) не́дра (-р) *pl*.

bowl[1] /bəʊl/ *n* ми́ска.

bowl[2] /bəʊl/ *n* (*ball*) шар; *vi* подава́ть *impf*, пода́ть *pf* мяч. **bowler** /ˈbəʊlə(r)/ *n* подаю́щий *sb* мяч; (*hat*) котело́к. **bowling-alley** /ˈbəʊlɪŋ ˈælɪ/ *n* кегельба́н. **bowls** /bəʊlz/ *n* игра́ в шары́.

box[1] /bɒks/ *n* коро́бка, я́щик; (*theat*) ло́жа; **~ office** ка́сса.

box[2] /bɒks/ *vi* бокси́ровать *impf*. **boxer** /ˈbɒksə(r)/ *n* боксёр. **boxing** /ˈbɒksɪŋ/ *n* бокс. **Boxing Day** *n* второ́й день Рождества́.

boy /bɔɪ/ *n* ма́льчик. **boyfriend** *n* друг, молодо́й челове́к. **boyhood** /ˈbɔɪhʊd/*n* о́трочество. **boyish** /ˈbɔɪɪʃ/ *adj* мальчи́шеский.

b

boycott /ˈbɔɪkɒt/ *n* бойкóт; *vt* бойкотúровать *impf* & *pf*.
bra /brɑː/ *n* лúфчик.
brace /breɪs/ *n* (*clamp*) скрéпа; *pl* подтя́жки *f pl*; (*dental*) шúна; *vt* скрепля́ть *impf*, скрепúть *pf*; ~ **o.s.** собирáться *impf*, собрáться *pf* с сúлами.
bracelet /ˈbreɪslɪt/ *n* браслéт.
bracing /ˈbreɪsɪŋ/ *adj* бодря́щий.
bracket /ˈbrækɪt/ *n* (*support*) кронштéйн; *pl* скóбки *f pl*; (*category*) категóрия.
brag /bræg/ *vi* хвáстаться *impf*, по~ *pf*.
braid /breɪd/ *n* тесьмá.
braille /breɪl/ *n* шрифт Брáйля.
brain /breɪn/ *n* мозг. **brainstorm** *n* припáдок безýмия. **brainwash** *vt* промывáть *impf*, промы́ть *pf* мозгú+*dat*. **brainwave** *n* блестя́щая идéя.
braise /breɪz/ *vt* тушúть *impf*, с~ *pf*.
brake /breɪk/ *n* тóрмоз; *vt* тормозúть *impf*, за~ *pf*.
bramble /ˈbræmb(ə)l/ *n* ежевúка.
bran /bræn/ *n* óтруби (-бéй) *pl*.
branch /brɑːntʃ/ *n* вéтка; (*fig*) óтрасль; (*comm*) филиáл; *vi* разветвля́ться *impf*, разветвúться *pf*; ~ **out** (*fig*) расширя́ть *impf*, расшúрить *pf* дéятельность.
brand /brænd/ *n* (*mark*) клеймó; (*make*) мáрка; (*sort*) сорт; *vt* клеймúть *impf*, за~ *pf*.
brandish /ˈbrændɪʃ/ *vt* размáхивать *impf* +*instr*.
brandy /ˈbrændɪ/ *n* конья́к.
brash /bræʃ/ *adj* нахáльный.
brass /brɑːs/ *n* латýнь, жёлтая медь; (*mus*) мéдные инструмéнты *m pl*; *adj* латýнный, мéдный; ~ **band** мéдный духовóй оркéстр; **top** ~ вы́сшее начáльство.
brassière /ˈbræzɪə(r)/ *n* бюстгáлтер.
brat /bræt/ *n* чертёнок.
bravado /brəˈvɑːdəʊ/ *n* бравáда.
brave /breɪv/ *adj* хрáбрый; *vt* покоря́ть *impf*, покорúть *pf*.
bravery /ˈbreɪvərɪ/ *n* хрáбрость.
bravo /brɑːˈvəʊ/ *int* брáво.
brawl /brɔːl/ *n* скандáл; *vi* дрáться *impf*, по~ *pf*.
brawny /ˈbrɔːnɪ/ *adj* мýскулистый.
bray /breɪ/ *n* крик ослá; *vi* кричáть *impf*.
brazen /ˈbreɪz(ə)n/ *adj* бесстыдный.
brazier /ˈbreɪzɪə(r)/ *n* жарóвня.
breach /briːtʃ/ *n* нарушéние; (*break*) пролóм; (*mil*) брешь; *vt* прорывáть *impf*, прорвáть *pf*; (*rule*) нарушáть *impf*, нарýшить *pf*.
bread /bred/ *n* хлеб; (*white*) бýлка. **breadcrumb** *n* крóшка. **breadwinner** *n* кормúлец.
breadth /bredθ/ *n* ширинá; (*fig*) широтá.
break /breɪk/ *n* пролóм, разры́в; (*pause*) переры́в, пáуза; *vt* (& *i*) ломáть(ся) *impf*, с~ *pf*; разбивáть(ся) *impf*, разбúть(ся) *pf*; *vt* (*violate*) нарушáть *impf*, нарýшить *pf*; ~ **away** вырывáться *impf*, вы́рваться *pf*; ~ **down** (*vi*) (*tech*) ломáться *impf*, с~ *pf*; (*talks*) срывáться *impf*, сорвáться *pf*; (*vt*) (*door*) вылáмывать *impf*, вы́ломать *pf*; ~ **in(to)** влáмываться *impf*, вломúться *pf* в+*acc*; ~ **off** (*vt* & *i*) отлáмывать(ся) *impf*, отломúть(ся) *pf*; (*vi*) (*speaking*) замолчáть *pf*; (*vt*) (*relations*) порывáть *impf*, порвáть *pf*; ~ **out** вырывáться *impf*, вы́рваться *pf*; (*fire*, *war*) вспы́хнуть *pf*; ~ **through** пробивáться *impf*, пробúться *pf*; ~ **up** (*vi*) (*marriage*) распадáться *impf*, распáсться *pf*; (*meeting*) прерывáться *impf*, прервáться *pf*; (*vt*) (*disperse*) разгоня́ть *impf*, разогнáть *pf*; (*vt* & *i*) разбивáть(ся) *impf*, разбúть(ся) *pf*; ~ **with** порывáть *impf*, порвáть *pf* с+*instr*. **breakage** /ˈbreɪkɪdʒ/ *n* полóмка. **breakdown** *n* полóмка; (*med*) нéрвный срыв. **breaker** /ˈbreɪkə(r)/ *n* бурýн. **breakfast** /ˈbrekfəst/ *n* зáвтрак; *vi* зáвтракать *impf*, по~

pf. **breakneck** *adj*: **at ~ speed** сломя́ го́лову. **breakthrough** *n* проры́в. **breakwater** *n* волноре́з.

breast /brest/ *n* грудь; **~-feeding** *n* кормле́ние гру́дью; **~ stroke** *n* брасс.

breath /breθ/ *n* дыха́ние; **be out of ~** запыха́ться *impf & pf.* **breathe** /bri:ð/ *vi* дыша́ть *impf*; **~ in** вдыха́ть *impf*, вдохну́ть *pf*; **~ out** выдыха́ть *impf*, вы́дохнуть *pf.* **breather** /ˈbri:ðə(r)/ *n* переды́шка. **breathless** /ˈbreθlɪs/ *adj* запыха́вшийся.

breeches /ˈbri:tʃɪz/ *n pl* бри́джи (-жей) *pl.*

breed /bri:d/ *n* поро́да; *vi* размножа́ться *impf*, размно́житься *pf*; *vt* разводи́ть *impf*, развести́ *pf.* **breeder** /ˈbri:də(r)/ *n* -во́д: **cattle ~** скотово́д. **breeding** /ˈbri:dɪŋ/ *n* разведе́ние, -во́дство; (*upbringing*) воспи́танность.

breeze /bri:z/ *n* ветеро́к; (*naut*) бриз. **breezy** /ˈbri:zɪ/ *adj* све́жий.

brevity /ˈbrevɪtɪ/ *n* кра́ткость.

brew /bru:/ *vt* (*beer*) вари́ть *impf*, с~ *pf*; (*tea*) зава́ривать *impf*, завари́ть *pf*; (*beer*) ва́рка; (*tea*) зава́рка. **brewer** /ˈbru:ə(r)/ *n* пивова́р. **brewery** /ˈbru:ərɪ/ *n* пивова́ренный заво́д.

bribe /braɪb/ *n* взя́тка; *vt* подкупа́ть *impf*, подкупи́ть *pf.* **bribery** /ˈbraɪbərɪ/ *n* по́дкуп.

brick /brɪk/ *n* кирпи́ч; *adj* кирпи́чный. **bricklayer** *n* ка́менщик.

bridal /ˈbraɪd(ə)l/ *adj* сва́дебный. **bride** /braɪd/ *n* неве́ста. **bridegroom** /ˈbraɪdgru:m/ *n* жени́х. **bridesmaid** /ˈbraɪdzmeɪd/ *n* подру́жка неве́сты.

bridge[1] /brɪdʒ/ *n* мост; (*of nose*) перено́сица; *vt* (*gap*) заполня́ть *impf*, запо́лнить *pf*; (*overcome*) преодолева́ть *impf*, преодоле́ть *pf.*

bridge[2] /brɪdʒ/ *n* (*game*) бридж.

bridle /ˈbraɪd(ə)l/ *n* узда́; *vi* возмуща́ться *impf*, возмути́ться *pf.*

brief /bri:f/ *adj* недо́лгий; (*concise*) кра́ткий; *n* инстру́кция; *vt* инструкти́ровать *impf & pf.* **briefcase** *n* портфе́ль *m.* **briefing** /ˈbri:fɪŋ/ *n* инструкта́ж. **briefly** /ˈbri:flɪ/ *adv* кра́тко. **briefs** /bri:fs/ *n pl* трусы́ (-со́в) *pl.*

brigade /brɪˈgeɪd/ *n* брига́да. **brigadier** /ˌbrɪgəˈdɪə(r)/ *n* генера́л-майо́р.

bright /braɪt/ *adj* я́ркий. **brighten** /ˈbraɪt(ə)n/ (*also* **~ up**) *vi* проясня́ться *impf*, проясни́ться *pf*; *vt* оживля́ть *impf*, оживи́ть *pf.* **brightness** /ˈbraɪtnɪs/ *n* я́ркость.

brilliant /ˈbrɪlɪənt/ *adj* блестя́щий.

brim /brɪm/ *n* край; (*hat*) поля́ (-ле́й) *pl.*

brine /braɪn/ *n* рассо́л.

bring /brɪŋ/ *vt* (*carry*) приноси́ть *impf*, принести́ *pf*; (*lead*) приводи́ть *impf*, привести́ *pf*; (*transport*) привози́ть *impf*, привезти́ *pf*; **~ about** приноси́ть *impf*, принести́ *pf*; **~ back** возвраща́ть *impf*, возврати́ть *pf*; **~ down** сва́ливать *impf*, свали́ть *pf*; **~ round** (*unconscious person*) приводи́ть *impf*, привести́ *pf* в себя́; (*deliver*) привози́ть *impf*, привезти́ *pf*; **~ up** (*educate*) воспи́тывать *impf*, воспита́ть *pf*; (*question*) поднима́ть *impf*, подня́ть *pf.*

brink /brɪŋk/ *n* край.

brisk /brɪsk/ *adj* (*air etc.*) све́жий; (*quick*) бы́стрый.

bristle /ˈbrɪs(ə)l/ *n* щети́на; *vi* щети́ниться *impf*, о~ *pf.*

Britain /ˈbrɪt(ə)n/ *n* Великобрита́ния, А́нглия. **British** /ˈbrɪtɪʃ/ *adj* брита́нский, англи́йский; **~ Isles** Брита́нские острова́ *m pl.* **Briton** /ˈbrɪt(ə)n/ *n* брита́нец, -нка; англича́нин, -а́нка.

brittle /ˈbrɪt(ə)l/ *adj* хру́пкий.

broach /brəʊtʃ/ *vt* затра́гивать *impf*, затро́нуть *pf.*

broad /brɔ:d/ *adj* широ́кий; **in ~ daylight** средь бе́ла дня; **in ~ outline** в о́бщих черта́х. **broadband** *n* (*comput*) широкополо́сная переда́ча да́нных. **broad-minded** /ˌbrɔ:dˈmaɪndɪd/ *adj* с широ́кими взгля́дами. **broadly** /ˈbrɔ:dlɪ/ *adv*:

b

~ speaking вообще́ говоря́.
broadcast /ˈbrɔːdkɑːst/ *n* переда́ча; *vt* передава́ть *impf*, переда́ть *pf* по ра́дио, по телеви́дению; (*seed*) се́ять *impf*, по~ *pf* вразбро́с. **broadcaster** /-stə(r)/ *n* ди́ктор. **broadcasting** /-stɪŋ/ *n* радио-, теле-, веща́ние.
brocade /brəˈkeɪd/ *n* парча́.
broccoli /ˈbrɒkəlɪ/ *n* бро́кколи *neut indecl.*
brochure /ˈbrəʊʃə(r)/ *n* брошю́ра.
broke /brəʊk/ *predic* без гроша́. **broken** /ˈbrəʊk(ə)n/ *adj* сло́манный; **~-hearted** с разби́тым се́рдцем.
broker /ˈbrəʊkə(r)/ *n* бро́кер, ма́клер.
bronchitis /brɒŋˈkaɪtɪs/ *n* бронхи́т.
bronze /brɒnz/ *n* бро́нза; *adj* бро́нзовый.
brooch /brəʊtʃ/ *n* брошь, бро́шка.
brood /bruːd/ *n* вы́водок; *vi* мра́чно размышля́ть *impf.*
brook[1] /brʊk/ *n* руче́й.
brook[2] /brʊk/ *vt* терпе́ть *impf.*
broom /bruːm/ *n* метла́. **broomstick** *n* (*witches'*) помело́.
broth /brɒθ/ *n* бульо́н.
brothel /ˈbrɒθ(ə)l/ *n* публи́чный дом.
brother /ˈbrʌðə(r)/ *n* брат; **~-in-law** *n* (*sister's husband*) зять; (*husband's brother*) де́верь; (*wife's brother*) шу́рин; (*wife's sister's husband*) своя́к. **brotherhood** /ˈbrʌðəhʊd/ *n* бра́тство. **brotherly** /ˈbrʌðəlɪ/ *adj* бра́тский.
brow /braʊ/ *n* (*eyebrow*) бровь; (*forehead*) лоб; (*of hill*) гре́бень *m.* **browbeaten** /ˈbraʊbiːt(ə)n/ *adj* запу́ганный.
brown /braʊn/ *adj* кори́чневый; (*eyes*) ка́рий; *n* кори́чневый цвет; *vt* (*cul*) подрумя́нивать *impf*, подрумя́нить *pf.*
browse /braʊz/ *vi* (*look around*) осма́триваться *impf*, осмотре́ться *pf*; (*in book*) просма́тривать *impf* просмотре́ть *pf* кни́гу.
bruise /bruːz/ *n* синя́к; *vt* ушиба́ть *impf*, ушиби́ть *pf.*
brunette /bruːˈnet/ *n* брюне́тка.
brunt /brʌnt/ *n* основна́я тя́жесть.
brush /brʌʃ/ *n* щётка; (*paint*) кисть; *vt* (*clean*) чи́стить *impf*, вы́~, по~ *pf* (щёткой); (*touch*) легко́ каса́ться *impf*, косну́ться *pf* +*gen*; (*hair*) расчёсывать *impf*, расчеса́ть *pf* щёткой; **~ aside, off** отма́хиваться *impf*, отмахну́ться *pf* от+*gen*; **~ up** смета́ть *impf*, смести́ *pf*; (*renew*) подчища́ть *impf*, подчи́стить *pf.*
brushwood /ˈbrʌʃwʊd/ *n* хво́рост.
Brussels sprouts /ˌbrʌs(ə)lz ˈspraʊts/ *n pl* брюссе́льская капу́ста.
brutal /ˈbruːt(ə)l/ *adj* жесто́кий. **brutality** /bruːˈtælɪtɪ/ *n* жесто́кость. **brutalize** /ˈbruːtəˌlaɪz/ *vt* ожесточа́ть *impf*, ожесточи́ть *pf.* **brute** /bruːt/ *n* живо́тное *sb*; (*person*) скоти́на. **brutish** /ˈbruːtɪʃ/ *adj* ха́мский.
B.Sc. *abbr* бакала́вр нау́к.
bubble /ˈbʌb(ə)l/ *n* пузы́рь *m*; *vi* пузы́риться *impf*; кипе́ть *impf*, вс~ *pf.*
buck /bʌk/ *n* саме́ц оле́ня, кро́лика *etc.*; *vi* брыка́ться *impf.*
bucket /ˈbʌkɪt/ *n* ведро́.
buckle /ˈbʌk(ə)l/ *n* пря́жка; *vt* застёгивать *impf*, застегну́ть *pf* (пря́жкой); *vi* (*warp*) коро́биться *impf*, по~, с~ *pf.*
bud /bʌd/ *n* по́чка.
Buddhism /ˈbʊdɪz(ə)m/ *n* будди́зм. **Buddhist** /ˈbʊdɪst/ *n* будди́ст; *adj* будди́йский.
budge /bʌdʒ/ *vt & i* шевели́ть(ся) *impf*, по~ *pf.*
budget /ˈbʌdʒɪt/ *n* бюдже́т; *vi*: **~ for** предусма́тривать *impf*, предусмотре́ть *pf* в бюдже́те.
buff /bʌf/ *adj* све́тло-кори́чневый.
buffalo /ˈbʌfəˌləʊ/ *n* бу́йвол.
buffet[1] /ˈbʊfeɪ/ *n* буфе́т.
buffet[2] /ˈbʌfɪt/ *vt* броса́ть *impf* (*impers*).
buffoon /bəˈfuːn/ *n* шут.
bug /bʌg/ *n* (*insect*) бука́шка;

(*germ*) инфе́кция; (*comput*) оши́бка в програ́мме; (*microphone*) потайно́й микрофо́н; *vt* (*install* ~) устана́вливать *impf*, установи́ть *pf* аппарату́ру для подслу́шивания в+*prep*; (*listen*) подслу́шивать *impf*.

bugle /ˈbjuːg(ə)l/ *n* горн.

build /bɪld/ *n* (*of person*) телосложе́ние; *vt* стро́ить *impf*, по~ *pf*; **~ on** пристра́ивать *impf*, пристро́ить *pf* (**to** к+*dat*); **~ up** (*vt*) создава́ть *impf*, созда́ть *pf*; (*vi*) накопля́ться *impf*; накопи́ться *pf*. **builder** /ˈbɪldə(r)/ *n* строи́тель *m*. **building** /ˈbɪldɪŋ/ *n* (*edifice*) зда́ние; (*action*) строи́тельство; **~ site** стро́йка; **~ society** жили́щно-строи́тельный кооперати́в.

built-up area /ˈbɪltʌp ˈeərɪə/ *n* застро́енный райо́н.

bulb /bʌlb/ *n* лу́ковица; (*electric*) ла́мпочка. **bulbous** /ˈbʌlbəs/ *adj* лу́ковичный.

Bulgaria /bʌlˈgeərɪə/ *n* Болга́рия. **Bulgarian** /-ən/ *n* болга́рин, -га́рка; *adj* болга́рский.

bulge /bʌldʒ/ *n* вы́пуклость; *vi* выпя́чиваться *impf*; выпира́ть *impf*. **bulging** /ˈbʌldʒɪŋ/ *adj* разбу́хший, оттопы́ривающийся.

bulk /bʌlk/ *n* (*size*) объём; (*greater part*) бо́льшая часть; **in ~** гурто́м. **bulky** /ˈbʌlkɪ/ *adj* громо́здкий.

bull /bʊl/ *n* бык; (*male*) саме́ц. **bulldog** *n* бульдо́г. **bulldoze** /-dəʊz/ *vt* расчища́ть *impf*, расчи́стить *pf* бульдо́зером. **bulldozer** /-dəʊzə(r)/ *n* бульдо́зер. **bullfinch** *n* снеги́рь *m*. **bullock** /ˈbʊlək/ *n* вол. **bull's-eye** *n* я́блоко.

bullet /ˈbʊlɪt/ *n* пу́ля. **bullet-proof** *adj* пулесто́йкий.

bulletin /ˈbʊlɪtɪn/ *n* бюллете́нь *m*.

bullion /ˈbʊlɪən/ *n*: **gold ~** зо́лото в сли́тках.

bully /ˈbʊlɪ/ *n* задира *m* & *f*; *vt* запу́гивать *impf*, запуга́ть *pf*.

bum /bʌm/ *n* зад.

bumble-bee /ˈbʌmb(ə)lˌbiː/ *n* шмель *m*.

bump /bʌmp/ *n* (*blow*) уда́р, толчо́к; (*swelling*) ши́шка; (*in road*) уха́б; *vi* ударя́ться *impf*, уда́риться *pf*; **~ into** ната́лкиваться *impf*, натолкну́ться *pf* на+*acc*. **bumper** /ˈbʌmpə(r)/ *n* ба́мпер.

bumpkin /ˈbʌmpkɪn/ *n* деревéнщина *m* & *f*.

bumptious /ˈbʌmpʃəs/ *adj* самоуве́ренный.

bumpy /ˈbʌmpɪ/ *adj* уха́бистый.

bun /bʌn/ *n* сдо́бная бу́лка; (*hair*) пучо́к.

bunch /bʌntʃ/ *n* (*of flowers*) буке́т; (*grapes*) гроздь; (*keys*) свя́зка.

bundle /ˈbʌnd(ə)l/ *n* у́зел; *vt* свя́зывать *impf*, связа́ть *pf* в у́зел; **~ off** спрова́живать *impf*, спрова́дить *pf*.

bungalow /ˈbʌŋgəˌləʊ/ *n* бу́нгало *neut indecl*.

bungle /ˈbʌŋg(ə)l/ *vt* по́ртить *impf*, ис~ *pf*.

bunk /bʌŋk/ *n* ко́йка.

bunker /ˈbʌŋkə(r)/ *n* бу́нкер.

buoy /bɔɪ/ *n* буй. **buoyancy** /ˈbɔɪənsɪ/ *n* плаву́честь; (*fig*) бо́дрость. **buoyant** /ˈbɔɪənt/ *adj* плаву́чий; (*fig*) бо́дрый.

burden /ˈbɜːd(ə)n/ *n* бре́мя *neut*; *vt* обременя́ть *impf*, обремени́ть *pf*.

bureau /ˈbjʊərəʊ/ *n* бюро́ *neut indecl*. **bureaucracy** /ˌbjːʊəˈrɒkrəsɪ/ *n* бюрократи́я. **bureaucrat** /ˈbjːʊərəˌkræt/ *n* бюрокра́т. **bureaucratic** /ˌbjːʊərəˈkrætɪk/ *adj* бюрократи́ческий.

burger /ˈbɜːgə(r)/ *n* котле́та.

burglar /ˈbɜːglə(r)/ *n* взло́мщик. **burglary** /-rɪ/ *n* кра́жа со взло́мом. **burgle** /ˈbɜːg(ə)l/ *vt* гра́бить *impf*, о~ *pf*.

burial /ˈberɪəl/ *n* погребе́ние.

burly /ˈbɜːlɪ/ *adj* здорове́нный.

burn /bɜːn/ *vt* жечь *impf*, с~ *pf*; *vt*

b

& *i* (*injure*) обжигáть(ся) *impf*, обжéчь(ся) *pf*; *vi* горéть *impf*, с~ *pf*; (*by sun*) загорáть *impf*, загорéть *pf*; *n* ожóг. **burner** /ˈbɜːnə(r)/ *n* горéлка.

burnish /ˈbɜːnɪʃ/ *vt* полировáть *impf*, от~ *pf*.

burp /bɜːp/ *vi* рыгáть *impf*, рыгнýть *pf*.

burrow /ˈbʌrəʊ/ *n* норá; *vi* рыть *impf*, вы́~ *pf* норý; (*fig*) ры́ться *impf*.

bursar /ˈbɜːsə/ *n* казначéй. **bursary** /-rɪ/ *n* стипéндия.

burst /bɜːst/ *n* разры́в, вспы́шка; *vi* разрывáться *impf*, разорвáться *pf*; (*bubble*) лóпаться *impf*, лóпнуть *pf*; *vt* разрывáть *impf*, разорвáть *pf*; ~ **into tears** расплáкаться *pf*.

bury /ˈberɪ/ *vt* (*dead*) хоронúть *impf*, по~ *pf*; (*hide*) зарывáть *impf*, зары́ть *pf*.

bus /bʌs/ *n* автóбус; ~ **stop** автóбусная останóвка.

bush /bʊʃ/ *n* куст. **bushy** /ˈbʊʃɪ/ *adj* густóй.

busily /ˈbɪzɪlɪ/ *adv* энергúчно.

business /ˈbɪznɪs/ *n* (*affair*, *dealings*) дéло; (*firm*) предприя́тие; **mind your own** ~ не вáше дéло; **on** ~ по дéлу. **businesslike** *adj* деловóй. **businessman** *n* бизнесмéн.

busker /ˈbʌskə(r)/ *n* ýличный музыкáнт.

bust /bʌst/ *n* бюст; (*bosom*) грудь.

bustle /ˈbʌs(ə)l/ *n* суетá; *vi* суетúться *impf*.

busy /ˈbɪzɪ/ *adj* занятóй; *vt*: ~ **o.s.** занимáться *impf*, заня́ться *pf* (**with** +*instr*). **busybody** *n* назóйливый человéк.

but /bʌt/ *conj* но, а; ~ **then** затó; *prep* крóме+*gen*.

butcher /ˈbʊtʃə(r)/ *n* мяснúк; *vt* рéзать *impf*, за~ *pf*; ~**'s shop** мяснáя *sb*.

butler /ˈbʌtlə(r)/ *n* дворéцкий *sb*.

butt¹ /bʌt/ *n* (*cask*) бóчка.

butt² /bʌt/ *n* (*of gun*) приклáд; (*cigarette*) окýрок.

butt³ /bʌt/ *n* (*target*) мишéнь.

butt⁴ /bʌt/ *vt* бодáть *impf*, за~ *pf*; ~ **in** вмéшиваться *impf*, вмешáться *pf*.

butter /ˈbʌtə(r)/ *n* (слúвочное) мáсло; *vt* намáзывать *impf*, намáзать *pf* мáслом; ~ **up** льстить *impf*, по~ *pf*. **buttercup** *n* лю́тик. **butterfly** *n* бáбочка.

buttock /ˈbʌtək/ *n* я́годица.

button /ˈbʌt(ə)n/ *n* пýговица; (*knob*) кнóпка; *vt* застёгивать *impf*, застегнýть *pf*. **buttonhole** *n* пéтля.

buttress /ˈbʌtrɪs/ *n* контрфóрс; *vt* подпирáть *impf*, подперéть *pf*.

buxom /ˈbʌksəm/ *adj* полногрýдая.

buy /baɪ/ *n* покýпка; *vt* покупáть *impf*, купúть *pf*. **buyer** /ˈbaɪə(r)/ *n* покупáтель *m*.

buzz /bʌz/ *n* жужжáние; *vi* жужжáть *impf*.

buzzard /ˈbʌzəd/ *n* каню́к.

buzzer /ˈbʌzə(r)/ *n* зýммер.

by /baɪ/ *adv* мúмо; *prep* (*near*) óколо+*gen*, у+*gen*; (*beside*) ря́дом с+*instr*; (*past*) мúмо +*gen*; (*time*) к+*dat*; (*means*) *instr without prep*; ~ **and large** в цéлом.

bye /baɪ/ *int* покá!

by-election /ˈbaɪɪˌlekʃ(ə)n/ *n* дополнúтельные вы́боры *m pl*.

Byelorussian /ˌbjeləʊˈrʌʃ(ə)n/ *see* **Belorussian**

bygone /ˈbaɪgɒn/ *adj* минýвший; **let** ~**s be** ~**s** что прошлó, то прошлó. **by-law** *n* постановлéние. **bypass** *n* обхóд; *vt* обходúть *impf*, обойтú *pf*. **by-product** *n* побóчный продýкт. **byroad** *n* небольшáя дорóга. **bystander** /ˈbaɪˌstændə(r)/ *n* свидéтель *m*. **byway** *n* просёлочная дорóга. **byword** *n* олицетворéние (**for** +*gen*).

Byzantine /bɪˈzæntaɪn/ *adj* византúйский.

C

cab /kæb/ *n* (*taxi*) такси́ *neut indecl*; (*of lorry*) каби́на.
cabaret /ˈkæbəˌreɪ/ *n* кабаре́ *neut indecl*.
cabbage /ˈkæbɪdʒ/ *n* капу́ста.
cabin /ˈkæbɪn/ *n* (*hut*) хи́жина; (*aeron*) каби́на; (*naut*) каю́та.
cabinet /ˈkæbɪnɪt/ *n* шкаф; (*Cabinet*) кабине́т; **~-maker** краснодере́вец; **~-minister** мини́стр-член кабине́та.
cable /ˈkeɪb(ə)l/ *n* (*rope*) кана́т; (*electric*) ка́бель *m*; (*cablegram*) телегра́мма; *vt* & *i* телеграфи́ровать *impf* & *pf*.
cache /kæʃ/ *n* потайно́й склад.
cackle /ˈkæk(ə)l/ *vi* гогота́ть *impf*.
cactus /ˈkæktəs/ *n* ка́ктус.
caddy /ˈkædɪ/ *n* (*box*) ча́йница.
cadet /kəˈdet/ *n* новобра́нец.
cadge /kædʒ/ *vt* стреля́ть *impf*, стрельну́ть *pf*.
cadres /ˈkɑːdəz/ *n pl* ка́дры *m pl*.
Caesarean (section) /sɪˈzeərɪən (ˈsekʃ(ə)n)/ *n* ке́сарево сече́ние.
cafe /ˈkæfeɪ/ *n* кафе́ *neut indecl*. **cafeteria** /ˌkæfɪˈtɪərɪə/ *n* кафете́рий.
caffeine /ˈkæfiːn/ *n* кофеи́н.
cage /keɪdʒ/ *n* кле́тка.
cajole /kəˈdʒəʊl/ *vt* зада́бривать *impf*, задо́брить *pf*.
cake /keɪk/ *n* (*large*) торт, (*small*) пиро́жное *sb*; (*fruit-~*) кекс; *vt*: **~d** обле́пленный (**in** +*instr*).
calamitous /kəˈlæmɪtəs/ *adj* бе́дственный. **calamity** /-ˈlæmɪtɪ/ *n* бе́дствие.
calcium /ˈkælsɪəm/ *n* ка́льций.
calculate /ˈkælkjʊˌleɪt/ *vt* вычисля́ть *impf*, вы́числить *pf*; *vi* рассчи́тывать *impf*, рассчита́ть *pf* (**on** на+*acc*). **calculation** /ˌkælkjʊˈleɪʃ(ə)n/ *n* вычисле́ние, расчёт. **calculator** /ˈkælkjʊˌleɪtə(r)/ *n* калькуля́тор.
calendar /ˈkælɪndə(r)/ *n* календа́рь *m*.
calf[1] /kɑːf/ *n* (*cow*) телёнок.
calf[2] /kɑːf/ *n* (*leg*) икра́.
calibrate /ˈkælɪˌbreɪt/ *vt* калиброва́ть *impf*. **calibre** /-bə(r)/ *n* кали́бр.
call /kɔːl/ *v* звать *impf*, по~ *pf*; (*name*) называ́ть *impf*, назва́ть *pf*; (*cry*) крича́ть *impf*, кри́кнуть *pf*; (*wake*) буди́ть *impf*, раз~ *pf*; (*visit*) заходи́ть *impf*, зайти́ *pf* (**on** к+*dat*; **at** в+*acc*); (*stop at*) остана́вливаться *impf*, останови́ться *pf* (**at** в, на, +*prep*); (*summon*) вызыва́ть *impf*, вы́звать *pf*; (*ring up*) звони́ть *impf*, по~ *pf* +*dat*; **~ for** (*require*) тре́бовать *impf*, по~ *pf* +*gen*; (*fetch*) заходи́ть *impf*, зайти́ *pf* за+*instr*; **~ off** отменя́ть *impf*, отмени́ть *pf*; **~ out** вскри́кивать *impf*, вскри́кнуть *pf*; **~ up** призыва́ть *impf*, призва́ть *pf*; *n* (*cry*) крик; (*summons*) зов, призы́в; (*telephone*) (телефо́нный) вы́зов, разгово́р; (*visit*) визи́т; (*signal*) сигна́л; **~-box** телефо́н-автома́т; **~ centre** колл-це́нтр, информацио́нно-спра́вочная слу́жба; **~-up** призы́в. **caller** /ˈkɔːlə(r)/ *n* посети́тель *m*, ~ница; (*tel*) позвони́вший *sb*. **calling** /ˈkɔːlɪŋ/ *n* (*vocation*) призва́ние.
callous /ˈkæləs/ *adj* (*person*) чёрствый.
callus /ˈkæləs/ *n* мозо́ль.
calm /kɑːm/ *adj* споко́йный; *n* споко́йствие; *vt* & *i* (**~ down**) успока́ивать(ся) *impf*, успоко́ить(ся) *pf*.
calorie /ˈkælərɪ/ *n* кало́рия.
camber /ˈkæmbə(r)/ *n* скат.
camcorder /ˈkæmˌkɔːdə(r)/ *n* камко́рдер.
camel /ˈkæm(ə)l/ *n* верблю́д.
camera /ˈkæmrə/ *n* фотоаппара́т. **cameraman** *n* кинооперато́р.
camouflage /ˈkæməˌflɑːʒ/ *n* камуфля́ж; *vt* маскирова́ть *impf*, за~ *pf*.
camp /kæmp/ *n* ла́герь *m*; *vi* (*set up* ~) располага́ться *impf*, рас-

положи́ться *pf* ла́герем; (*go camping*) жить *impf* в пала́тках; **~-bed** раскладу́шка; **~-fire** костёр.

C

campaign /kæm'peɪn/ *n* кампа́ния; *vi* проводи́ть *impf*, провести́ *pf* кампа́нию.

campsite /'kæmpsaɪt/ *n* ла́герь *m*, ке́мпинг.

campus /'kæmpəs/ *n* университе́тский городо́к.

can[1] /kæn/ *n* ба́нка; *vt* консерви́ровать *impf*, за~ *pf*.

can[2] /kæn/ *v aux* (*be able*) мочь *impf*, с~ *pf* +*inf*; (*know how*) уме́ть *impf*, с~ *pf* +*inf*.

Canada /'kænədə/ *n* Кана́да. **Canadian** /kə'neɪdɪən/ *n* кана́дец, -дка; *adj* кана́дский.

canal /kə'næl/ *n* кана́л.

canary /kə'neərɪ/ *n* канаре́йка.

cancel /'kæns(ə)l/ *vt* (*make void*) аннули́ровать *impf* & *pf*; (*call off*) отменя́ть *impf*, отмени́ть *pf*; (*stamp*) гаси́ть *impf*, по~ *pf*. **cancellation** /,kænsə'leɪʃ(ə)n/ *n* аннули́рование; отме́на.

cancer /'kænsə(r)/ *n* рак; (**C~**) Рак. **cancerous** /'kænsərəs/ *adj* ра́ковый.

candelabrum /,kændɪ'lɑːbrəm/ *n* канделя́бр.

candid /'kændɪd/ *adj* открове́нный.

candidate /'kændɪdət/ *n* кандида́т.

candied /'kændɪd/ *adj* заса́харенный.

candle /'kænd(ə)l/ *n* свеча́. **candlestick** *n* подсве́чник.

candour /'kændə(r)/ *n* открове́нность.

candy /'kændɪ/ *n* сла́дости *f pl*.

cane /keɪn/ *n* (*plant*) тростни́к; (*stick*) трость, па́лка; *vt* бить *impf*, по~ *pf* па́лкой.

canine /'keɪnaɪn/ *adj* соба́чий; *n* (*tooth*) клык.

canister /'kænɪstə(r)/ *n* ба́нка.

cannabis /'kænəbɪs/ *n* гаши́ш.

cannibal /'kænɪb(ə)l/ *n* людое́д. **cannibalism** /-,lɪz(ə)m/ *n* людое́дство.

cannon /'kænən/ *n* пу́шка; **~-ball** пу́шечное ядро́.

canoe /kə'nuː/ *n* кано́э *neut indecl*; *vi* пла́вать *indet*, плыть *det* на кано́э.

canon /'kænən/ *n* кано́н; (*person*) кано́ник. **canonize** /-,naɪz/ *vt* канонизова́ть *impf* & *pf*.

canopy /'kænəpɪ/ *n* балдахи́н.

cant /kænt/ *n* (*hypocrisy*) ха́нжество; (*jargon*) жарго́н.

cantankerous /kæn'tæŋkərəs/ *adj* сварли́вый.

cantata /kæn'tɑːtə/ *n* канта́та.

canteen /kæn'tiːn/ *n* столо́вая *sb*.

canter /'kæntə(r)/ *n* лёгкий гало́п; *vi* (*rider*) е́здить *indet*, е́хать *det* лёгким гало́пом; (*horse*) ходи́ть *indet*, идти́ *det* лёгким гало́пом.

canvas /'kænvəs/ *n* (*art*) холст; (*naut*) паруси́на; (*tent material*) брезе́нт.

canvass /'kænvəs/ *vi* агити́ровать *impf*, с~ *pf* (**for** за+*acc*); *n* собира́ние голосо́в; агита́ция. **canvasser** /'kænvəsə(r)/ *n* собира́тель *m* голосо́в.

canyon /'kænjən/ *n* каньо́н.

cap /kæp/ *n* (*of uniform*) фура́жка; (*cloth*) ке́пка; (*woman's*) чепе́ц; (*lid*) кры́шка; *vt* превосходи́ть *impf*, превзойти́ *pf*.

capability /,keɪpə'bɪlɪtɪ/ *n* спосо́бность. **capable** /'keɪpəb(ə)l/ *adj* спосо́бный (**of** на+*acc*).

capacious /kə'peɪʃəs/ *adj* вмести́тельный. **capacity** /kə'pæsɪtɪ/ *n* ёмкость; (*ability*) спосо́бность; **in the ~ of** в ка́честве +*gen*.

cape[1] /keɪp/ *n* (*geog*) мыс.

cape[2] /keɪp/ *n* (*cloak*) наки́дка.

caper /'keɪpə(r)/ *vi* скака́ть *impf*.

capers /'keɪpəz/ *n pl* (*cul*) ка́персы *m pl*.

capillary /kə'pɪlərɪ/ *adj* капилля́рный.

capital /'kæpɪt(ə)l/ *adj* (*letter*) прописно́й; **~ punishment** сме́ртная казнь; *n* (*town*) столи́ца; (*letter*) прописна́я бу́ква; (*econ*) капита́л. **capitalism** /-,lɪz(ə)m/ *n* капитали́зм. **capitalist** /-lɪst/ *n* капи-

C

та́лист; *adj* капиталисти́ческий. **capitalize** /-ˌlaɪz/ *vt* извлека́ть *impf*, извле́чь *pf* вы́году (**on** из+*gen*).

capitulate /kəˈpɪtjʊˌleɪt/ *vi* капитули́ровать *impf & pf*. **capitulation** /-ˈleɪʃ(ə)n/ *n* капитуля́ция.

caprice /kəˈpriːs/ *n* капри́з. **capricious** /-ˈprɪʃəs/ *adj* капри́зный.

Capricorn /ˈkæprɪˌkɔːn/ *n* Козеро́г.

capsize /kæpˈsaɪz/ *vt & i* опроки́дывать(ся) *impf*, опроки́нуть(ся) *pf*.

capsule /ˈkæpsjuːl/ *n* ка́псула.

captain /ˈkæptɪn/ *n* капита́н; *vt* быть капита́ном +*gen*.

caption /ˈkæpʃ(ə)n/ *n* по́дпись; (*cin*) титр.

captious /ˈkæpʃəs/ *adj* приди́рчивый.

captivate /ˈkæptɪˌveɪt/ *vt* пленя́ть *impf*, плени́ть *pf*. **captivating** /ˈkæptɪˌveɪtɪŋ/ *adj* плени́тельный. **captive** /ˈkæptɪv/ *adj & n* пле́нный. **captivity** /kæpˈtɪvɪtɪ/ *n* нево́ля; (*esp mil*) плен. **capture** /ˈkæptʃə(r)/ *n* взя́тие, захва́т, пои́мка; *vt* (*person*) брать *impf*, взять *pf* в плен; (*seize*) захва́тывать *impf*, захвати́ть *pf*.

car /kɑː(r)/ *n* маши́на; автомоби́ль *m*; **~ park** стоя́нка.

carafe /kəˈræf/ *n* графи́н.

caramel(s) /ˈkærəˌmel(z)/ *n* караме́ль.

carat /ˈkærət/ *n* кара́т.

caravan /ˈkærəˌvæn/ *n* фурго́н; (*convoy*) карава́н.

caraway (seeds) /ˈkærəˌweɪ (siːdz)/ *n* тмин.

carbohydrate /ˌkɑːbəˈhaɪdreɪt/ *n* углево́д. **carbon** /ˈkɑːb(ə)n/ *n* углеро́д; **~ copy** ко́пия; **~ dioxide** углекислота́; **~ monoxide** о́кись углеро́да; **~ paper** копирова́льная бума́га.

carburettor /ˌkɑːbjʊˈretə(r)/ *n* карбюра́тор.

carcass /ˈkɑːkəs/ *n* ту́ша.

card /kɑːd/ *n* (*stiff paper*) карто́н; (*visiting* **~**) ка́рточка; (*playing* **~**) ка́рта; (*greetings* **~**) откры́тка; (*ticket*) биле́т. **cardboard** *n* карто́н; *adj* карто́нный.

cardiac /ˈkɑːdɪˌæk/ *adj* серде́чный.

cardigan /ˈkɑːdɪgən/ *n* кардига́н.

cardinal /ˈkɑːdɪn(ə)l/ *adj* кардина́льный; **~ number** коли́чественное числи́тельное *sb*; *n* кардина́л.

care /keə(r)/ *n* (*trouble*) забо́та; (*caution*) осторо́жность; (*tending*) ухо́д; **in the ~ of** на попече́нии +*gen*; **take ~** осторо́жно!; смотри́(те)!; **take ~ of** забо́титься *impf*, по~ *pf* о+*prep*; *vi*: **I don't ~** мне всё равно́; **~ for** (*look after*) уха́живать *impf* за +*instr*; (*like*) нра́виться *impf*, по~ *pf impers* +*dat*.

career /kəˈrɪə(r)/ *n* карье́ра.

carefree /ˈkeəfriː/ *adj* беззабо́тный. **careful** /-fʊl/ *adj* (*cautious*) осторо́жный; (*thorough*) тща́тельный. **careless** /-lɪs/ *adj* (*negligent*) небре́жный; (*incautious*) неосторо́жный.

caress /kəˈres/ *n* ла́ска; *vt* ласка́ть *impf*.

caretaker /ˈkeəteɪkə(r)/ *n* смотри́тель *m*, ~ница; *attrib* вре́менный.

cargo /ˈkɑːgəʊ/ *n* груз.

caricature /ˈkærɪkətjʊə(r)/ *n* карикату́ра; *vt* изобража́ть *impf*, изобрази́ть *pf* в карикату́рном ви́де.

carnage /ˈkɑːnɪdʒ/ *n* резня́.

carnal /ˈkɑːn(ə)l/ *adj* пло́тский.

carnation /kɑːˈneɪʃ(ə)n/ *n* гвозди́ка.

carnival /ˈkɑːnɪv(ə)l/ *n* карнава́л.

carnivorous /kɑːˈnɪvərəs/ *adj* плотоя́дный.

carol /ˈkær(ə)l/ *n* (рожде́ственский) гимн.

carouse /kəˈraʊz/ *vi* кути́ть *impf*, кутну́ть *pf*.

carp[1] /kɑːp/ *n* карп.

carp[2] /kɑːp/ *vi* придира́ться *impf*, придра́ться *pf* (**at** к+*dat*).

carpenter /ˈkɑːpɪntə(r)/ *n* пло́тник. **carpentry** /-trɪ/ *n* пло́тничество.

carpet /ˈkɑːpɪt/ *n* ковёр; *vt* покрыва́ть *impf*, покры́ть *pf* ковро́м.

carping /'kɑːpɪŋ/ *adj* приди́рчивый.

carriage /'kærɪdʒ/ *n* (*vehicle*) каре́та; (*rly*) ваго́н; (*conveyance*) перево́зка; (*bearing*) оса́нка. **carriageway** *n* прое́зжая часть доро́ги. **carrier** /'kærɪə(r)/ *n* (*on bike*) бага́жник; (*firm*) тра́нспортная кампа́ния; (*med*) бациллоноси́тель *m*.

carrot /'kærət/ *n* морко́вка; *pl* морко́вь (*collect*).

carry /'kærɪ/ *vt* (*by hand*) носи́ть *indet*, нести́ *det*; переноси́ть *impf*, перенести́ *pf*; (*in vehicle*) вози́ть *indet*, везти́ *det*; (*sound*) передава́ть *impf*, переда́ть *pf*; *vi* (*sound*) быть слы́шен; **be carried away** увлека́ться *impf*, увле́чься *pf*; **~ on** (*continue*) продолжа́ть *impf*; **~ out** выполня́ть *impf*, вы́полнить *pf*; **~ over** переноси́ть *impf*, перенести́ *pf*.

cart /kɑːt/ *n* теле́га; *vt* (*lug*) таска́ть *impf*.

cartilage /'kɑːtɪlɪdʒ/ *n* хрящ.

carton /'kɑːt(ə)n/ *n* карто́нка

cartoon /kɑː'tuːn/ *n* карикату́ра; (*cin*) мультфи́льм. **cartoonist** /-nɪst/ *n* карикатури́ст, **~ка**.

cartridge /'kɑːtrɪdʒ/ *n* патро́н; (*for printer*) ка́ртридж.

carve /kɑːv/ *vt* ре́зать *impf* по+*dat*; (*in wood*) выреза́ть *impf*, вы́резать *pf*; (*in stone*) высека́ть *impf*, вы́сечь; (*slice*) нареза́ть *impf*, наре́зать *pf*. **carving** /'kɑːvɪŋ/ *n* резьба́; **~ knife** нож для нареза́ния мя́са.

cascade /kæs'keɪd/ *n* каска́д; *vi* па́дать *impf*.

case[1] /keɪs/ *n* (*instance*) слу́чай; (*law*) де́ло; (*med*) больно́й *sb*; (*gram*) паде́ж; **in ~** (в слу́чае) е́сли; **in any ~** во вся́ком слу́чае; **in no ~** ни в ко́ем слу́чае; **just in ~** на вся́кий слу́чай.

case[2] /keɪs/ *n* (*box*) я́щик; (*suitcase*) чемода́н; (*small box*) футля́р; (*cover*) чехо́л; (*display ~*) витри́на.

cash /kæʃ/ *n* нали́чные *sb*; (*money*) де́ньги *pl*; **~ on delivery** нало́женным платежо́м; **~ desk, register** ка́сса; **~ machine** банкома́т; *vt*: **~ a cheque** получа́ть *impf*, получи́ть *pf* де́ньги по че́ку. **cashier** /kæ'ʃɪə(r)/ *n* касси́р.

casing /'keɪsɪŋ/ *n* (*tech*) кожу́х.

casino /kə'siːnəʊ/ *n* казино́ *neut indecl*.

cask /kɑːsk/ *n* бо́чка.

casket /'kɑːskɪt/ *n* шкату́лка.

casserole /'kæsəˌrəʊl/ *n* (*pot*) ла́тка; (*stew*) рагу́ *neut indecl*.

cassette /kə'set/ *n* кассе́та; **~ recorder** кассе́тный магнитофо́н.

cassock /'kæsək/ *n* ря́са.

cast /kɑːst/ *vt* (*throw*) броса́ть *impf*, бро́сить *pf*; (*shed*) сбра́сывать *impf*, сбро́сить *pf*; (*theat*) распределя́ть *impf*, распредели́ть *pf* ро́ли +*dat*; (*found*) лить *impf*, с~ *pf*; **~ off** (*knitting*) спуска́ть *impf*, спусти́ть *pf* пе́тли; (*naut*) отплыва́ть *impf*, отплы́ть *pf*; **~ on** (*knitting*) набира́ть *impf*, набра́ть *pf* пе́тли; *n* (*of mind etc.*) склад; (*mould*) фо́рма; (*moulded object*) сле́пок; (*med*) ги́псовая повя́зка; (*theat*) де́йствующие ли́ца (-ц) *pl*. **castaway** /'kɑːstəweɪ/ *n* потерпе́вший *sb* кораблекруше́ние. **cast iron** *n* чугу́н. **cast-iron** *adj* чугу́нный. **cast-offs** *n pl* но́шеное пла́тье.

castanet /ˌkæstæ'net/ *n* кастанье́та.

caste /kɑːst/ *n* ка́ста.

castigate /'kæstɪˌgeɪt/ *vt* бичева́ть *impf*.

castle /'kɑːs(ə)l/ *n* за́мок; (*chess*) ладья́.

castor /'kɑːstə(r)/ *n* (*wheel*) ро́лик; **~ sugar** са́харная пу́дра.

castrate /kæ'streɪt/ *vt* кастри́ровать *impf* & *pf*. **castration** /-'streɪʃ(ə)n/ *n* кастра́ция.

casual /'kæʒʊəl/ *adj* (*chance*) случа́йный; (*offhand*) небре́жный; (*clothes*) обы́денный; (*unofficial*) неофициа́льный; (*informal*) лёгкий; (*labour*) подённый; **~ la-**

bourer подёнщик, -ица. **casualty** /'kæʒʊəltɪ/ *n* (*wounded*) ра́неный *sb*; (*killed*) уби́тый *sb*; *pl* поте́ри (-рь) *pl*; ~ **ward** пала́та ско́рой по́мощи.

cat /kæt/ *n* ко́шка; (*tom*) кот; ~**'s-eye** (*on road*) (доро́жный) рефле́ктор.

catalogue /'kætəˌlɒg/ *n* катало́г; (*price list*) прейскура́нт; *vt* каталогизи́ровать *impf* & *pf*.

catalyst /'kætəlɪst/ *n* катализа́тор. **catalytic** /ˌkætə'lɪtɪk/ *adj* каталити́ческий.

catapult /'kætəˌpʌlt/ *n* (*toy*) рога́тка; (*hist*, *aeron*) катапу́льта; *vt* & *i* катапульти́ровать(ся) *impf* & *pf*.

cataract /'kætəˌrækt/ *n* (*med*) катара́кта.

catarrh /kə'tɑː(r)/ *n* ката́р.

catastrophe /kə'tæstrəfɪ/ *n* катастро́фа. **catastrophic** /ˌkætə'strɒfɪk/ *adj* катастрофи́ческий.

catch /kætʃ/ *vt* (*ball*, *fish*, *thief*) лови́ть *impf*, пойма́ть *pf*; (*surprise*) застава́ть *impf*, заста́ть *pf*; (*disease*) заража́ться *impf*, зарази́ться *pf* +*instr*; (*be in time for*) успева́ть *impf*, успе́ть *pf* на+*acc*; *vt* & *i* (*snag*) зацепля́ть(ся) *impf*, зацепи́ть(ся) *pf* (**on** за+*acc*); ~ **on** (*become popular*) прививáться *impf*, приви́ться *pf*; ~ **up with** догоня́ть *impf*, догна́ть *pf*; *n* (*of fish*) уло́в; (*trick*) уло́вка; (*on door etc.*) защёлка. **catching** /'kætʃɪŋ/ *adj* зара́зный. **catchword** *n* мо́дное слове́чко. **catchy** /'kætʃɪ/ *adj* прили́пчивый.

categorical /ˌkætɪ'gɒrɪk(ə)l/ *adj* категори́ческий. **category** /'kætɪgərɪ/ *n* катего́рия.

cater /'keɪtə(r)/ *vi*: ~ **for** поставля́ть *impf*, поста́вить *pf* прови́зию для+*gen*; (*satisfy*) удовлетворя́ть *impf*, удовлетвори́ть *pf*. **caterer** /'keɪtərə(r)/ *n* поставщи́к (прови́зии).

caterpillar /'kætəˌpɪlə(r)/ *n* гу́сеница.

cathedral /kə'θiːdr(ə)l/ *n* собо́р.

catheter /'kæθɪtə(r)/ *n* кате́тер.

Catholic /'kæθəlɪk/ *adj* католи́ческий; *n* като́лик, -ичка. **Catholicism** /kə'θɒlɪˌsɪz(ə)m/ *n* католи́чество.

cattle /'kæt(ə)l/ *n* скот.

Caucasus /'kɔːkəsəs/ *n* Кавка́з.

cauldron /'kɔːldrən/ *n* котёл.

cauliflower /'kɒlɪˌflaʊə(r)/ *n* цветна́я капу́ста.

cause /kɔːz/ *n* причи́на, по́вод; (*law etc.*) де́ло; *vt* причиня́ть *impf*, причини́ть *pf*; вызыва́ть *impf*, вы́звать *pf*; (*induce*) заставля́ть *impf*, заста́вить *pf*.

caustic /'kɔːstɪk/ *adj* е́дкий.

cauterize /'kɔːtəˌraɪz/ *vt* прижига́ть *impf*, приже́чь *pf*.

caution /'kɔːʃ(ə)n/ *n* осторо́жность; (*warning*) предостереже́ние; *vt* предостерега́ть *impf*, предостере́чь *pf*. **cautious** /'kɔːʃəs/ *adj* осторо́жный. **cautionary** /'kɔːʃənərɪ/ *adj* предостерега́ющий.

cavalcade /ˌkævəl'keɪd/ *n* кавалька́да. **cavalier** /ˌkævə'lɪə(r)/ *adj* бесцеремо́нный. **cavalry** /'kævəlrɪ/ *n* кавале́рия.

cave /keɪv/ *n* пеще́ра; *vi*: ~ **in** обва́ливаться *impf*, обвали́ться *pf*; (*yield*) сдава́ться *impf*, сда́ться *pf*. **caveman** *n* пеще́рный челове́к. **cavern** /'kæv(ə)n/ *n* пеще́ра. **cavernous** /'kæv(ə)nəs/ *adj* пеще́ристый.

caviare /'kævɪˌɑː(r)/ *n* икра́.

cavity /'kævɪtɪ/ *n* впа́дина, по́лость; (*in tooth*) дупло́.

cavort /kə'vɔːt/ *vi* скака́ть *impf*.

caw /kɔː/ *vi* ка́ркать *impf*, ка́ркнуть *pf*.

CD *abbr* (*of* **compact disc**) компа́кт-ди́ск; ~ **player** прои́грыватель *m* компа́кт-ди́сков.

cease /siːs/ *vt* & *i* прекраща́ть(ся) *impf*, прекрати́ть(ся) *pf*; *vt* перестава́ть *impf*, переста́ть *pf* (+*inf*); ~**-fire** прекраще́ние огня́. **ceaseless** /'siːslɪs/ *adj* непреста́нный.

C

cedar /ˈsiːdə(r)/ *n* кедр.
cede /siːd/ *vt* уступа́ть *impf*, уступи́ть *pf*.
ceiling /ˈsiːlɪŋ/ *n* потоло́к; (*fig*) максима́льный у́ровень *m*.
celebrate /ˈselɪˌbreɪt/ *vt & i* пра́здновать *impf*, от~ *pf*; (*extol*) прославля́ть *impf*, просла́вить *pf*. **celebrated** /-tɪd/ *adj* знамени́тый. **celebration** /-ˈbreɪʃ(ə)n/ *n* пра́зднование. **celebrity** /sɪˈlebrɪtɪ/ *n* знамени́тость.
celery /ˈselərɪ/ *n* сельдере́й.
celestial /sɪˈlestɪəl/ *adj* небе́сный.
celibacy /ˈselɪbəsɪ/ *n* безбра́чие. **celibate** /ˈselɪbət/ *adj* холосто́й; *n* холостя́к.
cell /sel/ *n* (*prison*) ка́мера; (*biol*) кле́тка; ~ **phone** со́товый телефо́н.
cellar /ˈselə(r)/ *n* подва́л.
cello /ˈtʃeləʊ/ *n* виолонче́ль.
cellophane /ˈseləˌfeɪn/ *n* целлофа́н. **cellular** /ˈseljʊlə(r)/ *adj* кле́точный.
Celt /kelt/ *n* кельт. **Celtic** /ˈkeltɪk/ *adj* ке́льтский.
cement /sɪˈment/ *n* цеме́нт; *vt* цементи́ровать *impf*, за~ *pf*.
cemetery /ˈsemɪtərɪ/ *n* кла́дбище.
censor /ˈsensə(r)/ *n* це́нзор; *vt* подверга́ть *impf*, подве́ргнуть *pf* цензу́ре. **censorious** /senˈsɔːrɪəs/ *adj* сверхкрити́ческий. **censorship** /ˈsensərʃɪp/ *n* цензу́ра. **censure** /ˈsensjə(r)/ *n* порица́ние; *vt* порица́ть *impf*.
census /ˈsensəs/ *n* пе́репись.
cent /sent/ *n* цент; **per** ~ проце́нт.
centenary /senˈtiːnərɪ/ *n* столе́тие. **centennial** /-ˈtenɪəl/ *adj* столе́тний. **centigrade** /ˈsentɪˌgreɪd/ *adj*: **10°** ~ 10° по Це́льсию. **centimetre** /ˈsentɪˌmiːtə(r)/ *n* сантиме́тр. **centipede** /ˈsentɪˌpiːd/ *n* сороконо́жка.
central /ˈsentr(ə)l/ *adj* центра́льный; ~ **heating** центра́льное отопле́ние. **centralization** /ˌsentrəlaɪˈzeɪʃ(ə)n/ *n* централиза́ция. **centralize** /ˈsentrəˌlaɪz/ *vt* централизова́ть *impf & pf*.
centre /ˈsentə(r)/ *n* центр; середи́на; ~ **forward** центр нападе́ния; *vi & i*: ~ **on** сосредото́чивать(ся) *impf*, сосредото́чить(ся) *pf* на+*prep*. **centrifugal** /ˌsentrɪˈfjuːg(ə)l/ *adj* центробе́жный.
century /ˈsentʃərɪ/ *n* столе́тие, век.
ceramic /sɪˈræmɪk/ *adj* керами́ческий. **ceramics** /-mɪks/ *n pl* кера́мика.
cereals /ˈsɪərɪəlz/ *n pl* хле́бные зла́ки *m pl*; **breakfast** ~ зерновы́е хло́пья (-ев) *pl*.
cerebral /ˈserɪbr(ə)l/ *adj* мозгово́й.
ceremonial /ˌserɪˈməʊnɪəl/ *adj* церемониа́льный; *n* церемониа́л. **ceremonious** /-nɪəs/ *adj* церемо́нный. **ceremony** /ˈserɪmənɪ/ *n* церемо́ния.
certain /ˈsɜːt(ə)n/ *adj* (*confident*) уве́рен (-нна); (*undoubted*) несомне́нный; (*unspecified*) изве́стный; (*inevitable*) ве́рный; **for** ~ наверняка́. **certainly** /-lɪ/ *adv* (*of course*) коне́чно, безусло́вно; (*without doubt*) несомне́нно; ~ **not!** ни в ко́ем слу́чае. **certainty** /-tɪ/ *n* (*conviction*) уве́ренность; (*fact*) несомне́нный факт.
certificate /səˈtɪfɪkət/ *n* свиде́тельство; сертифика́т. **certify** /ˈsɜːtɪfaɪ/ *vt* удостоверя́ть *impf*, удостове́рить *pf*.
cervical /sɜːˈvaɪk(ə)l/ *n* ше́йный. **cervix** /ˈsɜːvɪks/ *n* ше́йка ма́тки.
cessation /seˈseɪʃ(ə)n/ *n* прекраще́ние.
cf. *abbr* ср., сравни́.
CFCs *abbr* (*of* **chlorofluorocarbons**) хлори́рованные фторуглеро́ды *m pl*.
chafe /tʃeɪf/ *vt* (*rub*) тере́ть *impf*; (*rub sore*) натира́ть *impf*, натере́ть *pf*.
chaff /tʃɑːf/ *n* (*husks*) мяки́на; (*straw*) се́чка.
chaffinch /ˈtʃæfɪntʃ/ *n* зя́блик.
chagrin /ˈʃægrɪn/ *n* огорче́ние.
chain /tʃeɪn/ *n* цепь; ~ **reaction** цепна́я реа́кция; ~ **smoker** заядлый кури́льщик.

chair /tʃeə(r)/ *n* стул, (*armchair*) крéсло; (*univ*) кáфедра; *vt* (*preside*) председáтельствовать *impf* на+*prep.* **chairman, -woman** *n* председáтель *m*, ~ница.
chalice /ˈtʃælɪs/ *n* чáша.
chalk /tʃɔːk/ *n* мел. **chalky** /ˈtʃɔːkɪ/ *adj* меловóй.
challenge /ˈtʃælɪndʒ/ *n* (*summons, fig*) вы́зов; (*sentry's*) óклик; (*law*) отвóд; *vt* вызывáть *impf*, вы́звать *pf*; (*sentry*) окликáть *impf*, окли́кнуть *pf*; (*law*) отводи́ть *impf*, отвести́ *pf.* **challenger** /-dʒə(r)/ *n* претендéнт. **challenging** /-dʒɪŋ/ *adj* интригу́ющий.
chamber /ˈtʃeɪmbə(r)/ *n* (*cavity*) кáмера; (*hall*) зал; (*parl*) палáта; *pl* (*law*) адвокáтская контóра, (*judge's*) кабинéт (судьи́); **~ music** кáмерная му́зыка; **~ pot** ночнóй горшóк. **chambermaid** *n* гóрничная *sb.*
chameleon /kəˈmiːlɪən/ *n* хамелеóн.
chamois /ˈʃæmwɑː/ *n* (*animal*) сéрна; (*~-leather*) зáмша.
champagne /ʃæmˈpeɪn/ *n* шампáнское *sb.*
champion /ˈtʃæmpɪən/ *n* чемпиóн, ~ка; (*upholder*) побóрник, -ица; *vt* борóться *impf* за +*acc*. **championship** *n* пéрвенство, чемпионáт.
chance /tʃɑːns/ *n* случáйность; (*opportunity*) возмóжность, (*favourable*) слу́чай; (*likelihood*) шанс (*usu pl*); **by ~** случáйно; *adj* случáйный; *vi*: **~ it** рискну́ть *pf.*
chancellery /ˈtʃɑːnsələrɪ/ *n* канцеля́рия. **chancellor** /ˈtʃɑːnsələ(r)/ *n* кáнцлер; (*univ*) рéктор; **C~ of the Exchequer** кáнцлер казначéйства.
chancy /ˈtʃɑːnsɪ/ *adj* рискóванный.
chandelier /ˌʃændɪˈlɪə(r)/ *n* лю́стра.
change /tʃeɪndʒ/ *n* перемéна; изменéние; (*of clothes etc.*) смéна; (*money*) сдáча; (*of trains etc.*) пересáдка; **for a ~** для разнообрáзия; *vt & i* меня́ть(ся) *impf*; изменя́ть(ся) *impf*, измени́ть(ся) *pf*; *vi* (*one's clothes*) переодевáться *impf*, переодéться *pf*; (*trains etc.*) пересáживаться *impf*, пересéсть *pf*; *vt* (*a baby*) перепелёнывать *impf*, перепеленáть *pf*; (*money*) обмéнивать *impf*, обменя́ть *pf*; (*give ~ for*) размéнивать *impf*, разменя́ть *pf*; **~ into** превращáться *impf*, преврати́ться *pf* в+*acc*; **~ over to** переходи́ть *impf*, перейти́ *pf* на+*acc*. **changeable** /ˈtʃeɪndʒəb(ə)l/ *adj* измéнчивый.
channel /ˈtʃæn(ə)l/ *n* (*water*) проли́в; (*also TV*) канáл; (*fig*) путь *m*; **the (English) C~** Ла-Мáнш; *vt* (*fig*) направля́ть *impf.*
chant /tʃɑːnt/ *n* (*eccl*) песнопéние; *vt & i* петь *impf*; (*slogans*) скандúровать *impf & pf.*
chaos /ˈkeɪɒs/ *n* хаóс. **chaotic** /-ˈɒtɪk/ *adj* хаоти́чный.
chap /tʃæp/ *n* (*person*) пáрень *m.*
chapel /ˈtʃæp(ə)l/ *n* часóвня; (*Catholic*) капéлла.
chaperone /ˈʃæpəˌrəʊn/ *n* компаньóнка.
chaplain /ˈtʃæplɪn/ *n* капеллáн.
chapped /tʃæpt/ *adj* потрескáвшийся.
chapter /ˈtʃæptə(r)/ *n* главá.
char /tʃɑː(r)/ *vt & i* обу́гливать(ся) *impf*, обу́глить(ся) *pf.*
character /ˈkærɪktə(r)/ *n* харáктер; (*theat*) дéйствующее лицó; (*letter*) бу́ква; (*Chinese etc.*) иерóглиф. **characteristic** /ˌkærɪktəˈrɪstɪk/ *adj* характéрный; *n* свóйство; (*of person*) чертá харáктера. **characterize** /ˈkærɪktəˌraɪz/ *vt* характеризовáть *impf & pf.*
charade /ʃəˈrɑːd/ *n* шарáда.
charcoal /ˈtʃɑːkəʊl/ *n* древéсный у́голь *m.*
charge /tʃɑːdʒ/ *n* (*for gun*; *electr*) заря́д; (*fee*) плáта; (*person*) питóмец, -мица; (*accusation*) обвинéние; (*mil*) атáка; **be in ~ of** за-

C

ве́довать *impf* +*instr*; **in the ~ of** на попече́нии +*gen*; *vt* (*gun*; *electr*) заряжа́ть *impf*, заряди́ть *pf*; (*accuse*) обвиня́ть *impf*, обвини́ть *pf* (**with** в+*prep*); (*mil*) атакова́ть *impf* & *pf*; *vi* броса́ться *impf*, бро́ситься *pf* в ата́ку; **~ (for)** брать *impf*, взять *pf* (за+*acc*); **~ to (the account of)** запи́сывать *impf*, записа́ть *pf* на счёт+*gen*.

chariot /'tʃærɪət/ *n* колесни́ца.

charisma /kə'rɪzmə/ *n* обая́ние. **charismatic** /ˌkærɪz'mætɪk/ *adj* обая́тельный.

charitable /'tʃærɪtəb(ə)l/ *adj* благотвори́тельный; (*kind*, *merciful*) милосе́рдный. **charity** /'tʃærɪtɪ/ *n* (*kindness*) милосе́рдие; (*organization*) благотвори́тельная организа́ция.

charlatan /'ʃɑːlət(ə)n/ *n* шарлата́н.

charm /tʃɑːm/ *n* очарова́ние; пре́лесть; (*spell*) за́говор; *pl* ча́ры (чар) *pl*; (*amulet*) талисма́н; (*trinket*) брело́к; *vt* очаро́вывать *impf*, очарова́ть *pf*. **charming** /-mɪŋ/ *adj* очарова́тельный, преле́стный.

chart /tʃɑːt/ *n* (*naut*) морска́я ка́рта; (*table*) гра́фик; *vt* наноси́ть *impf*, нанести́ *pf* на гра́фик **charter** /-tə(r)/ *n* (*document*) ха́ртия; (*statutes*) уста́в; *vt* нанима́ть *impf*, наня́ть *pf*.

charwoman /'tʃɑːwʊmən/ *n* приходя́щая убо́рщица.

chase /tʃeɪs/ *vt* гоня́ться *indet*, гна́ться *det* за+*instr*; *n* пого́ня; (*hunting*) охо́та.

chasm /'kæz(ə)m/ *n* (*abyss*) бе́здна.

chassis /'ʃæsɪ/ *n* шасси́ *neut indecl*.

chaste /tʃeɪst/ *adj* целому́дренный.

chastise /tʃæs'taɪz/ *vt* кара́ть *impf*, по~ *pf*.

chastity /'tʃæstɪtɪ/ *n* целому́дрие.

chat /tʃæt/ *n* бесе́да; *vi* бесе́довать *impf*; **~ room** (*comput*) разде́л ча́та; **~ show** телевизио́нная бесе́да-интервью́ *f*.

chatter /'tʃætə(r)/ *n* болтовня́; *vi* болта́ть *impf*; (*teeth*) стуча́ть *impf*. **chatterbox** *n* болту́н. **chatty** /'tʃætɪ/ *adj* разгово́рчивый.

chauffeur /'ʃəʊfə(r)/ *n* шофёр.

chauvinism /'ʃəʊvɪˌnɪz(ə)m/ *n* шовини́зм. **chauvinist** /-nɪst/ *n* шовини́ст; *adj* шовинисти́ческий.

cheap /tʃiːp/ *adj* дешёвый. **cheapen** /'tʃiːpən/ *vt* (*fig*) опошля́ть *impf*, опошли́ть *pf*. **cheaply** /'tʃiːplɪ/ *adv* дёшево.

cheat /tʃiːt/ *vt* обма́нывать *impf*, обману́ть *pf*; *vi* плутова́ть *impf*, на~, с~ *pf*; *n* обма́нщик, -ица; плут.

check¹ /tʃek/ *n* контро́ль *m*, прове́рка; (*chess*) шах; **~mate** шах и мат; *vt* (*examine*) проверя́ть *impf*, прове́рить *pf*; контроли́ровать *impf*, про~ *pf*; (*restrain*) сде́рживать *impf*, сдержа́ть *pf*; **~ in** регистри́роваться *impf*, за~ *pf*; **~ out** выпи́сываться *impf*, вы́писаться *pf*; **~-out** ка́сса; **~-up** осмо́тр.

check² /tʃek/ *n* (*pattern*) клётка. **check(ed)** /tʃekt/ *adj* клётчатый.

cheek /tʃiːk/ *n* щека́; (*impertinence*) на́глость. **cheeky** /tʃiːkɪ/ *adj* на́глый.

cheep /tʃiːp/ *vi* пища́ть *impf*, пи́скнуть *pf*.

cheer /'tʃɪə(r)/ *n* ободря́ющий во́зглас; **~s!** за (ва́ше) здоро́вье!; *vt* (*applaud*) приве́тствовать *impf* & *pf*; **~ up** ободря́ть(ся) *impf*, ободри́ть(ся) *pf*. **cheerful** /'tʃɪəfʊl/ *adj* весёлый. **cheerio** /ˌtʃɪərɪ'əʊ/ *int* пока́. **cheerless** /'tʃɪəlɪs/ *adj* уны́лый.

cheese /tʃiːz/ *n* сыр; **~-cake** ватру́шка.

cheetah /'tʃiːtə/ *n* гепа́рд.

chef /ʃef/ *n* (шеф-)по́вар.

chemical /'kemɪk(ə)l/ *adj* хими́ческий; *n* химика́т. **chemist** /'kemɪst/ *n* хи́мик; (*druggist*) апте́карь *m*; **~'s (shop)** апте́ка. **chemistry** /'kemɪstrɪ/ *n* хи́мия.

cheque /tʃek/ *n* чек; **~-book** чéковая кни́жка.

cherish /ˈtʃerɪʃ/ *vt* (*foster*) леле́ять *impf*; (*hold dear*) дорожи́ть *impf* +*instr*; (*love*) не́жно люби́ть *impf.*

cherry /ˈtʃerɪ/ *n* ви́шня; *adj* вишнёвый.

cherub /ˈtʃerəb/ *n* херуви́м.

chess /tʃes/ *n* ша́хматы (-т) *pl*; **~-board** ша́хматная доска́; **~-men** *n* ша́хматы (-т) *pl.*

chest /tʃest/ *n* сунду́к; (*anat*) грудь; **~ of drawers** комо́д.

chestnut /ˈtʃesnʌt/ *n* кашта́н; (*horse*) гнеда́я *sb.*

chew /tʃuː/ *vt* жева́ть *impf.* **chewing-gum** /ˈtʃuːɪŋ gʌm/ *n* жева́тельная рези́нка.

chic /ʃiːk/ *adj* элега́нтный.

chick /tʃɪk/ *n* цыплёнок. **chicken** /ˈtʃɪkɪn/ *n* ку́рица; цыплёнок; *adj* трусли́вый; **~ out** тру́сить *impf*, с~ *pf.* **chicken-pox** /ˈtʃɪkɪn pɒks/ *n* ветря́нка.

chicory /ˈtʃɪkərɪ/ *n* цико́рий.

chief /tʃiːf/ *n* глава́ *m* & *f*; (*boss*) нача́льник; (*of tribe*) вождь *m*; *adj* гла́вный. **chiefly** /ˈtʃiːflɪ/ *adv* гла́вным о́бразом. **chieftain** /ˈtʃiːft(ə)n/ *n* вождь *m.*

chiffon /ˈʃɪfɒn/ *n* шифо́н.

child /tʃaɪld/ *n* ребёнок; **~ birth** ро́ды (-дов) *pl.* **childhood** /ˈtʃaɪldhʊd/*n* де́тство. **childish** /ˈtʃaɪldɪʃ/ *adj* де́тский. **childless** /ˈtʃaɪldlɪs/ *adj* безде́тный. **childlike** /ˈtʃaɪldlaɪk/ *adj* де́тский. **childrens'** /ˈtʃɪldr(ə)nz/ *adj* де́тский.

chili /ˈtʃɪlɪ/ *n* стручко́вый пе́рец.

chill /tʃɪl/ *n* хо́лод; (*ailment*) просту́да; *vt* охлажда́ть *impf*, охлади́ть *pf.* **chilly** /ˈtʃɪlɪ/ *adj* прохла́дный.

chime /tʃaɪm/ *n* (*set of bells*) набо́р колоколо́в; *pl* (*sound*) перезво́н; (*of clock*) бой; *vt* & *i* (*clock*) бить *impf*, про~ *pf*; *vi* (*bell*) звони́ть *impf*, по~ *pf.*

chimney /ˈtʃɪmnɪ/ *n* труба́; **~-sweep** трубочи́ст.

chimpanzee /ˌtʃɪmpænˈziː/ *n* шимпанзе́ *m indecl.*

chin /tʃɪn/ *n* подборо́док.

china /ˈtʃaɪnə/ *n* фарфо́р.

China /ˈtʃaɪnə/ *n* Кита́й. **Chinese** /tʃaɪˈniːz/ *n* кита́ец, -ая́нка; *adj* кита́йский.

chink[1] /tʃɪŋk/ *n* (*sound*) звон; *vi* звене́ть *impf*, про~ *pf.*

chink[2] /tʃɪŋk/ *n* (*crack*) щель.

chintz /tʃɪnts/ *n* си́тец.

chip /tʃɪp/ *vt* & *i* отка́лывать(ся) *impf*, отколо́ть(ся) *pf*; *n* (*of wood*) ще́пка; (*in cup*) щерби́на; (*in games*) фи́шка; *pl* карто́фель-соло́мка (*collect*); (*electron*) чип, микросхе́ма.

chiropodist /kɪˈrɒpədɪst/ *n* челове́к, занима́ющийся педикю́ром. **chiropody** /-ˈrɒpədɪ/ *n* педикю́р.

chirp /tʃɜːp/ *vi* чири́кать *impf.*

chisel /ˈtʃɪz(ə)l/ *n* (*wood*) стаме́ска; (*masonry*) зуби́ло; *vt* высека́ть *impf*, вы́сечь *pf.*

chit /tʃɪt/ *n* (*note*) запи́ска.

chivalrous /ˈʃɪvəlrəs/ *adj* ры́царский. **chivalry** /-rɪ/ *n* ры́царство.

chlorine /ˈklɔːriːn/ *n* хлор. **chlorophyll** /ˈklɒrəfɪl/ *n* хлорофи́лл.

chock-full /ˈtʃɒkfʊl/ *adj* битко́м наби́тый.

chocolate /ˈtʃɒkələt/ *n* шокола́д; (*sweet*) шокола́дная конфе́та; **~ bar** шокола́дка.

choice /tʃɔɪs/ *n* вы́бор; *adj* отбо́рный.

choir /ˈkwaɪə(r)/ *n* хор *m*; **~-boy** пе́вчий *sb.*

choke /tʃəʊk/ *n* (*valve*) дро́ссель *m*; *vi* дави́ться *impf*, по~ *pf*; (*with anger etc.*) задыха́ться *impf*, задохну́ться *pf* (**with** от+*gen*); *vt* (*suffocate*) души́ть *impf*, за~ *pf*; (*of plants*) заглуша́ть, глуши́ть *impf*, заглуши́ть *pf.*

cholera /ˈkɒlərə/ *n* холе́ра.

cholesterol /kəˈlestəˌrɒl/ *n* холестери́н.

choose /tʃuːz/ *vt* (*select*) выбира́ть *impf*, вы́брать *pf*; (*decide*) решáть *impf*, решúть *pf*. **choosy** /ˈtʃuːzɪ/ *adj* разбóрчивый.

chop /tʃɒp/ *vt* (*also* ~ *down*) рубúть *impf*, рубнýть, рубанýть *pf*; ~ **off** отрубáть *impf*, отрубúть *pf*; *n* (*cul*) отбивнáя котлéта.

chopper /ˈtʃɒpə(r)/ *n* топóр. **choppy** /ˈtʃɒpɪ/ *adj* бурлúвый.

chop-sticks /ˈtʃɒpstɪks/ *n* пáлочки *f pl* для еды́.

choral /ˈkɔːr(ə)l/ *adj* хоровóй. **chorale** /kɔːˈrɑːl/ *n* хорáл.

chord /kɔːd/ *n* (*mus*) аккóрд.

chore /tʃɔː(r)/ *n* обя́занность.

choreographer /ˌkɒrɪˈɒgrəfə(r)/ *n* хореóграф. **choreography** /-grəfɪ/ *n* хореográфия.

chorister /ˈkɒrɪstə(r)/ *n* пéвчий *sb*.

chortle /ˈtʃɔːt(ə)l/ *vi* фы́ркать *impf*, фы́ркнуть *pf*.

chorus /ˈkɔːrəs/ *n* хор; (*refrain*) припéв.

christen /ˈkrɪs(ə)n/ *vt* крестúть *impf* & *pf*. **Christian** /ˈkrɪstɪən/ *n* христианúн, -áнка; *adj* христиáнский; ~ **name** úмя *neut*. **Christianity** /ˌkrɪstɪˈænɪtɪ/ *n* христиáнство. **Christmas** /ˈkrɪsməs/ *n* Рождествó; ~ **Day** пéрвый день Рождествá; ~ **Eve** сочéльник; ~ **tree** ёлка.

chromatic /krəˈmætɪk/ *adj* хроматúческий. **chrome** /krəʊm/ *n* хром. **chromium** /ˈkrəʊmɪəm/ *n* хром. **chromosome** /ˈkrəʊməˌsəʊm/ *n* хромосóма.

chronic /ˈkrɒnɪk/ *adj* хронúческий.

chronicle /ˈkrɒnɪk(ə)l/ *n* хрóника, лéтопись.

chronological /ˌkrɒnəˈlɒdʒɪk(ə)l/ *adj* хронологúческий.

chrysalis /ˈkrɪsəlɪs/ *n* кýколка.

chrysanthemum /krɪˈsænθəməm/ *n* хризантéма.

chubby /ˈtʃʌbɪ/ *adj* пýхлый.

chuck /tʃʌk/ *vt* бросáть *impf*, брóсить *pf*; ~ **out** вышибáть *impf*, вы́шибить *pf*.

chuckle /ˈtʃʌk(ə)l/ *vi* посмéиваться *impf*.

chum /tʃʌm/ *n* товáрищ.

chunk /tʃʌŋk/ *n* ломóть *m*.

church /tʃɜːtʃ/ *n* цéрковь. **churchyard** *n* клáдбище.

churlish /ˈtʃɜːlɪʃ/ *adj* грýбый.

churn /tʃɜːn/ *n* маслобóйка; *vt* сбивáть *impf*, сбить *pf*; *vi* (*foam*) пéниться *impf*, вс~ *pf*; (*stomach*) крутúть *impf*; ~ **out** выпекáть *impf*, вы́печь *pf*; ~ **up** взбить *pf*.

chute /ʃuːt/ *n* жёлоб.

cider /ˈsaɪdə(r)/ *n* сидр.

cigar /sɪˈgɑː(r)/ *n* сигáра. **cigarette** /ˌsɪgəˈret/ *n* сигарéта; папирóса; ~ **lighter** зажигáлка.

cinder /ˈsɪndə(r)/ *n* шлак; *pl* золá.

cine-camera /ˈsɪnɪˌkæmrə/ *n* киноаппарáт. **cinema** /ˈsɪnɪˌmɑː/ *n* кинó *neut indecl*.

cinnamon /ˈsɪnəmən/ *n* корúца.

cipher /ˈsaɪfə(r)/ *n* нуль *m*; (*code*) шифр.

circle /ˈsɜːk(ə)l/ *n* круг; (*theatre*) я́рус; *vi* кружúться *impf*; *vt* (*walking*) обходúть *impf*, обойтú *pf*; (*flying*) облетáть *impf*, облетéть *pf*. **circuit** /ˈsɜːkɪt/ *n* кругооборóт; объéзд, обхóд; (*electron*) схéма; (*electr*) цепь. **circuitous** /sɜːˈkjuːɪtəs/ *adj* окружнóй. **circular** /ˈsɜːkjʊlə(r)/ *adj* крýглый; (*moving in a circle*) круговóй; *n* циркуля́р. **circulate** /ˈsɜːkjʊˌleɪt/ *vi* циркулúровать *impf*; *vt* распространя́ть *impf*, распространúть *pf*. **circulation** /ˌsɜːkjuːˈleɪʃ(ə)n/ *n* (*air*) циркуля́ция; (*distribution*) распространéние; (*of newspaper*) тирáж; (*med*) кровообращéние.

circumcise /ˈsɜːkəmˌsaɪz/ *vt* обрезáть *impf*, обрéзать *pf*. **circumcision** /-ˈsɪʒ(ə)n/ *n* обрезáние.

circumference /sɜːˈkʌmfərəns/ *n* окрýжность.

circumspect /ˈsɜːkəmˌspekt/ *adj* осмотрúтельный.

circumstance /ˈsɜːkəmst(ə)ns/ *n* обстоя́тельство; **under the ~s** при дáнных обстоя́тельствах, в такóм слýчае; **under no ~s** ни при какúх обстоя́тельствах, ни в кóем слýчае.

circumvent /ˌsɜːkəm'vent/ *vt* обходи́ть *impf*, обойти́ *pf*.
circus /'sɜːkəs/ *n* цирк.
cirrhosis /sɪ'rəʊsɪs/ *n* цирро́з.
CIS *abbr* (*of* **Commonwealth of Independent States**) СНГ.
cistern /'sɪst(ə)n/ *n* бачо́к.
citadel /'sɪtəd(ə)l/ *n* цитаде́ль.
cite /saɪt/ *vt* ссыла́ться *impf*, сосла́ться *pf* на+*acc*.
citizen /'sɪtɪz(ə)n/ *n* граждани́н, -а́нка. **citizenship** /'sɪtɪz(ə)nʃɪp/ *n* гражда́нство.
citrus /'sɪtrəs/ *n* ци́трус; *adj* ци́трусовый.
city /'sɪtɪ/ *n* го́род.
civic /'sɪvɪk/ *adj* гражда́нский. **civil** /-v(ə)l/ *adj* гражда́нский; (*polite*) ве́жливый; ~ **engineer** гражда́нский инжене́р; ~ **engineering** гражда́нское строи́тельство; **C~ Servant** госуда́рственный слу́жащий *sb*; чино́вник; **C~ Service** госуда́рственная слу́жба. **civilian** /sɪ'vɪlɪən/ *n* шта́тский *sb*; *adj* шта́тский. **civility** /sɪ'vɪlɪtɪ/ *n* ве́жливость. **civilization** /ˌsɪvɪlaɪ'zeɪʃ(ə)n/ *n* цивилиза́ция. **civilize** /'sɪvɪˌlaɪz/ *vt* цивилизова́ть *impf* & *pf*. **civilized** /'sɪvɪˌlaɪzd/ *adj* цивилизо́ванный.
clad /klæd/ *adj* оде́тый.
claim /kleɪm/ *n* (*demand*) тре́бование, притяза́ние; (*assertion*) утвержде́ние; *vt* (*demand*) тре́бовать *impf* +*gen*; (*assert*) утвержда́ть *impf*, утверди́ть *pf*. **claimant** /'kleɪmənt/ *n* претенде́нт.
clairvoyant /kleə'vɔɪənt/ *n* ясновидец, -дица; *adj* ясновидящий.
clam /klæm/ *n* моллю́ск; *vi*: ~ **up** отка́зываться *impf*, отказа́ться *pf* разгова́ривать.
clamber /'klæmbə(r)/ *vi* кара́бкаться *impf*, вс~ *pf*.
clammy /'klæmɪ/ *adj* вла́жный.
clamour /'klæmə(r)/ *n* шум; *vi*: ~ **for** шу́мно тре́бовать *impf*, по~ *pf* +*gen*.
clamp /klæmp/ *n* зажи́м; *vt* скрепля́ть *impf*, скрепи́ть *pf*; ~ **down on** прижа́ть *pf*.
clan /klæn/ *n* клан.
clandestine /klæn'destɪn/ *adj* та́йный.
clang, clank /klæŋ, klæŋk/ *n* лязг; *vt* & *i* ля́згать *impf*, ля́згнуть *pf* (+*instr*).
clap /klæp/ *vt* & *i* хло́пать *impf*, хло́пнуть *pf* +*dat*; *n* хлопо́к; (*thunder*) уда́р.
claret /'klærət/ *n* бордо́ *neut indecl*.
clarification /ˌklærɪfɪ'keɪʃ(ə)n/ *n* (*explanation*) разъясне́ние. **clarify** /'klærɪˌfaɪ/ *vt* разъясня́ть *impf*, разъясни́ть *pf*.
clarinet /ˌklærɪ'net/ *n* кларне́т.
clarity /'klærɪtɪ/ *n* я́сность.
clash /klæʃ/ *n* (*conflict*) столкнове́ние; (*disharmony*) дисгармо́ния; *vi* ста́лкиваться *impf*, столкну́ться *pf*; (*coincide*) совпада́ть *impf*, совпа́сть *pf*; не гармони́ровать *impf*.
clasp /klɑːsp/ *n* застёжка; (*embrace*) объя́тие; *vt* обхва́тывать *impf*, обхвати́ть *pf*; ~ **one's hands** сплести́ *pf* па́льцы рук.
class /klɑːs/ *n* класс; **~-room** класс; *vt* классифици́ровать *impf* & *pf*.
classic /'klæsɪk/ *adj* класси́ческий; *n* кла́ссик; *pl* (*literature*) кла́ссика; (*Latin and Greek*) класси́ческие языки́ *m pl*. **classical** /-k(ə)l/ *adj* класси́ческий.
classification /ˌklæsɪfɪ'keɪʃ(ə)n/ *n* классифика́ция. **classified** /'klæsɪˌfaɪd/ *adj* засекре́ченный. **classify** /'klæsɪˌfaɪ/ *vt* классифици́ровать *impf* & *pf*.
classy /'klɑːsɪ/ *adj* кла́ссный.
clatter /'klætə(r)/ *n* стук; *vi* стуча́ть *impf*, по~ *pf*.
clause /klɔːz/ *n* статья́; (*gram*) предложе́ние.
claustrophobia /ˌklɔːstrə'fəʊbɪə/ *n* клаустрофо́бия.
claw /klɔː/ *n* ко́готь; *vt* цара́пать *impf* когтя́ми.
clay /kleɪ/ *n* гли́на; *adj* гли́няный.
clean /kliːn/ *adj* чи́стый; *adv*

C

C

(*fully*) совершéнно; **~-shaven** гла́дко вы́бритый; *vt* чи́стить *impf*, вы́~, по~ *pf*. **cleaner** /'kliːnə(r)/ *n* убо́рщик, -ица. **cleaner's** /'kliːnəz/ *n* химчи́стка. **clean(li)ness** /'klenlɪnɪs/ *n* чистота́. **cleanse** /klenz/ *vt* очища́ть *impf*, очи́стить *pf*.

clear /klɪə(r)/ *adj* я́сный; (*transparent*) прозра́чный; (*distinct*) отчётливый; (*free*) свобо́дный (**of** от+*gen*); (*pure*) чи́стый; *vt* & *i* очища́ть(ся) *impf*, очи́стить(ся) *pf*; *vt* (*jump over*) перепры́гивать *impf*, перепры́гнуть *pf*; (*acquit*) опра́вдывать *impf*, оправда́ть *pf*; **~ away** убира́ть *impf*, убра́ть *pf* со стола́; **~ off** (*go away*) убира́ться *impf*, убра́ться *pf*; **~ out** (*vt*) вычища́ть *impf*, вы́чистить *pf*; (*vi*) (*make off*) убира́ться *impf*, убра́ться *pf*; **~ up** (*tidy* (*away*)) убира́ть *impf*, убра́ть *pf*; (*weather*) проясня́ться *impf*, проясни́ться *pf*; (*explain*) выясня́ть *impf*, вы́яснить *pf*. **clearance** /'klɪərəns/ *n* расчи́стка; (*permission*) разреше́ние. **clearing** /'klɪərɪŋ/ *n* (*glade*) поля́на. **clearly** /'klɪəlɪ/ *adv* я́сно.

cleavage /'kliːvɪdʒ/ *n* разре́з груди́.

clef /klef/ *n* (*mus*) ключ.

cleft /kleft/ *n* тре́щина.

clemency /'klemənsɪ/ *n* милосе́рдие.

clench /klentʃ/ *vt* (*fist*) сжима́ть *impf*, сжать *pf*; (*teeth*) сти́скивать *impf*, сти́снуть *pf*.

clergy /'klɜːdʒɪ/ *n* духове́нство. **clergyman** *n* свяще́нник. **clerical** /'klerɪk(ə)l/ *adj* (*eccl*) духо́вный; (*of clerk*) канцеля́рский. **clerk** /klɑːk/ *n* конто́рский слу́жащий *sb*.

clever /'klevə(r)/ *adj* у́мный. **cleverness** /-nɪs/ *n* уме́ние.

cliche /'kliːʃeɪ/ *n* клише́ *neut indecl*.

click /klɪk/ *vt* щёлкать *impf*, щёлкнуть *pf* +*instr*.

client /'klaɪənt/ *n* клие́нт. **clientele** /ˌkliːɒn'tel/ *n* клиенту́ра.

cliff /klɪf/ *n* утёс.

climate /'klaɪmɪt/ *n* кли́мат. **climatic** /-'mætɪk/ *adj* климати́ческий.

climax /'klaɪmæks/ *n* кульмина́ция.

climb /klaɪm/ *vt* & *i* ла́зить *indet*, лезть *det* на+*acc*; влеза́ть *impf*, влезть *pf* на+*acc*; поднима́ться *impf*, подня́ться *pf* на+*acc*; **~ down** (*tree*) слеза́ть *impf*, слезть *pf* (с+*gen*); (*mountain*) спуска́ться *impf*, спусти́ться *pf* (с+*gen*); (*give in*) отступа́ть *impf*, отступи́ть *pf*; *n* подъём. **climber** /-mə(r)/ *n* альпини́ст, ~ка; (*plant*) вью́щееся расте́ние. **climbing** /-mɪŋ/ *n* альпини́зм.

clinch /klɪntʃ/ *vt*: **~ a deal** закрепи́ть *pf* сде́лку.

cling /klɪŋ/ *vi* (*stick*) прилипа́ть *impf*, прили́пнуть *pf* (**to** к+*dat*); (*grasp*) цепля́ться *impf*, цепи́ться *pf* (**to** за+*acc*).

clinic /'klɪnɪk/ *n* кли́ника. **clinical** /-k(ə)l/ *adj* клини́ческий.

clink /klɪŋk/ *vt* & *i* звене́ть *impf*, про~ *pf* (+*instr*); **~ glasses** чо́каться *impf*, чо́кнуться *pf*; *n* звон.

clip¹ /klɪp/ *n* скре́пка; зажи́м; *vt* скрепля́ть *impf*, скрепи́ть *pf*.

clip² /klɪp/ *vt* (*cut*) подстрига́ть *impf*, подстри́чь *pf*. **clippers** /-pəz/ *n pl* но́жницы *f pl*. **clipping** /-pɪŋ/ *n* (*extract*) вы́резка.

clique /kliːk/ *n* кли́ка.

cloak /kləʊk/ *n* плащ. **cloakroom** *n* гардеро́б; (*lavatory*) убо́рная *sb*.

clock /klɒk/ *n* часы́ *m pl*; **~wise** /-waɪz/ по часово́й стре́лке; **~-work** часово́й механи́зм; *vi*: **~ in, out** отмеча́ться *impf*, отме́титься *pf* приходя́ на рабо́ту/уходя́ с рабо́ты.

clod /klɒd/ *n* ком.

clog /klɒg/ *vt*: **~ up** засоря́ть *impf*, засори́ть *pf*.

cloister /'klɔɪstə(r)/ *n* арка́да.

clone /kləʊn/ *n* клон.

close *adj* /kləʊs/ (*near*) бли́зкий;

(*stuffy*) ду́шный; *vt* & *i* /kləʊz/ (*also* ~ *down*) закрыва́ть(ся) *impf*, закры́ть(ся) *pf*; (*conclude*) зака́нчивать *impf*, зако́нчить *pf*; *adv* бли́зко (**to** от+*gen*). **closed** /kləʊzd/ *adj* закры́тый. **closet** /'klɒzɪt/ *n* (стенно́й) шкаф. **close-up** *n* фотогра́фия сня́тая кру́пным пла́ном. **closing** /'kləʊzɪŋ/ *n* закры́тие; *adj* заключи́тельный. **closure** /'kləʊʒə(r)/ *n* закры́тие.

clot /klɒt/ *n* сгу́сток; *vi* сгуща́ться *impf*, сгусти́ться *pf*.

cloth /klɒθ/ *n* ткань; (*duster*) тря́пка; (*table-*~) ска́терть.

clothe /kləʊð/ *vt* одева́ть *impf*, оде́ть (**in** +*instr*, в+*acc*) *pf*. **clothes** /kləʊðz/ *n pl* оде́жда, пла́тье.

cloud /klaʊd/ *n* о́блако; (*rain* ~) ту́ча; *vt* затемня́ть *impf*, затемни́ть *pf*; омрача́ть *impf*, омрачи́ть *pf*; ~ **over** покрыва́ться *impf*, покры́ться *pf* облака́ми, ту́чами. **cloudy** /-dɪ/ *adj* о́блачный; (*liquid*) му́тный.

clout /klaʊt/ *vt* ударя́ть *impf*, уда́рить *pf*; *n* затре́щина; (*fig*) влия́ние.

clove /kləʊv/ *n* гвозди́ка; (*of garlic*) зубо́к.

cloven /'kləʊv(ə)n/ *adj* раздво́енный.

clover /'kləʊvə(r)/ *n* кле́вер.

clown /klaʊn/ *n* кло́ун.

club /klʌb/ *n* (*stick*) дуби́нка; *pl* (*cards*) тре́фы (треф) *pl*; (*association*) клуб; *vt* колоти́ть *impf*, по~ *pf* дуби́нкой; *vi*: ~ **together** скла́дываться *impf*, сложи́ться *pf*.

cluck /klʌk/ *vi* куда́хтать *impf*.

clue /kluː/ *n* (*evidence*) ули́ка; (*to puzzle*) ключ; (*hint*) намёк.

clump /klʌmp/ *n* гру́ппа.

clumsiness /'klʌmzɪnɪs/ *n* неуклю́жесть. **clumsy** /'klʌmzɪ/ *adj* неуклю́жий.

cluster /'klʌstə(r)/ *n* гру́ппа; *vi* собира́ться *impf*, собра́ться *pf* гру́ппами.

clutch /klʌtʃ/ *n* (*grasp*) хва́тка; ко́гти *m pl*; (*tech*) сцепле́ние; *vt* зажима́ть *impf*, зажа́ть *pf*; *vi*: ~ **at** хвата́ться *impf*, хвати́ться *pf* за+*acc*.

clutter /'klʌtə(r)/ *n* беспоря́док; *vt* загроможда́ть *impf*, загромозди́ть *pf*.

c/o *abbr* (*of* **care of**) по а́дресу +*gen*; че́рез+*acc*.

coach /kəʊtʃ/ *n* (*horse-drawn*) каре́та; (*rly*) ваго́н; (*bus*) авто́бус; (*tutor*) репети́тор; (*sport*) тре́нер; *vt* репети́ровать *impf*; тренирова́ть *impf*, на~ *pf*.

coagulate /kəʊ'ægjʊˌleɪt/ *vi* сгуща́ться *impf*, сгусти́ться *pf*.

coal /kəʊl/ *n* у́голь *m*; ~**mine** у́гольная ша́хта.

coalition /ˌkəʊə'lɪʃ(ə)n/ *n* коали́ция.

coarse /kɔːs/ *adj* гру́бый.

coast /kəʊst/ *n* побере́жье, бе́рег; ~ **guard** берегова́я охра́на; *vi* (*move without power*) дви́гаться *impf*, дви́нуться *pf* по ине́рции. **coastal** /-t(ə)l/ *adj* берегово́й, прибре́жный.

coat /kəʊt/ *n* пальто́ *neut indecl*; (*layer*) слой; (*animal*) шерсть, мех; ~ **of arms** герб; *vt* покрыва́ть *impf*, покры́ть *pf*.

coax /kəʊks/ *vt* угова́ривать *impf*, уговори́ть *pf*.

cob /kɒb/ *n* (*corn-*~) поча́ток кукуру́зы.

cobble /'kɒb(ə)l/ *n* булы́жник (*also collect*). **cobbled** /-b(ə)ld/ *adj* булы́жный.

cobbler /'kɒblə(r)/ *n* сапо́жник.

cobweb /'kɒbweb/ *n* паути́на.

Coca-Cola /ˌkəʊkə'kəʊlə/ *n* (*propr*) ко́ка-ко́ла.

cocaine /kə'keɪn/ *n* кокаи́н.

cock /kɒk/ *n* (*bird*) пету́х; (*tap*) кран; (*of gun*) куро́к; *vt* (*gun*) взводи́ть *impf*, взвести́ *pf* куро́к+*gen*.

cockerel /'kɒkər(ə)l/ *n* петушо́к.

cockle /'kɒk(ə)l/ *n* сердцеви́дка.

cockpit /'kɒkpɪt/ *n* (*aeron*) каби́на.

cockroach /'kɒkrəʊtʃ/ *n* тарака́н.

C

C

cocktail /ˈkɒkteɪl/ *n* коктéйль *m.*
cocky /ˈkɒkɪ/ *adj* чвáнный.
cocoa /ˈkəʊkəʊ/ *n* какáо *neut indecl.*
coco(a)nut /ˈkəʊkəˌnʌt/ *n* кокóс.
cocoon /kəˈkuːn/ *n* кóкон.
cod /kɒd/ *n* трескá.
code /kəʊd/ *n* (*of laws*) кóдекс; (*cipher*) код; *vt* шифровáть *impf*, за~ *pf.* **codify** /ˈkəʊdɪˌfaɪ/ *vt* кодифицúровать *impf* & *pf.*
co-education /ˌkəʊedjuːˈkeɪʃ(ə)n/ *n* совмéстное обучéние.
coefficient /ˌkəʊɪˈfɪʃ(ə)nt/ *n* коэффициéнт.
coerce /kəʊˈɜːs/ *vt* принуждáть *impf*, принýдить *pf.* **coercion** /kəʊˈɜːʃ(ə)n/ *n* принуждéние.
coexist /ˌkəʊɪgˈzɪst/ *vi* сосуществовáть *impf.* **coexistence** /-ˈzɪstəns/ *n* сосуществовáние.
coffee /ˈkɒfɪ/ *n* кóфе *m indecl*; **~-mill** *n* кофéйница; **~-pot** *n* кофéйник.
coffer /ˈkɒfə(r)/ *n pl* казнá.
coffin /ˈkɒfɪn/ *n* гроб.
cog /kɒg/ *n* зубéц. **cogwheel** *n* зубчáтое колесó.
cogent /ˈkəʊdʒ(ə)nt/ *adj* убедúтельный.
cohabit /kəʊˈhæbɪt/ *vi* сожúтельствовать *impf.*
coherent /kəʊˈhɪərənt/ *adj* свя́зный. **cohesion** /kəʊˈhiːʒ(ə)n/ *n* сплочённость. **cohesive** /kəʊˈhiːsɪv/ *adj* сплочённый.
coil /kɔɪl/ *vt* & *i* свёртывать(ся) *impf*, свернýть(ся) *pf* кольцóм; *n* кольцó; (*electr*) катýшка.
coin /kɔɪn/ *n* монéта; *vt* чекáнить *impf*, от~ *pf.*
coincide /ˌkəʊɪnˈsaɪd/ *vi* совпадáть *impf*, совпáсть *pf.* **coincidence** /kəʊˈɪnsɪdəns/ *n* совпадéние. **coincidental** /kəʊˌɪnsɪˈdent(ə)l/ *adj* случáйный.
coke /kəʊk/ *n* кокс.
colander /ˈkʌləndə(r)/ *n* дуршлáг.
cold /kəʊld/ *n* хóлод; (*med*) простýда, нáсморк; *adj* холóдный; **~-blooded** *adj* жестóкий; (*zool*) холоднокрóвный.
colic /ˈkɒlɪk/ *n* кóлики *f pl.*
collaborate /kəˈlæbəˌreɪt/ *vi* сотрýдничать *impf.* **collaboration** /kəˌlæbəˈreɪʃ(ə)n/ *n* сотрýдничество. **collaborator** /kəˈlæbəˌreɪtə(r)/ *n* сотрýдник, -ица; (*traitor*) коллаборационúст, -úстка.
collapse /kəˈlæps/ *vi* рýхнуть *pf*; *n* падéние; крушéние.
collar /ˈkɒlə(r)/ *n* воротнúк; (*dog's*) ошéйник; **~-bone** ключúца.
colleague /ˈkɒliːg/ *n* коллéга *m* & *f.*
collect /kəˈlekt/ *vt* собирáть *impf*, собрáть *pf*; (*as hobby*) коллекционúровать *impf*; (*fetch*) забирáть *impf*, забрáть *pf.* **collected** /-ˈlektɪd/ *adj* (*calm*) сóбранный; **~ works** собрáние сочинéний. **collection** /-ˈlekʃ(ə)n/ *n* (*stamps etc.*) коллéкция; (*church etc.*) сбор; (*post*) вы́емка. **collective** /-ˈlektɪv/ *n* коллектúв; *adj* коллектúвный; **~ farm** колхóз; **~ noun** собирáтельное существúтельное *sb.* **collectivization** /kəˌlektɪvaɪˈzeɪʃ(ə)n/ *n* коллективизáция. **collector** /-ˈlektə(r)/ *n* сбóрщик; коллекционéр.
college /ˈkɒlɪdʒ/ *n* коллéдж, учúлище.
collide /kəˈlaɪd/ *vi* стáлкиваться *impf*, столкнýться *pf.* **collision** /-ˈlɪʒ(ə)n/ *n* столкновéние.
colliery /ˈkɒlɪərɪ/ *n* каменноугóльная шáхта.
colloquial /kəˈləʊkwɪəl/ *adj* разговóрный. **colloquialism** /-ˌlɪz(ə)m/ *n* разговóрное выражéние.
collusion /kəˈluːʒ(ə)n/ *n* тáйный сгóвор.
colon[1] /ˈkəʊlən/ *n* (*anat*) тóлстая кишкá.
colon[2] /ˈkəʊlən/ *n* (*gram*) двоетóчие.
colonel /ˈkɜːn(ə)l/ *n* полкóвник.
colonial /kəˈləʊnɪəl/ *adj* колониáльный. **colonialism** /-ˌlɪz(ə)m/ *n* колониалúзм. **colonize** /ˈkɒləˌnaɪz/ *vt* колонизовáть *impf*

& *pf.* **colony** /ˈkɒlənɪ/ *n* коло́ния.

colossal /kəˈlɒs(ə)l/ *adj* колосса́льный.

colour /ˈkʌlə(r)/ *n* цвет, кра́ска; (*pl*) (*flag*) зна́мя *neut*; **~-blind** страда́ющий дальтони́змом; **~ film** цветна́я плёнка; *vt* раскра́шивать *impf*, раскра́сить *pf*; *vi* красне́ть *impf*, по~ *pf*. **coloured** /-ləd/ *adj* цветно́й. **colourful** /-fʊl/ *adj* я́ркий. **colourless** /-lɪs/ *adj* бесцве́тный.

colt /kəʊlt/ *n* жеребёнок.

column /ˈkɒləm/ *n* (*archit*, *mil*) коло́нна; (*of smoke etc.*) столб; (*of print*) столбе́ц. **columnist** /ˈkɒləmnɪst/ *n* журнали́ст.

coma /ˈkəʊmə/ *n* ко́ма.

comb /kəʊm/ *n* гребёнка; *vt* причёсывать *impf*, причеса́ть *pf*.

combat /ˈkɒmbæt/ *n* бой; *vt* боро́ться *impf* с+*instr*, про́тив+*gen*.

combination /ˌkɒmbɪˈneɪʃ(ə)n/ *n* сочета́ние; комбина́ция. **combine** *n* /ˈkɒmbaɪn/ комбина́т; (*~-harvester*) комба́йн; *vt* & *i* /kəmˈbaɪn/ совмеща́ть(ся) *impf*, совмести́ть(ся) *pf*. **combined** /kəmˈbaɪnd/ *adj* совме́стный.

combustion /kəmˈbʌstʃ(ə)n/ *n* горе́ние.

come /kʌm/ *vi* (*on foot*) приходи́ть *impf*, прийти́ *pf*; (*by transport*) приезжа́ть *impf*, прие́хать *pf*; **~ about** случа́ться *impf*, случи́ться *pf*; **~ across** случа́йно ната́лкиваться *impf*, натолкну́ться *pf* на+*acc*; **~ back** возвраща́ться *impf*, возврати́ться *pf*; **~ in** входи́ть *impf*, войти́ *pf*; **~ out** выходи́ть *impf*, вы́йти *pf*; **~ round** (*revive*) приходи́ть *impf*, прийти́ *pf* в себя́; (*visit*) заходи́ть *impf*, зайти́ *pf*; (*agree*) соглаша́ться *impf*, согласи́ться *pf*; **~ up to** (*approach*) подходи́ть *impf*, подойти́ *pf* к+*dat*; (*reach*) доходи́ть *impf*, дойти́ *pf* до+*gen*. **come-back** *n* возвраще́ние. **come-down** *n* униже́ние.

comedian /kəˈmiːdɪən/ *n* комедиа́нт. **comedy** /ˈkɒmɪdɪ/ *n* коме́дия.

comet /ˈkɒmɪt/ *n* коме́та.

comfort /ˈkʌmfət/ *n* комфо́рт; (*convenience*) удо́бство; (*consolation*) утеше́ние; *vt* утеша́ть *impf*, уте́шить *pf*. **comfortable** /ˈkʌmftəb(ə)l/ *adj* удо́бный.

comic /ˈkɒmɪk/ *adj* коми́ческий; *n* ко́мик; (*magazine*) ко́микс. **comical** /-k(ə)l/ *adj* смешно́й.

coming /ˈkʌmɪŋ/ *adj* сле́дующий.

comma /ˈkɒmə/ *n* запята́я *sb.*

command /kəˈmɑːnd/ *n* (*order*) прика́з; (*order*, *authority*) кома́нда; **have ~ of** (*master*) владе́ть *impf* +*instr*; *vt* прика́зывать *impf*, приказа́ть *pf* +*dat*; (*mil*) кома́ндовать *impf*, с~ *pf* +*instr.* **commandant** /ˌkɒmənˈdænt/ *n* коменда́нт. **commandeer** /ˌkɒmənˈdɪə(r)/ *vt* реквизи́ровать *impf* & *pf*. **commander** /kəˈmɑːndə(r)/ *n* команди́р; **~-in-chief** главнокома́ндующий *sb.* **commandment** /kəˈmɑːndmənt/ *n* за́поведь. **commando** /kəˈmɑːndəʊ/ *n* деса́нтник.

commemorate /kəˈmeməˌreɪt/ *vt* ознамено́вывать *impf*, ознаменова́ть *pf*. **commemoration** /kəˌmeməˈreɪʃ(ə)n/ *n* ознаменова́ние. **commemorative** /kəˈmemərəˌtɪv/ *adj* па́мятный.

commence /kəˈmens/ *vt* & *i* начина́ть(ся) *impf*, нача́ть(ся) *pf*. **commencement** /-mənt/ *n* нача́ло.

commend /kəˈmend/ *vt* хвали́ть *impf*, по~ *pf*; (*recommend*) рекомендова́ть *impf* & *pf*. **commendable** /-dəb(ə)l/ *adj* похва́льный. **commendation** /ˌkɒmenˈdeɪʃ(ə)n/ *n* похвала́.

commensurate /kəˈmenʃərət/ *adj* соразме́рный.

comment /ˈkɒment/ *n* замеча́ние; *vi* де́лать *impf*, с~ *pf* замеча́ния; **~ on** комменти́ровать *impf* & *pf*, про~ *pf*. **commentary** /-məntərɪ/ *n* коммента́рий. **com-**

C

mentator /-ˌteɪtə(r)/ *n* коммента́тор.

commerce /ˈkɒmɜːs/ *n* комме́рция. **commercial** /kəˈmɜːʃ(ə)l/ *adj* торго́вый; *n* рекла́ма.

C

commiserate /kəˈmɪzəˌreɪt/ *vi*: ~ **with** соболе́зновать *impf* +*dat*. **commiseration** /-ˈreɪʃ(ə)n/ *n* соболе́знование.

commission /kəˈmɪʃ(ə)n/ *n* (*order for work*) зака́з; (*agent's fee*) комиссио́нные *sb*; (*of inquiry etc.*) коми́ссия; (*mil*) офице́рское зва́ние; *vt* зака́зывать *impf*, заказа́ть *pf*. **commissionaire** /kəˌmɪʃ(ə)ˈneə(r)/ *n* швейца́р. **commissioner** /kəˈmɪʃənə(r)/ *n* комисса́р.

commit /kəˈmɪt/ *vt* соверша́ть *impf*, соверши́ть *pf*; ~ **o.s.** обя́зываться *impf*, обяза́ться *pf*. **commitment** /-mənt/ *n* обяза́тельство.

committee /kəˈmɪtɪ/ *n* комите́т.

commodity /kəˈmɒdɪtɪ/ *n* това́р.

commodore /ˈkɒməˌdɔː(r)/ *n* (*officer*) коммодо́р.

common /ˈkɒmən/ *adj* о́бщий; (*ordinary*) просто́й; *n* общи́нная земля́; ~ **sense** здра́вый смысл. **commonly** /-lɪ/ *adv* обы́чно. **commonplace** *adj* бана́льный. **commonwealth** *n* содру́жество.

commotion /kəˈməʊʃ(ə)n/ *n* сумато́ха.

communal /ˈkɒmjʊn(ə)l/ *adj* общи́нный, коммуна́льный. **commune** *n* /ˈkɒmjuːn/ комму́на; *vi* /kəˈmjuːn/ обща́ться *impf*.

communicate /kəˈmjuːnɪˌkeɪt/ *vt* передава́ть *impf*, переда́ть *pf*; сообща́ть *impf*, сообщи́ть *pf*. **communication** /-ˈkeɪʃ(ə)n/ *n* сообще́ние; связь. **communicative** /kəˈmjuːnɪkətɪv/ *adj* разгово́рчивый.

communion /kəˈmjuːnɪən/ *n* (*eccl*) прича́стие.

communiqué /kəˈmjuːnɪˌkeɪ/ *n* коммюнике́ *neut indecl*.

Communism /ˈkɒmjʊˌnɪz(ə)m/ *n* коммуни́зм. **Communist** /ˈkɒmjʊnɪst/ *n* коммуни́ст, ~ка; *adj* коммунисти́ческий.

community /kəˈmjuːnɪtɪ/ *n* о́бщина.

commute /kəˈmjuːt/ *vt* заменя́ть *impf*, замени́ть *pf*; (*travel*) добира́ться *impf*, добра́ться *pf* тра́нспортом. **commuter** /-tə(r)/ *n* регуля́рный пассажи́р.

compact[1] /ˈkɒmpækt/ *n* (*agreement*) соглаше́ние.

compact[2] /kəmˈpækt/ *adj* компа́ктный; ~ **disc** /ˈkɒmpækt dɪsk/ компа́кт-ди́ск; *n* /ˈkɒmpækt/ пу́дреница.

companion /kəmˈpænjən/ *n* това́рищ; (*handbook*) спра́вочник. **companionable** /-nəb(ə)l/ *adj* общи́тельный. **companionship** /-ʃɪp/*n* дру́жеское обще́ние. **company** /ˈkʌmpənɪ/ *n* о́бщество, (*also firm*) компа́ния; (*theat*) тру́ппа; (*mil*) ро́та.

comparable /ˈkɒmpərəb(ə)l/ *adj* сравни́мый. **comparative** /kəmˈpærətɪv/ *adj* сравни́тельный; *n* сравни́тельная сте́пень. **compare** /kəmˈpeə(r)/ *vt & i* сра́внивать(ся) *impf*, сравни́ть(ся) *pf* (**to, with** с+*instr*). **comparison** /kəmˈpærɪs(ə)n/ *n* сравне́ние.

compartment /kəmˈpɑːtmənt/ *n* отделе́ние; (*rly*) купе́ *neut indecl*.

compass /ˈkʌmpəs/ *n* ко́мпас; *pl* ци́ркуль *m*.

compassion /kəmˈpæʃ(ə)n/ *n* сострада́ние. **compassionate** /-nət/ *adj* сострада́тельный.

compatibility /kəmˌpætəˈbɪlɪtɪ/ *n* совмести́мость. **compatible** /kəmˈpætəb(ə)l/ *adj* совмести́мый.

compatriot /kəmˈpætrɪət/ *n* сооте́чественник, -ица.

compel /kəmˈpel/ *vt* заставля́ть *impf*, заста́вить *pf*.

compensate /ˈkɒmpenˌseɪt/ *vt* компенси́ровать *impf & pf* (**for** за+*acc*). **compensation** /-ˈseɪʃ(ə)n/ *n* компенса́ция.

compete /kəmˈpiːt/ *vi* конкури́ровать *impf*; соревнова́ться *impf*.

competence /ˈkɒmpɪtəns/ *n* компете́нтность. **competent** /-tənt/ *adj* компете́нтный.

competition /ˌkɒmpəˈtɪʃ(ə)n/ *n* (*contest*) соревнова́ние, состяза́ние; (*rivalry*) конкуре́нция. **competitive** /kəmˈpetɪtɪv/ *adj* (*comm*) конкурентоспосо́бный. **competitor** /kəmˈpetɪtə(r)/ *n* конкуре́нт, ~ка.

compilation /ˌkɒmpɪˈleɪʃ(ə)n/ *n* (*result*) компиля́ция; (*act*) составле́ние. **compile** /kəmˈpaɪl/ *vt* составля́ть *impf*, соста́вить *pf*. **compiler** /kəmˈpaɪlə(r)/ *n* состави́тель *m*, ~ница.

complacency /kəmˈpleɪsənsɪ/ *n* самодово́льство. **complacent** /kəmˈpleɪs(ə)nt/ *adj* самодово́льный.

complain /kəmˈpleɪn/ *vi* жа́ловаться *impf*, по~ *pf*. **complaint** /-ˈpleɪnt/ *n* жа́лоба.

complement /ˈkɒmplɪmənt/ *n* дополне́ние; (*full number*) (ли́чный) соста́в; *vt* дополня́ть *impf*, допо́лнить *pf*. **complementary** /ˌkɒmplɪˈmentərɪ/ *adj* дополни́тельный.

complete /kəmˈpliːt/ *vt* заверша́ть *impf*, заверши́ть *pf*; *adj* (*entire, thorough*) по́лный; (*finished*) зако́нченный. **completion** /-ˈpliːʃ(ə)n/ *n* заверше́ние.

complex /ˈkɒmpleks/ *adj* сло́жный; *n* ко́мплекс. **complexity** /kəmˈpleksɪtɪ/ *n* сло́жность.

complexion /kəmˈplekʃ(ə)n/ *n* цвет лица́.

compliance /kəmˈplaɪəns/ *n* усту́пчивость. **compliant** /-ˈplaɪənt/ *adj* усту́пчивый.

complicate /ˈkɒmplɪˌkeɪt/ *vt* осложня́ть *impf*, осложни́ть *pf*. **complicated** /-tɪd/ *adj* сло́жный. **complication** /ˌkɒmplɪˈkeɪʃ(ə)n/ *n* осложне́ние.

complicity /kəmˈplɪsɪtɪ/ *n* соуча́стие.

compliment /ˈkɒmplɪmənt/ *n* комплиме́нт; *pl* приве́т; *vt* говори́ть *impf* комплиме́нт(ы) +*dat*; хвали́ть *impf*, по~ *pf*. **complimentary** /ˌkɒmplɪˈmentərɪ/ *adj* ле́стный; (*free*) беспла́тный.

comply /kəmˈplaɪ/ *vi*: ~ **with** (*fulfil*) исполня́ть *impf*, испо́лнить *pf*; (*submit to*) подчиня́ться *impf*, подчини́ться *pf* +*dat*.

component /kəmˈpəʊnənt/ *n* дета́ль; *adj* составно́й.

compose /kəmˈpəʊz/ *vt* (*music etc.*) сочиня́ть *impf*, сочини́ть *pf*; (*draft; constitute*) составля́ть *impf*, соста́вить *pf*. **composed** /-ˈpəʊzd/ *adj* споко́йный; **be ~ of** состоя́ть *impf* из+*gen*. **composer** /-ˈpəʊzə(r)/ *n* компози́тор. **composition** /ˌkɒmpəˈzɪʃ(ə)n/ *n* сочине́ние; (*make-up*) соста́в.

compost /ˈkɒmpɒst/ *n* компо́ст.

composure /kəmˈpəʊʒə(r)/ *n* самооблада́ние.

compound¹ /ˈkɒmpaʊnd/ *n* (*chem*) соедине́ние; *adj* сло́жный.

compound² /ˈkɒmpaʊnd/ *n* (*enclosure*) огоро́женное ме́сто.

comprehend /ˌkɒmprɪˈhend/ *vt* понима́ть *impf*, поня́ть *pf*. **comprehensible** /-ˈhensɪb(ə)l/ *adj* поня́тный. **comprehension** /-ˈhenʃ(ə)n/ *n* понима́ние. **comprehensive** /-ˈhensɪv/ *adj* всеобъе́млющий; ~ **school** общеобразова́тельная шко́ла.

compress /kəmˈpres/ *vt* сжима́ть *impf*, сжать *pf*. **compressed** /-ˈprest/ *adj* сжа́тый.

comprise /kəmˈpraɪz/ *vt* состоя́ть *impf* из+*gen*.

compromise /ˈkɒmprəˌmaɪz/ *n* компроми́сс; *vt* компромети́ровать *impf*, с~ *pf*; *vi* идти́ *impf*, пойти́ *pf* на компроми́сс.

compulsion /kəmˈpʌlʃ(ə)n/ *n* принужде́ние. **compulsory** /-ˈpʌlsərɪ/ *adj* обяза́тельный.

compunction /kəmˈpʌŋkʃ(ə)n/ *n* угрызе́ние со́вести.

computer /kəmˈpjuːtə(r)/ *n* компью́тер. ~ **game** компью́терная игра́; ~ **science** электро́нно-вычисли́тельная нау́ка.

comrade /ˈkɒmreɪd/ *n* това́рищ.

C

comradeship *n* това́рищество.
con[1] /kɒn/ *see* **pro**[1]
con[2] /kɒn/ *vt* надува́ть *impf*, наду́ть *pf.*
concave /'kɒnkeɪv/ *adj* во́гнутый.
conceal /kən'siːl/ *vt* скрыва́ть *impf*, скрыть *pf.*
concede /kən'siːd/ *vt* уступа́ть *impf*, уступи́ть *pf*; (*admit*) признава́ть *impf*, призна́ть *pf*; (*goal*) пропуска́ть *impf*, пропусти́ть *pf.*
conceit /kən'siːt/ *n* самомне́ние. **conceited** /kən'siːtɪd/ *adj* самовлюблённый.
conceivable /kən'siːvəb(ə)l/ *adj* мы́слимый. **conceive** /kən'siːv/ *vt* (*plan, imagine*) заду́мывать *impf*, заду́мать *pf*; (*biol*) зачина́ть *impf* зача́ть *pf*; *vi* забере́менеть *pf.*
concentrate /'kɒnsən,treɪt/ *vt & i* сосредото́чивать(ся) *impf*, сосредото́чить(ся) *pf* (**on** на +*prep*); *vt* (*also chem*) концентри́ровать *impf*, с~ *pf.* **concentration** /,kɒnsən'treɪʃ(ə)n/ *n* сосредото́ченность, концентра́ция.
concept /'kɒnsept/ *n* поня́тие. **conception** /kən'sepʃ(ə)n/ *n* поня́тие; (*biol*) зача́тие.
concern /kən'sɜːn/ *n* (*worry*) забо́та; (*comm*) предприя́тие; *vt* каса́ться *impf* +*gen*; **~ o.s. with** занима́ться *impf*, заня́ться *pf* +*instr.* **concerned** /-'sɜːnd/ *adj* озабо́ченный; **as far as I'm ~** что каса́ется меня́. **concerning** /-'sɜːnɪŋ/ *prep* относи́тельно+*gen.*
concert /'kɒnsət/ *n* конце́рт. **concerted** /kən'sɜːtɪd/ *adj* согласо́ванный.
concertina /,kɒnsə'tiːnə/ *n* гармо́ника.
concession /kən'seʃ(ə)n/ *n* усту́пка; (*econ*) конце́ссия. **concessionary** /-nərɪ/ *adj* концессио́нный.
conciliation /kən,sɪlɪ'eɪʃ(ə)n/ *n* примире́ние. **conciliatory** /kən'sɪlɪətərɪ/ *adj* примири́тельный.
concise /kən'saɪs/ *adj* кра́ткий. **conciseness** /-nɪs/ *n* кра́ткость.
conclude /kən'kluːd/ *vt* заключа́ть *impf*, заключи́ть *pf.* **concluding** /-dɪŋ/ *adj* заключи́тельный. **conclusion** /-'kluːʒ(ə)n/ *n* заключе́ние; (*deduction*) вы́вод. **conclusive** /-'kluːsɪv/ *adj* реша́ющий.
concoct /kən'kɒkt/ *vt* стря́пать *impf*, со~ *pf.* **concoction** /-'kɒkʃ(ə)n/ *n* стряпня́.
concourse /'kɒŋkɔːs/ *n* зал.
concrete /'kɒŋkriːt/ *n* бето́н; *adj* бето́нный; (*fig*) конкре́тный.
concur /kən'kɜː(r)/ *vi* соглаша́ться *impf*, согласи́ться *pf.* **concurrent** /-'kʌrənt/ *adj* одновре́ме́нный.
concussion /kən'kʌʃ(ə)n/ *n* сотрясе́ние.
condemn /kən'dem/ *vt* осужда́ть *impf*, осуди́ть *pf*; (*as unfit for use*) бракова́ть *impf*, за~ *pf.* **condemnation** /,kɒndem'neɪʃ(ə)n/ *n* осужде́ние.
condensation /,kɒnden'seɪʃ(ə)n/ *n* конденса́ция. **condense** /kən'dens/ *vt* (*liquid etc.*) конденси́ровать *impf & pf*; (*text etc.*) сокраща́ть *impf*, сократи́ть *pf.* **condensed** /kən'denst/ *adj* сжа́тый; (*milk*) сгущённый. **condenser** /kən'densə(r)/ *n* конденса́тор.
condescend /,kɒndɪ'send/ *vi* снисходи́ть *impf*, снизойти́ *pf.* **condescending** /-'sendɪŋ/ *adj* снисходи́тельный. **condescension** /-'senʃ(ə)n/ *n* снисхожде́ние.
condiment /'kɒndɪmənt/ *n* припра́ва.
condition /kən'dɪʃ(ə)n/ *n* усло́вие; (*state*) состоя́ние; *vt* (*determine*) обусло́вливать *impf*, обусло́вить *pf*; (*psych*) приуча́ть *impf*, приучи́ть *pf.* **conditional** /-'dɪʃən(ə)l/ *adj* усло́вный.
condolence /kən'dəʊləns/ *n*: *pl* соболе́знование.
condom /'kɒndɒm/ *n* презервати́в.
condone /kən'dəʊn/ *vt* закрыва́ть *impf*, закры́ть *pf* глаза́ на+*acc.*
conducive /kən'djuːsɪv/ *adj* спо-

со́бствующий (**to** +*dat*).
conduct *n* /'kɒndʌkt/ (*behaviour*) поведе́ние; *vt* /kən'dʌkt/ вести́ *impf*, по~, про~ *pf*; (*mus*) дирижи́ровать *impf* +*instr*; (*phys*) проводи́ть *impf*. **conduction** /kən'dʌkʃ(ə)n/ *n* проводи́мость. **conductor** /kən'dʌktə(r)/ *n* (*bus*) конду́ктор; (*phys*) проводни́к; (*mus*) дирижёр.
conduit /'kɒndɪt/ *n* трубопрово́д.
cone /kəʊn/ *n* ко́нус; (*bot*) ши́шка.
confectioner /kən'fekʃənə(r)/ *n* конди́тер; **~'s** (*shop*) конди́терская *sb*. **confectionery** /-nərɪ/ *n* конди́терские изде́лия *neut pl*.
confederation /kənˌfedə'reɪʃ(ə)n/ *n* конфедера́ция.
confer /kən'fɜː(r)/ *vt* присужда́ть *impf*, присуди́ть (**on** +*dat*) *pf*; *vi* совеща́ться *impf*. **conference** /'kɒnfərəns/ *n* совеща́ние; конфере́нция.
confess /kən'fes/ *vt* & *i* (*acknowledge*) признава́ть(ся) *impf*, призна́ть(ся) *pf* (**to** в+*prep*); (*eccl*) испове́довать(ся) *impf* & *pf*. **confession** /-'feʃ(ə)n/ *n* призна́ние; и́споведь. **confessor** /-'fesə(r)/ *n* духовни́к.
confidant(e) /ˌkɒnfɪ'dænt/ *n* бли́зкий собесе́дник. **confide** /kən'faɪd/ *vt* доверя́ть *impf*, дове́рить *pf*; ~ **in** дели́ться *impf*, по~ *pf* с+*instr*. **confidence** /'kɒnfɪd(ə)ns/ *n* (*trust*) дове́рие; (*certainty*) уве́ренность; (*self-~*) самоуве́ренность. **confident** /'kɒnfɪd(ə)nt/ *adj* уве́ренный. **confidential** /ˌkɒnfɪ'denʃ(ə)l/ *adj* секре́тный.
confine /kən'faɪn/ *vt* ограни́чивать *impf*, ограни́чить *pf*; (*shut in*) заключа́ть *impf*, заключи́ть *pf*. **confinement** /-mənt/ *n* заключе́ние. **confines** /'kɒnfaɪnz/ *n pl* преде́лы *m pl*.
confirm /kən'fɜːm/ *vt* подтвержда́ть *impf*, подтверди́ть *pf*. **confirmation** /ˌkɒnfə'meɪʃ(ə)n/ *n* подтвержде́ние; (*eccl*) конфирма́ция. **confirmed** /-'fɜːmd/ *adj* закорене́лый.
confiscate /'kɒnfɪˌskeɪt/ *vt* конфискова́ть *impf* & *pf*. **confiscation** /ˌkɒnfɪ'skeɪʃ(ə)n/ *n* конфиска́ция.
conflict *n* /'kɒnflɪkt/ конфли́кт; противоре́чие; *vi*: /kən'flɪkt/ ~ **with** противоре́чить *impf* +*dat*. **conflicting** /kən'flɪktɪŋ/ *adj* противоречи́вый.
conform /kən'fɔːm/ *vi*: ~ **to** подчиня́ться *impf*, подчини́ться *pf* +*dat*. **conformity** /-'fɔːmɪtɪ/ *n* соотве́тствие; (*compliance*) подчине́ние.
confound /kən'faʊnd/ *vt* сбива́ть *impf*, сбить *pf* с то́лку. **confounded** /-dɪd/ *adj* прокля́тый.
confront /kən'frʌnt/ *vt* стоя́ть *impf* лицо́м к лицу́ с+*instr*; ~ (*person*) **with** ста́вить *impf*, по~ *pf* лицо́м к лицу́ с+*instr*. **confrontation** /ˌkɒnfrʌn'teɪʃ(ə)n/ *n* конфронта́ция.
confuse /kən'fjuːz/ *vt* смуща́ть *impf*, смути́ть *pf*; (*also mix up*) пу́тать *impf*, за~, с~ *pf*. **confusion** /-'fjuːʒ(ə)n/ *n* смуще́ние; пу́таница.
congeal /kən'dʒiːl/ *vt* густе́ть *impf*, за~ *pf*; (*blood*) свёртываться *impf*, сверну́ться *pf*.
congenial /kən'dʒiːnɪəl/ *adj* прия́тный.
congenital /kən'dʒenɪt(ə)l/ *adj* врождённый.
congested /kən'dʒestɪd/ *adj* перепо́лненный. **congestion** /-'dʒestʃ(ə)n/ *n* (*traffic*) зато́р.
congratulate /kən'grætjʊˌleɪt/ *vt* поздравля́ть *impf*, поздра́вить *pf* (**on** с+*instr*). **congratulation** /-'leɪʃ(ə)n/ *n* поздравле́ние; **~s!** поздравля́ю!
congregate /'kɒŋgrɪˌgeɪt/ *vi* собира́ться *impf*, собра́ться *pf*. **congregation** /-'geɪʃ(ə)n/ *n* (*eccl*) прихожа́не (-н) *pl*.
congress /'kɒŋgres/ *n* съезд. **Congressman** *n* конгрессме́н.
conic(al) /'kɒnɪk(ə)l/ *adj* кони́ческий.

C

C

conifer /'kɒnɪfə(r)/ *n* хвóйное дéрево. **coniferous** /kə'nɪfərəs/ *adj* хвóйный.
conjecture /kən'dʒektʃə(r)/ *n* догáдка; *vt* гадáть *impf.*
conjugal /'kɒndʒʊg(ə)l/ *adj* супрýжеский.
conjugate /'kɒndʒʊˌgeɪt/ *vt* спрягáть *impf*, про~ *pf.* **conjugation** /-'geɪʃ(ə)n/ *n* спряжéние.
conjunction /kən'dʒʌŋkʃ(ə)n/ *n* (*gram*) союз; **in ~ with** совмéстно с+*instr.*
conjure /'kʌndʒə(r)/ *vi*: **~ up** (*in mind*) вызывáть *impf*, вы́звать *pf* в воображéнии. **conjurer** /-rə(r)/ *n* фóкусник. **conjuring trick** /-rɪŋ/ *n* фóкус.
connect /kə'nekt/ *vt & i* свя́зывать(ся) *impf*, связáть(ся) *pf*; соединя́ть(ся) *impf*, соедини́ть(ся) *pf.* **connected** /-'nektɪd/ *adj* свя́занный. **connection, -exion** /-'nekʃ(ə)n/ *n* связь; (*rly etc.*) пересáдка.
connivance /kə'naɪv(ə)ns/ *n* попусти́тельство. **connive** /kə'naɪv/ *vi*: **~ at** попусти́тельствовать *impf* +*dat.*
connoisseur /ˌkɒnə'sɜː(r)/ *n* знатóк.
conquer /'kɒŋkə(r)/ *vt* (*country*) завоёвывать *impf*, завоевáть *pf*; (*enemy*) побеждáть *impf*, победи́ть *pf*; (*habit*) преодолевáть *impf*, преодолéть *pf.* **conqueror** /'kɒŋkərə(r)/ *n* завоевáтель *m.* **conquest** /'kɒŋkwest/ *n* завоевáние.
conscience /'kɒnʃ(ə)ns/ *n* сóвесть. **conscientious** /ˌkɒnʃɪ'enʃ(ə)s/ *adj* добросóвестный. **conscious** /'kɒnʃ(ə)s/ *adj* сознáтельный; *predic* в сознáнии; **be ~ of** сознавáть *impf* +*acc.* **consciousness** /'kɒnʃəsnɪs/ *n* сознáние.
conscript *vt* /kən'skrɪpt/ призывáть *impf*, призвáть *pf* на воéнную слýжбу; *n* /'kɒnskrɪpt/ призывни́к. **conscription** /kən'skrɪpʃ(ə)n/ *n* вóинская пови́нность.
consecrate /'kɒnsɪˌkreɪt/ *vt* освящáть *impf*, освяти́ть *pf.* **consecration** /-'kreɪʃ(ə)n/ *n* освящéние.
consecutive /kən'sekjʊtɪv/ *adj* послéдовательный.
consensus /kən'sensəs/ *n* соглáсие.
consent /kən'sent/ *vi* соглашáться *impf*, согласи́ться *pf* (**to** +*inf*, на+*acc*); *n* соглáсие.
consequence /'kɒnsɪkwəns/ *n* послéдствие; **of great ~** большóго значéния; **of some ~** довóльно вáжный. **consequent** /-kwənt/ *adj* вытекáющий. **consequential** /ˌkɒnsɪ'kwenʃ(ə)l/ *adj* вáжный. **consequently** /'kɒnsɪˌkwəntlɪ/ *adv* слéдовательно.
conservation /ˌkɒnsə'veɪʃ(ə)n/ *n* сохранéние; (*of nature*) охрáна прирóды. **conservative** /kən'sɜːvətɪv/ *adj* консервати́вный; *n* консервáтор. **conservatory** /kən'sɜːvətərɪ/ *n* оранжерéя. **conserve** /kən'sɜːv/ *vt* сохраня́ть *impf*, сохрани́ть *pf.*
consider /kən'sɪdə(r)/ *vt* (*think over*) обдýмывать *impf*, обдýмать *pf*; (*examine*) рассмáтривать *impf*, рассмотрéть *pf*; (*regard as, be of opinion that*) считáть *impf*, счесть *pf* +*instr*, за+*acc*, что; (*take into account*) считáться *impf* с+*instr.* **considerable** /-'sɪdərəb(ə)l/ *adj* значи́тельный. **considerate** /-'sɪdərət/ *adj* внимáтельный. **consideration** /kənˌsɪdə'reɪʃ(ə)n/ *n* рассмотрéние; внимáние; (*factor*) фáктор; **take into ~** принимáть *impf*, приня́ть *pf* во внимáние. **considering** /-'sɪdərɪŋ/ *prep* принимáя +*acc* во внимáние.
consign /kən'saɪn/ *vt* передавáть *impf*, передáть *pf.* **consignment** /-'saɪnmənt/ *n* (*goods*) пáртия; (*consigning*) отпрáвка товáров.
consist /kən'sɪst/ *vi*: **~ of** состоя́ть *impf* из+*gen.* **consistency** /-'sɪstənsɪ/ *n* послéдовательность; (*density*) консистéнция. **consistent** /-'sɪstənt/ *adj* послé-

довательный; ~ **with** совместимый с+*instr.*
consolation /ˌkɒnsəˈleɪʃ(ə)n/ *n* утешение. **console**[1] /kənˈsəʊl/ *vt* утешать *impf*, утешить *pf.*
console[2] /ˈkɒnsəʊl/ *n* (*control panel*) пульт управления.
consolidate /kənˈsɒlɪˌdeɪt/ *vt* укреплять *impf*, укрепить *pf.* **consolidation** /-ˈdeɪʃ(ə)n/ *n* укрепление.
consonant /ˈkɒnsənənt/ *n* согласный *sb.*
consort /ˈkɒnsɔːt/ *n* супруг, ~а.
conspicuous /kənˈspɪkjʊəs/ *adj* заметный.
conspiracy /kənˈspɪrəsɪ/ *n* заговор. **conspirator** /-ˈspɪrətə(r)/ *n* заговорщик, -ица. **conspiratorial** /-ˌspɪrəˈtɔːrɪəl/ *adj* заговорщицкий. **conspire** /-ˈspaɪə(r)/ *vi* устраивать *impf*, устроить *pf* заговор.
constable /ˈkʌnstəb(ə)l/ *n* полицейский *sb.*
constancy /ˈkɒnstənsɪ/ *n* постоянство. **constant** /-st(ə)nt/ *adj* постоянный. **constantly** /-st(ə)ntlɪ/ *adv* постоянно.
constellation /ˌkɒnstəˈleɪʃ(ə)n/ *n* созвездие.
consternation /ˌkɒnstəˈneɪʃ(ə)n/ *n* тревога.
constipation /ˌkɒnstɪˈpeɪʃ(ə)n/ *n* запор.
constituency /kənˈstɪtjʊənsɪ/ *n* избирательный округ. **constituent** /-ˈstɪtjʊənt/ *n* (*component*) составная часть; (*voter*) избиратель *m*; *adj* составной. **constitute** /ˈkɒnstɪˌtjuːt/ *vt* составлять *impf*, составить *pf.* **constitution** /ˌkɒnstɪˈtjuːʃ(ə)n/ *n* (*polit*, *med*) конституция; (*composition*) составление. **constitutional** /ˌkɒnstɪˈtjuːʃən(ə)l/ *adj* (*polit*) конституционный.
constrain /kənˈstreɪn/ *vt* принуждать *impf*, принудить *pf.* **constrained** /-ˈstreɪnd/ *adj* (*inhibited*) стеснённый. **constraint** /-ˈstreɪnt/ *n* принуждение; (*inhibition*) стеснение.
constrict /kənˈstrɪkt/ *vt* (*compress*) сжимать *impf*, сжать *pf*; (*narrow*) суживать *impf*, сузить *pf.* **constriction** /-ˈstrɪkʃ(ə)n/ *n* сжатие; сужение.
construct /kənˈstrʌkt/ *vt* строить *impf*, по~ *pf.* **construction** /-ˈstrʌkʃ(ə)n/ *n* строительство; (*also gram*) конструкция; (*interpretation*) истолкование; ~ **site** стройка. **constructive** /-ˈstrʌktɪv/ *adj* конструктивный.
construe /kənˈstruː/ *vt* истолковывать *impf*, истолковать *pf.*
consul /ˈkɒns(ə)l/ *n* консул. **consulate** /ˈkɒnsjʊlət/ *n* консульство.
consult /kənˈsʌlt/ *vt* советоваться *impf*, по~ *pf* с+*instr.* **consultant** /-ˈsʌlt(ə)nt/ *n* консультант. **consultation** /ˌkɒnsəlˈteɪʃ(ə)n/ *n* консультация.
consume /kənˈsjuːm/ *vt* потреблять *impf*, потребить *pf*; (*eat or drink*) съедать *impf*, съесть *pf.* **consumer** /-ˈsjuːmə(r)/ *n* потребитель *m*; ~ **goods** товары *m pl* широкого потребления.
consummate /ˈkɒnsjʊˌmeɪt/ *vt* завершать *impf*, завершить *pf*; ~ **a marriage** осуществлять *impf*, осуществить *pf* брачные отношения. **consummation** /-ˈmeɪʃ(ə)n/ *n* завершение; (*of marriage*) осуществление.
consumption /kənˈsʌmpʃ(ə)n/ *n* потребление.
contact /ˈkɒntækt/ *n* контакт; (*person*) связь; ~ **lens** контактная линза; *vt* связываться *impf*, связаться *pf* с+*instr.*
contagious /kənˈteɪdʒəs/ *adj* заразный.
contain /kənˈteɪn/ *vt* содержать *impf*; (*restrain*) сдерживать *impf*, сдержать *pf.* **container** /-nə(r)/ *n* (*vessel*) сосуд; (*transport*) контейнер.
contaminate /kənˈtæmɪˌneɪt/ *vt* загрязнять *impf*, загрязнить *pf.*

C

C

contamination /-'neɪʃ(ə)n/ *n* загрязнéние.

contemplate /'kɒntəm,pleɪt/ *vt* (*gaze*) созерцáть *impf*; размышлять *impf*; (*consider*) предполагáть *impf*, предположи́ть *pf*. **contemplation** /-'pleɪʃ(ə)n/ *n* созерцáние; размышлéние. **contemplative** /kən'templətɪv/ *adj* созерцáтельный.

contemporary /kən'tempərərɪ/ *n* совремéнник; *adj* совремéнный.

contempt /kən'tempt/ *n* презрéние; **~ of court** неуважéние к судý; **hold in ~** презирáть *impf*. **contemptible** /-'temptɪb(ə)l/ *adj* презрéнный. **contemptuous** /-'temptjʊəs/ *adj* презри́тельный.

contend /kən'tend/ *vi* (*compete*) состязáться *impf*; **~ for** оспáривать *impf*; **~ with** справля́ться *impf*, спрáвиться *pf* с+*instr*; *vt* утверждáть *impf*. **contender** /-də(r)/ *n* претендéнт.

content[1] /'kɒntent/ *n* содержáние; *pl* содержи́мое *sb*; **(table of) ~s** содержáние.

content[2] /kən'tent/ *predic* довóлен (-льна); *vt*: **~ o.s. with** довóльствоваться *impf*, у~ *pf* +*instr*. **contented** /-'tentɪd/ *adj* довóльный.

contention /kən'tenʃ(ə)n/ *n* (*claim*) утверждéние. **contentious** /-'tenʃəs/ *adj* спóрный.

contest *n* /'kɒntest/ состязáние; *vt* /kən'test/ (*dispute*) оспáривать *impf*, оспóрить *pf*. **contestant** /kən'test(ə)nt/ *n* учáстник, -ица, состязáния.

context /'kɒntekst/ *n* контéкст.

continent /'kɒntɪnənt/ *n* матери́к. **continental** /,kɒntɪ'nent(ə)l/ *adj* материкóвый.

contingency /kən'tɪndʒənsɪ/ *n* возмóжный слýчай; **~ plan** вариáнт плáна. **contingent** /-'tɪndʒənt/ *adj* случáйный; *n* контингéнт.

continual /kən'tɪnjʊəl/ *adj* непрестáнный. **continuation** /-,tɪnjʊ'eɪʃ(ə)n/ *n* продолжéние. **continue** /-'tɪnjuː/ *vt* & *i* продолжáть(ся) *impf*, продóлжить(ся) *pf*. **continuous** /-'tɪnjʊəs/ *adj* непреры́вный.

contort /kən'tɔːt/ *vt* искажáть *impf*, искази́ть *pf*. **contortion** /-'tɔːʃ(ə)n/ *n* искажéние.

contour /'kɒntʊə(r)/ *n* кóнтур; **~ line** горизонтáль.

contraband /'kɒntrə,bænd/ *n* контрабáнда.

contraception /,kɒntrə'sepʃ(ə)n/ *n* предупреждéние зачáтия. **contraceptive** /-'septɪv/ *n* противозачáточное срéдство; *adj* противозачáточный.

contract *n* /'kɒntrækt/ контрáкт, дóговóр; *vi* /kən'trækt/ (*make a* **~**) заключáть *impf*, заключи́ть *pf* контрáкт; *vt* & *i* /kən'trækt/ (*shorten*, *reduce*) сокращáть(ся) *impf*, сократи́ть(ся) *pf*; *vt* (*illness*) заболевáть *impf*, заболéть *pf* +*instr*. **contraction** /kən'trækʃ(ə)n/ *n* сокращéние; *pl* (*med*) схвáтки *f pl*. **contractor** /kən'træktə(r)/ *n* подря́дчик.

contradict /,kɒntrə'dɪkt/ *vt* противорéчить *impf* +*dat*. **contradiction** /-'dɪkʃ(ə)n/ *n* противорéчие. **contradictory** /-'dɪktərɪ/ *adj* противоречи́вый.

contraflow /'kɒntrəfləʊ/ *n* встрéчное движéние.

contralto /kən'træltəʊ/ *n* контрáльто (*voice*) *neut* & (*person*) *f indecl*.

contraption /kən'træpʃ(ə)n/ *n* приспособлéние.

contrary *adj* (*opposite*) /'kɒntrərɪ/ противополóжный; **~ to** вопреки́ +*dat*; (*perverse*) /kən'treərɪ/ капри́зный; *n* /'kɒntrərɪ/: **on the ~** наоборóт.

contrast /'kɒntrɑːst/ *n* контрáст, противополóжность; *vt* противопоставля́ть *impf*, противопостáвить *pf* (**with** +*dat*); *vi* контрасти́ровать *impf*.

contravene /,kɒntrə'viːn/ *vt* нарушáть *impf*, нарýшить *pf*. **contravention** /-'venʃ(ə)n/ *n* нарушéние.

contribute /kən'trɪbjuːt/ *vt* (*to fund*

etc.) же́ртвовать *impf*, по~ *pf* (**to** в+*acc*); **~ to** (*further*) соде́йствовать *impf* & *pf*, по~ *pf* +*dat*; (*write for*) сотру́дничать *impf* в+*prep*. **contribution** /ˌkɒntrɪ'bjuːʃ(ə)n/ *n* (*money*) поже́ртвование; (*fig*) вклад. **contributor** /kən'trɪbjʊtə(r)/ *n* (*donor*) же́ртвователь *m*; (*writer*) сотру́дник.

contrite /'kɒntraɪt/ *adj* ка́ющийся.

contrivance /kən'traɪv(ə)ns/ *n* приспособле́ние. **contrive** /kən'traɪv/ *vt* ухитря́ться *impf*, ухитри́ться *pf* +*inf*.

control /kən'trəʊl/ *n* (*mastery*) контро́ль *m*; (*operation*) управле́ние; *pl* управле́ния *pl*; *vt* (*dominate*; *verify*) контроли́ровать *impf*, про~ *pf*; (*regulate*) управля́ть *impf* +*instr*; **~ o.s.** сде́рживаться *impf*, сдержа́ться *pf*.

controversial /ˌkɒntrə'vɜːʃ(ə)l/ *adj* спо́рный. **controversy** /'kɒntrəˌvɜːsɪ/ *n* спор.

convalesce /ˌkɒnvə'les/ *vi* выздора́вливать *impf*. **convalescence** /-'les(ə)ns/ *n* выздоровле́ние.

convection /kən'vekʃ(ə)n/ *n* конве́кция. **convector** /-'vektə(r)/ *n* конве́ктор.

convene /kən'viːn/ *vt* созыва́ть *impf*, созва́ть *pf*.

convenience /kən'viːnɪəns/ *n* удо́бство; (*public* ~) убо́рная *sb*. **convenient** /-'viːnɪənt/ *adj* удо́бный.

convent /'kɒnv(ə)nt/ *n* же́нский монасты́рь *m*.

convention /kən'venʃ(ə)n/ *n* (*assembly*) съезд; (*agreement*) конве́нция; (*custom*) обы́чай; (*conventionality*) усло́вность. **conventional** /-ʃən(ə)l/ *adj* общепри́нятый; (*also mil*) обы́чный.

converge /kən'vɜːdʒ/ *vi* сходи́ться *impf*, сойти́сь *pf*. **convergence** /-dʒəns/ *n* сходи́мость.

conversant /kən'vɜːs(ə)nt/ *predic*: **~ with** знако́м с+*instr*.

conversation /ˌkɒnvə'seɪʃ(ə)n/ *n* разгово́р. **conversational** /-'seɪʃən(ə)l/ *adj* разгово́рный.

converse[1] /kən'vɜːs/ *vi* разгова́ривать *impf*.

converse[2] /'kɒnvɜːs/ *n* обра́тное *sb*. **conversely** /'kɒnvɜːslɪ/ *adv* наоборо́т. **conversion** /kən'vɜːʃ(ə)n/ *n* (*change*) превраще́ние; (*of faith*) обраще́ние; (*of building*) перестро́йка. **convert** /kən'vɜːt/ *vt* (*change*) превраща́ть *impf*, преврати́ть *pf* (**into** в+*acc*); (*to faith*) обраща́ть *impf*, обрати́ть *pf* (**to** в+*acc*); (*a building*) перестра́ивать *impf*, перестро́ить *pf*. **convertible** /kən'vɜːtɪb(ə)l/ *adj* обрати́мый; *n* автомоби́ль *m* со снима́ющейся кры́шей.

convex /'kɒnveks/ *adj* вы́пуклый.

convey /kən'veɪ/ *vt* (*transport*) перевози́ть *impf*, перевезти́ *pf*; (*communicate*) передава́ть *impf*, переда́ть *pf*. **conveyance** /-'veɪəns/ *n* перево́зка; переда́ча. **conveyancing** /-'veɪənsɪŋ/ *n* нотариа́льная переда́ча. **conveyor belt** /-'veɪə(r)/ *n* транспортёрная ле́нта.

convict /'kɒnvɪkt/ *n* осуждённый *sb*; *vt* /kən'vɪkt/ осужда́ть *impf*, осуди́ть *pf*. **conviction** /kən'vɪkʃ(ə)n/ *n* (*law*) осужде́ние; (*belief*) убежде́ние. **convince** /kən'vɪns/ *vt* убежда́ть *impf*, убеди́ть *pf*. **convincing** /kən'vɪnsɪŋ/ *adj* убеди́тельный.

convivial /kən'vɪvɪəl/ *adj* весёлый.

convoluted /'kɒnvəˌluːtɪd/ *adj* изви́листый; (*fig*) запу́танный.

convoy /'kɒnvɔɪ/ *n* конво́й.

convulse /kən'vʌls/ *vt*: **be ~d with** содрога́ться *impf*, содрогну́ться *pf* от+*gen*. **convulsion** /-'vʌlʃ(ə)n/ *n* (*med*) конву́льсия.

cook /kʊk/ *n* куха́рка, по́вар; *vt* гото́вить *impf*; *vi* вари́ться *impf*; с~ *pf*. **cooker** /'kʊkə(r)/ *n* плита́, печь. **cookery** /'kʊkərɪ/ *n* кулина́рия.

cool /kuːl/ *adj* прохла́дный; (*calm*) хладнокро́вный; (*unfriendly*) холо́дный; *vt* охлажда́ть *impf*, охлади́ть *pf*; **~ down, off** остыва́ть *impf*, осты́(ну)ть *pf*. **coolness** /'ku:lnɪs/ *n* прохла́да; (*calm*) хладнокро́вие; (*manner*) холодо́к.

coop /ku:p/ *n* куря́тник; *vt*: **~ up** держа́ть *impf* взаперти́.

cooperate /kəʊ'ɒpə,reɪt/ *vi* сотру́дничать *impf*. **cooperation** /kəʊ,ɒpə'reɪʃ(ə)n/ *n* сотру́дничество. **cooperative** /kəʊ'ɒpərətɪv/ *n* кооперати́в; *adj* кооперати́вный; (*helpful*) услу́жливый.

co-opt /kəʊ'ɒpt/ *vt* коопти́ровать *impf* & *pf*.

coordinate *vt* /kəʊ'ɔ:dɪ,neɪt/ координи́ровать *impf* & *pf*; *n* /kəʊ'ɔ:dɪnət/ координа́та. **coordination** /kəʊ,ɔ:dɪ'neɪʃ(ə)n/ *n* координа́ция.

cope /kəʊp/ *vi*: **~ with** справля́ться *impf*, спра́виться *pf* с+*instr*.

copious /'kəʊpɪəs/ *adj* оби́льный.

copper /'kɒpə(r)/ *n* (*metal*) медь; *adj* ме́дный.

coppice, copse /'kɒpɪs, kɒps/ *n* ро́щица.

copulate /'kɒpjʊ,leɪt/ *vi* совокупля́ться *impf*, совокупи́ться *pf*.

copy /'kɒpɪ/ *n* ко́пия; (*book*) экземпля́р; *vt* (*reproduce*) копи́ровать *impf*, с~ *pf*; (*transcribe*) переписывать *impf*, переписа́ть *pf*; (*imitate*) подража́ть *impf* +*dat*. **copyright** *n* а́вторское пра́во.

coral /'kɒr(ə)l/ *n* кора́лл.

cord /kɔ:d/ *n* (*string*) верёвка; (*electr*) шнур.

cordial /'kɔ:dɪəl/ *adj* серде́чный.

corduroy /'kɔ:də,rɔɪ/ *n* ру́бчатый вельве́т.

core /kɔ:(r)/ *n* сердцеви́на; (*fig*) суть.

cork /kɔ:k/ *n* (*material*; *stopper*) про́бка; (*float*) поплаво́к. **corkscrew** *n* што́пор.

corn[1] /kɔ:n/ *n* зерно́; (*wheat*) пшени́ца; (*maize*) кукуру́за. **cornflakes** *n pl* кукуру́зные хло́пья (-пьев) *pl*. **cornflour** *n* кукуру́зная мука́. **corny** /'kɔ:nɪ/ *adj* (*coll*) бана́льный.

corn[2] /kɔ:n/ *n* (*med*) мозо́ль.

cornea /'kɔ:nɪə/ *n* рогова́я оболо́чка.

corner /'kɔ:nə(r)/ *n* у́гол; **~-stone** *n* краеуго́льный ка́мень *m*; *vt* загоня́ть *impf*, загна́ть *pf* в у́гол.

cornet /'kɔ:nɪt/ *n* (*mus*) корне́т; (*ice-cream*) рожо́к.

cornice /'kɔ:nɪs/ *n* карни́з.

coronary (thrombosis) /'kɒrənərɪ (θrɒm'bəʊsɪs)/ *n* коронаротромбо́з. **coronation** /,kɒrə'neɪʃ(ə)n/ *n* корона́ция. **coroner** /'kɒrənə(r)/ *n* ме́дик суде́бной эксперти́зы.

corporal[1] /'kɔ:pr(ə)l/ *n* капра́л.

corporal[2] /'kɔ:pr(ə)l/ *adj* теле́сный; **~ punishment** теле́сное наказа́ние.

corporate /'kɔ:pərət/ *adj* корпорати́вный. **corporation** /,kɔ:pə'reɪʃ(ə)n/ *n* корпора́ция.

corps /kɔ:(r)/ *n* ко́рпус.

corpse /kɔ:ps/ *n* труп.

corpulent /'kɔ:pjʊlənt/ *adj* ту́чный.

corpuscle /'kɔ:pʌs(ə)l/ *n* кровяно́й ша́рик.

correct /kə'rekt/ *adj* пра́вильный; (*conduct*) корре́ктный; *vt* исправля́ть *impf*, испра́вить *pf*. **correction** /-'rekʃ(ə)n/ *n* исправле́ние.

correlation /,kɒrə'leɪʃ(ə)n/ *n* соотноше́ние.

correspond /,kɒrɪ'spɒnd/ *vi* соотве́тствовать *impf* (**to, with** +*dat*); (*by letter*) перепи́сываться *impf*. **correspondence** /-dəns/ *n* соотве́тствие; (*letters*) корреспонде́нция. **correspondent** /-dənt/ *n* корреспонде́нт. **corresponding** /-dɪŋ/ *adj* соотве́тствующий (**to** +*dat*).

corridor /'kɒrɪ,dɔ:(r)/ *n* коридо́р.

corroborate /kə'rɒbə,reɪt/ *vt* подтвержда́ть *impf*, подтверди́ть *pf*.

corrode /kə'rəʊd/ *vt* разъеда́ть *impf*, разъе́сть *pf*. **corrosion** /-'rəʊʒ(ə)n/ *n* корро́зия. **corrosive** /-'rəʊsɪv/ *adj* е́дкий.

corrugated iron /'kɒrʊ,geɪtɪd 'aɪən/ *n* рифлёное желе́зо.

corrupt /kə'rʌpt/ *adj* (*person*) развращённый; (*government*) продажный; *vt* развращать *impf*, развратить *pf*. **corruption** /-'rʌpʃ(ə)n/ *n* развращение; коррупция.
corset /'kɔːsɪt/ *n* корсет.
cortège /kɔː'teɪʒ/ *n* кортеж.
cortex /'kɔːteks/ *n* кора.
corundum /kə'rʌndəm/ *n* корунд.
cosmetic /kɒz'metɪk/ *adj* косметический. **cosmetics** /-tɪks/ *n pl* косметика.
cosmic /'kɒzmɪk/ *adj* космический. **cosmonaut** /'kɒzmə,nɔːt/ *n* космонавт.
cosmopolitan /,kɒzmə'pɒlɪt(ə)n/ *adj* космополитический.
cosmos /'kɒzmɒs/ *n* космос.
Cossack /'kɒsæk/ *n* казак, -ачка.
cosset /'kɒsɪt/ *vt* нежить *impf*.
cost /kɒst/ *n* стоимость, цена; *vt* стоить *impf*.
costly /'kɒstlɪ/ *adj* дорогой.
costume /'kɒstjuːm/ *n* костюм.
cosy /'kəʊzɪ/ *adj* уютный.
cot /kɒt/ *n* детская кроватка.
cottage /'kɒtɪdʒ/ *n* коттедж; **~ cheese** творог.
cotton /'kɒt(ə)n/ *n* хлопок; (*cloth*) хлопчатобумажная ткань; (*thread*) нитка; **~ wool** вата; *adj* хлопковый; хлопчатобумажный.
couch /kaʊtʃ/ *n* диван.
couchette /kuː'ʃet/ *n* спальное место.
cough /kɒf/ *n* кашель *m*; *vi* кашлять *impf*.
council /'kaʊns(ə)l/ *n* совет; **~ tax** местный налог; **~ house** жильё из общественного фонда. **councillor** /'kaʊnsələ(r)/ *n* член совета.
counsel /'kaʊns(ə)l/ *n* (*advice*) совет; (*lawyer*) адвокат; *vt* советовать *impf*, по~ *pf* +*dat*.
count[1] /kaʊnt/ *vt* считать *impf*, со~, счесть *pf*; **~ on** рассчитывать *impf* на+*acc*; *n* счёт. **countdown** *n* отсчёт времени.
count[2] /kaʊnt/ *n* (*title*) граф.
countenance /'kaʊntɪnəns/ *n* лицо; *vt* одобрять *impf*, одобрить *pf*.
counter /'kaʊntə(r)/ *n* прилавок; (*token*) фишка; *adv*: **run ~ to** идти *impf* вразрез с+*instr*; *vt* парировать *impf*, от~ *pf*. **counteract** *vt* противодействовать *impf* +*dat*. **counterbalance** *n* противовес; *vt* уравновешивать *impf*, уравновесить *pf*. **counterfeit** /-fɪt/ *adj* поддельный. **counterpart** *n* соответственная часть. **counterpoint** *n* контрапункт. **counter-revolutionary** *n* контрреволюционер; *adj* контрреволюционный. **countersign** *vt* ставить *impf*, по~ *pf* вторую подпись на+*prep*.
countess /'kaʊntɪs/ *n* графиня.
countless /'kaʊntlɪs/ *adj* бесчисленный.
country /'kʌntrɪ/ *n* (*nation*) страна; (*native land*) родина; (*rural areas*) деревня; *adj* деревенский, сельский. **countryman** *n* (*compatriot*) соотечественник; сельский житель *m*. **countryside** *n* природный ландшафт.
county /'kaʊntɪ/ *n* графство.
coup /kuː/ *n* (*polit*) переворот.
couple /'kʌp(ə)l/ *n* пара; (*a few*) несколько +*gen*; *vt* сцеплять *impf*, сцепить *pf*.
coupon /'kuːpɒn/ *n* купон; талон; ваучер.
courage /'kʌrɪdʒ/ *n* храбрость. **courageous** /kə'reɪdʒəs/ *adj* храбрый.
courier /'kʊrɪə(r)/ *n* (*messenger*) курьер; (*guide*) гид.
course /kɔːs/ *n* курс; (*process*) ход, течение; (*of meal*) блюдо; **of ~** конечно.
court /kɔːt/ *n* двор; (*sport*) корт, площадка; (*law*) суд; **~ martial** военный суд; *vt* ухаживать *impf* за+*instr*. **courteous** /'kɜːtɪəs/ *adj* вежливый. **courtesy** /'kɜːtɪsɪ/ *n* вежливость. **courtier** /'kɔːtɪə(r)/ *n* придворный *sb*. **courtyard** *n* двор.

C

cousin /ˈkʌz(ə)n/ *n* двоюродный брат, -ная сестра́.
cove /kəʊv/ *n* бу́хточка.
covenant /ˈkʌvənənt/ *n* догово́р.
cover /ˈkʌvə(r)/ *n* (*covering*; *lid*) покры́шка; (*shelter*) укры́тие; (*chair* ~; *soft case*) чехо́л; (*bed*) покрыва́ло; (*book*) переплёт, обло́жка; **under separate** ~ в отде́льном конве́рте; *vt* покрыва́ть *impf*, покры́ть *pf*; (*hide*, *protect*) закрыва́ть *impf*, закры́ть *pf*. **coverage** /-rɪdʒ/ *n* освеще́ние. **covert** /ˈkəʊvɜːt/ *adj* скры́тый.
covet /ˈkʌvɪt/ *vt* пожела́ть *pf* +*gen*.
cow[1] /kaʊ/ *n* коро́ва. **cowboy** *n* ковбо́й. **cowshed** *n* хлев.
cow[2] /kaʊ/ *vt* запу́гивать *impf*, запуга́ть *pf*.
coward /ˈkaʊəd/ *n* трус. **cowardice** /-dɪs/ *n* тру́сость. **cowardly** /-lɪ/ *adj* трусли́вый.
cower /ˈkaʊə(r)/ *vi* съёживаться *impf*, съёжиться *pf*.
cox(swain) /ˈkɒks(weɪn)/ *n* рулево́й *m*.
coy /kɔɪ/ *adj* жема́нно стыдли́вый.
crab /kræb/ *n* краб.
crack /kræk/ *n* (*in cup*, *ice*) тре́щина; (*in wall*) щель; (*noise*) треск; *adj* первокла́ссный; *vt* (*break*) коло́ть *impf*, рас~ *pf*; (*china*) де́лать *impf*, с~ *pf* тре́щину в+*acc*; *vi* тре́снуть *pf*. **crackle** /ˈkræk(ə)l/ *vi* потре́скивать *impf*.
cradle /ˈkreɪd(ə)l/ *n* колыбе́ль.
craft /krɑːft/ *n* (*trade*) ремесло́; (*boat*) су́дно. **craftiness** /ˈkrɑːftɪnɪs/ *n* хи́трость. **craftsman** *n* реме́сленник. **crafty** /ˈkrɑːftɪ/ *adj* хи́трый.
crag /kræg/ *n* утёс. **craggy** /ˈkrægɪ/ *adj* скали́стый.
cram /kræm/ *vt* (*fill*) набива́ть *impf*, наби́ть *pf*; (*stuff in*) впи́хивать *impf*, впихну́ть *pf*; *vi* (*study*) зубри́ть *impf*.
cramp[1] /kræmp/ *n* (*med*) су́дорога.
cramp[2] /kræmp/ *vt* стесня́ть *impf*, стесни́ть *pf*. **cramped** /kræmpt/ *adj* те́сный.
cranberry /ˈkrænbərɪ/ *n* клю́ква.
crane /kreɪn/ *n* (*bird*) жура́вль *m*; (*machine*) кран; *vt* (*one's neck*) вытя́гивать *impf*, вы́тянуть *pf* (ше́ю).
crank[1] /kræŋk/ *n* заводна́я ру́чка; ~**-shaft** коле́нчатый вал; *vt* заводи́ть *impf*, завести́ *pf*.
crank[2] /kræŋk/ *n* (*eccentric*) чуда́к.
cranny /ˈkrænɪ/ *n* щель.
crash /kræʃ/ *n* (*noise*) гро́хот, треск; (*accident*) ава́рия; (*financial*) крах; ~ **course** уско́ренный курс; ~ **helmet** защи́тный шлем; ~ **landing** авари́йная поса́дка; *vi* (~ *into*) вреза́ться *impf*, вре́заться *pf* в+*acc*; (*aeron*) разбива́ться *impf*, разби́ться *pf*; (*fall with* ~) гро́хнуться *pf*; (*comput*) зависа́ть *impf*, зави́снуть *pf*; *vt* (*bang down*) гро́хнуть *pf*.
crass /kræs/ *adj* гру́бый.
crate /kreɪt/ *n* я́щик.
crater /ˈkreɪtə(r)/ *n* кра́тер.
crave /kreɪv/ *vi*: ~ **for** жа́ждать *impf* +*gen*. **craving** /ˈkreɪvɪŋ/ *n* стра́стное жела́ние.
crawl /krɔːl/ *vi* по́лзать *indet*, ползти́ *det*; ~ **with** кише́ть +*instr*; *n* (*sport*) кроль *m*.
crayon /ˈkreɪən/ *n* цветно́й каранда́ш.
craze /kreɪz/ *n* ма́ния. **crazy** /ˈkreɪzɪ/ *adj* поме́шанный (**about** на+*prep*).
creak /kriːk/ *n* скрип; *vi* скрипе́ть *impf*.
cream /kriːm/ *n* сли́вки (-вок) *pl*; (*cosmetic*; *cul*) крем; ~ **cheese** сли́вочный сыр; **soured** ~ смета́на; *vt* сбива́ть *impf*, сбить *pf*; *adj* (*of cream*) сли́вочный; (*colour*) кре́мовый. **creamy** /ˈkriːmɪ/ *adj* сли́вочный, кре́мовый.
crease /kriːs/ *n* скла́дка; *vt* мять *impf*, из~, с~ *pf*. **creased** /kriːst/ *adj* мя́тый.
create /kriːˈeɪt/ *vt* создава́ть *impf*, созда́ть *pf*. **creation** /-ˈeɪʃ(ə)n/ *n*

создáние. **creative** /-'eɪtɪv/ *adj* твóрческий. **creator** /-'eɪtə(r)/ *n* создáтель *m*. **creature** /'kri:tʃə(r)/ *n* создáние.

crêche /kreʃ/ *n* (дéтские) я́сли (-лей) *pl.*

credence /'kri:d(ə)ns/ *n* вéра; **give ~** вéрить *impf* (**to** +*dat*). **credentials** /krɪ'denʃ(ə)lz/ *n pl* удостоверéние; (*diplomacy*) вери́тельные грáмоты *f pl.* **credibility** /ˌkredɪ'bɪlɪtɪ/ *n* правдоподóбие; (*of person*) спосóбность вызывáть довéрие. **credible** /'kredɪb(ə)l/ *adj* (*of thing*) правдоподóбный; (*of person*) заслу́живающий довéрия.

credit /'kredɪt/ *n* довéрие; (*comm*) креди́т; (*honour*) честь; **give ~** кредитовáть *impf* & *pf* +*acc*; отдавáть *impf*, отдáть *pf* дóлжное+*dat*; **~ card** креди́тная кáрточка; *vt*: **~ with** припи́сывать *impf*, приписáть *pf* +*dat*. **creditable** /-təb(ə)l/ *adj* похвáльный. **creditor** /-tə(r)/ *n* кредитóр.

credulity /krɪ'dju:lɪtɪ/ *n* легковéрие. **credulous** /'kredjʊləs/ *adj* легковéрный.

creed /kri:d/ *n* убеждéния *neut pl*; (*eccl*) вероисповедáние.

creep /kri:p/ *vi* пóлзать *indet*, ползти́ *det*. **creeper** /'kri:pə(r)/ *n* (*plant*) ползу́чее растéние.

cremate /krɪ'meɪt/ *vt* креми́ровать *impf* & *pf*. **cremation** /-'meɪʃ(ə)n/ *n* кремáция. **crematorium** /ˌkremə'tɔ:rɪəm/ *n* крематóрий.

crêpe /kreɪp/ *n* креп.

crescendo /krɪ'ʃendəʊ/ *adv*, *adj*, & *n* крещéндо *indecl.*

crescent /'krez(ə)nt/ *n* полумéсяц.

crest /krest/ *n* грéбень *m*; (*heraldry*) герб.

crevasse, crevice /krə'væs, 'krevɪs/ *n* расщéлина, рассéлина.

crew /kru:/ *n* бригáда; (*of ship, plane*) экипáж.

crib /krɪb/ *n* (*bed*) дéтская кровáтка; *vi* спи́сывать *impf*, списáть *pf*.

crick /krɪk/ *n* растяжéние мышц.

cricket[1] /'krɪkɪt/ *n* (*insect*) сверчóк.

cricket[2] /'krɪkɪt/ *n* (*sport*) кри́кет; **~ bat** битá.

crime /kraɪm/ *n* преступлéние.

Crimea /kraɪ'mɪə/ *n* Крым. **Crimean** /-ən/ *adj* кры́мский.

criminal /'krɪmɪn(ə)l/ *n* престу́пник; *adj* престу́пный; (*of crime*) уголóвный.

crimson /'krɪmz(ə)n/ *adj* мали́новый.

cringe /krɪndʒ/ *vi* (*cower*) съёживаться *impf*, съёжиться *pf*.

crinkle /'krɪŋk(ə)l/ *n* морщи́на; *vt* & *i* мóрщить(ся) *impf*, на~, с~ *pf*.

cripple /'krɪp(ə)l/ *n* калéка *m* & *f*; *vt* калéчить *impf*, ис~ *pf*; (*fig*) расшáтывать *impf*, расшатáть *pf*.

crisis /'kraɪsɪs/ *n* кри́зис.

crisp /krɪsp/ *adj* (*brittle*) хрустя́щий; (*fresh*) свéжий. **crisps** /krɪsps/ *n pl* хрустя́щий картóфель *m*.

criss-cross /'krɪskrɒs/ *adv* крест-нáкрест.

criterion /kraɪ'tɪərɪən/ *n* критéрий.

critic /'krɪtɪk/ *n* кри́тик. **critical** /-k(ə)l/ *adj* крити́ческий. **critically** /-kəlɪ/ *adv* (*ill*) тяжелó. **criticism** /-tɪˌsɪz(ə)m/ *n* кри́тика. **criticize** /-tɪˌsaɪz/ *vt* критиковáть *impf*. **critique** /krɪ'ti:k/ *n* кри́тика.

croak /krəʊk/ *vi* квáкать *impf*, квáкнуть *pf*; хрипéть *impf*.

Croat /'krəʊæt/ *n* хорвáт, ~ка. **Croatia** /krəʊ'eɪʃə/ *n* Хорвáтия. **Croatian** /krəʊ'eɪʃ(ə)n/ *adj* хорвáтский.

crochet /'krəʊʃeɪ/ *n* вязáние крючкóм; *vt* вязáть *impf*, с~ *pf* (крючкóм).

crockery /'krɒkərɪ/ *n* посу́да.

crocodile /'krɒkəˌdaɪl/ *n* крокоди́л.

crocus /'krəʊkəs/ *n* крóкус.

crony /'krəʊnɪ/ *n* закады́чный друг.

crook /krʊk/ *n* (*staff*) пóсох; (*swindler*) мошéнник. **crooked**

/ˈkrʊkɪd/ *adj* кривóй; (*dishonest*) нечéстный.

crop /krɒp/ *n* (*yield*) урожáй; *pl* культýры *f pl*; (*bird's*) зоб; *vt* (*cut*) подстригáть *impf*, подстрúчь *pf*; **~ up** возникáть *impf*, вознúкнуть *pf*.

croquet /ˈkrəʊkeɪ/ *n* крокéт.

cross /krɒs/ *n* крест; (*biol*) пóмесь; *adj* (*angry*) злой; *vt* (*on foot*) переходúть *impf*, перейтú *pf* (чéрез) +*acc*; (*by transport*) переезжáть *impf*, переéхать *pf* (чéрез) +*acc*; (*biol*) скрéщивать *impf*, скрестúть *pf*; **~ off, out** вычёркивать *impf*, вы́черкнуть *pf*; **~ o.s.** крестúться *impf*, пере~ *pf*; **~ over** переходúть *impf*, перейтú *pf* (чéрез) +*acc*. **~bar** поперéчина. **~-breed** пóмесь; **~-country race** кросс; **~-examination** перекрёстный допрóс; **~-examine, ~-question** подвергáть *impf*, подвéргнуть *pf* перекрёстному допрóсу; **~-eyed** косоглáзый; **~-legged: sit ~** сидéть *impf* по-турéцки; **~-reference** перекрёстная ссы́лка; **~road(s)** перекрёсток; **~-section** перекрёстное сечéние; **~word (puzzle)** кроссвóрд. **crossing** /ˈkrɒsɪŋ/ *n* (*intersection*) перекрёсток; (*foot*) перехóд; (*transport*; *rly*) переéзд.

crotch /krɒtʃ/ *n* (*anat*) промéжность.

crotchet /ˈkrɒtʃɪt/ *n* (*mus*) четвертнáя нóта.

crotchety /ˈkrɒtʃɪtɪ/ *adj* раздражúтельный.

crouch /kraʊtʃ/ *vi* приседáть *impf*, присéсть *pf*.

crow /krəʊ/ *n* ворóна; **as the ~ flies** по прямóй лúнии; *vi* кукарéкать *impf*. **crowbar** *n* лом.

crowd /kraʊd/ *n* толпá; *vi* теснúться *impf*, с~ *pf*; **~ into** втúскиваться *impf*, втúснуться *pf*. **crowded** /ˈkraʊdɪd/ *adj* переполненный.

crown /kraʊn/ *n* корóна; (*tooth*) корóнка; (*head*) тéма; (*hat*) тулья́; *vt* короновáть *impf* & *pf*.

crucial /ˈkruːʃ(ə)l/ *adj* (*important*) óчень вáжный; (*decisive*) решáющий; (*critical*) критúческий.

crucifix /ˈkruːsɪˌfɪks/ *n* распя́тие. **crucifixion** /-ˈfɪkʃ(ə)n/ *n* распя́тие. **crucify** /ˈkruːsɪˌfaɪ/ *vt* распинáть *impf*, распя́ть *pf*.

crude /kruːd/ *adj* (*rude*) грýбый; (*raw*) сырóй. **crudity** /ˈkruːdɪtɪ/ *n* грýбость.

cruel /ˈkruːəl/ *adj* жестóкий. **cruelty** /-tɪ/ *n* жестóкость.

cruise /kruːz/ *n* круи́з; *vi* крейсúровать *impf*. **cruiser** /ˈkruːzə(r)/ *n* крéйсер.

crumb /krʌm/ *n* крóшка.

crumble /ˈkrʌmb(ə)l/ *vt* крошúть *impf*, рас~ *pf*; *vi* обвáливаться *impf*, обвалúться *pf*. **crumbly** /ˈkrʌmblɪ/ *adj* рассы́пчатый.

crumple /ˈkrʌmp(ə)l/ *vt* мять *impf*, с~ *pf*; (*intentionally*) кóмкать *impf*, с~ *pf*.

crunch /krʌntʃ/ *n* (*fig*) решáющий момéнт; *vt* грызть *impf*, раз~ *pf*; *vi* хрустéть *impf*, хрýстнуть *pf*.

crusade /kruːˈseɪd/ *n* крестóвый похóд; (*fig*) кампáния. **crusader** /-ˈseɪdə(r)/ *n* крестонóсец; (*fig*) борéц (**for** за+*acc*).

crush /krʌʃ/ *n* дáвка; (*infatuation*) сúльное увлечéние; *vt* давúть *impf*, за~, раз~ *pf*; (*crease*) мять *impf*, с~ *pf*; (*fig*) подавля́ть *impf*, подавúть *pf*.

crust /krʌst/ *n* (*of earth*) корá; (*bread etc.*) кóрка.

crutch /krʌtʃ/ *n* косты́ль *m*.

crux /krʌks/ *n*: **~ of the matter** суть дéла.

cry /kraɪ/ *n* крик; **a far ~ from** далекó от+*gen*; *vi* (*weep*) плáкать *impf*; (*shout*) кричáть *impf*, крúкнуть *pf*.

crypt /krɪpt/ *n* склеп. **cryptic** /ˈkrɪptɪk/ *adj* загáдочный.

crystal /ˈkrɪst(ə)l/ *n* кристáлл; (*glass*) хрустáль *m*. **crystallize** /-laɪz/ *vt* & *i* кристаллизовáть(ся) *impf* & *pf*.

cub /kʌb/ *n* детёныш; **bear ~** медвежо́нок; **fox ~** лисёнок; **lion ~** львёнок; **wolf ~** волчо́нок
cube /kju:b/ *n* куб. **cubic** /ˈkju:bɪk/ *adj* куби́ческий.
cubicle /ˈkju:bɪk(ə)l/ *n* каби́на.
cuckoo /ˈkʊku:/ *n* куку́шка.
cucumber /ˈkju:kʌmbə(r)/ *n* огуре́ц.
cuddle /ˈkʌd(ə)l/ *vt* обнима́ть *impf*, обня́ть *pf*; *vi* обнима́ться *impf*, обня́ться *pf*; **~ up** прижима́ться *impf*, прижа́ться *pf* (**to** к+ *dat*).
cudgel /ˈkʌdʒ(ə)l/ *n* дуби́нка.
cue[1] /kju:/ *n* (*theat*) ре́плика.
cue[2] /kju:/ *n* (*billiards*) кий.
cuff[1] /kʌf/ *n* манже́та; **off the ~** экспро́мтом; **~-link** за́понка.
cuff[2] /kʌf/ *vt* (*hit*) шлёпать *impf*, шлёпнуть *pf*.
cul-de-sac /ˈkʌldəˌsæk/ *n* тупи́к.
culinary /ˈkʌlɪnərɪ/ *adj* кулина́рный.
cull /kʌl/ *vt* (*select*) отбира́ть *impf*, отобра́ть *pf*; (*slaughter*) бить *impf*.
culminate /ˈkʌlmɪˌneɪt/ *vi* конча́ться *impf*, ко́нчиться *pf* (**in** +*instr*). **culmination** /-ˈneɪʃ(ə)n/ *n* кульминацио́нный пункт.
culpability /ˌkʌlpəˈbɪlɪtɪ/ *n* вино́вность. **culpable** /ˈkʌlpəb(ə)l/ *adj* вино́вный. **culprit** /ˈkʌlprɪt/ *n* вино́вник.
cult /kʌlt/ *n* культ.
cultivate /ˈkʌltɪˌveɪt/ *vt* (*land*) обраба́тывать *impf*, обрабо́тать *pf*; (*crops*) выра́щивать *impf*; вы́растить *impf*; (*develop*) развива́ть *impf*, разви́ть *pf*.
cultural /ˈkʌltʃər(ə)l/ *adj* культу́рный. **culture** /ˈkʌltʃə(r)/ *n* культу́ра. **cultured** /ˈkʌltʃəd/ *adj* культу́рный.
cumbersome /ˈkʌmbəsəm/ *adj* громо́здкий.
cumulative /ˈkju:mjʊlətɪv/ *adj* кумуляти́вный.
cunning /ˈkʌnɪŋ/ *n* хи́трость; *adj* хи́трый.
cup /kʌp/ *n* ча́шка; (*prize*) ку́бок.
cupboard /ˈkʌbəd/ *n* шкаф.
cupola /ˈkju:pələ/ *n* ку́пол.
curable /ˈkjʊərəb(ə)l/ *adj* излечи́мый.
curative /ˈkjʊərətɪv/ *adj* целе́бный.
curator /kjʊəˈreɪtə(r)/ *n* храни́тель *m*.
curb /kɜ:b/ *vt* обу́здывать *impf*, обузда́ть *pf*.
curd /kɜ:d/ *n* (*cheese*) творо́г. **curdle** /ˈkɜ:d(ə)l/ *vt & i* свёртывать(ся) *impf*, сверну́ть(ся) *pf*.
cure /ˈkjʊə(r)/ *n* сре́дство (**for** про́тив+*gen*); *vt* выле́чивать *impf*, вы́лечить *pf*; (*smoke*) копти́ть *impf*, за~ *pf*; (*salt*) соли́ть *impf*, по~ *pf*.
curfew /ˈkɜ:fju:/ *n* коменда́нтский час.
curiosity /ˌkjʊərɪˈɒsɪtɪ/ *n* любопы́тство. **curious** /ˈkjʊərɪəs/ *adj* любопы́тный.
curl /kɜ:l/ *n* ло́кон; *vt* завива́ть *impf*, зави́ть *pf*; **~ up** свёртываться *impf*, сверну́ться *pf*. **curly** /ˈkɜ:lɪ/ *adj* кудря́вый.
currants /ˈkʌrənts/ *n pl* (*dried*) изю́м (*collect*).
currency /ˈkʌrənsɪ/ *n* валю́та; (*prevalence*) хожде́ние. **current** /ˈkʌrənt/ *adj* теку́щий; *n* тече́ние; (*air*) струя́; (*water*; *electr*) ток.
curriculum /kəˈrɪkjʊləm/ *n* курс обуче́ния; **~ vitae** /ˈvi:taɪ/ автобиогра́фия.
curry[1] /ˈkʌrɪ/ *n* ка́рри *neut indecl*.
curry[2] /ˈkʌrɪ/ *vt*: **~ favour with** зaи́скивать *impf* пе́ред+*instr*.
curse /kɜ:s/ *n* прокля́тие; (*oath*) руга́тельство; *vt* проклина́ть *impf*, прокля́сть *pf*; *vi* руга́ться *impf*, по~ *pf*.
cursor /ˈkɜ:sə(r)/ *n* (*comput*) курсо́р.
cursory /ˈkɜ:sərɪ/ *adj* бе́глый.
curt /kɜ:t/ *adj* ре́зкий.
curtail /kɜ:ˈteɪl/ *vt* сокраща́ть *impf*, сократи́ть *pf*.
curtain /ˈkɜ:t(ə)n/ *n* занаве́ска.
curts(e)y /ˈkɜ:tsɪ/ *n* featurereвера́нс; *vi* де́лать *impf*, с~ *pf*ревера́нс.
curve /kɜ:v/ *n* изги́б; (*line*) крива́я

C

sb; *vi* изгиба́ться *impf*, изогну́ться *pf*.
cushion /ˈkʊʃ(ə)n/ *n* поду́шка; *vt* смягча́ть *impf*, смягчи́ть *pf*.
custard /ˈkʌstəd/ *n* сла́дкий заварно́й крем.
custodian /kʌˈstəʊdɪən/ *n* храни́тель *m*. **custody** /ˈkʌstədɪ/ *n* опе́ка; (*of police*) аре́ст; **to take into ~** арестова́ть *pf*.
custom /ˈkʌstəm/ *n* обы́чай; (*comm*) клиенту́ра; *pl* (*duty*) тамо́женные по́шлины *f pl*; **go through ~s** проходи́ть *impf*, пройти́ *pf* тамо́женный осмо́тр; **~-house** тамо́жня; **~ officer** тамо́женник. **customary** /ˈkʌstəmərɪ/ *adj* обы́чный. **customer** /ˈkʌstəmə(r)/ *n* клие́нт; покупа́тель *m*.
cut /kʌt/ *vt* ре́зать *impf*, по~ *pf*; (*hair*) стричь *impf*, о~ *pf*; (*mow*) коси́ть *impf*, с~ *pf*; (*price*) снижа́ть *impf*, сни́зить *pf*; (*cards*) снима́ть *impf*, снять *pf* коло́ду; **~ back** (*prune*) подреза́ть *impf*, подре́зать *pf*; (*reduce*) сокраща́ть *impf*, сократи́ть *pf*; **~ down** сруба́ть *impf*, сруби́ть *pf*; **~ off** отреза́ть *impf*, отре́зать *pf*; (*interrupt*) прерыва́ть *impf*, прерва́ть *pf*; (*disconnect*) отключа́ть *impf*, отключи́ть *pf*; **~ out** выре́зывать *impf*, вы́резать *pf*; **~ out for** со́зданный для+*gen*; **~ up** разреза́ть *impf*, разре́зать *pf*; *n* (*gash*) поре́з; (*clothes*) покро́й; (*reduction*) сниже́ние; **~ glass** хруста́ль *m*.
cute /kjuːt/ *adj* симпати́чный.
cutlery /ˈkʌtlərɪ/ *n* ножи́, ви́лки и ло́жки *pl*.
cutlet /ˈkʌtlɪt/ *n* отбивна́я котле́та.
cutting /ˈkʌtɪŋ/ *n* (*press*) вы́резка; (*plant*) черено́к; *adj* ре́зкий.
CV *abbr* (*of* **curriculum vitae**) автобиогра́фия.
cycle /ˈsaɪk(ə)l/ *n* цикл; (*bicycle*) велосипе́д; *vi* е́здить *impf* на велосипе́де. **cyclic(al)** /ˈsɪklɪk((ə)l)/ *adj* цикли́ческий. **cyclist** /ˈsaɪklɪst/ *n* велосипеди́ст.
cylinder /ˈsɪlɪndə(r)/ *n* цили́ндр. **cylindrical** /sɪˈlɪndrɪk(ə)l/ *adj* цилиндри́ческий.
cymbals /ˈsɪmb(ə)lz/ *n pl* таре́лки *f pl*.
cynic /ˈsɪnɪk/ *n* ци́ник. **cynical** /-k(ə)l/ *adj* цини́чный. **cynicism** /ˈsɪnɪsɪz(ə)m/ *n* цини́зм.
cypress /ˈsaɪprəs/ *n* кипари́с.
Cyrillic /sɪˈrɪlɪk/ *n* кири́ллица.
cyst /sɪst/ *n* киста́.
Czech /tʃek/ *n* чех, че́шка; *adj* че́шский; **~ Republic** Че́шская Респу́блика.

D

dab /dæb/ *n* мазо́к; *vt* (*eyes etc.*) прикла́дывать *impf* плато́к к+*dat*; **~ on** накла́дывать *impf*, наложи́ть *pf* мазка́ми.
dabble /ˈdæb(ə)l/ *vi*: **~ in** пове́рхностно занима́ться *impf*, заня́ться *pf* +*instr*.
dachshund /ˈdækshʊnd/ *n* та́кса.
dad, daddy /dæd, ˈdædɪ/ *n* па́па; **~-long-legs** *n* долгоно́жка.
daffodil /ˈdæfədɪl/ *n* жёлтый нарци́сс.
daft /dɑːft/ *adj* глу́пый.
dagger /ˈdægə(r)/ *n* кинжа́л.
dahlia /ˈdeɪlɪə/ *n* георги́н.
daily /ˈdeɪlɪ/ *adv* ежедне́вно; *adj* ежедне́вный; *n* (*charwoman*) приходя́щая убо́рщица; (*newspaper*) ежедне́вная газе́та.
dainty /ˈdeɪntɪ/ *adj* изя́щный.
dairy /ˈdeərɪ/ *n* маслобо́йня; (*shop*) моло́чная *sb*; *adj* моло́чный.
dais /ˈdeɪɪs/ *n* помо́ст.
daisy /ˈdeɪzɪ/ *n* маргари́тка.
dale /deɪl/ *n* доли́на.
dally /ˈdælɪ/ *vi* (*dawdle*) ме́шкать *impf*; (*toy*) игра́ть *impf* +*instr*; (*flirt*) флиртова́ть *impf*.
dam /dæm/ *n* (*barrier*) плоти́на; *vt* запру́живать *impf*, запруди́ть *pf*.
damage /ˈdæmɪdʒ/ *n* поврежде́-

ние; *pl* убы́тки *m pl*; *vt* повреждáть *impf*, повреди́ть *pf*.

damn /dæm/ *vt* (*curse*) проклинáть *impf*, проклясть *pf*; (*censure*) осуждáть *impf*, осуди́ть *pf*; *int* чёрт возьми́!; **I don't give a ~** мне наплевáть. **damnation** /-ˈneɪʃ(ə)n/ *n* проклятие. **damned** /dæmd/ *adj* прокля́тый.

damp /dæmp/ *n* сы́рость; *adj* сырóй; *vt* (*also* **dampen**) смáчивать *impf*, смочи́ть *pf*; (*fig*) охлаждáть *impf*, охлади́ть *pf*.

dance /dɑːns/ *vi* танцевáть *impf*; *n* тáнец; (*party*) танцевáльный вéчер. **dancer** /-sə(r)/ *n* танцóр, ~ка; (*ballet*) танцóвщик, -ица; балери́на.

dandelion /ˈdændɪˌlaɪən/ *n* одувáнчик.

dandruff /ˈdændrʌf/ *n* пéрхоть.

Dane /deɪn/ *n* датчáнин, -áнка; **Great ~** дог. **Danish** /ˈdeɪnɪʃ/ *adj* дáтский.

danger /ˈdeɪndʒə(r)/ *n* опáсность. **dangerous** /-rəs/ *adj* опáсный.

dangle /ˈdæŋg(ə)l/ *vt* & *i* покáчивать(ся) *impf*.

dank /dæŋk/ *adj* промóзглый.

dapper /ˈdæpə(r)/ *adj* выхоленный.

dare /deə(r)/ *vi* (*have courage*) осмéливаться *impf*, осмéлиться *pf*; (*have impudence*) сметь *impf*, по~ *pf*; *vt* вызывáть *impf*, вы́звать *pf*; *n* вы́зов. **daredevil** *n* лихáч; *adj* отчáянный. **daring** /ˈdeərɪŋ/ *n* отвáга; *adj* отчáянный.

dark /dɑːk/ *adj* тёмный; **~ blue** тёмно-си́ний; *n* темнотá. **darken** /-kən/ *vt* затемня́ть *impf*, затемни́ть *pf*; *vi* темнéть *impf*, по~ *pf*. **darkly** /-lɪ/ *adv* мрáчно. **darkness** /-nɪs/ *n* темнотá.

darling /ˈdɑːlɪŋ/ *n* дорогóй *sb*, ми́лый *sb*; *adj* дорогóй.

darn /dɑːn/ *vt* штóпать *impf*, за~ *pf*.

dart /dɑːt/ *n* стрелá; (*for game*) метáтельная стрелá; (*tuck*) вы́тачка; *vi* броси́ться *pf*.

dash /dæʃ/ *n* (*hyphen*) тирé *neut indecl*; (*admixture*) при́месь; *vt* швыря́ть *impf*, швырнýть *pf*; *vi* бросáться *impf*, брóситься *pf*. **dashboard** *n* прибóрная доскá. **dashing** /ˈdæʃɪŋ/ *adj* лихóй.

data /ˈdeɪtə/ *n pl* дáнные *sb pl*. **database** *n* бáза дáнных.

date[1] /deɪt/ *n* (*fruit*) фи́ник.

date[2] /deɪt/ *n* числó, дáта; (*engagement*) свидáние; **out of ~** устарéлый; **up to ~** совремéнный; в кýрсе дéла; *vt* дати́ровать *impf* & *pf*; (*go out with*) встречáться *impf* с+*instr*; *vi* (*originate*) относи́ться *impf* (**from** к+*instr*).

dative /ˈdeɪtɪv/ *adj* (*n*) дáтельный (падéж).

daub /dɔːb/ *vt* мáзать *impf*, на~ *pf* (**with** +*instr*).

daughter /ˈdɔːtə(r)/ *n* дочь; **~-in-law** невéстка (*in relation to mother*), снохá (*in relation to father*).

daunting /ˈdɔːntɪŋ/ *adj* угрожáющий.

dawdle /ˈdɔːd(ə)l/ *vi* мéшкать *impf*.

dawn /dɔːn/ *n* рассвéт; (*also fig*) заря́; *vi* (*day*) рассветáть *impf*, рассвести́ *pf impers*; **~ (up)on** осеня́ть *impf*, осени́ть *pf*; **it ~ed on me** меня́ осени́ло.

day /deɪ/ *n* день *m*; (*24 hours*) сýтки *pl*; *pl* (*period*) пери́од, врéмя *neut*; **~ after ~** изо дня́ в дéнь; **the ~ after tomorrow** послезáвтра; **the ~ before** наканýне; **the ~ before yesterday** позавчерá; **the other ~** на днях; **by ~** днём; **every other ~** чéрез день; **~ off** выходнóй день *m*; **one ~** однáжды; **these ~s** в нáши дни. **daybreak** *n* рассвéт. **day-dreams** *n pl* мечты́ *f pl*. **daylight** *n* дневнóй свет; **in broad ~** средь бéла дня́. **daytime** *n*: **in the ~** днём.

daze /deɪz/ *n*: **in a ~**, **dazed** /deɪzd/ *adj* оглушён (-енá).

dazzle /ˈdæz(ə)l/ *vt* ослепля́ть *impf*, ослепи́ть *pf*.

deacon /ˈdiːkən/ *n* дья́кон.

dead /ded/ *adj* мёртвый; (*animals*)

до́хлый; (*plants*) увя́дший; (*numb*) онеме́вший; *n*: **the ~** мёртвые *sb pl*; **at ~ of night** глубо́кой но́чью; *adv* соверше́нно; **~ end** тупи́к; **~ heat** одновре́ме́нный фи́ниш; **~line** преде́льный срок; **~lock** тупи́к.

d

deaden /'ded(ə)n/ *vt* заглуша́ть *impf*, заглуши́ть *pf*.

deadly /'dedlɪ/ *adj* смерте́льный.

deaf /def/ *adj* глухо́й; **~ and dumb** глухонемо́й. **deafen** /-f(ə)n/ *vt* оглуша́ть *impf*, оглуши́ть *pf*. **deafness** /-nɪs/ *n* глухота́.

deal[1] /di:l/ *n*: **a great, good, ~** мно́го (+*gen*); (*with comp*) гора́здо.

deal[2] /di:l/ *n* (*bargain*) сде́лка; (*cards*) сда́ча; *vt* (*cards*) сдава́ть *impf*, сдать *pf*; (*blow*) наноси́ть *impf*, нанести́ *pf*; **~ in** торгова́ть *impf* +*instr*; **~ out** распределя́ть *impf*, распредели́ть *pf*; **~ with** (*take care of*) занима́ться *impf*, заня́ться *pf* +*instr*; (*handle a person*) поступа́ть *impf*, поступи́ть *pf* с+*instr*; (*treat a subject*) рассма́тривать *impf*, рассмотре́ть *pf*; (*cope with*) справля́ться *impf*, спра́виться *pf* с+*instr*. **dealer** /'di:lə(r)/ *n* торго́вец (**in** +*instr*).

dean /di:n/ *n* дека́н.

dear /dɪə(r)/ *adj* дорого́й; (*also n*) ми́лый (*sb*).

dearth /dɜ:θ/ *n* недоста́ток.

death /deθ/ *n* смерть; **put to ~** казни́ть *impf* & *pf*; **~bed** *n* сме́ртное ло́же; **~ certificate** свиде́тельство о сме́рти; **~ penalty** сме́ртная казнь. **deathly** /'deθlɪ/ *adj* смерте́льный.

debar /dɪ'bɑ:(r)/ *vt*: **~ from** не допуска́ть *impf* до+*gen*.

debase /dɪ'beɪs/ *vt* унижа́ть *impf*, уни́зить *pf*; (*coinage*) понижа́ть *impf*, пони́зить *pf* ка́чество +*gen*.

debatable /dɪ'beɪtəb(ə)l/ *adj* спо́рный. **debate** /dɪ'beɪθ/ *n* пре́ния (-ий) *pl*; *vt* обсужда́ть *impf*, обсуди́ть *pf*.

debauched /dɪ'bɔ:tʃt/ *adj* развращённый. **debauchery** /-'bɔ:tʃərɪ/ *n* развра́т.

debilitate /dɪ'bɪlɪˌteɪt/ *vt* ослабля́ть; *impf*, осла́бить *pf*. **debility** /-'bɪlɪtɪ/ *n* сла́бость.

debit /'debɪt/ *n* де́бет; *vt* дебетова́ть *impf* & *pf*.

debris /'debri:/ *n* обло́мки *m pl*.

debt /det/ *n* долг. **debtor** /'detə(r)/ *n* должни́к.

début /'deɪbju:/ *n* дебю́т; **make one's ~** дебюти́ровать *impf* & *pf*.

decade /'dekeɪd/ *n* десятиле́тие.

decadence /'dekəd(ə)ns/ *n* дека-де́нтство. **decadent** /-d(ə)nt/ *adj* декаде́нтский.

decaffeinated /di:'kæfɪˌneɪtɪd/ *adj* без кофеи́на.

decant /dɪ'kænt/ *vt* перелива́ть *impf*, перели́ть *pf*. **decanter** /-'kæntə(r)/ *n* графи́н.

decapitate /dɪ'kæpɪˌteɪt/ *vt* обезгла́вливать *impf*, обезгла́вить *pf*.

decay /dɪ'keɪ/ *vi* гнить *impf*, с~ *pf*; (*tooth*) разруша́ться *impf*, разру́шиться *pf*; *n* гние́ние; (*tooth*) разруше́ние.

decease /dɪ'si:s/ *n* конч́ина. **deceased** /-'si:st/ *adj* поко́йный; *n* поко́йник, -ица.

deceit /dɪ'si:t/ *n* обма́н. **deceitful** /-'si:tfʊl/ *adj* лжи́вый. **deceive** /-'si:v/ *vt* обма́нывать *impf*, обману́ть *pf*.

deceleration /di:ˌselə'reɪʃ(ə)n/ *n* замедле́ние.

December /dɪ'sembə(r)/ *n* дека́брь *m*; *adj* дека́брьский.

decency /'di:sənsɪ/ *n* прили́чие. **decent** /-s(ə)nt/ *adj* прили́чный.

decentralization /di:ˌsentrəlaɪ'zeɪʃ(ə)n/ *n* децентрализа́ция. **decentralize** /di:'sentrəˌlaɪz/ *vt* децентрализова́ть *impf* & *pf*.

deception /dɪ'sepʃ(ə)n/ *n* обма́н. **deceptive** /-'septɪv/ *adj* обма́нчивый.

decibel /'desɪˌbel/ *n* децибе́л.

decide /dɪ'saɪd/ *vt* реша́ть *impf*,

реши́ть *pf.* **decided** /-ˈsaɪdɪd/ *adj* реши́тельный.

deciduous /dɪˈsɪdjʊəs/ *adj* листопа́дный.

decimal /ˈdesɪm(ə)l/ *n* десяти́чная дробь; *adj* десяти́чный; **~ point** запята́я *sb.*

decimate /ˈdesɪˌmeɪt/ *vt* (*fig*) коси́ть *impf*, с~ *pf.*

decipher /dɪˈsaɪfə(r)/ *vt* расшифро́вывать *impf*, расшифрова́ть *pf.*

decision /dɪˈsɪʒ(ə)n/ *n* реше́ние. **decisive** /dɪˈsaɪsɪv/ *adj* (*firm*) реши́тельный, (*deciding*) реша́ющий.

deck /dek/ *n* па́луба; (*bus etc.*) эта́ж; **~-chair** *n* шезло́нг; *vt*: **~ out** украша́ть *impf*, укра́сить *pf.*

declaim /dɪˈkleɪm/ *vt* деклами́ровать *impf*, про~ *pf.*

declaration /ˌdekləˈreɪʃ(ə)n/ *n* объявле́ние; (*document*) деклара́ция. **declare** /dɪˈkleə(r)/ *vt* (*proclaim*) объявля́ть *impf*, объяви́ть *pf*; (*assert*) заявля́ть *impf*, заяви́ть *pf.*

declension /dɪˈklenʃ(ə)n/ *n* склоне́ние. **decline** /dɪˈklaɪn/ *n* упа́док; *vi* приходи́ть *impf*, прийти́ *pf* в упа́док; *vt* отклоня́ть *impf*, отклони́ть *pf*; (*gram*) склоня́ть *impf*, про~ *pf.*

decode /diːˈkəʊd/ *vt* расшифро́вывать *impf*, расшифрова́ть *pf.*

decompose /ˌdiːkəmˈpəʊz/ *vi* разлага́ться *impf*, разложи́ться *pf.*

décor /ˈdeɪkɔː(r)/ *n* эстети́ческое оформле́ние. **decorate** /ˈdekəˌreɪt/ *vt* украша́ть *impf*, укра́сить *pf*; (*room*) ремонти́ровать *impf*, от~ *pf*; (*with medal etc.*) награжда́ть *impf*, награди́ть *pf.* **decoration** /ˌdekəˈreɪʃ(ə)n/ *n* украше́ние; (*medal*) о́рден. **decorative** /ˈdekərətɪv/ *adj* декорати́вный. **decorator** /ˈdekəˌreɪtə(r)/ *n* маля́р.

decorous /ˈdekərəs/ *adj* прили́чный. **decorum** /dɪˈkɔːrəm/ *n* прили́чие.

decoy /ˈdiːkɔɪ/ *n* (*bait*) прима́нка; *vt* зама́нивать *impf*, замани́ть *pf.*

decrease *vt & i* /dɪˈkriːs/ уменьша́ть(ся) *impf*, уме́ньшить(ся) *pf*; *n* /ˈdiːkriːs/ уменьше́ние.

decree /dɪˈkriː/ *n* ука́з; *vt* постановля́ть *impf*, постанови́ть *pf.*

decrepit /dɪˈkrepɪt/ *adj* дря́хлый.

dedicate /ˈdedɪˌkeɪt/ *vt* посвяща́ть *impf*, посвяти́ть *pf.* **dedication** /ˌdedɪˈkeɪʃ(ə)n/ *n* посвяще́ние.

deduce /dɪˈdjuːs/ *vt* заключа́ть *impf*, заключи́ть *pf.*

deduct /dɪˈdʌkt/ *vt* вычита́ть *impf*, вы́честь *pf.* **deduction** /-ˈdʌkʃ(ə)n/ *n* (*subtraction*) вы́чет; (*inference*) вы́вод.

deed /diːd/ *n* посту́пок; (*heroic*) по́двиг; (*law*) акт.

deem /diːm/ *vt* счита́ть *impf*, счесть *pf +acc & instr.*

deep /diːp/ *adj* глубо́кий; (*colour*) тёмный; (*sound*) ни́зкий; **~ freeze** морози́льник. **deepen** /-pən/ *vt & i* углубля́ть(ся) *impf*, углуби́ть(ся) *pf.*

deer /dɪə(r)/ *n* оле́нь *m.*

deface /dɪˈfeɪs/ *vt* обезобра́живать *impf*, обезобра́зить *pf.*

defamation /ˌdefəˈmeɪʃ(ə)n/ *n* диффама́ция. **defamatory** /dɪˈfæmətərɪ/ *adj* клеветни́ческий.

default /dɪˈfɔːlt/ *n* (*failure to pay*) неупла́та; (*failure to appear*) нея́вка; (*comput*) автомати́ческий вы́бор; *vi* не выполня́ть *impf* обяза́тельств.

defeat /dɪˈfiːt/ *n* пораже́ние; *vt* побежда́ть *impf*, победи́ть *pf.* **defeatism** /-tɪz(ə)m/ *n* пораже́нчество. **defeatist** /-tɪst/ *n* пораже́нец; *adj* пораже́нческий.

defecate /ˈdefɪˌkeɪt/ *vi* испражня́ться *impf*, испражни́ться *pf.*

defect *n* /ˈdiːfekt/ дефе́кт; *vi* /dɪˈfekt/ перебега́ть *impf*, перебежа́ть *pf.* **defective** /dɪˈfektɪv/ *adj* неиспра́вный. **defector** /dɪˈfektə(r)/ *n* перебе́жчик.

defence /dɪˈfens/ *n* защи́та. **defenceless** /-ˈfenslɪs/ *adj* беззащи́тный. **defend** /-'fend/ *vt* защища́ть *impf*, защити́ть *pf.* **defendant** /-'fend(ə)nt/ *n* подсуди́мый *sb.* **defender** /-'fendə(r)/ *n* защи́тник. **defensive** /-'fensɪv/ *adj* оборони́тельный.

defer[1] /dɪ'fɜː(r)/ *vt* (*postpone*) отсро́чивать *impf*, отсро́чить *pf.*

defer[2] /dɪ'fɜː(r)/ *vi*: **~ to** подчиня́ться *impf* +*dat.* **deference** /'defərəns/ *n* уваже́ние. **deferential** /ˌdefə'renʃ(ə)l/ *adj* почти́тельный.

defiance /dɪ'faɪəns/ *n* неповинове́ние; **in ~ of** вопреки́+*dat.* **defiant** /-'faɪənt/ *adj* вызыва́ющий.

deficiency /dɪ'fɪʃənsɪ/ *n* недоста́ток. **deficient** /-'fɪʃ(ə)nt/ *adj* недоста́точный. **deficit** /'defɪsɪt/ *n* дефици́т.

defile /dɪ'faɪl/ *vt* оскверня́ть *impf*, оскверни́ть *pf.*

define /dɪ'faɪn/ *vt* определя́ть *impf*, определи́ть *pf.* **definite** /'defɪnɪt/ *adj* определённый **definitely** /'defɪnɪtlɪ/ *adv* несомне́нно. **definition** /ˌdefɪ'nɪʃ(ə)n/ *n* определе́ние. **definitive** /dɪ'fɪnɪtɪv/ *adj* оконча́тельный.

deflate /dɪ'fleɪt/ *vt* & *i* спуска́ть *impf*, спусти́ть *pf*; *vt* (*person*) сбива́ть *impf*, сбить *pf* спесь с+*gen.* **deflation** /-'fleɪʃ(ə)n/ *n* дефля́ция.

deflect /dɪ'flekt/ *vt* отклоня́ть *impf*, отклони́ть *pf.*

deforestation /diːˌfɒrɪ'steɪʃ(ə)n/ *n* обезле́сение.

deformed /dɪ'fɔːmd/ *adj* уро́дливый. **deformity** /-'fɔːmɪtɪ/ *n* уро́дство.

defraud /dɪ'frɔːd/ *vt* обма́нывать *impf*, обману́ть *pf*; **~ of** выма́нивать *impf*, вы́манить *pf* +*acc* & у+*gen* (*of person*).

defray /dɪ'freɪ/ *vt* опла́чивать *impf*, оплати́ть *pf.*

defrost /diː'frɒst/ *vt* размора́живать *impf*, разморо́зить *pf.*

deft /deft/ *adj* ло́вкий.

defunct /dɪ'fʌŋkt/ *adj* бо́льше не существу́ющий.

defy /dɪ'faɪ/ *vt* (*challenge*) вызыва́ть *impf*, вы́звать *pf*; (*disobey*) идти́ *impf*, по~ *pf* про́тив+*acc*; (*fig*) не поддава́ться *impf* +*dat.*

degenerate *vi* / dɪ'dʒenəˌreɪt/ вырожда́ться *impf*, вы́родиться *pf*; *adj* /dɪ'dʒenərət/ вы́родившийся.

degradation /ˌdegrə'deɪʃ(ə)n/ *n* униже́ние. **degrade** /dɪ'greɪd/ *vt* унижа́ть *impf*, уни́зить *pf.* **degrading** /dɪ'greɪdɪŋ/ *adj* унизи́тельный.

degree /dɪ'griː/ *n* сте́пень; (*math etc.*) гра́дус; (*univ*) учёная сте́пень.

dehydrate /diː'haɪdreɪt/ *vt* обезво́живать *impf*, обезво́дить *pf.* **dehydration** /-'dreɪʃ(ə)n/ *n* обезво́живание.

deign /deɪn/ *vi* снисходи́ть *impf*, снизойти́ *pf.*

deity /'diːɪtɪ/ *n* божество́.

dejected /dɪ'dʒektɪd/ *adj* удручённый.

delay /dɪ'leɪ/ *n* заде́ржка; **without ~** неме́дленно; *vt* заде́рживать *impf*, задержа́ть *pf.*

delegate *n* /'delɪgət/ делега́т; *vt* /'delɪˌgeɪt/ делеги́ровать *impf* & *pf.* **delegation** /-'geɪʃ(ə)n/ *n* делега́ция.

delete /dɪ'liːt/ *vt* вычёркивать *impf*, вы́черкнуть *pf.*

deliberate *adj* /dɪ'lɪbərət/ (*intentional*) преднаме́ренный; (*careful*) осторо́жный; *vt* & *i* /dɪ'lɪbəˌreɪt/ размышля́ть *impf*, размы́слить *pf* (о+*prep*); (*discuss*) совеща́ться *impf* (о+*prep*). **deliberation** /dɪˌlɪbə'reɪʃ(ə)n/ *n* размышле́ние; (*discussion*) совеща́ние.

delicacy /'delɪkəsɪ/ *n* (*tact*) делика́тность; (*dainty*) ла́комство. **delicate** /-kət/ *adj* то́нкий; (*tactful, needing tact*) делика́тный; (*health*) боле́зненный.

delicatessen /ˌdelɪkə'tes(ə)n/ *n* гастроно́м.

delicious /dɪ'lɪʃəs/ *adj* о́чень вку́сный.

delight /dɪ'laɪt/ *n* наслажде́ние;

(*delightful thing*) пре́лесть. **delightful** /-fʊl/ *adj* преле́стный.

delinquency /dɪ'lɪŋkwənsɪ/ *n* престу́пность. **delinquent** /-wənt/ *n* правонаруши́тель *m*, ~ница; *adj* вино́вный.

delirious /dɪ'lɪrɪəs/ *adj*: **be** ~ бре́дить *impf*. **delirium** /-rɪəm/ *n* бред.

deliver /dɪ'lɪvə(r)/ *vt* (*goods*) доставля́ть *impf*, доста́вить *pf*; (*save*) избавля́ть *impf*, изба́вить *pf* (**from** от+*gen*); (*lecture*) прочита́ть *impf*, проче́сть *pf*; (*letters*) разноси́ть *impf*, разнести́ *pf*; (*speech*) произноси́ть *impf*, произнести́ *pf*; (*blow*) наноси́ть *impf*, нанести́ *pf*. **deliverance** /-'lɪvərəns/ *n* избавле́ние. **delivery** /-'lɪvərɪ/ *n* доста́вка.

delta /'deltə/ *n* де́льта.

delude /dɪ'lu:d/ *vt* вводи́ть *impf*, ввести́ *pf* в заблужде́ние.

deluge /'delju:dʒ/ *n* (*flood*) пото́п; (*rain*) ли́вень *m*; (*fig*) пото́к.

delusion /dɪ'lu:ʒ(ə)n/ *n* заблужде́ние; ~**s of grandeur** ма́ния вели́чия.

de luxe /də 'lʌks/ *adj* -люкс (*added to noun*).

delve /delv/ *vi* углубля́ться *impf*, углуби́ться *pf* (**into** в+*acc*).

demand /dɪ'mɑ:nd/ *n* тре́бование; (*econ*) спрос (**for** на+*acc*); *vt* тре́бовать *impf*, по~ *pf* +*gen*. **demanding** /-dɪŋ/ *adj* тре́бовательный.

demarcation /ˌdi:mɑ:'keɪʃ(ə)n/ *n* демарка́ция.

demean /dɪ'mi:n/ *vt*: ~ **o.s.** унижа́ться *impf*, уни́зиться *pf*.

demeanour /dɪ'mi:nə(r)/ *n* мане́ра вести́ себя́.

demented /dɪ'mentɪd/ *adj* сумасше́дший. **dementia** /-'menʃə/ *n* слабоу́мие.

demise /dɪ'maɪz/ *n* кончи́на.

demobilize /di:'məʊbɪˌlaɪz/ *vt* демобилизова́ть *impf* & *pf*.

democracy /dɪ'mɒkrəsɪ/ *n* демокра́тия. **democrat** /'deməˌkræt/ *n* демокра́т. **democratic** /ˌdemə'krætɪk/ *adj* демократи́ческий. **democratization** /dɪˌmɒkrətaɪ'zeɪʃ(ə)n/ *n* демократиза́ция.

demolish /dɪ'mɒlɪʃ/ *vt* (*destroy*) разруша́ть *impf*, разру́шить *pf*; (*building*) сноси́ть *impf*, снести́ *pf*; (*refute*) опроверга́ть *impf*, опрове́ргнуть *pf*. **demolition** /ˌdemə'lɪʃ(ə)n/ *n* разруше́ние; снос.

demon /'di:mən/ *n* де́мон.

demonstrable /'demɒnstrəb(ə)l/ *adj* доказу́емый. **demonstrably** /dɪ'mɒnstrəblɪ/ *adv* нагля́дно. **demonstrate** /'demənˌstreɪt/ *vt* демонстри́ровать *impf* & *pf*; *vi* уча́ствовать *impf* в демонстра́ции. **demonstration** /ˌdemən'streɪʃ(ə)n/ *n* демонстра́ция. **demonstrative** /dɪ'mɒnstrətɪv/ *adj* экспанси́вный; (*gram*) указа́тельный. **demonstrator** /'demənˌstreɪtə(r)/ *n* демонстра́тор; (*polit*) демонстра́нт.

demoralize /dɪ'mɒrəˌlaɪz/ *vt* деморализова́ть *impf* & *pf*.

demote /dɪ'məʊt/ *vt* понижа́ть *impf*, пони́зить *pf* в до́лжности.

demure /dɪ'mjʊə(r)/ *adj* скро́мный.

den /den/ *n* берло́га.

denial /dɪ'naɪəl/ *n* отрица́ние; (*refusal*) отка́з.

denigrate /'denɪˌgreɪt/ *vt* черни́ть *impf*, о~ *pf*.

denim /'denɪm/ *adj* джинсо́вый; *n* джинсо́вая ткань.

Denmark /'denmɑ:k/ *n* Да́ния.

denomination /dɪˌnɒmɪ'neɪʃ(ə)n/ *n* (*money*) досто́инство; (*relig*) вероисповеда́ние. **denominator** /dɪ'nɒmɪˌneɪtə(r)/ *n* знамена́тель *m*.

denote /dɪ'nəʊt/ *vt* означа́ть *impf*, озна́чить *pf*.

denounce /dɪ'naʊns/ *vt* (*condemn*) осужда́ть *impf*, осуди́ть *pf*; (*inform on*) доноси́ть *impf*, донести́ *pf* на+*acc*.

dense /dens/ *adj* густо́й; (*stupid*)

d

тупой. **density** /ˈdensɪtɪ/ *n* плотность.

dent /dent/ *n* вмятина; *vt* делать *impf*, с~ *pf* вмятину в+*prep*.

dental /ˈdent(ə)l/ *adj* зубной. **dentist** /ˈdentɪst/ *n* зубной врач. **dentures** /ˈdentʃəz/ *n pl* зубной протез.

d

denunciation /dɪˌnʌnsɪˈeɪʃ(ə)n/ *n* (*condemnation*) осуждение; (*informing*) донос.

deny /dɪˈnaɪ/ *vt* отрицать *impf*; (*refuse*) отказывать *impf*, отказать *pf* +*dat* (*person*) в+*prep*.

deodorant /diːˈəʊdərənt/ *n* дезодорант.

depart /dɪˈpɑːt/ *vi* отбывать *impf*, отбыть *pf*; (*deviate*) отклоняться *impf*, отклониться *pf* (**from** от+*gen*).

department /dɪˈpɑːtmənt/ *n* отдел; (*univ*) кафедра; ~ **store** универмаг.

departure /dɪˈpɑːtʃə(r)/ *n* отбытие; (*deviation*) отклонение.

depend /dɪˈpend/ *vi* зависеть *impf* (**on** от+*gen*); (*rely*) полагаться *impf*, положиться *pf* (**on** на+*acc*). **dependable** /-ˈpendəb(ə)l/ *adj* надёжный. **dependant** /-ˈpend(ə)nt/ *n* иждивенец. **dependence** /-ˈpend(ə)ns/ *n* зависимость. **dependent** /-ˈpend(ə)nt/ *adj* зависимый.

depict /dɪˈpɪkt/ *vt* изображать *impf*, изобразить *pf*.

deplete /dɪˈpliːt/ *vt* истощать *impf*, истощить *pf*. **depleted** /-ˈpliːtɪd/ *adj* истощённый. **depletion** /-ˈpliːʃ(ə)n/ *n* истощение.

deplorable /dɪˈplɔːrəb(ə)l/ *adj* плачевный. **deplore** /dɪˈplɔː(r)/ *vt* сожалеть *impf* о+*prep*.

deploy /dɪˈplɔɪ/ *vt* развёртывать *impf*, развернуть *pf*. **deployment** /-mənt/ *n* развёртывание.

deport /dɪˈpɔːt/ *vt* депортировать *impf* & *pf*; высылать *impf*, выслать *pf*. **deportation** /ˌdiːpɔːˈteɪʃ(ə)n/ *n* депортация; высылка.

deportment /dɪˈpɔːtmənt/ *n* осанка.

depose /dɪˈpəʊz/ *vt* свергать *impf*, свергнуть *pf*. **deposit** /-ˈpɒzɪt/ *n* (*econ*) вклад; (*advance*) задаток; (*sediment*) осадок; (*coal etc.*) месторождение; *vt* (*econ*) вносить *impf*, внести *pf*.

depot /ˈdepəʊ/ *n* (*transport*) депо *neut indecl*; (*store*) склад.

deprave /dɪˈpreɪv/ *vt* развращать *impf*, развратить *pf*. **depraved** /-ˈpreɪvd/ *adj* развращённый. **depravity** /-ˈprævɪtɪ/ *n* разврат.

deprecate /ˈdeprɪˌkeɪt/ *vt* осуждать *impf*, осудить *pf*.

depreciate /dɪˈpriːʃɪˌeɪt/ *vt* & *i* (*econ*) обесценивать(ся) *impf*, обесценить(ся) *pf*. **depreciation** /-ˈeɪʃ(ə)n/ *n* обесценение.

depress /dɪˈpres/ *vt* (*dispirit*) удручать *impf*, удручить *pf*. **depressed** /-ˈprest/ *adj* удручённый. **depressing** /-ˈpresɪŋ/ *adj* угнетающий. **depression** /-ˈpreʃ(ə)n/ *n* (*hollow*) впадина; (*econ, med, meteorol, etc.*) депрессия.

deprivation /ˌdeprɪˈveɪʃ(ə)n/ *n* лишение. **deprive** /dɪˈpraɪv/ *vt* лишать *impf*, лишить *pf* (**of** +*gen*)

depth /depθ/ *n* глубина; **in the ~ of winter** в разгаре зимы.

deputation /ˌdepjʊˈteɪʃ(ə)n/ *n* депутация. **deputize** /ˈdepjʊˌtaɪz/ *vi* замещать *impf*, заместить *pf* (**for** +*acc*). **deputy** /ˈdepjʊtɪ/ *n* заместитель *m*; (*parl*) депутат.

derail /dɪˈreɪl/ *vt*: **be derailed** сходить *impf*, сойти *pf* с рельсов. **derailment** /-mənt/ *n* сход с рельсов.

deranged /dɪˈreɪndʒd/ *adj* сумасшедший.

derelict /ˈderəlɪkt/ *adj* заброшенный.

deride /dɪˈraɪd/ *vt* высмеивать *impf*, высмеять *pf*. **derision** /-ˈrɪʒ(ə)n/ *n* высмеивание. **derisive** /-ˈraɪsɪv/ *adj* (*mocking*) насмешливый. **derisory** /-ˈraɪsərɪ/ *adj* (*ridiculous*) смехотворный.

derivation /ˌderɪˈveɪʃ(ə)n/ *n* происхождéние. **derivative** /dəˈrɪvətɪv/ *n* производное *sb*; *adj* производный. **derive** /dɪˈraɪv/ *vt* извлекáть *impf*, извлéчь *pf*; *vi*: ~ **from** происходи́ть *impf*, произойти́ *pf* от+*gen*.

derogatory /dɪˈrɒgətərɪ/ *adj* отрицáтельный.

descend /dɪˈsend/ *vi* (& *t*) (*go down*) спускáться *impf*, спусти́ться *pf* (с+*gen*); **be descended from** происходи́ть *impf*, произойти́ *pf* из, от, +*gen*. **descendant** /-ˈsend(ə)nt/ *n* потóмок. **descent** /-ˈsent/ *n* спуск; (*lineage*) происхождéние.

describe /dɪˈskraɪb/ *vt* опи́сывать *impf*, описáть *pf*. **description** /-ˈskrɪpʃ(ə)n/ *n* описáние. **descriptive** /-ˈskrɪptɪv/ *adj* описáтельный.

desecrate /ˈdesɪˌkreɪt/ *vt* осквернять *impf*, оскверни́ть *pf*. **desecration** /ˌdesɪˈkreɪʃ(ə)n/ *n* осквернéние.

desert[1] /ˈdezət/ *n* (*waste*) пусты́ня.

desert[2] /dɪˈzɜːt/ *vt* покидáть *impf*, поки́нуть *pf*; (*mil*) дезерти́ровать *impf* & *pf*. **deserter** /-ˈzɜːtə(r)/ *n* дезерти́р. **desertion** /-ˈzɜːʃ(ə)n/ *n* дезерти́рство.

deserts /dɪˈzɜːts/ *n pl* заслу́ги *f pl*. **deserve** /-ˈzɜːv/ *vt* заслу́живать *impf*, заслужи́ть *pf*. **deserving** /-ˈzɜːvɪŋ/ *adj* достóйный (**of** +*gen*).

design /dɪˈzaɪn/ *n* (*pattern*) узóр; (*of car etc.*) констру́кция, проéкт; (*industrial*) дизáйн; (*aim*) у́мысел; *vt* проекти́ровать *impf*, с~ *pf*; (*intend*) предназначáть *impf*, предназнáчить *pf*.

designate /ˈdezɪgˌneɪt/ *vt* (*indicate*) обозначáть *impf*, обознáчить *pf*; (*appoint*) назначáть *impf*, назнáчить *pf*.

designer /dɪˈzaɪnə(r)/ *n* (*tech*) констру́ктор; (*industrial*) дизáйнер; (*of clothes*) модельéр.

desirable /dɪˈzaɪərəb(ə)l/ *adj* желáтельный. **desire** /-ˈzaɪə(r)/ *n* желáние; *vt* желáть *impf*, по~ *pf* +*gen*.

desist /dɪˈzɪst/ *vi* (*refrain*) воздéрживаться *impf*, воздержáться *pf* (**from** от+*gen*).

desk /desk/ *n* пи́сьменный стол; (*school*) пáрта.

desolate /ˈdesələt/ *adj* забрóшенный. **desolation** /ˌdesəˈleɪʃ(ə)n/ *n* забрóшенность.

despair /dɪˈspeə(r)/ *n* отчáяние; *vi* отчáиваться *impf*, отчáяться *pf*. **desperate** /ˈdespərət/ *adj* отчáянный. **desperation** /ˌdespəˈreɪʃ(ə)n/ *n* отчáяние.

despicable /dɪˈspɪkəb(ə)l/ *adj* презрéнный. **despise** /dɪˈspaɪz/ *vt* презирáть *impf*, презрéть *pf*.

despite /dɪˈspaɪt/ *prep* несмотря́ на+*acc*.

despondency /dɪˈspɒndənsɪ/ *n* уны́ние. **despondent** /-d(ə)nt/ *adj* уны́лый.

despot /ˈdespɒt/ *n* дéспот.

dessert /dɪˈzɜːt/ *n* десéрт.

destination /ˌdestɪˈneɪʃ(ə)n/ *n* (*of goods*) мéсто назначéния; (*of journey*) цель. **destiny** /ˈdestɪnɪ/ *n* судьбá.

destitute /ˈdestɪˌtjuːt/ *adj* без вся́ких средств.

destroy /dɪˈstrɔɪ/ *vt* разрушáть *impf*, разру́шить *pf*. **destroyer** /-ˈstrɔɪə(r)/ *n* (*naut*) эсми́нец. **destruction** /-ˈstrʌkʃ(ə)n/ *n* разрушéние. **destructive** /-ˈstrʌktɪv/ *adj* разруши́тельный.

detach /dɪˈtætʃ/ *vt* отделя́ть *impf*, отдели́ть *pf*. **detached** /-ˈtætʃt/ *adj* отдéльный; (*objective*) беспристрáстный; ~ **house** особня́к. **detachment** /-ˈtætʃmənt/ *n* (*objectivity*) беспристрáстие; (*mil*) отря́д.

detail /ˈdiːteɪl/ *n* детáль, подрóбность; **in detail** подрóбно; *vt* подрóбно расскáзывать *impf*, рассказáть *pf*. **detailed** /-teɪld/ *adj* подрóбный.

detain /dɪˈteɪn/ *vt* задéрживать *impf*, задержáть *pf*. **detainee** /ˌdiːteɪˈniː/ *n* задéржанный *sb*.

d

d

detect /dɪˈtekt/ *vt* обнару́живать *impf*, обнару́жить *pf.* **detection** /-ˈtekʃ(ə)n/ *n* обнаруже́ние; (*crime*) рассле́дование. **detective** /-ˈtektɪv/ *n* детекти́в; ~ **film, story,** *etc.* детекти́в. **detector** /-ˈtektə(r)/ *n* дете́ктор.

detention /dɪˈtenʃ(ə)n/ *n* задержа́ние; (*school*) заде́ржка в наказа́ние.

deter /dɪˈtɜː(r)/ *vt* уде́рживать *impf*, удержа́ть *pf* (**from** от+*gen*).

detergent /dɪˈtɜːdʒ(ə)nt/ *n* мо́ющее сре́дство.

deteriorate /dɪˈtɪərɪəˌreɪt/ *vi* ухудша́ться *impf*, уху́дшиться *pf.* **deterioration** /-ˈreɪʃ(ə)n/ *n* ухудше́ние.

determination /dɪˌtɜːmɪˈneɪʃ(ə)n/ *n* реши́мость. **determine** /dɪˈtɜːmɪn/ *vt* (*ascertain*) устана́вливать *impf*, установи́ть *pf*; (*be decisive factor*) определя́ть *impf*, определи́ть *pf*; (*decide*) реша́ть *impf*, реши́ть *pf.* **determined** /dɪˈtɜːmɪnd/ *adj* реши́тельный.

deterrent /dɪˈterənt/ *n* сре́дство устраше́ния.

detest /dɪˈtest/ *vt* ненави́деть *impf.* **detestable** /-ˈtestəb(ə)l/ *adj* отврати́тельный.

detonate /ˈdetəˌneɪt/ *vt & i* взрыва́ть(ся) *impf*, взорва́ть(ся) *pf.* **detonator** /-tə(r)/ *n* детона́тор.

detour /ˈdiːtʊə(r)/ *n* объе́зд.

detract /dɪˈtrækt/ *vi*: ~ **from** умаля́ть *impf*, умали́ть *pf* +*acc.*

detriment /ˈdetrɪmənt/ *n* уще́рб. **detrimental** /-ˈment(ə)l/ *adj* вре́дный.

deuce /djuːs/ *n* (*tennis*) ра́вный счёт.

devaluation /diːˌvæljuːˈeɪʃ(ə)n/ *n* девальва́ция. **devalue** /diːˈvæljuː/ *vt* девальви́ровать *impf & pf.*

devastate /ˈdevəˌsteɪt/ *vt* опустоша́ть *impf*, опустоши́ть *pf.* **devastated** /-ˌsteɪtɪd/ *adj* потрясённый. **devastating** /-ˌsteɪtɪŋ/ *adj* уничтожа́ющий. **devastation** /-ˈsteɪʃ(ə)n/ *n* опустоше́ние.

develop /dɪˈveləp/ *vt & i* развива́ть(ся) *impf*, разви́ть(ся) *pf*; *vt* (*phot*) проявля́ть *impf*, прояви́ть *pf.* **developer** /-pə(r)/ *n* (*of land etc.*) застро́йщик. **development** /-mənt/ *n* разви́тие.

deviant /ˈdiːvɪənt/ *adj* ненорма́льный. **deviate** /-vɪeɪt/ *vi* отклоня́ться *impf*, отклони́ться *pf* (**from** от+*gen*). **deviation** /ˌdiːvɪˈeɪʃ(ə)n/ *n* отклоне́ние.

device /dɪˈvaɪs/ *n* прибо́р.

devil /ˈdev(ə)l/ *n* чёрт. **devilish** /ˈdevəlɪʃ/ *adj* черто́вский.

devious /ˈdiːvɪəs/ *adj* (*circuitous*) окружно́й; (*person*) непоря́дочный.

devise /dɪˈvaɪz/ *vt* приду́мывать *impf*, приду́мать *pf.*

devoid /dɪˈvɔɪd/ *adj* лишённый (**of** +*gen*).

devolution /ˌdiːvəˈluːʃ(ə)n/ *n* переда́ча (вла́сти).

devote /dɪˈvəʊt/ *vt* посвяща́ть *impf*, посвяти́ть *pf.* **devoted** /-ˈvəʊtɪd/ *adj* пре́данный. **devotee** /ˌdevəˈtiː/ *n* покло́нник. **devotion** /dɪˈvəʊʃ(ə)n/ *n* пре́данность.

devour /dɪˈvaʊə(r)/ *vt* пожира́ть *impf*, пожра́ть *pf.*

devout /dɪˈvaʊt/ *adj* на́божный.

dew /djuː/ *n* роса́.

dexterity /dekˈsterɪtɪ/ *n* ло́вкость. **dext(e)rous** /ˈdekstrəs/ *adj* ло́вкий.

diabetes /ˌdaɪəˈbiːtiːz/ *n* диабе́т. **diabetic** /ˌdaɪəˈbetɪk/ *n* диабе́тик; *adj* диабети́ческий.

diabolic(al) /ˌdaɪəˈbɒlɪk((ə)l)/ *adj* дья́вольский.

diagnose /ˈdaɪəgˌnəʊz/ *vt* диагности́ровать *impf & pf.* **diagnosis** /ˌdaɪəgˈnəʊsɪs/ *n* диа́гноз.

diagonal /daɪˈægən(ə)l/ *n* диагона́ль; *adj* диагона́льный. **diagonally** /-ˈægənəlɪ/ *adv* по диагона́ли.

diagram /ˈdaɪəˌgræm/ *n* диагра́мма.

dial /ˈdaɪ(ə)l/ *n* (*clock*) цифербла́т;

(*tech*) шкала́; *vt* набира́ть *impf*, набра́ть *pf*.
dialect /ˈdaɪəˌlekt/ *n* диале́кт.
dialogue /ˈdaɪəˌlɒg/ *n* диало́г.
diameter /daɪˈæmɪtə(r)/ *n* диа́метр. **diametric(al)** /ˌdaɪəˈmetrɪk((ə)l)/ *adj* диаметра́льный; **~ly opposed** диаметра́льно противополо́жный.
diamond /ˈdaɪəmənd/ *n* алма́з; (*shape*) ромб; *pl* (*cards*) бу́бны (-бён, -бна́м) *pl*.
diaper /ˈdaɪəpə(r)/ *n* пелёнка.
diaphragm /ˈdaɪəˌfræm/ *n* диафра́гма.
diarrhoea /ˌdaɪəˈrɪə/ *n* поно́с.
diary /ˈdaɪərɪ/ *n* дневни́к.
dice /daɪs/ *see* **die**[1]
dicey /ˈdaɪsɪ/ *adj* риско́ванный.
dictate /dɪkˈteɪt/ *vt* диктова́ть *impf*, про~ *pf*. **dictation** /-ˈteɪʃ(ə)n/ *n* дикто́вка. **dictator** /-ˈteɪtə(r)/ *n* дикта́тор. **dictatorial** /ˌdɪktəˈtɔːrɪəl/ *adj* дикта́торский. **dictatorship** /dɪkˈteɪtəʃɪp/ *n* диктату́ра.
diction /ˈdɪkʃ(ə)n/ *n* ди́кция.
dictionary /ˈdɪkʃənrɪ/ *n* слова́рь *m*.
didactic /daɪˈdæktɪk/ *adj* дидакти́ческий.
die[1] /daɪ/ *n* (*pl* **dice** /daɪs/) игра́льная кость; (*pl* **dies** /daɪz/) (*stamp*) штамп.
die[2] /daɪ/ *vi* (*person*) умира́ть *impf*, умере́ть *pf*; (*animal*) до́хнуть *impf*, из~, по~ *pf*; (*plant*) вя́нуть *impf*, за~ *pf*; **be dying to** о́чень хоте́ть *impf*; **~ down** (*fire, sound*) угаса́ть *impf*, уга́снуть *pf*; **~ out** вымира́ть *impf*, вы́мереть *pf*.
diesel /ˈdiːz(ə)l/ *n* (*engine*) ди́зель *m*; *attrib* ди́зельный.
diet /ˈdaɪət/ *n* дие́та; (*habitual food*) пи́ща; *vi* быть на дие́те. **dietary** /ˈdaɪətrɪ/ *adj* диети́ческий.
differ /ˈdɪfə(r)/ *vi* отлича́ться *impf*; различа́ться *impf*; (*disagree*) расходи́ться *impf*, разойти́сь *pf*. **difference** /ˈdɪfrəns/ *n* ра́зница; (*disagreement*) разногла́сие. **different** /ˈdɪfrənt/ *adj* разли́чный, ра́зный. **differential** /ˌdɪfəˈrenʃ(ə)l/ *n* (*difference*) ра́зница. **differentiate** /ˌdɪfəˈrenʃɪˌeɪt/ *vt* различа́ть *impf*, различи́ть *pf*.
difficult /ˈdɪfɪkəlt/ *adj* тру́дный. **difficulty** /-kəltɪ/ *n* тру́дность; (*difficult situation*) затрудне́ние; **without ~** без труда́.
diffidence /ˈdɪfɪdəns/ *n* неуве́ренность в себе́. **diffident** /-d(ə)nt/ *adj* неуве́ренный в себе́.
diffused /dɪˈfjuːzd/ *adj* рассе́янный.
dig /dɪg/ *n* (*archaeol*) раско́пки *f pl*; (*poke*) тычо́к; (*gibe*) шпи́лька; *pl* (*lodgings*) кварти́ра; **give a ~ in the ribs** ткнуть *pf* ло́ктем под ребро́; *vt* копа́ть *impf*, вы́~ *pf*; рыть *impf*, вы́~ *pf*; **~ up** (*bone*) выка́пывать *impf*, вы́копать *pf*; (*land*) вска́пывать *impf*, вскопа́ть *pf*.
digest /daɪˈdʒest/ *vt* перева́ривать *impf*, перевари́ть *pf*. **digestible** /-ˈdʒestɪb(ə)l/ *adj* удобовари́мый. **digestion** /-ˈdʒestʃ(ə)n/ *n* пищеваре́ние.
digger /ˈdɪgə(r)/ *n* (*tech*) экскава́тор.
digit /ˈdɪdʒɪt/ *n* (*math*) знак.
digital /ˈdɪdʒɪt(ə)l/ *adj* цифрово́й.
dignified /ˈdɪgnɪˌfaɪd/ *adj* велича́вый. **dignitary** /-nɪtərɪ/ *n* сано́вник. **dignity** /-nɪtɪ/ *n* досто́инство.
digress /daɪˈgres/ *vi* отклоня́ться *impf*, отклони́ться *pf*. **digression** /-ˈgreʃ(ə)n/ *n* отклоне́ние.
dike /daɪk/ *n* да́мба; (*ditch*) ров.
dilapidated /dɪˈlæpɪˌdeɪtɪd/ *adj* ве́тхий.
dilate /daɪˈleɪt/ *vt & i* расширя́ть(ся) *impf*, расши́рить(ся) *pf*.
dilemma /daɪˈlemə/ *n* диле́мма.
dilettante /ˌdɪlɪˈtæntɪ/ *n* дилета́нт.
diligence /ˈdɪlɪdʒ(ə)ns/ *n* прилежа́ние. **diligent** /-lɪdʒ(ə)nt/ *adj* приле́жный.
dilute /daɪˈljuːt/ *vt* разбавля́ть *impf*, разба́вить *pf*.
dim /dɪm/ *adj* (*not bright*) ту́склый;

(*vague*) смýтный; (*stupid*) тупóй. **dimension** /daɪˈmenʃ(ə)n/ *n* (*pl*) размéры *m pl*; (*math*) измерéние. **-dimensional** /-ˈmenʃən(ə)l/ *in comb* -мéрный; **three-~** трёхмéрный.

diminish /dɪˈmɪnɪʃ/ *vt & i* уменьшáть(ся) *impf*, умéньшить(ся) *pf*. **diminutive** /-ˈmɪnjʊtɪv/ *adj* мáленький; *n* уменьшúтельное *sb*.

dimness /ˈdɪmnɪs/ *n* тýсклость.

dimple /ˈdɪmp(ə)l/ *n* я́мочка.

din /dɪn/ *n* грóхот; (*voices*) гам.

dine /daɪn/ *vi* обéдать *impf*, по~ *pf*. **diner** /ˈdaɪnə(r)/ *n* обéдающий *sb*.

dinghy /ˈdɪŋgɪ/ *n* шлю́пка; (*rubber* ~) надувнáя лóдка.

dingy /ˈdɪndʒɪ/ *adj* (*drab*) тýсклый; (*dirty*) гря́зный.

dining-car /ˈdaɪnɪŋ kɑː/ *n* вагóн-ресторáн. **dining-room** *n* столóвая *sb*. **dinner** /ˈdɪnə(r)/ *n* обéд; **~-jacket** смóкинг.

dinosaur /ˈdaɪnəˌsɔː(r)/ *n* динозáвр.

diocese /ˈdaɪəsɪs/ *n* епáрхия.

dip /dɪp/ *vt* (*immerse*) окунáть *impf*, окунýть *pf*; (*partially*) обмáкивать *impf*, обмакнýть *pf*; *vi* (*slope*) понижáться *impf*, понúзиться *pf*; *n* (*depression*) впáдина; (*slope*) уклóн; **have a ~** (*bathe*) купáться *impf*, вы́~ *pf*.

diphtheria /dɪfˈθɪərɪə/ *n* дифтерúя.

diphthong /ˈdɪfθɒŋ/ *n* дифтóнг.

diploma /dɪˈpləʊmə/ *n* диплóм. **diplomacy** /-ˈpləʊməsɪ/ *n* дипломáтия. **diplomat** /ˈdɪpləˌmæt/ *n* дипломáт. **diplomatic** /ˌdɪpləˈmætɪk/ *adj* дипломатúческий.

dire /ˈdaɪə(r)/ *adj* стрáшный; (*ominous*) зловéщий.

direct /daɪˈrekt/ *adj* прямóй; **~ current** постоя́нный ток; *vt* направля́ть *impf*, напрáвить *pf*; (*guide, manage*) руководúть *impf* +*instr*; (*film*) режиссúровать *impf*. **direction** /-ˈrekʃ(ə)n/ *n* направлéние; (*guidance*) руковóдство; (*instruction*) указáние; (*film*) режиссýра; **stage ~** ремáрка. **directive** /-ˈrektɪv/ *n* директúва. **directly** /-ˈrektlɪ/ *adv* пря́мо; (*at once*) срáзу. **director** /-ˈrektə(r)/ *n* дирéктор; (*film etc.*) режиссёр(-постанóвщик). **directory** /-ˈrektərɪ/ *n* спрáвочник, указáтель *m*; (*tel*) телефóнная кнúга.

dirt /dɜːt/ *n* грязь. **dirty** /ˈdɜːtɪ/ *adj* гря́зный; *vt* пáчкать *impf*, за~ *pf*.

disability /ˌdɪsəˈbɪlɪtɪ/ *n* физúческий/психúческий недостáток; (*disablement*) инвалúдность. **disabled** /dɪsˈeɪb(ə)ld/ *adj*: **he is ~** он инвалúд.

disadvantage /ˌdɪsədˈvɑːntɪdʒ/ *n* невы́годное положéние; (*defect*) недостáток. **disadvantageous** /dɪsˌædvənˈteɪdʒəs/ *adj* невы́годный.

disaffected /ˌdɪsəˈfektɪd/ *adj* недовóльный.

disagree /ˌdɪsəˈgriː/ *vi* не соглашáться *impf*, согласúться *pf*; (*not correspond*) не соотвéтствовать *impf* +*dat*. **disagreeable** /-ˈgriːəb(ə)l/ *adj* неприя́тный. **disagreement** /-ˈgriːmənt/ *n* разноглáсие; (*quarrel*) ссóра.

disappear /ˌdɪsəˈpɪə(r)/ *vi* исчезáть *impf*, исчéзнуть *pf*. **disappearance** /-ˈpɪərəns/ *n* исчезновéние.

disappoint /ˌdɪsəˈpɔɪnt/ *vt* разочарóвывать *impf*, разочаровáть *pf*. **disappointed** /-ˈpɔɪntɪd/ *adj* разочарóванный. **disappointing** /-ˈpɔɪntɪŋ/ *adj* разочарóвывающий. **disappointment** /-ˈpɔɪntmənt/ *n* разочаровáние.

disapproval /ˌdɪsəˈpruːv(ə)l/ *n* неодобрéние. **disapprove** /ˌdɪsəˈpruːv/ *vt & i* не одобря́ть *impf*.

disarm /dɪsˈɑːm/ *vt* (*mil*) разоружáть *impf*., разоружúть *pf*; (*criminal; also fig*) обезорýживать *impf*, обезорýжить *pf*. **disarmament** /-ˈɑːməmənt/ *n* разоружéние.

disarray /ˌdɪsəˈreɪ/ *n* беспоря́док.

disaster /dɪ'zɑːstə(r)/ *n* бе́дствие. **disastrous** /-'zɑːstrəs/ *adj* катастрофи́ческий.
disband /dɪs'bænd/ *vt* распуска́ть *impf*, распусти́ть *pf*; *vi* расходи́ться *impf*, разойти́сь *pf*.
disbelief /ˌdɪsbɪ'liːf/ *n* неве́рие.
disc, disk /dɪsk/ *n* диск; **~ drive** (*comput*) дисково́д; **~ jockey** диск-жоке́й, дидже́й.
discard /dɪ'skɑːd/ *vt* отбра́сывать *impf*, отбро́сить *pf*.
discern /dɪ'sɜːn/ *vt* различа́ть *impf*, различи́ть *pf*. **discernible** /-'sɜːnɪb(ə)l/ *adj* различи́мый. **discerning** /-'sɜːnɪŋ/ *adj* проница́тельный.
discharge *vt* / dɪs'tʃɑːdʒ/ (*gun*; *electr*) разряжа́ть *impf*, разряди́ть *pf*; (*dismiss*) увольня́ть *impf*, уво́лить *pf*; (*prisoner*) освобожда́ть *impf*, освободи́ть *pf*; (*debt*; *duty*) выполня́ть *impf*, вы́полнить *pf*; (*from hospital*) выпи́сывать *impf*, вы́писать *pf*; *n* /'dɪstʃɑːdʒ/ разгру́зка; (*electr*) разря́д; увольне́ние; освобожде́ние; выполне́ние; (*med*) выделе́ния *neut pl*.
disciple /dɪ'saɪp(ə)l/ *n* учени́к.
disciplinarian /ˌdɪsɪplɪ'neərɪən/ *n* сторо́нник дисципли́ны. **disciplinary** /ˌdɪsɪ'plɪnərɪ/ *adj* дисциплина́рный. **discipline** /'dɪsɪplɪn/ *n* дисципли́на; *vt* дисциплини́ровать *impf* & *pf*.
disclaim /dɪs'kleɪm/ *vt* (*deny*) отрица́ть *impf*; **~ responsibility** слага́ть *impf*, сложи́ть *pf* с себя́ отве́тственность.
disclose /dɪs'kləʊz/ *vt* обнару́живать *impf*, обнару́жить *pf*. **disclosure** /-'kləʊʒə(r)/ *n* обнару́же́ние.
discoloured /dɪs'kʌləd/ *adj* обесцве́ченный.
discomfit /dɪs'kʌmfɪt/ *vt* смуща́ть *impf*, смути́ть *pf*. **discomfiture** /-'kʌmfɪtjə(r)/ *n* смуще́ние.
discomfort /dɪs'kʌmfət/ *n* неудо́бство.
disconcert /ˌdɪskən'sɜːt/ *vt* смуща́ть *impf*, смути́ть *pf*.
disconnect /ˌdɪskə'nekt/ *vt* разъединя́ть *impf*, разъедини́ть *pf*; (*switch off*) выключа́ть *impf*, вы́ключить *pf*. **disconnected** /-tɪd/ *adj* (*incoherent*) бессвя́зный.
disconsolate /dɪs'kɒnsələt/ *adj* неуте́шный.
discontent /ˌdɪskən'tent/ *n* недово́льство. **discontented** /-'tentɪd/ *adj* недово́льный.
discontinue /ˌdɪskən'tɪnjuː/ *vt* прекраща́ть *impf*, прекрати́ть *pf*.
discord /'dɪskɔːd/ *n* разногла́сие; (*mus*) диссона́нс. **discordant** /dɪ'skɔːd(ə)nt/ *adj* несогласу́ющийся; диссони́рующий.
discotheque /'dɪskəˌtek/ *n* дискоте́ка.
discount *n* /'dɪskaʊnt/ ски́дка; *vt* /dɪs'kaʊnt/ (*disregard*) не принима́ть *impf*, приня́ть *pf* в расчёт.
discourage /dɪ'skʌrɪdʒ/ *vt* обескура́живать *impf*, обескура́жить *pf*; (*dissuade*) отгова́ривать *impf*, отговори́ть *pf*.
discourse /'dɪskɔːs/ *n* речь.
discourteous /dɪs'kɜːtɪəs/ *adj* неве́жливый.
discover /dɪ'skʌvə(r)/ *vt* открыва́ть *impf*, откры́ть *pf*; (*find out*) обнару́живать *impf*, обнару́жить *pf*. **discovery** /-'skʌvərɪ/ *n* откры́тие.
discredit /dɪs'kredɪt/ *n* позо́р; *vt* дискредити́ровать *impf* & *pf*.
discreet /dɪ'skriːt/ *adj* такти́чный. **discretion** /-'skreʃ(ə)n/ *n* (*judgement*) усмотре́ние; (*prudence*) благоразу́мие; **at one's ~** по своему́ усмотре́нию.
discrepancy /dɪs'krepənsɪ/ *n* несоотве́тствие.
discriminate /dɪ'skrɪmɪˌneɪt/ *vt* различа́ть *impf*, различи́ть *pf*; **~ against** дискримини́ровать *impf* & *pf*. **discrimination** /-'neɪʃ(ə)n/ *n* (*taste*) разбо́рчивость; (*bias*) дискримина́ция.
discus /'dɪskəs/ *n* диск.
discuss /dɪ'skʌs/ *vt* обсужда́ть

d

impf, обсуди́ть *pf.* **discussion** /-'skʌʃ(ə)n/ *n* обсужде́ние.

disdain /dɪs'deɪn/ *n* презре́ние. **disdainful** /-fʊl/ *adj* презри́тельный.

disease /dɪ'zi:z/ *n* боле́знь. **diseased** /-'zi:zd/ *adj* больно́й.

d

disembark /ˌdɪsɪm'bɑ:k/ *vi* выса́живаться *impf*, вы́садиться *pf.*

disenchantment /ˌdɪsɪn'tʃɑ:ntmənt/ *n* разочарова́ние.

disengage /ˌdɪsɪn'geɪdʒ/ *vt* освобожда́ть *impf*, освободи́ть *pf*; (*clutch*) отпуска́ть *impf*, отпусти́ть *pf.*

disentangle /ˌdɪsɪn'tæŋg(ə)l/ *vt* распу́тывать *impf*, распу́тать *pf.*

disfavour /dɪs'feɪvə(r)/ *n* неми́лость.

disfigure /dɪs'fɪgə(r)/ *vt* уро́довать *impf*, из~ *pf.*

disgrace /dɪs'greɪs/ *n* позо́р; (*disfavour*) неми́лость; *vt* позо́рить *impf*, о~ *pf.* **disgraceful** /-'greɪsfʊl/ *adj* позо́рный.

disgruntled /dɪs'grʌnt(ə)ld/ *adj* недово́льный.

disguise /dɪs'gaɪz/ *n* маскиро́вка; *vt* маскирова́ть *impf*, за~ *pf*; (*conceal*) скрыва́ть *impf*, скрыть *pf.* **disguised** /-'gaɪzd/ *adj* замаскиро́ванный.

disgust /dɪs'gʌst/ *n* отвраще́ние; *vt* внуша́ть *impf*, внуши́ть *pf.* отвраще́ние +*dat.* **disgusting** /-'gʌstɪŋ/ *adj* отврати́тельный.

dish /dɪʃ/ *n* блю́до; *pl* посу́да *collect*; **~-washer** посу́домо́ечная маши́на; *vt*: **~ up** подава́ть *impf*, пода́ть *pf.*

dishearten /dɪs'hɑ:t(ə)n/ *vt* обескура́живать *impf*, обескура́жить *pf.*

dishevelled /dɪ'ʃev(ə)ld/ *adj* растрёпанный.

dishonest /dɪs'ɒnɪst/ *adj* нече́стный. **dishonesty** /-'ɒnɪstɪ/ *n* нече́стность. **dishonour** /-'ɒnə(r)/ *n* бесче́стье; *vt* бесче́стить *impf*, о~ *pf.* **dishonourable** /-'ɒnərəb(ə)l/ *adj* бесче́стный.

disillusion /ˌdɪsɪ'lu:ʒ(ə)n/ *vt* разочаро́вывать *impf*, разочарова́ть *pf.* **disillusionment** /-mənt/ *n* разочаро́ванность.

disinclination /ˌdɪsɪnklɪ'neɪʃ(ə)n/ *n* несклонность, неохо́та. **disinclined** /-'klaɪnd/ *adj* **be ~** не хоте́ться *impers* +*dat.*

disinfect /ˌdɪsɪn'fekt/ *vt* дезинфици́ровать *impf* & *pf.* **disinfectant** /-t(ə)nt/ *n* дезинфици́рующее сре́дство.

disingenuous /ˌdɪsɪn'dʒenjʊəs/ *adj* нeíскренний.

disinherit /ˌdɪsɪn'herɪt/ *vt* лиша́ть *impf*, лиши́ть *pf* насле́дства.

disintegrate /dɪs'ɪntɪˌgreɪt/ *vi* распада́ться *impf*, распа́сться *pf.* **disintegration** /-'greɪʃ(ə)n/ *n* распа́д.

disinterested /dɪs'ɪntrɪstɪd/ *adj* бескоры́стный.

disjointed /dɪs'dʒɔɪntɪd/ *adj* бессвя́зный.

disk /dɪsk/ *see* **disc**

dislike /dɪs'laɪk/ *n* нелюбо́вь (**for** к+*dat*); *vt* не люби́ть *impf.*

dislocate /'dɪsləˌkeɪt/ *vt* (*med*) вы́вихнуть *pf.*

dislodge /dɪs'lɒdʒ/ *vt* смеща́ть *impf*, смести́ть *pf.*

disloyal /dɪs'lɔɪəl/ *adj* нелоя́льный. **disloyalty** /-tɪ/ *n* нелоя́льность.

dismal /'dɪzm(ə)l/ *adj* мра́чный.

dismantle /dɪs'mænt(ə)l/ *vt* разбира́ть *impf*, разобра́ть *pf.*

dismay /dɪs'meɪ/ *vt* смуща́ть *impf*, смути́ть *pf*; *n* смуще́ние.

dismiss /dɪs'mɪs/ *vt* (*sack*) увольня́ть *impf*, уво́лить *pf*; (*disband*) распуска́ть *impf*, распусти́ть *pf.* **dismissal** /-səl/ *n* увольне́ние; ро́спуск.

dismount /dɪs'maʊnt/ *vi* спе́шиваться *impf*, спе́шиться *pf.*

disobedience /ˌdɪsə'bi:dɪəns/ *n* непослуша́ние. **disobedient** /-ənt/ *adj* непослу́шный. **disobey** /ˌdɪsə'beɪ/ *vt* не слу́шаться *impf* +*gen.*

disorder /dɪs'ɔ:də(r)/ *n* беспоря́док. **disorderly** /-dəlɪ/ *adj* (*un-*

tidy) беспоря́дочный; (*unruly*) бу́йный.
disorganized /dɪsˈɔːgəˌnaɪzd/ *adj* неорганизо́ванный.
disorientation /dɪsˌɔːrɪənˈteɪʃ(ə)n/ *n* дезориента́ция. **disoriented** /dɪsˈɔːrɪəntɪd/ *adj*: **I am/was ~** я потеря́л(а) направле́ние.
disown /dɪsˈəʊn/ *vt* отка́зываться *impf*, отказа́ться *pf* от+*gen*.
disparaging /dɪˈspærɪdʒɪŋ/ *adj* оскорби́тельный.
disparity /dɪˈspærɪtɪ/ *n* нера́венство.
dispassionate /dɪˈspæʃənət/ *adj* беспристра́стный.
dispatch /dɪˈspætʃ/ *vt* (*send*) отправля́ть *impf*, отпра́вить *pf*; (*deal with*) расправля́ться *impf*, распра́виться *pf* с+*instr*; *n* отпра́вка; (*message*) донесе́ние; (*rapidity*) быстрота́; **~-rider** мотоцикли́ст свя́зи.
dispel /dɪˈspel/ *vt* рассе́ивать *impf*, рассе́ять *pf*.
dispensable /dɪˈspensəb(ə)l/ *adj* необяза́тельный.
dispensary /dɪˈspensərɪ/ *n* апте́ка.
dispensation /ˌdɪspenˈseɪʃ(ə)n/ *n* (*exemption*) освобожде́ние (от обяза́тельства). **dispense** /dɪˈspens/ *vt* (*distribute*) раздава́ть *impf*, разда́ть *pf*; **~ with** обходи́ться *impf*, обойти́сь *pf* без+*gen*.
dispersal /dɪˈspɜːsəl/ *n* распростране́ние. **disperse** /-ˈspɜːs/ *vt* (*drive away*) разгоня́ть *impf*, разогна́ть *pf*; (*scatter*) рассе́ивать *impf*, рассе́ять *pf*; *vi* расходи́ться *impf*, разойти́сь *pf*.
dispirited /dɪˈspɪrɪtɪd/ *adj* удручённый.
displaced /dɪsˈpleɪst/ *adj*: **~ persons** перемещённые ли́ца *neut pl*.
display /dɪˈspleɪ/ *n* пока́з; *vt* пока́зывать *impf*, показа́ть *pf*.
displeased /dɪsˈpliːzd/ *predic* недово́лен (-льна). **displeasure** /-ˈpleʒə(r)/ *n* недово́льство.
disposable /dɪˈspəʊzəb(ə)l/ *adj* однора́зовый. **disposal** /-ˈspəʊz(ə)l/ *n* удале́ние; **at your ~** в ва́шем распоряже́нии. **dispose** /-ˈspəʊz/ *vi*: **~ of** избавля́ться *impf*, изба́виться *pf* от+*gen*. **disposed** /-ˈspəʊzd/ *predic*: **~ to** располо́жен (-ена) к+*dat or* +*inf*. **disposition** /ˌdɪspəˈzɪʃ(ə)n/ *n* расположе́ние; (*temperament*) нрав.
disproportionate /ˌdɪsprəˈpɔːʃənət/ *adj* непропорциона́льный.
disprove /dɪsˈpruːv/ *vt* опроверга́ть *impf*, опрове́ргнуть *pf*.
dispute /dɪˈspjuːt/ *n* (*debate*) спор; (*quarrel*) ссо́ра; *vt* оспа́ривать *impf*, оспо́рить *pf*.
disqualification /dɪsˌkwɒlɪfɪˈkeɪʃ(ə)n/ *n* дисквалифика́ция. **disqualify** /dɪsˈkwɒlɪˌfaɪ/ *vt* дисквалифици́ровать *impf* & *pf*.
disquieting /dɪsˈkwaɪətɪŋ/ *adj* трево́жный.
disregard /ˌdɪsrɪˈgɑːd/ *n* пренебреже́ние +*instr*; *vt* игнори́ровать *impf* & *pf*; пренебрега́ть *impf*, пренебре́чь *pf* +*instr*.
disrepair /ˌdɪsrɪˈpeə(r)/ *n* неиспра́вность.
disreputable /dɪsˈrepjʊtəb(ə)l/ *adj* по́льзующийся дурно́й сла́вой. **disrepute** /ˌdɪsrɪˈpjuːt/ *n* дурна́я сла́ва.
disrespect /ˌdɪsrɪˈspekt/ *n* неуваже́ние. **disrespectful** /-fʊl/ *adj* непочти́тельный.
disrupt /dɪsˈrʌpt/ *vt* срыва́ть *impf*, сорва́ть *pf*. **disruptive** /tɪv/ *adj* подрывно́й.
dissatisfaction /ˌdɪsætɪsˈfækʃ(ə)n/ *n* недово́льство. **dissatisfied** /dɪˈsætɪsfaɪd/ *adj* недово́льный.
dissect /dɪˈsekt/ *vt* разреза́ть *impf*, разре́зать *pf*; (*med*) вскрыва́ть *impf*, вскрыть *pf*.
disseminate /dɪˈsemɪˌneɪt/ *vt* распространя́ть *impf*, распространи́ть *pf*; **dissemination** /-ˈneɪʃ(ə)n/ *n* распростране́ние.
dissension /dɪˈsenʃ(ə)n/ *n* раздо́р. **dissent** /-ˈsent/ *n* расхожде́ние; (*eccl*) раско́л.

d

dissertation /ˌdɪsəˈteɪʃ(ə)n/ *n* диссерта́ция.

disservice /dɪsˈsɜːvɪs/ *n* плоха́я услу́га.

dissident /ˈdɪsɪd(ə)nt/ *n* диссиде́нт.

dissimilar /dɪˈsɪmɪlə(r)/ *adj* несхо́дный.

dissipate /ˈdɪsɪˌpeɪt/ *vt* (*dispel*) рассе́ивать *impf*, рассе́ять *pf*; (*squander*) прома́тывать *impf*, промота́ть *pf*. **dissipated** /-tɪd/ *adj* распу́тный.

dissociate /ˌdɪˈsəʊʃɪˌeɪt/ *vt*: **~ o.s.** отмежёвываться *impf*, отмежева́ться *pf* (**from** от+*gen*).

dissolute /ˈdɪsəˌluːt/ *adj* распу́тный. **dissolution** /-ˈluːʃ(ə)n/ *n* расторже́ние; (*parl*) ро́спуск. **dissolve** /dɪˈzɒlv/ *vt* & *i* (*in liquid*) растворя́ть(ся) *impf*, раствори́ть(ся) *pf*; *vt* (*annul*) расторга́ть *impf*, расто́ргнуть *pf*; (*parl*) распуска́ть *impf*, распусти́ть *pf*.

dissonance /ˈdɪsənəns/ *n* диссона́нс. **dissonant** /-nənt/ *adj* диссони́рующий.

dissuade /dɪˈsweɪd/ *vt* отгова́ривать *impf*, отговори́ть *pf*.

distance /ˈdɪst(ə)ns/ *n* расстоя́ние; **from a ~** и́здали; **in the ~** вдалеке́. **distant** /-ˈt(ə)nt/ *adj* далёкий, (*also of relative*) да́льний; (*reserved*) сде́ржанный.

distaste /dɪsˈteɪst/ *n* отвраще́ние. **distasteful** /-fʊl/ *adj* проти́вный.

distended /dɪˈstendɪd/ *adj* наду́тый.

distil /dɪˈstɪl/ *vt* (*whisky*) перегоня́ть *impf*, перегна́ть *pf*; (*water*) дистилли́ровать *impf* & *pf*. **distillation** /ˌdɪstɪˈleɪʃ(ə)n/ *n* перего́нка; дистилля́ция. **distillery** /dɪˈstɪlərɪ/ *n* перего́нный заво́д.

distinct /dɪˈstɪŋkt/ *adj* (*different*) отли́чный; (*clear*) отчётливый; (*evident*) заме́тный. **distinction** /-ˈstɪŋkʃ(ə)n/ *n* (*difference*; *excellence*) отли́чие; (*discrimination*) разли́чие. **distinctive** /-ˈstɪŋktɪv/ *adj* отличи́тельный. **distinctly** /-ˈstɪŋktlɪ/ *adv* я́сно.

distinguish /dɪˈstɪŋgwɪʃ/ *vt* различа́ть *impf*, различи́ть *pf*; **~ o.s.** отлича́ться *impf*, отличи́ться *pf*. **distinguished** /-ˈstɪŋgwɪʃt/ *adj* выдаю́щийся.

distort /dɪˈstɔːt/ *vt* искажа́ть *impf*, искази́ть *pf*; (*misrepresent*) извраща́ть *impf*, изврати́ть *pf*. **distortion** /-ˈstɔːʃ(ə)n/ *n* искаже́ние; извраще́ние.

distract /dɪˈstrækt/ *vt* отвлека́ть *impf*, отвле́чь *pf*. **distraction** /-ˈstrækʃ(ə)n/ *n* (*amusement*) развлече́ние; (*madness*) безу́мие.

distraught /dɪˈstrɔːt/ *adj* обезу́мевший.

distress /dɪˈstres/ *n* (*suffering*) огорче́ние; (*danger*) бе́дствие; *vt* огорча́ть *impf*, огорчи́ть *pf*.

distribute /dɪˈstrɪbjuːt/ *vt* (*hand out*) раздава́ть *impf*, разда́ть *pf*; (*allocate*) распределя́ть *impf*, распредели́ть *pf*. **distribution** /ˌdɪstrɪˈbjuːʃ(ə)n/ *n* распределе́ние. **distributor** /dɪˈstrɪbjʊtə(r)/ *n* распредели́тель *m*.

district /ˈdɪstrɪkt/ *n* райо́н.

distrust /dɪsˈtrʌst/ *n* недове́рие; *vt* не доверя́ть *impf*. **distrustful** /-fʊl/ *adj* недове́рчивый.

disturb /dɪˈstɜːb/ *vt* беспоко́ить *impf*, о~ *pf*. **disturbance** /-bəns/ *n* наруше́ние поко́я; *pl* (*polit etc.*) беспоря́дки *m pl*.

disuse /dɪsˈjuːs/ *n* неупотребле́ние; **fall into ~** выходи́ть *impf*, вы́йти *pf* из употребле́ния. **disused** /-ˈjuːzd/ *adj* забро́шенный.

ditch /dɪtʃ/ *n* кана́ва, ров.

dither /ˈdɪðə(r)/ *vi* колеба́ться *impf*.

ditto /ˈdɪtəʊ/ *n* то же са́мое; *adv* так же.

divan /dɪˈvæn/ *n* дива́н.

dive /daɪv/ *vi* ныря́ть *impf*, нырну́ть *pf*; (*aeron*) пики́ровать *impf* & *pf*; *n* ныро́к, прыжо́к в во́ду. **diver** /-və(r)/ *n* водола́з.

diverge /daɪˈvɜːdʒ/ *vi* расходи́ться *impf*, разойти́сь *pf*. **divergent** /-dʒ(ə)nt/ *adj* расходя́щийся.

diverse /daɪˈvɜːs/ *adj* разнообра́зный. **diversification** /-vɜːsɪfɪˈkeɪʃ(ə)n/ *n* расшире́ние ассортиме́нта. **diversify** /-ˈvɜːsɪˌfaɪ/ *vt* разнообра́зить *impf*. **diversion** /-ˈvɜːʃ(ə)n/ *n* (*detour*) объе́зд; (*amusement*) развлече́ние. **diversity** /-ˈvɜːsɪtɪ/ *n* разнообра́зие. **divert** /-ˈvɜːt/ *vt* отклоня́ть *impf*, отклони́ть *pf*; (*amuse*) развлека́ть *impf*, развле́чь *pf*. **diverting** /-ˈvɜːtɪŋ/ *adj* заба́вный.

divest /daɪˈvest/ *vt* (*deprive*) лиша́ть *impf*, лиши́ть *pf* (**of** +*gen*); **~ o.s.** отка́зываться *impf*, отказа́ться *pf* (**of** от+*gen*).

divide /dɪˈvaɪd/ *vt* (*share*; *math*) дели́ть *impf*, по~ *pf*; (*separate*) разделя́ть *impf*, раздели́ть *pf*. **dividend** /ˈdɪvɪˌdend/ *n* дивиде́нд.

divine /dɪˈvaɪn/ *adj* боже́ственный.

diving /ˈdaɪvɪŋ/ *n* ныря́ние; **~-board** трампли́н.

divinity /dɪˈvɪnɪtɪ/ *n* (*quality*) боже́ственность; (*deity*) божество́; (*theology*) богосло́вие.

divisible /dɪˈvɪzɪb(ə)l/ *adj* дели́мый. **division** /-ˈvɪʒ(ə)n/ *n* (*dividing*) деле́ние, разделе́ние; (*section*) отде́л; (*mil*) диви́зия.

divorce /dɪˈvɔːs/ *n* разво́д; *vi* разводи́ться *impf*, развести́сь *pf*. **divorced** /-ˈvɔːst/ *adj* разведённый.

divulge /daɪˈvʌldʒ/ *vt* разглаша́ть *impf*, разгласи́ть *pf*.

DIY *abbr* (*of* **do-it-yourself**): **he is good at ~** у него́ золоты́е ру́ки; **~ shop** магази́н «сде́лай сам».

dizziness /ˈdɪzɪnɪs/ *n* головокруже́ние. **dizzy** /ˈdɪzɪ/ *adj* (*causing dizziness*) головокружи́тельный; **I am ~** у меня́ кру́жится голова́.

DNA *abbr* (*of* **deoxyribonucleic acid**) ДНК.

do /duː/ *vt* де́лать *impf*, с~ *pf*; *vi* (*be suitable*) годи́ться *impf*; (*suffice*) быть доста́точным; **~-it-yourself** *see* **DIY; that will ~!** хва́тит!; **how ~ you ~?** здра́вствуйте!; как вы пожива́ете?; **~ away with** (*abolish*) уничтожа́ть *impf*, уничто́жить *pf*; **~ in** (*kill*) убива́ть *impf*, уби́ть *pf*; **~ up** (*restore*) ремонти́ровать *impf*, от~ *pf*; (*wrap up*) завёртывать *impf*, заверну́ть *pf*; (*fasten*) застёгивать *impf*, застегну́ть *pf*; **~ without** обходи́ться *impf*, обойти́сь *pf* без+*gen*.

docile /ˈdəʊsaɪl/ *adj* поко́рный. **docility** /-ˈsɪlɪtɪ/ *n* поко́рность.

dock[1] /dɒk/ *n* (*naut*) док; *vt* ста́вить *impf*, по~ *pf* в док; *vi* входи́ть *impf*, войти́ *pf* в док; *vi* (*spacecraft*) стыкова́ться *impf*, со~ *pf*. **docker** /-kə(r)/ *n* до́кер. **dockyard** *n* верфь.

dock[2] /dɒk/ *n* (*law*) скамья́ подсуди́мых.

docket /ˈdɒkɪt/ *n* квита́нция; (*label*) ярлы́к.

doctor /ˈdɒktə(r)/ *n* врач; (*also univ*) до́ктор; *vt* (*castrate*) кастри́ровать *impf* & *pf*; (*spay*) удаля́ть *impf*, удали́ть *pf* яи́чники у+*gen*; (*falsify*) фальсифици́ровать *impf* & *pf*. **doctorate** /-rət/ *n* сте́пень до́ктора.

doctrine /ˈdɒktrɪn/ *n* доктри́на.

document /ˈdɒkjʊmənt/ *n* докуме́нт; *vt* документи́ровать *impf* & *pf*. **documentary** /ˌdɒkjʊˈmentərɪ/ *n* документа́льный фильм. **documentation** /ˌdɒkjʊmenˈteɪʃ(ə)n/ *n* документа́ция.

doddery /ˈdɒdərɪ/ *adj* дря́хлый.

dodge /dɒdʒ/ *n* увёртка; *vt* уклоня́ться *impf*, уклони́ться *pf* от+*gen*; (*jump to avoid*) отска́кивать *impf*, отскочи́ть *pf* (от+*gen*). **dodgy** /ˈdɒdʒɪ/ *adj* ка́верзный.

doe /dəʊ/ *n* са́мка.

dog /dɒg/ *n* соба́ка, пёс; (*fig*) пресле́довать *impf*. **dog-eared** /ˈdɒgɪəd/ *adj* захва́танный.

dogged /ˈdɒgɪd/ *adj* упо́рный.

dogma /ˈdɒgmə/ *n* до́гма. **dogmatic** /-ˈmætɪk/ *adj* догмати́ческий.

doings /ˈduːɪŋz/ *n pl* дела́ *neut pl*.

doldrums /ˈdɒldrəmz/ *n*: **be in the ~** хандри́ть *impf*.

d

d

dole /dəʊl/ *n* посо́бие по безрабо́тице; *vt* (~ *out*) выдава́ть *impf*, вы́дать *pf*.
doleful /'dəʊlfʊl/ *adj* ско́рбный.
doll /'dɒl/ *n* ку́кла.
dollar /'dɒlə(r)/ *n* до́ллар.
dollop /'dɒləp/ *n* соли́дная по́рция.
dolphin /'dɒlfɪn/ *n* дельфи́н.
domain /də'meɪn/ *n* (*estate*) владе́ние; (*field*) о́бласть.
dome /dəʊm/ *n* ку́пол.
domestic /də'mestɪk/ *adj* (*of household*; *animals*) дома́шний; (*of family*) семе́йный; (*polit*) вну́тренний; *n* прислу́га. **domesticate** /-'mestɪˌkeɪt/ *vt* прируча́ть *impf*, приручи́ть *pf*. **domesticity** /ˌdɒmə'stɪsɪtɪ/ *n* дома́шняя, семе́йная, жизнь.
domicile /'dɒmɪˌsaɪl/ *n* местожи́тельство.
dominance /'dɒmɪnəns/ *n* госпо́дство. **dominant** /-mɪnənt/ *adj* преоблада́ющий; госпо́дствующий. **dominate** /-mɪˌneɪt/ *vt* госпо́дствовать *impf* над +*instr*. **domineering** /-mɪ'nɪərɪŋ/ *adj* вла́стный.
dominion /də'mɪnɪən/ *n* влады́чество; (*realm*) владе́ние.
domino /'dɒmɪˌnəʊ/ *n* кость домино́; *pl* (*game*) домино́ *neut indecl*.
don /dɒn/ *vt* надева́ть *impf*, наде́ть *pf*.
donate /dəʊ'neɪt/ *vt* же́ртвовать *impf*, по~ *pf*. **donation** /-'neɪʃ(ə)n/ *n* поже́ртвование.
donkey /'dɒŋkɪ/ *n* осёл.
donor /'dəʊnə(r)/ *n* же́ртвователь *m*; (*med*) до́нор.
doom /du:m/ *n* (*ruin*) ги́бель; *vt* обрека́ть *impf*, обре́чь *pf*.
door /dɔ:(r)/ *n* дверь. **doorbell** *n* (дверно́й) звоно́к. **doorman** *n* швейца́р. **doormat** *n* полови́к. **doorstep** *n* поро́г. **doorway** *n* дверно́й проём.
dope /dəʊp/ *n* (*drug*) нарко́тик; *vt* дурма́нить *impf*, о~ *pf*.
dormant /'dɔ:mənt/ *adj* (*sleeping*) спя́щий; (*inactive*) безде́йствующий.
dormer window /'dɔ:mə 'wɪndəʊ/ *n* слухово́е окно́.
dormitory /'dɔ:mɪtərɪ/ *n* о́бщая спа́льня.
dormouse /'dɔ:maʊs/ *n* со́ня.
dorsal /'dɔ:s(ə)l/ *adj* спинно́й.
dosage /'dəʊsɪdʒ/ *n* дозиро́вка. **dose** /dəʊs/ *n* до́за.
dossier /'dɒsɪə(r)/ *n* досье́ *neut indecl*.
dot /dɒt/ *n* то́чка; *vt* ста́вить *impf*, по~ *pf* то́чки на+*acc*; (*scatter*) усе́ивать *impf*, усе́ять *pf* (**with** +*instr*); ~**ted line** пункти́р.
dote /dəʊt/ *vi*: ~ **on** обожа́ть *impf*.
double /'dʌb(ə)l/ *adj* двойно́й; (*doubled*) удво́енный; ~**-bass** контраба́с; ~ **bed** двуспа́льная крова́ть; ~**-breasted** двубо́ртный; ~**-cross** обма́нывать *impf*, обману́ть *pf*; ~**-dealing** двуру́шничество; ~**-decker** двухэта́жный авто́бус; ~**-edged** обоюдоо́стрый; ~ **glazing** двойны́е ра́мы *f pl*; ~ **room** ко́мната на двои́х; *adv* вдво́е; (*two together*) вдвоём; *n* двойно́е коли́чество; (*person's*) двойни́к; *pl* (*sport*) па́рная игра́; *vt* & *i* удва́ивать(ся) *impf*, удво́ить(ся) *pf*; ~ **back** возвраща́ться *impf*, верну́ться *pf* наза́д; ~ **up** (*in pain*) скрю́чиваться *impf*, скрю́читься *pf*; (*share a room*) помеща́ться *impf*, помести́ться *pf* вдвоём в одно́й ко́мнате; (~ *up as*) рабо́тать *impf* + *instr* по совмести́тельству.
doubt /daʊt/ *n* сомне́ние; *vt* сомнева́ться *impf* в+*prep*. **doubtful** /-fʊl/ *adj* сомни́тельный. **doubtless** /-lɪs/ *adv* несомне́нно.
dough /dəʊ/ *n* те́сто. **doughnut** *n* по́нчик.
douse /daʊs/ *vt* (*drench*) залива́ть *impf*, зали́ть *pf*.
dove /dʌv/ *n* го́лубь *m*. **dovetail** *n* ла́сточкин хвост.
dowdy /'daʊdɪ/ *adj* неэлега́нтный.
down[1] /daʊn/ *n* (*fluff*) пух.

down² /daʊn/ *adv* (*motion*) вниз; (*position*) внизу́; **be ~ with** (*ill*) боле́ть *impf* +*instr*; *prep* вниз с+*gen*, по+*dat*; (*along*) (вдоль) по+*dat*; *vt*: (*gulp*) опроки́дывать *impf*, опроки́нуть *pf*; **~-and-out** бродя́га *m*; **~cast, ~-hearted** уны́лый. **downfall** *n* ги́бель. **downhill** *adv* по́д гору. **download** *vt* (*comput*) за-гружа́ть *impf*, за-грузи́ть *pf*. **downpour** *n* ли́вень *m*. **downright** *adj* я́вный; *adv* соверше́нно. **downstairs** *adv* (*motion*) вниз; (*position*) внизу́. **downstream** *adv* вниз по тече́нию. **down-to-earth** *adj* реалисти́ческий. **downtrodden** /ˈdaʊnˌtrɒd(ə)n/ *adj* угнетённый.

dowry /ˈdaʊərɪ/ *n* прида́ное *sb*.

doze /dəʊz/ *vi* дрема́ть *impf*.

dozen /ˈdʌz(ə)n/ *n* дю́жина.

drab /dræb/ *adj* бесцве́тный.

draft /drɑːft/ *n* (*outline*, *rough copy*) набро́сок; (*document*) прое́кт; (*econ*) тра́тта; *see also* **draught**; *vt* составля́ть *impf*, соста́вить *pf* план, прое́кт, +*gen*.

drag /dræg/ *vt* тащи́ть *impf*; (*river etc.*) драги́ровать *impf* & *pf*; **~ on** (*vi*) затя́гиваться *impf*, затяну́ться *pf*; *n* (*burden*) обу́за; (*on cigarette*) затя́жка; **in ~** в же́нской оде́жде.

dragon /ˈdrægən/ *n* драко́н. **dragonfly** *n* стрекоза́.

drain /dreɪn/ *n* водосто́к; (*leakage*; *fig*) уте́чка; *vt* осуша́ть *impf*, осуши́ть *pf*; *vi* спуска́ться *impf*, спусти́ться *pf*. **drainage** /ˈdreɪnɪdʒ/ *n* дрена́ж; (*system*) канализа́ция.

drake /dreɪk/ *n* се́лезень *m*.

drama /ˈdrɑːmə/ *n* дра́ма; (*quality*) драмати́зм. **dramatic** /drəˈmætɪk/ *adj* драмати́ческий. **dramatist** /ˈdræmətɪst/ *n* драмату́рг. **dramatize** /ˈdræməˌtaɪz/ *vt* драматизи́ровать *impf* & *pf*.

drape /dreɪp/ *vt* драпирова́ть *impf*, за~ *pf*; *n* драпиро́вка.

drastic /ˈdræstɪk/ *adj* радика́льный.

draught /drɑːft/ *n* (*air*) сквозня́к; (*traction*) тя́га; *pl* (*game*) ша́шки *f pl*; *see also* **draft; there is a ~** сквози́т; **~ beer** пи́во из бо́чки. **draughtsman** /ˈdrɑːftsmən/ *n* чертёжник. **draughty** /ˈdrɑːftɪ/ *adj*: **it is ~ here** здесь ду́ет.

draw /drɔː/ *n* (*in lottery*) ро́зыгрыш; (*attraction*) прима́нка; (*drawn game*) ничья́; *vt* (*pull*) тяну́ть *impf*, по~ *pf*; таска́ть *indet*, тащи́ть *det*; (*curtains*) задёргивать *impf*, задёрнуть *pf* (занаве́ски); (*attract*) привлека́ть *impf*, привле́чь *pf*; (*pull out*) выта́скивать *impf*, вы́тащить *pf*; (*sword*) обнажа́ть *impf*, обнажи́ть *pf*; (*lots*) броса́ть *impf*, бро́сить *pf* (жре́бий); (*water*; *inspiration*) че́рпать *impf*, черпну́ть *pf*; (*evoke*) вызыва́ть *impf*, вы́звать *pf*; (*conclusion*) выводи́ть *impf*, вы́вести *pf* (заключе́ние); (*diagram*) черти́ть *impf*, на~ *pf*; (*picture*) рисова́ть *impf*, на~ *pf*; *vi* (*sport*) сыгра́ть *pf* вничью́; **~ aside** отводи́ть *impf*, отвести́ *pf* в сто́рону; **~ back** (*withdraw*) отступа́ть *impf*, отступи́ть *pf*; **~ in** втя́гивать *impf*, втяну́ть *pf*; (*train*) входи́ть *impf*, войти́ *pf* в ста́нцию; (*car*) подходи́ть *impf*, подойти́ *pf* (**to** к + *dat*); (*days*) стано́виться *impf* коро́че; **~ out** вытя́гивать *impf*, вы́тянуть *pf*; (*money*) выпи́сывать *impf*, вы́писать *pf*; (*train/car*) выходи́ть *impf*, вы́йти *pf* (со ста́нции/на доро́гу); **~ up** (*car*) подходи́ть *impf*, подойти́ *pf* (**to** к + *dat*); (*document*) составля́ть *impf*, соста́вить *pf*. **drawback** *n* недоста́ток. **drawbridge** *n* подъёмный мост. **drawer** /ˈdrɔːə(r)/ *n* я́щик. **drawing** /ˈdrɔːɪŋ/ *n* (*action*) рисова́ние, черче́ние; (*object*) рису́нок, чертёж; **~-board** чертёжная доска́; **~-pin** кно́пка; **~-room** гости́ная *sb*.

drawl /drɔːl/ *n* протя́жное произноше́ние.

dread /dred/ *n* страх; *vt* боя́ться

impf +*gen.* **dreadful** /ˈdredfʊl/ *adj* ужа́сный.

dream /driːm/ *n* сон; (*fantasy*) мечта́; *vi* ви́деть *impf*, у∼ *pf* сон; **∼ of** ви́деть *impf*, у∼ *pf* во сне́; (*fig*) мечта́ть *impf* о+*prep*.

d

dreary /ˈdrɪərɪ/ *adj* (*weather*) па́смурный; (*boring*) ску́чный.

dredge /dredʒ/ *vt* (*river etc.*) драги́ровать *impf* & *pf*. **dredger** /-dʒə(r)/ *n* дра́га.

dregs /dregz/ *n pl* оса́дки (-ков) *pl*.

drench /drentʃ/ *vt* прома́чивать *impf*, промочи́ть *pf*; **get ∼ed** промока́ть *impf*, промо́кнуть *pf*.

dress /dres/ *n* пла́тье; (*apparel*) оде́жда; **∼ circle** бельэта́ж; **∼maker** портни́ха; **∼ rehearsal** генера́льная репети́ция; *vt* & *i* одева́ть(ся) *impf*, оде́ть(ся) *pf*; *vt* (*cul*) приправля́ть *impf*, припра́вить *pf*; (*med*) перевя́зывать *impf*, перевяза́ть *pf*; **∼ up** наряжа́ться *impf*, наряди́ться *pf* (**as** + *instr*).

dresser /ˈdresə(r)/ *n* ку́хонный шкаф.

dressing /ˈdresɪŋ/ *n* (*cul*) припра́ва; (*med*) перевя́зка; **∼-gown** хала́т; **∼-room** убо́рная *sb*; **∼-table** туале́тный сто́лик.

dribble /ˈdrɪb(ə)l/ *vi* (*person*) пуска́ть *impf*, пусти́ть *pf* слю́ни; (*sport*) вести́ *impf* мяч.

dried /draɪd/ *adj* сушёный. **drier** /draɪə(r)/ *n* суши́лка.

drift /drɪft/ *n* (*meaning*) смысл; (*snow*) сугро́б; *vi* плыть *impf* по тече́нию; (*naut*) дрейфова́ть *impf*; (*snow etc.*) скопля́ться *impf*, скопи́ться *pf*; **∼ apart** расходи́ться *impf*, разойти́сь *pf*.

drill[1] /drɪl/ *n* сверло́; (*dentist's*) бур; *vt* сверли́ть *impf*, про∼ *pf*.

drill[2] /drɪl/ *vt* (*mil*) обуча́ть *impf*, обучи́ть *pf* стро́ю; *vi* проходи́ть *impf*, пройти́ *pf* строеву́ю подгото́вку; *n* строева́я подгото́вка.

drink /drɪŋk/ *n* напи́ток; *vt* пить *impf*, вы́∼ *pf*; **∼-driving** вожде́ние в нетре́звом состоя́нии. **drinking-water** /ˈdrɪŋkɪŋ ˈwɔːtə(r)/ *n* питьева́я вода́.

drip /drɪp/ *n* (*action*) ка́панье; (*drop*) ка́пля; *vi* ка́пать *impf*, ка́пнуть *pf*.

drive /draɪv/ *n* (*journey*) езда́; (*excursion*) прогу́лка; (*campaign*) похо́д, кампа́ния; (*energy*) эне́ргия; (*tech*) приво́д; (*driveway*) подъездна́я доро́га; *vt* (*urge*; *chase*) гоня́ть *indet*, гнать *det*; (*vehicle*) води́ть *indet*, вести́ *det*; управля́ть *impf* +*instr*; (*convey*) вози́ть *indet*, везти́ *det*, по∼ *pf*; *vi* (*travel*) е́здить *indet*, е́хать *det*, по∼ *pf*; *vt* доводи́ть *impf*, довести́ *pf* (**to** до+*gen*); (*nail etc.*) вбива́ть *impf*, вбить *pf* (**into** в+*acc*); **∼ away** *vt* прогоня́ть *impf*, прогна́ть *pf*; *vi* уезжа́ть *impf*, уе́хать *pf*; **∼ up** подъезжа́ть *impf*, подъе́хать *pf* (**to** к+*dat*).

driver /ˈdraɪvə(r)/ *n* (*of vehicle*) води́тель *m*, шофёр. **driving** /ˈdraɪvɪŋ/ *adj* (*force*) дви́жущий; (*rain*) проливно́й; **∼-licence** води́тельские права́ *neut pl*; **∼-test** экза́мен на получе́ние води́тельских прав; **∼-wheel** веду́щее колесо́.

drizzle /ˈdrɪz(ə)l/ *n* ме́лкий до́ждь *m*; *vi* мороси́ть *impf*.

drone /drəʊn/ *n* (*bee*; *idler*) тру́тень *m*; (*of voice*) жужжа́ние; (*of engine*) гул; *vi* (*buzz*) жужжа́ть *impf*; (**∼** *on*) бубни́ть *impf*.

drool /druːl/ *vi* пуска́ть *impf*, пусти́ть *pf* слю́ни.

droop /druːp/ *vi* поника́ть *impf*, пони́кнуть *pf*.

drop /drɒp/ *n* (*of liquid*) ка́пля; (*fall*) паде́ние, пониже́ние; *vt* & *i* (*price*) снижа́ть(ся) *impf*, сни́зить(ся) *pf*; *vi* (*fall*) па́дать *impf*, упа́сть *pf*; *vt* (*let fall*) роня́ть *impf*, урони́ть *pf*; (*abandon*) броса́ть *impf*, бро́сить *pf*; **∼ behind** отстава́ть *impf*, отста́ть *pf*; **∼ in** заходи́ть *impf*, зайти́ *pf* (**on** к+*dat*); **∼ off** (*fall asleep*) засыпа́ть *impf*, засну́ть *pf*; (*from car*) выса́живать *impf*, вы́садить *pf*; **∼ out** выбыва́ть *impf*, вы́быть *pf* (**of** из +*gen*). **droppings** /ˈdrɒpɪŋz/ *n pl* помёт.

drought /draʊt/ *n* за́суха.

droves /drəʊvz/ *n pl*: **in ~** то́лпами.

drown /draʊn/ *vt* топи́ть *impf*, у~ *pf*; (*sound*) заглуша́ть *impf*, заглуши́ть *pf*; *vi* тону́ть *impf*, у~ *pf*.

drowsy /ˈdraʊzɪ/ *adj* сонли́вый.

drudgery /ˈdrʌdʒərɪ/ *n* ну́дная рабо́та.

drug /drʌg/ *n* медикаме́нт; (*narcotic*) нарко́тик; **~ addict** наркома́н, ~ка; *vt* дава́ть *impf*, дать *pf* нарко́тик+*dat*.

drum /drʌm/ *n* бараба́н; *vi* бить *impf* в бараба́н; бараба́нить *impf*; **~ sth into s.o.** вда́лбливать *impf*, вдолби́ть *pf* + *dat of person* в го́лову. **drummer** /ˈdrʌmə(r)/ *n* бараба́нщик.

drunk /drʌŋk/ *adj* пья́ный. **drunkard** /ˈdrʌŋkəd/ *n* пья́ница *m* & *f*. **drunken** /ˈdrʌŋkən/ *adj* пья́ный; **~ driving** вожде́ние в нетре́звом состоя́нии. **drunkenness** /ˈdrʌŋkənnɪs/ *n* пья́нство.

dry /draɪ/ *adj* сухо́й; **~ land** су́ша; *vt* суши́ть *impf*, вы́~ *pf*; (*wipe dry*) вытира́ть *impf*, вы́тереть *pf*; *vi* со́хнуть *impf*, вы́~, про~ *pf*. **dry-cleaning** /draɪˈkli:nɪŋ/ *n* химчи́стка. **dryness** /ˈdraɪnɪs/ *n* су́хость.

dual /ˈdju:əl/ *adj* двойно́й; (*joint*) совме́стный; **~-purpose** двойно́го назначе́ния.

dub[1] /dʌb/ *vt* (*nickname*) прозыва́ть *impf*, прозва́ть *pf*.

dub[2] /dʌb/ *vt* (*cin*) дубли́ровать *impf* & *pf*.

dubious /ˈdju:bɪəs/ *adj* сомни́тельный.

duchess /ˈdʌtʃɪs/ *n* герцоги́ня. **duchy** /ˈdʌtʃɪ/ *n* ге́рцогство.

duck[1] /dʌk/ *n* (*bird*) у́тка.

duck[2] /dʌk/ *vt* (*immerse*) окуна́ть *impf*, окуну́ть *pf*; (*one's head*) нагну́ть *pf*; (*evade*) увёртываться *impf*, уверну́ться *pf* от+*gen*; *vi* (**~ down**) наклоня́ться *impf*, наклони́ться *pf*.

duckling /ˈdʌklɪŋ/ *n* утёнок

duct /ˈdʌkt/ *n* прохо́д; (*anat*) прото́к.

dud /dʌd/ *n* (*forgery*) подде́лка; (*shell*) неразорва́вшийся снаря́д; *adj* подде́льный; (*worthless*) него́дный.

due /dju:/ *n* (*credit*) до́лжное *sb*; *pl* взно́сы *m pl*; *adj* (*proper*) до́лжный, надлежа́щий; *predic* (*expected*) до́лжен (-жна́); **in ~ course** со вре́менем; **~ south** пря́мо на юг; **~ to** благодаря́+*dat*.

duel /ˈdju:əl/ *n* дуэ́ль.

duet /dju:ˈet/ *n* дуэ́т.

duke /dju:k/ *n* ге́рцог.

dull /dʌl/ *adj* (*tedious*) ску́чный; (*colour*) ту́склый, (*weather*) па́смурный; (*not sharp; stupid*) тупо́й; *vt* притупля́ть *impf*, притупи́ть *pf*.

duly /ˈdju:lɪ/ *adv* надлежа́щим о́бразом; (*punctually*) своевре́менно.

dumb /dʌm/ *adj* немо́й. **dumbfounded** /ˈdʌmfəʊndɪd/ *adj* ошара́шенный.

dummy /ˈdʌmɪ/ *n* (*tailor's*) манеке́н; (*baby's*) со́ска; **~ run** испыта́тельный рейс.

dump /dʌmp/ *n* сва́лка; *vt* сва́ливать *impf*, свали́ть *pf*.

dumpling /ˈdʌmplɪŋ/ *n* клёцка.

dumpy /ˈdʌmpɪ/ *adj* приземи́стый.

dune /dju:n/ *n* дю́на.

dung /dʌŋ/ *n* наво́з.

dungarees /ˌdʌŋgəˈri:z/ *n pl* комбинезо́н.

dungeon /ˈdʌndʒ(ə)n/ *n* темни́ца.

duo /ˈdju:əʊ/ *n* па́ра; (*mus*) дуэ́т.

dupe /dju:p/ *vt* надува́ть *impf*, наду́ть *pf*; *n* простофи́ля *m* & *f*.

duplicate *n* /ˈdju:plɪkət/ ко́пия; **in ~** в двух экземпля́рах; *adj* запасно́й; *vt* /ˈdju:plɪkeɪt/ размножа́ть *impf*, размно́жить *pf* **duplicity** /dju:ˈplɪsɪtɪ/ *n* двули́чность.

durability /ˌdjʊərəˈbɪlɪtɪ/ *n* про́чность. **durable** /ˈdjʊərəb(ə)l/ *adj* про́чный. **duration** /djʊə'reɪʃ(ə)n/ *n* продолжи́тельность.

duress /djʊə'res/ *n* принужде́ние; **under ~** под давле́нием.

during /'djʊərɪŋ/ *prep* во вре́мя *+gen*; (*throughout*) в тече́ние *+gen*.

dusk /dʌsk/ *n* су́мерки (-рек) *pl*.

dust /dʌst/ *n* пыль; **~bin** му́сорный я́щик; **~-jacket** суперобло́жка; **~man** му́сорщик; **~pan** сово́к; *vt & i* (*clean*) стира́ть *impf*, стере́ть *pf* пыль (с+*gen*); (*sprinkle*) посыпа́ть *impf*, посы́пать *pf sth +acc*, *with +instr*. **duster** /'dʌstə(r)/ *n* пы́льная тря́пка. **dusty** /'dʌstɪ/ *adj* пы́льный.

Dutch /dʌtʃ/ *adj* голла́ндский; *n*: **the ~** голла́ндцы *m pl*. **Dutchman** *n* голла́ндец. **Dutchwoman** *n* голла́ндка.

dutiful /'dju:tɪˌfʊl/ *adj* послу́шный. **duty** /'dju:tɪ/ *n* (*obligation*) долг; обя́занность; (*office*) дежу́рство; (*tax*) по́шлина; **be on ~** дежу́рить *impf*; **~-free** *adj* беспо́шлинный.

duvet /'du:veɪ/ *n* стёганое одея́ло.

DVD *abbr* (*of* **digital versatile disk**) DVD; **~ player** DVD-пле́ер.

dwarf /dwɔ:f/ *n* ка́рлик; *vt* (*tower above*) возвыша́ться *impf*, возвы́ситься *pf* над+*instr*.

dwell /dwel/ *vi* обита́ть *impf*; **~ upon** остана́вливаться *impf* на+*prep*. **dweller** /'dwelə(r)/ *n* жи́тель *m*. **dwelling** /'dwelɪŋ/ *n* жили́ще.

dwindle /'dwɪnd(ə)l/ *vi* убыва́ть *impf*, убы́ть *pf*.

dye /daɪ/ *n* краси́тель *m*; *vt* окра́шивать *impf*, окра́сить *pf*.

dynamic /daɪ'næmɪk/ *adj* динами́ческий. **dynamics** /-mɪks/ *n pl* дина́мика.

dynamite /'daɪnəˌmaɪt/ *n* динами́т.

dynamo /'daɪnəˌməʊ/ *n* дина́мо *neut indecl*.

dynasty /'dɪnəstɪ/ *n* дина́стия.

dysentery /'dɪsəntərɪ/ *n* дизентери́я.

dyslexia /dɪs'leksɪə/ *n* дисле́ксия. **dyslexic** /-'leksɪk/ *adj*: **he is ~** он дисле́ктик.

E

each /i:tʃ/ *adj & pron* ка́ждый; **~ other** друг дру́га (*dat* -гу, *etc*.).

eager /'i:gə(r)/ *adj* (*pupil*) усе́рдный; **I am ~ to** мне не те́рпится *+inf*; о́чень жела́ю *+inf*. **eagerly** /-lɪ/ *adv* с нетерпе́нием; жа́дно. **eagerness** /-nɪs/ *n* си́льное жела́ние.

eagle /'i:g(ə)l/ *n* орёл.

ear[1] /ɪə(r)/ *n* (*corn*) ко́лос.

ear[2] /ɪə(r)/ *n* (*anat*) у́хо; (*sense*) слух; **~-ache** боль в у́хе; **~drum** бараба́нная перепо́нка; **~mark** (*assign*) предназнача́ть *impf*, предназна́чить *pf*; **~phone** нау́шник; **~ring** серьга́; (*clip-on*) клипс; **~shot**: **within/out of ~** в преде́лах/вне преде́лов слы́шимости.

earl /ɜ:l/ *n* граф.

early /'ɜ:lɪ/ *adj* ра́нний; *adv* ра́но.

earn /ɜ:n/ *vt* зараба́тывать *impf*, зарабо́тать *pf*; (*deserve*) заслу́живать *impf*, заслужи́ть *pf*. **earnings** /'ɜ:nɪŋz/ *n pl* за́работок.

earnest /'ɜ:nɪst/ *adj* серьёзный; *n*: **in ~** всерьёз.

earth /ɜ:θ/ *n* земля́; (*soil*) по́чва; *vt* заземля́ть *impf*, заземли́ть *pf*. **earthenware** /'ɜ:θ(ə)nˌweə(r)/ *adj* гли́няный. **earthly** /'ɜ:θlɪ/ *adj* земно́й. **earthquake** *n* землетрясе́ние. **earthy** /'ɜ:θɪ/ *adj* земли́стый; (*coarse*) гру́бый.

earwig /'ɪəwɪg/ *n* уховёртка.

ease /i:z/ *n* (*facility*) лёгкость; (*unconstraint*) непринуждённость; **with ~** легко́; *vt* облегча́ть *impf*, облегчи́ть *pf*; *vi* успока́иваться *impf*, успоко́иться *pf*.

easel /'i:z(ə)l/ *n* мольбе́рт.

east /i:st/ *n* восто́к; (*naut*) ост; *adj*

восто́чный. **easterly** /ˈiːstəlɪ/ *adj* восто́чный. **eastern** /ˈiːst(ə)n/ *adj* восто́чный. **eastward(s)** /ˈiːstwəd(z)/ *adv* на восто́к, к восто́ку.

Easter /ˈiːstə(r)/ *n* Па́сха.

easy /ˈiːzɪ/ *adj* лёгкий; (*unconstrained*) непринуждённый; **~-going** ужи́вчивый.

eat /iːt/ *vt* есть *impf*, с~ *pf*; ку́шать *impf*, по~, с~ *pf*; **~ away** разъеда́ть *impf*, разъе́сть *pf*; **~ into** въеда́ться *impf*, въе́сться *pf* в+*acc*; **~ up** доеда́ть *impf*, дое́сть *pf*. **eatable** /iːtəb(ə)l/ *adj* съедо́бный.

eaves /iːvz/ *n pl* стреха́. **eavesdrop** /ˈiːvzdrɒp/ *vi* подслу́шивать *impf*.

ebb /eb/ *n* (*tide*) отли́в; (*fig*) упа́док.

ebony /ˈebənɪ/ *n* чёрное де́рево.

ebullient /ɪˈbʌlɪənt/ *adj* кипу́чий.

EC *abbr* (*of* **European Community**) Европе́йское соо́бщество.

eccentric /ɪkˈsentrɪk/ *n* чуда́к; *adj* эксцентри́чный.

ecclesiastical /ɪˌkliːzɪˈæstɪk(ə)l/ *adj* церко́вный.

echo /ˈekəʊ/ *n* э́хо; *vi* (*resound*) отража́ться *impf*, отрази́ться *pf*; *vt* (*repeat*) повторя́ть *impf*, повтори́ть *pf*.

eclipse /ɪˈklɪps/ *n* затме́ние; *vt* затмева́ть *impf*, затми́ть *pf*.

ecological /ˌiːkəˈlɒdʒɪk(ə)l/ *adj* экологи́ческий. **ecology** /ɪˈkɒlədʒɪ/ *n* эколо́гия.

economic /ˌiːkəˈnɒmɪk/ *adj* экономи́ческий. **economical** /ˌiːkəˈnɒmɪk(ə)l/ *adj* эконо́мный. **economist** /ɪˈkɒnəmɪst/ *n* экономи́ст. **economize** /ɪˈkɒnəˌmaɪz/ *vt & i* эконо́мить *impf*, с~ *pf*. **economy** /ɪˈkɒnəmɪ/ *n* эконо́мика; (*saving*) эконо́мия.

ecstasy /ˈekstəsɪ/ *n* экста́з. **ecstatic** /ekˈstætɪk/ *adj* экстати́ческий.

eddy /ˈedɪ/ *n* водоворо́т.

edge /edʒ/ *n* край; (*blade*) ле́звие; **on ~** в не́рвном состоя́нии; **have the ~ on** име́ть *impf* преиму́щество над+*instr*; *vt* (*border*) окаймля́ть *impf*, окайми́ть *pf*; *vi* пробира́ться *impf*, пробра́ться *pf*. **edging** /ˈedʒɪŋ/ *n* кайма́. **edgy** /ˈedʒɪ/ *adj* раздражи́тельный.

edible /ˈedɪb(ə)l/ *adj* съедо́бный.

edict /ˈiːdɪkt/ *n* ука́з.

edifice /ˈedɪfɪs/ *n* зда́ние. **edifying** /ˈedɪˌfaɪɪŋ/ *adj* назида́тельный.

edit /ˈedɪt/ *vt* редакти́ровать *impf*, от~ *pf*; (*cin*) монти́ровать *impf*, с~ *pf*. **edition** /ɪˈdɪʃ(ə)n/ *n* изда́ние; (*number of copies*) тира́ж. **editor** /ˈedɪtə(r)/ *n* реда́ктор. **editorial** /ˌedɪˈtɔːrɪəl/ *n* передова́я статья́; *adj* реда́кторский, редакцио́нный.

educate /ˈedjʊˌkeɪt/ *vt* дава́ть *impf*, дать *pf* образова́ние +*dat*; **where was he educated?** где он получи́л образова́ние? **educated** /-ˌkeɪtɪd/ *adj* образо́ванный. **education** /-ˈkeɪʃ(ə)n/ *n* образова́ние. **educational** /-ˈkeɪʃən(ə)l/ *adj* образова́тельный; (*instructive*) уче́бный.

eel /iːl/ *n* у́горь *m*.

eerie /ˈɪərɪ/ *adj* жу́ткий.

effect /ɪˈfekt/ *n* (*result*) сле́дствие; (*validity*; *influence*) де́йствие; (*impression*; *theat*) эффе́кт; **in ~** факти́чески; **take ~** вступа́ть *impf*, вступи́ть *pf* в си́лу; (*medicine*) начина́ть *impf*, нача́ть *pf* де́йствовать; *vt* производи́ть *impf*, произвести́ *pf*. **effective** /-ˈfektɪv/ *adj* эффекти́вный; (*striking*) эффе́ктный; (*actual*) факти́ческий. **effectiveness** /-ˈfektɪvnɪs/ *n* эффекти́вность.

effeminate /ɪˈfemɪnət/ *adj* женоподо́бный.

effervesce /ˌefəˈves/ *vi* пузы́риться *impf*. **effervescent** /-ˈvesənt/ *adj* (*fig*) и́скря́щийся.

efficiency /ɪˈfɪʃənsɪ/ *n* эффекти́вность. **efficient** /-ˈfɪʃ(ə)nt/ *adj* эффекти́вный; (*person*) организо́ванный.

effigy /ˈefɪdʒɪ/ *n* изображе́ние.

effort /ˈefət/ *n* уси́лие.

effrontery /ɪ'frʌntərɪ/ *n* нáглость.
effusive /ɪ'fjuːsɪv/ *adj* экспансúвный.
e.g. *abbr* напр.
egalitarian /ɪˌgælɪ'teərɪən/ *adj* эгалитáрный.
egg¹ /eg/ *n* яйцó; **~cup** рю́мка для яйцá; **~shell** яúчная скорлупá.
egg² /eg/ *vt*: **~ on** подстрекáть *impf*, подстрекнýть *pf*.
ego /'iːgəʊ/ *n* «Я». **egocentric** /ˌiːgəʊ'sentrɪk/ *adj* эгоцентрúческий. **egoism** /'iːgəʊˌɪz(ə)m/ *n* эгоúзм. **ego(t)ist** /'iːgəʊ(t)ɪst/ *n* эгоúст, **~**ка. **ego(t)istical** /ˌiːgə'(t)ɪstɪk(ə)l/ *adj* эгоцентрúческий. **egotism** /'iːgəˌtɪz(ə)m/ *n* эготúзм.
Egypt /'iːdʒɪpt/ *n* Егúпет. **Egyptian** /ɪ'dʒɪpʃ(ə)n/ *n* египтя́нин, -я́нка; *adj* егúпетский.
eiderdown /'aɪdəˌdaʊn/ *n* пухóвое одея́ло.
eight /eɪt/ *adj & n* вóсемь; (*number 8*) восьмёрка. **eighteen** /eɪ'tiːn/ *adj & n* восемнáдцать. **eighteenth** /eɪ'tiːnθ/ *adj & n* восемнáдцатый. **eighth** /eɪtθ/ *adj & n* восьмóй; (*fraction*) восьмáя *sb*. **eightieth** /'eɪtɪɪθ/ *adj & n* восьмидеся́тый. **eighty** /'eɪtɪ/ *adj & n* вóсемьдесят; *pl* (*decade*) восьмидеся́тые гóды (-дóв) *m pl*.
either /'aɪðə(r)/ *adj & pron* (*one of two*) одúн из двух, тот úли другóй; (*both*) и тот, и другóй; óба; (*one or other*) любóй; *adv & conj*: **~ ... or** úли… úли, лúбо… лúбо.
eject /ɪ'dʒekt/ *vt* выбрáсывать *impf*, вы́бросить *pf*; *vi* (*pilot*) катапультúроваться *impf & pf*.
eke /iːk/ *vt*: **~ out a living** перебивáться *impf*, перебúться *pf* кóе-как.
elaborate *adj* /ɪ'læbərət/ (*ornate*) витиевáтый; (*detailed*) подрóбный; *vt* /ɪ'læbəˌreɪt/ разрабáтывать *impf*, разрабóтать *pf*; (*detail*) уточня́ть *impf*, уточнúть *pf*.
elapse /ɪ'læps/ *vi* проходúть *impf*, пройтú *pf*; (*expire*) истекáть *impf*, истéчь *pf*.
elastic /ɪ'læstɪk/ *n* резúнка; *adj* эластúчный, **~ band** резúнка. **elasticity** /-'stɪsɪtɪ/ *n* эластúчность.
elated /ɪ'leɪtɪd/ *adj* в востóрге. **elation** /ɪ'leɪʃ(ə)n/ *n* востóрг.
elbow /'elbəʊ/ *n* лóкоть *m*; *vt*: **~ (one's way) through** протáлкиваться *impf*, протолкнýться *pf* чéрез+*acc*.
elder¹ /'eldə(r)/ *n* (*tree*) бузинá.
elder² /'eldə(r)/ *n* (*person*) стáрец; *pl* стáршие *sb*; *adj* стáрший. **elderly** /'eldəlɪ/ *adj* пожилóй. **eldest** /'eldɪst/ *adj* стáрший.
elect /ɪ'lekt/ *adj* úзбранный; *vt* избирáть *impf*, избрáть *pf*. **election** /ɪ'lekʃ(ə)n/ *n* вы́боры *m pl*. **elector** /ɪ'lektə(r)/ *n* избирáтель *m*. **electoral** /ɪ'lektər(ə)l/ *adj* избирáтельный. **electorate** /ɪ'lektərət/ *n* избирáтели *m pl*.
electric(al) /ɪ'lektrɪk((ə)l)/ *adj* электрúческий; **~ shock** удáр электрúческим тóком. **electrician** /ˌɪlek'trɪʃ(ə)n/ *n* элéктрик. **electricity** /ˌɪlek'trɪsɪtɪ/ *n* электрúчество. **electrify** /ɪ'lektrɪˌfaɪ/ *vt* (*convert to electricity*) электрифицúровать *impf & pf*; (*charge with electricity*; *fig*) электризовáть *impf*, на**~** *pf*. **electrode** /ɪ'lektrəʊd/ *n* электрóд. **electron** /ɪ'lektrɒn/ *n* электрóн. **electronic** /ˌɪlek'trɒnɪk/ *adj* электрóнный. **electronics** /ˌɪlek'trɒnɪks/ *n* электрóника.
electrocute /ɪ'lektrəˌkjuːt/ *vt* убивáть *impf*, убúть *pf* электрúческим тóком; (*execute*) казнúть *impf & pf* на электрúческом стýле. **electrolysis** /ˌɪlek'trɒlɪsɪs/ *n* электрóлиз.
elegance /'elɪgəns/ *n* элегáнтность. **elegant** /-gənt/ *adj* элегáнтный.
elegy /'elɪdʒɪ/ *n* элéгия.
element /'elɪmənt/ *n* элемéнт; (*earth, wind, etc.*) стихúя; **be in one's ~** быть в своéй стихúи. **elemental** /-'ment(ə)l/ *adj* стихúй-

ный. **elementary** /-'mentərɪ/ *adj* элементáрный; (*school etc.*) начáльный.
elephant /'elɪfənt/ *n* слон.
elevate /'elɪˌveɪt/ *vt* поднимáть *impf*, поднять *pf*. **elevated** /-ˌveɪtɪd/ *adj* возвы́шенный. **elevation** /-ˌveɪʃ(ə)n/ *n* (*height*) высотá. **elevator** /-ˌveɪtə(r)/ *n* (*lift*) лифт.
eleven /ɪ'lev(ə)n/ *adj* & *n* оди́ннадцать. **eleventh** /-'levənθ/ *adj* & *n* оди́ннадцатый; **at the ~ hour** в послéднюю минýту.
elf /elf/ *n* эльф.
elicit /ɪ'lɪsɪt/ *vt* (*obtain*) выявля́ть *impf*, вы́явить *pf*; (*evoke*) вызывáть *impf*, вы́звать *pf*.
eligible /'elɪdʒɪb(ə)l/ *adj* имéющий прáво (**for** на+*acc*); (*bachelor*) подходя́щий.
eliminate /ɪ'lɪmɪˌneɪt/ *vt* устраня́ть *impf*, устрани́ть *pf*; (*rule out*) исключáть *impf*, исключи́ть *pf*.
élite /eɪ'liːt/ *n* эли́та.
ellipse /ɪ'lɪps/ *n* э́ллипс. **elliptic(al)** /ɪ'lɪptɪk((ə)l)/ *adj* эллипти́ческий.
elm /elm/ *n* вяз.
elongate /'iːlɒŋˌgeɪt/ *vt* удлиня́ть *impf*, удлини́ть *pf*.
elope /ɪ'ləʊp/ *vi* бежáть *det* (с возлю́бленным).
eloquence /'eləkwəns/ *n* красноречие. **eloquent** /-kwənt/ *adj* красноречи́вый.
else /els/ *adv* (*besides*) ещё; (*instead*) другóй; (*with neg*) бóльше; **nobody ~** никтó бóльше; **or ~** и́наче; а (не) то; и́ли же; **s.o. ~** кто-нибýдь другóй; **something ~?** ещё чтó-нибудь? **elsewhere** *adv* (*place*) в другóм мéсте; (*direction*) в другóе мéсто.
elucidate /ɪ'luːsɪˌdeɪt/ *vt* разъясня́ть *impf*, разъясни́ть *pf*.
elude /ɪ'luːd/ *vt* избегáть *impf* +*gen*. **elusive** /-'luːsɪv/ *adj* неулови́мый.
emaciated /ɪ'meɪsɪˌeɪtɪd/ *adj* истощённый.
email /'iːmeɪl/ *n* (*system, letters*) электрóнная пóчта; (*letter*) электрóнное письмó; **~ address** электрóнный áдрес
emanate /'eməˌneɪt/ *vi* исходи́ть *impf* (**from** из, от, +*gen*).
emancipate /ɪ'mænsɪˌpeɪt/ *vt* эмансипи́ровать *impf* & *pf*. **emancipation** /-'peɪʃ(ə)n/ *n* эмансипáция.
embankment /ɪm'bæŋkmənt/ *n* (*river*) нáбережная *sb*; (*rly*) нáсыпь.
embargo /em'bɑːgəʊ/ *n* эмбáрго *neut indecl*.
embark /ɪm'bɑːk/ *vi* сади́ться *impf*, сесть *pf* на корáбль; **~ upon** предпринимáть *impf*, предприня́ть *pf*. **embarkation** /ˌembɑː'keɪʃ(ə)n/ *n* посáдка (на корáбль).
embarrass /ɪm'bærəs/ *vt* смущáть *impf*, смути́ть *pf*; **be ~ed** чýвствовать *impf* себя́ неудóбно. **embarrassing** /-sɪŋ/ *adj* неудóбный. **embarrassment** /-mənt/ *n* смущéние.
embassy /'embəsɪ/ *n* посóльство.
embedded /ɪm'bedɪd/ *adj* врéзанный.
embellish /ɪm'belɪʃ/ *vt* (*adorn*) украшáть *impf*, укрáсить *pf*; (*story*) прикрáшивать *impf*, прикрáсить *pf*. **embellishment** /-mənt/ *n* украшéние.
embers /'embəz/ *n pl* тлéющие угольки́ *m pl*.
embezzle /ɪm'bez(ə)l/ *vt* растрáчивать *impf*, растрáтить *pf*. **embezzlement** /-mənt/ *n* растрáта.
embittered /ɪm'bɪtəd/ *adj* озлóбленный.
emblem /'embləm/ *n* эмблéма.
embodiment /ɪm'bɒdɪmənt/ *n* воплощéние. **embody** /ɪm'bɒdɪ/ *vt* воплощáть *impf*, воплоти́ть *pf*.
emboss /ɪm'bɒs/ *vt* чекáнить *impf*, вы́~, от~ *pf*.
embrace /ɪm'breɪs/ *n* объя́тие; *vi* обнимáться *impf*, обня́ться *pf*; *vt* обнимáть *impf*, обня́ть *pf*; (*accept*) принимáть *impf*, приня́ть *pf*; (*include*) охвáтывать

impf, охвати́ть *pf.*
embroider /ɪm'brɔɪdə(r)/ *vt* вышива́ть *impf*, вы́шить *pf*; (*story*) прикра́шивать *impf*, прикра́сить *pf.* **embroidery** /-dərɪ/ *n* вы́шивка.
embroil /ɪm'brɔɪl/ *vt* впу́тывать *impf*, впу́тать *pf.*
e **embryo** /'embrɪəʊ/ *n* эмбрио́н.
emerald /'emər(ə)ld/ *n* изумру́д.
emerge /ɪ'mɜːdʒ/ *vi* появля́ться *impf*, появи́ться *pf.* **emergence** /-dʒəns/ *n* появле́ние. **emergency** /-dʒənsɪ/ *n* кра́йняя необходи́мость; **state of ~** чрезвыча́йное положе́ние; **~ exit** запасно́й вы́ход.
emery paper /'emərɪ 'peɪpə(r)/ *n* наждáчная бума́га.
emigrant /'emɪgrənt/ *n* эмигра́нт, **~**ка. **emigrate** /'emɪgreɪt/ *vi* эмигри́ровать *impf* & *pf.* **emigration** /ˌemɪ'greɪʃ(ə)n/ *n* эмигра́ция.
eminence /'emɪnəns/ *n* (*fame*) знамени́тость. **eminent** /-nənt/ *adj* выдаю́щийся. **eminently** /-nəntlɪ/ *adv* чрезвыча́йно.
emission /ɪ'mɪʃ(ə)n/ *n* испуска́ние. **emit** /ɪ'mɪt/ *vt* испуска́ть *impf*, испусти́ть *pf*; (*light*) излуча́ть *impf*, излучи́ть *pf*; (*sound*) издава́ть *impf*, изда́ть *pf.*
emotion /ɪ'məʊʃ(ə)n/ *n* эмо́ция, чу́вство. **emotional** /-n(ə)l/ *adj* эмоциона́льный.
empathize /'empəˌθaɪz/ *vt* сопережива́ть *impf*, сопережи́ть *pf.* **empathy** /-pəθɪ/ *n* эмпа́тия.
emperor /'empərə(r)/ *n* импера́тор.
emphasis /'emfəsɪs/ *n* ударе́ние. **emphasize** /'emfəˌsaɪz/ *vt* подчёркивать *impf*, подчеркну́ть *pf.* **emphatic** /em'fætɪk/ *adj* вырази́тельный; категори́ческий.
empire /'empaɪə(r)/ *n* импе́рия.
empirical /ɪm'pɪrɪk(ə)l/ *adj* эмпири́ческий.
employ /ɪm'plɔɪ/ *vt* (*use*) по́льзоваться *impf* +*instr*; (*person*) нанима́ть *impf*, наня́ть *pf.* **employee** /ˌemplɔɪ'iː/ *n* сотру́дник, рабо́чий *sb.* **employer** /ɪm'plɔɪə(r)/ *n* работода́тель *m.* **employment** /ɪm'plɔɪmənt/ *n* рабо́та, слу́жба; (*use*) испо́льзование.
empower /ɪm'paʊə(r)/ *vt* уполномо́чивать *impf*, уполномо́чить *pf* (**to** на+*acc*).
empress /'emprɪs/ *n* императри́ца.
emptiness /'emptɪnɪs/ *n* пустота́. **empty** /'emptɪ/ *adj* пусто́й; **~-headed** пустоголо́вый; *vt* (*container*) опорожня́ть *impf*, опоро́жни́ть *pf*; (*solid*) высыпа́ть *impf*, вы́сыпать *pf*; (*liquid*) вылива́ть *impf*, вы́лить *pf*; *vi* пусте́ть *impf*, о**~** *pf.*
emulate /'emjʊˌleɪt/ *vt* достига́ть *impf*, дости́гнуть, дости́чь *pf* +*gen*; (*copy*) подража́ть *impf* +*dat.*
emulsion /ɪ'mʌlʃ(ə)n/ *n* эму́льсия.
enable /ɪ'neɪb(ə)l/ *vt* дава́ть *impf*, дать *pf* возмо́жность +*dat* & *inf.*
enact /ɪ'nækt/ *vt* (*law*) принима́ть *impf*, приня́ть *pf*; (*theat*) разы́грывать *impf*, разыгра́ть *pf.* **enactment** /-'næktmənt/ *n* (*law*) постановле́ние; (*theat*) игра́.
enamel /ɪ'næm(ə)l/ *n* эма́ль; *adj* эма́левый; *vt* эмалирова́ть *impf* & *pf.*
encampment /ɪn'kæmpmənt/ *n* ла́герь *m.*
enchant /ɪn'tʃɑːnt/ *vt* очаро́вывать *impf*, очарова́ть *pf.* **enchanting** /-tɪŋ/ *adj* очарова́тельный. **enchantment** /-mənt/ *n* очарова́ние.
encircle /ɪn'sɜːk(ə)l/ *vt* окружа́ть *impf*, окружи́ть *pf.*
enclave /'enkleɪv/ *n* анкла́в.
enclose /ɪn'kləʊz/ *vt* огора́живать *impf*, огороди́ть *pf*; (*in letter*) прикла́дывать *impf*, приложи́ть *pf*; **please find ~d** прилага́ется (-а́ются) +*nom.* **enclosure** /ɪn'kləʊʒə(r)/ *n* огоро́женное ме́сто; (*in letter*) приложе́ние.

encode /ɪn'kəʊd/ *vt* шифровáть *impf*, за~ *pf*.
encompass /ɪn'kʌmpəs/ *vt* (*encircle*) окружáть *impf*, окружи́ть *pf*; (*contain*) заключáть *impf*, заключи́ть *pf*.
encore /'ɒŋkɔː(r)/ *int* бис!; *n* вы́зов на бис.
encounter /ɪn'kaʊntə(r)/ *n* встрéча; (*in combat*) столкновéние; *vt* встречáть *impf*, встрéтить *pf*; (*fig*) стáлкиваться *impf*, столкнýться *pf* с+*instr*.
encourage /ɪn'kʌrɪdʒ/ *vt* ободря́ть *impf*, ободри́ть *pf*. **encouragement** /-mənt/ *n* ободрéние. **encouraging** /-dʒɪŋ/ *adj* ободри́тельный.
encroach /ɪn'krəʊtʃ/ *vt* вторгáться *impf*, вто́ргнуться *pf* (**on** в+*acc*). **encroachment** /-mənt/ *n* вторжéние.
encumber /ɪn'kʌmbə(r)/ *vt* обременя́ть *impf*, обремени́ть *pf*. **encumbrance** /-brəns/ *n* обýза.
encyclopaedia /en,saɪklə'piːdɪə/ *n* энциклопéдия. **encyclopaedic** /-'piːdɪk/ *adj* энциклопеди́ческий.
end /end/ *n* конéц; (*death*) смерть; (*purpose*) цель; **an ~ in itself** самоцéль; **in the ~** в концé концо́в; **make ~s meet** своди́ть *impf*, свести́ *pf* концы́ с концáми; **no ~ of** мáсса+*gen*; **on ~** (*upright*) стоймя́, ды́бом; (*continuously*) подря́д; **put an ~ to** класть *impf*, положи́ть *pf* конéц +*dat*; *vt* кончáть *impf*, ко́нчить *pf*; (*halt*) прекращáть *impf*, прекрати́ть *pf*; *vi* кончáться *impf*, ко́нчиться *pf*.
endanger /ɪn'deɪndʒə(r)/ *vt* подвергáть *impf*, подвéргнуть *pf* опáсности.
endearing /ɪn'dɪərɪŋ/ *adj* привлекáтельный. **endearment** /-'dɪəmənt/ *n* лáска.
endeavour /ɪn'devə(r)/ *n* попы́тка; (*exertion*) уси́лие; (*undertaking*) дéло; *vi* старáться *impf*, по~ *pf*.
endemic /en'demɪk/ *adj* эндеми́ческий.
ending /'endɪŋ/ *n* окончáние. **endless** /'endlɪs/ *adj* бесконéчный.
endorse /ɪn'dɔːs/ *vt* (*document*) подпи́сывать *impf*, подписáть *pf*; (*support*) поддéрживать *impf*, поддержáть *pf*. **endorsement** /-mənt/ *n* по́дпись; поддéржка; (*on driving licence*) прóкол.
endow /ɪn'daʊ/ *vt* обеспéчивать *impf*, обеспéчить *pf* постоя́нным дохо́дом; (*fig*) одаря́ть *impf*, одари́ть *pf*. **endowment** /-mənt/ *n* пожéртвование; (*talent*) даровáние.
endurance /ɪn'djʊərəns/ *n* (*of person*) выно́сливость; (*of object*) про́чность. **endure** /-'djʊə(r)/ *vt* выноси́ть *impf*, вы́нести *pf*; терпéть *impf*, по~ *pf*; *vi* продолжáться *impf*, продо́лжиться *pf*.
enemy /'enəmɪ/ *n* враг; *adj* врáжеский.
energetic /,enə'dʒetɪk/ *adj* энерги́чный. **energy** /'enədʒɪ/ *n* энéргия; *pl* си́лы *f pl*.
enforce /ɪn'fɔːs/ *vt* (*law etc.*) следи́ть *impf* за выполнéнием +*gen*. **enforcement** /-mənt/ *n* наблюдéние за выполнéнием +*gen*.
engage /ɪn'geɪdʒ/ *vt* (*hire*) нанимáть *impf*, наня́ть *pf*; (*tech*) зацепля́ть *impf*, зацепи́ть *pf*. **engaged** /-'geɪdʒd/ *adj* (*occupied*) зáнятый; **be ~ in** занимáться *impf*, заня́ться *pf* +*instr*; **become ~** обручáться *impf*, обручи́ться *pf* (**to** с+*instr*). **engagement** /-'geɪdʒmənt/ *n* (*appointment*) свидáние; (*betrothal*) обручéние; (*battle*) бой; **~ ring** обручáльное кольцо́. **engaging** /-'geɪdʒɪŋ/ *adj* привлекáтельный.
engender /ɪn'dʒendə(r)/ *vt* порождáть *impf*, породи́ть *pf*.
engine /'endʒɪn/ *n* дви́гатель *m*; (*rly*) локомоти́в; **~-driver** (*rly*) машини́ст. **engineer** /,endʒɪ'nɪə(r)/ *n* инженéр; *vt* (*fig*) организовáть *impf* & *pf*. **engineering** /,endʒɪ'nɪərɪŋ/ *n* инженéрное дéло, тéхника.
England /'ɪŋglənd/ *n* Áнглия. **Eng-**

e

lish /ˈɪŋɡlɪʃ/ *adj* английский; *n*: **the ~** *pl* англичáне (-н) *pl*. **Englishman, -woman** *n* англичáнин, -áнка.

engrave /ɪnˈɡreɪv/ *vt* гравировáть *impf*, вы́~ *pf*; (*fig*) врезáть *impf*, врéзать *pf*. **engraver** /-ˈɡreɪvə(r)/ *n* гравёр. **engraving** /-ˈɡreɪvɪŋ/ *n* гравю́ра.

e

engross /ɪnˈɡrəʊs/ *vt* поглощáть *impf*, поглоти́ть *pf*; **be ~ed in** быть поглощённым +*instr*.

engulf /ɪnˈɡʌlf/ *vt* поглощáть *impf*, поглоти́ть *pf*.

enhance /ɪnˈhɑːns/ *vt* увели́чивать *impf*, увели́чить *pf*.

enigma /ɪˈnɪɡmə/ *n* загáдка. **enigmatic** /ˌenɪɡˈmætɪk/ *adj* загáдочный.

enjoy /ɪnˈdʒɔɪ/ *vt* получáть *impf*, получи́ть *pf* удовóльствие от+*gen*; наслаждáться *impf*, наслади́ться *pf* +*instr*; (*health etc.*) обладáть *impf* +*instr*; **~ o.s.** хорошó проводи́ть *impf*, провести́ *pf* врéмя. **enjoyable** /-əb(ə)l/ *adj* прия́тный. **enjoyment** /-mənt/ *n* удовóльствие.

enlarge /ɪnˈlɑːdʒ/ *vt* увели́чивать *impf*, увели́чить *pf*; **~ upon** распространя́ться *impf*, распространи́ться *pf* о+*prep*. **enlargement** /-mənt/ *n* увеличéние.

enlighten /ɪnˈlaɪt(ə)n/ *vt* просвещáть *impf*, просвети́ть *pf*. **enlightenment** /-mənt/ *n* просвещéние.

enlist /ɪnˈlɪst/ *vi* поступáть *impf*, поступи́ть *pf* на воéнную слу́жбу; *vt* (*mil*) вербовáть *impf*, за~ *pf*; (*support etc.*) заручáться *impf*, заручи́ться *pf* +*instr*.

enliven /ɪnˈlaɪv(ə)n/ *vt* оживля́ть *impf*, оживи́ть *pf*.

enmity /ˈenmɪtɪ/ *n* враждá.

ennoble /ɪˈnəʊb(ə)l/ *vt* облагорáживать *impf*, облагорóдить *pf*.

ennui /ɒnˈwiː/ *n* тоскá.

enormity /ɪˈnɔːmɪtɪ/ *n* чудóвищность. **enormous** /-ˈnɔːməs/ *adj* огрóмный. **enormously** /-ˈnɔːməslɪ/ *adv* чрезвычáйно.

enough /ɪˈnʌf/ *adj* достáточно +*gen*; *adv* достáточно, довóльно; **be ~** хватáть *impf*, хвати́ть *pf impers*+*gen*.

enquire, enquiry /ɪnˈkwaɪə(r), ɪnˈkwaɪərɪ/ *see* **inquire, inquiry**

enrage /ɪnˈreɪdʒ/ *vt* беси́ть *impf*, вз~ *pf*.

enrapture /ɪnˈræptʃə(r)/ *vt* восхищáть *impf*, восхити́ть *pf*.

enrich /ɪnˈrɪtʃ/ *vt* обогащáть *impf*, обогати́ть *pf*.

enrol /ɪnˈrəʊl/ *vt* & *i* запи́сывать(ся) *impf*, записáть(ся) *pf*. **enrolment** /-mənt/ *n* зáпись.

en route /ɑ̃ ˈruːt/ *adv* по пути́ (**to, for** в+*acc*).

ensconce /ɪnˈskɒns/ *vt*: **~ o.s.** засáживаться *impf*, засéсть *pf* (**with** за+*acc*).

ensemble /ɒnˈsɒmb(ə)l/ *n* (*mus*) ансáмбль *m*.

enshrine /ɪnˈʃraɪn/ *vt* (*fig*) охраня́ть *impf*, охрани́ть *pf*.

ensign /ˈensaɪn/ *n* (*flag*) флаг.

enslave /ɪnˈsleɪv/ *vt* порабощáть *impf*, поработи́ть *pf*.

ensue /ɪnˈsjuː/ *vi* слéдовать *impf*. **ensuing** /-ˈsjuːɪŋ/ *adj* послéдующий.

ensure /ɪnˈʃʊə(r)/ *vt* обеспéчивать *impf*, обеспéчить *pf*.

entail /ɪnˈteɪl/ *vt* (*necessitate*) влечь *impf* за собóй.

entangle /ɪnˈtæŋɡ(ə)l/ *vt* запу́тывать *impf*, запу́тать *pf*.

enter /ˈentə(r)/ *vt* & *i* входи́ть *impf*, войти́ *pf* в+*acc*; (*by transport*) въезжáть *impf*, въéхать *pf* в+*acc*; *vt* (*join*) поступáть *impf*, поступи́ть *pf* в, на, +*acc*; (*competition*) вступáть *impf*, вступи́ть *pf* в+*acc*; (*in list*) вноси́ть *impf*, внести́ *pf* в+*acc*.

enterprise /ˈentəˌpraɪz/ *n* (*undertaking*) предприя́тие; (*initiative*) предприи́мчивость. **enterprising** /-zɪŋ/ *adj* предприи́мчивый.

entertain /ˌentəˈteɪn/ *vt* (*amuse*) развлекáть *impf*, развлéчь *pf*; (*guests*) принимáть *impf*, приня́ть *pf*; угощáть *impf*, угости́ть *pf* (**to** +*instr*); (*hopes*) пита́ть *impf*. **entertaining** /-nɪŋ/ *adj* занима́тельный. **entertainment** /-mənt/ *n* развлече́ние; (*show*) представле́ние.

enthral /ɪn'θrɔːl/ *vt* порабоща́ть *impf*, поработи́ть *pf*.

enthusiasm /ɪn'θjuːzɪˌæz(ə)m/ *n* энтузиа́зм. **enthusiast** /-ˌæst/ *n* энтузиа́ст, ~ка. **enthusiastic** /-'æstɪk/ *adj* восто́рженный; по́лный энтузиа́зма.

entice /ɪn'taɪs/ *vt* зама́нивать *impf*, замани́ть *pf*. **enticement** /-mənt/ *n* прима́нка. **enticing** /-sɪŋ/ *adj* зама́нчивый.

entire /ɪn'taɪə(r)/ *adj* по́лный, це́лый, весь. **entirely** /-'taɪəlɪ/ *adv* вполне́, соверше́нно; (*solely*) исключи́тельно. **entirety** /-'taɪərətɪ/ *n*: **in its ~** по́лностью.

entitle /ɪn'taɪt(ə)l/ *vt* (*authorize*) дава́ть *impf*, дать *pf* пра́во+*dat* (**to** на+*acc*); **be ~d** (*book*) называ́ться *impf*; **be ~d to** име́ть *impf* пра́во на+*acc*.

entity /'entɪtɪ/ *n* объе́кт; феноме́н.

entomology /ˌentə'mɒlədʒɪ/ *n* энтомоло́гия.

entourage /ˌɒntʊə'rɑːʒ/ *n* сви́та.

entrails /'entreɪlz/ *n pl* вну́тренности (-тей) *pl*.

entrance[1] /'entrəns/ *n* вход, въезд; (*theat*) вы́ход; **~ exam** вступи́тельный экза́мен; **~ hall** вестибю́ль *m*.

entrance[2] /ɪn'trɑːns/ *vt* (*charm*) очаро́вывать *impf*, очарова́ть *pf*. **entrancing** /-'trɑːnsɪŋ/ *adj* очарова́тельный.

entrant /'entrənt/ *n* уча́стник (**for** +*gen*).

entreat /ɪn'triːt/ *vt* умоля́ть *impf*, умоли́ть *pf*. **entreaty** /-'triːtɪ/ *n* мольба́.

entrench /ɪn'trentʃ/ *vt* **be, become ~ed** (*fig*) укореня́ться *impf*, укорени́ться *pf*.

entrepreneur /ˌɒntrəprə'nɜː(r)/ *n* предпринима́тель *m*.

entrust /ɪn'trʌst/ *vt* (*secret*) вверя́ть *impf*, вве́рить *pf* (**to** +*dat*); (*object; person*) поруча́ть *impf*, поручи́ть *pf* (**to** +*dat*).

entry /'entrɪ/ *n* вход, въезд; вступле́ние; (*theat*) вы́ход; (*note*) за́пись; (*in reference book*) статья́.

entwine /ɪn'twaɪn/ *vt* (*interweave*) сплета́ть *impf*, сплести́ *pf*; (*wreathe*) обвива́ть *impf*, обви́ть *pf*.

enumerate /ɪ'njuːməˌreɪt/ *vt* перечисля́ть *impf*, перечи́слить *pf*.

enunciate /ɪ'nʌnsɪˌeɪt/ *vt* (*express*) излага́ть *impf*, изложи́ть *pf*; (*pronounce*) произноси́ть *impf*, произнести́ *pf*. **enunciation** /-'eɪʃ(ə)n/ *n* изложе́ние; произноше́ние.

envelop /ɪn'veləp/ *vt* оку́тывать *impf*, оку́тать *pf*. **envelope** /'envəˌləʊp/ *n* конве́рт.

enviable /'envɪəb(ə)l/ *adj* зави́дный. **envious** /'envɪəs/ *adj* зави́стливый.

environment /ɪn'vaɪərənmənt/ *n* среда́; (*the* ~) окружа́ющая среда́. **environs** /-'vaɪərənz/ *n pl* окре́стности *f pl*.

envisage /ɪn'vɪzɪdʒ/ *vt* предусма́тривать *impf*, предусмотре́ть *pf*.

envoy /'envɔɪ/ *n* посла́нник, аге́нт.

envy /'envɪ/ *n* за́висть; *vt* зави́довать *impf*, по~ *pf* +*dat*.

enzyme /'enzaɪm/ *n* энзи́м.

ephemeral /ɪ'femər(ə)l/ *adj* эфеме́рный.

epic /'epɪk/ *n* эпопе́я; *adj* эпи́ческий.

epidemic /ˌepɪ'demɪk/ *n* эпиде́мия.

epilepsy /'epɪˌlepsɪ/ *n* эпиле́псия. **epileptic** /-'leptɪk/ *n* эпиле́птик; *adj* эпилепти́ческий.

epilogue /'epɪˌlɒg/ *n* эпило́г.

episode /'epɪˌsəʊd/ *n* эпизо́д. **episodic** /-'sɒdɪk/ *adj* эпизоди́ческий.

epistle /ɪ'pɪs(ə)l/ *n* посла́ние.

epitaph /'epɪˌtɑːf/ *n* эпита́фия.

epithet /'epɪˌθet/ *n* эпи́тет.

epitome /ɪ'pɪtəmɪ/ *n* воплоще́ние. **epitomize** /-ˌmaɪz/ *vt* воплоща́ть *impf*, воплоти́ть *pf*.

epoch /'iːpɒk/ *n* эпо́ха.

e

equal /ˈiːkw(ə)l/ *adj* ра́вный, одина́ковый; (*capable of*) спосо́бный (**to** на+*acc*, +*inf*); *n* ра́вный *sb*; *vt* равня́ться *impf* +*dat*. **equality** /ɪˈkwɒlɪtɪ/ *n* ра́венство. **equalize** /ˈiːkwəˌlaɪz/ *vt* ура́внивать *impf*, уравня́ть *pf*; *vi* (*sport*) равня́ть *impf*, с~ *pf* счёт. **equally** /ˈiːkwəlɪ/ *adv* равно́, ра́вным о́бразом.

equanimity /ˌekwəˈnɪmɪtɪ/ *n* хладнокро́вие.

equate /ɪˈkweɪt/ *vt* прира́внивать *impf*, приравня́ть *pf* (**with** к+*dat*).

equation /ɪˈkweɪʒ(ə)n/ *n* (*math*) уравне́ние.

equator /ɪˈkweɪtə(r)/ *n* эква́тор. **equatorial** /ˌekwəˈtɔːrɪəl/ *adj* экваториа́льный.

equestrian /ɪˈkwestrɪən/ *adj* ко́нный.

equidistant /ˌiːkwɪˈdɪst(ə)nt/ *adj* равностоя́щий. **equilibrium** /ˌiːkwɪˈlɪbrɪəm/ *n* равнове́сие.

equip /ɪˈkwɪp/ *vt* обору́довать *impf* & *pf*; (*person*) снаряжа́ть *impf*, снаряди́ть *pf*; (*fig*) вооружа́ть *impf*, вооружи́ть *pf*. **equipment** /-mənt/ *n* обору́дование, снаряже́ние.

equitable /ˈekwɪtəb(ə)l/ *adj* справедли́вый. **equity** /ˈekwɪtɪ/ *n* справедли́вость; *pl* (*econ*) обыкнове́нные а́кции *f pl*.

equivalent /ɪˈkwɪvələnt/ *adj* эквивале́нтный; *n* эквивале́нт.

equivocal /ɪˈkwɪvək(ə)l/ *adj* двусмы́сленный.

era /ˈɪərə/ *n* э́ра.

eradicate /ɪˈrædɪˌkeɪt/ *vt* искореня́ть *impf*, искорени́ть *pf*.

erase /ɪˈreɪz/ *vt* стира́ть *impf*, стере́ть *pf*; (*from memory*) вычёркивать *impf*, вы́черкнуть *pf* (из па́мяти). **eraser** /-zə(r)/ *n* ла́стик.

erect /ɪˈrekt/ *adj* прямо́й; *vt* сооружа́ть *impf*, сооруди́ть *pf*. **erection** /ɪˈrekʃ(ə)n/ *n* сооруже́ние; (*biol*) эре́кция.

erode /ɪˈrəʊd/ *vt* разруша́ть *impf*, разру́шить *pf*. **erosion** /ɪˈrəʊʒ(ə)n/ *n* эро́зия; (*fig*) разруше́ние.

erotic /ɪˈrɒtɪk/ *adj* эроти́ческий.

err /ɜː(r)/ *vi* ошиба́ться *impf*, ошиби́ться *pf*; (*sin*) греши́ть *impf*, со~ *pf*.

errand /ˈerənd/ *n* поруче́ние; **run ~s** быть на посы́лках (**for** у+*gen*).

erratic /ɪˈrætɪk/ *adj* неро́вный.

erroneous /ɪˈrəʊnɪəs/ *adj* оши́бочный. **error** /ˈerə(r)/ *n* оши́бка.

erudite /ˈeruːˌdaɪt/ *adj* учёный. **erudition** /ˌeruːˈdɪʃ(ə)n/ *n* эруди́ция.

erupt /ɪˈrʌpt/ *vi* взрыва́ться *impf*, взорва́ться *pf*; (*volcano*) изверга́ться *impf*, изве́ргнуться *pf*. **eruption** /ɪˈrʌpʃ(ə)n/ *n* изверже́ние.

escalate /ˈeskəˌleɪt/ *vi* возраста́ть *impf*, возрасти́ *pf*; *vt* интенсифици́ровать *impf* & *pf*.

escalator /ˈeskəˌleɪtə(r)/ *n* эскала́тор.

escapade /ˈeskəˌpeɪd/ *n* вы́ходка. **escape** /ɪˈskeɪp/ *n* (*from prison*) побе́г; (*from danger*) спасе́ние; (*leak*) уте́чка; **have a narrow ~** едва́ спасти́сь; *vi* (*flee*) бежа́ть *impf* & *pf*; убега́ть *impf*, убежа́ть *pf*; (*save o.s.*) спаса́ться *impf*, спасти́сь *pf*; (*leak*) утека́ть *impf*, уте́чь *pf*; *vt* избега́ть *impf*, избежа́ть *pf* +*gen*; (*groan*) вырыва́ться *impf*, вы́рваться *pf* из, у, +*gen*.

escort *n* /ˈeskɔːt/ (*mil*) эско́рт; (*of lady*) кавале́р; *vt* /ɪˈskɔːt/ сопровожда́ть *impf*, сопроводи́ть *pf*; (*mil*) эскорти́ровать *impf* & *pf*.

Eskimo /ˈeskɪˌməʊ/ *n* эскимо́с, ~ка.

esoteric /ˌiːsəʊˈterɪk/ *adj* эзотери́ческий.

especially /ɪˈspeʃəlɪ/ *adv* осо́бенно.

espionage /ˈespɪəˌnɑːʒ/ *n* шпиона́ж.

espousal /ɪˈspaʊz(ə)l/ *n* подде́ржка. **espouse** /ɪˈspaʊz/ *vt* (*fig*) подде́рживать *impf*, поддержа́ть *pf*.

essay /'eseɪ/ *n* о́черк; (*in school*) сочине́ние.

essence /'es(ə)ns/ *n* (*philos*) су́щность; (*gist*) суть; (*extract*) эссе́нция. **essential** /ɪ'senʃ(ə)l/ *adj* (*fundamental*) суще́ственный; (*necessary*) необходи́мый; *n pl* (*necessities*) необходи́мое *sb*; (*crux*) суть; (*fundamentals*) осно́вы *f pl*. **essentially** /ɪ'senʃəlɪ/ *adv* по существу́.

establish /ɪ'stæblɪʃ/ *vt* (*set up*) учрежда́ть *impf*, учреди́ть *pf*; (*fact etc.*) устана́вливать *impf*, установи́ть *pf*. **establishment** /-mənt/ *n* (*action*) учрежде́ние, установле́ние; (*institution*) учрежде́ние.

estate /ɪ'steɪt/ *n* (*property*) име́ние; (*after death*) насле́дство; (*housing* ~) жило́й масси́в; ~ **agent** аге́нт по прода́же недви́жимости; ~ **car** автомоби́ль *m* с ку́зовом «универса́л».

esteem /ɪ'sti:m/ *n* уваже́ние; *vt* уважа́ть *impf*. **estimate** *n* /'estɪmət/ (*of quality*) оце́нка; (*of cost*) сме́та; *vt* /'estɪˌmeɪt/ оце́нивать *impf*, оцени́ть *pf*. **estimation** /ˌestɪ'meɪʃ(ə)n/ *n* оце́нка, мне́ние.

Estonia /ɪ'stəʊnɪə/ *n* Эсто́ния. **Estonian** /-nɪən/ *n* эсто́нец, -нка; *adj* эсто́нский.

estranged /ɪ'streɪndʒd/ *adj* отчуждённый.

estuary /'estjʊərɪ/ *n* у́стье.

etc. *abbr* и т.д. **etcetera** /et'setərə/ и так да́лее.

etch /etʃ/ *vt* трави́ть *impf*, вы́~ *pf*. **etching** /'etʃɪŋ/ *n* (*action*) травле́ние; (*object*) офо́рт.

eternal /ɪ'tɜ:n(ə)l/ *adj* ве́чный. **eternity** /-nɪtɪ/ *n* ве́чность.

ether /'i:θə(r)/ *n* эфи́р. **ethereal** /ɪ'θɪərɪəl/ *adj* эфи́рный.

ethical /'eθɪk(ə)l/ *adj* эти́ческий, эти́чный. **ethics** /'eθɪks/ *n* э́тика.

ethnic /'eθnɪk/ *adj* этни́ческий.

etiquette /'etɪˌket/ *n* этике́т.

etymology /ˌetɪ'mɒlədʒɪ/ *n* этимоло́гия.

EU *abbr* (*of* **European Union**) ЕС.

eucalyptus /ˌju:kə'lɪptəs/ *n* эвкали́пт.

Eucharist /'ju:kərɪst/ *n* прича́стие.

eulogy /'ju:lədʒɪ/ *n* похвала́.

euphemism /'ju:fɪˌmɪz(ə)m/ *n* эвфеми́зм. **euphemistic** /-'mɪstɪk/ *adj* эвфемисти́ческий.

euro /'jʊərəʊ/ *n* е́вро *neut indecl*.

Europe /'jʊərəp/ *n* Евро́па. **European** /-'pɪən/ *n* европе́ец; *adj* европе́йский; ~ **Community** Европе́йское соо́бщество; ~ **Union** Европе́йский сою́з.

evacuate /ɪ'vækjʊˌeɪt/ *vt* (*person, place*) эваку́ировать *impf* & *pf*. **evacuation** /-'eɪʃ(ə)n/ *n* эваку́ация.

evade /ɪ'veɪd/ *vt* уклоня́ться *impf*, уклони́ться *pf* от+*gen*.

evaluate /ɪ'væljʊˌeɪt/ *vt* оце́нивать *impf*, оцени́ть *pf*. **evaluation** /-'eɪʃ(ə)n/ *n* оце́нка.

evangelical /ˌi:væn'dʒelɪk(ə)l/ *adj* ева́нгельский. **evangelist** /ɪ'vændʒəlɪst/ *n* евангели́ст.

evaporate /ɪ'væpəˌreɪt/ *vt* & *i* испаря́ть(ся) *impf*, испари́ть(ся) *pf*. **evaporation** /-'reɪʃ(ə)n/ *n* испаре́ние.

evasion /ɪ'veɪʒ(ə)n/ *n* уклоне́ние (**of** от+*gen*). **evasive** /ɪ'veɪsɪv/ *adj* укло́нчивый.

eve /i:v/ *n* кану́н; **on the** ~ накану́не.

even /'i:v(ə)n/ *adj* ро́вный; (*number*) чётный; **get** ~ расквита́ться *pf* (**with** с+*instr*); *adv* да́же; (*just*) как раз; (*with comp*) ещё; ~ **if** да́же е́сли; ~ **though** хотя́; ~ **so** всё-таки; **not** ~ да́же не; *vt* выра́внивать *impf*, вы́ровнять *pf*.

evening /'i:vnɪŋ/ *n* ве́чер; *adj* вече́рний; ~ **class** вече́рние ку́рсы *m pl*.

evenly /'i:vənlɪ/ *adv* по́ровну, ро́вно. **evenness** /'i:vənnɪs/ *n* ро́вность.

event /ɪ'vent/ *n* собы́тие, происше́ствие; **in the** ~ **of** в слу́чае

+*gen*; **in any ~** во вся́ком слу́чае; **in the ~** в коне́чном счёте. **eventful** /ɪ'ventfʊl/ *adj* по́лный собы́тий. **eventual** /ɪ'ventjʊəl/ *adj* коне́чный. **eventuality** /ɪˌventjʊ'ælɪtɪ/ *n* возмо́жность. **eventually** /ɪ'ventjʊəlɪ/ *adv* в конце́ концо́в.

e **ever** /'evə(r)/ *adv* (*at any time*) когда́-либо, когда́-нибудь; (*always*) всегда́; (*emph*) же; **~ since** с тех пор (как); **~ so** о́чень; **for ~** навсегда́; **hardly ~** почти́ никогда́. **evergreen** *adj* вечнозелёный; *n* вечнозелёное расте́ние. **everlasting** /ˌevə'lɑːstɪŋ/ *adj* ве́чный. **evermore** *adv*: **for ~** навсегда́.

every /'evrɪ/ *adj* ка́ждый, вся́кий, все (*pl*); **~ now and then** вре́мя от вре́мени; **~ other** ка́ждый второ́й; **~ other day** че́рез день. **everybody, everyone** *pron* ка́ждый, все (*pl*). **everyday** *adj* (*daily*) ежедне́вный; (*commonplace*) повседне́вный. **everything** *pron* всё. **everywhere** *adv* всю́ду, везде́.

evict /ɪ'vɪkt/ *vt* выселя́ть *impf*, вы́селить *pf*. **eviction** /ɪ'vɪkʃ(ə)n/ *n* выселе́ние.

evidence /'evɪd(ə)ns/ *n* свиде́тельство, доказа́тельство; **give ~** свиде́тельствовать *impf* (о+*prep*; +*acc*; +что). **evident** /-d(ə)nt/ *adj* очеви́дный.

evil /'iːv(ə)l/ *n* зло; *adj* злой.

evoke /ɪ'vəʊk/ *vt* вызыва́ть *impf*, вы́звать *pf*.

evolution /ˌiːvə'luːʃ(ə)n/ *n* эволю́ция. **evolutionary** /-nərɪ/ *adj* эволюцио́нный. **evolve** /ɪ'vɒlv/ *vt* & *i* развива́ть(ся) *impf*, разви́ть(ся) *pf*.

ewe /juː/ *n* овца́.

ex- /eks/ *in comb* бы́вший.

exacerbate /ek'sæsəˌbeɪt/ *vt* обостря́ть *impf*, обостри́ть *pf*.

exact /ɪg'zækt/ *adj* то́чный; *vt* взы́скивать *impf*, взыска́ть *pf* (**from, of** с+*gen*). **exacting** /-'zæktɪŋ/ *adj* тре́бовательный. **exactitude,** **exactness** /-'zæktɪˌtjuːd, -'zæktnɪs/ *n* то́чность. **exactly** /-'zæktlɪ/ *adv* то́чно; (*just*) как раз; (*precisely*) и́менно.

exaggerate /ɪg'zædʒəˌreɪt/ *vt* преувели́чивать *impf*, преувели́чить *pf*. **exaggeration** /-'reɪʃ(ə)n/ *n* преувеличе́ние.

exalt /ɪg'zɔːlt/ *vt* возвыша́ть *impf*, возвы́сить *pf*; (*extol*) превозноси́ть *impf*, превознести́ *pf*.

examination /ɪgˌzæmɪ'neɪʃ(ə)n/ *n* (*inspection*) осмо́тр; (*exam*) экза́мен; (*law*) допро́с. **examine** /ɪg'zæmɪn/ *vt* (*inspect*) осма́тривать *impf*, осмотре́ть *pf*; (*test*) экзаменова́ть *impf*, про~ *pf*; (*law*) допра́шивать *impf*, допроси́ть *pf*. **examiner** /ɪg'zæmɪnə(r)/ *n* экзамена́тор.

example /ɪg'zɑːmp(ə)l/ *n* приме́р; **for ~** наприме́р.

exasperate /ɪg'zɑːspəˌreɪt/ *vt* раздража́ть *impf*, раздражи́ть *pf*. **exasperation** /-'reɪʃ(ə)n/ *n* раздраже́ние.

excavate /'ekskəˌveɪt/ *vt* раска́пывать *impf*, раскопа́ть *pf*. **excavations** /-'veɪʃ(ə)nz/ *n pl* раско́пки *f pl*. **excavator** /'ekskəˌveɪtə(r)/ *n* экскава́тор.

exceed /ɪk'siːd/ *vt* превыша́ть *impf*, превы́сить *pf*. **exceedingly** /-dɪŋlɪ/ *adv* чрезвыча́йно.

excel /ɪk'sel/ *vt* превосходи́ть *impf*, превзойти́ *pf*; *vi* отлича́ться *impf*, отличи́ться *pf* (**at, in** в+*prep*). **excellence** /'eksələns/ *n* превосхо́дство. **excellency** /'eksələnsɪ/ *n* превосходи́тельство. **excellent** /'eksələnt/ *adj* отли́чный.

except /ɪk'sept/ *vt* исключа́ть *impf*, исключи́ть *pf*; *prep* кро́ме+*gen*. **exception** /-'sepʃ(ə)n/ *n* исключе́ние; **take ~ to** возража́ть *impf*, возрази́ть *pf* про́тив+*gen*. **exceptional** /-'sepʃən(ə)l/ *adj* исключи́тельный.

excerpt /'eksɜːpt/ *n* отры́вок.

excess /ɪk'ses/ *n* избы́ток. **excessive** /-sɪv/ *adj* чрезме́рный.

exchange /ɪks'tʃeɪndʒ/ *n* обме́н (**of** +*instr*); (*of currency*) разме́н; (*building*) би́ржа; (*telephone*) центра́льная телефо́нная ста́нция; ~ **rate** курс; *vt* обме́нивать *impf*, обменя́ть *pf* (**for** на+*acc*); обме́ниваться *impf*, обменя́ться *pf* +*instr*.

excise[1] /'eksaɪz/ *n* (*duty*) акци́з(ный сбор).

excise[2] /ek'saɪz/ *vt* (*cut out*) выреза́ть *impf*, вы́резать *pf*.

excitable /ɪk'saɪtəb(ə)l/ *adj* возбуди́мый. **excite** /-'saɪt/ *vt* (*cause, arouse*) возбужда́ть *impf*, возбуди́ть *pf*; (*thrill, agitate*) волнова́ть *impf*, вз~ *pf*. **excitement** /-'saɪtmənt/ *n* возбужде́ние; волне́ние.

exclaim /ɪk'skleɪm/ *vi* восклица́ть *impf*, воскли́кнуть *pf*. **exclamation** /ˌekskləˈmeɪʃ(ə)n/ *n* восклица́ние; ~ **mark** восклица́тельный знак.

exclude /ɪk'sklu:d/ *vt* исключа́ть *impf*, исключи́ть *pf*. **exclusion** /-'sklu:ʒ(ə)n/ *n* исключе́ние. **exclusive** /-'sklu:sɪv/ *adj* исключи́тельный; (*high-class*) эксклюзи́вный.

excommunicate /ˌekskəˈmju:nɪˌkeɪt/ *vt* отлуча́ть *impf*, отлучи́ть *pf* (от це́ркви).

excrement /'ekskrɪmənt/ *n* экскреме́нты (-тов) *pl*.

excrete /ɪk'skri:t/ *vt* выделя́ть *impf*, вы́делить *pf*. **excretion** /-'skri:ʃ(ə)n/ *n* выделе́ние.

excruciating /ɪk'skru:ʃɪˌeɪtɪŋ/ *adj* мучи́тельный.

excursion /ɪk'skɜ:ʃ(ə)n/ *n* экску́рсия.

excusable /ɪk'skju:zəb(ə)l/ *adj* прости́тельный. **excuse** /-'skju:s/ *n* оправда́ние; (*pretext*) отгово́рка; /-'skju:z/ *vt* (*forgive*) извиня́ть *impf*, извини́ть *pf*; (*justify*) опра́вдывать *impf*, оправда́ть *pf*; (*release*) освобожда́ть *impf*, освободи́ть *pf* (**from** от+*gen*); ~ **me!** извини́те!; прости́те!

execute /'eksɪˌkju:t/ *vt* исполня́ть *impf*, испо́лнить *pf*; (*criminal*) казни́ть *impf* & *pf*. **execution** /-'kju:ʃ(ə)n/ *n* исполне́ние; казнь. **executioner** /-'kju:ʃənə(r)/ *n* пала́ч. **executive** /ɪg'zekjʊtɪv/ *n* исполни́тельный о́рган; (*person*) руководи́тель *m*; *adj* исполни́тельный.

exemplary /ɪg'zemplərɪ/ *adj* приме́рный. **exemplify** /-'zemplɪˌfaɪ/ *vt* (*illustrate by example*) приводи́ть *impf*, привести́ *pf* приме́р +*gen*; (*serve as example*) служи́ть *impf*, по~ *pf* приме́ром +*gen*.

exempt /ɪg'zempt/ *adj* освобождённый; *vt* освобожда́ть *impf*, освободи́ть *pf* (**from** от+*gen*). **exemption** /-'zempʃ(ə)n/ *n* освобожде́ние.

exercise /'eksəˌsaɪz/ *n* (*use*) примене́ние; (*physical* ~; *task*) упражне́ние; **take** ~ упражня́ться *impf*; ~ **book** тетра́дь; *vt* (*use*) применя́ть *impf*, примени́ть *pf*; (*dog*) прогу́ливать *impf*; (*train*) упражня́ть *impf*.

exert /ɪg'zɜ:t/ *vt* ока́зывать *impf*, оказа́ть *pf*; ~ **o.s.** стара́ться *impf*, по~ *pf*. **exertion** /-'zɜ:ʃ(ə)n/ *n* напряже́ние.

exhale /eks'heɪl/ *vt* выдыха́ть *impf*, вы́дохнуть *pf*.

exhaust /ɪg'zɔ:st/ *n* вы́хлоп; ~ **fumes** выхлопны́е га́зы *m pl*; ~ **pipe** выхлопна́я труба́; *vt* (*use up*) истоща́ть *impf*, истощи́ть *pf*; (*person*) изнуря́ть *impf*, изнури́ть *pf*; (*subject*) исче́рпывать *impf*, исче́рпать *pf*. **exhausted** /-stɪd/ *adj*: **be** ~ (*person*) быть измождённым. **exhausting** /-stɪŋ/ *adj* изнури́тельный. **exhaustion** /-stʃ(ə)n/ *n* изнуре́ние; (*depletion*) истоще́ние. **exhaustive** /-stɪv/ *adj* исче́рпывающий.

exhibit /ɪg'zɪbɪt/ *n* экспона́т; (*law*) веще́ственное доказа́тельство; *vt* (*manifest*) проявля́ть *impf*, прояви́ть *pf*; (*publicly*) выставля́ть *impf*, вы́ставить *pf*. **exhibition** /ˌeksɪ'bɪʃ(ə)n/ *n* вы́ставка.

exhibitor /ɪg'zɪbɪtə(r)/ *n* экспоне́нт.

exhilarated /ɪg'zɪlə,reɪtɪd/ *adj* в припо́днятом настрое́нии. **exhilarating** /-,reɪtɪŋ/ *adj* возбужда́ющий. **exhilaration** /-'reɪʃ(ə)n/ *n* возбужде́ние.

exhort /ɪg'zɔːt/ *vt* увещева́ть *impf.* **exhortation** /,egzɔː'teɪʃ(ə)n/ *n* увещева́ние.

exhume /eks'hjuːm/ *vt* выка́пывать *impf*, вы́копать *pf.*

exile /'eksaɪl/ *n* изгна́ние; (*person*) изгна́нник; *vt* изгоня́ть *impf*, изгна́ть *pf.*

exist /ɪg'zɪst/ *vi* существова́ть *impf.* **existence** /-st(ən)s/ *n* существова́ние. **existing** /-stɪŋ/ *adj* существу́ющий.

exit /'eksɪt/ *n* вы́ход; (*for vehicles*) вы́езд; (*theat*) ухо́д (со сце́ны); **~ visa** выездна́я ви́за; *vi* уходи́ть *impf*, уйти́ *pf.*

exonerate /ɪg'zɒnə,reɪt/ *vt* опра́вдывать *impf*, оправда́ть *pf.*

exorbitant /ɪg'zɔːbɪt(ə)nt/ *adj* непоме́рный.

exorcize /'eksɔː,saɪz/ *vt* (*spirits*) изгоня́ть *impf*, изгна́ть *pf.*

exotic /ɪg'zɒtɪk/ *adj* экзоти́ческий.

expand /ɪk'spænd/ *vt & i* расширя́ть(ся) *impf*, расши́рить(ся) *pf*; **~ on** распространя́ться *impf*, распространи́ться *pf* о+*prep.* **expanse** /-'spæns/ *n* простра́нство. **expansion** /-'spænʃ(ə)n/ *n* расшире́ние. **expansive** /-'spænsɪv/ *adj* экспанси́вный.

expatriate /eks'pætrɪət/ *n* экспатриа́нт, **~**ка.

expect /ɪk'spekt/ *vt* (*await*) ожида́ть *impf* +*gen*; ждать *impf* +*gen*, что; (*suppose*) полага́ть *impf*; (*require*) тре́бовать *impf* +*gen*, что́бы. **expectant** /-t(ə)nt/ *adj* выжида́тельный; **~ mother** бере́менная же́нщина. **expectation** /,ekspek'teɪʃ(ə)n/ *n* ожида́ние.

expediency /ɪk'spiːdɪənsɪ/ *n* целесообра́зность. **expedient** /-ənt/ *n* приём; *adj* целесообра́зный. **expedite** /'ekspɪ,daɪt/ *vt* ускоря́ть *impf*, уско́рить *pf.* **expedition** /,ekspɪ'dɪʃ(ə)n/ *n* экспеди́ция. **expeditionary** /,ekspɪ'dɪʃənərɪ/ *adj* экспедицио́нный.

expel /ɪk'spel/ *vt* (*drive out*) выгоня́ть *impf*, вы́гнать *pf*; (*from school etc.*) исключа́ть *impf*, исключи́ть *pf*; (*from country etc.*) изгоня́ть *impf*, изгна́ть *pf.*

expend /ɪk'spend/ *vt* тра́тить *impf*, ис**~**, по**~** *pf.* **expendable** /-'spendəb(ə)l/ *adj* необяза́тельный. **expenditure** /-'spendɪtʃə(r)/ *n* расхо́д. **expense** /-'spens/ *n* расхо́д; *pl* расхо́ды *m pl*, **at the ~ of** за счёт+*gen*; (*fig*) цено́ю+*gen.* **expensive** /-'spensɪv/ *adj* дорого́й.

experience /ɪk'spɪərɪəns/ *n* о́пыт; (*incident*) пережива́ние; *vt* испы́тывать *impf*, испыта́ть *pf*; (*undergo*) пережива́ть *impf*, пережи́ть *pf.* **experienced** /-ənst/ *adj* о́пытный.

experiment /ɪk'sperɪmənt/ *n* экспериме́нт; *vi* эксперименти́ровать *impf* (**on, with** над, с+*instr*). **experimental** /-'ment(ə)l/ эксперимента́льный.

expert /'ekspɜːt/ *n* экспе́рт; *adj* о́пытный. **expertise** /-'tiːz/ *n* специа́льные зна́ния *neut pl.*

expire /ɪk'spaɪə(r)/ *vi* (*period*) истека́ть *impf*, исте́чь *pf.* **expiry** /-rɪ/ *n* истече́ние.

explain /ɪk'spleɪn/ *vt* объясня́ть *impf*, объясни́ть *pf.* **explanation** /,eksplə'neɪʃ(ə)n/ *n* объясне́ние. **explanatory** /ɪk'splænətərɪ/ *adj* объясни́тельный.

expletive /ɪk'spliːtɪv/ *n* (*oath*) бра́нное сло́во.

explicit /ɪk'splɪsɪt/ *adj* я́вный; (*of person*) прямо́й.

explode /ɪk'spləʊd/ *vt & i* взрыва́ть(ся) *impf*, взорва́ть(ся) *pf*; *vt* (*discredit*) опроверга́ть *impf*, опрове́ргнуть *pf*; *vi* (*with anger etc.*) разража́ться *impf*, разрази́ться *pf.*

exploit *n* /'eksplɔɪt/ по́двиг; *vt*

/ɪk'splɔɪt/ эксплуати́ровать *impf*; (*use to advantage*) испо́льзовать *impf* & *pf*. **exploitation** /ˌeksplɔɪ'teɪʃ(ə)n/ *n* эксплуата́ция. **exploiter** /ɪk'splɔɪtə(r)/ *n* эксплуата́тор.

exploration /ˌeksplə'reɪʃ(ə)n/ *n* иссле́дование. **exploratory** /ɪk'splɒrətərɪ/ *adj* иссле́довательский. **explore** /ɪk'splɔː(r)/ *vt* иссле́довать *impf* & *pf*. **explorer** /ɪk'splɔːrə(r)/ *n* иссле́дователь *m*.

explosion /ɪk'spləʊʒ(ə)n/ *n* взрыв. **explosive** /-'spləʊsɪv/ *n* взры́вчатое вещество́; *adj* взры́вчатый; (*fig*) взрывно́й.

exponent /ɪk'spəʊnənt/ *n* (*interpreter*) истолкова́тель *m*; (*advocate*) сторо́нник.

export *n* /'ekspɔːt/ вы́воз, э́кспорт; *vt* /ek'spɔːt/ вывози́ть *impf*, вы́везти *pf*; экспорти́ровать *impf* & *pf*. **exporter** /ek'spɔːtə(r)/ *n* экспортёр.

expose /ɪk'spəʊz/ *vt* (*bare*) раскрыва́ть *impf*, раскры́ть *pf*; (*subject*) подверга́ть *impf*, подве́ргнуть *pf* (**to** +*dat*); (*discredit*) разоблача́ть *impf*, разоблачи́ть *pf*; (*phot*) экспони́ровать *impf* & *pf*.

exposition /ˌekspə'zɪʃ(ə)n/ *n* изложе́ние.

exposure /ɪk'spəʊʒə(r)/ *n* подверга́ние (**to** +*dat*); (*phot*) вы́держка; (*unmasking*) разоблаче́ние; (*med*) хо́лод.

expound /ɪk'spaʊnd/ *vt* излага́ть *impf*, изложи́ть *pf*.

express /ɪk'spres/ *n* (*train*) экспре́сс; *adj* (*clear*) то́чный; (*purpose*) специа́льный; (*urgent*) сро́чный; *vt* выража́ть *impf*, вы́разить *pf*. **expression** /-'spreʃ(ə)n/ *n* выраже́ние; (*expressiveness*) вырази́тельность. **expressive** /-'spresɪv/ *adj* вырази́тельный. **expressly** /-'spreslɪ/ *adv* (*clearly*) я́сно; (*specifically*) специа́льно.

expropriate /eks'prəʊprɪˌeɪt/ *vt* экспроприи́ровать *impf* & *pf*. **expropriation** /-'eɪʃ(ə)n/ *n* экспроприа́ция.

expulsion /ɪk'spʌlʃ(ə)n/ *n* (*from school etc.*) исключе́ние; (*from country etc.*) изгна́ние.

exquisite /'ekskwɪzɪt/ *adj* утончённый.

extant /ek'stænt/ *adj* сохрани́вшийся.

extempore /ɪk'stempərɪ/ *adv* экспро́мптом. **extemporize** /-'stempəˌraɪz/ *vt* & *i* импровизи́ровать *impf*, сымпровизи́ровать *pf*.

extend /ɪk'stend/ *vt* (*stretch out*) протя́гивать *impf*, протяну́ть *pf*; (*enlarge*) расширя́ть *impf*, расши́рить *pf*; (*prolong*) продлева́ть *impf*, продли́ть *pf*; *vi* простира́ться *impf*, простере́ться *pf*. **extension** /-'stenʃ(ə)n/ *n* (*enlarging*) расшире́ние; (*time*) продле́ние; (*to house*) пристро́йка; (*tel*) доба́вочный. **extensive** /-'stensɪv/ *adj* обши́рный. **extent** /-'stent/ *n* (*degree*) сте́пень.

extenuating /ɪk'stenjʊˌeɪtɪŋ/ *adj*: ~ **circumstances** смягча́ющие вину́ обстоя́тельства *neut pl.*

exterior /ɪk'stɪərɪə(r)/ *n* вне́шность; *adj* вне́шний.

exterminate /ɪk'stɜːmɪˌneɪt/ *vt* истребля́ть *impf*, истреби́ть *pf*. **extermination** /-'neɪʃ(ə)n/ *n* истребле́ние.

external /ɪk'stɜːn(ə)l/ *adj* вне́шний.

extinct /ɪk'stɪŋkt/ *adj* (*volcano*) поту́хший; (*species*) вы́мерший; **become** ~ вымира́ть *impf*, вы́мереть *pf*. **extinction** /-'stɪŋkʃ(ə)n/ *n* вымира́ние.

extinguish /ɪk'stɪŋgwɪʃ/ *vt* гаси́ть *impf*, по~ *pf*. **extinguisher** /-'stɪŋgwɪʃə(r)/ *n* огнетуши́тель *m*.

extol /ɪk'stəʊl/ *vt* превозноси́ть *impf*, превознести́ *pf*.

extort /ɪk'stɔːt/ *vt* вымога́ть *impf* (**from** у+*gen*). **extortion** /-'stɔːʃ(ə)n/ *n* вымога́тельство. **extortionate** /-'stɔːʃənət/ *adj* вымога́тельский.

e

extra /'ekstrə/ *n* (*theat*) статист, ~ка; (*payment*) приплата; *adj* дополнительный; (*special*) особый; *adv* особенно.
extract *n* /'ekstrækt/ экстракт; (*from book etc.*) выдержка; *vt* /ɪk'strækt/ извлекать *impf*, извлечь *pf*. **extraction** /ɪk'strækʃ(ə)n/ *n* извлечение; (*origin*) происхождение. **extradite** /'ekstrə,daɪt/ *vt* выдавать *impf*, выдать *pf*. **extradition** /-'dɪʃ(ə)n/ *n* выдача.
extramarital /,ekstrə'mærɪt(ə)l/ *adj* внебрачный.
extraneous /ɪk'streɪnɪəs/ *adj* посторонний.
extraordinary /ɪk'strɔːdɪnərɪ/ *adj* чрезвычайный.
extrapolate /ɪk'stræpə,leɪt/ *vt & i* экстраполировать *impf & pf*.
extravagance /ɪk'strævəgəns/ *n* расточительность. **extravagant** /-gənt/ *adj* расточительный; (*fantastic*) сумасбродный.
extreme /ɪk'striːm/ *n* крайность; *adj* крайний. **extremity** /-'stremɪtɪ/ *n* (*end*) край; (*adversity*) крайность; *pl* (*hands & feet*) конечности *f pl*.
extricate /'ekstrɪ,keɪt/ *vt* выпутывать *impf*, выпутать *pf*.
exuberance /ɪg'zjuːbərəns/ *n* жизнерадостность. **exuberant** /-rənt/ *adj* жизнерадостный.
exude /ɪg'zjuːd/ *vt & i* выделять(ся) *impf*, выделить(ся) *pf*; (*fig*) излучать(ся) *impf*, излучить(ся) *pf*.
exult /ɪg'zʌlt/ *vi* ликовать *impf*. **exultant** /-tənt/ *adj* ликующий. **exultation** /ɪg,zʌl'teɪʃ(ə)n/ *n* ликование.
eye /aɪ/ *n* глаз; (*needle etc.*) ушко; *vt* разглядывать *impf*, разглядеть *pf*. **eyeball** *n* глазное яблоко. **eyebrow** *n* бровь. **eyelash** *n* ресница. **eyelid** *n* веко. **eyeshadow** *n* тени *f pl* для век. **eyesight** *n* зрение. **eyewitness** *n* очевидец.

F

fable /'feɪb(ə)l/ *n* басня.
fabric /'fæbrɪk/ *n* (*structure*) структура; (*cloth*) ткань. **fabricate** /-,keɪt/ *vt* (*invent*) выдумывать *impf*, выдумать *pf*. **fabrication** /-'keɪʃ(ə)n/ *n* выдумка.
fabulous /'fæbjʊləs/ *adj* сказочный.
façade /fə'sɑːd/ *n* фасад.
face /feɪs/ *n* лицо; (*expression*) выражение; (*grimace*) гримаса; (*side*) сторона; (*surface*) поверхность; (*clock etc.*) циферблат; **make ~s** корчить *impf* рожи; **~ down** лицом вниз; **~ to ~** лицом к лицу; **in the ~ of** перед лицом+*gen*, вопреки+*dat*; **on the ~ of it** на первый взгляд; *vt* (*be turned towards*) быть обращённым к+*dat*; (*of person*) стоять *impf* лицом к+*dat*; (*meet firmly*) смотреть *impf* в лицо+*dat*; (*cover*) облицовывать *impf*, облицевать *pf*; **I can't ~ it** я даже думать об этом не могу. **faceless** /'feɪʃlɪs/ *adj* безличный.
facet /'fæsɪt/ *n* грань; (*fig*) аспект.
facetious /fə'siːʃəs/ *adj* шутливый.
facial /'feɪʃ(ə)l/ *adj* лицевой.
facile /'fæsaɪl/ *adj* поверхностный. **facilitate** /fə'sɪlɪ,teɪt/ *vt* облегчать *impf*, облегчить *pf*. **facility** /fə'sɪlɪtɪ/ *n* (*ease*) лёгкость; (*ability*) способность; *pl* (*conveniences*) удобства *neut pl*, (*opportunities*) возможности *f pl*.
facing /'feɪsɪŋ/ *n* облицовка; (*of garment*) отделка.
facsimile /fæk'sɪmɪlɪ/ *n* факсимиле *neut indecl*.
fact /fækt/ *n* факт; **the ~ is that** … дело в том, что…; **as a matter of ~** собственно говоря; **in ~** на самом деле.
faction /'fækʃ(ə)n/ *n* фракция.
factor /'fæktə(r)/ *n* фактор.
factory /'fæktərɪ/ *n* фабрика, завод.

factual /ˈfæktjʊəl/ *adj* факти́ческий.
faculty /ˈfækəltɪ/ *n* спосо́бность; (*univ*) факульте́т.
fade /feɪd/ *vi* (*wither*) вя́нуть *impf*, за~ *pf*; (*colour*) выцвета́ть *impf*, вы́цвести *pf*; (*sound*) замира́ть *impf*, замере́ть *pf*.
faeces /ˈfiːsiːz/ *n pl* кал.
fag /fæg/ *n* (*cigarette*) сигаре́тка.
fail /feɪl/ *n*: **without ~** обяза́тельно; *vi* (*weaken*) слабе́ть *impf*; (*break down*) отка́зывать *impf*, отказа́ть *pf*; (*not succeed*) терпе́ть *impf*, по~ *pf* неуда́чу; не удава́ться *impf*, уда́ться *pf impers* +*dat*; *vt* & *i* (*exam*) прова́ливать(ся) *impf*, провали́ть(ся) *pf*.; *vt* (*disappoint*) подводи́ть *impf*, подвести́ *pf*. **failing** /ˈfeɪlɪŋ/ *n* недоста́ток; *prep* за неиме́нием +*gen*. **failure** /ˈfeɪljə(r)/ *n* неуда́ча; (*person*) неуда́чник, -ица.
faint /feɪnt/ *n* о́бморок; *adj* (*weak*) сла́бый; (*pale*) бле́дный; **I feel ~** мне ду́рно; **~-hearted** малоду́шный; *vi* па́дать *impf*, упа́сть *pf* в о́бморок.
fair[1] /feə(r)/ *n* я́рмарка.
fair[2] /feə(r)/ *adj* (*hair, skin*) све́тлый; (*weather*) я́сный; (*just*) справедли́вый; (*average*) сно́сный; **a ~ amount** дово́льно мно́го +*gen*. **fairly** /ˈfeəlɪ/ *adv* дово́льно.
fairy /ˈfeərɪ/ *n* фе́я; **~-tale** ска́зка.
faith /feɪθ/ *n* ве́ра; (*trust*) дове́рие. **faithful** /ˈfeɪθfʊl/ *adj* ве́рный; **yours ~ly** с уваже́нием.
fake /feɪk/ *n* подде́лка; *vt* подде́лывать *impf*, подде́лать *pf*.
falcon /ˈfɔːlkən/ *n* со́кол.
fall /fɔːl/ *n* паде́ние; *vi* па́дать *impf*, упа́сть *pf*; **~ apart** распада́ться *impf*, распа́сться *pf*; **~ asleep** засыпа́ть *impf*, засну́ть *pf*; **~ back on** прибега́ть *impf*, прибе́гнуть *pf* к+*dat*; **~ down** па́дать *impf*, упа́сть *pf*; **~ in** ру́хнуть *pf*; **~ in love with** влюбля́ться *impf*, влюби́ться *pf* в+*acc*; **~ off** отпада́ть *impf*, отпа́сть *pf*; **~ out** выпа́дать *impf*, вы́пасть *pf*; (*quarrel*) поссо́риться *pf*; **~ over** опроки́дываться *impf*, опроки́нуться *pf*; **~ through** прова́ливаться *impf*, провали́ться *pf*; **~-out** радиоакти́вные оса́дки (-ков) *pl*.
fallacy /ˈfæləsɪ/ *n* оши́бка.
fallible /ˈfælɪb(ə)l/ *adj* подве́рженный оши́бкам.
fallow /ˈfæləʊ/ *n*: **lie ~** лежа́ть *impf* под па́ром.
false /fɒls/ *adj* ло́жный; (*teeth*) иску́сственный; **~ start** неве́рный старт. **falsehood** /ˈfɒlshʊd/ *n* ложь. **falsification** /ˌfɒlsɪfɪˈkeɪʃ(ə)n/ *n* фальсифика́ция. **falsify** /ˈfɒlsɪˌfaɪ/ *vt* фальсифици́ровать *impf* & *pf*. **falsity** /ˈfɒlsɪtɪ/ *n* ло́жность.
falter /ˈfɒltə(r)/ *vi* спотыка́ться *impf*, споткну́ться *pf*; (*stammer*) запина́ться *impf*, запну́ться *pf*.
fame /feɪm/ *n* сла́ва.
familiar /fəˈmɪlɪə(r)/ *adj* (*well known*) знако́мый; (*usual*) обы́чный; (*informal*) фамилья́рный. **familiarity** /fəˌmɪlɪˈærɪtɪ/ *n* знако́мство; фамилья́рность. **familiarize** /fəˈmɪlɪəˌraɪz/ *vt* ознакомля́ть *impf*, ознако́мить *pf* (**with** с+*instr*).
family /ˈfæmɪlɪ/ *n* семья́; *attrib* семе́йный; **~ tree** родосло́вная *sb*.
famine /ˈfæmɪn/ *n* го́лод. **famished** /ˈfæmɪʃd/ *adj*: **be ~** голода́ть *impf*.
famous /ˈfeɪməs/ *adj* знамени́тый.
fan[1] /fæn/ *n* ве́ер; (*ventilator*) вентиля́тор; **~-belt** реме́нь *m* вентиля́тора; *vt* обма́хивать *impf*, обмахну́ть *pf*; (*flame*) раздува́ть *impf*, разду́ть *pf*.
fan[2] /fæn/ *n* покло́нник, -ица; (*sport*) боле́льщик. **fanatic** /fəˈnætɪk/ *n* фана́тик. **fanatical** /fəˈnætɪkəl/ *adj* фанати́ческий.
fanciful /ˈfænsɪfʊl/ *adj* причу́дливый. **fancy** /ˈfænsɪ/ *n* фанта́зия; (*whim*) причу́да; **take a ~ to** увлека́ться *impf*, увле́чься *pf* +*instr*; *adj* витиева́тый; *vt* (*imagine*)

f

представля́ть *impf*, предста́вить *pf* себе́; (*suppose*) полага́ть *impf*; (*like*) нра́виться *impf*, по~ *pf impers+dat*; ~ **dress** маскара́дный костю́м; ~**-dress** костюмированный.

fanfare /'fænfeə(r)/ *n* фанфа́ра.

fang /fæŋ/ *n* клык; (*serpent's*) ядови́тый зуб.

fantasize /'fæntə,saɪz/ *vi* фантази́ровать *impf*. **fantastic** /fæn'tæstɪk/ *adj* фантасти́ческий. **fantasy** /'fæntəsɪ/ *n* фанта́зия.

far /fɑː(r)/ *adj* да́льний; **Russia is ~ away** Росси́я о́чень далеко́; *adv* далёко́; (*fig*) намно́го; **as ~ as** (*prep*) до+*gen*; (*conj*) поско́льку; **by ~** намно́го; **(in) so ~ as** поско́льку; **so ~** до сих пор; **~-fetched** притя́нутый за́ волосы; **~-reaching** далеко́ иду́щий; **~-sighted** дальнови́дный.

farce /fɑːs/ *n* фарс. **farcical** /'fɑːsɪk(ə)l/ *adj* смехотво́рный.

fare /feə(r)/ *n* (*price*) проездна́я пла́та; (*food*) пи́ща; *vi* пожива́ть *impf*. **farewell** /feə'wel/ *int* проща́й(те)!; *n* проща́ние; *attrib* проща́льный; **bid ~** проща́ться *impf*, прости́ться *pf* (**to** с+*instr*).

farm /fɑːm/ *n* фе́рма. **farmer** /'fɑːmə(r)/ *n* фе́рмер; **~ s' market**; ры́нок сельскохозя́йственной проду́кции. **farming** /'fɑːmɪŋ/ *n* се́льское хозя́йство.

fart /fɑːt/ *n* (*vulg*) пу́кание; *vi* пу́кать *impf*, пу́кнуть *pf*.

farther /'fɑːðə(r)/ *see* **further. farthest** /'fɑːðɪst/ *see* **furthest.**

fascinate /'fæsɪ,neɪt/ *vt* очаро́вывать *impf*, очарова́ть *pf*. **fascinating** /-,neɪtɪŋ/ *adj* очарова́тельный. **fascination** /-'neɪʃ(ə)n/ *n* очарова́ние.

Fascism /'fæʃɪz(ə)m/ *n* фаши́зм. **Fascist** /-ʃɪst/ *n* фаши́ст, ~ка; *adj* фаши́стский.

fashion /'fæʃ(ə)n/ *n* мо́да; (*manner*) мане́ра; **after a ~** не́которым о́бразом; *vt* придава́ть *impf*, прида́ть *pf* фо́рму +*dat*.

fashionable /'fæʃnəb(ə)l/ *adj* мо́дный.

fast[1] /fɑːst/ *n* пост; *vi* пости́ться *impf*.

fast[2] /fɑːst/ *adj* (*rapid*) ско́рый, бы́стрый; (*colour*) сто́йкий; (*shut*) пло́тно закры́тый; **be ~** (*timepiece*) спеши́ть *impf*.

fasten /'fɑːs(ə)n/ *vt* (*attach*) прикрепля́ть *impf*, прикрепи́ть *pf* (**to** к+*dat*); (*tie*) привя́зывать *impf*, привяза́ть *pf* (**to** к+*dat*); (*garment*) застёгивать *impf*, застегну́ть *pf*. **fastener, fastening** /'fɑːs(ə)nə(r), 'fɑːsnɪŋ/ *n* запо́р, задви́жка; (*on garment*) застёжка.

fastidious /fæ'stɪdɪəs/ *adj* брезгли́вый.

fat /fæt/ *n* жир; *adj* (*greasy*) жи́рный; (*plump*) то́лстый; **get ~** толсте́ть *impf*, по~ *pf*.

fatal /'feɪt(ə)l/ *adj* роково́й; (*deadly*) смерте́льный. **fatalism** /'feɪtə,lɪzəm/ *n* фатали́зм. **fatality** /fə'tælətɪ/ *n* (*death*) смерте́льный слу́чай. **fate** /feɪt/ *n* судьба́. **fateful** /'feɪtfʊl/ *adj* роково́й.

father /'fɑːðə(r)/ *n* оте́ц; **~-in-law** (*husband's* ~) свёкор; (*wife's* ~) тесть *m*. **fatherhood** *n* отцо́вство. **fatherland** *n* оте́чество. **fatherly** /'fɑːðəlɪ/ *adj* оте́ческий.

fathom /'fæð(ə)m/ *n* морска́я са́жень; *vt* (*fig*) понима́ть *impf*, поня́ть *pf*.

fatigue /fə'tiːg/ *n* утомле́ние; *vt* утомля́ть *impf*, утоми́ть *pf*.

fatten /'fæt(ə)n/ *vt* отка́рмливать *impf*, откорми́ть *pf*; *vi* толсте́ть *impf*, по~ *pf*. **fatty** /'fætɪ/ *adj* жи́рный.

fatuous /'fætjʊəs/ *adj* глу́пый.

fault /fɒlt/ *n* недоста́ток; (*blame*) вина́; (*geol*) сброс. **faultless** /-lɪs/ *adj* безупре́чный. **faulty** /-tɪ/ *adj* дефе́ктный.

fauna /'fɔːnə/ *n* фа́уна.

favour /'feɪvə(r)/ *n* (*kind act*) любе́зность; (*goodwill*) благоскло́нность; **in (s.o.'s) ~** в по́льзу +*gen*; **be in ~ of** быть за+*acc*; *vt* (*support*) благоприя́тствовать *impf* +*dat*; (*treat with partiality*) оказывать *impf*, оказа́ть *pf* предпочте́ние +*dat*. **favourable** /-rəb(ə)l/ *adj* (*propitious*) благоприя́тный; (*approving*) благоскло́нный. **favourite** /-rɪt/ *n* люби́мец, -мица; (*also sport*) фавори́т, ~ка; *adj* люби́мый.

fawn[1] /fɔːn/ *n* оленёнок; *adj* желтова́то-кори́чневый.

fawn[2] /fɔːn/ *vi* подли́зываться *impf*, подлиза́ться *pf* (**on** к+*dat*).

fax /fæks/ *n* факс; *vt* посыла́ть *impf*, посла́ть *pf* по фа́ксу.

fear /fɪə(r)/ *n* страх, боя́знь, опасе́ние; *vt* & *i* боя́ться *impf* +*gen*; опаса́ться *impf* +*gen*. **fearful** /-fʊl/ *adj* (*terrible*) стра́шный; (*timid*) пугли́вый. **fearless** /-lɪs/ *adj* бесстра́шный. **fearsome** /-səm/ *adj* гро́зный.

feasibility /ˌfiːzɪˈbɪlɪtɪ/ *n* осуществи́мость. **feasible** /ˈfiːzɪb(ə)l/ *adj* осуществи́мый.

feast /fiːst/ *n* (*meal*) пир; (*festival*) пра́здник; *vi* пирова́ть *impf*.

feat /fiːt/ *n* по́двиг.

feather /ˈfeðə(r)/ *n* перо́.

feature /ˈfiːtʃə(r)/ *n* черта́; (*newspaper*) (темати́ческая) статья́; ~ **film** худо́жественный фильм; *vt* помеща́ть *impf*, помести́ть *pf* на ви́дном ме́сте; (*in film*) пока́зывать *impf*, показа́ть *pf*; *vi* игра́ть *impf* сыгра́ть *pf* роль.

February /ˈfebrʊərɪ/ *n* февра́ль *m*; *adj* февра́льский.

feckless /ˈfeklɪs/ *adj* безала́берный.

federal /ˈfedər(ə)l/ *adj* федера́льный. **federation** /-ˈreɪʃ(ə)n/ *n* федера́ция.

fee /fiː/ *n* гонора́р; (*entrance* ~ *etc.*) взнос; *pl* (*regular payment, school, etc.*) пла́та.

feeble /ˈfiːb(ə)l/ *adj* сла́бый.

feed /fiːd/ *n* корм; *vt* корми́ть *impf*, на~, по~ *pf*; *vi* корми́ться *impf*, по~ *pf*; ~ **up** отка́рмливать *impf*, откорми́ть *pf*; **I am fed up with** мне надое́л (-а, -о; -и) +*nom*. **feedback** *n* обра́тная связь.

feel /fiːl/ *vt* чу́вствовать *impf*, по~ *pf*; (*think*) счита́ть *impf*, счесть *pf*; *vi* (~ *bad etc.*) чу́вствовать *impf*, по~ *pf* себя́ +*adv*, +*instr*; ~ **like** хоте́ться *impf impers*+*dat*. **feeling** /-lɪŋ/ *n* (*sense*) ощуще́ние; (*emotion*) чу́вство; (*impression*) впечатле́ние; (*mood*) настрое́ние.

feign /feɪn/ *vt* притворя́ться *impf*, притвори́ться *pf* +*instr*. **feigned** /feɪnd/ *adj* притво́рный.

feline /ˈfiːlaɪn/ *adj* коша́чий.

fell /fel/ *vt* (*tree*) сруба́ть *impf*, сруби́ть *pf*; (*person*) сбива́ть *impf*, сбить *pf* с ног.

fellow /ˈfeləʊ/ *n* па́рень *m*; (*of society etc.*) член; ~ **countryman** сооте́чественник. **fellowship** /-ʃɪp/ *n* това́рищество.

felt /felt/ *n* фетр; *adj* фе́тровый; ~**-tip pen** флома́стер.

female /ˈfiːmeɪl/ *n* (*animal*) са́мка; (*person*) же́нщина; *adj* же́нский. **feminine** /ˈfemɪnɪn/ *adj* же́нский, же́нственный; (*gram*) же́нского ро́да. **femininity** /-ˈnɪnɪtɪ/ *n* же́нственность. **feminism** /ˈfemɪˌnɪz(ə)m/ *n* femини́зм. **feminist** /-nɪst/ *n* фемини́ст, ~ка; *adj* фемини́стский.

fence /fens/ *n* забо́р; *vt*: ~ **in** огора́живать *impf*, огороди́ть *pf*; ~ **off** отгора́живать *impf*, отгороди́ть *pf*; *vi* (*sport*) фехтова́ть *impf*. **fencer** /-sə(r)/ *n* фехтова́льщик, -ица. **fencing** /-sɪŋ/ *n* (*enclosure*) забо́р; (*sport*) фехтова́ние.

fend /fend/ *vt*: ~ **off** отража́ть *impf*, отрази́ть *pf*; *vi*: ~ **for o.s.** забо́титься *impf*, по~ *pf* о себе́. **fender** /-də(r)/ *n* решётка.

fennel /ˈfen(ə)l/ *n* фе́нхель *m*.

ferment *n* /ˈfɜːment/ броже́ние; *vi* /fəˈment/ броди́ть *impf*; *vt* ква́сить *impf*, за~ *pf*; (*excite*) возбужда́ть *impf*, возбуди́ть *pf*. **fermentation** /ˌfɜːmenˈteɪʃ(ə)n/ *n* брожéние; (*excitement*) возбуждéние.

fern /fɜ:n/ *n* пáпоротник.

ferocious /fəˈrəʊʃəs/ *adj* свирéпый. **ferocity** /-ˈrɒsɪtɪ/ *n* свирéпость.

ferret /ˈferɪt/ *n* хорёк; *vt*: **~ out** (*search out*) разню́хивать *impf*, разню́хать *pf*; *vi*: **~ about** (*rummage*) ры́ться *impf*.

f

ferry /ˈferɪ/ *n* парóм; *vt* перевози́ть *impf*, перевезти́ *pf*.

fertile /ˈfɜ:taɪl/ *adj* плодорóдный. **fertility** /fəˈtɪlɪtɪ/ *n* плодорóдие. **fertilize** /ˈfɜ:tɪˌlaɪz/ *vt* (*soil*) удобря́ть *impf*, удóбрить *pf*; (*egg*) оплодотворя́ть *impf*, оплодотвори́ть *pf*. **fertilizer** /ˈfɜ:tɪˌlaɪzə(r)/ *n* удобрéние.

fervent /ˈfɜ:v(ə)nt/ *adj* горя́чий. **fervour** /-və(r)/ *n* жар.

fester /ˈfestə(r)/ *vi* гнои́ться *impf*.

festival /ˈfestɪv(ə)l/ *n* прáздник, (*music etc.*) фестивáль *m*. **festive** /ˈfestɪv/ *adj* прáздничный. **festivities** /fesˈtɪvɪtɪz/ *n pl* торжествá *neut pl*.

festoon /feˈstu:n/ *vt* украшáть *impf*, укрáсить *pf*.

fetch /fetʃ/ *vt* (*carrying*) приноси́ть *impf*, принести́ *pf*; (*leading*) приводи́ть *impf*, привести́ *pf*; (*go and come back with*) (*on foot*) идти́ *impf*, по~ *pf* за +*instr*; (*by vehicle*) заезжáть *impf*, заéхать *pf* за+*instr*; (*price*) выручáть *impf*, вы́ручить *pf*. **fetching** /ˈfetʃɪŋ/ *adj* привлекáтельный.

fetid /ˈfetɪd/ *adj* зловóнный.

fetish /ˈfetɪʃ/ *n* фети́ш.

fetter /ˈfetə(r)/ *vt* скóвывать *impf*, сковáть *pf*; *n*: *pl* кандалы́ (-лóв) *pl*; (*fig*) окóвы (-в) *pl*.

fettle /ˈfet(ə)l/ *n* состоя́ние.

feud /fju:d/ *n* крóвная месть.

feudal /ˈfju:d(ə)l/ *adj* феодáльный. **feudalism** /-dəˌlɪz(ə)m/ *n* феодали́зм.

fever /ˈfi:və(r)/ *n* лихорáдка. **feverish** /-rɪʃ/ *adj* лихорáдочный.

few /fju:/ *adj* & *pron* немнóгие *pl*; мáло+*gen*; **a ~** нéсколько +*gen*; **quite a ~** немáло +*gen*.

fiancé /fɪˈɒnseɪ/ *n* жени́х. **fiancée** /fɪˈɒnseɪ/ *n* невéста.

fiasco /fɪˈæskəʊ/ *n* провáл.

fib /fɪb/ *n* враньё; *vi* привирáть *impf*, приврáть *pf*.

fibre /ˈfaɪbə(r)/ *n* волокнó. **fibreglass** *n* стекловолокнó. **fibrous** /-brəs/ *adj* волокни́стый.

fickle /ˈfɪk(ə)l/ *adj* непостоя́нный.

fiction /ˈfɪkʃ(ə)n/ *n* худóжественная литератýра; (*invention*) вы́думка. **fictional** /ˈfɪkʃən(ə)l/ *adj* беллетристи́ческий. **fictitious** /fɪkˈtɪʃəs/ *adj* вы́мышленный.

fiddle /ˈfɪd(ə)l/ *n* (*violin*) скри́пка; (*swindle*) обмáн; *vi*: **~ about** бездéльничать *impf*; **~ with** вертéть *impf*; *vt* (*falsify*) поддéлывать *impf*, поддéлать *pf*; (*cheat*) жи́лить *impf*, у~ *pf*.

fidelity /fɪˈdelɪtɪ/ *n* вéрность.

fidget /ˈfɪdʒɪt/ *n* непосéда *m* & *f*; *vi* ёрзать *impf*; нéрвничать *impf*. **fidgety** /-tɪ/ *adj* непосéдливый.

field /fi:ld/ *n* пóле; (*sport*) площáдка; (*sphere*) óбласть; **~-glasses** полевóй бинóкль *m*. **~work** полевы́е рабóты *f pl*.

fiend /fi:nd/ *n* дья́вол. **fiendish** /ˈfi:ndɪʃ/ *adj* дья́вольский.

fierce /ˈfɪəs/ *adj* свирéпый; (*strong*) си́льный.

fiery /ˈfaɪərɪ/ *adj* óгненный.

fifteen /fɪfˈti:n/ *adj* & *n* пятнáдцать. **fifteenth** /fɪfˈti:nθ/ *adj* & *n* пятнáдцатый. **fifth** /fɪfθ/ *adj* & *n* пя́тый; (*fraction*) пя́тая *sb*. **fiftieth** /ˈfɪftɪɪθ/ *adj* & *n* пятидеся́тый. **fifty** /ˈfɪftɪ/ *adj* & *n* пятьдеся́т; *pl* (*decade*) пятидеся́тые гóды (-дóв) *m pl*.

fig /fɪg/ *n* инжи́р.

fight /faɪt/ *n* дрáка; (*battle*) бой; (*fig*) борьбá; *vt* борóться *impf* с+*instr*; *vi* дрáться *impf*; *vt* & *i* (*wage war*) воевáть *impf* с+*instr*. **fighter** /-tə(r)/ *n* боéц; (*aeron*) истреби́тель *m*. **fighting** /-tɪŋ/ *n* бои́ *m pl*.

figment /ˈfɪgmənt/ *n* плод воображéния.

figurative /ˈfɪgjʊrətɪv/ *adj* перено́сный. **figure** /ˈfɪgə(r)/ *n* (*form, body, person*) фигу́ра; (*number*) ци́фра; (*diagram*) рису́нок; (*image*) изображе́ние; (*of speech*) оборо́т ре́чи; **~-head** (*naut*) носово́е украше́ние; (*person*) номина́льная глава́; *vt* (*think*) полага́ть *impf*; *vi* фигури́ровать *impf*; **~ out** вычисля́ть *impf*, вы́числить *pf*.

filament /ˈfɪləmənt/ *n* волокно́; (*electr*) нить.

file[1] /faɪl/ *n* (*tool*) напи́льник; *vt* подпи́ливать *impf*, подпили́ть *pf*.

file[2] /faɪl/ *n* (*folder*) па́пка; (*comput*) файл; *vt* подшива́ть *impf*, подши́ть *pf*; (*complaint*) подава́ть *impf*, пода́ть *pf*.

file[3] /faɪl/ *n* (*row*) ряд; **in (single) ~** гусько́м.

filigree /ˈfɪlɪˌgriː/ *adj* филигра́нный.

fill /fɪl/ *vt & i* (*also* **~ up**) наполня́ть(ся) *impf*, напо́лнить(ся) *pf*; *vt* заполня́ть *impf*, запо́лнить *pf*; (*tooth*) пломбирова́ть *impf*, за~ *pf*; (*occupy*) занима́ть *impf*, заня́ть *pf*; (*satiate*) насыща́ть *impf*, насы́тить *pf*; **~ in** (*vt*) заполня́ть *impf*, запо́лнить *pf*; (*vi*) замеща́ть *impf*, замести́ть *pf*.

fillet /ˈfɪlɪt/ *n* (*cul*) филе́ *neut indecl*.

filling /ˈfɪlɪŋ/ *n* (*tooth*) пло́мба; (*cul*) начи́нка.

filly /ˈfɪlɪ/ *n* кобы́лка.

film /fɪlm/ *n* (*layer*; *phot*) плёнка; (*cin*) фильм; **~ star** кинозвезда́; *vt* снима́ть *impf*, снять *pf*.

filter /ˈfɪltə(r)/ *n* фильтр; *vt* фильтрова́ть *impf*, про~ *pf*; **~ through, out** проса́чиваться *impf*, просочи́ться *pf*.

filth /fɪlθ/ *n* грязь. **filthy** /-θɪ/ *adj* гря́зный.

fin /fɪn/ *n* плавни́к

final /ˈfaɪn(ə)l/ *n* фина́л; *pl* выпускны́е экза́мены *m pl*; *adj* после́дний; (*decisive*) оконча́тельный. **finale** /fɪˈnɑːlɪ/ *n* фина́л. **finalist** /ˈfaɪnəlɪst/ *n* финали́ст. **finality** /faɪˈnælɪtɪ/ *n* зако́нченность. **finalize** /ˈfaɪnəˌlaɪz/ *vt* (*complete*) заверша́ть *impf*, заверши́ть *pf*; (*settle*) ула́живать *impf*, ула́дить *pf*. **finally** /ˈfaɪnəlɪ/ *adv* (*at last*) наконе́ц; (*in the end*) в конце́ концо́в.

finance /ˈfaɪnæns/ *n* фина́нсы (-сов) *pl*; *vt* финанси́ровать *impf & pf*. **financial** /-ˈnænʃ(ə)l/ *adj* фина́нсовый. **financier** /-ˈnænsɪə(r)/ *n* финанси́ст.

finch /fɪntʃ/ *n see comb, e.g.* **bullfinch**

find /faɪnd/ *n* нахо́дка; *vt* находи́ть *impf*, найти́ *pf*; (*person*) застава́ть *impf*, заста́ть *pf*; **~ out** узнава́ть *impf*, узна́ть *pf*; **~ fault with** придира́ться *impf*, придра́ться *pf* к+*dat*. **finding** /-dɪŋ/ *n pl* (*of inquiry*) вы́воды *m pl*.

fine[1] /faɪn/ *n* (*penalty*) штраф; *vt* штрафова́ть *impf*, о~ *pf*.

fine[2] /faɪn/ *adj* (*weather*) я́сный; (*excellent*) прекра́сный; (*delicate*) то́нкий; (*of sand etc.*) ме́лкий; **~ arts** изобрази́тельные иску́сства *neut pl*; *adv* хорошо́. **finery** /-nərɪ/ *n* наря́д. **finesse** /fɪˈnes/ *n* то́нкость.

finger /ˈfɪŋgə(r)/ *n* па́лец; **~-nail** но́готь; **~-print** отпеча́ток па́льца; **~-tip** ко́нчик па́льца; **have at (one's) ~s** знать *impf* как свои́ пять па́льцев; *vt* щу́пать *impf*, по~ *pf*.

finish /ˈfɪnɪʃ/ *n* коне́ц; (*polish*) отде́лка; (*sport*) фи́ниш; *vt & i* конча́ть(ся) *impf*, ко́нчить(ся) *pf*; *vt* ока́нчивать *impf*, око́нчить *pf*.

finite /ˈfaɪnaɪt/ *adj* коне́чный.

Finland /ˈfɪnlənd/ *n* Финля́ндия. **Finn** /fɪn/ *n* финн, фи́нка. **Finnish** /ˈfɪnɪʃ/ *adj* фи́нский.

fir /fɜː(r)/ *n* ель, пи́хта.

fire /ˈfaɪə(r)/ *vt* (*bake*) обжига́ть *impf*, обже́чь *pf*; (*excite*) воспламеня́ть *impf*, воспламени́ть *pf*; (*gun*) стреля́ть *impf* из+*gen* (**at** в+*acc*, по+*dat*); (*dismiss*) увольня́ть *impf*, уво́лить *pf*; *n* ого́нь *m*; (*grate*) ками́н; (*conflagration*)

f

пожа́р; (*bonfire*) костёр; (*fervour*) пыл; **be on ~** горе́ть *impf*; **catch ~** загора́ться *impf*, загоре́ться *pf*; **set ~ to, set on ~** поджига́ть *impf*, подже́чь *pf*; **~-alarm** пожа́рная трево́га; **~arm(s)** огнестре́льное ору́жие; **~ brigade** пожа́рная кома́нда; **~-engine** пожа́рная маши́на; **~-escape** пожа́рная ле́стница; **~ extinguisher** огнетуши́тель *m*; **~-guard** ками́нная решётка; **~man** пожа́рный *sb*; **~ place** ками́н; **~side** ме́сто у ками́на; **~ station** пожа́рное депо́ *neut indecl*; **~wood** дрова́ (-в) *pl*; **~work** фейерве́рк. **firing** /ˈfaɪərɪŋ/ *n* (*shooting*) стрельба́.

firm[1] /fɜːm/ *n* (*business*) фи́рма.

firm[2] /fɜːm/ *adj* твёрдый. **firmness** /-nɪs/ *n* твёрдость.

first /fɜːst/ *adj* пе́рвый; *n* пе́рвый *sb*; *adv* сперва́, снача́ла; (*for the ~ time*) впервы́е; **in the ~ place** во-пе́рвых; **~ of all** пре́жде всего́; **at ~ sight** на пе́рвый взгляд; **~ aid** пе́рвая по́мощь; **~-class** первокла́ссный; **~-hand** из пе́рвых рук; **~-rate** первокла́ссный. **firstly** /-lɪ/ *adv* во-пе́рвых.

fiscal /ˈfɪsk(ə)l/ *adj* фина́нсовый.

fish /fɪʃ/ *n* ры́ба; *adj* ры́бный; *vi* лови́ть *impf* ры́бу; **~ out** вытаскивать *impf*, вы́таскать *pf*. **fisherman** /ˈfɪʃəmən/ *n* рыба́к. **fishery** /ˈfɪʃərɪ/ *n* ры́бный про́мысел. **fishing** /ˈfɪʃɪŋ/ *n* ры́бная ло́вля; **~ boat** рыболо́вное су́дно; **~ line** ле́са́; **~ rod** у́дочка. **fishmonger** /ˈfɪʃmʌŋgə(r)/ *n* торго́вец ры́бой. **fishmonger's** /ˈfɪʃmʌŋgəz/ *n* ры́бный магази́н. **fishy** /ˈfɪʃɪ/ *adj* ры́бный; (*dubious*) подозри́тельный.

fissure /ˈfɪʃə(r)/ *n* тре́щина.

fist /fɪst/ *n* кула́к.

fit[1] /fɪt/ *n*: **be a good ~** хорошо́ сиде́ть *impf*; *adj* (*suitable*) подходя́щий, го́дный; (*healthy*) здоро́вый; *vt* (*be suitable*) годи́ться *impf* +*dat*, на+*acc*, для +*gen*; *vt* & *i* (*be the right size* (*for*)) подходи́ть *impf*, подойти́ *pf* (+*dat*); (*adjust*) прила́живать *impf*, прила́дить *pf* (**to** к+*dat*); (*be small enough for*) входи́ть *impf*, войти́ *pf* в+*acc*; **~ out** снабжа́ть *impf*, снабди́ть *pf*.

fit[2] /fɪt/ *n* (*attack*) припа́док; (*fig*) поры́в. **fitful** /-fʊl/ *adj* поры́вистый.

fitter /ˈfɪtə(r)/ *n* монтёр. **fitting** /-tɪŋ/ *n* (*of clothes*) приме́рка; *pl* армату́ра; *adj* подходя́щий.

five /faɪv/ *adj* & *n* пять; (*number 5*) пятёрка; **~-year plan** пятиле́тка.

fix /fɪks/ *n* (*dilemma*) переде́лка; (*drugs*) уко́л; *vt* (*repair*) чини́ть *impf*, по~ *pf*; (*settle*) назнача́ть *impf*, назна́чить *pf*; (*fasten*) укрепля́ть *impf*, укрепи́ть *pf*; **~ up** (*organize*) организова́ть *impf* & *pf*; (*install*) устана́вливать *impf*, установи́ть *pf*. **fixation** /-ˈseɪʃ(ə)n/ *n* фикса́ция. **fixed** /fɪkst/ *adj* устано́вленный. **fixture** /ˈfɪkstʃə(r)/ *n* (*sport*) предстоя́щее спорти́вное мероприя́тие; (*fitting*) приспособле́ние.

fizz, fizzle /fɪz, ˈfɪz(ə)l/ *vi* шипе́ть *impf*; **fizzle out** выдыха́ться *impf*, вы́дохнуться *pf*. **fizzy** /ˈfɪzɪ/ *adj* шипу́чий.

flabbergasted /ˈflæbəˌgɑːstɪd/ *adj* ошеломлённый.

flabby /ˈflæbɪ/ *adj* дря́блый.

flag[1] /flæg/ *n* флаг, зна́мя *neut*; *vt*: **~ down** остана́вливать *impf*, останови́ть *pf*.

flag[2] /flæg/ *vi* (*weaken*) ослабева́ть *impf*, ослабе́ть *pf*.

flagon /ˈflægən/ *n* кувши́н.

flagrant /ˈfleɪgrənt/ *adj* вопию́щий.

flagship /ˈflægʃɪp/ *n* фла́гман.

flagstone /ˈflægstəʊn/ *n* плита́.

flair /ˈfleə(r)/ *n* чутьё.

flake /fleɪk/ *n* слой; *pl* хло́пья (-ьев) *pl*; *vi* шелуши́ться *impf*. **flaky** /ˈfleɪkɪ/ *adj* слои́стый.

flamboyant /flæmˈbɔɪənt/ *adj* цвети́стый.

flame /fleɪm/ *n* пла́мя *neut*, ого́нь

m; *vi* пылáть *impf*.

flange /flændʒ/ *n* флáнец.

flank /flæŋk/ *n* (*of body*) бок; (*mil*) фланг; *vt* быть сбóку +*gen*.

flannel /'flæn(ə)l/ *n* фланéль; (*for face*) мочáлка для лицá.

flap /flæp/ *n* (*board*) откиднáя доскá; (*pocket*, *tent* ~) клáпан; (*panic*) пáника; *vt* взмáхивать *impf*, взмахнýть *pf* +*instr*; *vi* развевáться *impf*.

flare /fleə(r)/ *n* вспы́шка; (*signal*) сигнáльная ракéта; *vi* вспы́хивать *impf*, вспы́хнуть *pf*; ~ **up** (*fire*) возгорáться *impf*, возгорéться *pf*; (*fig*) вспыли́ть *pf*.

flash /flæʃ/ *n* вспы́шка; **in a** ~ ми́гом; *vi* сверкáть *impf*, сверкнýть *pf*. **flashback** *n* ретроспéкция. **flashy** /'flæʃɪ/ *adj* показнóй.

flask /flɑːsk/ *n* фля́жка.

flat[1] /flæt/ *n* (*dwelling*) кварти́ра.

flat[2] /flæt/ *n* (*mus*) бемóль *m*; (*tyre*) спýщенная ши́на; **on the** ~ на плóскости; *adj* плóский; ~**-fish** кáмбала. **flatly** /-lɪ/ *adv* наотрéз. **flatten** /-t(ə)n/ *vt* & *i* вырáвнивать(ся) *impf*, вы́ровнять(ся) *pf*.

flatmate /'flætmeɪt/ *n* сосéд, ~ка по кварти́ре.

flatter /'flætə(r)/ *vt* льстить *impf*, по~ *pf* +*dat*. **flattering** /-rɪŋ/ *adj* льсти́вый. **flattery** /-rɪ/ *n* лесть.

flaunt /flɔːnt/ *vt* щеголя́ть *impf*, щегольнýть *pf* +*instr*.

flautist /'flɔːtɪst/ *n* флейти́ст.

flavour /'fleɪvə(r)/ *n* вкус; (*fig*) при́вкус; *vt* приправля́ть *impf*, приправи́ть *pf*.

flaw /flɔː/ *n* изъя́н.

flax /flæks/ *n* лён. **flaxen** /'flæks(ə)n/ *adj* (*colour*) solóменный.

flea /fliː/ *n* блохá; ~ **market** барахóлка.

fleck /flek/ *n* крáпинка.

flee /fliː/ *vi* бежáть *impf* & *pf* (**from** от+*gen*); *vt* бежáть *impf* из+*gen*.

fleece /fliːs/ *n* рунó; *vt* (*fig*) обдирáть *impf*, ободрáть *pf*. **fleecy** /-sɪ/ *adj* шерсти́стый.

fleet /fliːt/ *n* флот; (*vehicles*) парк.

fleeting /'fliːtɪŋ/ *adj* мимолётный.

flesh /fleʃ/ *n* (*as opposed to mind*) плоть; (*meat*) мя́со; **in the** ~ во плоти́. **fleshy** /-ʃɪ/ *adj* мяси́стый.

flex /fleks/ *n* шнур; *vt* сгибáть *impf*, согнýть *pf*. **flexibility** /ˌfleksɪ'bɪlɪtɪ/ *adj* ги́бкость. **flexible** /'fleksɪb(ə)l/ *adj* ги́бкий.

flick /flɪk/ *vt* & *i* щёлкать *impf*, щёлкнуть *pf* (+*instr*); ~ **through** пролистáть *pf*.

flicker /'flɪkə(r)/ *n* мерцáние; *vi* мерцáть *impf*.

flier /'flaɪə(r)/ *see* **flyer**

flight[1] /flaɪt/ *n* (*fleeing*) бéгство; **put (take) to** ~ обращáть(ся) *impf*, обрати́ть(ся) *pf* в бéгство.

flight[2] /flaɪt/ *n* (*flying*) полёт; (*trip*) рейс; ~ **of stairs** лéстничный марш. **flighty** /-tɪ/ *adj* вéтреный.

flimsy /'flɪmzɪ/ *adj* (*fragile*) непрóчный; (*dress*) лёгкий; (*excuse*) слáбый.

flinch /flɪntʃ/ *vi* (*recoil*) отпря́дывать *impf*, отпря́нуть *pf*; (*fig*) уклоня́ться *impf*, уклони́ться *pf* (**from** от+*gen*).

fling /flɪŋ/ *vt* швыря́ть *impf*, швырнýть *pf*; *vi* (*also* ~ *o.s.*) бросáться *impf*, брóситься *pf*.

flint /flɪnt/ *n* кремéнь *m*.

flip /flɪp/ *vt* щёлкать *impf*, щёлкнуть *pf* +*instr*.

flippant /'flɪpənt/ *adj* легкомы́сленный.

flipper /'flɪpə(r)/ *n* ласт.

flirt /flɜːt/ *n* кокéтка; *vi* флиртовáть *impf* (**with** с+*instr*). **flirtation** /-'teɪʃ(ə)n/ *n* флирт.

flit /flɪt/ *vi* порхáть *impf*, порхнýть *pf*.

float /fləʊt/ *n* поплавóк; *vi* плáвать *indet*, плыть *det*; *vt* (*company*) пускáть *impf*, пусти́ть *pf* в ход.

flock /flɒk/ *n* (*animals*) стáдо; (*birds*) стáя; *vi* стекáться *impf*, стéчься *pf*.

flog /flɒg/ *vt* сечь *impf*, вы́~ *pf*.

flood /flʌd/ *n* наводнéние; (*bibl*) потóп; (*fig*) потóк; *vi* (*river etc.*) выступáть *impf*, вы́ступить *pf* из берегóв; *vt* затопля́ть *impf*, затопи́ть *pf*. **floodgate** *n* шлюз. **floodlight** *n* прожéктор.

floor /flɔ:(r)/ *n* пол; (*storey*) этáж; **~board** полови́ца; *vt* (*confound*) стáвить *impf*, по~ *pf* в тупи́к.

flop /flɒp/ *vi* (*fall*) плю́хаться *impf*, плю́хнуться *pf*; (*fail*) провáливаться *impf*, провали́ться *pf*.

f

flora /ˈflɔ:rə/ *n* флóра. **floral** /-r(ə)l/ *adj* цветóчный.

florid /ˈflɒrɪd/ *adj* цвети́стый; (*ruddy*) румя́ный. **florist** /ˈflɒrɪst/ *n* торгóвец цветáми.

flounce[1] /flaʊns/ *vi* бросáться *impf*, брóситься *pf*.

flounce[2] /flaʊns/ *n* (*of skirt*) обóрка.

flounder[1] /ˈflaʊndə(r)/ *n* (*fish*) кáмбала.

flounder[2] /ˈflaʊndə(r)/ *vi* барáхтаться *impf*.

flour /ˈflaʊə(r)/ *n* мукá.

flourish /ˈflʌrɪʃ/ *n* (*movement*) размáхивание (+*instr*); (*of pen*) рóсчерк; *vi* (*thrive*) процветáть *impf*; *vt* (*wave*) размáхивать *impf*, размахнýть *pf* +*instr*.

flout /flaʊt/ *vt* попирáть *impf*, попрáть *pf*.

flow /fləʊ/ *vi* течь *impf*; ли́ться *impf*; *n* течéние.

flower /ˈflaʊə(r)/ *n* цветóк; **~-bed** клýмба; **~pot** цветóчный горшóк; *vi* цвести́ *impf*. **flowery** /-rɪ/ *adj* цвети́стый.

flu /flu:/ *n* грипп.

fluctuate /ˈflʌktjʊˌeɪt/ *vi* колебáться *impf*, по~ *pf*. **fluctuation** /-ˈeɪʃ(ə)n/ *n* колебáние.

flue /flu:/ *n* дымохóд.

fluent /ˈflu:ənt/ *adj* бéглый. **fluently** /-lɪ/ *adv* свобóдно.

fluff /flʌf/ *n* пух. **fluffy** /-fɪ/ *adj* пуши́стый.

fluid /ˈflu:ɪd/ *n* жи́дкость; *adj* жи́дкий.

fluke /flu:k/ *n* случáйная удáча.

fluorescent /flʊəˈres(ə)nt/ *adj* флюоресцéнтный.

fluoride /ˈflʊəraɪd/ *n* фтори́д.

flurry /ˈflʌrɪ/ *n* (*squall*) шквал; (*fig*) волнá.

flush /flʌʃ/ *n* (*redness*) румя́нец; *vi* (*redden*) краснéть *impf*, по~ *pf*; *vt* спускáть *impf*, спусти́ть *pf* вóду в+*acc*.

flustered /ˈflʌstəd/ *adj* сконфýженный.

flute /flu:t/ *n* флéйта.

flutter /ˈflʌtə(r)/ *vi* (*flit*) порхáть *impf*, порхнýть *pf*; (*wave*) развевáться *impf*.

flux /flʌks/ *n*: **in a state of ~** в состоя́нии изменéния.

fly[1] /flaɪ/ *n* (*insect*) мýха.

fly[2] /flaɪ/ *vi* летáть *indet*, летéть *det*, по~ *pf*; (*flag*) развевáться *impf*; (*hasten*) нести́сь *impf*, по~ *pf*; *vt* (*aircraft*) управля́ть *impf* +*instr*; (*transport*) перевози́ть *impf*, перевезти́ *pf* (самолётом); (*flag*) поднимáть *impf*, подня́ть *pf*. **flyer, flier** /ˈflaɪə(r)/ *n* лётчик. **flying** /ˈflaɪɪŋ/ *n* полёт.

foal /fəʊl/ *n* (*horse*) жеребёнок

foam /fəʊm/ *n* пéна; **~ plastic** пенопláст; **~ rubber** пенорези́на; *vi* пéниться *impf*, вс~ *pf*. **foamy** /-mɪ/ *adj* пéнистый.

focal /ˈfəʊk(ə)l/ *adj* фóкусный. **focus** /ˈfəʊkəs/ *n* фóкус; (*fig*) центр; *vt* фокуси́ровать *impf*, с~ *pf*; (*concentrate*) сосредотóчивать *impf*, сосредотóчить *pf*.

fodder /ˈfɒdə(r)/ *n* корм.

foe /fəʊ/ *n* враг.

foetus /ˈfi:təs/ *n* зарóдыш.

fog /fɒg/ *n* тумáн. **foggy** /-gɪ/ *adj* тумáнный.

foible /ˈfɔɪb(ə)l/ *n* слáбость.

foil[1] /fɔɪl/ *n* (*metal*) фольгá; (*contrast*) контрáст.

foil[2] /fɔɪl/ *vt* (*thwart*) расстрáивать *impf*, расстрóить *pf*.

foil[3] /fɔɪl/ *n* (*sword*) рапи́ра.

foist /fɔɪst/ *vt* навя́зывать *impf*, навязáть *pf* (**on** +*dat*).

fold[1] /fəʊld/ *n* (*sheep-~*) овчáрня.

fold[2] /fəʊld/ *n* склáдка, сгиб; *vt* склáдывать *impf*, сложи́ть *pf*. **folder** /-də(r)/ *n* пáпка. **folding** /-dɪŋ/ *adj* складнóй.

foliage /ˈfəʊlɪɪdʒ/ *n* листвá.
folk /fəʊk/ *n* нарóд, лю́ди *pl*; *pl* (*relatives*) родня́ *collect*; *attrib* нарóдный. **folklore** /ˈfəʊklɔː(r)/ *n* фольклóр.
follow /ˈfɒləʊ/ *vt* слéдовать *impf*, по~ *pf* +*dat*, за+*instr*; (*walk behind*) идти́ *det* за+*instr*; (*fig*) следи́ть *impf* за+*instr*. **follower** /ˈfɒləʊwə(r)/ *n* послéдователь *m*. **following** /ˈfɒləʊwɪŋ/ *adj* слéдующий.
folly /ˈfɒlɪ/ *n* глу́пость.
fond /fɒnd/ *adj* нéжный; **be ~ of** люби́ть *impf* +*acc*.
fondle /ˈfɒnd(ə)l/ *vt* ласкáть *impf*.
fondness /ˈfɒndnɪs/ *n* любóвь.
font /fɒnt/ *n* (*eccl*) купéль.
food /fuːd/ *n* пи́ща, едá. **foodstuff** *n* пищевóй проду́кт.
fool /fuːl/ *n* дурáк, ду́ра; *vt* дурáчить *impf*, о~ *pf*; *vi*: **~ about** дурáчиться *impf*. **foolhardy** /ˈfuːlˌhɑːdɪ/ *adj* безрассу́дно хрáбрый. **foolish** /ˈfuːlɪʃ/ *adj* глу́пый. **foolishness** /ˈfuːlɪʃnɪs/ *n* глу́пость. **foolproof** /ˈfuːlpruːf/ *adj* абсолю́тно надёжный.
foot /fʊt/ *n* ногá; (*measure*) фут; (*of hill etc.*) поднóжие; **on ~** пешкóм; **put one's ~ in it** сесть *pf* в лу́жу. **foot-and-mouth (disease)** *n* я́щур. **football** *n* футбóл; *attrib* футбóльный. **footballer** /ˈfʊtbɔːlə(r)/ *n* футболи́ст. **foothills** *n pl* предгóрье. **footing** /ˈfʊtɪŋ/ *n* (*fig*) бáзис; **lose one's ~** оступи́ться *pf*; **on an equal ~** на рáвной ногé. **footlights** *n pl* рáмпа. **footman** *n* лакéй. **footnote** *n* снóска. **footpath** *n* тропи́нка; (*pavement*) тротуáр. **footprint** *n* след. **footstep** *n* (*sound*) шаг; (*footprint*) след. **footwear** *n* óбувь.
for /fɔː(r)/ *prep* (*of time*) в течéние +*gen*, на+*acc*; (*of purpose*) для +*gen*, за+*acc*, +*instr*; (*price*) за+*acc*; (*on account of*) из-за +*gen*; (*in place of*) вмéсто+*gen*; **~ the sake of** рáди +*gen*; **as ~** что касáется+*gen*; *conj* так как.
forage /ˈfɒrɪdʒ/ *n* фурáж; *vi*: **~ for** разы́скивать *impf*.
foray /ˈfɒreɪ/ *n* набéг.
forbearance /fɔːˈbeərəns/ *n* воздéржанность.
forbid /fəˈbɪd/ *vt* запрещáть *impf*, запрети́ть *pf* (+*dat* (*person*) & *acc* (*thing*)). **forbidding** /-dɪŋ/ *adj* грóзный.
force /fɔːs/ *n* си́ла; *pl* (*armed ~*) вооружённые си́лы *f pl*; **by ~** си́лой; *vt* (*compel*) заставля́ть *impf*, застáвить *pf*; (*lock etc.*) взлáмывать *impf*, взломáть *pf*. **forceful** /-fʊl/ *adj* си́льный; (*speech*) убеди́тельный. **forcible** /ˈfɔːsɪb(ə)l/ *adj* наси́льственный.
forceps /ˈfɔːseps/ *n* щипцы́ (-цóв) *pl*.
ford /fɔːd/ *n* брод; *vt* переходи́ть *impf*, перейти́ *pf* вброд+*acc*.
fore /fɔː(r)/ *n*: **come to the ~** выдвигáться *impf*, вы́двинуться *pf* на перéдний план.
forearm *n* /ˈfɔːrɑːm/ предплéчье. **foreboding** /fɔːˈbəʊdɪŋ/ *n* предчу́вствие. **forecast** /ˈfɔːkɑːst/ *n* предсказáние; (*of weather*) прогнóз; *vt* /fɔːrˈɑːm/ предскáзывать *impf*, предсказáть *pf*. **forecourt** *n* перéдний двор. **forefather** *n* прéдок. **forefinger** *n* указáтельный пáлец. **forefront** *n* (*foreground*) перéдний план; (*leading position*) авангáрд. **foregone** /ˈfɔːgɒn/ *adj*: **~ conclusion** предрешённый исхóд. **foreground** *n* перéдний план. **forehead** /ˈfɒrɪd/ *n* лоб.
foreign /ˈfɒrɪn/ *adj* (*from abroad*) инострáнный; (*alien*) чу́ждый; (*external*) внéшний; **~ body** инорóдное тéло; **~ currency** валю́та. **foreigner** /ˈfɒrɪnə(r)/ *n* инострáнец, -нка.
foreman /ˈfɔːmən/ *n* мáстер.
foremost /ˈfɔːməʊst/ *adj* выдаю́щийся; **first and ~** прéжде всегó.
forename /ˈfɔːneɪm/ *n* и́мя.
forensic /fəˈrensɪk/ *adj* судéбный.
forerunner /ˈfɔːˌrʌnə(r)/ *n* предвéстник. **foresee** /fɔːˈsiː/ *vt* пред-

f

ви́деть *impf.* **foreshadow** /fɔː'ʃædəʊ/ *vt* предвеща́ть *impf.* **foresight**/'fɔːsaɪt/ *n* предви́дение; (*caution*) предусмотри́тельность.

forest /'fɒrɪst/ *n* лес.

forestall /fɔː'stɔːl/ *vt* предупрежда́ть *impf*, предупреди́ть *pf.*

forester /'fɒrɪstə(r)/ *n* лесни́чий *sb.* **forestry** /'fɒrɪstrɪ/ *n* лесово́дство.

f

foretaste /'fɔːteɪst/ *n* предвкуше́ние; *vt* предвкуша́ть *impf*, предвкуси́ть *pf.* **foretell** /fɔː'tel/ *vt* предска́зывать *impf*, предсказа́ть *pf.* **forethought** /'fɔːθɔːt/ *n* предусмотри́тельность. **forewarn** /fɔː'wɔːn/ *vt* предостерега́ть *impf*, предостере́чь *pf.* **foreword** /'fɔːwɜːd/ *n* предисло́вие.

forfeit /'fɔːfɪt/ *n* (*in game*) фант; *vt* лиша́ться *impf*, лиши́ться *pf* +*gen.*

forge[1] /fɔːdʒ/ *n* (*smithy*) ку́зница; (*furnace*) горн; *vt* кова́ть *impf*, вы́~ *pf*; (*fabricate*) подде́лывать *impf*, подде́лать *pf.*

forge[2] /fɔːdʒ/ *vi*: **~ ahead** продвига́ться *impf*, продви́нуться *pf* вперёд.

forger /'fɔːdʒə(r)/ *n* фальшивомоне́тчик. **forgery** /-rɪ/ *n* подде́лка.

forget /fə'get/ *vt* забыва́ть *impf*, забы́ть *pf.* **forgetful** /-fʊl/ *adj* забы́вчивый.

forgive /fə'gɪv/ *vt* проща́ть *impf*, прости́ть *pf.* **forgiveness** /-nɪs/ *n* проще́ние.

forgo /fɔː'gəʊ/ *vt* возде́рживаться *impf*, воздержа́ться *pf* от+*gen.*

fork /fɔːk/ *n* (*eating*) ви́лка; (*digging*) ви́лы (-л) *pl*; (*in road*) разветвле́ние; *vi* (*road*) разветвля́ться *impf*, разветви́ться *pf.*

forlorn /fɔː'lɔːn/ *adj* жа́лкий.

form /fɔːm/ *n* (*shape*; *kind*) фо́рма; (*class*) класс; (*document*) анке́та; *vt* (*make*, *create*) образо́вывать *impf*, образова́ть *pf*; (*develop*; *make up*) составля́ть *impf*, соста́вить *pf*; *vi* образо́вываться *impf*, образова́ться *pf.* **formal** /'fɔːm(ə)l/ *adj* форма́льный; (*official*) официа́льный. **formality** /fɔː'mælɪtɪ/ *n* форма́льность. **format** /'fɔːmæt/ *n* форма́т. **formation** /fɔː'meɪʃ(ə)n/ *n* образова́ние. **formative** /'fɔːmətɪv/ *adj*: **~ years** молоды́е го́ды (-до́в) *m pl.*

former /'fɔːmə(r)/ *adj* (*earlier*) пре́жний; (*ex*) бы́вший; **the ~** (*of two*) пе́рвый. **formerly** /'fɔːməlɪ/ *adv* пре́жде.

formidable /'fɔːmɪdəb(ə)l/ *adj* (*dread*) гро́зный; (*arduous*) тру́дный.

formless /'fɔːmlɪs/ *adj* бесфо́рменный.

formula /'fɔːmjʊlə/ *n* фо́рмула. **formulate** /-ˌleɪt/ *vt* формули́ровать *impf*, с~ *pf.* **formulation** /-'leɪʃ(ə)n/ *n* формулиро́вка.

forsake /fə'seɪk/ *vt* (*desert*) покида́ть *impf*, поки́нуть *pf*; (*renounce*) отка́зываться *impf*, отказа́ться *pf* от+*gen.*

fort /fɔːt/ *n* форт.

forth /fɔːθ/ *adv* вперёд, да́льше; **back and ~** взад и вперёд; **and so ~** и так да́лее. **forthcoming** /fɔːθ'kʌmɪŋ/ *adj* предстоя́щий; **be ~** (*available*) поступа́ть *impf*, поступи́ть *pf.* **forthwith** /fɔːθ'wɪθ/ *adv* неме́дленно.

fortieth /'fɔːtɪɪθ/ *adj* & *n* сороково́й.

fortification /ˌfɔːtɪfɪ'keɪʃ(ə)n/ *n* укрепле́ние. **fortify** /'fɔːtɪˌfaɪ/ *vt* укрепля́ть *impf*, укрепи́ть *pf*; (*fig*) подкрепля́ть *impf*, подкрепи́ть *pf.* **fortitude** /'fɔːtɪˌtjuːd/ *n* сто́йкость.

fortnight /'fɔːtnaɪt/ *n* две неде́ли *f pl.* **fortnightly** /-lɪ/ *adj* двухнеде́льный; *adv* раз в две неде́ли.

fortress /'fɔːtrɪs/ *n* кре́пость.

fortuitous /fɔː'tjuːɪtəs/ *adj* случа́йный.

fortunate /'fɔːtjʊnət/ *adj* счастли́вый. **fortunately** /-lɪ/ *adv* к сча́стью. **fortune** /'fɔːtjuːn/ *n* (*destiny*) судьба́; (*good ~*) сча́стье; (*wealth*) состоя́ние.

forty /'fɔːtɪ/ *adj* & *n* со́рок; *pl* (*decade*) сороковы́е го́ды (-до́в) *m pl.*

forward /'fɔːwəd/ *adj* пере́дний; (*presumptuous*) развя́зный; *n* (*sport*) напада́ющий *sb*; *adv* вперёд; *vt* (*letter*) пересыла́ть *impf*, пересла́ть *pf*.

fossil /'fɒs(ə)l/ *n* ископа́емое *sb*; *adj* ископа́емый. **fossilized** /'fɒsɪ͵laɪzd/ *adj* ископа́емый.

foster /'fɒstə(r)/ *vt* (*child*) приюти́ть *pf*; (*idea*) вына́шивать *impf*, вы́носить *pf*; (*create*) создава́ть *impf*, созда́ть *pf*; (*cherish*) леле́ять *impf*; **~-child** приёмыш.

foul /faʊl/ *adj* (*dirty*) гря́зный; (*repulsive*) отврати́тельный; (*obscene*) непристо́йный; *n* (*sport*) наруше́ние пра́вил; *vt* (*dirty*) па́чкать *impf*, за~, ис~ *pf*; (*entangle*) запу́тывать *impf*, запу́тать *pf*.

found /faʊnd/ *vt* осно́вывать *impf*, основа́ть *pf*.

foundation /faʊn'deɪʃ(ə)n/ *n* (*of building*) фунда́мент; (*basis*) осно́ва; (*institution*) учрежде́ние; (*fund*) фонд. **founder**[1] /'faʊndə(r)/ *n* основа́тель *m*.

founder[2] /'faʊndə(r)/ *vi* (*naut*, *fig*) тону́ть *impf*, по~ *pf*.

foundry /'faʊndrɪ/ *n* лите́йная *sb*.

fountain /'faʊntɪn/ *n* фонта́н; **~-pen** автору́чка.

four /fɔː(r)/ *adj* & *n* четы́ре; (*number 4*) четвёрка; **on all ~s** на четвере́ньках. **fourteen** /fɔː'tiːn/ *adj* & *n* четы́рнадцать. **fourteenth** /fɔː'tiːnθ/ *adj* & *n* четы́рнадцатый. **fourth** /fɔːθ/ *adj* & *n* четвёртый; (*quarter*) че́тверть.

fowl /faʊl/ *n* (*domestic*) дома́шняя пти́ца; (*wild*) дичь *collect*.

fox /fɒks/ *n* лиса́, лиси́ца; *vt* озада́чивать *impf*, озада́чить *pf*.

foyer /'fɔɪeɪ/ *n* фойе́ *neut indecl*.

fraction /'frækʃ(ə)n/ *n* (*math*) дробь; (*portion*) части́ца.

fractious /'frækʃəs/ *adj* раздражи́тельный.

fracture /'fræktʃə(r)/ *n* перело́м; *vt* & *i* лома́ть(ся) *impf*, с~ *pf*.

fragile /'frædʒaɪl/ *adj* ло́мкий.

fragment /'frægmənt/ *n* обло́мок; (*of conversation*) отры́вок; (*of writing*) фрагме́нт. **fragmentary** /-tərɪ/ *adj* отры́вочный.

fragrance /'freɪgrəns/ *n* арома́т. **fragrant** /-grənt/ *adj* арома́тный, души́стый.

frail /freɪl/ *adj* хру́пкий.

frame /freɪm/ *n* о́стов; (*build*) телосложе́ние; (*picture*) ра́ма; (*cin*) кадр; **~ of mind** настрое́ние; *vt* (*devise*) создава́ть *impf*, созда́ть *pf*; (*formulate*) формули́ровать *impf*, с~ *pf*; (*picture*) вставля́ть *impf*, вста́вить *pf* в ра́му; (*incriminate*) фабрикова́ть *impf*, с~ *pf* обвине́ние про́тив+*gen*. **framework** *n* о́стов; (*fig*) ра́мки *f pl*.

franc /fræŋk/ *n* франк.

France /frɑːns/ *n* Фра́нция.

franchise /'fræntʃaɪz/ *n* (*comm*) привиле́гия; (*polit*) пра́во го́лоса.

frank[1] /fræŋk/ *adj* открове́нный.

frank[2] /fræŋk/ *vt* (*letter*) франки́ровать *impf* & *pf*.

frantic /'fræntɪk/ *adj* неи́стовый.

fraternal /frə'tɜːn(ə)l/ *adj* бра́тский. **fraternity** /-'tɜːnɪtɪ/ *n* бра́тство.

fraud /frɔːd/ *n* обма́н; (*person*) обма́нщик. **fraudulent** /'frɔːdjʊlənt/ *adj* обма́нный.

fraught /frɔːt/ *adj*: **~ with** чрева́тый +*instr*.

fray[1] /freɪ/ *vt* & *i* обтрёпывать(ся) *impf*, обтрепа́ть(ся) *pf*.

fray[2] /freɪ/ *n* бой.

freak /friːk/ *n* уро́д; *attrib* необы́чный.

freckle /'frek(ə)l/ *n* весну́шка. **freckled** /'frekəld/ *adj* весну́шчатый.

free /friː/ *adj* свобо́дный; (*gratis*) беспла́тный; **~ kick** штрафно́й уда́р; **~ speech** свобо́да сло́ва; *vt* освобожда́ть *impf*, освободи́ть *pf*. **freedom** /'friːdəm/ *n* свобо́да. **freehold** *n* неограни́ченное пра́во со́бственности на недви́жимость. **freelance** /'friːlɑːns/ *adj* внешта́тный. **Free-**

f

mason *n* франкмасóн.
freeze /fri:z/ *vi* замерзáть *impf*, мёрзнуть *impf*, замёрзнуть *pf*; *vt* заморáживать *impf*, заморóзить *pf*. **freezer** /-zə(r)/ *n* морози́льник; (*compartment*) морози́лка. **freezing** /-zɪŋ/ *adj* морóзный; **below ~** ни́же нуля́.
freight /freɪt/ *n* фрахт. **freighter** /-tə(r)/ *n* (*ship*) грузовóе сýдно.
f **French** /frentʃ/ *adj* францýзский; **~ bean** фасóль; **~ horn** валтóрна; **~ windows** двуствóрчатое окнó до пóла. **Frenchman** *n* францýз. **Frenchwoman** *n* францýженка.
frenetic /frə'netɪk/ *adj* неи́стовый.
frenzied /'frenzɪd/ *adj* неи́стовый. **frenzy** /-zɪ/ *n* неи́стовство.
frequency /'fri:kwənsɪ/ *n* частотá. **frequent** *adj* /'fri:kwənt/ чáстый; *vt* /frɪ'kwent/ чáсто посещáть *impf*.
fresco /'freskəʊ/ *n* фрéска.
fresh /freʃ/ *adj* свéжий; (*new*) нóвый; **~ water** прéсная водá. **freshen** /-ʃ(ə)n/ *vt* освежáть *impf*, освежи́ть *pf*; *vi* свежéть *impf*, по~ *pf*. **freshly** /-lɪ/ *adv* свежó; (*recently*) недáвно. **freshness** /-nɪs/ *n* свéжесть. **freshwater** *adj* пресновóдный.
fret[1] /fret/ *vi* мýчиться *impf*. **fretful** /-fʊl/ *adj* раздражи́тельный.
fret[2] /fret/ *n* (*mus*) лад.
fretsaw /'fretsɔ:/ *n* лóбзик.
friar /'fraɪə(r)/ *n* монáх.
friction /'frɪkʃ(ə)n/ *n* трéние; (*fig*) трéния *neut pl*.
Friday /'fraɪdeɪ/ *n* пя́тница.
fridge /frɪdʒ/ *n* холоди́льник.
fried /fraɪd/ *adj*: **~ egg** яи́чница.
friend /frend/ *n* друг, подрýга; приятель *m*, ~ница. **friendly** /-lɪ/ *adj* дрýжеский. **friendship** *n* дрýжба.
frieze /fri:z/ *n* фриз.
frigate /'frɪgɪt/ *n* фрегáт.
fright /fraɪt/ *n* испýг. **frighten** /-t(ə)n/ *vt* пугáть *impf*, ис~, на~ *pf*. **frightful** /-fʊl/ *adj* стрáшный.
frigid /'frɪdʒɪd/ *adj* холóдный.
frill /frɪl/ *n* обóрка.
fringe /frɪndʒ/ *n* бахромá; (*of hair*) чёлка; (*edge*) край.
frisk /frɪsk/ *vi* (*frolic*) резви́ться *impf*; *vt* (*search*) шмонáть *impf*. **frisky** /-kɪ/ *adj* рéзвый.
fritter /'frɪtə(r)/ *vt*: **~ away** растрáчивать *impf*, растрáтить *pf*.
frivolity /frɪ'vɒlɪtɪ/ *n* легкомы́сленность. **frivolous** /'frɪvələs/ *adj* легкомы́сленный.
fro /frəʊ/ *adv*: **to and ~** взад и вперёд.
frock /frɒk/ *n* плáтье.
frog /frɒg/ *n* лягýшка.
frolic /'frɒlɪk/ *vi* резви́ться *impf*.
from /frɒm/ *prep* от+*gen*; (*~ off, down ~; in time*) с+*gen*; (*out of*) из+*gen*; (*according to*) по+*dat*; (*because of*) из-за+*gen*; **~ above** свéрху; **~ abroad** из-за грани́цы; **~ afar** и́здали; **~ among** из числá+*gen*; **~ behind** из-за+*gen*; **~ day to day** изо дня́ в день; **~ everywhere** отовсю́ду; **~ here** отсю́да; **~ memory** по пáмяти; **~ now on** отны́не; **~ there** оттýда; **~ time to time** врéмя от врéмени; **~ under** из-под+*gen*.
front /frʌnt/ *n* фасáд, перéдняя сторонá; (*mil*) фронт; **in ~ of** впереди́+*gen*, пéред+*instr*; *adj* перéдний; (*first*) пéрвый.
frontier /'frʌntɪə(r)/ *n* грани́ца.
frost /frɒst/ *n* морóз; **~-bite** отморожéние; **~-bitten** отморóженный. **frosted** /-tɪd/ *adj*: **~ glass** мáтовое стеклó. **frosty** /-tɪ/ *adj* морóзный; (*fig*) ледянóй.
froth /frɒθ/ *n* пéна; *vi* пéниться *impf*, вс~ *pf*. **frothy** /-θɪ/ *adj* пéнистый.
frown /fraʊn/ *n* хмýрый взгляд; *vi* хмýриться *impf*, на~ *pf*.
frugal /'fru:g(ə)l/ *adj* (*careful*) бережли́вый; (*scanty*) скýдный.
fruit /fru:t/ *n* плод; *collect* фрýкты *m pl*; *adj* фруктóвый. **fruitful** /-fʊl/ *adj* плодотвóрный. **fruition**

/fruːˈɪʃ(ə)n/ *n*: **come to ~** осуществи́ться *pf*. **fruitless** /ˈfruːtlɪs/ *adj* беспло́дный.

frustrate /frʌˈstreɪt/ *vt* фрустри́ровать *impf* & *pf*. **frustrating** /-ˈstreɪtɪŋ/ *adj* фрустри́рующий. **frustration** /-ˈstreɪʃ(ə)n/ *n* фрустра́ция.

fry[1] /fraɪ/ *n*: **small ~** мелюзга́.

fry[2] /fraɪ/ *vt* & *i* жа́рить(ся) *impf*, за~, из~ *pf*. **frying-pan** /ˈfraɪŋ pæn/ *n* сковорода́.

fuel /ˈfjuːəl/ *n* то́пливо.

fugitive /ˈfjuːdʒɪtɪv/ *n* бегле́ц.

fulcrum /ˈfʊlkrəm/ *n* то́чка опо́ры.

fulfil /fʊlˈfɪl/ *vt* (*perform*) выполня́ть *impf*, вы́полнить *pf*; (*dreams*) осуществля́ть *impf*, осуществи́ть *pf*. **fulfilling** /-lɪŋ/ *adj* удовлетворя́ющий. **fulfilment** /-mənt/ *n* выполне́ние; осуществле́ние; удовлетворе́ние.

full /fʊl/ *adj* по́лный (**of** +*gen*, *instr*); (*replete*) сы́тый; **~ stop** то́чка; **~ time: I work ~ time** я рабо́таю на по́лную ста́вку; *n*: **in ~** по́лностью; **to the ~** в по́лной ме́ре. **fullness** /ˈfʊlnɪs/ *n* полнота́. **fully** /ˈfʊlɪ/ *adv* вполне́.

fulsome /ˈfʊlsəm/ *adj* чрезме́рный.

fumble /ˈfʌmb(ə)l/ *vi*: **~ for** нащу́пывать *impf* +*acc*; **~ with** вози́ться *impf* с+*instr*.

fume /fjuːm/ *vi* (*with anger*) кипе́ть *impf*, вс~ *pf* гне́вом. **fumes** /fjuːmz/ *n pl* испаре́ния *neut pl*. **fumigate** /ˈfjuːmɪˌgeɪt/ *vt* оку́ривать *impf*, окури́ть *pf*.

fun /fʌn/ *n* заба́ва; **it was ~** бы́ло заба́вно; **have ~** забавля́ться *impf*; **make ~ of** смея́ться *impf*, по~ *pf* над +*instr*.

function /ˈfʌŋkʃ(ə)n/ *n* фу́нкция; (*event*) ве́чер; *vi* функциони́ровать *impf*; де́йствовать *impf*. **functional** /-n(ə)l/ *adj* функциона́льный. **functionary** /-nərɪ/ *n* чино́вник.

fund /fʌnd/ *n* фонд; (*store*) запа́с.

fundamental /ˌfʌndəˈment(ə)l/ *adj* основно́й; *n*: *pl* осно́вы *f pl*.

funeral /ˈfjuːnər(ə)l/ *n* по́хороны (-о́н, -она́м) *pl*.

fungus /ˈfʌŋgəs/ *n* гриб.

funnel /ˈfʌn(ə)l/ *n* воро́нка; (*chimney*) дымова́я труба́.

funny /ˈfʌnɪ/ *adj* смешно́й; (*odd*) стра́нный.

fur /fɜː(r)/ *n* мех; **~ coat** шу́ба.

furious /ˈfjʊərɪəs/ *adj* бе́шеный.

furnace /ˈfɜːnɪs/ *n* горн, печь.

furnish /ˈfɜːnɪʃ/ *vt* (*provide*) снабжа́ть *impf*, снабди́ть *pf* (**with** с+*instr*); (*house*) обставля́ть *impf*, обста́вить *pf*. **furniture** /ˈfɜːnɪtʃə(r)/ *n* ме́бель.

furrow /ˈfʌrəʊ/ *n* борозда́.

furry /ˈfɜːrɪ/ *adj* пуши́стый.

further, farther /ˈfɜːðə(r), ˈfɑːðə(r)/ *comp adj* дальне́йший; *adv* да́льше; *vt* продвига́ть *impf*, продви́нуть *pf*. **furthermore** *adv* к тому́ же. **furthest, farthest** /ˈfɜːðɪst, ˈfɑːðɪst/ *superl adj* са́мый да́льний.

furtive /ˈfɜːtɪv/ *adj* скры́тый, та́йный.

fury /ˈfjʊərɪ/ *n* я́рость.

fuse[1] /fjuːz/ *vt* & *i* (*of metal*) сплавля́ть(ся) *impf*, спла́вить(ся) *pf*.

fuse[2] /fjuːz/ *n* (*in bomb*) запа́л; (*detonating device*) взрыва́тель *m*.

fuse[3] /fjuːz/ *n* (*electr*) про́бка; *vi* перегора́ть *impf*, перегоре́ть *pf*.

fuselage /ˈfjuːzəˌlɑːʒ/ *n* фюзеля́ж.

fusion /ˈfjuːʒ(ə)n/ *n* пла́вка, слия́ние.

fuss /fʌs/ *n* суета́; *vi* суети́ться *impf*. **fussy** /-sɪ/ *adj* суетли́вый; (*fastidious*) разбо́рчивый.

futile /ˈfjuːtaɪl/ *adj* тще́тный. **futility** /-ˈtɪlɪtɪ/ *n* тще́тность.

future /ˈfjuːtʃə(r)/ *n* бу́дущее *sb*; (*gram*) бу́дущее вре́мя *neut*; *adj* бу́дущий. **futuristic** /ˌfjuːtʃəˈrɪstɪk/ *adj* футуристи́ческий.

fuzzy /ˈfʌzɪ/ *adj* (*hair*) пуши́стый; (*blurred*) расплы́вчатый.

G

gabble /ˈgæb(ə)l/ *vi* тарато́рить *impf.*

gable /ˈgeɪb(ə)l/ *n* щипе́ц.

gad /gæd/ *vi*: ~ **about** шата́ться *impf.*

gadget /ˈgædʒɪt/ *n* приспособле́ние.

gaffe /gæf/ *n* оплóшность.

gag /gæg/ *n* кляп; *vt* засóвывать *impf*, засу́нуть *pf* кляп в рот+*dat.*

gaiety /ˈgeɪətɪ/ *n* весёлость. **gaily** /ˈgeɪlɪ/ *adv* ве́село.

gain /geɪn/ *n* при́быль; *pl* дохóды *m pl*; (*increase*) прирóст; *vt* (*acquire*) получа́ть *impf*, получи́ть *pf*; ~ **on** нагоня́ть *impf*, нагна́ть *pf.*

gait /geɪt/ *n* похóдка.

gala /ˈgɑːlə/ *n* пра́зднество; *adj* пра́здничный.

galaxy /ˈgæləksɪ/ *n* гала́ктика; (*fig*) плея́да.

gale /geɪl/ *n* бу́ря, шторм.

gall[1] /gɔːl/ *n* (*bile*) жёлчь; (*cheek*) на́глость; ~**-bladder** жёлчный пузы́рь *m.*

gall[2] /gɔːl/ *vt* (*vex*) раздража́ть *impf*, раздражи́ть *pf.*

gallant /ˈgælənt/ *adj* (*brave*) хра́брый; (*courtly*) гала́нтный. **gallantry** /-trɪ/ *n* хра́брость; гала́нтность.

gallery /ˈgælərɪ/ *n* галере́я.

galley /ˈgælɪ/ *n* (*ship*) гале́ра; (*kitchen*) ка́мбуз.

gallon /ˈgælən/ *n* галлóн.

gallop /ˈgæləp/ *n* галóп; *vi* галопи́ровать *impf.*

gallows /ˈgæləʊz/ *n pl* ви́селица.

gallstone /ˈgɔːlstəʊn/ *n* жёлчный ка́мень *m.*

galore /gəˈlɔː(r)/ *adv* в изоби́лии.

galvanize /ˈgælvəˌnaɪz/ *vt* гальванизи́ровать *impf* & *pf.*

gambit /ˈgæmbɪt/ *n* гамби́т.

gamble /ˈgæmb(ə)l/ *n* (*undertaking*) риско́ванное предприя́тие; *vi* игра́ть *impf* в аза́ртные и́гры; (*fig*) рискова́ть *impf* (**with** +*instr*); ~ **away** проигрывать *impf*, проигра́ть *pf.* **gambler** /-blə(r)/ *n* игрóк. **gambling** /-blɪŋ/ *n* аза́ртные и́гры *f pl.*

game /geɪm/ *n* игра́; (*single* ~) па́ртия; (*collect, animals*) дичь; *adj* (*ready*) готóвый. **gamekeeper** /-ˌkiːpə(r)/ *n* лесни́к.

gammon /ˈgæmən/ *n* óкорок.

gamut /ˈgæmət/ *n* га́мма.

gang /gæŋ/ *n* ба́нда; (*workmen*) брига́да.

gangrene /ˈgæŋgriːn/ *n* гангре́на.

gangster /ˈgæŋstə(r)/ *n* га́нгстер.

gangway /ˈgæŋweɪ/ *n* (*passage*) прохóд; (*naut*) схóдни (-ней) *pl.*

gaol /dʒeɪl/ *n* тюрьма́; *vt* заключа́ть *impf*, заключи́ть *pf* в тюрьму́. **gaoler** /-lə(r)/ *n* тюре́мщик.

gap /gæp/ *n* (*empty space; deficiency*) пробе́л; (*in wall etc.*) брешь; (*fig*) разры́в.

gape /geɪp/ *vi* (*person*) зева́ть *impf* (*at* на+*acc*); (*chasm*) зия́ть *impf.*

garage /ˈgærɑːdʒ/ *n* гара́ж.

garb /gɑːb/ *n* одея́ние.

garbage /ˈgɑːbɪdʒ/ *n* му́сор.

garbled /ˈgɑːb(ə)ld/ *adj* искажённый.

garden /ˈgɑːd(ə)n/ *n* сад; *attrib* садóвый. **gardener** /ˈgɑːdnə(r)/ *n* садóвник. **gardening** /ˈgɑːdnɪŋ/ *n* садовóдство.

gargle /ˈgɑːg(ə)l/ *vi* полоска́ть *impf*, про~ *pf* гóрло.

gargoyle /ˈgɑːgɔɪl/ *n* горгу́лья.

garish /ˈgeərɪʃ/ *adj* крича́щий.

garland /ˈgɑːlənd/ *n* гирля́нда.

garlic /ˈgɑːlɪk/ *n* чеснóк.

garment /ˈgɑːmənt/ *n* предме́т оде́жды.

garnish /ˈgɑːnɪʃ/ *n* гарни́р; *vt* гарни́ровать *impf* & *pf.*

garret /ˈgærɪt/ *n* манса́рда.

garrison /ˈgærɪs(ə)n/ *n* гарнизóн.

garrulous /ˈgærʊləs/ *adj* болтли́вый.

gas /gæs/ *n* газ; *attrib* га́зовый; *vt* отравля́ть *impf*, отрави́ть *pf* га́зом. **gaseous** /'gæsɪəs/ *adj* газообра́зный.

gash /gæʃ/ *n* поре́з; *vt* поре́зать *pf*.

gasket /'gæskɪt/ *n* прокла́дка.

gasp /gɑːsp/ *vi* задыха́ться *impf*, задохну́ться *pf*.

gastric /'gæstrɪk/ *adj* желу́дочный.

gate /geɪt/ *n* (*large*) воро́та (-т) *pl*; (*small*) кали́тка. **gateway** *n* (*gate*) воро́та (-т) *pl*; (*entrance*) вход.

gather /'gæðə(r)/ *vt & i* собира́ть(ся) *impf*, собра́ть(ся) *pf*; *vt* заключа́ть *impf*, заключи́ть *pf*. **gathering** /-rɪŋ/ *n* (*assembly*) собра́ние.

gaudy /'gɔːdɪ/ *adj* крича́щий.

gauge /geɪdʒ/ *n* (*measure*) ме́ра; (*instrument*) кали́бр, измери́тельный прибо́р; (*rly*) колея́; (*criterion*) крите́рий; *vt* измеря́ть *impf*, изме́рить *pf*; (*estimate*) оце́нивать *impf*, оцени́ть *pf*.

gaunt /gɔːnt/ *adj* то́щий.

gauntlet /'gɔːntlɪt/ *n* рукави́ца.

gauze /gɔːz/ *n* ма́рля.

gay /geɪ/ *adj* весёлый; (*bright*) пёстрый; (*homosexual*) гомосексуа́льный.

gaze /geɪz/ *n* при́стальный взгляд; *vt* при́стально гляде́ть *impf* (**at** на+*acc*).

gazelle /gə'zel/ *n* газе́ль.

GCSE *abbr* (*of* **General Certificate of Secondary Education**) аттеста́т о сре́днем образова́нии.

gear /gɪə(r)/ *n* (*equipment*) принадле́жности *f pl*; (*in car*) ско́рость; **~ lever** рыча́г; *vt* приспособля́ть *impf*, приспосо́бить *pf* (**to** к+*dat*). **gearbox** *n* коро́бка переда́ч.

gel /dʒel/ *n* космети́ческое желе́ *neut indecl*. **gelatine** /'dʒelə,tiːn/ *n* желати́н.

gelding /'geldɪŋ/ *n* ме́рин.

gelignite /'dʒelɪg,naɪt/ *n* гелигни́т.

gem /dʒem/ *n* драгоце́нный ка́мень *m*.

Gemini /'dʒemɪ,naɪ/ *n* Близнецы́ *m pl*.

gender /'dʒendə(r)/ *n* род.

gene /dʒiːn/ *n* ген.

genealogy /,dʒiːnɪ'ælədʒɪ/ *n* генеало́гия.

general /'dʒenər(ə)l/ *n* генера́л; *adj* о́бщий; (*nationwide*) всео́бщий; **in ~** вообще́. **generalization** /,dʒenərəlaɪ'zeɪʃ(ə)n/ *n* обобще́ние. **generalize** /'dʒenərə,laɪz/ *vi* обобща́ть *impf*, обобщи́ть *pf*. **generally** /'dʒenərəlɪ/ *adv* (*usually*) обы́чно; (*in general*) вообще́.

generate /'dʒenə,reɪt/ *vt* порожда́ть *impf*, породи́ть *pf*. **generation** /-'reɪʃ(ə)n/ *n* (*in descent*) поколе́ние. **generator** /'dʒenə,reɪtə(r)/ *n* генера́тор.

generic /dʒɪ'nerɪk/ *adj* родово́й; (*general*) о́бщий.

generosity /,dʒenə'rɒsɪtɪ/ *n* (*magnanimity*) великоду́шие; (*munificence*) ще́дрость. **generous** /'dʒenərəs/ *adj* великоду́шный; ще́дрый.

genesis /'dʒenɪsɪs/ *n* происхожде́ние; (**G~**) Кни́га Бытия́.

genetic /dʒɪ'netɪk/ *adj* генети́ческий. **genetics** /-tɪks/ *n* гене́тика.

genial /'dʒiːnɪəl/ *adj* (*of person*) доброду́шный.

genital /'dʒenɪt(ə)l/ *adj* полово́й. **genitals** /-t(ə)lz/ *n pl* полов́ые о́рганы *m pl*.

genitive /'dʒenɪtɪv/ *adj* (*n*) роди́тельный (паде́ж).

genius /'dʒiːnɪəs/ *n* (*person*) ге́ний; (*ability*) гениа́льность.

genocide /'dʒenə,saɪd/ *n* геноци́д.

genome /'dʒiːnəʊm/ *n* гено́м.

genre /'ʒɑ̃rə/ *n* жанр.

genteel /dʒen'tiːl/ *adj* благовоспи́танный.

gentile /'dʒentaɪl/ *n* неевре́й, ~ка.

gentility /dʒen'tɪlɪtɪ/ *n* благовоспи́танность.

gentle /'dʒent(ə)l/ *adj* (*mild*) мя́гкий; (*quiet*) ти́хий; (*light*) лёгкий. **gentleman** *n* джентльме́н. **gentleness** /-nɪs/ *n* мя́гкость. **gents** /dʒents/ *n pl* мужска́я убо́рная *sb*.

genuine /'dʒenjʊɪn/ *adj* (*authentic*)

по́длинный; (*sincere*) и́скренний.

genus /'dʒiːnəs/ *n* род.

geographical /ˌdʒiːə'græfɪk(ə)l/ *adj* географи́ческий. **geography** /dʒɪ'ɒgrəfɪ/ *n* геогра́фия. **geological** /ˌdʒiːə'lɒdʒɪk(ə)l/ *adj* геологи́ческий. **geologist** /dʒɪ'ɒlədʒɪst/ *n* гео́лог. **geology** /dʒɪ'ɒlədʒɪ/ *n* геоло́гия. **geometric(al)** /ˌdʒɪə'metrɪk((ə)l)/ *adj* геометри́ческий. **geometry** /dʒɪ'ɒmɪtrɪ/ *n* геоме́трия.

g

Georgia /'dʒɔːdʒɪə/ *n* Гру́зия. **Georgian** /-dʒɪən/ *n* грузи́н, ~ка; *adj* грузи́нский.

geranium /dʒə'reɪnɪəm/ *n* гера́нь.

geriatric /ˌdʒerɪ'ætrɪk/ *adj* гериатри́ческий.

germ /dʒɜːm/ *n* микро́б.

German /'dʒɜːmən/ *n* не́мец, не́мка; *adj* неме́цкий; ~ **measles** красну́ха.

germane /dʒɜː'meɪn/ *adj* уме́стный.

Germanic /dʒɜː'mænɪk/ *adj* герма́нский.

Germany /'dʒɜːmənɪ/ *n* Герма́ния.

germinate /'dʒɜːmɪˌneɪt/ *vi* прораста́ть *impf*, прорасти́ *pf*.

gesticulate /dʒe'stɪkjʊˌleɪt/ *vi* жестикули́ровать *impf*. **gesture** /'dʒestʃə(r)/ *n* жест.

get /get/ *vt* (*obtain*) достава́ть *impf*, доста́ть *pf*; (*receive*) получа́ть *impf*, получи́ть *pf*; (*understand*) понима́ть *impf*, поня́ть *pf*; (*disease*) заража́ться *impf*, зарази́ться *pf* +*instr*; (*induce*) угова́ривать *impf*, уговори́ть *pf* (**to do** +*inf*); (*fetch*) приноси́ть *impf*, принести́ *pf*; *vi* (*become*) станови́ться *impf*, стать *pf* +*instr*; **have got** (*have*) име́ть *impf*; **have got to** быть до́лжен (-жна́) +*inf*; ~ **about** (*spread*) распространя́ться *impf*, распространи́ться *pf*; (*move around*) передвига́ться *impf*; (*travel*) разъезжа́ть *impf*; ~ **at** (*mean*) хоте́ть *impf* сказа́ть; ~ **away** (*slip off*) ускольза́ть *impf*, ускользну́ть *pf*; (*escape*) убега́ть *impf*, убежа́ть *pf*; (*leave*) уезжа́ть *impf*, уе́хать *pf*; ~ **away with** избега́ть *impf*, избежа́ть *pf* отве́тственности за+*acc*; ~ **back** (*recover*) получа́ть *impf*, получи́ть *pf* обра́тно; (*return*) возвраща́ться *impf*, верну́ться *pf*; ~ **by** (*manage*) справля́ться *impf*, спра́виться *pf*; ~ **down** сходи́ть *impf*, сойти́ *pf*; ~ **down to** принима́ться *impf*, приня́ться *pf* за+*acc*; ~ **off** слеза́ть *impf*, слезть *pf* с+*gen*; ~ **on** сади́ться *impf*, сесть *pf* в, на, +*acc*; (*prosper*) преуспева́ть *impf*, преуспе́ть *pf*; ~ **on with** (*person*) ужива́ться *impf*, ужи́ться *pf* с+*instr*; ~ **out of** (*avoid*) избавля́ться *impf*, изба́виться *pf* от+*gen*; (*car*) выходи́ть *impf*, вы́йти *pf* из+*gen*; ~ **round to** успева́ть *impf*, успе́ть *pf*; ~ **to** (*reach*) достига́ть *impf*, дости́гнуть & дости́чь *pf* +*gen*; ~ **up** (*from bed*) встава́ть *impf*, встать *pf*.

geyser /'giːzə(r)/ *n* (*spring*) ге́йзер; (*water-heater*) коло́нка.

ghastly /'gɑːstlɪ/ *adj* ужа́сный.

gherkin /'gɜːkɪn/ *n* огуре́ц.

ghetto /'getəʊ/ *n* ге́тто *neut indecl*.

ghost /gəʊst/ *n* привиде́ние. **ghostly** /-lɪ/ *adj* при́зрачный.

giant /'dʒaɪənt/ *n* гига́нт; *adj* гига́нтский.

gibberish /'dʒɪbərɪʃ/ *n* тараба́рщина.

gibbet /'dʒɪbɪt/ *n* ви́селица.

gibe /dʒaɪb/ *n* насме́шка; *vi* насмеха́ться *impf* (**at** над+*instr*).

giblets /'dʒɪblɪts/ *n pl* потроха́ (-хо́в) *pl*.

giddiness /'gɪdɪnɪs/ *n* головокруже́ние. **giddy** /'gɪdɪ/ *predic*: **I feel** ~ у меня́ кру́жится голова́.

gift /gɪft/ *n* (*present*) пода́рок; (*donation*; *ability*) дар. **gifted** /-tɪd/ *adj* одарённый.

gig /gɪg/ *n* (*theat*) выступле́ние.

gigantic /dʒaɪ'gæntɪk/ *adj* гига́нтский.

giggle /'gɪg(ə)l/ *n* хихи́канье; *vi* хихи́кать *impf*, хихи́кнуть *pf*.

gild /gɪld/ *vt* золоти́ть *impf*, вы́~, по~ *pf*.
gill /gɪl/ *n* (*of fish*) жа́бра.
gilt /gɪlt/ *n* позоло́та; *adj* золочённый.
gimmick /ˈgɪmɪk/ *n* трюк.
gin /dʒɪn/ *n* (*spirit*) джин.
ginger /ˈdʒɪndʒə(r)/ *n* имби́рь *m*; *adj* (*colour*) ры́жий.
gingerly /ˈdʒɪndʒəlɪ/ *adv* осторо́жно.
gipsy /ˈdʒɪpsɪ/ *n* цыга́н, ~ка.
giraffe /dʒɪˈrɑːf/ *n* жира́ф.
girder /ˈgɜːdə(r)/ *n* ба́лка. **girdle** /ˈgɜːd(ə)l/ *n* по́яс.
girl /gɜːl/ *n* (*child*) де́вочка; (*young woman*) де́вушка. **girlfriend** *n* подру́га. **girlish** /-lɪʃ/ *adj* де́вичий.
girth /gɜːθ/ *n* обхва́т; (*on saddle*) подпру́га.
gist /dʒɪst/ *n* суть.
give /gɪv/ *vt* дава́ть *impf*, дать *pf*; **~ away** выдава́ть *impf*, вы́дать *pf*; **~ back** возвраща́ть *impf*, возврати́ть *pf*; **~ in** (*yield*, *vi*) уступа́ть *impf*, уступи́ть *pf* (**to** +*dat*); (*hand in*, *vt*) вруча́ть *impf*, вручи́ть *pf*; **~ out** (*emit*) издава́ть *impf*, изда́ть *pf*; (*distribute*) раздава́ть *impf*, разда́ть *pf*; **~ up** отка́зываться *impf*, отказа́ться *pf* от+*gen*; (*habit etc.*) броса́ть *impf*, бро́сить *pf*; **~ o.s. up** сдава́ться *impf*, сда́ться *pf*. **given** /ˈgɪv(ə)n/ *predic* (*inclined*) скло́нен (-онна́, -о́нно) (**to** к+*dat*).
glacier /ˈglæsɪə(r)/ *n* ледни́к.
glad /glæd/ *adj* ра́достный; *predic* рад. **gladden** /-d(ə)n/ *vt* ра́довать *impf*, об~ *pf*.
glade /gleɪd/ *n* поля́на.
gladly /ˈglædlɪ/ *adv* охо́тно.
glamorous /ˈglæmərəs/ *adj* я́ркий; (*attractive*) привлека́тельный.
glamour /ˈglæmə(r)/ *n* я́ркость; привлека́тельность.
glance /glɑːns/ *n* (*look*) бе́глый взгляд; *vi*: **~ at** взгля́дывать *impf*, взгляну́ть *pf* на+*acc*.
gland /glænd/ *n* железа́. **glandular** /-djʊlə(r)/ *adj* желе́зистый.
glare /gleə(r)/ *n* (*light*) ослепи́тельный блеск; (*look*) свире́пый взгляд; *vi* свире́по смотре́ть *impf* (**at** на+*acc*). **glaring** /-rɪŋ/ *adj* (*dazzling*) ослепи́тельный; (*mistake*) гру́бый.
glasnost /ˈglæznɒst/ *n* гла́сность.
glass /glɑːs/ *n* (*substance*) стекло́; (*drinking vessel*) стака́н; (*wine* ~) рю́мка; (*mirror*) зе́ркало; *pl* (*spectacles*) очки́ (-ко́в) *pl*; *attrib* стекля́нный. **glassy** /-sɪ/ *adj* (*look*) ту́склый.
glaze /gleɪz/ *n* глазу́рь; *vt* (*with glass*) застекля́ть *impf*, застекли́ть *pf*; (*pottery*) глазурова́ть *impf* & *pf*; (*cul*) глази́ровать *impf* & *pf*. **glazier** /-zjə(r)/ *n* стеко́льщик.
gleam /gliːm/ *n* про́блеск; *vi* свети́ться *impf*.
glean /gliːn/ *vt* собира́ть *impf*, собра́ть *pf* по крупи́цам.
glee /gliː/ *n* весе́лье. **gleeful** /-fʊl/ *adj* лику́ющий.
glib /glɪb/ *adj* бо́йкий.
glide /glaɪd/ *vi* скользи́ть *impf*; (*aeron*) плани́ровать *impf*, с~ *pf*. **glider** /-də(r)/ *n* планёр.
glimmer /ˈglɪmə(r)/ *n* мерца́ние; *vi* мерца́ть *impf*.
glimpse /glɪmps/ *vt* мелько́м ви́деть *impf*, у~ *pf*.
glint /glɪnt/ *n* блеск; *vi* блесте́ть *impf*.
glisten, glitter /ˈglɪs(ə)n, ˈglɪtə(r)/ *vi* блесте́ть *impf*.
gloat /gləʊt/ *vi* злора́дствовать *impf*.
global /ˈgləʊb(ə)l/ *adj* (*world-wide*) глоба́льный; (*total*) всео́бщий. **globe** /gləʊb/ *n* (*sphere*) шар; (*the earth*) земно́й шар; (*chart*) гло́бус. **globule** /ˈglɒbjuːl/ *n* ша́рик.
gloom /gluːm/ *n* мрак. **gloomy** /-mɪ/ *adj* мра́чный.
glorify /ˈglɔːrɪˌfaɪ/ *vt* прославля́ть *impf*, просла́вить *pf*. **glorious** /ˈglɔːrɪəs/ *adj* сла́вный; (*splendid*) великоле́пный. **glory** /ˈglɔːrɪ/ *n* сла́ва; *vi* торжествова́ть *impf*.
gloss /glɒs/ *n* лоск; *vi*: **~ over** за-

g

ма́зывать *impf*, зама́зать *pf*.
glossary /'glɒsərɪ/ *n* глосса́рий.
glove /glʌv/ *n* перча́тка.
glow /gləʊ/ *n* за́рево; (*of cheeks*) румя́нец; *vi* (*incandesce*) нака-ля́ться *impf*, накали́ться *pf*; (*shine*) сия́ть *impf*.
glucose /'gluːkəʊs/ *n* глюко́за.
glue /gluː/ *n* клей; *vt* прикле́ивать *impf*, прикле́ить *pf* (**to** к+*dat*).
glum /glʌm/ *adj* угрю́мый.
glut /glʌt/ *n* избы́ток.
g **glutton** /'glʌt(ə)n/ *n* обжо́ра *m & f*. **gluttonous** /-nəs/ *adj* обжо́рливый. **gluttony** /-nɪ/ *n* обжо́рство.
GM *abbr* (*of* **genetically modified**) генети́чески модифици́рованный.
gnarled /nɑːld/ *adj* (*hands*) шишкова́тый; (*tree*) сучкова́тый.
gnash /næʃ/ *vt* скрежета́ть *impf* +*instr*.
gnat /næt/ *n* кома́р.
gnaw /nɔː/ *vt* грызть *impf*.
gnome /nəʊm/ *n* гном.
go /gəʊ/ *n* (*try*) попы́тка; **be on the ~** быть в движе́нии; **have a ~** пыта́ться *impf*, по~ *pf*; *vi* (*on foot*) ходи́ть *indet*, идти́ *det*, пойти́ *pf*; (*by transport*) е́здить *indet*, е́хать *det*, по~ *pf*; (*work*) рабо́тать *impf*; (*become*) станови́ться *impf*, стать *pf* +*instr*; (*belong*) идти́ *impf*; **be ~ing** (*to do*) собира́ться *impf*, собра́ться *pf* (+*inf*); **~ about** (*set to work at*) бра́ться *impf*, взя́ться *pf* за+*acc*; (*wander*) броди́ть *indet*; **~ away** (*on foot*) уходи́ть *impf*, уйти́ *pf*; (*by transport*) уезжа́ть *impf*, уе́хать *pf*; **~ down** спуска́ться *impf*, спусти́ться *pf* (с+*gen*); **~ in(to)** (*enter*) входи́ть *impf*, войти́ *pf* (в+*acc*); (*investigate*) рассле́довать *impf & pf*; **~ off** (*go away*) уходи́ть *impf*, уйти́ *pf*; (*deteriorate*) по́ртиться *impf*, ис~ *pf*; **~ on** (*continue*) продолжа́ть(ся) *impf*, продо́лжить(ся) *pf*; **~ out** выходи́ть *impf*, вы́йти *pf*; (*flame etc.*) га́снуть *impf*, по~ *pf*; **~ over** (*inspect*) пересма́тривать *impf*, пересмотре́ть *pf*; (*rehearse*) повторя́ть *impf*, повтори́ть *pf*; (*change allegiance etc.*) переходи́ть *impf*, перейти́ *pf* (**to** в, на, +*acc*, к+*dat*); **~ through** (*scrutinize*) разбира́ть *impf*, разобра́ть *pf*; **~ through with** доводи́ть *impf*, довести́ *pf* до конца́; **~ without** обходи́ться *impf*, обойти́сь *pf* без+*gen*; **~-ahead** предприи́мчивый; **~-between** посре́дник.
goad /gəʊd/ *vt* (*provoke*) подстрека́ть *impf*, подстрекну́ть *pf* (**into** к+*dat*).
goal /gəʊl/ *n* (*aim*) цель; (*sport*) воро́та (-т) *pl*; (*point won*) гол. **goalkeeper** *n* врата́рь *m*.
goat /gəʊt/ *n* коза́; (*male*) козёл.
gobble /'gɒb(ə)l/ *vt* (*eat*) жрать *impf*; **~ up** пожира́ть *impf*, пожра́ть *pf*.
goblet /'gɒblɪt/ *n* бока́л, ку́бок.
god /gɒd/ *n* бог; (**G~**) Бог. **godchild** *n* кре́стник, -ица. **goddaughter** *n* кре́стница. **goddess** /'gɒdɪs/ *n* боги́ня. **godfather** *n* крёстный *sb*. **God-fearing** /'gɒdfɪərɪŋ/ *adj* богобоя́зненный. **godless** /'gɒdlɪs/ *adj* безбо́жный. **godly** /'gɒdlɪ/ *adj* на́божный. **godmother** *n* крёстная *sb*. **godparent** *n* крёстный *sb*. **godsend** *n* бо́жий дар. **godson** *n* кре́стник.
goggle /'gɒg(ə)l/ *vi* тара́щить *impf* глаза́ (**at** на+*acc*); *n*: *pl* защи́тные очки́ (-ко́в) *pl*.
going /'gəʊɪŋ/ *adj* де́йствующий. **goings-on** /ˌgəʊɪŋ'zɒn/ *n pl* дела́ *neut pl*.
gold /gəʊld/ *n* зо́лото; *adj* золото́й; **~-plated** накладно́го зо́лота; **~-smith** золоты́х дел ма́стер. **golden** /-d(ə)n/ *adj* золото́й; **~ eagle** бе́ркут. **goldfish** *n* золота́я ры́бка.
golf /gɒlf/ *n* гольф; **~ club** (*implement*) клю́шка; **~ course** площа́дка для го́льфа. **golfer** /'gɒlfə(r)/ *n* игро́к в гольф.
gondola /'gɒndələ/ *n* гондо́ла.
gong /gɒŋ/ *n* гонг.

gonorrhoea /ˌɡɒnəˈrɪə/ *n* три́ппер.
good /ɡʊd/ *n* добро́; *pl* (*wares*) това́р(ы); **do ~** (*benefit*) идти́ *impf*, пойти́ *pf* на по́льзу +*dat*; *adj* хоро́ший, до́брый; **~-humoured** доброду́шный; **~-looking** краси́вый; **~ morning** до́брое у́тро!; **~ night** споко́йной но́чи! **goodbye** /ɡʊdˈbaɪ/ *int* проща́й(те)!; до свида́ния! **goodness** /ˈɡʊdnɪs/ *n* доброта́.
goose /ɡuːs/ *n* гусь *m*; **~-flesh** гуси́ная ко́жа.
gooseberry /ˈɡʊzbərɪ/ *n* крыжо́вник
gore[1] /ɡɔː(r)/ *n* (*blood*) запёкшаяся кровь.
gore[2] /ɡɔː(r)/ *vt* (*pierce*) бода́ть *impf*, за~ *pf*.
gorge /ɡɔːdʒ/ *n* (*geog*) уще́лье; *vi* & *t* объеда́ться *impf*, объе́сться *pf* (**on** +*instr*).
gorgeous /ˈɡɔːdʒəs/ *adj* великоле́пный.
gorilla /ɡəˈrɪlə/ *n* гори́лла.
gorse /ɡɔːs/ *n* утёсник.
gory /ˈɡɔːrɪ/ *adj* крова́вый.
gosh /ɡɒʃ/ *int* бо́же мой!
Gospel /ˈɡɒsp(ə)l/ *n* Ева́нгелие.
gossip /ˈɡɒsɪp/ *n* спле́тня; (*person*) спле́тник, -ица; *vi* спле́тничать *impf*, на~ *pf*.
Gothic /ˈɡɒθɪk/ *adj* готи́ческий.
gouge /ɡaʊdʒ/ *vt*: **~ out** выда́лбливать *impf*, вы́долбить *pf*; (*eyes*) выка́лывать *impf*, вы́колоть *pf*.
goulash /ˈɡuːlæʃ/ *n* гуля́ш.
gourmet /ˈɡʊəmeɪ/ *n* гурма́н.
gout /ɡaʊt/ *n* пода́гра.
govern /ˈɡʌv(ə)n/ *vt* пра́вить *impf* +*instr*; (*determine*) определя́ть *impf*, определи́ть *pf*. **governess** /ˈɡʌvənɪs/ *n* гуверна́нтка. **government** /ˈɡʌvənmənt/ *n* прави́тельство. **governmental** /ˌɡʌvənˈment(ə)l/ *adj* прави́тельственный. **governor** /ˈɡʌvənə(r)/ *n* губерна́тор; (*of school etc.*) член правле́ния.
gown /ɡaʊn/ *n* пла́тье; (*official's*) ма́нтия.
grab /ɡræb/ *vt* хвата́ть *impf*, схвати́ть *pf*.
grace /ɡreɪs/ *n* (*gracefulness*) гра́ция; (*refinement*) изя́щество; (*favour*) ми́лость; (*at meal*) моли́тва; **have the ~ to** быть насто́лько такти́чен, что; **with bad ~** нелюбе́зно; **with good ~** с досто́инством; *vt* (*adorn*) украша́ть *impf*, укра́сить *pf*; (*favour*) удоста́ивать *impf*, удосто́ить *pf* (**with** +*gen*). **graceful** /-fʊl/ *adj* грацио́зный.
gracious /ˈɡreɪʃəs/ *adj* ми́лостивый.
gradation /ɡrəˈdeɪʃ(ə)n/ *n* града́ция.
grade /ɡreɪd/ *n* (*level*) сте́пень; (*quality*) сорт; *vt* сортирова́ть *impf*, рас~ *pf*.
gradient /ˈɡreɪdɪənt/ *n* укло́н.
gradual /ˈɡrædjʊəl/ *adj* постепе́нный.
graduate *n* /ˈɡrædjʊət/ око́нчивший *sb* университе́т, вуз; *vi* /ˈɡrædjʊˌeɪt/ конча́ть *impf*, око́нчить *pf* (университе́т, вуз); *vt* градуи́ровать *impf* & *pf*.
graffiti /ɡrəˈfiːtiː/ *n* на́дписи *f pl*.
graft /ɡrɑːft/ *n* (*bot*) черено́к; (*med*) переса́дка (живо́й тка́ни); *vt* (*bot*) привива́ть *impf*, приви́ть *pf* (**to** +*dat*); (*med*) переса́живать *impf*, пересади́ть *pf*.
grain /ɡreɪn/ *n* (*seed*; *collect*) зерно́; (*particle*) крупи́нка; (*of sand*) песчи́нка; (*of wood*) (дре́весное) волокно́; **against the ~** не по нутру́.
gram(me) /ɡræm/ *n* грамм.
grammar /ˈɡræmə(r)/ *n* грамма́тика; **~ school** гимна́зия. **grammatical** /ɡrəˈmætɪk(ə)l/ *adj* граммати́ческий.
gramophone /ˈɡræməˌfəʊn/ *n* прои́грыватель *m*; **~ record** грампласти́нка.
granary /ˈɡrænərɪ/ *n* амба́р.
grand /ɡrænd/ *adj* великоле́пный; **~ piano** роя́ль *m*. **grandchild** *n* внук, вну́чка. **granddaughter** *n* вну́чка. **grandfather** *n* де́душка

g

m. **grandmother** *n* ба́бушка. **grandparents** *n* ба́бушка и де́душка. **grandson** *n* внук. **grandstand** *n* трибу́на.

grandeur /ˈgrændjə(r)/ *n* вели́чие.

grandiose /ˈgrændɪˌəʊs/ *adj* грандио́зный.

granite /ˈgrænɪt/ *n* грани́т.

granny /ˈgrænɪ/ *n* ба́бушка.

grant /grɑːnt/ *n* (*financial*) грант, дота́ция; (*univ*) стипе́ндия; *vt* дарова́ть *impf* & *pf*; (*concede*) допуска́ть *impf*, допусти́ть *pf*; **take for ~ed** (*assume*) счита́ть *impf*, счесть *pf* само́ собо́й разуме́ющимся; (*not appreciate*) принима́ть *impf* как до́лжное.

granular /ˈgrænjʊlə(r)/ *adj* зерни́стый.

granulated /ˈgrænʊˌleɪtɪd/ *adj*: **~ sugar** са́харный песо́к.

granule /ˈgrænjuːl/ *n* зёрнышко.

grape /greɪp/ *n* (*single grape*) вино́гра́дина; *collect* виногра́д. **grapefruit** *n* гре́йпфрут.

graph /grɑːf/ *n* гра́фик.

graphic /ˈgræfɪk/ *adj* графи́ческий; (*vivid*) я́ркий.

graphite /ˈgræfaɪt/ *n* графи́т.

grapple /ˈgræp(ə)l/ *vi* (*struggle*) боро́ться *impf* (**with** с+*instr*).

grasp /grɑːsp/ *n* (*grip*) хва́тка; (*comprehension*) понима́ние; *vt* (*clutch*) хвата́ть *impf*, схвати́ть *pf*; (*comprehend*) понима́ть *impf*, поня́ть *pf*. **grasping** /-spɪŋ/ *adj* жа́дный.

grass /grɑːs/ *n* трава́. **grasshopper** /ˈgrɑːsˌhɒpə(r)/ *n* кузне́чик. **grassy** /ˈgrɑːsɪ/ *adj* травяни́стый.

grate[1] /greɪt/ *n* (*fireplace*) решётка.

grate[2] /greɪt/ *vt* (*rub*) тере́ть *impf*, на~ *pf*; *vi* (*sound*) скрипе́ть *impf*; **~ (up)on** (*irritate*) раздража́ть *impf*, раздражи́ть *pf*.

grateful /ˈgreɪtfʊl/ *n* благода́рный.

grater /ˈgreɪtə(r)/ *n* тёрка.

gratify /ˈgrætɪˌfaɪ/ *vt* удовлетворя́ть *impf*, удовлетвори́ть *pf*.

grating /ˈgreɪtɪŋ/ *n* решётка.

gratis /ˈgrɑːtɪs/ *adv* беспла́тно.

gratitude /ˈgrætɪˌtjuːd/ *n* благода́рность.

gratuitous /grəˈtjuːɪtəs/ *adj* (*free*) даровóй; (*motiveless*) беспричи́нный.

gratuity /grəˈtjuːɪtɪ/ *n* (*tip*) чаевы́е *sb pl*.

grave[1] /greɪv/ *n* моги́ла. **gravedigger** /ˈgreɪvdɪgə(r)/ *n* моги́льщик. **gravestone** *n* надгро́бный ка́мень *m*. **graveyard** *n* кла́дбище.

grave[2] /greɪv/ *adj* серьёзный.

gravel /ˈgræv(ə)l/ *n* гра́вий.

gravitate /ˈgrævɪˌteɪt/ *vi* тяготе́ть *impf* (**towards** к+*dat*). **gravitational** /-ˈteɪʃən(ə)l/ *adj* гравитацио́нный. **gravity** /ˈgrævɪtɪ/ *n* (*seriousness*) серьёзность; (*force*) тя́жесть.

gravy /ˈgreɪvɪ/ *n* (мясна́я) подли́вка.

graze[1] /greɪz/ *vi* (*feed*) пасти́сь *impf*.

graze[2] /greɪz/ *n* (*abrasion*) цара́пина; *vt* (*touch*) задева́ть *impf*, заде́ть *pf*; (*abrade*) цара́пать *impf*, о~ *pf*.

grease /griːs/ *n* жир; (*lubricant*) сма́зка; **~-paint** грим; *vt* сма́зывать *impf*, сма́зать *pf*. **greasy** /-sɪ/ *adj* жи́рный.

great /greɪt/ *adj* (*large*) большо́й; (*eminent*) вели́кий; (*splendid*) замеча́тельный; **to a ~ extent** в большо́й сте́пени; **a ~ deal** мно́го (+*gen*); **a ~ many** мно́гие; **~-aunt** двоюро́дная ба́бушка; **~-granddaughter** пра́внучка; **~-grandfather** пра́дед; **~-grandmother** праба́бка; **~-grandson** пра́внук; **~-uncle** двоюро́дный де́душка *m*. **greatly** /-lɪ/ *adv* о́чень.

Great Britain /greɪt ˈbrɪt(ə)n/ *n* Великобрита́ния.

Greece /griːs/ *n* Гре́ция.

greed /griːd/ *n* жа́дность (**for** к+*dat*). **greedy** /-dɪ/ *adj* жа́дный (**for** к+*dat*).

Greek /griːk/ *n* грек, греча́нка; *adj* гре́ческий.

green /griːn/ *n* (*colour*) зелёный

цвет; (*grassy area*) лужáйка; *pl* зéлень *collect*; *adj* зелёный. **greenery** /-nərɪ/ *n* зéлень. **greenfly** *n* тля. **greengrocer** *n* зеленщи́к. **greengrocer's** *n* овощно́й магази́н. **greenhouse** *n* тепли́ца; ~ **effect** парнико́вый эффéкт.

greet /griːt/ *vt* здоро́ваться *impf*, по~ *pf* с+*instr*; (*meet*) встречáть *impf*, встрéтить *pf*. **greeting** /-tɪŋ/ *n* привéт(ствие).

gregarious /grɪ'geərɪəs/ *adj* общи́тельный.

grenade /grɪ'neɪd/ *n* гранáта.

grey /greɪ/ *adj* сéрый; (*hair*) седо́й.

greyhound /'greɪhaʊnd/ *n* борзáя *sb.*

grid /grɪd/ *n* (*grating*) решётка; (*electr*) сеть; (*map*) координáтная сéтка.

grief /griːf/ *n* го́ре; **come to** ~ терпéть *impf*, по~ *pf* неудáчу.

grievance /'griːv(ə)ns/ *n* жáлоба, оби́да.

grieve /griːv/ *vt* огорчáть *impf*, огорчи́ть *pf*; *vi* горевáть *impf* (**for** о+*prep*).

grievous /'griːvəs/ *adj* тя́жкий.

grill /grɪl/ *n* рáшпер; *vt* (*cook*) жáрить *impf*, за~, из~ *pf* (на рáшпере); (*question*) допрáшивать *impf*, допроси́ть *pf*.

grille /grɪl/ *n* (*grating*) решётка.

grim /grɪm/ *adj* (*stern*) суро́вый; (*unpleasant*) неприя́тный.

grimace /'grɪməs/ *n* гримáса; *vi* гримáсничать *impf*.

grime /graɪm/ *n* грязь. **grimy** /-mɪ/ *adj* гря́зный.

grin /grɪn/ *n* усмéшка; *vi* усмехáться *impf*, усмехну́ться *pf*.

grind /graɪnd/ *vt* (*flour etc.*) моло́ть *impf*, с~ *pf*; (*axe*) точи́ть *impf*, на~ *pf*; ~ **one's teeth** скрежетáть *impf* зубáми.

grip /grɪp/ *n* хвáтка; *vt* схвáтывать *impf*, схвати́ть *pf*.

gripe /graɪp/ *vi* ворчáть *impf*.

gripping /'grɪpɪŋ/ *adj* захвáтывающий.

grisly /'grɪzlɪ/ *adj* жу́ткий.

gristle /'grɪs(ə)l/ *n* хрящ.

grit /grɪt/ *n* песо́к; (*for building*) грáвий; (*firmness*) вы́держка.

grizzle /'grɪz(ə)l/ *vi* хны́кать *impf*.

groan /grəʊn/ *n* стон; *vi* стонáть *impf*.

grocer /'grəʊsə(r)/ *n* бакалéйщик; ~**'s (shop)** бакалéйная лáвка, гастроно́м. **groceries** /-sərɪz/ *n pl* бакалéя *collect*.

groggy /'grɒgɪ/ *adj* разби́тый.

groin /grɔɪn/ *n* (*anat*) пах.

groom /gruːm/ *n* ко́нюх; (*bridegroom*) жени́х; *vt* (*horse*) чи́стить *impf*, по~ *pf*; (*prepare*) гото́вить *impf*, под~ *pf* (**for** к+*dat*); **well-groomed** хорошо́ вы́глядящий.

groove /gruːv/ *n* желобо́к.

grope /grəʊp/ *vi* нащу́пывать *impf* (**for, after** +*acc*).

gross[1] /grəʊs/ *n* (*12 dozen*) гросс.

gross[2] /grəʊs/ *adj* (*fat*) ту́чный; (*coarse*) гру́бый; (*total*) валово́й; ~ **weight** вес бру́тто.

grotesque /grəʊ'tesk/ *adj* гротéскный.

grotto /'grɒtəʊ/ *n* грот.

ground /graʊnd/ *n* земля́; (*earth*) по́чва; *pl* (*dregs*) гу́ща; (*sport*) площáдка; *pl* (*of house*) парк; (*reason*) основáние; ~ **floor** пéрвый этáж; *vt* (*instruct*) обучáть *impf*, обучи́ть *pf* осно́вам (**in** +*gen*); (*aeron*) запрещáть *impf*, запрети́ть *pf* полёты +*gen*; *vi* (*naut*) сади́ться *impf*, сесть *pf* на мель. **groundless** /-lɪs/ *adj* необосно́ванный. **groundwork** *n* фундáмент.

group /gruːp/ *n* гру́ппа; *vt & i* группировáть(ся) *impf*, с~ *pf*.

grouse[1] /graʊs/ *n* шотлáндская куропáтка.

grouse[2] /graʊs/ *vi* (*grumble*) ворчáть *impf*.

grove /grəʊv/ *n* ро́ща.

grovel /'grɒv(ə)l/ *vi* пресмыкáться *impf* (**before** пéред +*instr*).

grow /grəʊ/ *vi* расти́ *impf*; (*become*) станови́ться *impf*, стать *pf* +*instr*; *vt* (*cultivate*) вырáщивать *impf*, вы́растить *pf*; (*hair*) отрá-

g

щивать *impf*, отрасти́ть *pf*; **~ up** (*person*) выраста́ть *impf*, вы́расти *pf*; (*custom*) возника́ть *impf*, возни́кнуть *pf*.

growl /graʊl/ *n* ворча́ние; *vi* ворча́ть *impf* (**at** на+*acc*).

grown-up /grəʊn'ʌp/ *adj* взро́слый *sb*.

growth /grəʊθ/ *n* рост; (*med*) о́пухоль.

grub /grʌb/ *n* (*larva*) личи́нка; (*food*) жратва́; *vi*: **~ about** ры́ться *impf*. **grubby** /'grʌbɪ/ *adj* запа́чканный.

grudge /grʌdʒ/ *n* зло́ба; **have a ~ against** име́ть *impf* зуб про́тив +*gen*; *vt* жале́ть *impf*, по~ *pf* +*acc*, +*gen*. **grudgingly** /-dʒɪŋglɪ/ *adv* неохо́тно.

gruelling /'gru:əlɪŋ/ *adj* изнури́тельный.

gruesome /'gru:səm/ *adj* жу́ткий.

gruff /grʌf/ *adj* (*surly*) грубова́тый; (*voice*) хри́плый.

grumble /'grʌmb(ə)l/ *vi* ворча́ть *impf* (**at** на+*acc*).

grumpy /'grʌmpɪ/ *adj* брюзгли́вый.

grunt /grʌnt/ *n* хрю́канье; *vi* хрю́кать *impf*, хрю́кнуть *pf*.

guarantee /ˌgærən'ti:/ *n* гара́нтия; *vt* гаранти́ровать *impf* & *pf* (**against** от+*gen*). **guarantor** /-'tɔ:(r)/ *n* поручи́тель *m*.

guard /gɑ:d/ *n* (*device*) предохрани́тель; (*watch*; *soldiers*) карау́л; (*sentry*) часово́й *sb*; (*watchman*) сто́рож; (*rly*) конду́ктор; *pl* (*prison*) надзира́тель *m*; *vt* охраня́ть *impf*, охрани́ть *pf*; *vi*: **~ against** остерега́ться *impf*, остере́чься *pf* +*gen*, *inf*.

guardian /'gɑ:dɪən/ *n* храни́тель *m*; (*law*) опеку́н.

guer(r)illa /gə'rɪlə/ *n* партиза́н; **~ warfare** партиза́нская война́.

guess /ges/ *n* дога́дка; *vt* & *i* дога́дываться *impf*, догада́ться *pf* (о+*prep*); *vt* (**~** *correctly*) уга́дывать *impf*, угада́ть *pf*. **guesswork** *n* дога́дки *f pl*.

guest /gest/ *n* гость *m*; **~ house** ма́ленькая гости́ница.

guffaw /gʌ'fɔ:/ *n* хо́хот; *vi* хохота́ть *impf*.

guidance /'gaɪd(ə)ns/ *n* руково́дство. **guide** /gaɪd/ *n* проводни́к, гид; (*guidebook*) путеводи́тель *m*; *vt* води́ть *indet*, вести́ *det*; (*direct*) руководи́ть *impf* +*instr*; **~d missile** управля́емая раке́та. **guidelines** *n pl* инстру́кции *f pl*; (*advice*) сове́т.

guild /gɪld/ *n* ги́льдия, цех.

guile /gaɪl/ *n* кова́рство. **guileless** /-lɪs/ *adj* простоду́шный.

guillotine /'gɪləˌti:n/ *n* гильоти́на.

guilt /gɪlt/ *n* вина́; (*guiltiness*) вино́вность. **guilty** /-tɪ/ *adj* (*of crime*) вино́вный (**of** в+*prep*); (*of wrong*) винова́тый.

guinea-pig /'gɪnɪpɪg/ *n* морска́я сви́нка; (*fig*) подо́пытный кро́лик.

guise /gaɪz/ *n*: **under the ~ of** под ви́дом+*gen*.

guitar /gɪ'tɑ:(r)/ *n* гита́ра. **guitarist** /-rɪst/ *n* гитари́ст.

gulf /gʌlf/ *n* (*geog*) зали́в; (*chasm*) про́пасть.

gull /gʌl/ *n* ча́йка.

gullet /'gʌlɪt/ *n* (*oesophagus*) пищево́д; (*throat*) го́рло.

gullible /'gʌlɪb(ə)l/ *adj* легкове́рный.

gully /'gʌlɪ/ *n* (*ravine*) овра́г.

gulp /gʌlp/ *n* глото́к; *vt* жа́дно глота́ть *impf*.

gum¹ /gʌm/ *n* (*anat*) десна́.

gum² /gʌm/ *n* каме́дь; (*glue*) клей; *vt* скле́ивать *impf*, скле́ить *pf*.

gumption /'gʌmpʃ(ə)n/ *n* инициати́ва.

gun /gʌn/ *n* (*piece of ordnance*) ору́дие, пу́шка; (*rifle etc.*) ружьё; (*pistol*) пистоле́т; *vt*: **~ down** расстре́ливать *impf*, расстреля́ть *pf*. **gunner** /-nə(r)/ *n* артиллери́ст. **gunpowder** *n* по́рох.

gurgle /'gɜ:g(ə)l/ *vi* бу́лькать *impf*.

gush /gʌʃ/ *vi* хлы́нуть *pf*.

gusset /'gʌsɪt/ *n* клин.

gust /gʌst/ *n* поры́в. **gusty** /-stɪ/ *adj* поры́вистый.

gusto /ˈgʌstəʊ/ *n* смак.
gut /gʌt/ *n* кишка́; *pl* (*entrails*) кишки́ *f pl*; *pl* (*bravery*) му́жество; *vt* потроши́ть *impf*, вы́~ *pf*; (*devastate*) опустоша́ть *impf*, опустоши́ть *pf*.
gutter /ˈgʌtə(r)/ *n* (*of roof*) (водосто́чный) жёлоб; (*of road*) сто́чная кана́ва.
guttural /ˈgʌtər(ə)l/ *adj* горта́нный.
guy[1] /gaɪ/ *n* (*rope*) оття́жка.
guy[2] /gaɪ/ *n* (*fellow*) па́рень *m*.
guzzle /ˈgʌz(ə)l/ *vt* (*food*) пожира́ть *impf*, пожра́ть *pf*; (*liquid*) хлеба́ть *impf*, хлебну́ть *pf*.
gym /dʒɪm/ *n* (*gymnasium*) гимнасти́ческий зал; (*gymnastics*) гимна́стика. **gymnasium** /dʒɪmˈneɪzɪəm/ *n* гимнасти́ческий зал. **gymnast** /ˈdʒɪmnæst/ *n* гимна́ст. **gymnastic** /dʒɪmˈnæstɪk/ *adj* гимнасти́ческий. **gymnastics** /dʒɪmˈnæstɪks/ *n* гимна́стика.
gynaecologist /ˌgaɪnɪˈkɒlədʒɪst/ *n* гинеко́лог. **gynaecology** /-dʒɪ/ *n* гинеколо́гия.
gyrate /ˌdʒaɪˈreɪt/ *vi* враща́ться *impf*.

H

haberdashery /ˈhæbəˌdæʃərɪ/ *n* галантере́я; (*shop*) галантере́йный магази́н.
habit /ˈhæbɪt/ *n* привы́чка; (*monk's*) ря́са.
habitable /ˈhæbɪtəb(ə)l/ *adj* приго́дный для жилья́. **habitat** /-tæt/ *n* есте́ственная среда́. **habitation** /-ˈteɪʃ(ə)n/ *n*: **unfit for ~** неприго́дный для жилья́.
habitual /həˈbɪtjʊəl/ *adj* привы́чный.
hack[1] /hæk/ *vt* руби́ть *impf*; **~saw** ножо́вка.
hack[2] /hæk/ *n* (*hired horse*) наёмная ло́шадь; (*writer*) халту́рщик. **hackneyed** /ˈhæknɪd/ *adj* изби́тый.
haddock /ˈhædək/ *n* пи́кша.
haemophilia /ˌhiːməˈfɪlɪə/ *n* гемофили́я. **haemorrhage** /ˈhemərɪdʒ/ *n* кровотече́ние. **haemorrhoids** /ˈheməˌrɔɪdz/ *n pl* геморро́й *collect*.
hag /hæg/ *n* карга́.
haggard /ˈhægəd/ *adj* измождённый.
haggle /ˈhæg(ə)l/ *vi* торгова́ться *impf*, с~ *pf*.
hail[1] /heɪl/ *n* град; *vi* **it is ~ing** идёт град. **hailstone** *n* гра́дина.
hail[2] /heɪl/ *vt* (*greet*) приве́тствовать *impf* (& *pf in past*); (*taxi*) подзыва́ть *impf*, подозва́ть *pf*.
hair /heə(r)/ *n* (*single ~*) во́лос; *collect* (*human*) во́лосы (-о́с, -оса́м) *pl*; (*animal*) шерсть. **hairbrush** *n* щётка для воло́с. **haircut** *n* стри́жка; **have a ~** постри́чься *pf*. **hair-do** /ˈheəduː/ *n* причёска. **hairdresser** /ˈheəˌdresə(r)/ *n* парикма́хер. **hairdresser's** /ˈheəˌdresəz/ *n* парикма́херская *sb*. **hair-dryer** /ˈheəˌdraɪə(r)/ *n* фен. **hairstyle** *n* причёска. **hairy** /ˈheərɪ/ *adj* волоса́тый.
hale /heɪl/ *adj*: **~ and hearty** здоро́вый и бо́дрый.
half /hɑːf/ *n* полови́на; (*sport*) тайм; *adj* полови́нный; **in ~** попола́м; **one and a ~** полтора́; **~ past** (*one etc.*) полови́на (второ́го и т.д.); **~-hearted** равноду́шный; **~ an hour** полчаса́; **~-time** переры́в ме́жду та́ймами; **~way** на полпути́; **~-witted** слабоу́мный.
hall /hɔːl/ *n* (*large room*) зал; (*entrance ~*) холл, вестибю́ль *m*; (*~ of residence*) общежи́тие. **hallmark** *n* пробирное клеймо́; (*fig*) при́знак.
hallo /həˈləʊ/ *int* здра́вствуй(те), приве́т; (*on telephone*) алло́.
hallucination /həˌluːsɪˈneɪʃ(ə)n/ *n* галлюцина́ция.
halo /ˈheɪləʊ/ *n* (*around Saint*) нимб.
halt /hɒlt/ *n* остано́вка; *vt* & *i* остана́вливать(ся) *impf*, остано-

ви́ть(ся) *pf*; *int* (*mil*) стой(те)!
halting /-tɪŋ/ *adj* запина́ющий.
halve /hɑːv/ *vt* дели́ть *impf*, раз~ *pf* попола́м.
ham /hæm/ *n* (*cul*) ветчина́.
hamburger /'hæm,bɜːgə(r)/ *n* котле́та.
hamlet /'hæmlɪt/ *n* дереву́шка.
hammer /'hæmə(r)/ *n* молото́к; *vt* бить *impf* молотко́м.
hammock /'hæmək/ *n* гама́к.
hamper[1] /'hæmpə(r)/ *n* (*basket*) корзи́на с кры́шкой.
hamper[2] /'hæmpə(r)/ *vt* (*hinder*) меша́ть *impf*, по~ *pf* +*dat*.
hamster /'hæmstə(r)/ *n* хомя́к.
hand /hænd/ *n* рука́; (*worker*) рабо́чий *sb*; (*writing*) по́черк; (*clock* ~) стре́лка; **at ~** под руко́й; **on ~s and knees** на четвере́ньках; *vt* передава́ть *impf*, переда́ть *pf*; **~ in** подава́ть *impf*, пода́ть *pf*; **~ out** раздава́ть *impf*, разда́ть *pf*. **handbag** *n* су́мка. **handbook** *n* руково́дство. **handcuffs** /-kʌfs/ *n pl* нару́чники *m pl*. **handful** /-fʊl/ *n* горсть.
handicap /'hændɪ,kæp/ *n* (*sport*) гандика́п; (*hindrance*) поме́ха. **handicapped** /-,kæpt/ *adj*: **~ person** инвали́д.
handicraft /'hændɪ,krɑːft/ *n* ремесло́.
handiwork /'hændɪ,wɜːk/ *n* ручна́я рабо́та.
handkerchief /'hæŋkə,tʃiːf/ *n* носово́й плато́к.
handle /'hænd(ə)l/ *n* ру́чка, рукоя́тка; *vt* (*people*) обраща́ться *impf* с+*instr*; (*situations*) справля́ться *impf*, спра́виться *pf* с+*instr*; (*touch*) тро́гать *impf*, тро́нуть *pf* руко́й, рука́ми. **handlebar(s)** /'hændəl,bɑːz/ *n* руль *m*.
handmade /'hændmeɪd/ *adj* ручно́й рабо́ты.
handout /'hændaʊt/ *n* пода́чка; (*document*) лифле́т.
handrail /'hændreɪl/ *n* пери́ла (-л) *pl*.
handshake /'hændʃeɪk/ *n* рукопожа́тие.
handsome /'hænsəm/ *adj* краси́вый; (*generous*) ще́дрый.
handwriting /'hænd,raɪtɪŋ/ *n* по́черк.
handy /'hændɪ/ *adj* (*convenient*) удо́бный; (*skilful*) ло́вкий; **come in ~** пригоди́ться *pf*.
hang /hæŋ/ *vt* ве́шать *impf*, пове́сить *pf*; *vi* висе́ть *impf*; **~ about** слоня́ться *impf*; **~ on** (*cling*) держа́ться *impf*; (*tel*) не ве́шать *impf* тру́бку; (*persist*) упо́рствовать *impf*; **~ out** выве́шивать *impf*, вы́весить *pf*; (*spend time*) болта́ться *impf*; **~ up** ве́шать *impf*, пове́сить *pf*; (*tel*) ве́шать *impf*, пове́сить *pf* тру́бку. **hanger** /'hæŋə(r)/ *n* ве́шалка. **hanger-on** /,hæŋə'rɒn/ *n* прилипа́ла *m* & *f*. **hangman** *n* пала́ч.
hangar /'hæŋə(r)/ *n* анга́р.
hangover /'hæŋəʊvə(r)/ *n* похме́лье.
hang-up /'hæŋʌp/ *n* ко́мплекс.
hanker /'hæŋkə(r)/ *vi*: **~ after** мечта́ть *impf* о+*prep*.
haphazard /hæp'hæzəd/ *adj* случа́йный.
happen /'hæpən/ *vi* (*occur*) случа́ться *impf*, случи́ться *pf*; происходи́ть *impf*, произойти́ *pf*; **~ upon** ната́лкиваться *impf*, натолкну́ться *pf* на+*acc*.
happiness /'hæpɪnɪs/ *n* сча́стье. **happy** /'hæpɪ/ *adj* счастли́вый; **~-go-lucky** беззабо́тный.
harass /'hærəs/ *vt* (*pester*) дёргать *impf*; (*persecute*) пресле́довать *impf*. **harassment** /-mənt/ *n* тра́вля; пресле́дование.
harbinger /'hɑːbɪndʒə(r)/ *n* предве́стник.
harbour /'hɑːbə(r)/ *n* га́вань, порт; *vt* (*person*) укрыва́ть *impf*, укры́ть *pf*; (*thoughts*) зата́ивать *impf*, затаи́ть *pf*.
hard /hɑːd/ *adj* твёрдый; (*difficult*) тру́дный; (*difficult to bear*) тяжёлый; (*severe*) суро́вый; *adv* (*work*) мно́го; (*hit*) си́льно; (*try*)

о́чень; **~-boiled egg** яйцо́ вкруту́ю; **~ disk** (*comput*) жёсткий диск; **~-headed** практи́чный; **~-hearted** жестокосе́рдный; **~-up** стеснённый в сре́дствах; **~-working** трудолюби́вый. **hardboard** *n* строи́тельный карто́н.

harden /'hɑːd(ə)n/ *vi* затвердева́ть *impf*, затверде́ть *pf*; (*fig*) ожесточа́ться *impf*, ожесточи́ться *pf.*

hardly /'hɑːdlɪ/ *adv* едва́ (ли).

hardship /'hɑːdʃɪp/ *n* (*privation*) нужда́.

hardware /'hɑːdweə(r)/ *n* скобяны́е изде́лия *neut pl*; (*comput*) аппарату́ра.

hardy /'hɑːdɪ/ *adj* (*robust*) выно́сливый; (*plant*) морозосто́йкий.

hare /heə(r)/ *n* за́яц.

hark /hɑːk/ *vi*: **~ back to** возвраща́ться *impf*, верну́ться *pf* к+*dat*; *int* слу́шай(те)!

harm /hɑːm/ *n* вред; *vt* вреди́ть *impf*, по~ *pf* +*dat*. **harmful** /-fʊl/ *adj* вре́дный. **harmless** /-lɪs/ *adj* безвре́дный.

harmonic /hɑː'mɒnɪk/ *adj* гармони́ческий. **harmonica** /-'mɒnɪkə/ *n* губна́я гармо́ника. **harmonious** /-'məʊnɪəs/ *adj* гармони́чный. **harmonize** /'hɑːməˌnaɪz/ *vi* гармони́ровать *impf* (**with** с+*instr*). **harmony** /'hɑːmənɪ/ *n* гармо́ния.

harness /'hɑːnɪs/ *n* у́пряжь; *vt* запряга́ть *impf*, запря́чь *pf*; (*fig*) испо́льзовать *impf* & *pf*.

harp /hɑːp/ *n* а́рфа; *vi*: **~ on** тверди́ть *impf* о+*prep*.

harpoon /hɑː'puːn/ *n* гарпу́н.

harpsichord /'hɑːpsɪˌkɔːd/ *n* клавеси́н.

harrowing /'hærəʊɪŋ/ *adj* душераздира́ющий.

harsh /hɑːʃ/ *adj* (*sound, colour*) ре́зкий; (*cruel*) суро́вый.

harvest /'hɑːvɪst/ *n* жа́тва, сбор (плодо́в); (*yield*) урожа́й; (*fig*) плоды́ *m pl*; *vt & abs* собира́ть *impf*, собра́ть *pf* (урожа́й).

hash /hæʃ/ *n*: **make a ~ of** напу́тать *pf* +*acc*, в+*prep*.

hashish /'hæʃiːʃ/ *n* гаши́ш.

hassle /'hæs(ə)l/ *n* беспоко́йство.

hassock /'hæsək/ *n* поду́шечка.

haste /heɪst/ *n* спе́шка. **hasten** /'heɪs(ə)n/ *vi* спеши́ть *impf*, по~ *pf*; *vt & i* торопи́ть(ся) *impf*, по~ *pf*; *vt* ускоря́ть *impf*, уско́рить *pf*. **hasty** /'heɪstɪ/ *adj* (*hurried*) поспе́шный; (*quick-tempered*) вспы́льчивый.

hat /hæt/ *n* ша́пка; (*stylish*) шля́па.

hatch[1] /hætʃ/ *n* люк; **~-back** маши́на-пика́п.

hatch[2] /hætʃ/ *vi* вылу́пливаться, вылупля́ться *impf*, вы́лупиться *pf*.

hatchet /'hætʃɪt/ *n* топо́рик.

hate /heɪt/ *n* не́нависть; *vt* ненави́деть *impf*. **hateful** /-fʊl/ *adj* ненави́стный. **hatred** /-trɪd/ *n* не́нависть.

haughty /'hɔːtɪ/ *adj* надме́нный.

haul /hɔːl/ *n* (*fish*) уло́в; (*loot*) добы́ча; (*distance*) езда́; *vt* (*drag*) тяну́ть *impf*; таска́ть *indet*, тащи́ть *det*. **haulage** /-lɪdʒ/ *n* перево́зка.

haunt /hɔːnt/ *n* люби́мое ме́сто; *vt* (*ghost*) обита́ть *impf*; (*memory*) пресле́довать *impf*. **haunted** /-tɪd/ *adj*: **~ house** дом с привиде́ниями. **haunting** /-tɪŋ/ *adj* навя́зчивый.

have /hæv/ *vt* име́ть *impf*; **I ~** (*possess*) у меня́ (есть; был, -а́, -о) +*nom*; **I ~ not** у меня́ нет (*past* не́ было) +*gen*; **I ~ (got) to** я до́лжен +*inf*; **you had better** вам лу́чше бы +*inf*; **~ on** (*wear*) быть оде́тым в +*prep*; (*be engaged in*) быть за́нятым +*instr*.

haven /'heɪv(ə)n/ *n* (*refuge*) убе́жище.

haversack /'hævəˌsæk/ *n* рюкза́к.

havoc /'hævək/ *n* (*devastation*) опустоше́ние; (*disorder*) беспоря́док.

hawk[1] /hɔːk/ *n* (*bird*) я́стреб.

hawk[2] /hɔːk/ *vt* (*trade*) торгова́ть *impf* вразно́с+*instr*. **hawker** /-kə(r)/ *n* разно́счик.

hawser /'hɔːzə(r)/ *n* трос.

hawthorn /ˈhɔːθɔːn/ *n* боя́рышник.
hay /heɪ/ *n* се́но; **make ~** коси́ть *impf*, c~ *pf* се́но; **~ fever** се́нная лихора́дка. **haystack** *n* стог.
hazard /ˈhæzəd/ *n* риск; *vt* рискова́ть *impf* +*instr*. **hazardous** /-dəs/ *adj* риско́ванный.
haze /heɪz/ *n* ды́мка.
hazel /ˈheɪz(ə)l/ *n* лещи́на. **hazelnut** *n* лесно́й оре́х.
hazy /ˈheɪzɪ/ *adj* тума́нный; (*vague*) сму́тный.
he /hiː/ *pron* он.
head /hed/ *n* голова́; (*mind*) ум; (*~ of coin*) лицева́я сторона́ моне́ты; **~s or tails?** орёл и́ли ре́шка?; (*chief*) глава́ *m*, нача́льник; *attrib* гла́вный; *vt* (*lead*) возглавля́ть *impf*, возгла́вить *pf*; (*ball*) забива́ть *impf*, заби́ть *pf* голово́й; *vi*: **~ for** направля́ться *impf*, напра́виться *pf* в, на, +*acc*, к+*dat*. **headache** *n* головна́я боль. **head-dress** *n* головно́й убо́р. **header** /-də(r)/ *n* уда́р голово́й. **heading** /-dɪŋ/ *n* (*title*) заголо́вок. **headland** *n* мыс. **headlight** *n* фа́ра. **headline** *n* заголо́вок. **headlong** *adv* стремгла́в. **headmaster, -mistress** *n* дире́ктор шко́лы. **head-on** *adj* голово́й; *adv* в лоб. **headphone** *n* нау́шник. **headquarters** *n* штаб-кварти́ра. **headscarf** *n* косы́нка. **headstone** *n* надгро́бный ка́мень *m*. **headstrong** *adj* своево́льный. **headway** *n* движе́ние вперёд. **heady** /-dɪ/ *adj* опьяня́ющий.
heal /hiːl/ *vt* излечи́вать *impf*, излечи́ть *pf*; *vi* зажива́ть *impf*, зажи́ть *pf*. **healing**/ -lɪŋ/ *adj* целе́бный.
health /helθ/ *n* здоро́вье; **~ care** здравохране́ние. **healthy** /-θɪ/ *adj* здоро́вый; (*beneficial*) поле́зный.
heap /hiːp/ *n* ку́ча; *vt* нагромажда́ть *impf*, нагромозди́ть *pf*.
hear /hɪə(r)/ *vt* слы́шать *impf*, у~ *pf*; (*listen to*) слу́шать *impf*, по~ *pf*; **~ out** выслу́шивать *impf*, вы́слушать *pf*. **hearing** /-rɪŋ/ *n* слух; (*law*) слу́шание. **hearsay** *n* слух.
hearse /hɜːs/ *n* катафа́лк.
heart /hɑːt/ *n* се́рдце; (*essence*) суть; *pl* (*cards*) че́рви (-ве́й) *pl*; **by ~** наизу́сть; **~ attack** серде́чный при́ступ. **heartburn** *n* изжо́га. **hearten** /-t(ə)n/ *vt* ободря́ть *impf*, ободри́ть *pf*. **heartfelt** *adj* серде́чный. **heartless** /-lɪs/ *adj* бессерде́чный. **heart-rending** /-ˌrendɪŋ/ *adj* душераздира́ющий. **hearty** /-tɪ/ *adj* (*cordial*) серде́чный; (*vigorous*) здоро́вый.
hearth /hɑːθ/ *n* оча́г.
heat /hiːt/ *n* жара́; (*phys*) теплота́; (*of feeling*) пыл; (*sport*) забе́г, заёзд; *vt & i* (*heat up*) нагрева́ть(ся) *impf*, нагре́ть(ся) *pf*; *vt* (*house*) топи́ть *impf*. **heater** /-tə(r)/ *n* нагрева́тель *m*. **heating** /-tɪŋ/ *n* отопле́ние.
heath /hiːθ/ *n* пу́стошь.
heathen /ˈhiːð(ə)n/ *n* язы́чник; *adj* язы́ческий.
heather /ˈheðə(r)/ *n* ве́реск.
heave /hiːv/ *vt* (*lift*) поднима́ть *impf*, подня́ть *pf*; (*pull*) тяну́ть *impf*, по~ *pf*.
heaven /ˈhev(ə)n/ *n* (*sky*) не́бо; (*paradise*) рай; *pl* небеса́ *neut pl*. **heavenly** /-lɪ/ *adj* небе́сный; (*divine*) боже́ственный.
heavy /ˈhevɪ/ *adj* тяжёлый; (*strong, intense*) си́льный. **heavyweight** *n* тяжелове́с.
Hebrew /ˈhiːbruː/ *adj* (древне)евре́йский.
heckle /ˈhek(ə)l/ *vt* препека́ться *impf* с+*instr*.
hectic /ˈhektɪk/ *adj* лихора́дочный.
hedge /hedʒ/ *n* жива́я и́згородь. **hedgerow** *n* шпале́ра.
hedgehog /ˈhedʒhɒg/ *n* ёж.
heed /hiːd/ *vt* обраща́ть *impf*, обрати́ть *pf* внима́ние на+*acc*. **heedless** /-lɪs/ *adj* небре́жный.
heel[1] /hiːl/ *n* (*of foot*) пята́; (*of foot, sock*) пя́тка; (*of shoe*) каблу́к.

heel² /hi:l/ *vi* крени́ться *impf*, на~ *pf*.
hefty /ˈheftɪ/ *adj* дю́жий.
heifer /ˈhefə(r)/ *n* тёлка.
height /haɪt/ *n* высота́; (*of person*) рост. **heighten** /-t(ə)n/ *vt* (*strengthen*) уси́ливать *impf*, уси́лить *pf*.
heinous /ˈheɪnəs/ *adj* гну́сный.
heir /eə(r)/ *n* насле́дник. **heiress** /ˈeərɪs/ *n* насле́дница. **heirloom** /ˈeəlu:m/ *n* фами́льная вещь.
helicopter /ˈhelɪˌkɒptə(r)/ *n* вертолёт.
helium /ˈhi:lɪəm/ *n* ге́лий.
hell /hel/ *n* ад. **hellish** /-lɪʃ/ *adj* а́дский.
hello /həˈləʊ/ *see* **hallo**
helm /helm/ *n* руль.
helmet /ˈhelmɪt/ *n* шлем.
help /help/ *n* по́мощь; *vt* помога́ть *impf*, помо́чь *pf* +*dat*; (*can't* ~) не мочь *impf* не +*inf*; ~ **o.s.** брать *impf*, взять *pf* себе́; ~ **yourself!** бери́те! **helpful** /-fʊl/ *adj* поле́зный; (*obliging*) услу́жливый. **helping** /-pɪŋ/ *n* (*of food*) по́рция. **helpless** /-lɪs/ *adj* беспо́мощный.
helter-skelter /ˌheltəˈskeltə(r)/ *adv* как попа́ло.
hem /hem/ *n* рубе́ц; *vt* подруба́ть *impf*, подруби́ть *pf*; ~ **in** окружа́ть *impf*, окружи́ть *pf*.
hemisphere /ˈhemɪˌsfɪə(r)/ *n* полуша́рие.
hemp /hemp/ *n* (*plant*) конопля́; (*fibre*) пенька́.
hen /hen/ *n* (*female bird*) са́мка; (*domestic fowl*) ку́рица.
hence /hens/ *adv* (*from here*) отсю́да; (*as a result*) сле́довательно; **3 years** ~ че́рез три го́да. **henceforth** /-ˈfɔ:θ/ *adv* отны́не.
henchman /ˈhentʃmən/ *n* присп́ешник.
henna /ˈhenə/ *n* хна.
hepatitis /ˌhepəˈtaɪtɪs/ *n* гепати́т.
her /hɜ:(r)/ *poss pron* её; свой.
herald /ˈher(ə)ld/ *n* ве́стник; *vt* возвеща́ть *impf*, возвести́ть *pf*.
herb /hɜ:b/ *n* трава́. **herbaceous** /hɜ:ˈbeɪʃ(ə)s/ *adj* травяно́й; ~ **border** цвето́чный бордю́р. **herbal** /ˈhɜ:b(ə)l/ *adj* травяно́й.
herd /hɜ:d/ *n* ста́до; (*people*) толпи́ться *impf*, с~ *pf*; *vt* (*tend*) пасти́ *impf*; (*drive*) загоня́ть *impf*, загна́ть *pf* в ста́до.
here /hɪə(r)/ *adv* (*position*) здесь, тут; (*direction*) сюда́; ~ **is ...** вот (+*nom*); ~ **and there** там и сям; ~ **you are!** пожа́луйста. **hereabout(s)** /ˌhɪərəˈbaʊts/ *adv* побли́зости. **hereafter** /ˌhɪərˈɑ:ftə(r)/ *adv* в бу́дущем. **hereby** /ˌhɪəˈbaɪ/ *adv* э́тим. **hereupon** /ˌhɪərəˈpɒn/ *adv* (*in consequence*) вследствие э́того; (*after*) по́сле э́того. **herewith** /hɪəˈwɪð/ *adv* при сём.
hereditary /hɪˈredɪtərɪ/ *adj* насле́дственный. **heredity** /-ˈredɪtɪ/ *n* насле́дственность.
heresy /ˈherəsɪ/ *n* е́ресь. **heretic** /ˈherətɪk/ *n* ерети́к. **heretical** /hɪˈretɪk(ə)l/ *adj* ерети́ческий.
heritage /ˈherɪtɪdʒ/ *n* насле́дие.
hermetic /hɜ:ˈmetɪk/ *adj* гермети́ческий.
hermit /ˈhɜ:mɪt/ *n* отше́льник.
hernia /ˈhɜ:nɪə/ *n* гры́жа.
hero /ˈhɪərəʊ/ *n* геро́й. **heroic** /hɪˈrəʊɪk/ *adj* герои́ческий.
heroin /ˈherəʊɪn/ *n* герои́н.
heroine /ˈherəʊɪn/ *n* герои́ня. **heroism** /ˈherəʊɪz(ə)m/ *n* герои́зм.
heron /ˈherən/ *n* ца́пля.
herpes /ˈhɜ:pi:z/ *n* лиша́й.
herring /ˈherɪŋ/ *n* сельдь; (*food*) селёдка.
hers /hɜ:z/ *poss pron* её; свой.
herself /həˈself/ *pron* (*emph*) (она́) сама́; (*refl*) себя́.
hertz /hɜ:ts/ *n* герц.
hesitant /ˈhezɪt(ə)nt/ *adj* нереши́тельный. **hesitate** /-ˌteɪt/ *vi* колеба́ться *impf*, по~ *pf*; (*in speech*) запина́ться *impf*, запну́ться *pf*. **hesitation** /-ˈteɪʃ(ə)n/ *n* колеба́ние.
hessian /ˈhesɪən/ *n* мешкови́на.
heterogeneous /ˌhetərəʊˈdʒi:nɪəs/

h

adj разноро́дный.
heterosexual /ˌhetərəʊˈseksjʊəl/ *adj* гетеросексуа́льный.
hew /hjuː/ *vt* руби́ть *impf.*
hexagon /ˈheksəgən/ *n* шестиуго́льник.
hey /heɪ/ *int* эй!
heyday /ˈheɪdeɪ/ *n* расцве́т.
hi /haɪ/ *int* приве́т!
hiatus /haɪˈeɪtəs/ *n* пробе́л.
hibernate /ˈhaɪbəˌneɪt/ *vi* быть *impf* в спя́чке; впада́ть *impf*, впасть *pf* в спя́чку. **hibernation** /-ˈneɪʃ(ə)n/ *n* спя́чка.
hiccup /ˈhɪkʌp/ *vi* ика́ть *impf*, икну́ть *pf*; *n*: *pl* ико́та.
hide[1] /haɪd/ *n* (*skin*) шку́ра.
hide[2] /ˈhɪd(ə)n/ *vt & i* (*conceal*) пря́тать(ся) *impf*, с~ *pf*; скрыва́ть(ся) *impf*, скры́ть(ся) *pf.*
hideous /ˈhɪdɪəs/ *adj* отврати́тельный.
hideout /ˈhaɪdaʊt/ *n* укры́тие.
hiding /ˈhaɪdɪŋ/ *n* (*flogging*) по́рка.
hierarchy /ˈhaɪəˌrɑːkɪ/ *n* иера́рхия.
hieroglyphics /ˌhaɪərəˈglɪfɪks/ *n pl* иеро́глифы *m pl.*
hi-fi /ˈhaɪfaɪ/ *n* проигрыватель *m* с высокока́чественным воспроизведе́нием зву́ка за́писи.
higgledy-piggledy /ˌhɪgəldɪˈpɪgəldɪ/ *adv* как придётся.
high /haɪ/ *adj* высо́кий; (*wind*) си́льный; (*on drugs*) в наркоти́ческом дурма́не; **~er education** вы́сшее образова́ние; **~-handed** своево́льный; **~-heeled** на высо́ких каблука́х; **~ jump** прыжо́к в высоту́; **~-minded** благоро́дный; иде́йный; **~-pitched** высо́кий; **~-rise** высо́тный. **highbrow** *adj* интеллектуа́льный. **highland(s)** *n* го́рная страна́. **highlight** *n* (*fig*) вы́сшая то́чка; *vt* обраща́ть *impf*, обрати́ть *pf* внима́ние на+*acc.* **highly** /-lɪ/ *adv* весьма́; **~-strung** легко́ возбужда́емый. **highness** /-nɪs/ *n* (*title*) высо́чество. **highstreet** *n* гла́вная у́лица. **highway** *n* магистра́ль.
hijack /ˈhaɪdʒæk/ *vt* похища́ть *impf*, похи́тить *pf.* **hijacker** /-kə(r)/ *n* похити́тель *m.*
hike /haɪk/ *n* похо́д.
hilarious /hɪˈleərɪəs/ *adj* умори́тельный. **hilarity** /-ˈlærɪtɪ/ *n* весе́лье.
hill /hɪl/ *n* холм. **hillock** /ˈhɪlək/ *n* хо́лмик. **hillside** *n* склон холма́. **hilly** /ˈhɪlɪ/ *adj* холми́стый.
hilt /hɪlt/ *n* рукоя́тка.
himself /hɪmˈself/ *pron* (*emph*) (он) сам; (*refl*) себя́.
hind /haɪnd/ *adj* (*rear*) за́дний.
hinder /ˈhɪndə(r)/ *vt* меша́ть *impf*, по~ *pf* +*dat.* **hindrance** /-drəns/ *n* поме́ха.
Hindu /ˈhɪnduː/ *n* инду́с; *adj* инду́сский.
hinge /hɪndʒ/ *n* шарни́р; *vi* (*fig*) зави́сеть *impf* от+*gen.*
hint /hɪnt/ *n* намёк; *vi* намека́ть *impf*, намекну́ть *pf* (**at** на+*acc*)
hip /hɪp/ *n* (*anat*) бедро́.
hippie /ˈhɪpɪ/ *n* хи́ппи *neut indecl.*
hippopotamus /ˌhɪpəˈpɒtəməs/ *n* гиппопота́м.
hire /ˈhaɪə(r)/ *n* наём, прока́т; **~-purchase** поку́пка в рассро́чку; *vt* нанима́ть *impf*, наня́ть *pf*; **~ out** сдава́ть *impf*, сдать *pf* напрока́т.
his /hɪz/ *poss pron* его́; свой.
hiss /hɪs/ *n* шипе́ние; *vi* шипе́ть *impf*; *vt* (*performer*) осви́стывать *impf*, освиста́ть *pf.*
historian /hɪˈstɔːrɪən/ *n* исто́рик. **historic(al)** /hɪˈstɒrɪk(ə)l/ *adj* истори́ческий. **history** /ˈhɪstərɪ/ *n* исто́рия.
histrionic /ˌhɪstrɪˈɒnɪk/ *adj* театра́льный.
hit /hɪt/ *n* (*blow*) уда́р; (*on target*) попада́ние (в цель); (*success*) успе́х; *vt* (*strike*) ударя́ть *impf*, уда́рить *pf*; (*target*) попада́ть *impf*, попа́сть *pf* (в цель); **~ (up)on** находи́ть *impf*, найти́ *pf.*
hitch /hɪtʃ/ *n* (*stoppage*) заде́ржка; *vt* (*fasten*) привя́зывать *impf*, привяза́ть *pf*; **~ up** подтя́гивать *impf*, подтяну́ть *pf*; **~-hike** éз-

дить *indet*, éхать *det*, по~ *pf* автостóпом.

hither /ˈhɪðə(r)/ *adv* сюдá. **hitherto** /ˈhɪðətuː/ *adv* до сих пор.

HIV *abbr* (*of* **human immunodeficiency virus**) ВИЧ.

hive /haɪv/ *n* ýлей.

hoard /hɔːd/ *n* запáс; *vt* скáпливать *impf*, скопи́ть *pf*.

hoarding /ˈhɔːdɪŋ/ *n* реклáмный щит.

hoarse /hɔːs/ *adj* хри́плый.

hoax /həʊks/ *n* надувáтельство.

hobble /ˈhɒb(ə)l/ *vi* ковылять *impf*.

hobby /ˈhɒbɪ/ *n* хóбби *neut indecl*.

hock /hɒk/ *n* (*wine*) рейнвéйн.

hockey /ˈhɒkɪ/ *n* хоккéй.

hoe /həʊ/ *n* моты́га; *vt* моты́жить *impf*.

hog /hɒg/ *n* бóров.

hoist /hɔɪst/ *n* подъёмник; *vt* поднимáть *impf*, подня́ть *pf*.

hold[1] /həʊld/ *n* (*naut*) трюм.

hold[2] /həʊld/ *n* (*grasp*) захвáт; (*influence*) влия́ние (**on** на+*acc*); **catch ~ of** ухвати́ться *pf* за+*acc*; *vt* (*grasp*) держáть *impf*; (*contain*) вмещáть *impf*, вмести́ть *pf*; (*possess*) владéть *impf* +*instr*; (*conduct*) проводи́ть *impf*, провести́ *pf*; (*consider*) считáть *impf*, счесть *pf* (+*acc* & *instr*, за+*acc*); *vi* держáться *impf*; (*weather*) продéрживаться *impf*, продержáться *pf*; **~ back** сдéрживать(ся) *impf*, сдержáть(ся) *pf*; **~ forth** разглагóльствовать *impf*; **~ on** (*wait*) подождáть *pf*; (*tel*) не вéшать *impf* трýбку; (*grip*) держáться *impf* (**to** за+*acc*); **~ out** (*stretch out*) протя́гивать *impf*, протянýть *pf*; (*resist*) не сдавáться *impf*; **~ up** (*support*) поддéрживать *impf*, поддержáть *pf*; (*impede*) задéрживать *impf*, задержáть *pf*. **holdall** *n* сýмка. **hold-up** *n* (*robbery*) налёт; (*delay*) задéржка.

hole /həʊl/ *n* дырá; (*animal's*) норá; (*golf*) лýнка.

holiday /ˈhɒlɪˌdeɪ/ *n* (*day off*) выходнóй день; (*festival*) прáздник; (*annual leave*) óтпуск; *pl* (*school*) кани́кулы (-л) *pl*; **~-maker** тури́ст; **on ~** в óтпуске.

holiness /ˈhəʊlɪnɪs/ *n* святость.

Holland /ˈhɒlənd/ *n* Голлáндия.

hollow /ˈhɒləʊ/ *n* впáдина; (*valley*) лощи́на; *adj* пустóй; (*sunken*) впáлый; (*sound*) глухóй; *vt* (**~** *out*) выдáлбливать *impf*, вы́долбить *pf*.

holly /ˈhɒlɪ/ *n* остроли́ст.

holocaust /ˈhɒləˌkɔːst/ *n* мáссовое уничтожéние.

holster /ˈhəʊlstə(r)/ *n* кобурá.

holy /ˈhəʊlɪ/ *adj* святóй, свящéнный.

homage /ˈhɒmɪdʒ/ *n* почтéние; **pay ~ to** преклоня́ться *impf*, преклони́ться *pf* пéред+*instr*.

home /həʊm/ *n* дом; (*also* **homeland**) рóдина; **at ~** дóма; **feel at ~** чýвствовать *impf* себя́ как дóма; *adj* домáшний; (*native*) роднóй; **H~ Affairs** внýтренние делá *neut pl*; *adv* (*direction*) домóй; (*position*) дóма. **homeless** /-lɪs/ *adj* бездóмный. **homemade** *adj* (*food*) домáшний; (*object*) самодéльный. **homesick** *adj*: **be ~** скучáть *impf* по дóму. **homewards** /-wədz/ *adv* домóй. **homework** *n* домáшние задáния *neut pl*.

homely /ˈhəʊmlɪ/ *adj* простóй.

homicide /ˈhɒmɪˌsaɪd/ *n* (*action*) уби́йство.

homogeneous /ˌhɒməʊˈdʒiːnɪəs/ *adj* однорóдный.

homosexual /ˌhɒməʊˈseksjʊəl/ *n* гомосексуали́ст; *adj* гомосексуáльный.

honest /ˈɒnɪst/ *n* чéстный. **honesty** /-tɪ/ *n* чéстность.

honey /ˈhʌnɪ/ *n* мёд. **honeymoon** *n* медóвый мéсяц. **honeysuckle** *n* жи́молость.

honk /hɒŋk/ *vi* гудéть *impf*.

honorary /ˈɒnərərɪ/ *adj* почётный.

honour /ˈɒnə(r)/ *n* честь; *vt* (*respect*) почитáть *impf*; (*confer*) удостáивать *impf*, удостóить *pf* (**with** +*gen*); (*fulfil*) выполня́ть *impf*, вы́полнить *pf*. **honourable** /-rəb(ə)l/ *adj* че́стный.

hood /hʊd/ *n* капюшо́н; (*tech*) капо́т.

hoodwink /ˈhʊdwɪŋk/ *vt* обма́нывать *impf*, обману́ть *pf*.

hoof /huːf/ *n* копы́то.

hook /hʊk/ *n* крючо́к; *vt* (*hitch*) зацепля́ть *impf*, зацепи́ть *pf*; (*fasten*) застёгивать *impf*, застегну́ть *pf*.

hooligan /ˈhuːlɪgən/ *n* хулига́н.

hoop /huːp/ *n* о́бруч.

hoot /huːt/ *vi* (*owl*) у́хать *impf*, у́хнуть *pf*; (*horn*) гуде́ть *impf*. **hooter** /ˈhuːtə(r)/ *n* гудо́к.

hop[1] /hɒp/ *n* (*plant*; *collect*) хмель *m*.

hop[2] /hɒp/ *n* (*jump*) прыжо́к; *vi* пры́гать *impf*, пры́гнуть *pf* (на одно́й ноге́).

hope /həʊp/ *n* наде́жда; *vi* наде́яться *impf*, по~ *pf* (**for** на+*acc*). **hopeful** /-fʊl/ *adj* (*promising*) обнадёживающий; **I am ~** я наде́юсь. **hopefully** /-fʊlɪ/ *adv* с наде́ждой; (*it is hoped*) надо наде́яться. **hopeless** /-lɪs/ *adj* безнадёжный.

horde /hɔːd/ *n* (*hist*; *fig*) орда́.

horizon /həˈraɪz(ə)n/ *n* горизо́нт. **horizontal** /ˌhɒrɪˈzɒnt(ə)l/ *adj* горизонта́льный.

hormone /ˈhɔːməʊn/ *n* гормо́н.

horn /hɔːn/ *n* рог; (*French horn*) валто́рна; (*car*) гудо́к.

hornet /ˈhɔːnɪt/ *n* ше́ршень *m*.

horny /ˈhɔːnɪ/ *adj* (*calloused*) мозо́листый.

horoscope /ˈhɒrəˌskəʊp/ *n* гороско́п.

horrible, horrid /ˈhɒrɪb(ə)l, ˈhɒrɪd/ *adj* ужа́сный. **horrify** /ˈhɒrɪˌfaɪ/ *vt* ужаса́ть *impf*, ужасну́ть *pf*. **horror** /ˈhɒrə(r)/ *n* у́жас.

hors-d'oeuvre /ɔːˈdɜːv/ *n* заку́ска.

horse /hɔːs/ *n* ло́шадь. **horse-chestnut** *n* ко́нский кашта́н. **horseman, -woman** *n* вса́дник, -ица. **horseplay** *n* возня́. **horsepower** *n* лошади́ная си́ла. **horse-racing** /ˈhɔːsˌreɪsɪŋ/ *n* ска́чки (-чек) *pl*. **horse-radish** *n* хрен. **horseshoe** *n* подко́ва.

horticulture /ˈhɔːtɪˌkʌltʃə(r)/ *n* садово́дство.

hose /həʊz/ *n* (**~-*pipe***) шланг.

hosiery /ˈhəʊzɪərɪ/ *n* чуло́чные изде́лия *neut pl*.

hospitable /ˈhɒspɪtəb(ə)l/ *adj* гостеприи́мный.

hospital /ˈhɒspɪt(ə)l/ *n* больни́ца.

hospitality /ˌhɒspɪˈtælɪtɪ/ *n* гостеприи́мство.

host[1] /həʊst/ *n* (*multitude*) мно́жество.

host[2] /həʊst/ *n* (*entertaining*) хозя́ин.

hostage /ˈhɒstɪdʒ/ *n* зало́жник.

hostel /ˈhɒst(ə)l/ *n* общежи́тие.

hostess /ˈhəʊstɪs/ *n* хозя́йка; (*air ~*) стюарде́сса.

hostile /ˈhɒstaɪl/ *adj* вражде́бный. **hostility** /hɒˈstɪlɪtɪ/ *n* вражде́бность; *pl* вое́нные де́йствия *neut pl*.

hot /hɒt/ *adj* горя́чий, жа́ркий; (*pungent*) о́стрый; **~-headed** вспы́льчивый; **~-water bottle** гре́лка. **hotbed** *n* (*fig*) оча́г. **hothouse** *n* тепли́ца. **hotplate** *n* пли́тка.

hotel /həʊˈtel/ *n* гости́ница.

hound /haʊnd/ *n* охо́тничья соба́ка; *vt* трави́ть *impf*, за~ *pf*.

hour /aʊə(r)/ *n* час. **hourly** /ˈaʊəlɪ/ *adj* ежеча́сный.

house *n* /haʊs/ дом; (*parl*) пала́та; *attrib* дома́шний; *vt* /haʊz/ помеща́ть *impf*, помести́ть *pf*. **household** *n* семья́; *adj* хозя́йственный; дома́шний. **housekeeper** /ˈhaʊsˌkiːpə(r)/ *n* эконо́мка. **house-warming** /ˈhaʊsˌwɔːmɪŋ/ *n* новосе́лье. **housewife** *n* хозя́йка. **housework** *n* дома́шняя рабо́та. **housing** /ˈhaʊzɪŋ/ *n* (*accommodation*) жильё; (*casing*) кожу́х; **~ estate** жило́й масси́в.

hovel /ˈhɒv(ə)l/ *n* лачу́га.

hover /ˈhɒvə(r)/ *vi* (*bird*) пари́ть *impf*; (*helicopter*) висе́ть *impf*;

(*person*) мая́чить *impf.* **hovercraft** *n* су́дно на возду́шной поду́шке, СВП.

how /haʊ/ *adv* как, каки́м о́бразом; ~ **do you do?** здра́вствуйте!; ~ **many,** ~ **much** ско́лько (+*gen*). **however** /haʊ'evə(r)/ *adv* как бы ни (+*past*); *conj* одна́ко, тем не ме́нее; ~ **much** ско́лько бы ни (+*gen* & *past*).

howl /haʊl/ *n* вой; *vi* выть *impf.* **howler** /'haʊlə(r)/ *n* грубе́йшая оши́бка.

hub /hʌb/ *n* (*of wheel*) ступи́ца; (*fig*) центр, средото́чие.

hubbub /'hʌbʌb/ *n* шум, гам.

huddle /'hʌd(ə)l/ *vi*: ~ **together** прижима́ться *impf*, прижа́ться *pf* друг к дру́гу.

hue /hju:/ *n* (*tint*) отте́нок.

huff /hʌf/ *n*: **in a** ~ оскорблённый.

hug /hʌg/ *n* объя́тие; *vt* (*embrace*) обнима́ть *impf*, обня́ть *pf.*

huge /hju:dʒ/ *adj* огро́мный.

hulk /hʌlk/ *n* ко́рпус (корабля́). **hulking** /-kɪŋ/ *adj* (*bulky*) грома́дный; (*clumsy*) неуклю́жий.

hull /hʌl/ *n* (*of ship*) ко́рпус.

hum /hʌm/ *n* жужжа́ние; *vi* (*buzz*) жужжа́ть *impf*; *vt* & *i* (*person*) напева́ть *impf.*

human /'hju:mən/ *adj* челове́ческий, людско́й; *n* челове́к. **humane, humanitarian** /hju:'meɪn, hju:,mænɪ'teərɪən/ *adj* челове́чный. **humanity** /hju:'mænɪtɪ/ *n* (*human race*) челове́чество; (*humaneness*) гума́нность; **the Humanities** гуманита́рные нау́ки *f pl.*

humble /'hʌmb(ə)l/ *adj* (*person*) смире́нный; (*abode*) скро́мный; *vt* унижа́ть *impf*, уни́зить *pf.*

humdrum /'hʌmdrʌm/ *adj* однообра́зный.

humid /'hju:mɪd/ *adj* вла́жный. **humidity** /hju:'mɪdɪtɪ/ *n* вла́жность.

humiliate /hju:'mɪlɪ,eɪt/ *vt* унижа́ть *impf*, уни́зить *pf.* **humiliation** /-'eɪʃ(ə)n/ *n* униже́ние.

humility /hju:'mɪlɪtɪ/ *n* смире́ние.

humorous /'hju:mərəs/ *adj* юмористи́ческий. **humour** /'hju:mə(r)/ *n* ю́мор; (*mood*) настрое́ние; *vt* потака́ть *impf* +*dat.*

hump /hʌmp/ *n* горб; (*of earth*) буго́р.

humus /'hju:məs/ *n* перегно́й.

hunch /hʌntʃ/ *n* (*idea*) предчу́вствие; *vt* го́рбить *impf*, с~ *pf.* **hunchback** *n* (*person*) горбу́н, ~ья. **hunchbacked** /'hʌntʃbækt/ *adj* горба́тый.

hundred /'hʌndrəd/ *adj* & *n* сто; ~**s of** со́тни *f pl* +*gen*; **two** ~ две́сти; **three** ~ три́ста; **four** ~ четы́реста; **five** ~ пятьсо́т. **hundredth** /'hʌndrədθ/ *adj* & *n* со́тый.

Hungarian /hʌŋ'geərɪən/ *n* венгр, венге́рка; *adj* венге́рский. **Hungary** /'hʌŋgərɪ/ *n* Ве́нгрия.

hunger /'hʌŋgə(r)/ *n* го́лод; (*fig*) жа́жда (**for** +*gen*); ~ **strike** голодо́вка; *vi* голода́ть *impf*; ~ **for** жа́ждать *impf* +*gen.* **hungry** /'hʌŋgrɪ/ *adj* голо́дный.

hunk /hʌŋk/ *n* ломо́ть *m.*

hunt /hʌnt/ *n* охо́та; (*fig*) по́иски *m pl* (**for** +*gen*); *vt* охо́титься *impf* на+*acc*, за+*instr*; (*persecute*) трави́ть *impf*, за~ *pf*; ~ **down** вы́следить *pf*; ~ **for** иска́ть *impf* +*acc or gen*; ~ **out** отыска́ть *pf.* **hunter** /-tə(r)/ *n* охо́тник. **hunting** /-tɪŋ/ *n* охо́та.

hurdle /'hɜ:d(ə)l/ *n* (*sport*; *fig*) барье́р. **hurdler** /'hɜ:dlə(r)/ *n* барьери́ст. **hurdles** /'hɜ:d(ə)lz/ *n pl* (*sport*) барье́рный бег.

hurl /hɜ:l/ *vt* швыря́ть *impf*, швырну́ть *pf.*

hurly-burly /'hɜ:lɪ,bɜ:lɪ/ *n* сумато́ха.

hurrah, hurray /hʊ'rɑ:, hʊ'reɪ/ *int* ура́!

hurricane /'hʌrɪkən/ *n* урага́н.

hurried /'hʌrɪd/ *adj* торопли́вый. **hurry** /'hʌrɪ/ *n* спе́шка; **be in a** ~ спеши́ть *impf*; *vt* & *i* торопи́ть(ся) *impf*, по~ *pf*; *vi* спеши́ть *impf*, по~ *pf.*

hurt /hɜ:t/ *n* уще́рб; *vi* боле́ть

impf; *vt* повреждáть *impf*, повредúть *pf*; (*offend*) обижáть *impf*, обúдеть *pf*.
hurtle /'hɜːt(ə)l/ *vi* нестúсь *impf*, по~ *pf*.
husband /'hʌzbənd/ *n* муж.
hush /hʌʃ/ *n* тишинá; *vt*: ~ **up** заминáть *impf*, замя́ть *pf*; *int* тúше!
husk /hʌsk/ *n* шелухá.
husky /'hʌskɪ/ *adj* (*voice*) хрúплый.
hustle /'hʌs(ə)l/ *n* толкотня́; *vt* (*push*) затолкáть *impf*, затолкнýть *pf*; (*herd people*) загоня́ть *impf*, загнáть *pf*; *vt* & *i* (*hurry*) торопúть(ся) *impf*, по~ *pf*.
hut /hʌt/ *n* хúжина.
hutch /hʌtʃ/ *n* клéтка.
hyacinth /'haɪəsɪnθ/ *n* гиацúнт.
hybrid /'haɪbrɪd/ *n* гибрúд; *adj* гибрúдный.
hydrangea /haɪ'dreɪndʒə/ *n* гортéнзия.
hydrant /'haɪdrənt/ *n* гидрáнт.
hydraulic /haɪ'drɒlɪk/ *adj* гидравлúческий.
hydrochloric acid /ˌhaɪdrə'klɔːrɪk 'æsɪd/ *n* соля́ная кислотá. **hydroelectric** /ˌhaɪdrəʊɪ'lektrɪk/ *adj* гидроэлектрúческий; ~ **power station** гидроэлектростáнция, ГЭС *f indecl.* **hydrofoil** /'haɪdrəˌfɔɪl/ *n* сýдно на подвóдных кры́льях, СПК.
hydrogen /'haɪdrədʒ(ə)n/ *n* водорóд.
hyena /haɪ'iːnə/ *n* гиéна.
hygiene /'haɪdʒiːn/ *n* гигиéна. **hygienic** /-'dʒiːnɪk/ *adj* гигиенúческий.
hymn /hɪm/ *n* гимн.
hyperbole /haɪ'pɜːbəlɪ/ *n* гипéрбола.
hyphen /'haɪf(ə)n/ *n* дефúс. **hyphen(ate)** /'haɪfəˌneɪt/ *vt* писáть *impf*, на~ *pf* чéрез дефúс.
hypnosis /hɪp'nəʊsɪs/ *n* гипнóз. **hypnotic** /hɪp'nɒtɪk/ *adj* гипнотúческий. **hypnotism** /'hɪpnəˌtɪz(ə)m/ *n* гипнотúзм. **hypnotist** /'hɪpnətɪst/ *n* гипнотизёр. **hypnotize** /'hɪpnəˌtaɪz/ *vt* гипнотизúровать *impf*, за~ *pf*.
hypochondria /ˌhaɪpə'kɒndrɪə/ *n* ипохóндрия. **hypochondriac** /-rɪˌæk/ *n* ипохóндрик.
hypocrisy /hɪ'pɒkrɪsɪ/ *n* лицемéрие. **hypocrite** /'hɪpəkrɪt/ *n* лицемéр. **hypocritical** /ˌhɪpə'krɪtɪk(ə)l/ *adj* лицемéрный.
hypodermic /ˌhaɪpə'dɜːmɪk/ *adj* подкóжный.
hypothesis /haɪ'pɒθɪsɪs/ *n* гипóтеза. **hypothesize** /-'pɒθɪˌsaɪz/ *vi* стрóить *impf*, по~ *pf* гипотéзу. **hypothetical** /ˌhaɪpə'θetɪk(ə)l/ *adj* гипотетúческий.
hysterectomy /ˌhɪstə'rektəmɪ/ *n* гистерэктомúя, удалéние мáтки.
hysteria /hɪ'stɪərɪə/ *n* истерúя. **hysterical** /-'sterɪk(ə)l/ *adj* истерúческий. **hysterics** /-'sterɪks/ *n pl* истéрика.

I

I /aɪ/ *pron* я.
ibid(em) /'ɪbɪˌd(em)/ *adv* там же.
ice /aɪs/ *n* лёд; ~**-age** ледникóвый перúод; ~**-axe** ледорýб; ~**-cream** морóженое *sb*; ~ **hockey** хоккéй (с шáйбой); ~ **rink** катóк; ~ **skate** конёк; *vi* катáться *impf* на конькáх; *vt* (*chill*) заморáживать *impf*, заморóзить *pf*; (*cul*) глазировáть *impf* & *pf*; *vi*: ~ **over, up** обледеневáть *impf*, обледенéть *pf*. **iceberg** /'aɪsbɜːg/ *n* áйсберг. **icicle** /'aɪsɪk(ə)l/ *n* сосýлька. **icing** /'aɪsɪŋ/ *n* (*cul*) глазýрь. **icy** /'aɪsɪ/ *adj* ледянóй.
icon /'aɪkɒn/ *n* икóна.
ID *abbr* (*of* **identification**) удостоверéние лúчности.
idea /aɪ'dɪə/ *n* идéя, мысль; (*conception*) поня́тие.
ideal /aɪ'diːəl/ *n* идеáл; *adj* идеáльный. **idealism** /-'diːəˌlɪz(ə)m/ *n* идеализм. **idealist** /-'dɪəlɪst/ *n* идеалúст. **idealize** /-'dɪəˌlaɪz/ *vt* идеализúровать *impf* & *pf*.

identical /aɪ'dentɪk(ə)l/ *adj* тождéственный, одинáковый. **identification** /aɪˌdentɪfɪ'keɪʃ(ə)n/ *n* (*recognition*) опознáние; (*of person*) установлéние лúчности. **identify** /aɪ'dentɪˌfaɪ/ *vt* опознавáть *impf*, опознáть *pf*. **identity** /aɪ'dentɪtɪ/ *n* (*of person*) лúчность; **~ card** удостоверéние лúчности.

ideological /ˌaɪdɪə'lɒdʒɪk(ə)l/ *adj* идеологúческий. **ideology** /ˌaɪdɪ'ɒlədʒɪ/ *n* идеолóгия.

idiom /'ɪdɪəm/ *n* идиóма. **idiomatic** /-'mætɪk/ *adj* идиоматúческий.

idiosyncrasy /ˌɪdɪəʊ'sɪŋkrəsɪ/ *n* идиосинкразúя.

idiot /'ɪdɪət/ *n* идиóт. **idiotic** /-'ɒtɪk/ *adj* идиóтский.

idle /'aɪd(ə)l/ *adj* (*unoccupied*; *lazy*; *purposeless*) прáздный; (*vain*) тщéтный; (*empty*) пустóй; (*machine*) недéйствующий; *vi* бездéльничать *impf*; (*engine*) рабóтать *impf* вхолостýю; *vt*: **~ away** прáздно проводúть *impf*, провестú *pf*. **idleness** /-nɪs/ *n* прáздность.

idol /'aɪd(ə)l/ *n* úдол. **idolatry** /aɪ'dɒlətrɪ/ *n* идолопоклóнство; (*fig*) обожáние. **idolize** /'aɪdəˌlaɪz/ *vt* боготворúть *impf*.

idyll /'ɪdɪl/ *n* идúллия. **idyllic** /ɪ'dɪlɪk/ *adj* идиллúческий.

i.e. *abbr* т.е., то есть.

if /ɪf/ *conj* éсли, éсли бы; (*whether*) ли; **as ~** как бýдто; **even ~** дáже éсли; **~ only** éсли бы тóлько.

ignite /ɪg'naɪt/ *vt* зажигáть *impf*, зажéчь *pf*; *vi* загорáться *impf*, загорéться *pf*. **ignition** /-'nɪʃ(ə)n/ *n* зажигáние.

ignoble /ɪg'nəʊb(ə)l/ *adj* нúзкий.

ignominious /ˌɪgnə'mɪnɪəs/ *adj* позóрный.

ignoramus /ˌɪgnə'reɪməs/ *n* невéжда *m*. **ignorance** /'ɪgnərəns/ *n* невéжество, (*of certain facts*) невéдение. **ignorant** /'ɪgnərənt/ *adj* невéжественный; (*uninformed*) несвéдущий (**of** в+*prep*).

ignore /ɪg'nɔː(r)/ *vt* не обращáть *impf* внимáния на+*acc*; игнорúровать *impf* & *pf*.

ilk /ɪlk/ *n*: **of that ~** такóго рóда.

ill /ɪl/ *n* (*evil*) зло; (*harm*) вред; *pl* (*misfortunes*) несчáстья (-тий) *pl*; *adj* (*sick*) больнóй; (*bad*) дурнóй; *adv* плóхо, дýрно; **fall ~** заболевáть *impf*, заболéть *pf*; **~-advised** неблагоразýмный; **~-mannered** невéжливый; **~-treat** *vt* плóхо обращáться *impf* с+*instr*.

illegal /ɪ'liːg(ə)l/ *adj* нелегáльный. **illegality** /ˌɪliː'gælɪtɪ/ *n* незакóнность, нелегáльность.

illegible /ɪ'ledʒɪb(ə)l/ *adj* неразбóрчивый.

illegitimacy /ˌɪlɪ'dʒɪtɪməsɪ/ *n* незакóнность; (*of child*) незаконнорождённость. **illegitimate** /-mət/ *adj* незакóнный; незаконнорождённый.

illicit /ɪ'lɪsɪt/ *adj* незакóнный, недозвóленный.

illiteracy /ɪ'lɪtərəsɪ/ *n* негрáмотность. **illiterate** /-rət/ *adj* негрáмотный.

illness /'ɪlnɪs/ *n* болéзнь.

illogical /ɪ'lɒdʒɪk(ə)l/ *adj* нелогúчный.

illuminate /ɪ'luːmɪˌneɪt/ *vt* освещáть *impf*, осветúть *pf*. **illumination** /-'neɪʃ(ə)n/ *n* освещéние.

illusion /ɪ'luːʒ(ə)n/ *n* иллюзия. **illusory** /ɪ'luːsərɪ/ *adj* иллюзóрный.

illustrate /'ɪləˌstreɪt/ *vt* иллюстрúровать *impf* & *pf*, про~ *pf*. **illustration** /-'streɪʃ(ə)n/ *n* иллюстрáция. **illustrative** /'ɪləstrətɪv/ *adj* иллюстратúвный.

illustrious /ɪ'lʌstrɪəs/ *adj* знаменúтый.

image /'ɪmɪdʒ/ *n* (*phys*; *statue etc.*) изображéние; (*optical ~*) отражéние; (*likeness*) кóпия; (*metaphor*; *conception*) óбраз; (*reputation*) репутáция. **imagery** /-dʒərɪ/ *n* óбразность.

imaginable /ɪ'mædʒɪnəb(ə)l/ *adj* вообразúмый. **imaginary** /-'mædʒɪnərɪ/ *adj* воображáемый.

i

imagination /-'neɪʃ(ə)n/ *n* воображе́ние. **imagine** /ɪ'mædʒɪn/ *vt* вообража́ть *impf*, вообрази́ть *pf*; (*conceive*) представля́ть *impf*, предста́вить *pf* себе́.
imbecile /'ɪmbɪˌsiːl/ *n* слабоу́мный *sb*; (*fool*) глупе́ц.
imbibe /ɪm'baɪb/ *vt* (*absorb*) впи́тывать *impf*, впита́ть *pf*.
imbue /ɪm'bjuː/ *vt* внуша́ть *impf*, внуши́ть *pf* +*dat* (**with** +*acc*).
imitate /'ɪmɪˌteɪt/ *vt* подража́ть *impf* +*dat*. **imitation** /-'teɪʃ(ə)n/ *n* подража́ние (**of** +*dat*); *attrib* иску́сственный. **imitative** /'ɪmɪtətɪv/ *adj* подража́тельный.
immaculate /ɪ'mækjʊlət/ *adj* безупре́чный.
immaterial /ˌɪmə'tɪərɪəl/ *adj* (*unimportant*) несуще́ственный.
immature /ˌɪmə'tjʊə(r)/ *adj* незре́лый.
immeasurable /ɪ'meʒərəb(ə)l/ *adj* неизмери́мый.
immediate /ɪ'miːdɪət/ *adj* (*direct*) непосре́дственный; (*swift*) неме́дленный. **immediately** /-lɪ/ *adv* то́тчас, сра́зу.
immemorial /ˌɪmɪ'mɔːrɪəl/ *adj*: **from time ~** с незапа́мятных времён.
immense /ɪ'mens/ *adj* огро́мный.
immerse /ɪ'mɜːs/ *vt* погружа́ть *impf*, погрузи́ть *pf*. **immersion** /ɪ'mɜːʃ(ə)n/ *n* погруже́ние.
immigrant /'ɪmɪgrənt/ *n* иммигра́нт, ~ка. **immigration** /-'greɪʃ(ə)n/ *n* иммигра́ция.
imminent /'ɪmɪnənt/ *adj* надвига́ющийся; (*danger*) грозя́щий.
immobile /ɪ'məʊbaɪl/ *adj* неподви́жный. **immobilize** /-bɪˌlaɪz/ *vt* парализова́ть *impf* & *pf*.
immoderate /ɪ'mɒdərət/ *adj* неуме́ренный.
immodest /ɪ'mɒdɪst/ *adj* нескро́мный.
immoral /ɪ'mɒr(ə)l/ *adj* безнра́вственный. **immorality** /ˌɪmə'rælɪtɪ/ *n* безнра́вственность.
immortal /ɪ'mɔːt(ə)l/ *adj* бессме́ртный. **immortality** /-'tælɪtɪ/ *n* бессме́ртие. **immortalize** /ɪ'mɔːtəˌlaɪz/ *vt* обессме́ртить *pf*.
immovable /ɪ'muːvəb(ə)l/ *adj* неподви́жный; (*fig*) непоколеби́мый.
immune /ɪ'mjuːn/ *adj* (*to illness*) невосприи́мчивый (**to** к+*dat*); (*free from*) свобо́дный (**from** от+*gen*). **immunity** /ɪ'mjuːnɪtɪ/ *n* иммуните́т (**from** к+*dat*); освобожде́ние (**from** от+*gen*). **immunize** /'ɪmjuːˌnaɪz/ *vt* иммунизи́ровать *impf* & *pf*.
immutable /ɪ'mjuːtəb(ə)l/ *adj* неизме́нный.
imp /ɪmp/ *n* бесёнок.
impact /'ɪmpækt/ *n* уда́р; (*fig*) влия́ние.
impair /ɪm'peə(r)/ *vt* вреди́ть *impf*, по~ *pf*.
impale /ɪm'peɪl/ *vt* протыка́ть *impf*, проткну́ть *pf*.
impart /ɪm'pɑːt/ *vt* дели́ться *impf*, по~ *pf* +*instr* (**to** с+*instr*).
impartial /ɪm'pɑːʃ(ə)l/ *adj* беспристра́стный.
impassable /ɪm'pɑːsəb(ə)l/ *adj* непроходи́мый; (*for vehicles*) непрое́зжий.
impasse /'æmpæs/ *n* тупи́к.
impassioned /ɪm'pæʃ(ə)nd/ *adj* стра́стный.
impassive /ɪm'pæsɪv/ *adj* бесстра́стный.
impatience /ɪm'peɪʃəns/ *n* нетерпе́ние. **impatient** /-ʃənt/ *adj* нетерпели́вый.
impeach /ɪm'piːtʃ/ *vt* обвиня́ть *impf*, обвини́ть *pf* (**for** в+*prep*).
impeccable /ɪm'pekəb(ə)l/ *adj* безупре́чный.
impecunious /ˌɪmpɪ'kjuːnɪəs/ *adj* безде́нежный.
impedance /ɪm'piːd(ə)ns/ *n* по́лное сопротивле́ние. **impede** /-'piːd/ *vt* препя́тствовать *impf*, вос~ *pf* +*dat*. **impediment** /-'pedɪmənt/ *n* препя́тствие; (*in speech*) заика́ние.
impel /ɪm'pel/ *vt* побужда́ть *impf*, побуди́ть *pf* (**to** +*inf*, к+*dat*).

impending /ɪm'pendɪŋ/ *adj* предстоя́щий.

impenetrable /ɪm'penɪtrəb(ə)l/ *adj* непроница́емый.

imperative /ɪm'perətɪv/ *adj* необходи́мый; *n* (*gram*) повели́тельное наклоне́ние.

imperceptible /ˌɪmpə'septɪb(ə)l/ *adj* незаме́тный.

imperfect /ɪm'pɜːfɪkt/ *n* импerфе́кт; *adj* несоверше́нный. **imperfection** /ˌɪmpə'fekʃ(ə)n/ *n* несоверше́нство; (*fault*) недоста́ток. **imperfective** /ˌɪmpə'fektɪv/ *adj* (*n*) несоверше́нный (вид).

imperial /ɪm'pɪərɪəl/ *adj* импе́рский. **imperialism** /-'pɪərɪəˌlɪz(ə)m/ *n* империали́зм. **imperialist** /-'pɪərɪəlɪst/ *n* империали́ст; *attrib* империалисти́ческий.

imperil /ɪm'perɪl/ *vt* подверга́ть *impf*, подве́ргнуть *pf* опа́сности.

imperious /ɪm'pɪərɪəs/ *adj* вла́стный.

impersonal /ɪm'pɜːsən(ə)l/ *adj* безли́чный.

impersonate /ɪm'pɜːsəˌneɪt/ *vt* (*imitate*) подража́ть *impf*; (*pretend to be*) выдава́ть *impf*, вы́дать *pf* себя́ за+*acc*. **impersonation** /-'neɪʃ(ə)n/ *n* подража́ние.

impertinence /ɪm'pɜːtɪnəns/ *n* де́рзость. **impertinent** /-nənt/ *adj* де́рзкий.

imperturbable /ˌɪmpə'tɜːbəb(ə)l/ *adj* невозмути́мый.

impervious /ɪm'pɜːvɪəs/ *adj* (*fig*) глухо́й (**to** к+*dat*).

impetuous /ɪm'petjʊəs/ *adj* стреми́тельный.

impetus /'ɪmpɪtəs/ *n* дви́жущая си́ла.

impinge /ɪm'pɪndʒ/ *vi*: ~ **(up)on** ока́зывать *impf*, оказа́ть *pf* (отрица́тельный) эффе́кт на+*acc*.

implacable /ɪm'plækəb(ə)l/ *adj* неумоли́мый.

implant /'ɪmplɑːnt/ *vt* вводи́ть *impf*, ввести́ *pf*; (*fig*) се́ять *impf*, по~ *pf*.

implement[1] /'ɪmplɪmənt/ *n* ору́дие, инструме́нт.

implement[2] /'ɪmplɪˌment/ *vt* (*fulfil*) выполня́ть *impf*, вы́полнить *pf*.

implicate /'ɪmplɪˌkeɪt/ *vt* впу́тывать *impf*, впу́тать *pf*. **implication** /-'keɪʃ(ə)n/ *n* (*inference*) намёк; *pl* значе́ние.

implicit /ɪm'plɪsɪt/ *adj* подразумева́емый; (*absolute*) безогово́рочный.

implore /ɪm'plɔː(r)/ *vt* умоля́ть *impf*.

imply /ɪm'plaɪ/ *vt* подразумева́ть *impf*.

impolite /ˌɪmpə'laɪt/ *adj* неве́жливый.

imponderable /ɪm'pɒndərəb(ə)l/ *adj* неопределённый.

import *n* /'ɪmpɔːt/ (*meaning*) значе́ние; (*of goods*) и́мпорт; *vt* /ɪm'pɔːt/ импорти́ровать *impf* & *pf*. **importer** /ɪm'pɔːtə(r)/ *n* импортёр.

importance /ɪm'pɔːt(ə)ns/ *n* ва́жность. **important** /-t(ə)nt/ *adj* ва́жный.

impose /ɪm'pəʊz/ *vt* (*tax*) облага́ть *impf*, обложи́ть *pf* +*instr* (**on** +*acc*); (*obligation*) налага́ть *impf*, наложи́ть *pf* (**on** на+*acc*); ~ **(o.s.) on** налега́ть *impf* на+*acc*. **imposing** /-'pəʊzɪŋ/ *adj* внуши́тельный. **imposition** /ˌɪmpə'zɪʃ(ə)n/ *n* обложе́ние, наложе́ние.

impossibility /ɪmˌpɒsɪ'bɪlɪtɪ/ *n* невозмо́жность. **impossible** /ɪm'pɒsɪb(ə)l/ *adj* невозмо́жный.

impostor /ɪm'pɒstə(r)/ *n* самозва́нец.

impotence /'ɪmpət(ə)ns/ *n* бесси́лие; (*med*) импоте́нция. **impotent** /-t(ə)nt/ *adj* бесси́льный; (*med*) импоте́нтный.

impound /ɪm'paʊnd/ *vt* (*confiscate*) конфискова́ть *impf* & *pf*.

impoverished /ɪm'pɒvərɪʃt/ *adj* обедне́вший.

impracticable /ɪm'præktɪkəb(ə)l/ *adj* невыполни́мый.

imprecise /ˌɪmprɪˈsaɪs/ *n* нето́чный.
impregnable /ɪmˈpregnəb(ə)l/ *adj* непристу́пный.
impregnate /ˈɪmpregˌneɪt/ *vt* (*fertilize*) оплодотворя́ть *impf*, оплодотвори́ть *pf*; (*saturate*) пропи́тывать *impf*, пропита́ть *pf*.
impresario /ˌɪmprɪˈsɑːrɪəʊ/ *n* аге́нт.
impress *vt* /ɪmˈpres/ производи́ть *impf*, произвести́ *pf* (како́е-либо) впечатле́ние на+*acc*; ~ **upon (s.o.)** внуша́ть *impf*, внуши́ть *pf* (+*dat*). **impression** /-ˈpreʃ(ə)n/ *n* впечатле́ние; (*imprint*) отпеча́ток; (*reprint*) (стереоти́пное) изда́ние.
impressionism /ɪmˈpreʃəˌnɪz(ə)m/ *n* импрессиони́зм. **impressionist** /-nɪst/ *n* импрессиони́ст.
impressive /ɪmˈpresɪv/ *adj* впечатля́ющий.
imprint *n* /ˈɪmprɪnt/ отпеча́ток; *vt* /ɪmˈprɪnt/ отпеча́тывать *impf*, отпеча́тать *pf*; (*on memory*) запечатлева́ть *impf*, запечатле́ть *pf*.
imprison /ɪmˈprɪz(ə)n/ *vt* заключа́ть *impf*, заключи́ть *pf* (в тюрьму́). **imprisonment** /-mənt/ *n* тюре́мное заключе́ние.
improbable /ɪmˈprɒbəb(ə)l/ *adj* невероя́тный.
impromptu /ɪmˈprɒmptjuː/ *adj* импровизи́рованный; *adv* без подгото́вки, экспро́мтом.
improper /ɪmˈprɒpə(r)/ *adj* (*incorrect*) непра́вильный; (*indecent*) неприли́чный. **impropriety** /ˌɪmprəˈpraɪətɪ/ *n* неуме́стность.
improve /ɪmˈpruːv/ *vt & i* улучша́ть(ся) *impf*, улу́чшить(ся) *pf*. **improvement** /-mənt/ *n* улучше́ние.
improvisation /ˌɪmprəvaɪˈzeɪʃ(ə)n/ *n* импровиза́ция. **improvise** /ˈɪmprəˌvaɪz/ *vt* импровизи́ровать *impf*, сымпровизи́ровать *pf*.
imprudent /ɪmˈpruːd(ə)nt/ *adj* неосторо́жный.
impudence /ˈɪmpjʊd(ə)ns/ *n* на́глость. **impudent** /-d(ə)nt/ *adj* на́глый.
impulse /ˈɪmpʌls/ *n* толчо́к, и́мпульс; (*sudden tendency*) поры́в. **impulsive** /ɪmˈpʌlsɪv/ *adj* импульси́вный.
impunity /ɪmˈpjuːnɪtɪ/ *n*: **with ~** безнака́занно.
impure /ɪmˈpjʊə(r)/ *adj* нечи́стый.
impute /ɪmˈpjuːt/ *vt* припи́сывать *impf*, приписа́ть *pf* (**to** +*dat*).
in /ɪn/ *prep* (*place*) в+*prep*, на +*prep*; (*into*) в+*acc*, на+*acc*; (*point in time*) в+*prep*, на+*prep*; **in the morning** (*etc.*) у́тром (*instr*); **in spring** (*etc.*) весно́й (*instr*); (*at some stage in; throughout*) во вре́мя +*gen*; (*duration*) за+*acc*; (*after interval of*) че́рез+*acc*; (*during course of*) в тече́ние+*gen*; (*circumstance*) в+*prep*, при+*prep*; *adv* (*place*) внутри́; (*motion*) вну́трь; (*at home*) до́ма; (*in fashion*) в мо́де; **in here, there** (*place*) здесь, там; (*motion*) сюда́, туда́; *adj* вну́тренний; (*fashionable*) мо́дный; *n*: **the ins and outs** все ходы́ и вы́ходы.
inability /ˌɪnəˈbɪlɪtɪ/ *n* неспосо́бность.
inaccessible /ˌɪnækˈsesɪb(ə)l/ *adj* недосту́пный.
inaccurate /ɪnˈækjʊrət/ *adj* нето́чный.
inaction /ɪnˈækʃ(ə)n/ *n* безде́йствие. **inactive** /-ˈæktɪv/ *adj* безде́йственный. **inactivity** /ˌɪnækˈtɪvɪtɪ/ *n* безде́йственность.
inadequate /ɪnˈædɪkwət/ *adj* недоста́точный.
inadmissible /ˌɪnədˈmɪsɪb(ə)l/ *adj* недопусти́мый.
inadvertent /ˌɪnədˈvɜːt(ə)nt/ *adj* нечая́нный.
inalienable /ɪnˈeɪlɪənəb(ə)l/ *adj* неотъе́млемый.
inane /ɪˈneɪn/ *adj* глу́пый.
inanimate /ɪnˈænɪmət/ *adj* неодушевлённый.
inappropriate /ˌɪnəˈprəʊprɪət/ *adj* неуме́стный.
inarticulate /ˌɪnɑːˈtɪkjʊlət/ *adj* (*per-*

i

son) косноязы́чный; (*indistinct*) невня́тный.
inasmuch /ˌɪnəz'mʌtʃ/ *adv*: **~ as** так как; ввиду́ того́, что.
inattentive /ˌɪnə'tentɪv/ *adj* невнима́тельный.
inaudible /ɪn'ɔːdɪb(ə)l/ *adj* неслы́шный.
inaugural /ɪ'nɔːgjʊr(ə)l/ *adj* вступи́тельный. **inaugurate** /-ˌreɪt/ *vt* (*admit to office*) торже́ственно вводи́ть *impf*, ввести́ *pf* в до́лжность; (*open*) открыва́ть *impf*, откры́ть *pf*; (*introduce*) вводи́ть *impf*, ввести́ *pf*. **inauguration** /-'reɪʃ(ə)n/ *n* введе́ние в до́лжность; откры́тие; нача́ло.
inauspicious /ˌɪnɔː'spɪʃəs/ *adj* неблагоприя́тный.
inborn, inbred /'ɪnbɔːn, 'ɪnbred/ *adj* врождённый.
incalculable /ɪn'kælkjʊləb(ə)l/ *adj* неисчисли́мый.
incandescent /ˌɪnkæn'des(ə)nt/ *adj* накалённый.
incantation /ˌɪnkæn'teɪʃ(ə)n/ *n* заклина́ние.
incapability /ɪnˌkeɪpə'bɪlɪtɪ/ *n* неспосо́бность. **incapable** /ɪn'keɪpəb(ə)l/ *adj* неспосо́бный (**of** к+*dat*, на+*acc*).
incapacitate /ˌɪnkə'pæsɪˌteɪt/ *vt* де́лать *impf*, с~ *pf* неспосо́бным. **incapacity** /-'pæsɪtɪ/ *n* неспосо́бность.
incarcerate /ɪn'kɑːsəˌreɪt/ *vt* заключа́ть *impf*, заключи́ть *pf* (в тюрьму́). **incarceration** /-'reɪʃ(ə)n/ *n* заключе́ние (в тюрьму́).
incarnate /ɪn'kɑːnət/ *adj* воплощённый. **incarnation** /-'neɪʃ(ə)n/ *n* воплоще́ние.
incendiary /ɪn'sendɪərɪ/ *adj* зажига́тельный.
incense[1] /'ɪnsens/ *n* фимиа́м, ла́дан.
incense[2] /ɪn'sens/ *vt* разгнева́ть *pf*.
incentive /ɪn'sentɪv/ *n* побужде́ние.
inception /ɪn'sepʃ(ə)n/ *n* нача́ло.
incessant /ɪn'ses(ə)nt/ *adj* непреста́нный.
incest /'ɪnsest/ *n* кровосмеше́ние.
inch /ɪntʃ/ *n* дюйм; **~ by ~** ма́ло-пома́лу; *vi* ползти́ *impf*.
incidence /'ɪnsɪd(ə)ns/ *n* (*phys*) паде́ние; (*prevalence*) распростране́ние. **incident** /-d(ə)nt/ *n* слу́чай, инциде́нт. **incidental** /ˌɪnsɪ'dent(ə)l/ *adj* (*casual*) случа́йный; (*inessential*) несуще́ственный. **incidentally** /ˌɪnsɪ'dentəlɪ/ *adv* ме́жду про́чим.
incinerate /ɪn'sɪnəˌreɪt/ *vt* испепеля́ть *impf*, испепели́ть *pf*. **incinerator** /-tə(r)/ *n* мусоросжига́тельная печь.
incipient /ɪn'sɪpɪənt/ *adj* начина́ющийся.
incision /ɪn'sɪʒ(ə)n/ *n* надре́з (**in** на+*acc*). **incisive** /ɪn'saɪsɪv/ *adj* (*fig*) о́стрый. **incisor** /ɪn'saɪzə(r)/ *n* резе́ц.
incite /ɪn'saɪt/ *vt* подстрека́ть *impf*, подстрекну́ть *pf* (**to** к+*dat*). **incitement** /-mənt/ *n* подстрека́тельство.
inclement /ɪn'klemənt/ *adj* суро́вый.
inclination /ˌɪnklɪ'neɪʃ(ə)n/ *n* (*slope*) накло́н; (*propensity*) скло́нность (**for, to** к+*dat*). **incline** *n* /'ɪnklaɪn/ накло́н; *vt & i* /ɪn'klaɪn/ склоня́ть(ся) *impf*, склони́ть(ся) *pf*. **inclined** /ɪn'klaɪnd/ *predic* (*disposed*) скло́нен (-онна́, -о́нно) (**to** к+*dat*).
include /ɪn'kluːd/ *vt* включа́ть *impf*, включи́ть *pf* (**in** в+*acc*); (*contain*) заключа́ть *impf*, заключи́ть *pf* в себе́. **including** /-'kluːdɪŋ/ *prep* включа́я+*acc*. **inclusion** /-'kluːʃ(ə)n/ *n* включе́ние. **inclusive** /-'kluːsɪv/ *adj* включа́ющий (в себе́); *adv* включи́тельно.
incognito /ˌɪnkɒg'niːtəʊ/ *adv* инко́гнито.
incoherent /ˌɪnkəʊ'hɪərənt/ *adj* бессвя́зный.
income /'ɪnkʌm/ *n* дохо́д; **~ tax** подохо́дный нало́г.

incommensurate /ˌɪnkəˈmenʃərət/ *adj* несоразме́рный.
incomparable /ɪnˈkɒmpərəb(ə)l/ *adj* несравни́мый (**to, with** с+*instr*); (*matchless*) несравне́нный.
incompatible /ˌɪnkəmˈpætɪb(ə)l/ *adj* несовмести́мый.
incompetence /ɪnˈkɒmpɪt(ə)ns/ *n* некомпете́нтность. **incompetent** /-t(ə)nt/ *adj* некомпете́нтный.
incomplete /ˌɪnkəmˈpliːt/ *adj* непо́лный, незако́нченный.
incomprehensible /ɪnˌkɒmprɪˈhensɪb(ə)l/ *adj* непоня́тный.
inconceivable /ˌɪnkənˈsiːvəb(ə)l/ *adj* невообрази́мый.
inconclusive /ˌɪnkənˈkluːsɪv/ *adj* (*evidence*) недоста́точный; (*results*) неопределённый.
incongruity /ˌɪnkɒŋˈɡruːɪtɪ/ *n* несоотве́тствие. **incongruous** /ɪnˈkɒŋɡrʊəs/ *adj* несоотве́тствующий.
inconsequential /ɪnˌkɒnsɪˈkwenʃ(ə)l/ *adj* незначи́тельный.
inconsiderable /ˌɪnkənˈsɪdərəb(ə)l/ *adj* незначи́тельный.
inconsiderate /ˌɪnkənˈsɪdərət/ *adj* невнима́тельный.
inconsistency /ˌɪnkənˈsɪst(ə)nsɪ/ *n* непосле́довательность. **inconsistent** /-t(ə)nt/ *adj* непосле́довательный.
inconsolable /ˌɪnkənˈsəʊləb(ə)l/ *adj* безуте́шный.
inconspicuous /ˌɪnkənˈspɪkjʊəs/ *adj* незаме́тный.
incontinence /ɪnˈkɒntɪnəns/ *n* (*med*) недержа́ние. **incontinent** /-nənt/ *adj*: **be ~** страда́ть *impf* недержа́нием.
incontrovertible /ˌɪnkɒntrəˈvɜːtɪb(ə)l/ *adj* неопроверroutineжи́мый.
inconvenience /ˌɪnkənˈviːnɪəns/ *n* неудо́бство; *vt* затрудня́ть *impf*, затрудни́ть *pf*. **inconvenient** /-ənt/ *adj* неудо́бный.
incorporate /ɪnˈkɔːpəˌreɪt/ *vt* (*include*) включа́ть *impf*, включи́ть *pf*; (*unite*) объединя́ть *impf*, объедини́ть *pf*.
incorrect /ˌɪnkəˈrekt/ *adj* непра́вильный.
incorrigible /ɪnˈkɒrɪdʒɪb(ə)l/ *adj* неисправи́мый.
incorruptible /ˌɪnkəˈrʌptɪb(ə)l/ *adj* неподку́пный.
increase *n* /ˈɪnkriːs/ рост, увеличе́ние; (*in pay etc.*) приба́вка; *vt & i* /ɪnˈkriːs/ увели́чивать(ся) *impf*, увели́чить(ся) *pf*.
incredible /ɪnˈkredɪb(ə)l/ *adj* невероя́тный.
incredulous /ɪnˈkredjʊləs/ *adj* недове́рчивый.
increment /ˈɪnkrɪmənt/ *n* приба́вка.
incriminate /ɪnˈkrɪmɪˌneɪt/ *vt* изоблича́ть *impf*, изобличи́ть *pf*.
incubate /ˈɪŋkjʊbeɪt/ *vt* (*eggs*) выводи́ть *impf*, вы́вести *pf* (в инкуба́торе). **incubator** /-tə(r)/ *n* инкуба́тор.
inculcate /ˈɪnkʌlˌkeɪt/ *vt* внедря́ть *impf*, внедри́ть *pf*.
incumbent /ɪnˈkʌmbənt/ *adj* (*in office*) стоя́щий у вла́сти; **it is ~ (up)on you** вы обя́заны.
incur /ɪnˈkɜː(r)/ *vt* навлека́ть *impf*, навле́чь *pf* на себя́.
incurable /ɪnˈkjʊərəb(ə)l/ *adj* неизлечи́мый.
incursion /ɪnˈkɜːʃ(ə)n/ *n* (*invasion*) вторже́ние; (*attack*) набе́г.
indebted /ɪnˈdetɪd/ *predic* в долгу́ (**to** у+*gen*).
indecency /ɪnˈdiːs(ə)nsɪ/ *n* неприли́чие. **indecent** /-ˈdiːs(ə)nt/ *adj* неприли́чный.
indecision /ˌɪndɪˈsɪʒ(ə)n/ *n* нереши́тельность. **indecisive** /-ˈsaɪsɪv/ *adj* нереши́тельный.
indeclinable /ˌɪndɪˈklaɪnəb(ə)l/ *adj* несклоня́емый.
indeed /ɪnˈdiːd/ *adv* в са́мом де́ле, действи́тельно; (*interrog*) неуже́ли?
indefatigable /ˌɪndɪˈfætɪɡəb(ə)l/ *adj* неутоми́мый.
indefensible /ˌɪndɪˈfensɪb(ə)l/ *adj*

не имéющий оправдáния.

indefinable /ˌɪndɪˈfaɪnəb(ə)l/ *adj* неопределимый. **indefinite** /ɪnˈdefɪnɪt/ *adj* неопределённый.

indelible /ɪnˈdelɪb(ə)l/ *adj* несмывáемый.

indemnify /ɪnˈdemnɪˌfaɪ/ *vt*: ~ **against** страховáть *impf*, за~ *pf* от+*gen*; ~ **for** (*compensate*) компенсúровать *impf* & *pf*. **indemnity** /-ˈdemnɪtɪ/ *n* (*against loss*) гарáнтия от убы́тков; (*compensation*) компенсáция.

indent /ɪnˈdent/ *vt* (*printing*) писáть *impf*, с~ *pf* с óтступом. **indentation** /-ˈteɪʃ(ə)n/ *n* (*notch*) зубéц; (*printing*) óтступ.

independence /ˌɪndɪˈpend(ə)ns/ *n* независимость, самостоятельность. **independent** /-d(ə)nt/ *adj* независимый, самостоятельный.

indescribable /ˌɪndɪˈskraɪbəb(ə)l/ *adj* неописýемый.

indestructible /ˌɪndɪˈstrʌktɪb(ə)l/ *adj* неразрушимый.

indeterminate /ˌɪndɪˈtɜːmɪnət/ *adj* неопределённый.

index /ˈɪndeks/ *n* (*alphabetical*) указáтель *m*; (*econ*) и́ндекс; (*pointer*) стрéлка; ~ **finger** указáтельный пáлец.

India /ˈɪndɪə/ *n* И́ндия. **Indian** /-ən/ *n* индиец, индиáнка; (*American*) индéец, индиáнка; *adj* индийский; (*American*) индéйский; ~ **summer** бáбье лéто.

indicate /ˈɪndɪˌkeɪt/ *vt* укáзывать *impf*, указáть *pf*; (*be a sign of*) свидéтельствовать *impf* о+*prep*. **indication** /-ˈkeɪʃ(ə)n/ *n* указáние; (*sign*) при́знак. **indicative** /ɪnˈdɪkətɪv/ *adj* укáзывающий; (*gram*) изъяви́тельный; *n* изъяви́тельное наклонéние. **indicator** /ˈɪndɪˌkeɪtə(r)/ *n* указáтель *m*.

indict /ɪnˈdaɪt/ *vt* обвинять *impf*, обвини́ть *pf* (**for** в+*prep*).

indifference /ɪnˈdɪfrəns/ *n* равнодýшие. **indifferent** /-frənt/ *adj* равнодýшный; (*mediocre*) посрéдственный.

indigenous /ɪnˈdɪdʒɪnəs/ *adj* тузéмный.

indigestible /ˌɪndɪˈdʒestɪb(ə)l/ *adj* неудобовари́мый. **indigestion** /-ˈdʒestʃ(ə)n/ *n* несварéние желýдка.

indignant /ɪnˈdɪgnənt/ *adj* негодýющий; **be** ~ негодовáть *impf* (**with** на+*acc*). **indignation** /-ˈneɪʃ(ə)n/ *n* негодовáние.

indignity /ɪnˈdɪgnɪtɪ/ *n* оскорблéние.

indirect /ˌɪndaɪˈrekt/ *adj* непрямóй; (*econ*; *gram*) кóсвенный.

indiscreet /ˌɪndɪˈskriːt/ *adj* нескрóмный. **indiscretion** /-ˈskreʃ(ə)n/ *n* нескрóмность.

indiscriminate /ˌɪndɪˈskrɪmɪnət/ *adj* неразбóрчивый. **indiscriminately** /-lɪ/ *adv* без разбóра.

indispensable /ˌɪndɪˈspensəb(ə)l/ *adj* необходи́мый.

indisposed /ˌɪndɪˈspəʊzd/ *predic* (*unwell*) нездорóв.

indisputable /ˌɪndɪˈspjuːtəb(ə)l/ *adj* бесспóрный.

indistinct /ˌɪndɪˈstɪŋkt/ *adj* неясный.

indistinguishable /ˌɪndɪˈstɪŋgwɪʃəb(ə)l/ *adj* неразличи́мый.

individual /ˌɪndɪˈvɪdjʊəl/ *n* ли́чность; *adj* индивидуáльный. **individualism** /-ˈvɪdjʊəˌlɪz(ə)m/ *n* индивидуали́зм. **individualist** /-ˈvɪdjʊəlɪst/ *n* индивидуали́ст. **individualistic** /ˌɪndɪˌvɪdjʊəˈlɪstɪk/ *adj* индивидуалисти́ческий. **individuality** /ˌɪndɪˌvɪdjʊˈælɪtɪ/ *n* индивидуáльность.

indivisible /ˌɪndɪˈvɪzɪb(ə)l/ *adj* недели́мый.

indoctrinate /ɪnˈdɒktrɪˌneɪt/ *vt* внушáть *impf*, внуши́ть *pf* +*dat* (**with** +*acc*).

indolence /ˈɪndələns/ *n* лéность. **indolent** /-lənt/ *adj* лени́вый.

indomitable /ɪnˈdɒmɪtəb(ə)l/ *adj* неукроти́мый.

Indonesia /ˌɪndəʊˈniːzɪə/ *n* Индонéзия.

indoor /ˈɪndɔː(r)/ *adj* кóмнатный.

I

indoors /ɪn'dɔːz/ *adv* (*position*) в до́ме; (*motion*) в дом.

induce /ɪn'djuːs/ *vt* (*prevail on*) убежда́ть *impf*, убеди́ть *pf*; (*bring about*) вызыва́ть *impf*, вы́звать *pf*. **inducement** /-mənt/ *n* побужде́ние.

induction /ɪn'dʌkʃ(ə)n/ *n* (*logic*, *electr*) инду́кция; (*in post*) введе́ние в до́лжность.

indulge /ɪn'dʌldʒ/ *vt* потво́рствовать *impf* +*dat*; *vi* предава́ться *impf*, преда́ться *pf* (**in** +*dat*). **indulgence** /-dʒ(ə)ns/ *n* потво́рство; (*tolerance*) снисходи́тельность. **indulgent** /-dʒ(ə)nt/ *adj* снисходи́тельный.

i

industrial /ɪn'dʌstrɪəl/ *adj* промы́шленный. **industrialist** /-'dʌstrɪəlɪst/ *n* промы́шленник. **industrious** /-'dʌstrɪəs/ *adj* трудолюби́вый. **industry** /'ɪndəstrɪ/ *n* промы́шленность; (*zeal*) трудолю́бие.

inebriated /ɪ'niːbrɪˌeɪtɪd/ *adj* пья́ный.

inedible /ɪn'edɪb(ə)l/ *adj* несъедо́бный.

ineffective, ineffectual /ˌɪnɪ'fektɪv, ˌɪnɪ'fektjʊəl/ *adj* безрезульта́тный; (*person*) неспосо́бный.

inefficiency /ˌɪnɪ'fɪʃ(ə)nsɪ/ *n* неэффекти́вность. **inefficient** /-'fɪʃ(ə)nt/ *adj* неэффекти́вный.

ineligible /ɪn'elɪdʒɪb(ə)l/ *adj* не име́ющий пра́во (**for** на+*acc*).

inept /ɪ'nept/ *adj* неуме́лый.

inequality /ˌɪnɪ'kwɒlɪtɪ/ *n* нера́венство.

inert /ɪ'nɜːt/ *adj* ине́ртный. **inertia** /ɪ'nɜːʃə/ *n* (*phys*) ине́рция; (*sluggishness*) ине́ртность.

inescapable /ˌɪnɪ'skeɪpəb(ə)l/ *adj* неизбе́жный.

inevitability /ɪnˌevɪtə'bɪlɪtɪ/ *n* неизбе́жность. **inevitable** /ɪn'evɪtəb(ə)l/ *adj* неизбе́жный.

inexact /ˌɪnɪg'zækt/ *adj* нето́чный.

inexcusable /ˌɪnɪk'skjuːzəb(ə)l/ *adj* непрости́тельный.

inexhaustible /ˌɪnɪg'zɔːstɪb(ə)l/ *adj* неистощи́мый.

inexorable /ɪn'eksərəb(ə)l/ *adj* неумоли́мый.

inexpensive /ˌɪnɪk'spensɪv/ *adj* недорого́й.

inexperience /ˌɪnɪk'spɪərɪəns/ *n* нео́пытность. **inexperienced** /-ənst/ *adj* нео́пытный.

inexplicable /ˌɪnɪk'splɪkəb(ə)l/ *adj* необъясни́мый.

infallible /ɪn'fælɪb(ə)l/ *adj* непогреши́мый.

infamous /'ɪnfəməs/ *adj* позо́рный. **infamy** /-mɪ/ *n* позо́р.

infancy /'ɪnfənsɪ/ *n* младе́нчество. **infant** /'ɪnfənt/ *n* младе́нец. **infantile** /'ɪnfənˌtaɪl/ *adj* де́тский.

infantry /'ɪnfəntrɪ/ *n* пехо́та.

infatuate /ɪn'fætjʊˌeɪt/ *vt* вскружи́ть *pf* го́лову +*dat*. **infatuation** /-'eɪʃ(ə)n/ *n* увлече́ние.

infect /ɪn'fekt/ *vt* заража́ть *impf*, зарази́ть *pf* (**with** +*instr*). **infection** /-'fekʃ(ə)n/ *n* зара́за, инфе́кция. **infectious** /-'fekʃəs/ *adj* зара́зный; (*fig*) зарази́тельный.

infer /ɪn'fɜː(r)/ *vt* заключа́ть *impf*, заключи́ть *pf*. **inference** /'ɪnfərəns/ *n* заключе́ние.

inferior /ɪn'fɪərɪə(r)/ *adj* (*in rank*) ни́зший; (*in quality*) ху́дший, плохо́й; *n* подчинённый *sb*. **inferiority** /ɪnˌfɪərɪ'ɒrɪtɪ/ *n* бо́лее ни́зкое ка́чество; **~ complex** ко́мплекс неполноце́нности.

infernal /ɪn'fɜːn(ə)l/ *adj* а́дский. **inferno** /-nəʊ/ *n* ад.

infertile /ɪn'fɜːtaɪl/ *adj* неплодоро́дный.

infested /ɪn'festɪd/ *adj*: **be ~ with** кише́ть *impf* +*instr*.

infidelity /ˌɪnfɪ'delɪtɪ/ *n* неве́рность.

infiltrate /'ɪnfɪlˌtreɪt/ *vt* постепе́нно проника́ть *impf*, прони́кнуть *pf* в+*acc*.

infinite /'ɪnfɪnɪt/ *adj* бесконе́чный. **infinitesimal** /ˌɪnfɪnɪ'tesɪməl/ *adj* бесконе́чно ма́лый. **infinitive** /ɪn'fɪnɪtɪv/ *n* инфинити́в. **infinity** /ɪn'fɪnɪtɪ/ *n* бесконе́чность.

infirm /ɪn'fɜːm/ *adj* не́мощный. **infirmary** /-mərɪ/ *n* больни́ца. **in-**

firmity /-mɪtɪ/ *n* немощь.
inflame /ɪn'fleɪm/ *vt & i* (*excite*) возбуждать(ся) *impf*, возбудить(ся) *pf*; (*med*) воспалять(ся) *impf*, воспалить(ся) *pf*. **inflammable** /-'flæməb(ə)l/ *adj* огнеопасный. **inflammation** /ˌɪnflə'meɪʃ(ə)n/ *n* воспаление. **inflammatory** /ɪn'flæmətərɪ/ *adj* подстрекательский.
inflate /ɪn'fleɪt/ *vt* надувать *impf*, надуть *pf*. **inflation** /-'fleɪʃ(ə)n/ *n* (*econ*) инфляция.
inflection /ɪn'flekʃ(ə)n/ *n* (*gram*) флексия.
inflexible /ɪn'fleksɪb(ə)l/ *adj* негибкий; (*fig*) непреклонный.
inflict /ɪn'flɪkt/ *vt* (*blow*) наносить *impf*, нанести *pf* (**(up)on** +*dat*); (*suffering*) причинять *impf*, причинить *pf* (**(up)on** +*dat*); (*penalty*) налагать *impf*, наложить *pf* (**(up)on** на+*acc*); **~ o.s. (up)on** навязываться *impf*, навязаться *pf* +*dat*.
inflow /'ɪnfləʊ/ *n* втекание, приток.
influence /'ɪnflʊəns/ *n* влияние; *vt* влиять *impf*, по~ *pf* на+*acc*. **influential** /ˌɪnflʊ'enʃ(ə)l/ *adj* влиятельный.
influenza /ˌɪnflʊ'enzə/ *n* грипп.
influx /'ɪnflʌks/ *n* (*fig*) наплыв.
inform /ɪn'fɔːm/ *vt* сообщать *impf*, сообщить *pf* +*dat* (**of, about** +*acc*, о+*prep*); *vi* доносить *impf*, донести *pf* (**against** на+*acc*).
informal /ɪn'fɔːm(ə)l/ *adj* (*unofficial*) неофициальный; (*casual*) обыденный.
informant /ɪn'fɔːmənt/ *n* осведомитель *m*. **information** /ˌɪnfə'meɪʃ(ə)n/ *n* информация. **informative** /ɪn'fɔːmətɪv/ *adj* поучительный. **informer** /ɪn'fɔːmə(r)/ *n* доносчик.
infra-red /ˌɪnfrə'red/ *adj* инфракрасный.
infrequent /ɪn'friːkwənt/ *adj* редкий.
infringe /ɪn'frɪndʒ/ *vt* (*violate*) нарушать *impf*, нарушить *pf*; *vi*: **~ (up)on** посягать *impf*, посягнуть *pf* на+*acc*. **infringement** /-mənt/ *n* нарушение; посягательство.
infuriate /ɪn'fjʊərɪˌeɪt/ *vt* разъярять *impf*, разъярить *pf*.
infuse /ɪn'fjuːz/ *vt* (*fig*) внушать *impf*, внушить *pf* (**into** +*dat*). **infusion** /-'fjuːʒ(ə)n/ *n* (*fig*) внушение; (*herbs etc*) настой.
ingenious /ɪn'dʒiːnɪəs/ *adj* изобретательный. **ingenuity** /ˌɪndʒɪ'njuːɪtɪ/ *n* изобретательность.
ingenuous /ɪn'dʒenjʊəs/ *adj* бесхитростный.
ingot /'ɪŋgɒt/ *n* слиток.
ingrained /ɪn'greɪnd/ *adj* закоренелый.
ingratiate /ɪn'greɪʃɪˌeɪt/ *vt* **~ o.s.** вкрадываться *impf*, вкрасться *pf* в милость (**with** +*dat*).
ingratitude /ɪn'grætɪˌtjuːd/ *n* неблагодарность.
ingredient /ɪn'griːdɪənt/ *n* ингредиент, составляющее *sb*.
inhabit /ɪn'hæbɪt/ *vt* жить *impf* в, на, +*prep*; обитать *impf* в, на, +*prep*. **inhabitant** /-t(ə)nt/ *n* житель *m*, ~ница.
inhalation /ˌɪnhə'leɪʃ(ə)n/ *n* вдыхание. **inhale** /ɪn'heɪl/ *vt* вдыхать *impf*, вдохнуть *pf*.
inherent /ɪn'hɪərənt/ *adj* присущий (**in** +*dat*).
inherit /ɪn'herɪt/ *vt* наследовать *impf & pf*, у~ *pf*. **inheritance** /-təns/ *n* наследство.
inhibit /ɪn'hɪbɪt/ *vt* стеснять *impf*, стеснить *pf*. **inhibited** /-tɪd/ *adj* стеснительный. **inhibition** /ˌɪnhɪ'bɪʃ(ə)n/ *n* стеснение.
inhospitable /ˌɪnhɒ'spɪtəb(ə)l/ *adj* негостеприимный; (*fig*) недружелюбный.
inhuman(e) /ɪn'hjuːmən, ˌɪnhjuː'meɪn/ *adj* бесчеловечный.
inimical /ɪ'nɪmɪk(ə)l/ *adj* враждебный; (*harmful*) вредный.
inimitable /ɪ'nɪmɪtəb(ə)l/ *adj* неподражаемый.
iniquity /ɪ'nɪkwɪtɪ/ *n* несправедливость.

initial /ɪ'nɪʃ(ə)l/ *adj* (перво)нача́льный; *n* нача́льная бу́ква; *pl* инициа́лы *m pl*; *vt* ста́вить *impf*, по~ *pf* инициа́лы на+*acc*. **initially** /-ʃəlɪ/ *adv* в нача́ле.
initiate /ɪ'nɪʃɪˌeɪt/ *vt* вводи́ть *impf*, ввести́ *pf* (**into** в+*acc*). **initiation** /-'eɪʃ(ə)n/ *n* введе́ние.
initiative /ɪ'nɪʃətɪv/ *n* инициати́ва.
inject /ɪn'dʒekt/ *vt* вводи́ть *impf*, ввести́ *pf* (*person* +*dat*, *substance* +*acc*). **injection** /-'dʒekʃ(ə)n/ *n* уко́л; (*fig*) инъе́кция.
injunction /ɪn'dʒʌŋkʃ(ə)n/ *n* (*law*) суде́бный запре́т.
injure /'ɪndʒə(r)/ *vt* поврежда́ть *impf*, повреди́ть *pf*. **injury** /'ɪndʒərɪ/ *n* ра́на.
injustice /ɪn'dʒʌstɪs/ *n* несправедли́вость.
ink /ɪŋk/ *n* черни́ла (-л).
inkling /'ɪŋklɪŋ/ *n* представле́ние.
inland /'ɪnlənd/ *adj* вну́тренний; *adv* (*motion*) внутрь страны́; (*place*) внутри́ страны́; **I~ Revenue** управле́ние нало́говых сбо́ров.
in-laws /'ɪnlɔːz/ *n pl* ро́дственники *m pl* супру́га, -ги.
inlay /'ɪnleɪ/ *n* инкруста́ция; /-'leɪ/ *vt* инкрусти́ровать *impf* & *pf*.
inlet /'ɪnlet/ *n* (*of sea*) у́зкий зали́в.
inmate /'ɪnmeɪt/ *n* (*prison*) заключённый *sb*; (*hospital*) больно́й *sb*.
inn /ɪn/ *n* гости́ница.
innate /ɪ'neɪt/ *adj* врождённый.
inner /'ɪnə(r)/ *adj* вну́тренний. **innermost** *adj* глубоча́йший; (*fig*) сокрове́ннейший.
innocence /'ɪnəs(ə)ns/ *n* неви́нность; (*guiltlessness*) невино́вность. **innocent** /-s(ə)nt/ *adj* неви́нный; (*not guilty*) невино́вный (**of** в+*prep*).
innocuous /ɪ'nɒkjʊəs/ *adj* безвре́дный.
innovate /'ɪnəˌveɪt/ *vi* вводи́ть *impf*, ввести́ *pf* но́вшества. **innovation** /-'veɪʃ(ə)n/ *n* нововведе́ние. **innovative** /'ɪnəvətɪv/ *adj* нова́торский. **innovator** /'ɪnəˌveɪtə(r)/ *n* нова́тор.
innuendo /ˌɪnjʊ'endəʊ/ *n* намёк, инсинуа́ция.
innumerable /ɪ'njuːmərəb(ə)l/ *adj* бесчи́сленный.
inoculate /ɪ'nɒkjʊˌleɪt/ *vt* привива́ть *impf*, приви́ть *pf* +*dat* (**against** +*acc*). **inoculation** /-'leɪʃ(ə)n/ *n* приви́вка.
inoffensive /ˌɪnə'fensɪv/ *adj* безоби́дный.
inopportune /ɪn'ɒpəˌtjuːn/ *adj* несвоевре́менный.
inordinate /ɪn'ɔːdɪnət/ *adj* чрезме́рный.
inorganic /ˌɪnɔː'gænɪk/ *adj* неоргани́ческий.
in-patient /'ɪnˌpeɪʃ(ə)nt/ *n* стациона́рный больно́й *sb*.
input /'ɪnpʊt/ *n* ввод.
inquest /'ɪnkwest/ *n* суде́бное сле́дствие, дозна́ние.
inquire /ɪn'kwaɪə(r)/ *vt* спра́шивать *impf*, спроси́ть *pf*; *vi* справля́ться *impf*, спра́виться *pf* (**about** о+*prep*); рассле́довать *impf* & *pf* (**into** +*acc*). **inquiry** /-'kwaɪərɪ/ *n* вопро́с, спра́вка; (*investigation*) рассле́дование.
inquisition /ˌɪnkwɪ'zɪʃ(ə)n/ *n* инквизи́ция. **inquisitive** /ɪn'kwɪzɪtɪv/ *adj* пытли́вый, любозна́тельный.
inroad /'ɪnrəʊd/ *n* (*attack*) набе́г; (*fig*) посяга́тельство (**on, into** на+*acc*).
insane /ɪn'seɪn/ *adj* безу́мный. **insanity** /-'sænɪtɪ/ *n* безу́мие.
insatiable /ɪn'seɪʃəb(ə)l/ *adj* ненасы́тный.
inscribe /ɪn'skraɪb/ *vt* надпи́сывать *impf*, надписа́ть *pf*; (*engrave*) вреза́ть *impf*, вы́резать *pf*. **inscription** /-'skrɪpʃ(ə)n/ *n* на́дпись.
inscrutable /ɪn'skruːtəb(ə)l/ *adj* непостижи́мый, непроница́емый.
insect /'ɪnsekt/ *n* насеко́мое *sb*. **insecticide** /ɪn'sektɪˌsaɪd/ *n* инсектици́д.
insecure /ˌɪnsɪ'kjʊə(r)/ *adj* (*unsafe*) небезопа́сный; (*not confident*) не-

уве́ренный (в себе́).

insemination /ɪn͵semɪˈneɪʃ(ə)n/ *n* оплодотворе́ние.

insensible /ɪnˈsensɪb(ə)l/ *adj* (*unconscious*) потеря́вший созна́ние.

insensitive /ɪnˈsensɪtɪv/ *adj* нечувстви́тельный.

inseparable /ɪnˈsepərəb(ə)l/ *adj* неотдели́мый; (*people*) неразлу́чный.

insert /ɪnˈsɜːt/ *vt* вставля́ть *impf*, вста́вить *pf*; вкла́дывать *impf*, вложи́ть *pf*; (*coin*) опуска́ть *impf*, опусти́ть *pf*. **insertion** /-ˈsɜːʃ(ə)n/ *n* (*inserting*) вставле́ние, вкла́дывание; (*thing inserted*) вста́вка.

inshore /ɪnˈʃɔː(r)/ *adj* прибре́жный; *adv* бли́зко к бе́регу.

inside /ɪnˈsaɪd/ *n* вну́тренняя часть; *pl* (*anat*) вну́тренности *f pl*; **turn ~ out** вывёртывать *impf*, вы́вернуть *pf* наизна́нку; *adj* вну́тренний; *adv* (*place*) внутри́; (*motion*) внутрь; *prep* (*place*) внутри́+*gen*, в+*prep*; (*motion*) внутрь+*gen*, в+*acc*.

insidious /ɪnˈsɪdɪəs/ *adj* кова́рный.

insight /ˈɪnsaɪt/ *n* проница́тельность.

insignia /ɪnˈsɪgnɪə/ *n* зна́ки *m pl* разли́чия.

insignificant /͵ɪnsɪgˈnɪfɪkənt/ *adj* незначи́тельный.

insincere /͵ɪnsɪnˈsɪə(r)/ *adj* нейскренний.

insinuate /ɪnˈsɪnjʊ͵eɪt/ *vt* (*hint*) намека́ть *impf*, намекну́ть *pf* на+*acc*. **insinuation** /-ˈeɪʃ(ə)n/ *n* инсинуа́ция.

insipid /ɪnˈsɪpɪd/ *adj* пре́сный.

insist /ɪnˈsɪst/ *vt* & *i* наста́ивать *impf*, настоя́ть *pf* (**on** на+*prep*). **insistence** /-t(ə)ns/ *n* насто́йчивость. **insistent** /-t(ə)nt/ *adj* насто́йчивый.

insolence /ˈɪnsələns/ *n* на́глость. **insolent** /-lənt/ *adj* на́глый.

insoluble /ɪnˈsɒljʊb(ə)l/ *adj* (*problem*) неразреши́мый; (*in liquid*) нераствори́мый.

insolvent /ɪnˈsɒlv(ə)nt/ *adj* несостоя́тельный.

insomnia /ɪnˈsɒmnɪə/ *n* бессо́нница.

inspect /ɪnˈspekt/ *vt* инспекти́ровать *impf*, про~ *pf*. **inspection** /-ˈspekʃ(ə)n/ *n* инспе́кция. **inspector** /-ˈspektə(r)/ *n* инспе́ктор; (*ticket* ~) контролёр.

inspiration /͵ɪnspɪˈreɪʃ(ə)n/ *n* вдохнове́ние. **inspire** /ɪnˈspaɪə(r)/ *vt* вдохновля́ть *impf*, вдохнови́ть *pf*; внуша́ть *impf*, внуши́ть *pf* +*dat* (**with** +*acc*).

instability /͵ɪnstəˈbɪlɪtɪ/ *n* неусто́йчивость; (*of character*) неуравнове́шенность.

install /ɪnˈstɔːl/ *vt* (*person in office*) вводи́ть *impf*, ввести́ *pf* в до́лжность; (*apparatus*) устана́вливать *impf*, установи́ть *pf*. **installation** /͵ɪnstəˈleɪʃ(ə)n/ *n* введе́ние в до́лжность; устано́вка; *pl* сооруже́ния *neut pl*.

instalment /ɪnˈstɔːlmənt/ *n* (*comm*) взнос; (*publication*) вы́пуск; часть; **by ~s** в рассро́чку.

instance /ˈɪnst(ə)ns/ *n* (*example*) приме́р; (*case*) слу́чай; **for ~** наприме́р.

instant /ˈɪnst(ə)nt/ *n* мгнове́ние, моме́нт; *adj* неме́дленный; (*coffee etc.*) раствори́мый. **instantaneous** /͵ɪnstənˈteɪnɪəs/ *adj* мгнове́нный. **instantly** /ˈɪnstəntlɪ/ *adv* неме́дленно, то́тчас.

instead /ɪnˈsted/ *adv* вме́сто (**of** +*gen*); **~ of going** вме́сто того́, что́бы пойти́.

instep /ˈɪnstep/ *n* подъём.

instigate /ˈɪnstɪ͵geɪt/ *vt* подстрека́ть *impf*, подстрекну́ть *pf* (**to** к+*dat*). **instigation** /-ˈgeɪʃ(ə)n/ *n* подстрека́тельство. **instigator** /ˈɪnstɪ͵geɪtə(r)/ *n* подстрека́тель *m*, ~ница.

instil /ɪnˈstɪl/ *vt* (*ideas etc.*) внуша́ть *impf*, внуши́ть *pf* (**into** +*dat*).

instinct /ˈɪnstɪŋkt/ *n* инсти́нкт. **instinctive** /ɪnˈstɪŋktɪv/ *adj* инстинкти́вный.

institute /'ɪnstɪˌtju:t/ *n* инститýт; *vt* (*establish*) устанáвливать *impf*, установи́ть *pf*; (*introduce*) вводи́ть *impf*, ввести́ *pf*; (*reforms*) проводи́ть *impf*, провести́ *pf*. **institution** /-'tju:ʃ(ə)n/ *n* учреждéние.

instruct /ɪn'strʌkt/ *vt* (*teach*) обучáть *impf*, обучи́ть *pf* (**in** +*dat*); (*inform*) сообщáть *impf*, сообщи́ть *pf* +*dat*; (*command*) прикáзывать *impf*, приказáть *pf* +*dat*. **instruction** /-'strʌkʃ(ə)n/ *n* (*in pl*) инстрýкция; (*teaching*) обучéние. **instructive** /-'strʌktɪv/ *adj* поучи́тельный. **instructor** /-'strʌktə(r)/ *n* инстрýктор.

i

instrument /'ɪnstrəmənt/ *n* орýдие, инструмéнт. **instrumental** /-'ment(ə)l/ *adj* (*mus*) инструментáльный; (*gram*) твори́тельный; **be ~ in** способствовать *impf*, по~ *pf* +*dat*; *n* (*gram*) твори́тельный падéж. **instrumentation** /ˌɪnstrəmen'teɪʃ(ə)n/ *n* (*mus*) инструментóвка.

insubordinate /ˌɪnsə'bɔ:dɪnət/ *adj* неподчиня́ющийся.

insufferable /ɪn'sʌfərəb(ə)l/ *adj* невыноси́мый.

insular /'ɪnsjʊlə(r)/ *adj* (*fig*) ограни́ченный.

insulate /'ɪnsjʊˌleɪt/ *vt* изоли́ровать *impf* & *pf*. **insulation** /-'leɪʃ(ə)n/ *n* изоля́ция. **insulator** /'ɪnsjʊˌleɪtə(r)/ *n* изоля́тор.

insulin /'ɪnsjʊlɪn/ *n* инсули́н.

insult *n* /'ɪnsʌlt/ оскорблéние; *vt* /ɪn'sʌlt/ оскорбля́ть *impf*, оскорби́ть *pf*. **insulting** /ɪn'sʌltɪŋ/ *adj* оскорби́тельный.

insuperable /ɪn'su:pərəb(ə)l/ *adj* непреодоли́мый.

insurance /ɪn'ʃʊərəns/ *n* страховáние; *attrib* страховóй. **insure** /-'ʃʊə(r)/ *vt* страховáть *impf*, за~ *pf* (**against** от+*gen*).

insurgent /ɪn'sɜ:dʒ(ə)nt/ *n* повстáнец.

insurmountable /ˌɪnsə'maʊntəb(ə)l/ *adj* непреодоли́мый.

insurrection /ˌɪnsə'rekʃ(ə)n/ *n* восстáние.

intact /ɪn'tækt/ *adj* цéлый.

intake /'ɪnteɪk/ *n* (*of persons*) набóр; (*consumption*) потреблéние.

intangible /ɪn'tændʒɪb(ə)l/ *adj* неосязáемый.

integral /'ɪntɪgr(ə)l/ *adj* неотъéмлемый. **integrate** /-ˌgreɪt/ *vt* & *i* интегри́роваться *impf* & *pf*. **integration** /-'greɪʃ(ə)n/ *n* интегрáция.

integrity /ɪn'tegrɪtɪ/ *n* (*honesty*) чéстность.

intellect /'ɪntɪˌlekt/ *n* интеллéкт. **intellectual** /-'lektjʊəl/ *n* интеллигéнт; *adj* интеллектуáльный.

intelligence /ɪn'telɪdʒ(ə)ns/ *n* (*intellect*) ум; (*information*) свéдения *neut pl*; (**~** *service*) развéдка. **intelligent** /-dʒ(ə)nt/ *adj* ýмный.

intelligentsia /ɪnˌtelɪ'dʒentsɪə/ *n* интеллигéнция.

intelligible /ɪn'telɪdʒɪb(ə)l/ *adj* поня́тный.

intemperate /ɪn'tempərət/ *adj* невоздéржанный.

intend /ɪn'tend/ *vt* собирáться *impf*, собрáться *pf*; (*design*) предназначáть *impf*, предназнáчить *pf* (**for** для+*gen*, на+*acc*).

intense /ɪn'tens/ *adj* си́льный. **intensify** /-'tensɪˌfaɪ/ *vt* & *i* уси́ливать(ся) *impf*, уси́лить(ся) *pf*. **intensity** /-'tensɪtɪ/ *n* интенси́вность, си́ла. **intensive** /-'tensɪv/ *adj* интенси́вный.

intent /ɪn'tent/ *n* намéрение; *adj* (*resolved*) стремя́щийся (**on** к+*dat*); (*occupied*) погружённый (**on** в+*acc*); (*earnest*) внимáтельный. **intention** /-'tenʃ(ə)n/ *n* намéрение. **intentional** /-'tenʃən(ə)l/ *adj* намéренный.

inter /ɪn'tɜ:(r)/ *vt* хорони́ть *impf*, по~ *pf*.

interact /ˌɪntər'ækt/ *vi* взаимодéйствовать *impf*. **interaction** /-'ækʃ(ə)n/ *n* взаимодéйствие. **interactive** /-tɪv/ *adj* (*comput*) интеракти́вный.

intercede /ˌɪntəˈsiːd/ *vi* хода́тайствовать *impf*, по~ *pf* (**for** за+*acc*; **with** пе́ред+*instr*).

intercept /ˌɪntəˈsept/ *vt* перехва́тывать *impf*, перехвати́ть *pf*. **interception** /-ˈsepʃ(ə)n/ *n* перехва́т.

interchange /ˈɪntəˌtʃeɪndʒ/ *n* обме́н (**of** +*instr*); (*junction*) тра́нспортная развя́зка; *vt* обме́ниваться *impf*, обменя́ться *pf* +*instr*. **interchangeable** /-ˈtʃeɪndʒəb(ə)l/ *adj* взаимозаменя́емый.

inter-city /ˌɪntəˈsɪtɪ/ *adj* междугоро́дный.

intercom /ˈɪntəˌkɒm/ *n* селе́ктор; (*to get into house*) домофо́н.

interconnected /ˌɪntəkəˈnektɪd/ *adj* взаимосвя́занный.

intercourse /ˈɪntəˌkɔːs/ *n* (*social*) обще́ние; (*trade*; *sexual*) сноше́ния *neut pl*.

interdisciplinary /ˌɪntədɪsɪˈplɪnərɪ/ *adj* межотраслево́й.

interest /ˈɪntrəst/ *n* интере́с (**in** к+*dat*); (*econ*) проце́нты *m pl*; *vt* интересова́ть *impf*; (~ *person in*) заинтересо́вывать *impf*, заинтересова́ть *pf* (**in** +*instr*); **be ~ed in** интересова́ться *impf* +*instr*. **interesting** /-stɪŋ/ *adj* интере́сный.

interfere /ˌɪntəˈfɪə(r)/ *vi* вме́шиваться *impf*, вмеша́ться *pf* (**in** в+*acc*). **interference** /-ˈfɪərəns/ *n* вмеша́тельство; (*radio*) поме́хи *f pl*.

interim /ˈɪntərɪm/ *n*: **in the ~** тем вре́менем; *adj* промежу́точный; (*temporary*) вре́менный.

interior /ɪnˈtɪərɪə(r)/ *n* (*of building*) интерье́р; (*of object*) вну́тренность; *adj* вну́тренний.

interjection /ˌɪntəˈdʒekʃ(ə)n/ *n* восклица́ние; (*gram*) междоме́тие.

interlock /ˌɪntəˈlɒk/ *vt & i* сцепля́ть(ся) *impf*, сцепи́ть(ся) *pf*.

interloper /ˈɪntəˌləʊpə(r)/ *n* незва́ный гость *m*.

interlude /ˈɪntəˌluːd/ *n* (*theat*) антра́кт; (*mus, fig*) интерлю́дия.

intermediary /ˌɪntəˈmiːdɪərɪ/ *n* посре́дник.

intermediate /ˌɪntəˈmiːdɪət/ *adj* промежу́точный.

interminable /ɪnˈtɜːmɪnəb(ə)l/ *adj* бесконе́чный.

intermission /ˌɪntəˈmɪʃ(ə)n/ *n* (*theat*) антра́кт.

intermittent /ˌɪntəˈmɪt(ə)nt/ *adj* преры́вистый.

intern /ɪnˈtɜːn/ *vt* интерни́ровать *impf & pf*.

internal /ɪnˈtɜːn(ə)l/ *adj* вну́тренний; **~ combustion engine** дви́гатель *m* вну́треннего сгора́ния.

international /ˌɪntəˈnæʃən(ə)l/ *adj* междунаро́дный; *n* (*contest*) междунаро́дные состяза́ния *neut pl*.

Internet /ˈɪntəˌnet/ *n* Интерне́т; **on the ~** в Интерне́те.

internment /ɪnˈtɜːnmənt/ *n* интерни́рование.

interplay /ˈɪntəˌpleɪ/ *n* взаимоде́йствие.

interpret /ɪnˈtɜːprɪt/ *vt* (*explain*) толкова́ть *impf*; (*understand*) истолко́вывать *impf*, истолкова́ть *pf*; *vi* переводи́ть *impf*, перевести́ *pf*. **interpretation** /-ˈteɪʃ(ə)n/ *n* толкова́ние. **interpreter** /ɪnˈtɜːprɪtə(r)/ *n* перево́дчик, -ица.

interrelated /ˌɪntərɪˈleɪtɪd/ *adj* взаимосвя́занный.

interrogate /ɪnˈterəˌgeɪt/ *vt* допра́шивать *impf*, допроси́ть *pf*. **interrogation** /-ˈgeɪʃ(ə)n/ *n* допро́с. **interrogative** /ˌɪntəˈrɒgətɪv/ *adj* вопроси́тельный.

interrupt /ˌɪntəˈrʌpt/ *vt* прерыва́ть *impf*, прерва́ть *pf*. **interruption** /-ˈrʌpʃ(ə)n/ *n* переры́в.

intersect /ˌɪntəˈsekt/ *vt & i* пересека́ть(ся) *impf*, пересе́чь(ся) *pf*. **intersection** /-ˈsekʃ(ə)n/ *n* пересече́ние.

intersperse /ˌɪntəˈspɜːs/ *vt* (*scatter*) рассыпа́ть *impf*, рассы́пать *pf* (**between, among** ме́жду+*instr*, среди́+*gen*).

intertwine /ˌɪntəˈtwaɪn/ *vt & i* переплета́ть(ся) *impf*, переплести́(сь) *pf*.

interval /ˈɪntəv(ə)l/ *n* интерва́л; (*theat*) антра́кт.

intervene /ˌɪntəˈviːn/ *vi* (*occur*) происходи́ть *impf*, произойти́ *pf*; ~ **in** вме́шиваться *impf*, вмеша́ться *pf* в+*acc*. **intervention** /-ˈvenʃ(ə)n/ *n* вмеша́тельство; (*polit*) интерве́нция.

interview /ˈɪntəˌvjuː/ *n* интервью́ *neut indecl*; *vt* интервьюи́ровать *impf* & *pf*, про~ *pf*. **interviewer** /-ˌvjuːə(r)/ *n* интервьюе́р.

interweave /ˌɪntəˈwiːv/ *vt* вотка́ть *pf*.

i

intestate /ɪnˈtesteɪt/ *adj* без завеща́ния.

intestine /ɪnˈtestɪn/ *n* кишка́; *pl* кише́чник.

intimacy /ˈɪntɪməsɪ/ *n* инти́мность. **intimate**[1] /ˈɪntɪmət/ *adj* инти́мный.

intimate[2] /ˈɪntɪˌmeɪt/ *vt* (*hint*) намека́ть *impf*, намекну́ть *pf* на+*acc*. **intimation** /-ˈmeɪʃ(ə)n/ *n* намёк.

intimidate /ɪnˈtɪmɪˌdeɪt/ *vt* запу́гивать *impf*, запуга́ть *pf*.

into /ˈɪntʊ/ *prep* в, во+*acc*, на+*acc*.

intolerable /ɪnˈtɒlərəb(ə)l/ *adj* невыноси́мый. **intolerance** /-rəns/ *n* нетерпи́мость. **intolerant** /-rənt/ *adj* нетерпи́мый.

intonation /ˌɪntəˈneɪʃ(ə)n/ *n* интона́ция.

intoxicated /ɪnˈtɒksɪˌkeɪtɪd/ *adj* пья́ный. **intoxication** /-ˈkeɪʃ(ə)n/ *n* опьяне́ние.

intractable /ɪnˈtræktəb(ə)l/ *adj* непода́тливый.

intransigent /ɪnˈtrænsɪdʒ(ə)nt/ *adj* непримири́мый.

intransitive /ɪnˈtrænsɪtɪv/ *adj* неперехо́дный.

intrepid /ɪnˈtrepɪd/ *adj* неустраши́мый.

intricacy /ˈɪntrɪkəsɪ/ *n* запу́танность. **intricate** /ˈɪntrɪkət/ *adj* запу́танный.

intrigue /ˈɪntriːg/ *n* интри́га; *vi* интригова́ть *impf*; *vt* интригова́ть *impf*, за~ *pf*.

intrinsic /ɪnˈtrɪnzɪk/ *adj* прису́щий; (*value*) вну́тренний.

introduce /ˌɪntrəˈdjuːs/ *vt* вводи́ть *impf*, ввести́ *pf*; (*person*) представля́ть *impf*, предста́вить *pf*. **introduction** /-ˈdʌkʃ(ə)n/ *n* введе́ние; представле́ние; (*to book*) предисло́вие. **introductory** /-ˈdʌktərɪ/ *adj* вступи́тельный.

introspection /ˌɪntrəˈspekʃ(ə)n/ *n* интроспе́кция.

intrude /ɪnˈtruːd/ *vi* вторга́ться *impf*, вто́ргнуться *pf* (**into** в+*acc*); (*disturb*) меша́ть *impf*, по~ *pf*. **intruder** /-ˈtruːdə(r)/ *n* (*burglar*) граби́тель *m*. **intrusion** /-ˈtruːʒ(ə)n/ *n* вторже́ние.

intuition /ˌɪntjuːˈɪʃ(ə)n/ *n* интуи́ция. **intuitive** /ɪnˈtjuːɪtɪv/ *adj* интуити́вный.

inundate /ˈɪnənˌdeɪt/ *vt* наводня́ть *impf*, наводни́ть *pf*. **inundation** /-ˈdeɪʃ(ə)n/ *n* наводне́ние.

invade /ɪnˈveɪd/ *vt* вторга́ться *impf*, вто́ргнуться *pf* в+*acc*. **invader** /-də(r)/ *n* захва́тчик.

invalid[1] /ˈɪnvəlɪd/ *n* (*person*) инвали́д.

invalid[2] /ɪnˈvælɪd/ *adj* недействи́тельный. **invalidate** /-ˈvælɪˌdeɪt/ *vt* де́лать *impf*, с~ *pf* недействи́тельным.

invaluable /ɪnˈvæljʊəb(ə)l/ *adj* неоцени́мый.

invariable /ɪnˈveərɪəb(ə)l/ *adj* неизме́нный.

invasion /ɪnˈveɪʒ(ə)n/ *n* вторже́ние.

invective /ɪnˈvektɪv/ *n* брань.

invent /ɪnˈvent/ *vt* изобрета́ть *impf*, изобрести́ *pf*; (*think up*) выду́мывать *impf*, вы́думать *pf*. **invention** /-ˈvenʃ(ə)n/ *n* изобрете́ние; вы́думка. **inventive** /-ˈventɪv/ *adj* изобрета́тельный. **inventor** /-ˈventə(r)/ *n* изобрета́тель *m*.

inventory /ˈɪnvəntərɪ/ *n* инвента́рь *m*.

inverse /ˈɪnvɜːs/ *adj* обра́тный; *n* противополо́жность. **invert** /ɪnˈvɜːt/ *vt* перевора́чивать *impf*, переверну́ть *pf*. **inverted**

commas *n pl* кавы́чки *f pl*.
invest /ɪn'vest/ *vt & i* (*econ*) вкла́дывать *impf*, вложи́ть *pf* (де́ньги) (**in** в+*acc*).
investigate /ɪn'vestɪˌgeɪt/ *vt* иссле́довать *impf & pf*; (*law*) рассле́довать *impf & pf*. **investigation** /-'geɪʃ(ə)n/ *n* иссле́дование; рассле́дование.
investment /ɪn'vestmənt/ *n* инвести́ция, вклад. **investor** /-'vestə(r)/ *n* вкла́дчик.
inveterate /ɪn'vetərət/ *adj* закорене́лый.
invidious /ɪn'vɪdɪəs/ *adj* оскорби́тельный.
invigorate /ɪn'vɪgəˌreɪt/ *vt* оживля́ть *impf*, оживи́ть *pf*.
invincible /ɪn'vɪnsɪb(ə)l/ *adj* непобеди́мый.
inviolable /ɪn'vaɪələb(ə)l/ *adj* неруши́мый.
invisible /ɪn'vɪzɪb(ə)l/ *adj* неви́димый.
invitation /ˌɪnvɪ'teɪʃ(ə)n/ *n* приглаше́ние. **invite** /ɪn'vaɪt/ *vt* приглаша́ть *impf*, пригласи́ть *pf*. **inviting**/ɪn'vaɪtɪŋ/ *adj* привлека́тельный.
invoice /'ɪnvɔɪs/ *n* факту́ра.
invoke /ɪn'vəʊk/ *vt* обраща́ться *impf*, обрати́ться *pf* к+*dat*.
involuntary /ɪn'vɒləntərɪ/ *adj* нево́льный.
involve /ɪn'vɒlv/ *vt* (*entangle*) вовлека́ть *impf*, вовле́чь *pf*; (*entail*) влечь *impf* за собо́й. **involved** /-'vɒlvd/ *adj* сло́жный.
invulnerable /ɪn'vʌlnərəb(ə)l/ *adj* неуязви́мый.
inward /'ɪnwəd/ *adj* вну́тренний. **inwardly** /-lɪ/ *adv* внутри́. **inwards** /'ɪnwədz/ *adv* внутрь.
iodine /'aɪəˌdiːn/ *n* йод.
iota /aɪ'əʊtə/ *n*: **not an** ~ ни на йо́ту.
IOU /ˌaɪəʊ'juː/ *n* долгова́я распи́ска.
Iran /ɪ'rɑːn/ *n* Ира́н. **Iranian** /-'reɪnɪən/ *n* ира́нец, -нка; *adj* ира́нский.
Iraq /ɪ'rɑːk/ *n* Ира́к. **Iraqi** /-kɪ/ *n* ира́кец; жи́тель *m*, ~ница Ира́ка; *adj* ира́кский.
irascible /ɪ'ræsɪb(ə)l/ *adj* раздражи́тельный.
irate /aɪ'reɪt/ *adj* гне́вный.
Ireland /'aɪələnd/ *n* Ирла́ндия.
iris /'aɪərɪs/ *n* (*anat*) ра́дужная оболо́чка; (*bot*) каса́тик.
Irish /'aɪərɪʃ/ *adj* ирла́ндский. **Irishman** *n* ирла́ндец. **Irishwoman** *n* ирла́ндка.
irk /ɜːk/ *vt* раздража́ть *impf*, раздражи́ть *pf* +*dat*. **irksome** /-səm/ *adj* раздражи́тельный.
iron /'aɪən/ *n* желе́зо; (*for clothes*) утю́г; *adj* желе́зный; *vt* гла́дить *impf*, вы́~ *pf*.
ironic(al) /aɪ'rɒnɪkəl/ *adj* ирони́ческий. **irony** /'aɪrənɪ/ *n* иро́ния.
irradiate /ɪ'reɪdɪˌeɪt/ *vt* (*subject to radiation*) облуча́ть *impf*, облучи́ть *pf*. **irradiation** /-'eɪʃ(ə)n/ *n* облуче́ние.
irrational /ɪ'ræʃən(ə)l/ *adj* неразу́мный.
irreconcilable /ɪ'rekənˌsaɪləb(ə)l/ *adj* непримири́мый.
irrefutable /ˌɪrɪ'fjuːtəb(ə)l/ *adj* неопровержи́мый.
irregular /ɪ'regjʊlə(r)/ *adj* нерегуля́рный; (*gram*) непра́вильный; (*not even*) неро́вный.
irrelevant /ɪ'relɪv(ə)nt/ *adj* неуме́стный.
irreparable /ɪ'repərəb(ə)l/ *adj* непоправи́мый.
irreplaceable /ˌɪrɪ'pleɪsəb(ə)l/ *adj* незамени́мый.
irrepressible /ˌɪrɪ'presɪb(ə)l/ *adj* неудержи́мый.
irreproachable /ˌɪrɪ'prəʊtʃəb(ə)l/ *adj* безупре́чный.
irresistible /ˌɪrɪ'zɪstɪb(ə)l/ *adj* неотрази́мый.
irresolute /ɪ'rezəˌluːt/ *adj* нереши́тельный.
irrespective /ˌɪrɪ'spektɪv/ *adj*: ~ **of** несмотря́ на+*acc*.
irresponsible /ˌɪrɪ'spɒnsɪb(ə)l/ *adj* безотве́тственный.
irretrievable /ˌɪrɪ'triːvəb(ə)l/ *adj* непоправи́мый.

irreverent /ɪ'revərənt/ *adj* непочти́тельный.

irreversible /ˌɪrɪ'vɜːsɪb(ə)l/ *adj* необрати́мый.

irrevocable /ɪ'revəkəb(ə)l/ *adj* неотменя́емый.

irrigate /'ɪrɪˌgeɪt/ *vt* ороша́ть *impf*, ороси́ть *pf*. **irrigation** /-'geɪʃ(ə)n/ *n* ороше́ние.

irritable /'ɪrɪtəb(ə)l/ *adj* раздражи́тельный. **irritate** /'ɪrɪˌteɪt/ *vt* раздража́ть *impf*, раздражи́ть *pf*. **irritation** /-'teɪʃ(ə)n/ *n* раздраже́ние.

Islam /'ɪzlɑːm/ *n* исла́м. **Islamic** /-'læmɪk/ *adj* мусульма́нский.

island, isle /'aɪlənd, aɪl/ *n* о́стров. **islander** /'aɪləndə(r)/ *n* островитя́нин, -я́нка.

isolate /'aɪsəˌleɪt/ *vt* изоли́ровать *impf* & *pf*. **isolation** /-'leɪʃ(ə)n/ *n* изоля́ция.

Israel /'ɪzreɪl/ *n* Изра́иль *m*. **Israeli** /-'reɪlɪ/ *n* израильтя́нин, -я́нка; *adj* изра́ильский.

issue /'ɪʃuː/ *n* (*question*) (спо́рный) вопро́с; (*of bonds etc.*) вы́пуск; (*of magazine*) но́мер; *vt* выпуска́ть *impf*, вы́пустить *pf*; (*give out*) выдава́ть *impf*, вы́дать *pf*.

isthmus /'ɪsməs/ *n* переше́ек.

IT *abbr* (*of* **information technology**) информа́тика.

it /ɪt/ *pron* он, она́, оно́; *demonstrative* э́то.

Italian /ɪ'tæljən/ *n* италья́нец, -нка; *adj* италья́нский.

italics /ɪ'tælɪks/ *n pl* курси́в; **in ~** курси́вом.

Italy /'ɪtəlɪ/ *n* Ита́лия.

itch /ɪtʃ/ *n* зуд; *vi* чеса́ться *impf*.

item /'aɪtəm/ *n* (*on list*) предме́т; (*in account*) статья́; (*on agenda*) пункт; (*in programme*) но́мер. **itemize** /-ˌmaɪz/ *vt* перечисля́ть *impf*, перечи́слить *pf*.

itinerant /aɪ'tɪnərənt/ *adj* стра́нствующий. **itinerary** /aɪ'tɪnərərɪ/ *n* маршру́т.

its /ɪts/ *poss pron* его́, её; свой.

itself /ɪt'self/ *pron* (*emph*) (он(о́)) сам(о́), (она́) сама́; (*refl*) себя́; -ся (*suffixed to vt*).

IVF *abbr* (*of* **in vitro fertilization**) экстракорпора́льное оплодотворе́ние.

ivory /'aɪvərɪ/ *n* слоно́вая кость.

ivy /'aɪvɪ/ *n* плющ.

J

jab /dʒæb/ *n* толчо́к; (*injection*) уко́л; *vt* ты́кать *impf*, ткнуть *pf*.

jabber /'dʒæbə(r)/ *vi* тарато́рить *impf*.

jack /dʒæk/ *n* (*cards*) вале́т; (*lifting device*) домкра́т; *vt* (~ *up*) поднима́ть *impf*, подня́ть *pf* домкра́том.

jackdaw /'dʒækdɔː/ *n* га́лка.

jacket /'dʒækɪt/ *n* (*tailored*) пиджа́к; (*anorak*) ку́ртка; (*on book*) (супер)обло́жка.

jackpot /'dʒækpɒt/ *n* банк.

jade /dʒeɪd/ *n* (*mineral*) нефри́т.

jaded /'dʒeɪdɪd/ *adj* утомлённый.

jagged /'dʒægɪd/ *adj* зазу́бренный.

jaguar /'dʒægjʊə(r)/ *n* ягуа́р.

jail /dʒeɪl/ *see* **gaol**

jam¹ /dʒæm/ *n* (*crush*) да́вка; (*in traffic*) про́бка; *vt* (*thrust*) впи́хивать *impf*, впихну́ть *pf* (**into** в+*acc*); (*wedge open; block*) закли́нивать *impf*, заклини́ть *pf*; (*radio*) заглуша́ть *impf*, заглуши́ть *pf*; *vi* (*machine*) закли́нивать *impf*, заклини́ть *pf* *impers*+*acc*.

jam² /dʒæm/ *n* (*conserve*) варе́нье, джем.

jangle /'dʒæŋg(ə)l/ *vi* (& *t*) звя́кать (+*instr*).

janitor /'dʒænɪtə(r)/ *n* приврáтник.

January /'dʒænjʊərɪ/ *n* янва́рь; *adj* янва́рский.

Japan /dʒə'pæn/ *n* Япо́ния. **Japanese** /ˌdʒæpə'niːz/ *n* япо́нец, -нка; *adj* япо́нский.

jar¹ /dʒɑː(r)/ *n* (*container*) ба́нка.

jar² /dʒɑː(r)/ *vi* (*irritate*) раздража́ть *impf*, раздражи́ть *pf* (**upon** +*acc*).

jargon /ˈdʒɑːgən/ *n* жаргóн.
jasmin(e) /ˈdʒæzmɪn/ *n* жасмúн.
jaundice /ˈdʒɔːndɪs/ *n* желтýха. **jaundiced** /-dɪst/ *adj* (*fig*) ци-нúчный.
jaunt /dʒɔːnt/ *n* прогýлка.
jaunty /ˈdʒɔːntɪ/ *adj* бóдрый.
javelin /ˈdʒævəlɪn/ *n* копьё.
jaw /dʒɔː/ *n* чéлюсть; *pl* пасть, рот.
jay /dʒeɪ/ *n* сóйка.
jazz /dʒæz/ *n* джаз; *adj* джáзовый.
jealous /ˈdʒeləs/ *adj* ревнúвый; (*envious*) завúстливый; **be ~ of** (*person*) ревновáть *impf*; (*thing*) завúдовать *impf*, по~ *pf* +*dat*; (*rights*) ревнúво оберегáть *impf*, оберéчь *pf.* **jealousy** /-sɪ/ *n* рé-вность; зáвисть.
jeans /dʒiːnz/ *n pl* джúнсы (-сов) *pl.*
jeer /dʒɪə(r)/ *n* насмéшка; *vt* & *i* насмехáться *impf* (**at** над+*instr*).
jelly /ˈdʒelɪ/ *n* (*sweet*) желé *neut in-decl*; (*aspic*) стýдень *m.* **jellyfish** *n* медýза.
jeopardize /ˈdʒepəˌdaɪz/ *vt* подвер-гáть *impf*, подвéргнуть *pf* опáс-ности. **jeopardy** /-dɪ/ *n* опáс-ность.
jerk /dʒɜːk/ *n* рывóк; *vt* дёргать *impf* +*instr*; *vi* (*twitch*) дёргаться *impf*, дёрнуться *pf.* **jerky** /-kɪ/ *adj* нерóвный.
jersey /ˈdʒɜːzɪ/ *n* (*garment*) джéм-пер; (*fabric*) джéрсú *neut indecl.*
jest /dʒest/ *n* шýтка; **in ~** в шýтку; *vi* шутúть *impf*, по~ *pf.* **jester** /-stə(r)/ *n* шут.
jet[1] /dʒet/ *n* (*stream*) струя́; (*nozzle*) сóпло́; **~ engine** реактúвный двúгатель *m*; **~ plane** реактúв-ный самолёт.
jet[2] /dʒet/ *n* (*mineralogy*) гагáт; **~-black** чёрный как смоль.
jettison /ˈdʒetɪs(ə)n/ *vt* выбрáсы-вать *impf*, вы́бросить *pf* зá борт.
jetty /ˈdʒetɪ/ *n* прúстань.
Jew /dʒuː/ *n* еврéй, еврéйка. **Jew-ish** /-ɪʃ/ *adj* еврéйский.
jewel /ˈdʒuːəl/ *n* драгоцéнность, драгоцéнный кáмень *m.* **jeweller** /-lə(r)/ *n* ювелúр. **jewellery** /-lərɪ/ *n* драгоцéнности *f pl.*
jib /dʒɪb/ *n* (*naut*) клúвер; *vi*: **~ at** уклоня́ться *impf* от+*gen.*
jigsaw /ˈdʒɪgsɔː/ *n* (*puzzle*) мо-зáика.
jingle /ˈdʒɪŋg(ə)l/ *n* звя́канье; *vi* (& *t*) звя́кать *impf*, звя́кнуть *pf* (+*instr*).
job /dʒɒb/ *n* (*work*) рабóта; (*task*) задáние; (*position*) мéсто. **job-less** /-lɪs/ *adj* безрабóтный.
jockey /ˈdʒɒkɪ/ *n* жокéй; *vi* отти-рáть *impf* друг дрýга.
jocular /ˈdʒɒkjʊlə(r)/ *adj* шут-лúвый.
jog /dʒɒg/ *n* (*push*) толчóк; *vt* под-тáлкивать *impf*, подтолкнýть *pf*; *vi* бéгать *impf* трусцóй. **jogger** /-gə(r)/ *n* занимáющийся оздо-ровúтельным бéгом. **jogging** /-gɪŋ/ *n* оздоровúтельный бег.
join /dʒɔɪn/ *vt* & *i* соединя́ть(ся) *impf*, соединúть(ся) *pf*; *vt* (*a group of people*) присоединя́ться *impf*, присоединúться *pf* к+*dat*; (*as member*) вступáть *impf*, всту-пúть *pf* в+*acc*; *vi*: **~ in** прини-мáть *impf*, приня́ть *pf* учáстие (в+*prep*); **~ up** вступáть *impf*, вступúть *pf* в áрмию.
joiner /ˈdʒɔɪnə(r)/ *n* столя́р.
joint /dʒɔɪnt/ *n* соединéние; (*anat*) сустáв; (*meat*) кусóк; *adj* со-вмéстный; (*common*) óбщий.
joist /dʒɔɪst/ *n* переклáдина.
joke /dʒəʊk/ *n* шýтка; *vi* шутúть *impf*, по~ *pf.* **joker** /-kə(r)/ *n* шутнúк; (*cards*) джóкер.
jollity /ˈdʒɒlɪtɪ/ *n* весéлье. **jolly** /-lɪ/ *adj* весёлый; *adv* óчень.
jolt /dʒəʊlt/ *n* толчóк; *vt* & *i* тря-стú(сь) *impf.*
jostle /ˈdʒɒs(ə)l/ *vt* & *i* толкáть(ся) *impf*, толкнýть(ся) *pf.*
jot /dʒɒt/ *n* йóта; **not a ~** ни на йóту; *vt* (**~** *down*) запúсывать *impf*, записáть *pf.*
journal /ˈdʒɜːn(ə)l/ *n* журнáл;

J

(*diary*) дневни́к. **journalese** /-'li:z/ *n* газе́тный язы́к. **journalism** /-lɪz(ə)m/ *n* журнали́стика. **journalist** /-lɪst/ *n* журнали́ст.

journey /'dʒɜ:nɪ/ *n* путеше́ствие; *vi* путеше́ствовать *impf.*

jovial /'dʒəʊvɪəl/ *adj* весёлый.

joy /dʒɔɪ/ *n* ра́дость. **joyful, joyous** /-fʊl, -əs/ *adj* ра́достный. **joyless** /-lɪs/ *adj* безра́достный. **joystick** *n* рыча́г управле́ния; (*comput*) джо́йстик.

jubilant /'dʒu:bɪlənt/ *adj* лику́ющий; **be ~** ликова́ть *impf.* **jubilation** /-'leɪʃ(ə)n/ *n* ликова́ние.

jubilee /'dʒu:bɪˌli:/ *n* юбиле́й.

Judaism /'dʒu:deɪˌɪz(ə)m/ *n* иудаи́зм.

j

judge /dʒʌdʒ/ *n* судья́ *m*; (*connoisseur*) цени́тель *m*; *vt & i* суди́ть *impf.* **judgement** /-mənt/ *n* (*legal decision*) реше́ние; (*opinion*) мне́ние; (*discernment*) рассуди́тельность.

judicial /dʒu:'dɪʃ(ə)l/ *adj* суде́бный. **judiciary** /-'dɪʃɪərɪ/ *n* судьи́ *m pl.* **judicious** /-'dɪʃəs/ *adj* здравомы́слящий.

judo /'dʒu:dəʊ/ *n* дзюдо́ *neut indecl.*

jug /dʒʌg/ *n* кувши́н.

juggernaut /'dʒʌgəˌnɔ:t/ *n* (*lorry*) многото́нный грузови́к; (*fig*) неумоли́мая си́ла.

juggle /'dʒʌg(ə)l/ *vi* жонгли́ровать *impf.* **juggler** /'dʒʌglə(r)/ *n* жонглёр.

jugular /'dʒʌgjʊlə(r)/ *n* яре́мная ве́на.

juice /dʒu:s/ *n* сок. **juicy** /-sɪ/ *adj* со́чный.

July /dʒu:'laɪ/ *n* ию́ль *m*; *adj* ию́льский.

jumble /'dʒʌmb(ə)l/ *n* (*disorder*) беспоря́док; (*articles*) барахло́; *vt* перепу́тывать *impf*, перепу́тать *pf.*

jump /dʒʌmp/ *n* прыжо́к, скачо́к; *vi* пры́гать *impf*, пры́гнуть *pf*; скака́ть *impf*; (*from shock*) вздра́гивать *impf*, вздро́гнуть *pf*; *vt* (**~** *over*) перепры́гивать *impf*, перепры́гнуть *pf*; **~ at** (*offer*) ухва́тываться *impf*, ухвати́ться *pf* за+*acc*; **~ up** вска́кивать *impf*, вскочи́ть *pf.*

jumper /'dʒʌmpə(r)/ *n* дже́мпер.

jumpy /'dʒʌmpɪ/ *adj* не́рвный.

junction /'dʒʌŋkʃ(ə)n/ *n* (*rly*) у́зел; (*roads*) перекрёсток.

juncture /'dʒʌŋktʃə(r)/ *n*: **at this ~** в э́тот моме́нт.

June /dʒu:n/ *n* ию́нь *m*; *adj* ию́ньский.

jungle /'dʒʌŋg(ə)l/ *n* джу́нгли (-лей) *pl.*

junior /'dʒu:nɪə(r)/ *adj* мла́дший; **~ school** нача́льная шко́ла.

juniper /'dʒu:nɪpə(r)/ *n* можжеве́льник.

junk /dʒʌŋk/ *n* (*rubbish*) барахло́.

jurisdiction /ˌdʒʊərɪs'dɪkʃ(ə)n/ *n* юрисди́кция.

jurisprudence /ˌdʒʊərɪs'pru:d(ə)ns/ *n* юриспруде́нция.

juror /'dʒʊərə(r)/ *n* прися́жный *sb.* **jury** /'dʒʊərɪ/ *n* прися́жные *sb*; (*in competition*) жюри́ *neut indecl.*

just /dʒʌst/ *adj* (*fair*) справедли́вый; (*deserved*) заслу́женный; *adv* (*exactly*) как раз, и́менно; (*simply*) про́сто; (*barely*) едва́; (*very recently*) то́лько что; **~ in case** на вся́кий слу́чай.

justice /'dʒʌstɪs/ *n* (*proceedings*) правосу́дие; (*fairness*) справедли́вость; **do ~ to** отдава́ть *impf*, отда́ть *pf* до́лжное +*dat.*

justify /'dʒʌstɪˌfaɪ/ *vt* опра́вдывать *impf*, оправда́ть *pf.* **justification** /-fɪ'keɪʃ(ə)n/ *n* оправда́ние.

jut /dʒʌt/ *vi* (**~** *out*) выдава́ться *impf*; выступа́ть *impf.*

juvenile /'dʒu:vəˌnaɪl/ *n & adj* несовершенноле́тний *sb & adj.*

juxtapose /ˌdʒʌkstə'pəʊz/ *vt* помеща́ть *impf*, помести́ть *pf* ря́дом; (*for comparison*) сопоставля́ть *impf*, сопоста́вить *pf* (**with** c+*instr*).

K

kaleidoscope /kə'laɪdə,skəʊp/ *n* калейдоскóп.
kangaroo /,kæŋgə'ruː/ *n* кенгурý *m indecl.*
Kazakhstan /,kæzæk'stɑːn/ *n* Казахстáн.
keel /kiːl/ *n* киль *m*; *vi*: ~ **over** опрокúдываться *impf*, опрокúнуться *pf.*
keen /kiːn/ *adj* (*enthusiastic*) пóлный энтузиáзма; (*sharp*) óстрый; (*strong*) сúльный; **be ~ on** увлекáться *impf*, увлéчься *pf* +*instr*; (*want to do*) óчень хотéть *impf* +*inf.*
keep[1] /kiːp/ *n* (*tower*) глáвная бáшня; (*maintenance*) содержáние.
keep[2] /kiːp/ *vt* (*possess, maintain*) держáть *impf*; хранúть *impf*; (*observe*) соблюдáть *impf*, соблюстú *pf* (*the law*); сдéрживать *impf*, сдержáть *pf* (*one's word*); (*family*) содержáть *impf*; (*diary*) вестú *impf*; (*detain*) задéрживать *impf*, задержáть *pf*; (*retain, reserve*) сохранять *impf*, сохранúть *pf*; *vi* (*remain*) оставáться *impf*, остáться *pf*; (*of food*) не пóртиться *impf*; ~ **back** (*vt*) (*hold back*) удéрживать *impf*, удержáть *pf*; (*vi*) держáться *impf* сзáди; ~ **doing sth** всё +*verb*: **she ~s giggling** онá всё хихúкает; ~ **from** удéрживаться *impf*, удержáться *pf* от+*gen*; ~ **on** продолжáть *impf*, продóлжить *pf* (+*inf*); ~ **up (with)** (*vi*) не отставáть *impf* (от+*gen*).
keepsake /'kiːpseɪk/ *n* подáрок на пáмять.
keg /keg/ *n* бочóнок.
kennel /'ken(ə)l/ *n* конурá.
kerb /kɜːb/ *n* край тротуáра.
kernel /'kɜːn(ə)l/ *n* (*nut*) ядрó; (*grain*) зернó; (*fig*) суть.
kerosene /'kerə,siːn/ *n* керосúн.
kettle /'ket(ə)l/ *n* чáйник.
key /kiː/ *n* ключ; (*piano, typewriter*) клáвиш(а); (*mus*) тонáльность; *attrib* ведýщий, ключевóй. **keyboard** *n* клавиатýра. **keyhole** *n* замóчная сквáжина.
KGB *abbr* КГБ.
khaki /'kɑːkɪ/ *n* & *adj* хáки *neut, adj indecl.*
kick /kɪk/ *n* удáр ногóй, пинóк; *vt* ударять *impf*, удáрить *pf* ногóй; пинáть *impf*, пнуть *pf*; *vi* (*of horse etc.*) лягáться *impf.* **kick-off** /'kɪkɒf/ *n* начáло (игры́).
kid[1] /kɪd/ *n* (*goat*) козлёнок; (*child*) малы́ш.
kid[2] /kɪd/ *vt* (*deceive*) обмáнывать *impf*, обманýть *pf*; *vi* (*joke*) шутúть *impf*, по~ *pf.*
kidnap /'kɪdnæp/ *vt* похищáть *impf*, похúтить *pf.*
kidney /'kɪdnɪ/ *n* пóчка.
kill /kɪl/ *vt* убивáть *impf*, убúть *pf.* **killer** /-lə(r)/ *n* убúйца *m* & *f.* **killing** /-lɪŋ/ *n* убúйство; *adj* (*murderous, fig*) убúйственный; (*amusing*) уморúтельный.
kiln /kɪln/ *n* óбжиговая печь.
kilo /'kiːləʊ/ *n* килó *neut indecl.* **kilohertz** /'kɪlə,hɜːts/ *n* килогéрц. **kilogram(me)** /'kɪlə,græm/ *n* килогрáмм. **kilometre** /'kɪlə,miːtə(r)/ *n* киломéтр. **kilowatt** /'kɪlə,wɒt/ *n* киловáтт.
kilt /kɪlt/ *n* шотлáндская ю́бка.
kimono /kɪ'məʊnəʊ/ *n* кимонó *neut indecl.*
kin /kɪn/ *n* (*family*) семья́; (*collect, relatives*) родня́.
kind[1] /kaɪnd/ *n* сорт, род; **a ~ of** чтó-то врóде+*gen*; **this ~ of** такóй; **what ~ of** что (э́то, он, *etc.*) за +*nom*; **~ of** (*adv*) как бýдто, кáк-то.
kind[2] /kaɪnd/ *adj* дóбрый.
kindergarten /'kɪndə,gɑːt(ə)n/ *n* дéтский сад.
kindle /'kɪnd(ə)l/ *vt* зажигáть *impf*, зажéчь *pf.* **kindling** /-dlɪŋ/ *n* растóпка.
kindly /'kaɪndlɪ/ *adj* дóбрый; *adv* любéзно; (*with imper*) (*request*)

k

бу́дьте добры́, +*imper.* **kindness** /ˈkaɪndnɪs/ *n* доброта́.
kindred /ˈkɪndrɪd/ *adj*: ~ **spirit** родна́я душа́.
kinetic /kɪˈnetɪk/ *adj* кинети́ческий.
king /kɪŋ/ *n* коро́ль *m* (*also chess, cards, fig*); (*draughts*) да́мка. **kingdom** /ˈkɪŋdəm/ *n* короле́вство; (*fig*) ца́рство. **kingfisher** /ˈkɪŋfɪʃə(r)/ *n* зиморо́док.
kink /kɪŋk/ *n* переги́б.
kinship /ˈkɪnʃɪp/ *n* родство́; (*similarity*) схо́дство. **kinsman, -woman** *n* ро́дственник, -ица.
kiosk /ˈkiːɒsk/ *n* кио́ск; (*telephone*) бу́дка.
kip /kɪp/ *n* сон; *vi* дры́хнуть *impf.*
kipper /ˈkɪpə(r)/ *n* копчёная селёдка.

k

Kirghizia /kɜːˈgiːzɪə/ *n* Кирги́зия.
kiss /kɪs/ *n* поцелу́й; *vt & i* целова́ть(ся) *impf*, по~ *pf.*
kit /kɪt/ *n* (*clothing*) снаряже́ние; (*tools*) набо́р, компле́кт; *vt*: ~ **out** снаряжа́ть *impf*, снаряди́ть *pf.* **kitbag** *n* вещево́й мешо́к.
kitchen /ˈkɪtʃɪn/ *n* ку́хня; *attrib* ку́хонный; ~ **garden** огоро́д.
kite /kaɪt/ *n* (*toy*) змей.
kitsch /kɪtʃ/ *n* дешёвка.
kitten /ˈkɪt(ə)n/ *n* котёнок.
knack /næk/ *n* снoро́вка.
knapsack /ˈnæpsæk/ *n* рюкза́к.
knead /niːd/ *vt* меси́ть *impf*, с~ *pf.*
knee /niː/ *n* коле́но. **kneecap** *n* коле́нная ча́шка.
kneel /niːl/ *vi* стоя́ть *impf* на коле́нях; (~ *down*) станови́ться *impf*, стать *pf* на коле́ни.
knickers /ˈnɪkəz/ *n pl* тру́сики (-ов) *pl.*
knick-knack /ˈnɪknæk/ *n* безделу́шка.
knife /naɪf/ *n* нож; *vt* коло́ть *impf*, за~ *pf* ножо́м.
knight /naɪt/ *n* (*hist*) ры́царь *m*; (*holder of order*) кавале́р; (*chess*) конь *m.* **knighthood** /-hʊd/ *n* ры́царское зва́ние.
knit /nɪt/ *vt* (*garment*) вяза́ть *impf*, с~ *pf*; *vi* (*bones*) сраста́ться *impf*, срасти́сь *pf*; ~ **one's brows** хму́рить *impf*, на~ *pf* бро́ви. **knitting** /-tɪŋ/ *n* (*action*) вяза́ние; (*object*) вяза́нье; **~-needle** спи́ца. **knitwear** *n* трикота́ж.
knob /nɒb/ *n* ши́шка, кно́пка; (*door handle*) ру́чка. **knobb(l)y** /ˈnɒb(l)ɪ/ *adj* шишкова́тый.
knock /nɒk/ *n* (*noise*) стук; (*blow*) уда́р; *vt & i* (*strike*) ударя́ть *impf*, уда́рить *pf*; (*strike door etc.*) стуча́ть *impf*, по~ *pf* (**at** в+*acc*); ~ **about** (*treat roughly*) колоти́ть *impf*, по~ *pf*; (*wander*) шата́ться *impf*; ~ **down** (*person*) сбива́ть *impf*, сбить *pf* с ног; (*building*) сноси́ть *impf*, снести́ *pf*; ~ **off** сбива́ть *impf*, сбить *pf*; (*stop work*) шаба́шить *impf* (рабо́ту); (*deduct*) сбавля́ть *impf*, сба́вить *pf*; ~ **out** выбива́ть *impf*, вы́бить *pf*; (*sport*) нокаути́ровать *impf* & *pf*; **~-out** нока́ут; ~ **over** опроки́дывать *impf*, опроки́нуть *impf.* **knocker** /ˈnɒkə(r)/ *n* дверно́й молото́к.
knoll /nəʊl/ *n* буго́р.
knot /nɒt/ *n* у́зел; *vt* завя́зывать *impf*, завяза́ть *pf* узло́м. **knotty** /-tɪ/ *adj* (*fig*) запу́танный.
know /nəʊ/ *vt* знать *impf*; (~ *how to*) уме́ть *impf*, с~ *pf* +*inf*; **~-how** уме́ние. **knowing** /ˈnəʊɪŋ/ *adj* многозначи́тельный. **knowingly** /ˈnəʊɪŋlɪ/ *adv* созна́тельно. **knowledge** /ˈnɒlɪdʒ/ *n* зна́ние; **to my** ~ наско́лько мне изве́стно.
knuckle /ˈnʌk(ə)l/ *n* суста́в па́льца; *vi*: ~ **down to** впряга́ться *impf*, впря́чься *pf* в+*acc*; ~ **under** уступа́ть *impf*, уступи́ть *pf* (**to** +*dat*).
Korea /kəˈriːə/ *n* Коре́я.
ko(w)tow /kaʊˈtaʊ/ *vi* (*fig*) раболе́пствовать *impf* (**to** пе́ред +*instr*).
Kremlin /ˈkremlɪn/ *n* Кремль *m.*
kudos /ˈkjuːdɒs/ *n* сла́ва.

L

label /'leɪb(ə)l/ *n* этике́тка, ярлы́к; *vt* прикле́ивать *impf*, прикле́ить *pf* ярлы́к к+*dat*.
laboratory /lə'bɒrətərɪ/ *n* лаборато́рия.
laborious /lə'bɔːrɪəs/ *adj* кропотли́вый.
labour /'leɪbə(r)/ *n* труд; (*med*) ро́ды (-дов) *pl*; *attrib* трудово́й; **~ force** рабо́чая си́ла; **~-intensive** трудоёмкий; **L~ Party** лейбори́стская па́ртия; *vi* труди́ться *impf*; *vt*: **~ a point** входи́ть *impf*, войти́ *pf* в изли́шние подро́бности. **laboured** /-bəd/ *adj* затруднённый; (*style*) вы́мученный. **labourer** /-bərə(r)/ *n* чернорабо́чий *sb*. **labourite** /-bəˌraɪt/ *n* лейбори́ст.
labyrinth /'læbərɪnθ/ *n* лабири́нт.
lace /leɪs/ *n* (*fabric*) кру́жево; (*cord*) шнуро́к; *vt* (**~** *up*) шнурова́ть *impf*, за**~** *pf*.
lacerate /'læsəˌreɪt/ *vt* (*also fig*) терза́ть *impf*, ис**~** *pf*. **laceration** /-'reɪʃ(ə)n/ *n* (*wound*) рва́ная ра́на.
lack /læk/ *n* недоста́ток (**of** +*gen*, в+*prep*), отсу́тствие; *vt & i* не хвата́ть *impf*, хвати́ть *pf impers* +*dat* (*person*), +*gen* (*object*).
lackadaisical /ˌlækə'deɪzɪk(ə)l/ *adj* то́мный.
laconic /lə'kɒnɪk/ *adj* лакони́чный.
lacquer /'lækə(r)/ *n* лак; *vt* лакирова́ть *impf*, от**~** *pf*.
lad /læd/ *n* па́рень *m*.
ladder /'lædə(r)/ *n* ле́стница.
laden /'leɪd(ə)n/ *adj* нагружённый.
ladle /'leɪd(ə)l/ *n* (*spoon*) поло́вник; *vt* че́рпать *impf*, черпну́ть *pf*.
lady /'leɪdɪ/ *n* да́ма, ле́ди *f indecl*. **ladybird** *n* бо́жья коро́вка.
lag[1] /læg/ *vi*: **~ behind** отстава́ть *impf*, отста́ть *pf* (от+*gen*).
lag[2] /læg/ *vt* (*insulate*) изоли́ровать *impf & pf*.
lagoon /lə'guːn/ *n* лагу́на.
lair /leə(r)/ *n* ло́говище.
laity /'leɪɪtɪ/ *n* (*in religion*) миря́не (-н) *pl*.
lake /leɪk/ *n* о́зеро.
lamb /læm/ *n* ягнёнок; (*meat*) бара́нина.
lame /leɪm/ *adj* хромо́й; **be ~** хрома́ть *impf*; **go ~** хроме́ть *impf*, о**~** *pf*; *vt* кале́чить *impf*, о**~** *pf*.
lament /lə'ment/ *n* плач; *vt* сожале́ть *impf* о+*prep*. **lamentable** /'læməntəb(ə)l/ *adj* приско́рбный.
laminated /'læmɪˌneɪtɪd/ *adj* слои́стый.
lamp /læmp/ *n* ла́мпа; (*in street*) фона́рь *m*. **lamp-post** *n* фона́рный столб. **lampshade** *n* абажу́р.
lance /lɑːns/ *n* пи́ка; *vt* (*med*) вскрыва́ть *impf*, вскрыть *pf* (ланце́том).
land /lænd/ *n* земля́; (*dry* **~**) су́ша; (*country*) страна́; *vi* (*naut*) прича́ливать *impf*, прича́лить *pf*; *vt & i* (*aeron*) приземля́ть(ся) *impf*, приземли́ть(ся) *pf*; (*find o.s.*) попада́ть *impf*, попа́сть *pf*. **landing** /-dɪŋ/ *n* (*aeron*) поса́дка; (*on stairs*) площа́дка; **~-stage** при́стань. **landlady** *n* хозя́йка. **landlord** *n* хозя́ин. **landmark** *n* (*conspicuous object*) ориенти́р; (*fig*) ве́ха. **landowner** *n* землевладе́лец. **landscape** /'lændskeɪp/ *n* ландша́фт; (*also picture*) пейза́ж. **landslide** *n* о́ползень *m*.
lane /leɪn/ *n* (*in country*) доро́жка; (*street*) переу́лок; (*passage*) прохо́д; (*on road*) ряд; (*in race*) доро́жка.
language /'læŋgwɪdʒ/ *n* язы́к; (*style, speech*) речь.
languid /'læŋgwɪd/ *adj* то́мный.
languish /'læŋgwɪʃ/ *vi* томи́ться *impf*.
languor /'læŋgə(r)/ *n* то́мность.
lank /læŋk/ *adj* (*hair*) гла́дкий. **lanky** /-kɪ/ *adj* долговя́зый.
lantern /'lænt(ə)n/ *n* фона́рь *m*.
lap[1] /læp/ *n* (*of person*) коле́ни (-ней) *pl*; (*sport*) круг.

lap² /læp/ *vt* (*drink*) лака́ть *impf*, вы́~ *pf*; *vi* (*water*) плеска́ться *impf*.
lapel /ləˈpel/ *n* отворо́т.
lapse /læps/ *n* (*mistake*) оши́бка; (*interval*) промежу́ток; (*expiry*) истече́ние; *vi* впада́ть *impf*, впасть *pf* (**into** в+*acc*); (*expire*) истека́ть *impf*, исте́чь *pf*.
laptop /ˈlæptɒp/ *n* портати́вный компью́тер.
lapwing /ˈlæpwɪŋ/ *n* чи́бис.
larch /lɑːtʃ/ *n* ли́ственница.
lard /lɑːd/ *n* свино́е са́ло.
larder /ˈlɑːdə(r)/ *n* кладова́я *sb*.
large /lɑːdʒ/ *adj* большо́й; *n*: **at ~** (*free*) на свобо́де; **by and ~** вообще́ говоря́. **largely** /-lɪ/ *adj* в значи́тельной сте́пени.
largesse /lɑːˈʒes/ *n* ще́дрость.
lark¹ /lɑːk/ *n* (*bird*) жа́воронок.
lark² /lɑːk/ *n* прока́за; *vi* (**~** *about*) резви́ться *impf*.
larva /ˈlɑːvə/ *n* личи́нка.
laryngitis /ˌlærɪnˈdʒaɪtɪs/ *n* ларинги́т. **larynx** /ˈlærɪŋks/ *n* горта́нь.
lascivious /ləˈsɪvɪəs/ *adj* похотли́вый.
laser /ˈleɪzə(r)/ *n* ла́зер.
lash /læʃ/ *n* (*blow*) уда́р плётью; (*eyelash*) ресни́ца; *vt* (*beat*) хлеста́ть *impf*, хлестну́ть *pf*; (*tie*) привя́зывать *impf*, привяза́ть *pf* (**to** к+*dat*).
last¹ /lɑːst/ *adj* (*final*) после́дний; (*most recent*) про́шлый; **the year** (*etc.*) **before ~** позапро́шлый год (и т.д.); **~ but one** предпосле́дний; **~ night** вчера́ ве́чером; **at ~** наконе́ц; *adv* (*after all others*) по́сле всех; (*on the last occasion*) в после́дний раз; (*lastly*) наконе́ц.
last² /lɑːst/ *vi* (*go on*) продолжа́ться *impf*, продо́лжиться *pf*; дли́ться *impf*, про~ *pf*; (*be preserved*) сохраня́ться *impf*, сохрани́ться *pf*; (*suffice*) хвата́ть *impf*, хвати́ть *pf*. **lasting** /-tɪŋ/ *adj* (*permanent*) постоя́нный; (*durable*) про́чный.
lastly /ˈlɑːstlɪ/ *adv* в заключе́ние; наконе́ц.
latch /lætʃ/ *n* щеко́лда.
late /leɪt/ *adj* по́здний; (*recent*) неда́вний; (*dead*) поко́йный; **be ~ for** опа́здывать *impf*, опозда́ть *pf* на+*acc*; *adv* по́здно. **lately** /-lɪ/ *adv* в после́днее вре́мя. **later** /-tə(r)/ *adv* (*after vv*) по́зже; **a year ~** год спустя́; **see you ~!** пока́!
latent /ˈleɪt(ə)nt/ *adj* скры́тый.
lateral /ˈlætər(ə)l/ *adj* боково́й.
lath /lɑːθ/ *n* ре́йка.
lathe /leɪð/ *n* тока́рный стано́к.
lather /ˈlɑːðə(r/ *n* (мы́льная) пе́на; *vt & i* мы́лить(ся) *impf*, на~ *pf*.
Latin /ˈlætɪn/ *adj* лати́нский; *n* лати́нский язы́к; **~-American** латиноамерика́нский.
latitude /ˈlætɪˌtjuːd/ *n* свобо́да; (*geog*) широта́.
latter /ˈlætə(r)/ *adj* после́дний; **~-day** совреме́нный. **latterly** /-lɪ/ *adv* в после́днее вре́мя.
lattice /ˈlætɪs/ *n* решётка.
Latvia /ˈlætvɪə/ *n* Ла́твия. **Latvian** /-ən/ *n* латви́ец, -и́йка; латы́ш, ~ка; *adj* латви́йский, латы́шский.
laud /lɔːd/ *vt* хвали́ть *impf*, по~ *pf*. **laudable** /-dəb(ə)l/ *adj* похва́льный.
laugh /lɑːf/ *n* смех; *vi* смея́ться *impf* (**at** над+*instr*); **~ it off** отшу́чиваться *impf*, отшути́ться *pf*; **~ing-stock** посме́шище. **laughable** /-fəb(ə)l/ *adj* смешно́й. **laughter** /-tə(r)/ *n* смех.
launch¹ /lɔːntʃ/ *vt* (*ship*) спуска́ть *impf*, спусти́ть *pf* на́ воду; (*rocket*) запуска́ть *impf*, запусти́ть *pf*; (*undertake*) начина́ть *impf*, нача́ть *pf*; *n* спуск на́ воду; за́пуск. **launcher** /-tʃə(r)/ *n* (*for rocket*) пускова́я устано́вка. **launching pad** /ˈlɔːntʃɪŋ pæd/ *n* пускова́я площа́дка.
launch² /lɔːntʃ/ *n* (*naut*) ка́тер.
launder /ˈlɔːndə(r)/ *vt* стира́ть *impf*, вы́~ *pf*. **laund(e)rette** /-ˈdret/ *n* пра́чечная *sb* самообслу́живания. **laundry** /ˈlɔːndrɪ/ *n*

(*place*) прачечная *sb*; (*articles*) бельё.

laurel /ˈlɒr(ə)l/ *n* лавр(овое дерево).

lava /ˈlɑːvə/ *n* лава.

lavatory /ˈlævətərɪ/ *n* уборная *sb*.

lavender /ˈlævɪndə(r)/ *n* лаванда.

lavish /ˈlævɪʃ/ *adj* щедрый; (*abundant*) обильный; *vt* расточать *impf* (**upon** +*dat*).

law /lɔː/ *n* закон; (*system*) право; **~ and order** правопорядок. **law-court** *n* суд. **lawful** /-fʊl/ *adj* законный. **lawless** /-lɪs/ *adj* беззаконный.

lawn /lɔːn/ *n* газон; **~-mower** газонокосилка.

lawsuit /ˈlɔːsuːt/ *n* процесс.

lawyer /ˈlɔɪə(r)/ *n* адвокат, юрист.

lax /læks/ *adj* слабый. **laxative** /-sətɪv/ *n* слабительное *sb*. **laxity** /-sɪtɪ/ *n* слабость.

lay[1] /leɪ/ *adj* (*non-clerical*) светский.

lay[2] /leɪ/ *vt* (*place*) класть *impf*, положить *pf*; (*cable, pipes*) прокладывать *impf*, проложить *pf*; (*carpet*) стлать *impf*, по~ *pf*; (*trap etc.*) устраивать *impf*, устроить *pf*; (*eggs*) класть *impf*, положить *pf*; *v abs* (*lay eggs*) нестись *impf*, с~ *pf*; **~ aside** откладывать *impf*, отложить *pf*; **~ bare** раскрывать *impf*, раскрыть *pf*; **~ a bet** держать *impf* пари (**on** на+*acc*); **~ down** (*relinquish*) отказываться *impf*, отказаться *pf* от+*gen*; (*rule etc.*) устанавливать *impf*, установить *pf*; **~ off** (*workmen*) увольнять *impf*, уволить *pf*; **~ out** (*spread*) выкладывать *impf*, выложить *pf*; (*garden*) разбивать *impf*, разбить *pf*; **~ the table** накрывать *impf*, накрыть *pf* стол (**for** (*meal*) к+*dat*); **~ up** запасать *impf*, запасти *pf* +*acc*, +*gen*; **be laid up** быть прикованным к постели. **layabout** *n* бездельник.

layer /ˈleɪə(r)/ *n* слой, пласт.

layman /ˈleɪmən/ *n* мирянин; (*non-expert*) неспециалист.

laze /leɪz/ *vi* бездельничать *impf*. **laziness** /-zɪnɪs/ *n* лень. **lazy** /-zɪ/ *adj* ленивый; **~-bones** лентяй, **~**ка.

lead[1] /liːd/ *n* (*example*) пример; (*leadership*) руководство; (*position*) первое место; (*theat*) главная роль; (*electr*) провод; (*dog's*) поводок; *vt* водить *indet*, вести *det*; (*be in charge of*) руководить *impf* +*instr*; (*induce*) побуждать *impf*, побудить *pf*; *vt* & *i* (*cards*) ходить *impf* (с+*gen*); *vi* (*sport*) занимать *impf*, занять *pf* первое место; **~ away** уводить *impf*, увести *pf*; **~ to** (*result in*) приводить *impf*, привести *pf* к+*dat*.

lead[2] /led/ *n* (*metal*) свинец. **leaden** /ˈled(ə)n/ *adj* свинцовый.

leader /ˈliːdə(r)/ *n* руководитель *m*, **~**ница, лидер; (*mus*) первая скрипка; (*editorial*) передовая статья. **leadership** *n* руководство.

leading /ˈliːdɪŋ/ *adj* ведущий, выдающийся; **~ article** передовая статья.

leaf /liːf/ *n* лист; (*of table*) откидная доска; *vi*: **~ through** перелистывать *impf*, перелистать *pf*. **leaflet** /ˈliːflɪt/ *n* листовка.

league /liːg/ *n* лига; **in ~ with** в союзе с +*instr*.

leak /liːk/ *n* течь, утечка; *vi* (*escape*) течь *impf*; (*allow water to* **~**) пропускать *impf* воду; **~ out** просачиваться *impf*, просочиться *pf*.

lean[1] /liːn/ *adj* (*thin*) худой; (*meat*) постный.

lean[2] /liːn/ *vt* & *i* прислонять(ся) *impf*, прислонить(ся) *pf* (**against** к+*dat*); (*be inclined*) быть склонным (**to(wards)** к+*dat*); **~ back** откидываться *impf*, откинуться *pf*; **~ out of** высовываться *impf*, высунуться *pf* в +*acc*. **leaning** /-nɪŋ/ *n* склонность.

leap /liːp/ *n* прыжок, скачок; *vi* прыгать *impf*, прыгнуть *pf*; скакать *impf*; **~ year** високосный год.

l

learn /lɜːn/ *vt* (*a subject*) учи́ть *impf*, вы́~ *pf*; (*to do sth*) учи́ться *impf*, на~ *pf* +*inf*; (*find out*) узнава́ть *impf*, узна́ть *pf*. **learned** /-nɪd/ *adj* учёный. **learner** /-nə(r)/ *n* учени́к, -и́ца. **learning** /-nɪŋ/ *n* (*studies*) уче́ние; (*erudition*) учёность.

lease /liːs/ *n* аре́нда; *vt* (*of owner*) сдава́ть *impf*, сдать *pf* в аре́нду; (*of tenant*) брать *impf*, взять *pf* в аре́нду. **leaseholder** /-ˌhəʊldə(r)/ *n* аренда́тор.

leash /liːʃ/ *n* при́вязь.

least /liːst/ *adj* наиме́ньший, мале́йший; *adv* ме́нее всего́; **at ~** по кра́йней ме́ре; **not in the ~** ничу́ть.

leather /ˈleðə(r)/ *n* ко́жа; *attrib* ко́жаный.

leave[1] /liːv/ *n* (*permission*) разреше́ние; (*holiday*) о́тпуск; **on ~** в о́тпуске; **take (one's) ~** проща́ться *impf*, прости́ться *pf* (**of** с+*instr*).

leave[2] /liːv/ *vt* & *i* оставля́ть *impf*, оста́вить *pf*; (*abandon*) покида́ть *impf*, поки́нуть *pf*; (*go away*) уходи́ть *impf*, уйти́ *pf* (**from** от+*gen*); уезжа́ть *impf*, уе́хать *pf* (**from** от+*gen*); (*go out of*) выходи́ть *impf*, вы́йти *pf* из+*gen*; (*entrust*) предоставля́ть *impf*, предоста́вить *pf* (**to** +*dat*); **~ out** пропуска́ть *impf*, пропусти́ть *pf*.

lecherous /ˈletʃərəs/ *adj* развра́тный.

lectern /ˈlektɜːn/ *n* анало́й; (*in lecture room*) пюпи́тр.

lecture /ˈlektʃə(r)/ *n* (*discourse*) ле́кция; (*reproof*) нота́ция; *vi* (*deliver ~(s)*) чита́ть *impf*, про~ *pf* ле́кцию (-ии) (**on** по+*dat*); *vt* (*admonish*) чита́ть *impf*, про~ *pf* нота́цию+*dat*; **~ room** аудито́рия. **lecturer** /-tʃərə(r)/ *n* ле́ктор; (*univ*) преподава́тель *m*, ~ница.

ledge /ledʒ/ *n* вы́ступ; (*shelf*) по́лочка.

ledger /ˈledʒə(r)/ *n* гла́вная кни́га.

lee /liː/ *n* защи́та; *adj* подве́тренный.

leech /liːtʃ/ *n* (*worm*) пия́вка.

leek /liːk/ *n* лук-поре́й.

leer /lɪə(r)/ *vi* криви́ться *impf*, с~ *pf*.

leeward /ˈliːwəd/ *n* подве́тренная сторона́; *adj* подве́тренный.

leeway /ˈliːweɪ/ *n* (*fig*) свобо́да де́йствий.

left /left/ *n* ле́вая сторона́; (**the L~**; *polit*) ле́вые *sb pl*; *adj* ле́вый; *adv* нале́во, сле́ва (**of** от+*gen*); **~-hander** левша́ *m* & *f*; **~-wing** ле́вый.

left-luggage office /left ˈlʌgɪdʒ ˈɒfɪs/ *n* ка́мера хране́ния.

leftovers /ˈleftˌəʊvəz/ *n pl* оста́тки *m pl*; (*food*) объе́дки (-ков) *pl*.

leg /leg/ *n* нога́; (*of furniture etc.*) но́жка; (*of journey etc.*) эта́п.

legacy /ˈlegəsɪ/ *n* насле́дство.

legal /ˈliːg(ə)l/ *adj* (*of the law*) правово́й; (*lawful*) лега́льный. **legality** /lɪˈgælɪtɪ/ *n* лега́льность. **legalize** /ˈliːgəlaɪz/ *vt* легализи́ровать *impf* & *pf*.

legend /ˈledʒ(ə)nd/ *n* леге́нда. **legendary** /-dʒəndərɪ/ *adj* легенда́рный.

leggings /ˈlegɪŋz/ *n pl* вя́заные рейту́зы (-з) *pl*.

legible /ˈledʒɪb(ə)l/ *adj* разбо́рчивый.

legion /ˈliːdʒ(ə)n/ *n* легио́н.

legislate /ˈledʒɪsˌleɪt/ *vi* издава́ть *impf*, изда́ть *pf* зако́ны. **legislation** /-ˈleɪʃ(ə)n/ *n* законода́тельство. **legislative** /ˈledʒɪslətɪv/ *adj* законода́тельный. **legislator** /ˈledʒɪsˌleɪtə(r)/ *n* законода́тель *m*. **legislature** /ˈledʒɪsˌlətʃə(r)/ *n* законода́тельные учрежде́ния *neut pl*.

legitimacy /lɪˈdʒɪtɪməsɪ/ *n* зако́нность; (*of child*) законнорождённость. **legitimate** /-mət/ *adj* зако́нный; (*child*) законнорождённый. **legitimize** /-ˌmaɪz/ *vt* узако́нивать *impf*, узако́нить *pf*.

leisure /ˈleʒə(r)/ *n* свобо́дное вре́мя, досу́г; **at ~** на досу́ге. **leisurely** /-lɪ/ *adj* неторопли́вый.

l

lemon /'lemən/ *n* лимóн. **lemonade** /ˌlemə'neɪd/ *n* лимонáд.

lend /lend/ *vt* давáть *impf*, дать *pf* взаймы́ (**to** +*dat*); одáлживать *impf*, одолжи́ть *pf* (**to** +*dat*).

length /leŋkθ/ *n* длинá; (*of time*) продолжи́тельность; (*of cloth*) отрéз; **at ~** подрóбно. **lengthen** /'leŋθ(ə)n/ *vt & i* удлиня́ть(ся) *impf*, удлини́ть(ся) *pf*. **lengthways** *adv* в длину́, вдоль. **lengthy** /'leŋθɪ/ *adj* дли́нный.

leniency /'liːnɪənsɪ/ *n* снисходи́тельность. **lenient** /-ənt/ *adj* снисходи́тельный.

lens /lenz/ *n* ли́нза; (*phot*) объекти́в; (*anat*) хрустáлик.

Lent /lent/ *n* вели́кий пост.

lentil /'lentɪl/ *n* чечеви́ца.

Leo /'liːəʊ/ *n* Лев.

leopard /'lepəd/ *n* леопáрд.

leotard /'liːəˌtɑːd/ *n* трикó *neut indecl*.

leper /'lepə(r)/ *n* прокажённый *sb*. **leprosy** /'leprəsɪ/ *n* прокáза.

lesbian /'lezbɪən/ *n* лесбия́нка; *adj* лесби́йский.

lesion /'liːʒ(ə)n/ *n* повреждéние.

less /les/ *adj* мéньший; *adv* мéньше, мéнее; *prep* за вы́четом +*gen*.

lessee /le'siː/ *n* арендáтор.

lessen /'les(ə)n/ *vt & i* умéньшáть(ся) *impf*, умéньшить(ся) *pf*.

lesser /'lesə(r)/ *adj* мéньший.

lesson /'les(ə)n/ *n* урóк.

lest /lest/ *conj* (*in order that not*) чтóбы не; (*that*) как бы не.

let /let/ *n* (*lease*) сдáча в наём; *vt* (*allow*) позволя́ть *impf*, позвóлить *pf* +*dat*; разрешáть *impf*, разреши́ть *pf* +*dat*; (*rent out*) сдавáть *impf*, сдать *pf* внаём (**to** +*dat*); *v aux* (*imperative*) (*1st person*) давáй(те); (*3rd person*) пусть; **~ alone** не говоря́ ужé о+*prep*; **~ down** (*lower*) опускáть *impf*, опусти́ть *pf*; (*fail*) подводи́ть *impf*, подвести́ *pf*; (*disappoint*) разочарóвывать *impf*, разочаровáть *pf*; **~ go** выпускáть *impf*, вы́пустить *pf*; **~'s go** пойдёмте!; пошли́!; поéхали!; **~ in(to)** (*admit*) впускáть *impf*, впусти́ть *pf* в+*acc*; (*into secret*) посвящáть *impf*, посвяти́ть *pf* в+*acc*; **~ know** давáть *impf*, дать *pf* знать +*dat*; **~ off** (*gun*) вы́стрелить *pf* из+*gen*; (*not punish*) отпускáть *impf*, отпусти́ть *pf* без наказáния; **~ out** (*release, loosen*) выпускáть *impf*, вы́пустить *pf*; **~ through** пропускáть *impf*, пропусти́ть *pf*; **~ up** затихáть *impf*, зати́хнуть *pf*.

lethal /'liːθ(ə)l/ *adj* (*fatal*) смертéльный; (*weapon*) смертонóсный.

lethargic /lɪ'θɑːdʒɪk/ *adj* летарги́ческий. **lethargy** /'leθədʒɪ/ *n* летарги́я.

letter /'letə(r)/ *n* письмó; (*symbol*) бу́ква; (*printing*) ли́тера; **~-box** почтóвый я́щик. **lettering** /-rɪŋ/ *n* шрифт.

lettuce /'letɪs/ *n* салáт.

leukaemia /luː'kiːmɪə/ *n* лейкеми́я.

level /'lev(ə)l/ *n* у́ровень; *adj* рóвный; **~ crossing** (железнодорóжный) переéзд; **~-headed** уравновéшенный; *vt* (*make ~*) вырáвнивать *impf*, вы́ровнять *pf*; (*sport*) срáвнивать *impf*, сравня́ть *pf*; (*gun*) наводи́ть *impf*, навести́ *pf* (**at** в, на, +*acc*); (*criticism*) направля́ть *impf*, напрáвить *pf* (**at** прóтив+*gen*).

lever /'liːvə(r)/ *n* рычáг. **leverage** /-rɪdʒ/ *n* дéйствие рычагá; (*influence*) влия́ние.

levity /'levɪtɪ/ *n* легкомы́слие.

levy /'levɪ/ *n* (*tax*) сбор; *vt* (*tax*) взимáть *impf* (**from** с+*gen*).

lewd /ljuːd/ *adj* (*lascivious*) похотли́вый; (*indecent*) сáльный.

lexicon /'leksɪkən/ *n* словáрь *m*.

liability /ˌlaɪə'bɪlɪtɪ/ *n* (*responsibility*) ответственность (**for** за+*acc*); (*burden*) обу́за. **liable** /'laɪəb(ə)l/ *adj* ответственный (**for** за+*acc*); (*susceptible*) подвéрженный (**to** +*dat*).

liaise /lɪ'eɪz/ *vi* поддéрживать *impf*

связь (с+*instr*). **liaison** /-'eɪzɒn/ *n* связь; (*affair*) любо́вная связь.
liar /'laɪə(r)/ *n* лгун, ~ья.
libel /'laɪb(ə)l/ *n* клевета́; *vt* клевета́ть *impf*, на~ *pf* на+*acc*. **libellous** /-bələs/ *adj* клеветни́ческий.
liberal /'lɪbər(ə)l/ *n* либера́л; *adj* либера́льный; (*generous*) ще́дрый.
liberate /'lɪbə,reɪt/ *vt* освобожда́ть *impf*, освободи́ть *pf*. **liberation** /-'reɪʃ(ə)n/ *n* освобожде́ние. **liberator** /'lɪbə,reɪtə(r)/ *n* освободи́тель *m*.
libertine /'lɪbə,tiːn/ *n* распу́тник.
liberty /'lɪbətɪ/ *n* свобо́да; **at ~** на свобо́де.
Libra /'liːbrə/ *n* Весы́ (-со́в) *pl*.
librarian /laɪ'breərɪən/ *n* библиоте́карь *m*. **library** /'laɪbrərɪ/ *n* библиоте́ка.
libretto /lɪ'bretəʊ/ *n* либре́тто *neut indecl*.
licence[1] /'laɪs(ə)ns/ *n* (*permission, permit*) разреше́ние, лице́нзия; (*liberty*) (изли́шняя) во́льность. **license, -ce**[2] /'laɪs(ə)ns/ *vt* (*allow*) разреша́ть *impf*, разреши́ть *pf* +*dat*; дава́ть *impf*, дать *pf* пра́во +*dat*.
licentious /laɪ'senʃəs/ *adj* распу́щенный.
lichen /'laɪkən/ *n* лиша́йник.
lick /lɪk/ *n* лиза́ние; *vt* лиза́ть *impf*, лизну́ть *pf*.
lid /lɪd/ *n* кры́шка; (*eyelid*) ве́ко.
lie[1] /laɪ/ *n* (*untruth*) ложь; *vi* лгать *impf*, со~ *pf*.
lie[2] /laɪ/ *n*: **~ of the land** (*fig*) положе́ние веще́й; *vi* лежа́ть *impf*; (*be situated*) находи́ться *impf*; **~ down** ложи́ться *impf*, лечь *pf*; **~ in** остава́ться *impf* в посте́ли.
lieu /ljuː/ *n*: **in ~ of** вме́сто+*gen*.
lieutenant /lef'tenənt/ *n* лейтена́нт.
life /laɪf/ *n* жизнь; (*way of ~*) о́браз жи́зни; (*energy*) жи́вость. **lifebelt** *n* спаса́тельный по́яс. **lifeboat** *n* спаса́тельная ло́дка. **lifebuoy** *n* спаса́тельный круг. **lifeguard** *n* спаса́тель *m*, -ница. **life-jacket** *n* спаса́тельный жиле́т. **lifeless** /-lɪs/ *adj* безжи́зненный. **lifelike** /-laɪk/ *adj* реалисти́чный. **lifeline** *n* спаса́тельный коне́ц. **lifelong** *adj* пожи́зненный. **life-size(d)** /-saɪz(d)/ *adj* в натура́льную величину́. **lifetime** *n* жизнь.
lift /lɪft/ *n* (*machine*) лифт, подъёмник; (*force*) подъёмная си́ла; **give s.o. a ~** подвози́ть *impf*, подвезти́ *pf*; *vt* & *i* поднима́ть(ся) *impf*, подня́ть(ся) *pf*.
ligament /'lɪgəmənt/ *n* свя́зка.
light[1] /laɪt/ *n* свет, освеще́ние; (*source of ~*) ого́нь *m*, ла́мпа, фона́рь *m*; *pl* (*traffic ~*) светофо́р; **can I have a ~?** мо́жно прикури́ть?; **~-bulb** ла́мпочка; *adj* (*bright*) све́тлый; (*pale*) бле́дный; *vt* & *i* (*ignite*) зажига́ть(ся) *impf*, заже́чь(ся) *pf*; *vt* (*illuminate*) освеща́ть *impf*, освети́ть *pf*; **~ up** освеща́ть(ся) *impf*, освети́ть(ся) *pf*; (*begin to smoke*) закури́ть *pf*.
light[2] /laɪt/ *adj* (*not heavy*) лёгкий; **~-hearted** беззабо́тный.
lighten[1] /'laɪt(ə)n/ *vt* (*make lighter*) облегча́ть *impf*, облегчи́ть *pf*; (*mitigate*) смягча́ть *impf*, смягчи́ть *pf*.
lighten[2] /'laɪt(ə)n/ *vt* (*illuminate*) освеща́ть *impf*, освети́ть *pf*; *vi* (*grow bright*) светле́ть *impf*, по~ *pf*.
lighter /'laɪtə(r)/ *n* зажига́лка.
lighthouse /'laɪthaʊs/ *n* мая́к.
lighting /'laɪtɪŋ/ *n* освеще́ние.
lightning /'laɪtnɪŋ/ *n* мо́лния.
lightweight /'laɪtweɪt/ *n* (*sport*) легкове́с; *adj* легкове́сный.
like[1] /laɪk/ *adj* (*similar*) похо́жий (на+*acc*); **what is he ~?** что он за челове́к?
like[2] /laɪk/ *vt* нра́виться *impf*, по~ *pf impers*+*dat*: **I ~ him** он мне нра́вится; люби́ть *impf*; *vi* (*wish*) хоте́ть *impf*; **if you ~** е́сли хоти́те; **I should ~** я хоте́л бы; мне хоте́лось бы. **likeable** /'laɪkəb(ə)l/ *adj* симпати́чный.

likelihood /ˈlaɪklɪˌhʊd/ *n* вероя́тность. **likely** /ˈlaɪklɪ/ *adj* (*probable*) вероя́тный; (*suitable*) подходя́щий.

liken /ˈlaɪkən/ *vt* уподобля́ть *impf*, уподо́бить *pf* (**to** +*dat*).

likeness /ˈlaɪknɪs/ *n* (*resemblance*) схо́дство; (*portrait*) портре́т.

likewise /ˈlaɪkwaɪz/ *adv* (*similarly*) подо́бно; (*also*) то́же, та́кже.

liking /ˈlaɪkɪŋ/ *n* вкус (**for** к+*dat*).

lilac /ˈlaɪlək/ *n* сире́нь; *adj* сире́невый.

lily /ˈlɪlɪ/ *n* ли́лия; **~ of the valley** ла́ндыш.

limb /lɪm/ *n* член.

limber /ˈlɪmbə(r)/ *vi*: **~ up** размина́ться *impf*, размя́ться *pf*.

limbo /ˈlɪmbəʊ/ *n* (*fig*) состоя́ние неопределённости.

lime[1] /laɪm/ *n* (*mineralogy*) и́звесть. **limelight** *n*: **in the ~** (*fig*) в це́нтре внима́ния. **limestone** *n* известня́к.

lime[2] /laɪm/ *n* (*fruit*) лайм.

lime[3] /laɪm/ *n* (**~**-*tree*) ли́па.

limit /ˈlɪmɪt/ *n* грани́ца, преде́л; *vt* ограни́чивать *impf*, ограни́чить *pf*. **limitation** /-ˈteɪʃ(ə)n/ *n* ограниче́ние. **limitless** /ˈlɪmɪtlɪs/ *adj* безграни́чный.

limousine /ˈlɪməˌziːn/ *n* лимузи́н.

limp[1] /lɪmp/ *n* хромота́; *vi* хрома́ть *impf*.

limp[2] /lɪmp/ *adj* мя́гкий; (*fig*) вя́лый.

limpid /ˈlɪmpɪd/ *adj* прозра́чный.

linchpin /ˈlɪntʃpɪn/ *n* чека́.

line[1] /laɪn/ *n* (*long mark*) ли́ния, черта́; (*transport*, *tel*) ли́ния; (*cord*) верёвка; (*wrinkle*) морщи́на; (*limit*) грани́ца; (*row*) ряд; (*of words*) строка́; (*of verse*) стих; *vt* (*paper*) линова́ть *impf*, раз**~** *pf*; *vt* & *i* (**~** *up*) выстра́ивать(ся) *impf*, вы́строить(ся) *pf* в ряд.

line[2] /laɪn/ *vt* (*clothes*) класть *impf*, положи́ть *pf* на подкла́дку.

lineage /ˈlɪnɪɪdʒ/ *n* происхожде́ние.

linear /ˈlɪnɪə(r)/ *adj* лине́йный.

lined[1] /laɪnd/ *adj* (*paper*) лино́ванный; (*face*) морщи́нистый.

lined[2] /laɪnd/ *adj* (*garment*) на подкла́дке.

linen /ˈlɪnɪn/ *n* полотно́; *collect* бельё.

liner /ˈlaɪnə(r)/ *n* ла́йнер.

linesman /ˈlaɪnzmən/ *n* боково́й судья́ *m*.

linger /ˈlɪŋgə(r)/ *vi* заде́рживаться *impf*, задержа́ться *pf*.

lingerie /ˈlæ̃ʒərɪ/ *n* да́мское бельё.

lingering /ˈlɪŋgərɪŋ/ *adj* (*illness*) затяжно́й.

lingo /ˈlɪŋgəʊ/ *n* жарго́н.

linguist /ˈlɪŋgwɪst/ *n* лингви́ст. **linguistic** /-ˈgwɪstɪk/ *adj* лингвисти́ческий. **linguistics** /-ˈgwɪstɪks/ *n* лингви́стика.

lining /ˈlaɪnɪŋ/ *n* (*clothing etc.*) подкла́дка; (*tech*) облицо́вка.

link /lɪŋk/ *n* (*of chain*) звено́; (*connection*) связь; *vt* соединя́ть *impf*, соедини́ть *pf*; свя́зывать *impf*, связа́ть *pf*.

lino(leum) /lɪˈnəʊlɪəm/ *n* лино́леум.

lintel /ˈlɪnt(ə)l/ *n* перемы́чка.

lion /ˈlaɪən/ *n* лев. **lioness** /-nɪs/ *n* льви́ца.

lip /lɪp/ *n* губа́; (*of vessel*) край. **lipstick** *n* губна́я пома́да.

liquefy /ˈlɪkwɪˌfaɪ/ *vt* & *i* превраща́ть(ся) *impf*, преврати́ть(ся) *pf* в жи́дкое состоя́ние.

liqueur /lɪˈkjʊə(r)/ *n* ликёр.

liquid /ˈlɪkwɪd/ *n* жи́дкость; *adj* жи́дкий.

liquidate /ˈlɪkwɪˌdeɪt/ *vt* ликвиди́ровать *impf* & *pf*. **liquidation** /-ˈdeɪʃ(ə)n/ *n* ликвида́ция; **go into ~** ликвиди́роваться *impf* & *pf*.

liquor /ˈlɪkə(r)/ *n* (спиртно́й) напи́ток.

liquorice /ˈlɪkərɪs/ *n* лакри́ца.

list[1] /lɪst/ *n* спи́сок; *vt* составля́ть *impf*, соста́вить *pf* спи́сок +*gen*; (*enumerate*) перечисля́ть *impf*, перечи́слить *pf*.

list[2] /lɪst/ *vi* (*naut*) накреня́ться *impf*, крени́ться *impf*, накрени́ться *pf*.

l

listen /ˈlɪs(ə)n/ *vi* слу́шать *impf*, по~ *pf* (**to** +*acc*). **listener** /-nə(r)/ *n* слу́шатель *m*.
listless /ˈlɪstlɪs/ *adj* апати́чный.
litany /ˈlɪtənɪ/ *n* лита́ния.
literacy /ˈlɪtərəsɪ/ *n* гра́мотность.
literal /ˈlɪtər(ə)l/ *adj* буква́льный.
literary /ˈlɪtərərɪ/ *adj* литерату́рный.
literate /ˈlɪtərət/ *adj* гра́мотный.
literature /ˈlɪtərətʃə(r)/ *n* литерату́ра.
lithe /laɪð/ *adj* ги́бкий.
lithograph /ˈlɪθəˌgrɑːf/ *n* литогра́фия.
Lithuania /ˌlɪθuːˈeɪnɪə/ *n* Литва́. **Lithuanian** /-nɪən/ *n* лито́вец, -вка; *adj* лито́вский.
litigation /ˌlɪtɪˈgeɪʃ(ə)n/ *n* тя́жба.
litre /ˈliːtə(r)/ *n* литр.
litter /ˈlɪtə(r)/ *n* (*rubbish*) сор; (*brood*) помёт; *vt* (*make untidy*) сори́ть *impf*, на~ *pf* (**with** +*instr*).
little /ˈlɪt(ə)l/ *n* немно́гое; **~ by ~** ма́ло-пома́лу; **a ~** немно́го +*gen*; *adj* ма́ленький, небольшо́й; (*in height*) небольшо́го ро́ста; (*in distance, time*) коро́ткий; *adv* ма́ло, немно́го.
liturgy /ˈlɪtədʒɪ/ *n* литурги́я.
live[1] /laɪv/ *adj* живо́й; (*coals*) горя́щий; (*mil*) боево́й; (*electr*) под напряже́нием; (*broadcast*) прямо́й.
live[2] /lɪv/ *vi* жить *impf*; **~ down** загла́живать *impf*, загла́дить *pf*; **~ on** (*feed on*) пита́ться *impf* +*instr*; **~ through** пережива́ть *impf*, пережи́ть *pf*; **~ until, to see** дожива́ть *impf*, дожи́ть *pf* до+*gen*; **~ up to** жить *impf* согла́сно +*dat*.
livelihood /ˈlaɪvlɪˌhʊd/ *n* сре́дства *neut pl* к жи́зни.
lively /ˈlaɪvlɪ/ *adj* живо́й.
liven (up) /ˈlaɪv(ə)n (ʌp)/ *vt & i* оживля́ть(ся) *impf*, оживи́ть(ся) *pf*.
liver /ˈlɪvə(r)/ *n* пе́чень; (*cul*) печёнка.
livery /ˈlɪvərɪ/ *n* ливре́я.
livestock /ˈlaɪvstɒk/ *n* скот.
livid /ˈlɪvɪd/ *adj* (*angry*) взбешённый.
living /ˈlɪvɪŋ/ *n* сре́дства *neut pl* к жи́зни; **earn a ~** зараба́тывать *impf*, зарабо́тать *pf* на жизнь; *adj* живо́й; **~-room** гости́ная *sb*.
lizard /ˈlɪzəd/ *n* я́щерица.
load /ləʊd/ *n* груз; (*also fig*) бре́мя *neut*; (*electr*) нагру́зка; *pl* (*lots*) ку́ча; *vt* (*goods*) грузи́ть *impf*, по~ *pf*; (*vehicle*) грузи́ть *impf*, на~ *pf*; (*fig*) обременя́ть *impf*, обремени́ть *pf*; (*gun, camera*) заряжа́ть *impf*, заряди́ть *pf*.
loaf[1] /ləʊf/ *n* буха́нка.
loaf[2] /ləʊf/ *vi* безде́льничать *impf*. **loafer** /ˈləʊfə(r)/ *n* безде́льник.
loan /ləʊn/ *n* заём; *vt* дава́ть *impf*, дать *pf* взаймы́.
loath, loth /ləʊθ/ *predic*: **be ~ to** не хоте́ть *impf* +*inf*.
loathe /ləʊð/ *vt* ненави́деть *impf*. **loathing** /ˈləʊðɪŋ/ *n* отвраще́ние. **loathsome** *adj* отврати́тельный.
lob /lɒb/ *vt* высоко́ подбра́сывать *impf*, подбро́сить *pf*.
lobby /ˈlɒbɪ/ *n* вестибю́ль *m*; (*parl*) кулуа́ры (-ров) *pl*.
lobe /ləʊb/ *n* (*of ear*) мо́чка.
lobster /ˈlɒbstə(r)/ *n* ома́р.
local /ˈləʊk(ə)l/ *adj* ме́стный.
locality /ləʊˈkælɪtɪ/ *n* ме́стность.
localized /ˈləʊkəˌlaɪzd/ *adj* локализо́ванный.
locate /ləʊˈkeɪt/ *vt* (*place*) помеща́ть *impf*, помести́ть *pf*; (*find*) находи́ть *impf*, найти́ *pf*; **be ~d** находи́ться *impf*.
location /ləʊˈkeɪʃ(ə)n/ *n* (*position*) местонахожде́ние; **on ~** (*cin*) на нату́ре.
locative /ˈlɒkətɪv/ *adj* (*n*) ме́стный (паде́ж).
lock[1] /lɒk/ *n* (*of hair*) ло́кон; *pl* во́лосы (-о́с, -оса́м) *pl*.
lock[2] /lɒk/ *n* замо́к; (*canal*) шлюз; *vt & i* запира́ть(ся) *impf*, запере́ть(ся) *pf*; **~ out** не впуска́ть *impf*; **~ up** (*imprison*) сажа́ть *impf*, посади́ть *pf*; (*close*) закрыва́ть(ся) *impf*, закры́ть(ся) *pf*.

l

locker /ˈlɒkə(r)/ *n* шка́фчик.
locket /ˈlɒkɪt/ *n* медальо́н.
locksmith /ˈlɒksmɪθ/ *n* сле́сарь *m.*
locomotion /ˌləʊkəˈməʊʃ(ə)n/ *n* передвиже́ние. **locomotive** /-ˈməʊtɪv/ *n* локомоти́в.
lodge /lɒdʒ/ *n* (*hunting*) (охо́тничий) до́мик; (*porter's*) сторо́жка; (*Masonic*) ло́жа; *vt* (*complaint*) подава́ть *impf*, пода́ть *pf*; *vi* (*reside*) жить *impf* (**with** у+*gen*); (*stick*) заса́живать *impf*, засе́сть *pf.* **lodger** /-dʒə(r)/ *n* жиле́ц, жили́ца. **lodging** /-dʒɪŋ/ *n* (*also pl*) кварти́ра, (снима́емая) ко́мната.
loft /lɒft/ *n* (*attic*) черда́к.
lofty /ˈlɒftɪ/ *adj* о́чень высо́кий; (*elevated*) возвы́шенный.
log /lɒg/ *n* бревно́; (*for fire*) поле́но; **~-book** (*naut*) ва́хтенный журна́л.; *vi*: **~ off** (*comput*) выходи́ть *impf*, вы́йти *pf* из систе́мы; **~ on** (*comput*) входи́ть *impf*, войти́ *pf* в систе́му.
logarithm /ˈlɒgəˌrɪð(ə)m/ *n* логари́фм.
loggerhead /ˈlɒgəˌhed/ *n*: **be at ~s** быть в ссо́ре.
logic /ˈlɒdʒɪk/ *n* ло́гика. **logical** /-k(ə)l/ *adj* (*of logic*) логи́ческий; (*consistent*) логи́чный.
logistics /ləˈdʒɪstɪks/ *n pl* организа́ция; (*mil*) материа́льно-техни́ческое обеспе́чение.
logo /ˈləʊgəʊ/ *n* эмбле́ма.
loin /lɔɪn/ *n* (*pl*) поясни́ца; (*cul*) филе́йная часть.
loiter /ˈlɔɪtə(r)/ *vi* слоня́ться *impf.*
lone, lonely /ləʊn, ˈləʊnlɪ/ *adj* одино́кий. **loneliness** /ˈləʊnlɪnɪs/ *n* одино́чество.
long[1] /lɒŋ/ *vi* (*want*) стра́стно жела́ть *impf*, по~ *pf* (**for** +*gen*); (*miss*) тоскова́ть *impf* (**for** по+*dat*).
long[2] /lɒŋ/ *adj* (*space*) дли́нный; (*time*) до́лгий; (*in measurements*) длино́й в+*acc*; **in the ~ run** в коне́чном счёте; **~-sighted** дальнозо́ркий; **~-suffering** долготерпели́вый; **~-term** долгосро́чный; **~-winded** многоречи́вый; *adv* до́лго; **~ ago** (уже́) давно́; **as ~ as** пока́; **~ before** задо́лго до+*gen.*
longevity /lɒnˈdʒevɪtɪ/ *n* долгове́чность.
longing /ˈlɒŋɪŋ/ *n* стра́стное жела́ние (**for** +*gen*); тоска́ (**for** по+*dat*); *adj* тоску́ющий.
longitude /ˈlɒŋgɪˌtjuːd/ *n* долгота́.
longways /ˈlɒŋweɪz/ *adv* в длину́.
look /lʊk/ *n* (*glance*) взгляд; (*appearance*) вид; (*expression*) выраже́ние; *vi* смотре́ть *impf*, по~ *pf* (**at** на, в, +*acc*); (*appear*) вы́глядеть *impf* +*instr*; (*face*) выходи́ть *impf* (**towards, onto** на+*acc*); **~ about** осма́триваться *impf*, осмотре́ться *pf*; **~ after** (*attend to*) присма́тривать *impf*, присмотре́ть *pf* за+*instr*; **~ down on** презира́ть *impf*; **~ for** иска́ть *impf* +*acc*, +*gen*; **~ forward to** предвкуша́ть *impf*, предвкуси́ть *pf*; **~ in on** загля́дывать *impf*, загляну́ть *pf* к+*dat*; **~ into** (*investigate*) рассма́тривать *impf*, рассмотре́ть *pf*; **~ like** быть похо́жим на+*acc*; **it ~s like rain** похо́же на (то, что бу́дет) дождь; **~ on** (*regard*) счита́ть *impf*, счесть *pf* (**as** +*instr*, за+*instr*); **~ out** выгля́дывать *impf*, вы́глянуть *pf* (в окно́); быть настороже́; *imper* осторо́жно!; **~ over, through** просма́тривать *impf*, просмотре́ть *pf*; **~ round** (*inspect*) осма́тривать *impf*, осмотре́ть *pf*; **~ up** (*raise eyes*) поднима́ть *impf*, подня́ть *pf* глаза́; (*in dictionary etc.*) иска́ть *impf*; (*improve*) улучша́ться *impf*, улу́чшиться *pf*; **~ up to** уважа́ть *impf.*
loom[1] /luːm/ *n* тка́цкий стано́к.
loom[2] /luːm/ *vi* вырисо́вываться *impf*, вы́рисоваться; (*fig*) надвига́ться *impf.*
loop /luːp/ *n* пе́тля; *vi* образо́вывать *impf*, образова́ть *pf* пе́тлю; (*fasten with loop*) закрепля́ть *impf*, закрепи́ть *pf* пе́тлей; (*wind*) обма́тывать *impf*, обмо-

l

та́ть *pf* (**around** вокру́г+*gen*).

loophole /'lu:phəʊl/ *n* бойни́ца; (*fig*) лазе́йка.

loose /lu:s/ *adj* (*free*; *not tight*) свобо́дный; (*not fixed*) неприкреплённый; (*connection*, *screw*) сла́бый; (*lax*) распу́щенный; **at a ~ end** без де́ла. **loosen** /-s(ə)n/ *vt* & *i* ослабля́ть(ся) *impf*, осла́бить(ся) *pf*.

loot /lu:t/ *n* добы́ча; *vt* гра́бить *impf*, о~ *pf*.

lop /lɒp/ *vt* (*tree*) подреза́ть *impf*, подре́зать *pf*; (~ *off*) отруба́ть *impf*, отруби́ть *pf*.

lope /ləʊp/ *vi* бе́гать *indet*, бежа́ть *det* вприпры́жку.

lopsided /lɒp'saɪdɪd/ *adj* кривобо́кий.

loquacious /lɒ'kweɪʃəs/ *adj* болтли́вый.

lord /lɔ:d/ *n* (*master*) господи́н; (*eccl*) Госпо́дь; (*peer*; *title*) лорд; *vt*: **~ it over** помыка́ть *impf* +*instr*. **lordship** *n* (*title*) све́тлость.

lore /lɔ:(r)/ *n* зна́ния *neut pl*.

lorry /'lɒrɪ/ *n* грузови́к.

lose /lu:z/ *vt* теря́ть *impf*, по~ *pf*; *vt* & *i* (*game etc.*) прои́грывать *impf*, проигра́ть *pf*; *vi* (*clock*) отстава́ть *impf*, отста́ть *pf*. **loss** /lɒs/ *n* поте́ря; (*monetary*) убы́ток; (*in game*) про́игрыш.

lot /lɒt/ *n* жре́бий; (*destiny*) у́часть; (*of goods*) па́ртия; **a ~, ~s** мно́го; **the ~** всё, все *pl*.

loth /ləʊθ/ *see* **loath**

lotion /'ləʊʃ(ə)n/ *n* лосьо́н.

lottery /'lɒtərɪ/ *n* лотере́я.

loud /laʊd/ *adj* (*sound*) гро́мкий; (*noisy*) шу́мный; (*colour*) крича́щий; **out ~** вслух. **loudspeaker** *n* громкоговори́тель *m*.

lounge /laʊndʒ/ *n* гости́ная *sb*; *vi* сиде́ть *impf* разваля́сь; (*idle*) безде́льничать *impf*.

louse /laʊs/ *n* вошь. **lousy** /'laʊzɪ/ *adj* (*coll*) парши́вый.

lout /laʊt/ *n* балбе́с, у́валень *m*.

lovable /'lʌvəb(ə)l/ *adj* ми́лый.

love /lʌv/ *n* любо́вь (**of, for** к+*dat*); **in ~ with** влюблённый в+*acc*; *vt* люби́ть *impf*. **lovely** /'lʌvlɪ/ *adj* прекра́сный; (*delightful*) преле́стный. **lover** /'lʌvə(r)/ *n* любо́вник, -ица.

low /ləʊ/ *adj* ни́зкий, невысо́кий; (*quiet*) ти́хий.

lower[1] /'ləʊə(r)/ *vt* опуска́ть *impf*, опусти́ть *pf*; (*price*, *voice*, *standard*) понижа́ть *impf*, пони́зить *pf*.

lower[2] /'ləʊə(r)/ *adj* ни́жний.

lowland /'ləʊlənd/ *n* ни́зменность.

lowly /'ləʊlɪ/ *adj* скро́мный.

loyal /'lɔɪəl/ *adj* ве́рный. **loyalty** /-tɪ/ *n* ве́рность.

LP *abbr* (*of* **long-playing record**) долгоигра́ющая пласти́нка.

Ltd. *abbr* (*of* **Limited**) с ограни́ченной отве́тственностью.

lubricant /'lu:brɪkənt/ *n* сма́зка. **lubricate** /-ˌkeɪt/ *vt* сма́зывать *impf*, сма́зать *pf*. **lubrication** /-'keɪʃ(ə)n/ *n* сма́зка.

lucid /'lu:sɪd/ *adj* я́сный. **lucidity** /ˌlu:'sɪdɪtɪ/ *n* я́сность.

luck /lʌk/ *n* (*chance*) слу́чай; (*good ~*) сча́стье, уда́ча; (*bad ~*) неуда́ча. **luckily** /-kɪlɪ/ *adv* к сча́стью. **lucky** /-kɪ/ *adj* счастли́вый; **be ~** везти́ *imp*, по~ *pf impers* +*dat*: **I was ~** мне повезло́.

lucrative /'lu:krətɪv/ *adj* при́быльный.

ludicrous /'lu:dɪkrəs/ *adj* смехотво́рный.

lug /lʌg/ *vt* (*drag*) таска́ть *indet*, тащи́ть *det*.

luggage /'lʌgɪdʒ/ *n* бага́ж.

lugubrious /lʊ'gu:brɪəs/ *adj* печа́льный.

lukewarm /lu:k'wɔ:m/ *adj* теплова́тый; (*fig*) прохла́дный.

lull /lʌl/ *n* (*in storm*) зати́шье; (*interval*) переры́в; *vt* (*to sleep*) убаю́кивать *impf*, убаю́кать *pf*; (*suspicions*) усыпля́ть *impf*, усыпи́ть *pf*.

lullaby /'lʌləˌbaɪ/ *n* колыбе́льная пе́сня.

l

lumbar /'lʌmbə(r)/ *adj* поясни́чный.
lumber[1] /'lʌmbə(r)/ *vi* (*move*) брести́ *impf.*
lumber[2] /'lʌmbə(r)/ *n* (*domestic*) ру́хлядь; *vt* обременя́ть *impf*, обремени́ть *pf.* **lumberjack** /'lʌmbədʒæk/ *n* лесору́б.
luminary /'lu:mɪnərɪ/ *n* свети́ло.
luminous /'lu:mɪnəs/ *adj* светя́щийся.
lump /lʌmp/ *n* ком; (*swelling*) о́пухоль; *vt*: **~ together** сме́шивать *impf*, смеша́ть *pf* (в одно́).
lunacy /'lu:nəsɪ/ *n* безу́мие.
lunar /'lu:nə(r)/ *adj* лу́нный.
lunatic /'lu:nətɪk/ *adj* (*n*) сумасше́дший (*sb*).
lunch /lʌntʃ/ *n* обе́д; **~-hour, ~-time** обе́денный переры́в; *vi* обе́дать *impf*, по~ *pf.*
lung /lʌŋ/ *n* лёгкое *sb.*
lunge /lʌndʒ/ *vi* де́лать *impf*, с~ *pf* вы́пад (**at** про́тив+*gen*).
lurch[1] /lɜ:tʃ/ *n*: **leave in the ~** покида́ть *impf*, поки́нуть *pf* в беде́.
lurch[2] /lɜ:tʃ/ *vi* (*stagger*) ходи́ть *indet*, идти́ *det* шата́ясь.
lure /ljʊə(r)/ *n* прима́нка; *vt* прима́нивать *impf*, примани́ть *pf.*
lurid /'ljʊərɪd/ *adj* (*gaudy*) крича́щий; (*details*) жу́ткий.
lurk /lɜ:k/ *vi* зата́иваться *impf*, зата́иться *pf.*
luscious /'lʌʃəs/ *adj* со́чный.
lush /lʌʃ/ *adj* пы́шный, со́чный.
lust /lʌst/ *n* по́хоть (**of, for** к+*dat*); *vi* стра́стно жела́ть *impf*, по~ *pf* (**for** +*gen*). **lustful** /-fʊl/ *adj* похотли́вый.
lustre /'lʌstə(r)/ *n* гля́нец. **lustrous** /'lʌstrəs/ *adj* глянцеви́тый.
lusty /'lʌstɪ/ *adj* (*healthy*) здоро́вый; (*lively*) живо́й.
lute /lu:t/ *n* (*mus*) лю́тня.
luxuriant /lʌg'zjʊərɪənt/ *adj* пы́шный.
luxuriate /lʌg'zjʊərɪˌeɪt/ *vi* наслажда́ться *impf*, наслади́ться *pf* (**in** +*instr*).
luxurious /lʌg'zjʊərɪəs/ *adj* роско́шный. **luxury** /'lʌgʒərɪ/ *n* ро́скошь.
lymph /lɪmf/ *attrib* лимфати́ческий.
lynch /lɪntʃ/ *vt* линчева́ть *impf* & *pf.*
lyric /'lɪrɪk/ *n* ли́рика; *pl* слова́ *neut pl* пе́сни. **lyrical** /-k(ə)l/ *adj* лири́ческий.

M

MA *abbr* (*of* **Master of Arts**) маги́стр гуманита́рных нау́к.
macabre /mə'kɑ:br(ə)/ *adj* жу́ткий.
macaroni /ˌmækə'rəʊnɪ/ *n* макаро́ны (-н) *pl.*
mace /meɪs/ *n* (*of office*) жезл.
machination /ˌmækɪ'neɪʃ(ə)n/ *n* махина́ция.
machine /mə'ʃi:n/ *n* маши́на; (*state* ~) аппара́т; *attrib* маши́нный; **~-gun** пулемёт; **~ tool** стано́к; *vt* обраба́тывать *impf*, обрабо́тать *pf* на станке́; (*sew*) шить *impf*, с~ *pf* (на маши́не). **machinery** /-nərɪ/ *n* (*machines*) маши́ны *f pl*; (*of state*) аппара́т. **machinist** /-nɪst/ *n* машини́ст; (*sewing*) шве́йник, -ица, швея́.
mackerel /'mækr(ə)l/ *n* ску́мбрия, макре́ль.
mackintosh /'mækɪnˌtɒʃ/ *n* плащ.
mad /mæd/ *adj* сумасше́дший. **madden** /'mæd(ə)n/ *vt* беси́ть *impf*, вз~ *pf.* **madhouse** *n* сумасше́дший дом. **madly** /-lɪ/*adv* безу́мно. **madman** *n* сумасше́дший *sb.* **madness** /-nɪs/ *n* сумасше́ствие. **madwoman** *n* сумасше́дшая *sb.*
madrigal /'mædrɪg(ə)l/ *n* мадрига́л.
maestro /'maɪstrəʊ/ *n* маэ́стро *m indecl.*
Mafia /'mæfɪə/ *n* ма́фия.
magazine /ˌmægə'zi:n/ *n* журна́л; (*of gun*) магази́н.
maggot /'mægət/ *n* личи́нка.
magic /'mædʒɪk/ *n* ма́гия, волшеб-

ство́; *adj* (*also* **magical**) волше́бный. **magician** /mə'dʒɪʃ(ə)n/ *n* волше́бник; (*conjurer*) фо́кусник.

magisterial /ˌmædʒɪ'stɪərɪəl/ *adj* авторите́тный.

magistrate /'mædʒɪstrət/ *n* судья́ *m*.

magnanimity /ˌmægnə'nɪmɪtɪ/ *n* великоду́шие. **magnanimous** /mæg'nænɪməs/ *adj* великоду́шный.

magnate /'mægneɪt/ *n* магна́т.

magnesium /mæg'niːzɪəm/ *n* ма́гний.

magnet /'mægnɪt/ *n* магни́т. **magnetic** /-'netɪk/ *adj* магни́тный; (*attractive*) притяга́тельный. **magnetism** /'mægnɪˌtɪz(ə)m/ *n* магнети́зм; притяга́тельность. **magnetize** /'mægnɪˌtaɪz/ *vt* намагни́чивать *impf*, намагни́тить *pf*.

magnification /ˌmægnɪfɪ'keɪʃ(ə)n/ *n* увеличе́ние.

m

magnificence /mæg'nɪfɪs(ə)ns/ *n* великоле́пие. **magnificent** /-s(ə)nt/ *adj* великоле́пный.

magnify /'mægnɪˌfaɪ/ *vt* увели́чивать *impf*, увели́чить *pf*; (*exaggerate*) преувели́чивать *impf*, преувели́чить *pf*. **magnifying glass** /-ˌfaɪɪŋ glɑːs/ *n* увеличи́тельное стекло́.

magnitude /'mægnɪˌtjuːd/ *n* величина́; (*importance*) ва́жность.

magpie /'mægpaɪ/ *n* соро́ка.

mahogany /mə'hɒgənɪ/ *n* кра́сное де́рево.

maid /meɪd/ *n* прислу́га. **maiden** /'meɪd(ə)n/ *adj* (*aunt etc.*) незаму́жняя; (*first*) пе́рвый; ~ **name** де́вичья фами́лия.

mail /meɪl/ *n* (*letters*) по́чта; ~ **order** почто́вый зака́з; *vt* посыла́ть *impf*, посла́ть *pf* по по́чте.

maim /meɪm/ *vt* кале́чить *impf*, ис~ *pf*.

main /meɪn/ *n* (*gas* ~; *pl*) магистра́ль; **in the** ~ в основно́м; *adj* основно́й, гла́вный; (*road*) магистра́льный. **mainland** *n* матери́к. **mainly** /-lɪ/ *adv* в основно́м. **mainstay** *n* (*fig*) гла́вная опо́ра.

maintain /meɪn'teɪn/ *vt* (*keep up*) подде́рживать *impf*, поддержа́ть *pf*; (*family*) содержа́ть *impf*; (*machine*) обслу́живать *impf*, обслужи́ть *pf*; (*assert*) утвержда́ть *impf*. **maintenance** /'meɪntənəns/ *n* подде́ржка; содержа́ние; обслу́живание.

maize /meɪz/ *n* кукуру́за.

majestic /mə'dʒestɪk/ *adj* вели́чественный. **majesty** /'mædʒɪstɪ/ *n* вели́чественность; (*title*) вели́чество.

major[1] /'meɪdʒə(r)/ *n* (*mil*) майо́р.

major[2] /'meɪdʒə(r)/ *adj* (*greater*) бо́льший; (*more important*) бо́лее ва́жный; (*main*) гла́вный; (*mus*) мажо́рный; *n* (*mus*) мажо́р. **majority** /mə'dʒɒrɪtɪ/ *n* большинство́; (*full age*) совершенноле́тие.

make /meɪk/ *vt* де́лать *impf*, с~ *pf*; (*produce*) производи́ть *impf*, произвести́ *pf*; (*prepare*) гото́вить *impf*, при~ *pf*; (*amount to*) равня́ться *impf* +*dat*; (*earn*) зараба́тывать *impf*, зарабо́тать *pf*; (*compel*) заставля́ть *impf*, заста́вить *pf*; (*reach*) добира́ться *impf*, добра́ться *pf* до+*gen*; (*be in time for*) успева́ть *impf*, успе́ть *pf* на+*acc*; **be made of** состоя́ть *impf* из+*gen*; ~ **as if, though** де́лать *impf*, с~ *pf* вид, что; ~ **a bed** стели́ть *impf*, по~ *pf* посте́ль; ~ **believe** притворя́ться *impf*, притвори́ться *pf*; ~**-believe** притво́рство; ~ **do with** дово́льствоваться *impf*, у~ *pf* +*instr*; ~ **off** удира́ть *impf*, удра́ть *pf*; ~ **out** (*cheque*) выпи́сывать *impf*, вы́писать *pf*; (*assert*) утвержда́ть *impf*, утверди́ть *pf*; (*understand*) разбира́ть *impf*, разобра́ть *pf*; ~ **over** передава́ть *impf*, переда́ть *pf*; ~ **up** (*form, compose, complete*) составля́ть *impf*, соста́вить *pf*; (*invent*) выду́мывать *impf*, вы́думать *pf*; (*theat*) гримирова́ть(ся) *impf*, за~ *pf*; ~**-up**

(*theat*) грим; (*cosmetics*) космéтика; (*composition*) состáв; **~ it up** мирúться *impf*, по~ *pf* (**with** с+*instr*); **~ up for** возмещáть *impf*, возместúть *pf*; **~ up one's mind** решáться *impf*, решúться *pf*. **make** /meɪk/ *n* мáрка. **makeshift** *adj* врéменный.

malady /'mælədɪ/ *n* болéзнь.

malaise /mə'leɪz/ *n* (*fig*) беспокóйство.

malaria /mə'leərɪə/ *n* малярúя.

male /meɪl/ *n* (*animal*) самéц; (*person*) мужчúна *m*; *adj* мужскóй.

malevolence /mə'levələns/ *n* недоброжелáтельность. **malevolent** /-lənt/ *adj* недоброжелáтельный.

malice /'mælɪs/ *n* злóба. **malicious** /mə'lɪʃ(ə)s/ *adj* злóбный.

malign /mə'laɪn/ *vt* клеветáть *impf*, на~ *pf* на+*acc*. **malignant** /-'lɪgnənt/ *adj* (*harmful*) зловрéдный; (*malicious*) злóбный; (*med*) злокáчественный.

malinger /mə'lɪŋgə(r)/ *vi* притворя́ться *impf*, притворúться *pf* больны́м. **malingerer** /-rə(r)/ *n* симуля́нт.

mallard /'mælɑːd/ *n* кря́ква.

malleable /'mælɪəb(ə)l/ *adj* кóвкий; (*fig*) подáтливый.

mallet /'mælɪt/ *n* (деревя́нный) молотóк.

malnutrition /ˌmælnjuː'trɪʃ(ə)n/ *n* недоедáние.

malpractice /mæl'præktɪs/ *n* престу́пная небрéжность.

malt /mɔːlt/ *n* сóлод.

maltreat /mæl'triːt/ *vt* плóхо обращáться *impf* с+*instr*.

mammal /'mæm(ə)l/ *n* млекопитáющее *sb*.

mammoth /'mæməθ/ *adj* громáдный.

man /mæn/ *n* (*human*, *person*) человéк; (*human race*) человéчество; (*male*) мужчúна *m*; (*labourer*) рабóчий *sb*; *pl* (*soldiers*) солдáты *m pl*; *vt* (*furnish with men*) укомплектóвывать *impf*, укомплектовáть *pf* лúчным состáвом; стáвить *impf*, по~ *pf* людéй к+*dat*; (*stall etc.*) обслу́живать *impf*, обслужúть *pf*; (*gate*, *checkpoint*) стоя́ть *impf* на+*prep*.

manacle /'mænək(ə)l/ *n* нару́чник; *vt* надевáть *impf*, надéть *pf* нару́чники на+*acc*.

manage /'mænɪdʒ/ *vt* (*control*) управля́ть *impf* +*instr*; *vi*(& *t*) (*cope*) справля́ться *impf*, спрáвиться *pf* (с+*instr*); (*succeed*) сумéть *pf*. **management** /-mənt/ *n* управлéние (**of** +*instr*); (*the* ~) администрáция. **manager** /-dʒə(r)/ *n* управля́ющий *sb* (**of** +*instr*); мéнеджер. **managerial** /-'dʒɪərɪəl/ *adj* администратúвный. **managing director** /'mænɪdʒɪŋ daɪ'rektə(r)/ *n* дирéктор-распорядúтель *m*.

mandarin /'mændərɪn/ *n* мандарúн.

mandate /'mændeɪt/ *n* мандáт. **mandated** /-tɪd/ *adj* подмандáтный. **mandatory** /-dətərɪ/ *adj* обязáтельный.

mane /meɪn/ *n* грúва.

manful /'mænfʊl/ *adj* му́жественный.

manganese /'mæŋgəˌniːz/ *n* мáрганец.

manger /'meɪndʒə(r)/ *n* я́сли (-лей) *pl*; **dog in the ~** собáка на сéне.

mangle /'mæŋg(ə)l/ *vt* (*mutilate*) калéчить *impf*, ис~ *pf*.

mango /'mæŋgəʊ/ *n* мáнго *neut indecl*.

manhandle /'mænˌhænd(ə)l/ *vt* гру́бо обращáться *impf* с+*instr*.

manhole /'mænhəʊl/ *n* смотровóй колóдец.

manhood /'mænhʊd/ *n* возмужáлость.

mania /'meɪnɪə/ *n* мáния. **maniac** /'meɪnɪˌæk/ *n* манья́к, -я́чка. **manic** /'mænɪk/ *adj* маниакáльный.

manicure /'mænɪˌkjʊə(r)/ *n* маникю́р; *vt* дéлать *impf*, с~ *pf* маникю́р +*dat*. **manicurist** /-ˌkjʊərɪst/ *n* маникю́рша.

m

manifest /'mænɪˌfest/ *adj* очеви́дный; *vt* (*display*) проявля́ть *impf*, прояви́ть *pf*; *n* манифе́ст. **manifestation** /-'teɪʃ(ə)n/ *n* проявле́ние. **manifesto** /-'festəʊ/ *n* манифе́ст.
manifold /'mænɪˌfəʊld/ *adj* разнообра́зный.
manipulate /mə'nɪpjʊˌleɪt/ *vt* манипули́ровать *impf* +*instr*. **manipulation** /-'leɪʃ(ə)n/ *n* манипуля́ция.
manly /'mænlɪ/ *adj* му́жественный.
mankind /mæn'kaɪnd/ *n* челове́чество.
manner /'mænə(r)/ *n* (*way*) о́браз; (*behaviour*) мане́ра; *pl* мане́ры *f pl*. **mannerism** /'mænərɪz(ə)m/ *n* мане́ра.
mannish /'mænɪʃ/ *adj* мужепо-до́бный.
manoeuvrable /mə'nuːvrəb(ə)l/ *adj* манёвренный. **manoeuvre** /-'nuːvə(r)/ *n* манёвр; *vt & i* маневри́ровать *impf*.
manor /'mænə(r)/ *n* поме́стье; (*house*) поме́щичий дом.
manpower /'mænˌpaʊə(r)/ *n* челове́ческие ресу́рсы *m pl*.
manservant /'mænˌsɜːv(ə)nt/ *n* слуга́ *m*.
mansion /'mænʃ(ə)n/ *n* особня́к.
manslaughter /'mænˌslɔːtə(r)/ *n* непредуму́шленное убийство.
mantelpiece /'mænt(ə)lˌpiːs/ *n* ками́нная доска́.
manual /'mænjʊəl/ *adj* ручно́й; *n* руково́дство. **manually** /-lɪ/ *adv* вручну́ю.
manufacture /ˌmænjʊ'fæktʃə(r)/ *n* произво́дство; *vt* производи́ть *impf*, произвести́ *pf*. **manufacturer** /-'fæktʃərə(r)/ *n* фабрика́нт.
manure /mə'njʊə(r)/ *n* наво́з.
manuscript /'mænjʊskrɪpt/ *n* ру́копись.
many /'menɪ/ *adj & n* мно́го +*gen*, мно́гие *pl*; **how ~** ско́лько +*gen*.
map /mæp/ *n* ка́рта; (*of town*) план; *vt*: **~ out** намеча́ть *impf*, наме́тить *pf*.
maple /'meɪp(ə)l/ *n* клён.
mar /mɑː(r)/ *vt* по́ртить *impf*, ис~ *pf*.
marathon /'mærəθ(ə)n/ *n* марафо́н.
marauder /mə'rɔːdə(r)/ *n* мародёр. **marauding** /-dɪŋ/ *adj* мародёрский.
marble /'mɑːb(ə)l/ *n* мра́мор; (*toy*) ша́рик; *attrib* мра́морный.
March /mɑːtʃ/ *n* март; *adj* ма́ртовский.
march /mɑːtʃ/ *vi* марширова́ть *impf*, про~ *pf*; *n* марш.
mare /meə(r)/ *n* кобы́ла.
margarine /ˌmɑːdʒə'riːn/ *n* маргари́н.
margin /'mɑːdʒɪn/ *n* (*on page*) по́ле; (*edge*) край; **profit ~** при́быль; **safety ~** запа́с про́чности.
marigold /'mærɪˌgəʊld/ *n* ноготки́ (-ко́в) *pl*.
marijuana /ˌmærɪ'wɑːnə/ *n* марихуа́на.
marina /mə'riːnə/ *n* мари́на.
marinade /ˌmærɪ'neɪd/ *n* марина́д; *vt* маринова́ть *impf*, за~ *pf*.
marine /mə'riːn/ *adj* морско́й; *n* (*soldier*) солда́т морско́й пехо́ты; *pl* морска́я пехо́та. **mariner** /'mærɪnə(r)/ *n* моря́к.
marital /'mærɪt(ə)l/ *adj* супру́жеский, бра́чный.
maritime /'mærɪˌtaɪm/ *adj* морско́й; (*near sea*) примо́рский.
mark[1] /mɑːk/ *n* (*coin*) ма́рка.
mark[2] /mɑːk/ *n* (*for distinguishing*) ме́тка; (*sign*) знак; (*school*) отме́тка; (*trace*) след; **on your ~s** на старт!; *vt* (*indicate; celebrate*) отмеча́ть *impf*, отме́тить *pf*; (*school etc.*) проверя́ть *impf*, прове́рить *pf*; (*stain*) па́чкать *impf*, за~ *pf*; (*sport*) закрыва́ть *impf*, закры́ть *pf*; **~ my words** по́мни(те) мои́ слова́!; **~ out** размеча́ть *impf*, разме́тить *pf*. **marker** /-kə(r)/ *n* знак; (*in book*) закла́дка.
market /'mɑːkɪt/ *n* ры́нок; **~ garden** огоро́д; **~-place** база́рная пло́щадь; *vt* продава́ть *impf*,

продáть *pf.* **marketing** /-tɪŋ/ *n* маркетинг.

marksman /ˈmɑːksmən/ *n* стрелóк.

marmalade /ˈmɑːməˌleɪd/ *n* апельсиновый джем.

maroon[1] /məˈruːn/ *adj* (*n*) (*colour*) тёмно-бордóвый (цвет).

maroon[2] /məˈruːn/ *vt* (*put ashore*) высáживать *impf*, вы́садить *pf* (на необитáемый óстров); (*cut off*) отрезáть *impf*, отрéзать *pf.*

marquee /mɑːˈkiː/ *n* тэнт.

marquis /ˈmɑːkwɪs/ *n* марки́з.

marriage /ˈmærɪdʒ/ *n* брак; (*wedding*) свáдьба; *attrib* брáчный. **marriageable** /-dʒəb(ə)l/ *adj*: **~ age** брáчный вóзраст. **married** /ˈmærɪd/ *adj* (*man*) женáтый; (*woman*) замýжняя, зáмужем; (*to each other*) женáты; (*of ~ persons*) супрýжеский.

marrow /ˈmærəʊ/ *n* кóстный мозг; (*vegetable*) кабачóк.

marry /ˈmærɪ/ *vt* (*of man*) жени́ться *impf* & *pf* на +*prep*; (*of woman*) выходи́ть *impf*, вы́йти *pf* зáмуж за +*acc*; *vi* (*of couple*) пожени́ться *pf.*

marsh /mɑːʃ/ *n* болóто. **marshy** /-ʃɪ/ *adj* болóтистый.

marshal /ˈmɑːʃ(ə)l/ *n* мáршал; *vt* выстрáивать *impf*, вы́строить *pf*; (*fig*) собирáть *impf*, собрáть *pf.*

marsupial /mɑːˈsuːpɪəl/ *n* сýмчатое живóтное *sb.*

martial /ˈmɑːʃ(ə)l/ *adj* воéнный; **~ law** воéнное положéние.

martyr /ˈmɑːtə(r)/ *n* мýченик, -ица; *vt* мýчить *impf*, за~ *pf.* **martyrdom** /-dəm/ *n* мýченичество.

marvel /ˈmɑːv(ə)l/ *n* чýдо; *vi* изумля́ться *impf*, изуми́ться *pf.* **marvellous** /-ləs/ *adj* чудéсный.

Marxist /ˈmɑːksɪst/ *n* маркси́ст; *adj* маркси́стский. **Marxism** /-sɪz(ə)m/ *n* маркси́зм.

marzipan /ˈmɑːzɪˌpæn/ *n* марципáн.

mascara /mæˈskɑːrə/ *n* тушь.

mascot /ˈmæskɒt/ *n* талисмáн.

masculine /ˈmæskjʊlɪn/ *adj* мужскóй; (*gram*) мужскóго рóда; (*of woman*) мужеподóбный.

mash /mæʃ/ *n* картóфельное пюрé *neut indecl*; *vt* разминáть *impf*, размя́ть *pf.*

mask /mɑːsk/ *n* мáска; *vt* маскировáть *impf*, за~ *pf.*

masochism /ˈmæsəˌkɪz(ə)m/ *n* мазохи́зм. **masochist** /-kɪst/ *n* мазохи́ст. **masochistic** /-ˈkɪstɪk/ *adj* мазохи́стский.

mason /ˈmeɪs(ə)n/ *n* кáменщик; (**M~**) масóн. **Masonic** /məˈsɒnɪk/ *adj* масóнский. **masonry** /ˈmeɪʃənrɪ/ *n* кáменная клáдка.

masquerade /ˌmæskəˈreɪd/ *n* маскарáд; *vi*: **~ as** выдавáть *impf*, вы́дать *pf* себя́ за+*acc.*

Mass /mæs/ *n* (*eccl*) мéсса.

mass /mæs/ *n* мáсса; (*majority*) большинствó; *attrib* мáссовый; **~ media** срéдства *neut pl* мáссовой информáции; **~-produced** мáссового произвóдства; **~ production** мáссовое произвóдство; *vt* масси́ровать *impf* & *pf.*

massacre /ˈmæsəkə(r)/ *n* резня́; *vt* вырезáть *impf*, вы́резать *pf.*

massage /ˈmæsɑːʒ/ *n* массáж; *vt* масси́ровать *impf* & *pf.* **masseur, -euse** /mæˈsɜː(r), -ˈsɜːz/ *n* массажи́ст, ~ка.

massive /ˈmæsɪv/ *adj* масси́вный; (*huge*) огрóмный.

mast /mɑːst/ *n* мáчта.

master /ˈmɑːstə(r)/ *n* (*owner*) хозя́ин; (*of ship*) капитáн; (*teacher*) учи́тель *m*; (**M~**, *univ*) маги́стр; (*workman*; *artist*) мáстер; (*original*) пóдлинник, оригинáл; **be ~ of** владéть *impf* +*instr*; **~-key** отмы́чка; *vt* (*overcome*) преодолевáть *impf*, преодолéть *pf*; справля́ться *impf*, спрáвиться *pf* с+*instr*; (*a subject*) овладевáть *impf*, овладéть *pf* +*instr.* **masterful** /-fʊl/ *adj* влáстный. **masterly** /-lɪ/ *adj* мастерскóй. **masterpiece** *n* шедéвр. **mastery** /-rɪ/ *n* (*of a subject*) владéние (**of** +*instr*).

masturbate /ˈmæstəˌbeɪt/ *vi* ма-

m

стурбировать *impf.*

mat /mæt/ *n* коврик, (*at door*) половик; (*on table*) подставка.

match[1] /mætʃ/ *n* спичка. **matchbox** *n* спичечная коробка.

match[2] /mætʃ/ *n* (*equal*) ровня *m* & *f*; (*contest*) матч, состязание; (*marriage*) партия; *vi* & *t* (*go well* (*with*)) гармонировать *impf* (с+*instr*); подходить *impf*, подойти *pf* (к+*dat*).

mate[1] /meɪt/ *n* (*chess*) мат.

mate[2] /meɪt/ *n* (*one of pair*) самец, самка; (*fellow worker*) товарищ; (*naut*) помощник капитана; *vi* (*of animals*) спариваться *impf*, спариться *pf.*

material /məˈtɪərɪəl/ *n* материал; (*cloth*) материя; *pl* (*necessary articles*) принадлежности *f pl.* **materialism** /-ˈtɪərɪəˌlɪz(ə)m/ *n* материализм. **materialistic** /-ˌtɪərɪəˈlɪstɪk/ *adj* материалистический. **materialize** /-ˈtɪərɪəˌlaɪz/ *vi* осуществляться *impf*, осуществиться *pf.*

m

maternal /məˈtɜːn(ə)l/ *adj* материнский; **~ grandfather** дедушка с материнской стороны. **maternity** /-ˈtɜːnɪtɪ/ *n* материнство; **~ leave** декретный отпуск; **~ ward** родильное отделение.

mathematical /ˌmæθɪˈmætɪk(ə)l/ *adj* математический. **mathematician** /ˌmæθɪməˈtɪʃ(ə)n/ *n* математик. **mathematics, maths** /mæθəˈmætɪks, mæθs/ *n* математика.

matinée /ˈmætɪˌneɪ/ *n* дневной спектакль *m.*

matriarchal /ˌmeɪtrɪˈɑːk(ə)l/ *adj* матриархальный. **matriarchy** /ˈmeɪtrɪˌɑːkɪ/ *n* матриархат.

matriculate /məˈtrɪkjʊˌleɪt/ *vi* быть принятым в вуз. **matriculation** /-ˈleɪʃ(ə)n/ *n* зачисление в вуз.

matrimonial /ˌmætrɪˈməʊnɪəl/ *adj* супружеский. **matrimony** /ˈmætrɪmənɪ/ *n* брак.

matrix /ˈmeɪtrɪks/ *n* матрица.

matron /ˈmeɪtrən/ *n* старшая сестра.

matt /mæt/ *adj* матовый.

matted /ˈmætɪd/ *adj* спутанный.

matter /ˈmætə(r)/ *n* (*affair*) дело; (*question*) вопрос; (*substance*) вещество; (*philos*; *med*) материя; (*printed*) материал; **a ~ of life and death** вопрос жизни и смерти; **a ~ of opinion** спорное дело; **a ~ of taste** дело вкуса; **as a ~ of fact** фактически; собственно говоря; **what's the ~?** в чём дело?; **what's the ~ with him?** что с ним?; **~-of-fact** прозаичный; *vi* иметь *impf* значение; **it doesn't ~** это не имеет значения; **it ~s a lot to me** для меня это очень важно.

matting /ˈmætɪŋ/ *n* рогожа.

mattress /ˈmætrɪs/ *n* матрас.

mature /məˈtjʊə(r)/ *adj* зрелый; *vi* зреть *impf*, со~ *pf.* **maturity** /-rɪtɪ/ *n* зрелость.

maul /mɔːl/ *vt* терзать *impf.*

mausoleum /ˌmɔːsəˈliːəm/ *n* мавзолей.

mauve /məʊv/ *adj* (*n*) розовато-лиловый (цвет).

maxim /ˈmæksɪm/ *n* сентенция.

maximum /ˈmæksɪməm/ *n* максимум; *adj* максимальный.

may /meɪ/ *v aux* (*possibility, permission*) мочь *impf*, с~ *pf*; (*possibility*) возможно, что +*indicative*; (*wish*) пусть +*indicative.*

May /meɪ/ *n* (*month*) май; *adj* майский **~ Day** Первое *sb* мая.

maybe /ˈmeɪbiː/ *adv* может быть.

mayonnaise /ˌmeɪəˈneɪz/ *n* майонез.

mayor /meə(r)/ *n* мэр. **mayoress** /ˈmeərɪs/ *n* жена мэра; женщина-мэр.

maze /meɪz/ *n* лабиринт.

meadow /ˈmedəʊ/ *n* луг.

meagre /ˈmiːgə(r)/ *adj* скудный.

meal[1] /miːl/ *n* еда; **at ~times** во время еды.

meal[2] /miːl/ *n* (*grain*) мука. **mealy** /ˈmiːlɪ/ *adj*: **~-mouthed** сладкоречивый.

mean[1] /miːn/ *adj* (*average*) средний; *n* (*middle point*) середина; *pl* (*method*) сре́дство, спо́соб; *pl* (*resources*) сре́дства *neut pl*; **by all ~s** коне́чно, пожа́луйста; **by ~s of** при по́мощи +*gen*, посре́дством +*gen*; **by no ~s** совсе́м не; **~s test** прове́рка нужда́емости.

mean² /miːn/ *adj* (*ignoble*) по́длый; (*miserly*) скупо́й; (*poor*) убо́гий.

mean³ /miːn/ *vt* (*have in mind*) име́ть *impf* в виду́; (*intend*) намерева́ться *impf* +*inf*; (*signify*) зна́чить *impf*.

meander /mɪˈændə(r)/ *vi* (*stream*) извива́ться *impf*; (*person*) броди́ть *impf*. **meandering** /-rɪŋ/ *adj* изви́листый.

meaning /ˈmiːnɪŋ/ *n* значе́ние. **meaningful** /-fʊl/ *adj* (много)значи́тельный. **meaningless** /-lɪs/ *adj* бессмы́сленный.

meantime, meanwhile /ˈmiːntaɪm, ˈmiːnwaɪl/ *adv* ме́жду тем.

measles /ˈmiːz(ə)lz/ *n* корь. **measly** /-zlɪ/ *adj* ничто́жный.

measurable /ˈmeʒərəb(ə)l/ *adj* измери́мый. **measure** /ˈmeʒə(r)/ *n* ме́ра; **made to ~** сши́тый по ме́рке; сде́ланный на зака́з; *vt* измеря́ть *impf*, изме́рить *pf*; (*for clothes*) снима́ть *impf*, снять *pf* ме́рку с+*gen*; *vi* име́ть *impf* +*acc*: **the room ~s 30 feet in length** ко́мната име́ет три́дцать фу́тов в длину́; **~ off, out** отмеря́ть *impf*, отме́рить *pf*; **~ up to** соотве́тствовать *impf* +*dat*. **measured** /ˈmeʒəd/ *adj* (*rhythmical*) ме́рный. **measurement** /ˈmeʒəmənt/ *n* (*action*) измере́ние; *pl* (*dimensions*) разме́ры *m pl*.

meat /miːt/ *n* мя́со. **meatball** *n* котле́та. **meaty** /-tɪ/ *adj* мяси́стый; (*fig*) содержа́тельный.

mechanic /mɪˈkænɪk/ *n* меха́ник. **mechanical** /-k(ə)l/ *adj* механи́ческий; (*fig*; *automatic*) машина́льный; **~ engineer** инжене́р-меха́ник; **~ engineering** машинострое́ние. **mechanics** /-nɪks/ *n* меха́ника. **mechanism** /ˈmekəˌnɪz(ə)m/ *n* механи́зм. **mechanization** /ˌmekənaɪˈzeɪʃ(ə)n/ *n* механиза́ция. **mechanize** /ˈmekəˌnaɪz/ *vt* механизи́ровать *impf* & *pf*.

medal /ˈmed(ə)l/ *n* меда́ль. **medallion** /mɪˈdæljən/ *n* медальо́н. **medallist** /ˈmedəlɪst/ *n* медали́ст.

meddle /ˈmed(ə)l/ *vi* вме́шиваться *impf*, вмеша́ться *pf* (**in, with** в+*acc*).

media /ˈmiːdɪə/ *pl of* **medium**

mediate /ˈmiːdɪˌeɪt/ *vi* посре́дничать *impf*. **mediation** /-ˈeɪʃ(ə)n/ *n* посре́дничество. **mediator** /-ˌeɪtə(r)/ *n* посре́дник.

medical /ˈmedɪk(ə)l/ *adj* медици́нский; **~ student** ме́дик, -и́чка. **medicated** /ˈmedɪˌkeɪtɪd/ *adj* (*impregnated*) пропи́танный лека́рством. **medicinal** /mɪˈdɪsɪn(ə)l/ *adj* (*of medicine*) лека́рственный; (*healing*) целе́бный. **medicine** /ˈmedsɪn/ *n* медици́на; (*substance*) лека́рство.

medieval /ˌmedɪˈiːv(ə)l/ *adj* средневеко́вый.

mediocre /ˌmiːdɪˈəʊkə(r)/ *adj* посре́дственный. **mediocrity** /-ˈɒkrɪtɪ/ *n* посре́дственность.

meditate /ˈmedɪˌteɪt/ *vi* размышля́ть *impf*. **meditation** /-ˈteɪʃ(ə)n/ *n* размышле́ние. **meditative** /ˈmedɪtətɪv/ *adj* заду́мчивый.

Mediterranean /ˌmedɪtəˈreɪnɪən/ *adj* средиземномо́рский; *n* Средизе́мное мо́ре.

medium /ˈmiːdɪəm/ *n* (*means*) сре́дство; (*phys*) среда́; (*person*) ме́диум; *pl* (*mass media*) сре́дства *neut pl* ма́ссовой информа́ции; *adj* сре́дний; **happy ~** золота́я середи́на.

medley /ˈmedlɪ/ *n* смесь; (*mus*) попурри́ *neut indecl*.

meek /miːk/ *adj* кро́ткий.

meet /miːt/ *vt & i* встреча́ть(ся) *impf*, встре́тить(ся) *pf*; *vt* (*make acquaintance*) знако́миться *impf*, по~ *pf* с+*instr*; *vi* (*assemble*) собира́ться *impf*, собра́ться *pf*.

m

meeting /-tɪŋ/ *n* встре́ча; (*of committee*) заседа́ние, ми́тинг.
megalomania /ˌmegələ'meɪnɪə/ *n* мегалома́ния.
megaphone /'megəˌfəʊn/ *n* мегафо́н.
melancholic /ˌmelən'kɒlɪk/ *adj* меланхоли́ческий. **melancholy** /'melənkəlɪ/ *n* грусть; *adj* уны́лый, гру́стный.
mellow /'meləʊ/ *adj* (*colour, sound*) со́чный; (*person*) доброду́шный; *vi* смягча́ться *impf*, смягчи́ться *pf*.
melodic /mɪ'lɒdɪk/ *adj* мелоди́ческий. **melodious** /-'ləʊdɪəs/ *adj* мелоди́чный. **melody** /'melədɪ/ *n* мело́дия.
melodrama /'meləˌdrɑːmə/ *n* мелодра́ма. **melodramatic** /ˌmelədrə'mætɪk/ *adj* мелодрамати́ческий.
melon /'melən/ *n* ды́ня; (*water-*~) арбу́з.

m

melt /melt/ *vt & i* раста́пливать(ся) *impf*, растопи́ть(ся) *pf*; (*smelt*) пла́вить(ся) *impf*, рас~ *pf*; (*dissolve*) растворя́ть(ся) *impf*, раствори́ть(ся) *pf*; *vi* (*thaw*) та́ять *impf*, рас~ *pf*; **~ing point** то́чка плавле́ния.
member /'membə(r)/ *n* член. **membership** /-ʃɪp/ *n* чле́нство; (*number of* ~) коли́чество чле́нов; *attrib* чле́нский.
membrane /'membreɪn/ *n* перепо́нка.
memento /mɪ'mentəʊ/ *n* сувени́р.
memoir /'memwɑː(r)/ *n pl* мемуа́ры (-ров) *pl*; воспомина́ния *neut pl.* **memorable** /'memərəb(ə)l/ *adj* достопа́мятный. **memorandum** /ˌmemə'rændəm/ *n* запи́ска. **memorial** /mɪ'mɔːrɪəl/ *adj* мемориа́льный; *n* па́мятник. **memorize** /'meməˌraɪz/ *vt* запомина́ть *impf*, запо́мнить *pf*. **memory** /'memərɪ/ *n* па́мять; (*recollection*) воспомина́ние.
menace /'menɪs/ *n* угро́за; *vt* угрожа́ть *impf* +*dat.* **menacing** /-sɪŋ/ *adj* угрожа́ющий.
menagerie /mɪ'nædʒərɪ/ *n* звери́нец.
mend /mend/ *vt* чини́ть *impf*, по~ *pf*; (*clothes*) што́пать *impf*, за~ *pf*; ~ **one's ways** исправля́ться *impf*, испра́виться *pf*.
menial /'miːnɪəl/ *adj* ни́зкий, чёрный.
meningitis /ˌmenɪn'dʒaɪtɪs/ *n* менинги́т.
menopause /'menəˌpɔːz/ *n* кли́макс.
menstrual /'menstrʊəl/ *adj* менструа́льный. **menstruation** /-strʊ'eɪʃ(ə)n/ *n* менструа́ция.
mental /'ment(ə)l/ *adj* у́мственный; (*of* ~ *illness*) психи́ческий; ~ **arithmetic** счёт в уме́. **mentality** /men'tælɪtɪ/ *n* ум; (*character*) склад ума́.
mention /'menʃ(ə)n/ *vt* упомина́ть *impf*, упомяну́ть *pf*; **don't ~ it** не́ за что!; **not to ~** не говоря́ уже́ о+*prep*.
menu /'menjuː/ *n* меню́ *neut indecl.*
mercantile /'mɜːkənˌtaɪl/ *adj* торго́вый.
mercenary /'mɜːsɪnərɪ/ *adj* коры́стный; (*hired*) наёмный; *n* наёмник.
merchandise /'mɜːtʃənˌdaɪz/ *n* това́ры *m pl.* **merchant** /'mɜːtʃənt/ *n* купе́ц; торго́вец; ~ **navy** торго́вый флот.
merciful /'mɜːsɪˌfʊl/ *adj* милосе́рдный. **mercifully** /-lɪ/ *adv* к сча́стью. **merciless** /'mɜːsɪlɪs/ *adj* беспоща́дный.
mercurial /mɜː'kjʊərɪəl/ *adj* (*person*) изме́нчивый. **mercury** /'mɜːkjʊrɪ/ *n* ртуть.
mercy /'mɜːsɪ/ *n* милосе́рдие; **at the ~ of** во вла́сти +*gen.*
mere /mɪə(r)/ *adj* просто́й; **a ~ £40** всего́ лишь со́рок фу́нтов. **merely** /'mɪəlɪ/ *adv* то́лько, про́сто.
merge /mɜːdʒ/ *vt & i* слива́ть(ся) *impf*, сли́ть(ся) *pf.* **merger** /-dʒə(r)/ *n* объедине́ние.
meridian /mə'rɪdɪən/ *n* меридиа́н.

meringue /mə'ræŋ/ *n* мере́нга.

merit /'merɪt/ *n* заслу́га, досто́инство; *vt* заслу́живать *impf*, заслужи́ть *pf +gen.*

mermaid /'mɜːmeɪd/ *n* руса́лка.

merrily /'merɪlɪ/ *adv* ве́село. **merriment** /'merɪmənt/ *n* весе́лье. **merry** /'merɪ/ *adj* весёлый; **~-go-round** карусе́ль; **~-making** весе́лье.

mesh /meʃ/ *n* сеть; *vi* сцепля́ться *impf*, сцепи́ться *pf.*

mesmerize /'mezməˌraɪz/ *vt* гипнотизи́ровать *impf*, за~ *pf.*

mess /mes/ *n* (*disorder*) беспоря́док; (*trouble*) беда́; (*eating-place*) столо́вая *sb*; *vi*: **~ about** вози́ться *impf*; **~ up** по́ртить *impf*, ис~ *pf.*

message /'mesɪdʒ/ *n* сообще́ние. **messenger** /'mesɪndʒə(r)/ *n* курье́р.

Messiah /mɪ'saɪə/ *n* месси́я *m.* **Messianic** /ˌmesɪ'ænɪk/ *adj* мессиа́нский.

Messrs /'mesəz/ *abbr* господа́ (*gen* -д) *m pl.*

messy /'mesɪ/ *adj* (*untidy*) беспоря́дочный; (*dirty*) гря́зный.

metabolism /mɪ'tæbəˌlɪz(ə)m/ *n* обме́н веще́ств.

metal /'met(ə)l/ *n* мета́лл; *adj* металли́ческий. **metallic** /mɪ'tælɪk/ *adj* металли́ческий. **metallurgy** /mɪ'tælədʒɪ/ *n* металлу́рги́я.

metamorphosis /ˌmetə'mɔːfəsɪs/ *n* метаморфо́за.

metaphor /'metəˌfɔː(r)/ *n* мета́фора. **metaphorical** /ˌmetə'fɒrɪk(ə)l/ *adj* метафори́ческий.

metaphysical /ˌmetə'fɪzɪk(ə)l/ *adj* метафизи́ческий. **metaphysics** /-'fɪzɪks/ *n* метафи́зика.

meteor /'miːtɪə(r)/ *n* метео́р. **meteoric** /ˌmiːtɪ'ɒrɪk/ *adj* метеори́ческий. **meteorite** /'miːtɪəˌraɪt/ *n* метеори́т. **meteorological** /ˌmiːtɪərə'lɒdʒɪk(ə)l/ *adj* метеорологи́ческий. **meteorology** /ˌmiːtɪə'rɒlədʒɪ/ *n* метеороло́гия.

meter /'miːtə(r)/ *n* счётчик; *vt* измеря́ть *impf*, изме́рить *pf.*

methane /'miːθeɪn/ *n* мета́н.

method /'meθəd/ *n* ме́тод. **methodical** /mɪ'θɒdɪk(ə)l/ *adj* методи́чный.

Methodist /'meθədɪst/ *n* методи́ст; *adj* методи́стский.

methodology /ˌmeθə'dɒlədʒɪ/ *n* методоло́гия.

methylated /'meθɪˌleɪtɪd/ *adj*: **~ spirit(s)** денатура́т.

meticulous /mə'tɪkjʊləs/ *adj* тща́тельный.

metre /'miːtə(r)/ *n* ме́тр. **metric(al)** /'metrɪk((ə)l)/ *adj* метри́ческий.

metronome /'metrəˌnəʊm/ *n* метроно́м.

metropolis /mɪ'trɒpəlɪs/ *n* столи́ца. **metropolitan** /ˌmetrə'pɒlɪt(ə)n/ *adj* столи́чный; *n* (*eccl*) митрополи́т.

mettle /'met(ə)l/ *n* хара́ктер.

Mexican /'meksɪkən/ *adj* мексика́нский; *n* мексика́нец, -а́нка. **Mexico** /'meksɪˌkəʊ/ *n* Ме́ксика.

mezzanine /'metsəˌniːn/ *n* антресо́ли *f pl.*

miaow /miː'aʊ/ *int* мя́у; *n* мяу́канье; *vi* мяу́кать *impf*, мяу́кнуть *pf.*

mica /'maɪkə/ *n* слюда́.

microbe /'maɪkrəʊb/ *n* микро́б. **microchip** /'maɪkrəʊˌtʃɪp/ *n* чип, микросхе́ма. **microcomputer** /'maɪkrəʊkəmˌpjuːtə(r)/ *n* микрокомпью́тер. **microcosm** /'maɪkrəˌkɒz(ə)m/ *n* микроко́см. **microfilm** /'maɪkrəʊˌfɪlm/ *n* микрофи́льм. **micro-organism** /ˌmaɪkrəʊ'ɔːgəˌnɪz(ə)m/ *n* микрооргани́зм. **microphone** /'maɪkrəˌfəʊn/ *n* микрофо́н. **microscope** *n* /'maɪkrəˌskəʊp/ микроско́п. **microscopic** /ˌmaɪkrə'skɒpɪk/ *adj* микроскопи́ческий. **microwave** /'maɪkrəʊˌweɪv/*n* микроволна́; **~ oven** микрово́лновая печь.

mid /mɪd/ *adj*: **~ May** середи́на ма́я. **midday** /'mɪddeɪ/ *n* по́лдень *m*; *attrib* полу́денный. **middle** /'mɪd(ə)l/ *n* середи́на; *adj* сре́д-

m

ний; **~-aged** сре́дних лет; **M~ Ages** сре́дние века́ *m pl*; **~-class** буржуа́зный; **~man** посре́дник; **~-sized** сре́днего разме́ра. **middleweight** *n* сре́дний вес.

midge /mɪdʒ/ *n* мо́шка.

midget /ˈmɪdʒɪt/ *n* ка́рлик, -ица.

midnight /ˈmɪdnaɪt/ *n* по́лночь; *attrib* полу́но́чный. **midriff** /ˈmɪdrɪf/ *n* диафра́гма. **midst** /mɪdst/ *n* середи́на. **midsummer** *n* середи́на ле́та. **midway** *adv* на полпути́. **mid-week** *n* середи́на неде́ли. **midwinter** *n* середи́на зимы́.

midwife /ˈmɪdwaɪf/ *n* акуше́рка. **midwifery** /ˌmɪdˈwɪfərɪ/ *n* акуше́рство.

might /maɪt/ *n* мощь; **with all one's ~** изо всех сил. **mighty** /ˈmaɪtɪ/ *adj* мо́щный.

migraine /ˈmiːɡreɪn/ *n* мигре́нь.

migrant /ˈmaɪɡrənt/ *adj* кочу́ющий; (*bird*) перелётный; *n* (*person*) переселе́нец; (*bird*) перелётная пти́ца. **migrate** /maɪˈɡreɪt/ *vi* мигри́ровать *impf* & *pf*. **migration** /-ˈɡreɪʃ(ə)n/ *n* мигра́ция. **migratory** /-ˈɡreɪtərɪ/ *adj* кочу́ющий; (*bird*) перелётный.

mike /maɪk/ *n* микрофо́н.

mild /maɪld/ *adj* мя́гкий.

mildew /ˈmɪldjuː/ *n* пле́сень.

mile /maɪl/ *n* ми́ля. **mileage** /-lɪdʒ/ *n* расстоя́ние в ми́лях; (*of car*) пробе́г. **milestone** *n* верстово́й столб; (*fig*) ве́ха.

militancy /ˈmɪlɪt(ə)nsɪ/ *n* вои́нственность. **militant** /-t(ə)nt/ *adj* вои́нствующий; *n* активи́ст. **military** /-tərɪ/ *adj* вое́нный; *n* вое́нные *sb pl*. **militate** /-ˌteɪt/ *vi*: **~ against** говори́ть *impf* про́тив +*gen*. **militia** /mɪˈlɪʃə/ *n* мили́ция. **militiaman** *n* милиционе́р.

milk /mɪlk/ *n* молоко́; *attrib* моло́чный; *vt* дои́ть *impf*, по~ *pf*. **milkman** *n* продаве́ц молока́. **milky** /-kɪ/ *adj* моло́чный; **M~ Way** Мле́чный Путь *m*.

mill /mɪl/ *n* ме́льница; (*factory*) фа́брика; *vt* (*grain etc.*) моло́ть *impf*, с~ *pf*; (*metal*) фрезерова́ть *impf*, от~ *pf*; (*coin*) гурти́ть *impf*; *vi*: **~ around** толпи́ться *impf*. **miller** /ˈmɪlə(r)/ *n* ме́льник.

millennium /mɪˈlenɪəm/ *n* тысячеле́тие.

millet /ˈmɪlɪt/ *n* (*plant*) про́со; (*grain*) пшено́.

milligram(me) /ˈmɪlɪˌɡræm/ *n* миллигра́мм. **millimetre** /-ˌmiːtə(r)/ *n* миллиме́тр.

million /ˈmɪljən/ *n* миллио́н. **millionaire** /-ˈneə(r)/ *n* миллионе́р. **millionth** /-jənθ/ *adj* миллио́нный.

millstone /ˈmɪlstəʊn/ *n* жёрнов; (*fig*) ка́мень *m* на ше́е.

mime /maɪm/ *n* мим; (*dumb-show*) пантоми́ма; *vt* изобража́ть *impf*, изобрази́ть *pf* мими́чески. **mimic** /ˈmɪmɪk/ *n* мими́ст; *vt* передра́знивать *impf*, передразни́ть *pf*. **mimicry** /ˈmɪmɪkrɪ/ *n* имита́ция.

minaret /ˌmɪnəˈret/ *n* минаре́т.

mince /mɪns/ *n* (*meat*) фарш; *vt* руби́ть *impf*; (*in machine*) пропуска́ть *impf*, пропусти́ть *pf* че́рез мясору́бку; *vi* (*walk*) семени́ть *impf*; **not ~ matters** говори́ть *impf* без обиняко́в. **mincemeat** *n* начи́нка из изю́ма, миндаля́ и т.п.

mind /maɪnd/ *n* ум; **bear in ~** име́ть *impf* в виду́; **change one's ~** переду́мывать *impf*, переду́мать *pf*; **make up one's ~** реша́ться *impf*, реши́ться *pf*; **you're out of your ~** вы с ума́ сошли́; *vt* (*give heed to*) обраща́ть *impf*, обрати́ть *pf* внима́ние на+*acc*; (*look after*) присма́тривать *impf*, присмотре́ть *pf* за+*instr*; **I don't ~** я ничего́ не име́ю про́тив; **don't ~ me** не обраща́й(те) внима́ния на меня́!; **~ you don't forget** смотри́ не забу́дь!; **~ your own business** не вме́шивайтесь в чужи́е дела́!; **never ~** ничего́! **mindful** /-fʊl/ *adj* по́мнящий. **mindless** /-lɪs/ *adj* бессмы́сленный.

mine[1] /maɪn/ *poss pron* мой; свой.

mine[2] /maɪn/ *n* ша́хта, рудни́к; (*fig*) исто́чник; (*mil*) ми́на; *vt* (*obtain from* ~) добыва́ть *impf*, добы́ть *pf*; (*mil*) мини́ровать *impf* & *pf*. **minefield** *n* ми́нное по́ле. **miner** /ˈmaɪnə(r)/ *n* шахтёр.

mineral /ˈmɪnər(ə)l/ *n* минера́л; *adj* минера́льный; **~ water** минера́льная вода́. **mineralogy** /-ˈrælədʒɪ/ *n* минерало́гия.

mingle /ˈmɪŋg(ə)l/ *vt* & *i* сме́шивать(ся) *impf*, смеша́ть(ся) *pf*.

miniature /ˈmɪnɪtʃə(r)/ *n* миниатю́ра; *adj* миниатю́рный.

minibus /ˈmɪnɪˌbʌs/ *n* микроавто́бус.

minim /ˈmɪnɪm/ *n* (*mus*) полови́нная но́та. **minimal** /-məl/ *adj* минима́льный. **minimize** /-ˌmaɪz/ *vt* (*reduce*) доводи́ть *impf*, довести́ *pf* до ми́нимума. **minimum** /-məm/ *n* ми́нимум; *adj* минима́льный.

mining /ˈmaɪnɪŋ/ *n* го́рное де́ло.

minister /ˈmɪnɪstə(r)/ *n* мини́стр; (*eccl*) свяще́нник. **ministerial** /-ˈstɪərɪəl/ *adj* министе́рский. **ministration** /-ˈstreɪʃ(ə)n/ *n* по́мощь. **ministry** /ˈmɪnɪstrɪ/ *n* (*polit*) министе́рство; (*eccl*) духове́нство.

mink /mɪŋk/ *n* но́рка; *attrib* но́рковый.

minor /ˈmaɪnə(r)/ *adj* (*unimportant*) незначи́тельный; (*less important*) второстепе́нный; (*mus*) мино́рный; *n* (*person under age*) несовершенноле́тний *n*; (*mus*) мино́р. **minority** /-ˈnɒrɪtɪ/ *n* меньшинство́; (*age*) несовершенноле́тие.

minstrel /ˈmɪnstr(ə)l/ *n* менестре́ль *m*.

mint[1] /mɪnt/ *n* (*plant*) мя́та; (*peppermint*) пе́речная мя́та.

mint[2] /mɪnt/ *n* (*econ*) моне́тный двор; **in ~ condition** но́венький; *vt* чека́нить *impf*, от~, вы́~ *pf*.

minuet /ˌmɪnjʊˈet/ *n* менуэ́т.

minus /ˈmaɪnəs/ *prep* ми́нус +*acc*; без+*gen*; *n* ми́нус.

minuscule /ˈmɪnəˌskjuːl/ *adj* малю́сенький.

minute[1] /ˈmɪnɪt/ *n* мину́та; *pl* протоко́л.

minute[2] /maɪˈnjuːt/ *adj* ме́лкий. **minutiae** /-ˈnjuːʃɪˌaɪ/ *n pl* ме́лочи (-че́й) *f pl*.

miracle /ˈmɪrək(ə)l/ *n* чу́до. **miraculous** /-ˈrækjʊləs/ *adj* чуде́сный.

mirage /ˈmɪrɑːʒ/ *n* мира́ж.

mire /ˈmaɪə(r)/ *n* (*mud*) грязь; (*swamp*) боло́то.

mirror /ˈmɪrə(r)/ *n* зе́ркало; *vt* отража́ть *impf*, отрази́ть *pf*.

mirth /mɜːθ/ *n* весе́лье.

misadventure /ˌmɪsədˈventʃə(r)/ *n* несча́стный слу́чай.

misapprehension /ˌmɪsæprɪˈhenʃ(ə)n/ *n* недопонима́ние. **misappropriate** /ˌmɪsəˈprəʊprɪˌeɪt/ *vt* незако́нно присва́ивать *impf*, присво́ить *pf*.

misbehave /ˌmɪsbɪˈheɪv/ *vi* ду́рно вести́ *impf* себя́. **misbehaviour** /ˌmɪsbɪˈheɪvɪə(r)/ *n* дурно́е поведе́ние.

miscalculate /ˌmɪsˈkælkjʊˌleɪt/ *vt* непра́вильно рассчи́тывать *impf*, рассчита́ть *pf*; (*fig*, *abs*) просчи́тываться *impf*, просчита́ться *pf*. **miscalculation** /-ˈleɪʃ(ə)n/ *n* просчёт. **miscarriage** /ˈmɪsˌkærɪdʒ/ *n* (*med*) вы́кидыш; **~ of justice** суде́бная оши́бка. **miscarry** /mɪsˈkærɪ/ *vi* (*med*) име́ть *impf* вы́кидыш.

miscellaneous /ˌmɪsəˈleɪnɪəs/ *adj* ра́зный, разнообра́зный. **miscellany** /mɪˈselənɪ/ *n* смесь.

mischief /ˈmɪstʃɪf/ *n* (*harm*) вред; (*naughtiness*) озорство́. **mischievous** /ˈmɪstʃɪvəs/ *adj* озорно́й. **misconception** /ˌmɪskənˈsepʃ(ə)n/ *n* непра́вильное представле́ние. **misconduct** /mɪsˈkɒndʌkt/ *n* дурно́е поведе́ние. **misconstrue** /ˌmɪskənˈstruː/ *vt* непра́вильно истолко́вывать *impf*, истолкова́ть *pf*.

misdeed, misdemeanour /mɪsˈdiːd, ˌmɪsdɪˈmiːnə(r)/ *n* просту́пок. **misdirect** /ˌmɪsdaɪˈrekt/ *vt* непра́вильно направля́ть *impf*, напра́вить *pf*; (*letter*) непра́вильно адресова́ть *impf* & *pf*.

miser /ˈmaɪzə(r)/ *n* скупе́ц. **miserable** /ˈmɪzərəb(ə)l/ *adj* (*unhappy, wretched*) несча́стный, жа́лкий; (*weather*) скве́рный. **miserly** /ˈmaɪzəlɪ/ *adj* скупо́й. **misery** /ˈmɪzərɪ/ *n* страда́ние.

misfire /mɪsˈfaɪə(r)/ *vi* дава́ть *impf*, дать *pf* осе́чку. **misfit** /ˈmɪsfɪt/ *n* (*person*) неуда́чник. **misfortune** /mɪsˈfɔːtjuːn/ *n* несча́стье. **misgiving** /mɪsˈgɪvɪŋ/ *n* опасе́ние. **misguided** /mɪsˈgaɪdɪd/ *adj* обма́нутый.

mishap /ˈmɪshæp/ *n* неприя́тность. **misinform** /ˌmɪsɪnˈfɔːm/ *vt* непра́вильно информи́ровать *impf* & *pf*. **misinterpret** /ˌmɪsɪnˈtɜːprɪt/ *vt* неве́рно истолко́вывать *impf*, истолкова́ть *pf*. **misjudge** /mɪsˈdʒʌdʒ/ *vt* неве́рно оце́нивать *impf*, оцени́ть *pf*. **misjudgement** /mɪsˈdʒʌdʒmənt/ *n* неве́рная оце́нка. **mislay** /mɪsˈleɪ/ *vt* затеря́ть *pf*. **mislead** /mɪsˈliːd/ *vt* вводи́ть *impf*, ввести́ *pf* в заблужде́ние. **mismanage** /mɪsˈmænɪdʒ/ *vt* пло́хо управля́ть *impf* +*instr*. **mismanagement** /mɪsˈmænɪdʒmənt/ *n* плохо́е управле́ние. **misnomer** /mɪsˈnəʊmə(r)/ *n* непра́вильное назва́ние.

misogynist /mɪˈsɒdʒɪnɪst/ *n* женоненави́стник. **misogyny** /-nɪ/ *n* женоненави́стничество.

misplaced /mɪsˈpleɪst/ *adj* неуме́стный. **misprint** /ˈmɪsprɪnt/ *n* опеча́тка. **misquote** /mɪsˈkwəʊt/ *vt* непра́вильно цити́ровать *impf*, про~ *pf*. **misread** /mɪsˈriːd/ *vt* (*fig*) непра́вильно истолко́вывать *impf*, истолкова́ть *pf*. **misrepresent** /ˌmɪsreprɪˈzent/ *vt* искажа́ть *impf*, искази́ть *pf*. **misrepresentation** /mɪsˌreprɪzenˈteɪʃ(ə)n/ *n* искаже́ние.

Miss /mɪs/ *n* (*title*) мисс.

miss /mɪs/ *n* про́мах; *vi* прома́хиваться *impf*, промахну́ться *pf*; *vt* (*fail to hit, see, hear*) пропуска́ть *impf*, пропусти́ть *pf*; (*train*) опа́здывать *impf*, опозда́ть *pf* на+*acc*; (*regret absence of*) скуча́ть *impf* по+*dat*; **~ out** пропуска́ть *impf*, пропусти́ть *pf*; **~ the point** не понима́ть *impf*, поня́ть *pf* су́ти.

misshapen /mɪsˈʃeɪpən/ *adj* уро́дливый.

missile /ˈmɪsaɪl/ *n* снаря́д, раке́та.

missing /ˈmɪsɪŋ/ *adj* отсу́тствующий, недостаю́щий; (*person*) пропа́вший бе́з ве́сти.

mission /ˈmɪʃ(ə)n/ *n* ми́ссия; команриро́вка. **missionary** /ˈmɪʃənərɪ/ *n* миссионе́р. **missive** /ˈmɪsɪv/ *n* посла́ние.

misspell /mɪsˈspel/ *vt* непра́вильно писа́ть *impf*, на~ *pf*. **misspelling** /-lɪŋ/ *n* непра́вильное написа́ние.

mist /mɪst/ *n* тума́н; *vt* & *i* затума́нивать(ся) *impf*, затума́нить(ся) *pf*.

mistake /mɪˈsteɪk/ *vt* непра́вильно понима́ть *impf*, поня́ть *pf*; **~ for** принима́ть *impf*, приня́ть *pf* за+*acc*; *n* оши́бка; **make a ~** ошиба́ться *impf*, ошиби́ться *pf*. **mistaken** /-kən/ *adj* оши́бочный; **be ~** ошиба́ться *impf*, ошиби́ться *pf*.

mister /ˈmɪstə(r)/ *n* ми́стер, господи́н.

mistletoe /ˈmɪs(ə)lˌtəʊ/ *n* оме́ла.

mistress /ˈmɪstrɪs/ *n* хозя́йка; (*teacher*) учи́тельница; (*lover*) любо́вница.

mistrust /mɪsˈtrʌst/ *vt* не доверя́ть *impf* +*dat*; *n* недове́рие. **mistrustful** /-fʊl/ *adj* недове́рчивый.

misty /ˈmɪstɪ/ *adj* тума́нный.

misunderstand /ˌmɪsʌndəˈstænd/ *vt* непра́вильно понима́ть *impf*, поня́ть *pf*. **misunderstanding** /-dɪŋ/ *n* недоразуме́ние.

misuse *vt* /mɪsˈjuːz/ непра́вильно употребля́ть *impf*, употреби́ть *pf*; (*ill-treat*) ду́рно обраща́ться *impf* с+*instr*; *n* /-'ju:s/ непра́вильное употребле́ние.

mite /maɪt/ *n* (*insect*) клещ.

mitigate /'mɪtɪˌgeɪt/ *vt* смягча́ть *impf*, смягчи́ть *pf*. **mitigation** /-'geɪʃ(ə)n/ *n* смягче́ние.

mitre /'maɪtə(r)/ *n* ми́тра.

mitten /'mɪt(ə)n/ *n* рукави́ца.

mix /mɪks/ *vt* меша́ть *impf*, с~ *pf*; *vi* сме́шиваться *impf*, смеша́ться *pf*; (*associate*) обща́ться *impf*; ~ **up** (*confuse*) пу́тать *impf*, с~ *pf*; **get ~ed up in** заме́шиваться *impf*, замеша́ться *pf* в+*acc*; *n* смесь. **mixer** /'mɪksə(r)/ *n* смеси́тель *m*; (*cul*) ми́ксер. **mixture** /'mɪkstʃə(r)/ *n* смесь; (*medicine*) миксту́ра.

moan /məʊn/ *n* стон; *vi* стона́ть *impf*, про~ *pf*.

moat /məʊt/ *n* (крепостно́й) ров.

mob /mɒb/ *n* толпа́; *vt* (*attack*) напада́ть *impf*, напа́сть *pf* толпо́й на+*acc*. **mobster** /-stə(r)/ *n* банди́т.

mobile /'məʊbaɪl/ *adj* подвижно́й, передвижно́й; ~ **phone** портати́вный телефо́н. **mobility** /mə'bɪlɪtɪ/ *n* подви́жность. **mobilize** /'məʊbɪˌlaɪz/ *vt* & *i* мобилизова́ть(ся) *impf* & *pf*.

moccasin /'mɒkəsɪn/ *n* мокаси́н (*gen pl* -н).

mock /mɒk/ *vt* & *i* издева́ться *impf* над+*instr*; *adj* (*sham*) подде́льный; (*pretended*) мни́мый; **~-up** *n* маке́т. **mockery** /'mɒkərɪ/ *n* издева́тельство; (*travesty*) паро́дия.

mode /məʊd/ *n* (*manner*) о́браз; (*method*) ме́тод.

model /'mɒd(ə)l/ *n* (*representation*) моде́ль; (*pattern, ideal*) образе́ц; (*artist's*) нату́рщик, -ица; (*fashion*) манеке́нщик, -ица; (*make*) моде́ль; *adj* образцо́вый; *vt* лепи́ть *impf*, вы́~, с~ *pf*; (*clothes*) демонстри́ровать *impf* & *pf*; *vi* (*act as* ~) быть нату́рщиком, -ицей; быть манеке́нщиком, -ицей; ~ **after, on** создава́ть *impf*, созда́ть *pf* по образцу́ +*gen*.

modem /'məʊdem/ *n* моде́м.

moderate *adj* /'mɒdərət/ (*various senses; polit*) уме́ренный; (*medium*) сре́дний; *vt* /'mɒdəˌreɪt/ умеря́ть *impf*, уме́рить *pf*; *vi* стиха́ть *impf*, сти́хнуть *pf*. **moderation** /ˌmɒdə'reɪʃ(ə)n/ *n* уме́ренность; **in ~** уме́ренно.

modern /'mɒd(ə)n/ *adj* совреме́нный; (*language, history*) но́вый. **modernization** /ˌmɒdənaɪ'zeɪʃ(ə)n/ *n* модерниза́ция. **modernize** /'mɒdəˌnaɪz/ *vt* модернизи́ровать *impf* & *pf*.

modest /'mɒdɪst/ *adj* скро́мный. **modesty** /-stɪ/ *n* скро́мность.

modification /ˌmɒdɪfɪ'keɪʃ(ə)n/ *n* модифика́ция. **modify** /'mɒdɪˌfaɪ/ *vt* модифици́ровать *impf* & *pf*.

modish /'məʊdɪʃ/ *adj* мо́дный.

modular /'mɒdjʊlə(r)/ *adj* мо́дульный. **modulate** /-ˌleɪt/ *vt* модули́ровать *impf*. **modulation** /-'leɪʃ(ə)n/ *n* модуля́ция. **module** /'mɒdju:l/ *n* мо́дуль *m*.

mohair /'məʊheə(r)/ *n* мохе́р.

moist /mɔɪst/ *adj* вла́жный. **moisten** /'mɔɪs(ə)n/ *vt* & *i* увлажня́ть(ся) *impf*, увлажни́ть(ся) *pf*. **moisture** /'mɔɪstʃə(r)/ *n* вла́га.

molar /'məʊlə(r)/ *n* (*tooth*) коренно́й зуб.

mole[1] /məʊl/ *n* (*on skin*) ро́динка.

mole[2] /məʊl/ *n* (*animal; agent*) крот.

molecular /mə'lekjʊlə(r)/ *adj* молекуля́рный. **molecule** /'mɒlɪˌkju:l/ *n* моле́кула.

molest /mə'lest/ *vt* пристава́ть *impf*, приста́ть *pf* к+*dat*.

mollify /'mɒlɪˌfaɪ/ *vt* смягча́ть *impf*, смягчи́ть *pf*.

mollusc /'mɒləsk/ *n* моллю́ск.

molten /'məʊlt(ə)n/ *adj* распла́вленный.

moment /'məʊmənt/ *n* моме́нт, миг; **at the ~** сейча́с; **at the last ~** в после́днюю мину́ту; **just a ~** сейча́с! **momentarily** /-'terɪlɪ/ *adv* на мгнове́ние. **momentary** /'məʊməntərɪ/ *adj* мгнове́нный. **momentous** /mə'mentəs/ *adj* ва́ж-

m

ный. **momentum** /mə'mentəm/ *n* количество движе́ния; (*impetus*) дви́жущая си́ла; **gather ~** набира́ть *impf*, набра́ть *pf* ско́рость.

monarch /'mɒnək/ *n* мона́рх. **monarchy** /-kɪ/ *n* мона́рхия.

monastery /'mɒnəstərɪ/ *n* монасты́рь *m*. **monastic** /mə'næstɪk/ *adj* мона́шеский.

Monday /'mʌndeɪ/ *n* понеде́льник.

monetary /'mʌnɪtərɪ/ *adj* де́нежный. **money** /'mʌnɪ/ *n* де́ньги (-нег, -ньга́м) *pl*; **~-lender** ростовщи́к.

mongrel /'mʌŋgr(ə)l/ *n* дворня́жка.

monitor /'mɒnɪt(ə)r/ *n* (*naut*; *TV*) монито́р; *vt* проверя́ть *impf*, прове́рить *pf*.

monk /mʌŋk/ *n* мона́х.

monkey /'mʌŋkɪ/ *n* обезья́на.

mono /'mɒnəʊ/ *n* мо́но *neut indecl*. **monochrome** *adj* одноцве́тный. **monogamous** /mə'nɒgəməs/ *adj* единобра́чный. **monogamy** /mə'nɒgəmɪ/ *n* единобра́чие. **monogram** /'mɒnə,græm/ *n* моногра́мма. **monograph** *n* моногра́фия. **monolith** /'mɒnəlɪθ/ *n* моноли́т. **monolithic** /,mɒnə'lɪθɪk/ *adj* моноли́тный. **monologue** /'mɒnə,lɒg/ *n* моноло́г. **monopolize** /mə'nɒpə,laɪz/ *vt* монополизи́ровать *impf* & *pf*. **monopoly** /mə'nɒpəlɪ/ *n* монопо́лия. **monosyllabic** /,mɒnəsɪ'læbɪk/ *adj* односло́жный. **monosyllable** /'mɒnə,sɪləb(ə)l/ *n* односло́жное сло́во. **monotone** *n* моното́нность; **in a ~** моното́нно. **monotonous** /mə'nɒtən(ə)s/ *adj* моното́нный. **monotony** /mə'nɒtənɪ/ *n* моното́нность.

monsoon /mɒn'su:n/ *n* (*wind*) муссо́н; (*rainy season*) дождли́вый сезо́н.

monster /'mɒnstə(r)/ *n* чудо́вище. **monstrosity** /mɒn'strɒsɪtɪ/ *n* чудо́вище. **monstrous** /'mɒnstrəs/ *adj* чудо́вищный; (*huge*) грома́дный.

montage /mɒn'tɑ:ʒ/ *n* монта́ж.

month /mʌnθ/ *n* ме́сяц. **monthly** /-lɪ/ *adj* ме́сячный; *n* ежеме́сячник; *adv* ежеме́сячно.

monument /'mɒnjʊmənt/ *n* па́мятник. **monumental** /-'ment(ə)l/ *adj* монумента́льный.

moo /mu:/ *vi* мыча́ть *impf*.

mood[1] /mu:d/ *n* (*gram*) наклоне́ние.

mood[2] /mu:d/ *n* настрое́ние. **moody** /-dɪ/ *adj* капри́зный.

moon /mu:n/ *n* луна́. **moonlight** *n* лу́нный свет; *vi* халту́рить *impf*. **moonlit** /-lɪt/ *adj* лу́нный.

moor[1] /mʊə(r)/ *n* ме́стность, поро́сшая ве́реском. **moorland** *n* ве́ресковая пу́стошь.

moor[2] /mʊə(r)/ *vt* & *i* швартова́ть(ся) *impf*, при~ *pf*. **mooring** /-rɪŋ/ *n* (*place*) прича́л; *pl* (*cables*) шварто́вы *m pl*.

Moorish /'mʊərɪʃ/ *adj* маврита́нский.

moose /mu:s/ *n* америка́нский лось *m*.

moot /mu:t/ *adj* спо́рный.

mop /mɒp/ *n* шва́бра; *vt* протира́ть *impf*, протере́ть *pf* (шва́брой); **~ one's brow** вытира́ть *impf*, вы́тереть *pf* лоб; **~ up** вытира́ть *impf*, вы́тереть *pf*.

mope /məʊp/ *vi* хандри́ть *impf*.

moped /'məʊped/ *n* мопе́д.

moraine /mə'reɪn/ *n* море́на.

moral /'mɒr(ə)l/ *adj* мора́льный; *n* мора́ль; *pl* нра́вы *m pl*. **morale** /mə'rɑ:l/ *n* мора́льное состоя́ние. **morality** /mə'rælɪtɪ/ *n* нра́вственность, мора́ль. **moralize** /'mɒrə,laɪz/ *vi* морализи́ровать *impf*.

morass /mə'ræs/ *n* боло́то.

moratorium /,mɒrə'tɔ:rɪəm/ *n* морато́рий.

morbid /'mɔ:bɪd/ *adj* боле́зненный.

more /mɔ:(r)/ *adj* (*greater quantity*) бо́льше +*gen*; (*additional*) ещё; *adv* бо́льше; (*forming comp*) бо́лее; **and what is ~** и бо́льше того́; **~ or less** бо́лее и́ли ме́нее;

once ~ ещё раз. **moreover** /mɔːˈrəʊvə(r)/ *adv* сверх того́; кро́ме того́.

morgue /mɔːg/ *n* морг.

moribund /ˈmɒrɪˌbʌnd/ *adj* умира́ющий.

morning /ˈmɔːnɪŋ/ *n* у́тро; **in the ~** у́тром; **in the ~s** по утра́м; *attrib* у́тренний.

moron /ˈmɔːrɒn/ *n* слабоу́мный *sb.*

morose /məˈrəʊs/ *adj* угрю́мый.

morphine /ˈmɔːfiːn/ *n* мо́рфий.

Morse (code) /mɔːs (kəʊd)/ *n* а́збука Мо́рзе.

morsel /ˈmɔːs(ə)l/ *n* кусо́чек.

mortal /ˈmɔːt(ə)l/ *adj* сме́ртный; (*fatal*) смерте́льный; *n* сме́ртный *sb.* **mortality** /-ˈtælɪtɪ/ *n* сме́ртность.

mortar /ˈmɔːtə(r)/ *n* (*vessel*) сту́п(к)а; (*cannon*) миномёт; (*cement*) (известко́вый) раство́р.

mortgage /ˈmɔːgɪdʒ/ *n* ссу́да на поку́пку до́ма; *vt* закла́дывать *impf*, заложи́ть *pf.*

mortify /ˈmɔːtɪˌfaɪ/ *vt* унижа́ть *impf*, уни́зить *pf.*

mortuary /ˈmɔːtjʊərɪ/ *n* морг.

mosaic /məʊˈzeɪɪk/ *n* моза́ика; *adj* моза́ичный.

mosque /mɒsk/ *n* мече́ть.

mosquito /mɒˈskiːtəʊ/ *n* кома́р.

moss /mɒs/ *n* мох. **mossy** /-sɪ/ *adj* мши́стый.

most /məʊst/ *adj* наибо́льший; *n* наибо́льшее коли́чество; *adj* & *n* (*majority*) большинство́ +*gen*; бо́льшая часть +*gen*; *adv* бо́льше всего́, наибо́лее; (*forming superl*) са́мый. **mostly** /-lɪ/ *adv* гла́вным о́бразом.

MOT (test) *n* техосмо́тр.

motel /məʊˈtel/ *n* моте́ль *m.*

moth /mɒθ/ *n* мотылёк; (*clothes-~*) моль.

mother /ˈmʌðə(r)/ *n* мать; *vt* относи́ться *impf* по-матери́нски к +*dat*; **~-in-law** (*wife's ~*) тёща; (*husband's ~*) свекро́вь; **~-of-pearl** перламу́тр; *adj* перламу́тровый; **~ tongue** родно́й язы́к. **motherhood** *n* матери́нство. **motherland** *n* ро́дина. **motherly** /-lɪ/ *adj* матери́нский.

motif /məʊˈtiːf/ *n* моти́в.

motion /ˈməʊʃ(ə)n/ *n* движе́ние; (*gesture*) жест; (*proposal*) предложе́ние; *vt* пока́зывать *impf*, показа́ть *pf* +*dat* же́стом, что́бы +*past*. **motionless** /-lɪs/ *adj* неподви́жный. **motivate** /ˈməʊtɪˌveɪt/ *vt* побужда́ть *impf*, побуди́ть *pf.* **motivation** /ˌməʊtɪˈveɪʃ(ə)n/ *n* побужде́ние. **motive** /ˈməʊtɪv/ *n* моти́в; *adj* дви́жущий.

motley /ˈmɒtlɪ/ *adj* пёстрый.

motor /ˈməʊtə(r)/ *n* дви́гатель *m*, мото́р; **~ bike** мотоци́кл; **~ boat** мото́рная ло́дка; **~ car** автомоби́ль *m*; **~ cycle** мотоци́кл; **~-cyclist** мотоцикли́ст; **~ racing** автомоби́льные го́нки *f pl*; **~ scooter** моторо́ллер; **~ vehicle** автомаши́на. **motoring** /-rɪŋ/ *n* автомобили́зм. **motorist** /-rɪst/ *n* автомобили́ст, **~**ка. **motorize** /-ˌraɪz/ *vt* моторизова́ть *impf* & *pf.* **motorway** *n* автостра́да.

mottled /ˈmɒtəld/ *adj* кра́пчатый.

motto /ˈmɒtəʊ/ *n* деви́з.

mould[1] /məʊld/ *n* (*shape*) фо́рма, фо́рмочка; *vt* формова́ть *impf*, с**~** *pf.* **moulding** /-dɪŋ/ *n* (*archit*) лепно́е украше́ние.

mould[2] /məʊld/ *n* (*fungi*) пле́сень. **mouldy** /-dɪ/ *adj* заплесневе́лый.

moulder /ˈməʊldə(r)/ *vi* разлага́ться *impf*, разложи́ться *pf.*

moult /məʊlt/ *vi* линя́ть *impf*, вы́**~** *pf.*

mound /maʊnd/ *n* холм; (*heap*) на́сыпь.

Mount /maʊnt/ *n* (*in names*) гора́.

mount /maʊnt/ *vt* (*ascend*) подниматься *impf*, подня́ться *pf* на+*acc*; (*~ a horse etc.*) сади́ться *impf*, сесть *pf* на+*acc*; (*picture*) накле́ивать *impf*, накле́ить *pf* на карто́н; (*gun*) устана́вливать *impf*, установи́ть *pf*; **~ up** (*accumulate*) нака́пливаться *impf*, накопи́ться *pf*; *n* (*for pic-*

m

ture) картóн; (*horse*) верховáя лóшадь.

mountain /ˈmaʊntɪn/ *n* горá; *attrib* гóрный. **mountaineer** /-ˈnɪə(r)/ *n* альпинúст, ~ка. **mountaineering** /-ˈnɪərɪŋ/ *n* альпинúзм. **mountainous** /ˈmaʊntɪnəs/ *adj* горúстый.

mourn /mɔːn/ *vt* оплáкивать *impf*, оплáкать *pf*; *vi* скорбéть *impf* (**over** о+*prep*). **mournful** /-fʊl/ *adj* скóрбный. **mourning** /-nɪŋ/ *n* трáур.

mouse /maʊs/ *n* мышь.

mousse /muːs/ *n* мусс.

moustache /məˈstɑːʃ/ *n* усы́ (усóв) *pl*.

mousy /ˈmaʊsɪ/ *adj* мышúный; (*timid*) рóбкий.

mouth *n* /maʊθ/ рот; (*poetical*) устá (-т) *pl*; (*entrance*) вход; (*of river*) ýстье; *vt* /maʊð/ говорúть *impf*, сказáть *pf* однúми губáми. **mouthful** /-fʊl/ *n* глотóк. **mouth-organ** *n* губнáя гармóника. **mouthpiece** *n* мундштýк; (*person*) рýпор.

movable /ˈmuːvəb(ə)l/ *adj* подвижнóй.

move /muːv/ *n* (*in game*) ход; (*change of residence*) переéзд; (*movement*) движéние; (*step*) шаг; *vt & i* двúгать(ся) *impf*, двúнуться *pf*; *vt* (*affect*) трóгать *impf*, трóнуть *pf*; (*propose*) вносúть *impf*, внестú *pf*; *vi* (*develop*) развивáться *impf*, развúться *pf*; (~ *house*) переезжáть *impf*, переéхать *pf*; ~ **away** (*vt & i*) удалять(ся) *impf*, удалúть(ся) *pf*; (*vi*) уезжáть *impf*, уéхать *pf*; ~ **in** въезжáть *impf*, въéхать *pf*; ~ **on** идтú *impf*, пойтú *pf* дáльше; ~ **out** съезжáть *impf*, съéхать *pf* (**of** с+*gen*). **movement** /-mənt/ *n* движéние; (*mus*) часть. **moving** /-vɪŋ/ *n* двúжущийся; (*touching*) трóгательный.

mow /məʊ/ *vt* (*also* ~ *down*) косúть *impf*, с~ *pf*. **mower** /ˈməʊə(r)/ *n* косúлка.

MP *abbr* (*of* **Member of Parliament**) член парлáмента.

Mr /ˈmɪstə(r)/ *abbr* мúстер, господúн. **Mrs** /ˈmɪsɪz/ *abbr* мúссис *f indecl*, госпожá.

Ms /mɪz/ *n* миз, госпожá.

much /mʌtʃ/ *adj & n* мнóго +*gen*; мнóгое *sb*; *adv* óчень; (*with comp adj*) горáздо.

muck /mʌk/ *n* (*dung*) навóз; (*dirt*) грязь; ~ **about** возúться *impf*; ~ **out** чúстить *impf*, вы́~ *pf*; ~ **up** изгáживать *impf*, изгáдить *pf*.

mucous /ˈmjuːkəs/ *adj* слúзистый. **mucus** /ˈmjuːkəs/ *n* слизь.

mud /mʌd/ *n* грязь. **mudguard** *n* крылó.

muddle /ˈmʌd(ə)l/ *vt* пýтать *impf*, с~ *pf*; *vi*: ~ **through** кóе-кáк справляться *impf*, спрáвиться *pf*; *n* беспорядок.

muddy /ˈmʌdɪ/ *adj* гря́зный; *vt* обры́згивать *impf*, обры́згать *pf* гря́зью.

muff /mʌf/ *n* мýфта.

muffle /ˈmʌf(ə)l/ *vt* (*for warmth*) закýтывать *impf*, закýтать *pf*; (*sound*) глушúть *impf*, за~ *pf*.

mug /mʌg/ *n* (*vessel*) крýжка; (*face*) мóрда.

muggy /ˈmʌgɪ/ *adj* сырóй и тёплый.

mulch /mʌltʃ/ *n* мýльча; *vt* мульчúровать *impf & pf*.

mule /mjuːl/ *n* мул.

mull /mʌl/ *vt*: ~ **over** обдýмывать *impf*, обдýмать *pf*. **mulled** /mʌld/ *adj*: ~ **wine** глинтвéйн.

mullet /ˈmʌlɪt/ *n* (*grey* ~) кефáль; (*red* ~) барабýлька.

multicoloured /ˈmʌltɪˌkʌləd/ *adj* многокрáсочный. **multifarious** /ˌmʌltɪˈfeərɪəs/ *adj* разнообрáзный. **multilateral** /ˌmʌltɪˈlætər(ə)l/ *adj* многосторóнний. **multimillionaire** /ˌmʌltɪˌmɪljəˈneə(r)/ *n* мультимиллионéр. **multinational** /ˌmʌltɪˈnæʃ(ə)n(ə)l/ *adj* многонационáльный.

multiple /ˈmʌltɪp(ə)l/ *adj* составнóй; (*numerous*) многочúсленный; ~ **sclerosis** рассéянный склерóз; *n* крáтное числó; **least**

m

common ~ общее наиме́ньшее кра́тное *sb.* **multiplication** /ˌmʌltɪplɪ'keɪʃ(ə)n/ *n* умноже́ние. **multiplicity** /ˌmʌltɪ'plɪsɪtɪ/ *n* многочи́сленность. **multiply** /'mʌltɪˌplaɪ/ *vt* (*math*) умножа́ть *impf*, умно́жить *pf*; *vi* размножа́ться *impf*, размно́житься *pf*.

multi-storey /ˌmʌltɪ'stɔːrɪ/ *adj* многоэта́жный.

multitude /'mʌltɪˌtjuːd/ *n* мно́жество; (*crowd*) толпа́.

mum[1] /mʌm/ *adj*: **keep ~** молча́ть *impf*.

mum[2] /mʌm/ *n* (*mother*) ма́ма.

mumble /'mʌmb(ə)l/ *vt* & *i* бормота́ть *impf*, про~ *pf*.

mummy[1] /'mʌmɪ/ *n* (*archaeol*) му́мия.

mummy[2] /'mʌmɪ/ *n* (*mother*) ма́ма, ма́мочка.

mumps /mʌmps/ *n* сви́нка.

munch /mʌntʃ/ *vt* жева́ть *impf*.

mundane /mʌn'deɪn/ *adj* земно́й.

municipal /mjuː'nɪsɪp(ə)l/ *adj* муниципа́льный. **municipality** /-'pælɪtɪ/ *n* муниципалите́т.

munitions /mjuː'nɪʃ(ə)ns/ *n pl* вое́нное иму́щество.

mural /'mjʊər(ə)l/ *n* стенна́я ро́спись.

murder /'mɜːdə(r)/ *n* уби́йство; *vt* убива́ть *impf*, уби́ть *pf*; (*language*) кове́ркать *impf*, ис~ *pf*. **murderer, murderess** /'mɜːdərə(r), 'mɜːdərɪs/ *n* уби́йца *m* & *f*. **murderous** /'mɜːdərəs/ *adj* уби́йственный.

murky /'mɜːkɪ/ *adj* тёмный, мра́чный.

murmur /'mɜːmə(r)/ *n* шёпот; *vt* & *i* шепта́ть *impf*, шепну́ть *pf*.

muscle /'mʌs(ə)l/ *n* му́скул. **muscular** /'mʌskjʊlə(r)/ *adj* мы́шечный; (*person*) му́скулистый.

Muscovite /'mʌskəˌvaɪt/ *n* москви́ч, ~ка.

muse /mjuːz/ *vi* размышля́ть *impf*.

museum /mjuː'zɪəm/ *n* музе́й.

mush /mʌʃ/ *n* ка́ша.

mushroom /'mʌʃrʊm/ *n* гриб.

music /'mjuːzɪk/ *n* му́зыка; (*sheet ~*) но́ты *f pl*; **~-hall** мю́зик-хо́лл; **~ stand** пюпи́тр. **musical** /-k(ə)l/ *adj* музыка́льный; *n* опере́тта. **musician** /mjuː'zɪʃ(ə)n/ *n* музыка́нт.

musk /mʌsk/ *n* му́скус.

musket /'mʌskɪt/ *n* мушке́т.

Muslim /'mʊzlɪm/ *n* мусульма́нин, -а́нка; *adj* мусульма́нский.

muslin /'mʌzlɪn/ *n* мусли́н.

mussel /'mʌs(ə)l/ *n* ми́дия.

must /mʌst/ *v aux* (*obligation*) до́лжен (-жна́) *predic+inf*; на́до *impers+dat* & *inf*; (*necessity*) ну́жно *impers+dat* & *inf*; **~ not** (*prohibition*) нельзя́ *impers+dat* & *inf*.

mustard /'mʌstəd/ *n* горчи́ца.

muster /'mʌstə(r)/ *vt* собира́ть *impf*, собра́ть *pf*; (*courage etc.*) собира́ться *impf*, собра́ться *pf* с+*instr*.

musty /'mʌstɪ/ *adj* за́тхлый.

mutation /mjuː'teɪʃ(ə)n/ *n* мута́ция.

mute /mjuːt/ *adj* немо́й; *n* немо́й *sb*; (*mus*) серди́нка. **muted** /-tɪd/ *adj* приглушённый.

mutilate /'mjuːtɪˌleɪt/ *vt* уве́чить *impf*, из~ *pf*. **mutilation** /-'leɪʃ(ə)n/ *n* уве́чье.

mutineer /ˌmjuːtɪ'nɪə(r)/ *n* мятéжник. **mutinous** /'mjuːtɪnəs/ *adj* мятéжный. **mutiny** /'mjuːtɪnɪ/ *n* мятéж; *vi* бунтова́ть *impf*, взбунтова́ться *pf*.

mutter /'mʌtə(r)/ *vi* бормота́ть *impf*; *impf*; *n* бормота́ние.

mutton /'mʌt(ə)n/ *n* бара́нина.

mutual /'mjuːtʃʊəl/ *adj* взаи́мный; (*common*) о́бщий.

muzzle /'mʌz(ə)l/ *n* (*animal's*) мо́рда; (*on animal*) намо́рдник; (*of gun*) ду́ло; *vt* надева́ть *impf*, наде́ть *pf* намо́рдник на+*acc*; (*fig*) заставля́ть *impf*, заста́вить *pf* молча́ть.

my /maɪ/ *poss pron* мой; свой.

myopia /maɪ'əʊpɪə/ *n* близору́кость. **myopic** /-'ɒpɪk/ *adj* близору́кий.

myriad /'mɪrɪəd/ *n* мириа́ды (-д)

m

pl; *adj* бесчи́сленный.
myrtle /ˈmɜːt(ə)l/ *n* мирт; *attrib* ми́ртовый.
myself /maɪˈself/ *pron* (*emph*) (я) сам, сама́; (*refl*) себя́; -ся (*suffixed to vt*).
mysterious /mɪˈstɪərɪəs/ *adj* таи́нственный. **mystery** /ˈmɪstərɪ/ *n* та́йна.
mystic(al) /ˈmɪstɪk(ə)l/ *adj* мисти́ческий; *n* ми́стик. **mysticism** /ˈmɪstɪˌsɪz(ə)m/ *n* мистици́зм. **mystification** /ˌmɪstɪfɪˈkeɪʃ(ə)n/ *n* озада́ченность. **mystify** /ˈmɪstɪˌfaɪ/ *vt* озада́чивать *impf*, озада́чить *pf*.
myth /mɪθ/ *n* миф. **mythical** /ˈmɪθɪk(ə)l/ *adj* мифи́ческий. **mythological** /ˌmɪθəˈlɒdʒɪk(ə)l/ *adj* мифологи́ческий. **mythology** /mɪˈθɒlədʒɪ/ *n* мифоло́гия.

N

nag[1] /næg/ *n* (*horse*) ло́шадь.
nag[2] /næg/ *vt* (*also* ~ *at*) пили́ть *impf* +*acc*; *vi* (*of pain*) ныть *impf*.
nail /neɪl/ *n* (*finger-*, *toe-*~) но́готь *m*; (*metal spike*) гвоздь *m*; **~ varnish** лак для ногте́й; *vt* прибива́ть *impf*, приби́ть *pf* (гвоздя́ми).
naive /naɪˈiːv/ *adj* наи́вный. **naivety** /-tɪ/ *n* наи́вность.
naked /ˈneɪkɪd/ *adj* го́лый; **~ eye** невооружённый глаз. **nakedness** /-nɪs/ *n* нагота́.
name /neɪm/ *n* назва́ние; (*forename*) и́мя *neut*; (*surname*) фами́лия; (*reputation*) репута́ция; **what is his ~?** как его́ зову́т?; **~-plate** доще́чка с фами́лией; **~sake** тёзка *m* & *f*; *vt* называ́ть *impf*, назва́ть *pf*; (*appoint*) назнача́ть *impf*, назна́чить *pf*. **nameless** /-lɪs/ *adj* безымя́нный. **namely** /-lɪ/ *adv* (а) и́менно; то есть.
nanny /ˈnænɪ/ *n* ня́ня.
nap /næp/ *n* коро́ткий сон; *vi* вздремну́ть *pf*.
nape /neɪp/ *n* загри́вок.
napkin /ˈnæpkɪn/ *n* салфе́тка.
nappy /ˈnæpɪ/ *n* пелёнка.
narcissus /nɑːˈsɪsəs/ *n* нарци́сс.
narcotic /nɑːˈkɒtɪk/ *adj* наркоти́ческий; *n* нарко́тик.
narrate /nəˈreɪt/ *vt* расска́зывать *impf*, рассказа́ть *pf*. **narration** /-ˈreɪʃ(ə)n/ *n* расска́з. **narrative** /ˈnærətɪv/ *n* расска́з; *adj* повествова́тельный. **narrator** /nəˈreɪtə(r)/ *n* расска́зчик
narrow /ˈnærəʊ/ *adj* у́зкий; *vt & i* су́живать(ся) *impf*, су́зить(ся) *pf*. **narrowly** /-lɪ/ *adv* (*hardly*) чуть, е́ле-е́ле; **he ~ escaped drowning** он чуть не утону́л. **narrow-minded** /ˌnærəʊˈmaɪndɪd/ *adj* ограни́ченный. **narrowness** /ˈnærəʊnɪs/ *n* у́зость.
nasal /ˈneɪz(ə)l/ *adj* носово́й; (*voice*) гнуса́вый.
nasturtium /nəˈstɜːʃəm/ *n* насту́рция.
nasty /ˈnɑːstɪ/ *adj* неприя́тный, проти́вный; (*person*) злой.
nation /ˈneɪʃ(ə)n/ *n* (*people*) наро́д; (*country*) страна́. **national** /ˈnæʃən(ə)l/ *adj* национа́льный, наро́дный; (*of the state*) госуда́рственный; *n* по́дданный *sb*. **nationalism** /ˈnæʃənəˌlɪz(ə)m/ *n* национали́зм. **nationalist** /ˈnæʃənəlɪst/ *n* национали́ст, ~ка. **nationalistic** /ˌnæʃənəˈlɪstɪk/ *adj* националисти́ческий. **nationality** /ˌnæʃəˈnælɪtɪ/ *n* национа́льность; (*citizenship*) гражда́нство, по́дданство. **nationalization** /ˌnæʃənəlaɪˈzeɪʃ(ə)n/ *n* национализа́ция. **nationalize** /ˈnæʃənəˌlaɪz/ *vt* национализи́ровать *impf* & *pf*.
native /ˈneɪtɪv/ *n* (~ *of*) уроже́нец, -нка (+*gen*); (*aborigine*) тузе́мец, -мка; *adj* (*innate*) приро́дный; (*of one's birth*) родно́й; (*indigenous*) тузе́мный; **~ land** ро́дина; **~ language** родно́й язы́к; **~ speaker** носи́тель *m* языка́.

nativity /nəˈtɪvɪtɪ/ *n* Рождество́ (Христо́во).
natter /ˈnætə(r)/ *vi* болта́ть *impf*.
natural /ˈnætʃər(ə)l/ *adj* есте́ственный, приро́дный; ~ **resources** приро́дные бога́тства *neut pl*; ~ **selection** есте́ственный отбо́р; *n* (*mus*) бека́р. **naturalism** /-ˌlɪz(ə)m/ *n* натурали́зм. **naturalist** /-lɪst/ *n* натурали́ст. **naturalistic** /ˌnætʃərəˈlɪstɪk/ *adj* натуралисти́ческий. **naturalization** /ˌnætʃərəlaɪˈzeɪʃ(ə)n/ *n* натурализа́ция. **naturalize** /ˈnætʃərəˌlaɪz/ *vt* натурализи́ровать *impf* & *pf*. **naturally** /ˈnætʃərəlɪ/ *adv* есте́ственно. **nature** /ˈneɪtʃə(r)/ *n* приро́да; (*character*) хара́ктер; **by** ~ по приро́де.
naught /nɔːt/ *n*: **come to** ~ своди́ться *impf*, свести́сь *pf* к нулю́.
naughty /ˈnɔːtɪ/ *adj* шаловли́вый.
nausea /ˈnɔːzɪə/ *n* тошнота́. **nauseate** /-zɪˌeɪt/ *vt* тошни́ть *impf impers* от +*gen*. **nauseating** /-zɪˌeɪtɪŋ/ *adj* тошнотво́рный. **nauseous** /-zɪəs/ *adj*: **I feel** ~ меня́ тошни́т.
nautical /ˈnɔːtɪk(ə)l/ *n* морско́й.
naval /ˈneɪv(ə)l/ *adj* (вое́нно-)морско́й.
nave /neɪv/ *n* неф.
navel /ˈneɪv(ə)l/ *n* пупо́к.
navigable /ˈnævɪgəb(ə)l/ *adj* судохо́дный. **navigate** /-ˌgeɪt/ *vt* (*ship*) вести́ *impf*; (*sea*) пла́вать *impf* по+*dat*. **navigation** /ˌnævɪˈgeɪʃ(ə)n/ *n* навига́ция. **navigator** /ˈnævɪˌgeɪtə(r)/ *n* шту́рман.
navvy /ˈnævɪ/ *n* землеко́п.
navy /ˈneɪvɪ/ *n* вое́нно-морско́й флот; ~ **blue** тёмно-си́ний.
Nazi /ˈnɑːtsɪ/ *n* наци́ст, ~ка; *adj* наци́стский. **Nazism** /ˈnɑːtsɪz(ə)m/ *n* наци́зм.
NB *abbr* нотабе́не.
near /nɪə(r)/ *adv* бли́зко; ~ **at hand** под руко́й; ~ **by** ря́дом; *prep* во́зле+*gen*, о́коло+*gen*, у+*gen*; *adj* бли́зкий; ~**-sighted** близору́кий; *vt* & *i* приближа́ться *impf*, прибли́зиться *pf* к+*dat*. **nearly** /-lɪ/ *adv* почти́.
neat /niːt/ *adj* (*tidy*) опря́тный, аккура́тный; (*clear*) чёткий; (*undiluted*) неразба́вленный.
nebulous /ˈnebjʊləs/ *adj* нея́сный.
necessarily /ˈnesəsərɪlɪ/ *adv* обяза́тельно. **necessary** /ˈnesəsərɪ/ *adj* необходи́мый; (*inevitable*) неизбе́жный. **necessitate** /nɪˈsesɪˌteɪt/ *vt* де́лать *impf*, с~ *pf* необходи́мым. **necessity** /-ˈsesɪtɪ/ *n* необходи́мость; неизбе́жность; (*object*) предме́т пе́рвой необходи́мости.
neck /nek/ *n* ше́я; (*of garment*) вы́рез; ~ **and** ~ голова́ в го́лову. **necklace** /ˈneklɪs/ *n* ожере́лье. **neckline** *n* вы́рез.
nectar /ˈnektə(r)/ *n* некта́р.
née /neɪ/ *adj* урождённая.
need /niːd/ *n* нужда́; *vt* нужда́ться *impf* в+*prep*; **I** (*etc.*) ~ мне (*dat*) ну́жен (-жна́, -жно, -жны́) +*nom*; **I** ~ **five roubles** мне ну́жно пять рубле́й.
needle /ˈniːd(ə)l/ *n* игла́, иго́лка; (*knitting*) спи́ца; (*pointer*) стре́лка; *vt* придира́ться *impf*, придра́ться *pf* к+*dat*.
needless /ˈniːdlɪs/ *adj* нену́жный; ~ **to say** разуме́ется. **needy** /ˈniːdɪ/ *adj* нужда́ющийся.
negation /nɪˈgeɪʃ(ə)n/ *n* отрица́ние. **negative** /ˈnegətɪv/ *adj* отрица́тельный; *n* отрица́ние; (*phot*) негати́в.
neglect /nɪˈglekt/ *vt* пренебрега́ть *impf*, пренебре́чь *pf* +*instr*; не забо́титься *impf* о+*prep*; *n* пренебреже́ние; (*condition*) забро́шенность. **neglectful** /-fʊl/ *adj* небре́жный, невнима́тельный (**of** к+*dat*). **negligence** /ˈneglɪdʒ(ə)ns/ *n* небре́жность. **negligent** /-dʒ(ə)nt/ *adj* небре́жный. **negligible** /-dʒɪb(ə)l/ *adj* незначи́тельный.
negotiate /nɪˈgəʊʃɪˌeɪt/ *vi* вести́ *impf* перегово́ры; *vt* (*arrange*) заключа́ть *impf*, заключи́ть *pf*; (*overcome*) преодолева́ть *impf*,

преодоле́ть *pf.* **negotiation** /nɪˌɡəʊʃɪ'eɪʃ(ə)n/ *n* (*discussion*) перегово́ры *m pl.*

Negro /'ni:ɡrəʊ/ *n* негр; *adj* негритя́нский.

neigh /neɪ/ *n* ржа́ние; *vi* ржать *impf.*

neighbour /'neɪbə(r)/ *n* сосе́д, ~ка. **neighbourhood** /-hʊd/ *n* ме́стность; **in the ~ of** о́коло +*gen.* **neighbouring** /-rɪŋ/ *adj* сосе́дний. **neighbourly** /-lɪ/ *adj* добрососе́дский.

neither /'naɪðə(r)/ *adv* та́кже не, то́же не; *pron* ни тот, ни друго́й; **~ ... nor** ни... ни.

neon /'ni:ɒn/ *n* нео́н; *attrib* нео́новый.

nephew /'nevju:/ *n* племя́нник.

nepotism /'nepəˌtɪz(ə)m/ *n* кумовство́.

nerve /nɜ:v/ *n* нерв; (*courage*) сме́лость; (*impudence*) на́глость; **get on the ~s of** де́йствовать *impf*, по~ *pf* +*dat* на не́рвы. **nervous** /'nɜ:vəs/ *adj* не́рвный; **~ breakdown** не́рвное расстро́йство. **nervy** /'nɜ:vɪ/ *adj* нерво́зный.

nest /nest/ *n* гнездо́; **~ egg** сбереже́ния *neut pl*; *vi* гнезди́ться *impf.* **nestle** /'nes(ə)l/ *vi* льнуть *impf*, при~ *pf.*

net[1] /net/ *n* сеть, се́тка; *vt* (*catch*) лови́ть *impf*, пойма́ть *pf* сетя́ми.

net[2], **nett** /net/ *adj* чи́стый; *vt* получа́ть *impf*, получи́ть *pf* ... чи́стого дохо́да.

Netherlands /'neðələndz/ *n* Нидерла́нды (-ов) *pl.*

nettle /'net(ə)l/ *n* крапи́ва.

network /'netwɜ:k/ *n* сеть.

neurologist /njʊə'rɒlədʒɪst/ *n* невро́лог. **neurology** /-dʒɪ/ *n* невроло́гия. **neurosis** /-'rəʊsɪs/ *n* невро́з. **neurotic** /-'rɒtɪk/ *adj* невроти́ческий.

neuter /'nju:tə(r)/ *adj* сре́дний, сре́днего ро́да; *n* сре́дний род; *vt* кастри́ровать *impf* & *pf.* **neutral** /-tr(ə)l/ *adj* нейтра́льный; *n* (*gear*) нейтра́льная ско́рость. **neutrality** /nju:'trælɪtɪ/ *n* нейтралите́т. **neutralize** /'nju:trəˌlaɪz/ *vt* нейтрализова́ть *impf* & *pf.* **neutron** /'nju:trɒn/ *n* нейтро́н.

never /'nevə(r)/ *adv* никогда́; **~ again** никогда́ бо́льше; **~ mind** ничего́!; всё равно́!; **~ once** ни ра́зу. **nevertheless** /ˌnevəðə'les/ *conj*, *adv* тем не ме́нее.

new /nju:/ *adj* но́вый; (*moon*, *potatoes*) молодо́й. **new-born** *adj* новорождённый. **newcomer** /'nju:kʌmə(r)/ *n* пришéлец. **new-fangled** /'nju:fæŋɡ(ə)ld/ *adj* новомо́дный. **newly** /'nju:lɪ/ *adv* то́лько что, неда́вно. **newness** /'nju:nɪs/ *n* новизна́.

news /nju:z/ *n* но́вость, -ти *pl*, изве́стие, -ия *pl.* **newsagent** *n* продаве́ц газе́т. **newsletter** *n* информацио́нный бюллете́нь *m.* **newspaper** *n* газе́та. **newsprint** *n* газе́тная бума́га. **newsreel** *n* кинохро́ника.

newt /nju:t/ *n* трито́н.

New Zealand /nju: 'zi:lənd/ *n* Но́вая Зела́ндия; *adj* новозела́ндский.

next /nekst/ *adj* сле́дующий, бу́дущий; *adv* (**~** *time*) в сле́дующий раз; (*then*) пото́м, зате́м; **~ door** (*house*) в сосе́днем до́ме; (*flat*) в сосе́дней кварти́ре; **~ of kin** ближа́йший ро́дственник; **~ to** ря́дом с+*instr*; (*fig*) почти́. **next-door** *adj* сосе́дний; **~ neighbour** ближа́йший сосе́д.

nib /nɪb/ *n* перо́.

nibble /'nɪb(ə)l/ *vt* & *i* грызть *impf*; *vt* обгрыза́ть *impf*, обгры́зть *pf*; (*grass*) щипа́ть *impf*; (*fish*) клева́ть *impf.*

nice /naɪs/ *adj* (*pleasant*) прия́тный, хоро́ший; (*person*) ми́лый. **nicety** /'naɪsɪtɪ/ *n* то́нкость.

niche /ni:ʃ/ *n* ни́ша; (*fig*) своё ме́сто.

nick /nɪk/ *n* (*scratch*) цара́пина; (*notch*) зару́бка; **in the ~ of time** в са́мый после́дний моме́нт; *vt* (*scratch*) цара́пать *impf*, о~ *pf*; (*steal*) сти́брить *pf.*

n

nickel /ˈnɪk(ə)l/ *n* ни́кель *m.*
nickname /ˈnɪkneɪm/ *n* про́звище; *vt* прозыва́ть *impf*, прозва́ть *pf.*
nicotine /ˈnɪkə͵tiːn/ *n* никоти́н.
niece /niːs/ *n* племя́нница.
niggardly /ˈnɪgədlɪ/ *adj* скупо́й.
niggling /ˈnɪglɪŋ/ *adj* ме́лочный.
night /naɪt/ *n* ночь; (*evening*) ве́чер; **at ~** но́чью; **last ~** вчера́ ве́чером; *attrib* ночно́й; **~-club** ночно́й клуб. **nightcap** *n* ночно́й колпа́к; (*drink*) стака́нчик спиртно́го на́ ночь. **nightdress** *n* ночна́я руба́шка. **nightfall** *n* наступле́ние но́чи. **nightingale** /ˈnaɪtɪŋ͵geɪl/ *n* солове́й. **nightly** /ˈnaɪtlɪ/ *adj* ежено́щный; *adv* ежено́щно. **nightmare** /ˈnaɪtmeə(r)/ *n* кошма́р. **nightmarish** /ˈnaɪtmeərɪʃ/ *adj* кошма́рный.
nil /nɪl/ *n* нуль *m.*
nimble /ˈnɪmb(ə)l/ *adj* прово́рный.
nine /naɪn/ *adj* & *n* де́вять; (*number 9*) девя́тка. **nineteen** /naɪnˈtiːn/ *adj* & *n* девятна́дцать. **nineteenth** /naɪnˈtiːnθ/ *adj* & *n* девятна́дцатый. **ninetieth** /ˈnaɪntɪəθ/ *adj* & *n* девяно́стый. **ninety** /ˈnaɪntɪ/ *adj* & *n* девяно́сто; *pl* (*decade*) девяно́стые го́ды (-до́в) *m pl.* **ninth** /ˈnaɪnθ/ *adj* & *n* девя́тый.
nip /nɪp/ *vt* (*pinch*) щипа́ть *impf*, щипну́ть *pf*; (*bite*) куса́ть *impf*, укуси́ть *pf*; **~ in the bud** пресека́ть *impf*, пресе́чь *pf* в заро́дыше; *n* щипо́к; уку́с; **there's a ~ in the air** во́здух па́хнет моро́зцем.
nipple /ˈnɪp(ə)l/ *n* сосо́к.
nirvana /nɪəˈvɑːnə/ *n* нирва́на.
nit /nɪt/ *n* гни́да.
nitrate /ˈnaɪtreɪt/ *n* нитра́т. **nitrogen** /ˈnaɪtrədʒ(ə)n/ *n* азо́т.
no /nəʊ/ *adj* (*not any*) никако́й, не оди́н; (*not a* (*fool etc.*)) (совсе́м) не; *adv* нет; (нисколько) не+*comp*; *n* отрица́ние, отка́з; (*in vote*) го́лос «про́тив»; **~ doubt** коне́чно, несомне́нно; **~ longer** уже́ не, бо́льше не; **no one** никто́; **~ wonder** не удиви́тельно.
Noah's ark /͵nəʊəz ˈɑːk/ *n* Но́ев ковче́г.
nobility /nəʊˈbɪlɪtɪ/ *n* (*class*) дворя́нство; (*quality*) благоро́дство. **noble** /ˈnəʊb(ə)l/ *adj* дворя́нский; благоро́дный. **nobleman** *n* дворяни́н.
nobody /ˈnəʊbədɪ/ *pron* никто́; *n* ничто́жество.
nocturnal /nɒkˈtɜːn(ə)l/ *adj* ночно́й.
nod /nɒd/ *vi* кива́ть *impf*, кивну́ть *pf* голово́й; *n* киво́к.
nodule /ˈnɒdjuːl/ *n* узело́к.
noise /nɔɪz/ *n* шум. **noiseless** /-lɪs/ *adj* бесшу́мный. **noisy** /ˈnɔɪzɪ/ *adj* шу́мный.
nomad /ˈnəʊmæd/ *n* коче́вник. **nomadic** /-ˈmædɪk/ *adj* кочево́й.
nomenclature /nəʊˈmenklətʃə(r)/ *n* номенклату́ра. **nominal** /ˈnɒmɪn(ə)l/ *adj* номина́льный. **nominate** /ˈnɒmɪ͵neɪt/ *vt* (*propose*) выдвига́ть *impf*, вы́двинуть *pf*; (*appoint*) назнача́ть *impf*, назна́чить *pf.* **nomination** /͵nɒmɪˈneɪʃ(ə)n/ *n* выдвиже́ние; назначе́ние. **nominative** /ˈnɒmɪnətɪv/ *adj* (*n*) имени́тельный (паде́ж). **nominee** /͵nɒmɪˈniː/ *n* кандида́т.
non-alcoholic /͵nɒnælkəˈhɒlɪk/ *adj* безалкого́льный. **non-aligned** /͵nɒnəˈlaɪnd/ *adj* неприсоедини́вшийся.
nonchalance /ˈnɒnʃələns/ *n* беззабо́тность. **nonchalant** /-lənt/ *n* беззабо́тный.
non-commissioned /͵nɒnkəˈmɪʃ(ə)nd/ *adj*: **~ officer** у́нтер-офице́р. **non-committal** /-ˈmɪt(ə)l/ *adj* укло́нчивый.
non-conformist /͵nɒnkənˈfɔːmɪst/ *n* нонконформи́ст; *adj* нонконформи́стский.
nondescript /ˈnɒndɪskrɪpt/ *adj* неопределённый.
none /nʌn/ *pron* (*no one*) никто́; (*nothing*) ничто́; (*not one*) не оди́н; *adv* ниско́лько не; **~ the**

n

less тем не ме́нее.

nonentity /nɒ'nentɪtɪ/ *n* ничто́жество.

non-existent /ˌnɒnɪg'zɪst(ə)nt/ *adj* несуществу́ющий. **non-fiction** /nɒn'fɪkʃ(ə)n/ *adj* документа́льный. **non-intervention** /ˌnɒnɪntə'venʃ(ə)n/ *n* невмеша́тельство. **non-party** *adj* беспарти́йный. **non-payment** /nɒn'peɪmənt/ *n* неплатёж.

nonplus /nɒn'plʌs/ *vt* ста́вить *impf*, по~ *pf* в тупи́к.

non-productive /ˌnɒnprə'dʌktɪv/ *adj* непроизводи́тельный. **non-resident** /nɒn'rezɪd(ə)nt/ *adj* не прожива́ющий (где́-нибудь).

nonsense /'nɒns(ə)ns/ *n* ерунда́. **nonsensical** /nɒn'sensɪk(ə)l/ *adj* бессмы́сленный.

non-smoker /nɒn'sməʊkə(r)/ *n* (*person*) некуря́щий *sb*; (*compartment*) купе́ *neut indecl*, для некуря́щих. **non-stop** /nɒn'stɒp/ *adj* безостано́вочный; (*flight*) беспоса́дочный; *adv* без остано́вок; без поса́док. **non-violent** /nɒn'vaɪələnt/ *adj* ненаси́льственный.

noodles /'nu:d(ə)lz/ *n pl* лапша́.

nook /nʊk/ *n* уголо́к.

noon /nu:n/ *n* по́лдень *m*.

no one /'nəʊwʌn/ *see* **no**

noose /nu:s/ *n* пе́тля.

nor /nɔ:(r)/ *conj* и не; то́же; **neither ... ~** ни… ни.

norm /nɔ:m/ *n* но́рма. **normal** /'nɔ:m(ə)l/ *adj* норма́льный. **normality** /nɔ:'mælɪtɪ/ *n* норма́льность. **normalize** /'nɔ:məˌlaɪz/ *vt* нормализова́ть *impf* & *pf*.

north /nɔ:θ/ *n* се́вер; (*naut*) норд; *adj* се́верный; *adv* к се́веру, на се́вер; **~-east** се́веро-восто́к; **~-easterly, -eastern** се́веро-восто́чный; **~-west** се́веро-за́пад; **~-westerly, -western** се́веро-за́падный. **northerly** /'nɔ:ðəlɪ/ *adj* се́верный. **northern** /'nɔ:ð(ə)n/ *adj* се́верный. **northerner** /'nɔ:ðənə(r)/ *n* северя́нин, -я́нка. **northward(s)** /'nɔ:θwəd(z)/ *adv* на се́вер, к се́веру.

Norway /'nɔ:weɪ/ *n* Норве́гия. **Norwegian** /nɔ:'wi:dʒ(ə)n/ *adj* норве́жский; *n* норве́жец, -жка.

nose /nəʊz/ *n* нос; *vt*: **~ about, out** разню́хивать *impf*, разню́хать *pf*. **nosebleed** *n* кровотече́ние и́з носу. **nosedive** *n* пике́ *neut indecl.*

nostalgia /nɒ'stældʒə/ *n* ностальги́я. **nostalgic** /-dʒɪk/ *adj* ностальги́ческий.

nostril /'nɒstrɪl/ *n* ноздря́.

not /nɒt/ *adv* не; нет; ни; **~ at all** нисколько, ничу́ть; (*reply to thanks*) не сто́ит (благода́рности); **~ once** ни ра́зу; **~ that** не то, что́бы; **~ too** дово́льно *+neg*; **~ to say** что́бы не сказа́ть; **~ to speak of** не говоря́ уже́ о*+prep.*

notable /'nəʊtəb(ə)l/ *adj* заме́тный; (*remarkable*) замеча́тельный. **notably** /-blɪ/ *adv* (*especially*) осо́бенно; (*perceptibly*) заме́тно.

notary (public) /'nəʊtərɪ ('pʌblɪk)/ *n* нота́риус.

notation /nəʊ'teɪʃ(ə)n/ *n* нота́ция; (*mus*) но́тное письмо́.

notch /nɒtʃ/ *n* зару́бка; *vt*: **~ up** выи́грывать *impf*, вы́играть *pf*.

note /nəʊt/ *n* (*record*) заме́тка, за́пись; (*annotation*) примеча́ние; (*letter*) запи́ска; (*banknote*) банкно́т; (*mus*) но́та; (*tone*) тон; (*attention*) внима́ние; *vt* отмеча́ть *impf*, отме́тить *pf*; **~ down** запи́сывать *impf*, записа́ть *pf*. **notebook** *n* записна́я кни́жка. **noted** /'nəʊtɪd/ *adj* знамени́тый; изве́стный (**for** *+instr*). **notepaper** *n* почто́вая бума́га. **noteworthy** /'nəʊtwɜ:ðɪ/ *adj* досто́йный внима́ния.

nothing /'nʌθɪŋ/ *n* ничто́, ничего́; **~ but** ничего́ кро́ме*+gen*, то́лько; **~ of the kind** ничего́ подо́бного; **come to ~** конча́ться *impf*, ко́нчиться *pf* ниче́м; **for ~** (*free*) да́ром; (*in vain*) зря, напра́сно; **have ~ to do with** не име́ть *impf* никако́го отноше́-

ния к+*dat*; **there is (was) ~ for it (but to)** ничего́ друго́го не остаётся (остава́лось) (как); **to say ~ of** не говоря́ уже́ о+*prep*.

notice /'nəʊtɪs/ *n* (*sign*) объявле́ние; (*warning*) предупрежде́ние; (*attention*) внима́ние; (*review*) о́тзыв; **give (in) one's ~** подава́ть *impf*, пода́ть *pf* заявле́ние об ухо́де с рабо́ты; **give s.o. ~** предупрежда́ть *impf*, предупреди́ть *pf* об увольне́нии; **take ~ of** обраща́ть *impf*, обрати́ть *pf* внима́ния на+*acc*; **~-board** доска́ для объявле́ний; *vt* замеча́ть *impf*, заме́тить *pf*. **noticeable** /-səb(ə)l/ *adj* заме́тный. **notification** /ˌnəʊtɪfɪ'keɪʃ(ə)n/ *n* извеще́ние. **notify** /'nəʊtɪˌfaɪ/ *vt* извеща́ть *impf*, извести́ть *pf* (**of** о+*prep*).

notion /'nəʊʃ(ə)n/ *n* поня́тие.

notoriety /ˌnəʊtə'raɪətɪ/ *n* дурна́я сла́ва. **notorious** /nəʊ'tɔːrɪəs/ *adj* преслову́тый.

notwithstanding /ˌnɒtwɪθ'stændɪŋ/ *prep* несмотря́ на+*acc*; *adv* те́м не ме́нее.

nought /nɔːt/ *n* (*nothing*) *see* **naught;** (*zero*) нуль *m*; (*figure 0*) ноль *m*.

noun /naʊn/ *n* (и́мя *neut*) существи́тельное *sb*.

nourish /'nʌrɪʃ/ *vt* пита́ть *impf*, на~ *pf*. **nourishing** /-ʃɪŋ/ *adj* пита́тельный. **nourishment** /-mənt/ *n* пита́ние.

novel /'nɒv(ə)l/ *adj* но́вый; (*unusual*) необыкнове́нный; *n* рома́н. **novelist** /-lɪst/ *n* романи́ст. **novelty** /-tɪ/ *n* (*newness*) новизна́; (*new thing*) нови́нка.

November /nə'vembə(r)/ *n* ноя́брь *m*; *adj* ноя́брьский.

novice /'nɒvɪs/ *n* (*eccl*) по́слушник, -ица; (*beginner*) новичо́к.

now /naʊ/ *adv* тепе́рь, сейча́с; (*immediately*) то́тчас же; (*next*) тогда́; *conj*: **~ (that)** раз, когда́; **(every) ~ and again, then** вре́мя от вре́мени; **by ~** уже́; **from ~ on** впредь. **nowadays** /'naʊəˌdeɪz/ *adv* в на́ше вре́мя.

nowhere /'nəʊweə(r)/ *adv* (*place*) нигде́; (*direction*) никуда́; *pron*: **I have ~ to go** мне не́куда пойти́.

noxious /'nɒkʃəs/ *adj* вре́дный.

nozzle /'nɒz(ə)l/ *n* со́пло́.

nuance /'njuːɑ̃s/ *n* нюа́нс.

nuclear /'njuːklɪə(r)/ *adj* я́дерный. **nucleus** /-klɪəs/ *n* ядро́.

nude /njuːd/ *adj* обнажённый, наго́й; *n* обнажённая фигу́ра.

nudge /nʌdʒ/ *vt* подта́лкивать *impf*, подтолкну́ть *pf* ло́ктем; *n* толчо́к ло́ктем.

nudity /'njuːdɪtɪ/ *n* нагота́.

nugget /'nʌgɪt/ *n* саморо́док.

nuisance /'njuːs(ə)ns/ *n* доса́да; (*person*) раздража́ющий челове́к.

null /nʌl/ *adj*: **~ and void** недействи́тельный. **nullify** /'nʌlɪˌfaɪ/ *vt* аннули́ровать *impf* & *pf*. **nullity** /'nʌlɪtɪ/ *n* недействи́тельность.

numb /nʌm/ *adj* онеме́лый; (*from cold*) окочене́лый; **go ~** онеме́ть *pf*; (*from cold*) окочене́ть *pf*.

number /'nʌmbə(r)/ *n* (*total*) коли́чество; (*total*; *symbol*; *math*; *gram*) число́; (*identifying numeral*; *item*) но́мер; **~-plate** номерна́я доще́чка; *vt* (*assign ~ to*) нумерова́ть *impf*, за~, про~ *pf*; (*contain*) насчи́тывать *impf*; **~ among** причисля́ть *impf*, причи́слить *pf* к+*dat*; **his days are ~ed** его́ дни сочтены́.

numeral /'njuːmər(ə)l/ *n* ци́фра; (*gram*) (и́мя *neut*) числи́тельное *sb*. **numerical** /njuː'merɪk(ə)l/ *adj* числово́й. **numerous** /'njuːmərəs/ *adj* многочи́сленный; (*many*) мно́го +*gen pl*.

nun /nʌn/ *n* мона́хиня. **nunnery** /'nʌnərɪ/ *n* (же́нский) монасты́рь *m*.

nuptial /'nʌpʃ(ə)l/ *adj* сва́дебный; *n*: *pl* сва́дьба.

nurse /nɜːs/ *n* (*child's*) ня́ня; (*medical*) медсестра́; *vt* (*suckle*) корми́ть *impf*, на~, по~ *pf*; (*tend sick*) уха́живать *impf* за +*instr*; **nursing home** санато́рий; дом

n

престаре́лых. **nursery** /ˈnɜːsərɪ/ *n* (*room*) де́тская *sb*; (*day* ~) я́сли (-лей) *pl*; (*for plants*) пито́мник; ~ **rhyme** де́тские прибау́тки *f pl*; ~ **school** де́тский сад.

nut /nʌt/ *n* оре́х; (*for bolt etc.*) га́йка. **nutshell** *n*: **in a** ~ в двух слова́х.

nutmeg /ˈnʌtmeg/ *n* муска́тный оре́х.

nutrient /ˈnjuːtrɪənt/ *n* пита́тельное вещество́. **nutrition** /njuːˈtrɪʃ(ə)n/ *n* пита́ние. **nutritious** /-ˈtrɪʃəs/ *adj* пита́тельный.

nylon /ˈnaɪlɒn/ *n* нейло́н; *pl* нейло́новые чулки́ (-ло́к) *pl*.

nymph /nɪmf/ *n* ни́мфа.

O

O /əʊ/ *int* o!; ах!

oaf /əʊf/ *n* неуклю́жий челове́к.

oak /əʊk/ *n* дуб; *attrib* дубо́вый.

oar /ɔː(r)/ *n* весло́. **oarsman** /ˈɔːzmən/ *n* гребе́ц.

oasis /əʊˈeɪsɪs/ *n* оа́зис.

oath /əʊθ/ *n* прися́га; (*expletive*) руга́тельство.

oatmeal /ˈəʊtmiːl/ *n* овся́нка. **oats** /əʊts/ *n pl* овёс (овса́) *collect.*

obdurate /ˈɒbdjʊrət/ *adj* упря́мый.

obedience /əʊˈbiːdɪəns/ *n* послуша́ние. **obedient** /-ənt/ *adj* послу́шный.

obese /əʊˈbiːs/ *n* ту́чный. **obesity** /-sɪtɪ/ *n* ту́чность.

obey /əʊˈbeɪ/ *vt* слу́шаться *impf*, по~ *pf* +*gen*; (*law*, *order*) подчиня́ться *impf*, подчини́ться *pf* +*dat.*

obituary /əˈbɪtjʊərɪ/ *n* некроло́г.

object *n* /ˈɒbdʒɪkt/ (*thing*) предме́т; (*aim*) цель; (*gram*) дополне́ние; *vi* /əbˈdʒekt/ возража́ть *impf*, возрази́ть *pf* (**to** про́тив +*gen*); **I don't** ~ я не про́тив. **objection** /əbˈdʒekʃ(ə)n/ *n* возраже́ние; **I have no** ~ я не возража́ю. **objectionable** /əbˈdʒekʃənəb(ə)l/ *adj* неприя́тный. **objective** /əbˈdʒektɪv/ *adj* объекти́вный; *n* цель. **objectivity** /ˌɒbdʒekˈtɪvɪtɪ/ *n* объекти́вность. **objector** /əbˈdʒektə(r)/ *n* возража́ющий *sb.*

obligation /ˌɒblɪˈgeɪʃ(ə)n/ *n* обяза́тельство; **I am under an** ~ я обя́зан(а). **obligatory** /əˈblɪgətərɪ/ *adj* обяза́тельный. **oblige** /əˈblaɪdʒ/ *vt* обя́зывать *impf*, обяза́ть *pf*; **be ~d to** (*grateful*) быть обя́занным+*dat.* **obliging** /əˈblaɪdʒɪŋ/ *adj* услу́жливый.

oblique /əˈbliːk/ *adj* косо́й; (*fig*; *gram*) ко́свенный.

obliterate /əˈblɪtəˌreɪt/ *vt* (*efface*) стира́ть *impf*, стере́ть *pf*; (*destroy*) уничтожа́ть *impf*, уничто́жить *pf.* **obliteration** /-ˈreɪʃ(ə)n/ *n* стира́ние; уничтоже́ние.

oblivion /əˈblɪvɪən/ *n* забве́ние. **oblivious** /-vɪəs/ *adj* (*forgetful*) забы́вчивый; **to be** ~ **of** не замеча́ть *impf* +*gen.*

oblong /ˈɒblɒŋ/ *adj* продолгова́тый.

obnoxious /əbˈnɒkʃəs/ *adj* проти́вный.

oboe /ˈəʊbəʊ/ *n* гобо́й.

obscene /əbˈsiːn/ *adj* непристо́йный. **obscenity** /-ˈsenɪtɪ/ *n* непристо́йность.

obscure /əbˈskjʊə(r)/ *adj* (*unclear*) нея́сный; (*little known*) малоизве́стный; *vt* затемня́ть *impf*, затемни́ть *pf*; де́лать *impf*, с~ *pf* нея́сным. **obscurity** /-rɪtɪ/ *n* нея́сность; неизве́стность.

obsequious /əbˈsiːkwɪəs/ *adj* подобостра́стный.

observance /əbˈzɜːv(ə)ns/ *n* соблюде́ние; (*rite*) обря́д. **observant** /-v(ə)nt/ *adj* наблюда́тельный. **observation** /ˌɒbzəˈveɪʃ(ə)n/ *n* наблюде́ние; (*remark*) замеча́ние. **observatory** /əbˈzɜːvətərɪ/ *n* обсервато́рия. **observe** /əbˈzɜːv/ *vt* (*law etc.*) соблюда́ть *impf*, соблюсти́ *pf*; (*watch*) наблюда́ть *impf*; (*remark*) замеча́ть *impf*, заме́тить *pf.* **observer** /əbˈzɜːvə(r)/ *n* наблюда́тель *m.*

obsess /əbˈses/ *vt* пресле́довать

impf; **obsessed by** одержи́мый +*instr.* **obsession** /-ˈseʃ(ə)n/ *n* одержи́мость; (*idea*) навя́зчивая иде́я. **obsessive** /-ˈsesɪv/ *adj* навя́зчивый.

obsolete /ˈɒbsəˌliːt/ *adj* устаре́лый, вы́шедший из употребле́ния.

obstacle /ˈɒbstək(ə)l/ *n* препя́тствие.

obstetrician /ˌɒbstəˈtrɪʃ(ə)n/ *n* акуше́р. **obstetrics** /əbˈstetrɪks/ *n* акуше́рство.

obstinacy /ˈɒbstɪnəsɪ/ *n* упря́мство. **obstinate** /ˈɒbstɪnət/ *adj* упря́мый.

obstreperous /əbˈstrepərəs/ *adj* бу́йный.

obstruct /əbˈstrʌkt/ *vt* заграждáть *impf*, загради́ть *pf*; (*hinder*) препя́тствовать *impf*, вос~ *pf* +*dat.* **obstruction** /-ˈstrʌkʃ(ə)n/ *n* загражде́ние; (*obstacle*) препя́тствие. **obstructive** /-ˈstrʌktɪv/ *adj* заграждáющий; препя́тствующий.

obtain /əbˈteɪn/ *vt* получáть *impf*, получи́ть *pf*; доставáть *impf*, достáть *pf*.

obtrusive /əbˈtruːsɪv/ *adj* навя́зчивый; (*thing*) бросáющийся в глазá.

obtuse /əbˈtjuːs/ *adj* тупо́й.

obviate /ˈɒbvɪˌeɪt/ *vt* устраня́ть *impf*, устрани́ть *pf*.

obvious /ˈɒbvɪəs/ *adj* очеви́дный.

occasion /əˈkeɪʒ(ə)n/ *n* слу́чай; (*cause*) по́вод; (*occurrence*) собы́тие; *vt* причиня́ть *impf*, причини́ть *pf*. **occasional** /-nəl/ *adj* ре́дкий. **occasionally** /-nəlɪ/ *adv* иногдá, вре́мя от вре́мени.

occult /ɒˈkʌlt/ *adj* окку́льтный; *n*: **the ~** окку́льт.

occupancy /ˈɒkjʊpənsɪ/ *n* заня́тие. **occupant** /-pənt/ *n* жи́тель *m*, ~ница. **occupation** /ˌɒkjʊˈpeɪʃ(ə)n/ *n* заня́тие; (*military ~*) оккупáция; (*profession*) профе́ссия. **occupational** /-ˈpeɪʃən(ə)l/ *adj* профессионáльный; **~ therapy** трудотерапи́я. **occupy** /ˈɒkjʊˌpaɪ/ *vt* занимáть *impf*, заня́ть *pf*; (*mil*) оккупи́ровать *impf & pf.*

occur /əˈkɜː(r)/ *vi* (*happen*) случáться *impf*, случи́ться *pf*; (*be found*) встречáться *impf*; **~ to** приходи́ть *impf*, прийти́ *pf* в го́лову+*dat.* **occurrence** /-ˈkʌrəns/ *n* слу́чай, происше́ствие.

ocean /ˈəʊʃ(ə)n/ *n* океáн. **oceanic** /ˌəʊʃɪˈænɪk/ *adj* океáнский.

o'clock /əˈklɒk/ *adv*: **(at) six ~** (в) шесть часо́в.

octagonal /ɒkˈtægən(ə)l/ *adj* восьмиуго́льный.

octave /ˈɒktɪv/ *n* (*mus*) октáва.

October /ɒkˈtəʊbə(r)/ *n* октя́брь *m*; *adj* октя́брьский.

octopus /ˈɒktəpəs/ *n* осьмино́г.

odd /ɒd/ *adj* (*strange*) стрáнный; (*not in a set*) разро́зненный; (*number*) нечётный; (*not paired*) непáрный; (*casual*) случáйный; **five hundred ~** пятьсо́т с ли́шним; **~ job** случáйная рабо́та. **oddity** /ˈɒdɪtɪ/ *n* стрáнность; (*person*) чудáк, -áчка. **oddly** /ˈɒdlɪ/ *adv* стрáнно; **~ enough** как э́то ни стрáнно. **oddment** /ˈɒdmənt/ *n* остáток. **odds** /ɒdz/ *n pl* шáнсы *m pl*; **be at ~ with** (*person*) не лáдить с+*instr*; (*things*) не соотве́тствовать *impf* +*dat*; **long (short) ~** нерáвные (почти́ рáвные) шáнсы *m pl*; **the ~ are that** вероя́тнее всего́, что; **~ and ends** обры́вки *m pl.*

ode /əʊd/ *n* о́да.

odious /ˈəʊdɪəs/ *adj* ненави́стный.

odour /ˈəʊdə(r)/ *n* зáпах.

oesophagus /iːˈsɒfəgəs/ *n* пищево́д.

of /ɒv/ *prep expressing* **1.** *origin*: из+*gen*: **he comes ~ a working-class family** он из рабо́чей семьи́; **2.** *cause*: от+*gen*: **he died ~ hunger** он у́мер от го́лода; **3.** *authorship*: *gen*: **the works ~ Pushkin** сочине́ния Пу́шкина; **4.** *material*: из+*gen*: **made ~ wood** сде́ланный из де́рева; **5.** *reference*: о+*prep*: **he talked ~ Lenin** он говори́л о Ле́нине; **6.** *partition*: *gen* (*often in* -ý(-ю)): **a glass ~ milk, tea** стака́н молока́, ча́ю; из+*gen*: **one ~ them** оди́н из них; **7.** *belonging*: *gen*: **the capital ~ England** столи́ца А́нглии.

off /ɒf/ *adv*: *in phrasal vv, see v, e.g.* **clear ~** убира́ться; *prep* (*from surface of*) с+*gen*; (*away from*) от+*gen*; **~ and on** вре́мя от вре́мени; **~-white** не совсе́м бе́лый.

offal /'ɒf(ə)l/ *n* требуха́.

offence /ə'fens/ *n* (*insult*) оби́да; (*against law*) просту́пок, преступле́ние; **take ~** обижа́ться *impf*, оби́деться *pf* (**at** на+*acc*). **offend** /ə'fend/ *vt* обижа́ть *impf*, оби́деть *pf*; **~ against** наруша́ть *impf*, нару́шить *pf*. **offender** /ə'fendə(r)/ *n* правонаруши́тель *m*, ~ница. **offensive** /ə'fensɪv/ *adj* (*attacking*) наступа́тельный; (*insulting*) оскорби́тельный; (*repulsive*) проти́вный; *n* нападе́ние.

offer /'ɒfə(r)/ *vt* предлага́ть *impf*, предложи́ть *pf*; *n* предложе́ние; **on ~** в прода́же.

offhand /ɒf'hænd/ *adj* бесцеремо́нный.

O

office /'ɒfɪs/ *n* (*position*) до́лжность; (*place, room etc.*) бюро́ *neut indecl*, конто́ра, канцеля́рия. **officer** /'ɒfɪsə(r)/ *n* должностно́е лицо́; (*mil*) офице́р. **official** /ə'fɪʃ(ə)l/ *adj* служе́бный; (*authorized*) официа́льный; *n* должностно́е лицо́. **officiate** /ə'fɪʃɪˌeɪt/ *vi* (*eccl*) соверша́ть *impf*, соверши́ть *pf* богослуже́ние. **officious** /ə'fɪʃəs/ *adj* (*intrusive*) навя́зчивый.

offing /'ɒfɪŋ/ *n*: **be in the ~** предстоя́ть *impf*.

off-licence /'ɒflaɪs(ə)ns/ *n* ви́нный магази́н. **off-load** *vt* разгружа́ть *impf*, разгрузи́ть *pf*. **off-putting** /'ɒfpʊtɪŋ/ *adj* отта́лкивающий. **offset** *vt* возмеща́ть *impf*, возмести́ть *pf*. **offshoot** *n* о́тпрыск. **offshore** *adj* прибре́жный. **offside** *adv* вне игры́. **offspring** *n* пото́мок; (*collect*) пото́мки *m pl*.

often /'ɒf(ə)n/ *adv* ча́сто.

ogle /'əʊg(ə)l/ *vt & i* смотре́ть *impf* с вожделе́нием на+*acc*.

ogre /'əʊgə(r)/ *n* велика́н-людое́д.

oh /əʊ/ *int* о!; ах!

ohm /əʊm/ *n* ом.

oil /ɔɪl/ *n* ма́сло; (*petroleum*) нефть; (*paint*) ма́сло, ма́сляные кра́ски *f pl*; *vt* сма́зывать *impf*, сма́зать *pf*; **~-painting** карти́на, напи́санная ма́сляными кра́сками; **~ rig** нефтяна́я вы́шка; **~-tanker** та́нкер; **~-well** нефтяна́я сква́жина. **oilfield** *n* месторожде́ние не́фти. **oilskin** *n* клеёнка; *pl* непромока́емый костю́м. **oily** /'ɔɪlɪ/ *adj* масляни́стый.

ointment /'ɔɪntmənt/ *n* мазь.

OK /əʊ'keɪ/ *adv & adj* хорошо́, норма́льно; *int* ла́дно!; *vt* одобря́ть *impf*, одо́брить *pf*.

old /əʊld/ *adj* ста́рый; (*ancient*; *of long standing*) стари́нный; (*former*) бы́вший; **how ~ are you?** ско́лько тебе́, вам, (*dat*) лет?; **~ age** ста́рость; **~-age pension** пе́нсия по ста́рости; **old-fashioned** старомо́дный; **~ maid** ста́рая де́ва; **~ man** (*also father, husband*) стари́к; **~-time** стари́нный; **~ woman** стару́ха; (*coll*) стару́шка.

olive /'ɒlɪv/ *n* (*fruit*) оли́вка; (*colour*) оли́вковый цвет; *adj* оли́вковый; **~ oil** оли́вковое ма́сло.

Olympic /ə'lɪmpɪk/ *adj* олимпи́йский; **~ games** Олимпи́йские и́гры *f pl*.

omelette /'ɒmlɪt/ *n* омле́т.

omen /'əʊmən/ *n* предзнаменова́ние. **ominous** /'ɒmɪnəs/ *adj* злове́щий.

omission /ə'mɪʃ(ə)n/ *n* про́пуск; (*neglect*) упуще́ние. **omit** /ə'mɪt/ *vt* (*leave out*) пропуска́ть *impf*, пропусти́ть *pf*; (*neglect*) упуска́ть *impf*, упусти́ть *pf*.

omnibus /'ɒmnɪbəs/ *n* (*bus*) авто́бус; (*collection*) колле́кция.

omnipotence /ɒm'nɪpət(ə)ns/ *n*

всемогу́щество. **omnipotent** /-t(ə)nt/ *adj* всемогу́щий. **omnipresent** /ˌɒmnɪ'prez(ə)nt/ *adj* вездесу́щий. **omniscient** /ɒm'nɪsɪənt/ *adj* всеве́дущий.

on /ɒn/ *prep* (*position*) на+*prep*; (*direction*) на+*acc*; (*time*) в+*acc*; **~ the next day** на сле́дующий день; **~ Mondays** (*repeated action*) по понеде́льникам (*dat pl*); **~ the first of June** пе́рвого ию́ня (*gen*); (*concerning*) по+*prep*, о+*prep*, на+*acc*; *adv* да́льше, вперёд; *in phrasal vv, see vv, e.g.* **move ~** идти́ да́льше; **and so ~** и так да́лее, и т.д.; **be ~** (*film etc.*) идти́ *impf*; **further ~** да́льше; **later ~** по́зже.

once /wʌns/ *adv* (оди́н) раз; (*on past occasion*) одна́жды; (*formerly*) не́когда; **all at ~** неожи́данно; **at ~** сра́зу, неме́дленно; (*if, when*) **~** как то́лько; **~ again, more** ещё раз; **~ and for all** раз и навсегда́; **~ or twice** не́сколько раз; **~ upon a time there lived ...** жил-бы́л... .

oncoming /'ɒnˌkʌmɪŋ/ *adj*: **~ traffic** встре́чное движе́ние.

one /wʌn/ *adj* оди́н (одна́, -но́); (*only, single*) еди́нственный; *n* оди́н; *pron*: *not usu translated*; *v translated in 2nd pers sg or by impers construction*: **~ never knows** никогда́ не зна́ешь; **where can ~ buy this book?** где мо́жно купи́ть э́ту кни́гу?; **~ after another** оди́н за други́м; **~ and all** все до одного́; все как оди́н; **~ and only** еди́нственный; **~ and the same** оди́н и тот же; **~ another** друг дру́га (*dat* -гу, *etc.*); **~ fine day** в оди́н прекра́сный день; **~ o'clock** час; **~-parent family** семья́ с одни́м роди́телем; **~-sided, -track, -way** односторо́нний; **~-time** бы́вший; **~-way street** у́лица односторо́ннего движе́ния.

onerous /'əʊnərəs/ *adj* тя́гостный.

oneself /wʌn'self/ *pron* себя́; -ся (*suffixed to vt*).

onion /'ʌnjən/ *n* (*plant; pl collect*) лук; (*single ~*) лу́ковица.

onlooker /'ɒnˌlʊkə(r)/ *n* наблюда́тель *m*.

only /'əʊnlɪ/ *adj* еди́нственный; *adv* то́лько; **if ~** е́сли бы то́лько; **~ just** то́лько что; *conj* но.

onset /'ɒnset/ *n* нача́ло.

onslaught /'ɒnslɔːt/ *n* на́тиск.

onus /'əʊnəs/ *n* отве́тственность.

onward(s) /'ɒnwəd(z)/ *adv* вперёд.

ooze /uːz/ *vt & i* сочи́ться *impf.*

opal /'əʊp(ə)l/ *n* опа́л.

opaque /əʊ'peɪk/ *adj* непрозра́чный.

open /'əʊpən/ *adj* откры́тый; (*frank*) открове́нный; **in the ~ air** на откры́том во́здухе; **~-minded** *adj* непредупреждённый; *vt & i* открыва́ть(ся) *impf*, откры́ть(ся) *pf*; *vi* (*begin*) начина́ться *impf*, нача́ться *pf*; (*flowers*) распуска́ться *impf*, распусти́ться *pf.* **opening** /-ɪŋ/ *n* откры́тие; (*aperture*) отве́рстие; (*beginning*) нача́ло; *adj* нача́льный, пе́рвый; (*introductory*) вступи́тельный.

opera /'ɒpərə/ *n* о́пера; *attrib* о́перный; **~-house** о́перный теа́тр.

operate /'ɒpəˌreɪt/ *vi* де́йствовать *impf* (**upon** на+*acc*); (*med*) опери́ровать *impf & pf* (**on** +*acc*); *vt* управля́ть *impf* +*instr.*

operatic /ˌɒpə'rætɪk/ *adj* о́перный.

operating-theatre /'ɒpəreɪtɪŋˌθɪətə(r)/ *n* операцио́нная *sb.* **operation** /ˌɒpə'reɪʃ(ə)n/ *n* де́йствие; (*med; mil*) опера́ция. **operational** /-'reɪʃən(ə)l/ *adj* (*in use*) де́йствующий; (*mil*) операти́вный. **operative** /'ɒpərətɪv/ *adj* де́йствующий. **operator** /'ɒpəˌreɪtə(r)/ *n* опера́тор; (*telephone ~*) телефони́ст, ~ка.

operetta /ˌɒpə'retə/ *n* опере́тта.

ophthalmic /ɒf'θælmɪk/ *adj* глазно́й.

opinion /ə'pɪnjən/ *n* мне́ние; **in my ~** по-мо́ему; **~ poll** опро́с обще́ственного мне́ния. **opinionated**

O

/-ˌneɪtɪd/ *adj* догмати́чный.
opium /ˈəʊpɪəm/ *n* о́пиум.
opponent /əˈpəʊnənt/ *n* проти́вник.
opportune /ˈɒpəˌtjuːn/ *adj* своевре́менный. **opportunism** /-ˈtjuːnɪz(ə)m/ *n* оппортуни́зм. **opportunist** /-ˈtjuːnɪst/ *n* оппортуни́ст. **opportunistic** /-tjuːˈnɪstɪk/ *n* оппортунисти́ческий. **opportunity** /-ˈtjuːnɪtɪ/ *n* слу́чай, возмо́жность.
oppose /əˈpəʊz/ *vt* (*resist*) проти́виться *impf*, вос~ *pf* +*dat*; (*speak etc. against*) выступа́ть *impf*, вы́ступить *pf* про́тив+*gen*. **opposed** /-ˈpəʊzd/ *adj* про́тив (**to** +*gen*); **as ~ to** в противополо́жность+*dat*. **opposing** /-ˈpəʊzɪŋ/ *adj* проти́вный; (*opposite*) противополо́жный. **opposite** /ˈɒpəzɪt/ *adj* противополо́жный; (*reverse*) обра́тный; *n* противополо́жность; **just the ~** как раз наоборо́т; *adv* напро́тив; *prep* (на)про́тив+*gen*. **opposition** /ˌɒpəˈzɪʃ(ə)n/ *n* (*resistance*) сопротивле́ние; (*polit*) оппози́ция.
oppress /əˈpres/ *vt* угнета́ть *impf*. **oppression** /-ˈpreʃ(ə)n/ *n* угнете́ние. **oppressive** /-ˈpresɪv/ *adj* угнета́ющий. **oppressor** /-ˈpresə(r)/ *n* угнета́тель *m*.
opt /ɒpt/ *vi* выбира́ть *impf*, вы́брать *pf* (**for** +*acc*); **~ out** не принима́ть *impf* уча́стия (**of** в+*prep*).
optic /ˈɒptɪk/ *adj* зри́тельный. **optical** /ˈɒptɪk(ə)l/ *adj* опти́ческий. **optician** /ɒpˈtɪʃ(ə)n/ *n* о́птик. **optics** /ˈɒptɪks/ *n* о́птика.
optimism /ˈɒptɪˌmɪz(ə)m/ *n* оптими́зм. **optimist** /-mɪst/ *n* оптими́ст. **optimistic** /-ˈmɪstɪk/ *adj* оптимисти́ческий. **optimum** /ˈɒptɪməm/ *adj* оптима́льный.
option /ˈɒpʃ(ə)n/ *n* вы́бор. **optional** /-nəl/ *adj* необяза́тельный.
opulence /ˈɒpjʊləns/ *n* бога́тство. **opulent** /-lənt/ *adj* бога́тый.
opus /ˈəʊpəs/ *n* о́пус.
or /ɔː(r)/ *conj* и́ли; **~ else** ина́че; **~ so** приблизи́тельно.
oracle /ˈɒrək(ə)l/ *n* ора́кул.
oral /ˈɔːr(ə)l/ *adj* у́стный; *n* у́стный экза́мен.
orange /ˈɒrɪndʒ/ *n* (*fruit*) апельси́н; (*colour*) ора́нжевый цвет; *attrib* апельси́новый; *adj* ора́нжевый.
oration /ɔːˈreɪʃ(ə)n/ *n* речь. **orator** /ˈɒrətə(r)/ *n* ора́тор.
oratorio /ˌɒrəˈtɔːrɪəʊ/ *n* орато́рия.
oratory /ˈɒrətərɪ/ *n* (*speech*) красноре́чие.
orbit /ˈɔːbɪt/ *n* орби́та; *vt* враща́ться *impf* по орби́те вокру́г +*gen*. **orbital** /-təl/ *adj* орбита́льный.
orchard /ˈɔːtʃəd/ *n* фрукто́вый сад.
orchestra /ˈɔːkɪstrə/ *n* орке́стр. **orchestral** /-ˈkestr(ə)l/ *adj* оркестро́вый. **orchestrate** /ˈɔːkɪˌstreɪt/ *vt* оркестрова́ть *impf* & *pf*. **orchestration** /ˌɔːkɪˈstreɪʃ(ə)n/ *n* оркестро́вка.
orchid /ˈɔːkɪd/ *n* орхиде́я.
ordain /ɔːˈdeɪn/ *vt* предпи́сывать *impf*, предписа́ть *pf*; (*eccl*) посвяща́ть *impf*, посвяти́ть *pf* (в духо́вный сан).
ordeal /ɔːˈdiːl/ *n* тяжёлое испыта́ние.
order /ˈɔːdə(r)/ *n* поря́док; (*command*) прика́з; (*for goods*) зака́з; (*insignia, medal; fraternity*) о́рден; (*archit*) о́рдер; *pl* (*holy* ~) духо́вный сан; **in ~ to** (для того́) что́бы +*inf*; *vt* (*command*) прика́зывать *impf*, приказа́ть *pf* +*dat*; (*goods etc.*) зака́зывать *impf*, заказа́ть *pf*. **orderly** /-lɪ/ *adj* аккура́тный; (*quiet*) ти́хий; *n* (*med*) санита́р; (*mil*) ордина́рец.
ordinance /ˈɔːdɪnəns/ *n* декре́т.
ordinary /ˈɔːdɪnərɪ/ *adj* обыкнове́нный, обы́чный.
ordination /ˌɔːdɪˈneɪʃ(ə)n/ *n* посвяще́ние.
ore /ɔː(r)/ *n* руда́.
organ /ˈɔːgən/ *n* о́рган; (*mus*) орга́н. **organic** /-ˈgænɪk/ *adj* органи́ческий. **organism**

/ˈɔːɡəˌnɪz(ə)m/ *n* органи́зм. **organist** /-nɪst/ *n* органи́ст. **organization** /ˌɔːɡənaɪˈzeɪʃ(ə)n/ *n* организа́ция. **organize** /ˈɔːɡəˌnaɪz/ *vt* организо́вывать *impf* (*pres not used*), организова́ть *impf* (*in pres*) & *pf*; устра́ивать *impf*, устро́ить *pf*. **organizer** /-ˌnaɪzə(r)/ *n* организа́тор.

orgy /ˈɔːdʒɪ/ *n* о́ргия.

Orient /ˈɔːrɪənt/ *n* Восто́к. **oriental** /ˌɔːrɪˈent(ə)l/ *adj* восто́чный.

orient, orientate /ˈɔːrɪənt, ˈɔːrɪənˌteɪt/ *vt* ориенти́ровать *impf* & *pf* (**o.s.** -ся). **orientation** /ˌɔːrɪənˈteɪʃ(ə)n/ *n* ориента́ция.

orifice /ˈɒrɪfɪs/ *n* отве́рстие.

origin /ˈɒrɪdʒɪn/ *n* происхожде́ние, нача́ло. **original** /əˈrɪdʒɪn(ə)l/ *adj* оригина́льный; (*initial*) первонача́льный; (*genuine*) по́длинный; *n* оригина́л. **originality** /əˌrɪdʒɪˈnælɪtɪ/ *n* оригина́льность. **originate** /əˈrɪdʒɪˌneɪt/ *vt* порожда́ть *impf*, породи́ть *pf*; *vi* брать *impf*, взять *pf* нача́ло (**from, in** в+*prep*, от+*gen*); (*arise*) возника́ть *impf*, возни́кнуть *pf*. **originator** /-ˈrɪdʒɪˌneɪtə(r)/ *n* а́втор, инициа́тор.

ornament *n* /ˈɔːnəmənt/ украше́ние; *vt* /ˈɔːnəment/ украша́ть *impf*, укра́сить *pf*. **ornamental** /-ˈment(ə)l/ *adj* декорати́вный.

ornate /ɔːˈneɪt/ *adj* витиева́тый.

ornithologist /ˌɔːnɪˈθɒlədʒɪst/ *n* орнито́лог. **ornithology** /-dʒɪ/ *n* орнитоло́гия.

orphan /ˈɔːf(ə)n/ *n* сирота́ *m* & *f*; *vt*: **be ~ed** сироте́ть *impf*, о~ *pf*. **orphanage** /-nɪdʒ/ *n* сиро́тский дом. **orphaned** /ˈɔːf(ə)nd/ *adj* осироте́лый.

orthodox /ˈɔːθəˌdɒks/ *adj* ортодокса́льный; (*eccl*, **O~**) правосла́вный. **orthodoxy** /-ˌdɒksɪ/ *n* ортодо́ксия; (**O~**) правосла́вие.

orthopaedic /ˌɔːθəˈpiːdɪk/ *adj* ортопеди́ческий.

oscillate /ˈɒsɪˌleɪt/ *vi* колеба́ться *impf*, по~ *pf*. **oscillation** /-ˈleɪʃ(ə)n/ *n* колеба́ние.

osmosis /ɒzˈməʊsɪs/ *n* о́смос.

ostensible /ɒˈstensɪb(ə)l/ *adj* мни́мый. **ostensibly** /-blɪ/ *adv* я́кобы.

ostentation /ˌɒstenˈteɪʃ(ə)n/ *n* выставле́ние напока́з. **ostentatious** /-ʃəs/ *adj* показно́й.

osteopath /ˈɒstɪəˌpæθ/ *n* остеопа́т. **osteopathy** /ˌɒstɪˈɒpəθɪ/ *n* остеопа́тия.

ostracize /ˈɒstrəˌsaɪz/ *vt* подверга́ть *impf*, подве́ргнуть *pf* остраки́зму.

ostrich /ˈɒstrɪtʃ/ *n* стра́ус.

other /ˈʌðə(r)/ *adj* друго́й, ино́й; тот; **every ~** ка́ждый второ́й; **every ~ day** че́рез день; **on the ~ hand** с друго́й стороны́; **on the ~ side** на той стороне́, по ту сто́рону; **one or the ~** тот и́ли ино́й; **the ~ day** на днях, неда́вно; **the ~ way round** наоборо́т; **the ~s** остальны́е *sb pl*. **otherwise** *adv* & *conj* ина́че, а то.

otter /ˈɒtə(r)/ *n* вы́дра.

ouch /aʊtʃ/ *int* ой!, ай!

ought /ɔːt/ *v aux* до́лжен (-жна́) (бы) +*inf*.

ounce /aʊns/ *n* у́нция.

our, ours /ˈaʊə(r), ˈaʊəz/ *poss pron* наш; свой. **ourselves** /ˌaʊəˈselvz/ *pron* (*emph*) (мы) са́ми; (*refl*) себя́; -ся (*suffixed to vt*).

oust /aʊst/ *vt* вытесня́ть *impf*, вы́теснить *pf*.

out /aʊt/ *adv* **1.** *in phrasal vv often rendered by pref* вы-; **2.: to be ~** *in various senses*: **he is ~** (*not at home*) его́ нет до́ма; (*not in office etc.*) он вы́шел; (*sport*) выходи́ть *impf*, вы́йти *pf* из игры́; (*of fashion*) вы́йти *pf* из мо́ды; (*be published*) вы́йти *pf* из печа́ти; (*of candle etc.*) поту́хнуть *pf*; (*of flower*) распусти́ться *pf*; (*be unconscious*) потеря́ть *pf* созна́ние; **3.: ~-and-~** отъя́вленный; **4.: ~ of** из+*gen*, вне+*gen*; **~ of date** устаре́лый, старомо́дный; **~ of doors** на откры́том во́здухе; **~ of work** безрабо́тный.

outbid /aʊtˈbɪd/ *vt* предлага́ть

O

impf, предложи́ть *pf* бо́лее высо́кую це́ну, чем+*nom.* **outboard** *adj*: **~ motor** подвесно́й мото́р *m.* **outbreak** *n* (*of anger, disease*) вспы́шка; (*of war*) нача́ло. **outbuilding** *n* надво́рная постро́йка. **outburst** *n* взрыв. **outcast** *n* изгна́нник. **outcome** *n* результа́т. **outcry** *n* (шу́мные) проте́сты *m pl.* **outdated** /aʊt'deɪtɪd/ *adj* устаре́лый. **outdo** *vt* превосходи́ть *impf*, превзойти́ *pf.*

outdoor /'aʊtdɔ:(r)/ *adj*, **outdoors** /-'dɔ:z/ *adv* на откры́том во́здухе, на у́лице.

outer /'aʊtə(r)/ *adj* (*external*) вне́шний, нару́жный; (*far from centre*) да́льний. **outermost** *adj* са́мый да́льний.

outfit /'aʊtfɪt/ *n* (*equipment*) снаряже́ние; (*set of things*) набо́р; (*clothes*) наря́д. **outgoing** *adj* уходя́щий; (*sociable*) общи́тельный. **outgoings** *n pl* изде́ржки *f pl.* **outgrow** *vt* вырата́ть *impf*, вы́расти *pf* из+*gen.* **outhouse** *n* надво́рная постро́йка.

O

outing /'aʊtɪŋ/ *n* прогу́лка, экску́рсия.

outlandish /aʊt'lændɪʃ/ *adj* дико́винный. **outlaw** *n* лицо́ вне зако́на; банди́т; *vt* объявля́ть *impf*, объяви́ть *pf* вне зако́на. **outlay** *n* изде́ржки *f pl.* **outlet** /'aʊtlɪt/ *n* выходно́е отве́рстие; (*fig*) вы́ход; (*market*) ры́нок; (*shop*) торго́вая то́чка. **outline** *n* очерта́ние, ко́нтур; (*sketch, summary*) набро́сок; *vt* оче́рчивать *impf*, очерти́ть *pf*; (*plans etc.*) набра́сывать *impf*, наброса́ть *pf.* **outlive** *vt* пережи́ть *pf.* **outlook** *n* перспекти́вы *f pl*; (*attitude*) кругозо́р. **outlying** /'aʊtˌlaɪɪŋ/ *adj* перифери́йный. **outmoded** /aʊt'məʊdɪd/ *adj* старомо́дный. **outnumber** *vt* чи́сленно превосходи́ть *impf*, превзойти́ *pf.* **outpatient** *n* амбулато́рный больно́й *sb.* **outpost** *n* форпо́ст. **output** *n* вы́пуск, проду́кция.

outrage /'aʊtreɪdʒ/ *n* безобра́зие; (*indignation*) возмуще́ние; *vt* оскорбля́ть *impf*, оскорби́ть *pf.* **outrageous** /-'reɪdʒəs/ *adj* возмути́тельный.

outright /'aʊtraɪt/ *adv* (*entirely*) вполне́; (*once for all*) раз (и) навсегда́; (*openly*) откры́то; *adj* прямо́й. **outset** *n* нача́ло; **at the ~** внача́ле; **from the ~** с са́мого нача́ла.

outside /aʊt'saɪd/ *n* нару́жная сторона́; **at the ~** са́мое бо́льшее; **from the ~** извне́; **on the ~** снару́жи; *adj* нару́жный, вне́шний; (*sport*) кра́йний; *adv* (*on the ~*) снару́жи; (*to the ~*) нару́жу; (*out of doors*) на откры́том во́здухе, на у́лице; *prep* вне+*gen*; за преде́лами +*gen.* **outsider** /-də(r)/ *n* посторо́нний *sb*; (*sport*) аутса́йдер.

outsize /'aʊtsaɪz/ *adj* бо́льше станда́ртного разме́ра. **outskirts** *n pl* окра́ина. **outspoken** /aʊt'spəʊkən/ *adj* прямо́й. **outstanding** /aʊt'stændɪŋ/ *adj* (*remarkable*) выдаю́щийся; (*unpaid*) неупла́ченный. **outstay** *vt*: **~ one's welcome** заси́живаться *impf*, засиде́ться *pf.* **outstretched** /'aʊtstretʃt/ *adj* распростёртый. **outstrip** *vt* обгоня́ть *impf*, обогна́ть *pf.*

outward /'aʊtwəd/ *adj* (*external*) вне́шний, нару́жный. **outwardly** /-lɪ/ *adv* вне́шне, на вид. **outwards** /-wədz/ *adv* нару́жу.

outweigh /aʊt'weɪ/ *vt* переве́шивать *impf*, переве́сить *pf.* **outwit** *vt* перехитри́ть *pf.*

oval /'əʊv(ə)l/ *adj* ова́льный; *n* ова́л.

ovary /'əʊvərɪ/ *n* яи́чник.

ovation /əʊ'veɪʃ(ə)n/ *n* ова́ция.

oven /'ʌv(ə)n/ *n* (*industrial*) печь; (*domestic*) духо́вка.

over /'əʊvə(r)/ *adv & prep with vv*: *see vv*; *prep* (*above*) над+*instr*; (*through; covering*) по+*dat*; (*concerning*) о+*prep*; (*across*) че́рез+*acc*; (*on the other side of*) по ту сто́рону+*gen*; (*more than*) свы́ше+*gen*; бо́лее+*gen*; (*with age*) за+*acc*; **all ~** (*finished*) всё ко́нчено; (*everywhere*) повсю́ду; **all ~ the country** по всей стране́; **~ again** ещё раз; **~ against** по сравне́нию с+*instr*; **~ and above** не говоря́ уже́ о+*prep*; **~ the telephone** по телефо́ну; **~ there** вон там.

overall /'əʊvər,ɔːl/ *n* хала́т; *pl* комбинезо́н; *adj* о́бщий. **overawe** *vt* внуша́ть *impf*, внуши́ть *pf* благогове́йный страх+*dat*. **overbalance** *vi* теря́ть *impf*, по~ *pf* равнове́сие. **overbearing** /,əʊvə'beərɪŋ/ *adj* вла́стный. **overboard** *adv* (*motion*) за́ борт; (*position*) за бо́ртом. **overcast** *adj* о́блачный. **overcoat** *n* пальто́ *neut indecl.* **overcome** *vt* преодолева́ть *impf*, преодоле́ть *pf*; *adj* охва́ченный. **overcrowded** /,əʊvə'kraʊdɪd/ *adj* перепо́лненный. **overcrowding** /,əʊvə'kraʊdɪŋ/ *n* переполне́ние. **overdo** *vt* (*cook*) пережа́ривать *impf*, пережа́рить *pf*; **~ it, things** (*work too hard*) переутомля́ться *impf*, переутоми́ться *pf*; (*go too far*) переба́рщивать *impf*, переборщи́ть *pf*.

overdose /'əʊvə,dəʊs/ *n* чрезме́рная до́за. **overdraft** *n* превыше́ние креди́та; (*amount*) долг ба́нку. **overdraw** *vi* превыша́ть *impf*, превы́сить *pf* креди́т (в ба́нке). **overdue** *adj* просро́ченный; **be ~** (*late*) запа́здывать *impf*, запозда́ть *pf*. **overestimate** *vt* переоце́нивать *impf*, переоцени́ть *pf*. **overflow** *vi* перелива́ться *impf*, перели́ться *pf*; (*river etc.*) разлива́ться *impf*, разли́ться *pf*; (*outlet*) перели́в. **overgrown** /,əʊvə'grəʊn/ *adj* заро́сший. **overhang** *vt* & *i* выступа́ть *impf* над+*instr*; *n* свес, вы́ступ.

overhaul /'əʊvə,hɔːl/ *vt* ремонти́ровать *impf* & *pf*; *n*: ремо́нт. **overhead** *adv* наверху́, над голово́й; *adj* возду́шный, подвесно́й; *n*: *pl* накладны́е расхо́ды *m pl.* **overhear** *vt* нечаа́нно слы́шать *impf*, у~ *pf.* **overheat** *vt* & *i* перегрева́ть(ся) *impf*, перегре́ть(ся) *pf.* **overjoyed** /,əʊvə'dʒɔɪd/ *adj* в восто́рге (**at** от+*gen*). **overland** *adj* сухопу́тный; *adv* по су́ше. **overlap** *vt* части́чно покрыва́ть *impf*, покры́ть *pf*; *vi* части́чно совпада́ть *impf*, совпа́сть *pf.*

overleaf /,əʊvə'liːf/ *adv* на оборо́те. **overload** *vt* перегружа́ть *impf*, перегрузи́ть *pf.* **overlook** *vt* (*look down on*) смотре́ть *impf* све́рху на+*acc*; (*of window*) выходи́ть *impf* на, в, +*acc*; (*not notice*) не замеча́ть *impf*, заме́тить *pf* +*gen*; (*~ offence etc.*) проща́ть *impf*, прости́ть *pf.*

overly /'əʊvəlɪ/ *adv* сли́шком.

overnight /,əʊvə'naɪt/ *adv* (*during the night*) за́ ночь; (*suddenly*) неожи́данно; **stay ~** ночева́ть *impf*, пере~ *pf*; *adj* ночно́й. **overpay** *vt* перепла́чивать *impf*, переплати́ть *pf.*

over-populated /,əʊvə'pɒpjʊ,leɪtɪd/ *adj* перенаселённый. **over-population** *n* перенаселённость. **overpower** *vt* одолева́ть *impf*, одоле́ть *pf.* **overpriced** /,əʊvə'praɪst/ *adj* завы́шенный в цене́. **over-production** *n* перепроизво́дство. **overrate** /,əʊvə'reɪt/ *vt* переоце́нивать *impf*, переоцени́ть *pf.* **override** *vt* (*fig*) отверга́ть *impf*, отве́ргнуть *pf.* **overriding** /,əʊvə'raɪdɪŋ/ *adj* гла́вный, реша́ющий. **overrule** *vt* отверга́ть *impf*, отве́ргнуть *pf.* **overrun** *vt* (*conquer*) завоёвывать *impf*, завоева́ть *pf*; **be ~ with** кише́ть *impf* +*instr.*

overseas /,əʊvə'siːz/ *adv* за мо́рем, че́рез мо́ре; *adj* замо́рский. **oversee** /,əʊvə'siː/ *vt* надзира́ть *impf* за+*instr.* **overseer** /'əʊvə,siːə(r)/ *n* надзира́тель *m*, ~ница. **overshadow** *vt* затмева́ть *impf*, затми́ть *pf.* **overshoot** *vi* переходи́ть *impf*, перейти́ *pf* грани́цу. **oversight** *n* случа́йный

O

недосмо́тр. **oversleep** *vi* просыпа́ть *impf*, проспа́ть *pf*. **overspend** *vi* тра́тить *impf* сли́шком мно́го. **overstate** *vt* преувели́чивать *impf*, преувели́чить *pf*. **overstep** *vt* переступа́ть *impf*, переступи́ть *pf* +*acc*, че́рез+*acc*.

overt /əʊ'vɜːt/ *adj* я́вный, откры́тый.

overtake /ˌəʊvə'teɪk/ *vt* обгоня́ть *impf*, обогна́ть *pf*. **overthrow** *vt* сверга́ть *impf*, све́ргнуть *pf*. **overtime** *n* (*work*) сверхуро́чная рабо́та; (*payment*) сверхуро́чное *sb*; *adv* сверхуро́чно.

overtone /'əʊvəˌtəʊn/ *n* скры́тый намёк.

overture /'əʊvəˌtjʊə(r)/ *n* предложе́ние; (*mus*) увертю́ра.

overturn /ˌəʊvə'tɜːn/ *vt* & *i* опроки́дывать(ся) *impf*, опроки́нуть(ся) *pf*. **overwhelm** /ˌəʊvə'welm/ *vt* подавля́ть *impf*, подави́ть *pf*. **overwhelming** /ˌəʊvə'welmɪŋ/ *adj* подавля́ющий. **overwork** *vt* & *i* переутомля́ть(ся) *impf*, переутоми́ть(ся) *pf*; *n* переутомле́ние.

owe /əʊ/ *vt* (~ *money*) быть до́лжным +*acc* & *dat*; (*be indebted*) быть обя́занным +*instr* & *dat*; **he, she, ~s me three roubles** он до́лжен, она́ должна́, мне три рубля́; **she ~s him her life** она́ обя́зана ему́ жи́знью. **owing** /'əʊɪŋ/ *adj*: **be ~** причита́ться *impf* (**to** +*dat*); **~ to** из-за+*gen*, по причи́не+*gen*.

owl /aʊl/ *n* сова́.

own /əʊn/ *adj* свой; (свой) со́бственный; **on one's ~** самостоя́тельно; (*alone*) оди́н; *vt* (*possess*) владе́ть *impf* +*instr*; (*admit*) признава́ть *impf*, призна́ть *pf*; **~ up** признава́ться *impf*, призна́ться *pf*. **owner** /'əʊnə(r)/ *n* владе́лец. **ownership** /'əʊnəʃɪp/ *n* владе́ние (**of** +*instr*), со́бственность.

ox /ɒks/ *n* вол.

oxidation /ˌɒksɪ'deɪʃ(ə)n/ *n* окисле́ние. **oxide** /'ɒksaɪd/ *n* о́кись. **oxidize** /'ɒksɪˌdaɪz/ *vt* & *i* окисля́ть(ся) *impf*, оки́слить(ся) *pf*. **oxygen** /'ɒksɪdʒ(ə)n/ *n* кислоро́д.

oyster /'ɔɪstə(r)/ *n* у́стрица.

ozone /'əʊzəʊn/ *n* озо́н.

P

pace /peɪs/ *n* шаг; (*fig*) темп; **keep ~ with** идти́ *impf* в но́гу с+*instr*; **set the ~** задава́ть *impf*, зада́ть *pf* темп; *vi*: **~ up and down** ходи́ть *indet* взад и вперёд. **pacemaker** *n* (*med*) электро́нный стимуля́тор.

pacifism /'pæsɪˌfɪz(ə)m/ *n* пацифи́зм. **pacifist** /-fɪst/ *n* пацифи́ст. **pacify** /-ˌfaɪ/ *vt* усмиря́ть *impf*, усмири́ть *pf*.

pack /pæk/ *n* у́зел, вьюк; (*soldier's*) ра́нец; (*hounds*) сво́ра; (*wolves*) ста́я; (*cards*) коло́да; *vt* (& *i*) упако́вывать(ся) *impf*, упакова́ть(ся) *pf*; (*cram*) набива́ть *impf*, наби́ть *pf*. **package** /'pækɪdʒ/ *n* посы́лка, паке́т; **~ holiday** организо́ванная туристи́ческая пое́здка. **packaging** /-dʒɪŋ/ *n* упако́вка. **packet** /'pækɪt/ *n* паке́т; па́чка; (*large sum of money*) ку́ча де́нег. **packing-case** /'pækɪŋ keɪs/ *n* я́щик.

pact /pækt/ *n* пакт.

pad /pæd/ *n* (*cushion*) поду́шечка; (*shin ~ etc.*) щито́к; (*of paper*) блокно́т; *vt* подбива́ть *impf*, подби́ть *pf*. **padding** /'pædɪŋ/ *n* наби́вка.

paddle[1] /'pæd(ə)l/ *n* (*oar*) весло́; *vi* (*row*) грести́ *impf*.

paddle[2] /'pæd(ə)l/ *vi* (*wade*) ходи́ть *indet*, идти́ *det*, пойти́ *pf* босико́м по воде́.

paddock /'pædək/ *n* вы́гон.

padlock /'pædlɒk/ *n* вися́чий замо́к; *vt* запира́ть *impf*, запере́ть *pf* на вися́чий замо́к.

paediatric /ˌpiːdɪ'ætrɪk/ *adj* педиатри́ческий. **paediatrician** /ˌpiːdɪə'trɪʃ(ə)n/ *n* педиа́тор.

pagan /ˈpeɪgən/ *n* язы́чник, -ица; *adj* язы́ческий. **paganism** /-ˌnɪz(ə)m/ *n* язы́чество.
page[1] /peɪdʒ/ *n* (*~-boy*) паж; *vt* (*summon*) вызыва́ть *impf*, вы́звать *pf*.
page[2] /peɪdʒ/ *n* (*of book*) страни́ца.
pageant /ˈpædʒ(ə)nt/ *n* пы́шная проце́ссия. **pageantry** /-trɪ/ *n* пы́шность.
pail /peɪl/ *n* ведро́.
pain /peɪn/ *n* бо́ль; *pl* (*efforts*) уси́лия *neut pl*; **~-killer** болеутоля́ющее сре́дство; *vt* (*fig*) огорча́ть *impf*, огорчи́ть *pf*. **painful** /-fʊl/ *adj* боле́зненный; **be ~** (*part of body*) боле́ть *impf*. **painless** /-lɪs/ *adj* безболе́зненный. **painstaking** /ˈpeɪnzˌteɪkɪŋ/ *adj* стара́тельный.
paint /peɪnt/ *n* кра́ска; *vt* кра́сить *impf*, по~ *pf*; (*portray*) писа́ть *impf*, на~ *pf* кра́сками. **paintbrush** *n* кисть. **painter** /-tə(r)/ *n* (*artist*) худо́жник, -ица; (*decorator*) маля́р. **painting** /-tɪŋ/ *n* (*art*) жи́вопись; (*picture*) карти́на.
pair /peə(r)/ *n* па́ра; *often not translated with nn denoting a single object, e.g.* **a ~ of scissors** но́жницы (-ц) *pl*; **a ~ of trousers** па́ра брюк; *vt* спа́ривать *impf*, спа́рить *pf*; **~ off** разделя́ться *impf*, раздели́ться *pf* по па́рам.
Pakistan /ˌpɑːkɪˈstɑːn/ *n* Пакиста́н. **Pakistani** /-nɪ/ *n* пакиста́нец, -а́нка; *adj* пакиста́нский.
pal /pæl/ *n* прия́тель *m*, ~ница.
palace /ˈpælɪs/ *n* дворе́ц.
palatable /ˈpælətəb(ə)l/ *adj* вку́сный; (*fig*) прия́тный. **palate** /ˈpælət/ *n* нёбо; (*fig*) вкус.
palatial /pəˈleɪʃ(ə)l/ *adj* великоле́пный.
palaver /pəˈlɑːvə(r)/ *n* (*trouble*) беспоко́йство; (*nonsense*) чепуха́.
pale[1] /peɪl/ *n* (*stake*) кол; **beyond the ~** невообрази́мый.
pale[2] /peɪl/ *adj* бле́дный; *vi* бледне́ть *impf*, по~ *pf*.
palette /ˈpælɪt/ *n* пали́тра.
pall[1] /pɔːl/ *n* покро́в.
pall[2] /pɔːl/ *vi*: **~ on** надоеда́ть *impf*, надое́сть *pf* +*dat*.
palliative /ˈpælɪətɪv/ *adj* паллиати́вный; *n* паллиати́в.
pallid /ˈpælɪd/ *adj* бле́дный. **pallor** /ˈpælə(r)/ *n* бле́дность.
palm[1] /pɑːm/ *n* (*tree*) па́льма; **P~ Sunday** Ве́рбное воскресе́нье.
palm[2] /pɑːm/ *n* (*of hand*) ладо́нь; *vt*: **~ off** всу́чивать *impf*, всучи́ть *pf* (**on** +*dat*).
palpable /ˈpælpəb(ə)l/ *adj* осяза́емый.
palpitations /ˌpælpɪˈteɪʃ(ə)nz/ *n pl* сердцебие́ние.
paltry /ˈpɔːltrɪ/ *adj* ничто́жный.
pamper /ˈpæmpə(r)/ *vt* балова́ть *impf*, из~ *pf*.
pamphlet /ˈpæmflɪt/ *n* брошю́ра.
pan[1] /pæn/ *n* (*saucepan*) кастрю́ля; (*frying-~*) сковорода́; (*of scales*) ча́шка; *vt*: **~ out** промыва́ть *impf*, промы́ть *pf*; (*fig*) выходи́ть *impf*, вы́йти *pf*.
pan[2] /pæn/ *vi* (*cin*) панорами́ровать *impf* & *pf*.
panacea /ˌpænəˈsiːə/ *n* панаце́я.
panache /pəˈnæʃ/ *n* рисо́вка.
pancake /ˈpæŋkeɪk/ *n* блин.
pancreas /ˈpæŋkrɪəs/ *n* поджелу́дочная железа́.
panda /ˈpændə/ *n* па́нда.
pandemonium /ˌpændɪˈməʊnɪəm/ *n* гвалт.
pander /ˈpændə(r)/ *vi*: **~ to** потво́рствовать *impf* +*dat*.
pane /peɪn/ *n* око́нное стекло́.
panel /ˈpæn(ə)l/ *n* пане́ль; (*control-~*) щит управле́ния; (*of experts*) гру́ппа специали́стов; (*of judges*) жюри́ *neut indecl*. **panelling** /-lɪŋ/ *n* пане́льная обши́вка.
pang /pæŋ/ *n pl* му́ки (-к) *pl*.
panic /ˈpænɪk/ *n* па́ника; **~-stricken** охва́ченный па́никой; *vi* впада́ть *impf*, впасть *pf* в па́нику. **panicky** /-kɪ/ *adj* пани́ческий.
pannier /ˈpænɪə(r)/ *n* корзи́нка.

P

panorama /ˌpænəˈrɑːmə/ *n* панора́ма. **panoramic** /-ˈræmɪk/ *adj* панора́мный.

pansy /ˈpænzɪ/ *n* аню́тины гла́зки (-зок) *pl.*

pant /pænt/ *vi* дыша́ть *impf* с оды́шкой.

panther /ˈpænθə(r)/ *n* панте́ра.

panties /ˈpæntɪz/ *n pl* тру́сики (-ков) *pl.*

pantomime /ˈpæntəˌmaɪm/ *n* рожде́ственское представле́ние; (*dumb show*) пантоми́ма.

pantry /ˈpæntrɪ/ *n* кладова́я *sb.*

pants /pænts/ *n pl* трусы́ (-со́в) *pl*; (*trousers*) брю́ки (-к) *pl.*

papal /ˈpeɪp(ə)l/ *adj* па́пский.

paper /ˈpeɪpə(r)/ *n* бума́га; *pl* докуме́нты *m pl*; (*newspaper*) газе́та; (*wallpaper*) обо́и (-о́ев) *pl*; (*treatise*) докла́д; *adj* бума́жный; *vt* окле́ивать *impf*, окле́ить *pf* обо́ями. **paperback** *n* кни́га в бума́жной обло́жке. **paperclip** *n* скре́пка. **paperwork** *n* канцеля́рская рабо́та.

par /pɑː(r)/ *n*: **feel below ~** чу́вствовать *impf* себя́ нева́жно; **on a ~ with** наравне́ с+*instr.*

parable /ˈpærəb(ə)l/ *n* при́тча.

parabola /pəˈræbələ/ *n* пара́бола.

parachute /ˈpærəˌʃuːt/ *n* парашю́т; *vi* спуска́ться *impf*, спусти́ться *pf* с парашю́том. **parachutist** /-tɪst/ *n* парашюти́ст.

parade /pəˈreɪd/ *n* пара́д; *vi* шестова́ть *impf*; *vt* (*show off*) выставля́ть *impf*, вы́ставить *pf* напока́з.

paradise /ˈpærəˌdaɪs/ *n* рай.

paradox /ˈpærəˌdɒks/ *n* парадо́кс. **paradoxical** /ˌpærəˈdɒksɪk(ə)l/ *adj* парадокса́льный.

paraffin /ˈpærəfɪn/ *n* (**~** *oil*) кероси́н.

paragon /ˈpærəgən/ *n* образе́ц.

paragraph /ˈpærəˌgrɑːf/ *n* абза́ц.

parallel /ˈpærəˌlel/ *adj* паралле́льный; *n* паралле́ль.

paralyse /ˈpærəˌlaɪz/ *vt* парализова́ть *impf* & *pf.* **paralysis** /pəˈrælɪsɪs/ *n* парали́ч.

paramedic /ˌpærəˈmedɪk/ *n* медрабо́тник (без вы́сшего образова́ния).

parameter /pəˈræmɪtə(r)/ *n* пара́метр.

paramilitary /ˌpærəˈmɪlɪtərɪ/ *adj* полувое́нный.

paramount /ˈpærəˌmaʊnt/ *adj* первостепе́нный.

paranoia /ˌpærəˈnɔɪə/ *n* парано́йя. **paranoid** /ˈpærəˌnɔɪd/ *adj*: **he is ~** он парано́ик.

parapet /ˈpærəpɪt/ *n* (*mil*) бру́ствер.

paraphernalia /ˌpærəfəˈneɪlɪə/ *n* принадле́жности *f pl.*

paraphrase /ˈpærəˌfreɪz/ *n* переска́з; *vt* переска́зывать *impf*, пересказа́ть *pf.*

parasite /ˈpærəˌsaɪt/ *n* парази́т. **parasitic** /ˌpærəˈsɪtɪk/ *adj* паразити́ческий.

parasol /ˈpærəˌsɒl/ *n* зо́нтик.

paratrooper /ˈpærəˌtruːpə(r)/ *n* парашюти́ст-деса́нтник.

parcel /ˈpɑːs(ə)l/ *n* паке́т, посы́лка.

parch /pɑːtʃ/ *vt* иссуша́ть *impf*, иссуши́ть *pf*; **become ~ed** пересыха́ть *impf*, пересо́хнуть *pf.*

parchment /ˈpɑːtʃmənt/ *n* перга́мент.

pardon /ˈpɑːd(ə)n/ *n* проще́ние; (*law*) поми́лование; *vt* проща́ть *impf*, прости́ть *pf*; (*law*) поми́ловать *pf.*

pare /peə(r)/ *vt* (*fruit*) чи́стить *impf*, о~ *pf*; **~ away, down** уре́зывать *impf*, уре́зать *pf.*

parent /ˈpeərənt/ *n* роди́тель *m*, ~ница. **parentage** /-tɪdʒ/ *n* происхожде́ние. **parental** /pəˈrent(ə)l/ *adj* роди́тельский.

parentheses /pəˈrenθəˌsiːz/ *n pl* (*brackets*) ско́бки *f pl.*

parish /ˈpærɪʃ/ *n* прихо́д. **parishioner** /pəˈrɪʃənə(r)/ *n* прихожа́нин, -а́нка.

parity /ˈpærɪtɪ/ *n* ра́венство.

park /pɑːk/ *n* парк; (*for cars etc.*) стоя́нка; *vt* & *abs* ста́вить *impf*, по~ *pf* (маши́ну). **parking** /-kɪŋ/ *n* стоя́нка.

parliament /ˈpɑːləmənt/ *n* парла́мент. **parliamentarian** /ˌpɑːləmenˈteərɪən/ *n* парламента́рий. **parliamentary** /-ˈmentərɪ/ *adj* парла́ментский.

parlour /ˈpɑːlə(r)/ *n* гости́ная *sb.*

parochial /pəˈrəʊkɪəl/ *adj* прихо́дский; (*fig*) ограни́ченный. **parochialism** /-ˌlɪz(ə)m/ *n* ограни́ченность.

parody /ˈpærədɪ/ *n* паро́дия; *vt* пароди́ровать *impf* & *pf.*

parole /pəˈrəʊl/ *n* че́стное сло́во; **on ~** освобождённый под че́стное сло́во.

paroxysm /ˈpærəkˌsɪz(ə)m/ *n* парокси́зм.

parquet /ˈpɑːkeɪ/ *n* парке́т; *attrib* парке́тный.

parrot /ˈpærət/ *n* попуга́й.

parry /ˈpærɪ/ *vt* пари́ровать *impf* & *pf*, от~ *pf.*

parsimonious /ˌpɑːsɪˈməʊnɪəs/ *adj* скупо́й.

parsley /ˈpɑːslɪ/ *n* петру́шка.

parsnip /ˈpɑːsnɪp/ *n* пастерна́к.

parson /ˈpɑːs(ə)n/ *n* свяще́нник.

part /pɑːt/ *n* часть; (*in play*) роль; (*mus*) па́ртия; **for the most ~** бо́льшей ча́стью; **in ~** ча́стью; **for my ~** что каса́ется меня́; **take ~ in** уча́ствовать *impf* в+*prep*; **~-time** (за́нятый) непо́лный рабо́чий день; *vt* & *i* (*divide*) разделя́ть(ся) *impf*, раздели́ть(ся) *pf*; *vi* (*leave*) расстава́ться *impf*, расста́ться *pf* (**from, with** с+*instr*); **~ one's hair** де́лать *impf*, с~ *pf* себе́ пробо́р.

partake /pɑːˈteɪk/ *vi* принима́ть *impf*, приня́ть *pf* уча́стие (**in, of** в+*prep*); (*eat*) есть *impf*, съ~ *pf* (**of** +*acc*).

partial /ˈpɑːʃ(ə)l/ *adj* части́чный; (*biased*) пристра́стный; **~ to** неравноду́шный к+*dat.* **partiality** /ˌpɑːʃɪˈælɪtɪ/ *n* (*bias*) пристра́стность. **partially** /ˈpɑːʃəlɪ/ *adv* части́чно.

participant /pɑːˈtɪsɪpənt/ *n* уча́стник, -ица (**in** +*gen*). **participate** /-ˌpeɪt/ *vi* уча́ствовать *impf* (**in** в+*prep*). **participation** /-ˈpeɪʃ(ə)n/ *n* уча́стие.

participle /ˈpɑːtɪˌsɪp(ə)l/ *n* прича́стие.

particle /ˈpɑːtɪk(ə)l/ *n* части́ца.

particular /pəˈtɪkjʊlə(r)/ *adj* осо́бый, осо́бенный; (*fussy*) разбо́рчивый; *n* подро́бность; **in ~** в ча́стности.

parting /ˈpɑːtɪŋ/ *n* (*leave-taking*) проща́ние; (*of hair*) пробо́р.

partisan /ˈpɑːtɪˌzæn/ *n* (*adherent*) сторо́нник; (*mil*) партиза́н; *attrib* (*biased*) пристра́стный; партиза́нский.

partition /pɑːˈtɪʃ(ə)n/ *n* (*wall*) перего́родка; (*polit*) разде́л; *vt* разделя́ть *impf*, раздели́ть *pf*; **~ off** отгора́живать *impf*, отгороди́ть *pf*.

partly /ˈpɑːtlɪ/ *adv* части́чно.

partner /ˈpɑːtnə(r)/ *n* (*in business*) компаньо́н; (*in dance, game*) партнёр, ~ша. **partnership** *n* това́рищество.

partridge /ˈpɑːtrɪdʒ/ *n* куропа́тка.

party /ˈpɑːtɪ/ *n* (*polit*) па́ртия; (*group*) гру́ппа; (*social gathering*) вечери́нка; (*law*) сторона́; **be a ~ to** принима́ть *impf*, приня́ть *pf* уча́стие в+*prep*; *attrib* парти́йный; **~ line** (*polit*) ли́ния па́ртии; (*telephone*) о́бщий телефо́нный про́вод; **~ wall** о́бщая стена́.

pass /pɑːs/ *vt* & *i* (*go past*; *of time*) проходи́ть *impf*, пройти́ *pf* (**by** ми́мо+*gen*); (*travel past*) проезжа́ть *impf*, прое́хать *pf* (**by** ми́мо+*gen*); (**~** *examination*) сдать *pf* (экза́мен); *vt* (*sport*) пасова́ть *impf*, пасну́ть *pf*; (*overtake*) обгоня́ть *impf*, обогна́ть *pf*; (*time*) проводи́ть *impf*, провести́ *pf*; (*hand on*) передава́ть *impf*, переда́ть *pf*; (*law, resolution*) утвержда́ть *impf*, утверди́ть *pf*; (*sentence*) выноси́ть *impf*, вы́нести *pf* (**upon** +*dat*); **~ as, for** слыть *impf*, про~ *pf* +*instr*, за+*acc*; **~ away** (*die*) сконча́ться *pf*; **~ o.s. off as** выдава́ть *impf*, вы́дать *pf*

P

себя́ за+*acc*; ~ **out** теря́ть *impf*, по~ *pf* созна́ние; ~ **over** (*in silence*) обходи́ть *impf*, обойти́ *pf* молча́нием; ~ **round** передава́ть *impf*, переда́ть *pf*; ~ **up** подава́ть *impf*, пода́ть *pf*; (*miss*) пропуска́ть *impf*, пропусти́ть *pf*; *n* (*permit*) про́пуск; (*sport*) пас; (*geog*) перева́л; **come to** ~ случа́ться *impf*, случи́ться *pf*; **make a** ~ **at** пристава́ть *impf*, приста́ть *pf* к+*dat*.

passable /'pɑːsəb(ə)l/ *adj* проходи́мый, прое́зжий; (*not bad*) неплохо́й.

passage /'pæsɪdʒ/ *n* прохо́д; (*of time*) тече́ние; (*sea trip*) рейс; (*in house*) коридо́р; (*in book*) отры́вок; (*mus*) пасса́ж.

passenger /'pæsɪndʒə(r)/ *n* пасса́жи́р.

passer-by /ˌpɑːsə'baɪ/ *n* прохо́жий *sb*.

passing /'pɑːsɪŋ/ *adj* (*transient*) мимолётный; *n*: **in** ~ мимохо́дом.

passion /'pæʃ(ə)n/ *n* страсть (**for** к+*dat*). **passionate** /-nət/ *adj* стра́стный.

passive /'pæsɪv/ *adj* пасси́вный; (*gram*) страда́тельный; *n* страда́тельный зало́г. **passivity** /-'sɪvɪtɪ/ *n* пасси́вность.

Passover /'pɑːsəʊvə(r)/ *n* евре́йская Па́сха.

passport /'pɑːspɔːt/ *n* па́спорт.

password /'pɑːswɜːd/ *n* паро́ль *m*.

past /pɑːst/ *adj* про́шлый; (*gram*) проше́дший; *n* про́шлое *sb*; (*gram*) проше́дшее вре́мя *neut*; *prep* ми́мо+*gen*; (*beyond*) за +*instr*; *adv* ми́мо.

pasta /'pæstə/ *n* макаро́нные изде́лия *neut pl*.

paste /peɪst/ *n* (*of flour*) те́сто; (*creamy mixture*) па́ста; (*glue*) клей́; (*jewellery*) страз; *vt* накле́ивать *impf*, накле́ить *pf*.

pastel /'pæst(ə)l/ *n* (*crayon*) пасте́ль; (*drawing*) рису́нок пасте́лью; *attrib* пасте́льный.

pasteurize /'pɑːstjəˌraɪz/ *vt* пастеризова́ть *impf* & *pf*.

pastime /'pɑːstaɪm/ *n* времяпрепровожде́ние.

pastor /'pɑːstə(r)/ *n* па́стор. **pastoral** /-r(ə)l/ *adj* (*bucolic*) пастора́льный; (*of pastor*) па́сторский.

pastry /'peɪstrɪ/ *n* (*dough*) те́сто; (*cake*) пиро́жное *sb*.

pasture /'pɑːstjə(r)/ *n* (*land*) па́стбище.

pasty[1] /'pæstɪ/ *n* пирожо́к.

pasty[2] /'peɪstɪ/ *adj* (~-*faced*) бле́дный.

pat /pæt/ *n* шлепо́к; (*of butter etc.*) кусо́к; *vt* хлопа́ть *impf*, по~ *pf*.

patch /pætʃ/ *n* запла́та; (*over eye*) повя́зка (на глазу́); (*spot*) пятно́; (*of land*) уча́сток земли́; *vt* ста́вить *impf*, по~ *pf* запла́ту на+*acc*; ~ **up** (*fig*) ула́живать *impf*, ула́дить *pf*. **patchwork** *n* лоску́тная рабо́та; *attrib* лоску́тный. **patchy** /'pætʃɪ/ *adj* неро́вный.

pâté /'pæteɪ/ *n* паштéт.

patent /'peɪt(ə)nt/ *adj* я́вный; ~ **leather** лакиро́ванная ко́жа; *n* пате́нт; *vt* патентова́ть *impf*, за~ *pf*.

paternal /pə'tɜːn(ə)l/ *adj* отцо́вский. **paternity** /-'tɜːnɪtɪ/ *n* отцо́вство.

path /pɑːθ/ *n* тропи́нка, тропа́; (*way*) путь *m*.

pathetic /pə'θetɪk/ *adj* жа́лкий.

pathological /ˌpæθə'lɒdʒɪk(ə)l/ *adj* патологи́ческий. **pathologist** /pə'θɒlədʒɪst/ *n* пато́лог.

pathos /'peɪθɒs/ *n* па́фос.

pathway /'pæθweɪ/ *n* тропи́нка, тропа́.

patience /'peɪʃ(ə)ns/ *n* терпе́ние; (*cards*) пасья́нс. **patient** /-ʃ(ə)nt/ *adj* терпели́вый; *n* больно́й *sb*, пацие́нт, ~ка.

patio /'pætɪəʊ/ *n* терра́са.

patriarch /'peɪtrɪˌɑːk/ *n* патриа́рх. **patriarchal** /-'ɑːk(ə)l/ *adj* патриарха́льный.

patriot /'pætrɪət/ *n* патрио́т, ~ка. **patriotic** /-trɪ'ɒtɪk/ *adj* патриоти́-

ческий. **patriotism** /ˈpætrɪəˌtɪz(ə)m/ *n* патриоти́зм.

patrol /pəˈtrəʊl/ *n* патру́ль *m*; **on ~** на дозо́ре; *vt & i* патрули́ровать *impf*.

patron /ˈpeɪtrən/ *n* покрови́тель *m*; (*of shop*) клие́нт. **patronage** /ˈpætrənɪdʒ/ *n* покрови́тельство. **patroness** /ˈpeɪtrənɪs/ *n* покрови́тельница. **patronize** /ˈpætrəˌnaɪz/ *vt* (*treat condescendingly*) снисходи́тельно относи́ться *impf* к+*dat*. **patronizing** /ˈpætrəˌnaɪzɪŋ/ *adj* покрови́тельственный.

patronymic /ˌpætrəˈnɪmɪk/ *n* о́тчество.

patter /ˈpætə(r)/ *vi* (*sound*) бараба́нить *impf*; *n* посту́кивание.

pattern /ˈpæt(ə)n/ *n* (*design*) узо́р; (*model*) образе́ц; (*sewing*) вы́кройка.

paunch /pɔːntʃ/ *n* брюшко́.

pauper /ˈpɔːpə(r)/ *n* бедня́к

pause /pɔːz/ *n* па́уза, переры́в; (*mus*) ферма́та; *vi* остана́вливаться *impf*, останови́ться *pf*.

pave /peɪv/ *vt* мости́ть *impf*, вы́~ *pf*; **~ the way** подготовля́ть *impf*, подгото́вить *pf* по́чву (**for** для +*gen*). **pavement** /-mənt/ *n* тротуа́р.

pavilion /pəˈvɪljən/ *n* павильо́н.

paw /pɔː/ *n* ла́па; *vt* тро́гать *impf* ла́пой; (*horse*) бить *impf* копы́том.

pawn[1] /pɔːn/ *n* (*chess*) пе́шка.

pawn[2] /pɔːn/ *vt* закла́дывать *impf*, заложи́ть *pf*. **pawnbroker** /-ˌbrəʊkə(r)/ *n* ростовщи́к. **pawnshop** *n* ломба́рд.

pay /peɪ/ *vt* плати́ть *impf*, за~, у~ *pf* (**for** за+*acc*); (*bill etc.*) опла́чивать *impf*, оплати́ть *pf*; *vi* (*be profitable*) окупа́ться *impf*, окупи́ться *pf*; *n* жа́лованье, зарпла́та; **~ packet** полу́чка; **~-roll** платёжная ве́домость. **payable** /ˈpeɪəb(ə)l/ *adj* подлежа́щий упла́те. **payee** /peɪˈiː/ *n* получа́тель *m*. **payment** /ˈpeɪmənt/ *n* упла́та, платёж.

PC *abbr* (*of* **personal computer**) ПК (персона́льный компью́тер); (*of* **politically correct**) полити́чески корре́ктный.

pea /piː/ *n* (*also pl, collect*) горо́х.

peace /piːs/ *n* мир; **in ~** в поко́е; **~ and quiet** мир и тишина́. **peaceable, peaceful** /ˈpiːsəb(ə)l, ˈpiːsfʊl/ *adj* ми́рный.

peach /piːtʃ/ *n* пе́рсик.

peacock /ˈpiːkɒk/ *n* павли́н.

peak /piːk/ *n* (*of cap*) козырёк; (*summit; fig*) верши́на; **~ hour** часы́ *m pl* пик.

peal /piːl/ *n* (*sound*) звон, трезво́н; (*of laughter*) взрыв.

peanut /ˈpiːnʌt/ *n* ара́хис.

pear /peə(r)/ *n* гру́ша.

pearl /pɜːl/ *n* (*also fig*) жемчу́жина; *pl* (*collect*) же́мчуг.

peasant /ˈpez(ə)nt/ *n* крестья́нин, -я́нка; *attrib* крестья́нский.

peat /piːt/ *n* торф.

pebble /ˈpeb(ə)l/ *n* га́лька.

peck /pek/ *vt & i* клева́ть *impf*, клю́нуть *pf*; *n* клево́к.

pectoral /ˈpektər(ə)l/ *adj* грудно́й.

peculiar /pɪˈkjuːlɪə(r)/ *adj* (*distinctive*) своеобра́зный; (*strange*) стра́нный; **~ to** сво́йственный +*dat*. **peculiarity** /-lɪˈærɪtɪ/ *n* осо́бенность; стра́нность.

pecuniary /pɪˈkjuːnɪərɪ/ *adj* де́нежный.

pedagogical /ˌpedəˈgɒgɪk(ə)l/ *adj* педагоги́ческий.

pedal /ˈped(ə)l/ *n* педа́ль; *vi* нажима́ть *impf*, нажа́ть *pf* педа́ль; (*ride bicycle*) е́хать *impf*, по~ *pf* на велосипе́де.

pedant /ˈped(ə)nt/ *n* педа́нт. **pedantic** /pɪˈdæntɪk/ *adj* педанти́чный.

peddle /ˈped(ə)l/ *vt* торгова́ть *impf* вразно́с+*instr*.

pedestal /ˈpedɪst(ə)l/ *n* пьедеста́л.

pedestrian /pɪˈdestrɪən/ *adj* пешехо́дный; (*prosaic*) прозаи́ческий; *n* пешехо́д; **~ crossing** перехо́д.

pedigree /ˈpedɪˌgriː/ *n* родосло́вная *sb*; *adj* поро́дистый.

pedlar /ˈpedlə(r)/ *n* разно́счик.

pee /piː/ *n* пи-пи́ *neut indecl*; *vi* мо-

P

чи́ться *impf*, по~ *pf*.
peek /piːk/ *vi* (~ *in*) загля́дывать *impf*, загляну́ть *pf*; (~ *out*) выгля́дывать *impf*, вы́глянуть *pf*.
peel /piːl/ *n* кожура́; *vt* очища́ть *impf*, очи́стить *pf*; *vi* (*skin*) шелуши́ться *impf*; (*paint*, ~ *off*) сходи́ть *impf*, сойти́ *pf*. **peelings** /-lɪŋz/ *n pl* очи́стки (-ков) *pl*.
peep /piːp/ *vi* (~ *in*) загля́дывать *impf*, загляну́ть *pf*; (~ *out*) выгля́дывать *impf*, вы́глянуть *pf*; *n* (*glance*) бы́стрый взгляд; **~-hole** глазо́к.
peer[1] /pɪə(r)/ *vi* всма́триваться *impf*, всмотре́ться *pf* (**at** в+*acc*).
peer[2] /pɪə(r)/ *n* (*noble*) пэр; (*person one's age*) све́рстник.
peeved /piːvd/ *adj* раздражённый. **peevish** /'piːvɪʃ/ *adj* раздражи́тельный.
peg /peg/ *n* ко́лышек; (*clothes* ~) крючо́к; (*for hat etc.*) ве́шалка; **off the ~** гото́вый; *vt* прикрепля́ть *impf*, прикрепи́ть *pf* ко́лышком, -ками.
pejorative /pɪ'dʒɒrətɪv/ *adj* уничижи́тельный.
pelican /'pelɪkən/ *n* пелика́н.
pellet /'pelɪt/ *n* ша́рик; (*shot*) дроби́на.
pelt[1] /pelt/ *n* (*skin*) шку́ра.
pelt[2] /pelt/ *vt* забра́сывать *impf*, заброса́ть *pf*; *vi* (*rain*) бараба́нить *impf*.
pelvis /'pelvɪs/ *n* таз.
pen[1] /pen/ *n* (*for writing*) ру́чка; **~-friend** друг по перепи́ске.
pen[2] /pen/ *n* (*enclosure*) заго́н.
penal /'piːn(ə)l/ *adj* уголо́вный. **penalize** /-ˌlaɪz/ *vt* штрафова́ть *impf*, о~ *pf*. **penalty** /'penəltɪ/ *n* наказа́ние; (*sport*) штраф; **~ area** штрафна́я площа́дка; **~ kick** штрафно́й уда́р. **penance** /'penəns/ *n* епитимья́.
penchant /'pɑ̃ʃɑ̃/ *n* скло́нность (**for** к+*dat*).
pencil /'pensɪl/ *n* каранда́ш; **~-sharpener** точи́лка.
pendant /'pend(ə)nt/ *n* подве́ска.
pending /'pendɪŋ/ *adj* (*awaiting decision*) ожида́ющий реше́ния; *prep* (*until*) в ожида́нии +*gen*, до+*gen*.
pendulum /'pendjʊləm/ *n* ма́ятник.
penetrate /'penɪˌtreɪt/ *vt* проника́ть *impf*, прони́кнуть *pf* в+*acc*. **penetrating** /-ˌtreɪtɪŋ/ *adj* проница́тельный; (*sound*) пронзи́тельный. **penetration** /ˌpenɪ'treɪʃ(ə)n/ *n* проникнове́ние; (*insight*) проница́тельность.
penguin /'peŋgwɪn/ *n* пингви́н.
penicillin /ˌpenɪ'sɪlɪn/ *n* пеницилли́н.
peninsula /pɪ'nɪnsjʊlə/ *n* полуо́стров.
penis /'piːnɪs/ *n* пе́нис.
penitence /'penɪt(ə)ns/ *n* раска́яние. **penitent** /-t(ə)nt/ *adj* раска́ивающийся; *n* ка́ющийся гре́шник.
penknife /'pennaɪf/ *n* перочи́нный нож.
pennant /'penənt/ *n* вы́мпел.
penniless /'penɪlɪs/ *adj* без гроша́.
penny /'penɪ/ *n* пе́нни *neut indecl*, пенс.
pension /'penʃ(ə)n/ *n* пе́нсия; *vt*: **~ off** увольня́ть *impf*, уво́лить *pf* на пе́нсию. **pensionable** /-nəb(ə)l/ *adj* (*age*) пенсио́нный. **pensioner** /-nə(r)/ *n* пенсионе́р, ~ка.
pensive /'pensɪv/ *adj* заду́мчивый.
pentagon /'pentəgən/ *n* пятиуго́льник; **the P~** Пентаго́н.
Pentecost /'pentɪˌkɒst/ *n* Пятидеся́тница.
penthouse /'penthaʊs/ *n* шика́рная кварти́ра на ве́рхнем этаже́.
pent-up /'pentʌp/ *adj* (*anger etc.*) сде́рживаемый.
penultimate /pɪ'nʌltɪmət/ *adj* предпосле́дний.
penury /'penjʊrɪ/ *n* нужда́.
peony /'piːənɪ/ *n* пио́н.
people /'piːp(ə)l/ *n pl* (*persons*) лю́ди *pl*; *sg* (*nation*) наро́д; *vt* населя́ть *impf*, насели́ть *pf*.
pepper /'pepə(r)/ *n* пе́рец; *vt* пе́рчить *impf*, на~, по~ *pf*. **pepper-**

corn *n* перчи́нка.
peppermint /ˈpepəˌmɪnt/ *n* пе́речная мя́та; (*sweet*) мя́тная конфе́та.
per /pɜː(r)/ *prep* (*for each*) (*person*) на+*acc*; **as ~** согла́сно+*dat*; **~ annum** в год; **~ capita** на челове́ка; **~ hour** в час; **~ se** сам по себе́.
perceive /pəˈsiːv/ *vt* воспринима́ть *impf*, восприня́ть *pf*.
per cent /pə ˈsent/ *adv* & *n* проце́нт. **percentage** /pəˈsentɪdʒ/ *n* проце́нт; (*part*) часть.
perceptible /pəˈseptɪb(ə)l/ *adj* заме́тный. **perception** /-ˈsepʃ(ə)n/ *n* восприя́тие; (*quality*) понима́ние. **perceptive** /-ˈseptɪv/ *adj* то́нкий.
perch¹ /pɜːtʃ/ *n* (*fish*) о́кунь *m*.
perch² /pɜːtʃ/ *n* (*roost*) насе́ст; *vi* сади́ться *impf*, сесть *pf*. **perched** /-d/ *adj* высоко́ сидя́щий, располо́женный.
percussion /pəˈkʌʃ(ə)n/ *n* (**~** *instruments*) уда́рные инструме́нты *m pl*.
peremptory /pəˈremptərɪ/ *adj* повели́тельный.
perennial /pəˈrenɪəl/ *adj* (*enduring*) ве́чный; *n* (*bot*) многоле́тнее расте́ние.
perestroika /ˌperɪˈstrɔɪkə/ *n* перестро́йка.
perfect *adj* /ˈpɜːfɪkt/ соверше́нный; (*gram*) перфе́ктный; *n* перфе́кт; *vt* /pəˈfekt/ соверше́нствовать *impf*, у~ *pf*. **perfection** /pəˈfekʃ(ə)n/ *n* соверше́нство. **perfective** /-ˈfektɪv/ *adj* (*n*) соверше́нный (вид).
perforate /ˈpɜːfəˌreɪt/ *vt* перфори́ровать *impf* & *pf*. **perforation** /-ˈreɪʃ(ə)n/ *n* перфора́ция.
perform /pəˈfɔːm/ *vt* (*carry out*) исполня́ть *impf*, испо́лнить *pf*; (*theat*, *mus*) игра́ть *impf*, сыгра́ть *pf*; *vi* выступа́ть *impf*, вы́ступить *pf*; (*function*) рабо́тать *impf*. **performance** /-məns/ *n* исполне́ние; (*of person*, *device*) де́йствие; (*of play etc.*) представле́ние, спекта́кль *m*; (*of engine etc.*) эксплуатацио́нные ка́чества *neut pl*. **performer** /-mə(r)/ *n* исполни́тель *m*.
perfume /ˈpɜːfjuːm/ *n* духи́ (-хо́в) *pl*; (*smell*) арома́т.
perfunctory /pəˈfʌŋktərɪ/ *adj* пове́рхностный.
perhaps /pəˈhæps/ *adv* мо́жет быть.
peril /ˈperɪl/ *n* опа́сность, риск. **perilous** /-ləs/ *adj* опа́сный, риско́ванный.
perimeter /pəˈrɪmɪtə(r)/ *n* вне́шняя грани́ца; (*geom*) пери́метр.
period /ˈpɪərɪəd/ *n* пери́од; (*epoch*) эпо́ха; (*menstrual*) ме́сячные *sb pl*. **periodic** /ˌpɪərɪˈɒdɪk/ *adj* периоди́ческий. **periodical** /-ˈɒdɪk(ə)l/ *adj* периоди́ческий; *n* периоди́ческое изда́ние.
peripheral /pəˈrɪfər(ə)l/ *adj* перифери́йный. **periphery** /-ˈrɪfərɪ/ *n* перифери́я.
periscope /ˈperɪˌskəʊp/ *n* периско́п.
perish /ˈperɪʃ/ *vi* погиба́ть *impf*, поги́бнуть *pf*; (*spoil*) по́ртиться *impf*, ис~ *pf*. **perishable** /-ʃəb(ə)l/ *adj* скоропо́ртящийся.
perjure /ˈpɜːdʒə(r)/ *v*: **~ o.s.** наруша́ть *impf*, нару́шить *pf* кля́тву. **perjury** /-dʒərɪ/ *n* лжесвиде́тельство.
perk¹ /pɜːk/ *n* льго́та.
perk² /pɜːk/ *vi*: **~ up** оживля́ться *impf*, оживи́ться *pf*. **perky** /-kɪ/ *adj* бо́йкий.
perm /pɜːm/ *n* пермане́нт. **permanence** /ˈpɜːmənəns/ *n* постоя́нство. **permanent** /-nənt/ *adj* постоя́нный.
permeable /ˈpɜːmɪəb(ə)l/ *adj* проница́емый. **permeate** /ˈpɜːmɪˌeɪt/ *vt* проника́ть *impf*, прони́кнуть *pf* в+*acc*.
permissible /pəˈmɪsɪb(ə)l/ *adj* допусти́мый. **permission** /-ˈmɪʃ(ə)n/ *n* разреше́ние. **permissive** /-ˈmɪsɪv/ *adj* (сли́шком) либера́льный; **~ society** о́бщество вседозво́ленности. **permis-**

P

siveness /-ˈmɪsɪvnɪs/ *n* вседозво́ленность. **permit** /ˈpɜːmɪt/ *vt* разреша́ть *impf*, разреши́ть *pf* +*dat*; *n* про́пуск.

permutation /ˌpɜːmjʊˈteɪʃ(ə)n/ *n* перестано́вка.

pernicious /pəˈnɪʃəs/ *adj* па́губный.

perpendicular /ˌpɜːpənˈdɪkjʊlə(r)/ *adj* перпендикуля́рный; *n* перпендикуля́р.

perpetrate /ˈpɜːpɪˌtreɪt/ *vt* соверша́ть *impf*, соверши́ть *pf*. **perpetrator** /-ˌtreɪtə(r)/ *n* вино́вник.

perpetual /pəˈpetjʊəl/ *adj* ве́чный. **perpetuate** /-tjʊˌeɪt/ *vt* увекове́чивать *impf*, увекове́чить *pf*. **perpetuity** /ˌpɜːpɪˈtjuːɪtɪ/ *n* ве́чность; **in ~** навсегда́, наве́чно.

perplex /pəˈpleks/ *vt* озада́чивать *impf*, озада́чить *pf*. **perplexity** /-ˈpleksɪtɪ/ *n* озада́ченность.

persecute /ˈpɜːsɪˌkjuːt/ *vt* пресле́довать *impf*. **persecution** /-ˌkjuːʃ(ə)n/ *n* пресле́дование.

perseverance /ˌpɜːsɪˈvɪərəns/ *n* насто́йчивость. **persevere** /ˌpɜːsɪˈvɪə(r)/ *vi* насто́йчиво, продолжа́ть *impf* (**in, at** *etc.* +*acc*, *inf*).

P **Persian** /ˈpɜːʃ(ə)n/ *n* перс, ~ия́нка; *adj* перси́дский.

persist /pəˈsɪst/ *vi* упо́рствовать *impf* (**in** в+*prep*); насто́йчиво продолжа́ть *impf* (**in** +*acc*, *inf*). **persistence** /-t(ə)ns/ *n* упо́рство. **persistent** /-t(ə)nt/ *adj* упо́рный.

person /ˈpɜːs(ə)n/ *n* челове́к; (*in play*; *gram*) лицо́; **in ~** ли́чно. **personable** /-nəb(ə)l/ *adj* привлека́тельный. **personage** /-nɪdʒ/ *n* ли́чность. **personal** /-n(ə)l/ *adj* ли́чный. **personality** /ˌpɜːsəˈnælɪtɪ/ *n* ли́чность. **personally** /-nəlɪ/ *adv* ли́чно. **personification** /pəˌsɒnɪfɪˈkeɪʃ(ə)n/ *n* олицетворе́ние. **personify** /-ˈsɒnɪˌfaɪ/ *vt* олицетворя́ть *impf*, олицетвори́ть *pf*.

personnel /ˌpɜːsəˈnel/ *n* ка́дры (-ров) *pl*, персона́л; **~ department** отде́л ка́дров.

perspective /pəˈspektɪv/ *n* перспекти́ва.

perspiration /ˌpɜːspɪˈreɪʃ(ə)n/ *n* пот. **perspire** /pəˈspaɪə(r)/ *vi* поте́ть *impf*, вс~ *pf*.

persuade /pəˈsweɪd/ *vt* (*convince*) убежда́ть *impf*, убеди́ть *pf* (**of** в+*prep*); (*induce*) угова́ривать *impf*, уговори́ть *pf*. **persuasion** /-ˈsweɪʒ(ə)n/ *n* убежде́ние. **persuasive** /-ˈsweɪsɪv/ *adj* убеди́тельный.

pertain /pəˈteɪn/ *vi*: **~ to** относи́ться *impf* отнести́сь *pf* к+*dat*.

pertinent /ˈpɜːtɪnənt/ *adj* уме́стный.

perturb /pəˈtɜːb/ *vt* трево́жить *impf*, вс~ *pf*.

peruse /pəˈruːz/ *vt* (*read*) внима́тельно чита́ть *impf*, про~ *pf*; (*fig*) рассма́тривать *impf*, рассмотре́ть *pf*.

pervade /pəˈveɪd/ *vt* наполня́ть *impf*. **pervasive** /-ˈveɪsɪv/ *adj* распространённый.

perverse /pəˈvɜːs/ *adj* капри́зный. **perversion** /-ˈvɜːʒ(ə)n/ *n* извраще́ние. **pervert** *vt* /pəˈvɜːt/ извраща́ть *impf*, изврати́ть *pf*; *n* /ˈpɜːvɜːt/ извращённый челове́к.

pessimism /ˈpesɪˌmɪz(ə)m/ *n* песси́мизм. **pessimist** /-mɪst/ *n* пессими́ст. **pessimistic** /-ˈmɪstɪk/ *adj* пессимисти́ческий.

pest /pest/ *n* вреди́тель *m*; (*fig*) зану́да. **pester** /ˈpestə(r)/ *vt* пристава́ть *impf*, приста́ть *pf* к+*dat*. **pesticide** /ˈpestɪˌsaɪd/ *n* пестици́д.

pet /pet/ *n* (*animal*) дома́шнее живо́тное *sb*; (*favourite*) люби́мец, -мица; **~ shop** зоомагази́н; *vt* ласка́ть *impf*.

petal /ˈpet(ə)l/ *n* лепесто́к.

peter /ˈpiːtə(r)/ *vi*: **~ out** (*road*) исчеза́ть *impf*, исче́знуть *pf*; (*stream*; *enthusiasm*) иссяка́ть *impf*, исся́кнуть *pf*.

petite /pəˈtiːt/ *adj* ма́ленькая.

petition /pɪˈtɪʃ(ə)n/ *n* пети́ция; *vt* подава́ть *impf*, пода́ть *pf* проше́ние +*dat*. **petitioner** /-nə(r)/ *n* проси́тель *m*.

petrified /ˈpetrɪˌfaɪd/ *adj* окамене́лый; **be ~** (*fig*) оцепене́ть *pf* (**with** от+*gen*).
petrol /ˈpetr(ə)l/ *n* бензи́н; **~ pump** бензоколо́нка; **~ station** бензозапра́вочная ста́нция; **~ tank** бензоба́к. **petroleum** /pɪˈtrəʊlɪəm/ *n* нефть.
petticoat /ˈpetɪˌkəʊt/ *n* ни́жняя ю́бка.
petty /ˈpetɪ/ *adj* ме́лкий; **~ cash** де́ньги (де́нег, -ньга́м) *pl* на ме́лкие расхо́ды.
petulant /ˈpetjʊlənt/ *adj* раздражи́тельный.
pew /pjuː/ *n* (церко́вная) скамья́.
phallic /ˈfælɪk/ *adj* фалли́ческий. **phallus** /ˈfæləs/ *n* фа́ллос.
phantom /ˈfæntəm/ *n* фанто́м.
pharmaceutical /ˌfɑːməˈsjuːtɪk(ə)l/ *adj* фармацевти́ческий. **pharmacist** /ˈfɑːməsɪst/ *n* фармаце́вт. **pharmacy** /-məsɪ/ *n* фармаци́я; (*shop*) апте́ка.
phase /feɪz/ *n* фа́за; *vt*: **~ in, out** постепе́нно вводи́ть *impf*, упраздня́ть *impf*.
Ph.D. *abbr* (*of* **Doctor of Philosophy**) кандида́т нау́к.
pheasant /ˈfez(ə)nt/ *n* фаза́н.
phenomenal /fɪˈnɒmɪn(ə)l/ *adj* феномена́льный. **phenomenon** /fɪˈnɒmɪnən/ *n* фено́мен.
phial /ˈfaɪəl/ *n* пузырёк.
philanderer /fɪˈlændərə(r)/ *n* волоки́та *m*.
philanthropic /ˌfɪlənˈθrɒpɪk/ *adj* филантропи́ческий. **philanthropist** /fɪˈlænθrəpɪst/ *n* филантро́п. **philanthropy** /-ˈlænθrəpɪ/ *n* филантро́пия.
philately /fɪˈlætəlɪ/ *n* филатели́я.
philharmonic /ˌfɪlhɑːˈmɒnɪk/ *adj* филармони́ческий.
Philistine /ˈfɪlɪˌstaɪn/ *n* (*fig*) фили́стер.
philosopher /fɪˈlɒsəfə(r)/ *n* фило́соф. **philosophical** /ˌfɪləˈsɒfɪk(ə)l/ *adj* филосо́фский. **philosophize** /fɪˈlɒsəfaɪz/ *vi* филосо́фствовать *impf*. **philosophy** /fɪˈlɒsəfɪ/ *n* филосо́фия.
phlegm /flem/ *n* мокрота́. **phlegmatic** /flegˈmætɪk/ *adj* флегмати́ческий.
phobia /ˈfəʊbɪə/ *n* фо́бия.
phone /fəʊn/ *n* телефо́н; *vt & i* звони́ть *impf*, по~ *pf* +*dat*. *See also* **telephone**
phonetic /fəˈnetɪk/ *adj* фонети́ческий. **phonetics** /-tɪks/ *n* фоне́тика.
phoney /ˈfəʊnɪ/ *n* подде́льный.
phosphorus /ˈfɒsfərəs/ *n* фо́сфор.
photo /ˈfəʊtəʊ/ *n* фо́то *neut indecl*. **photocopier** /ˈfəʊtəˌkɒpɪə(r)/ *n* копирова́льная маши́на. **photocopy** /-ˌkɒpɪ/ *n* фотоко́пия; *vt* де́лать *impf*, с~ *pf* фотоко́пию +*gen*. **photogenic** /ˌfəʊtəʊˈdʒenɪk/ *adj* фотогени́чный. **photograph** /ˈfəʊtəˌgrɑːf/ *n* фотогра́фия; *vt* фотографи́ровать *impf*, с~ *pf*. **photographer** /fəˈtɒgrəfə(r)/ *n* фото́граф. **photographic** /ˌfəʊtəˈgræfɪk/ *adj* фотографи́ческий. **photography** /fəˈtɒgrəfɪ/ *n* фотогра́фия.
phrase /freɪz/ *n* фра́за; *vt* формули́ровать *impf*, с~ *pf*.
physical /ˈfɪzɪk(ə)l/ *adj* физи́ческий; **~ education** физкульту́ра; **~ exercises** заря́дка. **physician** /fɪˈzɪʃ(ə)n/ *n* врач. **physicist** /ˈfɪzɪsɪst/ *n* фи́зик. **physics** /ˈfɪzɪks/ *n* фи́зика.
physiological /ˌfɪzɪəˈlɒdʒɪk(ə)l/ *n* физиологи́ческий. **physiologist** /ˌfɪzɪˈɒlədʒɪst/ *n* физио́лог. **physiology** /ˌfɪzɪˈɒlədʒɪ/ *n* физиоло́гия. **physiotherapist** /ˌfɪzɪəʊˈθerəpɪst/ *n* физиотерапе́вт. **physiotherapy** /ˌfɪzɪəʊˈθerəpɪ/ *n* физиотерапи́я.
physique /fɪˈziːk/ *n* телосложе́ние.
pianist /ˈpɪənɪst/ *n* пиани́ст, ~ка. **piano** /pɪˈænəʊ/ *n* фортепья́но *neut indecl*; (*grand*) роя́ль *m*; (*upright*) пиани́но *neut indecl*.
pick[1] /pɪk/ *vt* (*flower*) срыва́ть *impf*, сорва́ть *pf*; (*gather*) собира́ть *impf*, собра́ть *pf*; (*select*) выбира́ть *impf*, вы́брать *pf*; **~ one's nose, teeth** ковыря́ть *impf*,

P

ковырну́ть *pf* в носу́, в зуба́х; **~ a quarrel** иска́ть *impf* ссо́ры (**with** с+*instr*); **~ one's way** выбира́ть *impf*, вы́брать *pf* доро́гу; **~ on** (*nag*) придира́ться *impf* к+*dat*; **~ out** отбира́ть *impf*, отобра́ть *pf*; **~ up** (*lift*) поднима́ть *impf*, подня́ть *pf*; (*acquire*) приобрета́ть *impf*, приобрести́ *pf*; (*fetch*) (*on foot*) заходи́ть *impf*, зайти́ *pf* за +*instr*; (*in vehicle*) заезжа́ть *impf*, зае́хать *pf* за+*instr*; (*a cold*; *a girl*) подцепля́ть *impf*, подцепи́ть *pf*; **~ o.s. up** поднима́ться *impf*, подня́ться *pf*; **~-up** (*truck*) пика́п; (*electron*) звукоснима́тель *m*.

pick² /pɪk/ *n* вы́бор; (*best part*) лу́чшая часть; **take your ~** выбира́й(те)!

pick³ /pɪk/, **pickaxe** /ˈpɪkæks/ *n* кирка́.

picket /ˈpɪkɪt/ *n* (*person*) пике́тчик, -ица; (*collect*) пике́т; *vt* пикети́ровать *impf*.

pickle /ˈpɪk(ə)l/ *n* соле́нье; *vt* соли́ть *impf*, по~ *pf*. **pickled** /-k(ə)ld/ *adj* солёный.

pickpocket /ˈpɪkpɒkɪt/ *n* карма́нник.

P

picnic /ˈpɪknɪk/ *n* пикни́к.

pictorial /pɪkˈtɔːrɪəl/ *adj* изобрази́тельный; (*illustrated*) иллюстри́рованный. **picture** /ˈpɪktʃə(r)/ *n* карти́на; (*of health etc.*) воплоще́ние; (*film*) фильм; **the ~s** кино́ *neut indecl*; *vt* (*to o.s.*) представля́ть *impf*, предста́вить *pf* себе́. **picturesque** /ˌpɪktʃəˈresk/ *adj* живопи́сный.

pie /paɪ/ *n* пиро́г.

piece /piːs/ *n* кусо́к, часть; (*one of set*) шту́ка; (*of paper*) листо́к; (*mus, literature*) произведе́ние; (*chess*) фигу́ра; (*coin*) моне́та; **take to ~s** разбира́ть *impf*, разобра́ть *pf* (на ча́сти); **~ of advice** сове́т; **~ of information** све́дение; **~ of news** но́вость; **~-work** сде́льщина; **~-worker** сде́льщик; *vt*: **~ together** воссоздава́ть *impf*, воссозда́ть *pf* карти́ну +*gen*.

piecemeal *adv* по частя́м.

pier /pɪə(r)/ *n* (*mole*) мол; (*projecting into sea*) пирс; (*of bridge*) бык; (*between windows etc.*) просте́нок.

pierce /pɪəs/ *vt* пронза́ть *impf*, пронзи́ть *pf*; (*ears*) прока́лывать *impf*, проколо́ть *pf*. **piercing** /-sɪŋ/ *adj* пронзи́тельный.

piety /ˈpaɪɪtɪ/ *n* на́божность.

pig /pɪg/ *n* свинья́. **pigheaded** /pɪgˈhedɪd/ *adj* упря́мый. **piglet** /ˈpɪglɪt/ *n* поросёнок. **pigsty** /ˈpɪgˌstaɪ/ *n* свина́рник. **pigtail** *n* коси́чка.

pigeon /ˈpɪdʒɪn/ *n* го́лубь; **~-hole** отделе́ние для бума́г.

pigment /ˈpɪgmənt/ *n* пигме́нт. **pigmentation** /-ˈteɪʃ(ə)n/ *n* пигмента́ция.

pike /paɪk/ *n* (*fish*) щу́ка.

pilchard /ˈpɪltʃəd/ *n* сарди́н(к)а.

pile¹ /paɪl/ *n* (*heap*) ку́ча, ки́па; *vt*: **~ up** сва́ливать *impf*, свали́ть *pf* в ку́чу; (*load*) нагружа́ть *impf*, нагрузи́ть *pf* (**with** +*instr*); *vi*: **~ in(to), on** забира́ться *impf*, забра́ться *pf* в+*acc*; **~ up** накопля́ться, нака́пливаться *impf*, накопи́ться *pf*.

pile² /paɪl/ *n* (*on cloth etc.*) ворс.

piles /paɪlz/ *n pl* геморро́й *collect*.

pilfer /ˈpɪlfə(r)/ *vt* ворова́ть *impf*.

pilgrim /ˈpɪlgrɪm/ *n* пилигри́м. **pilgrimage** /-mɪdʒ/ *n* пало́мничество.

pill /pɪl/ *n* пилю́ля; **the ~** противозача́точная пилю́ля.

pillage /ˈpɪlɪdʒ/ *vt* гра́бить *impf*, о~ *pf*; *v abs* мародёрствовать *impf*.

pillar /ˈpɪlə(r)/ *n* столб; **~-box** стоя́чий почто́вый я́щик.

pillion /ˈpɪljən/ *n* за́днее сиде́нье (мотоци́кла).

pillory /ˈpɪlərɪ/ *n* позо́рный столб; *vt* (*fig*) пригвожда́ть *impf*, пригвозди́ть *pf* к позо́рному столбу́.

pillow /ˈpɪləʊ/ *n* поду́шка. **pillowcase** *n* на́волочка.

pilot /ˈpaɪlət/ *n* (*naut*) ло́цман;

(*aeron*) пило́т; *adj* о́пытный, про́бный; *vt* пилоти́ровать *impf*.
pimp /pɪmp/ *n* сво́дник.
pimple /ˈpɪmp(ə)l/ *n* прыщ.
pin /pɪn/ *n* була́вка; (*peg*) па́лец; **~-point** то́чно определя́ть *impf*, определи́ть *pf*; **~-stripe** то́нкая поло́ска; *vt* прика́лывать *impf*, приколо́ть *pf*; (*press*) прижима́ть *impf*, прижа́ть *pf* (**against** к+*dat*).
pinafore /ˈpɪnəˌfɔː(r)/ *n* пере́дник.
pincers /ˈpɪnsəz/ *n pl* (*tool*) клещи́ (-щей́) *pl*, пинце́т; (*claw*) клешни́ *f pl*.
pinch /pɪntʃ/ *vt* щипа́ть *impf*, (у)щипну́ть *pf*; (*finger in door etc.*) прищемля́ть *impf*, прищеми́ть *pf*; (*of shoe*) жать *impf*; (*steal*) стяну́ть *pf*; *n* щипо́к; (*of salt*) щепо́тка; **at a ~** в кра́йнем слу́чае.
pine[1] /paɪn/ *vi* томи́ться *impf*; **~ for** тоскова́ть *impf* по+*dat*, *prep*.
pine[2] /paɪn/ *n* (*tree*) сосна́.
pineapple /ˈpaɪnæp(ə)l/ *n* анана́с.
ping-pong /ˈpɪŋpɒŋ/ *n* пинг-по́нг.
pink /pɪŋk/ *n* (*colour*) ро́зовый цвет; *adj* ро́зовый.
pinnacle /ˈpɪnək(ə)l/ *n* верши́на.
pint /paɪnt/ *n* пи́нта.
pioneer /ˌpaɪəˈnɪə(r)/ *n* пионе́р, **~**ка; *vt* прокла́дывать *impf*, проложи́ть *pf* путь к+*dat*.
pious /ˈpaɪəs/ *adj* на́божный.
pip[1] /pɪp/ *n* (*seed*) зёрнышко.
pip[2] /pɪp/ *n* (*sound*) бип.
pipe /paɪp/ *n* труба́; (*mus*) ду́дка; (*for smoking*) тру́бка; **~-dream** пуста́я мечта́; *vt* пуска́ть *impf*, пусти́ть *pf* по труба́м; *vi* **~ down** затиха́ть *impf*, зати́хнуть *pf*. **pipeline** *n* трубопрово́д; (*oil* **~**) нефтепрово́д. **piper** /ˈpaɪpə(r)/ *n* волы́нщик. **piping** /ˈpaɪpɪŋ/ *adj*: **~ hot** с пы́лу.
piquant /ˈpiːkənt/ *adj* пика́нтный.
pique /piːk/ *n*: **in a fit of ~** в поры́ве раздраже́ния.
pirate /ˈpaɪərət/ *n* пира́т.
pirouette /ˌpɪrʊˈet/ *n* пиру́эт; *vi* де́лать *impf*, с**~** *pf* пиру́эт(ы).
Pisces /ˈpaɪsiːz/ *n* Ры́бы *f pl*.
pistol /ˈpɪst(ə)l/ *n* пистоле́т.
piston /ˈpɪst(ə)n/ *n* по́ршень *m*.
pit /pɪt/ *n* я́ма; (*mine*) ша́хта; (*orchestra* **~**) орке́стр; (*motor-racing*) запра́вочно-ремо́нтный пункт; *vt*: **~ against** выставля́ть *impf*, вы́ставить *pf* про́тив+*gen*.
pitch[1] /pɪtʃ/ *n* (*resin*) смола́; **~-black** чёрный как смоль; **~-dark** о́чень тёмный.
pitch[2] /pɪtʃ/ *vt* (*camp, tent*) разбива́ть *impf*, разби́ть *pf*; (*throw*)броса́ть *impf*, бро́сить *pf*; *vi* (*fall*) па́дать *impf*, (у)па́сть *pf*; (*ship*) кача́ть *impf*, *n* (*football* **~** *etc.*) по́ле; (*degree*) у́ровень *m*; (*mus*) высота́; (*slope*) укло́н.
pitcher /ˈpɪtʃə(r)/ *n* (*vessel*) кувши́н.
pitchfork /ˈpɪtʃfɔːk/ *n* ви́лы (-л) *pl*.
piteous /ˈpɪtɪəs/ *adj* жа́лкий.
pitfall /ˈpɪtfɔːl/ *n* западня́.
pith /pɪθ/ *n* сердцеви́на; (*essence*) суть. **pithy** /ˈpɪθɪ/ *adj* (*fig*) содержа́тельный.
pitiful /ˈpɪtɪˌfʊl/ *adj* жа́лкий. **pitiless** /ˈpɪtɪlɪs/ *adj* безжа́лостный.
pittance /ˈpɪt(ə)ns/ *n* жа́лкие гроши́ (-ше́й) *pl*.
pity /ˈpɪtɪ/ *n* жа́лость; **it's a ~** жа́лко, жаль; **take ~ on** сжа́литься *pf* над+*instr*; **what a ~** как жа́лко!; *vt* жале́ть *impf*, по**~** *pf*; **I ~ you** мне жаль тебя́.
pivot /ˈpɪvət/ *n* сте́ржень *m*; (*fig*) центр; *vi* враща́ться *impf*.
pixie /ˈpɪksɪ/ *n* эльф.
pizza /ˈpiːtsə/ *n* пи́цца.
placard /ˈplækɑːd/ *n* афи́ша, плака́т.
placate /pləˈkeɪt/ *vt* умиротворя́ть *impf*, умиротвори́ть *pf*.
place /pleɪs/ *n* ме́сто; **in ~ of** вме́сто+*gen*; **in the first, second, ~** во-пе́рвых, во-вторы́х; **out of ~** не на ме́сте; (*unsuitable*) неуме́стный; **take ~** случа́ться *impf*, случи́ться *pf*; (*pre-arranged event*) состоя́ться *pf*; **take the ~ of** заменя́ть *impf*, замени́ть *pf*; *vt* (*stand*) ста́вить *impf*, по**~** *pf*;

P

(*lay*) класть *impf*, положи́ть *pf*; (*an order etc.*) помеща́ть *impf*, помести́ть *pf*.

placenta /plə'sentə/ *n* плаце́нта.

placid /'plæsɪd/ *adj* споко́йный.

plagiarism /'pleɪdʒəˌrɪz(ə)m/ *n* плагиа́т. **plagiarize** /-ˌraɪz/ *vt* заи́мствовать *impf* & *pf*.

plague /pleɪg/ *n* чума́; *vt* му́чить *impf*, за~, из~ *pf*.

plaice /pleɪs/ *n* ка́мбала.

plain /pleɪn/ *n* равни́на; *adj* (*clear*) я́сный; (*simple*) просто́й; (*ugly*) некраси́вый; **~-clothes policeman** переоде́тый полице́йский *sb*.

plaintiff /'pleɪntɪf/ *n* исте́ц, исти́ца.

plaintive /'pleɪntɪv/ *adj* жа́лобный.

plait /plæt/ *n* коса́; *vt* плести́ *impf*, с~ *pf*.

plan /plæn/ *n* план; *vt* плани́ровать *impf*, за~, с~ *pf*; (*intend*) намерева́ться *impf* +*inf*.

plane[1] /pleɪn/ *n* (*tree*) плата́н.

plane[2] /pleɪn/ *n* (*tool*) руба́нок; *vt* строга́ть *impf*, вы́~ *pf*.

plane[3] /pleɪn/ *n* (*surface*) пло́скость; (*level*) у́ровень *m*; (*aeroplane*) самолёт.

planet /'plænɪt/ *n* плане́та.

plank /plæŋk/ *n* доска́.

plant /plɑːnt/ *n* расте́ние; (*factory*) заво́д; *vt* сажа́ть *impf*, посади́ть *pf*; (*fix firmly*) про́чно ста́вить *impf*, по~ *pf*; (*garden etc.*) заса́живать *impf*, засади́ть *pf* (**with** +*instr*).

plantation /plɑːn'teɪʃ(ə)n/ *n* (*of trees*) (лесо)насажде́ние; (*of cotton etc.*) планта́ция.

plaque /plæk/ *n* доще́чка.

plasma /'plæzmə/ *n* пла́зма.

plaster /'plɑːstə(r)/ *n* пла́стырь *m*; (*for walls etc.*) штукату́рка; (*of Paris*) гипс; *vt* (*wall*) штукату́рить *impf*, от~, о~ *pf*; (*cover*) облепля́ть *impf*, облепи́ть *pf*. **plasterboard** *n* суха́я штукату́рка. **plasterer** /-rə(r)/ *n* штукату́р.

plastic /'plæstɪk/ *n* пластма́сса; *adj* (*malleable*) пласти́чный; (*made of ~*) пластма́ссовый; **~ surgery** пласти́ческая хирурги́я.

plate /pleɪt/ *n* таре́лка; (*metal sheet*) лист; (*in book*) (вкладна́я) иллюстра́ция; (*name ~ etc.*) доще́чка.

plateau /'plætəʊ/ *n* плато́ *neut indecl*.

platform /'plætfɔːm/ *n* платфо́рма; (*rly*) перро́н.

platinum /'plætɪnəm/ *n* пла́тина.

platitude /'plætɪˌtjuːd/ *n* бана́льность.

platoon /plə'tuːn/ *n* взвод.

plausible /'plɔːzɪb(ə)l/ *adj* правдоподо́бный.

play /pleɪ/ *vt* & *i* игра́ть *impf*, сыгра́ть *pf* (*game*) в+*acc*, (*instrument*) на+*prep*, (*record*) ста́вить *impf*, по~ *pf*; **~ down** преуменьша́ть *impf*, преуме́ньшить *pf*; **~ a joke, trick, on** подшу́чивать *impf*, подшути́ть *pf* над+*instr*; **~ off** игра́ть *impf*, сыгра́ть *pf* реша́ющую па́ртию; **~-off** реша́ющая встре́ча; **~ safe** де́йствовать *impf* наверняка́; *n* игра́; (*theat*) пье́са. **player** /'pleɪə(r)/ *n* игро́к; (*actor*) актёр, актри́са; (*musician*) музыка́нт. **playful** /'pleɪfʊl/ *adj* игри́вый. **playground** *n* площа́дка для игр. **playgroup, playschool** *n* де́тский сад. **playing** /'pleɪɪŋ/ *n*: **~-card** игра́льная ка́рта; **~-field** игрова́я площа́дка. **playmate** *n* друг де́тства. **plaything** *n* игру́шка. **playwright** /'pleɪraɪt/ *n* драмату́рг.

plea /pliː/ *n* (*entreaty*) мольба́; (*law*) заявле́ние. **plead** /pliːd/ *vi* умоля́ть *impf* (**with** +*acc*; **for** о+*prep*); *vt* (*offer as excuse*) ссыла́ться *impf*, сосла́ться *pf* на+*acc*; **~ (not) guilty** (не) признава́ть *impf*, призна́ть *pf* себя́ вино́вным.

pleasant /'plez(ə)nt/ *adj* прия́тный. **pleasantry** /-trɪ/ *n* любе́зность. **please** /pliːz/ *vt* нра́виться *impf*, по~ *pf* +*dat*; *imper* пожа́луйста; бу́дьте добры́.

pleased /pliːzd/ *adj* дово́льный; *predic* рад. **pleasing, pleasurable** /ˈpliːzɪŋ, ˈpleʒərəb(ə)l/ *adj* прия́тный. **pleasure** /ˈpleʒə(r)/ *n* удово́льствие.

pleat /pliːt/ *n* скла́дка; *vt* плиссирова́ть *impf*.

plebiscite /ˈplebɪsɪt/ *n* плебисци́т.

plectrum /ˈplektrəm/ *n* плектр.

pledge /pledʒ/ *n* (*security*) зало́г; (*promise*) заро́к, обеща́ние; *vt* отдава́ть *impf*, отда́ть *pf* в зало́г; ~ **o.s.** обя́зываться *impf*, обяза́ться *pf*; ~ **one's word** дава́ть *impf*, дать *pf* сло́во.

plentiful /ˈplentɪˌfʊl/ *adj* оби́льный. **plenty** /ˈplentɪ/ *n* изоби́лие; ~ **of** мно́го+*gen*.

plethora /ˈpleθərə/ *n* (*fig*) изоби́лие.

pleurisy /ˈplʊərɪsɪ/ *n* плеври́т.

pliable /ˈplaɪəb(ə)l/ *adj* ги́бкий.

pliers /ˈplaɪəz/ *n pl* плоскогу́бцы (-цев) *pl*.

plight /plaɪt/ *n* незави́дное положе́ние.

plimsolls /ˈplɪms(ə)lz/ *n pl* спорти́вные та́почки *f pl*.

plinth /plɪnθ/ *n* пли́нтус.

plod /plɒd/ *vi* тащи́ться *impf*.

plonk /plɒŋk/ *vt* плю́хнуть *pf*.

plot /plɒt/ *n* (*of land*) уча́сток; (*of book etc.*) фа́була; (*conspiracy*) за́говор; *vt* (*on graph, map, etc.*) наноси́ть *impf*, нанести́ на гра́фик, на ка́рту; *v abs* (*conspire*) составля́ть *impf*, соста́вить *pf* за́говор.

plough /plaʊ/ *n* плуг; *vt* паха́ть *impf*, вс~ *pf*; *vi*: ~ **through** пробива́ться *impf*, проби́ться *pf* сквозь+*acc*.

ploy /plɔɪ/ *n* уло́вка.

pluck /plʌk/ *n* (*courage*) сме́лость; *vt* (*chicken*) щипа́ть *impf*, об~ *pf*; (*mus*) щипа́ть *impf*; (*flower*) срыва́ть *impf*, сорва́ть *pf*; ~ **up courage** собира́ться *impf*, собра́ться *pf* с ду́хом; *vi*: ~ **at** дёргать *impf*, дёрнуть *pf*. **plucky** /ˈplʌkɪ/ *adj* сме́лый.

plug /plʌg/ *n* (*stopper*) про́бка; (*electr*) ви́лка; (*electr socket*) розе́тка; *vt* (~ *up*) затыка́ть *impf*, заткну́ть *pf*; ~ **in** включа́ть *impf*, включи́ть *pf*.

plum /plʌm/ *n* сли́ва.

plumage /ˈpluːmɪdʒ/ *n* опере́ние.

plumb /plʌm/ *n* лот; *adv* вертика́льно; (*fig*) то́чно; *vt* измеря́ть *impf*, изме́рить *pf* глубину́+*gen*; (*fig*) проника́ть *impf*, прони́кнуть *pf* в+*acc*; ~ **in** подключа́ть *impf*, подключи́ть *pf*.

plumber /ˈplʌmə(r)/ *n* водопрово́дчик. **plumbing** /-mɪŋ/ *n* водопрово́д.

plume /pluːm/ *n* (*feather*) перо́; (*on hat etc.*) султа́н.

plummet /ˈplʌmɪt/ *vi* па́дать *impf*, (у)па́сть *pf*.

plump[1] /plʌmp/ *adj* пу́хлый.

plump[2] /plʌmp/ *vi*: ~ **for** выбира́ть *impf*, вы́брать *pf*.

plunder /ˈplʌndə(r)/ *vt* гра́бить *impf*, о~ *pf*; *n* добы́ча.

plunge /plʌndʒ/ *vt & i* (*immerse*) погружа́ть(ся) *impf*, погрузи́ть(ся) *pf* (**into** в+*acc*); *vi* (*dive*) ныря́ть *impf*, нырну́ть *pf*; (*rush*) броса́ться *impf*, бро́ситься *pf*. **plunger** /ˈplʌndʒə(r)/ *n* плу́нжер.

pluperfect /pluːˈpɜːfɪkt/ *n* давнопроше́дшее вре́мя *neut*.

plural /ˈplʊər(ə)l/ *n* мно́жественное число́. **pluralism** /-ˌlɪz(ə)m/ *n* плюрали́зм. **pluralistic** /-ˈlɪstɪk/ *adj* плюралисти́ческий.

plus /plʌs/ *prep* плюс+*acc*; *n* (знак) плюс.

plushy /ˈplʌʃɪ/ *adj* шика́рный.

plutonium /pluːˈtəʊnɪəm/ *n* плуто́ний.

ply /plaɪ/ *vt* (*tool*) рабо́тать *impf* +*instr*; (*task*) занима́ться *impf* +*instr*; (*keep supplied*) по́тчевать *impf* (**with** +*instr*); ~ **with questions** засыпа́ть *impf*, засы́пать *pf* вопро́сами.

plywood /ˈplaɪwʊd/ *n* фане́ра.

p.m. *adv* по́сле полу́дня.

pneumatic /njuːˈmætɪk/ *adj* пневмати́ческий; ~ **drill** отбо́йный молото́к.

pneumonia /nju:'məʊnɪə/ *n* воспале́ние лёгких.

poach[1] /pəʊtʃ/ *vt* (*cook*) вари́ть *impf*; **~ed egg** яйцо́-пашо́т.

poach[2] /pəʊtʃ/ *vi* браконье́рствовать *impf*. **poacher** /-tʃə(r)/ *n* браконье́р.

pocket /'pɒkɪt/ *n* карма́н; **out of ~** в убы́тке; **~ money** карма́нные де́ньги (-нег, -ньга́м) *pl*; *vt* класть *impf*, положи́ть *pf* в карма́н.

pock-marked /'pɒkma:kt/ *adj* рябо́й.

pod /pɒd/ *n* стручо́к.

podgy /'pɒdʒɪ/ *adj* то́лстенький.

podium /'pəʊdɪəm/ *n* трибу́на; (*conductor's*) пульт.

poem /'pəʊɪm/ *n* стихотворе́ние; (*longer ~*) поэ́ма. **poet** /'pəʊɪt/ *n* поэ́т. **poetess** /'pəʊɪtɪs/ *n* поэте́сса. **poetic(al)** /pəʊ'etɪk/ *adj* поэти́ческий. **poetry** /'pəʊɪtrɪ/ *n* поэ́зия, стихи́ *m pl*.

pogrom /'pɒgrəm/ *n* погро́м.

poignancy /'pɔɪnjənsɪ/ *n* острота́. **poignant** /'pɔɪnjənt/ *adj* о́стрый.

point[1] /pɔɪnt/ *n* то́чка; (*place*; *in list*) пункт; (*in score*) очко́; (*in time*) моме́нт; (*in space*) ме́сто; (*essence*) суть; (*sense*) смысл; (*sharp ~*) остриё; (*tip*) ко́нчик; (*power ~*) ште́псель *m*; *pl* (*rly*) стре́лка; **be on the ~ of** (*doing*) собира́ться *impf*, собра́ться *pf* +*inf*; **beside, off, the ~** некста́ти; **that is the ~** в э́том и де́ло; **the ~ is that** де́ло в том, что; **there is no ~** (*in doing*) не име́ет смы́сла (+*inf*); **to the ~** кста́ти; **~-blank** прямо́й; **~ of view** то́чка зре́ния.

point[2] /pɔɪnt/ *vt* (*wall*) расшива́ть *impf*, расши́ть *pf* швы +*gen*; (*gun etc.*) наводи́ть *impf*, навести́ *pf* (**at** на+*acc*); *vi* по-, у-, ка́зывать *impf*, по-, у-, каза́ть *pf* (**at, to** на+*acc*). **pointed** /'pɔɪntɪd/ *adj* (*sharp*) о́стрый. **pointer** /'pɔɪntə(r)/ *n* указа́тель *m*, стре́лка. **pointless** /'pɔɪntlɪs/ *adj* бессмы́сленный.

poise /pɔɪz/ *n* уравнове́шенность. **poised** /pɔɪzd/ *adj* (*composed*) уравнове́шенный; (*ready*) гото́вый (**to** к+*dat*).

poison /'pɔɪz(ə)n/ *n* яд; *vt* отравля́ть *impf*, отрави́ть *pf*. **poisonous** /'pɔɪzənəs/ *adj* ядови́тый.

poke /pəʊk/ *vt* (*prod*) ты́кать *impf*, ткнуть *pf*; **~ fun at** подшу́чивать *impf*, подшути́ть *pf* над +*instr*; (*thrust*) сова́ть *impf*, су́нуть *pf*; **~ the fire** меша́ть *impf*, по~ *pf* у́гли в ками́не; *n* тычо́к. **poker**[1] /'pəʊkə(r)/ *n* (*rod*) кочерга́.

poker[2] /'pəʊkə(r)/ *n* (*cards*) по́кер.

poky /'pəʊkɪ/ *adj* те́сный.

Poland /'pəʊlənd/ *n* По́льша.

polar /'pəʊlə(r)/ *adj* поля́рный; **~ bear** бе́лый медве́дь *m*. **polarity** /pə'lærɪtɪ/ *n* поля́рность. **polarize** /'pəʊlə,raɪz/ *vt* поляризова́ть *impf* & *pf*. **pole**[1] /pəʊl/ *n* (*geog*; *phys*) по́люс; **~-star** Поля́рная звезда́.

pole[2] /pəʊl/ *n* (*rod*) столб, шест; **~-vaulting** прыжо́к с шесто́м.

Pole /pəʊl/ *n* поля́к, по́лька.

polecat /'pəʊlkæt/ *n* хорёк.

polemic /pə'lemɪk/ *adj* полеми́ческий; *n* поле́мика.

police /pə'li:s/ *n* поли́ция; (*as pl*) полице́йские *sb*; (*in Russia*) мили́ция; **~ station** полице́йский уча́сток. **policeman** *n* полице́йский *sb*, полисме́н; (*in Russia*) милиционе́р. **policewoman** *n* же́нщина-полице́йский *sb*; (*in Russia*) же́нщина-милиционе́р.

policy[1] /'pɒlɪsɪ/ *n* поли́тика.

policy[2] /'pɒlɪsɪ/ *n* (*insurance*) по́лис.

polio /'pəʊlɪəʊ/ *n* полиомиели́т.

Polish /'pəʊlɪʃ/ *adj* по́льский.

polish /'pɒlɪʃ/ *n* (*gloss, process*) полиро́вка; (*substance*) политу́ра; (*fig*) лоск; *vt* полирова́ть *impf*, от~ *pf*; **~ off** расправля́ться *impf*, распра́виться *pf* с+*instr*. **polished** /-lɪʃt/ *adj* отто́ченный.

polite /pə'laɪt/ *adj* ве́жливый. **politeness** /-nɪs/ *n* ве́жливость.

politic /'pɒlɪtɪk/ *adj* полити́чный. **political** /pə'lɪtɪkəl/ *adj* полити́ческий; ~ **economy** политэконо́мика; ~ **prisoner** политзаключённый *sb.* **politician** /ˌpɒlɪˈtɪʃ(ə)n/ *n* поли́тик. **politics** /ˈpɒlɪtɪks/ *n* поли́тика.

poll /pəʊl/ *n* (*voting*) голосова́ние; (*opinion* ~) опро́с; **go to the** ~**s** голосова́ть *impf*, про~ *pf*; *vt* получа́ть *impf*, получи́ть *pf*.

pollen /ˈpɒlən/ *n* пыльца́. **pollinate** /ˈpɒlɪˌneɪt/ *vt* опыля́ть *impf*, опыли́ть *pf*.

polling /ˈpəʊlɪŋ/ *attrib*: ~ **booth** каби́на для голосова́ния; ~ **station** избира́тельный уча́сток.

pollutant /pəˈluːtənt/ *n* загрязни́тель *m*. **pollute** /-ˈluːt/ *vt* загрязня́ть *impf*, загрязни́ть *pf*. **pollution** /-ˈluːʃ(ə)n/ *n* загрязне́ние.

polo /ˈpəʊləʊ/ *n* по́ло *neut indecl*; ~**-neck sweater** водола́зка.

polyester /ˌpɒlɪˈestə(r)/ *n* полиэфи́р. **polyethylene** /ˌpɒlɪˈeθəliːn/ *n* полиэтиле́н. **polyglot** /ˈpɒlɪˌglɒt/ *n* полигло́т; *adj* многоязы́чный. **polygon** /ˈpɒlɪgɒn/ *n* многоуго́льник. **polymer** /ˈpɒlɪmə(r)/ *n* полиме́р. **polystyrene** /ˌpɒlɪˈstaɪəˌriːn/ *n* полистиро́л. **polytechnic** /ˌpɒlɪˈteknɪk/ *n* техни́ческий вуз. **polythene** /ˈpɒlɪθiːn/ *n* полиэтиле́н. **polyunsaturated** /ˌpɒlɪʌnˈsætʃəˌreɪtɪd/ *adj*: ~ **fats** полиненасы́щенные жиры́ *m pl*. **polyurethane** /ˌpɒlɪˈjʊərəˌθeɪn/ *n* полиурета́н.

pomp /pɒmp/ *n* пы́шность. **pomposity** /pɒmˈpɒsɪtɪ/ *n* напы́щенность. **pompous** /ˈpɒmpəs/ *adj* напы́щенный.

pond /pɒnd/ *n* пруд.

ponder /ˈpɒndə(r)/ *vt* обду́мывать *impf*, обду́мать *pf*; *vi* размышля́ть *impf*, размы́слить *pf*.

ponderous /ˈpɒndərəs/ *adj* тяжелове́сный.

pony /ˈpəʊnɪ/ *n* по́ни *m indecl*.

poodle /ˈpuːd(ə)l/ *n* пу́дель *m*.

pool[1] /puːl/ *n* (*of water*) прудо́к; (*puddle*) лу́жа; (*swimming* ~) бассе́йн.

pool[2] /puːl/ *n* (*collective stakes*) совоку́пность ста́вок; (*common fund*) о́бщий фонд; *vt* объединя́ть *impf*, объедини́ть *pf*.

poor /pʊə(r)/ *adj* бе́дный; (*bad*) плохо́й; *n*: **the** ~ бедняки́ *m pl*. **poorly** /ˈpʊəlɪ/ *predic* нездоро́в.

pop[1] /pɒp/ *vi* хло́пать *impf*, хло́пнуть *pf*; *vt* (*put*) бы́стро всу́нуть *pf* (**into** в+*acc*); ~ **in on** забега́ть *impf*, забежа́ть *pf* к+*dat*; *n* хлопо́к.

pop[2] /pɒp/ *adj* поп-; ~ **concert** поп-конце́рт; ~ **music** поп-му́зыка.

pope /pəʊp/ *n* Па́па *m*.

poplar /ˈpɒplə(r)/ *n* то́поль *m*.

poppy /ˈpɒpɪ/ *n* мак.

populace /ˈpɒpjʊləs/ *n* просто́й наро́д. **popular** /-lə(r)/ *adj* наро́дный; (*liked*) популя́рный. **popularity** /-ˈlærɪtɪ/ *n* популя́рность. **popularize** /ˈpɒpjʊləˌraɪz/ *vt* популяризи́ровать *impf* & *pf*. **populate** /ˈpɒpjʊˌleɪt/ *vt* населя́ть *impf*, насели́ть *pf*. **population** /-ˈleɪʃ(ə)n/ *n* населе́ние. **populous** /ˈpɒpjʊləs/ *adj* (много)лю́дный.

porcelain /ˈpɔːsəlɪn/ *n* фарфо́р.

porch /pɔːtʃ/ *n* крыльцо́.

porcupine /ˈpɔːkjʊˌpaɪn/ *n* дикобра́з.

pore[1] /pɔː(r)/ *n* по́ра.

pore[2] /pɔː(r)/ *vi*: ~ **over** погружа́ться *impf*, погрузи́ться *pf* в+*acc*.

pork /pɔːk/ *n* свини́на.

pornographic /ˌpɔːnəˈgræfɪk/ *adj* порнографи́ческий. **pornography** /pɔːˈnɒgrəfɪ/ *n* порногра́фия.

porous /ˈpɔːrəs/ *adj* по́ристый.

porpoise /ˈpɔːpəs/ *n* морска́я свинья́.

porridge /ˈpɒrɪdʒ/ *n* овся́ная ка́ша.

port[1] /pɔːt/ *n* (*harbour*) порт; (*town*) порто́вый го́род.

port[2] /pɔːt/ *n* (*naut*) ле́вый борт.

port[3] /pɔːt/ *n* (*wine*) портве́йн.

portable /ˈpɔːtəb(ə)l/ *adj* порта́тивный.

portend /pɔːˈtend/ *vt* предвеща́ть

impf. **portent** /ˈpɔːt(ə)nt/ *n* предзнаменова́ние. **portentous** /-ˈtentəs/ *adj* злове́щий.

porter[1] /ˈpɔːtə(r)/ *n* (*at door*) швейца́р.

porter[2] /ˈpɔːtə(r)/ *n* (*carrier*) носи́льщик.

portfolio /pɔːtˈfəʊlɪəʊ/ *n* портфе́ль *m*; (*artist's*) па́пка.

porthole /ˈpɔːthəʊl/ *n* иллюмина́тор.

portion /ˈpɔːʃ(ə)n/ *n* часть, до́ля; (*of food*) по́рция.

portly /ˈpɔːtlɪ/ *adj* доро́дный.

portrait /ˈpɔːtrɪt/ *n* портре́т. **portray** /pɔːˈtreɪ/ *vt* изобража́ть *impf*, изобрази́ть *pf.* **portrayal** /-ˈtreɪəl/ *n* изображе́ние.

Portugal /ˈpɔːtjʊg(ə)l/ *n* Португа́лия. **Portuguese** /ˌpɔːtjʊˈgiːz/ *n* португа́лец, -лка; *adj* португа́льский.

pose /pəʊz/ *n* по́за; *vt* (*question*) ста́вить *impf*, по~ *pf*; (*a problem*) представля́ть *impf*, предста́вить *pf*; *vi* пози́ровать *impf*; **~ as** выдава́ть *impf*, вы́дать *pf* себя́ за+*acc.*

posh /pɒʃ/ *adj* шика́рный.

posit /ˈpɒzɪt/ *vt* постули́ровать *impf* & *pf.*

position /pəˈzɪʃ(ə)n/ *n* положе́ние, пози́ция; **in a ~ to** в состоя́нии +*inf*; *vt* ста́вить *impf*, по~ *pf.*

positive /ˈpɒzɪtɪv/ *adj* положи́тельный; (*convinced*) уве́ренный; (*proof*) несомне́нный; *n* (*phot*) позити́в.

possess /pəˈzes/ *vt* облада́ть *impf* +*instr*; владе́ть *impf* +*instr*; (*of feeling etc.*) овладева́ть *impf*, овладе́ть *pf* +*instr.* **possessed** /-ˈzest/ *adj* одержи́мый. **possession** /-ˈzeʃ(ə)n/ *n* владе́ние (**of** +*instr*); *pl* со́бственность. **possessive** /-ˈzesɪv/ *adj* со́бственнический. **possessor** /-ˈzesə(r)/ *n* облада́тель *m.*

possibility /ˌpɒsɪˈbɪlɪtɪ/ *n* возмо́жность. **possible** /ˈpɒsɪb(ə)l/ *adj* возмо́жный; **as much as ~** ско́лько возмо́жно; **as soon as ~** как мо́жно скоре́е. **possibly** /ˈpɒsɪblɪ/ *adv* возмо́жно, мо́жет (быть).

post[1] /pəʊst/ *n* (*pole*) столб; *vt* (**~** *up*) выве́шивать *impf*, вы́весить *pf.*

post[2] /pəʊst/ *n* (*station*) пост; (*job*) до́лжность; *vt* (*station*) расставля́ть *impf*, расста́вить *pf*; (*appoint*) назнача́ть *impf*, назна́чить *pf.*

post[3] /pəʊst/ *n* (*letters*, **~** *office*) по́чта; **by ~** по́чтой; *attrib* почто́вый; **~-box** почто́вый я́щик; **~-code** почто́вый и́ндекс; **~ office** по́чта; *vt* (*send by* **~**) отправля́ть *impf*, отпра́вить *pf* по по́чте; (*put in* **~***-box*) опуска́ть *impf*, опусти́ть *pf* в почто́вый я́щик. **postage** /ˈpəʊstɪdʒ/ *n* почто́вый сбор, почто́вые расхо́ды *m pl*; **~ stamp** почто́вая ма́рка. **postal** /ˈpəʊst(ə)l/ *adj* почто́вый; **~-order** почто́вый перево́д. **postcard** *n* откры́тка.

poster /ˈpəʊstə(r)/ *n* афи́ша, плака́т.

poste restante /ˌpəʊst reˈstɑ̃t/ *n* до востре́бования.

posterior /pɒˈstɪərɪə(r)/ *adj* за́дний; *n* зад.

posterity /pɒˈsterɪtɪ/ *n* пото́мство.

post-graduate /pəʊstˈgrædjʊət/ *n* аспира́нт.

posthumous /ˈpɒstjʊməs/ *adj* посме́ртный.

postman /ˈpəʊstmən/ *n* почтальо́н. **postmark** *n* почто́вый ште́мпель *m.*

post-mortem /pəʊstˈmɔːtəm/ *n* вскры́тие тру́па.

postpone /pəʊstˈpəʊn/ *vt* отсро́чивать *impf*, отсро́чить *pf.* **postponement** /-mənt/ *n* отсро́чка.

postscript /ˈpəʊstskrɪpt/ *n* постскри́птум.

postulate /ˈpɒstjʊˌleɪt/ *vt* постули́ровать *impf* & *pf.*

posture /ˈpɒstʃə(r)/ *n* по́за, положе́ние.

post-war /pəʊstˈwɔː(r)/ *adj* послевое́нный.

posy /ˈpəʊzɪ/ *n* букéтик.

pot /pɒt/ *n* горшóк; (*cooking* ~) кастрю́ля; **~-shot** вы́стрел наугáд; *vt* (*food*) консерви́ровать *impf*, за~ *pf*; (*plant*) сажáть *impf*, посади́ть *pf* в горшóк; (*billiards*) загоня́ть *impf*, загнáть *pf* в лу́зу.

potash /ˈpɒtæʃ/ *n* потáш. **potassium** /pəˈtæsɪəm/ *n* кáлий.

potato /pəˈteɪtəʊ/ *n* (*also collect*) картóшка (*no pl*); (*plant*; *also collect*) картóфель *m* (*no pl*).

potency /ˈpəʊt(ə)nsɪ/ *n* си́ла. **potent** /ˈpəʊt(ə)nt/ *adj* си́льный.

potential /pəˈtenʃ(ə)l/ *adj* потенциáльный; *n* потенциáл. **potentiality** /pəˌtenʃɪˈælɪtɪ/ *n* потенциáльность.

pot-hole /ˈpɒthəʊl/ *n* (*in road*) вы́боина.

potion /ˈpəʊʃ(ə)n/ *n* зéлье.

potter[1] /ˈpɒtə(r)/ *vi*: **~ about** вози́ться *impf*.

potter[2] /ˈpɒtə(r)/ *n* гончáр. **pottery** /ˈpɒtərɪ/ *n* (*goods*) гончáрные издéлия *neut pl*; (*place*) гончáрная *sb*.

potty[1] /ˈpɒtɪ/ *adj* (*crazy*) помéшанный (**about** на+*prep*).

potty[2] /ˈpɒtɪ/ *n* ночнóй горшóк.

pouch /paʊtʃ/ *n* су́мка.

poultry /ˈpəʊltrɪ/ *n* домáшняя пти́ца.

pounce /paʊns/ *vi*: **~ (up)on** набрáсываться *impf*, наброси́ться *pf* на+*acc*.

pound[1] /paʊnd/ *n* (*measure*) фунт; **~ sterling** фунт стéрлингов.

pound[2] /paʊnd/ *vt* (*strike*) колоти́ть *impf*, по~ *pf* по+*dat*, в+*acc*; *vi* (*heart*) колоти́ться *impf*; **~ along** (*run*) мчáться *impf* с грóхотом.

pour /pɔː(r)/ *vt* лить *impf*; **~ out** наливáть *impf*, нали́ть *pf*; *vi* ли́ться *impf*; **it is ~ing (with rain)** дождь льёт как из ведрá.

pout /paʊt/ *vi* ду́ть(ся) *impf*, на~ *pf*.

poverty /ˈpɒvətɪ/ *n* бéдность; **~-stricken** убóгий.

POW *abbr* военноплéнный *sb*.

powder /ˈpaʊdə(r)/ *n* порошóк; (*cosmetic*) пу́дра; *vt* пу́дрить *impf*, на~ *pf*. **powdery** /-rɪ/ *adj* порошкообрáзный.

power /ˈpaʊə(r)/ *n* (*vigour*) си́ла; (*might*) могу́щество; (*ability*) спосóбность; (*control*) власть; (*authorization*) полномóчие; (*State*) держáва; **~ cut** переры́в электропитáния; **~ point** розéтка; **~ station** электростáнция. **powerful** /-fʊl/ *adj* си́льный. **powerless** /-lɪs/ *adj* бесси́льный.

practicable /ˈpræktɪkəb(ə)l/ *adj* осуществи́мый. **practical** /-tɪk(ə)l/ *adj* (*help, activities*) практи́ческий; (*person, object*) практи́чный. **practically** /-klɪ/ *adv* практи́чески. **practice** /ˈpræktɪs/ *n* прáктика; (*custom*) обы́чай; (*mus*) заня́тия *neut pl*; **in ~** на прáктике; **put into ~** осуществля́ть *impf*, осуществи́ть *pf*.

practise /ˈpræktɪs/ *vt* (*also abs of doctor etc.*) практиковáть *impf*; упражня́ться *impf* в+*prep*; (*mus*) занимáться *impf*, заня́ться *pf* на+*prep*. **practised** /ˈpræktɪst/ *adj* óпытный. **practitioner** /prækˈtɪʃənə(r)/ *n* (*doctor*) практику́ющий врач; **general ~** врач óбщей прáктики.

pragmatic /prægˈmætɪk/ *adj* прагмати́ческий. **pragmatism** /ˈprægməˌtɪz(ə)m/ *n* прагмати́зм. **pragmatist** /ˈprægmətɪst/ *n* прагмáтик.

prairie /ˈpreərɪ/ *n* прéрия.

praise /preɪz/ *vt* хвали́ть *impf*, по~ *pf*; *n* похвалá. **praiseworthy** /ˈpreɪzˌwɜːðɪ/ *adj* похвáльный.

pram /præm/ *n* дéтская коля́ска.

prance /prɑːns/ *vi* гарцевáть *impf*.

prank /præŋk/ *n* вы́ходка.

prattle /ˈpræt(ə)l/ *vi* лепетáть; *n* лéпет.

prawn /prɔːn/ *n* кревéтка.

pray /preɪ/ *vi* моли́ться *impf*, по~ *pf* (**to** +*dat*; **for** о+*prep*). **prayer** /ˈpreə(r)/ *n* моли́тва.

preach /priːtʃ/ *vt* & *i* проповéды-

P

вать *impf*. **preacher** /'priːtʃə(r)/ *n* проповéдник.

preamble /priː'æmb(ə)l/ *n* преáмбула.

pre-arrange /ˌpriːə'reɪndʒ/ *vt* зарáнее организóвывать *impf*, организовáть *pf*.

precarious /prɪ'keərɪəs/ *adj* опáсный.

precaution /prɪ'kɔːʃ(ə)n/ *n* предосторóжность. **precautionary** /-ʃənərɪ/ *adj*: ~ **measures** мéры предосторóжности.

precede /prɪ'siːd/ *vt* предшéствовать *impf* +*dat*. **precedence** /'presɪd(ə)ns/ *n* предпочтéние. **precedent** /'presɪd(ə)nt/ *n* прецедéнт. **preceding** /prɪ'siːdɪŋ/ *adj* предыдýщий.

precept /'priːsept/ *n* наставлéние.

precinct /'priːsɪŋkt/ *n* двор; *pl* окрéстности *f pl*. **pedestrian** ~ учáсток для пешехóдов; **shopping** ~ торгóвый пассáж.

precious /'preʃəs/ *adj* драгоцéнный; (*style*) манéрный; *adv* óчень.

precipice /'presɪpɪs/ *n* обры́в. **precipitate** *adj* /prɪ'sɪpɪtət/ (*person*) опромéтчивый; *vt* /prɪ'sɪpɪˌteɪt/ (*throw down*) низвергáть *impf*, низвéргнуть *pf*; (*hurry*) ускорять *impf*, ускóрить *pf*. **precipitation** /prɪˌsɪpɪ'teɪʃ(ə)n/ *n* (*meteorol*) осáдки *m pl*. **precipitous** /prɪ'sɪpɪtəs/ *adj* обры́вистый.

précis /'preɪsiː/ *n* конспéкт.

precise /prɪ'saɪs/ *adj* тóчный. **precisely** /-'saɪslɪ/ *adv* тóчно; (*in answer*) и́менно. **precision** /-'sɪʒ(ə)n/ *n* тóчность.

preclude /prɪ'kluːd/ *vt* предотвращáть *impf*, предотврати́ть *pf*.

precocious /prɪ'kəʊʃəs/ *adj* рáно разви́вшийся.

preconceived /ˌpriːkən'siːvd/ *adj* предвзя́тый. **preconception** /ˌpriːkən'sepʃ(ə)n/ *n* предвзя́тое мнéние.

pre-condition /ˌpriːkən'dɪʃ(ə)n/ *n* предпосы́лка.

precursor /priː'kɜːsə(r)/ *n* предшéственник.

predator /'predətə(r)/ *n* хи́щник. **predatory** /-tərɪ/ *adj* хи́щный.

predecessor /'priːdɪˌsesə(r)/ *n* предшéственник.

predestination /priːˌdestɪ'neɪʃ(ə)n/ *n* предопределéние.

predetermine /ˌpriːdɪ'tɜːmɪn/ *vt* предрешáть *impf*, предреши́ть *pf*.

predicament /prɪ'dɪkəmənt/ *n* затрудни́тельное положéние.

predicate /'predɪkət/ *n* (*gram*) сказýемое *sb*. **predicative** /prɪ'dɪkətɪv/ *adj* предикати́вный.

predict /prɪ'dɪkt/ *vt* предскáзывать *impf*, предсказáть *pf*. **predictable** /-'dɪktəb(ə)l/ *adj* предсказýемый. **prediction** /-'dɪkʃ(ə)n/ *n* предсказáние.

predilection /ˌpriːdɪ'lekʃ(ə)n/ *n* пристрáстие (**for** к+*dat*).

predispose /ˌpriːdɪ'spəʊz/ *vt* предрасполагáть *impf*, предрасполoжи́ть *pf* (**to** к+*dat*). **predisposition** /ˌpriːdɪspə'zɪʃ(ə)n/ *n* предрасположéние (**to** к+*dat*).

predominance /prɪ'dɒmɪnəns/ *n* преобладáние. **predominant** /-nənt/ *adj* преобладáющий. **predominate** /-ˌneɪt/ *vi* преобладáть *impf*.

pre-eminence /priː'emɪnəns/ *n* превосхóдство. **pre-eminent** /-nənt/ *adj* выдаю́щийся.

pre-empt /priː'empt/ *vt* (*fig*) завладевáть *impf*, завладéть *pf* +*instr* прéжде други́х. **pre-emptive** /-tɪv/ *adj* (*mil*) упреждáющий.

preen /priːn/ *vt* (*of bird*) чи́стить *impf*, по~ *pf* клю́вом; ~ **o.s.** (*be proud*) горди́ться *impf* собóй.

pre-fab /'priːfæb/ *n* сбóрный дом. **pre-fabricated** /priː'fæbrɪˌkeɪtɪd/ *adj* сбóрный.

preface /'prefəs/ *n* предисловие.

prefect /'priːfekt/ *n* префéкт; (*school*) стáроста *m*.

prefer /prɪ'fɜː(r)/ *vt* предпочитáть *impf*, предпочéсть *pf*. **preferable**

/ˈprefərəb(ə)l/ *adj* предпочти́тельный. **preference** /ˈprefərəns/ *n* предпочте́ние. **preferential** /ˌprefəˈrenʃ(ə)l/ *adj* предпочти́тельный.

prefix /ˈpriːfɪks/ *n* приста́вка.

pregnancy /ˈpregnənsɪ/ *n* бере́менность. **pregnant** /ˈpregnənt/ *adj* бере́менная.

prehistoric /ˌpriːhɪˈstɒrɪk/ *adj* доистори́ческий.

prejudice /ˈpredʒʊdɪs/ *n* предубежде́ние; (*detriment*) уще́рб; *vt* наноси́ть *impf*, нанести́ *pf* уще́рб+*dat*; **~ against** предубежда́ть *impf*, предубеди́ть *pf* про́тив+*gen*; **be ~d against** име́ть *impf* предубежде́ние про́тив +*gen*.

preliminary /prɪˈlɪmɪnərɪ/ *adj* предвари́тельный.

prelude /ˈpreljuːd/ *n* прелю́дия.

premarital /priːˈmærɪt(ə)l/ *adj* добра́чный.

premature /ˌpreməˈtjʊə(r)/ *adj* преждевре́менный.

premeditated /priːˈmedɪˌteɪtɪd/ *adj* преднаме́ренный.

premier /ˈpremɪə(r)/ *adj* пе́рвый; *n* премье́р-мини́стр. **première** /ˈpremɪˌeə(r)/ *n* премье́ра.

premise, premiss /ˈpremɪs/ *n* (*logic*) (пред)посы́лка. **premises** /ˈpremɪsɪz/ *n pl* помеще́ние.

premium /ˈpriːmɪəm/ *n* пре́мия.

premonition /ˌpreməˈnɪʃ(ə)n/ *n* предчу́вствие.

preoccupation /priːˌɒkjʊˈpeɪʃ(ə)n/ *n* озабо́ченность; (*absorbing subject*) забо́та. **preoccupied** /-ˈɒkjʊˌpaɪd/ *adj* озабо́ченный. **preoccupy** /-ˈɒkjʊˌpaɪ/ *vt* поглоща́ть *impf*, поглоти́ть *pf*.

preparation /ˌprepəˈreɪʃ(ə)n/ *n* приготовле́ние; *pl* подгото́вка (**for** к+*dat*); (*substance*) препара́т. **preparatory** /prɪˈpærətərɪ/ *adj* подготови́тельный. **prepare** /prɪˈpeə(r)/ *vt* & *i* при-, под-, гота́вливать(ся) *impf*, при-, под-, гото́вить(ся) *pf* (**for** к+*dat*). **prepared** /prɪˈpeəd/ *adj* гото́вый.

preponderance /prɪˈpɒndərəns/ *n* переве́с.

preposition /ˌprepəˈzɪʃ(ə)n/ *n* предло́г.

prepossessing /ˌpriːpəˈzesɪŋ/ *adj* привлека́тельный.

preposterous /prɪˈpɒstərəs/ *adj* неле́пый.

prerequisite /priːˈrekwɪzɪt/ *n* предпосы́лка.

prerogative /prɪˈrɒgətɪv/ *n* прерогати́ва.

presage /ˈpresɪdʒ/ *vt* предвеща́ть *impf*.

Presbyterian /ˌprezbɪˈtɪərɪən/ *n* пресвитериа́нин, -а́нка; *adj* пресвитериа́нский.

prescribe /prɪˈskraɪb/ *vt* предпи́сывать *impf*, предписа́ть *pf*; (*med*) пропи́сывать *impf*, прописа́ть *pf*. **prescription** /prɪˈskrɪpʃ(ə)n/ *n* (*med*) реце́пт.

presence /ˈprez(ə)ns/ *n* прису́тствие; **~ of mind** прису́тствие ду́ха. **present** /ˈprez(ə)nt/ *adj* прису́тствующий; (*being dealt with*) да́нный; (*existing now*) ны́нешний; (*also gram*) настоя́щий; *predic* налицо́; **be ~** прису́тствовать *impf* (**at** на+*prep*); **~-day** ны́нешний; *n*: **the ~** настоя́щее *sb*; (*gram*) настоя́щее вре́мя *neut*; (*gift*) пода́рок; **at ~** в настоя́щее вре́мя *neut*; **for the ~** пока́; *vt* (*introduce*) представля́ть *impf*, предста́вить *pf* (**to** +*dat*); (*award*) вруча́ть *impf*, вручи́ть *pf*; (*a play*) ста́вить *impf*, по~ *pf*; (*a gift*) преподноси́ть *impf*, преподнести́ *pf* +*dat* (**with** +*acc*); **~ o.s.** явля́ться *impf*, яви́ться *pf*. **presentable** /prɪˈzentəb(ə)l/ *adj* прили́чный. **presentation** /ˌprezənˈteɪʃ(ə)n/ *n* (*introducing*) представле́ние; (*awarding*) подноше́ние.

presentiment /prɪˈzentɪmənt/ *n* предчу́вствие.

presently /ˈprezəntlɪ/ *adv* вско́ре.

preservation /ˌprezəˈveɪʃ(ə)n/ *n* сохране́ние. **preservative** /prɪˈzɜːvətɪv/ *n* консерва́нт. **pre-**

serve /prɪ'zɜːv/ *vt* (*keep safe*) сохраня́ть *impf*, сохрани́ть *pf*; (*maintain*) храни́ть *impf*; (*food*) консерви́ровать *impf*, за~ *pf*; *n* (*for game etc*) запове́дник; (*jam*) варе́нье.

preside /prɪ'zaɪd/ *vi* председа́тельствовать *impf* (**at** на+*prep*). **presidency** /'prezɪdənsɪ/ *n* президе́нтство. **president** /'prezɪd(ə)nt/ *n* президе́нт. **presidential** /,prezɪ'denʃ(ə)l/ *adj* президе́нтский. **presidium** /prɪ'sɪdɪəm/ *n* прези́диум.

press /pres/ *n* (*machine*) пресс; (*printing firm*) типогра́фия; (*publishing house*) изда́тельство; (*the* ~) пре́сса, печа́ть; ~ **conference** пресс-конфере́нция; *vt* (*button etc*) нажима́ть *impf*, нажа́ть *pf*; (*clasp*) прижима́ть *impf*, прижа́ть *pf* (**to** к+*dat*); (*iron*) гла́дить *impf*, вы́~ *pf*; (*insist on*) наста́ивать *impf*, настоя́ть *pf* на+*prep*; (*urge*) угова́ривать *impf*; ~ **on** (*make haste*) потора́пливаться *impf*.

pressing /'presɪŋ/ *adj* неотло́жный. **pressure** /'preʃə(r)/ *n* давле́ние; ~**-cooker** скорова́рка; ~ **group** инициати́вная гру́ппа. **pressurize** /'preʃə,raɪz/ *vt* (*fig*) ока́зывать *impf*, оказа́ть *pf* давле́ние на+*acc*. **pressurized** /'preʃə,raɪzd/ *adj* гермети́ческий.

prestige /pre'stiːʒ/ *n* прести́ж. **prestigious** /pre'stɪdʒəs/ *adj* прести́жный.

presumably /prɪ'zjuːməblɪ/ *adv* предположи́тельно. **presume** /-'zjuːm/ *vt* полага́ть *impf*; (*venture*) позволя́ть *impf*, позво́лить *pf* себе́. **presumption** /-'zʌmpʃ(ə)n/ *n* предположе́ние; (*arrogance*) самонаде́янность. **presumptuous** /-'zʌmptjʊəs/ *adj* самонаде́янный.

presuppose /,priːsə'pəʊz/ *vt* предполага́ть *impf*.

pretence /prɪ'tens/ *n* притво́рство. **pretend** /-'tend/ *vt* притворя́ться *impf*, притвори́ться *pf* (**to be** +*instr*); де́лать *impf*, с~ *pf* вид (что); *vi*: ~ **to** претендова́ть *impf* на+*acc*. **pretender** /-'tendə(r)/ *n* претенде́нт. **pretension** /-'tenʃ(ə)n/ *n* прете́нзия. **pretentious** /-'tenʃəs/ *adj* претенцио́зный.

pretext /'priːtekst/ *n* предло́г.

prettiness /'prɪtɪnɪs/ *n* милови́дность. **pretty** /'prɪtɪ/ *adj* хоро́шенький; *adv* дово́льно.

prevail /prɪ'veɪl/ *vi* (*predominate*) преоблада́ть *impf*; ~ **(up)on** угова́ривать *impf*, уговори́ть *pf*. **prevalence** /'prevələns/ *n* распростране́ние. **prevalent** /'prevələnt/ *adj* распространённый.

prevaricate /prɪ'værɪ,keɪt/ *vi* увиливать *impf* увильну́ть *pf*.

prevent /prɪ'vent/ *vt* (*stop from happening*) предупрежда́ть *impf*, предупреди́ть *pf*; (*stop from doing*) меша́ть *impf*, по~ *pf* +*dat*. **prevention** /-'venʃ(ə)n/ *n* предупрежде́ние. **preventive** /-'ventɪv/ *adj* предупреди́тельный.

preview /'priːvjuː/ *n* предвари́тельный просмо́тр.

previous /'priːvɪəs/ *adj* предыду́щий; *adv*: ~ **to** до+*gen*; пре́жде чем +*inf*. **previously** /-lɪ/ *adv* ра́ньше.

pre-war /priː'wɔː(r)/ *adj* довое́нный.

prey /preɪ/ *n* (*animal*) добы́ча; (*victim*) же́ртва (**to** +*gen*); **bird of** ~ хи́щная пти́ца; *vi*: ~ **(up)on** (*emotion etc.*) му́чить *impf*.

price /praɪs/ *n* цена́; ~**-list** прейскура́нт; *vt* назнача́ть *impf*, назна́чить *pf* це́ну +*gen*. **priceless** /-lɪs/ *adj* бесце́нный.

prick /prɪk/ *vt* коло́ть *impf*, у~ *pf*; (*conscience*) му́чить *impf*; ~ **up one's ears** навостри́ть *pf* у́ши; *n* уко́л. **prickle** /'prɪk(ə)l/ *n* (*thorn*) колю́чка; (*spine*) игла́. **prickly** /-klɪ/ *adj* колю́чий.

pride /praɪd/ *n* го́рдость; ~ **o.s. on** горди́ться *impf* +*instr*.

priest /priːst/ *n* свяще́нник; (*non-Christian*) жрец.
prig /prɪg/ *n* педа́нт.
prim /prɪm/ *adj* чо́порный.
primarily /ˈpraɪmərɪlɪ/ *adv* первонача́льно; (*above all*) пре́жде всего́. **primary** /ˈpraɪmərɪ/ *adj* основно́й; ~ **school** нача́льная шко́ла. **prime** /praɪm/ *n*: **in one's** ~ в расцве́те сил; *adj* (*chief*) гла́вный; ~ **minister** премье́р-мини́стр; *vt* (*engine*) заправля́ть *impf*, запра́вить *pf*; (*bomb*) активизи́ровать *impf* & *pf*; (*with facts*) инструкти́ровать *impf* & *pf*; (*with paint etc.*) грунтова́ть *impf*, за~ *pf*. **primer** /ˈpraɪmə(r)/ *n* (*paint etc.*) грунт. **prim(a)eval** /praɪˈmiːv(ə)l/ *adj* первобы́тный. **primitive** /ˈprɪmɪtɪv/ *adj* первобы́тный; (*crude*) примити́вный. **primordial** /praɪˈmɔːdɪəl/ *adj* иско́нный.
primrose /ˈprɪmrəʊz/ *n* первоцве́т; (*colour*) бле́дно-жёлтый цвет.
prince /prɪns/ *n* принц; (*in Russia*) князь. **princely** /ˈprɪnslɪ/ *adj* кня́жеский; (*sum*) огро́мный. **princess** /ˈprɪnses/ *n* принце́сса; (*wife*) княги́ня; (*daughter*) княжна́.
principal /ˈprɪnsɪp(ə)l/ *n* гла́вный; *n* дире́ктор. **principality** /ˌprɪnsɪˈpælɪtɪ/ *n* кня́жество. **principally** /ˈprɪnsɪpəlɪ/ *adv* гла́вным о́бразом.
principle /ˈprɪnsɪp(ə)l/ *n* при́нцип; **in** ~ в при́нципе; **on** ~ принципиа́льно. **principled** /-p(ə)ld/ *adj* принципиа́льный.
print /prɪnt/ *n* (*mark*) след; (*also phot*) отпеча́ток; (*printing*) печа́ть; (*picture*) о́ттиск; **in** ~ в прода́же; **out of** ~ распро́данный; *vt* (*impress*) запечатлева́ть *impf*, запечатле́ть *pf*; (*book etc.*) печа́тать *impf*, на~ *pf*; (*write*) писа́ть *impf*, на~ *pf* печа́тными бу́квами; (*phot*; ~ *out*, *off*) отпеча́тывать *impf*, отпеча́тать *pf*; ~ **out** (*of computer etc.*) распеча́тывать *impf*, распеча́тать *pf*; ~**-out** распеча́тка. **printer** /-tə(r)/ *n* (*person*) печа́тник, типо́гаф; (*of computer*) при́нтер. **printing** /-tɪŋ/ *n* печа́тание; ~**-press** печа́тный стано́к.
prior /ˈpraɪə(r)/ *adj* пре́жний; *adv*: ~ **to** до+*gen*. **priority** /praɪˈɒrɪtɪ/ *n* приорите́т. **priory** /ˈpraɪərɪ/ *n* монасты́рь *m*.
prise /praɪz/ *vt*: ~ **open** взла́мывать *impf*, взлома́ть *pf*.
prism /ˈprɪz(ə)m/ *n* при́зма.
prison /ˈprɪz(ə)n/ *n* тюрьма́; *attrib* тюре́мный; ~ **camp** ла́герь *m*. **prisoner** /-nə(r)/ *n* заключённый *sb*; (~ *of war*) (военно)пле́нный *sb*.
pristine /ˈprɪstiːn/ *adj* нетро́нутый.
privacy /ˈprɪvəsɪ/ *n* уедине́ние; (*private life*) ча́стная жизнь. **private** /ˈpraɪvət/ *adj* (*personal*) ча́стный, ли́чный; (*confidential*) конфиденциа́льный; **in** ~ наедине́; в ча́стной жи́зни; *n* рядово́й *sb*.
privation /praɪˈveɪʃ(ə)n/ *n* лише́ние.
privilege /ˈprɪvɪlɪdʒ/ *n* привиле́гия. **privileged** /-lɪdʒd/ *adj* привилегиро́ванный.
privy /ˈprɪvɪ/ *adj*: ~ **to** посвящённый в+*acc*.
prize /praɪz/ *n* пре́мия, приз; ~**-winner** призёр; *vt* высоко́ цени́ть *impf*.
pro[1] /prəʊ/ *n*: ~**s and cons** до́воды *m pl* за и про́тив.
pro[2] /prəʊ/ *n* (*professional*) профессиона́л.
probability /ˌprɒbəˈbɪlɪtɪ/ *n* вероя́тность. **probable** /ˈprɒbəb(ə)l/ *adj* вероя́тный. **probably** /-blɪ/ *adv* вероя́тно.
probate /ˈprəʊbeɪt/ *n* утвержде́ние завеща́ния.
probation /prəˈbeɪʃ(ə)n/ *n* испыта́тельный срок; (*law*) усло́вный пригово́р; **got two years** ~ получи́л два го́да усло́вно. **probationary** /-nərɪ/ *adj* испыта́тельный.
probe /prəʊb/ *n* (*med*) зонд; (*fig*)

p

расслéдование; *vt* зондúровать *impf*; (*fig*) расслéдовать *impf* & *pf*.

probity /'prəʊbɪtɪ/ *n* чéстность.

problem /'prɒbləm/ *n* проблéма, вопрóс; (*math*) задáча. **problematic** /-'mætɪk/ *adj* проблематúчный.

procedural /prə'siːdjərəl/ *adj* процедýрный. **procedure** /-'siːdjə(r)/ *n* процедýра. **proceed** /-'siːd/ *vi* (*go further*) идтú *impf*, пойтú *pf* дáльше; (*act*) поступáть *impf*, поступúть *pf*; (*abs*, ~ *to say*; *continue*) продолжáть *impf*, продóлжить *pf*; (*of action*) продолжáться *impf*, продóлжиться *pf*; ~ **from** исходúть *impf*. из, от+*gen*; ~ **to** (*begin to*) принимáться *impf*, принятся *pf* +*inf*. **proceedings** /-'siːdɪŋz/ *n pl* (*activity*) дéятельность; (*legal* ~) судопроизвóдство; (*published report*) трудь́ *m pl*, запúски *f pl*. **proceeds** /'prəʊsiːdz/ *n pl* вы́ручка. **process** /'prəʊses/ *n* процéсс; *vt* обрабáтывать *impf*, обрабóтать *pf*. **procession** /prə'seʃ(ə)n/ *n* процéссия, шéствие.

P

proclaim /prə'kleɪm/ *vt* провозглашáть *impf*, провозгласúть *pf*. **proclamation** /ˌprɒklə'meɪʃ(ə)n/ *n* провозглашéние.

procure /prə'kjʊə(r)/ *vt* доставáть *impf*, достáть *pf*.

prod /prɒd/ *vt* ты́кать *impf*, ткнуть *pf*; *n* тычóк.

prodigal /'prɒdɪg(ə)l/ *adj* расточúтельный.

prodigious /prə'dɪdʒəs/ *adj* огрóмный. **prodigy** /'prɒdɪdʒɪ/ *n*: **child** ~ вундеркúнд.

produce *vt* /prə'djuːs/ (*evidence etc.*) представлять *impf*, предстáвить *pf*; (*ticket etc.*) предъявлять *impf*, предъявúть *pf*; (*play etc.*) стáвить *impf*, по~ *pf*; (*manufacture*; *cause*) производúть *impf*, произвестú *pf*; *n* /'prɒdjuːs/ (*collect*) продýкты *m pl*. **producer** /prə'djuːsə(r)/ *n* (*econ*) производúтель *m*; (*of play etc.*) режиссёр. **product** /'prɒdʌkt/ *n* продýкт; (*result*) результáт. **production** /prə'dʌkʃ(ə)n/ *n* произвóдство; (*of play etc.*) постанóвка. **productive** /prə'dʌktɪv/ *adj* продуктúвный; (*fruitful*) плодотвóрный. **productivity** /ˌprɒdʌk'tɪvɪtɪ/ *n* производúтельность.

profane /prə'feɪn/ *adj* свéтский; (*blasphemous*) богохýльный. **profanity** /-'fænɪtɪ/ *n* богохýльство.

profess /prə'fes/ *vt* (*pretend*) притворяться *impf*, притворúться *pf* (**to be** +*instr*); (*declare*) заявлять *impf*, заявúть *pf*; (*faith*) исповéдовать *impf*. **profession** /-'feʃ(ə)n/ *n* (*job*) профéссия. **professional** /-'feʃən(ə)l/ *adj* профессионáльный; *n* профессионáл. **professor** /-'fesə(r)/ *n* профéссор.

proffer /'prɒfə(r)/ *vt* предлагáть *impf*, предложúть *pf*.

proficiency /prə'fɪʃ(ə)nsɪ/ *n* умéние. **proficient** /-ʃ(ə)nt/ *adj* умéлый.

profile /'prəʊfaɪl/ *n* прóфиль *m*.

profit /'prɒfɪt/ *n* (*benefit*) пóльза; (*monetary*) прúбыль; *vt* приносúть *impf*, принестú *pf* пóльзу +*dat*; *vi*: ~ **from** пóльзоваться *impf*, вос~ *pf* +*instr*; (*financially*) получáть *impf*, получúть *pf* прúбыль на +*prep*. **profitable** /'prɒfɪtəb(ə)l/ *adj* (*lucrative*) прúбыльный; (*beneficial*) полéзный. **profiteering** /-'tɪərɪŋ/ *n* спекуляция.

profligate /'prɒflɪgət/ *adj* распýтный.

profound /prə'faʊnd/ *adj* глубóкий.

profuse /prə'fjuːs/ *adj* обúльный. **profusion** /-'fjuːʒ(ə)n/ *n* изобúлие.

progeny /'prɒdʒɪnɪ/ *n* потóмство.

prognosis /prɒg'nəʊsɪs/ *n* прогнóз.

program(me) /'prəʊgræm/ *n* прогрáмма; *vt* программúровать *impf*, за~ *pf*. **programmer**

/-mə(r)/ *n* программи́ст.
progress *n* /ˈprəʊgres/ прогре́сс; (*success*) успе́хи *m pl*; **make ~** де́лать *impf*, с~ *pf* успе́хи; *vi* /prəˈgres/ продвига́ться *impf*, продви́нуться *pf* вперёд. **progression** /prəˈgreʃ(ə)n/ *n* продвиже́ние. **progressive** /prəˈgresɪv/ *adj* прогресси́вный.
prohibit /prəˈhɪbɪt/ *vt* запреща́ть *impf*, запрети́ть *pf*. **prohibition** /ˌprəʊhɪˈbɪʃ(ə)n/ *n* запреще́ние; (*on alcohol*) сухо́й зако́н. **prohibitive** /prəʊˈhɪbɪtɪv/ *adj* запрети́тельный; (*price*) недосту́пный.
project *vt* /prəˈdʒekt/ (*plan*) проекти́ровать *impf*, с~ *pf*; (*a film*) демонстри́ровать *impf*, про~ *pf*; *vi* (*jut out*) выступа́ть *impf*; *n* /ˈprɒdʒekt/ прое́кт. **projectile** /prəˈdʒektaɪl/ *n* снаря́д. **projection** /prəˈdʒekʃ(ə)n/ *n* (*cin*) прое́кция; (*protrusion*) вы́ступ; (*forecast*) прогно́з. **projector** /prəˈdʒektə(r)/ *n* прое́ктор.
proletarian /ˌprəʊlɪˈteərɪən/ *adj* пролета́рский. **proletariat** /-rɪət/ *n* пролетариа́т.
proliferate /prəˈlɪfəˌreɪt/ *vi* распространя́ться *impf*, распространи́ться *pf*. **proliferation** /-ˈreɪʃ(ə)n/ *n* распростране́ние.
prolific /prəˈlɪfɪk/ *adj* плодови́тый.
prologue /ˈprəʊlɒg/ *n* проло́г.
prolong /prəˈlɒŋ/ *vt* продлева́ть *impf*, продли́ть *pf*.
promenade /ˌprɒməˈnɑːd/ *n* ме́сто для гуля́нья; (*at seaside*) на́бережная *sb*; *vi* прогу́ливаться *impf*, прогуля́ться *pf*.
prominence /ˈprɒmɪnəns/ *n* изве́стность. **prominent** /ˈprɒmɪnənt/ *adj* выступа́ющий; (*distinguished*) выдаю́щийся.
promiscuity /ˌprɒmɪˈskjuːɪtɪ/ *n* лёгкое поведе́ние. **promiscuous** /prəˈmɪskjʊəs/ *adj* лёгкого поведе́ния.
promise /ˈprɒmɪs/ *n* обеща́ние; *vt* обеща́ть *impf* & *pf*. **promising** /-sɪŋ/ *adj* многообеща́ющий.
promontory /ˈprɒməntərɪ/ *n* мыс.
promote /prəˈməʊt/ *vt* (*in rank*) продвига́ть *impf*, продви́нуть *pf*; (*assist*) спосо́бствовать *impf* & *pf* +*dat*; (*publicize*) реклами́ровать *impf*. **promoter** /-ˈməʊtə(r)/ *n* (*of event etc.*) аге́нт. **promotion** /-ˈməʊʃ(ə)n/ *n* (*in rank*) продвиже́ние; (*comm*) рекла́ма.
prompt /prɒmpt/ *adj* бы́стрый, неме́дленный; *adv* ро́вно; *vt* (*incite*) побужда́ть *impf*, побуди́ть *pf* (**to** к+*dat*; +*inf*); (*speaker*; *also fig*) подска́зывать *impf*, подсказа́ть *pf* +*dat*; (*theat*) суфли́ровать *impf* +*dat*; *n* подска́зка. **prompter** /-tə(r)/ *n* суфлёр.
prone /prəʊn/ *adj* (лежа́щий) ничко́м; *predic*: **~ to** скло́нен (-онна́, -о́нно) к+*dat*.
prong /prɒŋ/ *n* зубе́ц.
pronoun /ˈprəʊnaʊn/ *n* местоиме́ние.
pronounce /prəˈnaʊns/ *vt* (*declare*) объявля́ть *impf*, объяви́ть *pf*; (*articulate*) произноси́ть *impf*, произнести́ *pf*. **pronounced** /-ˈnaʊnst/ *adj* я́вный; заме́тный. **pronouncement** /-ˈnaʊnsmənt/ *n* заявле́ние. **pronunciation** /prəˌnʌnsɪˈeɪʃ(ə)n/ *n* произноше́ние.
proof /pruːf/ *n* доказа́тельство; (*printing*) корректу́ра; **~-reader** корре́ктор; *adj* (*impenetrable*) непроница́емый (**against** для+*gen*); (*not yielding*) неподдаю́щийся (**against** +*dat*).
prop[1] /prɒp/ *n* (*support*) подпо́рка; (*fig*) опо́ра; *vt* (**~** *open*, *up*) подпира́ть *impf*, подпере́ть *pf*; (*fig*) подде́рживать *impf*, поддержа́ть *pf*.
prop[2] /prɒp/ *n* (*theat*) *see* **props**
propaganda /ˌprɒpəˈgændə/ *n* пропага́нда.
propagate /ˈprɒpəˌgeɪt/ *vt* & *i* размножа́ть(ся) *impf*, размно́жить(ся) *pf*; (*disseminate*) распространя́ть(ся) *impf*, распространи́ть(ся) *pf*. **propagation** /-ˈgeɪʃ(ə)n/ *n* размноже́-

P

ние; распространéние.

propel /prə'pel/ *vt* приводи́ть *impf*, привести́ *pf* в движéние. **propeller** /-'pelə(r)/ *n* винт.

propensity /prə'pensɪtɪ/ *n* наклóнность (**to** к+*dat*; +*inf*).

proper /'prɒpə(r)/ *adj* (*correct*) прáвильный; (*suitable*) подходя́щий; (*decent*) пристóйный; ~ **noun** и́мя сóбственное. **properly** /'prɒpəlɪ/ *adv* как слéдует.

property /'prɒpətɪ/ *n* (*possessions*) сóбственность, иму́щество; (*attribute*) свóйство; *pl* (*theat*) реквизи́т.

prophecy /'prɒfɪsɪ/ *n* прорóчество. **prophesy** /'prɒfɪˌsaɪ/ *vt* прорóчить *impf*, на~ *pf*. **prophet** /'prɒfɪt/ *n* прорóк. **prophetic** /prə'fetɪk/ *adj* прорóческий.

propitious /prə'pɪʃəs/ *adj* благоприя́тный.

proponent /prə'pəʊnənt/ *n* сторóнник.

proportion /prə'pɔːʃ(ə)n/ *n* прорóрция; (*due relation*) соразмéрность; *pl* размéры *m pl*. **proportional** /-n(ə)l/ *adj* пропорционáльный. **proportionate** /-'pɔːʃən(ə)t/ *adj* соразмéрный (**to** +*dat*; с+*instr*).

proposal /prə'pəʊz(ə)l/ *n* предложéние. **propose** /-'pəʊz/ *vt* предлагáть *impf*, предложи́ть *pf*; (*intend*) предполагáть *impf*; *vi* (~ *marriage*) дéлать *impf*, с~ *pf* предложéние (**to** +*dat*). **proposition** /ˌprɒpə'zɪʃ(ə)n/ *n* предложéние.

propound /prə'paʊnd/ *vt* предлагáть *impf*, предложи́ть *pf* на обсуждéние.

proprietor /prə'praɪətə(r)/ *n* сóбственник, хозя́ин.

propriety /prə'praɪɪtɪ/ *n* прили́чие.

props /prɒps/ *n pl* (*theat*) реквизи́т.

propulsion /prə'pʌlʃ(ə)n/ *n* движéние вперёд.

prosaic /prə'zeɪɪk/ *adj* прозаи́ческий.

proscribe /prə'skraɪb/ *vt* (*forbid*) запрещáть *impf*, запрети́ть *pf*.

prose /prəʊz/ *n* прóза.

prosecute /'prɒsɪˌkjuːt/ *vt* преслéдовать *impf*. **prosecution** /-'kjuːʃ(ə)n/ *n* судéбное преслéдование; (*prosecuting party*) обвинéние. **prosecutor** /'prɒsəˌkjuːtə(r)/ *n* обвини́тель *m*.

prospect *n* /'prɒspekt/ вид; (*fig*) перспекти́ва; *vi*: /prə'spekt/ ~ **for** искáть *impf*. **prospective** /prə'spektɪv/ *adj* бу́дущий. **prospector** /prə'spektə(r)/ *n* развéдчик. **prospectus** /prə'spektəs/ *n* проспéкт.

prosper /'prɒspə(r)/ *vi* процветáть *impf*. **prosperity** /prɒ'sperɪtɪ/ *n* процветáние. **prosperous** /'prɒspərəs/ *adj* процветáющий; (*wealthy*) зажи́точный.

prostate (gland) /'prɒsteɪt (glænd)/ *n* простáта.

prostitute /'prɒstɪˌtjuːt/ *n* проститу́тка. **prostitution** /-'tjuːʃ(ə)n/ *n* проститу́ция.

prostrate /'prɒstreɪt/ *adj* распростёртый, (лежáщий) ничкóм; (*exhausted*) обесси́ленный; (*with grief*) уби́тый (**with** +*instr*).

protagonist /prəʊ'tægənɪst/ *n* глáвный герóй; (*in contest*) протагони́ст.

protect /prə'tekt/ *vt* защищáть *impf*, защити́ть. **protection** /-'tekʃ(ə)n/ *n* защи́та. **protective** /-'tektɪv/ *adj* защи́тный. **protector** /-'tektə(r)/ *n* защи́тник.

protégé(e) /'prɒtɪˌʒeɪ/ *n* протежé *m* & *f indecl*.

protein /'prəʊtiːn/ *n* белóк.

protest *n* /'prəʊtest/ протéст; *vi* /prə'test/ протестовáть *impf*; *vt* (*affirm*) утверждáть *impf*.

Protestant /'prɒtɪst(ə)nt/ *n* протестáнт, ~ка; *adj* протестáнтский.

protestation /ˌprɒtɪ'steɪʃ(ə)n/ *n* (торжéственное) заявлéние (о+*prep*; что); (*protest*) протéст.

protocol /ˌprəʊtə'kɒl/ *n* протокóл.

proton /'prəʊtɒn/ *n* протóн.

prototype /'prəʊtəˌtaɪp/ *n* прототи́п.

P

protract /prə'trækt/ *vt* тяну́ть *impf.* **protracted** /-'træktɪd/ *adj* дли́тельный.

protrude /prə'truːd/ *vi* выдава́ться *impf*, вы́даться *pf.*

proud /praʊd/ *adj* го́рдый; **be ~ of** горди́ться *impf +instr.*

prove /pruːv/ *vt* дока́зывать *impf*, доказа́ть *pf*; *vi* ока́зываться *impf*, оказа́ться *pf* (**to be** *+instr*). **proven** /'pruːv(ə)n/ *adj* дока́занный.

provenance /'prɒvɪnəns/ *n* происхожде́ние.

proverb /'prɒvɜːb/ *n* посло́вица. **proverbial** /prə'vɜːbɪəl/ *adj* воше́дший в погово́рку; (*well-known*) общеизве́стный.

provide /prə'vaɪd/ *vt* (*supply person*) снабжа́ть *impf*, снабди́ть *pf* (**with** *+instr*); (*supply thing*) предоставля́ть *impf*, предоста́вить *pf* (**to, for** *+dat*); дава́ть *impf*, дать *pf* (**to, for** *+dat*); *vi*: **~ for** предусма́тривать *impf*, предусмотре́ть *pf +acc*; (**~** *for family etc.*) содержа́ть *impf +acc.* **provided (that)** /-'vaɪdɪd/ *conj* при усло́вии, что; е́сли то́лько. **providence** /'prɒvɪd(ə)ns/ *n* провиде́ние; (*foresight*) предусмотри́тельность. **provident** /'prɒvɪd(ə)nt/ *adj* предусмотри́тельный. **providential** /-'denʃ(ə)l/ *adj* счастли́вый. **providing** /prə'vaɪdɪŋ/ *see* **provided (that)**

province /'prɒvɪns/ *n* о́бласть; *pl* (*the* **~**) прови́нция. **provincial** /prə'vɪnʃ(ə)l/ *adj* провинциа́льный.

provision /prə'vɪʒ(ə)n/ *n* снабже́ние; *pl* (*food*) прови́зия; (*in agreement etc.*) положе́ние; **make ~ against** принима́ть *impf*, приня́ть *pf* ме́ры про́тив*+gen.* **provisional** /-'vɪʒən(ə)l/ *adj* вре́менный. **proviso** /-'vaɪzəʊ/ *n* усло́вие.

provocation /ˌprɒvə'keɪʃ(ə)n/ *n* провока́ция. **provocative** /prə'vɒkətɪv/ *adj* провокацио́нный. **provoke** /prə'vəʊk/ *vt* провоци́ровать *impf*, с**~** *pf*; (*call forth, cause*) вызыва́ть *impf*, вы́звать *pf.*

prow /praʊ/ *n* нос.

prowess /'praʊɪs/ *n* уме́ние.

prowl /praʊl/ *vi* ры́скать *impf.*

proximity /prɒk'sɪmɪtɪ/ *n* бли́зость.

proxy /'prɒksɪ/ *n* полномо́чие; (*person*) уполномо́ченный *sb*, замести́тель *m*; **by ~** по дове́ренности; **stand ~ for** быть *impf* замести́телем *+gen.*

prudence /'pruːd(ə)ns/ *n* благоразу́мие. **prudent** /-d(ə)nt/ *adj* благоразу́мный.

prudery /'pruːdərɪ/ *n* притво́рная стыдли́вость. **prudish** /-dɪʃ/ *adj* ни в ме́ру стыдли́вый.

prune[1] /pruːn/ *n* (*plum*) черносли́в.

prune[2] /pruːn/ *vt* (*trim*) об-, под-, реза́ть *impf*, об-, под-, ре́зать *pf.*

pry /praɪ/ *vi* сова́ть *impf* нос (**into** в*+acc*).

PS *abbr* (*of* **postscript**) постскри́птум.

psalm /sɑːm/ *n* псало́м.

pseudonym /'sjuːdənɪm/ *n* псевдони́м.

psyche /'saɪkɪ/ *n* пси́хика. **psychiatric** /ˌsaɪkɪ'ætrɪk/ *adj* психиатри́ческий. **psychiatrist** /saɪ'kaɪətrɪst/ *n* психиа́тр. **psychiatry** /saɪ'kaɪətrɪ/ *n* психиатри́я. **psychic** /'saɪkɪk/ *adj* ясновидя́щий. **psychoanalysis** /ˌsaɪkəʊə'nælɪsɪs/ *n* психоана́лиз. **psychoanalyst** /ˌsaɪkəʊ'ænəlɪst/ *n* психоанали́тик. **psychoanalytic(al)** /ˌsaɪkəʊˌænə'lɪtɪk((ə)l)/ *adj* психоаналити́ческий. **psychological** /ˌsaɪkə'lɒdʒɪk(ə)l/ *adj* психологи́ческий. **psychologist** /saɪ'kɒlədʒɪst/ *n* психо́лог. **psychology** /saɪ'kɒlədʒɪ/ *n* психоло́гия. **psychopath** /'saɪkəˌpæθ/ *n* психопа́т. **psychopathic** /ˌsaɪkə'pæθɪk/ *adj* психопати́ческий. **psychosis** /saɪ'kəʊsɪs/ *n* психо́з. **psychotherapy** /ˌsaɪkəʊ'θerəpɪ/ *n* психотерапи́я.

PTO *abbr* (*of* **please turn over**) см.

на об., смотри́ на оборо́те.
pub /pʌb/ *n* пивна́я *sb.*
puberty /ˈpjuːbətɪ/ *n* полова́я зре́лость.
public /ˈpʌblɪk/ *adj* обще́ственный; (*open*) публи́чный, откры́тый; ~ **school** ча́стная сре́дняя шко́ла; *n* пу́блика, обще́ственность; **in** ~ откры́то, публи́чно. **publication** /-ˈkeɪʃ(ə)n/ *n* изда́ние. **publicity** /-ˈlɪsɪtɪ/ *n* рекла́ма. **publicize** /ˈpʌblɪˌsaɪz/ *vt* реклами́ровать *impf & pf.* **publicly** /pʌbˈlɪsɪtɪ/ *adv* публи́чно, откры́то. **publish** /ˈpʌblɪʃ/ *vt* публикова́ть *impf*, о~ *pf*; (*book*) издава́ть *impf*, изда́ть *pf.* **publisher** /ˈpʌblɪʃə(r)/ *n* изда́тель *m.* **publishing** /ˈpʌblɪʃɪŋ/ *n* (*business*) изда́тельское де́ло; ~ **house** изда́тельство.
pucker /ˈpʌkə(r)/ *vt & i* мо́рщить(ся) *impf*, с~ *pf.*
pudding /ˈpʊdɪŋ/ *n* пу́динг, запека́нка; (*dessert*) сла́дкое *sb.*
puddle /ˈpʌd(ə)l/ *n* лу́жа.
puff /pʌf/ *n* (*of wind*) поры́в; (*of smoke*) дымо́к; ~ **pastry** слоёное те́сто; *vi* пыхте́ть *impf*; ~ **at** (*pipe etc.*) попы́хивать *impf* +*instr*; *vt*: ~ **up, out** (*inflate*) надува́ть *impf*, наду́ть *pf.*
pugnacious /pʌgˈneɪʃəs/ *adj* драчли́вый.
puke /pjuːk/ *vi* рвать *impf*, вы~ *pf impers*+*acc*.
pull /pʊl/ *vt* тяну́ть *impf*, по~ *pf*; таска́ть *indet*, тащи́ть *det*, по~ *pf*; (*a muscle*) растя́гивать *impf*, растяну́ть *pf*; *vt & i* дёргать *impf*, дёрнуть *pf* (**at** (за)+*acc*); ~ **s.o's leg** разы́грывать *impf*, разыгра́ть *pf*; ~ **the trigger** спуска́ть *impf*, спусти́ть *pf* куро́к; ~ **apart, to pieces** разрыва́ть *impf*, разорва́ть *pf*; (*fig*) раскритикова́ть *pf*; ~ **down** (*demolish*) сноси́ть *impf*, снести́ *pf*; ~ **in** (*of train*) прибыва́ть *impf*, прибы́ть *pf*; (*of vehicle*) подъезжа́ть *impf*, подъе́хать *pf* к обо́чине (доро́ги); ~ **off** (*garment*) стя́гивать *impf*, стяну́ть *pf*; (*achieve*) успе́шно заверша́ть *impf*, заверши́ть *pf*; ~ **on** (*garment*) натя́гивать *impf*, натяну́ть *pf*; ~ **out** (*vt*) (*remove*) вытаскивать *impf*, вы́тащить *pf*; (*vi*) (*withdraw*) отка́зываться *impf*, отказа́ться *pf* от уча́стия (**of** в+*prep*); (*of vehicle*) отъезжа́ть *impf*, отъе́хать *pf* от обо́чины (доро́ги); (*of train*) отходи́ть *impf*, отойти́ *pf* (от ста́нции); ~ **through** выжива́ть *impf*, вы́жить *pf*; ~ **o.s. together** брать *impf*, взять *pf* себя́ в ру́ки; ~ **up** (*vt*) подтя́гивать *impf*, подтяну́ть *pf*; (*vt & i*) (*stop*) остана́вливать(ся) *impf*, останови́ть(ся) *pf*; *n* тя́га; (*fig*) блат.
pulley /ˈpʊlɪ/ *n* блок.
pullover /ˈpʊləʊvə(r)/ *n* пуло́вер.
pulp /pʌlp/ *n* пу́льпа.
pulpit /ˈpʊlpɪt/ *n* ка́федра.
pulsate /pʌlˈseɪt/ *vi* пульси́ровать *impf.* **pulse** /pʌls/ *n* пульс.
pulses /ˈpʌlsɪz/ *n pl* (*food*) бобо́вые *sb.*
pulverize /ˈpʌlvəˌraɪz/ *vt* размельча́ть *impf*, размельчи́ть *pf.*
pummel /ˈpʌm(ə)l/ *vt* колоти́ть *impf*, по~ *pf.*
pump /pʌmp/ *n* насо́с; *vt* кача́ть *impf*; ~ **in(to)** вка́чивать *impf*, вкача́ть *pf*; ~ **out** выка́чивать *impf*, вы́качать *pf*; ~ **up** нака́чивать *impf*, накача́ть *pf.*
pumpkin /ˈpʌmpkɪn/ *n* ты́ква.
pun /pʌn/ *n* каламбу́р.
punch[1] /pʌntʃ/ *vt* (*with fist*) ударя́ть *impf*, уда́рить *pf* кулако́м; (*hole*) пробива́ть *impf*, проби́ть *pf*; (*a ticket*) компости́ровать *impf*, про~ *pf*; ~**-up** дра́ка; *n* (*blow*) уда́р кулако́м; (*for tickets*) компо́стер; (*for piercing*) перфора́тор.
punch[2] /pʌntʃ/ *n* (*drink*) пунш.
punctilious /pʌŋkˈtɪlɪəs/ *adj* щепети́льный.
punctual /ˈpʌŋktjʊəl/ *adj* пунктуа́льный. **punctuality** /ˌpʌŋktjʊˈælɪtɪ/ *n* пунктуа́льность.

punctuate /ˈpʌŋktjʊˌeɪt/ *vt* ста́вить *impf*, по~ *pf* зна́ки препина́ния в+*acc*; (*fig*) прерыва́ть *impf*, прерва́ть *pf*. **punctuation** /-ˈeɪʃ(ə)n/ *n* пунктуа́ция; **~ marks** зна́ки *m pl* препина́ния.

puncture /ˈpʌŋktʃə(r)/ *n* проко́л; *vt* прока́лывать *impf*, проколо́ть *pf*.

pundit /ˈpʌndɪt/ *n* (*fig*) знато́к.

pungent /ˈpʌndʒ(ə)nt/ *adj* е́дкий.

punish /ˈpʌnɪʃ/ *vt* нака́зывать *impf*, наказа́ть *pf*. **punishable** /-ʃəb(ə)l/ *adj* наказу́емый. **punishment** /-mənt/ *n* наказа́ние. **punitive** /ˈpju:nɪtɪv/ *adj* кара́тельный.

punter /ˈpʌntə(r)/ *n* (*gambler*) игро́к; (*client*) клие́нт.

puny /ˈpju:nɪ/ *adj* хи́лый.

pupil /ˈpju:pɪl/ *n* учени́к, -и́ца; (*of eye*) зрачо́к.

puppet /ˈpʌpɪt/ *n* марионе́тка, ку́кла.

puppy /ˈpʌpɪ/ *n* щено́к.

purchase /ˈpɜ:tʃɪs/ *n* поку́пка; (*leverage*) то́чка опо́ры; *vt* покупа́ть *impf*, купи́ть *pf*. **purchaser** /-sə(r)/ *n* покупа́тель *m*.

pure /pjʊə(r)/ *adj* чи́стый.

purée /ˈpjʊəreɪ/ *n* пюре́ *neut indecl*.

purely /ˈpjʊəlɪ/ *adv* чи́сто.

purgatory /ˈpɜ:gətərɪ/ *n* чисти́лище; (*fig*) ад. **purge** /pɜ:dʒ/ *vt* очища́ть *impf*, очи́стить *pf*; *n* очище́ние; (*polit*) чи́стка.

purification /ˌpjʊərɪfɪˈkeɪʃ(ə)n/ *n* очи́стка. **purify** /ˈpjʊərɪˌfaɪ/ *vt* очища́ть *impf*, очи́стить *pf*.

purist /ˈpjʊərɪst/ *n* пури́ст.

puritan, P., /ˈpjʊərɪt(ə)n/ *n* пурита́нин, -а́нка. **puritanical** /-ˈtænɪk(ə)l/ *adj* пурита́нский.

purity /ˈpjʊərɪtɪ/ *n* чистота́.

purple /ˈpɜ:p(ə)l/ *adj* (*n*) пу́рпу́рный, фиоле́товый (цвет).

purport /pəˈpɔ:t/ *vt* претендова́ть *impf*.

purpose /ˈpɜ:pəs/ *n* цель, намере́ние; **on ~** наро́чно; **to no ~** напра́сно. **purposeful** /-fʊl/ *adj* целеустремлённый. **purposeless** /-lɪs/ *adj* бесце́льный. **purposely** /-lɪ/ *adv* наро́чно.

purr /pɜ:(r)/ *vi* мурлы́кать *impf*.

purse /pɜ:s/ *n* кошелёк; *vt* поджима́ть *impf*, поджа́ть *pf*.

pursue /pəˈsju:/ *vt* пресле́довать *impf*. **pursuit** /-ˈsju:t/ *n* пресле́дование; (*pastime*) заня́тие.

purveyor /pəˈveɪə(r)/ *n* поставщи́к.

pus /pʌs/ *n* гной.

push /pʊʃ/ *vt* толка́ть *impf*, толкну́ть *pf*; (*press*) нажима́ть *impf*, нажа́ть *pf*; (*urge*) подта́лкивать *impf*, подтолкну́ть *pf*; *vi* толка́ться *impf*; **be ~ed for** име́ть *impf* ма́ло+*gen*; **he is ~ing fifty** ему́ ско́ро сту́кнет пятьдеся́т; **~ one's way** прота́лкиваться *impf*, протолкну́ться *pf*; **~ around** (*person*) помыка́ть *impf* +*instr*; **~ aside** (*also fig*) отстраня́ть *impf*, отстрани́ть *pf*; **~ away** отта́лкивать *impf*, оттолкну́ть *pf*; **~ off** (*vi*) (*in boat*) отта́лкиваться *impf*, оттолкну́ться *pf* (от бе́рега); (*go away*) убира́ться *impf*, убра́ться *pf*; **~ on** (*vi*) продолжа́ть *impf* путь; *n* толчо́к; (*energy*) эне́ргия. **pushchair** *n* коля́ска. **pusher** /-ʃə(r)/ *n* (*drugs*) продаве́ц нарко́тиков. **pushy** /-ʃɪ/ *adj* напо́ристый.

puss, pussy(-cat) /pʊs, ˈpʊsɪ(kæt)/ *n* ки́ска.

put /pʊt/ *vt* класть *impf*, положи́ть *pf*; (*upright*) ста́вить *impf*, по~ *pf*; помеща́ть *impf*, помести́ть *pf*; (*into specified state*) приводи́ть *impf*, привести́ *pf*; (*express*) выража́ть *impf*, вы́разить *pf*; (*a question*) задава́ть *impf*, зада́ть *pf*; **~ an end, a stop, to** класть *impf*, положи́ть *pf* коне́ц +*dat*; **~ o.s. in another's place** ста́вить *impf*, по~ *pf* себя́ на ме́сто +*gen*; **~ about** (*rumour etc.*) распространя́ть *impf*, распространи́ть *pf*; **~ away** (*tidy*) убира́ть *impf*, убра́ть *pf*; (*save*) откла́дывать *impf*, отложи́ть *pf*; **~ back** (*in place*) ста́вить *impf*, по~ *pf* на ме́сто; (*clock*) перево-

P

ди́ть *impf*, перевести́ *pf* наза́д; **~ by** (*money*) откла́дывать *impf*, отложи́ть *pf*; **~ down** класть *impf*, положи́ть *pf*; (*suppress*) подавля́ть *impf*, подави́ть *pf*; (*write down*) запи́сывать *impf*, записа́ть *pf*; (*passengers*) выса́живать *impf*, вы́садить *pf*; (*attribute*) припи́сывать *impf*, приписа́ть *pf* (**to** +*dat*); **~ forward** (*proposal*) предлага́ть *impf*, предложи́ть *pf*; (*clock*) переводи́ть *impf*, перевести́ *pf* вперёд; **~ in** (*install*) устана́вливать *impf*, установи́ть *pf*; (*a claim*) предъявля́ть *impf*, предъяви́ть *pf*; (*interpose*) вставля́ть *impf*, вста́вить *pf*; **~ in an appearance** появля́ться *impf*, появи́ться *pf*; **~ off** (*postpone*) откла́дывать *impf*, отложи́ть *pf*; (*repel*) отта́лкивать *impf*, оттолкну́ть *pf*; (*dissuade*) отгова́ривать *impf*, отговори́ть *pf* от+*gen*, +*inf*; **~ on** (*clothes*) надева́ть *impf*, наде́ть *pf*; (*kettle, a record, a play*) ста́вить *impf*, по~ *pf*; (*turn on*) включа́ть *impf*, включи́ть *pf*; (*add to*) прибавля́ть *impf*, приба́вить *pf*; **~ on airs** ва́жничать *impf*; **~ on weight** толсте́ть *impf*, по~ *pf*; **~ out** (*vex*) обижа́ть *impf*, оби́деть *pf*; (*inconvenience*) затрудня́ть *impf*, затрудни́ть *pf*; (*a fire etc.*) туши́ть *impf*, по~ *pf*; **~ through** (*tel*) соединя́ть *impf*, соедини́ть *pf* по телефо́ну; **~ up** (*building*) стро́ить *impf*, по~ *pf*; (*hang up*) ве́шать *impf*, пове́сить *pf*; (*price*) повыша́ть *impf*, повы́сить *pf*; (*a guest*) дава́ть *impf*, дать *pf* ночле́г +*dat*; (*as guest*) ночева́ть *impf*, пере~ *pf*; **~ up to** (*instigate*) подбива́ть *impf*, подби́ть *pf* на+*acc*; **~ up with** терпе́ть *impf*.

putative /ˈpjuːtətɪv/ *adj* предполага́емый.

putrefy /ˈpjuːtrɪˌfaɪ/ *vi* гнить *impf*, с~ *pf*. **putrid** /ˈpjuːtrɪd/ *adj* гнило́й.

putty /ˈpʌtɪ/ *n* зама́зка.

puzzle /ˈpʌz(ə)l/ *n* (*enigma*) зага́дка; (*toy etc.*) головоло́мка; (*jigsaw*) моза́ика; *vt* озада́чивать *impf*, озада́чить *pf*; **~ out** разгада́ть *pf*; *vi*: **~ over** лома́ть *impf* себе́ го́лову над+*instr*.

pygmy /ˈpɪgmɪ/ *n* пигме́й.

pyjamas /pɪˈdʒɑːməz/ *n pl* пижа́ма.

pylon /ˈpaɪlən/ *n* пило́н.

pyramid /ˈpɪrəmɪd/ *n* пирами́да.

pyre /ˈpaɪə(r)/ *n* погреба́льный костёр.

python /ˈpaɪθ(ə)n/ *n* пито́н.

Q

quack[1] /kwæk/ *n* (*sound*) кря́канье; *vi* кря́кать *impf*, кря́кнуть *pf*.

quack[2] /kwæk/ *n* шарлата́н.

quad /kwɒd/ *n* (*court*) четырёхуго́льный двор; *pl* (*quadruplets*) че́тверо близнецо́в. **quadrangle** /ˈkwɒdˌræŋg(ə)l/ *n* (*figure*) четырёхуго́льник; (*court*) четырёхуго́льный двор. **quadrant** /ˈkwɒdrənt/ *n* квадра́нт.

quadruped /ˈkwɒdrʊˌped/ *n* четвероно́гое живо́тное *sb*. **quadruple** /ˈkwɒdrʊp(ə)l/ *adj* четверно́й; *vt & i* учетверя́ть(ся) *impf*, учетвери́ть(ся) *pf*. **quadruplets** /ˈkwɒdrʊplɪts/ *n pl* че́тверо близнецо́в.

quagmire /ˈkwɒgˌmaɪə(r)/ *n* боло́то.

quail /kweɪl/ *n* (*bird*) пе́репел.

quaint /kweɪnt/ *adj* причу́дливый.

quake /kweɪk/ *vi* дрожа́ть *impf* (**with** от+*gen*).

Quaker /ˈkweɪkə(r)/ *n* ква́кер, ~ка.

qualification /ˌkwɒlɪfɪˈkeɪʃ(ə)n/ *n* (*for post etc.*) квалифика́ция; (*reservation*) огово́рка. **qualified** /ˈkwɒlɪˌfaɪd/ *adj* компете́нтный; (*limited*) ограни́ченный. **qualify** /ˈkwɒlɪˌfaɪ/ *vt & i* (*prepare for job*) гото́вить(ся) *impf* (**for** к+*dat*; +*inf*); *vt* (*render fit*) де́лать *impf*, с~ *pf* приго́дным; (*entitle*) дава́ть *impf*, дать *pf* пра́во +*dat* (**to**

на+*acc*); (*limit*): **~ what one says** сде́лать *pf* огово́рку; *vi* получа́ть *impf*, получи́ть *pf* дипло́м; **~ for** (*be entitled to*) име́ть *impf* пра́во на+*acc*.

qualitative /'kwɒlɪtətɪv/ *adj* ка́чественный. **quality** /'kwɒlɪtɪ/ *n* ка́чество.

qualm /kwɑːm/ *n* сомне́ние; (*of conscience*) угрызе́ние со́вести.

quandary /'kwɒndərɪ/ *n* затрудни́тельное положе́ние.

quantify /'kwɒntɪˌfaɪ/ *vt* определя́ть *impf*, определи́ть *pf* коли́чество +*gen*. **quantitative** /'kwɒntɪtətɪv/ *adj* коли́чественный. **quantity** /'kwɒntɪtɪ/ *n* коли́чество.

quarantine /'kwɒrənˌtiːn/ *n* каранти́н.

quarrel /'kwɒr(ə)l/ *n* ссо́ра; *vi* ссо́риться *impf*, по~ *pf* (**with** с+*instr*; **about, for** из-за+*gen*). **quarrelsome** /-səm/ *adj* вздо́рный.

quarry[1] /'kwɒrɪ/ *n* (*for stone etc.*) каменоло́мня; *vt* добыва́ть *impf*, добы́ть *pf*.

quarry[2] /'kwɒrɪ/ *n* (*prey*) добы́ча.

quart /kwɔːt/ *n* ква́рта. **quarter** /'kwɔːtə(r)/ *n* че́тверть; (*of year*; *of town*) кварта́л; *pl* кварти́ры *f pl*; **a ~ to one** без че́тверти час; **~-final** четверть-фина́л; *vt* (*divide*) дели́ть *impf*, раз~ *pf* на четы́ре ча́сти; (*lodge*) расквартиро́вывать *impf*, расквартирова́ть *pf*. **quarterly** /'kwɔːtəlɪ/ *adj* кварта́льный; *adv* раз в кварта́л. **quartet** /kwɔː'tet/ *n* кварте́т.

quartz /kwɔːts/ *n* кварц.

quash /kwɒʃ/ *vt* (*annul*) аннули́ровать *impf* & *pf*; (*crush*) подавля́ть *impf*, подави́ть *pf*.

quasi- /'kweɪzaɪ/ *in comb* квази-.

quaver /'kweɪvə(r)/ *vi* дрожа́ть *impf*; *n* (*mus*) восьма́я *sb* но́ты.

quay /kiː/ *n* на́бережная *sb*.

queasy /'kwiːzɪ/ *adj*: **I feel ~** меня́ тошни́т.

queen /kwiːn/ *n* короле́ва; (*cards*) да́ма; (*chess*) ферзь *m*.

queer /kwɪə(r)/ *adj* стра́нный.

quell /kwel/ *vt* подавля́ть *impf*, подави́ть *pf*.

quench /kwentʃ/ *vt* (*thirst*) утоля́ть *impf*, утоли́ть *pf*; (*fire, desire*) туши́ть *impf*, по~ *pf*.

query /'kwɪərɪ/ *n* вопро́с; *vt* (*express doubt*) выража́ть *impf* вы́разить *pf* сомне́ние в+*prep*. **quest** /kwest/ *n* по́иски *m pl*; **in ~ of** в по́исках+*gen*. **question** /'kwestʃ(ə)n/ *n* вопро́с; **beyond ~** вне сомне́ния; **it is a ~ of** э́то вопро́с+*gen*; **it is out of the ~** об э́том не мо́жет быть и ре́чи; **the person in ~** челове́к, о кото́ром идёт речь; **the ~ is this** де́ло в э́том; **~ mark** вопроси́тельный знак; *vt* расспра́шивать *impf*, распроси́ть *pf*; (*interrogate*) допра́шивать *impf* допроси́ть *pf*; (*doubt*) сомнева́ться *impf* в+*prep*. **questionable** /'kwestʃənəb(ə)l/ *adj* сомни́тельный. **questionnaire** /ˌkwestʃə'neə(r)/ *n* вопро́сник.

queue /kjuː/ *n* о́чередь; *vi* стоя́ть *impf* в о́череди.

quibble /'kwɪb(ə)l/ *n* софи́зм; (*minor criticism*) приди́рка; *vi* придира́ться *impf*; (*argue*) спо́рить *impf*.

quick /kwɪk/ *adj* ско́рый, бы́стрый; **~-tempered** вспы́льчивый; **~-witted** нахо́дчивый; *n*: **to the ~** за живо́е; *adv* ско́ро, бы́стро; *as imper* скоре́е! **quicken** /'kwɪkən/ *vt* & *i* ускоря́ть(ся) *impf*, уско́рить(ся) *pf*. **quickness** /'kwɪknɪs/ *n* быстрота́. **quicksand** *n* зыбу́чий песо́к. **quicksilver** *n* ртуть.

quid /kwɪd/ *n* фунт.

quiet /'kwaɪət/ *n* (*silence*) тишина́; (*calm*) споко́йствие; *adj* ти́хий; споко́йный; *int* ти́ше!; *vt* & *i* успока́ивать(ся) *impf*, успоко́ить(ся) *pf*.

quill /kwɪl/ *n* перо́; (*spine*) игла́.

quilt /kwɪlt/ *n* (стёганое) одея́ло; *vt* стега́ть *impf*, вы́~ *pf*. **quilted**

q

/ˈkwɪltɪd/ *adj* стёганый.
quintessential /ˌkwɪntɪˈsenʃ(ə)l/ *adj* наибо́лее суще́ственный.
quintet /kwɪnˈtet/ *n* квинте́т.
quins, quintuplets /kwɪnz, ˈkwɪntjʊplɪts/ *n pl* пять близнецо́в.
quip /kwɪp/ *n* острота́; *vi* остри́ть *impf*, с~ *pf*.
quirk /kwɜːk/ *n* причу́да. **quirky** /-kɪ/ *adj* с причу́дами.
quit /kwɪt/ *vt* (*leave*) покида́ть *impf*, поки́нуть *pf*; (*stop*) перестава́ть *impf*, переста́ть *pf*; (*give up*) броса́ть *impf*, бро́сить *pf*; (*resign*) уходи́ть *impf*, уйти́ *pf* с+*gen*.
quite /kwaɪt/ *adv* (*wholly*) совсе́м; (*rather*) дово́льно; **~ a few** дово́льно мно́го.
quits /kwɪts/ *predic*: **we are ~** мы с тобо́й квиты́; **I am ~ with him** я расквита́лся (*past*) с ним.
quiver /ˈkwɪvə(r)/ *vi* (*tremble*) трепета́ть *impf*; *n* тре́пет.
quiz /kwɪz/ *n* виктори́на. **quizzical** /ˈkwɪzɪk(ə)l/ *adj* насме́шливый.
quorum /ˈkwɔːrəm/ *n* кво́рум.
quota /ˈkwəʊtə/ *n* но́рма.
quotation /kwəʊˈteɪʃ(ə)n/ *n* цита́та; (*of price*) цена́; **~ marks** кавы́чки (-чек) *pl*. **quote** /kwəʊt/ *vt* цити́ровать *impf*, про~ *pf*; ссыла́ться *impf*, сосла́ться *pf* на+*acc*; (*price*) назнача́ть *impf*, назна́чить *pf*.

R

rabbi /ˈræbaɪ/ *n* равви́н.
rabbit /ˈræbɪt/ *n* кро́лик.
rabble /ˈræb(ə)l/ *n* сброд.
rabid /ˈræbɪd/ *adj* бе́шеный. **rabies** /ˈreɪbiːz/ *n* бе́шенство.
race[1] /reɪs/ *n* (*ethnic ~*) ра́са; род.
race[2] /reɪs/ *n* (*contest*) (*on foot*) бег; (*of cars etc.*; *fig*) го́нка, го́нки *f pl*; (*of horses*) ска́чки *f pl*; **~-track** трек; (*for horse ~*) скакова́я доро́жка; *vi* (*compete*) состяза́ться *impf* в ско́рости; (*rush*) мча́ться *impf*; *vt* бежа́ть *impf* наперегонки́ с+*instr*. **racecourse** *n* ипподро́м. **racehorse** *n* скакова́я ло́шадь.
racial /ˈreɪʃ(ə)l/ *adj* ра́совый. **rac(ial)ism** /ˈreɪʃəˌlɪz(ə)m, ˈreɪsɪz(ə)m/ *n* раси́зм. **rac(ial)ist** /ˈreɪʃəlɪst, ˈreɪsɪst/ *n* раси́ст, ~ка; *adj* раси́стский.
racing /ˈreɪsɪŋ/ *n* (*horses*) ска́чки *f pl*; (*cars*) го́нки *f pl*; **~ car** го́ночный автомоби́ль *m*; **~ driver** го́нщик.
rack /ræk/ *n* (*for hats etc.*) ве́шалка; (*for plates etc.*) стелла́ж; (*in train etc.*) се́тка; *vt*: **~ one's brains** лома́ть *impf* себе́ го́лову.
racket[1] /ˈrækɪt/ *n* (*bat*) раке́тка.
racket[2] /ˈrækɪt/ *n* (*uproar*) шум; (*illegal activity*) ре́кет. **racketeer** /ˌrækɪˈtɪə(r)/ *n* рэкети́р.
racy /ˈreɪsɪ/ *adj* колори́тный.
radar /ˈreɪdɑː(r)/ *n* (*system*) радиолока́ция; (*apparatus*) радиолока́тор, рада́р; *attrib* рада́рный.
radiance /ˈreɪdɪəns/ *n* сия́ние. **radiant** /-dɪənt/ *adj* сия́ющий. **radiate** /-dɪˌeɪt/ *vt & i* излуча́ть(ся) *impf*, излучи́ться *pf*. **radiation** /-dɪˈeɪʃ(ə)n/ *n* излуче́ние. **radiator** /ˈreɪdɪˌeɪtə(r)/ *n* батаре́я; (*in car*) радиа́тор.
radical /ˈrædɪk(ə)l/ *adj* радика́льный; *n* радика́л.
radio /ˈreɪdɪəʊ/ *n* ра́дио *neut indecl*; (*set*) радиоприёмник; *vt* ради́ровать *impf & pf* +*dat*.
radioactive /ˌreɪdɪəʊˈæktɪv/ *adj* радиоакти́вный. **radioactivity** /-ækˈtɪvɪtɪ/ *n* радиоакти́вность. **radiologist** /ˌreɪdɪˈɒlədʒɪst/ *n* радио́лог; рентгено́лог. **radiotherapy** /ˌreɪdɪəʊˈθerəpɪ/ *n* радиотерапи́я.
radish /ˈrædɪʃ/ *n* реди́ска.
radius /ˈreɪdɪəs/ *n* ра́диус.
raffle /ˈræf(ə)l/ *n* лотере́я; *vt* разы́грывать *impf*, разыгра́ть *pf* в лотере́е.
raft /rɑːft/ *n* плот.

q r

rafter /ˈrɑːftə(r)/ *n* (*beam*) стропи́ло.

rag /ræg/ *n* тря́пка; *pl* (*clothes*) лохмо́тья (-ьев) *pl*.

rage /reɪdʒ/ *n* я́рость; **all the ~** после́дний крик мо́ды; *vi* беси́ться *impf*; (*storm etc.*) бушева́ть *impf*.

ragged /ˈrægɪd/ *adj* (*jagged*) зазу́бренный; (*of clothes*) рва́ный.

raid /reɪd/ *n* налёт; (*by police*) обла́ва; *vt* де́лать *impf*, с~ *pf* налёт на+*acc*.

rail /reɪl/ *n* пери́ла (-л) *pl*; (*rly*) рельс; **by ~** по́ездом. **railing** /ˈreɪlɪŋ/ *n* пери́ла (-л) *pl*.

railway /ˈreɪlweɪ/ *n* желе́зная доро́га; *attrib* железнодоро́жный. **railwayman** *n* железнодоро́жник.

rain /reɪn/ *n* дождь *m*; *v impers*: **it is (was) ~ing** идёт (шёл) дождь; *vt* осыпа́ть *impf*, осы́пать *pf* +*instr* (**upon** +*acc*); *vi* осыпа́ться *impf*, осы́паться *pf*. **rainbow** *n* ра́дуга. **raincoat** *n* плащ. **raindrop** *n* дождева́я ка́пля. **rainfall** *n* (*amount of rain*) коли́чество оса́дков. **rainy** /ˈreɪnɪ/ *adj* дождли́вый; **~ day** чёрный день *m*.

raise /reɪz/ *vt* (*lift*) поднима́ть *impf*, подня́ть *pf*; (*heighten*) повыша́ть *impf*, повы́сить *pf*; (*provoke*) вызыва́ть *impf*, вы́звать *pf*; (*money*) собира́ть *impf*, собра́ть *pf*; (*children*) расти́ть *impf*.

raisin /ˈreɪz(ə)n/ *n* изю́минка; *pl* (*collect*) изю́м.

rake /reɪk/ *n* (*tool*) гра́бли (-бель & -блей) *pl*; *vt* грести́ *impf*; (**~** *together*, *up*) сгреба́ть *impf*, сгрести́ *pf*.

rally /ˈrælɪ/ *vt* & *i* спла́чивать(ся) *impf*, сплоти́ть(ся) *pf*; *vi* (*after illness etc.*) оправля́ться *impf*, опра́виться *pf*; *n* (*meeting*) слёт; ми́тинг; (*motoring ~*) (авто-) ра́лли *neut indecl*; (*tennis*) обме́н уда́рами.

ram /ræm/ *n* (*sheep*) бара́н; *vt* (*beat down*) трамбова́ть *impf*, у~ *pf*; (*drive in*) вбива́ть *impf*, вбить *pf*.

ramble /ˈræmb(ə)l/ *vi* (*walk*) прогу́ливаться *impf*, прогуля́ться *pf*; (*speak*) бубни́ть *impf*; *n* прогу́лка. **rambling** /ˈræmblɪŋ/ *adj* (*incoherent*) бессвя́зный.

ramification /ˌræmɪfɪˈkeɪʃ(ə)n/ *n* (*fig*) после́дствие.

ramp /ræmp/ *n* скат.

rampage /ræmˈpeɪdʒ/ *vi* бу́йствовать *impf*.

rampant /ˈræmpənt/ *adj* (*plant*) бу́йный; (*unchecked*) безу́держный.

rampart /ˈræmpɑːt/ *n* вал.

ramshackle /ˈræmˌʃæk(ə)l/ *adj* ве́тхий.

ranch /rɑːntʃ/ *n* ра́нчо *neut indecl*.

rancid /ˈrænsɪd/ *adj* прого́рклый.

rancour /ˈræŋkə(r)/ *n* зло́ба.

random /ˈrændəm/ *adj* случа́йный; **at ~** наудачу.

range /reɪndʒ/ *n* (*of mountains*) цепь; (*artillery ~*) полиго́н; (*of voice*) диапазо́н; (*scope*) круг, преде́лы *m pl*; (*operating distance*) да́льность; *vi* (*vary*) колеба́ться *impf*, по~ *pf*; (*wander*) броди́ть *impf*; **~ over** (*include*) охва́тывать *impf*, охвати́ть *pf*.

rank[1] /ræŋk/ *n* (*row*) ряд; (*taxi ~*) стоя́нка такси́; (*grade*) зва́ние, чин, ранг; *vt* (*classify*) классифици́ровать *impf* & *pf*; (*consider*) счита́ть *impf* (**as** +*instr*); *vi*: **~ with** быть в числе́+*gen*.

rank[2] /ræŋk/ *adj* (*luxuriant*) бу́йный; (*in smell*) зловóнный; (*gross*) я́вный.

rankle /ˈræŋk(ə)l/ *vi* боле́ть *impf*.

ransack /ˈrænsæk/ *vt* (*search*) обша́ривать *impf*, обша́рить *pf*; (*plunder*) гра́бить *impf*, о~ *pf*.

ransom /ˈrænsəm/ *n* вы́куп; *vt* выкупа́ть *impf*, вы́купить *pf*.

rant /rænt/ *vi* вопи́ть *impf*.

rap /ræp/ *n* стук; *vt* (ре́зко) ударя́ть *impf*, уда́рить *pf*; *vi* стуча́ть *impf*, сту́кнуть *pf*.

rape[1] /reɪp/ *vt* наси́ловать *impf*, из~ *pf*; *n* изнаси́лование.

rape[2] /reɪp/ *n* (*plant*) рапс.

rapid /ˈræpɪd/ *adj* бы́стрый; *n*: *pl* поро́г, быстрина́. **rapidity**

r

/rəˈpɪdɪtɪ/ *n* быстрота́.
rapt /ræpt/ *adj* восхищённый; (*absorbed*) поглощённый. **rapture** /ˈræptʃə(r)/ *n* восто́рг. **rapturous** /ˈræptʃərəs/ *adj* восто́рженный.
rare[1] /reə(r)/ *adj* (*of meat*) недожа́ренный.
rare[2] /reə(r)/ *adj* ре́дкий. **rarity** /ˈreərɪtɪ/ *n* ре́дкость.
rascal /ˈrɑːsk(ə)l/ *n* плут.
rash[1] /ræʃ/ *n* сыпь.
rash[2] /ræʃ/ *adj* опроме́тчивый.
rasher /ˈræʃə(r)/ *n* ло́мтик (беко́на).
rasp /rɑːsp/ *n* (*file*) ра́шпиль *m*; (*sound*) скре́жет; *vt*: **~ out** га́ркнуть *pf*.
raspberry /ˈrɑːzbərɪ/ *n* мали́на (*no pl*; *usu collect*).
rasping /ˈrɑːspɪŋ/ *adj* (*sound*) скрипу́чий.
rat /ræt/ *n* кры́са; **~ race** го́нка за успе́хом.
ratchet /ˈrætʃɪt/ *n* храпови́к.
rate /reɪt/ *n* но́рма, ста́вка; (*speed*) ско́рость; *pl* ме́стные нало́ги *m pl*; **at any ~** во вся́ком слу́чае; *vt* оце́нивать *impf*, оцени́ть *pf*; (*consider*) счита́ть *impf*; *vi* счита́ться *impf* (**as** +*instr*).
rather /ˈrɑːðə(r)/ *adv* скоре́е; (*somewhat*) дово́льно; **he (she) had (would) ~** он (она́) предпочёл (-чла́) бы+*inf*.
ratification /ˌrætɪfɪˈkeɪʃ(ə)n/ *n* ратифика́ция. **ratify** /ˈrætɪˌfaɪ/ *vt* ратифици́ровать *impf* & *pf*.
rating /ˈreɪtɪŋ/ *n* оце́нка.
ratio /ˈreɪʃɪəʊ/ *n* пропо́рция.
ration /ˈræʃ(ə)n/ *n* паёк, рацио́н; *vt* норми́ровать *impf* & *pf*; **be ~ed** выдава́ться *impf*, вы́даться *pf* по ка́рточкам.
rational /ˈræʃən(ə)l/ *adj* разу́мный. **rationalism** /-ˌlɪz(ə)m/ *n* рационали́зм. **rationality** /ˌræʃəˈnælɪtɪ/ *n* разу́мность. **rationalize** /ˈræʃənəˌlaɪz/ *vt* обосно́вывать *impf*, обоснова́ть *pf*; (*industry etc.*) рационализи́ровать *impf* & *pf*.
rattle /ˈræt(ə)l/ *vi* & *t* (*sound*) греме́ть *impf* (+*instr*); **~ along** (*move*) грохота́ть *impf*; **~ off** (*utter*) отбараба́нить *pf*; *n* (*sound*) треск, гро́хот; (*toy*) погрему́шка. **rattlesnake** *n* грему́чая змея́.
raucous /ˈrɔːkəs/ *adj* ре́зкий.
ravage /ˈrævɪdʒ/ *vt* опустоша́ть *impf*, опустоши́ть *pf*; *n*: *pl* разруши́тельное де́йствие.
rave /reɪv/ *vi* бре́дить *impf*; **~ about** быть в восто́рге от+*gen*.
raven /ˈreɪv(ə)n/ *n* во́рон.
ravenous /ˈrævənəs/ *adj* голо́дный как волк.
ravine /rəˈviːn/ *n* уще́лье.
ravishing /ˈrævɪʃɪŋ/ *adj* восхити́тельный.
raw /rɔː/ *adj* сыро́й; (*inexperienced*) нео́пытный; **~ material(s)** сырьё (*no pl*).
ray /reɪ/ *n* луч.
raze /reɪz/ *vt*: **~ to the ground** ровня́ть *impf*, с~ *pf* с землёй.
razor /ˈreɪzə(r)/ *n* бри́тва; **~-blade** ле́звие.
reach /riːtʃ/ *vt* (*attain, extend to, arrive at*) достига́ть *impf*, дости́чь & дости́гнуть *pf* +*gen*, до+*gen*; доходи́ть *impf*, дойти́ *pf* до+*gen*; (*with hand*) дотя́гиваться *impf*, дотяну́ться *pf* до+*gen*; *vi* (*extend*) простира́ться *impf*; *n* досяга́емость; (*pl, of river*) тече́ние.
react /rɪˈækt/ *vi* реаги́ровать *impf*, от~, про~ *pf* (**to** на+*acc*). **reaction** /-ˈækʃən/ *n* реа́кция. **reactionary** /-ˈækʃənərɪ/ *adj* реакцио́нный; *n* реакционе́р. **reactor** /-ˈæktə(r)/ *n* реа́ктор.
read /riːd/ *vt* чита́ть *impf*, про~, проче́сть *pf*; (*mus*) разбира́ть *impf*, разобра́ть *pf*; (*~ a meter etc.*) снима́ть *impf*, снять *pf* показа́ния +*gen*; (*univ*) изуча́ть *impf*; (*interpret*) толкова́ть *impf*. **readable** /ˈriːdəb(ə)l/ *adj* интере́сный. **reader** /ˈriːdə(r)/ *n* чита́тель *m*, ~ница; (*book*) хрестома́тия.
readily /ˈredɪlɪ/ *adv* (*willingly*) охо́тно; (*easily*) легко́. **readiness**

/ˈredɪnɪs/ *n* готóвность.

reading /ˈriːdɪŋ/ *n* чтéние; (*on meter*) показáние.

ready /ˈredɪ/ *adj* готóвый (**for** к+*dat*, на+*acc*); **get ~** готóвиться *impf*; **~-made** готóвый; **~ money** налúчные дéньги (-нег, -ньгáм) *pl.*

real /rɪəl/ *adj* настоя́щий, реáльный; **~ estate** недвúжимость. **realism** /-ˌlɪz(ə)m/ *n* реалúзм. **realist** /ˈrɪəlɪst/ *n* реалúст. **realistic** /ˌrɪəˈlɪstɪk/ *adj* реалистúчный, -úческий. **reality** /rɪˈælɪtɪ/ *n* действúтельность; **in ~** действúтельно. **realization** /ˌrɪəlaɪˈzeɪʃ(ə)n/ *n* (*of plan etc.*) осуществлéние; (*of assets*) реализáция; (*understanding*) осознáние. **realize** /ˈrɪəlaɪz/ *vt* (*plan etc.*) осуществля́ть *impf*, осуществúть *pf*; (*assets*) реализовáть *impf & pf*; (*apprehend*) осознавáть *impf*, осознáть *pf.* **really** /ˈrɪəlɪ/ *adv* действúтельно, в сáмом дéле.

realm /relm/ *n* (*kingdom*) королéвство; (*sphere*) óбласть.

reap /riːp/ *vt* жать *impf*, сжать *pf*; (*fig*) пожинáть *impf*, пожáть *pf.*

rear[1] /rɪə(r)/ *vt* (*lift*) поднимáть *impf*, подня́ть *pf*; (*children*) воспúтывать *impf*, воспитáть *pf*; *vi* (*of horse*) становúться *impf*, стать *pf* на дыбы́.

rear[2] /rɪə(r)/ *n* зáдняя часть; (*mil*) тыл; **bring up the ~** замыкáть *impf*, замкнýть *pf* шéствие; *adj* зáдний; (*also mil*) ты́льный. **rearguard** *n* арьергáрд; **~ action** арьергáрдный бой.

rearmament /riːˈɑːməmənt/ *n* перевооружéние.

rearrange /ˌriːəˈreɪndʒ/ *vt* меня́ть *impf.*

reason /ˈriːz(ə)n/ *n* (*cause*) причúна, основáние; (*intellect*) рáзум, рассýдок; *vi* рассуждáть *impf*; **~ with** (*person*) уговáривать *impf* +*acc.* **reasonable** /-nəb(ə)l/ *adj* разýмный; (*inexpensive*) недорогóй.

reassurance /ˌriːəˈʃʊərəns/ *n* успокáивание. **reassure** /-ˈʃʊə(r)/ *vt* успокáивать *impf*, успокóить *pf.*

rebate /ˈriːbeɪt/ *n* скúдка.

rebel *n* /ˈreb(ə)l/ повстáнец; *vi* /rɪˈbel/ восставáть *impf*, восстáть *pf.* **rebellion** /rɪˈbeljən/ *n* восстáние. **rebellious** /rɪˈbeljəs/ *adj* мятéжный.

rebound *vi* /rɪˈbaʊnd/ отскáкивать *impf*, отскочúть *pf*; *n* /ˈriːbaʊnd/ рикошéт.

rebuff /rɪˈbʌf/ *n* отпóр; *vt* давáть *impf*, дать *pf* +*dat* отпóр.

rebuild /riːˈbɪld/ *vt* перестрáивать *impf*, перестрóить *pf.*

rebuke /rɪˈbjuːk/ *vt* упрекáть *impf*, упрекнýть *pf*; *n* упрёк.

rebuttal /rɪˈbʌtəl/ *n* опровержéние.

recalcitrant /rɪˈkælsɪtrənt/ *adj* непокóрный.

recall *vt* /rɪˈkɔːl/ (*an official*) отзывáть *impf*, отозвáть *pf*; (*remember*) вспоминáть *impf*, вспóмнить *pf*; *n* /ˈriːkɔːl/ óтзыв; (*memory*) пáмять.

recant /rɪˈkænt/ *vi* отрекáться *impf*, отрéчься *pf.*

recapitulate /ˌriːkəˈpɪtjʊˌleɪt/ *vt* резюмúровать *impf & pf.*

recast /riːˈkɑːst/ *vt* передéлывать *impf*, передéлать *pf.*

recede /rɪˈsiːd/ *vi* отходúть *impf*, отойтú *pf.*

receipt /rɪˈsiːt/ *n* (*receiving*) получéние; *pl* (*amount*) вы́ручка; (*written ~*) квитáнция; (*from till*) чек. **receive** /-ˈsiːv/ *vt* (*admit, entertain*) принимáть *impf*, приня́ть *pf*; (*get, be given*) получáть *impf*, получúть *pf.* **receiver** /-ˈsiːvə(r)/ *n* (*radio, television*) приёмник; (*tel*) трýбка.

recent /ˈriːs(ə)nt/ *adj* недáвний; (*new*) нóвый. **recently** /-lɪ/ *adv* недáвно.

receptacle /rɪˈseptək(ə)l/ *n* вместúлище. **reception** /-ˈsepʃ(ə)n/ *n* приём; **~ room** приёмная *sb.* **receptionist** /-ˈsepʃənɪst/ *n* секретáрь *m*, -рша, в приёмной. **receptive** /-ˈseptɪv/ *adj*

r

восприимчивый.

recess /rɪ'ses/ *n* (*parl*) каникулы (-л) *pl*; (*niche*) ниша. **recession** /-'seʃ(ə)n/ *n* спад.

recipe /'resɪpɪ/ *n* рецепт.

recipient /rɪ'sɪpɪənt/ *n* получатель *m*.

reciprocal /rɪ'sɪprək(ə)l/ *adj* взаимный. **reciprocate** /-ˌkeɪt/ *vt* отвечать *impf* (взаимностью) на+*acc*.

recital /rɪ'saɪt(ə)l/ *n* (сольный) концерт. **recitation** /ˌresɪ'teɪʃ(ə)n/ *n* публичное чтение. **recite** /rɪ'saɪt/ *vt* декламировать *impf*, про~ *pf*; (*list*) перечислять *impf*, перечислить *pf*.

reckless /'reklɪs/ *adj* (*rash*) опрометчивый; (*careless*) неосторожный.

reckon /'rekən/ *vt* подсчитывать *impf*, подсчитать *pf*; (*also regard as*) считать *impf*, счесть *pf* (**to be** +*instr*); *vi*: ~ **on** рассчитывать *impf*, рассчитать *pf* на+*acc*; ~ **with** считаться *impf* с+*instr*. **reckoning** /'rekənɪŋ/ *n* счёт; **day of** ~ час расплаты.

reclaim /rɪ'kleɪm/ *vt* требовать *impf*, по~ *pf* обратно; (*land*) осваивать *impf*, освоить *pf*.

recline /rɪ'klaɪn/ *vi* полулежать *impf*.

recluse /rɪ'klu:s/ *n* затворник.

recognition /ˌrekəg'nɪʃ(ə)n/ *n* узнавание; (*acknowledgement*) признание. **recognize** /'rekəgˌnaɪz/ *vt* узнавать *impf*, узнать *pf*; (*acknowledge*) признавать *impf*, признать *pf*.

recoil /'ri:kɔɪl/ *vi* отпрядывать *impf*, отпрянуть *pf*.

recollect /ˌrekə'lekt/ *vt* вспоминать *impf*, вспомнить *pf*. **recollection** /-'lekʃ(ə)n/ *n* воспоминание.

recommend /ˌrekə'mend/ *vt* рекомендовать *impf* & *pf*. **recommendation** /ˌrekəmen'deɪʃ(ə)n/ *n* рекомендация.

recompense /'rekəmˌpens/ *n* вознаграждение; *vt* вознаграждать *impf*, вознаградить *pf*.

reconcile /'rekənˌsaɪl/ *vt* примирять *impf*, примирить *pf*; ~ **o.s.** примиряться *impf*, примириться *pf* (**to** с+*instr*). **reconciliation** /ˌrekənˌsɪlɪ'eɪʃ(ə)n/ *n* примирение.

reconnaissance /rɪ'kɒnɪs(ə)ns/ *n* разведка. **reconnoitre** /ˌrekə'nɔɪtə(r)/ *vt* разведывать *impf*, разведать *pf*.

reconstruct /ˌri:kən'strʌkt/ *vt* перестраивать *impf*, перестроить *pf*. **reconstruction** /-'strʌkʃən/ *n* перестройка.

record *vt* /rɪ'kɔ:d/ записывать *impf*, записать *pf*; *n* /'rekɔ:d/ запись; (*minutes*) протокол; (*gramophone* ~) грампластинка; (*sport etc.*) рекорд; **off the** ~ неофициально; *adj* рекордный; **~-breaker, -holder** рекордсмен, ~ка; **~-player** проигрыватель *m*. **recorder** /rɪ'kɔ:də(r)/ *n* (*mus*) блок-флейта. **recording** /-dɪŋ/ *n* запись.

recount[1] /rɪ'kaʊnt/ *vt* (*narrate*) пересказывать *impf*, пересказать *pf*.

re-count[2] /'ri:kaʊnt/ *vt* (*count again*) пересчитывать *impf*, пересчитать *pf*; *n* пересчёт.

recoup /rɪ'ku:p/ *vt* возвращать *impf*, вернуть *pf* (**losses** потерянное).

recourse /rɪ'kɔ:s/ *n*: **have ~ to** прибегать *impf*, прибегнуть *pf* к+*dat*.

recover /rɪ'kʌvə(r)/ *vt* (*regain possession*) получать *impf*, получить *pf* обратно; возвращать *impf*, вернуть *pf*; *vi* (~ *health*) поправляться *impf*, поправиться *pf* (**from** после +*gen*). **recovery** /-rɪ/ *n* возвращение; выздоровление.

recreate /ˌri:krɪ'eɪt/ *vt* воссоздавать *impf*, воссоздать *pf*.

recreation /ˌrekrɪ'eɪʃ(ə)n/ *n* развлечение, отдых.

recrimination /rɪˌkrɪmɪ'neɪʃ(ə)n/ *n* взаимное обвинение.

recruit /rɪ'kru:t/ *n* новобранец; *vt*

вербова́ть *impf*, за~ *pf*. **recruitment** /-mənt/ *n* вербо́вка.

rectangle /ˈrektæŋg(ə)l/ *n* прямоуго́льник. **rectangular** /rekˈtæŋgjʊlə(r)/ *adj* прямоуго́льный.

rectify /ˈrektɪˌfaɪ/ *vt* исправля́ть *impf*, испра́вить *pf*.

rector /ˈrektə(r)/ *n* (*priest*) прихо́дский свяще́нник; (*univ*) ре́ктор. **rectory** /-rɪ/ *n* дом прихо́дского свяще́нника.

rectum /ˈrektəm/ *n* пряма́я кишка́.

recuperate /rɪˈkuːpəˌreɪt/ *vi* поправля́ться *impf*, попра́виться *pf*. **recuperation** /-ˌkuːpəˈreɪʃ(ə)n/ *n* выздоровле́ние.

recur /rɪˈkɜː(r)/ *vi* повторя́ться *impf*, повтори́ться *pf*. **recurrence** /-ˈkʌrəns/ *n* повторе́ние. **recurrent** /-ˈkʌrənt/ *adj* повторя́ющийся.

recycle /riːˈsaɪk(ə)l/ *vt* перераба́тывать *impf*, перерабо́тать *pf*.

red /red/ *adj* кра́сный; (*of hair*) ры́жий; *n* кра́сный цвет; (*polit*) кра́сный *sb*; **in the ~** в долгу́; **~-handed** с поли́чным; **~ herring** ло́жный след; **~-hot** раскалённый до́красна́; **R~ Indian** инде́ец, индиа́нка; **~ tape** волоки́та. **redcurrant** *n* кра́сная сморо́дина (*no pl*; *usu collect*). **redden** /ˈred(ə)n/ *vt* окра́шивать *impf*, окра́сить *pf* в кра́сный цвет; *vi* красне́ть *impf*, по~ *pf*. **reddish** /ˈredɪʃ/ *adj* красноватый; (*hair*) рыжева́тый.

redecorate /riːˈdekəˌreɪt/ *vt* отде́лывать *impf*, отде́лать *pf*.

redeem /rɪˈdiːm/ *vt* (*buy back*) выкупа́ть *impf*, вы́купить *pf*; (*from sin*) искупа́ть *impf*, искупи́ть *pf*. **redeemer** /-ˈdiːmə(r)/ *n* искупи́тель *m*. **redemption** /-ˈdempʃ(ə)n/ *n* вы́куп; искупле́ние.

redeploy /ˌriːdɪˈplɔɪ/ *vt* передислоци́ровать *impf* & *pf*.

redo /riːˈduː/ *vt* переде́лывать *impf*, переде́лать *pf*.

redouble /riːˈdʌb(ə)l/ *vt* удва́ивать *impf*, удво́ить *pf*.

redress /rɪˈdres/ *vt* исправля́ть *impf*, испра́вить *pf*; **~ the balance** восстана́вливать *impf*, восстанови́ть *pf* равнове́сие; *n* возмеще́ние.

reduce /rɪˈdjuːs/ *vt* (*decrease*) уменьша́ть *impf*, уме́ньшить *pf*; (*lower*) снижа́ть *impf*, сни́зить *pf*; (*shorten*) сокраща́ть *impf*, сократи́ть *pf*; (*bring to*) доводи́ть *impf*, довести́ *pf* (**to** в+*acc*). **reduction** /-ˈdʌkʃ(ə)n/ *n* уменьше́ние, сниже́ние, сокраще́ние; (*discount*) ски́дка.

redundancy /rɪˈdʌnd(ə)nsɪ/ *n* (*dismissal*) увольне́ние. **redundant** /-d(ə)nt/ *adj* изли́шний; **make ~** увольня́ть *impf*, уво́лить *pf*.

reed /riːd/ *n* (*plant*) тростни́к; (*in oboe etc.*) язычо́к.

reef /riːf/ *n* риф.

reek /riːk/ *n* вонь; *vi*: **~ (of)** воня́ть *impf* (+*instr*).

reel[1] /riːl/ *n* кату́шка; *vt*: **~ off** (*story etc.*) отбараба́нить *pf*.

reel[2] /riːl/ *vi* (*stagger*) поша́тываться *impf*, пошатну́ться *pf*.

refectory /rɪˈfektərɪ/ *n* (*monastery*) тра́пезная *sb*; (*univ*) столо́вая *sb*.

refer /rɪˈfɜː(r)/ *vt* (*direct*) отсыла́ть *impf*, отосла́ть *pf* (**to** к+*dat*); *vi*: **~ to** (*cite*) ссыла́ться *impf*, сосла́ться *pf* на+*acc*; (*mention*) упомина́ть *impf*, упомяну́ть *pf* +*acc*. **referee** /ˌrefəˈriː/ *n* судья́ *m*; *vt* суди́ть *impf*. **reference** /ˈrefərəns/ *n* (*to book etc.*) ссы́лка; (*mention*) упомина́ние; (*testimonial*) характери́стика; **~ book** спра́вочник. **referendum** /ˌrefəˈrendəm/ *n* рефере́ндум.

refine /rɪˈfaɪn/ *vt* очища́ть *impf*, очи́стить *pf*. **refined** /-d/ *adj* (*in style etc.*) утончённый; (*in manners*) культу́рный. **refinement** /-mənt/ *n* утончённость. **refinery** /-nərɪ/ *n* (*oil ~*) нефтеочисти́тельный заво́д.

refit /riːˈfɪt/ *vt* переобору́довать *impf* & *pf*.

reflect /rɪˈflekt/ *vt* отража́ть *impf*, отрази́ть *pf*; *vi* размышля́ть

r

impf, размы́слить *pf* (**on** о+*prep*). **reflection** /-'flekʃ(ə)n/ *n* отраже́ние; размышле́ние; **on ~** поду́мав. **reflective** /-'flektɪv/ *adj* (*thoughtful*) серьёзный. **reflector** /-'flektə(r)/ *n* рефле́ктор. **reflex** /'riːfleks/ *n* рефле́кс; *adj* рефле́кторный. **reflexive** /rɪ'fleksɪv/ *adj* (*gram*) возвра́тный.

reform /rɪ'fɔːm/ *vt* реформи́ровать *impf* & *pf*; *vt* & *i* (*of people*) исправля́ть(ся) *impf*, испра́вить(ся) *pf*; *n* рефо́рма; исправле́ние. **Reformation** /ˌrefə'meɪʃ(ə)n/ *n* Реформа́ция.

refract /rɪ'frækt/ *vt* преломля́ть *impf*, преломи́ть *pf*.

refrain[1] /rɪ'freɪn/ *n* припе́в.

refrain[2] /rɪ'freɪn/ *vi* возде́рживаться *impf*, воздержа́ться *pf* (**from** от+*gen*).

refresh /rɪ'freʃ/ *vt* освежа́ть *impf*, освежи́ть *pf*. **refreshments** /-mənts/ *n pl* напи́тки *m pl*.

refrigerate /rɪ'frɪdʒəˌreɪt/ *vt* охлажда́ть *impf*, охлади́ть *pf*. **refrigeration** /-'reɪʃ(ə)n/ *n* охлажде́ние. **refrigerator** /rɪ'frɪdʒəˌreɪtə(r)/ *n* холоди́льник.

refuge /'refjuːdʒ/ *n* убе́жище; **take ~** находи́ть *impf*, найти́ *pf* убе́жище. **refugee** /ˌrefjʊ'dʒiː/ *n* бе́женец, -нка.

refund *vt* /rɪ'fʌnd/ возвраща́ть *impf*, возврати́ть *pf*; (*expenses*) возмеща́ть *impf*, возмести́ть *pf*; *n* /'riːfʌnd/ возвраще́ние (де́нег); возмеще́ние.

refusal /rɪ'fjuːz(ə)l/ *n* отка́з. **refuse**[1] /rɪ'fjuːz/ *vt* (*decline to accept*) отка́зываться *impf*, отказа́ться *pf* от+*gen*; (*decline to do sth*) отка́зываться *impf*, отказа́ться *pf* +*inf*; (*deny s.o. sth*) отка́зывать *impf*, отказа́ть *pf* +*dat*+в+*prep*.

refuse[2] /'refjuːs/ *n* му́сор.

refute /rɪ'fjuːt/ *vt* опроверга́ть *impf*, опрове́ргнуть *pf*.

regain /rɪ'geɪn/ *vt* возвраща́ть *impf*, верну́ть *pf*.

regal /'riːg(ə)l/ *adj* короле́вский.

regalia /rɪ'geɪlɪə/ *n pl* рега́лии *f pl*.

regard /rɪ'gɑːd/ *vt* смотре́ть *impf*, по~ *pf* на+*acc*; (*take into account*) счита́ться *impf* с+*instr*; **~ as** счита́ть *impf* +*instr*, за+*instr*; **as ~s** что каса́ется+*gen*; *n* (*esteem*) уваже́ние; *pl* приве́т. **regarding** /-dɪŋ/ *prep* относи́тельно +*gen*. **regardless** /-lɪs/ *adv* не обраща́я внима́ния; **~ of** не счита́ясь с+*instr*.

regatta /rɪ'gætə/ *n* рега́та.

regenerate /rɪ'dʒenəˌreɪt/ *vt* перерожда́ть *impf*, переродить *pf*.

regent /'riːdʒ(ə)nt/ *n* ре́гент.

régime /reɪ'ʒiːm/ *n* режи́м.

regiment /'redʒɪmənt/ *n* полк. **regimental** /-'ment(ə)l/ *adj* полково́й. **regimentation** /ˌredʒɪmən'teɪʃ(ə)n/ *n* регламента́ция.

region /'riːdʒ(ə)n/ *n* регио́н. **regional** /-nəl/ *adj* региона́льный.

register /'redʒɪstə(r)/ *n* рее́стр; (*also mus*) реги́стр; *vt* регистри́ровать *impf*, за~ *pf*; (*a letter*) отправля́ть *impf*, отпра́вить *pf* заказны́м. **registered** /-təd/ *adj* (*letter*) заказно́й. **registrar** /ˌredʒɪs'trɑː(r)/ *n* регистра́тор. **registration** /ˌredʒɪ'streɪʃ(ə)n/ *n* регистра́ция; **~ number** но́мер маши́ны. **registry** /'redʒɪstrɪ/ *n* регистрату́ра; **~ office** загс.

regret /rɪ'gret/ *vt* сожале́ть *impf* о+*prep*; *n* сожале́ние. **regretful** /-fʊl/ *adj* по́лный сожале́ния. **regrettable** /-'gretəb(ə)l/ *adj* приско́рбный. **regrettably** /-'gretəblɪ/ *adv* к сожале́нию.

regular /'regjʊlə(r)/ *adj* регуля́рный; (*also gram*) пра́вильный; *n* (*coll*) завсегда́тай. **regularity** /ˌregjʊ'lærɪtɪ/ *n* регуля́рность. **regulate** /'regjʊˌleɪt/ *vt* регули́ровать *impf*, у~ *pf*. **regulation** /ˌregjʊ'leɪʃ(ə)n/ *n* регули́рование; *pl* пра́вила *neut pl*.

rehabilitate /ˌriːhə'bɪlɪˌteɪt/ *vt* реабилити́ровать *impf* & *pf*. **rehabilitation** /-ˌbɪlɪ'teɪʃ(ə)n/ *n* реабилита́ция.

rehearsal /rɪ'hɜːs(ə)l/ *n* репети́ция.

rehearse /-ˈhɜːs/ *vt* репетировать *impf*, от~ *pf.*
reign /reɪn/ *n* царствование; *vi* царствовать *impf*; (*fig*) царить *impf.*
reimburse /ˌriːɪmˈbɜːs/ *vt* возмещать *impf*, возместить *pf* (+*dat of person*). **reimbursement** /-mənt/ *n* возмещение.
rein /reɪn/ *n* повод.
reincarnation /ˌriːɪnkɑːˈneɪʃ(ə)n/ *n* перевоплощение.
reindeer /ˈreɪndɪə(r)/ *n* северный олень *m.*
reinforce /ˌriːɪnˈfɔːs/ *vt* подкреплять *impf*, подкрепить *pf*. **reinforcement** /-mənt/ *n* (*also pl*) подкрепление.
reinstate /ˌriːɪnˈsteɪt/ *vt* восстанавливать *impf*, восстановить *pf.* **reinstatement** /-mənt/ *n* восстановление.
reiterate /riːˈɪtəˌreɪt/ *vt* повторять *impf*, повторить *pf.*
reject *vt* /rɪˈdʒekt/ отвергать *impf*, отвергнуть *pf*; (*as defective*) браковать *impf*, за~ *pf*; *n* /ˈriːdʒekt/ брак. **rejection** /-ˈdʒekʃ(ə)n/ *n* отказ (**of** от+*gen*).
rejoice /rɪˈdʒɔɪs/ *vi* радоваться *impf*, об~ *pf* (**in, at** +*dat*). **rejoicing** /-sɪŋ/ *n* радость.
rejoin /riːˈdʒɔɪn/ *vt* (вновь) присоединяться *impf*, присоединиться *pf* к+*dat.*
rejuvenate /rɪˈdʒuːvɪˌneɪt/ *vt* омолаживать *impf*, омолодить *pf.*
relapse /rɪˈlæps/ *n* рецидив; *vi* снова впадать *impf*, впасть *pf* (**into** в+*acc*); (*into illness*) снова заболевать *impf*, заболеть *pf.*
relate /rɪˈleɪt/ *vt* (*tell*) рассказывать *impf*, рассказать *pf*; (*connect*) связывать *impf*, связать *pf*; *vi* относиться *impf* (**to** к+*dat*). **related** /-tɪd/ *adj* родственный. **relation** /-ˈleɪʃ(ə)n/ *n* отношение; (*person*) родственник, -ица. **relationship** *n* (*connection*; *liaison*) связь; (*kinship*) родство. **relative** /ˈrelətɪv/ *adj* относительный; *n* родственник, -ица. **relativity** /ˌreləˈtɪvɪtɪ/ *n* относительность.
relax /rɪˈlæks/ *vt* ослаблять *impf*, ослабить *pf*; *vi* (*rest*) расслабляться *impf*, расслабиться *pf.* **relaxation** /ˌriːlækˈseɪʃ(ə)n/ *n* ослабление; (*rest*) отдых.
relay /ˈriːleɪ/ *n* (*shift*) смена; (*sport*) эстафета; (*electr*) реле *neut indecl*; *vt* передавать *impf*, передать *pf.*
release /rɪˈliːs/ *vt* (*set free*) освобождать *impf*, освободить *pf*; (*unfasten, let go*) отпускать *impf*, отпустить *pf*; (*film etc.*) выпускать *impf*, выпустить *pf*; *n* освобождение; выпуск.
relegate /ˈrelɪˌgeɪt/ *vt* переводить *impf*, перевести *pf* (в низшую группу). **relegation** /-ˈgeɪʃ(ə)n/ *n* перевод (в низшую группу).
relent /rɪˈlent/ *vi* смягчаться *impf*, смягчиться *pf.* **relentless** /-lɪs/ *adj* непрестанный.
relevance /ˈrelɪv(ə)ns/ *n* уместность. **relevant** /-v(ə)nt/ *adj* относящийся к делу; уместный.
reliability /rɪˌlaɪəˈbɪlɪtɪ/ *n* надёжность. **reliable** /-ˈlaɪəb(ə)l/ *adj* надёжный. **reliance** /-ˈlaɪəns/ *n* доверие. **reliant** /-ˈlaɪənt/ *adj*: **be ~ upon** зависеть *impf* от+*gen.*
relic /ˈrelɪk/ *n* остаток, реликвия.
relief[1] /rɪˈliːf/ *n* (*art, geol*) рельеф.
relief[2] /rɪˈliːf/ *n* (*alleviation*) облегчение; (*assistance*) помощь; (*in duty*) смена. **relieve** /-ˈliːv/ *vt* (*alleviate*) облегчать *impf*, облегчить *pf*; (*replace*) сменять *impf*, сменить *pf*; (*unburden*) освобождать *impf*, освободить *pf* (**of** от+*gen*).
religion /rɪˈlɪdʒ(ə)n/ *n* религия. **religious** /-ˈlɪdʒəs/ *adj* религиозный.
relinquish /rɪˈlɪŋkwɪʃ/ *vt* оставлять *impf*, оставить *pf*; (*right etc.*) отказываться *impf*, отказаться *pf* от+*gen.*
relish /ˈrelɪʃ/ *n* (*enjoyment*) смак; (*cul*) приправа; *vt* смаковать *impf.*
relocate /ˌriːləʊˈkeɪt/ *vt & i* пере-

мещáть(ся) *impf*, переместúть(ся) *pf*.

reluctance /rɪ'lʌkt(ə)ns/ *n* неохóта. **reluctant** /-t(ə)nt/ *adj* неохóтный; **be ~ to** не желáть *impf* +*inf*.

rely /rɪ'laɪ/ *vi* полагáться *impf*, положúться *pf* (**on** на+*acc*).

remain /rɪ'meɪn/ *vi* оставáться *impf*, остáться *pf*. **remainder** /-'meɪndə(r)/ *n* остáток. **remains** /-'meɪnz/ *n pl* остáтки *m pl*; (*human* ~) остáнки (-ков) *pl*.

remand /rɪ'mɑːnd/ *vt* содержáть *impf* под стрáжей; **be on ~** содержáться *impf* под стрáжей.

remark /rɪ'mɑːk/ *vt* замечáть *impf*, замéтить *pf*; *n* замечáние. **remarkable** /-'mɑːkəb(ə)l/ *adj* замечáтельный.

remarry /riː'mærɪ/ *vi* вступáть *impf*, вступúть *pf* в нóвый брак.

remedial /rɪ'miːdɪəl/ *adj* лечéбный. **remedy** /'remɪdɪ/ *n* срéдство (**for** от, прóтив+*gen*); *vt* исправлять *impf*, испрáвить *pf*.

remember /rɪ'membə(r)/ *vt* пóмнить *impf*, вспоминáть *impf*, вспóмнить *pf*; (*greet*) передавáть *impf*, передáть *pf* привéт от+*gen* (**to** +*dat*). **remembrance** /-'membrəns/ *n* пáмять.

remind /rɪ'maɪnd/ *vt* напоминáть *impf*, напóмнить *pf* +*dat* (**of** +*acc*, о+*prep*). **reminder** /-də(r)/ *n* напоминáние.

reminiscence /ˌremɪ'nɪs(ə)ns/ *n* воспоминáние. **reminiscent** /-'nɪs(ə)nt/ *adj* напоминáющий.

remiss /rɪ'mɪs/ *predic* небрéжный. **remission** /-'mɪʃ(ə)n/ *n* (*pardon*) отпущéние; (*med*) ремúссия. **remit** /'riːmɪt/ *vt* пересылáть *impf*, переслáть *pf*. **remittance** /rɪ'mɪt(ə)ns/ *n* перевóд дéнег; (*money*) дéнежный перевóд.

remnant /'remnənt/ *n* остáток.

remonstrate /'remənˌstreɪt/ *vi*: ~ **with** увещевáть *impf* +*acc*.

remorse /rɪ'mɔːs/ *n* угрызéния *neut pl* сóвести. **remorseful** /-fʊl/ *adj* пóлный раскáяния. **remorseless** /-lɪs/ *adj* безжáлостный.

remote /rɪ'məʊt/ *adj* отдалённый; **~ control** дистанциóнное управлéние.

removal /rɪ'muːv(ə)l/ *n* (*taking away*) удалéние; (*of obstacles*) устранéние. **remove** /-'muːv/ *vt* (*take away*) убирáть *impf*, убрáть *pf*; (*get rid of*) устранять *impf*, устранúть *pf*.

remuneration /rɪˌmjuːnə'reɪʃ(ə)n/ *n* вознаграждéние. **remunerative** /-'mjuːnərətɪv/ *adj* вы́годный.

renaissance /rɪ'neɪs(ə)ns/ *n* возрождéние; **the R~** Возрождéние.

render /'rendə(r)/ *vt* воздавáть *impf*, воздáть *pf*; (*help etc.*) окáзывать *impf*, оказáть *pf*; (*role etc.*) исполнять *impf*, испóлнить *pf*; (*stone*) штукатýрить *impf*, о~, от~ *pf*. **rendering** /-rɪŋ/ *n* исполнéние.

rendezvous /'rɒndɪˌvuː/ *n* (*meeting*) свидáние.

renegade /'renɪˌgeɪd/ *n* ренегáт, ~ка.

renew /rɪ'njuː/ *vt* (*extend*; *continue*) возобновлять *impf*, возобновúть *pf*; (*replace*) обновлять *impf*, обновúть *pf*. **renewal** /-'njuːəl/ *n* (воз)обновлéние.

renounce /rɪ'naʊns/ *vt* отвергáть *impf*, отвéргнуть *pf*; (*claim*) откáзываться *impf*, отказáться *pf* от+*gen*.

renovate /'renəˌveɪt/ *vt* ремонтúровать *impf*, от~ *pf*. **renovation** /-'veɪʃ(ə)n/ *n* ремóнт.

renown /rɪ'naʊn/ *n* слáва. **renowned** /-'naʊnd/ *adj* извéстный; **be ~ for** слáвиться *impf* +*instr*.

rent /rent/ *n* (*for home*) квартплáта; (*for premises*) (арéндная) плáта; *vt* (*of tenant*) арендовáть *impf* & *pf*; (*of owner*) сдавáть *impf*, сдать *pf*.

renunciation /rɪˌnʌnsɪ'eɪʃ(ə)n/ *n* (*repudiation*) отрицáние; (*of claim*) откáз.

rep /rep/ *n* (*comm*) агéнт.

repair /rɪ'peə(r)/ *vt* ремонтúровать *impf*, от~ *pf*; *n* (*also pl*) ремóнт

r

(*only sg*); почи́нка; **in good/bad ~** в хоро́шем/плохо́м состоя́нии.

reparations /ˌrepəˈreɪʃ(ə)nz/ *n pl* репара́ции *f pl.*

repatriate /riːˈpætrɪˌeɪt/ *vt* репатрии́ровать *impf* & *pf.* **repatriation** /-ˌpætrɪˈeɪʃ(ə)n/ *n* репатриа́ция.

repay /riːˈpeɪ/ *vt* отпла́чивать *impf*, отплати́ть *pf* (*person +dat*). **repayment** /-mənt/ *n* отпла́та.

repeal /rɪˈpiːl/ *vt* отменя́ть *impf*, отмени́ть *pf*; *n* отме́на.

repeat /rɪˈpiːt/ *vt* & *i* повторя́ть(ся) *impf*, повтори́ть(ся) *pf*; *n* повторе́ние. **repeatedly** /-tɪdlɪ/ *adv* неоднокра́тно.

repel /rɪˈpel/ *vt* отта́лкивать *impf*, оттолкну́ть *pf*; (*enemy*) отража́ть *impf*, отрази́ть *pf.*

repent /rɪˈpent/ *vi* раска́иваться *impf*, раска́яться *pf.* **repentance** /-ˈpent(ə)ns/ *n* раска́яние. **repentant** /-ˈpent(ə)nt/ *adj* раска́ивающийся.

repercussion /ˌriːpəˈkʌʃ(ə)n/ *n* после́дствие.

repertoire /ˈrepəˌtwɑː(r)/ *n* реперту́ар. **repertory** /ˈrepətərɪ/ *n* (*store*) запа́с; (*repertoire*) реперту́ар; **~ company** постоя́нная тру́ппа.

repetition /ˌrepɪˈtɪʃ(ə)n/ *n* повторе́ние. **repetitious, repetitive** /ˌrepɪˈtɪʃəs, rɪˈpetɪtɪv/ *adj* повторя́ющийся.

replace /rɪˈpleɪs/ *vt* (*put back*) класть *impf*, положи́ть *pf* обра́тно; (*substitute*) заменя́ть *impf*, замени́ть *pf* (**by** *+instr*). **replacement** /-mənt/ *n* заме́на.

replay /ˈriːpleɪ/ *n* переигро́вка.

replenish /rɪˈplenɪʃ/ *vt* пополня́ть *impf*, попо́лнить *pf.*

replete /rɪˈpliːt/ *adj* насы́щенный; (*sated*) сы́тый.

replica /ˈreplɪkə/ *n* ко́пия.

reply /rɪˈplaɪ/ *vt* & *i* отвеча́ть *impf*, отве́тить *pf* (**to** на*+acc*); *n* отве́т.

report /rɪˈpɔːt/ *vt* сообща́ть *impf*, сообщи́ть *pf*; *vi* докла́дывать *impf*, доложи́ть *pf*; (*present o.s.*) явля́ться *impf*, яви́ться *pf*; *n* сообще́ние; докла́д; (*school*) та́бель *m*; (*sound*) звук взры́ва, вы́стрела. **reporter** /-tə(r)/ *n* корреспонде́нт.

repose /rɪˈpəʊz/ *n* (*rest*) о́тдых; (*peace*) поко́й.

repository /rɪˈpɒzɪtərɪ/ *n* храни́лище.

repossess /ˌriːpəˈzes/ *vt* изыма́ть *impf*, изъя́ть *pf* за неплатёж.

reprehensible /ˌreprɪˈhensɪb(ə)l/ *adj* предосуди́тельный.

represent /ˌreprɪˈzent/ *vt* представля́ть *impf*; (*portray*) изобража́ть *impf*, изобрази́ть *pf.* **representation** /-zenˈteɪʃ(ə)n/ *n* (*being represented*) представи́тельство; (*statement of case*) представле́ние; (*portrayal*) изображе́ние. **representative** /ˈzentətɪv/ *adj* изобража́ющий (**of** *+acc*); (*typical*) типи́чный; *n* представи́тель *m.*

repress /rɪˈpres/ *vt* подавля́ть *impf*, подави́ть *pf.* **repression** /-ˈpreʃ(ə)n/ *n* подавле́ние, репре́ссия. **repressive** /-ˈpresɪv/ *adj* репресси́вный.

reprieve /rɪˈpriːv/ *vt* отсро́чивать *impf*, отсро́чить *pf +dat* приведе́ние в исполне́ние (сме́ртного) пригово́ра; *n* отсро́чка приведе́ния в исполне́ние (сме́ртного) пригово́ра; (*fig*) переды́шка.

reprimand /ˈreprɪˌmɑːnd/ *n* вы́говор; *vt* де́лать *impf*, с~ *pf* вы́говор *+dat.*

reprint *vt* /riːˈprɪnt/ переиздава́ть *impf*, переизда́ть *pf*; *n* /ˈriːprɪnt/ переизда́ние.

reprisal /rɪˈpraɪz(ə)l/ *n* отве́тная ме́ра.

reproach /rɪˈprəʊtʃ/ *vt* упрека́ть *impf*, упрекну́ть *pf* (**with** в*+prep*). **reproachful** /-fʊl/ *adj* укори́зненный.

reproduce /ˌriːprəˈdjuːs/ *vt* воспроизводи́ть *impf*, воспроизвести́ *pf*; *vi* размножа́ться *impf*, размно́житься *pf.* **reproduction** /-ˈdʌkʃ(ə)n/ *n* (*action*) воспроизведе́ние; (*object*) репроду́кция;

(*of offspring*) размноже́ние. **reproductive** /-ˈdʌktɪv/ *adj* воспроизводи́тельный.

reproof /rɪˈpruːf/ *n* вы́говор. **reprove** /-ˈpruːv/ *vt* де́лать *impf* с~ *pf* вы́говор *+dat*.

reptile /ˈreptaɪl/ *n* пресмыка́ющееся *sb*.

republic /rɪˈpʌblɪk/ *n* респу́блика. **republican** /-kən/ *adj* республика́нский; *n* республика́нец, -нка.

repudiate /rɪˈpjuːdɪˌeɪt/ *vt* (*renounce*) отка́зываться *impf*, отказа́ться *pf* от+*gen*; (*reject*) отверга́ть *impf*, отве́ргнуть *pf*. **repudiation** /-ˌpjuːdɪˈeɪʃ(ə)n/ *n* отка́з (**of** от+*gen*).

repugnance /rɪˈpʌgnəns/ *n* отвраще́ние. **repugnant** /-nənt/ *adj* проти́вный.

repulse /rɪˈpʌls/ *vt* отража́ть *impf*, отрази́ть *pf*. **repulsion** /-ˈpʌlʃ(ə)n/ *n* отвраще́ние. **repulsive** /-ˈpʌlsɪv/ *adj* отврати́тельный.

reputable /ˈrepjʊtəb(ə)l/ *adj* по́льзующийся хоро́шей репута́цией. **reputation, repute** /ˌrepjʊˈteɪʃ(ə)n, rɪˈpjuːt/ *n* репута́ция. **reputed** /-ˈpjuːtɪd/ *adj* предполага́емый. **reputedly** /-ˈpjuːtɪdlɪ/ *adv* по о́бщему мне́нию.

request /rɪˈkwest/ *n* про́сьба; **by, on, ~** по про́сьбе; *vt* проси́ть *impf*, по~ *pf* *+acc*, *+gen* (*person* *+acc*).

requiem /ˈrekwɪˌem/ *n* ре́квием.

require /rɪˈkwaɪə(r)/ *vt* (*demand*; *need*) тре́бовать *impf*, по~ *pf* *+gen*; (*need*) нужда́ться *impf* в+*prep*. **requirement** /-mənt/ *n* тре́бование; (*necessity*) потре́бность. **requisite** /ˈrekwɪzɪt/ *adj* необходи́мый; *n* необходи́мая вещь. **requisition** /ˌrekwɪˈzɪʃ(ə)n/ *n* реквизи́ция; *vt* реквизи́ровать *impf* & *pf*.

resale /riːˈseɪl/ *n* перепрода́жа.

rescind /rɪˈsɪnd/ *vt* отменя́ть *impf*, отмени́ть *pf*.

rescue /ˈreskjuː/ *vt* спаса́ть *impf*, спасти́ *pf*; *n* спасе́ние. **rescuer** /ˈreskjuːə(r)/ *n* спаси́тель *m*.

research /rɪˈsɜːtʃ/ *n* иссле́дование (*+gen*); (*occupation*) иссле́довательская рабо́та; *vi*: **~ into** иссле́довать *impf* & *pf* *+acc*. **researcher** /-tʃə(r)/ *n* иссле́дователь *m*.

resemblance /rɪˈzembləns/ *n* схо́дство. **resemble** /-ˈzemb(ə)l/ *vt* походи́ть *impf* на+*acc*.

resent /rɪˈzent/ *vt* возмуща́ться *impf*, возмути́ться *pf*. **resentful** /-fʊl/ *adj* возмущённый. **resentment** /-mənt/ *n* возмуще́ние.

reservation /ˌrezəˈveɪʃ(ə)n/ *n* (*doubt*) огово́рка; (*booking*) предвари́тельный зака́з; (*land*) резерва́ция. **reserve** /rɪˈzɜːv/ *vt* (*keep*) резерви́ровать *impf* & *pf*; (*book*) зака́зывать *impf*, заказа́ть *pf*; *n* (*stock*; *mil*) запа́с, резе́рв; (*sport*) запасно́й игро́к; (*nature ~ etc.*) запове́дник; (*proviso*) огово́рка; (*self-restraint*) сде́ржанность; *attrib* запасно́й. **reserved** /-ˈzɜːvd/ *adj* (*person*) сде́ржанный. **reservist** /-ˈzɜːvɪst/ *n* резерви́ст. **reservoir** /ˈrezəˌvwɑː(r)/ *n* (*for water*) водохрани́лище; (*for other fluids*) резервуа́р.

resettle /riːˈset(ə)l/ *vt* переселя́ть *impf*, пересели́ть *pf*. **resettlement** /-mənt/ *n* переселе́ние.

reshape /riːˈʃeɪp/ *vt* видоизменя́ть *impf*, видоизмени́ть *pf*.

reshuffle /riːˈʃʌf(ə)l/ *n* перестано́вка.

reside /rɪˈzaɪd/ *vi* прожива́ть *impf*. **residence** /ˈrezɪd(ə)ns/ *n* (*residing*) прожива́ние; (*abode*) местожи́тельство; (*official ~ etc.*) резиде́нция. **resident** /ˈrezɪd(ə)nt/ *n* (постоя́нный) жи́тель *m*, ~ница; *adj* прожива́ющий; (*population*) постоя́нный. **residential** /ˌrezɪˈdenʃ(ə)l/ *adj* жило́й.

residual /rɪˈzɪdjʊəl/ *adj* оста́точный. **residue** /ˈrezɪˌdjuː/ *n* оста́ток.

resign /rɪˈzaɪn/ *vt* отка́зываться

impf, отказа́ться *pf* от+*gen*; *vi* уходи́ть *impf*, уйти́ *pf* в отста́вку; ~ **o.s. to** покоря́ться *impf*, покори́ться *pf* +*dat*. **resignation** /ˌrezɪɡˈneɪʃ(ə)n/ *n* отста́вка, заявле́ние об отста́вке; (*being resigned*) поко́рность. **resigned** /rɪˈzaɪnd/ *adj* поко́рный.

resilient /rɪˈzɪlɪənt/ *adj* выно́сливый.

resin /ˈrezɪn/ *n* смола́.

resist /rɪˈzɪst/ *vt* сопротивля́ться *impf* +*dat*; (*temptation*) устоя́ть *pf* пе́ред+*instr*. **resistance** /-ˈzɪst(ə)ns/ *n* сопротивле́ние. **resistant** /-ˈzɪst(ə)nt/ *adj* сто́йкий.

resolute /ˈrezəˌluːt/ *adj* реши́тельный. **resolution** /ˌrezəˈluːʃ(ə)n/ *n* (*character*) реши́тельность; (*vow*) заро́к; (*at meeting etc.*) резолю́ция; (*of problem*) разреше́ние. **resolve** /rɪˈzɒlv/ *vt* (*decide*) реша́ть *impf*, реши́ть *pf*; (*settle*) разреша́ть *impf*, разреши́ть *pf*; *n* реши́тельность; (*decision*) реше́ние.

resonance /ˈrezənəns/ *n* резона́нс. **resonant** /ˈrezənənt/ *adj* зву́чный.

resort /rɪˈzɔːt/ *vi*: ~ **to** прибега́ть *impf*, прибе́гнуть *pf* к+*dat*; *n* (*place*) куро́рт; **in the last** ~ в кра́йнем слу́чае.

resound /rɪˈzaʊnd/ *vi* (*of sound etc.*) раздава́ться *impf*, разда́ться *pf*; (*of place*) оглаша́ться *impf*, огласи́ться *pf* (**with** +*instr*).

resource /rɪˈsɔːs/ *n* (*usu pl*) ресу́рс. **resourceful** /-fʊl/ *adj* нахо́дчивый.

respect /rɪˈspekt/ *n* (*relation*) отноше́ние; (*esteem*) уваже́ние; **with** ~ **to** что каса́ется+*gen*; *vt* уважа́ть *impf*. **respectability** /-ˌspektəˈbɪlɪtɪ/ *n* респекта́бельность. **respectable** /-ˈspektəb(ə)l/ *adj* прили́чный. **respectful** /-ˈspektfʊl/ *adj* почти́тельный. **respective** /-ˈspektɪv/ *adj* свой. **respectively** /-ˈspektɪvlɪ/ *adv* соотве́тственно.

respiration /ˌrespɪˈreɪʃ(ə)n/ *n* дыха́ние. **respirator** /ˈrespɪˌreɪtə(r)/ *n* респира́тор. **respiratory** /rɪˈspɪrətərɪ/ *adj* дыха́тельный.

respite /ˈrespaɪt/ *n* передышка.

resplendent /rɪˈsplend(ə)nt/ *adj* блиста́тельный.

respond /rɪˈspɒnd/ *vi*: ~ **to** отвеча́ть *impf*, отве́тить *pf* на+*acc*; (*react*) реаги́ровать *impf*, про~, от~ *pf* на+*acc*. **response** /-ˈspɒns/ *n* отве́т; (*reaction*) о́тклик. **responsibility** /-ˌspɒnsɪˈbɪlɪtɪ/ *n* отве́тственность; (*duty*) обя́занность. **responsible** /-ˈspɒnsɪb(ə)l/ *adj* отве́тственный (**to** пе́ред +*instr*; **for** за+*acc*); (*reliable*) надёжный. **responsive** /-ˈspɒnsɪv/ *adj* отзы́вчивый.

rest[1] /rest/ *vi* отдыха́ть *impf*, отдохну́ть *pf*; *vt* (*place*) класть *impf*, положи́ть *pf*; (*allow to* ~) дава́ть *impf*, дать *pf* о́тдых+*dat*; *n* (*repose*) о́тдых; (*peace*) поко́й; (*mus*) па́уза; (*support*) опо́ра.

rest[2] /rest/ *n* (*remainder*) оста́ток; (*the others*) остальны́е *sb pl*.

restaurant /ˈrestəˌrɒnt/ *n* ресторáн.

restful /ˈrestfʊl/ *adj* успока́ивающий.

restitution /ˌrestɪˈtjuːʃ(ə)n/ *n* возвраще́ние.

restive /ˈrestɪv/ *adj* беспоко́йный.

restless /ˈrestlɪs/ *adj* беспоко́йный.

restoration /ˌrestəˈreɪʃ(ə)n/ *n* реставра́ция; (*return*) восстановле́ние. **restore** /rɪˈstɔː(r)/ *vt* реставри́ровать *impf* & *pf*; (*return*) восстана́вливать *impf*, восстанови́ть *pf*.

restrain /rɪˈstreɪn/ *vt* уде́рживать *impf*, удержа́ть *pf* (**from** от+*gen*). **restraint** /-ˈstreɪnt/ *n* сде́ржанность.

restrict /rɪˈstrɪkt/ *vt* ограни́чивать *impf*, ограни́чить *pf*. **restriction** /-ˈstrɪkʃ(ə)n/ *n* ограниче́ние. **restrictive** /-ˈstrɪktɪv/ *adj* ограничи́тельный.

result /rɪˈzʌlt/ *vi* сле́довать *impf*; происходи́ть *impf* (**from** из+*gen*);

r

~ in конча́ться *impf*, ко́нчиться *pf* +*instr*; *n* результа́т; **as a ~** в результа́те (**of** +*gen*).

resume /rɪ'zju:m/ *vt* & *i* возобновля́ть(ся) *impf*, возобнови́ть(ся) *pf*. **résumé** /'rezjʊ,meɪ/ *n* резюме́ *neut indecl*. **resumption** /rɪ'zʌmpʃ(ə)n/ *n* возобновле́ние.

resurrect /,rezə'rekt/ *vt* (*fig*) воскреша́ть *impf*, воскреси́ть *pf*. **resurrection** /-'rekʃ(ə)n/ *n* (*of the dead*) воскресе́ние; (*fig*) воскреше́ние.

resuscitate /rɪ'sʌsɪ,teɪt/ *vt* приводи́ть *impf*, привести́ *pf* в созна́ние.

retail /'ri:teɪl/ *n* ро́зничная прода́жа; *attrib* ро́зничный; *adv* в ро́зницу; *vt* продава́ть *impf*, прода́ть *pf* в ро́зницу; *vi* продава́ться *impf* в ро́зницу. **retailer** /-lə(r)/ *n* ро́зничный торго́вец.

retain /rɪ'teɪn/ *vt* уде́рживать *impf*, удержа́ть *pf*.

retaliate /rɪ'tælɪ,eɪt/ *vi* отпла́чивать *impf*, отплати́ть *pf* тем же. **retaliation** /-,tælɪ'eɪʃ(ə)n/ *n* отпла́та, возме́здие.

retard /rɪ'tɑ:d/ *vt* замедля́ть *impf*, заме́длить *pf*. **retarded** /-dɪd/ *adj* отста́лый.

retention /rɪ'tenʃ(ə)n/ *n* удержа́ние. **retentive** /-'tentɪv/ *adj* (*memory*) хоро́ший.

r

reticence /'retɪs(ə)ns/ *n* сде́ржанность. **reticent** /-s(ə)nt/ *adj* сде́ржанный.

retina /'retɪnə/ *n* сетча́тка.

retinue /'retɪ,nju:/ *n* сви́та.

retire /rɪ'taɪə(r)/ *vi* (*withdraw*) удаля́ться *impf*, удали́ться *pf*; (*from office etc.*) уходи́ть *impf*, уйти́ *pf* в отста́вку. **retired** /-'taɪəd/ *adj* в отста́вке. **retirement** /-'taɪəmənt/ *n* отста́вка. **retiring** /-'taɪrɪŋ/ *adj* скро́мный.

retort[1] /rɪ'tɔ:t/ *vt* отвеча́ть *impf*, отве́тить *pf* ре́зко; *n* возраже́ние.

retort[2] /rɪ'tɔ:t/ *n* (*vessel*) рето́рта.

retrace /rɪ'treɪs/ *vt*: **~ one's steps** возвраща́ться *impf*, возврати́ться *pf*.

retract /rɪ'trækt/ *vt* (*draw in*) втя́гивать *impf*, втяну́ть *pf*; (*take back*) брать *impf*, взять *pf* наза́д.

retreat /rɪ'tri:t/ *vi* отступа́ть *impf*, отступи́ть *pf*; *n* отступле́ние; (*withdrawal*) уедине́ние; (*place*) убе́жище.

retrenchment /rɪ'trentʃmənt/ *n* сокраще́ние расхо́дов.

retrial /'ri:traɪəl/ *n* повто́рное слу́шание де́ла.

retribution /,retrɪ'bju:ʃ(ə)n/ *n* возме́здие.

retrieval /rɪ'tri:v(ə)l/ *n* возвраще́ние; (*comput*) поиск (информа́ции); *vt* брать *impf*, взять *pf* обра́тно.

retrograde /'retrə,greɪd/ *adj* (*fig*) реакцио́нный. **retrospect** /'retrə,spekt/ *n*: **in ~** ретроспекти́вно. **retrospective** /-'spektɪv/ *adj* (*law*) име́ющий обра́тную си́лу.

return /rɪ'tɜ:n/ *vt* & *i* (*give back*; *come back*) возвраща́ть(ся) *impf*, возврати́ть(ся) *impf*, верну́ть(ся) *pf*; *vt* (*elect*) избира́ть *impf*, избра́ть *pf*; *n* возвраще́ние; возвра́т; (*profit*) при́быль; **by ~** обра́тной по́чтой; **in ~** взаме́н (**for** +*gen*); **many happy ~s!** с днём рожде́ния!; **~ match** отве́тный матч; **~ ticket** обра́тный биле́т.

reunion /ri:'ju:njən/ *n* встре́ча (друзе́й и т. п.); **family ~** сбор всей семьи́. **reunite** /,ri:ju:'naɪt/ *vt* воссоединя́ть *impf*, воссоедини́ть *pf*.

reuse /ri:'ju:z/ *vt* сно́ва испо́льзовать *impf* & *pf*.

rev /rev/ *n* оборо́т; *vt* & *i*: **~ up** рвану́ть(ся) *pf*.

reveal /rɪ'vi:l/ *vt* обнару́живать *impf*, обнару́жить *pf*. **revealing** /-lɪŋ/ *adj* показа́тельный.

revel /'rev(ə)l/ *vi* пирова́ть *impf*; **~ in** наслажда́ться *impf* +*instr*.

revelation /,revə'leɪʃ(ə)n/ *n* открове́ние.

revenge /rɪ'vendʒ/ *vt*: ~ **o.s.** мстить *impf*, ото~ *pf* (**for** за+*acc*; **on** +*dat*); *n* месть.
revenue /'revəˌnjuː/ *n* дохо́д.
reverberate /rɪ'vɜːbəˌreɪt/ *vi* отража́ться *impf*. **reverberation** /-'reɪʃ(ə)n/ *n* отраже́ние; (*fig*) о́тзвук.
revere /rɪ'vɪə(r)/ *vt* почита́ть *impf*. **reverence** /'revərəns/ *n* почте́ние. **Reverend** /'reverənd/ *adj* (*in title*) (его́) преподо́бие. **reverent(ial)** /'revərənt/, /ˌrevə'renʃ(ə)l/ *adj* почти́тельный.
reverie /'revərɪ/ *n* мечта́ние.
reversal /rɪ'vɜːs(ə)l/ *n* (*change*) измене́ние; (*of decision*) отме́на. **reverse** /-'vɜːs/ *adj* обра́тный; ~ **gear** за́дний ход; *vt* (*change*) изменя́ть *impf*, измени́ть *pf*; (*decision*) отменя́ть *impf*, отмени́ть *pf*; *vi* дава́ть *impf*, дать *pf* за́дний ход; *n* (*the* ~) обра́тное *sb*, противополо́жное *sb*; (~ *gear*) за́дний ход; (~ *side*) обра́тная сторона́. **reversible** /-'vɜːsɪb(ə)l/ *adj* обрати́мый; (*cloth*) двусторо́нний. **reversion** /-'vɜːʃ(ə)n/ *n* возвраще́ние. **revert** /-'vɜːt/ *vi* возвраща́ться *impf* (**to** в+*acc*, к+*dat*); (*law*) переходи́ть *impf*, перейти́ *pf* (**to** к+*dat*).
review /rɪ'vjuː/ *n* (*re-examination*) пересмо́тр; (*mil*) пара́д; (*survey*) обзо́р; (*criticism*) реце́нзия; *vt* (*re-examine*) пересма́тривать *impf*, пересмотре́ть *pf*; (*survey*) обозрева́ть *impf*, обозре́ть *pf*; (*troops etc.*) принима́ть *impf*, приня́ть *pf* пара́д+*gen*; (*book etc.*) рецензи́ровать *impf*, про~ *pf*. **reviewer** /-'vjuːə(r)/ *n* рецензе́нт.
revise /rɪ'vaɪz/ *vt* пересма́тривать *impf*, пересмотре́ть *pf*; исправля́ть *impf*, испра́вить *pf*; *vi* (*for exam*) гото́виться *impf* (**for** к+*dat*). **revision** /-'vɪʒ(ə)n/ *n* пересмо́тр, исправле́ние.
revival /rɪ'vaɪv(ə)l/ *n* возрожде́ние; (*to life etc.*) оживле́ние. **revive** /-'vaɪv/ *vt* возрожда́ть *impf*, возроди́ть *pf*; (*resuscitate*) оживля́ть *impf*, оживи́ть *pf*; *vi* ожива́ть *impf*, ожи́ть *pf*.
revoke /rɪ'vəʊk/ *vt* отменя́ть *impf*, отмени́ть *pf*.
revolt /rɪ'vəʊlt/ *n* бунт; *vt* вызыва́ть *impf*, вы́звать *pf* отвраще́ние у+*gen*; *vi* бунтова́ть *impf*, взбунтова́ться *pf*. **revolting** /-'vəʊltɪŋ/ *adj* отврати́тельный.
revolution /ˌrevə'luːʃ(ə)n/ *n* (*single turn*) оборо́т; (*polit*) револю́ция. **revolutionary** /-'luːʃənərɪ/ *adj* революцио́нный; *n* революционе́р. **revolutionize** /-'luːʃəˌnaɪz/ *vt* революционизи́ровать *impf* & *pf*. **revolve** /rɪ'vɒlv/ *vt* & *i* враща́ть(ся) *impf*. **revolver** /rɪ'vɒlvə(r)/ *n* револьве́р.
revue /rɪ'vjuː/ *n* ревю́ *neut indecl*.
revulsion /rɪ'vʌlʃ(ə)n/ *n* отвраще́ние.
reward /rɪ'wɔːd/ *n* вознагражде́ние; *vt* (воз)награжда́ть *impf*, (воз)награди́ть *pf*.
rewrite /riː'raɪt/ *vt* перепи́сывать *impf*, переписа́ть *pf*; (*recast*) переде́лывать *impf*, переде́лать *pf*.
rhapsody /'ræpsədɪ/ *n* рапсо́дия.
rhetoric /'retərɪk/ *n* рито́рика. **rhetorical** /rɪ'tɒrɪk(ə)l/ *adj* ритори́ческий.
rheumatic /ruː'mætɪk/ *adj* ревмати́ческий. **rheumatism** /'ruːməˌtɪz(ə)m/ *n* ревмати́зм.
rhinoceros /raɪ'nɒsərəs/ *n* носоро́г.
rhododendron /ˌrəʊdə'dendrən/ *n* рододе́ндрон.
rhubarb /'ruːbɑːb/ *n* реве́нь *m*.
rhyme /raɪm/ *n* ри́фма; *pl* (*verse*) стихи́ *m pl*; *vt* & *i* рифмова́ть(ся) *impf*.
rhythm /'rɪð(ə)m/ *n* ритм. **rhythmic(al)** /'rɪðmɪk(əl)/ *adj* ритми́ческий, -чный.
rib /rɪb/ *n* ребро́.
ribald /'rɪb(ə)ld/ *adj* непристо́йный.
ribbon /'rɪbən/ *n* ле́нта.
rice /raɪs/ *n* рис.
rich /rɪtʃ/ *adj* бога́тый; (*soil*) ту́ч-

ный; (*food*) жи́рный. **riches** /'rɪtʃɪz/ *n pl* бога́тство. **richly** /'rɪtʃlɪ/ *adv* (*fully*) вполне́.

rickety /'rɪkɪtɪ/ *adj* (*shaky*) расша́танный.

ricochet /'rɪkə,ʃeɪ/ *vi* рикошети́ровать *impf* & *pf*.

rid /rɪd/ *vt* освобожда́ть *impf*, освободи́ть *pf* (**of** от+*gen*); **get ~ of** избавля́ться *impf*, изба́виться *pf* от+*gen*. **riddance** /'rɪd(ə)ns/ *n*: **good ~!** ска́тертью доро́га!

riddle /'rɪd(ə)l/ *n* (*enigma*) зага́дка.

riddled /'rɪd(ə)ld/ *adj*: **~ with** изрешечённый; (*fig*) прони́занный.

ride /raɪd/ *vi* е́здить *indet*, е́хать *det*, по~ *pf* (**on horseback** верхо́м); *vt* е́здить *indet*, е́хать *det*, по~ *pf* в, на+*prep*; *n* пое́здка, езда́. **rider** /-də(r)/ *n* вса́дник, -ица; (*clause*) дополне́ние.

ridge /rɪdʒ/ *n* хребе́т; (*on cloth*) ру́бчик; (*of roof*) конёк.

ridicule /'rɪdɪ,kjuːl/ *n* насме́шка; *vt* осме́ивать *impf*, осмея́ть *pf*. **ridiculous** /rɪ'dɪkjʊləs/ *adj* смешно́й.

riding /'raɪdɪŋ/ *n* (*horse-~*) (верхова́я) езда́.

rife /raɪf/ *predic* распространённый.

riff-raff /'rɪfræf/ *n* подо́нки (-ков) *pl*.

rifle /'raɪf(ə)l/ *n* винто́вка; *vt* (*search*) обы́скивать *impf*, обыска́ть *pf*.

rift /rɪft/ *n* тре́щина (*also fig*).

rig /rɪg/ *vt* оснаща́ть *impf*, оснасти́ть *pf*; **~ out** наряжа́ть *impf*, наряди́ть *pf*; **~ up** скола́чивать *impf*, сколоти́ть *pf*; *n* бурова́я устано́вка. **rigging** /-gɪŋ/ *n* такела́ж.

right /raɪt/ *adj* (*position*; *justified*; *polit*) пра́вый; (*correct*) пра́вильный; (*the one wanted*) тот; (*suitable*) подходя́щий; **~ angle** прямо́й у́гол; *vt* исправля́ть *impf*, испра́вить *pf*; *n* пра́во; (*what is just*) справедли́вость; (*~ side*) пра́вая сторона́; (**the R~**; *polit*) пра́вые *sb pl*; **be in the ~** быть пра́вым; **by ~s** по пра́ву; **~ of way** пра́во прохо́да, прое́зда; *adv* (*straight*) пря́мо; (*exactly*) то́чно, как раз; (*to the full*) соверше́нно; (*correctly*) пра́вильно; как сле́дует; (*on the ~*) спра́во (**of** от+*gen*); (*to the ~*) напра́во; **~ away** сейча́с.

righteous /'raɪtʃəs/ *adj* (*person*) пра́ведный; (*action*) справедли́вый.

rightful /'raɪtfʊl/ *adj* зако́нный.

rigid /'rɪdʒɪd/ *adj* жёсткий; (*strict*) стро́гий. **rigidity** /rɪ'dʒɪdɪtɪ/ *n* жёсткость; стро́гость.

rigmarole /'rɪgmə,rəʊl/ *n* канитéль.

rigorous /'rɪgərəs/ *adj* стро́гий. **rigour** /'rɪgə(r)/ *n* стро́гость.

rim /rɪm/ *n* (*of wheel*) о́бод; (*spectacles*) опра́ва. **rimless** /-lɪs/ *adj* без опра́вы.

rind /raɪnd/ *n* кожура́.

ring[1] /rɪŋ/ *n* кольцо́; (*circle*) круг; (*boxing*) ринг; (*circus*) (циркова́я) аре́на; **~ road** кольцева́я доро́га; *vt* (*encircle*) окружа́ть *impf*, окружи́ть *pf*.

ring[2] /rɪŋ/ *vi* (*sound*) звони́ть *impf*, по~ *pf*; (*ring out, of shot etc.*) раздава́ться *impf*, разда́ться *pf*; (*of place*) оглаша́ться *impf*, огласи́ться *pf* (**with** +*instr*); *vt* звони́ть *impf*, по~ *pf* в+*acc*; **~ back** перезва́нивать *impf*, перезвони́ть *pf*; **~ off** пове́сить *pf* тру́бку; **~ up** звони́ть *impf*, по~ *pf* +*dat*; *n* звон, звоно́к.

ringleader *n* глава́рь *m*.

ringtone *n* мело́дия звонка́, рингто́н (в моби́льном телефо́не).

rink /rɪŋk/ *n* като́к.

rinse /rɪns/ *vt* полоска́ть *impf*, вы́~ *pf*; *n* полоска́ние.

riot /'raɪət/ *n* бунт; **run ~** бу́йствовать *impf*; (*of plants*) бу́йно разраста́ться *impf*, разрасти́сь *pf*; *vi* бунтова́ть *impf*, взбунтова́ться *pf*. **riotous** /'raɪətəs/ *adj* бу́йный.

rip /rɪp/ *vt* & *i* рва́ть(ся) *impf*; разо~ *pf*; **~ up** разрыва́ть *impf*, разорва́ть *pf*; *n* проре́ха, разре́з.

r

ripe /raɪp/ *adj* зре́лый, спе́лый. **ripen** /ˈraɪpən/ *vt* де́лать *impf*, с~ *pf* зре́лым; *vi* созрева́ть *impf*, созре́ть *pf*. **ripeness** /-nɪs/ *n* зре́лость.

ripple /ˈrɪp(ə)l/ *n* рябь; *vt* & *i* покрыва́ть(ся) *impf*, покры́ть(ся) *pf* ря́бью.

rise /raɪz/ *vi* поднима́ться *impf*, подня́ться *pf*; повыша́ться *impf*, повы́ситься *pf*; (*get up*) встава́ть *impf*, встать *pf*; (*rebel*) восстава́ть *impf*, восста́ть *pf*; (*sun etc.*) в(о)сходи́ть *impf*, взойти́; *n* подъём, возвыше́ние; (*in pay*) приба́вка; (*of sun etc.*) восхо́д. **riser** /-zə(r)/ *n*: **he is an early ~** он ра́но встаёт.

risk /rɪsk/ *n* риск; *vt* рискова́ть *impf*, рискну́ть *pf* +*instr.* **risky** /-kɪ/ *adj* риско́ванный.

risqué /ˈrɪskeɪ/ *adj* непристо́йный.

rite /raɪt/ *n* обря́д. **ritual** /ˈrɪtjʊəl/ *n* ритуа́л; *adj* ритуа́льный.

rival /ˈraɪv(ə)l/ *n* сопе́рник, -ица; *adj* сопе́рничающий; *vt* сопе́рничать *impf* с+*instr.* **rivalry** /-rɪ/ *n* сопе́рничество.

river /ˈrɪvə(r)/ *n* река́. **riverside** *attrib* прибре́жный.

rivet /ˈrɪvɪt/ *n* заклёпка; *vt* заклёпывать *impf*, заклепа́ть *pf*; (*fig*) прико́вывать *impf*, прикова́ть *pf* (**on** к+*dat*).

road /rəʊd/ *n* доро́га; (*street*) у́лица; **~-block** загражде́ние на доро́ге; **~-map** (доро́жная) ка́рта; **~ sign** доро́жный знак. **roadside** *n* обо́чина; *attrib* придоро́жный. **roadway** *n* мостова́я *sb.*

roam /rəʊm/ *vt* & *i* броди́ть *impf* (по+*dat*).

roar /rɔː(r)/ *n* (*animal's*) рёв; *vi* реве́ть *impf.*

roast /rəʊst/ *vt* & *i* жа́рить(ся) *impf*, за~, из~ *pf*; *adj* жа́реный; **~ beef** ро́стбиф; *n* жарко́е *sb.*

rob /rɒb/ *vt* гра́бить *impf*, о~ *pf*; красть *impf*, у~ *pf* у+*gen* (**of** +*acc*); (*deprive*) лиша́ть *impf*, лиши́ть *pf* (**of** +*gen*). **robber** /ˈrɒbə(r)/ *n* граби́тель *m.* **robbery** /ˈrɒbərɪ/ *n* грабёж.

robe /rəʊb/ *n* (*also pl*) ма́нтия.

robin /ˈrɒbɪn/ *n* мали́новка.

robot /ˈrəʊbɒt/ *n* ро́бот.

robust /rəʊˈbʌst/ *adj* кре́пкий.

rock[1] /rɒk/ *n* (*geol*) (го́рная) поро́да; (*cliff etc.*) скала́; (*large stone*) большо́й ка́мень *m*; **on the ~s** (*in difficulty*) на мели́; (*drink*) со льдом.

rock[2] /rɒk/ *vt* & *i* кача́ть(ся) *impf*, качну́ть(ся) *pf*; *n* (*mus*) рок; **~ing-chair** кача́лка; **~ and roll** рок-н-ро́лл.

rockery /ˈrɒkərɪ/ *n* альпина́рий.

rocket /ˈrɒkɪt/ *n* раке́та; *vi* подска́кивать *impf*, подскочи́ть *pf.*

rocky /ˈrɒkɪ/ *adj* скали́стый; (*shaky*) ша́ткий.

rod /rɒd/ *n* (*stick*) прут; (*bar*) сте́ржень *m*; (*fishing-~*) у́дочка.

rodent /ˈrəʊd(ə)nt/ *n* грызу́н.

roe[1] /rəʊ/ *n* икра́; (*soft*) моло́ки (-о́к) *pl.*

roe[2] /rəʊ/ **(-deer)** // *n* косу́ля.

rogue /rəʊg/ *n* плут.

role /rəʊl/ *n* роль.

roll[1] /rəʊl/ *n* (*cylinder*) руло́н; (*register*) рее́стр; (*bread*) бу́лочка; **~-call** перекли́чка.

roll[2] /rəʊl/ *vt* & *i* ката́ть(ся) *indet*, кати́ть(ся) *det*, по~ *pf*; (**~ *up***) свёртывать(ся) *impf*, сверну́ть(ся) *pf*; *vt* (**~ *out***) (*dough*) раска́тывать *impf*, раската́ть *pf*; *vi* (*sound*) греме́ть *impf*; **~ over** перевора́чиваться *impf*, переверну́ться *pf*; *n* (*of drums*) бараба́нная дробь; (*of thunder*) раска́т.

roller /ˈrəʊlə(r)/ *n* (*small*) ро́лик; (*large*) като́к; (*for hair*) бигуди́ *neut indecl*; **~-skates** коньки́ *m pl* на ро́ликах.

rolling /ˈrəʊlɪŋ/ *adj* (*of land*) холми́стый; **~-pin** ска́лка. **~-stock** подвижно́й соста́в.

Roman /ˈrəʊmən/ *n* ри́млянин, -янка; *adj* ри́мский; **~ Catholic** (*n*) като́лик, -и́чка; (*adj*) ри́мско-католи́ческий.

romance /rəʊˈmæns/ *n* (*tale*; *love*

affair) рома́н; (*quality*) рома́нтика.

Romanesque /ˌrəʊmə'nesk/ *adj* рома́нский.

Romania /rəʊ'meɪnɪə/ *n* Румы́ния. **Romanian** /-nɪən/ *n* румы́н, ~ка; *adj* румы́нский.

romantic /rəʊ'mæntɪk/ *adj* романти́чный, -ческий. **romanticism** /-tɪˌsɪz(ə)m/ *n* романти́зм.

romp /rɒmp/ *vi* вози́ться *impf*.

roof /ruːf/ *n* кры́ша; **~ of the mouth** нёбо; *vt* крыть *impf*, покры́ть *pf*.

rook[1] /rʊk/ *n* (*chess*) ладья́.

rook[2] /rʊk/ *n* (*bird*) грач.

room /ruːm/ *n* ко́мната; (*in hotel*) но́мер; (*space*) ме́сто. **roomy** /'ruːmɪ/ *adj* просто́рный.

roost /ruːst/ *n* насе́ст.

root[1] /ruːt/ *n* ко́рень *m*; **take ~** укореня́ться *impf*, укорени́ться *pf*; *vi* пуска́ть *impf*, пусти́ть *pf* ко́рни; **~ out** вырыва́ть *impf*, вы́рвать *pf* с ко́рнем; **rooted to the spot** прико́ванный к ме́сту.

root[2] /ruːt/ *vi* (*rummage*) ры́ться *impf*; **~ for** боле́ть *impf* за +*acc*.

rope /rəʊp/ *n* верёвка; **~-ladder** верёвочная ле́стница; *vt*: **~ in** (*enlist*) втя́гивать *impf*, втя́нуть *pf*; **~ off** о(т)гора́живать *impf*, о(т)городи́ть *pf* верёвкой.

rosary /'rəʊzərɪ/ *n* чётки (-ток) *pl*.

rose /rəʊz/ *n* ро́за; (*nozzle*) се́тка.

r

rosemary /'rəʊzmərɪ/ *n* розмари́н.

rosette /rəʊ'zet/ *n* розе́тка.

rosewood /'rəʊzwʊd/ *n* ро́зовое де́рево.

roster /'rɒstə(r)/ *n* расписа́ние дежу́рств.

rostrum /'rɒstrəm/ *n* трибу́на.

rosy /'rəʊzɪ/ *adj* ро́зовый; (*cheeks*) румя́ный.

rot /rɒt/ *n* гниль; (*nonsense*) вздор; *vi* гнить *impf*, с~ *pf*; *vt* гнои́ть *impf*, с~ *pf*.

rota /'rəʊtə/ *n* расписа́ние дежу́рств. **rotary** /'rəʊtərɪ/ *adj* враща́тельный, ротацио́нный. **rotate** /rəʊ'teɪt/ *vt* & *i* враща́ть(ся) *impf*. **rotation** /-'teɪʃ(ə)n/ *n* враще́ние; **in ~** по о́череди.

rote /rəʊt/ *n*: **by ~** наизу́сть.

rotten /'rɒt(ə)n/ *adj* гнило́й; (*fig*) отврати́тельный.

rotund /rəʊ'tʌnd/ *adj* (*round*) кру́глый; (*plump*) по́лный.

rouble /'ruːb(ə)l/ *n* рубль *m*.

rough /rʌf/ *adj* (*uneven*) неро́вный; (*coarse*) гру́бый; (*sea*) бу́рный; (*approximate*) приблизи́тельный; **~ copy** чернови́к; *n*: **the ~** тру́дности *f pl*; *vt*: **~ it** жить *impf* без удо́бств. **roughage** /'rʌfɪdʒ/ *n* гру́бая пи́ща. **roughly** /'rʌflɪ/ *adv* гру́бо; (*approximately*) приблизи́тельно.

roulette /ruː'let/ *n* руле́тка.

round /raʊnd/ *adj* кру́глый; **~-shouldered** суту́лый; *n* (**~** *object*) круг; (*circuit*; *also pl*) обхо́д; (*sport*) тур, ра́унд; (*series*) ряд; (*ammunition*) патро́н; (*of applause*) взрыв; *adv* вокру́г; (*in a circle*) по кру́гу; **all ~** круго́м; **all the year ~** кру́глый год; *prep* вокру́г+*gen*; круго́м +*gen*; по+*dat*; **~ the corner** (*motion*) за́ угол, (*position*) за угло́м; *vt* (*go ~*) огиба́ть *impf*, обогну́ть *pf*; **~ off** (*complete*) заверша́ть *impf*, заверши́ть *pf*; **~ up** сгоня́ть *impf*, согна́ть *pf*; **~-up** заго́н; (*raid*) обла́ва. **roundabout** *n* (*merry-go-round*) карусе́ль; (*road junction*) кольцева́я тра́нспортная развя́зка; *adj* око́льный.

rouse /raʊz/ *vt* буди́ть *impf*, раз~ *pf*; (*to action etc.*) побужда́ть *impf*, побуди́ть *pf* (**to** к+*dat*). **rousing** /'raʊzɪŋ/ *adj* восто́рженный.

rout /raʊt/ *n* (*defeat*) разгро́м.

route /ruːt/ *n* маршру́т, путь *m*.

routine /ruː'tiːn/ *n* заведённый поря́док, режи́м; *adj* устано́вленный; очередно́й.

rove /rəʊv/ *vi* скита́ться *impf*.

row[1] /rəʊ/ *n* (*line*) ряд.

row[2] /rəʊ/ *vi* (*in boat*) грести́ *impf*.

row[3] /raʊ/ *n* (*dispute*) ссо́ра; (*noise*) шум; *vi* ссо́риться *impf*, по~ *pf*.

rowdy /ˈraʊdɪ/ *adj* бу́йный.
royal /ˈrɔɪəl/ *adj* короле́вский; (*majestic*) великоле́пный. **royalist** /-lɪst/ *n* роялист; *adj* роялистский. **royalty** /-tɪ/ *n* член, чле́ны *pl*, короле́вской семьи́; (*fee*) а́вторский гонора́р.
rub /rʌb/ *vt* & *i* тере́ть(ся) *impf*; *vt* (*polish*; *chafe*) натира́ть *impf*, натере́ть *pf*; (**~** *dry*) вытира́ть *impf*, вы́тереть *pf*; **~ in, on** втира́ть *impf*, втере́ть *pf*; **~ out** стира́ть *impf*, стере́ть *pf*; **~ it in** растравля́ть *impf*, растрави́ть *pf* ра́ну.
rubber /ˈrʌbə(r)/ *n* рези́на; (*eraser, also* **~** *band*) рези́нка; *attrib* рези́новый; **~-stamp** (*fig*) штампова́ть *impf*.
rubbish /ˈrʌbɪʃ/ *n* му́сор; (*nonsense*) чепуха́.
rubble /ˈrʌb(ə)l/ *n* щёбень *m*.
rubella /ruːˈbelə/ *n* красну́ха.
ruby /ˈruːbɪ/ *n* руби́н.
ruck /rʌk/ *vt* (**~** *up*) мять *impf*, из**~**, с**~** *pf*.
rucksack /ˈrʌksæk/ *n* рюкза́к.
rudder /ˈrʌdə(r)/ *n* руль *m*.
ruddy /ˈrʌdɪ/ *adj* (*face*) румя́ный; (*damned*) проклятый.
rude /ruːd/ *adj* гру́бый. **rudeness** /-nɪs/ *n* гру́бость.
rudimentary /ˌruːdɪˈmentərɪ/ *adj* рудимента́рный. **rudiments** /ˈruːdɪmənts/ *n pl* осно́вы *f pl*.
rueful /ˈruːfʊl/ *adj* печа́льный.
ruff /rʌf/ *n* (*frill*) бры́жи (-жей) *pl*; (*of feathers, hair*) кольцо́ (пе́рьев, ше́рсти) вокру́г ше́и.
ruffian /ˈrʌfɪən/ *n* хулига́н.
ruffle /ˈrʌf(ə)l/ *n* обо́рка; *vt* (*hair*) еро́шить *impf*, взъ**~** *pf*; (*water*) рябить *impf*; (*person*) смуща́ть *impf*, смути́ть *pf*.
rug /rʌg/ *n* (*mat*) ковёр; (*wrap*) плед.
rugby /ˈrʌgbɪ/ *n* ре́гби *neut indecl*.
rugged /ˈrʌgɪd/ *adj* (*rocky*) скали́стый.
ruin /ˈruːɪn/ *n* (*downfall*) ги́бель; (*building, ruins*) разва́лины *f pl*, руи́ны *f pl*; *vt* губи́ть *impf*, по**~** *pf*. **ruinous** /-nəs/ *adj* губи́тельный.
rule /ruːl/ *n* пра́вило; (*for measuring*) лине́йка; (*government*) правле́ние; **as a ~** как пра́вило; *vt* & *i* пра́вить *impf* (+*instr*); (*decree*) постановля́ть *impf*, постанови́ть *pf*; **~ out** исключа́ть *impf*, исключи́ть *pf*. **ruled** /ruːld/ *adj* лино́ванный. **ruler** /ˈruːlə(r)/ *n* (*person*) прави́тель *m*, **~**ница; (*object*) лине́йка. **ruling** /ˈruːlɪŋ/ *n* (*of court etc.*) постановле́ние.
rum /rʌm/ *n* (*drink*) ром.
Rumania(n) /rəˈmeɪnɪə(n)/ *see* **Romania(n)**
rumble /ˈrʌmb(ə)l/ *vi* громыха́ть *impf*; *n* громыха́ние.
ruminant /ˈruːmɪnənt/ *n* жва́чное (живо́тное) *sb*. **ruminate** /-ˌneɪt/ *vi* (*fig*) размышля́ть *impf* (**over, on** о+*prep*).
rummage /ˈrʌmɪdʒ/ *vi* ры́ться *impf*.
rumour /ˈruːmə(r)/ *n* слух; *vt*: **it is ~ed that** хо́дят слу́хи (*pl*), что.
rump /rʌmp/ *n* кресте́ц; **~ steak** ромште́кс.
rumple /ˈrʌmp(ə)l/ *vt* мять *impf*, из**~**, с**~** *pf*; (*hair*) еро́шить *impf*, взъ**~** *pf*.
run /rʌn/ *vi* бе́гать *indet*, бежа́ть *det*, по**~** *pf*; (*work, of machines*) рабо́тать *impf*; (*ply, of bus etc.*) ходи́ть *indet*, идти́ *det*; (*seek election*) выставля́ть *impf*, вы́ставить *pf* свою́ кандидату́ру; (*of play etc.*) идти́ *impf*; (*of ink, dye*) расплыва́ться *impf*, расплы́ться *pf*; (*flow*) течь *impf*; (*of document*) гласи́ть *impf*; *vt* (*manage; operate*) управля́ть *impf* +*instr*; (*a business etc.*) вести́ *impf*; **~ dry, low** иссяка́ть *impf*, исся́кнуть *pf*; **~ risks** рискова́ть *impf*; **~ across, into** (*meet*) встреча́ться *impf*, встре́титься *pf* с+*instr*; **~ away** (*flee*) убега́ть *impf*, убежа́ть *pf*; **~ down** (*knock down*) задави́ть *pf*; (*disparage*) принижа́ть *impf*, прини́зить *pf*; **be ~ down** (*of person*) переутоми́ться *pf* (*in past*

r

tense); **~-down** (*decayed*) запу́щенный; **~ in** (*engine*) обка́тывать *impf*, обката́ть *pf*; **~ into** *see* **~ across; ~ out** конча́ться *impf*, ко́нчиться *pf*; **~ out of** истоща́ть *impf*, истощи́ть *pf* свой запа́с +*gen*; **~ over** (*glance over*) бе́гло просма́тривать *impf*, просмотре́ть *pf*; (*injure*) задави́ть *pf*; **~ through** (*pierce*) прока́лывать *impf*, проколо́ть *pf*; (*money*) прома́тывать *impf*, промота́ть *pf*; (*review*) повторя́ть *impf*, повтори́ть *pf*; **~ to** (*reach*) (*of money*) хвата́ть *impf*, хвати́ть *pf impers* +*gen* на+*acc*; **the money won't ~ to a car** э́тих де́нег не хва́тит на маши́ну; **~ up against** ната́лкиваться *impf*, натолкну́ться *pf* на+*acc*; *n* бег; (*sport*) перебе́жка; (*journey*) пое́здка; (*period*) полоса́; **at a ~** бего́м; **on the ~** в бега́х; **~ on** большо́й спрос на+*acc*; **in the long ~** в конце́ концо́в.

rung /rʌŋ/ *n* ступе́нька.

runner /ˈrʌnə(r)/ *n* (*also tech*) бегу́н; (*of sledge*) по́лоз; (*bot*) побе́г; **~ bean** фасо́ль; **~-up** уча́стник, заня́вший второ́е ме́сто. **running** /ˈrʌnɪŋ/ *n* бег; (*management*) управле́ние (**of** +*instr*); **be in the ~** име́ть *impf* ша́нсы; *adj* бегу́щий; (*of ~*) бегово́й; (*after pl n, in succession*) подря́д; **~ commentary** репорта́ж; **~ water** водопрово́д. **runway** *n* взлётно-поса́дочная полоса́.

rupee /ruːˈpiː/ *n* ру́пия.

rupture /ˈrʌptʃə(r)/ *n* разры́в; *vt & i* прорыва́ть(ся) *impf*, прорва́ть(ся) *pf*.

rural /ˈrʊər(ə)l/ *adj* се́льский.

ruse /ruːz/ *n* уло́вка.

rush¹ /rʌʃ/ *n* (*bot*) тростни́к.

rush² /rʌʃ/ *vt & i* (*hurry*) торопи́ть(ся) *impf*, по~ *pf*; *vi* (*dash*) броса́ться *impf*, бро́ситься *pf*; (*of water*) нести́сь *impf*, по~ *pf*; *vt* (*to hospital etc.*) умча́ть *pf*; *n* (*of blood etc.*) прили́в; (*hurry*) спе́шка; **be in a ~** торопи́ться *impf*; **~-hour(s)** часы́ *m pl* пик.

Russia /ˈrʌʃə/ *n* Росси́я. **Russian** /-ʃən/ *n* ру́сский *sb*; *adj* (*of ~ nationality, culture*) ру́сский; (*of ~ State*) росси́йский.

rust /rʌst/ *n* ржа́вчина; *vi* ржаве́ть *impf*, за~, по~ *pf*.

rustic /ˈrʌstɪk/ *adj* дереве́нский.

rustle /ˈrʌs(ə)l/ *n* ше́лест, шо́рох, шурша́ние; *vi & t* шелесте́ть *impf* (+*instr*); **~ up** раздобыва́ть *impf*; раздобы́ть *pf*.

rusty /ˈrʌstɪ/ *adj* ржа́вый.

rut /rʌt/ *n* колея́.

ruthless /ˈruːθlɪs/ *adj* безжа́лостный.

rye /raɪ/ *n* рожь; *attrib* ржано́й.

S

Sabbath /ˈsæbəθ/ *n* (*Jewish*) суббо́та; (*Christian*) воскресе́нье. **sabbatical** /səˈbætɪk(ə)l/ *n* годи́чный о́тпуск.

sable /ˈseɪb(ə)l/ *n* со́боль.

sabotage /ˈsæbəˌtɑːʒ/ *n* дивéрсия; *vt* саботи́ровать *impf & pf*. **saboteur** /ˌsæbəˈtɜː(r)/ *n* диверса́нт.

sabre /ˈseɪbə(r)/ *n* са́бля.

sachet /ˈsæʃeɪ/ *n* упако́вка.

sack¹ /sæk/ *vt* (*plunder*) разгра́бить *pf*.

sack² /sæk/ *n* мешо́к; (*dismissal*): **get the ~** быть уво́ленным; *vt* увольня́ть *impf*, уво́лить *pf*. **sacking** /-kɪŋ/ *n* (*hessian*) мешкови́на.

sacrament /ˈsækrəmənt/ *n* та́инство; (*Eucharist*) прича́стие. **sacred** /ˈseɪkrɪd/ *adj* свяще́нный, свято́й. **sacrifice** /ˈsækrɪˌfaɪs/ *n* же́ртва; *vt* же́ртвовать *impf*, по~ *pf* +*instr*. **sacrilege** /ˈsækrɪlɪdʒ/ *n* святота́тство. **sacrosanct** /ˈsækrəʊˌsæŋkt/ *adj* свяще́нный.

sad /sæd/ *adj* печа́льный, гру́стный. **sadden** /-d(ə)n/ *vt* печа́лить *impf*, о~ *pf*.

saddle /'sæd(ə)l/ *n* седло́; *vt* седла́ть *impf*, о~ *pf*; (*burden*) обременя́ть *impf*, обремени́ть *pf* (**with** +*instr*).

sadism /'seɪdɪz(ə)m/ *n* сади́зм. **sadist** /-dɪst/ *n* сади́ст. **sadistic** /sə'dɪstɪk/ *adj* сади́стский.

sadness /'sædnɪs/ *n* печа́ль, грусть.

safe /seɪf/ *n* сейф; *adj* (*unharmed*) невреди́мый; (*out of danger*) в безопа́сности; (*secure*) безопа́сный; (*reliable*) надёжный; ~ **and sound** цел и невреди́м. **safeguard** *n* предохрани́тельная ме́ра; *vt* предохраня́ть *impf*, предохрани́ть *pf*. **safety** /-tɪ/ *n* безопа́сность; ~**-belt** реме́нь *m* безопа́сности; ~ **pin** англи́йская була́вка; ~**-valve** предохрани́тельный кла́пан.

sag /sæg/ *vi* (*of rope, curtain*) провиса́ть *impf*, прови́снуть *pf*; (*of ceiling*) прогиба́ться *impf*, прогну́ться *pf*.

saga /'sɑːgə/ *n* са́га.

sage[1] /seɪdʒ/ *n* (*herb*) шалфе́й.

sage[2] /seɪdʒ/ *n* (*person*) мудре́ц; *adj* му́дрый.

Sagittarius /ˌsædʒɪ'teərɪəs/ *n* Стреле́ц.

sail /seɪl/ *n* па́рус; *vt* (*a ship*) управля́ть *impf* +*instr*; *vi* пла́вать *indet*, плыть *det*; (*depart*) отплыва́ть *impf*, отплы́ть *pf*. **sailing** /-lɪŋ/ *n* (*sport*) па́русный спорт; ~**-ship** па́русное су́дно. **sailor** /-lə(r)/ *n* матро́с, моря́к.

saint /seɪnt/ *n* свято́й *sb*. **saintly** /-lɪ/ *adj* свято́й.

sake /seɪk/ *n*: **for the ~ of** ра́ди+*gen*.

salad /'sæləd/ *n* сала́т; ~**-dressing** припра́ва к сала́ту.

salami /sə'lɑːmɪ/ *n* саля́ми *f indecl*.

salary /'sælərɪ/ *n* жа́лованье.

sale /seɪl/ *n* прода́жа; (*also amount sold*) сбыт (*no pl*); (*with reduced prices*) распрода́жа; **be for ~** продава́ться *impf*. **saleable** /-ləb(ə)l/ *adj* хо́дкий. **salesman** /'seɪlzmən/ *n* продаве́ц. **saleswoman** /'seɪlzˌwʊmən/*n* продавщи́ца.

salient /'seɪlɪənt/ *adj* основно́й.

saliva /sə'laɪvə/ *n* слюна́.

sallow /'sæləʊ/ *adj* желтова́тый.

salmon /'sæmən/ *n* ло́со́сь *m*.

salon /'sælɒn/ *n* сало́н. **saloon** /sə'luːn/ *n* (*on ship*) сало́н; (*car*) седа́н; (*bar*) бар.

salt /sɔːlt/ *n* соль; ~**-cellar** соло́нка; ~ **water** морска́я вода́; ~**-water** морско́й; *adj* солёный; *vt* соли́ть *impf*, по~ *pf*. **salty** /-tɪ/ *adj* солёный.

salutary /'sæljʊtərɪ/ *adj* благотво́рный. **salute** /sə'luːt/ *n* отда́ча че́сти; (*with guns*) салю́т; *vt & i* отдава́ть *impf*, отда́ть *pf* честь (+*dat*).

salvage /'sælvɪdʒ/ *n* спасе́ние; *vt* спаса́ть *impf*, спасти́ *pf*.

salvation /sæl'veɪʃ(ə)n/ *n* спасе́ние; **S~ Army** А́рмия спасе́ния.

salve /sælv/ *n* мазь; *vt*: ~ **one's conscience** успока́ивать *impf*, успоко́ить *pf* со́весть.

salvo /'sælvəʊ/ *n* залп.

same /seɪm/ *adj*: **the ~** тот же (са́мый); (*applying to both or all*) оди́н; (*identical*) одина́ковый; *pron*: **the ~** одно́ и то́ же, то же са́мое; *adv*: **the ~** таки́м же о́бразом, так же; **all the ~** всё-таки, тем не ме́нее. **sameness** /-nɪs/ *n* однообра́зие.

samovar /'sæməˌvɑː(r)/ *n* самова́р.

sample /'sɑːmp(ə)l/ *n* образе́ц; *vt* про́бовать *impf*, по~ *pf*.

sanatorium /ˌsænə'tɔːrɪəm/ *n* санато́рий.

sanctify /'sæŋktɪˌfaɪ/ *vt* освяща́ть *impf*, освяти́ть *pf*. **sanctimonious** /ˌsæŋktɪ'məʊnɪəs/ *adj* ха́нжеский. **sanction** /'sæŋkʃ(ə)n/ *n* са́нкция; *vt* санкциони́ровать *impf & pf*. **sanctity** /'sæŋktɪtɪ/ *n* (*holiness*) свя́тость; (*sacredness*) свяще́нность. **sanctuary** /'sæŋktjʊərɪ/ *n* святи́лище; (*ref-*

uge) убе́жище; (*for wild life*) запове́дник.

sand /sænd/ *n* песо́к; *vt* (~ *down*) шку́рить *impf*, по~ *pf*; **~-dune** дю́на.

sandal /'sænd(ə)l/ *n* санда́лия.

sandalwood /'sænd(ə)lwʊd/ *n* санда́ловое де́рево.

sandbank /'sændbæŋk/ *n* о́тмель.

sandpaper /'sænd,peɪpə(r)/ *n* шку́рка; *vt* шлифова́ть *impf*, от~ *pf* шку́ркой.

sandstone /'sændstəʊn/ *n* песча́ник.

sandwich /'sænwɪdʒ/ *n* бутербро́д; *vt*: ~ **between** вти́скивать *impf*, вти́снуть *pf* ме́жду +*instr*.

sandy /'sændɪ/ *adj* (*of sand*) песча́ный; (*like sand*) песо́чный; (*hair*) рыжева́тый.

sane /seɪn/ *adj* норма́льный; (*sensible*) разу́мный.

sang-froid /sɑ̃'frwɑː/ *n* самооблада́ние.

sanguine /'sæŋgwɪn/ *adj* оптимисти́ческий.

sanitary /'sænɪtərɪ/ *adj* санита́рный; гигиени́ческий; ~ **towel** гигиени́ческая поду́шка. **sanitation** /,sænɪ'teɪʃ(ə)n/ *n* (*conditions*) санита́рные усло́вия *neut pl*; (*system*) водопрово́д и канализа́ция. **sanity** /'sænɪtɪ/ *n* психи́ческое здоро́вье; (*good sense*) здра́вый смысл.

sap /sæp/ *n* (*bot*) сок; *vt* (*exhaust*) истоща́ть *impf*, истощи́ть *pf*.

sapling /'sæplɪŋ/ *n* са́женец.

sapphire /'sæfaɪə(r)/ *n* сапфи́р.

sarcasm /'sɑː,kæz(ə)m/ *n* сарка́зм. **sarcastic** /sɑː'kæstɪk/ *adj* саркасти́ческий.

sardine /sɑː'diːn/ *n* сарди́на.

sardonic /sɑː'dɒnɪk/ *adj* сардони́ческий.

sash[1] /sæʃ/ *n* (*scarf*) куша́к.

sash[2] /sæʃ/ *n* (*frame*) скользя́щая ра́ма; **~-window** подъёмное окно́.

satanic /sə'tænɪk/ *adj* сатани́нский.

satchel /'sætʃ(ə)l/ *n* ра́нец, су́мка.

satellite /'sætə,laɪt/ *n* спу́тник, сателли́т (*also fig*); ~ **dish** параболи́ческая анте́нна; таре́лка (*coll*); ~ **TV** спу́тниковое телеви́дение.

satiate /'seɪʃɪ,eɪt/ *vt* насыща́ть *impf*, насы́тить *pf*.

satin /'sætɪn/ *n* атла́с.

satire /'sætaɪə(r)/ *n* сати́ра. **satirical** /sə'tɪrɪk(ə)l/ *adj* сатири́ческий. **satirist** /'sætərɪst/ *n* сати́рик. **satirize** /-,raɪz/ *vt* высме́ивать *impf*, вы́смеять *pf*.

satisfaction /,sætɪs'fækʃ(ə)n/ *n* удовлетворе́ние. **satisfactory** /-'fæktərɪ/ *adj* удовлетвори́тельный. **satisfy** /'sætɪs,faɪ/ *vt* удовлетворя́ть *impf*, удовлетвори́ть *pf*; (*hunger, curiosity*) утоля́ть *impf*, утоли́ть *pf*.

saturate /'sætʃə,reɪt/ *vt* насыща́ть *impf*, насы́тить *pf*; **I got ~d** (*by rain*) я промо́к до ни́тки. **saturation** /,sætʃə'reɪʃ(ə)n/ *n* насыще́ние.

Saturday /'sætə,deɪ/ *n* суббо́та.

sauce /sɔːs/ *n* со́ус; (*cheek*) на́глость. **saucepan** *n* кастрю́ля. **saucer** /'sɔːsə(r)/ *n* блю́дце. **saucy** /'sɔːsɪ/ *adj* на́глый.

Saudi /'saʊdɪ/ *n* сау́довец, -вка; *adj* сау́довский. **Saudi Arabia** /,saʊdɪ ə'reɪbɪə/ *n* Сау́довская Ара́вия.

sauna /'sɔːnə/ *n* фи́нская ба́ня.

saunter /'sɔːntə(r)/ *vi* прогу́ливаться *impf*.

sausage /'sɒsɪdʒ/ *n* соси́ска; (*salami-type*) колбаса́.

savage /'sævɪdʒ/ *adj* ди́кий; (*fierce*) свире́пый; (*cruel*) жесто́кий; *n* дика́рь *m*; *vt* искуса́ть *pf*. **savagery** /-rɪ/ *n* ди́кость; жесто́кость.

save /seɪv/ *vt* (*rescue*) спаса́ть *impf*, спасти́ *pf*; (*money*) копи́ть *impf*, на~ *pf*; (*put aside, keep*) бере́чь *impf*; (*avoid using*) эконо́мить *impf*, с~ *pf*; *vi*: ~ **up** копи́ть *impf*, на~ *pf* де́ньги. **savings** /-vɪŋz/ *n pl* сбереже́ния *neut pl*; ~ **bank** сберега́тельная

S

ка́сса. **saviour** /-vjə(r)/ *n* спаси́тель *m*.

savour /ˈseɪvə(r)/ *vt* смакова́ть *impf*.

savoury /ˈseɪvərɪ/ *adj* пика́нтный; (*fig*) поря́дочный.

saw /sɔː/ *n* пила́; *vt* пили́ть *impf*; **~ up** распи́ливать *impf*, распили́ть *pf*. **sawdust** *n* опи́лки (-лок) *pl*.

saxophone /ˈsæksəˌfəʊn/ *n* саксофо́н.

say /seɪ/ *vt* говори́ть *impf*, сказа́ть *pf*; **to ~ nothing of** не говоря́ уже́ о+*prep*; **that is to ~** то есть; (*let us*) **~** ска́жем; **it is said (that)** говоря́т (что); *n* (*opinion*) мне́ние; (*influence*) влия́ние; **have one's ~** вы́сказаться *pf*. **saying** /ˈseɪɪŋ/ *n* погово́рка.

scab /skæb/ *n* (*on wound*) струп; (*polit*) штрейкбре́хер.

scabbard /ˈskæbəd/ *n* но́жны (*gen* -жен) *pl*.

scaffold /ˈskæfəʊld/ *n* эшафо́т. **scaffolding** /-dɪŋ/ *n* леса́ (-со́в) *pl*.

scald /skɔːld/ *vt* обва́ривать *impf*, обвари́ть *pf*.

scale /skeɪl/ *n* (*ratio*) масшта́б; (*grading*) шкала́; (*mus*) га́мма; *vt* (*climb*) взбира́ться *impf*, взобра́ться *pf* на+*acc*; **~ down** понижа́ть *impf*, пони́зить *pf*.

scales[1] /skeɪlz/ *n pl* (*of fish*) чешуя́ (*collect*).

scales[2] /skeɪlz/ *n pl* весы́ (-со́в) *pl*.

scallop /ˈskɒləp/ *n* гребешо́к; (*decoration*) фесто́н.

scalp /skælp/ *n* ко́жа головы́.

scalpel /ˈskælp(ə)l/ *n* ска́льпель *m*.

scaly /ˈskeɪlɪ/ *adj* чешу́йчатый; (*of boiler etc.*) покры́тый на́кипью.

scamper /ˈskæmpə(r)/ *vi* бы́стро бе́гать *impf*; (*frolic*) резви́ться *impf*.

scan /skæn/ *vt* (*intently*) рассма́тривать *impf*; (*quickly*) просма́тривать *impf*, просмотре́ть *pf*; (*med*) просве́чивать *impf*, просвети́ть *pf*; *n* просве́чивание.

scandal /ˈskænd(ə)l/ *n* сканда́л; (*gossip*) спле́тни (-тен) *pl*. **scandalize** /-ˌlaɪz/ *vt* шоки́ровать *impf* & *pf*. **scandalous** /-ləs/ *adj* сканда́льный.

Scandinavia /ˌskændɪˈneɪvɪə/ *n* Скандина́вия. **Scandinavian** /-vɪən/ *adj* скандина́вский.

scanner /ˈskænə(r)/ *n* (*comput*, *med*) ска́нер.

scanty /ˈskæntɪ/ *adj* ску́дный.

scapegoat /ˈskeɪpgəʊt/ *n* козёл отпуще́ния.

scar /skɑː(r)/ *n* шрам; *vt* оставля́ть *impf*, оста́вить *pf* шрам на+*prep*.

scarce /skeəs/ *adj* дефици́тный; (*rare*) ре́дкий. **scarcely** /-lɪ/ *adv* едва́. **scarcity** /-sɪtɪ/ *n* дефици́т; ре́дкость.

scare /skeə(r)/ *vt* пуга́ть *impf*, ис~, на~ *pf*; **~ away, off** отпу́гивать *impf*, отпугну́ть *pf*; *n* па́ника. **scarecrow** *n* пу́гало.

scarf /skɑːf/ *n* шарф.

scarlet /ˈskɑːlɪt/ *adj* (*n*) а́лый (цвет).

scathing /ˈskeɪðɪŋ/ *adj* уничтожа́ющий.

scatter /ˈskætə(r)/ *vt* & *i* рассыпа́ть(ся) *impf*, рассы́пать(ся) *pf*; (*disperse*) рассе́ивать(ся) *impf*, рассе́ять(ся) *pf*; **~-brained** ве́треный. **scattered** /-təd/ *adj* разбро́санный; (*sporadic*) отде́льный.

scavenge /ˈskævɪndʒ/ *vi* ры́ться *impf* в отбро́сах. **scavenger** /-dʒə(r)/ *n* (*person*) му́сорщик; (*animal*) живо́тное *sb*, пита́ющееся па́далью.

scenario /sɪˈnɑːrɪəʊ/ *n* сцена́рий. **scene** /siːn/ *n* (*place of disaster etc.*) ме́сто; (*place of action*) ме́сто де́йствия; (*view*) вид, пейза́ж; (*picture*) карти́на; (*theat*) сце́на, явле́ние; (*incident*) сце́на; **behind the ~s** за кули́сами; **make a ~** устра́ивать *impf*, устро́ить *pf* сце́ну. **scenery** /ˈsiːnərɪ/ *n* (*theat*) декора́ция; (*landscape*) пейза́ж. **scenic** /ˈsiːnɪk/ *adj* живопи́сный.

scent /sent/ *n* (*smell*) арома́т;

S

(*perfume*) духи́ (-хо́в) *pl*; (*trail*) след. **scented** /-tɪd/ *adj* души́стый.

sceptic /'skeptɪk/ *n* ске́птик. **sceptical** /-k(ə)l/ *adj* скепти́ческий. **scepticism** /-tɪˌsɪz(ə)m/ *n* скептици́зм.

schedule /'ʃedju:l/ *n* (*timetable*) расписа́ние; *vt* составля́ть *impf*, соста́вить *pf* расписа́ние +*gen.*

schematic /skɪ'mætɪk/ *adj* схемати́ческий. **scheme** /ski:m/ *n* (*plan*) прое́кт; (*intrigue*) махина́ция; *vi* интригова́ть *impf.*

schism /'skɪz(ə)m/ *n* раско́л.

schizophrenia /ˌskɪtsə'fri:nɪə/ *n* шизофрени́я. **schizophrenic** /-'frenɪk/ *adj* шизофрени́ческий; *n* шизофре́ник.

scholar /'skɒlə(r)/ *n* учёный *sb*: **scholarly** /-lɪ/ *adj* учёный. **scholarship** *n* учёность; (*payment*) стипе́ндия.

school /sku:l/ *n* шко́ла; *attrib* шко́льный; *vt* (*train*) приуча́ть *impf*, приучи́ть *pf* (**to** к+*dat*, +*inf*). **school-book** *n* уче́бник. **schoolboy** *n* шко́льник. **schoolgirl** *n* шко́льница. **schooling** /-lɪŋ/ *n* обуче́ние. **school-leaver** /-ˌli:və(r)/ *n* выпускни́к, -и́ца. **school teacher** *n* учи́тель *m*, ~ница.

schooner /'sku:nə(r)/ *n* шху́на.

sciatica /saɪ'ætɪkə/ *n* и́шиас.

science /'saɪəns/ *n* нау́ка; ~ **fiction** нау́чная фанта́стика. **scientific** /ˌsaɪən'tɪfɪk/ *adj* нау́чный. **scientist** /'saɪəntɪst/ *n* учёный *sb*.

scintillating /'sɪntɪˌleɪtɪŋ/ *adj* блиста́тельный.

scissors /'sɪzəz/ *n pl* но́жницы (-ц) *pl.*

scoff /skɒf/ *vi* (*mock*) смея́ться *impf* (**at** над+*instr*).

scold /skəʊld/ *vt* брани́ть *impf*, вы́~ *pf.*

scoop /sku:p/ *n* (*large*) черпа́к; (*ice-cream* ~) ло́жка для моро́женого; *vt* (~ *out*, *up*) вычё́рпывать *impf*, вы́черпать *pf.*

scooter /'sku:tə(r)/ *n* (*motor* ~) моторо́ллер.

scope /skəʊp/ *n* (*range*) преде́лы *m pl*; (*chance*) возмо́жность.

scorch /skɔ:tʃ/ *vt* (*fingers*) обжига́ть *impf*, обже́чь *pf*; (*clothes*) сжига́ть *impf*, сжечь *pf.*

score /skɔ:(r)/ *n* (*of points etc.*) счёт; (*mus*) партиту́ра; *pl* (*great numbers*) мно́жество; *vt* (*notch*) де́лать *impf*, с~ *pf* зару́бки на +*prep*; (*points etc.*) получа́ть *impf*, получи́ть *pf*; (*mus*) оркестрова́ть *impf* & *pf*; *vi* (*keep* ~) вести́ *impf*, с~ *pf* счёт. **scorer** /-rə(r)/ *n* счётчик.

scorn /skɔ:n/ *n* презре́ние; *vt* презира́ть *impf* презре́ть *pf.* **scornful** /-fʊl/ *adj* презри́тельный.

Scorpio /'skɔ:pɪəʊ/ *n* Скорпио́н.

scorpion /'skɔ:pɪən/ *n* скорпио́н.

Scot /skɒt/ *n* шотла́ндец, -дка. **Scotch** /skɒtʃ/ *n* (*whisky*) шотла́ндское ви́ски *neut indecl.* **Scotland** *n* Шотла́ндия. **Scots, Scottish** /skɒts, 'skɒtɪʃ/ *adj* шотла́ндский.

scoundrel /'skaʊndr(ə)l/ *n* подле́ц.

scour[1] /'skaʊə(r)/ *vt* (*cleanse*) отчища́ть *impf*, отчи́стить *pf.*

scour[2] /'skaʊə(r)/ *vt* & *i* (*rove*) ры́скать *impf* (по+*dat*).

scourge /skɜ:dʒ/ *n* бич.

scout /skaʊt/ *n* разве́дчик; (**S**~) бойска́ут; *vi*: ~ **about** разы́скивать *impf* (**for** +*acc*).

scowl /skaʊl/ *vi* хму́риться *impf*, на~ *pf*; *n* хму́рый взгляд.

scrabble /'skræb(ə)l/ *vi*: ~ **about** ры́ться *impf.*

scramble /'skræmb(ə)l/ *vi* кара́бкаться *impf*, вс~ *pf*; (*struggle*) дра́ться *impf* (**for** за+*acc*); ~**d eggs** яи́чница-болту́нья.

scrap[1] /skræp/ *n* (*fragment etc.*) кусо́чек; *pl* оста́тки *m pl*; *pl* (*of food*) объе́дки (-ков) *pl*; ~ **metal** металлоло́м; *vt* сдава́ть *impf*, сдать *pf* в ути́ль.

scrap[2] /skræp/ *n* (*fight*) дра́ка; *vi* дра́ться *impf.*

scrape /skreɪp/ *vt* скрести́ *impf*;

(*graze*) цара́пать *impf*, о~ *pf*; ~ **off** отскреба́ть *impf*, отскрести́ *pf*; ~ **through** (*exam*) с трудо́м выде́рживать *impf*, вы́держать *pf*; ~ **together** наскреба́ть *impf*, наскрести́ *pf*.

scratch /skrætʃ/ *vt* цара́пать *impf*, о~ *pf*; *vt & i* (*when itching*) чеса́ть(ся) *impf*, по~ *pf*; *n* цара́пина.

scrawl /skrɔːl/ *n* кара́кули *f pl*; *vt* писа́ть *impf*, на~ *pf* кара́кулями.

scrawny /ˈskrɔːnɪ/ *adj* сухопа́рый.

scream /skriːm/ *n* крик; *vi* крича́ть *impf*, кри́кнуть *pf*.

screech /skriːtʃ/ *n* визг; *vi* визжа́ть *impf*.

screen /skriːn/ *n* ши́рма; (*cin, TV*) экра́н; ~**-play** сцена́рий; *vt* (*protect*) защища́ть *impf*, защити́ть *pf*; (*hide*) укрыва́ть *impf*, укры́ть *pf*; (*show film etc.*) демонстри́ровать *impf & pf*; (*check on*) проверя́ть *impf*, прове́рить *pf*; ~ **off** отгора́живать *impf*, отгороди́ть *pf* ши́рмой.

screw /skruː/ *n* винт; *vt* (~ *on*) приви́нчивать *impf*, привинти́ть *pf*; (~ *up*) зави́нчивать *impf*, завинти́ть *pf*; (*crumple*) ко́мкать *impf*, с~ *pf*; ~ **up one's eyes** щу́риться *impf*, со~ *pf*. **screwdriver** *n* отвёртка.

scribble /ˈskrɪb(ə)l/ *vt* строчи́ть *impf*, на~ *pf*; *n* кара́кули *f pl*.

script /skrɪpt/ *n* (*of film etc.*) сцена́рий; (*of speech etc.*) текст; (*writing system*) письмо́; ~**-writer** сценари́ст.

Scripture /ˈskrɪptʃə(r)/ *n* свяще́нное писа́ние.

scroll /skrəʊl/ *n* сви́ток; (*design*) завито́к; *vi* (*comput*) прокру́чивать *impf*, прокрути́ть *pf*.

scrounge /skraʊndʒ/ *vt* (*cadge*) стреля́ть *impf*, стрельну́ть *pf*; *vi* попроша́йничать *impf*.

scrub[1] /skrʌb/ *n* (*brushwood*) куста́рник; (*area*) за́росли *f pl*.

scrub[2] /skrʌb/ *vt* мыть *impf*, вы~ *pf* щёткой.

scruff /skrʌf/ *n*: **by the ~ of the neck** за ши́ворот.

scruffy /ˈskrʌfɪ/ *adj* обо́дранный.

scrum /skrʌm/ *n* схва́тка вокру́г мяча́.

scruple /ˈskruːp(ə)l/ *n* (*also pl*) колеба́ния *neut pl*; угрызе́ния *neut pl* со́вести. **scrupulous** /-pjʊləs/ *adj* скрупулёзный.

scrutinize /ˈskruːtɪˌnaɪz/ *vt* рассма́тривать *impf*. **scrutiny** /ˈskruːtɪnɪ/ *n* рассмотре́ние.

scuffed /skʌft/ *adj* поцара́панный.

scuffle /ˈskʌf(ə)l/ *n* потасо́вка.

sculpt /skʌlpt/ *vt* ваять *impf*, из~ *pf*. **sculptor** /-tə(r)/ *n* ску́льптор. **sculpture** /-tʃə(r)/ *n* скульпту́ра.

scum /skʌm/ *n* на́кипь.

scurrilous /ˈskʌrɪləs/ *adj* непристо́йный.

scurry /ˈskʌrɪ/ *vi* поспе́шно бе́гать *indet*, бежа́ть *det*.

scuttle /ˈskʌt(ə)l/ *vi* (*run away*) удира́ть *impf*, удра́ть *pf*.

scythe /saɪð/ *n* коса́.

sea /siː/ *n* мо́ре; *attrib* морско́й; ~ **front** на́бережная *sb*; ~**-gull** ча́йка; ~**-level** у́ровень *m* мо́ря; ~**-lion** морско́й лев; ~**-shore** побере́жье. **seaboard** *n* побере́жье. **seafood** *n* проду́кты *m pl* мо́ря.

seal[1] /siːl/ *n* (*on document etc.*) печа́ть; *vt* скрепля́ть *impf*, скрепи́ть *pf* печа́тью; (*close*) запеча́тывать *impf*, запеча́тать *pf*; ~ **up** заде́лывать *impf*, заде́лать *pf*

seal[2] /siːl/ *n* (*zool*) тюле́нь *m*; (*fur-*~) ко́тик.

seam /siːm/ *n* шов; (*geol*) пласт.

seaman /ˈsiːm(ə)n/ *n* моря́к, матро́с.

seamless /ˈsiːmlɪs/ *adj* без шва.

seamstress /ˈsemstrɪs/ *n* швея́.

seance /ˈseɪɑ̃s/ *n* спирити́ческий сеа́нс.

seaplane /ˈsiːpleɪn/ *n* гидросамолёт.

searing /ˈsɪərɪŋ/ *adj* паля́щий.

search /sɜːtʃ/ *vt* обы́скивать *impf*, обыска́ть *pf*; *vi* иска́ть *impf* (**for** +*acc*); *n* по́иски *m pl*; о́быск;

S

~-party поисковая гру́ппа. **searching** /-tʃɪŋ/ *adj* (*look*) испыту́ющий. **searchlight** *n* проже́ктор.

seasick /'siːsɪk/ *adj*: **I was ~** меня́ укача́ло. **seaside** *n* бе́рег мо́ря.

season /'siːz(ə)n/ *n* сезо́н; (*one of four*) вре́мя *neut* го́да; **~ ticket** сезо́нный биле́т; *vt* (*flavour*) приправля́ть *impf*, припра́вить *pf*. **seasonable** /-nəb(ə)l/ *adj* по сезо́ну; (*timely*) своевре́менный. **seasonal** /-n(ə)l/ *adj* сезо́нный. **seasoning** /-nɪŋ/ *n* припра́ва.

seat /siːt/ *n* (*place*) ме́сто; (*of chair*) сиде́нье; (*chair*) стул; (*bench*) скаме́йка; (*of trousers*) зад; **~ belt** привязно́й реме́нь *m*; *vt* сажа́ть *impf*, посади́ть *pf*; (*of room etc.*) вмеща́ть *impf*, вмести́ть *pf*; **be ~ed** сади́ться *impf*, сесть *pf*.

seaweed /'siːwiːd/ *n* морска́я во́доросль.

secateurs /ˌsekə'tɜːz/ *n pl* сека́тор.

secede /sɪ'siːd/ *vi* отка́лываться *impf*, отколо́ться *pf*. **secession** /-'seʃ(ə)n/ *n* отко́л.

secluded /sɪ'kluːdɪd/ *adj* укро́мный. **seclusion** /-'kluːʒ(ə)n/ *n* укро́мность.

second[1] /'sekənd/ *adj* второ́й; **~-class** второкла́ссный; **~-hand** подержанный; (*of information*) из вторы́х рук; **~-rate** второразря́дный; **~ sight** ясновиде́ние; **on ~ thoughts** взве́сив всё ещё раз; **have ~ thoughts** переду́мывать *impf*, переду́мать *pf* (**about** +*acc*); *n* второ́й *sb*; (*date*) второ́е (число́) *sb*; (*time*) секу́нда; *pl* (*comm*) това́р второ́го со́рта; **~ hand** (*of clock*) секу́ндная стре́лка; *vt* (*support*) подде́рживать *impf*, поддержа́ть *pf*; (*transfer*) откомандиро́вывать *impf* откомандирова́ть *pf*. **secondary** /-dərɪ/ *adj* втори́чный, второстепе́нный; (*education*) сре́дний. **secondly** /-lɪ/ *adv* во-вторы́х.

secrecy /'siːkrɪsɪ/ *n* секре́тность. **secret** /'siːkrɪt/ *n* та́йна, секре́т; *adj* та́йный, секре́тный; (*hidden*) потайно́й.

secretarial /ˌsekrɪ'teərɪəl/ *adj* секрета́рский. **secretariat** /-'teərɪət/ *n* секретариа́т. **secretary** /'sekrɪtərɪ/ *n* секрета́рь *m*, -рша; (*minister*) мини́стр.

secrete /sɪ'kriːt/ *vt* (*conceal*) укрыва́ть *impf*, укры́ть *pf*; (*med*) выделя́ть *impf*, вы́делить *pf*. **secretion** /-'kriːʃ(ə)n/ *n* укрыва́ние; (*med*) выделе́ние.

secretive /'siːkrɪtɪv/ *adj* скры́тный.

sect /sekt/ *n* се́кта. **sectarian** /sek'teərɪən/ *adj* секта́нтский.

section /'sekʃ(ə)n/ *n* се́кция; (*of book*) разде́л; (*geom*) сече́ние. **sector** /'sektə(r)/ *n* се́ктор.

secular /'sekjʊlə(r)/ *adj* све́тский. **secularization** /ˌsekjʊləraɪ'zeɪʃ(ə)n/ *n* секуляриза́ция.

secure /sɪ'kjʊə(r)/ *adj* (*safe*) безопа́сный; (*firm*) надёжный; (*emotionally*) уве́ренный; *vt* (*fasten*) закрепля́ть *impf*, закрепи́ть *pf*; (*guarantee*) обеспе́чивать *impf*, обеспе́чить *pf*; (*obtain*) достава́ть *impf*, доста́ть *pf*. **security** /-'kjʊərɪtɪ/ *n* безопа́сность; (*guarantee*) зало́г; *pl* це́нные бума́ги *f pl*.

sedate /sɪ'deɪt/ *adj* степе́нный.

sedation /sɪ'deɪʃ(ə)n/ *n* успокое́ние. **sedative** /'sedətɪv/ *n* успока́ивающее сре́дство.

sedentary /'sedəntərɪ/ *adj* сидя́чий.

sediment /'sedɪmənt/ *n* оса́док.

seduce /sɪ'djuːs/ *vt* соблазня́ть *impf*, соблазни́ть *pf*. **seduction** /-'dʌkʃ(ə)n/ *n* обольще́ние. **seductive** /-'dʌktɪv/ *adj* соблазни́тельный.

see /siː/ *vt & i* ви́деть *impf*, у~ *pf*; *vt* (*watch, look*) смотре́ть *impf*, по~ *pf*; (*find out*) узнава́ть *impf*, узна́ть *pf*; (*understand*) понима́ть *impf*, поня́ть *pf*; (*meet*) ви́деться *impf*, у~ *pf* с+*instr*; (*imagine*) представля́ть *impf*, предста́вить *pf* себе́; (*escort*, ~

S

off) провожа́ть *impf*, проводи́ть *pf*; **~ about** (*attend to*) забо́титься *impf*, по~ *pf* о+*prep*; **~ through** (*fig*) ви́деть *impf*, насквозь+*acc*.

seed /siːd/ *n* се́мя *neut*. **seedling** /-lɪŋ/ *n* се́янец; *pl* расса́да. **seedy** /-dɪ/ *adj* (*shabby*) потрёпанный.

seeing (that) /ˈsiːɪŋ (ðæt)/ *conj* ввиду́ того́, что.

seek /siːk/ *vt* иска́ть *impf* +*acc*, *gen*.

seem /siːm/ *vi* каза́ться *impf*, по~ *pf* (+*instr*). **seemingly** /-mɪŋlɪ/ *adv* по-ви́димому.

seemly /ˈsiːmlɪ/ *adj* прили́чный.

seep /siːp/ *vi* проса́чиваться *impf*, просочи́ться *pf*.

seethe /siːð/ *vi* кипе́ть *impf*, вс~ *pf*.

segment /ˈsegmənt/ *n* отре́зок; (*of orange etc.*) до́лька; (*geom*) сегме́нт.

segregate /ˈsegrɪˌgeɪt/ *vt* отделя́ть *impf*, отдели́ть *pf*. **segregation** /ˌsegrɪˈgeɪʃ(ə)n/ *n* сегрега́ция.

seismic /ˈsaɪzmɪk/ *adj* сейсми́ческий.

seize /siːz/ *vt* хвата́ть *impf*, схвати́ть *pf*; *vi*: **~ up** заеда́ть *impf*, зае́сть *pf impers*+*acc*; **~ upon** ухва́тываться *impf*, ухвати́ться *pf* за+*acc*. **seizure** /ˈsiːʒə(r)/ *n* захва́т; (*med*) припа́док.

seldom /ˈseldəm/ *adv* ре́дко.

select /sɪˈlekt/ *adj* и́збранный; *vt* отбира́ть *impf*, отобра́ть *pf*. **selection** /-ˈlekʃ(ə)n/ *n* (*choice*) вы́бор. **selective** /-ˈlektɪv/ *adj* разбо́рчивый.

self /self/ *n* со́бственное «я» *neut indecl*.

self- /self/ *in comb* само-; **~-absorbed** эгоцентри́чный; **~-assured** самоуве́ренный; **~-catering (accommodation)** жильё с ку́хней; **~-centred** эгоцентри́чный; **~-confessed** открове́нный; **~-confidence** самоуве́ренность; **~-confident** самоуве́ренный; **~-conscious** засте́нчивый; **~-contained** (*person*) незави́симый; (*flat etc.*) отде́льный; **~-control** самооблада́ние; **~-defence** самозащи́та; **~-denial** самоотрече́ние; **~-determination** самоопределе́ние; **~-effacing** скро́мный; **~-employed person** незави́симый предпринима́тель *m*; **~-esteem** самоуваже́ние; **~-evident** очеви́дный; **~-governing** самоуправля́ющий; **~-help** самопо́мощь; **~-importance** самомне́ние; **~-imposed** доброво́льный; **~-indulgent** избало́ванный; **~-interest** со́бственный интере́с; **~-pity** жа́лость к себе́; **~-portrait** автопортре́т; **~-preservation** самосохране́ние; **~-reliance** самостоя́тельность; **~-respect** самоуваже́ние; **~-righteous** *adj* ха́нжеский; **~-sacrifice** самопоже́ртвование; **~-satisfied** самодово́льный; **~-service** самообслу́живание (*attrib*: *in gen after n*); **~-styled** самозва́нный; **~-sufficient** самостоя́тельный.

selfish /ˈselfɪʃ/ *adj* эгоисти́чный. **selfless** /ˈselflɪs/ *adj* самоотве́рженный.

sell /sel/ *vt & i* продава́ть(ся) *impf*, прода́ть(ся) *pf*; *vt* (*deal in*) торгова́ть *impf* +*instr*; **~ out of** распродава́ть *impf*, распрода́ть *pf*. **seller** /-lə(r)/ *n* продаве́ц. **selling** /-lɪŋ/ *n* прода́жа. **sell-out** /-aʊt/ *n*: **the play was a ~** пье́са прошла́ с аншла́гом.

Sellotape /ˈseləˌteɪp/ *n* (*propr*) ли́пкая ле́нта.

semantic /sɪˈmæntɪk/ *adj* семанти́ческий. **semantics** /-tɪks/ *n* сема́нтика.

semblance /ˈsembləns/ *n* ви́димость.

semen /ˈsiːmən/ *n* се́мя *neut*.

semi- /ˈsemɪ/ *in comb* полу-; **~-detached house** дом, разделённый о́бщей стено́й. **semibreve** /-ˌbriːv/ *n* це́лая но́та. **semicircle** *n* полукру́г. **semicircular** /-ˈsɜːkjʊlə(r)/ *adj* полукру́глый. **semicolon** /-ˈkəʊlɒn/ *n*

S

то́чка с запято́й. **semiconductor** /-kənˌdʌktə(r)/ *n* полупроводни́к. **semifinal** /-ˈfaɪnəl/ *n* полуфина́л.

seminar /ˈsemɪˌnɑː(r)/ *n* семина́р. **seminary** /-nərɪ/ *n* семина́рия.

semiquaver /ˈsemɪˌkweɪvə(r)/ *n* шестна́дцатая но́та.

semitone /ˈsemɪˌtəʊn/ *n* полуто́н.

senate /ˈsenɪt/ *n* сена́т; (*univ*) сове́т. **senator** /ˈsenətə(r)/ *n* сена́тор.

send /send/ *vt* посыла́ть *impf*, посла́ть *pf* (**for** за+*instr*); ~ **off** отправля́ть *impf*, отпра́вить *pf*; ~-**off** про́воды (-дов) *pl*. **sender** /-də(r)/ *n* отправи́тель *m*.

senile /ˈsiːnaɪl/ *adj* ста́рческий. **senility** /sɪˈnɪlɪtɪ/ *n* ста́рческое слабоу́мие.

senior /ˈsiːnɪə(r)/ *adj* (*n*) ста́рший (*sb*); ~ **citizen** стари́к, стару́ха. **seniority** /ˌsiːnɪˈɒrɪtɪ/ *n* старшинство́.

sensation /senˈseɪʃ(ə)n/ *n* сенса́ция; (*feeling*) ощуще́ние. **sensational** /-ˈseɪʃən(ə)l/ *adj* сенсацио́нный.

sense /sens/ *n* чу́вство; (*good* ~) здра́вый смысл; (*meaning*) смысл; *pl* (*sanity*) ум; *vt* чу́вствовать *impf*. **senseless** /-lɪs/ *adj* бессмы́сленный.

sensibility /ˌsensɪˈbɪlɪtɪ/ *n* чувстви́тельность; *pl* самолю́бие. **sensible** /ˈsensɪb(ə)l/ *adj* благоразу́мный. **sensitive** /ˈsensɪtɪv/ *adj* чувстви́тельный; (*touchy*) оби́дчивый. **sensitivity** /ˌsensɪˈtɪvɪtɪ/ *n* чувстви́тельность.

sensory /ˈsensərɪ/ *adj* чувстви́тельный.

sensual, sensuous /ˈsensjʊəl, ˈsensjʊəs/ *adj* чу́вственный.

sentence /ˈsent(ə)ns/ *n* (*gram*) предложе́ние; (*law*) пригово́р; *vt* пригова́ривать *impf*, приговори́ть *pf* (**to** к+*dat*).

sentiment /ˈsentɪmənt/ *n* (*feeling*) чу́вство; (*opinion*) мне́ние. **sentimental** /ˌsentɪˈment(ə)l/ *adj* сентимента́льный. **sentimentality** /ˌsentɪmenˈtælɪtɪ/ *n* сентимента́льность.

sentry /ˈsentrɪ/ *n* часово́й *sb*.

separable /ˈsepərəb(ə)l/ *adj* отдели́мый. **separate** /ˈsepərət/ *adj* отде́льный; *vt* & *i* отделя́ть(ся) *impf*, отдели́ть(ся) *pf*. **separation** /ˌsepəˈreɪʃ(ə)n/ *n* отделе́ние. **separatism** /ˈsepərəˌtɪz(ə)m/ *n* сепарати́зм. **separatist** /ˈsepərətɪst/ *n* сепарати́ст.

September /sepˈtembə(r)/ *n* сентя́брь *m*; *adj* сентя́брьский.

septic /ˈseptɪk/ *adj* септи́ческий.

sepulchre /ˈsepəlkə(r)/ *n* моги́ла.

sequel /ˈsiːkw(ə)l/ *n* (*result*) после́дствие; (*continuation*) продолже́ние. **sequence** /-kwəns/ *n* после́довательность; ~ **of events** ход собы́тий.

sequester /sɪˈkwestə(r)/ *vt* секвестрова́ть *impf* & *pf*.

sequin /ˈsiːkwɪn/ *n* блёстка.

Serb(ian) /ˈsɜːb(ɪən)/ *adj* се́рбский; *n* серб, ~ка. **Serbia** /ˈsɜːbɪə/ *n* Се́рбия. **Serbo-Croat(ian)** /ˌsɜːbəʊˈkrəʊæt, ˌsɜːbəʊkrəʊˈeɪʃ(ə)n/ *adj* сербскохорва́тский.

serenade /ˌserəˈneɪd/ *n* серена́да.

serene /sɪˈriːn/ *adj* споко́йный. **serenity** /-ˈrenɪtɪ/ *n* споко́йствие.

serf /sɜːf/ *n* крепостно́й *sb*. **serfdom** /-dəm/ *n* крепостно́е пра́во.

sergeant /ˈsɑːdʒ(ə)nt/ *n* сержа́нт.

serial /ˈsɪərɪəl/ *adj*: ~ **number** сери́йный но́мер; *n* (*story*) рома́н с продолже́нием; (*broadcast*) сери́йная постано́вка. **serialize** /-ˌlaɪz/ *vt* ста́вить *impf*, по~ *pf* в не́скольких частя́х. **series** /ˈsɪəriːz/ *n* (*succession*) ряд; (*broadcast*) се́рия переда́ч.

serious /ˈsɪərɪəs/ *adj* серьёзный. **seriousness** /-nɪs/ *n* серьёзность.

sermon /ˈsɜːmən/ *n* про́поведь.

serpent /ˈsɜːpənt/ *n* змея́.

serrated /seˈreɪtɪd/ *adj* зазу́бренный.

serum /ˈsɪərəm/ *n* сы́воротка.

servant /ˈsɜːv(ə)nt/ *n* слуга́ *m*, служа́нка. **serve** /sɜːv/ *vt* служи́ть *impf*, по~ *pf* +*dat* (**as, for** +*instr*); (*attend to*) обслу́живать *impf*, обслужи́ть *pf*; (*food*; *ball*) подава́ть *impf*, пода́ть *pf*; (*sentence*) отбыва́ть *impf*, отбы́ть *pf*; (*writ etc.*) вруча́ть *impf*, вручи́ть *pf* (**on** +*dat*); *vi* (*be suitable*) годи́ться (**for** на +*acc*, для+*gen*); (*sport*) подава́ть *impf*, пода́ть *pf* мя́ч; **it ~s him right** подело́м ему́ (*dat*). **server** /'sɜːvə(r)/ *n* (*comput*) се́рвер. **service** /'sɜːvɪs/ *n* (*act of serving*; *branch of public work*; *eccl*) слу́жба; (*quality of* ~) обслу́живание; (*of car etc.*) техобслу́живание; (*set of dishes*) серви́з; (*sport*) пода́ча; (*transport*) сообще́ние; **at your ~** к ва́шим услу́гам; *vt* (*car*) проводи́ть *impf*, провести́ *pf* техобслу́живание +*gen*; **~ charge** пла́та за обслу́живание; **~ station** ста́нция обслу́живания. **serviceable** /-səb(ə)l/ *n* (*useful*) поле́зный; (*durable*) про́чный. **serviceman** *n* военнослу́жащий *sb*.

serviette /ˌsɜːvɪ'et/ *n* салфе́тка.

servile /'sɜːvaɪl/ *adj* раболе́пный.

session /'seʃ(ə)n/ *n* заседа́ние, се́ссия.

set[1] /set/ *vt* (*put*; ~ *clock*, *trap*) ста́вить *impf*, по- *pf*; (*table*) накрыва́ть *impf*, накры́ть *pf*; (*bone*) вправля́ть *impf*, впра́вить *pf*; (*hair*) укла́дывать *impf*, уложи́ть *pf*; (*bring into state*) приводи́ть *impf*, привести́ *pf* (**in, to** в+*acc*); (*example*) подава́ть *impf*, пода́ть *pf*; (*task*) задава́ть *impf*, зада́ть *pf*; *vi* (*solidify*) тверде́ть *impf*, за~ *pf*; застыва́ть *impf*, засты́(ну)ть *pf*; (*sun etc.*) заходи́ть *impf*, зайти́ *pf*; сади́ться *impf*, сесть *pf*; **~ about** (*begin*) начина́ть *impf*, нача́ть *pf*; (*attack*) напада́ть *impf*, напа́сть *pf* на+*acc*; **~ back** (*impede*) препя́тствовать *impf*, вос~ *pf* +*dat*; **~-back** неуда́ча; **~ in** наступа́ть *impf*, наступи́ть *pf*; **~ off** (*on journey*) отправля́ться *impf*, отпра́виться *pf*; (*enhance*) оттеня́ть *impf*, оттени́ть *pf*; **~ out** (*state*) излага́ть *impf*, изложи́ть *pf*; (*on journey*) *see* **~ off; ~ up** (*business*) осно́вывать *impf*, основа́ть *pf*.

set[2] /set/ *n* набо́р, компле́кт; (*of dishes*) серви́з; (*radio*) приёмник; (*television*) телеви́зор; (*tennis*) сет; (*theat*) декора́ция; (*cin*) съёмочная площа́дка.

set[3] /set/ *adj* (*established*) устано́вленный.

settee /se'tiː/ *n* дива́н.

setting /'setɪŋ/ *n* (*frame*) опра́ва; (*surroundings*) обстано́вка; (*of mechanism etc.*) устано́вка; (*of sun etc.*) захо́д.

settle /'set(ə)l/ *vt* (*decide*) реша́ть *impf*, реши́ть *pf*; (*reconcile*) ула́живать *impf*, ула́дить *pf*; (*a bill etc.*) опла́чивать *impf*, оплати́ть *pf*; (*calm*) успока́ивать *impf*, успоко́ить *pf*; *vi* поселя́ться *impf*, посели́ться *pf*; (*subside*) оседа́ть *impf*, осе́сть *pf*; **~ down** уса́живаться *impf*, усе́сться *pf* (**to** за+*acc*). **settlement** /-mənt/ *n* поселе́ние; (*agreement*) соглаше́ние; (*payment*) упла́та. **settler** /'setlə(r)/ *n* поселе́нец.

seven /'sev(ə)n/ *adj* & *n* семь; (*number 7*) семёрка. **seventeen** /ˌsev(ə)n'tiːn/ *adj* & *n* семна́дцать. **seventeenth** /ˌsev(ə)n'tiːnθ/ *adj* & *n* семна́дцатый. **seventh** /'sev(ə)nθ/ *adj* & *n* седьмо́й; (*fraction*) седьма́я *sb*. **seventieth** /'sev(ə)ntɪɪθ/ *adj* & *n* семидеся́тый. **seventy** /'sev(ə)ntɪ/ *adj* & *n* се́мьдесят; *pl* (*decade*) семидеся́тые го́ды (-до́в) *m pl*.

sever /'sevə(r)/ *vt* (*cut off*) отреза́ть *impf*, отре́зать *pf*; (*relations*) разрыва́ть *impf*, разорва́ть *pf*.

several /'sevr(ə)l/ *pron* (*adj*) не́сколько (+*gen*).

severance /'sevərəns/ *n* разры́в; **~ pay** выходно́е посо́бие.

severe /sɪ'vɪə(r)/ *adj* стро́гий, суро́вый; (*pain*, *frost*) си́льный; (*illness*) тяжёлый. **severity** /-'verɪtɪ/ *n* стро́гость, суро́вость.

S

sew /səʊ/ *vt* шить *impf*, с~ *pf*; ~ **on** пришивáть *impf*, пришúть *pf*; ~ **up** зашивáть *impf*, зашúть *pf*.

sewage /'suːɪdʒ/ *n* стóчные вóды *f pl*; **~-farm** поля́ *neut pl* орошéния. **sewer** /'suːə(r)/ *n* стóчная трубá. **sewerage** /-rɪdz/ *n* канализáция.

sewing /'səʊɪŋ/ *n* шитьё; **~-machine** швéйная машúна.

sex /seks/ *n* (*gender*) пол; (*sexual activity*) секс; **have ~** имéть *impf* сношéние. **sexual** /'seksjʊəl/ *adj* половóй, сексуáльный; **~ intercourse** половóе сношéние. **sexuality** /,seksjʊ'ælɪtɪ/ *n* сексуáльность. **sexy** /'seksɪ/ *adj* эротúческий.

sh /ʃ/ *int* тúше!; тсс!

shabby /'ʃæbɪ/ *adj* вéтхий.

shack /ʃæk/ *n* лачýга.

shackles /'ʃæk(ə)lz/ *n pl* окóвы (-в) *pl*.

shade /ʃeɪd/ *n* тень; (*of colour, meaning*) оттéнок; (*lamp-~*) абажýр; **a ~** чуть-чýть; *vt* затеня́ть *impf*, затенúть *pf*; (*eyes etc.*) заслоня́ть *impf* заслонúть *pf*; (*drawing*) тушевáть *impf*, за~ *pf*. **shadow** /'ʃædəʊ/ *n* тень; *vt* (*follow*) тáйно следúть *impf* за +*instr*. **shadowy** /'ʃædəʊɪ/ *adj* тёмный. **shady** /'ʃeɪdɪ/ *adj* тенúстый; (*suspicious*) подозрúтельный.

shaft /ʃɑːft/ *n* (*of spear*) дрéвко; (*arrow*; *fig*) стрелá; (*of light*) луч; (*of cart*) оглóбля; (*axle*) вал; (*mine, lift*) шáхта.

shaggy /'ʃægɪ/ *adj* лохмáтый.

shake /'ʃeɪk(ə)n/ *vt* & *i* трястú(сь) *impf*; *vi* (*tremble*) дрожáть *impf*; *vt* (*weaken*) колебáть *impf*, по~ *pf*; (*shock*) потрясáть *impf* потрястú *pf*; **~ hands** пожимáть *impf*, пожáть *pf* рýку (**with** +*dat*); **~ one's head** покачáть *pf* головóй; **~ off** стря́хивать *impf*, стряхнýть *pf*; (*fig*) избавля́ться *impf*, избáвиться *pf* от+*gen*.

shaky /'ʃeɪkɪ/ *adj* шáткий.

shallow /'ʃæləʊ/ *adj* мéлкий; (*fig*) повéрхностный.

sham /ʃæm/ *vt* & *i* притворя́ться *impf*, притворúться *pf* +*instr*; *n* притвóрство; (*person*) притвóрщик, -ица; *adj* притвóрный.

shambles /'ʃæmb(ə)lz/ *n* хаóс.

shame /ʃeɪm/ *n* (*guilt*) стыд; (*disgrace*) позóр; **what a ~!** как жаль!; *vt* стыдúть *impf*, при~ *pf*. **shameful** /-fʊl/ *adj* позóрный. **shameless** /-lɪs/ *adj* бесстыдный.

shampoo /ʃæm'puː/ *n* шампýнь *m*.

shanty[1] /'ʃæntɪ/ *n* (*hut*) хибáрка; **~ town** трущóба.

shanty[2] /'ʃæntɪ/ *n* (*song*) матрóсская пéсня.

shape /ʃeɪp/ *n* фóрма; *vt* придавáть *impf*, придáть *pf* фóрму+*dat*; *vi*: **~ up** склáдываться *impf*, сложúться *pf*. **shapeless** /-lɪs/ *adj* бесфóрменный. **shapely** /-lɪ/ *adj* стрóйный.

share /ʃeə(r)/ *n* дóля; (*econ*) áкция; *vt* делúть *impf*, по~ *pf*; (*opinion etc.*; *~ out*) разделя́ть *impf*, разделúть *pf*. **shareholder** /-,həʊldə(r)/ *n* акционéр.

shark /ʃɑːk/ *n* акýла.

sharp /ʃɑːp/ *adj* óстрый; (*steep*) крутóй; (*sudden*; *harsh*) рéзкий; *n* (*mus*) диéз; *adv* (*with time*) рóвно; (*of angle*) крýто. **sharpen** /-pən/ *vt* точúть *impf*, на~ *pf*.

shatter /'ʃætə(r)/ *vt* & *i* разбивáть(ся) *impf*, разбúть(ся) *pf* вдрéбезги; *vt* (*hopes etc.*) разрушáть *impf*, разрýшить *pf*.

shave /ʃeɪv/ *vt* & *i* брúть(ся) *impf*, по~ *pf*; *n* бритьё. **shaver** /-və(r)/ *n* электрúческая брúтва.

shawl /ʃɔːl/ *n* шаль.

she /ʃiː/ *pron* онá.

sheaf /ʃiːf/ *n* сноп; (*of papers*) связка.

shear /ʃɪə(r)/ *vt* стричь *impf*, о~ *pf*. **shears** /ʃɪəz/ *n pl* нóжницы (-ц) *pl*.

sheath /ʃiːθ/ *n* нóжны (*gen* -жен) *pl*.

shed[1] /ʃed/ *n* сарáй.

shed² /ʃed/ *vt* (*tears, blood, light*) проливáть *impf*, пролѝть *pf*; (*skin, clothes*) сбрáсывать *impf*, сбрóсить *pf*.
sheen /ʃiːn/ *n* блеск.
sheep /ʃiːp/ *n* овцá. **sheepish** /-pɪʃ/ *adj* сконфýженный. **sheepskin** *n* овчѝна; ~ **coat** дублёнка.
sheer /ʃɪə(r)/ *adj* (*utter*) сýщий; (*textile*) прозрáчный; (*rock etc.*) отвéсный.
sheet /ʃiːt/ *n* (*on bed*) простынꙗ́; (*of glass, paper, etc.*) лист.
sheikh /ʃeɪk/ *n* шейх.
shelf /ʃelf/ *n* пóлка.
shell /ʃel/ *n* (*of mollusc*) рáковина; (*seashell*) ракýшка; (*of tortoise*) щит; (*of egg, nut*) скорлупá; (*of building*) óстов; (*explosive* ~) снарꙗ́д; *vt* (*peas etc.*) лущѝть *impf*, об~ *pf*; (*bombard*) обстрéливать *impf*, обстрелꙗ́ть *pf*.
shellfish /ˈʃelfɪʃ/ *n* (*mollusc*) моллю́ск; (*crustacean*) ракообрáзное *sb*.
shelter /ˈʃeltə(r)/ *n* убéжище; *vt* (*provide with refuge*) приютѝть *pf*; *vt & i* укрывáть(ся) *impf*, укры́ть(ся) *pf*.
shelve¹ /ʃelv/ *vt* (*defer*) отклáдывать *impf*, отложѝть *pf*.
shelve² /ʃelv/ *vi* (*slope*) отлóго спускáться *impf*.
shelving /ˈʃelvɪŋ/ *n* (*shelves*) стеллáж.
shepherd /ˈʃepəd/ *n* пастýх; *vt* проводѝть *impf*, провестѝ *pf*.
sherry /ˈʃerɪ/ *n* хéрес.
shield /ʃiːld/ *n* щит; *vt* защищáть *impf*, защитѝть *pf*.
shift /ʃɪft/ *vt & i* (*change position*) перемещáть(ся) *impf*, переместѝть(ся) *pf*; (*change*) менꙗ́ть(ся) *impf*; *n* перемещéние; перемéна; (*of workers*) смéна; ~ **work** смéнная рабóта. **shifty** /-tɪ/ *adj* скóльзкий.
shimmer /ˈʃɪmə(r)/ *vi* мерцáть *impf*; *n* мерцáние.
shin /ʃɪn/ *n* гóлень.
shine /ʃaɪn/ *vi* светѝть(ся) *impf*; (*glitter*) блестéть *impf*; (*excel*) блистáть *impf*; (*sun, eyes*) сиꙗ́ть *impf*; *vt* (*a light*) освещáть *impf*, осветѝть *pf* фонарём (**on** +*acc*); *n* глꙗ́нец.
shingle /ˈʃɪŋg(ə)l/ *n* (*pebbles*) гáлька.
shingles /ˈʃɪŋg(ə)lz/ *n* опоꙗ́сывающий лишáй.
shiny /ˈʃaɪnɪ/ *adj* блестꙗ́щий.
ship /ʃɪp/ *n* корáбль *m*; сýдно; *vt* (*transport*) перевозѝть *impf*, перевезтѝ *pf*; (*dispatch*) отправлꙗ́ть *impf*, отпрáвить *pf*. **shipbuilding** *n* судостроѝтельство. **shipment** /-mənt/ *n* (*dispatch*) отпрáвка; (*goods*) пáртия. **shipping** /-pɪŋ/ *n* судá (-дóв) *pl*. **shipshape** *adv* в пóлном порꙗ́дке. **shipwreck** *n* кораблекрушéние; **be** ~**ed** терпéть *impf*, по~ *pf* кораблекрушéние. **shipyard** *n* верфь.
shirk /ʃɜːk/ *vt* увѝливать *impf*, увильнýть *pf* от+*gen*.
shirt /ʃɜːt/ *n* рубáшка.
shit /ʃɪt/ *n* (*vulg*) говнó; *vi* срать *impf*, по~ *pf*.
shiver /ˈʃɪvə(r)/ *vi* (*tremble*) дрожáть *impf*; *n* дрожь.
shoal /ʃəʊl/ *n* (*of fish*) стáя.
shock /ʃɒk/ *n* (*emotional*) потрꙗсéние; (*impact*) удáр, толчóк; (*electr*) удáр тóком; (*med*) шок; *vt* шокѝровать *impf*. **shocking** /-kɪŋ/ *adj* (*outrageous*) скандáльный; (*awful*) ужáсный.
shoddy /ˈʃɒdɪ/ *adj* халтýрный.
shoe /ʃuː/ *n* тýфля; *vt* подкóвывать *impf*, подковáть *pf*. **shoelace** *n* шнурóк. **shoemaker** /-ˌmeɪkə(r)/ *n* сапóжник. **shoestring** *n*: **on a** ~ с небольшѝми срéдствами.
shoo /ʃuː/ *int* кш!; *vt* прогонꙗ́ть *impf*, прогнáть *pf*.
shoot /ʃuːt/ *vt & i* стрелꙗ́ть *impf*, вы́стрелить *pf* (*a gun* из +*gen*; **at** в+*acc*); (*arrow*) пускáть *impf*, пустѝть *pf*; (*kill*) застрелѝть *pf*; (*execute*) расстрéливать *impf*, расстрелꙗ́ть *pf*; (*hunt*) охóтиться *impf* на+*acc*; (*football*) бить

S

impf (по воро́там); (*cin*) снима́ть *impf*, снять *pf* (фильм); *vi* (*go swiftly*) проноси́ться *impf*, пронести́сь *pf*; ~ **down** (*aircraft*) сбива́ть *impf*, сбить *pf*; ~ **up** (*grow*) бы́стро расти́ *impf*, по~ *pf*; (*prices*) подска́кивать *impf*, подскочи́ть *pf*; *n* (*branch*) росто́к, побе́г; (*hunt*) охо́та. **shooting** /-tɪŋ/ *n* стрельба́; (*hunting*) охо́та; ~**-gallery** тир.

shop /ʃɒp/ *n* магази́н; (*workshop*) мастерска́я *sb*, цех; ~ **assistant** продаве́ц, -вщи́ца; ~**-lifter** магази́нный вор; ~**-lifting** воровство́ в магази́нах; ~ **steward** цехово́й ста́роста *m*; ~**-window** витри́на; *vi* де́лать *impf*, с~ *pf* поку́пки (*f pl*). **shopkeeper** /-ˌkiːpə(r)/ *n* ла́вочник. **shopper** /ˈʃɒpə(r)/ *n* покупа́тель *m*, ~ница. **shopping** /ˈʃɒpɪŋ/ *n* поку́пки *f pl*; **go, do one's** ~ де́лать *impf*, с~ *pf* поку́пки; ~ **centre** торго́вый центр.

shore[1] /ʃɔː(r)/ *n* бе́рег.

shore[2] /ʃɔː(r)/ *vt*: ~ **up** подпира́ть *impf*, подпере́ть *pf*.

short /ʃɔːt/ *adj* коро́ткий; (*not tall*) ни́зкого ро́ста; (*deficient*) недоста́точный; **be ~ of** испы́тывать *impf*, испыта́ть *pf* недоста́ток в+*prep*; (*curt*) ре́зкий; **in ~** одни́м сло́вом; ~**-change** обсчи́тывать *impf*, обсчита́ть *pf*; ~ **circuit** коро́ткое замыка́ние; ~ **cut** коро́ткий путь *m*; ~ **list** оконча́тельный спи́сок; ~**-list** включа́ть *impf*, включи́ть *pf* в оконча́тельный спи́сок; ~**-lived** недолгове́чный; ~**-sighted** близору́кий; (*fig*) недальнови́дный; ~ **story** расска́з; **in ~ supply** дефици́тный; ~**-tempered** вспы́льчивый; ~**-term** краткосро́чный; ~**-wave** коротково́лно́вый. **shortage** /-tɪdʒ/ *n* недоста́ток. **shortcoming** /-ˌkʌmɪŋ/ *n* недоста́ток. **shorten** /-t(ə)n/ *vt & i* укора́чивать(ся) *impf*, укороти́ть(ся) *pf*. **shortfall** *n* дефици́т. **shorthand** *n* стеногра́фия; ~ **typist** машини́стка-стенографи́стка. **shortly** /-lɪ/ *adv*: ~ **after** вско́ре (по́сле+*gen*); ~ **before** незадо́лго (до+*gen*). **shorts** /ʃɔːts/ *n pl* шо́рты (-т) *pl*.

shot /ʃɒt/ *n* (*discharge of gun*) вы́стрел; (*pellets*) дробь; (*person*) стрело́к; (*attempt*) попы́тка; (*phot*) сни́мок; (*cin*) кадр; (*sport*) (*stroke*) уда́р; (*throw*) бросо́к; **like a ~** неме́дленно; ~**-gun** дробови́к.

should /ʃʊd/ *v aux* (*ought*) до́лжен (бы) +*inf*: **you ~ know that** вы должны́ э́то знать; **he ~ be here soon** он до́лжен бы быть тут ско́ро; (*conditional*) бы +*past*: **I ~ say** я бы сказа́л(а); **I ~ like** я бы хоте́л(а).

shoulder /ˈʃəʊldə(r)/ *n* плечо́; ~**-blade** лопа́тка; ~**-strap** брете́лька; взва́ливать *impf*, взвали́ть *pf* на пле́чи; (*fig*) брать *impf*, взять *pf* на себя́.

shout /ʃaʊt/ *n* крик; *vi* крича́ть *impf*, кри́кнуть *pf*; ~ **down** перекри́кивать *impf*, перекрича́ть *pf*.

shove /ʃʌv/ *n* толчо́к; *vt & i* толка́ть(ся) *impf*, толкну́ть *pf*; ~ **off** (*coll*) убира́ться *impf*, убра́ться *pf*.

shovel /ˈʃʌv(ə)l/ *n* лопа́та; *vt* (~ *up*) сгреба́ть *impf*, сгрести́ *pf*.

show /ʃəʊ/ *vt* пока́зывать *impf*, показа́ть *pf*; (*exhibit*) выставля́ть *impf*, вы́ставить *pf*; (*film etc.*) демонстри́ровать *impf*, про~ *pf*; *vi* (*also* ~ *up*) быть ви́дным, заме́тным; ~ **off** (*vi*) привлека́ть *impf*; привле́чь *pf* к себе́ внима́ние; ~ **up** *see vi*; (*appear*) появля́ться *impf*; появи́ться *pf*; *n* (*exhibition*) вы́ставка; (*theat*) спекта́кль *m*, шо́у *neut indecl*; (*effect*) ви́димость; ~ **of hands** голосова́ние подня́тием руки́; ~ **business** шо́у-би́знес; ~**-case** витри́на; ~**-jumping** соревнова́ние по ска́чкам; ~**-room** сало́н. **showdown** *n* развя́зка.

shower /ˈʃaʊə(r)/ *n* (*rain*) до́ждик; (*hail*; *fig*) град; (~*-bath*) душ; *vt*

S

осыпа́ть *impf*, осы́пать *pf* +*instr* (**on** +*acc*); *vi* принима́ть *impf*, приня́ть *pf* душ. **showery** /-rɪ/ *adj* дождли́вый.

showpiece /'ʃəʊpi:s/ *n* образе́ц.

showy /'ʃəʊɪ/ *adj* показно́й.

shrapnel /'ʃræpn(ə)l/ *n* шрапне́ль.

shred /ʃred/ *n* клочо́к; **not a ~** ни ка́пли; *vt* мельчи́ть *impf*, из~ *pf*.

shrewd /ʃru:d/ *adj* проница́тельный.

shriek /ʃri:k/ *vi* визжа́ть *impf*; взви́гнуть *pf*.

shrill /ʃrɪl/ *adj* пронзи́тельный.

shrimp /ʃrɪmp/ *n* креве́тка.

shrine /ʃraɪn/ *n* святы́ня.

shrink /ʃrɪŋk/ *vi* сади́ться *impf*, сесть *pf*; (*recoil*) отпря́нуть *pf*; *vt* вызыва́ть *impf*, вы́звать *pf* уса́дку у+*gen*; **~ from** избега́ть *impf* +*gen*. **shrinkage** /-kɪdʒ/ *n* уса́дка.

shrivel /'ʃrɪv(ə)l/ *vi* смо́рщиваться *impf*, смо́рщиться *pf*.

shroud /ʃraʊd/ *n* са́ван; *vt* (*fig*) оку́тывать *impf*, оку́тать *pf* (**in** +*instr*).

Shrove Tuesday /ʃrəʊv/ *n* вто́рник на ма́сленой неде́ле.

shrub /ʃrʌb/ *n* куст. **shrubbery** /-bərɪ/ *n* кустა́рник.

shrug /ʃrʌg/ *vt* & *i* пожима́ть *impf*, пожа́ть *pf* (плеча́ми).

shudder /'ʃʌdə(r)/ *n* содрога́ние; *vi* содрога́ться *impf*, содрогну́ться *pf*.

shuffle /'ʃʌf(ə)l/ *vt* & *i* (*one's feet*) ша́ркать *impf* (нога́ми); *vt* (*cards*) тасова́ть *impf*, с~ *pf*.

shun /ʃʌn/ *vt* избега́ть *impf* +*gen*.

shunt /ʃʌnt/ *vi* (*rly*) маневри́ровать *impf*, с~ *pf*; *vt* (*rly*) переводи́ть *impf*, перевести́ *pf* на запасно́й путь.

shut /ʃʌt/ *vt* & *i* (*also* **~** *down*) закрыва́ть(ся) *impf*, закры́ть(ся) *pf*; **~ out** (*exclude*) исключа́ть *impf*, исключи́ть *pf*; (*fence off*) загора́живать *impf*, загороди́ть *pf*; (*keep out*) не пуска́ть *impf*, пусти́ть *pf*; **~ up** (*vi*) замолча́ть *pf*; (*imper*) заткни́сь!

shutter /'ʃʌtə(r)/ *n* ста́вень *m*; (*phot*) затво́р.

shuttle /'ʃʌt(ə)l/ *n* челно́к.

shy[1] /ʃaɪ/ *adj* засте́нчивый.

shy[2] /ʃaɪ/ *vi* (*in alarm*) отпря́дывать *impf*, отпря́нуть *pf*.

Siberia /saɪ'bɪərɪə/ *n* Сиби́рь. **Siberian** /-rɪən/ *adj* сиби́рский; *n* сибиря́к, -я́чка.

sick /sɪk/ *adj* больно́й; **be ~** (*vomit*) рвать *impf*, вы́~ *pf impers* +*acc*: **he was ~** его́ вы́рвало; **feel ~** тошни́ть *impf impers* +*acc*; **be ~ of** надоеда́ть *impf*, надое́сть *pf* +*nom* (*object*) & *dat* (*subject*): **I'm ~ of her** она́ мне надое́ла; **~-leave** о́тпуск по боле́зни. **sicken** /-kən/ *vt* вызыва́ть *impf*, вы́звать *pf* тошноту́, (*disgust*) отвраще́ние, у+*gen*; *vi* заболева́ть *impf*, заболе́ть *pf*. **sickening** /-kənɪŋ/ *adj* отврати́тельный.

sickle /'sɪk(ə)l/ *n* серп.

sickly /'sɪklɪ/ *adj* боле́зненный; (*nauseating*) тошнотво́рный. **sickness** /'sɪknɪs/ *n* боле́знь; (*vomiting*) тошнота́.

side /saɪd/ *n* сторона́; (*of body*) бок; **~ by ~** ря́дом (**with** с+*instr*); **on the ~** на стороне́; *vi*: **~ with** встава́ть *impf*, встать *pf* на сто́рону+*gen*; **~-effect** побо́чное де́йствие; **~-step** (*fig*) уклоня́ться *impf*, уклони́ться *pf* от+*gen*; **~-track** (*distract*) отвлека́ть *impf*, отвле́чь *pf*. **sideboard** *n* буфе́т; *pl* ба́ки (-к) *pl*. **sidelight** *n* боково́й фона́рь *m*. **sideline** *n* (*work*) побо́чная рабо́та.

sidelong /'saɪdlɒŋ/ *adj* (*glance*) косо́й.

sideways /'saɪdweɪz/ *adv* бо́ком.

siding /'saɪdɪŋ/ *n* запасно́й путь *m*.

sidle /'saɪd(ə)l/ *vi*: **~ up to** подходи́ть *impf*, подойти́ *pf* к (+*dat*) бочко́м.

siege /si:dʒ/ *n* оса́да; **lay ~ to** осажда́ть *impf*, осади́ть *pf*; **raise the ~ of** снима́ть *impf*, снять *pf* оса́ду с+*gen*.

S

sieve /sɪv/ *n* си́то; *vt* просе́ивать *impf*, просе́ять *pf*.
sift /sɪft/ *vt* просе́ивать *impf*, просе́ять *pf*; (*fig*) тща́тельно рассма́тривать *impf*, рассмотре́ть *pf*.
sigh /saɪ/ *vi* вздыха́ть *impf*, вздохну́ть *pf*; *n* вздох.
sight /saɪt/ *n* (*faculty*) зре́ние; (*view*) вид; (*spectacle*) зре́лище; *pl* достопримеча́тельности *f pl*; (*on gun*) прице́л; **at first ~** с пе́рвого взгля́да; **catch ~ of** уви́деть *pf*; **know by ~** знать *impf* в лицо́; **lose ~ of** теря́ть *impf*, по~ *pf* из виду; (*fig*) упуска́ть *impf*, упусти́ть *pf* из виду.
sign /saɪn/ *n* знак; (*indication*) при́знак; (*~board*) вы́веска; *vt & abs* подпи́сывать(ся) *impf*, подписа́ть(ся) *pf*; *vi* (*give ~*) подава́ть *impf*, пода́ть *pf* знак; **~ on** (*as unemployed*) запи́сываться *impf*, записа́ться *pf* в спи́ски безрабо́тных; (*~ up*) нанима́ться *impf*, наня́ться *pf*.
signal /'sɪgn(ə)l/ *n* сигна́л; *vt & i* сигнализи́ровать *impf & pf*. **signal-box** *n* сигна́льная бу́дка.
signatory /'sɪgnətərɪ/ *n* подписа́вший *sb*; (*of treaty*) сторона́, подписа́вшая до́говор.
signature /'sɪgnətʃə(r)/ *n* по́дпись.
significance /sɪg'nɪfɪkəns/ *n* значе́ние. **significant** /-kənt/ *adj* значи́тельный. **signify** /'sɪgnɪˌfaɪ/ *vt* означа́ть *impf*.
signpost /'saɪnpəʊst/ *n* указа́тельный столб.
silage /'saɪlɪdʒ/ *n* си́лос.
silence /'saɪləns/ *n* молча́ние, тишина́; *vt* заста́вить *pf* замолча́ть. **silencer** /-sə(r)/ *n* глуши́тель *m*. **silent** /'saɪlənt/ *adj* (*not speaking*) безмо́лвный; (*of film*) немо́й; (*without noise*) ти́хий; **be ~** молча́ть *impf*.
silhouette /ˌsɪluː'et/ *n* силуэ́т; *vt*: **be ~d** вырисо́вываться *impf*, вы́рисоваться *pf* (**against** на фо́не+*gen*).
silicon /'sɪlɪkən/ *n* кре́мний. **silicone** /-ˌkəʊn/ *n* силико́н.
silk /sɪlk/ *n* шёлк; *attrib* шёлковый. **silky** /-kɪ/ *adj* шелкови́стый.
sill /sɪl/ *n* подоко́нник.
silly /'sɪlɪ/ *adj* глу́пый.
silo /'saɪləʊ/ *n* си́лос.
silt /sɪlt/ *n* ил.
silver /'sɪlvə(r)/ *n* серебро́; (*cutlery*) столо́вое серебро́; *adj* (*of ~*) сере́бряный; (*silvery*) серебри́стый; **~-plated** посеребрённый. **silversmith** *n* сере́бряных дел ма́стер. **silverware** /'sɪlvəˌweə(r)/ *n* столо́вое серебро́. **silvery** /'sɪlvərɪ/ *adj* серебри́стый.
SIM (card) /sɪm/ *n* сим-ка́рта.
similar /'sɪmɪlə(r)/ *adj* подо́бный (**to** +*dat*). **similarity** /ˌsɪmɪ'lærɪtɪ/ *n* схо́дство. **similarly** /'sɪmɪləlɪ/ *adv* подо́бным о́бразом.
simile /'sɪmɪlɪ/ *n* сравне́ние.
simmer /'sɪmə(r)/ *vt* кипяти́ть *impf* на ме́дленном огне́; *vi* кипе́ть *impf* на ме́дленном огне́; **~ down** успока́иваться *impf*, успоко́иться *pf*.
simper /'sɪmpə(r)/ *vi* жема́нно улыба́ться *impf*, улыбну́ться *pf*.
simple /'sɪmp(ə)l/ *adj* просто́й; **~-minded** тупова́тый. **simplicity** /sɪm'plɪsɪtɪ/ *n* простота́. **simplify** /'sɪmplɪˌfaɪ/ *vt* упроща́ть *impf*, упрости́ть *pf*. **simply** /'sɪmplɪ/ *adv* про́сто.
simulate /'sɪmjʊˌleɪt/ *vt* притворя́ться *impf*, притвори́ться *pf* +*instr*; (*conditions etc.*) модели́ровать *impf & pf*. **simulated** /-ˌleɪtɪd/ *adj* (*pearls etc.*) иску́сственный.
simultaneous /ˌsɪməl'teɪnɪəs/ *adj* одновре́ме́нный.
sin /sɪn/ *n* грех; *vi* греши́ть *impf*, со~ *pf*.
since /sɪns/ *adv* с тех пор; *prep* с+*gen*; *conj* с тех пор как; (*reason*) так как.
sincere /sɪn'sɪə(r)/ *adj* и́скренний. **sincerely** /-'sɪəlɪ/ *adv* и́скренне; **yours ~** и́скренне Ваш. **sincerity** /-'serɪtɪ/ *n* и́скренность.

sinew /ˈsɪnjuː/ *n* сухожи́лие.
sinful /ˈsɪnfʊl/ *adj* гре́шный.
sing /sɪŋ/ *vt & i* петь *impf*, про~, с~ *pf*.
singe /sɪndʒ/ *vt* пали́ть *impf*, о~ *pf*.
singer /ˈsɪŋə(r)/ *n* певе́ц, -ви́ца.
single /ˈsɪŋg(ə)l/ *adj* оди́н; (*unmarried*) (*of man*) неженáтый; (*of woman*) незаму́жняя; (*bed*) односпáльный; **~-handed** без посторóнней пóмощи; **~-minded** целеустремлённый; **~ parent** мать/отéц-одинóчка; **~ room** кóмната на одногó; *n* (*ticket*) билéт в оди́н конéц; *pl* (*tennis etc.*) одинóчная игрá *vt*: **~ out** выделя́ть *impf*, вы́делить *pf*. **singly** /ˈsɪŋglɪ/ *adv* по-одномý.
singular /ˈsɪŋgjʊlə(r)/ *n* еди́нственное числó; *adj* еди́нственный; (*unusual*) необычáйный. **singularly** /-ləlɪ/ *adv* необычáйно.
sinister /ˈsɪnɪstə(r)/ *adj* зловéщий.
sink /sɪŋk/ *vi* (*descend slowly*) опускáться *impf*, опусти́ться *pf*; (*in mud etc.*) погружáться *impf*, погрузи́ться *pf*; (*in water*) тонýть *impf*, по~ *pf*; *vt* (*ship*) топи́ть *impf*, по~ *pf*; (*pipe, post*) вкáпывать *impf*, вкопáть *pf*; *n* рáковина.
sinner /ˈsɪnə(r)/ *n* грéшник, -ица.
sinus /ˈsaɪnəs/ *n* пáзуха.
sip /sɪp/ *vt* пить *impf*, мáленькими глоткáми; *n* малéнький глотóк.
siphon /ˈsaɪf(ə)n/ *n* сифóн; **~ off** (*also fig*) перекáчивать *impf*, перекачáть *pf*.
sir /sɜː(r)/ *n* сэр.
siren /ˈsaɪərən/ *n* сирéна.
sister /ˈsɪstə(r)/ *n* сестрá; **~-in-law** (*husband's sister*) золóвка; (*wife's sister*) своя́ченица; (*brother's wife*) невéстка.
sit /sɪt/ *vi* (*be sitting*) сидéть *impf*; (*~ down*) сади́ться *impf*, сесть *pf*; (*parl, law*) заседáть *impf*; *vt* усáживать *impf*, усади́ть *pf*; (*exam*) сдавáть *impf*; **~ back** откиды́ваться *impf*, отки́нуться *pf*; **~ down** сади́ться *impf*, сесть *pf*; **~ up** приподнимáться *impf*, приподня́ться *pf*; (*not go to bed*) не ложи́ться *impf* спать.
site /saɪt/ *n* (*where a thing takes place*) мéсто; (*where a thing is*) местоположéние.
sitting /ˈsɪtɪŋ/ *n* (*parl etc.*) заседáние; (*for meal*) смéна; **~-room** гости́ная *sb*.
situated /ˈsɪtjʊˌeɪtɪd/ *adj*: **be ~** находи́ться *impf*. **situation** /ˌsɪtjʊˈeɪʃ(ə)n/ *n* местоположéние; (*circumstances*) положéние; (*job*) мéсто.
six /sɪks/ *adj & n* шесть; (*number 6*) шестёрка. **sixteen** /ˌsɪksˈtiːn/ *adj & n* шестнáдцать. **sixteenth** /-ˈtiːnθ/ *adj & n* шестнáдцатый. **sixth** /sɪksθ/ *adj & n* шестóй; (*fraction*) шестáя *sb*. **sixtieth** /ˈsɪkstɪɪθ/ *adj & n* шестидеся́тый. **sixty** /ˈsɪkstɪ/ *adj & n* шестьдеся́т; *pl* (*decade*) шестидеся́тые гóды (-дóв) *m pl*.
size /saɪz/ *n* размéр; *vt*: **~ up** оцéнивать *impf*, оцени́ть *pf*. **sizeable** /ˈsaɪzəb(ə)l/ *adj* значи́тельный.
sizzle /ˈsɪz(ə)l/ *vi* шипéть *impf*.
skate[1] /skeɪt/ *n* (*fish*) скат.
skate[2] /skeɪt/ *n* (*ice-~*) конёк; (*roller-~*) конёк на рóликах; *vi* катáться *impf* на конькáх; **skating-rink** катóк.
skeleton /ˈskelɪt(ə)n/ *n* скелéт.
sketch /sketʃ/ *n* зарисóвка; (*theat*) скетч; *vt & i* зарисóвывать *impf*, зарисовáть *pf*. **sketchy** /-tʃɪ/ *adj* схемати́ческий; (*superficial*) повéрхностный.
skew /skjuː/ *adj* косóй; **on the ~** кóсо.
skewer /ˈskjuːə(r)/ *n* вéртел.
ski /skiː/ *n* лы́жа; **~-jump** трампли́н; *vi* ходи́ть *impf* на лы́жах.
skid /skɪd/ *n* занóс; *vi* заноси́ть *impf*, занести́ *pf impers+acc*.
skier /ˈskiːə(r)/ *n* лы́жник. **skiing** /ˈskiːɪŋ/ *n* лы́жный спорт.
skilful /ˈskɪlfʊl/ *adj* искýсный. **skill** /skɪl/ *n* мастерствó; (*countable*)

поле́зный на́вык. **skilled** /skɪld/ *adj* иску́сный; (*trained*) квалифици́рованный.
skim /skɪm/ *vt* снима́ть *impf*, снять *pf* (*cream* сли́вки *pl*, *scum* на́кипь) с+*gen*; *vi* скользи́ть *impf* (**over, along** по+*dat*); **~ through** бе́гло просма́тривать *impf*, просмотре́ть *pf*; *adj*: **~ milk** снято́е молоко́.
skimp /skɪmp/ *vt* & *i* скупи́ться *impf* (на+*acc*). **skimpy** /-pɪ/ *adj* ску́дный.
skin /skɪn/ *n* ко́жа; (*hide*) шку́ра; (*of fruit etc.*) кожура́; (*on milk*) пе́нка; *vt* сдира́ть *impf*, содра́ть *pf* ко́жу, шку́ру, с+*gen*; (*fruit*) снима́ть *impf*, снять *pf* кожуру́ с+*gen*. **skinny** /-nɪ/ *adj* то́щий.
skip¹ /skɪp/ *vi* скака́ть *impf*; (*with rope*) пры́гать *impf* че́рез скака́лку; *vt* (*omit*) пропуска́ть *impf*, пропусти́ть *pf*.
skip² /skɪp/ *n* (*container*) скип.
skipper /'skɪpə(r)/ *n* (*naut*) шки́пер.
skirmish /'skɜːmɪʃ/ *n* схва́тка.
skirt /skɜːt/ *n* ю́бка; *vt* обходи́ть *impf*, обойти́ *pf* стороно́й; **~ing-board** пли́нтус.
skittle /'skɪt(ə)l/ *n* ке́гля; *pl* ке́гли *f pl*.
skulk /skʌlk/ *vi* (*hide*) скрыва́ться *impf*; (*creep*) кра́сться *impf*.
skull /skʌl/ *n* че́реп.
skunk /skʌŋk/ *n* скунс.
sky /skaɪ/ *n* не́бо. **skylark** *n* жа́воронок. **skylight** *n* окно́ в кры́ше. **skyline** *n* горизо́нт. **skyscraper** /-ˌskreɪpə(r)/ *n* небоскрёб.
slab /slæb/ *n* плита́; (*of cake etc.*) кусо́к.
slack /slæk/ *adj* (*loose*) сла́бый; (*sluggish*) вя́лый; (*negligent*) небре́жный; *n* (*of rope*) слабина́; *pl* брю́ки (-к) *pl*. **slacken** /-kən/ *vt* ослабля́ть *impf*, осла́бить *pf*; *vt* & *i* (*slow down*) замедля́ть(ся) *impf*, заме́длить(ся) *pf*; *vi* ослабева́ть *impf*, ослабе́ть *pf*.
slag /slæg/ *n* шлак.
slam /slæm/ *vt* & *i* захло́пывать(ся) *impf*, захло́пнуть(ся) *pf*.
slander /'slɑːndə(r)/ *n* клевета́; *vt* клевета́ть *impf*, на**~** *pf* на+*acc*. **slanderous** /-rəs/ *adj* клеветни́ческий.
slang /slæŋ/ *n* жарго́н. **slangy** /slæŋɪ/ *adj* жарго́нный.
slant /slɑːnt/ *vt* & *i* наклоня́ть(ся) *impf*, наклони́ть(ся) *pf*; *n* укло́н. **slanting** /-tɪŋ/ *adj* косо́й.
slap /slæp/ *vt* шлёпать *impf*, шлёпнуть *pf*; *n* шлепо́к; *adv* пря́мо. **slapdash** *adj* небре́жный. **slapstick** *n* фарс.
slash /slæʃ/ *vt* (*cut*) поро́ть *impf*, рас**~** *pf*; (*fig*) уре́зывать *impf*, уре́зать *pf*; *n* разре́з; (*sign*) дробь.
slat /slæt/ *n* пла́нка.
slate¹ /sleɪt/ *n* сла́нец; (*for roofing*) (кро́вельная) пли́тка.
slate² /sleɪt/ *vt* (*criticize*) разноси́ть *impf*, разнести́ *pf*.
slaughter /'slɔːtə(r)/ *n* (*of animals*) убо́й; (*massacre*) резня́; *vt* (*animals*) ре́зать *impf*, за**~** *pf*; (*people*) убива́ть *impf*, уби́ть *pf*. **slaughterhouse** *n* бо́йня.
Slav /slɑːv/ *n* славяни́н, -я́нка; *adj* славя́нский.
slave /sleɪv/ *n* раб, рабы́ня; *vi* рабо́тать *impf* как раб. **slavery** /-vərɪ/ *n* ра́бство.
Slavic /'slɑːvɪk/ *adj* славя́нский.
slavish /'sleɪvɪʃ/ *adj* ра́бский.
Slavonic /slə'vɒnɪk/ *adj* славя́нский.
slay /sleɪ/ *vt* убива́ть *impf*, уби́ть *pf*.
sleazy /'sliːzɪ/ *adj* убо́гий.
sledge /sledʒ/ *n* са́ни (-не́й) *pl*.
sledge-hammer /'sledʒˌhæmə(r)/ *n* кува́лда.
sleek /sliːk/ *adj* гла́дкий.
sleep /sliːp/ *n* сон; **go to ~** засыпа́ть *impf*, засну́ть *pf*; *vi* спать *impf*; (*spend the night*) ночева́ть *impf*, пере**~** *pf*. **sleeper** /-pə(r)/ *n* спя́щий *sb*; (*on track*) шпа́ла; (*sleeping-car*) спа́льный ваго́н. **sleeping** /-pɪŋ/ *adj* спя́щий; **~-bag** спа́льный мешо́к; **~-car**

спа́льный ваго́н; **~-pill** снотво́рная табле́тка. **sleepless** /-lɪs/ *adj* бессо́нный. **sleepy** /-pɪ/ *adj* со́нный.

sleet /sliːt/ *n* мо́крый снег.

sleeve /sliːv/ *n* рука́в; (*of record*) конве́рт.

sleigh /sleɪ/ *n* са́ни (-не́й) *pl.*

sleight-of-hand /ˌslaɪtəvˈhænd/ *n* ло́вкость рук.

slender /ˈslendə(r)/ *adj* (*slim*) то́нкий; (*meagre*) ску́дный; (*of hope etc.*) сла́бый.

sleuth /sluːθ/ *n* сы́щик.

slice /slaɪs/ *n* кусо́к; *vt* (*~ up*) нареза́ть *impf*, наре́зать *pf.*

slick /slɪk/ *adj* (*dextrous*) ло́вкий; (*crafty*) хи́трый; *n* нефтяна́я плёнка.

slide /slaɪd/ *vi* скользи́ть *impf*; *vt* (*drawer etc.*) задвига́ть *impf*, задви́нуть *pf*; *n* (*children's ~*) го́рка; (*microscope ~*) предме́тное стекло́; (*phot*) диапозити́в, слайд; (*for hair*) зако́лка. **sliding** /-dɪŋ/ *adj* (*door*) задвижно́й.

slight[1] /slaɪt/ *adj* (*slender*) то́нкий; (*inconsiderable*) небольшо́й; (*light*) лёгкий; **not the ~est** ни мале́йшего, -шей (*gen*); **not in the ~est** ничу́ть.

slight[2] /slaɪt/ *vt* пренебрега́ть *impf*, пренебре́чь *pf* +*instr*; *n* оби́да.

slightly /ˈslaɪtlɪ/ *adv* слегка́, немно́го.

slim /slɪm/ *adj* то́нкий; (*chance etc.*) сла́бый; *vi* худе́ть *impf*, по~ *pf.*

slime /slaɪm/ *n* слизь. **slimy** /-mɪ/ *adj* сли́зистый; (*person*) ско́льзкий.

sling /slɪŋ/ *vt* (*throw*) швыря́ть *impf*, швырну́ть *pf*; (*suspend*) подве́шивать *impf*, подве́сить *pf*; *n* (*med*) пе́ревязь.

slink /slɪŋk/ *vi* кра́сться *impf.*

slip /slɪp/ *n* (*mistake*) оши́бка; (*garment*) комбина́ция; (*pillow-case*) на́волочка; (*paper*) листо́чек; **~ of the tongue** обмо́лвка; **give the ~** ускользну́ть *pf* от+*gen*; *vi* скользи́ть *impf*, скользну́ть *pf*; (*fall over*) поскользну́ться *pf*; (*from hands etc.*) выска́льзывать *impf*, вы́скользнуть *pf*; *vt* (*insert*) сова́ть *impf*, су́нуть *pf*; **~ off** (*depart*) ускольза́ть *impf*, ускользну́ть *pf*; **~ up** (*make mistake*) ошиба́ться *impf*, ошиби́ться *pf.* **slipper** /-pə(r)/ *n* та́пка. **slippery** /-pərɪ/ *adj* ско́льзкий.

slit /slɪt/ *vt* разреза́ть *impf*, разре́зать *pf*; (*throat*) пере́резать *pf*; *n* щель; (*cut*) разре́з.

slither /ˈslɪðə(r)/ *vi* скользи́ть *impf.*

sliver /ˈslɪvə(r)/ *n* ще́пка.

slob /slɒb/ *n* неря́ха *m* & *f.*

slobber /ˈslɒbə(r)/ *vi* пуска́ть *impf*, пусти́ть *pf* слю́ни.

slog /slɒg/ *vt* (*hit*) си́льно ударя́ть *impf*, уда́рить *pf*; (*work*) упо́рно рабо́тать *impf.*

slogan /ˈsləʊgən/ *n* ло́зунг.

slop /slɒp/ *n*: *pl* помо́и (-о́ев) *pl*; *vt* & *i* выплёскивать(ся) *impf*, вы́плескать(ся) *pf.*

slope /sləʊp/ *n* (*artificial*) накло́н; (*geog*) склон; *vi* име́ть *impf* накло́н. **sloping** /-pɪŋ/ *adj* накло́нный.

sloppy /ˈslɒpɪ/ *adj* (*work*) неря́шливый; (*sentimental*) сентимента́льный.

slot /slɒt/ *n* отве́рстие; **~-machine** автома́т; *vt*: **~ in** вставля́ть *impf*, вста́вить *pf.*

sloth /sləʊθ/ *n* лень.

slouch /slaʊtʃ/ *vi* (*stoop*) суту́литься *impf.*

slovenly /ˈslʌvənlɪ/ *adj* неря́шливый.

slow /sləʊ/ *adj* ме́дленный; (*tardy*) медли́тельный; (*stupid*) тупо́й; (*business*) вя́лый; **be ~** (*clock*) отстава́ть *impf*, отста́ть *pf*; *adv* ме́дленно; *vt* & *i* (*~ down, up*) замедля́ть(ся) *impf*, заме́длить(ся) *pf.*

sludge /slʌdʒ/ *n* (*mud*) грязь; (*sediment*) отсто́й.

slug /slʌg/ *n* (*zool*) слизня́к.

sluggish /ˈslʌgɪʃ/ *adj* вя́лый.

S

sluice /sluːs/ *n* шлюз.
slum /slʌm/ *n* трущо́ба.
slumber /ˈslʌmbə(r)/ *n* сон; *vi* спать *impf*.
slump /slʌmp/ *n* спад; *vi* ре́зко па́дать *impf*, (у)па́сть *pf*; (*of person*) сва́ливаться *impf*, свали́ться *pf*.
slur /slɜː(r)/ *vt* говори́ть *impf* невня́тно; *n* (*stigma*) пятно́.
slush /slʌʃ/ *n* сля́коть.
slut /slʌt/ *n* (*sloven*) неря́ха; (*trollop*) потаску́ха.
sly /slaɪ/ *adj* хи́трый; **on the ~** тайко́м.
smack[1] /smæk/ *vi*: **~ of** па́хнуть *impf* +*instr*.
smack[2] /smæk/ *n* (*slap*) шлепо́к; *vt* шлёпать *impf*, шлёпнуть *pf*.
small /smɔːl/ *adj* ма́ленький, небольшо́й, ма́лый; (*of agent, particles; petty*) ме́лкий; **~ change** ме́лочь; **~-scale** мелкомасшта́бный; **~ talk** све́тская бесе́да.
smart[1] /smɑːt/ *vi* са́днить *impf impers*.
smart[2] /smɑːt/ *adj* элега́нтный; (*brisk*) бы́стрый; (*cunning*) ло́вкий; (*sharp*) смека́листый (*coll*).
smash /smæʃ/ *vt* & *i* разбива́ть(ся) *impf*, разби́ть(ся) *pf*; *vi*: **~ into** вреза́ться *impf*, вре́заться *pf* в+*acc*; *n* (*crash*) гро́хот; (*collision*) столкнове́ние; (*blow*) си́льный уда́р.
smattering /ˈsmætərɪŋ/ *n* пове́рхностное зна́ние.
smear /smɪə(r)/ *vt* сма́зывать *impf*, сма́зать *pf*; (*dirty*) па́чкать *impf*, за~, ис~ *pf*; (*discredit*) поро́чить *impf*, о~ *pf*; *n* (*spot*) пятно́; (*slander*) клевета́; (*med*) мазо́к.
smell /smel/ *n* (*sense*) обоня́ние; (*odour*) за́пах; *vt* чу́вствовать *impf* за́пах+*gen*; (*sniff*) ню́хать *impf*, по~ *pf*; *vi*: **~ of** па́хнуть *impf* +*instr*. **smelly** /-lɪ/ *adj* воню́чий.
smelt /smelt/ *vt* (*ore*) пла́вить *impf*; (*metal*) выплавля́ть *impf*, вы́плавить *pf*.
smile /smaɪl/ *vi* улыба́ться *impf*, улыбну́ться *pf*; *n* улы́бка.
smirk /smɜːk/ *vi* ухмыля́ться *impf*, ухмыльну́ться *pf*; *n* ухмы́лка.
smith /smɪθ/ *n* кузне́ц.
smithereens /ˌsmɪðəˈriːnz/ *n*: **(in)to ~** вдре́безги.
smithy /ˈsmɪðɪ/ *n* ку́зница.
smock /smɒk/ *n* блу́за.
smog /smɒg/ *n* тума́н (с ды́мом).
smoke /sməʊk/ *n* дым; **~-screen** дымова́я заве́са; *vt* & *i* (*cigarette etc.*) кури́ть *impf*, по~ *pf*; *vt* (*cure; colour*) копти́ть *impf*, за~ *pf*; *vi* (*abnormally*) дыми́ть *impf*; (*of fire*) дыми́ться *impf*. **smoker** /-kə(r)/ *n* кури́льщик, -ица, куря́щий *sb*. **smoky** /-kɪ/ *adj* ды́мный.
smooth /smuːð/ *adj* (*surface etc.*) гла́дкий; (*movement etc.*) пла́вный; *vt* пригла́живать *impf*, пригла́дить *pf*; **~ over** сгла́живать *impf*, сгла́дить *pf*.
smother /ˈsmʌðə(r)/ *vt* (*stifle, also fig*) души́ть *impf*, за~ *pf*; (*cover*) покрыва́ть *impf*, покры́ть *pf*.
smoulder /ˈsməʊldə(r)/ *vi* тлеть *impf*.
smudge /smʌdʒ/ *n* пятно́; *vt* сма́зывать *impf*, сма́зать *pf*.
smug /smʌg/ *adj* самодово́льный.
smuggle /ˈsmʌg(ə)l/ *vt* провози́ть *impf*, провезти́ *pf* контраба́ндой; (*convey secretly*) проноси́ть *impf*, пронести́ *pf*. **smuggler** /-glə(r)/ *n* контрабанди́ст. **smuggling** /-glɪŋ/ *n* контраба́нда.
smut /smʌt/ *n* са́жа; (*indecency*) непристо́йность. **smutty** /-tɪ/ *adj* гря́зный; непристо́йный.
snack /snæk/ *n* заку́ска; **~ bar** заку́сочная *sb*, (*within institution*) буфе́т.
snag /snæg/ *n* (*fig*) загво́здка; *vt* зацепля́ть *impf*, зацепи́ть *pf*.
snail /sneɪl/ *n* ули́тка.
snake /sneɪk/ *n* змея́.
snap /snæp/ *vi* (*of dog or person*) огрыза́ться *impf*, огрызну́ться *pf* (**at** на+*acc*); *vt* & *i* (*break*) обрыва́ть(ся) *impf*, оборва́ть(ся)

S

pf; *vt* (*make sound*) щёлкать *impf*, щёлкнуть *pf* +*instr*; **~ up** (*buy*) расхва́тывать *impf*, расхвата́ть *pf*; *n* (*sound*) щёлк; (*photo*) сни́мок; *adj* (*decision*) скоропали́тельный. **snappy** /-pɪ/ *adj* (*brisk*) живо́й; (*stylish*) шика́рный. **snapshot** /ˈsnæpʃɒt/ *n* сни́мок.

snare /sneə(r)/ *n* лову́шка.

snarl /snɑːl/ *vi* рыча́ть *impf*, за~ *pf*; *n* рыча́ние.

snatch /snætʃ/ *vt* хвата́ть *impf*, (с)хвати́ть *pf*; *vi*: **~ at** хвата́ться *impf*, (с)хвати́ться *pf* за+*acc*; *n* (*fragment*) обры́вок.

sneak /sniːk/ *vi* (*slink*) кра́сться *impf*; *vt* (*steal*) стащи́ть *pf*; *n* я́бедник, -ица (*coll*). **sneaking** /-kɪŋ/ *adj* та́йный. **sneaky** /-kɪ/ *adj* лука́вый.

sneer /snɪə(r)/ *vi* насмеха́ться *impf* (**at** над+*instr*).

sneeze /sniːz/ *vi* чиха́ть *impf*, чихну́ть *pf*; *n* чиха́нье.

snide /snaɪd/ *adj* ехи́дный.

sniff /snɪf/ *vi* шмы́гать *impf*, шмыгну́ть *pf* но́сом; *vt* ню́хать *impf*, по~ *pf*.

snigger /ˈsnɪgə(r)/ *vi* хихи́кать *impf*, хихи́кнуть *pf*; *n* хихи́канье.

snip /snɪp/ *vt* ре́зать *impf* (но́жницами); **~ off** среза́ть *impf*, сре́зать *pf*.

snipe /snaɪp/ *vi* стреля́ть *impf* из укры́тия (**at** в+*acc*); (*fig*) напада́ть *impf*, напа́сть *pf* на+*acc*. **sniper** /-pə(r)/ *n* сна́йпер.

snippet /ˈsnɪpɪt/ *n* отре́зок; *pl* (*of news etc.*) обры́вки *m pl*.

snivel /ˈsnɪv(ə)l/ *vi* (*run at nose*) распуска́ть *impf*, распусти́ть *pf* со́пли; (*whimper*) хны́кать *impf*.

snob /snɒb/ *n* сноб. **snobbery** /-bərɪ/ *n* сноби́зм. **snobbish** /-bɪʃ/ *adj* снobи́стский.

snoop /snuːp/ *vi* шпио́нить *impf*; **~ about** разню́хивать *impf*, разню́хать *pf*.

snooty /ˈsnuːtɪ/ *adj* чва́нный.

snooze /snuːz/ *vi* вздремну́ть *pf*; *n* коро́ткий сон.

snore /snɔː(r)/ *vi* храпе́ть *impf*.

snorkel /ˈsnɔːk(ə)l/ *n* шно́ркель *m*.

snort /snɔːt/ *vi* фы́ркать *impf*, фы́ркнуть *pf*.

snot /snɒt/ *n* со́пли (-ле́й) *pl*.

snout /snaʊt/ *n* ры́ло, мо́рда.

snow /snəʊ/ *n* снег; **~-white** белосне́жный; *vi*: **it is ~ing, it snows** идёт снег; **~ed under** зава́ленный рабо́той; **we were ~ed up, in** нас занесло́ сне́гом. **snowball** *n* снежо́к. **snowdrop** *n* подсне́жник. **snowflake** *n* снежи́нка. **snowman** *n* сне́жная ба́ба. **snowstorm** *n* мете́ль. **snowy** /-ɪ/ *adj* сне́жный; (*snow-white*) белосне́жный.

snub /snʌb/ *vt* игнори́ровать *impf* & *pf*.

snuff[1] /snʌf/ *n* (*tobacco*) ню́хательный таба́к.

snuff[2] /snʌf/ *vt*: **~ out** туши́ть *impf*, по~ *pf*.

snuffle /ˈsnʌf(ə)l/ *vi* сопе́ть *impf*.

snug /snʌg/ *adj* ую́тный.

snuggle /ˈsnʌg(ə)l/ *vi*: **~ up to** прижима́ться *impf*, прижа́ться *pf* к+*dat*.

so /səʊ/ *adv* так; (*in this way*) так; (*thus, at beginning of sentence*) ита́к; (*also*) та́кже, то́же; *conj* (*therefore*) так что, поэ́тому; **and ~ on** и так да́лее; **if ~** в тако́м слу́чае; **~ ... as** так(о́й)… как; **~ as to** с тем что́бы; **~-called** так называ́емый; **(in) ~ far as** наско́лько; **~ long!** пока́!; **~ long as** поско́льку; **~ much** насто́лько; **~ much ~** до тако́й сте́пени; **~ much the better** тем лу́чше; **~ that** что́бы; **~... that** так… что; **~ to say, speak** так сказа́ть; **~ what?** ну и что?

soak /səʊk/ *vt* мочи́ть *impf*, на~ *pf*; (*drench*) прома́чивать *impf*, промочи́ть *pf*; **~ up** впи́тывать *impf*, впита́ть *pf*; *vi*: **~ through** проса́чиваться *impf*, просочи́ться *pf*; **get ~ed** промока́ть *impf*, промо́кнуть *pf*.

soap /səʊp/ *n* мы́ло; *vt* мы́лить *impf*, на~ *pf*; **~ opera** многосе-

S

ри́йная переда́ча; ~ **powder** стира́льный порошо́к. **soapy** /-pɪ/ *adj* мы́льный.

soar /sɔː(r)/ *vi* пари́ть *impf*; (*prices*) подска́кивать *impf*, подскочи́ть *pf*.

sob /sɒb/ *vi* рыда́ть *impf*; *n* рыда́ние.

sober /'səʊbə(r)/ *adj* тре́звый; *vt* & *i*: ~ **up** отрезвля́ть(ся) *impf*, отрезви́ть(ся) *pf*. **sobriety** /sə'braɪɪtɪ/ *n* тре́звость.

soccer /'sɒkə(r)/ *n* футбо́л.

sociable /'səʊʃəb(ə)l/ *adj* общи́тельный. **social** /'səʊʃ(ə)l/ *adj* обще́ственный, социа́льный; **S~ Democrat** социа́л-демокра́т; ~ **sciences** обще́ственные нау́ки *f pl*; ~ **security** социа́льное обеспе́чение. **socialism** /-ˌlɪz(ə)m/ *n* социали́зм. **socialist** /-lɪst/ *n* социали́ст; *adj* социалисти́ческий. **socialize** /-ˌlaɪz/ *vt* обща́ться *impf*. **society** /sə'saɪətɪ/ *n* о́бщество. **sociological** /ˌsəʊsɪə'lɒdʒɪk(ə)l/ *adj* социологи́ческий. **sociologist** /ˌsəʊsɪ'ɒlɪdʒɪst/ *n* социо́лог. **sociology** /ˌsəʊsɪ'ɒlədʒɪ/ *n* социоло́гия.

sock /sɒk/ *n* носо́к.

socket /'sɒkɪt/ *n* (*eye*) впа́дина; (*electr*) ште́псель *m*; (*for bulb*) патро́н.

soda /'səʊdə/ *n* со́да; **~-water** со́довая вода́.

S

sodden /'sɒd(ə)n/ *adj* промо́кший.

sodium /'səʊdɪəm/ *n* на́трий.

sodomy /'sɒdəmɪ/ *n* педера́стия.

sofa /'səʊfə/ *n* дива́н.

soft /sɒft/ *adj* мя́гкий; (*sound*) ти́хий; (*colour*) нея́ркий; (*malleable*) ко́вкий; (*tender*) не́жный; ~ **drink** безалкого́льный напи́ток. **soften** /'sɒf(ə)n/ *vt* & *i* смягча́ть(ся) *impf*, смягчи́ть(ся) *pf*. **softness** /'sɒftnɪs/ *n* мя́гкость. **software** /-weə(r)/ *n* програ́ммное обеспе́чение.

soggy /'sɒgɪ/ *adj* сыро́й.

soil[1] /sɔɪl/ *n* по́чва.

soil[2] /sɔɪl/ *vt* па́чкать *impf*, за~, ис~ *pf*.

solace /'sɒləs/ *n* утеше́ние.

solar /'səʊlə(r)/ *adj* со́лнечный.

solder /'səʊldə(r)/ *n* припо́й; *vt* пая́ть *impf*; (~ *together*) спа́ивать *impf*, спая́ть *pf*. **soldering iron** /-rɪŋ 'aɪən/ *n* пая́льник.

soldier /'səʊldʒə(r)/ *n* солда́т.

sole[1] /səʊl/ *n* (*of foot, shoe*) подо́шва.

sole[2] /səʊl/ *n* (*fish*) морско́й язы́к.

sole[3] /səʊl/ *adj* еди́нственный.

solemn /'sɒləm/ *adj* торже́ственный. **solemnity** /sə'lemnɪtɪ/ *n* торже́ственность.

solicit /sə'lɪsɪt/ *vt* проси́ть *impf*, по~ *pf* +*acc*, *gen*, о+*prep*; *vi* (*of prostitute*) пристава́ть *impf* к мужчи́нам. **solicitor** /-'lɪsɪtə(r)/ *n* адвока́т. **solicitous** /-'lɪsɪtəs/ *adj* забо́тливый.

solid /'sɒlɪd/ *adj* (*not liquid*) твёрдый; (*not hollow*; *continuous*) сплошно́й; (*firm*) про́чный; (*pure*) чи́стый; *n* твёрдое те́ло; *pl* твёрдая пи́ща. **solidarity** /ˌsɒlɪ'dærɪtɪ/ *n* солида́рность. **solidify** /sə'lɪdɪˌfaɪ/ *vi* затвердева́ть *impf*, затверде́ть *pf*. **solidity** /-'lɪdɪtɪ/ *n* твёрдость; про́чность.

soliloquy /sə'lɪləkwɪ/ *n* моноло́г.

solitary /'sɒlɪtərɪ/ *adj* одино́кий, уединённый; ~ **confinement** одино́чное заключе́ние. **solitude** /'sɒlɪˌtjuːd/ *n* одино́чество, уедине́ние.

solo /'səʊləʊ/ *n* со́ло *neut indecl*; *adj* со́льный; *adv* со́ло. **soloist** /-ɪst/ *n* соли́ст, ~ка.

solstice /'sɒlstɪs/ *n* солнцестоя́ние.

soluble /'sɒljʊb(ə)l/ *adj* раствори́мый. **solution** /sə'luːʃ(ə)n/ *n* раство́р; (*of puzzle etc.*) реше́ние. **solve** /sɒlv/ *vt* реша́ть *impf*, реши́ть *pf*. **solvent** /'sɒlv(ə)nt/ *adj* растворя́ющий; (*financially*) платёжеспосо́бный; *n* раствори́тель *m*.

sombre /'sɒmbə(r)/ *adj* мра́чный.

some /sʌm/ *adj* & *pron* (*any*)

какóй-нибудь; (*a certain*) какóй-то; (*a certain amount or number of*) нéкоторый, *or often expressed by noun in* (*partitive*) *gen*; (*several*) нéсколько+*gen*; (~ *people, things*) нéкоторые *pl*; ~ **day** когдá-нибудь; ~ **more** ещё; ~ **... others** одни́... другие. **somebody, someone** /'sʌmbədɪ, 'sʌmwʌn/ *n, pron* (*def*) ктó-то; (*indef*) ктó-нибудь. **somehow** /'sʌmhaʊ/ *adv* кáк-то; кáк-нибудь; (*for some reason*) почемý-то; ~ **or other** так и́ли инáче.

somersault /'sʌməˌsɒlt/ *n* сáльто *neut indecl*; *vi* кувыркáться *impf*, кувыр(к)нýться *pf.*

something /'sʌmθɪŋ/ *n* & *pron* (*def*) чтó-то; (*indef*) чтó-нибудь; ~ **like** (*approximately*) приблизи́тельно; (*a thing like*) чтó-то врóде+*gen.* **sometime** /'sʌmtaɪm/ *adv* нéкогда; *adj* бы́вший. **sometimes** /-taɪmz/ *adv* иногдá. **somewhat** /'sʌmwɒt/ *adv* нéсколько, довóльно. **somewhere** /'sʌmweə(r)/ *adv* (*position*) (*def*) гдé-то; (*indef*) гдé-нибудь; (*motion*) кудá-то; кудá-нибудь.

son /sʌn/ *n* сын; ~**-in-law** зять *m.*

sonata /sə'nɑːtə/ *n* сонáта.

song /sɒŋ/ *n* пéсня.

sonic /'sɒnɪk/ *adj* звуковóй.

sonnet /'sɒnɪt/ *n* сонéт.

soon /suːn/ *adv* скóро; (*early*) рáно; **as ~ as** как тóлько; **as ~ as possible** как мóжно скорéе; ~**er or later** рáно и́ли пóздно; **the ~er the better** чем рáньше, тем лýчше.

soot /sʊt/ *n* сáжа, кóпоть.

soothe /suːð/ *vt* успокáивать *impf*, успокóить *pf*; (*pain*) облегчáть *impf*, облегчи́ть *pf.*

sophisticated /sə'fɪstɪˌkeɪtɪd/ *adj* (*person*) искушённый; (*equipment*) слóжный.

soporific /ˌsɒpə'rɪfɪk/ *adj* снотвóрный.

soprano /sə'prɑːnəʊ/ *n* сопрáно (*voice*) *neut* & (*person*) *f indecl.*

sorcerer /'sɔːsərə(r)/ *n* колдýн. **sorcery** /'sɔːsərɪ/ *n* колдовствó.

sordid /'sɔːdɪd/ *adj* гря́зный.

sore /sɔː(r)/ *n* болячка; *adj* больнóй; **my throat is ~** у меня́ боли́т гóрло.

sorrow /'sɒrəʊ/ *n* печáль. **sorrowful** /-fʊl/ *adj* печáльный. **sorry** /'sɒrɪ/ *adj* жáлкий; *predic*: **be ~** жалéть *impf* (**about** о+*prep*); жаль *impers+dat* (**for** +*gen*); **~!** извини́(те)!

sort /sɔːt/ *n* род, вид, сорт; *vt* (*also ~ out*) сортировáть *impf*, рас~ *pf*; (*also fig*) разбирáть *impf*, разобрáть *pf.*

sortie /'sɔːtɪ/ *n* вы́лазка.

SOS *n* (радио)сигнáл бéдствия.

soul /səʊl/ *n* душá.

sound[1] /saʊnd/ *adj* (*healthy, thorough*) здорóвый; (*in good condition*) испрáвный; (*logical*) здрáвый, разýмный; (*of sleep*) крéпкий.

sound[2] /saʊnd/ *n* (*noise*) звук, шум; *attrib* звуковóй; ~ **effects** звуковы́е эффéкты *m pl*; *vi* звучáть *impf*, про~ *pf.*

sound[3] /saʊnd/ *vt* (*naut*) измеря́ть *impf*, измéрить *pf* глубинý +*gen*; ~ **out** (*fig*) зонди́ровать *impf*, по~ *pf*; *n* зонд.

sound[4] /saʊnd/ *n* (*strait*) проли́в.

soup /suːp/ *n* суп; *vt*: ~**ed up** форси́рованный.

sour /'saʊə(r)/ *adj* ки́слый; ~ **cream** сметáна; *vt* & *i* (*fig*) озлобля́ть(ся) *impf*, озлóбить(ся) *pf.*

source /sɔːs/ *n* истóчник; (*of river*) истóк

south /saʊθ/ *n* юг; (*naut*) зюйд; *adj* ю́жный; *adv* к ю́гу, на юг; ~**-east** ю́го-востóк; ~**-west** ю́го-зáпад. **southerly** /'sʌðəlɪ/ *adj* ю́жный. **southern** /'sʌð(ə)n/ *adj* ю́жный. **southerner** /'sʌðənə(r)/ *n* южáнин, -áнка. **southward(s)** /'saʊθwədz/ *adv* на юг, к ю́гу.

souvenir /ˌsuːvə'nɪə(r)/ *n* сувени́р.

sovereign /'sɒvrɪn/ *adj* суверéнный; *n* монáрх. **sovereignty** /-tɪ/ *n* суверенитéт.

S

soviet /ˈsəʊvɪət/ *n* совéт; **S~ Union** Совéтский Сою́з; *adj* (**S~**) совéтский.

sow¹ /saʊ/ *n* свинья́.

sow² /səʊ/ *vt* (*seed*) сéять *impf*, по~ *pf*; (*field*) засéивать *impf*, засéять *pf*.

soya /ˈsɔɪə/ *n*: **~ bean** сóевый боб.

spa /spɑː/ *n* курóрт.

space /speɪs/ *n* (*place*, *room*) мéсто; (*expanse*) простра́нство; (*interval*) промежу́ток; (*outer ~*) кóсмос; *attrib* косми́ческий; *vt* расставля́ть *impf*, расста́вить *pf* с промежу́тками. **spacecraft, -ship** *n* косми́ческий кора́бль *m*. **spacious** /ˈspeɪʃəs/ *adj* простóрный.

spade /speɪd/ *n* (*tool*) лопа́та; *pl* (*cards*) пи́ки (пик) *pl*.

spaghetti /spəˈgetɪ/ *n* спагéтти *neut indecl*.

Spain /speɪn/ *n* Испа́ния.

span /spæn/ *n* (*of bridge*) пролёт; (*aeron*) разма́х; *vt* (*of bridge*) соединя́ть *impf*, соедини́ть *pf* стóроны *+gen*, (*river*) берега́ *+gen*; (*fig*) охва́тывать *impf*, охвати́ть *pf*.

Spaniard /ˈspænjəd/ *n* испа́нец, -нка. **Spanish** /ˈspænɪʃ/ *adj* испа́нский.

spank /spæŋk/ *vt* шлёпать *impf*, шлёпнуть *pf*.

spanner /ˈspænə(r)/ *n* га́ечный ключ.

spar¹ /spɑː(r)/ *n* (*aeron*) лонжерóн.

spar² /spɑː(r)/ *vi* бокси́ровать *impf*; (*fig*) препира́ться *impf*.

spare /speə(r)/ *adj* (*in reserve*) запаснóй; (*extra*, *to ~*) ли́шний; (*of seat*, *time*) свобóдный; **~ parts** запасны́е ча́сти *f pl*; **~ room** кóмната для гостéй; *n*: *pl* запча́сти *f pl*; *vt* (*grudge*) жалéть *impf*, по~ *pf* *+acc*, *gen*; **he ~d no pains** он не жалéл трудóв; (*do without*) обходи́ться *impf*, обойти́сь *pf* без*+gen*; (*time*) уделя́ть *impf*, удели́ть *pf*; (*show mercy towards*) щади́ть *impf*, по~ *pf*; (*save from*) избавля́ть *impf*, изба́вить *pf* от*+gen*: **~ me the details** изба́вьте меня́ от подрóбностей.

spark /spɑːk/ *n* и́скра; **~-plug** запа́льная свеча́; *vt* (*~ off*) вызыва́ть *impf*, вы́звать *pf*.

sparkle /ˈspɑːk(ə)l/ *vi* сверка́ть *impf*.

sparrow /ˈspærəʊ/ *n* воробéй.

sparse /spɑːs/ *adj* рéдкий.

Spartan /ˈspɑːt(ə)n/ *adj* спарта́нский.

spasm /ˈspæz(ə)m/ *n* спазм. **spasmodic** /spæzˈmɒdɪk/ *adj* спазмоди́ческий.

spastic /ˈspæstɪk/ *n* парали́тик.

spate /speɪt/ *n* разли́в; (*fig*) потóк.

spatial /ˈspeɪʃ(ə)l/ *adj* простра́нственный.

spatter, splatter /ˈspætə(r), ˈsplætə(r)/ *vt* (*liquid*) бры́згать *impf* *+instr*; (*person etc.*) забры́згивать *impf*, забры́згать *pf* (**with** *+instr*); *vi* плеска́ть(ся) *impf*, плесну́ть *pf*.

spatula /ˈspætjʊlə/ *n* шпа́тель *m*.

spawn /spɔːn/ *vt & i* мета́ть *impf* (икру́); *vt* (*fig*) порожда́ть *impf*, породи́ть *pf*.

speak /spiːk/ *vt & i* говори́ть *impf*, сказа́ть *pf*; *vi* (*make speech*) выступа́ть *impf*, вы́ступить *pf* (с рéчью); (*~ out*) выска́зываться *impf*, вы́сказаться *pf* (**for** за*+acc*; **against** прóтив*+gen*). **speaker** /-kə(r)/ *n* говоря́щий *sb*; (*giving speech*) выступа́ющий *sb*; (*orator*) ора́тор; (**S~**, *parl*) спи́кер; (*loud-~*) громкоговори́тель *m*.

spear /ˈspɪə(r)/ *n* копьё; *vt* пронза́ть *impf*, пронзи́ть *pf* копьём. **spearhead** *vt* возглавля́ть *impf*, возгла́вить *pf*.

special /ˈspeʃ(ə)l/ *adj* осóбый, специа́льный. **specialist** /ˈspeʃəlɪst/ *n* специали́ст, ~ка. **speciality** /ˌspeʃɪˈælɪtɪ/ *n* (*dish*) фи́рменное блю́до; (*subject*) специа́льность. **specialization** /ˌspeʃəlaɪˈzeɪʃ(ə)n/ *n* специализа́ция. **specialize** /ˈspeʃəˌlaɪz/ *vt & i* специализи́ровать(ся) *impf* & *pf.* **specially** /'speʃəlɪ/ *adv* осо́бенно.

species /'spiːʃɪz/ *n* вид.

specific /spɪ'sɪfɪk/ *adj* осо́бенный. **specification(s)** /ˌspesɪfɪ'keɪʃ(ə)nz/ *n* специфика́ция. **specify** /'spesɪˌfaɪ/ *vt* уточня́ть *impf*, уточни́ть *pf.*

specimen /'spesɪmən/ *n* образе́ц, экземпля́р.

speck /spek/ *n* кра́пинка, пя́тнышко. **speckled** /-k(ə)ld/ *adj* кра́пчатый.

spectacle /'spektək(ə)l/ *n* зре́лище; *pl* очки́ (-ко́в) *pl.*

spectacular /spek'tækjʊlə(r)/ *adj* эффе́ктный; (*amazing*) потряса́ющий.

spectator /spek'teɪtə(r)/ *n* зри́тель *m.*

spectre /'spektə(r)/ *n* при́зрак.

spectrum /'spektrəm/ *n* спектр.

speculate /'spekjʊˌleɪt/ *vi* (*meditate*) размышля́ть *impf*, размы́слить *pf* (**on** о+*prep*); (*conjecture*) гада́ть *impf*; (*comm*) спекули́ровать *impf.* **speculation** /ˌspekjʊ'leɪʃ(ə)n/ *n* (*conjecture*) дога́дка; (*comm*) спекуля́ция. **speculative** /'spekjʊlətɪv/ *adj* гипотети́ческий; спекуляти́вный. **speculator** /'spekjʊˌleɪtə(r)/ *n* спекуля́нт.

speech /spiːtʃ/ *n* речь. **speechless** /-lɪs/ *adj* (*fig*) онеме́вший.

speed /spiːd/ *n* ско́рость; *vi* мча́ться *impf*, про~ *pf*; (*illegally*) превыша́ть *impf*, превы́сить *pf* ско́рость; **~ up** ускоря́ть(ся) *impf*, уско́рить(ся) *pf.* **speedboat** *n* быстрохо́дный ка́тер. **speedometer** /spiː'dɒmɪtə(r)/ *n* спидо́метр. **speedy** /'spiːdɪ/ *adj* бы́стрый.

spell[1] /spel/ *n* (*charm*) загово́р.

spell[2] /spel/ *vt* (*say*) произноси́ть *impf*, произнести́ *pf* по бу́квам; (*write*) пра́вильно писа́ть *impf*, на~ *pf*; **how do you ~ that word?** как пи́шется э́то сло́во?

spell[3] /spel/ *n* (*period*) пери́од.

spellbound /'spelbaʊnd/ *adj* зачаро́ванный.

spelling /'spelɪŋ/ *n* правописа́ние.

spend /spend/ *vt* (*money*; *effort*) тра́тить *impf*, ис~, по~ *pf*; (*time*) проводи́ть *impf*, провести́ *pf.*

sperm /spɜːm/ *n* спе́рма.

sphere /sfɪə(r)/ *n* сфе́ра; (*ball*) шар. **spherical** /'sferɪk(ə)l/ *adj* сфери́ческий.

spice /spaɪs/ *n* пря́ность; *vt* приправля́ть *impf*, припра́вить *pf.* **spicy** /-sɪ/ *adj* пря́ный; (*fig*) пика́нтный.

spider /'spaɪdə(r)/ *n* пау́к.

spike /spaɪk/ *n* (*point*) остриё; (*on fence*) зубе́ц; (*on shoes*) шип.

spill /spɪl/ *vt* & *i* (*liquid*) пролива́ть(ся) *impf*, проли́ть(ся) *pf*; (*dry substance*) рассыпа́ть(ся) *impf*, рассы́пать(ся) *pf.*

spin /spɪn/ *vt* (*thread etc.*) прясть *impf*, с~ *pf*; (*coin*) подбра́сывать *impf*, подбро́сить *pf*; *vt* & *i* (*turn*) кружи́ть(ся) *impf*; **~ out** (*prolong*) затя́гивать *impf*, затяну́ть *pf.*

spinach /'spɪnɪdʒ/ *n* шпина́т.

spinal /'spaɪn(ə)l/ *adj* спинно́й; **~ column** спинно́й хребе́т; **~ cord** спинно́й мозг.

spindle /'spɪnd(ə)l/ *n* ось *m.* **spindly** /-dlɪ/ *adj* дли́нный и то́нкий.

spine /spaɪn/ *n* (*anat*) позвоно́чник, хребе́т; (*prickle*) игла́; (*of book*) корешо́к. **spineless** /-lɪs/ *adj* (*fig*) бесхара́ктерный.

spinning /'spɪnɪŋ/ *n* пряде́ние; **~-wheel** пря́лка.

spinster /'spɪnstə(r)/ *n* незаму́жняя же́нщина.

spiral /'spaɪər(ə)l/ *adj* спира́льный; (*staircase*) винтово́й; *n* спира́ль; *vi* (*rise sharply*) ре́зко возраста́ть *impf*, возрасти́ *pf.*

spire /'spaɪə(r)/ *n* шпиль *m.*

spirit /'spɪrɪt/ *n* дух, душа́; *pl* (*mood*) настрое́ние; *pl* (*drinks*) спиртно́е *sb*; **~-level** ватерпа́с; *vt*: **~ away** та́йно уноси́ть *impf*, унести́ *pf.* **spirited** /-tɪd/ *adj* живо́й. **spiritual** /-tjʊəl/ *adj* духо́вный. **spiritualism** /-tjʊəˌlɪz(ə)m/ *n* спирити́зм. **spiritualist** /-tjʊəlɪst/ *n* спири́т.

spit[1] /spɪt/ *n* (*skewer*) ве́ртел.

spit[2] /spɪt/ *vi* плева́ть *impf*, плю́нуть *pf*; (*of rain*) мороси́ть *impf*; (*of fire*) разбры́згивать *impf*, разбры́згать *pf* и́скры; (*sizzle*) шипе́ть *impf*; *vt*: **~ out** выплёвывать *impf*, вы́плюнуть *pf*; **~ing image** то́чная ко́пия; *n* слюна́.

spite /spaɪt/ *n* зло́ба; **in ~ of** несмотря́ на+*acc.* **spiteful** /-fʊl/ *adj* зло́бный.

spittle /'spɪt(ə)l/ *n* слюна́.

splash /splæʃ/ *vt* (*person*) забры́згивать *impf*, забры́згать *pf* (**with** +*instr*); (**~** *liquid*) бры́згать *impf* +*instr*; *vi* плеска́ть(ся) *impf*, плесну́ть *pf*; (*move*) шлёпать *impf*, шлёпнуть *pf* (**through** по+*dat*); *n* (*act, sound*) плеск; (*mark made*) пятно́.

splatter /'splætə(r)/ *see* **spatter**

spleen /spliːn/ *n* селезёнка.

splendid /'splendɪd/ *adj* великоле́пный. **splendour** /'splendə(r)/ *n* великоле́пие.

splice /splaɪs/ *vt* (*ropes etc.*) сра́щивать *impf*, срасти́ть *pf*; (*film, tape*) скле́ивать *impf*, скле́ить *pf* концы́+*gen.*

splint /splɪnt/ *n* ши́на.

splinter /'splɪntə(r)/ *n* оско́лок; (*in skin*) зано́за; *vt & i* расщепля́ть(ся) *impf*, расщепи́ть(ся) *pf.*

split /splɪt/ *n* расще́лина, расще́п; (*schism*) раско́л; *pl* шпага́т; *vt & i* расщепля́ть(ся) *impf*, расщепи́ть(ся) *pf*; раска́лывать(ся) *impf*, расколо́ть(ся) *pf*; *vt* (*divide*) дели́ть *impf*, раз**~** *pf*; **~ second** мгнове́ние о́ка; **~ up** (*part company*) расходи́ться *impf*, разойти́сь *pf.*

splutter /'splʌtə(r)/ *vi* бры́згать *impf* слюно́й; *vt* (*utter*) говори́ть *impf* захлёбываясь.

spoil /spɔɪl/ *n* (*booty*) добы́ча; *vt & i* (*damage; decay*) по́ртить(ся) *impf*, ис**~** *pf*; *vt* (*indulge*) балова́ть *impf*, из**~** *pf.*

spoke /spəʊk/ *n* спи́ца.

spokesman, -woman /'spəʊksmən, -ˌwʊmən/ *n* представи́тель *m*, **~**ница.

sponge /spʌndʒ/ *n* гу́бка; **~ cake** бискви́т; *vt* (*wash*) мыть *impf*, вы́**~**, по**~** *pf* гу́бкой; *vi*: **~ on** жить *impf* на счёт+*gen.* **sponger** /-dʒə(r)/ *n* прижива́льщик. **spongy** /-dʒɪ/ *adj* гу́бчатый.

sponsor /'spɒnsə(r)/ *n* спо́нсор; *vt* финанси́ровать *impf & pf.*

spontaneity /ˌspɒntə'niːɪtɪ/ *n* спонта́нность. **spontaneous** /spɒn'teɪnɪəs/ *adj* спонта́нный.

spoof /spuːf/ *n* паро́дия.

spooky /'spuːkɪ/ *adj* жу́ткий.

spool /spuːl/ *n* кату́шка.

spoon /spuːn/ *n* ло́жка; *vt* че́рпать *impf*, черпну́ть *pf* ло́жкой. **spoonful** /-fʊl/ *n* ло́жка.

sporadic /spə'rædɪk/ *adj* споради́ческий.

sport /spɔːt/ *n* спорт; **~s car** спорти́вный автомоби́ль *m*; *vt* щеголя́ть *impf*, щегольну́ть *pf* +*instr.* **sportsman** *n* спортсме́н. **sporty** /-tɪ/ *adj* спорти́вный.

spot /spɒt/ *n* (*place*) ме́сто; (*mark*) пятно́; (*pimple*) пры́щик; **on the ~** на ме́сте; (*at once*) сра́зу; **~ check** вы́борочная прове́рка; *vt* (*notice*) замеча́ть *impf*, заме́тить *pf.* **spotless** /-lɪs/ *adj* абсолю́тно чи́стый. **spotlight** *n* проже́ктор; (*fig*) внима́ние. **spotty** /-tɪ/ *adj* прыщева́тый.

spouse /spaʊz/ *n* супру́г, **~**а.

spout /spaʊt/ *vi* бить *impf* струёй; хлы́нуть *pf*; (*pontificate*) ора́торствовать *impf*; *vt* изверга́ть *impf*, изве́ргнуть *pf*; (*verses etc.*) деклами́ровать *impf*, про**~** *pf*; *n* (*tube*) но́сик; (*jet*) струя́.

sprain /spreɪn/ *vt* растя́гивать *impf*, растяну́ть *pf*; *n* растяже́ние.

sprawl /sprɔːl/ *vi* (*of person*) разва́ливаться *impf*, развали́ться *pf*;

S

(*of town*) раски́дываться *impf*, раски́нуться *pf*.
spray[1] /spreɪ/ *n* (*flowers*) ве́т(оч)ка.
spray[2] /spreɪ/ *n* бры́зги (-г) *pl*; (*atomizer*) пульвериза́тор; *vt* опры́скивать *impf*, опры́скать *pf* (**with** +*instr*); (*cause to scatter*) распыля́ть *impf*, распыли́ть *pf*.
spread /spred/ *vt & i* (*news, disease, etc.*) распространя́ть(ся) *impf*, распространи́ть(ся) *pf*; *vt* (~ *out*) расстила́ть *impf*, разостла́ть *pf*; (*unfurl, unroll*) развёртывать *impf*, разверну́ть *pf*; (*bread etc.* +*acc*; *butter etc.* +*instr*) нама́зывать *impf*, нама́зать *pf*; *n* (*expansion*) распростране́ние; (*span*) разма́х; (*feast*) пир; (*paste*) па́ста.
spree /spriː/ *n* кутёж; **go on a ~** кути́ть *impf*, кутну́ть *pf*.
sprig /sprɪɡ/ *n* ве́точка.
sprightly /ˈspraɪtlɪ/ *adj* бо́дрый.
spring /sprɪŋ/ *vi* (*jump*) пры́гать *impf*, пры́гнуть *pf*; *vt* (*tell unexpectedly*) неожи́данно сообща́ть *impf*, сообщи́ть *pf* (**on** +*dat*); **~ a leak** дава́ть *impf*, дать *pf* течь; **~ from** (*originate*) происходи́ть *impf*, произойти́ *pf* из+*gen*; *n* (*jump*) прыжо́к; (*season*) весна́, *attrib* весе́нний; (*water*) исто́чник; (*elasticity*) упру́гость; (*coil*) пружи́на; **~-clean** генера́льная убо́рка. **springboard** *n* трампли́н.
sprinkle /ˈsprɪŋk(ə)l/ *vt* (*with liquid*) опры́скивать *impf*, опры́скать *pf* (**with** +*instr*); (*with solid*) посыпа́ть *impf*, посы́пать *pf* (**with** +*instr*). **sprinkler** /-klə(r)/ *n* разбры́згиватель *m*.
sprint /sprɪnt/ *vi* бежа́ть *impf* на коро́ткую диста́нцию; (*rush*) рвану́ться *pf*; *n* спринт. **sprinter** /-tə(r)/ *n* спри́нтер.
sprout /spraʊt/ *vi* пуска́ть *impf*, пусти́ть *pf* ростки́; *n* росто́к; *pl* брюссе́льская капу́ста.
spruce[1] /spruːs/ *adj* наря́дный, элега́нтный; *vt*: **~ o.s. up** приводи́ть *impf*, привести́ *pf* себя́ в поря́док.
spruce[2] /spruːs/ *n* ель.
spur /spɜː(r)/ *n* шпо́ра; (*fig*) сти́мул; **on the ~ of the moment** под влия́нием мину́ты; *vt*: **~ on** подхлёстывать *impf*, подхлестну́ть *pf*.
spurious /ˈspjʊərɪəs/ *adj* подде́льный.
spurn /spɜːn/ *vt* отверга́ть *impf*, отве́ргнуть *pf*.
spurt /spɜːt/ *n* (*jet*) струя́; (*effort*) рыво́к; *vi* бить *impf* струёй; (*make an effort*) де́лать *impf*, с~ *pf* рыво́к.
spy /spaɪ/ *n* шпио́н; *vi* шпио́нить *impf* (**on** за+*instr*). **spying** /-ɪŋ/ *n* шпиона́ж.
squabble /ˈskwɒb(ə)l/ *n* перебра́нка; *vi* вздо́рить *impf*, по~ *pf*.
squad /skwɒd/ *n* кома́нда, гру́ппа.
squadron /ˈskwɒdrən/ *n* (*mil*) эскадро́н; (*naut*) эска́дра; (*aeron*) эскадри́лья.
squalid /ˈskwɒlɪd/ *adj* убо́гий.
squall /skwɔːl/ *n* шквал.
squalor /ˈskwɒlə(r)/ *n* убо́жество.
squander /ˈskwɒndə(r)/ *vt* растра́чивать *impf*, растра́тить *pf*.
square /skweə(r)/ *n* (*shape*) квадра́т; (*in town*) пло́щадь; (*on paper, material*) кле́тка; (*instrument*) науго́льник; *adj* квадра́тный; (*meal*) пло́тный; **~ root** квадра́тный ко́рень *m*; *vt* (*accounts*) своди́ть *impf*, свести́ *pf*; (*math*) возводи́ть *impf*, возвести́ *pf* в квадра́т; *vi* (*correspond*) соотве́тствовать *impf* (**with** +*dat*).
squash /skwɒʃ/ *n* (*crowd*) толку́чка; (*drink*) сок; *vt* разда́вливать *impf*, раздави́ть *pf*; (*suppress*) подавля́ть *impf*, подави́ть *pf*; *vi* вти́скиваться *impf*, вти́снуться *pf*.
squat /skwɒt/ *adj* призе́мистый; *vi* сиде́ть *impf* на ко́рточках; **~ down** сади́ться *impf*, сесть *pf* на ко́рточки.

squatter /ˈskwɒtə(r)/ *n* незако́нный жиле́ц.

squawk /skwɔːk/ *n* клёкот; *vi* клекота́ть *impf*.

squeak /skwiːk/ *n* писк; (*of object*) скрип; *vi* пища́ть *impf*, пи́скнуть *pf*; (*of object*) скрипе́ть *impf*, скри́пнуть *pf*. **squeaky** /-kɪ/ *adj* пискли́вый, скрипу́чий.

squeal /skwiːl/ *n* визг; *vi* визжа́ть *impf*, ви́згнуть *pf*.

squeamish /ˈskwiːmɪʃ/ *adj* брезгли́вый.

squeeze /skwiːz/ *n* (*crush*) да́вка; (*pressure*) сжа́тие; (*hand*) пожа́тие; *vt* дави́ть *impf*; сжима́ть *impf*, сжать *pf*; ~ **in** впи́хивать(ся) *impf*, впихну́ть(ся) *pf*; вти́скивать(ся) *impf*, вти́снуть(ся) *pf*; ~ **out** выжима́ть *impf*, вы́жать *pf*; ~ **through** проти́скивать(ся) *impf*, проти́снуть(ся) *pf*.

squelch /skweltʃ/ *vi* хлю́пать *impf*, хлю́пнуть *pf*.

squid /skwɪd/ *n* кальма́р.

squint /skwɪnt/ *n* косогла́зие; *vi* коси́ть *impf*; (*screw up eyes*) щу́риться *impf*.

squire /ˈskwaɪə(r)/ *n* сквайр, поме́щик.

squirm /skwɜːm/ *vi* (*wriggle*) извива́ться *impf*, изви́ться *pf*.

squirrel /ˈskwɪr(ə)l/ *n* бе́лка.

squirt /skwɜːt/ *n* струя́; *vi* бить *impf* струёй; *vt* пуска́ть *impf*, пусти́ть *pf* струю́ (*substance* +*gen*; **at** на+*acc*).

St. *abbr* (*of* **Street**) ул., у́лица; (*of* **Saint**) св., Свято́й, -а́я.

stab /stæb/ *n* уда́р (ножо́м *etc.*); (*pain*) внеза́пная о́страя боль; *vt* наноси́ть *impf*, нанести́ *pf* уда́р (ножо́м *etc.*) (*person* +*dat*).

stability /stəˈbɪlɪtɪ/ *n* усто́йчивость, стаби́льность. **stabilize** /ˈsteɪbɪˌlaɪz/ *vt* стабилизи́ровать *impf* & *pf*.

stable /ˈsteɪb(ə)l/ *adj* усто́йчивый, стаби́льный; (*psych*) уравнове́шенный; *n* коню́шня.

staccato /stəˈkɑːtəʊ/ *n* стакка́то *neut indecl*; *adv* стакка́то; *adj* оты́вистый.

stack /stæk/ *n* ку́ча; *vt* скла́дывать *impf*, сложи́ть *pf* в ку́чу.

stadium /ˈsteɪdɪəm/ *n* стадио́н.

staff /stɑːf/ *n* (*personnel*) штат, сотру́дники *m pl*; (*stick*) посо́х, жезл; *adj* шта́тный; (*mil*) штабно́й.

stag /stæg/ *n* саме́ц-оле́нь *m*.

stage /steɪdʒ/ *n* (*theat*) сце́на; (*period*) ста́дия; *vt* (*theat*) ста́вить *impf*, по~ *pf*; (*organize*) организова́ть *impf* & *pf*; ~**-manager** режиссёр.

stagger /ˈstægə(r)/ *vi* шата́ться *impf*, шатну́ться *pf*; *vt* (*hours of work etc.*) распределя́ть *impf*, распредели́ть *pf*. **be staggered** /-gəd/ *vi* поража́ться *impf*, порази́ться *pf*. **staggering** /-gərɪŋ/ *adj* потряса́ющий.

stagnant /ˈstægnənt/ *adj* (*water*) стоя́чий; (*fig*) засто́йный. **stagnate** /stægˈneɪt/ *vi* заста́иваться *impf*, застоя́ться *pf*; (*fig*) косне́ть *impf*, за~ *pf*.

staid /steɪd/ *adj* степе́нный.

stain /steɪn/ *n* пятно́; (*dye*) кра́ска; *vt* па́чкать *impf*, за~, ис~ *pf*; (*dye*) окра́шивать *impf*, окра́сить *pf*; ~**ed glass** цветно́е стекло́. **stainless** /-lɪs/ *adj*: ~ **steel** нержаве́ющая сталь.

stair /steə(r)/ *n* ступе́нька. **staircase, stairs** /ˈsteəkeɪs, steəz/ *n pl* ле́стница.

stake /steɪk/ *n* (*stick*) кол; (*bet*) ста́вка; (*comm*) до́ля; **be at** ~ быть поста́вленным на ка́рту; *vt* (*mark out*) огора́живать *impf*, огороди́ть *pf* ко́льями; (*support*) укрепля́ть *impf*, укрепи́ть *pf* коло́м; (*risk*) ста́вить *impf*, по~ *pf* на ка́рту.

stale /steɪl/ *adj* несве́жий; (*musty, damp*) за́тхлый; (*hackneyed*) изби́тый.

stalemate /ˈsteɪlmeɪt/ *n* пат; (*fig*) тупи́к.

stalk /stɔːk/ *n* сте́бель *m*; *vt* высле́живать *impf*; *vi* (& *t*) (*stride*) ше́-

S

ствовать *impf* (по+*dat*).

stall /stɔːl/ *n* стóйло; (*booth*) ларёк; *pl* (*theat*) партéр; *vi* (*of engine*) глóхнуть *impf*, за~ *pf*; (*play for time*) оттягивать *impf*, оттянуть *pf* врéмя; *vt* (*engine*) нечáянно заглушáть *impf*, заглушить *pf*.

stallion /ˈstæljən/ *n* жеребéц.

stalwart /ˈstɔːlwət/ *adj* стóйкий; *n* стóйкий привéрженец.

stamina /ˈstæmɪnə/ *n* выносливость.

stammer /ˈstæmə(r)/ *vi* заикáться *impf*; *n* заикáние.

stamp /stæmp/ *n* печáть; (*postage*) (почтóвая) мáрка; *vt* штамповáть *impf*; *vi* тóпать *impf*, тóпнуть *pf* (ногáми); **~ out** побороть *pf*.

stampede /stæmˈpiːd/ *n* панúческое бéгство; *vi* обращáться *impf* в панúческое бéгство.

stance /stɑːns/ *n* позúция.

stand /stænd/ *n* (*hat, coat*) вéшалка; (*music*) пюпúтр; (*umbrella, support*) подстáвка; (*booth*) ларёк; (*taxi*) стоянка; (*at stadium*) трибýна; (*position*) позúция; (*resistance*) сопротивлéние; *vi* стоять *impf*; (**~** *up*) вставáть *impf*, встать *pf*; (*remain in force*) оставáться *impf*, остáться в сúле; *vt* (*put*) стáвить *impf*, по~ *pf*; (*endure*) терпéть *impf*, по~ *pf*; **~ back** отходúть *impf*, отойтú *pf* (**from** от+*gen*); (*not go forward*) держáться *impf* позадú; **~ by** (*vi*) (*not interfere*) не вмéшиваться *impf*, вмешáться *pf*; (*be ready*) быть *impf* на готóве; (*vt*) (*support*) поддéрживать *impf*, поддержáть *pf*; (*stick to*) придéрживаться *impf* +*gen*; **~ down** (*resign*) уходúть *impf*, уйтú *pf* с пóста (**as** +*gen*); **~ for** (*signify*) означáть *impf*; (*tolerate*): **I shall not ~ for it** я не потерплю; **~-in** заместúтель *m*; **~ in** (*for*) замещáть *impf*, заместúть *pf*; **~ out** выделяться *impf*, вы́делиться *pf*; **~ up** вставáть *impf*, встать *pf*; **~ up for** (*defend*) отстáивать *impf*, отстоять *pf*; **~ up to** (*endure*) выдéрживать *impf*, вы́держать *pf*; (*not give in to*) противостоять *impf* +*dat*.

standard /ˈstændəd/ *n* (*norm*) стандáрт, норм; (*flag*) знáмя *neut*; **~ of living** жúзненный ýровень *m*; *adj* нормáльный, стандáртный. **standardization** /ˌstændədaɪˈzeɪʃ(ə)n/ *n* нормализáция, стандартизáция. **standardize** /ˈstændəˌdaɪz/ *vt* стандартизúровать *impf* & *pf*; нормализовáть *impf* & *pf*.

standing /ˈstændɪŋ/ *n* положéние; *adj* (*upright*) стоячий; (*permanent*) постоянный.

standpoint /ˈstændpɔɪnt/ *n* тóчка зрéния.

standstill /ˈstændstɪl/ *n* остановка, застóй, пáуза; **be at a ~** стоять *impf* на мёртвой тóчке; **bring (come) to a ~** останáвливать(ся) *impf*, остановúть(ся) *pf*.

stanza /ˈstænzə/ *n* строфá.

staple[1] /ˈsteɪp(ə)l/ *n* (*metal bar*) скобá; (*for paper*) скрéпка; *vt* скреплять *impf*, скрепúть *pf*.

staple[2] /ˈsteɪp(ə)l/ *n* (*product*) глáвный продýкт; *adj* основнóй.

star /stɑː(r)/ *n* звездá; (*asterisk*) звёздочка; *vi* игрáть *impf*, сыгрáть *pf* глáвную роль. **starfish** *n* морскáя звездá.

starboard /ˈstɑːbəd/ *n* прáвый борт.

starch /stɑːtʃ/ *n* крахмáл; *vt* крахмáлить *impf*, на~ *pf*. **starchy** /-tʃɪ/ *adj* крахмáлистый; (*prim*) чóпорный.

stare /steə(r)/ *n* прúстальный взгляд; *vi* прúстально смотрéть *impf* (**at** на+*acc*).

stark /stɑːk/ *adj* (*bare*) гóлый; (*desolate*) пусты́нный; (*sharp*) рéзкий; *adv* совершéнно.

starling /ˈstɑːlɪŋ/ *n* скворéц.

starry /ˈstɑːrɪ/ *adj* звёздный.

start /stɑːt/ *n* начáло; (*sport*) старт; *vi* начинáться *impf*, начáться *pf*; (*engine*) заводúться *impf*, завести́сь *pf*; (*set out*) отправля́ться *impf*, отпра́виться *pf*; (*shudder*) вздра́гивать *impf*, вздро́гнуть *pf*; (*sport*) стартова́ть *impf* & *pf*; *vt* начина́ть *impf*, нача́ть *pf* (*gerund*, *inf*, +*inf*; *by*, +*gerund* с того́, что…; **with** +*instr*, с+*gen*); (*car, engine*) заводи́ть *impf*, завести́ *pf*; (*fire, rumour*) пуска́ть *impf*, пусти́ть *pf*; (*found*) осно́вывать *impf*, основа́ть *pf*. **starter** /-tə(r)/ *n* (*tech*) ста́ртёр; (*cul*) заку́ска. **starting-point** /-tɪŋ pɔɪnt/ *n* отправно́й пункт.

startle /'stɑːt(ə)l/ *vt* испуга́ть *pf*.

starvation /stɑː'veɪʃ(ə)n/ *n* го́лод. **starve** /stɑːv/ *vi* голода́ть *impf*; (*to death*) умира́ть *impf*, умере́ть с го́лоду; *vt* мори́ть *impf*, по~, у~ *pf* го́лодом. **starving** /'stɑːvɪŋ/ *adj* голода́ющий; (*hungry*) о́чень голо́дный.

state /steɪt/ *n* (*condition*) состоя́ние; (*polit*) госуда́рство, штат; *adj* (*ceremonial*) торже́ственный; пара́дный; (*polit*) госуда́рственный; *vt* (*announce*) заявля́ть *impf*, заяви́ть *pf*; (*expound*) излага́ть *impf*, изложи́ть *pf*. **stateless** /-lɪs/ *adj* не име́ющий гражда́нства. **stately** /-lɪ/ *adj* вели́чественный. **statement** /-mənt/ *n* заявле́ние; (*comm*) отчёт. **statesman** *n* госуда́рственный де́ятель *m*.

static /'stætɪk/ *adj* неподви́жный.

station /'steɪʃ(ə)n/ *n* (*rly*) вокза́л, ста́нция; (*social*) обще́ственное положе́ние; (*meteorological, hydro-electric power, radio etc.*) ста́нция; (*post*) пост; *vt* размеща́ть *impf*, размести́ть *pf*.

stationary /'steɪʃənərɪ/ *adj* неподви́жный.

stationery /'steɪʃənərɪ/ *n* канцеля́рские принадле́жности *f pl*; (*writing-paper*) почто́вая бума́га; **~ shop** канцеля́рский магази́н.

statistic /stə'tɪstɪk/ *n* статисти́ческое да́нное. **statistical** /-'tɪstɪk(ə)l/ *adj* статисти́ческий. **statistician** /ˌstætɪ'stɪʃ(ə)n/ *n* стати́стик. **statistics** /stə'tɪstɪks/ *n* стати́стика.

statue /'stætjuː/ *n* ста́туя. **statuette** /ˌstætjʊ'et/ *n* статуэ́тка.

stature /'stætʃə(r)/ *n* рост; (*merit*) кали́бр.

status /'steɪtəs/ *n* ста́тус. **status quo** /ˌsteɪtəs 'kwəʊ/ *n* ста́тус-кво́ *neut indecl*.

statute /'stætjuːt/ *n* стату́т. **statutory** /-tərɪ/ *adj* устано́вленный зако́ном.

staunch /stɔːntʃ/ *adj* ве́рный.

stave /steɪv/ *vt*: **~ off** предотвраща́ть *impf*, предотврати́ть *pf*.

stay /steɪ/ *n* (*time spent*) пребыва́ние; *vi* (*remain*) остава́ться *impf*, оста́ться *pf* (**to dinner** обе́дать); (*put up*) остана́вливаться *impf*, останови́ться *pf* (**at** (*place*) в+*prep*; **at** (*friends' etc;*) у+*gen*); (*live*) жить; **~ behind** остава́ться *impf*, оста́ться *pf*; **~ in** остава́ться *impf*, оста́ться *pf* до́ма; **~ up** не ложи́ться *impf* спать; (*trousers*) держа́ться *impf*. **staying-power** /'steɪɪŋ ˌpaʊə(r)/ *n* выно́сливость.

stead /sted/ *n*: **stand s.o. in good ~** ока́зываться *impf*, оказа́ться *pf* поле́зным кому́-л.

steadfast /'stedfɑːst/ *adj* сто́йкий, непоколеби́мый.

steady /'stedɪ/ *adj* (*firm*) усто́йчивый; (*continuous*) непреры́вный; (*wind, temperature*) ро́вный; (*speed*) постоя́нный; (*unshakeable*) непоколеби́мый; *vt* (*boat etc.*) приводи́ть *impf*, привести́ *pf* в равнове́сие.

steak /steɪk/ *n* бифште́кс.

steal /stiːl/ *vt* & *abs* ворова́ть *impf*, с~ *pf*; красть *impf*, у~ *pf*; *vi* (*creep*) кра́сться *impf*; подкра́дываться *impf*, подкра́сться *pf*. **stealth** /stelθ/ *n*: **by ~** укра́дкой. **stealthy** /-θɪ/ *adj* ворова́тый, та́йный, скры́тый.

steam /stiːm/ *n* пар; **at full ~** на всех пара́х; **let off ~** (*fig*) дава́ть *impf*, дать *pf* вы́ход свои́м чу́вствам; *vt* па́рить *impf*; *vi* па́риться *impf*, по~ *pf*; (*vessel*) ходи́ть *indet*, идти́ *det* на пара́х; ~ **up** (*mist over*) запотева́ть *impf*, запоте́ть *pf*; поте́ть *impf*, за~, от~ *pf*; ~ **engine** парова́я маши́на. **steamer, steamship** /-mə(r), -ʃɪp/ *n* парохо́д. **steamy** /-mɪ/ *adj* напо́лненный па́ром; (*passionate*) горя́чий.

steed /stiːd/ *n* конь *m*.

steel /stiːl/ *n* сталь; *adj* стально́й; *vt*: ~ **o.s.** ожесточа́ться *impf*, ожесточи́ться *pf*; ~ **works** сталелите́йный заво́д. **steely** /-lɪ/ *adj* стально́й.

steep[1] /stiːp/ *adj* круто́й; (*excessive*) чрезме́рный.

steep[2] /stiːp/ *vt* (*immerse*) погружа́ть *impf*, погрузи́ть *pf* (**in** в+*acc*); (*saturate*) пропи́тывать *impf*, пропита́ть *pf* (**in** +*instr*).

steeple /ˈstiːp(ə)l/ *n* шпиль *m*. **steeplechase** *n* ска́чки *f pl* с препя́тствиями.

steer /stɪə(r)/ *vt* управля́ть *impf*, пра́вить *impf* +*instr*; *v abs* рули́ть *impf*; ~ **clear of** избега́ть *impf*, избежа́ть *pf* +*gen*. **steering-wheel** /ˈstɪərɪŋˌwiːl/ *n* руль *m*.

stem[1] /stem/ *n* сте́бель *m*; (*of wine-glass*) но́жка; (*ling*) осно́ва; *vi*: ~ **from** происходи́ть *impf*, произойти́ *pf* от+*gen*.

stem[2] /stem/ *vt* (*stop*) остана́вливать *impf*, останови́ть *pf*.

stench /stentʃ/ *n* злово́ние.

stencil /ˈstensɪl/ *n* трафаре́т; (*tech*) шабло́н; *vt* наноси́ть *impf*, нанести́ *pf* по трафаре́ту. **stencilled** /-sɪld/ *adj* трафаре́тный.

step /step/ *n* (*pace, action*) шаг; (*dance*) па *neut indecl*; (*of stairs, ladder*) ступе́нь; ~ **by** ~ шаг за ша́гом; **in** ~ в но́гу; **out of** ~ не в но́гу; **take** ~**s** принима́ть *impf*, приня́ть *pf* ме́ры *vi* шага́ть *impf*, шагну́ть *pf*; ступа́ть *impf*, ступи́ть *pf*; ~ **aside** сторони́ться *impf*, по~ *pf*; ~ **back** отступа́ть *impf*, отступи́ть *pf*; ~ **down** (*resign*) уходи́ть *impf*, уйти́ *pf* в отста́вку; ~ **forward** выступа́ть *impf*, вы́ступить *pf*; ~ **in** (*intervene*) вме́шиваться *impf*, вмеша́ться *pf*; ~ **on** наступа́ть *impf*, наступи́ть *pf* на+*acc* (**s.o.'s foot** кому́-л. на́ ногу); ~ **over** переша́гивать *impf*, перешагну́ть *pf* +*acc*, че́рез+*acc*; ~ **up** (*increase*) повыша́ть *impf*, повы́сить *pf*. **step-ladder** *n* стремя́нка. **stepping-stone** /ˈstepɪŋˌstəʊn/ *n* ка́мень *m* для перехо́да; (*fig*) сре́дство. **steps** /steps/ *n pl* ле́стница.

stepbrother /ˈstepˌbrʌθə(r)/ *n* сво́дный брат. **stepdaughter** /ˈstepˌdɔːtə(r)/ *n* па́дчерица. **stepfather** /ˈstepˌfɑːðə(r)/ *n* о́тчим. **stepmother** /ˈstepˌmʌðə(r)/ *n* ма́чеха. **stepsister** /ˈstepˌsɪstə(r)/ *n* сво́дная сестра́. **stepson** /ˈstepsʌn/ *n* па́сынок.

steppe /step/ *n* степь.

stereo /ˈsterɪəʊ/ *n* (*system*) стереофони́ческая систе́ма; (*stereophony*) стереофо́ния; *adj* (*recorded in* ~) сте́рео *indecl*. **stereophonic** /-ˈfɒnɪk/ *adj* стереофони́ческий. **stereotype** /-ˌtaɪp/ *n* стереоти́п. **stereotyped** /-ˌtaɪpt/ *adj* стереоти́пный.

sterile /ˈsteraɪl/ *adj* стери́льный. **sterility** /stəˈrɪlɪtɪ/ *n* стери́льность. **sterilization** /ˌsterɪlaɪˈzeɪʃ(ə)n/ *n* стерилиза́ция. **sterilize** /ˈsterɪˌlaɪz/ *vt* стерилизова́ть *impf* & *pf*.

sterling /ˈstɜːlɪŋ/ *n* сте́рлинг; **pound** ~ фунт сте́рлингов; *adj* сте́рлинговый.

stern[1] /stɜːn/ *n* корма́.

stern[2] /stɜːn/ *adj* суро́вый, стро́гий.

stethoscope /ˈsteθəˌskəʊp/ *n* стетоско́п.

stew /stjuː/ *n* (*cul*) мя́со тушёное вме́сте с овоща́ми; *vt* & *i* (*cul*) туши́ть(ся) *impf*, с~ *pf*; (*fig*) томи́ть(ся) *impf*.

steward /ˈstjuːəd/ *n* бортпроводни́к. **stewardess** /-dɪs/ *n* стюарде́сса.

stick[1] /stɪk/ *n* па́лка; (*of chalk etc.*) па́лочка; (*hockey*) клю́шка.

stick[2] /stɪk/ *vt* (*spear*) зака́лывать *impf*, заколо́ть *pf*; (*make adhere*) прикле́ивать *impf*, прикле́ить *pf* (**to** к+*dat*); (*coll*) (*put*) ста́вить *impf*, по~ *pf*; (*lay*) класть *impf*, положи́ть *pf*; (*endure*) терпе́ть *impf*, вы́~ *pf*; *vi* (*adhere*) ли́пнуть *impf* (**to** к+*dat*); прилипа́ть *impf*, прили́пнуть *pf* (**to** к+*dat*); **~ in** (*thrust in*) втыка́ть *impf*, воткну́ть *pf*; (*into opening*) всо́вывать *impf*, всу́нуть *pf*; **~ on** (*glue on*) накле́ивать *impf*, накле́ить *pf*; **~ out** (*thrust out*) высо́вывать *impf*, вы́сунуть *pf* (**from** из+*gen*); (*project*) торча́ть *impf*; **~ to** (*keep to*) приде́рживаться *impf*, придержа́ться *pf* +*gen*; (*remain at*) не отвлека́ться *impf* от+*gen*; **~ together** держа́ться *impf* вме́сте; **~ up for** защища́ть *impf*, защити́ть *pf*; **be, get, stuck** застрева́ть *impf*, застря́ть *pf*. **sticker** /-kə(r)/ *n* накле́йка.

sticky /ˈstɪkɪ/ *adj* ли́пкий.

stiff /stɪf/ *adj* жёсткий, неги́бкий; (*prim*) чо́порный; (*difficult*) тру́дный; (*penalty*) суро́вый; **be ~** (*ache*) боле́ть *impf*. **stiffen** /-f(ə)n/ *vt* де́лать *impf*, с~ *pf* жёстким; *vi* станови́ться *impf*, стать *pf* жёстким. **stiffness** /-nɪs/ *n* жёсткость; (*primness*) чо́порность.

stifle /ˈstaɪf(ə)l/ *vt* души́ть *impf*, за~ *pf*; (*suppress*) подавля́ть *impf*, подави́ть *pf*; (*sound*) заглуша́ть *impf*, заглуши́ть *pf*; *vi* задыха́ться *impf*, задохну́ться *pf*. **stifling** /-lɪŋ/ *adj* уду́шливый.

stigma /ˈstɪgmə/ *n* клеймо́.

stile /staɪl/ *n* перела́з (*coll*).

stilettos /stɪˈletəʊz/ *n pl* ту́фли *f pl* на шпи́льках.

still /stɪl/ *adv* (всё) ещё; (*nevertheless*) тем не ме́нее; (*motionless*) неподви́жно; **stand ~** не дви́гаться *impf*, дви́нуться *pf*; *n* (*quiet*) тишина́; *adj* ти́хий; (*immobile*) неподви́жный. **still-born** *adj* мертворождённый. **still life** *n* натюрмо́рт. **stillness** /-nɪs/ *n* тишина́.

stilted /ˈstɪltɪd/ *adj* ходу́льный.

stimulant /ˈstɪmjʊlənt/ *n* возбужда́ющее сре́дство. **stimulate** /-ˌleɪt/ *vt* возбужда́ть *impf*, возбуди́ть *pf*. **stimulating** /-ˌleɪtɪŋ/ *adj* возбуди́тельный. **stimulation** /-ˈleɪʃ(ə)n/ *n* возбужде́ние. **stimulus** /ˈstɪmjʊləs/ *n* сти́мул.

sting /stɪŋ/ *n* (*wound*) уку́с; (*stinger*; *fig*) жа́ло; *vt* жа́лить *impf*, у~ *pf*; *vi* (*burn*) жечь *impf*. **stinging** /ˈstɪŋɪŋ/ *adj* (*caustic*) язви́тельный.

stingy /ˈstɪndʒɪ/ *adj* скупо́й.

stink /stɪŋk/ *n* вонь; *vi* воня́ть *impf* (**of** +*instr*). **stinking** /-kɪŋ/ *adj* воню́чий.

stint /stɪnt/ *n* срок; *vi*: **~on** скупи́ться *impf*, по~ *pf* на+*acc*.

stipend /ˈstaɪpend/ *n* (*salary*) жа́лование; (*grant*) стипе́ндия.

stipulate /ˈstɪpjʊˌleɪt/ *vt* обусло́вливать *impf*, обусло́вить *pf*. **stipulation** /-ˈleɪʃ(ə)n/ *n* усло́вие.

stir /stɜː(r)/ *n* (*commotion*) шум; *vt* (*mix*) меша́ть *impf*, по~ *pf*; (*excite*) волнова́ть *impf*, вз~ *pf*; *vi* (*move*) шевели́ться *impf*, шевельну́ться *pf*; **~ up** возбужда́ть *impf*, возбуди́ть *pf*. **stirring** /-rɪŋ/ *adj* волну́ющий.

stirrup /ˈstɪrəp/ *n* стре́мя *neut*.

stitch /stɪtʃ/ *n* стежо́к; (*knitting*) пе́тля; (*med*) шов; (*pain*) ко́лики *f pl*; *vt* (*embroider, make line of ~es*) строчи́ть *impf*, про~ *pf*; (*join by sewing, make, suture*) сшива́ть *impf*, сшить *pf*; **~ up** зашива́ть *impf*, заши́ть *pf*. **stitching** /-tʃɪŋ/ *n* (*stitches*) стро́чка.

stoat /stəʊt/ *n* горноста́й.

stock /stɒk/ *n* (*store*) запа́с; (*of shop*) ассортиме́нт; (*live~*) скот; (*cul*) бульо́н; (*lineage*) семья́; (*fin*) а́кции *f pl*; **in ~** в нали́чии; **out of ~** распро́дан; **take ~ of**

S

крити́чески оце́нивать *impf*, оцени́ть *pf*; *adj* станда́ртный; *vt* име́ть в нали́чии; **~ up** запаса́ться *impf*, запасти́сь *pf* (**with** +*instr*). **stockbroker** *n* биржево́й ма́клер. **stock-exchange** *n* би́ржа. **stockpile** *n* запа́с; *vt* нака́пливать *impf*, накопи́ть *pf*. **stock-taking** *n* переучёт.

stocking /ˈstɒkɪŋ/ *n* чуло́к

stocky /ˈstɒkɪ/ *adj* призе́мистый.

stodgy /ˈstɒdʒɪ/ *adj* тяжёлый.

stoic(al) /ˈstəʊɪk((ə)l)/ *adj* стоя́ческий. **stoicism** /ˈstəʊɪˌsɪz(ə)m/ *n* стоици́зм.

stoke /stəʊk/ *vt* топи́ть *impf*.

stolid /ˈstɒlɪd/ *adj* флегмати́чный.

stomach /ˈstʌmək/ *n* желу́док, (*also surface of body*) живо́т; *vt* терпе́ть *impf*, по~ *pf*. **stomach ache** /ˈstʌmək eɪk/ *n* боль в животе́.

stone /stəʊn/ *n* ка́мень *m*; (*of fruit*) ко́сточка; *adj* ка́менный; *vt* побива́ть *impf*, поби́ть *pf* камня́ми; (*fruit*) вынима́ть *impf*, вы́нуть *pf* ко́сточки из+*gen*. **Stone Age** *n* ка́менный век **stone-deaf** *adj* соверше́нно глухо́й. **stone-mason** *n* ка́менщик. **stonily** /-nɪlɪ/ *adv* с ка́менным выраже́нием, хо́лодно. **stony** /-nɪ/ *adj* камени́стый; (*fig*) ка́менный.

stool /stuːl/ *n* табуре́т, табуре́тка.

stoop /stuːp/ *n* суту́лость; *vt & i* суту́лить(ся) *impf*, с~ *pf*; (*bend* (*down*)) наклоня́ть(ся) *impf*, наклони́ть(ся) *pf*; **~ to** (*abase o.s.*) унижа́ться *impf*, уни́зиться *pf* до+*gen*; (*condescend*) снисходи́ть *impf*, снизойти́ *pf* до+*gen*. **stooped, stooping** /stuːpt, ˈstuːpɪŋ/ *adj* суту́лый.

stop /stɒp/ *n* остано́вка; **put a ~ to** положи́ть *pf* коне́ц +*dat*; *vt* остана́вливать *impf*, останови́ть *pf*; (*discontinue*) прекраща́ть *impf*, прекрати́ть *pf*; (*restrain*) уде́рживать *impf*, удержа́ть *pf* (**from** от+*gen*); *vi* остана́вливаться *impf*, останови́ться *pf*; (*discontinue*) прекраща́ться *impf*, прекрати́ться *pf*; (*cease*) перестава́ть *impf*, переста́ть *pf* (+*inf*); **~ up** *vt* затыка́ть *impf*, заткну́ть *pf*. **stoppage** /-pɪdʒ/ *n* остано́вка; (*strike*) забасто́вка. **stopper** /-pə(r)/ *n* про́бка. **stop-press** *n* э́кстренное сообще́ние в газе́те. **stop-watch** *n* секундоме́р.

storage /ˈstɔːrɪdʒ/ *n* хране́ние. **store** /stɔː(r)/ *n* запа́с; (*storehouse*) склад; (*shop*) магази́н; **set ~ by** цени́ть *impf*; **what is in ~ for me?** что ждёт меня́ впереди́?; *vt* запаса́ть *impf*, запасти́ *pf*; (*put into storage*) сдава́ть *impf*, сдать *pf* на хране́ние. **storehouse** *n* склад. **store-room** кладова́я *sb*.

storey /ˈstɔːrɪ/ *n* эта́ж.

stork /stɔːk/ *n* а́ист.

storm /stɔːm/ *n* бу́ря, (*thunder* ~) гроза́; *vt* (*mil*) штурмова́ть *impf*; *vi* бушева́ть *impf*. **stormy** /-mɪ/ *adj* бу́рный.

story /ˈstɔːrɪ/ *n* расска́з, по́весть; (*anecdote*) анекдо́т; (*plot*) фа́була; **~-teller** расска́зчик.

stout /staʊt/ *adj* (*strong*) кре́пкий; (*staunch*) сто́йкий; (*portly*) доро́дный.

stove /stəʊv/ *n* (*with fire inside*) печь; (*cooker*) плита́.

stow /stəʊ/ *vt* укла́дывать *impf*, уложи́ть *pf*. **stowaway** /ˈstəʊəˌweɪ/ *n* безбиле́тный пассажи́р.

straddle /ˈstræd(ə)l/ *vt* (*sit astride*) сиде́ть *impf* верхо́м на+*prep*; (*stand astride*) стоя́ть *impf*, расста́вив но́ги над +*instr*.

straggle /ˈstræg(ə)l/ *vi* отстава́ть *impf*, отста́ть *pf*. **straggler** /-glə(r)/ *n* отста́вший *sb*. **straggling** /-glɪŋ/ *adj* разбро́санный. **straggly** /-glɪ/ *adj* растрёпанный.

straight /streɪt/ *adj* прямо́й; (*undiluted*) неразба́вленный; *predic* (*in order*) в поря́дке; *adv* пря́мо; **~ away** сра́зу. **straighten** /-t(ə)n/ *vt & i* выпрямля́ть(ся) *impf*, вы-

S

прямить(ся) *pf*; *vt* (*put in order*) поправлять *impf*, поправить *pf*. **straightforward** *adj* прямой; (*simple*) простой.

strain[1] /streɪn/ *n* (*tension*) натяжение; (*sprain*) растяжение; (*effort, exertion*) напряжение; (*tendency*) склонность; (*sound*) звук; *vt* (*stretch*) натягивать *impf*, натянуть *pf*; (*sprain*) растягивать *impf*, растянуть *pf*; (*exert*) напрягать *impf*, напрячь *pf*; (*filter*) процеживать *impf*, процедить *pf*; *vi* (*also exert o.s.*) напрягаться *impf*, напрячься *pf*. **strained** /streɪnd/ *adj* натянутый. **strainer** /-nə(r)/ *n* (*tea* ~) ситечко; (*sieve*) сито.

strain[2] /streɪn/ *n* (*breed*) порода.

strait(s) /streɪt(s)/ *n* (*geog*) пролив. **strait-jacket** *n* смирительная рубашка. **straits** *n pl* (*difficulties*) затруднительное положение.

strand[1] /strænd/ *n* (*hair, rope*) прядь; (*thread, also fig*) нить.

strand[2] /strænd/ *vt* сажать *impf*, посадить *pf* на мель. **stranded** /-dɪd/ *adj* на мели.

strange /streɪndʒ/ *adj* странный; (*unfamiliar*) незнакомый; (*alien*) чужой. **strangely** /-lɪ/ *adv* странно. **strangeness** /-nɪs/ *n* странность. **stranger** /ˈstreɪndʒə(r)/ *n* незнакомец.

strangle /ˈstræŋg(ə)l/ *vt* душить *impf*, за~ *pf*. **stranglehold** *n* мёртвая хватка. **strangulation** /ˌstræŋgjʊˈleɪʃ(ə)n/ *n* удушение.

strap /stræp/ *n* ремень *m*; *vt* (*tie up*) стягивать *impf*, стянуть *pf* ремнём. **strapping** /-pɪŋ/ *adj* рослый.

stratagem /ˈstrætədʒəm/ *n* хитрость. **strategic** /strəˈtiːdʒɪk/ *adj* стратегический. **strategist** /ˈstrætɪdʒɪst/ *n* стратег. **strategy** /ˈstrætɪdʒɪ/ *n* стратегия.

stratum /ˈstrɑːtəm/ *n* слой.

straw /strɔː/ *n* солома; (*drinking*) соломинка; **the last** ~ последняя капля; *adj* соломенный.

strawberry /ˈstrɔːbərɪ/ *n* клубника (*no pl*; *usu collect*); (*wild* ~) земляника (*no pl*; *usu collect*).

stray /streɪ/ *vi* сбиваться *impf*, сбиться *pf*; (*digress*) отклоняться *impf*, отклониться *pf*; *adj* (*lost*) заблудившийся; (*homeless*) бездомный; *n* (*from flock*) отбившееся от стада животное *sb*; ~ **bullet** шальная пуля.

streak /striːk/ *n* полоса (**of luck** везения); (*tendency*) жилка; *vi* (*rush*) проноситься *impf*, пронестись *pf*. **streaked** /striːkt/ *adj* с полосами (**with** +*gen*). **streaky** /-kɪ/ *adj* полосатый; (*meat*) с прослойками жира.

stream /striːm/ *n* (*brook, tears*) ручей; (*brook, flood, tears, people etc.*) поток; (*current*) течение; **up/down** ~ вверх/вниз по течению; *vi* течь *impf*; струиться *impf*; (*rush*) проноситься *impf*, пронестись *pf*; (*blow*) развеваться *impf*. **streamer** /-mə(r)/ *n* вымпел. **stream-lined** *adj* обтекаемый; (*fig*) хорошо налаженный.

street /striːt/ *n* улица; *adj* уличный; ~ **lamp** уличный фонарь *m*.

strength /streŋθ/ *n* сила; (*numbers*) численность; **on the** ~ **of** в силу +*gen*. **strengthen** /-θ(ə)n/ *vt* усиливать *impf*, усилить *pf*.

strenuous /ˈstrenjʊəs/ *adj* (*work*) трудный; (*effort*) напряжённый.

stress /stres/ *n* напряжение; (*mental*) стресс; (*emphasis*) ударение; *vt* (*accent*) ставить *impf*, по~ *pf* ударение на+*acc*; (*emphasize*) подчёркивать *impf* подчеркнуть *pf*. **stressful** /-fʊl/ *adj* стрессовый.

stretch /stretʃ/ *n* (*expanse*) отрезок; **at a** ~ (*in succession*) подряд; *vt & i* (*widen, spread out*) растягивать(ся) *impf*, растянуть(ся) *pf*; (*in length*, ~ *out limbs*) вытягивать(ся) *impf*, вытянуть(ся) *pf*; (*tauten*) натягивать(ся) *impf*, натянуть(ся) *pf*; (*extend, e.g. rope*, ~ *forth limbs*) протягивать(ся) *impf*, протя-

S

ну́ть(ся) *pf*; *vi* (*material*, *land*) тяну́ться *impf*; ~ **one's legs** (*coll*) размина́ть *impf*, размя́ть *pf* но́ги. **stretcher** /-tʃə(r)/ *n* носи́лки (-лок) *pl*.

strew /struː/ *vt* разбра́сывать *impf*, разброса́ть *pf*; ~ **with** посыпа́ть *impf*, посы́пать *pf* +*instr*.

stricken /'strɪkən/ *adj* поражённый.

strict /strɪkt/ *adj* стро́гий. **stricture(s)** /'strɪktʃəz/ *n* (стро́гая) кри́тика.

stride /'straɪd/ *n* (большо́й) шаг; *pl* (*fig*) успе́хи *m pl*; **to take sth in one's** ~ преодолева́ть *impf*, преодоле́ть *pf* что-л. без уси́лий; *vi* шага́ть *impf*.

strident /'straɪd(ə)nt/ *adj* ре́зкий.

strife /straɪf/ *n* раздо́р.

strike /straɪk/ *n* (*refusal to work*) забасто́вка; (*mil*) уда́р; *vi* (*be on* ~) бастова́ть *impf*; (*go on* ~) забастова́ть *pf*; (*attack*) ударя́ть *impf*, уда́рить *pf*; (*the hour*) бить *impf*, про~ *pf*; *vt* (*hit*) ударя́ть *impf*, уда́рить *pf*; (*impress*) поража́ть *impf*, порази́ть *pf*; (*discover*) открыва́ть *impf*, откры́ть *pf*; (*match*) зажига́ть *impf*, заже́чь *pf*; (*the hour*) бить *impf*, про~ *pf*; (*occur to*) приходи́ть *impf*, прийти́ *pf* в го́лову+*dat*; ~ **off** вычёркивать *impf*, вы́черкнуть *pf*; ~ **up** начина́ть *impf*, нача́ть *pf*. **striker** /-kə(r)/ *n* забасто́вщик. **striking** /-kɪŋ/ *adj* порази́тельный.

string /strɪŋ/ *n* бечёвка; (*mus*) струна́; (*series*) ряд; *pl* (*mus*) стру́нные инструме́нты *m pl*; ~ **bag,** ~ **vest** се́тка; *vt* (*thread*) низа́ть *impf*, на~ *pf*; ~ **along** (*coll*) води́ть *impf* за нос; ~ **out** (*prolong*) растя́гивать *impf*, растяну́ть *pf*; **strung up** (*tense*) напряжённый. **stringed** /strɪŋd/ *adj* стру́нный. **stringy** /'strɪŋɪ/ *adj* (*fibrous*) волокни́стый; (*meat*) жи́листый.

stringent /'strɪndʒ(ə)nt/ *adj* стро́гий.

strip[1] /strɪp/ *n* полоса́, поло́ска.

strip[2] /strɪp/ *vt* (*undress*) раздева́ть *impf*, разде́ть *pf*; (*deprive*) лиша́ть *impf*, лиши́ть *pf* (**of** +*gen*); ~ **off** (*tear off*) сдира́ть *impf*, содра́ть *pf*; *vi* раздева́ться *impf*, разде́ться *pf*. **strip-tease** *n* стрипти́з.

stripe /straɪp/ *n* полоса́. **striped** /straɪpt/ *adj* полоса́тый.

strive /'strɪv(ə)n/ *vi* (*endeavour*) стреми́ться *impf* (**for** к+*dat*); (*struggle*) боро́ться *impf* (**for** за+*acc*; **against** про́тив+*gen*).

stroke /strəʊk/ *n* (*blow*, *med*) уда́р; (*of oar*) взмах; (*swimming*) стиль *m*; (*of pen etc.*) штрих; (*piston*) ход; *vt* гла́дить *impf*, по~ *pf*.

stroll /strəʊl/ *n* прогу́лка; *vi* прогу́ливаться *impf*, прогуля́ться *pf*.

strong /strɒŋ/ *adj* си́льный; (*stout*; *of drinks*) кре́пкий; (*healthy*) здоро́вый; (*opinion etc.*) твёрдый. **stronghold** *n* кре́пость. **strong-minded, strong-willed** /-'maɪndɪd, -'wɪld/ *adj* реши́тельный.

structural /'strʌktʃər(ə)l/ *adj* структу́рный. **structure** /'strʌktʃə(r)/ *n* структу́ра; (*building*) сооруже́ние; *vt* организова́ть *impf* & *pf*.

struggle /'strʌg(ə)l/ *n* борьба́; *vi* боро́ться *impf* (**for** за+*acc*; **against** про́тив+*gen*); (*writhe*, ~ *with* (*fig*)) би́ться (**with** над +*instr*).

strum /strʌm/ *vi* бренча́ть *impf* (**on** на+*prep*).

strut[1] /strʌt/ *n* (*vertical*) сто́йка; (*horizontal*) распо́рка.

strut[2] /strʌt/ *vi* ходи́ть *indet*, идти́ *det* го́голем.

stub /stʌb/ *n* огры́зок; (*cigarette*) оку́рок; (*counterfoil*) корешо́к; *vt*: ~ **one's toe** ударя́ться *impf*, уда́риться *pf* ного́й (**on** на+*acc*); ~ **out** гаси́ть *impf*, по~ *pf*.

stubble /'stʌb(ə)l/ *n* жнивьё; (*hair*) щети́на.

stubborn /'stʌbən/ *adj* упря́мый. **stubbornness** /-nɪs/ *n* упря́мство.

stucco /ˈstʌkəʊ/ *n* штукатýрка. **stud**[1] /stʌd/ *n* (*collar, cuff*) зáпонка; (*nail*) гвоздь *m* с большóй шля́пкой; *vt* (*bestrew*) усéивать *impf*, усéять *pf* (**with** +*instr*).

stud[2] /stʌd/ *n* (*horses*) кóнный завóд.

student /ˈstjuːd(ə)nt/ *n* студéнт, ~ка.

studied /ˈstʌdɪd/ *adj* напускнóй.

studio /ˈstjuːdɪəʊ/ *n* стýдия.

studious /ˈstjuːdɪəs/ *adj* лю́бящий наýку; (*diligent*) старáтельный.

study /ˈstʌdɪ/ *n* изучéние; *pl* заня́тия *neut pl*; (*investigation*) исслéдование; (*art, mus*) этю́д; (*room*) кабинéт; *vt* изучáть *impf*, изучи́ть *pf*; учи́ться *impf*, об~ *pf* +*dat*; (*scrutinize*) рассмáтривать *impf*, рассмотрéть *pf*; *vi* (*take lessons*) учи́ться *impf*, об~ *pf*; (*do one's studies*) занимáться *impf*.

stuff /stʌf/ *n* (*material*) материáл; (*things*) вéщи *f pl*; *vt* набивáть *impf*, наби́ть *pf*; (*cul*) начиня́ть *impf*, начини́ть *pf*; (*cram into*) запи́хивать *impf*, запихáть *pf* (**into** в+*acc*); (*shove into*) совáть *impf*, сýнуть *pf* (**into** в+*acc*); *vi* (*overeat*) объедáться *impf*, объéсться *pf*. **stuffiness** /-fɪnɪs/ *n* духотá. **stuffing** /-fɪŋ/ *n* наби́вка; (*cul*) начи́нка. **stuffy** /-fɪ/ *adj* дýшный.

stumble /ˈstʌmb(ə)l/ *vi* (*also fig*) спотыкáться *impf*, споткнýться *pf* (**over** о+*acc*); ~ **upon** натыкáться *impf*, наткнýться *pf* на+*acc*. **stumbling-block** *n* кáмень *m* преткновéния.

stump /stʌmp/ *n* (*tree*) пень *m*; (*pencil*) огры́зок; (*limb*) культя́; *vt* (*perplex*) стáвить *impf*, по~ *pf* в тупи́к.

stun /stʌn/ *vt* (*also fig*) оглушáть *impf*, оглуши́ть *pf*. **stunning** /-nɪŋ/ *adj* потрясáющий.

stunt[1] /stʌnt/ *n* трюк.

stunt[2] /stʌnt/ *vt* задéрживать *impf*, задержáть *pf* рост+*gen*. **stunted** /-tɪd/ *adj* низкорóслый.

stupefy /ˈstjuːpɪˌfaɪ/ *vt* оглушáть *impf*, оглуши́ть *pf*. **stupendous** /stjuːˈpendəs/ *adj* колоссáльный. **stupid** /ˈstjuːpɪd/ *adj* глýпый. **stupidity** /stjuːˈpɪdɪtɪ/ *n* глýпость. **stupor** /ˈstjuːpə(r)/ *n* оцепенéние.

sturdy /ˈstɜːdɪ/ *adj* крéпкий.

stutter /ˈstʌtə(r)/ *n* заикáние; *vi* заикáться *impf*.

sty[1] /staɪ/ *n* (*pig*~) свинáрник.

sty[2] /staɪ/ *n* (*on eye*) ячмéнь *m*.

style /staɪl/ *n* стиль *m*; (*taste*) вкус; (*fashion*) мóда; (*sort*) род; (*of hair*) причёска. **stylish** /-lɪʃ/ *adj* мóдный. **stylist** /-lɪst/ *n* (*of hair*) парикмáхер. **stylistic** /-ˈlɪstɪk/ *adj* стилисти́ческий. **stylize** /-laɪz/ *vt* стилизовáть *impf* & *pf*.

stylus /ˈstaɪləs/ *n* иглá звукоснимáтеля.

suave /swɑːv/ *adj* обходи́тельный.

subconscious /sʌbˈkɒnʃəs/ *adj* подсознáтельный; *n* подсознáние. **subcontract** *vt* давáть *impf*, дать *pf* подря́дчику. **subcontractor** *n* подря́дчик. **subdivide** *vt* подразделя́ть *impf*, подраздели́ть *pf*. **subdivision** *n* подразделéние. **subdue** /səbˈdjuː/ *vt* покоря́ть *impf*, покори́ть *pf*. **subdued** /səbˈdjuːd/ *adj* (*suppressed, dispirited*) подáвленный; (*soft*) мя́гкий; (*indistinct*) приглушённый. **sub-editor** *n* помóщник редáктора.

subject *n* /ˈsʌbdʒɪkt/ (*theme*) тéма; (*discipline, theme*) предмéт; (*question*) вопрóс; (*thing on to which action is directed*) объéкт; (*gram*) подлежáщее *sb*; (*national*) пóдданный *sb*; *adj*: ~ **to** (*susceptible to*) подвéрженный+*dat*; (*on condition that*) при услóвии, что…; éсли; **be ~ to** (*change etc.*) подлежáть *impf* +*dat*; *vt*: /səbˈdʒekt/ ~ **to** подвергáть *impf*, подвéргнуть *pf* +*dat*. **subjection** /səbˈdʒekʃ(ə)n/ *n* подчинéние. **subjective** /səbˈdʒektɪv/ *adj* субъекти́вный. **subjectivity** /ˌsʌbdʒekˈtɪvɪtɪ/ *n* субъекти́вность. **subject-matter** *n* (*of book,*

S

lecture) содержа́ние, те́ма; (*of discussion*) предме́т.

subjugate /ˈsʌbdʒʊˌgeɪt/ *vt* покоря́ть *impf*, покори́ть *pf*. **subjugation** /ˌsʌbdʒʊˈgeɪʃ(ə)n/ *n* покоре́ние.

subjunctive (mood) /səbˈdʒʌŋktɪv (muːd)/ *n* сослага́тельное наклоне́ние.

sublet /ˈsʌblet/ *vt* передава́ть *impf*, переда́ть *pf* в субаре́нду.

sublimate /ˈsʌblɪˌmeɪt/ *vt* сублими́ровать *impf* & *pf*. **sublimation** /ˌsʌblɪˈmeɪʃ(ə)n/ *n* сублима́ция. **sublime** /səˈblaɪm/ *adj* возвы́шенный.

subliminal /səbˈlɪmɪn(ə)l/ *adj* подсозна́тельный. **sub-machine-gun** /ˌsʌbməˈʃiːnˌgʌn/ *n* автома́т. **submarine** /ˌsvbməˈriːn/ *n* подво́дная ло́дка. **submerge** /səbˈmɜːdʒ/ *vt* погружа́ть *impf*, погрузи́ть *pf*. **submission** /-ˈmɪʃ(ə)n/ *n* подчине́ние; (*for inspection*) представле́ние. **submissive** /-ˈmɪsɪv/ *adj* поко́рный. **submit** /-ˈmɪt/ *vi* подчиня́ться *impf*, подчини́ться *pf* (**to** +*dat*); *vt* представля́ть *impf*, предста́вить *pf*. **subordinate** *n* /səˈbɔːdɪnət/ подчинённый *sb*; *adj* подчинённый; (*secondary*) второстепе́нный; (*gram*) прида́точный; *vt* /səˈbɔːdɪˌneɪt/ подчиня́ть *impf*, подчини́ть *pf*. **subscribe** /səbˈskraɪb/ *vi* подпи́сываться *impf*, подписа́ться *pf* (**to** на+*acc*); **~ to** (*opinion*) присоединя́ться *impf*, присоедини́ться *pf* к+*dat*. **subscriber** /-ˈskraɪbə(r)/ *n* подпи́счик; абоне́нт. **subscription** /-ˈskrɪpʃ(ə)n/ *n* подпи́ска, абонеме́нт; (*fee*) взнос. **subsection** /ˈsʌbˌsekʃ(ə)n/ *n* подразде́л. **subsequent** /ˈsʌbsɪkwənt/ *adj* после́дующий. **subsequently** /ˈsʌbsɪkwəntlɪ/ *adv* впосле́дствии. **subservient** /səbˈsɜːvɪənt/ *adj* рабо́ле́пный. **subside** /səbˈsaɪd/ *vi* убыва́ть *impf*, убы́ть *pf*; (*soil*) оседа́ть *impf*, осе́сть *pf*. **subsidence** /səbˈsaɪd(ə)ns/ *n* (*soil*) оседа́ние. **subsidiary** /səbˈsɪdɪərɪ/ *adj* вспомога́тельный; (*secondary*) второстепе́нный; *n* филиа́л. **subsidize** /ˈsʌbsɪˌdaɪz/ *vt* субсиди́ровать *impf* & *pf*. **subsidy** /ˈsʌbsɪdɪ/ *n* субси́дия. **subsist** /səbˈsɪst/ *vi* (*live*) жить *impf* (**on** +*instr*). **substance** /ˈsʌbst(ə)ns/ *n* вещество́; (*essence*) су́щность, суть; (*content*) содержа́ние. **substantial** /səbˈstænʃ(ə)l/ *adj* (*durable*) про́чный; (*considerable*) значи́тельный; (*food*) пло́тный. **substantially** /səbˈstænʃəlɪ/ *adv* (*basically*) в основно́м; (*considerably*) значи́тельно. **substantiate** /səbˈstænʃɪˌeɪt/ *vt* обосно́вывать *impf*, обоснова́ть *pf*. **substitute** /ˈsʌbstɪˌtjuːt/ *n* (*person*) замести́тель *m*; (*thing*) заме́на; *vt* заменя́ть *impf*, замени́ть *pf* +*instr* (**for** +*acc*); **I ~ water for milk** заменя́ю молоко́ водо́й. **substitution** /ˌsʌbstɪˈtjuːʃ(ə)n/ *n* заме́на. **subsume** /səbˈsjuːm/ *vt* относи́ть *impf*, отнести́ *pf* к како́й-л. катего́рии. **subterfuge** /ˈsʌbtəˌfjuːdʒ/ *n* увёртка. **subterranean** /ˌsʌbtəˈreɪnɪən/ *adj* подзе́мный. **subtitle** /ˈsʌbˌtaɪt(ə)l/ *n* подзаголо́вок; (*cin*) субти́тр.

subtle /ˈsʌt(ə)l/ *adj* то́нкий. **subtlety** /ˈsʌtəltɪ/ *n* то́нкость.

subtract /səbˈtrækt/ *vt* вычита́ть *impf*, вы́честь *pf*. **subtraction** /-ˈtrækʃ(ə)n/ *n* вычита́ние. **suburb** /ˈsʌbɜːb/ *n* при́город. **suburban** /səˈbɜːbən/ *adj* при́городный. **subversion** /səbˈvɜːʃ(ə)n/ *n* подрывна́я де́ятельность. **subversive** /səbˈvɜːsɪv/ *adj* подрывно́й. **subway** /ˈsʌbweɪ/ *n* подзе́мный перехо́д.

succeed /səkˈsiːd/ *vi* удава́ться *impf*, уда́ться *pf*; **the plan will ~** план уда́стся; **he ~ed in buying the book** ему́ удало́сь купи́ть кни́гу; (*be successful*) преуспева́ть *impf*, преуспе́ть *pf* (**in** в+*prep*); (*follow*) сменя́ть *impf*, смени́ть *pf*; (*be heir*) насле́довать *impf* & *pf* (**to** +*dat*). **suc-**

S

ceeding /-dɪŋ/ *adj* послéдующий. **success** /sək'ses/ *n* успéх. **successful** /sək'sesfʊl/ *adj* успéшный. **succession** /sək'seʃ(ə)n/ *n* (*series*) ряд; (*to throne*) престолонаслéдие; **right of ~** прáво наслéдования; **in ~** подря́д, оди́н за други́м. **successive** /sək'sesɪv/ *adj* (*consecutive*) последовáтельный. **successor** /sək'sesə(r)/ *n* преéмник.

succinct /sək'sɪŋkt/ *adj* сжáтый.

succulent /'sʌkjʊlənt/ *adj* сóчный.

succumb /sə'kʌm/ *vi* (*to pressure*) уступáть *impf*, уступи́ть *pf* (**to** +*dat*); (*to temptation*) поддавáться *impf*, поддáться *pf* (**to** +*dat*).

such /sʌtʃ/ *adj* такóй; **~ people** таки́е лю́ди; **~ as** (*for example*) так напримéр; (*of ~ a kind as*) такóй как; **~ beauty as yours** такáя красотá как вáша; (*that which*) тот, котóрый; **I shall read ~ books as I like** я бу́ду читáть те кни́ги, котóрые мне нрáвятся; **~ as to** такóй, чтóбы; **his illness was not ~ as to cause anxiety** егó болéзнь былá не такóй (серьёзной), чтóбы вы́звать беспокóйство; **~ and ~** такóй-то; *pron* такóв; **~ was his character** такóв был егó харáктер; **as ~** сам по себé; **~ is not the case** э́то не так. **suchlike** *pron* (*inanimate*) томý подóбное; (*people*) такие лю́ди *pl.*

suck /sʌk/ *vt* сосáть *impf*; **~ in** всáсывать *impf*, всосáть *pf*; (*engulf*) засáсывать *impf*, засосáть *pf*; **~ out** высáсывать *impf*, вы́сосать *pf*; **~ up to** (*coll*) подли́зываться *impf*, подлизáться *pf* к+*dat*. **sucker** /-kə(r)/ *n* (*biol*, *rubber device*) присóска; (*bot*) корневóй побéг. **suckle** /-k(ə)l/ *vt* корми́ть *impf*, на~ *pf* грýдью. **suction** /'sʌkʃ(ə)n/ *n* всáсывание.

sudden /'sʌd(ə)n/ *adj* внезáпный. **suddenly** /-lɪ/ *adv* вдруг. **suddenness** /-nɪs/ *n* внезáпность.

sue /suː/ *vt* & *i* подавáть *impf*, подáть *pf* в суд (на+*acc*); **~ s.o. for damages** предъявля́ть *impf*, предъяви́ть *pf* (к) комý-л. иск о возмещéнии ущéрба.

suede /sweɪd/ *n* зáмша; *adj* зáмшевый.

suet /'suːɪt/ *n* нутрянóе сáло.

suffer /'sʌfə(r)/ *vt* страдáть *impf*, по~ *pf* +*instr*, от+*gen*; (*loss*, *defeat*) терпéть *impf*, по~ *pf*; (*tolerate*) терпéть *impf*; *vi* страдáть *impf*, по~ *pf* (**from** +*instr*, от+*gen*). **sufferance** /-rəns/ *n*: **he is here on ~** егó здесь тéрпят. **suffering** /-rɪŋ/ *n* страдáние.

suffice /sə'faɪs/ *vi* & *t* быть достáточным (для+*gen*); хватáть *impf*, хвати́ть *pf impers*+*gen* (+*dat*). **sufficient** /-fɪʃ(ə)nt/ *adj* достáточный.

suffix /'sʌfɪks/ *n* сýффикс.

suffocate /'sʌfəˌkeɪt/ *vt* удушáть *impf*, удуши́ть *pf*; *vi* задыхáться *impf*, задохнýться *pf.* **suffocating** /-tɪŋ/ *adj* удýшливый. **suffocation** /ˌsʌfə'keɪʃ(ə)n/ *n* удушéние.

suffrage /'sʌfrɪdʒ/ *n* избирáтельное прáво.

suffuse /sə'fjuːz/ *vt* заливáть *impf*, зали́ть *pf* (**with** +*instr*).

sugar /'ʃʊgə(r)/ *n* сáхар; *adj* сáхарный; *vt* подслáщивать *impf*, подсласти́ть *pf*; **~ basin** сáхарница; **~ beet** сáхарная свёкла; **~ cane** сáхарный трóстник. **sugary** /-rɪ/ *adj* сáхарный; (*fig*) слащáвый.

suggest /sə'dʒest/ *vt* предлагáть *impf*, предложи́ть *pf*; (*evoke*) напоминáть *impf*, напóмнить *pf*; (*imply*) намекáть *impf*, намекнýть *pf* на+*acc*; (*indicate*) говори́ть *impf* о+*prep*. **suggestion** /-'dʒestʃ(ə)n/ *n* предложéние; (*psych*) внушéние. **suggestive** /-'dʒestɪv/ *adj* вызывáющий мы́сли (**of** о+*prep*); (*indecent*) соблазни́тельный.

suicidal /ˌsuːɪ'saɪd(ə)l/ *adj* самоуби́йственный; (*fig*) губи́тельный. **suicide** /'suːɪˌsaɪd/ *n* самоуби́йство; **commit ~** совершáть

S

impf, совершить *pf* самоубийство.
suit /suːt/ *n* (*clothing*) костюм; (*law*) иск; (*cards*) масть; **follow ~** (*fig*) следовать *impf*, по~ *pf* примеру; *vt* (*be convenient for*) устраивать *impf*, устроить *pf*; (*adapt*) приспосабливать *impf*, приспособить *pf*; (*be ~able for, match*) подходить *impf*, подойти *pf* (+*dat*); (*look attractive on*) идти *impf* +*dat*. **suitability** /ˌsuːtəˈbɪlɪtɪ/ *n* пригодность. **suitable** /ˈsuːtəb(ə)l/ *adj* (*fitting*) подходящий; (*convenient*) удобный. **suitably** /ˈsuːtəblɪ/ *adv* соответственно. **suitcase** *n* чемодан.
suite /swiːt/ *n* (*retinue*) свита; (*furniture*) гарнитур; (*rooms*) апартаменты *m pl*; (*mus*) сюита.
suitor /ˈsuːtə(r)/ *n* поклонник.
sulk /sʌlk/ *vi* дуться *impf*. **sulky** /-kɪ/ *adj* надутый.
sullen /ˈsʌlən/ *adj* угрюмый.
sully /ˈsʌlɪ/ *vt* пятнать *impf*, за~ *pf*.
sulphur /ˈsʌlfə(r)/ *n* сера. **sulphuric** /sʌlˈfjʊərɪk/ *adj*: **~ acid** серная кислота.
sultana /sʌlˈtɑːnə/ *n* (*raisin*) изюминка; *pl* кишмиш (*collect*).
sultry /ˈsʌltrɪ/ *adj* знойный.
sum /sʌm/ *n* сумма; (*arithmetical problem*) арифметическая задача; *pl* арифметика; *v*: **~ up** *vi* & *t* (*summarize*) подводить *impf*, подвести *pf* итоги (+*gen*); *vt* (*appraise*) оценивать *impf*, оценить *pf*.
summarize /ˈsʌməˌraɪz/ *vt* суммировать *impf* & *pf*. **summary** /ˈsʌmərɪ/ *n* резюме *neut indecl*, сводка; *adj* суммарный; (*dismissal*) бесцеремонный.
summer /ˈsʌmə(r)/ *n* лето; *attrib* летний. **summer-house** *n* беседка.
summit /ˈsʌmɪt/ *n* вершина; **~ meeting** встреча на верхах.
summon /ˈsʌmən/ *vt* вызывать *impf*, вызвать *pf*; **~ up one's courage** собираться *impf*, собраться *pf* с духом. **summons** /-mənz/ *n* вызов; (*law*) повестка в суд; *vt* вызывать *impf*, вызвать *pf* в суд.
sumptuous /ˈsʌmptjʊəs/ *adj* роскошный.
sun /sʌn/ *n* солнце; **in the ~** на солнце. **sunbathe** *vi* загорать *impf*. **sunbeam** *n* солнечный луч. **sunburn** *n* загар; (*inflammation*) солнечный ожог. **sunburnt** /-bɜːnt/ *adj* загорелый; **become ~** загорать *impf*, загореть *pf*.
Sunday /ˈsʌndeɪ/ *n* воскресенье.
sundry /ˈsʌndrɪ/ *adj* разный; **all and ~** всё и вся.
sunflower /ˈsʌnflaʊə(r)/ *n* подсолнечник. **sun-glasses** *n pl* очки (-ков) *pl* от солнца.
sunken /ˈsʌŋkən/ *adj* (*cheeks, eyes*) впалый; (*submerged*) погружённый; (*ship*) затопленный; (*below certain level*) ниже (какого-л. уровня).
sunlight /ˈsʌnlaɪt/ *n* солнечный свет. **sunny** /ˈsʌnɪ/ *adj* солнечный. **sunrise** *n* восход солнца. **sunset** *n* закат. **sunshade** *n* (*parasol*) зонтик; (*awning*) навес. **sunshine** *n* солнечный свет. **sunstroke** *n* солнечный удар. **suntan** *n* загар. **sun-tanned** /ˈsʌntænd/ *adj* загорелый.
super /ˈsuːpə(r)/ *adj* замечательный. **superb** /suːˈpɜːb/ *adj* превосходный. **supercilious** /ˌsuːpəˈsɪlɪəs/ *adj* высокомерный. **superficial** /-ˈfɪʃ(ə)l/ *adj* поверхностный. **superficiality** /-ˌfɪʃɪˈælɪtɪ/ *n* поверхностность. **superfluous** /suːˈpɜːflʊəs/ *adj* лишний. **superhuman** /ˌsuːpəˈhjuːmən/ *adj* сверхчеловеческий. **superintendent** /ˌsuːpərɪnˈtendənt/ *n* заведующий *sb* (**of** +*instr*); (*police*) старший полицейский офицер. **superior** /suːˈpɪərɪə(r)/ *n* старший *sb*; *adj* (*better*) превосходный; (*in rank*) старший; (*haughty*) высокомерный. **superiority** /suːˌpɪərɪˈɒrɪtɪ/ *n* превосходство. **superlative**

/suːˈpɜːlətɪv/ *adj* превосхóдный; *n* (*gram*) превосхóдная стéпень. **superman** *n* сверхчеловéк. **supermarket** *n* универсáм. **supernatural** *adj* сверхъестéственный. **superpower** *n* сверхдержáва. **supersede** /ˌsuːpəˈsiːd/ *vt* заменя́ть *impf*, замени́ть *pf*. **supersonic** *adj* сверхзвуковóй. **superstition** /ˌsuːpəˈstɪʃ(ə)n/ *n* суевéрие. **superstitious** /ˌsuːpəˈstɪʃ(ə)s/ *adj* суевéрный. **superstructure** *n* надстрóйка. **supervise** /ˈsuːpəˌvaɪz/ *vt* наблюдáть *impf* за +*instr*. **supervision** /ˌsuːpəˈvɪʒ(ə)n/ *n* надзóр. **supervisor** /ˈsuːpəˌvaɪzə(r)/ *n* начáльник; (*of studies*) руководи́тель *m*.

supper /ˈsʌpə(r)/ *n* у́жин; **have ~** у́жинать *impf*, по~ *pf*.

supple /ˈsʌp(ə)l/ *adj* ги́бкий. **suppleness** /-nɪs/ *n* ги́бкость.

supplement *n* /ˈsʌplɪmənt/ (*to book*) дополнéние; (*to periodical*) приложéние; *vt* /ˈsʌplɪˌment/ дополня́ть *impf*, допóлнить *pf*. **supplementary** /ˌsʌplɪˈmentərɪ/ *adj* дополни́тельный.

supplier /səˈplaɪə(r)/ *n* поставщи́к **supply** /səˈplaɪ/ *n* (*stock*) запáс; (*econ*) предложéние; *pl* (*mil*) припáсы (-ов) *pl*, *vt* снабжáть *impf*, снабди́ть *pf* (**with** +*instr*).

support /səˈpɔːt/ *n* поддéржка; *vt* поддéрживать *impf*, поддержáть *pf*; (*family*) содержáть *impf*. **supporter** /-tə(r)/ *n* сторóнник; (*sport*) болéльщик. **supportive** /-tɪv/ *adj* учáстливый.

suppose /səˈpəʊz/ *vt* (*think*) полагáть *impf*; (*presuppose*) предполагáть *impf*, предположи́ть *pf*; (*assume*) допускáть *impf*, допусти́ть *pf*. **supposed** /-ˈpəʊzd/ *adj* (*assumed*) предполагáемый. **supposition** /ˌsʌpəˈzɪʃ(ə)n/ *n* предположéние.

suppress /səˈpres/ *vt* подавля́ть *impf*, подави́ть *pf*. **suppression** /-ˈpreʃ(ə)n/ *n* подавлéние.

supremacy /suːˈpreməsɪ/ *n* госпóдство. **supreme** /-ˈpriːm/ *adj* верхóвный.

surcharge /ˈsɜːtʃɑːdʒ/ *n* нацéнка.

sure /ʃʊə(r)/ *adj* увéренный (**of** в+*prep*; **that** что); (*reliable*) вéрный; **~ enough** действи́тельно; **he is ~ to come** он обязáтельно придёт; **make ~ of** (*convince o.s.*) убеждáться *impf*, убеди́ться *pf* в+*prep*; **make ~ that** (*check up*) проверя́ть *impf*, провéрить *pf* что. **surely** /ˈʃʊəlɪ/ *adv* навернякá. **surety** /ˈʃʊərɪtɪ/ *n* порýка; **stand ~ for** ручáться *impf*, поручи́ться *pf* за+*acc*.

surf /sɜːf/ *n* прибóй; *vi* занимáться *impf*, заня́ться *pf* сéрфингом.

surface /ˈsɜːfɪs/ *n* повéрхность; (*exterior*) внéшность; **on the ~** (*fig*) внéшне; **under the ~** (*fig*) по существý; *adj* повéрхностный; *vi* всплывáть *impf*, всплыть *pf*.

surfeit /ˈsɜːfɪt/ *n* (*surplus*) изли́шек

surge /sɜːdʒ/ *n* волнá; *vi* (*rise, heave*) вздымáться *impf*; (*emotions*) нахлы́нуть *pf*; **~ forward** ри́нуться *pf* вперёд.

surgeon /ˈsɜːdʒ(ə)n/ *n* хирýрг. **surgery** /ˈsɜːdʒərɪ/ *n* (*treatment*) хирурги́я; (*place*) кабинéт; (**~** *hours*) приёмные часы́ *m pl* (врачá). **surgical** /ˈsɜːdʒɪk(ə)l/ *adj* хирурги́ческий.

surly /ˈsɜːlɪ/ *adj* (*morose*) угрю́мый; (*rude*) грýбый.

surmise /səˈmaɪz/ *vt* & *i* предполагáть *impf*, предположи́ть *pf*.

surmount /səˈmaʊnt/ *vt* преодолевáть *impf*, преодолéть *pf*.

surname /ˈsɜːneɪm/ *n* фами́лия.

surpass /səˈpɑːs/ *vt* превосходи́ть *impf*, превзойти́ *pf*.

surplus /ˈsɜːpləs/ *n* изли́шек; *adj* изли́шний.

surprise /səˈpraɪz/ *n* (*astonishment*) удивлéние; (*surprising thing*) сюрпри́з; *vt* удивля́ть *impf*, удиви́ть *pf*; (*come upon suddenly*) заставáть *impf*, застáть *pf* врасплóх; **be ~d** (*at*) удивля́ться *impf*, удиви́ться *pf* (+*dat*). **sur-**

prising /-zɪŋ/ *adj* удиви́тельный.
surreal /sə'rɪəl/ *adj* сюрреалисти́ческий. **surrealism** /-lɪz(ə)m/ *n* сюрреали́зм. **surrealist** /-lɪst/ *n* сюрреали́ст; *adj* сюрреалисти́ческий.
surrender /sə'rendə(r)/ *n* сда́ча; (*renunciation*) отка́з; *vt* сдава́ть *impf*, сдать *pf*; (*give up*) отка́зываться *impf*, отказа́ться *pf* от+*gen*; *vi* сдава́ться *impf*, сда́ться *pf*; **~ o.s. to** предава́ться *impf*, преда́ться *pf* +*dat*.
surreptitious /ˌsʌrəp'tɪʃəs/ *adj* та́йный.
surrogate /'sʌrəgət/ *n* замени́тель *m*.
surround /sə'raʊnd/ *vt* окружа́ть *impf*, окружи́ть *pf* (**with** +*instr*). **surrounding** /-dɪŋ/ *adj* окружа́ющий. **surroundings** /-dɪŋz/ *n* (*environs*) окре́стности *f pl*; (*milieu*) среда́.
surveillance /sɜː'veɪləns/ *n* надзо́р.
survey *n* /'sɜːveɪ/ (*review*) обзо́р; (*inspection*) инспе́кция; (*poll*) опро́с; *vt* /sə'veɪ/ (*review*) обозрева́ть *impf*, обозре́ть *pf*; (*inspect*) инспекти́ровать *impf*, про~ *pf*; (*poll*) опра́шивать *impf*, опроси́ть *pf*. **surveyor** /sə'veɪə(r)/ *n* инспе́ктор.
survival /sə'vaɪv(ə)l/ *n* (*surviving*) выжива́ние; (*relic*) пережи́ток. **survive** /-'vaɪv/ *vt* пережива́ть *impf*, пережи́ть *pf*; *vi* выжива́ть *impf*, вы́жить *pf*. **survivor** /-'vaɪvə(r)/ *n* уцеле́вший *sb*; (*fig*) боре́ц.
susceptible /sə'septɪb(ə)l/ *adj* подве́рженный (**to** влия́нию +*gen*); (*sensitive*) чувстви́тельный (**to** к+*dat*); (*impressionable*) впечатли́тельный.
suspect *n* /'sʌspekt/ подозрева́емый *sb*; *adj* подозри́тельный; *vt* /sə'spekt/ подозрева́ть *impf* (**of** в+*prep*); (*assume*) полага́ть *impf*.
suspend /sə'spend/ *vt* (*hang*) подве́шивать *impf*, подве́сить *pf*; (*delay*) приостана́вливать *impf*, приостанови́ть *pf*; (*debar temporarily*) вре́менно отстраня́ть *impf*, отстрани́ть *pf*; **~ed sentence** усло́вный пригово́р. **suspender** /-'spendə(r)/ *n* (*stocking*) подвя́зка. **suspense** /-'spens/ *n* неизве́стность. **suspension** /-'spenʃ(ə)n/ *n* (*halt*) приостано́вка; (*of car*) рессо́ры *f pl*; **~ bridge** вися́чий мост.
suspicion /sə'spɪʃ(ə)n/ *n* подозре́ние; **on ~** по подозре́нию (**of** в+*loc*); (*trace*) отте́нок. **suspicious** /-'spɪʃəs/ *adj* подозри́тельный.
sustain /sə'steɪn/ *vt* (*support*) подде́рживать *impf*, поддержа́ть *pf*; (*suffer*) потерпе́ть *pf*. **sustained** /-'steɪnd/ *adj* непреры́вный. **sustenance** /'sʌstɪnəns/ *n* пи́ща.
swab /swɒb/ *n* (*mop*) шва́бра; (*med*) тампо́н; (*specimen*) мазо́к.
swagger /'swægə(r)/ *vi* расха́живать *impf* с ва́жным ви́дом.
swallow[1] /'swɒləʊ/ *n* глото́к; *vt* прогла́тывать *impf*, проглоти́ть *pf*; **~ up** поглоща́ть *impf*, поглоти́ть *pf*.
swallow[2] /'swɒləʊ/ *n* (*bird*) ла́сточка.
swamp /swɒmp/ *n* боло́та; *vt* залива́ть *impf*, зали́ть *pf*; (*fig*) зава́ливать *impf*, завали́ть *pf* (**with** +*instr*). **swampy** /-pɪ/ *adj* боло́тистый.
swan /swɒn/ *n* ле́бедь *m*.
swap /swɒp/ *n* обме́н; *vt* (*for different thing*) меня́ть *impf*, об~, по~ *pf* (**for** на+*acc*); (*for similar thing*) обме́ниваться *impf*, обменя́ться *pf* +*instr*.
swarm /swɔːm/ *n* рой; (*crowd*) толпа́; *vi* рои́ться *impf*; толпи́ться *impf*; (*teem*) кише́ть *impf* (**with** +*instr*).
swarthy /'swɔːðɪ/ *adj* сму́глый.
swastika /'swɒstɪkə/ *n* сва́стика.
swat /swɒt/ *vt* прихло́пывать *impf*, прихло́пнуть *pf*.
swathe /sweɪð/ *n* (*expanse*) простра́нство; *vt* (*wrap*) заку́тывать *impf*, заку́тать *pf*.
sway /sweɪ/ *n* (*influence*) влия́ние;

(*power*) власть *vt* & *i* кача́ть(ся) *impf*, качну́ть(ся) *pf*; *vt* (*influence*) име́ть *impf* влия́ние на+*acc*.

swear /sweə(r)/ *vi* (*vow*) кля́сться *impf*, по~ *pf*; (*curse*) руга́ться *impf*, ругну́ться *pf*; **~-word** руга́тельство.

sweat /swet/ *n* пот; *vi* поте́ть *impf*, вс~ *pf*. **sweater** /-tə(r)/ *n* сви́тер. **sweatshirt** *n* тёплая футбо́лка с дли́нными рукава́ми. **sweaty** /-tɪ/ *adj* по́тный.

swede /swi:d/ *n* брю́ква.

Swede /swi:d/ *n* швед, ~дка. **Sweden** /-d(ə)n/ *n* Шве́ция. **Swedish** /-dɪʃ/ *adj* шве́дский.

sweep /swi:p/ *n* (*span*) разма́х; (*chimney-~*) трубочи́ст; *vt* подмета́ть *impf*, подмести́ *pf*; *vi* (*go majestically*) ходи́ть *indet*, идти́ *det*, пойти́ *pf* велича́во; (*move swiftly*) мча́ться *impf*; **~ away** смета́ть *impf*, смести́ *pf*. **sweeping** /-pɪŋ/ *adj* (*changes*) радика́льный; (*statement*) огу́льный.

sweet /swi:t/ *n* (*sweetmeat*) конфе́та; (*dessert*) сла́дкое *sb*; *adj* сла́дкий; (*fragrant*) души́стый; (*dear*) ми́лый. **sweeten** /-t(ə)n/ *vt* подсла́щивать *impf*, подсласти́ть *pf*. **sweetheart** *n* возлю́бленный, -нная *sb*. **sweetness** /-nɪs/ *n* сла́дость.

swell /swel/ *vi* (*up*) опуха́ть *impf*, опу́хнуть *pf*; *vt* & *i* (*a sail*) надува́ть(ся) *impf*, наду́ть(ся) *pf*; *vt* (*increase*) увели́чивать *impf*, увели́чить *pf*; *n* (*of sea*) зыбь. **swelling** /-lɪŋ/ *n* о́пухоль.

swelter /ˈsweltə(r)/ *vi* изнемога́ть *impf* от жары́. **sweltering** /-rɪŋ/ *adj* зно́йный.

swerve /swɜ:v/ *vi* ре́зко свёртывать, свора́чивать *impf*, сверну́ть *pf*.

swift /swɪft/ *adj* бы́стрый.

swig /swɪg/ *n* глото́к; *vt* хлеба́ть *impf*.

swill /swɪl/ *n* по́йло; *vt* (*rinse*) полоска́ть *impf*, вы́~ *pf*.

swim /swɪm/ *vi* пла́вать *indet*, плыть *det*; *vt* (*across*) переплыва́ть *impf*, переплы́ть *pf* +*acc*, че́рез+*acc*. **swimmer** /-mə(r)/ *n* плове́ц, пловчи́ха. **swimming** /-mɪŋ/ *n* пла́вание. **swimming-pool** *n* бассе́йн для пла́вания. **swim-suit** *n* купа́льный костю́м.

swindle /ˈswɪnd(ə)l/ *vt* обма́нывать *impf*, обману́ть *pf*; *n* обма́н. **swindler** /-dlə(r)/ *n* моше́нник.

swine /swaɪn/ *n* свинья́.

swing /swɪŋ/ *vi* кача́ться *impf*, качну́ться *pf*; *vt* кача́ть *impf*, качну́ть *pf* +*acc*, *instr*; (*arms*) разма́хивать *impf* +*instr*; *n* кача́ние; (*shift*) крен; (*seat*) каче́ли (-лей) *pl*; **in full ~** в по́лном разга́ре.

swingeing /ˈswɪndʒɪŋ/ *adj* (*huge*) грома́дный; (*forcible*) си́льный.

swipe /swaɪp/ *n* си́льный уда́р; *vt* с сило́й ударя́ть *impf*, уда́рить *pf*.

swirl /swɜ:l/ *vi* крути́ться *impf*; *n* (*of snow*) вихрь *m*.

swish /swɪʃ/ *vi* (*cut the air*) рассека́ть *impf*, рассе́чь *pf* во́здух со сви́стом; (*rustle*) шелесте́ть *impf*; *vt* (*tail*) взма́хивать *impf*, взмахну́ть *pf* +*instr*; (*brandish*) разма́хивать *impf* +*instr*; *n* (*of whip*) свист; (*rustle*) ше́лест.

Swiss /swɪs/ *n* швейца́рец, -ца́рка; *adj* швейца́рский.

switch /swɪtʃ/ *n* (*electr*) выключа́тель *m*; (*change*) измене́ние; *vt* & *i* (*also ~ over*) переключа́ть(ся) *impf*, переключи́ть(ся) *pf*; *vt* (*swap*) меня́ться *impf*, об~, по~ *pf* +*instr*; **~ off** выключа́ть *impf*, вы́ключить *pf*; **~ on** включа́ть *impf*, включи́ть *pf*. **switchboard** *n* коммута́тор.

Switzerland /ˈswɪtsələnd/ *n* Швейца́рия.

swivel /ˈswɪv(ə)l/ *vt* & *i* враща́ть(ся) *impf*.

swollen /ˈswəʊlən/ *adj* взду́тый.

swoon /swu:n/ *n* о́бморок; *vi* па́дать *impf*, упа́сть *pf* в о́бморок.

swoop /swu:p/ *vi*: **~ down** налета́ть *impf*, налете́ть *pf* (**on**

S

на+*acc*); *n* налёт; **at one fell ~** одни́м уда́ром.

sword /sɔːd/ *n* меч.

sycophantic /ˌsɪkə'fæntɪk/ *adj* льсти́вый.

syllable /'sɪləb(ə)l/ *n* слог.

syllabus /'sɪləbəs/ *n* програ́мма.

symbol /'sɪmb(ə)l/ *n* си́мвол. **symbolic(al)** /sɪm'bɒlɪ(k(ə)l)/ *adj* символи́ческий. **symbolism** /'sɪmbəˌlɪz(ə)m/ *n* символи́зм. **symbolize** /'sɪmbəˌlaɪz/ *vt* символизи́ровать *impf.*

symmetrical /sɪ'metrɪk(ə)l/ *adj* симметри́ческий. **symmetry** /'sɪmɪtrɪ/ *n* симметри́я.

sympathetic /ˌsɪmpə'θetɪk/ *adj* сочу́вственный. **sympathize** /'sɪmpəˌθaɪz/ *vi* сочу́вствовать *impf* (**with** +*dat*). **sympathizer** /'sɪmpəˌθaɪzə(r)/ *n* сторо́нник. **sympathy** /'sɪmpəθɪ/ *n* сочу́вствие.

symphony /'sɪmfənɪ/ *n* симфо́ния.

symposium /sɪm'pəʊzɪəm/ *n* симпо́зиум.

symptom /'sɪmptəm/ *n* симпто́м. **symptomatic** /ˌsɪmptə'mætɪk/ *adj* симтомати́чный.

synagogue /'sɪnəˌgɒg/ *n* синаго́га.

synchronization /ˌsɪŋkrənaɪ'zeɪʃ(ə)n/ *n* синхрониза́ция. **synchronize** /'sɪŋkrəˌnaɪz/ *vt* синхронизи́ровать *impf & pf.*

syndicate /'sɪndɪkət/ *n* синдика́т.

syndrome /'sɪndrəʊm/ *n* синдро́м.

synonym /'sɪnənɪm/ *n* сино́ним. **synonymous** /sɪ'nɒnɪməs/ *adj* синоними́ческий.

synopsis /sɪ'nɒpsɪs/ *n* конспе́кт.

syntax /'sɪntæks/ *n* си́нтаксис.

synthesis /'sɪnθɪsɪs/ *n* си́нтез. **synthetic** /sɪn'θetɪk/ *adj* синтети́ческий.

syphilis /'sɪfɪlɪs/ *n* си́филис.

Syria /'sɪrɪə/ *n* Си́рия. **Syrian** /-rɪən/ *n* сири́ец, сири́йка; *adj* сири́йский.

syringe /sɪ'rɪndʒ/ *n* шприц; *vt* спринцева́ть *impf.*

syrup /'sɪrəp/ *n* сиро́п; (*treacle*) па́тока.

system /'sɪstəm/ *n* систе́ма; (*network*) сеть; (*organism*) органи́зм. **systematic** /ˌsɪstə'mætɪk/ *adj* системати́ческий. **systematize** /'sɪstəməˌtaɪz/ *vt* систематизи́ровать *impf & pf.*

T

tab /tæb/ *n* (*loop*) пе́телька; (*on uniform*) петли́ца; (*of boot*) ушко́; **keep ~s on** следи́ть *impf* за+*instr.*

table /'teɪb(ə)l/ *n* стол; (*chart*) табли́ца; **~cloth** ска́терть; **~spoon** столо́вая ло́жка; **~ tennis** насто́льный те́ннис; *vt* (*for discussion*) предлага́ть *impf*, предложи́ть *pf* на обсужде́ние.

tableau /'tæbləʊ/ *n* жива́я карти́на.

tablet /'tæblɪt/ *n* (*pill*) табле́тка; (*of stone*) плита́; (*memorial ~*) мемориа́льная доска́; (*name plate*) доще́чка.

tabloid /'tæblɔɪd/ *n* (*newspaper*) малоформа́тная газе́та; (*derog*) бульва́рная газе́та.

taboo /tə'buː/ *n* табу́ *neut indecl*; *adj* запрещённый.

tacit /'tæsɪt/ *adj* молчали́вый. **taciturn** /'tæsɪˌtɜːn/ *adj* неразгово́рчивый.

tack[1] /tæk/ *n* (*nail*) гво́здик; (*stitch*) намётка; (*naut*) галс; (*fig*) курс; *vt* (*fasten*) прикрепля́ть *impf*, прикрепи́ть *pf* гво́здиками; (*stitch*) смётывать *impf*, смета́ть *pf* на живу́ю ни́тку; (*fig*) добавля́ть *impf*, доба́вить *pf* (**(on)to** +*dat*); *vi* (*naut*; *fig*) лави́ровать *impf.*

tack[2] /tæk/ *n* (*riding*) сбру́я (*collect*).

tackle /'tæk(ə)l/ *n* (*requisites*) снасть (*collect*); (*sport*) блокиро́вка; *vt* (*problem*) бра́ться *impf*, взя́ться *pf* за+*acc*; (*sport*) блоки́ровать *impf & pf.*

tacky /'tækɪ/ *adj* ли́пкий.

tact /tækt/ *n* такт(и́чность). **tactful** /-fʊl/ *adj* такти́чный.
tactical /ˈtæktɪk(ə)l/ *adj* такти́ческий. **tactics** /ˈtæktɪks/ *n pl* та́ктика.
tactless /ˈtæktlɪs/ *adj* беста́ктный.
tadpole /ˈtædpəʊl/ *n* голова́стик.
Tadzhikistan /ˌtædʒɪkɪˈstɑːn/ *n* Таджикиста́н.
tag /tæg/ *n* (*label*) ярлы́к; (*of lace*) наконе́чник; *vt* (*label*) прикрепля́ть *impf*, прикрепи́ть *pf* ярлы́к на+*acc*; *vi*: **~ along** (*follow*) тащи́ться *impf* сзади́; **may I ~ along?** мо́жно с ва́ми?
tail /teɪl/ *n* хвост; (*of shirt*) ни́жний коне́ц; (*of coat*) фа́лда; (*of coin*) обра́тная сторона́ моне́ты; **heads or ~s?** орёл и́ли ре́шка?; *pl* (*coat*) фрак; *vt* (*shadow*) высле́живать *impf*; *vi*: **~ away, off** постепе́нно уменьша́ться *impf*; (*grow silent, abate*) затиха́ть *impf*. **tailback** *n* хвост. **tailcoat** *n* фрак.
tailor /ˈteɪlə(r)/ *n* портно́й *sb*; **~-made** сши́тый на зака́з; (*fig*) сде́ланный индивидуа́льно.
taint /teɪnt/ *vt* по́ртить *impf*, ис~ *pf*.
Taiwan /taɪˈwɑːn/ *n* Тайва́нь *m*.
take /teɪk/ *vt* (*various senses*) брать *impf*, взять *pf*; (*also seize, capture*) захва́тывать *impf*, захвати́ть *pf*; (*receive, accept*; **~** *breakfast*; **~** *medicine*; **~** *steps*) принима́ть *impf*, приня́ть *pf*; (*convey, escort*) провожа́ть *impf*, проводи́ть *pf*; (*public transport*) е́здить *indet*, е́хать *det*, по~ *pf* +*instr*, на+*prep*; (*photograph*) снима́ть *impf*, снять *pf*; (*occupy*; **~** *time*) занима́ть *impf*, заня́ть *pf*; (*impers*) **how long does it ~?** ско́лько вре́мени ну́жно?; (*size in clothing*) носи́ть *impf*; (*exam*) сдава́ть *impf*; *vi* (*be successful*) име́ть *impf* успе́х (*of injection*) прививáться *impf*, приви́ться *pf*; **~ after** походи́ть *impf* на+*acc*; **~ away** (*remove*) убира́ть *impf*, убра́ть *pf*; (*subtract*) вычита́ть *impf*, вы́честь *pf*; **~-away** магази́н, где продаю́т на вы́нос; **~ back** (*return*) возвраща́ть *impf*, возврати́ть *pf*; (*retrieve, retract*) брать *impf*, взять *pf* наза́д; **~ down** (*in writing*) запи́сывать *impf*, записа́ть *pf*; (*remove*) снима́ть *impf*, снять *pf*; **~ s.o., sth for, to be** принима́ть *impf*, приня́ть *pf* за+*acc*; **~ from** отнима́ть *impf*, отня́ть *pf* у, от+*gen*; **~ in** (*carry in*) вноси́ть *impf*, внести́ *pf*; (*lodgers*; *work*) брать *impf*, взять *pf*; (*clothing*) ушива́ть *impf*, уши́ть *pf*; (*understand*) понима́ть *impf*, поня́ть *pf*; (*deceive*) обма́нывать *impf*, обману́ть *pf*; **~ off** (*clothing*) снима́ть *impf*, снять *pf*; (*mimic*) передра́знивать *impf*, передразни́ть *pf*; (*aeroplane*) взлета́ть *impf*, взлете́ть *pf*; **~-off** (*imitation*) подража́ние; (*aeron*) взлёт; **~ on** (*undertake*; *hire*) брать *impf*, взять *pf* на себя́; (*acquire*) приобрета́ть *impf*, приобрести́ *pf*; (*at game*) сража́ться *impf*, срази́ться *pf* с+*instr* (**at** в+*acc*); **~ out** вынима́ть *impf*, вы́нуть *pf*; (*dog*) выводи́ть *impf*, вы́вести *pf* (**for a walk** на прогу́лку); (*to theatre, restaurant etc.*) приглаша́ть *impf*, пригласи́ть *pf* (**to** в+*acc*); **we took them out every night** мы приглаша́ли их куда́-нибудь ка́ждый ве́чер; **~ it out on** срыва́ть *impf*, сорва́ть *pf* всё на +*prep*; **~ over** принима́ть *impf*, приня́ть *pf* руково́дство +*instr*; **~ to** (*thing*) пристрасти́ться *pf* к+*dat*; (*person*) привя́зываться *impf*, привяза́ться *pf* к+*dat*; (*begin*) стано́виться *impf*, стать *pf* +*inf*; **~ up** (*interest oneself in*) занима́ться *impf*, заня́ться *pf*; (*with an official etc.*) обраща́ться *impf*, обрати́ться *pf* с+*instr*, к+*dat*; (*challenge*) принима́ть *impf*, приня́ть *pf*; (*time, space*) занима́ть *impf*, заня́ть *pf*; **~ up with** (*person*) свя́зываться *impf*,

t

связа́ться *pf* с+*instr*; *n* (*cin*) дубль *m*.
taking /ˈteɪkɪŋ/ *adj* привлека́тельный.
takings /ˈteɪkɪŋz/ *n pl* сбор.
talcum powder /ˈtælkəm ˈpaʊdə(r)/ *n* тальк.
tale /teɪl/ *n* расска́з.
talent /ˈtælənt/ *n* тала́нт. **talented** /-tɪd/ *adj* тала́нтливый.
talk /tɔːk/ *vi* разгова́ривать *impf* (**to, with** с+*instr*); (*gossip*) сплётничать *impf*, на~ *pf*; *vt* & *i* говори́ть *impf*, по~ *pf*; ~ **down to** говори́ть *impf* свысока́ с+*instr*; ~ **into** угова́ривать *impf*, уговори́ть *pf* +*inf*; ~ **out of** отгова́ривать *impf*, отговори́ть *pf* +*inf*, от+*gen*; ~ **over** (*discuss*) обсужда́ть *impf*, обсуди́ть *pf*; ~ **round** (*persuade*) переубежда́ть *impf*, переубеди́ть *pf*; *n* (*conversation*) разгово́р; (*lecture*) бесе́да; *pl* перегово́ры (-ров) *pl*. **talkative** /ˈtɔːkətɪv/ *adj* разгово́рчивый; (*derog*) болтли́вый. **talker** /ˈtɔːkə(r)/ *n* говоря́щий *sb*; (*chatterer*) болту́н (*coll*); (*orator*) ора́тор. **talking-to** *n* (*coll*) вы́говор.
tall /tɔːl/ *adj* высо́кий; (*in measurements*) ро́стом в+*acc*.
tally /ˈtælɪ/ *n* (*score*) счёт; *vi* соотве́тствовать (**with** +*dat*).
talon /ˈtælən/ *n* ко́готь *m*.
tambourine /ˌtæmbəˈriːn/ *n* бу́бен.
tame /teɪm/ *adj* ручно́й; (*insipid*) пре́сный; *vt* прируча́ть *impf*, приручи́ть *pf*. **tamer** /ˈteɪmə(r)/ *n* укроти́тель *m*.
tamper /ˈtæmpə(r)/ *vi*: ~ **with** (*meddle*) тро́гать *impf*, тро́нуть *pf*; (*forge*) подде́лывать *impf*, подде́лать *pf*.
tampon /ˈtæmpɒn/ *n* тампо́н.
tan /tæn/ *n* (*sun*~) зага́р; *adj* желтова́то-кори́чневый; *vt* (*hide*) дуби́ть *impf*, вы́~ *pf*; (*beat*) (*coll*) дуба́сить *impf*, от~ *pf*; *vi* загора́ть *impf*, загоре́ть *pf*; (*of sun*): **tanned** загоре́лый.
tang /tæŋ/ *n* (*taste*) ре́зкий при́вкус; (*smell*) о́стрый за́пах.
tangent /ˈtændʒ(ə)nt/ *n* (*math*) каса́тельная *sb*; (*trigonometry*) та́нгенс; **go off at a** ~ отклоня́ться *impf*, отклони́ться *pf* от те́мы.
tangerine /ˌtændʒəˈriːn/ *n* мандари́н.
tangible /ˈtændʒɪb(ə)l/ *adj* осяза́емый.
tangle /ˈtæŋg(ə)l/ *vt* & *i* запу́тывать(ся) *impf*, запу́таться *pf*; *n* пу́таница.
tango /ˈtæŋgəʊ/ *n* та́нго *neut indecl*.
tangy /ˈtæŋɪ/ *adj* о́стрый; ре́зкий.
tank /tæŋk/ *n* бак; (*mil*) танк.
tankard /ˈtæŋkəd/ *n* кру́жка.
tanker /ˈtæŋkə(r)/ *n* (*sea*) та́нкер; (*road*) автоцисте́рна.
tantalize /ˈtæntəˌlaɪz/ *vt* дразни́ть *impf*.
tantamount /ˈtæntəˌmaʊnt/ *predic* равноси́лен (-льна) (**to** +*dat*).
tantrum /ˈtæntrəm/ *n* при́ступ раздраже́ния.
tap[1] /tæp/ *n* кран; *vt* (*resources*) испо́льзовать *impf* & *pf*; (*telephone conversation*) подслу́шивать *impf*.
tap[2] /tæp/ *n* (*knock*) стук; *vt* стуча́ть *impf*, по~ *pf* в+*acc*, по+*dat*; ~**-dance** (*vi*) отбива́ть *impf*, отби́ть *pf* чечётку; (*n*) чечётка; ~**-dancer** чечёточник, -ица.
tape /teɪp/ *n* (*cotton strip*) тесьма́; (*adhesive*, *magnetic*, *measuring*, *etc.*) ле́нта; ~**-measure** руле́тка; ~ **recorder** магнитофо́н; ~ **recording** за́пись; *vt* (*seal*) закле́ивать *impf*, закле́ить *pf*; (*record*) запи́сывать *impf*, записа́ть *pf* на ле́нту.
taper /ˈteɪpə(r)/ *vt* & *i* су́живать(ся) *impf*, су́зить(ся) *pf*.
tapestry /ˈtæpɪstrɪ/ *n* гобеле́н.
tar /tɑː(r)/ *n* дёготь *m*.
tardy /ˈtɑːdɪ/ *adj* (*slow*) медли́тельный; (*late*) запозда́лый.
target /ˈtɑːgɪt/ *n* мише́нь, цель.
tariff /ˈtærɪf/ *n* тари́ф.
tarmac /ˈtɑːmæk/ *n* (*material*) гудро́н; (*road*) гудрони́рованное шоссе́ *neut indecl*; (*runway*) бето-

ни́рованная площа́дка; *vt* гудрони́ровать *impf* & *pf*.

tarnish /ˈtɑːnɪʃ/ *vt* де́лать *impf*, с~ *pf* ту́склым; (*fig*) пятна́ть *impf*, за~ *pf*; *vi* тускне́ть *impf*, по~ *pf*.

tarpaulin /tɑːˈpɔːlɪn/ *n* брезе́нт.

tarragon /ˈtærəgən/ *n* эстраго́н.

tart[1] /tɑːt/ *adj* (*taste*) ки́слый; (*fig*) ко́лкий.

tart[2] /tɑːt/ *n* (*pie*) сла́дкий пиро́г.

tart[3] /tɑːt/ *n* (*prostitute*) шлю́ха.

tartan /ˈtɑːt(ə)n/ *n* шотла́ндка.

tartar /ˈtɑːtə(r)/ *n* ви́нный ка́мень *m*.

task /tɑːsk/ *n* зада́ча; **take to ~** де́лать *impf*, с~ *pf* вы́говор+*dat*; **~ force** операти́вная гру́ппа.

Tass /tæs/ *abbr* ТАСС, Телегра́фное аге́нтство Сове́тского Сою́за.

tassel /ˈtæs(ə)l/ *n* ки́сточка.

taste /teɪst/ *n* (*also fig*) вкус; **take a ~ of** про́бовать *impf*, по~ *pf*; *vt* чу́вствовать *impf*, по~ *pf* вкус +*gen*; (*sample*) про́бовать *impf*, по~ *pf*; (*fig*) вкуша́ть *impf*, вкуси́ть *pf*; (*wine etc.*) дегусти́ровать *impf* & *pf*; *vi* име́ть *impf* вкус, при́вкус (**of** +*gen*). **tasteful** /-fʊl/ *adj* (сде́ланный) со вку́сом. **tasteless** /-lɪs/ *adj* безвку́сный. **tasting** /-tɪŋ/ *n* дегуста́ция. **tasty** /-tɪ/ *adj* вку́сный.

tatter /ˈtætə(r)/ *n pl* лохмо́тья (-ьев) *pl*. **tattered** /-d/ *adj* обо́рванный.

tattoo /təˈtuː/ *n* (*design*) татуиро́вка; *vt* тату́ировать *impf* & *pf*.

taunt /tɔːnt/ *n* насме́шка; *vt* насмеха́ться *impf* над+*instr*.

Taurus /ˈtɔːrəs/ *n* Теле́ц.

taut /tɔːt/ *adj* ту́го натя́нутый; туго́й.

tavern /ˈtæv(ə)n/ *n* тавéрна.

tawdry /ˈtɔːdrɪ/ *adj* мишу́рный.

tawny /ˈtɔːnɪ/ *adj* рыжева́то-кори́чневый.

tax /tæks/ *n* нало́г; **~-free** освобождённый от нало́га; *vt* облага́ть *impf*, обложи́ть *pf* нало́гом; (*strain*) напряга́ть *impf*, напря́чь *pf*; (*patience*) испы́тывать *impf*, испыта́ть *pf*. **taxable** /ˈtæksəb(ə)l/ *adj* подлежа́щий обложе́нию нало́гом. **taxation** /tækˈseɪʃ(ə)n/ *n* обложе́ние нало́гом. **taxing** /ˈtæksɪŋ/ *adj* утоми́тельный. **taxpayer** *n* налогоплате́льщик.

taxi /ˈtæksɪ/ *n* такси́ *neut indecl*; **~-driver** води́тель *m* такси́; **~-rank** стоя́нка такси́; *vi* (*aeron*) рули́ть *impf*.

tea /tiː/ *n* чай; **~ bag** паке́тик с сухи́м ча́ем; **~ cloth, ~ towel** полоте́нце для посу́ды; **~ cosy** чехо́льщик (для ча́йника); **~cup** ча́йная ча́шка; **~-leaf** ча́йный лист; **~-pot** ча́йник; **~spoon** ча́йная ло́жка; **~ strainer** ча́йное си́течко.

teach /tiːtʃ/ *vt* учи́ть *impf*, на~ *pf* (*person* +*acc*; *subject* +*dat*, *inf*); преподава́ть *impf* (*subject* +*acc*); (*coll*) проу́чивать *impf*, проучи́ть *pf*. **teacher** /ˈtiːtʃə(r)/ *n* учи́тель *m*, ~ница; преподава́тель *m*, ~ница; **~-training college** педогоги́ческий институ́т. **teaching** /ˈtiːtʃɪŋ/ *n* (*instruction*) обуче́ние; (*doctrine*) уче́ние.

teak /tiːk/ *n* тик; *attrib* ти́ковый.

team /tiːm/ *n* (*sport*) кома́нда; (*of people*) брига́да; (*of horses etc.*) упря́жка; **~-mate** член той же кома́нды; **~work** сотру́дничество; *vi* (**~ up**) объединя́ться *impf*, объедини́ться *pf*.

tear[1] /teə(r)/ *n* (*rent*) проре́ха; *vt* (*also* **~ up**) рвать *impf*; (*also* **~ up**) разрыва́ть *impf*, разорва́ть *pf*; *vi* рва́ться *impf*; (*rush*) мча́ться *impf*; **~ down, off** срыва́ть *impf*, сорва́ть *pf*; **~ out** вырыва́ть *impf*, вы́рвать *pf*.

tear[2] /tɪə(r)/ *n* (**~-drop**) слеза́; **~-gas** слезоточи́вый газ. **tearful** /-fʊl/ *adj* слезли́вый.

tease /tiːz/ *vt* дразни́ть *impf*.

teat /tiːt/ *n* сосо́к.

technical /ˈteknɪk(ə)l/ *adj* техни́ческий; **~ college** техни́ческое учи́лище. **technicality** /ˌteknɪˈkælɪtɪ/ *n* форма́льность. **technically**

/ˈteknɪklɪ/ *adv* (*strictly*) формáльно. **technician** /tekˈnɪʃən/ *n* тéхник. **technique** /-ˈniːk/ *n* тéхника; (*method*) мéтод. **technology** /-ˈnɒlədʒɪ/ *n* технолóгия, тéхника. **technological** /ˌteknəˈlɒdʒɪkəl/ *adj* технологи́ческий. **technologist** /tekˈnɒlədʒɪst/ *n* технóлог.

teddy-bear /ˈtedɪˌbeə(r)/ *n* медвежóнок.

tedious /ˈtiːdɪəs/ *adj* скýчный. **tedium** /ˈtiːdɪəm/ *n* скýка.

teem¹ /tiːm/ *vi* (*swarm*) кишéть *impf* (**with** +*instr*).

teem² /tiːm/ *vi*: **it is ~ing (with rain)** дождь льёт как из ведрá.

teenage /ˈtiːneɪdʒ/ *adj* ю́ношеский. **teenager** /-dʒə(r)/ *n* подрóсток. **teens** /tiːnz/ *n pl* вóзраст от тринáдцати до девятнáдцати лет.

teeter /ˈtiːtə(r)/ *vi* качáться *impf*, качнýться *pf*.

teethe /tiːð/ *vi*: **the child is teething** у ребёнка прорéзываются зýбы; **teething troubles** (*fig*) начáльные проблéмы *f pl*.

teetotal /tiːˈtəʊt(ə)l/ *adj* трéзвый. **teetotaller** /-lə(r)/ *n* трéзвенник.

telecommunication(s) /ˌtelɪkəˌmjuːnɪˈkeɪʃ(ə)nz/ *n* дáльняя связь. **telegram** /ˈtelɪˌgræm/ *n* телегрáмма. **telegraph** /ˈtelɪˌgrɑːf/ *n* телегрáф; **~ pole** телегрáфный столб. **telepathic** /ˌtelɪˈpæθɪk/ *adj* телепати́ческий. **telepathy** /tɪˈlepəθɪ/ *n* телепáтия. **telephone** /ˈtelɪˌfəʊn/ *n* телефóн; *vt* (*message*) телефони́ровать *impf* & *pf* +*acc*, о+*prep*; (*person*) звони́ть *impf*, по~ *pf* (по телефóну) +*dat*; **~ box** телефóнная бýдка; **~ directory** телефóнная кни́га; **~ exchange** телефóнная стáнция; **~ number** нóмер телефóна. **telephonist** /tɪˈlefənɪst/ *n* телефони́ст, ~ка. **telephoto lens** /ˈtelɪˌfəʊtəʊ lenz/ *n* телеобъекти́в. **telescope** /ˈtelɪˌskəʊp/ *n* телескóп. **telescopic** /ˌtelɪˈskɒpɪk/ *adj* телескопи́ческий. **televise** /ˈtelɪˌvaɪz/ *vt* покáзывать *impf*, показáть *pf* по телеви́дению. **television** /ˈtelɪˌvɪʒ(ə)n/ *n* телеви́дение; (*set*) телеви́зор; *attrib* телевизиóнный. **telex** /ˈteleks/ *n* тéлекс.

tell /tel/ *vt* & *i* (*relate*) расскáзывать *impf*, рассказáть *pf* (*thing told* +*acc*, о+*prep*; *person told* +*dat*); *vt* (*utter, inform*) говори́ть *impf*, сказáть *pf* (*thing uttered* +*acc*; *thing informed about* о+*prep*; *person informed* +*dat*); (*order*) велéть *impf* & *pf* +*dat*; **~ one thing from another** отличáть *impf*, отличи́ть *pf* +*acc* от+*gen*; *vi* (*have an effect*) скáзываться *impf*, сказáться *pf* (**on** на+*prep*); **~ off** отчи́тывать *impf*, отчитáть *pf*; **~ on, ~ tales about** ябéдничать *impf*, на~ *pf* на+*acc*. **teller** /ˈtelə(r)/ *n* (*of story*) расскáзчик; (*of votes*) счётчик; (*in bank*) касси́р. **telling** /ˈtelɪŋ/ *adj* (*effective*) эффекти́вный; (*significant*) многозначи́тельный. **telltale** *n* сплéтник; *adj* предáтельский.

temerity /tɪˈmerɪtɪ/ *n* дéрзость.

temp /temp/ *n* рабóтающий *sb* врéменно; *vi* рабóтать *impf* врéменно.

temper /ˈtempə(r)/ *n* (*character*) нрав; (*mood*) настроéние; (*anger*) гнев; **lose one's ~** выходи́ть *impf*, вы́йти *pf* из себя́; *vt* (*fig*) смягчáть *impf*, смягчи́ть *pf*.

temperament /ˈtemprəmənt/ *n* темперáмент. **temperamental** /ˌtemprəˈment(ə)l/ *adj* темперáментный.

temperance /ˈtempərəns/ *n* (*moderation*) умéренность; (*sobriety*) трéзвенность.

temperate /ˈtempərət/ *adj* умéренный.

temperature /ˈtemprɪtʃə(r)/ *n* температýра; (*high ~*) повы́шенная температýра; **take s.o.'s ~** измеря́ть *impf*, измéрить *pf* температýру +*dat*.

tempest /ˈtempɪst/ *n* бýря. **tem-**

t

pestuous /tem'pestjʊəs/ *adj* бу́рный.
template /'templeɪt/ *n* шабло́н.
temple[1] /'temp(ə)l/ *n* (*religion*) храм.
temple[2] /'temp(ə)l/ *n* (*anat*) висо́к.
tempo /'tempəʊ/ *n* темп.
temporal /'tempər(ə)l/ *adj* (*of time*) временно́й; (*secular*) мирско́й.
temporary /'tempərərɪ/ *adj* вре́менный.
tempt /tempt/ *vt* соблазня́ть *impf*, соблазни́ть *pf*; **~ fate** испы́тывать *impf*, испыта́ть *pf* судьбу́. **temptation** /temp'teɪʃ(ə)n/ *n* собла́зн. **tempting** /'temptɪŋ/ *adj* соблазни́тельный.
ten /ten/ *adj* & *n* де́сять; (*number 10*) деся́тка. **tenth** /tenθ/ *adj* & *n* деся́тый.
tenable /'tenəb(ə)l/ *adj* (*logical*) разу́мный.
tenacious /tɪ'neɪʃəs/ *adj* це́пкий. **tenacity** /-'næsɪtɪ/ *n* це́пкость.
tenancy /'tenənsɪ/ *n* (*renting*) наём помеще́ния; (*period*) срок аре́нды. **tenant** /'tenənt/ *n* аренда́тор.
tend[1] /tend/ *vi* (*be apt*) име́ть скло́нность (**to** к+*dat*, +*inf*).
tend[2] /tend/ *vt* (*look after*) уха́живать *impf* за+*instr.*
tendency /'tendənsɪ/ *n* тенде́нция. **tendentious** /ten'denʃəs/ *adj* тенденцио́зный.
tender[1] /'tendə(r)/ *vt* (*offer*) предлага́ть *impf*, предложи́ть *pf*; *vi* (*make ~ for*) подава́ть *impf*, пода́ть *pf* зая́вку (на торга́х); *n* предложе́ние; **legal ~** зако́нное платёжное сре́дство.
tender[2] /'tendə(r)/ *adj* (*delicate, affectionate*) не́жный. **tenderness** /-nɪs/ *n* не́жность.
tendon /'tend(ə)n/ *n* сухожи́лие.
tendril /'tendrɪl/ *n* у́сик.
tenement /'tenɪmənt/ *n* (*dwelling-house*) жило́й дом; **~-house** многокварти́рный дом.
tenet /'tenɪt/ *n* до́гмат, при́нцип.
tennis /'tenɪs/ *n* те́ннис.
tenor /'tenə(r)/ *n* (*direction*) направле́ние; (*purport*) смысл; (*mus*) те́нор.
tense[1] /tens/ *n* вре́мя *neut.*
tense[2] /tens/ *vt* напряга́ть *impf*, напря́чь *pf*; *adj* напряжённый. **tension** /'tenʃ(ə)n/ *n* напряже́ние.
tent /tent/ *n* пала́тка.
tentacle /'tentək(ə)l/ *n* щу́пальце.
tentative /'tentətɪv/ *adj* (*experimental*) про́бный; (*preliminary*) предвари́тельный.
tenterhooks /'tentəˌhʊks/ *n pl*: **be on ~** сиде́ть *impf* как на иго́лках.
tenth /tenθ/ *see* **ten**
tenuous /'tenjʊəs/ *adj* (*fig*) неубеди́тельный.
tenure /'tenjə(r)/ *n* (*of property*) владе́ние; (*of office*) пребыва́ние в до́лжности; (*period*) срок; (*guaranteed employment*) несменя́емость.
tepid /'tepɪd/ *adj* теплова́тый.
term /tɜːm/ *n* (*period*) срок; (*univ*) семе́стр; (*school*) че́тверть; (*technical word*) те́рмин; (*expression*) выраже́ние; *pl* (*conditions*) усло́вия *neut pl*; (*relations*) отноше́ния *neut pl*; **on good ~s** в хоро́ших отноше́ниях; **come to ~s with** (*resign o.s. to*) покоря́ться *impf*, покори́ться *pf* к+*dat*; *vt* называ́ть *impf*, назва́ть *pf*.
terminal /'tɜːmɪn(ə)l/ *adj* коне́чный; (*med*) смерте́льный; *n* (*electr*) зажи́м; (*computer, aeron*) термина́л; (*terminus*) коне́чная остано́вка.
terminate /'tɜːmɪˌneɪt/ *vt* & *i* конча́ть(ся) *impf*, ко́нчить(ся) *pf* (**in** +*instr*). **termination** /-'neɪʃ(ə)n/ *n* прекраще́ние.
terminology /ˌtɜːmɪ'nɒlədʒɪ/ *n* терминоло́гия.
terminus /'tɜːmɪnəs/ *n* коне́чная остано́вка.
termite /'tɜːmaɪt/ *n* терми́т.
terrace /'terəs/ *n* терра́са; (*houses*) ряд домо́в.
terracotta /ˌterə'kɒtə/ *n* терракóта.
terrain /te'reɪn/ *n* ме́стность.

terrestrial /tə'restrɪəl/ *adj* земно́й.
terrible /'terɪb(ə)l/ *adj* ужа́сный. **terribly** /-blɪ/ *adv* ужа́сно.
terrier /'terɪə(r)/ *n* терье́р.
terrific /tə'rɪfɪk/ *adj* (*huge*) огро́мный; (*splendid*) потряса́ющий. **terrify** /'terɪˌfaɪ/ *vt* ужаса́ть *impf*, ужасну́ть *pf*.
territorial /ˌterɪ'tɔːrɪəl/ *adj* территориа́льный. **territory** /'terɪtərɪ/ *n* террито́рия.
terror /'terə(r)/ *n* у́жас; (*person*; *polit*) терро́р. **terrorism** /'terəˌrɪz(ə)m/ *n* террори́зм. **terrorist** /'terərɪst/ *n* террори́ст, ~ка. **terrorize** /'terəˌraɪz/ *vt* терроризи́ровать *impf* & *pf*.
terse /tɜːs/ *adj* кра́ткий.
tertiary /'tɜːʃərɪ/ *adj* трети́чный; (*education*) вы́сший.
test /test/ *n* испыта́ние, про́ба; (*exam*) экза́мен; контро́льная рабо́та; (*analysis*) ана́лиз; **~-tube** проби́рка; *vt* (*try out*) испы́тывать *impf*, испыта́ть *pf*; (*check up on*) проверя́ть *impf*, прове́рить *pf*; (*give exam to*) экзаменова́ть *impf*, про~ *pf*.
testament /'testəmənt/ *n* завеща́ние; **Old, New T~** Ве́тхий, Но́вый заве́т.
testicle /'testɪk(ə)l/ *n* яи́чко.
testify /'testɪˌfaɪ/ *vi* свиде́тельствовать *impf* (**to** в по́льзу +*gen*; **against** про́тив+*gen*); *vt* (*declare*) заявля́ть *impf*, заяви́ть *pf*; (*be evidence of*) свиде́тельствовать о+*prep*.
testimonial /ˌtestɪ'məʊnɪəl/ *n* рекоменда́ция. **testimony** /'testɪmənɪ/ *n* свиде́тельство.
tetanus /'tetənəs/ *n* столбня́к.
tetchy /'tetʃɪ/ *adj* раздражи́тельный.
tête-à-tête /ˌteɪtɑː'teɪt/ *n* & *adv* тет-а-те́т.
tether /'teðə(r)/ *n*: **be at, come to the end of one's ~** дойти́ *pf* до то́чки; *vt* привя́зывать *impf*, привяза́ть *pf*.
text /tekst/ *n* текст; **~ message** SMS/СМС-сообще́ние; *vt* посыла́ть *impf*, посла́ть *pf* SMS (+*dat*). **textbook** *n* уче́бник.
textile /'tekstaɪl/ *adj* тексти́льный; *n* ткань; *pl* тексти́ль *m* (*collect*).
textual /'tekstjʊəl/ *adj* текстово́й.
texture /'tekstʃə(r)/ *n* тексту́ра.
than /ðæn/ *conj* (*comparison*) чем; **other ~** (*except*) кро́ме+*gen*.
thank /θæŋk/ *vt* благодари́ть *impf*, по~ *pf* (**for** за+*acc*); **~ God** сла́ва Бо́гу; **~ you** спаси́бо; благодарю́ вас; *n pl* благода́рность; **~s to** (*good result*) благодаря́ +*dat*; (*bad result*) из-за+*gen*. **thankful** /-fʊl/ *adj* благода́рный. **thankless** /-lɪs/ *adj* неблагода́рный. **thanksgiving** /'θæŋksˌgɪvɪŋ/ *n* благодаре́ние.
that /ðæt/ *demonstrative adj* & *pron* тот; **~ which** тот кото́рый; *rel pron* кото́рый; *conj* что; (*purpose*) что́бы; *adv* так, до тако́й сте́пени.
thatched /θætʃt/ *adj* соло́менный.
thaw /θɔː/ *vt* раста́пливать *impf*, растопи́ть *pf*; *vi* та́ять *impf*, рас~ *pf*; *n* о́ттепель.
the /ðə, ðiː/ *def article, not translated*; *adv* тем; **the ... the ...** чем ...тем; **~ more ~ better** чем бо́льше, тем лу́чше.
theatre /'θɪətə(r)/ *n* теа́тр; (*lecture ~*) аудито́рия; (*operating ~*) операцио́нная *sb*; **~-goer** театра́л. **theatrical** /θɪ'ætrɪk(ə)l/ *adj* театра́льный.
theft /θeft/ *n* кра́жа.
their, theirs /ðeə(r), ðeəz/ *poss pron* их; свой.
theme /θiːm/ *n* те́ма.
themselves /ðəm'selvz/ *pron* (*emph*) (они́) са́ми; (*refl*) себя́; -ся (*suffixed to vt*).
then /ðen/ *adv* (*at that time*) тогда́; (*after that*) пото́м; **now and ~** вре́мя от вре́мени; *conj* в тако́м слу́чае, тогда́; *adj* тогда́шний; **by ~** к тому́ вре́мени; **since ~** с тех пор.
thence /ðens/ *adv* отту́да. **thenceforth, -forward** /ðens'fɔːθ, -'fɔːwəd/ *adv* с того́/э́того вре́мени.

t

theologian /ˌθɪəˈləʊdʒ(ə)n/ *n* теóлог. **theological** /-ˈlɒdʒɪk(ə)l/ *adj* теологи́ческий. **theology** /θɪˈɒlədʒɪ/ *n* теолóгия.

theorem /ˈθɪərəm/ *n* теорéма. **theoretical** /ˌθɪəˈretɪk(ə)l/ *adj* теорети́ческий. **theorize** /ˈθɪəraɪz/ *vi* теоретизи́ровать *impf.* **theory** /ˈθɪərɪ/ *n* теóрия.

therapeutic /ˌθerəˈpjuːtɪk/ *adj* терапевти́ческий. **therapist** /ˈθerəpɪst/ *n* (*psychotherapist*) психотерапéвт. **therapy** /ˈθerəpɪ/ *n* терапи́я.

there /ðeə(r)/ *adv* (*place*) там; (*direction*) тудá; *int* вот!; ну!; **~ is, are** есть, имéется (-éются); **~ you are** (*on giving sth*) пожáлуйста. **thereabouts** /ˈðeərəˌbaʊts/ *adv* (*near*) побли́зости; (*approximately*) приблизи́тельно. **thereafter** *adv* пóсле э́того. **thereby** *adv* таки́м óбразом. **therefore** *adv* поэ́тому. **therein** *adv* в э́том. **thereupon** *adv* затéм.

thermal /ˈθɜːm(ə)l/ *adj* теплово́й, терми́ческий; (*underwear*) тёплый.

thermometer /θəˈmɒmɪtə(r)/ *n* термóметр, грáдусник. **thermos** /ˈθɜːm(ə)l/ *n* тéрмос. **thermostat** /ˈθɜːməˌstæt/ *n* термостáт.

thesis /ˈθiːsɪs/ *n* (*proposition*) тéзис; (*dissertation*) диссертáция.

they /ðeɪ/ *pron* они́.

thick /θɪk/ *adj* тóлстый, (*in measurements*) толщинóй в+*acc*; (*dense*) густóй; (*stupid*) тупóй; **~-skinned** толстокóжий. **thicken** /ˈθɪkən/ *vt & i* утолщáть(ся) *impf*, утолсти́ть(ся) *pf*; (*make, become denser*) сгущáть(ся) *impf*, сгусти́ть(ся) *pf*; *vi* (*become more intricate*) усложня́ться *impf*, усложни́ться *pf.* **thicket** /ˈθɪkɪt/ *n* чáща. **thickness** /ˈθɪknɪs/ *n* (*also dimension*) толщинá; (*density*) густотá; (*layer*) слой. **thickset** *adj* коренáстый.

thief /θiːf/ *n* вор. **thieve** /θiːv/ *vi* ворова́ть *impf.* **thievery** /ˈθiːvərɪ/ *n* воровствó.

thigh /θaɪ/ *n* бедрó.

thimble /ˈθɪmb(ə)l/ *n* напёрсток.

thin /θɪn/ *adj* (*slender; not thick*) тóнкий; (*lean*) худóй; (*too liquid*) жи́дкий; (*sparse*) рéдкий; *vt & i* дéлать(ся) *impf*, с~ *pf* тóнким, жи́дким; *vi*: (*also* ~ *out*) редéть *impf*, по~ *pf*; *vt*: **~ out** прорéживать *impf*, прореди́ть *pf.*

thing /θɪŋ/ *n* вещь; (*object*) предмéт; (*matter*) дéло.

think /θɪŋk/ *vt & i* дýмать *impf*, по~ *pf* (**about, of** о+*prep*); (*consider*) считáть *impf*, счесть *pf* (**to be** +*instr*, за+*acc*; **that** что); *vi* (*reflect, reason*) мы́слить *impf*; (*intend*) намеревáться *impf* (*of doing* +*inf*); **~ out** продýмывать *impf*, продýмать *pf*; **~ over** обдýмывать *impf*, обдýмать *pf*; **~ up, of** придýмывать *impf*, придýмать *pf.* **thinker** /ˈθɪŋkə(r)/ *n* мысли́тель *m.* **thinking** /ˈθɪŋkɪŋ/ *adj* мы́слящий; *n* (*reflection*) размышлéние; **to my way of ~** по моемý мнéнию.

third /θɜːd/ *adj & n* трéтий; (*fraction*) треть; **T~ World** стрáны *f pl* трéтьего ми́ра.

thirst /θɜːst/ *n* жáжда (**for** +*gen* (*fig*)); *vi* (*fig*) жáждать *impf* (**for** +*gen*). **thirsty** /ˈθɜːstɪ/ *adj*: **be ~** хотéть *impf* пить.

thirteen /θɜːˈtiːn/ *adj & n* тринáдцать. **thirteenth** /-ˈtiːnθ/ *adj & n* тринáдцатый.

thirtieth /ˈθɜːtɪɪθ/ *adj & n* тридцáтый. **thirty** /ˈθɜːtɪ/ *adj & n* три́дцать; *pl* (*decade*) тридцáтые гóды (-дóв) *m pl.*

this /ðɪs/ *demonstrative adj & pron* э́тот; **like ~** вот так; **~ morning** сегóдня ýтром.

thistle /ˈθɪs(ə)l/ *n* чертополóх.

thither /ˈðɪðə(r)/ *adv* тудá.

thorn /θɔːn/ *n* шип. **thorny** /ˈθɔːnɪ/ *adj* колю́чий; (*fig*) терни́стый.

thorough /ˈθʌrə/ *adj* основáтельный; (*complete*) совершéнный. **thoroughbred** /-ˌbred/ *adj* чистокро́вный. **thoroughfare** /-ˌfeə(r)/*n* проéзд; (*walking*) прохо́д. **thoroughgoing** /-ˌɡəʊɪŋ/ *adj* радика́льный. **thoroughly** /-lɪ/ *adv* (*completely*) соверше́нно. **thoroughness** /-nɪs/ *n* основа́тельность.

though /ðəʊ/ *conj* хотя́; несмотря́ на то, что; **as ~** как бу́дто; *adv* одна́ко.

thought /θɔːt/ *n* мысль; (*meditation*) размышле́ние; (*intention*) наме́рение; *pl* (*opinion*) мне́ние. **thoughtful** /-fʊl/ *adj* заду́мчивый; (*considerate*) внима́тельный. **thoughtless** /-lɪs/ *adj* необду́манный; (*inconsiderate*) невнима́тельный.

thousand /ˈθaʊz(ə)nd/ *adj* & *n* ты́сяча. **thousandth** /ˈθaʊz(ə)ntθ/ *adj* & *n* ты́сячный.

thrash /θræʃ/ *vt* бить *impf*, по~ *pf*; **~ out** (*discuss*) обстоя́тельно обсужда́ть *impf*, обсуди́ть *pf*; *vi*: **~ about** мета́ться *impf*. **thrashing** /-ʃɪŋ/ *n* (*beating*) взбу́чка (*coll*).

thread /θred/ *n* ни́тка, нить (*also fig*); (*of screw etc.*) резьба́; *vt* (*needle*) продева́ть *impf*, проде́ть *pf* ни́тку в+*acc*; (*beads*) нани́зывать *impf*, наниза́ть *pf*; **~ one's way** пробира́ться *impf*, пробра́ться *pf* (**through** че́рез+*acc*). **threadbare** *adj* потёртый.

threat /θret/ *n* угро́за. **threaten** /-t(ə)n/ *vt* угрожа́ть *impf*, грози́ть *impf*, при~ *pf* (*person* +*dat*; **with** +*instr*; *to do* +*inf*).

three /θriː/ *adj* & *n* три; (*number 3*) тро́йка; **~-dimensional** трёхме́рный; **~-quarters** три че́тверти. **threefold** *adj* тройно́й; *adv* втройне́. **threesome** *n* тро́йка.

thresh /θreʃ/ *vt* молоти́ть *impf*.

threshold /ˈθreʃəʊld/ *n* поро́г.

thrice /θraɪs/ *adv* три́жды.

thrift /θrɪft/ *n* бережли́вость. **thrifty** /-tɪ/ *adj* бережли́вый.

thrill /θrɪl/ *n* тре́пет; *vt* восхища́ть *impf*, восхити́ть *pf*; **be thrilled** быть в восто́рге. **thriller** /-lə(r)/ *n* приключе́нческий, детекти́вный (*novel*) рома́н, (*film*) фильм. **thrilling** /-lɪŋ/ *adj* захва́тывающий.

thrive /θraɪv/ *vi* процвета́ть *impf*.

throat /θrəʊt/ *n* го́рло.

throb /θrɒb/ *vi* (*heart*) си́льно би́ться *impf*; пульси́ровать *impf*; *n* бие́ние; пульса́ция.

throes /θrəʊz/ *n pl*: **in the ~** в мучи́тельных попы́тках.

thrombosis /θrɒmˈbəʊsɪs/ *n* тромбо́з.

throne /θrəʊn/ *n* трон, престо́л; **come to the ~** вступа́ть *impf*, вступи́ть *pf* на престо́л.

throng /θrɒŋ/ *n* толпа́; *vi* толпи́ться *impf*; *vt* заполня́ть *impf*, запо́лнить *pf*.

throttle /ˈθrɒt(ə)l/ *n* (*tech*) дро́ссель *m*; *vt* (*strangle*) души́ть *impf*, за~ *pf*; (*tech*) дроссели́ровать *impf* & *pf*; **~ down** сбавля́ть *impf*, сба́вить *pf* газ.

through /θruː/ *prep* (*across, via, ~ opening*) че́рез+*acc*; (*esp ~ thick of*) сквозь+*acc*; (*air, streets etc.*) по+*dat*; (*agency*) посре́дством +*gen*; (*reason*) из-за+*gen*; *adv* насквозь; (*from beginning to end*) до конца́; **be ~ with** (*sth*) ока́нчивать *impf*, око́нчить *pf*; (*s.o.*) порыва́ть *impf*, порва́ть *pf* с+*instr*; **put ~** (*on telephone*) соединя́ть *impf*, соедини́ть *pf*; **~ and ~** соверше́нно; *adj* (*train*) прямо́й; (*traffic*) сквозно́й. **throughout** *adv* повсю́ду, во всех отноше́ниях; *prep* по всему́ (всей, всему́; *pl* всем)+*dat*; (*from beginning to end*) с нача́ла до конца́+*gen*.

throw /θrəʊ/ *n* бросо́к; *vt* броса́ть *impf*, бро́сить *pf*; (*confuse*) смуща́ть *impf*, смути́ть *pf*; (*rider*) сбра́сывать *impf*, сбро́сить *pf*; (*party*) устра́ивать *impf*, устро́ить *pf*; **~ o.s. into** броса́ться *impf*, бро́ситься *pf* в+*acc*; **~ away, out** выбра́сывать *impf*, вы́бросить *pf*; **~ down** сбра́сывать *impf*, сбро́сить *pf*; **~ in** (*add*) до-

t

бавля́ть *impf*, доба́вить *pf*; (*sport*) вбра́сывать *impf*, вбро́сить *pf*; **~-in** вбра́сывание мяча́; **~ off** сбра́сывать *impf*, сбро́сить *pf*; **~ open** распа́хивать *impf*, распахну́ть *pf*; **~ out** (*see also ~ away*) (*expel*) выгоня́ть *impf*, вы́гнать *pf*; (*reject*) отверга́ть *impf*, отве́ргнуть *pf*; **~ over, ~ up** (*abandon*) броса́ть *impf*, бро́сить *pf*; **~ up** подбра́сывать *impf*, подбро́сить *pf*; (*vomit*) рвать *impf*, вы́~ *pf impers*; **he threw up** его́ вы́рвало.

thrush /θrʌʃ/ *n* (*bird*) дрозд.

thrust /θrʌst/ *n* (*shove*) толчо́к; (*tech*) тя́га; *vt* (*shove*) толка́ть *impf*, толкну́ть *pf*; (*~ into, out of; give quickly, carelessly*) сова́ть *impf*, су́нуть *pf*.

thud /θʌd/ *n* глухо́й звук; *vi* па́дать *impf*, *pf* с глухи́м сту́ком.

thug /θʌg/ *n* головоре́з (*coll*).

thumb /θʌm/ *n* большо́й па́лец; **under the ~ of** под башмако́м у+*gen*; *vt*: **~ through** перели́стывать *impf*, перелиста́ть *pf*; **~ a lift** голосова́ть *impf*, про~ *pf*.

thump /θʌmp/ *n* (*blow*) тяжёлый уда́р; (*thud*) глухо́й звук, стук; *vt* колоти́ть *impf*, по~ *pf* в+*acc*, по+*dat*; *vi* колоти́ться *impf*.

thunder /ˈθʌndə(r)/ *n* гром; *vi* греме́ть *impf*; **it thunders** гром греми́т. **thunderbolt** *n* уда́р мо́лнии. **thunderous** /-rəs/ *adj* громово́й. **thunderstorm** *n* гроза́. **thundery** /-rɪ/ *adj* грозово́й.

Thursday /ˈθɜːzdeɪ/ *n* четве́рг.

thus /ðʌs/ *adv* так, таки́м о́бразом.

thwart /θwɔːt/ *vt* меша́ть *impf*, по~ *pf* +*dat*; (*plans*) расстра́ивать *impf*, расстро́ить *pf*.

thyme /taɪm/ *n* тимья́н.

thyroid /ˈθaɪrɔɪd/ *n* (*~ gland*) щитови́дная железа́.

tiara /tɪˈɑːrə/ *n* тиа́ра.

tick /tɪk/ *n* (*noise*) ти́канье; (*mark*) пти́чка; *vi* ти́кать *impf*, ти́кнуть *pf*; *vt* отмеча́ть *impf*, отме́тить *pf* пти́чкой; **~ off** (*scold*) отде́лывать *impf*, отде́лать *pf*.

ticket /ˈtɪkɪt/ *n* биле́т; (*label*) ярлы́к; (*season ~*) ка́рточка; (*cloakroom ~*) номеро́к; (*receipt*) квита́нция; **~ collector** контролёр; **~ office** (биле́тная) ка́сса.

tickle /ˈtɪk(ə)l/ *n* щеко́тка; *vt* щекота́ть *impf*, по~ *pf*; (*amuse*) весели́ть *impf*, по~, раз~ *pf*; *vi* щекота́ть *impf*, по~ *pf impers*; **my throat ~s** у меня́ щеко́чет в го́рле. **ticklish** /ˈtɪklɪʃ/ *adj* (*fig*) щекотли́вый; **to be ~** боя́ться *impf* щеко́тки.

tidal /ˈtaɪd(ə)l/ *adj* прили́во-отли́вный; **~ wave** прили́вная волна́.

tide /taɪd/ *n* прили́в и отли́в; **high ~** прили́в; **low ~** отли́в; (*current, tendency*) тече́ние; **the ~ turns** (*fig*) собы́тия принима́ют друго́й оборо́т; *vt*: **~ over** помога́ть *impf*, помо́чь *pf* +*dat of person* спра́виться (*difficulty* с+*instr*); **will this money ~ you over?** вы протя́нете с э́тими деньга́ми?

tidiness /ˈtaɪdɪnɪs/ *n* аккура́тность. **tidy** /-dɪ/ *adj* аккура́тный; (*considerable*) поря́дочный; *vt* убира́ть *impf*, убра́ть *pf*; приводи́ть *impf*, привести́ *pf* в поря́док.

tie /taɪ/ *n* (*garment*) га́лстук; (*cord*) завя́зка; (*link; tech*) связь; (*equal points etc.*) ра́вный счёт; **end in a ~** зака́нчиваться *impf*, зако́нчиться *pf* вничью́; (*burden*) обу́за; *pl* (*bonds*) у́зы (уз) *pl*; *vt* свя́зывать *impf*, связа́ть *pf* (*also fig*); (*~ up*) завя́зывать *impf*, завяза́ть *pf*; (*restrict*) ограни́чивать *impf*, ограни́чить *pf*; **~ down** (*fasten*) привя́зывать *impf*, привяза́ть *pf*; **~ up** (*tether*) привя́зывать *impf*, привяза́ть *pf*; (*parcel*) перевя́зывать *impf*, перевяза́ть *pf*; *vi* (*be ~d*) завя́зываться *impf*, завяза́ться *pf*; (*sport*) сыгра́ть *pf* вничью́; **~ in, up, with** совпада́ть *impf*, совпа́сть *pf* с+*instr*.

tier /tɪə(r)/ *n* ряд, я́рус.

tiff /tɪf/ *n* размо́лвка.
tiger /ˈtaɪɡə(r)/ *n* тигр.
tight /taɪt/ *adj* (*cramped*) те́сный; у́зкий; (*strict*) стро́гий; (*taut*) туго́й; **~ corner** (*fig*) тру́дное положе́ние. **tighten** /-t(ə)n/ *vt* & *i* натя́гиваться *impf*, натяну́ться *pf*; (*clench, contract*) сжима́ть(ся) *impf*, сжа́ться *pf*; **~ one's belt** поту́же затя́гивать *impf*, затяну́ть *pf* по́яс (*also fig*); **~ up** (*discipline etc.*) подтя́гивать *impf*, подтяну́ть *pf* (*coll*). **tightly** /-lɪ/ *adv* (*strongly*) про́чно; (*closely, cramped*) те́сно. **tightrope** *n* натя́нутый кана́т. **tights** /taɪts/ *n pl* колго́тки (-ток) *pl*.
tile /taɪl/ *n* (*roof*) черепи́ца (*also collect*); (*decorative*) ка́фель *m* (*also collect*); *vt* крыть *impf*, по~ *pf* черепи́цей, ка́фелем. **tiled** /-d/ *adj* (*roof*) черепи́чный; (*floor*) ка́фельный.
till[1] /tɪl/ *prep* до+*gen*; **not ~** то́лько (**Friday** в пя́тницу; **the next day** на сле́дующий день); *conj* пока́ не; **not ~** то́лько когда́.
till[2] /tɪl/ *n* ка́сса.
till[3] /tɪl/ *vt* возде́лывать *impf*, возде́лать *pf*.
tiller /ˈtɪlə(r)/ *n* (*naut*) ру́мпель *m*.
tilt /tɪlt/ *n* накло́н; **at full ~** по́лным хо́дом; *vt* & *i* наклоня́ть(ся) *impf*, наклони́ть(ся) *pf*; (*heel (over)*) крени́ть(ся) *impf*, на~ *pf*.
timber /ˈtɪmbə(r)/ *n* лесоматериа́л.
time /taɪm/ *n* вре́мя *neut*; (*occasion*) раз; (*mus*) такт; (*sport*) тайм; *pl* (*period*) времена́ *pl*; (*in comparison*) раз; **five ~s as big** в пять раз бо́льше; (*multiplication*) **four ~s four** четы́режды четы́ре; **~ and ~ again, ~ after ~** не раз, ты́сячу раз; **at a ~** ра́зом, одновре́ме́нно; **at the ~** в э́то вре́мя; **at ~s** времена́ми; **at the same ~** в то же вре́мя; **before my ~** до меня́; **for a long ~** до́лго; (*up to now*) давно́; **for the ~ being** пока́; **from ~ to ~** вре́мя от вре́мени; **in ~** (*early enough*) во́время; (*with ~*) со вре́менем; **in good ~** заблаговре́менно; **in ~ with** в такт +*dat*; **in no ~** момента́льно; **on ~** во́-время; **one at a ~** по одному́; **be in ~** успева́ть *impf*, успе́ть *pf* (**for** к+*dat*, на+*acc*); **have ~ to** (*manage*) успева́ть *impf*, успе́ть *pf* +*inf*; **have a good ~** хорошо́ проводи́ть *impf*, провести́ *pf* вре́мя; **it is ~** пора́ (**to** +*inf*); **what is the ~?** кото́рый час?; **~ bomb** бо́мба заме́дленного де́йствия; **~-consuming** отнима́ющий мно́го вре́мени; **~ difference** ра́зница во вре́мени; **~-lag** отстава́ние во вре́мени; **~ zone** часово́й по́яс; *vt* (*choose ~*) выбира́ть *impf*, вы́брать *pf* вре́мя +*gen*; (*ascertain ~ of*) измеря́ть *impf*, изме́рить *pf* вре́мя +*gen*. **timeless** /-lɪs/ *adj* ве́чный. **timely** /-lɪ/ *adj* своевре́менный. **timetable** *n* расписа́ние; гра́фик.
timid /ˈtɪmɪd/ *adj* ро́бкий.
tin /tɪn/ *n* (*metal*) о́лово; (*container*) ба́нка; (*cake-~*) фо́рма; (*baking ~*) про́тивень *m*; **~ foil** оловя́нная фольга́; **~-opener** консе́рвный нож; **~ned food** консе́рвы (-вов) *pl*.
tinge /tɪndʒ/ *n* отте́нок; *vt* (*also fig*) слегка́ окра́шивать *impf*, окра́сить *pf*.
tingle /ˈtɪŋɡlɪŋ/ *vi* (*sting*) коло́ть *impf impers*; **my fingers ~** у меня́ ко́лет па́льцы; **his nose ~d with the cold** моро́з пощи́пывал ему́ нос; (*burn*) горе́ть *impf*.
tinker /ˈtɪŋkə(r)/ *vi*: **~ with** вози́ться *impf* с+*instr*.
tinkle /ˈtɪŋk(ə)l/ *n* звон, звя́канье; *vi* (& *t*) звене́ть *impf* (+*instr*).
tinsel /ˈtɪns(ə)l/ *n* мишура́.
tint /tɪnt/ *n* отте́нок; *vt* подкра́шивать *impf*, подкра́сить *pf*.
tiny /ˈtaɪnɪ/ *adj* кро́шечный.
tip[1] /tɪp/ *n* (*end*) ко́нчик
tip[2] /tɪp/ *n* (*money*) чаевы́е (-ы́х) *pl*; (*advice*) сове́т; (*dump*) сва́лка; *vt* & *i* (*tilt*) наклоня́ть(ся) *impf*, наклони́ть(ся) *pf*; (*give ~*) дава́ть

t

impf, дать *pf* (*person* +*dat*; *money* де́ньги на чай, *information* ча́стную информа́цию); ~ **out** выва́ливать *impf*, вы́валить *pf*; ~ **over, up** (*vt* & *i*) опроки́дывать(ся) *impf*, опроки́нуть(ся) *pf*.

Tippex /ˈtɪpeks/ *n* (*propr*) бели́ла.

tipple /ˈtɪp(ə)l/ *n* напи́ток.

tipsy /ˈtɪpsɪ/ *adj* подвы́пивший.

tiptoe /ˈtɪptəʊ/ *n*: **on ~** на цы́почках.

tip-top /ˈtɪptɒp/ *adj* превосхо́дный.

tirade /taɪˈreɪd/ *n* тира́да.

tire /ˈtaɪə(r)/ *vt* (*weary*) утомля́ть *impf*, утоми́ть *pf*; *vi* утомля́ться *impf*, утоми́ться *pf*. **tired** /ˈtaɪəd/ *adj* уста́лый; **be ~ of: I am ~ of him** он мне надое́л; **I am ~ of playing** мне надое́ло игра́ть; **~ out** изму́ченный. **tiredness** /ˈtaɪədnɪs/ *n* уста́лость. **tireless** /ˈtaɪəlɪs/ *adj* неутоми́мый. **tiresome** /ˈtaɪəsəm/ *adj* надое́дливый. **tiring** /ˈtaɪərɪŋ/ *adj* утоми́тельный.

tissue /ˈtɪʃuː/ *n* ткань; (*handkerchief*) бума́жная салфе́тка. **tissue-paper** *n* папиро́сная бума́га.

tit[1] /tɪt/ *n* (*bird*) сини́ца.

tit[2] /tɪt/ *n*: **~ for tat** зуб за́ зуб.

titbit /ˈtɪtbɪt/ *n* ла́комый кусо́к; (*news*) пика́нтная но́вость.

titillate /ˈtɪtɪˌleɪt/ *vt* щекота́ть *impf*, по~ *pf*.

title /ˈtaɪt(ə)l/ *n* (*of book etc.*) загла́вие; (*rank*) зва́ние; (*sport*) зва́ние чемпио́на; **~-holder** чемпио́н; **~-page** ти́тульный лист; **~ role** загла́вная роль. **titled** /ˈtaɪt(ə)ld/ *adj* титуло́ванный.

titter /ˈtɪtə(r)/ *n* хихи́канье; *vi* хихи́кать *impf*, хихи́кнуть *pf*.

to /tuː/ *prep* (*town*, *a country*, *theatre*, *school*, *etc.*) в+*acc*; (*the sea*, *the moon*, *the ground*, *post-office*, *meeting*, *concert*, *north*, *etc.*) на+*acc*; (*the doctor*; *towards*, *up* ~; ~ *one's surprise etc.*) к+*dat*; (*with accompaniment of*) под+*acc*; (*in toast*) за+*acc*; (*time*): **ten minutes ~ three** без десяти́ три; (*compared with*) в сравне́нии с+*instr*; **it is ten ~ one that** де́вять из десяти́ за то, что; **~ the left (right)** нале́во (напра́во); (*in order to*) что́бы +*inf*; *adv*: **shut the door ~** закро́йте дверь; **come ~** приходи́ть *impf*, прийти́ *pf* в созна́ние; **~ and fro** взад и вперёд.

toad /təʊd/ *n* жа́ба. **toadstool** *n* пога́нка.

toast /təʊst/ *n* (*bread*) поджа́ренный хлеб; (*drink*) тост; *vt* (*bread*) поджа́ривать *impf*, поджа́рить *pf*; (*drink*) пить *impf*, вы́~ *pf* за здоро́вье +*gen*. **toaster** /ˈtəʊstə(r)/ *n* то́стер.

tobacco /təˈbækəʊ/ *n* таба́к. **tobacconist's** /-kənɪsts/ *n* (*shop*) таба́чный магази́н.

toboggan /təˈbɒgən/ *n* са́ни (-не́й) *pl*; *vi* ката́ться *impf* на саня́х.

today /təˈdeɪ/ *adv* сего́дня; (*nowadays*) в на́ши дни; *n* сего́дняшний день *m*; **~'s newspaper** сего́дняшняя газе́та.

toddler /ˈtɒdlə(r)/ *n* малы́ш.

toe /təʊ/ *n* па́лец ноги́; (*of sock etc.*) носо́к; *vt*: **~ the line** (*fig*) ходи́ть *indet* по стру́нке.

toffee /ˈtɒfɪ/ *n* (*substance*) ири́с; (*a single* ~) ири́ска.

together /təˈgeðə(r)/ *adv* вме́сте; (*simultaneously*) одновре́ме́нно.

toil /tɔɪl/ *n* тяжёлый труд; *vi* труди́ться *impf*.

toilet /ˈtɔɪlɪt/ *n* туале́т; **~ paper** туале́тная бума́га. **toiletries** /-trɪz/ *n pl* туале́тные принадле́жности *f pl*.

token /ˈtəʊkən/ *n* (*sign*) знак; (*coin substitute*) жето́н; **as a ~ of** в знак +*gen*; *attrib* символи́ческий.

tolerable /ˈtɒlərəb(ə)l/ *adj* терпи́мый; (*satisfactory*) удовлетвори́тельный. **tolerance** /ˈtɒlərəns/ *n* терпи́мость. **tolerant** /-rənt/ *adj* терпи́мый. **tolerate** /-ˌreɪt/ *vt* терпе́ть *impf*, по~ *pf*; (*allow*) до-

t

пуска́ть *impf*, допусти́ть *pf*. **toleration** /ˌtɒləˈreɪʃ(ə)n/ *n* терпи́мость.
toll[1] /təʊl/ *n* (*duty*) по́шлина; **take its ~** ска́зываться *impf*, сказа́ться *pf* (**on** на+*prep*).
toll[2] /təʊl/ *vi* звони́ть *impf*, по~ *pf*.
tom(-cat) /ˈtɒm(kæt)/ *n* кот.
tomato /təˈmɑːtəʊ/ *n* помидо́р; *attrib* тома́тный.
tomb /tuːm/ *n* моги́ла. **tombstone** *n* надгро́бный ка́мень *m*.
tomboy /ˈtɒmbɔɪ/ *n* сорване́ц.
tome /təʊm/ *n* том.
tomorrow /təˈmɒrəʊ/ *adv* за́втра; *n* за́втрашний день *m*; **~ morning** за́втра у́тром; **the day after ~** послеза́втра; **see you ~** до за́втра.
ton /tʌn/ *n* то́нна; (*pl*, *lots*) ма́сса.
tone /təʊn/ *n* тон; *vt*: **~ down** смягча́ть *impf*, смягчи́ть *pf*; **~ up** тонизи́ровать *impf* & *pf*.
tongs /tɒŋz/ *n* щипцы́ (-цо́в) *pl*.
tongue /tʌŋ/ *n* язы́к; **~-in-cheek** с насме́шкой, ирони́чески; **~-tied** косноязы́чный; **~-twister** скорогово́рка.
tonic /ˈtɒnɪk/ *n* (*med*) тонизи́рующее сре́дство; (*mus*) то́ника; (*drink*) напи́ток «то́ник».
tonight /təˈnaɪt/ *adv* сего́дня ве́чером.
tonnage /ˈtʌnɪdʒ/ *n* тонна́ж.
tonsil /ˈtɒns(ə)l/ *n* минда́лина. **tonsillitis** /ˌtɒnsɪˈlaɪtɪs/ *n* тонзилли́т.
too /tuː/ *adv* сли́шком; (*also*) та́кже, то́же; (*very*) о́чень; (*moreover*) к тому́ же; **none ~** не сли́шком.
tool /tuːl/ *n* инструме́нт; (*fig*) ору́дие.
toot /tuːt/ *n* гудо́к; *vi* гуде́ть *impf*.
tooth /tuːθ/ *n* зуб; (*tech*) зубе́ц; *attrib* зубно́й; **~-brush** зубна́я щётка. **toothache** *n* зубна́я боль. **toothless** /-lɪs/ *adj* беззу́бый. **toothpaste** *n* зубна́я па́ста. **toothpick** *n* зубочи́стка. **toothy** /-θɪ/ *adj* зуба́стый (*coll*).
top[1] /tɒp/ *n* (*toy*) волчо́к.
top[2] /tɒp/ *n* (*of object*; *fig*) верх; (*of hill etc.*) верши́на; (*of tree*) верху́шка; (*of head*) маку́шка; (*lid*) кры́шка; (*upper part*) ве́рхняя часть; **~ hat** цили́ндр; **~-heavy** переве́шивающий в свое́й ве́рхней ча́сти; **~-secret** соверше́нно секре́тный; **on ~ of** (*position*) на +*prep*, сверх +*gen*; (*on to*) на+*acc*; **on ~ of everything** сверх всего́; **from ~ to bottom** све́рху до́низу; **at the ~ of one's voice** во весь го́лос; **at ~ speed** во весь опо́р; *adj* ве́рхний, вы́сший, са́мый высо́кий; (*foremost*) пе́рвый; *vt* (*cover*) покрыва́ть *impf*, покры́ть *pf*; (*exceed*) превосходи́ть *impf*, превзойти́ *pf*; (*cut ~ off*) обреза́ть *impf*, обре́зать *pf* верху́шку +*gen*; **~ up** (*with liquid*) долива́ть *impf*, доли́ть *pf*.
topic /ˈtɒpɪk/ *n* те́ма, предме́т. **topical** /ˈtɒpɪk(ə)l/ *adj* актуа́льный.
topless /ˈtɒplɪs/ *adj* с обнажённой гру́дью.
topmost /ˈtɒpməʊst/ *adj* са́мый ве́рхний; са́мый ва́жный.
topographical /ˌtɒpəˈgræfɪk(ə)l/ *adj* топографи́ческий. **topography** /təˈpɒgrəfɪ/ *n* топогра́фия.
topple /ˈtɒp(ə)l/ *vt* & *i* опроки́дывать(ся) *impf*, опроки́нуть(ся) *pf*.
topsy-turvy /ˌtɒpsɪˈtɜːvɪ/ *adj* повёрнутый вверх дном; (*disorderly*) беспоря́дочный; *adv* вверх дном.
torch /tɔːtʃ/ *n* электри́ческий фона́рь *m*; (*flaming*) фа́кел.
torment /ˈtɔːment/ *n* муче́ние, му́ка; *vt* му́чить *impf*, за~, из~ *pf*.
tornado /tɔːˈneɪdəʊ/ *n* торна́до *neut indecl*.
torpedo /tɔːˈpiːdəʊ/ *n* торпе́да; *vt* торпеди́ровать *impf* & *pf*.
torrent /ˈtɒrənt/ *n* пото́к **torrential** /təˈrenʃ(ə)l/ *adj* (*rain*) проливно́й.
torso /ˈtɔːsəʊ/ *n* ту́ловище; (*art*) торс.
tortoise /ˈtɔːtəs/ *n* черепа́ха.

t

tortoise-shell *n* черепа́ха.

tortuous /ˈtɔːtjʊəs/ *adj* изви́листый.

torture /ˈtɔːtʃə(r)/ *n* пы́тка; (*fig*) му́ка; *vt* пыта́ть *impf*; (*torment*) му́чить *impf*, за~, из~ *pf*.

toss /tɒs/ *n* бросо́к; **win (lose) the ~** (не) выпада́ть *impf*, вы́пасть *pf* жре́бий *impers* (**I won the ~** мне вы́пал жре́бий); *vt* броса́ть *impf*, бро́сить *pf*; (*coin*) подбра́сывать *impf*, подбро́сить *pf*; (*head*) вски́дывать *impf*, вски́нуть *pf*; (*salad*) переме́шивать *impf*, перемеша́ть *pf*; *vi* (*in bed*) мета́ться *impf*; **~ aside, away** отбра́сывать *impf*, отбро́сить *pf*; **~ up** броса́ть *impf*, бро́сить *pf* жре́бий.

tot[1] /tɒt/ *n* (*child*) малы́ш; (*of liquor*) глото́к.

tot[2] /tɒt/ *vt* & *i* : **~ up** (*vt*) скла́дывать *impf*, сложи́ть *pf*; (*vi*) равня́ться *impf* (**to** *+dat*).

total /ˈtəʊt(ə)l/ *n* ито́г, су́мма; *adj* о́бщий; (*complete*) по́лный; **in ~** в це́лом, вме́сте; *vt* подсчи́тывать *impf*, подсчита́ть *pf*; *vi* равня́ться *impf +dat*. **totalitarian** /təʊˌtælɪˈteərɪən/ *adj* тоталита́рный. **totality** /təʊˈtælɪtɪ/ *n* вся су́мма целико́м; **the ~ of** весь. **totally** /ˈtəʊtəlɪ/ *adv* соверше́нно.

totter /ˈtɒtə(r)/ *vi* шата́ться *impf*.

touch /tʌtʃ/ *n* прикоснове́ние; (*sense*) осяза́ние; (*shade*) отте́нок; (*taste*) при́вкус; (*small amount*) чу́точка; (*of illness*) лёгкий при́ступ; **get in ~ with** свя́зываться *impf*, связа́ться *pf* с*+instr*; **keep in (lose) ~ with** подде́рживать *impf*, поддержа́ть *pf* (теря́ть *impf*, по~ *pf*) связь, конта́кт с*+instr*; **put the finishing ~es to** отде́лывать *impf*, отде́лать *pf*; *vt* (*lightly*) прикаса́ться *impf*, прикосну́ться *pf* к*+dat*; каса́ться *impf*, косну́ться *pf +gen*; (*also disturb*; *affect*) тро́гать *impf*, тро́нуть *pf*; (*be comparable with*) идти́ *impf* в сравне́нии с*+instr*; *vi* (*be contiguous*; *come into contact*) соприкаса́ться *impf*, соприкосну́ться *pf*; **~ down** приземля́ться *impf*, приземли́ться *pf*; **~down** поса́дка; **~ (up)on** (*fig*) каса́ться *impf*, косну́ться *pf +gen*; **~ up** поправля́ть *impf*, попра́вить *pf*. **touched** /tʌtʃt/ *adj* тро́нутый. **touchiness** /ˈtʌtʃɪnɪs/ *n* оби́дчивость. **touching** /ˈtʌtʃɪŋ/ *adj* тро́гательный. **touchstone** *n* про́бный ка́мень *m*. **touchy** /ˈtʌtʃɪ/ *adj* оби́дчивый.

tough /tʌf/ *adj* жёсткий; (*durable*) про́чный; (*difficult*) тру́дный; (*hardy*) выно́сливый. **toughen** /ˈtʌf(ə)n/ *vt* & *i* де́лать(ся) *impf*, с~ *pf* жёстким.

tour /tʊə(r)/ *n* (*journey*) путеше́ствие, пое́здка; (*excursion*) экску́рсия; (*of artistes*) гастро́ли *f pl*; (*of duty*) объе́зд; *vi* (& *t*) путеше́ствовать *impf* (по *+dat*); (*theat*) гастроли́ровать *impf*. **tourism** /ˈtʊərɪz(ə)m/ *n* тури́зм. **tourist** /ˈtʊərɪst/ *n* тури́ст, ~ка.

tournament /ˈtʊənəmənt/ *n* турни́р.

tousle /ˈtaʊz(ə)l/ *vt* взъеро́шивать *impf*, взъеро́шить *pf* (*coll*).

tout /taʊt/ *n* зазыва́ла *m*; (*ticket ~*) жучо́к

tow /təʊ/ *vt* букси́ровать *impf*; *n*: **on ~** на букси́ре.

towards /təˈwɔːdz/ *prep* к*+dat*.

towel /ˈtaʊəl/ *n* полоте́нце.

tower /ˈtaʊə(r)/ *n* ба́шня; *vi* вы́ситься *impf*, возвыша́ться *impf* (**above** над*+instr*).

town /taʊn/ *n* го́род; *attrib* городско́й; **~ hall** ра́туша. **townsman** *n* горожа́нин.

toxic /ˈtɒksɪk/ *adj* токси́ческий.

toy /tɔɪ/ *n* игру́шка; *vi*: **~ with** (*sth in hands*) верте́ть *impf* в рука́х; (*trifle with*) игра́ть *impf* (с)*+instr*.

trace /treɪs/ *n* след; *vt* (*track (down)*) выousле́живать *impf*, вы́следить *pf*; (*copy*) кальки́ровать *impf*, с~ *pf*; **~ out** (*plan*) набра́сывать *impf*, наброса́ть *pf*; (*map, diagram*) черти́ть *impf*, на~ *pf*.

t

tracing-paper /'treɪsɪŋ,peɪpə(r)/ *n* ка́лька.

track /træk/ *n* (*path*) доро́жка; (*mark*) след; (*rly*) путь *m*, (*sport, on tape*) доро́жка; (*on record*) за́пись; **~ suit** трениро́вочный костю́м; **off the beaten ~** в глуши́; **go off the ~** (*fig*) отклоня́ться *impf*, отклони́ться *pf* от те́мы; **keep ~ of** следи́ть *impf* за+*instr*; **lose ~ of** теря́ть *impf*, по~ *pf* след+*gen*; *vt* просле́живать *impf*, проследи́ть *pf*; **~ down** высле́живать *impf*, вы́следить *pf*.

tract[1] /trækt/ *n* (*land*) простра́нство.

tract[2] /trækt/ *n* (*pamphlet*) брошю́ра.

tractor /'træktə(r)/ *n* тра́ктор.

trade /treɪd/ *n* торго́вля; (*occupation*) профе́ссия, ремесло́; **~ mark** фабри́чная ма́рка; **~ union** профсою́з; **~-unionist** член профсою́за; *vi* торгова́ть *impf* (**in** +*instr*); *vt* (*swap like things*) обме́ниваться *impf*, обменя́ться *pf* +*instr*; (*~ for sth different*) обме́нивать *impf*, обменя́ть *pf* (**for** на+*acc*); **~ in** сдава́ть *impf*, сдать *pf* в счёт поку́пки но́вого. **trader, tradesman** /-də(r), -dzmən/ *n* торго́вец. **trading** /-dɪŋ/ *n* торго́вля.

tradition /trə'dɪʃ(ə)n/ *n* тради́ция. **traditional** /-n(ə)l/ *adj* традицио́нный. **traditionally** /-nəlɪ/ *adv* по тради́ции.

traffic /'træfɪk/ *n* движе́ние; (*trade*) торго́вля; **~ jam** про́бка; *vi* торгова́ть *impf* (**in** +*instr*). **trafficker** /-kə(r)/ *n* торго́вец (**in** +*instr*). **traffic-lights** *n pl* светофо́р.

tragedy /'trædʒɪdɪ/ *n* траге́дия. **tragic** /'trædʒɪk/ *adj* траги́ческий.

trail /treɪl/ *n* (*trace, track*) след; (*path*) тропи́нка; *vt* (*track*) высле́живать *impf*, вы́следить *pf*; *vt & i* (*drag*) таска́ть(ся) *indet*, тащи́ть(ся) *det*. **trailer** /-lə(r)/ *n* (*on vehicle*) прице́п; (*cin*) (кино-)ро́лик.

train /treɪn/ *n* по́езд; (*of dress*) шлейф; *vt* (*instruct*) обуча́ть *impf*, обучи́ть *pf* (**in** +*dat*); (*prepare*) гото́вить *impf* (**for** к+*dat*); (*sport*) тренирова́ть *impf*, на~ *pf*; (*animals*) дрессирова́ть *impf*, вы́~ *pf*; (*aim*) наводи́ть *impf*, навести́ *pf*; (*plant*) направля́ть *impf*, напра́вить *pf* рост+*gen*; *vi* пригота́вливаться *impf*, пригото́виться *pf* (**for** к+*dat*); (*sport*) тренирова́ться *impf*, на~ *pf*. **trainee** /-'niː/ *n* стажёр, практика́нт. **trainer** /-nə(r)/ *n* (*sport*) тре́нер; (*of animals*) дрессиро́вщик; (*shoe*) кроссо́вка. **training** /-nɪŋ/ *n* обуче́ние; (*sport*) трениро́вка; (*of animals*) дрессиро́вка; **~-college** (*teachers'*) педагоги́ческий институ́т.

traipse /treɪps/ *vi* таска́ться *indet*, тащи́ться *det*.

trait /treɪ/ *n* черта́.

traitor /'treɪtə(r)/ *n* преда́тель *m*, ~ница.

trajectory /trə'dʒektərɪ/ *n* траекто́рия.

tram /træm/ *n* трамва́й.

tramp /træmp/ *n* (*vagrant*) бродя́га *m*; *vi* (*walk heavily*) то́пать *impf*. **trample** /-p(ə)l/ *vt* топта́ть *impf*, по~, ис~ *pf*; **~ down** выта́птывать *impf*, вы́топтать *pf*; **~ on** (*fig*) попира́ть *impf*, попра́ть *pf*.

trampoline /,træmpə'liːn/ *n* бату́т.

trance /trɑːns/ *n* транс.

tranquil /'træŋkwɪl/ *adj* споко́йный. **tranquillity** /-'kwɪlɪtɪ/ *n* споко́йствие. **tranquillize** /'trænkwɪ,laɪz/ *vt* успока́ивать *impf*, успоко́ить *pf*. **tranquillizer** /-,laɪzə(r)/ *n* транквилиза́тор.

transact /træn'zækt/ *vt* (*business*) вести́ *impf*; (*a deal*) заключа́ть *impf*, заключи́ть *pf*. **transaction** /-'zækʃ(ə)n/ *n* де́ло, сде́лка; *pl* (*publications*) труды́ *m pl*.

transatlantic /,trænzət'læntɪk/ *adj* трансатланти́ческий.

transcend /træn'send/ *vt* превосходи́ть *impf*, превзойти́ *pf*. **transcendental** /,trænsen'dent(ə)l/ *adj* (*philos.*) трансцендента́льный.

transcribe /træn'skraɪb/ *vt* (*copy out*) переписывать *impf*, переписа́ть *pf.* **transcript** /'trænskrɪpt/ *n* ко́пия. **transcription** /træn'skrɪpʃ(ə)n/ *n* (*copy*) ко́пия.

transfer *n* /'trænsfɜː(r)/ (*of objects*) перено́с, перемеще́ние; (*of money*; *of people*) перево́д; (*of property*) переда́ча; (*design*) переводна́я карти́нка; *vt* /træns'fɜː(r)/ (*objects*) переноси́ть *impf*, перенести́ *pf*; перемеща́ть *impf*, перемести́ть *pf*; (*money*; *people*; *design*) переводи́ть *impf*, перевести́ *pf*; (*property*) передава́ть *impf*, переда́ть *pf*; *vi* (*to different job*) переходи́ть *impf*, перейти́ *pf*; (*change trains etc.*) переса́живаться *impf*, пересе́сть *pf.* **transferable** /træns'fɜːrəb(ə)l/ *adj* допуска́ющий переда́чу.

transfix /træns'fɪks/ *vt* (*fig*) прико́вывать *impf*, прикова́ть *pf* к ме́сту.

transform /træns'fɔːm/ *vt* & *i* преобразо́вывать(ся) *impf*, преобразова́ть(ся) *pf*; ~ **into** *vt* (*i*) превраща́ть(ся) *impf*, преврати́ть(ся) *pf* в+*acc.* **transformation** /ˌtrænsfə'meɪʃ(ə)n/ *n* преобразова́ние; превраще́ние. **transformer** /træns'fɔːmə(r)/ *n* трансформа́тор.

transfusion /træns'fjuːʒ(ə)n/ *n* перелива́ние (кро́ви).

transgress /trænz'gres/ *vt* наруша́ть *impf*, нару́шить *pf*; *vi* (*sin*) греши́ть *impf*, за~ *pf.* **transgression** /-'greʃ(ə)n/ *n* наруше́ние; (*sin*) грех.

transience /'trænzɪəns/ *n* мимолётность. **transient** /'trænzɪənt/ *adj* мимолётный.

transistor /træn'zɪstə(r)/ *n* транзи́стор; ~ **radio** транзи́сторный приёмник.

transit /'trænzɪt/ *n* транзи́т; **in** ~ (*goods*) при перево́зке; (*person*) по пути́; ~ **camp** транзи́тный ла́герь *m*. **transition** /-'zɪʃ(ə)n/ *n* перехо́д. **transitional** /-'zɪʃənəl/ *adj* перехо́дный. **transitive** /'trænsɪtɪv/ *adj* перехо́дный. **transitory** /'trænsɪtərɪ/ *adj* мимолётный.

translate /træn'sleɪt/ *vt* переводи́ть *impf*, перевести́ *pf.* **translation** /-'leɪʃən/ *n* перево́д. **translator** /-'leɪtə(r)/ *n* перево́дчик.

translucent /trænz'luːs(ə)nt/ *adj* полупрозра́чный.

transmission /trænz'mɪʃ(ə)n/ *n* переда́ча. **transmit** /-'mɪt/ *vt* передава́ть *impf*, переда́ть *pf.* **transmitter** /-'mɪtə(r)/ *n* (радио)переда́тчик.

transparency /træns'pærənsɪ/ *n* (*phot*) диапозити́в. **transparent** /-rənt/ *adj* прозра́чный.

transpire /træn'spaɪə(r)/ *vi* (*become known*) обнару́живаться *impf*, обнару́житься *pf*; (*occur*) случа́ться *impf*, случи́ться *pf.*

transplant *vt* /træns'plɑːnt/ переса́живать *impf*, пересади́ть *pf*; (*med*) де́лать *impf*, с~ *pf* переса́дку+*gen*; *n* /'trænsplɑːnt/ (*med*) переса́дка.

transport *n* /'trænspɔːt/ (*various senses*) тра́нспорт; (*conveyance*) перево́зка; *attrib* тра́нспортный; *vt* /træns'pɔːt/ перевози́ть *impf*, перевезти́ *pf.* **transportation** /ˌtrænspɔː'teɪʃ(ə)n/ *n* тра́нспорт, перево́зка.

transpose /træns'pəʊz/ *vt* переставля́ть *impf*, переста́вить *pf*; (*mus*) транспони́ровать *impf* & *pf.* **transposition** /ˌtrænspə'zɪʃ(ə)n/ *n* перестано́вка; (*mus*) транспони́ро́вка.

transverse /'trænzvɜːs/ *adj* попере́чный.

transvestite /trænz'vestaɪt/ *n* трансвести́т.

trap /træp/ *n* лову́шка (*also fig*), западня́; *vt* (*catch*) лови́ть *impf*, пойма́ть *pf* (в лову́шку); (*jam*) защемля́ть *impf*, защеми́ть *pf.* **trapdoor** *n* люк.

trapeze /trə'piːz/ *n* трапе́ция.

trapper /'træpə(r)/ *n* зверело́в.

trappings /'træpɪŋz/ *n pl* (*fig*) (*ex-*

t

terior attributes) внéшние атрибу́ты *m pl*; (*adornments*) украшéния *neut pl*.

trash /træʃ/ *n* дрянь (*coll*). **trashy** /-ʃɪ/ *adj* дрянно́й.

trauma /ˈtrɔːmə/ *n* трáвма. **traumatic** /-ˈmætɪk/ *adj* травмати́ческий.

travel /ˈtræv(ə)l/ *n* путешéствие; **~ agency** бюро́ *neut indecl* путешéствий; **~ sick: be ~-sick** укáчивать *impf*; укачáть *pf impers* +*acc*; **I am ~-sick in cars** меня́ в маши́не укáчивает; *vi* путешéствовать *impf*; *vt* объезжáть *impf*, объéхать *pf*. **traveller** /-lə(r)/ *n* путешéственник; (*salesman*) коммивояжёр; **~'s cheque** тури́стский чек.

traverse /ˈtrævəs/ *vt* пересекáть *impf*, пересéчь *pf*.

travesty /ˈtrævɪstɪ/ *n* паро́дия.

trawler /ˈtrɔːlə(r)/ *n* трáулер.

tray /treɪ/ *n* подно́с; **in- (out-)~** корзи́нка для входя́щих (исходя́щих) бумáг.

treacherous /ˈtretʃərəs/ *adj* предáтельский; (*unsafe*) ненадёжный. **treachery** /ˈtretʃərɪ/ *n* предáтельство.

treacle /ˈtriːk(ə)l/ *n* пáтока.

tread /tred/ *n* похо́дка; (*stair*) ступéнька; (*of tyre*) протéктор; *vi* ступáть *impf*, ступи́ть *pf*; **~ on** наступáть *impf*, наступи́ть *pf* на+*acc*; *vt* топтáть *impf*.

treason /ˈtriːz(ə)n/ *n* измéна.

treasure /ˈtreʒə(r)/ *n* сокро́вище; *vt* высоко́ цени́ть *impf*. **treasurer** /ˈtreʒərə(r)/ *n* казначéй. **treasury** /ˈtreʒərɪ/ *n* (*also fig*) сокро́вищница; **the T~** госудáрственное казначéйство.

treat /triːt/ *n* (*pleasure*) удово́льствие; (*entertainment*) угощéние; *vt* (*have as guest*) угощáть *impf*, угости́ть *pf* (**to** +*instr*); (*med*) лечи́ть *impf* (**for** от+*gen*; **with** +*instr*); (*behave towards*) обращáться *impf* с+*instr*; (*process*) обрабáтывать *impf*, обрабо́тать *pf* (**with** +*instr*); (*discuss*) трактовáть *impf* о+*prep*; (*regard*) относи́ться *impf*, отнести́сь *pf* к+*dat* (**as** как к+*dat*). **treatise** /-tɪs/ *n* трактáт. **treatment** /-mənt/ *n* (*behaviour*) обращéние; (*med*) лечéние; (*processing*) обрабо́тка; (*discussion*) тракто́вка. **treaty** /-tɪ/ *n* догово́р.

treble /ˈtreb(ə)l/ *adj* тройно́й; (*trebled*) утро́енный; *adv* втро́е; *n* (*mus*) ди́скáнт; *vt & i* утрáивать(ся) *impf*, утро́ить(ся) *pf*.

tree /triː/ *n* дéрево.

trek /trek/ *n* (*migration*) переселéние; (*journey*) путешéствие; *vi* (*migrate*) переселя́ться *impf*, пересели́ться *pf*; (*journey*) путешéствовать *impf*.

trellis /ˈtrelɪs/ *n* шпалéра; (*for creepers*) решётка.

tremble /ˈtremb(ə)l/ *vi* дрожáть *impf* (**with** от+*gen*). **trembling** /-blɪŋ/ *n* дрожь; **in fear and ~** трепещá.

tremendous /trɪˈmendəs/ *adj* (*huge*) огро́мный; (*excellent*) потрясáющий.

tremor /ˈtremə(r)/ *n* дрожь; (*earthquake*) толчо́к. **tremulous** /-mjʊləs/ *adj* дрожáщий.

trench /trentʃ/ *n* канáва, ров; (*mil*) око́п.

trend /trend/ *n* направлéние, тендéнция. **trendy** /-dɪ/ *adj* мо́дный.

trepidation /ˌtrepɪˈdeɪʃ(ə)n/ *n* трéпет.

trespass /ˈtrespəs/ *n* (*on property*) нарушéние грани́ц; *vi* нарушáть *impf*, нару́шить *pf* грани́цу (**on** +*gen*); (*fig*) вторгáться *impf*, вто́ргнуться *pf* (**on** в+*acc*). **trespasser** /-sə(r)/ *n* наруши́тель *m*.

trestle /ˈtres(ə)l/ *n* ко́злы (-зел, -злам) *pl*; **~ table** стол на ко́злах.

trial /ˈtraɪəl/ *n* (*test*) испытáние (*also ordeal*), про́ба; (*law*) процéсс, суд; (*sport*) попы́тка; **on ~** (*probation*) на испытáнии; (*of objects*) взя́тый на про́бу; (*law*) под судо́м; **~ and error** мéтод проб и оши́бок.

triangle /ˈtraɪˌæŋg(ə)l/ *n* треуго́льник. **triangular** /-ˈæŋgjʊlə(r)/ *adj* треуго́льный.

tribal /ˈtraɪb(ə)l/ *adj* племенно́й. **tribe** /traɪb/ *n* пле́мя *neut*.

tribulation /ˌtrɪbjʊˈleɪʃ(ə)n/ *n* го́ре, несча́стье.

tribunal /traɪˈbjuːn(ə)l/ *n* трибуна́л.

tributary /ˈtrɪbjʊtərɪ/ *n* прито́к. **tribute** /ˈtrɪbjuːt/ *n* дань; **pay ~** (*fig*) отдава́ть *impf*, отда́ть *pf* дань (уваже́ния) (**to** +*dat*).

trice /traɪs/ *n*: **in a ~** мгнове́нно.

trick /trɪk/ *n* (*ruse*) хи́трость; (*deception*) обма́н; (*conjuring ~*) фо́кус; (*stunt*) трюк; (*joke*) шу́тка; (*habit*) привы́чка; (*cards*) взя́тка; **play a ~ on** игра́ть *impf*, сыгра́ть *pf* шу́тку с+*instr*; *vt* обма́нывать *impf*, обману́ть *pf*. **trickery** /-kərɪ/ *n* обма́н.

trickle /ˈtrɪk(ə)l/ *vi* сочи́ться *impf*.

trickster /ˈtrɪkstə(r)/ *n* обма́нщик. **tricky** /-kɪ/ *adj* сло́жный.

tricycle /ˈtraɪsɪk(ə)l/ *n* трёхколёсный велосипе́д.

trifle /ˈtraɪf(ə)l/ *n* пустя́к; **a ~** (*adv*) немно́го +*gen*; *vi* шути́ть *impf*, по~ *pf* (**with** с+*instr*). **trifling** /-flɪŋ/ *adj* пустяко́вый.

trigger /ˈtrɪgə(r)/ *n* (*of gun*) куро́к; *vt*: **~ off** вызыва́ть *impf*, вы́звать *pf*.

trill /trɪl/ *n* трель.

trilogy /ˈtrɪlədʒɪ/ *n* трило́гия.

trim /trɪm/ *n* поря́док, гото́вность; **in fighting ~** в боево́й гото́вности; **in good ~** (*sport*) в хоро́шей фо́рме; (*haircut*) подстри́жка; *adj* опря́тный; *vt* (*cut, clip, cut off*) подреза́ть *impf*, подре́зать *pf*; (*hair*) подстрига́ть *impf*, подстри́чь *pf*; (*a dress etc.*) отде́лывать *impf*, отде́лать *pf*. **trimming** /-mɪŋ/ *n* (*on dress*) отде́лка; (*to food*) гарни́р.

Trinity /ˈtrɪnɪtɪ/ *n* Тро́ица.

trinket /ˈtrɪŋkɪt/ *n* безделу́шка.

trio /ˈtriːəʊ/ *n* три́о *neut indecl*; (*of people*) тро́йка.

trip /trɪp/ *n* пое́здка, путеше́ствие, экску́рсия; (*business ~*) командиро́вка; *vi* (*stumble*) спотыка́ться *impf*, споткну́ться *pf* (**over** о+*acc*); *vt* (*also ~ up*) подставля́ть *impf*, подста́вить *pf* но́жку +*dat* (*also fig*); (*confuse*) запу́тывать *impf*, запу́тать *pf*.

triple /ˈtrɪp(ə)l/ *adj* тройно́й; (*tripled*) утро́енный; *vt & i* утра́ивать(ся) *impf*, утро́ить(ся) *pf*. **triplet** /ˈtrɪplɪt/ *n* (*mus*) трио́ль; (*one of ~s*) близне́ц (из тро́йни); *pl* тро́йня.

tripod /ˈtraɪpɒd/ *n* трено́жник.

trite /traɪt/ *adj* бана́льный.

triumph /ˈtraɪəmf/ *n* торжество́, побе́да; *vi* торжествова́ть *impf*, вос~ *pf* (**over** над+*instr*). **triumphal** /traɪˈʌmf(ə)l/ *adj* триумфа́льный. **triumphant** /traɪˈʌmf(ə)nt/ *adj* (*exultant*) торжеству́ющий; (*victorious*) победоно́сный.

trivia /ˈtrɪvɪə/ *n pl* ме́лочи (-че́й) *pl*. **trivial** /-vɪəl/ *adj* незначи́тельный. **triviality** /ˌtrɪvɪˈælɪtɪ/ *n* тривиа́льность. **trivialize** /ˈtrɪvɪəˌlaɪz/ *vt* опошля́ть *impf*, опо́шлить *pf*.

trolley /ˈtrɒlɪ/ *n* теле́жка; (*table on wheels*) сто́лик на колёсиках. **trolley-bus** *n* тролле́йбус.

trombone /trɒmˈbəʊn/ *n* тромбо́н.

troop /truːp/ *n* гру́ппа, отря́д; *pl* (*mil*) войска́ *neut pl*; *vi* идти́ *impf*, по~ *pf* стро́ем.

trophy /ˈtrəʊfɪ/ *n* трофе́й; (*prize*) приз.

tropic /ˈtrɒpɪk/ *n* тро́пик. **tropical** /-k(ə)l/ *adj* тропи́ческий.

trot /trɒt/ *n* рысь; *vi* рыси́ть *impf*; (*rider*) е́здить *indet*, е́хать *det*, по~ *pf* ры́сью; (*horse*) ходи́ть *indet*, идти́ *det*, пойти́ *pf* ры́сью.

trouble /ˈtrʌb(ə)l/ *n* (*worry*) беспоко́йство, трево́га; (*misfortune*) беда́; (*unpleasantness*) неприя́тности *f pl*; (*effort, pains*) труд; (*care*) забо́та; (*disrepair*) неиспра́вность (**with** в+*prep*); (*illness*) боле́знь; **heart ~** больно́е се́рдце; **~-maker** наруши́тель *m*, **~**ница споко́йствия; **ask for ~** напра́шиваться *impf*, напроси́ться *pf* на неприя́тности; **be in ~** име́ть *impf* неприя́тности; **get into ~** попа́сть *pf* в беду́; **take ~** стара́ться *impf*, по~ *pf*; **take the ~** труди́ться *impf*, по~ *pf* (**to** +*inf*); **the ~ is (that)** беда́ в том, что; *vt* (*make anxious, disturb, give pain*) беспоко́ить *impf*; **may I ~ you for ...?** мо́жно попроси́ть у вас +*acc*?; *vi* (*take the ~*) труди́ться *impf*. **troubled** /ˈtrʌb(ə)ld/ *adj* беспоко́йный. **troublesome** *adj* (*restless, fidgety*) беспоко́йный; (*capricious*) капри́зный; (*difficult*) тру́дный.

trough /trɒf/ *n* (*for food*) корму́шка.

trounce /traʊns/ *vt* (*beat*) поро́ть *impf*, вы́~ *pf*; (*defeat*) разбива́ть *impf*, разби́ть *pf*.

troupe /tru:p/ *n* тру́ппа.

trouser-leg /ˈtraʊzəˌleg/ *n* штани́на (*coll*). **trousers** /ˈtraʊzəz/ *n pl* брю́ки (-к) *pl*, штаны́ (-но́в) *pl*.

trout /traʊt/ *n* форе́ль.

trowel /ˈtraʊəl/ *n* (*for building*) мастеро́к; (*garden ~*) садо́вый сово́к.

truancy /ˈtru:ənsɪ/ *n* прогу́л. **truant** /ˈtru:ənt/ *n* прогу́льщик; **play ~** прогу́ливать *impf*, прогуля́ть *pf*.

truce /tru:s/ *n* переми́рие.

truck[1] /trʌk/ *n*: **have no ~ with** не име́ть никаки́х дел с+*instr*.

truck[2] /trʌk/ *n* (*lorry*) грузови́к; (*rly*) ваго́н-платфо́рма.

truculent /ˈtrʌkjʊlənt/ *adj* свире́пый.

trudge /trʌdʒ/ *vi* уста́ло тащи́ться *impf*.

true /tru:/ *adj* (*faithful, correct*) ве́рный; (*correct*) пра́вильный; (*story*) правди́вый; (*real*) настоя́щий; **come ~** сбыва́ться *impf*, сбы́ться *pf*.

truism /ˈtru:ɪz(ə)m/ *n* трюи́зм.

truly /ˈtru:lɪ/ *adv* (*sincerely*) и́скренне; (*really, indeed*) действи́тельно; **yours ~** пре́данный Вам.

trump /trʌmp/ *n* ко́зырь *m*; *vt* бить *impf*, по~ *pf* ко́зырем; **~ up** фабрикова́ть *impf*, с~ *pf*.

trumpet /ˈtrʌmpɪt/ *n* труба́; *vt* (*proclaim*) труби́ть *impf* о+*prep*. **trumpeter** /-tə(r)/ *n* труба́ч.

truncate /trʌŋˈkeɪt/ *vt* усека́ть *impf*, усе́чь *pf*.

truncheon /ˈtrʌntʃ(ə)n/ *n* дуби́нка.

trundle /ˈtrʌnd(ə)l/ *vt & i* ката́ть(ся) *indet*, кати́ть(ся) *det*, по~ *pf*.

trunk /trʌŋk/ *n* (*stem*) ствол; (*anat*) ту́ловище; (*elephant's*) хо́бот; (*box*) сунду́к; *pl* (*swimming*) пла́вки (-вок) *pl*; (*boxing etc.*) трусы́ (-со́в) *pl*; **~ call** вы́зов по междугоро́дному телефо́ну; **~ road** магистра́льная доро́га.

truss /trʌs/ *n* (*girder*) фе́рма; (*med*) грыжево́й банда́ж; *vt* (*tie (up), bird*) свя́зывать *impf*, связа́ть *pf*; (*reinforce*) укрепля́ть *impf*, укрепи́ть *pf*.

trust /trʌst/ *n* дове́рие; (*body of trustees*) опе́ка; (*property held in ~*) довери́тельная со́бственность; (*econ*) трест; **take on ~** принима́ть *impf*, приня́ть *pf* на ве́ру; *vt* доверя́ть *impf*, дове́рить *pf* +*dat* (**with** +*acc*; **to** +*inf*); *vi* (*hope*) наде́яться *impf*, по~ *pf*. **trustee** /trʌsˈti:/ *n* опеку́н. **trustful, trusting** /-fʊl, tɪŋ/ *adj* дове́рчивый. **trustworthy, trusty** /-ˌwɜ:ðɪ, -tɪ/ *adj* надёжный, ве́рный.

truth /tru:θ/ *n* пра́вда; **tell the ~** говори́ть *impf*, сказа́ть *pf* пра́вду; **to tell you the ~** по пра́вде говоря́. **truthful** /-fʊl/ *adj* правди́вый.

try /traɪ/ *n* (*attempt*) попы́тка; (*test, trial*) испыта́ние, про́ба; *vt* (*taste; sample*) про́бовать *impf*, по~ *pf*; (*patience*) испы́тывать *impf*, испыта́ть *pf*; (*law*) суди́ть *impf* (**for** за+*acc*); *vi* (*endeavour*) стара́ться *impf*, по~ *pf*; **~ on** (*clothes*) примеря́ть *impf*, приме́рить *pf*. **trying** /ˈtraɪɪŋ/ *adj* тру́дный.

tsar /zɑ:(r)/ *n* царь *m*. **tsarina**

/zɑːˈriːnə/ *n* цари́ца.
T-shirt /ˈtiːʃɜːt/ *n* футбо́лка.
tub /tʌb/ *n* ка́дка; (*bath*) ва́нна; (*of margarine etc.*) упако́вка.
tubby /ˈtʌbɪ/ *adj* то́лстенький.
tube /tjuːb/ *n* тру́бка, труба́; (*toothpaste etc.*) тю́бик; (*underground*) метро́ *neut indecl*.
tuber /ˈtjuːbə(r)/ *n* клу́бень *m*. **tuberculosis** /tjʊˌbɜːkjʊˈləʊsɪs/ *n* туберкулёз.
tubing /ˈtjuːbɪŋ/ *n* тру́бы *m pl*. **tubular** /ˈtjuːbjʊlə(r)/ *adj* тру́бчатый.
tuck /tʌk/ *n* (*in garment*) скла́дка; *vt* (*thrust into*, ~ *away*) засо́вывать *impf*, засу́нуть *pf*; (*hide away*) пря́тать *impf*, с~ *pf*; ~ **in** (*shirt etc.*) заправля́ть *impf*, запра́вить *pf*; ~ **in, up** (*blanket, skirt*) подтыка́ть *impf*, подоткну́ть *pf*; ~ **up** (*sleeves*) засу́чивать *impf*, засучи́ть *pf*; (*in bed*) укрыва́ть *impf*, укры́ть *pf*.
Tuesday /ˈtjuːzdeɪ/ *n* вто́рник.
tuft /tʌft/ *n* пучо́к.
tug /tʌg/ *vt* тяну́ть *impf*, по~ *pf*; *vi* (*sharply*) дёргать *impf*, дёрнуть *pf* (**at** за+*acc*); *n* рыво́к; (*tugboat*) букси́р.
tuition /tjuːˈɪʃ(ə)n/ *n* обуче́ние (**in** +*dat*).
tulip /ˈtjuːlɪp/ *n* тюльпа́н.
tumble /ˈtʌmb(ə)l/ *vi* (*fall*) па́дать *impf*, (у)па́сть *pf*; *n* паде́ние. **tumbledown** *adj* полуразру́шенный. **tumbler** /-blə(r)/ *n* стака́н.
tumour /ˈtjuːmə(r)/ *n* о́пухоль.
tumult /ˈtjuːmʌlt/ *n* (*uproar*) сумато́ха; (*agitation*) волне́ние. **tumultuous** /tjʊˈmʌltjʊəs/ *adj* шу́мный.
tuna /ˈtjuːnə/ *n* туне́ц.
tundra /ˈtʌndrə/ *n* ту́ндра.
tune /tjuːn/ *n* мело́дия; **in** ~ в тон, (*of instrument*) настро́енный; **out of** ~ не в тон, фальши́вый, (*of instrument*) расстро́енный; **change one's** ~ (пере)меня́ть *impf*, перемени́ть *pf* тон; *vt* (*instrument*; *radio*) настра́ивать *impf*, настро́ить *pf*; (*engine etc.*) регули́ровать *impf*, от~ *pf*; ~ **in** настра́ивать *impf*, настро́ить (*radio*) ра́дио (**to** на+*acc*); *vi*: ~ **up** настра́ивать *impf*, настро́ить *pf* инструме́нт(ы). **tuneful** /-fʊl/ *adj* мелоди́чный. **tuner** /ˈtjuːnə(r)/ *n* (*mus*) настро́йщик; (*receiver*) приёмник.
tunic /ˈtjuːnɪk/ *n* туни́ка; (*of uniform*) ки́тель *m*.
tuning /ˈtjuːnɪŋ/ *n* настро́йка; (*of engine*) регулиро́вка; **~-fork** камерто́н.
tunnel /ˈtʌn(ə)l/ *n* тунне́ль *m*; *vi* прокла́дывать *impf*, проложи́ть *pf* тунне́ль *m*.
turban /ˈtɜːbən/ *n* тюрба́н.
turbine /ˈtɜːbaɪn/ *n* турби́на.
turbulence /ˈtɜːbjʊləns/ *n* бу́рность; (*aeron*) турбуле́нтность. **turbulent** /-lənt/ *adj* бу́рный.
tureen /tjʊˈriːn/ *n* су́пник.
turf /tɜːf/ *n* дёрн.
turgid /ˈtɜːdʒɪd/ *adj* (*pompous*) напы́щенный.
Turk /tɜːk/ *n* ту́рок, турча́нка. **Turkey** /ˈtɜːkɪ/ *n* Ту́рция.
turkey /ˈtɜːkɪ/ *n* индю́к, *f* инде́йка; (*dish*) индю́шка.
Turkish /ˈtɜːkɪʃ/ *adj* туре́цкий. **Turkmenistan** /tɜːkˌmenɪˈstɑːn/ *n* Туркмениста́н.
turmoil /ˈtɜːmɔɪl/ *n* (*disorder*) беспоря́док; (*uproar*) сумато́ха.
turn /tɜːn/ *n* (*change of direction*) поворо́т; (*revolution*) оборо́т; (*service*) услу́га; (*change*) измене́ние; (*one's ~ to do sth*) о́чередь; (*theat*) но́мер; ~ **of phrase** оборо́т ре́чи; **at every** ~ на ка́ждом шагу́; **by, in turn(s)** по о́череди; *vt* (*handle, key, car around, etc.*) повора́чивать *impf*, поверну́ть *pf*; (*revolve, rotate*) враща́ть *impf*; (*page*; *on its face*) перевёртывать *impf*, переверну́ть *pf*; (*direct*) направля́ть *impf*, напра́вить *pf*; (*cause to become*) де́лать *impf*, с~ *pf* +*instr*; (*on lathe*) точи́ть *impf*; *vi* (*change direction*) повора́чивать *impf*, поверну́ть *pf*; (*rotate*) враща́ться *impf*; (~ *round*)

повора́чиваться *impf*, поверну́ться *pf*; (*become*) станови́ться *impf*, стать *pf* +*instr*; ~ **against** ополча́ться *impf*, ополчи́ться *pf* на+*acc*, про́тив+*gen*; ~ **around** *see* ~ **round;** ~ **away** (*vt* & *i*) отвора́чивать(ся) *impf*, отверну́ть(ся) *pf*; (*refuse admittance*) прогоня́ть *impf*, прогна́ть *pf*; ~ **back** (*vi*) повора́чивать *impf*, поверну́ть *pf* наза́д; (*vt*) (*bend back*) отгиба́ть *impf*, отогну́ть *pf*; ~ **down** (*refuse*) отклоня́ть *impf*, отклони́ть *pf*; (*collar*) отгиба́ть *impf*, отогну́ть *pf*; (*make quieter*) де́лать *impf*, с~ *pf* ти́ше; ~ **grey** (*vi*) седе́ть *impf*, по~ *pf*; ~ **in** (*so as to face inwards*) повора́чивать *impf*, поверну́ть *pf* вовну́трь; ~ **inside out** вывора́чивать *impf*, вы́вернуть *pf* наизна́нку; ~ **into** (*change into*) (*vt* & *i*) превраща́ть(ся) *impf*, преврати́ть(ся) *pf* в+*acc*; (*street*) свора́чивать *impf*, сверну́ть *pf* на+*acc*; ~ **off** (*light, radio etc.*) выключа́ть *impf*, вы́ключить *pf*; (*tap*) закрыва́ть *impf*, закры́ть *pf*; (*vi*) (*branch off*) свора́чивать *impf*, сверну́ть *pf*; ~ **on** (*light, radio etc.*) включа́ть *impf*, включи́ть *pf*; (*tap*) открыва́ть *impf*, откры́ть *pf*; (*attack*) напада́ть *impf*, напа́сть *pf* на+*acc*; ~ **out** (*light etc.*): *see* ~ **off**; (*prove to be*) ока́зываться *impf*, оказа́ться *pf* (**to be** +*instr*); (*drive out*) выгоня́ть *impf*, вы́гнать *pf*; (*pockets*) вывёртывать *impf*, вы́вернуть *pf*; (*be present*) приходи́ть *impf*, прийти *pf*; (*product*) выпуска́ть *impf*, вы́пустить *pf*; ~ **over** (*page, on its face, roll over*) (*vt* & *i*) перевёртывать(ся) *impf*, переверну́ть(ся) *pf*; (*hand over*) передава́ть *impf*, переда́ть *pf*; (*think about*) обду́мывать *impf*, обду́мать *pf*; (*overturn*) (*vt* & *i*) опроки́дывать(ся) *impf*, опроки́нуть(ся) *pf*; ~ **pale** бледне́ть *impf*, по~ *pf*; ~ **red** красне́ть *impf*, по~ *pf*; ~ **round** (*vi*) (*rotate*; ~ *one's back*; ~ *to face sth*) повёртываться *impf*, поверну́ться *pf*; (~ *to face*) обора́чиваться *impf*, оберну́ться *pf*; (*vt*) повёртывать *impf*, поверну́ть *pf*; ~ **sour** скиса́ть *impf*, ски́снуть *pf*; ~ **to** обраща́ться *impf*, обрати́ться *pf* к+*dat* (**for** за +*instr*); ~ **up** (*appear*) появля́ться *impf*, появи́ться *pf*; (*be found*) находи́ться *impf*, найти́сь *pf*; (*shorten garment*) подшива́ть *impf*, подши́ть *pf*; (*crop up*) подвёртываться *impf*, подверну́ться *pf*; (*bend up; stick up*) (*vt* & *i*) загиба́ть(ся) *impf*, загну́ть(ся) *pf*; (*make louder*) де́лать *impf*, с~ *pf* гро́мче; ~ **up one's nose** вороти́ть *impf* нос (**at** от+*gen*) (*coll*); ~ **upside down** перевора́чивать *impf*, переверну́ть *pf* вверх дном. **turn-out** *n* коли́чество приходя́щих. **turn-up** *n* (*on trousers*) обшла́г.

turner /'tɜːnə(r)/ *n* то́карь *m*.

turning /'tɜːnɪŋ/ *n* (*road*) поворо́т. **turning-point** *n* поворо́тный пункт.

turnip /'tɜːnɪp/ *n* ре́па.

turnover /'tɜːnəʊvə(r)/ *n* (*econ*) оборо́т; (*of staff*) теку́честь рабо́чей си́лы.

turnpike /'tɜːnpaɪk/ *n* доро́жная заста́ва.

turnstile /'tɜːnstaɪl/ *n* турнике́т.

turntable /'tɜːnteɪb(ə)l/ *n* (*rly*) поворо́тный круг; (*gramophone*) диск.

turpentine /'tɜːpən,taɪn/ *n* скипида́р.

turquoise /'tɜːkwɔɪz/ *n* (*material, stone*) бирюза́; *adj* бирюзо́вый.

turret /'tʌrɪt/ *n* ба́шенка.

turtle /'tɜːt(ə)l/ *n* черепа́ха.

turtle-dove /'tɜt(ə)l,dʌv/ *n* го́рлица.

tusk /tʌsk/ *n* би́вень *m*, клык.

tussle /'tʌs(ə)l/ *n* дра́ка; *vi* дра́ться *impf* (**for** за+*acc*).

tutor /'tjuːtə(r)/ *n* (*private teacher*) ча́стный дома́шний учи́тель *m*, ~ница; (*univ*) преподава́тель *m*,

~ница; (*primer*) учёбник; *vt* (*instruct*) обучáть *impf*, обучи́ть *pf* (**in** +*dat*); (*give lessons to*) давáть *impf*, дать *pf* урóки+*dat*; (*guide*) руководи́ть *impf* +*instr*. **tutorial** /tjuːˈtɔːrɪəl/ *n* консультáция.

tutu /ˈtuːtuː/ *n* (*ballet*) пáчка.

TV *abbr* (*of* **television**) ТВ, телеви́дение; (*set*) телеви́зор.

twang /twæŋ/ *n* (*of string*) рéзкий звук (натя́нутой струны́); (*voice*) гнусáвый гóлос.

tweak /twiːk/ *n* щипóк; *vt* щипáть *impf*, (у)щипну́ть *pf*.

tweed /twiːd/ *n* твид.

tweezers /ˈtwiːzəz/ *n pl* пинцéт.

twelfth /twelfθ/ *adj* & *n* двенáдцатый. **twelve** /twelv/ *adj* & *n* двенáдцать.

twentieth /ˈtwentɪɪθ/ *adj* & *n* двадцáтый. **twenty** /ˈtwentɪ/ *adj* & *n* двáдцать; *pl* (*decade*) двадцáтые гóды (-дóв) *m pl*.

twice /twaɪs/ *adv* двáжды; **~ as** вдвóе, в два рáза +*comp*.

twiddle /ˈtwɪd(ə)l/ *vt* (*turn*) вертéть *impf* +*acc*, *instr*; (*toy with*) игрáть *impf* +*instr*; **~ one's thumbs** (*fig*) бездéльничать *impf*.

twig /twɪg/ *n* вéточка, прут.

twilight /ˈtwaɪlaɪt/ *n* су́мерки (-рек) *pl*.

twin /twɪn/ *n* близнéц; *pl* (*Gemini*) Близнецы́ *m pl*; **~ beds** пáра односпáльных кровáтей; **~ brother** брат-близнéц; **~ town** гóрод-побрати́м.

twine /twaɪn/ *n* бечёвка, шпагáт; *vt* (*twist*, *weave*) вить *impf*, с~ *pf*; *vt* & *i* (**~** *round*) обвивáть(ся) *impf*, обви́ть(ся) *pf*.

twinge /twɪndʒ/ *n* при́ступ (бóли); (*of conscience*) угрызéние.

twinkle /ˈtwɪŋk(ə)l/ *n* мерцáние; (*of eyes*) огонёк; *vi* мерцáть *impf*, сверкáть *impf*. **twinkling** /-klɪŋ/ *n* мерцáние; **in the ~ of an eye** в мгновéние óка.

twirl /twɜːl/ *vt* & *i* (*twist*, *turn*) вертéть(ся) *impf*; (*whirl*, *spin*) кружи́ть(ся) *impf*.

twist /twɪst/ *n* (*bend*) изги́б, поворóт; (**~***ing*) кручéние; (*in story*) поворóт фáбулы; *vt* скру́чивать *impf*, крути́ть *impf*, с~ *pf*; (*distort*) искажáть *impf*, искази́ть *pf*; (*sprain*) подвёртывать *impf*, подверну́ть *pf*; *vi* (*climb*, *meander*, *twine*) ви́ться *impf*. **twisted** /-tɪd/ *adj* искривлённый (*also fig*).

twit /twɪt/ *n* дурáк.

twitch /twɪtʃ/ *n* подёргивание; *vt* & *i* дёргать(ся) *impf*, дёрнуть(ся) *pf* (**at** за+*acc*).

twitter /ˈtwɪtə(r)/ *n* щéбет; *vi* щебетáть *impf*, чири́кать *impf*.

two /tuː/ *adj* & *n* два, две (*f*); (*collect*; *2 pairs*) двóе; (*number 2*) двóйка; **in ~** (*in half*) нáдвое, пополáм; **~-seater** двухмéстный (автомоби́ль); **~-way** двустороóнний. **twofold** *adj* двойнóй; *adv* вдвойнé. **twosome** *n* пáра.

tycoon /taɪˈkuːn/ *n* магнáт.

type /taɪp/ *n* тип, род; (*printing*) шрифт; *vt* писáть *impf*, на~ *pf* на маши́нке. **typescript** *n* маши́нопись. **typewriter** *n* пи́шущая маши́нка. **typewritten** /ˈtaɪpˌrɪt(ə)n/ *adj* машинопи́сный.

typhoid /ˈtaɪfɔɪd/ *n* брюшнóй тиф.

typical /ˈtɪpɪk(ə)l/ *adj* типи́чный. **typify** /ˈtɪpɪˌfaɪ/ *vt* служи́ть *impf*, по~ *pf* типи́чным примéром +*gen*.

typist /ˈtaɪpɪst/ *n* машини́стка.

typography /taɪˈpɒgrəfɪ/ *n* книгопечáтание; (*style*) оформлéние.

tyrannical /tɪˈrænɪk(ə)l/ *adj* тиранúческий. **tyrant** /ˈtaɪrənt/ *n* тирáн.

tyre /ˈtaɪə(r)/ *n* ши́на.

U

ubiquitous /juːˈbɪkwɪtəs/ *adj* вездесу́щий.

udder /ˈʌdə(r)/ *n* вы́мя *neut*.

UFO *abbr* (*of* **unidentified flying object**) НЛО, неопóзнанный летáющий объéкт.

ugh /əx/ *int* тьфу!

ugliness /ˈʌglɪnɪs/ *n* урóдство. **ugly** /-lɪ/ *adj* некраси́вый, урóдливый; (*unpleasant*) непри́ятный.

UK *abbr* (*of* **United Kingdom**) Соединённое Королéвство.

Ukraine /juːˈkreɪn/ *n* Украи́на. **Ukrainian** /-nɪən/ *n* украи́нец, -нка; *adj* украи́нский.

ulcer /ˈʌlsə(r)/ *n* я́зва.

ulterior /ʌlˈtɪərɪə(r)/ *adj* скры́тый.

ultimate /ˈʌltɪmət/ *adj* (*final*) послéдний, окончáтельный; (*purpose*) конéчный. **ultimately** /-lɪ/ *adv* в конéчном счёте, в концé концóв. **ultimatum** /ˌʌltɪˈmeɪtəm/ *n* ультимáтум.

ultrasound /ˈʌltrəˌsaʊnd/ *n* ультразвýк. **ultra-violet** /ˌʌltrəˈvaɪələt/ *adj* ультрафиолéтовый.

umbilical /ʌmˈbɪlɪk(ə)l/ *adj*: **~ cord** пуповѝна.

umbrella /ʌmˈbrelə/ *n* зóнтик, зонт.

umpire /ˈʌmpaɪə(r)/ *n* судья́ *m*; *vt* & *i* суди́ть *impf*.

umpteenth /ʌmpˈtiːnθ/ *adj*: **for the ~ time** в котóрый раз.

unabashed /ˌʌnəˈbæʃt/ *adj* без вся́кого смущéния. **unabated** /ˌʌnəˈbeɪtɪd/ *adj* неослáбленный. **unable** /ʌnˈeɪb(ə)l/ *adj*: **be ~ to** не мочь *impf*, с~ *pf*; быть не в состоя́нии; (*not know how to*) не умéть *impf*, с~ *pf*. **unabridged** /ˌʌnəˈbrɪdʒd/ *adj* несокращённый. **unaccompanied** /ˌʌnəˈkʌmpənɪd/ *adj* без сопровождéния; (*mus*) без аккомпанемéнта. **unaccountable** /ˌʌnəˈkaʊntəb(ə)l/ *adj* необъясни́мый. **unaccustomed** /ˌʌnəˈkʌstəmd/ *adj* (*not accustomed*) непривы́кший (**to** к+*dat*); (*unusual*) непривы́чный. **unadulterated** /ˌʌnəˈdʌltəreɪtɪd/ *adj* настоя́щий; (*utter*) чистéйший. **unaffected** /ˌʌnəˈfektɪd/ *adj* непринуждённый. **unaided** /ʌnˈeɪdɪd/ *adj* без пóмощи, самостоя́тельный. **unambiguous** /ˌʌnæmˈbɪgjʊəs/ *adj* недвусмы́сленный. **unanimity** /ˌjuːnəˈnɪmɪtɪ/ *n* единодýшие. **unanimous** /juːˈnænɪməs/ *adj* единодýшный. **unanswerable** /ʌnˈɑːnsərəb(ə)l/ *adj* (*irrefutable*) неопровержи́мый. **unarmed** /ʌnˈɑːmd/ *adj* невооружённый. **unashamed** /ˌʌnəˈʃeɪmd/ *adj* бессóвестный. **unassailable** /ˌʌnəˈseɪləb(ə)l/ *adj* непристýпный; (*irrefutable*) неопровержи́мый. **unassuming** /ˌʌnəˈsjuːmɪŋ/ *adj* скрóмный. **unattainable** /ˌʌnəˈteɪnəb(ə)l/ *adj* недосягáемый. **unattended** /ˌʌnəˈtendɪd/ *adj* без присмóтра. **unattractive** /ˌʌnəˈtræktɪv/ *adj* непривлекáтельный. **unauthorized** /ʌnˈɔːθəˌraɪzd/ *adj* неразрешённый. **unavailable** /ˌʌnəˈveɪləb(ə)l/ *adj* не имéющийся в нали́чии, недостýпный. **unavoidable** /ˌʌnəˈvɔɪdəb(ə)l/ *adj* неизбéжный. **unaware** /ˌʌnəˈweə(r)/ *predic*: **be ~ of** не сознавáть *impf* +*acc*; не знать *impf* о+*prep*. **unawares** /ˌʌnəˈweəz/ *adv* врасплóх.

unbalanced /ʌnˈbælənst/ *adj* (*psych*) неуравновéшенный. **unbearable** /ʌnˈbeərəb(ə)l/ *adj* невыноси́мый. **unbeatable** /ʌnˈbiːtəb(ə)l/ *adj* (*unsurpassable*) не могýщий быть превзойдённым; (*invincible*) непобеди́мый. **unbeaten** /ʌnˈbiːtən/ *adj* (*undefeated*) непокорённый; (*unsurpassed*) непревзойдённый. **unbelief** /ˌʌnbɪˈliːf/ *n* невéрие. **unbelievable** /ˌʌnbɪˈliːvəb(ə)l/ *adj* невероя́тный. **unbeliever** /ˌʌnbɪlˈliːvə(r)/ *n* невéрующий *sb*. **unbiased** /ʌnˈbaɪəst/ *adj* беспристрáстный. **unblemished** /ʌnˈblemɪʃt/ *adj* незапя́тнанный. **unblock** /ʌnˈblɒk/ *vt* прочищáть *impf*, прочи́стить *pf*. **unbolt** /ʌnˈbəʊlt/ *vt* отпирáть *impf*, отперéть *pf*. **unborn** /ʌnˈbɔːn/ *adj* ещё не рождённый. **unbounded** /ʌnˈbaʊndɪd/ *adj* неограни́ченный. **unbreakable** /ʌnˈbreɪkəb(ə)l/ *adj* небью́щийся. **unbridled** /ʌnˈbraɪd(ə)ld/ *adj* разнýзданный.

unbroken /ʌn'brəʊkən/ *adj* (*intact*) неразби́тый, це́лый; (*continuous*) непреры́вный; (*unsurpassed*) непоби́тый; (*horse*) необъе́зженный. **unbuckle** /ʌn'bʌk(ə)l/ *vt* расстёгивать *impf*, расстегну́ть *pf*. **unburden** /ʌn'bɜːd(ə)n/ *vt*: **~ o.s.** отводи́ть *impf*, отвести́ *pf* ду́шу. **unbutton** /ʌn'bʌt(ə)n/ *vt* расстёгивать *impf*, расстегну́ть *pf*.

uncalled-for /ʌn'kɔːldfɔː(r)/ *adj* неуме́стный. **uncanny** /ʌn'kænɪ/ *adj* жу́ткий, сверхъесте́ственный. **unceasing** /ʌn'siːsɪŋ/ *adj* непреры́вный. **unceremonious** /ˌʌnserɪ'məʊnɪəs/ *adj* бесцеремо́нный. **uncertain** /ʌn'sɜːt(ə)n/ *adj* (*not sure, hesitating*) неуве́ренный; (*indeterminate*) неопределённый, нея́сный; **be ~** (*not know for certain*) то́чно не знать *impf*; **in no ~ terms** недвусмы́сленно. **uncertainty** /ʌn'sɜːt(ə)ntɪ/ *n* неизве́стность; неопределённость. **unchallenged** /ʌn'tʃælɪndʒd/ *adj* не вызыва́ющий возраже́ний. **unchanged** /ʌn'tʃeɪndʒd/ *adj* неизмени́вшийся. **unchanging** /ʌn'tʃeɪndʒɪŋ/ *adj* неизменя́ющийся. **uncharacteristic** /ˌʌnkærəktə'rɪstɪk/ *adj* нетипи́чный. **uncharitable** /ʌn'tʃærɪtəb(ə)l/ *adj* немилосе́рдный, жесто́кий. **uncharted** /ʌn'tʃɑːtɪd/ *adj* неиссле́дованный. **unchecked** /ʌn'tʃekt/ *adj* (*unrestrained*) необу́зданный. **uncivilized** /ʌn'sɪvɪˌlaɪzd/ *adj* нецивилизо́ванный. **unclaimed** /ʌn'kleɪmd/ *adj* невостре́бованный.

uncle /'ʌŋk(ə)l/ *n* дя́дя *m*.

unclean /ʌn'kliːn/ *adj* нечи́стый. **unclear** /ʌn'klɪə(r)/ *adj* нея́сный. **uncomfortable** /ʌn'kʌmftəb(ə)l/ *adj* неудо́бный. **uncommon** /ʌn'kɒmən/ *adj* необыкнове́нный; (*rare*) ре́дкий. **uncommunicative** /ˌʌnkə'mjuːnɪkətɪv/ *adj* неразгово́рчивый, сде́ржанный. **uncomplaining** /ˌʌnkəm'pleɪnɪŋ/ *adj* безро́потный. **uncomplicated** /ʌn'kɒmplɪˌkeɪtɪd/ *adj* несло́жный. **uncompromising** /ʌn'kɒmprəˌmaɪzɪŋ/ *adj* бескомпроми́ссный. **unconcealed** /ˌʌnkən'siːld/ *adj* нескрыва́емый. **unconcerned** /ˌʌnkən'sɜːnd/ *adj* (*unworried*) беззабо́тный; (*indifferent*) равноду́шный. **unconditional** /ˌʌnkən'dɪʃən(ə)l/ *adj* безогово́рочный, безусло́вный. **unconfirmed** /ˌʌnkən'fɜːmd/ *adj* неподтверждённый. **unconnected** /ˌʌnkə'nektɪd/ *adj* **~ with** не свя́занный с+*instr*. **unconscious** /ʌn'kɒnʃəs/ *adj* (*also unintentional*) бессозна́тельный; (*predic*) без созна́ния; **be ~ of** не сознава́ть *impf* +*gen*; *n* подсозна́тельное *sb*. **unconsciousness** /ʌn'kɒnʃəsnɪs/ *n* бессозна́тельное состоя́ние. **unconstitutional** /ˌʌnkɒnstɪ'tjuːʃən(ə)l/ *adj* неконституцио́нный. **uncontrollable** /ˌʌnkən'trəʊləb(ə)l/ *adj* неудержи́мый. **uncontrolled** /ˌʌnkən'trəʊld/ *adj* бесконтро́льный. **unconventional** /ˌʌnkən'venʃən(ə)l/ *adj* необы́чный; оригина́льный. **unconvincing** /ˌʌnkən'vɪnsɪŋ/ *adj* неубеди́тельный. **uncooked** /ʌn'kʊkt/ *adj* сыро́й. **uncooperative** /ˌʌnkəʊ'ɒpərətɪv/ *adj* неотзы́вчивый. **uncouth** /ʌn'kuːθ/ *adj* гру́бый. **uncover** /ʌn'kʌvə(r)/ *vt* раскрыва́ть *impf*, раскры́ть *pf*. **uncritical** /ʌn'krɪtɪk(ə)l/ *adj* некрити́чный.

unctuous /'ʌŋktjʊəs/ *adj* еле́йный.

uncut /ʌn'kʌt/ *adj* неразре́занный; (*unabridged*) несокращённый.

undamaged /ʌn'dæmɪdʒd/ *adj* неповреждённый. **undaunted** /ʌn'dɔːntɪd/ *adj* бесстра́шный. **undecided** /ˌʌndɪ'saɪdɪd/ *adj* (*not settled*) нерешённый; (*irresolute*) нереши́тельный. **undefeated** /ˌʌndɪ'fiːtɪd/ *adj* непокорённый. **undemanding** /ˌʌndɪ'mɑːndɪŋ/ *adj* нетре́бовательный. **undemocratic** /ˌʌndemə'krætɪk/ *adj* неде-

u

мократи́ческий. **undeniable** /ˌʌndɪˈnaɪəb(ə)l/ *adj* неоспори́мый.

under /ˈʌndə(r)/ *prep* (*position*) под+*instr*; (*direction*) под+*acc*; (*fig*) под +*instr*; (*less than*) ме́ньше+*gen*; (*in view of, in the reign, time of*) при+*prep*; **~-age** несовершенноле́тний; **~ way** на ходу́; *adv* (*position*) внизу́; (*direction*) вниз; (*less*) ме́ньше.

undercarriage /ˈʌndəˌkærɪdʒ/ *n* шасси́ *neut indecl.* **underclothes** /ˈʌndəˌkləʊðz/ *n pl* ни́жнее бельё. **undercoat** /ˈʌndəˌkəʊt/ *n* (*of paint*) грунто́вка. **undercover** /ˌʌndəˈkʌvə(r)/ *adj* та́йный. **undercurrent** /ˈʌndəˌkʌrənt/ *n* подво́дное тече́ние; (*fig*) скры́тая тенде́нция. **undercut** /ˌʌndəˈkʌt/ *vt* (*price*) назнача́ть *impf*, назна́чить *pf* бо́лее ни́зкую це́ну чем+*nom.* **underdeveloped** /ˌʌndədɪˈveləpt/ *adj* слабора́звитый. **underdog** /ˈʌndəˌdɒg/ *n* неуда́чник.

underdone /ˌʌndəˈdʌn/ *adj* недожа́ренный. **underemployment** /ˌʌndərɪmˈplɔɪmənt/ *n* непо́лная за́нятость. **underestimate** *vt* /ˌʌndərˈestɪˌmeɪt/ недооце́нивать *impf*, недооцени́ть *pf*; *n* /ˌʌndərˈestɪmət/недооце́нка. **underfoot** /ˌʌndəˈfʊt/ *adv* под нога́ми.

undergo /ˌʌndəˈgəʊ/ *vt* подверга́ться *impf*, подве́ргнуться *pf* +*dat*; (*endure*) переноси́ть *impf*, перенести́ *pf.* **undergraduate** /ˌʌndəˈgrædjʊət/ *n* студе́нт, ~ка. **underground** /ˈʌndəˌgraʊnd/ *n* (*rly*) метро́ *neut indecl*; (*fig*) подпо́лье; *adj* подзе́мный; (*fig*) подпо́льный; *adv* под землёй; (*fig*) подпо́льно. **undergrowth** /ˈʌndəˌgrəʊθ/ *n* подле́сок. **underhand** /ˈʌndəˌhænd/ *adj* закули́сный. **underlie** /ˌʌndəˈlaɪ/ *vt* (*fig*) лежа́ть *impf* в осно́ве +*gen.* **underline** /ˌʌndəˈlaɪn/ *vt* подчёркивать *impf*, подчеркну́ть *pf.* **underling** /ˈʌndəlɪŋ/ *n* подчинённый *sb.* **underlying** /ˈʌndəˌlaɪɪŋ/ *adj* лежа́щий в осно́ве.

undermine /ˌʌndəˈmaɪn/ *vt* (*authority*) подрыва́ть *impf*, подорва́ть *pf*; (*health*) разруша́ть *impf*, разру́шить *pf.*

underneath /ˌʌndəˈniːθ/ *adv* (*position*) внизу́; (*direction*) вниз; *prep* (*position*) под+*instr*; (*direction*) под+*acc*; *n* ни́жняя часть; *adj* ни́жний.

undernourished /ˌʌndəˈnʌrɪʃt/ *adj* исхуда́лый; **be ~** недоеда́ть *impf.*

underpaid /ˌʌndəˈpeɪd/ *adj* низкоопла́чиваемый. **underpants** /ˈʌndəˌpænts/ *n pl* трусы́ (-со́в) *pl.* **underpass** /ˈʌndəˌpɑːs/ *n* прое́зд под полотно́м доро́ги; тонне́ль *m.* **underpin** /ˌʌndəˈpɪn/ *vt* подводи́ть *impf*, подвести́ *pf* фунда́мент под+*acc*; (*fig*) подде́рживать *impf*, поддержа́ть *pf.* **underprivileged** /ˌʌndəˈprɪvɪlɪdʒd/ *adj* обделённый; (*poor*) бе́дный. **underrate** /ˌʌndəˈreɪt/ *vt* недооце́нивать *impf*, недооцени́ть *pf.*

underscore /ˌʌndəˈskɔː(r)/ *vt* подчёркивать *impf*, подчеркну́ть *pf.* **under-secretary** /ˌʌndəˈsekrətərɪ/ *n* замести́тель *m* мини́стра. **underside** /ˈʌndəˌsaɪd/ *n* ни́жняя сторона́, низ. **undersized** /ˈʌndəˌsaɪzd/ *adj* малоро́слый. **understaffed** /ˌʌndəˈstɑːft/ *adj* неукомплекто́ванный.

understand /ˌʌndəˈstænd/ *vt* понима́ть *impf*, поня́ть *pf*; (*have heard say*) слы́шать *impf.* **understandable** /ˌʌndəˈstændəb(ə)l/ *adj* поня́тный. **understanding** /ˌʌndəˈstændɪŋ/ *n* понима́ние; (*agreement*) соглаше́ние; *adj* (*sympathetic*) отзы́вчивый.

understate /ˌʌndəˈsteɪt/ *vt* преуменьша́ть *impf*, преуме́ньшить *pf.* **understatement** /ˈʌndəˌsteɪtmənt/ *n* преуменьше́ние.

understudy /ˈʌndəˌstʌdɪ/ *n* дублёр.

undertake /ˌʌndəˈteɪk/ *vt* (*enter upon*) предпринима́ть *impf*, предприня́ть *pf*; (*responsibility*)

u

брать *impf*, взять *pf* на себя́; (+*inf*) обя́зываться *impf*, обяза́ться *pf*. **undertaker** /ˈʌndəˌteɪkə(r)/ *n* гробовщи́к. **undertaking** /ˌʌndəˈteɪkɪŋ/ *n* предприя́тие; (*pledge*) гара́нтия.

undertone /ˈʌndəˌtəʊn/ *n* (*fig*) подте́кст; **in an ~** вполго́лоса. **underwater** /ˌʌndəˈwɔːtə(r)/ *adj* подво́дный. **underwear** /ˈʌndəˌweə(r)/ *n* ни́жнее бельё. **underweight** /ˌʌndəˈweɪt/ *adj* исхуда́лый. **underworld** /ˈʌndəˌwɜːld/ *n* (*mythology*) преиспо́дняя *sb*; (*criminals*) престу́пный мир. **underwrite** /ˌʌndəˈraɪt/ *vt* (*guarantee*) гаранти́ровать *impf* & *pf*. **underwriter** /ˈʌndəˌraɪtə(r)/ *n* страхо́вщик.

undeserved /ˌʌndɪˈzɜːvd/ *adj* незаслу́женный. **undesirable** /ˌʌndɪˈzaɪərəb(ə)l/ *adj* нежела́тельный; *n* нежела́тельное лицо́. **undeveloped** /ˌʌndɪˈveləpt/ *adj* нера́звитый; (*land*) незастро́енный. **undignified** /ʌnˈdɪgnɪˌfaɪd/ *adj* недосто́йный. **undiluted** /ˌʌndaɪˈljuːtɪd/ *adj* неразба́вленный. **undisciplined** /ʌnˈdɪsɪplɪnd/ *adj* недисциплини́рованный. **undiscovered** /ˌʌndɪˈskʌvəd/ *adj* неоткры́тый. **undisguised** /ˌʌndɪsˈgaɪzd/ *adj* я́вный. **undisputed** /ˌʌndɪˈspjuːtɪd/ *adj* бесспо́рный. **undistinguished** /ˌʌndɪˈstɪŋgwɪʃt/ *adj* зауря́дный. **undisturbed** /ˌʌndɪˈstɜːbd/ *adj* (*untouched*) нетро́нутый; (*peaceful*) споко́йный. **undivided** /ˌʌndɪˈvaɪdɪd/ *adj*: **~ attention** по́лное внима́ние

undo /ʌnˈduː/ *vt* (*open*) открыва́ть *impf*, откры́ть *pf*; (*untie*) развя́зывать *impf*, развяза́ть *pf*; (*unbutton*, *unhook*, *unbuckle*) расстёгивать *impf*, расстегну́ть *pf*; (*destroy*, *cancel*) уничтожа́ть *impf*, уничто́жить *pf*. **undoubted** /ʌnˈdaʊtɪd/ *adj* несомне́нный. **undoubtedly** /ʌnˈdaʊtɪdlɪ/ *adv* несомне́нно. **undress** /ʌnˈdres/ *vt* & *i* раздева́ть(ся) *impf*, разде́ть(ся) *pf*. **undue** /ʌnˈdjuː/ *adj* чрезме́рный. **unduly** /ʌnˈdjuːlɪ/ *adv* чрезме́рно.

undulating /ˈʌndjʊˌleɪtɪŋ/ *adj* волни́стый; (*landscape*) холми́стый.

undying /ʌnˈdaɪɪŋ/ *adj* (*eternal*) ве́чный.

unearth /ʌnˈɜːθ/ *vt* (*dig up*) выка́пывать *impf*, вы́копать *pf* из земли́; (*fig*) раска́пывать *impf*, раскопа́ть *pf*. **uneasiness** /ʌnˈiːzɪnɪs/ *n* (*anxiety*) беспоко́йство; (*awkwardness*) нело́вкость. **uneasy** /ʌnˈiːzɪ/ *adj* беспоко́йный; нело́вкий. **uneconomic** /ˌʌniːkəˈnɒmɪk/ *adj* нерента́бельный. **uneconomical** /ˌʌniːkəˈnɒmɪk(ə)l/ *adj* (*car etc.*) неэкономи́чный; (*person*) неэконо́мный. **uneducated** /ʌnˈedjʊˌkeɪtɪd/ *adj* необразо́ванный. **unemployed** /ˌʌnɪmˈplɔɪd/ *adj* безрабо́тный. **unemployment** /ˌʌnɪmˈplɔɪmənt/ *n* безрабо́тица; **~ benefit** посо́бие по безрабо́тице. **unending** /ʌnˈendɪŋ/ *adj* бесконе́чный. **unenviable** /ʌnˈenvɪəb(ə)l/ *adj* незави́дный. **unequal** /ʌnˈiːkw(ə)l/ *adj* нера́вный. **unequalled** /ʌnˈiːkw(ə)ld/ *adj* непревзойдённый. **unequivocal** /ˌʌnɪˈkwɪvək(ə)l/ *adj* недвусмы́сленный. **unerring** /ʌnˈɜːrɪŋ/ *adj* безоши́бочный.

uneven /ʌnˈiːv(ə)n/ *adj* неро́вный. **uneventful** /ˌʌnɪˈventfʊl/ *adj* непримеча́тельный. **unexceptional** /ˌʌnɪkˈsepʃən(ə)l/ *adj* обы́чный. **unexpected** /ˌʌnɪkˈspektɪd/ *adj* неожи́данный. **unexplored** /ˌʌnɪkˈsplɔːd/ *adj* неиссле́дованный.

unfailing /ʌnˈfeɪlɪŋ/ *adj* неизме́нный; (*inexhaustible*) неисчерпа́емый. **unfair** /ʌnˈfeə(r)/ *adj* несправедли́вый. **unfaithful** /ʌnˈfeɪθfʊl/ *adj* неве́рный. **unfamiliar** /ˌʌnfəˈmɪljə(r)/ *adj* незнако́мый; (*unknown*) неве́домый. **unfashionable** /ʌnˈfæʃənəb(ə)l/ *adj* немо́дный. **unfasten** /ʌnˈfɑːs(ə)n/ *vt* (*detach*, *untie*) открепля́ть *impf*, открепи́ть *pf*; (*undo*, *unbutton*, *unhook*) расстёгивать *impf*, расстегну́ть *pf*; (*open*) открыва́ть *impf*, откры́ть *pf*. **unfavourable** /ʌn'feɪvərəb(ə)l/ *adj* неблагоприя́тный. **unfeeling** /ʌn'fi:lɪŋ/ *adj* бесчу́вственный. **unfinished** /ʌn'fɪnɪʃt/ *adj* незако́нченный. **unfit** /ʌn'fɪt/ *adj* него́дный; (*unhealthy*) нездоро́вый. **unflagging** /ʌn'flægɪŋ/ *adj* неослабева́ющий. **unflattering** /ʌn'flætərɪŋ/ *adj* нele´стный. **unflinching** /ʌn'flɪntʃɪŋ/ *adj* непоколеби́мый. **unfold** /ʌn'fəʊld/ *vt* & *i* развёртывать(ся) *impf*, разверну́ть(ся) *pf*; *vi* (*fig*) раскрыва́ться *impf*, раскры́ться *pf*. **unforeseen** /ˌʌnfɔ:'si:n/ *adj* непредви́денный. **unforgettable** /ˌʌnfə'getəb(ə)l/ *adj* незабыва́емый. **unforgivable** /ˌʌnfə'gɪvəb(ə)l/ *adj* непрости́тельный. **unforgiving** /ˌʌnfə'gɪvɪŋ/ *adj* непроща́ющий. **unfortunate** /ʌn'fɔ:tjʊnət/ *adj* несча́стный; (*regrettable*) неуда́чный; *n* неуда́чник. **unfortunately** /ʌn'fɔ:tjʊnətlɪ/ *adv* к сожале́нию. **unfounded** /ʌn'faʊndɪd/ *adj* необосно́ванный. **unfriendly** /ʌn'frendlɪ/ *adj* недружелю́бный. **unfulfilled** /ˌʌnfʊl'fɪld/ *adj* (*hopes etc.*) неосуществлённый; (*person*) неудовлетворённый. **unfurl** /ʌn'fɜ:l/ *vt* & *i* развёртывать(ся) *impf*, разверну́ть(ся) *pf*. **unfurnished** /ʌn'fɜ:nɪʃt/ *adj* немеблиро́ванный.

ungainly /ʌn'geɪnlɪ/ *adj* неуклю́жий. **ungovernable** /ʌn'gʌvənəb(ə)l/ *adj* неуправля́емый. **ungracious** /ʌn'greɪʃəs/ *adj* нелюбе́зный. **ungrateful** /ʌn'greɪtfʊl/ *adj* неблагода́рный. **unguarded** /ʌn'gɑ:dɪd/ *adj* (*incautious*) неосторо́жный.

unhappiness /ʌn'hæpɪnɪs/ *n* несча́стье. **unhappy** /ʌn'hæpɪ/ *adj* несчастли́вый. **unharmed** /ʌn'hɑ:md/ *adj* невреди́мый. **unhealthy** /ʌn'helθɪ/ *adj* нездоро́вый; (*harmful*) вре́дный. **unheard-of** /ʌn'hɜ:dɒv/ *adj* неслы́ханный. **unheeded** /ʌn'hi:dɪd/ *adj* незаме́ченный. **unheeding** /ʌn'hi:dɪŋ/ *adj* невнима́тельный. **unhelpful** /ʌn'helpfʊl/ *adj* бесполе́зный; (*person*) неотзы́вчивый. **unhesitating** /ʌn'hezɪˌteɪtɪŋ/ *adj* реши́тельный. **unhesitatingly** /ʌn'hezɪˌteɪtɪŋlɪ/ *adv* без колеба́ния. **unhindered** /ʌn'hɪndəd/ *adj* беспрепя́тственный. **unhinge** /ʌn'hɪndʒ/ *vt* (*fig*) расстра́ивать *impf*, расстро́ить *pf*. **unholy** /ʌn'həʊlɪ/ *adj* (*impious*) нечести́вый; (*awful*) ужа́сный. **unhook** /ʌn'hʊk/ *vt* (*undo hooks of*) расстёгивать *impf*, расстегну́ть *pf*; (*uncouple*) расцепля́ть *impf*, расцепи́ть *pf*. **unhurt** /ʌn'hɜ:t/ *adj* невреди́мый.

unicorn /'ju:nɪˌkɔ:n/ *n* единоро́г.

unification /ˌju:nɪfɪ'keɪʃ(ə)n/ *n* объедине́ние.

uniform /'ju:nɪˌfɔ:m/ *n* фо́рма; *adj* единообра́зный; (*unchanging*) постоя́нный. **uniformity** /ˌju:nɪ'fɔ:mɪtɪ/ *n* единообра́зие.

unify /'ju:nɪˌfaɪ/ *vt* объединя́ть *impf*, объедини́ть *pf*.

unilateral /ˌju:nɪ'lætər(ə)l/ *adj* односторо́нний.

unimaginable /ˌʌnɪ'mædʒɪnəb(ə)l/ *adj* невообрази́мый. **unimaginative** /ˌʌnɪ'mædʒɪnətɪv/ *adj* лишённый воображе́ния, прозаи́чный. **unimportant** /ˌʌnɪm'pɔ:t(ə)nt/ *adj* нева́жный. **uninformed** /ˌʌnɪn'fɔ:md/ *adj* (*ignorant*) несве́дущий (**about** в+*prep*); (*ill-informed*) неосведомлённый. **uninhabited** /ˌʌnɪn'hæbɪtɪd/ *adj* необита́емый. **uninhibited** /ˌʌnɪn'hɪbɪtɪd/ *adj* нестеснённый. **uninspired** /ˌʌnɪn'spaɪəd/ *adj* бана́льный. **unintelligible** /ˌʌnɪn'telɪdʒɪb(ə)l/ *adj* непоня́тный. **unintentional** /ˌʌnɪn'tenʃən(ə)l/ *adj* нечая́нный. **unintentionally** /ˌʌnɪn'tenʃənəlɪ/ *adv* нечая́нно. **uninterested**

U

/ʌn'ɪntrəstɪd/ *adj* незаинтересо́ванный. **uninteresting** /ʌn'ɪntrəstɪŋ/ *adj* неинтере́сный. **uninterrupted** /ˌʌnɪntə'rʌptɪd/ *adj* непреры́вный.

union /'ju:njən/ *n* (*alliance*) сою́з; (*joining together, alliance*) объедине́ние; (*trade* ~) профсою́з. **unionist** /'ju:njənɪst/ *n* член профсою́за; (*polit*) унион́ист.

unique /jʊ'ni:k/ *adj* уника́льный.

unison /'ju:nɪs(ə)n/ *n*: **in** ~ (*mus*) в унисо́н; (*fig*) в согла́сии.

unit /'ju:nɪt/ *n* едини́ца; (*mil*) часть.

unite /jʊ'naɪt/ *vt & i* соединя́ть(ся) *impf*, соедини́ть(ся) *pf*; объединя́ть(ся) *impf*, объедини́ть(ся) *pf*. **united** /jʊ'naɪtɪd/ *adj* соединённый, объединённый; **U~ Kingdom** Соединённое Короле́вство; **U~ Nations** Организа́ция Объединённых На́ций; **U~ States** Соединённые Шта́ты *m pl* Аме́рики. **unity** /'ju:nɪtɪ/ *n* еди́нство.

universal /ˌju:nɪ'vɜ:s(ə)l/ *adj* всео́бщий; (*many-sided*) универса́льный. **universe** /'ju:nɪˌvɜ:s/ *n* вселе́нная *sb*; (*world*) мир.

university /ˌju:nɪ'vɜ:sɪtɪ/ *n* университе́т; *attrib* университе́тский.

unjust /ʌn'dʒʌst/ *adj* несправедли́вый. **unjustifiable** /ʌnˌdʒʌstɪ'faɪəb(ə)l/ *adj* непрости́тельный. **unjustified** /ʌn'dʒʌstɪˌfaɪd/ *adj* неопра́вданный.

unkempt /ʌn'kempt/ *adj* нечёсаный. **unkind** /ʌn'kaɪnd/ *adj* недо́брый, злой. **unknown** /ʌn'nəʊn/ *adj* неизве́стный.

unlawful /ʌn'lɔ:fʊl/ *adj* незако́нный. **unleaded** /ʌn'ledɪd/ *adj* неэтили́рованный. **unleash** /ʌn'li:ʃ/ *vt* (*also fig*) развя́зывать *impf*, развяза́ть *pf*.

unless /ən'les/ *conj* е́сли... не.

unlike /ʌn'laɪk/ *adj* непохо́жий (на+*acc*); (*in contradistinction to*) в отли́чие от+*gen*. **unlikely** /ʌn'laɪklɪ/ *adj* маловероя́тный; **it is ~ that** вряд ли. **unlimited** /ʌn'lɪmɪtɪd/ *adj* неограни́ченный. **unlit** /ʌn'lɪt/ *adj* неосвещённый. **unload** /ʌn'ləʊd/ *vt* (*vehicle etc.*) разгружа́ть *impf*, разгрузи́ть *pf*; (*goods etc.*) выгружа́ть *impf*, вы́грузить *pf*. **unlock** /ʌn'lɒk/ *vt* отпира́ть *impf*, отпере́ть *pf*; открыва́ть *impf*, откры́ть *pf*. **unlucky** /ʌn'lʌkɪ/ *adj* (*number etc.*) несчастли́вый; (*unsuccessful*) неуда́чный.

unmanageable /ʌn'mænɪdʒəb(ə)l/ *adj* тру́дный, непоко́рный. **unmanned** /ʌn'mænd/ *adj* автомати́ческий. **unmarried** /ʌn'mærɪd/ *adj* холосто́й; (*of man*) нежена́тый; (*of woman*) незаму́жняя. **unmask** /ʌn'mɑ:sk/ *vt* (*fig*) разоблача́ть *impf*, разоблачи́ть *pf*. **unmentionable** /ʌn'menʃənəb(ə)l/ *adj* неупомина́емый. **unmistakable** /ˌʌnmɪ'steɪkəb(ə)l/ *adj* несомне́нный, я́сный. **unmitigated** /ʌn'mɪtɪgeɪtɪd/ *adj* (*thorough*) отъя́вленный. **unmoved** /ʌn'mu:vd/ *adj*: **be** ~ остава́ться *impf*, оста́ться *pf* равноду́шен, -шна.

unnatural /ʌn'nætʃər(ə)l/ *adj* неесте́ственный. **unnecessary** /ʌn'nesəsərɪ/ *adj* нену́жный. **unnerve** /ʌn'nɜ:v/ *vt* лиша́ть *impf*, лиши́ть *pf* му́жества; (*upset*) расстра́ивать *impf*, расстро́ить *pf*. **unnoticed** /ʌn'nəʊtɪst/ *adj* незаме́ченный.

unobserved /ˌʌnəb'zɜ:vd/ *adj* незаме́ченный. **unobtainable** /ˌʌnəb'teɪnəb(ə)l/ *adj* недосту́пный. **unobtrusive** /ˌʌnəb'tru:sɪv/ *adj* скро́мный, ненавя́зчивый. **unoccupied** /ʌn'ɒkjʊˌpaɪd/ *adj* неза́нятый, свобо́дный; (*house*) пусто́й. **unofficial** /ˌʌnə'fɪʃ(ə)l/ *adj* неофициа́льный. **unopposed** /ˌʌnə'pəʊzd/ *adj* не встре́тивший сопротивле́ния. **unorthodox** /ʌn'ɔ:θəˌdɒks/ *adj* неортодокса́льный.

unpack /ʌn'pæk/ *vt* распако́вывать *impf*, распакова́ть *pf*. **unpaid** /ʌn'peɪd/ *adj* (*bill*) неупла́-

U

ченный; (*person*) не получа́ющий пла́ты; (*work*) беспла́тный. **unpalatable** /ʌn'pælətəb(ə)l/ *adj* невку́сный; (*unpleasant*) неприя́тный. **unparalleled** /ʌn'pærə,leld/ *adj* несравни́мый. **unpleasant** /ʌn'plez(ə)nt/ *adj* неприя́тный. **unpleasantness** /ʌn'plez(ə)ntnɪs/ *n* неприя́тность. **unpopular** /ʌn'pɒpjʊlə(r)/ *adj* непопуля́рный. **unprecedented** /ʌn'presɪ,dentɪd/ *adj* беспрецеде́нтный. **unpredictable** /,ʌnprɪ'dɪktəb(ə)l/ *adj* непредсказу́емый. **unprejudiced** /ʌn'predʒʊdɪst/ *adj* беспристра́стный. **unprepared** /,ʌnprɪ'peəd/ *adj* неподгото́вленный, негото́вый. **unprepossessing** /,ʌnpri:pə'zesɪŋ/ *adj* непривлека́тельный. **unpretentious** /,ʌnprɪ'tenʃəs/ *adj* просто́й, без прете́нзий. **unprincipled** /ʌn'prɪnsɪp(ə)ld/ *adj* беспринци́пный. **unproductive** /,ʌnprə'dʌktɪv/ *adj* непродукти́вный. **unprofitable** /ʌn'prɒfɪtəb(ə)l/ *adj* невы́годный. **unpromising** /ʌn'prɒmɪsɪŋ/ *adj* малообеща́ющий. **unprotected** /,ʌnprə'tektɪd/ *adj* незащищённый. **unproven** /ʌn'pru:vən/ *adj* недока́занный. **unprovoked** /,ʌnprə'vəʊkt/ *adj* неспровоци́рованный. **unpublished** /ʌn'pʌblɪʃt/ *adj* неопублико́ванный, неи́зданный. **unpunished** /ʌn'pʌnɪʃt/ *adj* безнака́занный.

unqualified /ʌn'kwɒlɪ,faɪd/ *adj* неквалифици́рованный; (*unconditional*) безогово́рочный. **unquestionable** /ʌn'kwestʃənəb(ə)l/ *adj* несомне́нный, неоспори́мый. **unquestionably** /ʌn'kwestʃənəblɪ/ *adv* несомне́нно, бесспо́рно.

unravel /ʌn'ræv(ə)l/ *vt & i* распу́тывать(ся) *impf*, распу́тать(ся) *pf*; *vt* (*solve*) разга́дывать *impf*, разгада́ть *pf*. **unread** /ʌn'red/ *adj* (*book etc.*) непрочи́танный. **unreadable** /ʌn'ri:dəb(ə)l/ *adj* (*illegible*) неразбо́рчивый; (*boring*) неудобочита́емый. **unreal** /ʌn'rɪəl/ *adj* нереа́льный. **unrealistic** /,ʌnrɪə'lɪstɪk/ *adj* нереа́льный. **unreasonable** /ʌn'ri:zənəb(ə)l/ *adj* (*person*) неразу́мный; (*behaviour, demand, price*) необосно́ванный. **unrecognizable** /ʌn'rekəg,naɪzəb(ə)l/ *adj* неузнава́емый. **unrecognized** /ʌn'rekəg,naɪzd/ *adj* непри́знанный. **unrefined** /,ʌnrɪ'faɪnd/ *adj* неочи́щенный; (*manners etc.*) гру́бый. **unrelated** /,ʌnrɪ'leɪtɪd/ *adj* не име́ющий отноше́ния (**to** к+*dat*), несвя́занный (**to** с+*instr*); **we are ~** мы не ро́дственники. **unrelenting** /,ʌnrɪ'lentɪŋ/ *adj* (*ruthless*) безжа́лостный; (*unremitting*) неосла́бный. **unreliable** /,ʌnrɪ'laɪəb(ə)l/ *adj* ненадёжный. **unremarkable** /,ʌnrɪ'mɑ:kəb(ə)l/ *adj* невыдаю́щийся. **unremitting** /,ʌnrɪ'mɪtɪŋ/ *adj* неосла́бный; (*incessant*) беспреста́нный. **unrepentant** /,ʌnrɪ'pent(ə)nt/ *adj* нераска́явшийся. **unrepresentative** /,ʌnreprɪ'zentətɪv/ *adj* нетипи́чный. **unrequited** /,ʌnrə'kwaɪtɪd/ *adj*: **~ love** неразделённая любо́вь. **unreserved** /,ʌnrɪ'zɜ:vd/ *adj* (*full*) по́лный; (*open*) открове́нный; (*unconditional*) безогово́рочный; (*seat*) незаброни́рованный. **unresolved** /,ʌnrɪ'zɒlvd/ *adj* нерешённый. **unrest** /ʌn'rest/ *n* беспоко́йство; (*polit*) волне́ния *neut pl*. **unrestrained** /,ʌnrɪ'streɪnd/ *adj* несде́ржанный. **unrestricted** /,ʌnrɪ'strɪktɪd/ *adj* неограни́ченный. **unripe** /ʌn'raɪp/ *adj* незре́лый. **unrivalled** /ʌn'raɪv(ə)ld/ *adj* беспо до́бный. **unroll** /ʌn'rəʊl/ *vt & i* развёртывать(ся) *impf*, разверну́ть(ся) *pf*. **unruffled** /ʌn'rʌf(ə)ld/ *adj* (*smooth*) гла́дкий; (*calm*) споко́йный. **unruly** /ʌn'ru:lɪ/ *adj* непоко́рный.

unsafe /ʌn'seɪf/ *adj* опа́сный; (*insecure*) ненадёжный. **unsaid** /ʌn'sed/ *adj*: **leave ~** молча́ть

U

impf o+*prep*. **unsaleable** /ʌn'seɪləb(ə)l/ *adj* нехо́дкий. **unsalted** /ʌn'sɔːltɪd/ *adj* несолённый. **unsatisfactory** /ˌʌnsætɪs'fæktərɪ/ *adj* неудовлетвори́тельный. **unsatisfied** /ʌn'sætɪsfaɪd/ *adj* неудовлетворённый. **unsavoury** /ʌn'seɪvərɪ/ *adj* (*unpleasant*) неприя́тный; (*disreputable*) сомни́тельный. **unscathed** /ʌn'skeɪðd/ *adj* невреди́мый; (*predic*) цел и невреди́м. **unscheduled** /ʌn'ʃedjuːld/ *adj* (*transport*) внеочередно́й; (*event*) незаплани́рованный. **unscientific** /ˌʌnsaɪən'tɪfɪk/ *adj* ненау́чный. **unscrew** /ʌn'skruː/ *vt* & *i* отви́нчивать(ся) *impf*, отвинти́ть(ся) *pf*. **unscrupulous** /ʌn'skruːpjʊləs/ *adj* беспринци́пный. **unseat** /ʌn'siːt/ *vt* (*of horse*) сбра́сывать *impf*, сбро́сить *pf* с седла́; (*parl*) лиша́ть *impf*, лиши́ть *pf* парла́ментского манда́та.

unseemly /ʌn'siːmlɪ/ *adj* неподоба́ющий. **unseen** /ʌn'siːn/ *adj* неви́данный. **unselfconscious** /ˌʌnself'kɒnʃəs/ *adj* непосре́дственный. **unselfish** /ʌn'selfɪʃ/ *adj* бескоры́стный. **unsettle** /ʌn'set(ə)l/ *vt* выбива́ть *impf*, вы́бить *pf* из колеи́; (*upset*) расстра́ивать *impf*, расстро́ить *pf*. **unsettled** /ʌn'set(ə)ld/ *adj* (*weather*) неусто́йчивый; (*unresolved*) нерешённый. **unsettling** /-'setlɪŋ/ *adj* волну́ющий. **unshakeable** /ʌn'ʃeɪkəb(ə)l/ *adj* непоколеби́мый. **unshaven** /ʌn'ʃeɪv(ə)n/ *adj* небри́тый. **unsightly** /ʌn'saɪtlɪ/ *adj* непригля́дный, уро́дливый. **unsigned** /ʌn'saɪnd/ *adj* неподпи́санный. **unskilful** /ʌn'skɪlfʊl/ *adj* неуме́лый. **unskilled** /ʌn'skɪld/ *adj* неквалифици́рованный. **unsociable** /ʌn'səʊʃəb(ə)l/ *adj* необщи́тельный. **unsold** /ʌn'səʊld/ *adj* непро́данный. **unsolicited** /ˌʌnsə'lɪsɪtɪd/ *adj* непро́шеный. **unsolved** /ʌn'sɒlvd/ *adj* нерешённый. **unsophisticated** /ˌʌnsə'fɪstɪˌkeɪtɪd/ *adj* просто́й. **unsound** /ʌn'saʊnd/ *adj* (*unhealthy, unwholesome*) нездоро́вый; (*not solid*) непро́чный; (*unfounded*) необосно́ванный; **of ~ mind** душевнобольно́й. **unspeakable** /ʌn'spiːkəb(ə)l/ *adj* (*inexpressible*) невырази́мый; (*very bad*) отврати́тельный. **unspecified** /ʌn'spesɪˌfaɪd/ *adj* то́чно не ука́занный, неопределённый. **unspoilt** /ʌn'spɔɪlt/ *adj* неиспо́рченный. **unspoken** /ʌn'spəʊkən/ *adj* невы́сказанный. **unstable** /ʌn'steɪb(ə)l/ *adj* неусто́йчивый; (*mentally*) неуравнове́шенный. **unsteady** /ʌn'stedɪ/ *adj* неусто́йчивый. **unstuck** /ʌn'stʌk/ *adj*: **come ~** откле́иваться *impf*, откле́иться *pf*; (*fig*) прова́ливаться *impf*, провали́ться *pf*. **unsuccessful** /ˌʌnsək'sesfʊl/ *adj* неуда́чный, безуспе́шный. **unsuitable** /ʌn'suːtəb(ə)l/ *adj* неподходя́щий. **unsuited** /ʌn'suːtɪd/ *adj* непри́годный. **unsung** /ʌn'sʌŋ/ *adj* невоспе́тый. **unsupported** /ˌʌnsə'pɔːtɪd/ *adj* неподде́ржанный. **unsure** /ʌn'ʃʊə(r)/ *adj* неуве́ренный (**of o.s.** в себе́). **unsurpassed** /ˌʌnsə'pɑːst/ *adj* непревзойдённый. **unsurprising** /ˌʌnsə'praɪzɪŋ/ *adj* неудиви́тельный. **unsuspected** /ˌʌnsə'spektɪd/ *adj* (*unforeseen*) непредви́денный. **unsuspecting** /ˌʌnsə'spektɪŋ/ *adj* неподозрева́ющий. **unsweetened** /ʌn'swiːt(ə)nd/ *adj* неподсла́щенный. **unswerving** /ʌn'swɜːvɪŋ/ *adj* непоколеби́мый. **unsympathetic** /ˌʌnsɪmpə'θetɪk/ *adj* несочу́вствующий. **unsystematic** /ˌʌnsɪstə'mætɪk/ *adj* несистемати́чный.

untainted /ʌn'teɪntɪd/ *adj* неиспо́рченный. **untangle** /ʌn'tæŋg(ə)l/ *vt* распу́тывать *impf*, распу́тать *pf*. **untapped** /ʌn'tæpt/ *adj*: **~ resources** неиспо́льзованные ресу́рсы *m pl*. **untenable** /ʌn'tenəb(ə)l/ *adj* несостоя́тельный. **untested** /ʌn'testɪd/ *adj* неиспы́танный. **unthinkable** /ʌn'θɪŋkəb(ə)l/ *adj* невообрази́мый. **unthinking** /ʌn'θɪŋkɪŋ/ *adj* безду́мный. **untidiness** /ʌn'taɪdɪnɪs/ *n* неопря́тность; (*disorder*) беспоря́док. **untidy** /ʌn'taɪdɪ/ *adj* неопря́тный; (*in disorder*) в беспоря́дке. **untie** /ʌn'taɪ/ *vt* развя́зывать *impf*, развяза́ть *pf*; (*set free*) освобожда́ть *impf*, освободи́ть *pf*.

until /ən'tɪl/ *prep* до+*gen*; **not ~** не ра́ньше+*gen*; **~ then** до тех пор; *conj* пока́, пока́... не; **not ~** то́лько когда́.

untimely /ʌn'taɪmlɪ/ *adj* (*premature*) безвре́менный; (*inappropriate*) неуме́стный. **untiring** /ʌn'taɪərɪŋ/ *adj* неутоми́мый. **untold** /ʌn'təʊld/ *adj* (*incalculable*) бессчётный, несме́тный; (*inexpressible*) невырази́мый. **untouched** /ʌn'tʌtʃt/ *adj* нетро́нутый; (*indifferent*) равноду́шный. **untoward** /ˌʌntə'wɔːd/ *adj* неблагоприя́тный. **untrained** /ʌn'treɪnd/ *adj* необу́ченный. **untried** /ʌn'traɪd/ *adj* неиспы́танный. **untroubled** /ʌn'trʌb(ə)ld/ *adj* споко́йный. **untrue** /ʌn'truː/ *adj* неве́рный. **untrustworthy** /ʌn'trʌstˌwɜːðɪ/ *adj* ненадёжный. **untruth** /ʌn'truːθ/ *n* непра́вда, ложь. **untruthful** /ʌn'truːθfʊl/ *adj* лжи́вый.

unusable /ʌn'juːzəb(ə)l/ *adj* неприго́дный. **unused** /ʌn'juːzd/ *adj* неиспо́льзованный; (*unaccustomed*) /ʌn'juːst/ непривы́кший (**to** к+*dat*); **I am ~ to this** я к э́тому не привы́к. **unusual** /ʌn'juːʒʊəl/ *adj* необыкнове́нный, необы́чный. **unusually** /ʌn'juːʒʊəlɪ/ *adv* необыкнове́нно. **unutterable** /ʌn'ʌtərəb(ə)l/ *adj* невырази́мый.

unveil /ʌn'veɪl/ *vt* (*statue*) торже́ственно открыва́ть *impf*, откры́ть *pf*; (*disclose*) обнаро́довать *impf* & *pf*.

unwanted /ʌn'wɒntɪd/ *adj* нежела́нный. **unwarranted** /ʌn'wɒrəntɪd/ *adj* неопра́вданный. **unwary** /ʌn'weərɪ/ *adj* неосторо́жный. **unwavering** /ʌn'weɪvərɪŋ/ *adj* непоколеби́мый. **unwelcome** /ʌn'welkəm/ *adj* нежела́тельный; (*unpleasant*) неприя́тный. **unwell** /ʌn'wel/ *adj* нездоро́вый. **unwieldy** /ʌn'wiːldɪ/ *adj* громо́здкий. **unwilling** /ʌn'wɪlɪŋ/ *adj* несклóнный; **be ~** не хоте́ть *impf*, за~ *pf* (**to** +*inf*). **unwillingly** /ʌn'wɪlɪŋlɪ/ *adv* неохо́тно. **unwillingness** /ʌn'wɪlɪŋnɪs/ *n* неохо́та. **unwind** /ʌn'waɪnd/ *vt* & *i* разма́тывать(ся) *impf*, размота́ть(ся) *pf*; (*rest*) отдыха́ть *impf*, отдохну́ть *pf*. **unwise** /ʌn'waɪz/ *adj* не(благо)разу́мный. **unwitting** /ʌn'wɪtɪŋ/ *adj* нево́льный. **unwittingly** /ʌn'wɪtɪŋlɪ/ *adv* нево́льно. **unworkable** /ʌn'wɜːkəb(ə)l/ *adj* неприме́нимый. **unworldly** /ʌn'wɜːldlɪ/ *adj* не от ми́ра сего́. **unworthy** /ʌn'wɜːðɪ/ *adj* недосто́йный. **unwrap** /ʌn'ræp/ *vt* развёртывать *impf*, разверну́ть *pf*. **unwritten** /ʌn'rɪt(ə)n/ *adj*: **~ law** непи́саный зако́н.

unyielding /ʌn'jiːldɪŋ/ *adj* упо́рный, непода́тливый.

unzip /ʌn'zɪp/ *vt* расстёгивать *impf*, расстегну́ть *pf* (мо́лнию+*gen*).

up /ʌp/ *adv* (*motion*) наве́рх, вверх; (*position*) наверху́, вверху́; **~ and down** вверх и вниз; (*back and forth*) взад и вперёд; **~ to** (*towards*) к+*dat*; (*as far as, until*) до+*gen*; **~ to now** до сих пор; **be ~ against** име́ть *impf* де́ло с+*instr*; **it is ~ to you**+*inf*, э́то вам+*inf*, вы должны́+*inf*; **what's ~?** что случи́лось?; в чём де́ло?; **your time is ~** ва́ше вре́мя истекло́; **~ and about** на нога́х; **he isn't ~ yet** он ещё не встал; **he isn't ~ to this job** он не годи́тся для э́той рабо́ты; *prep* вверх по+*dat*; (*along*) (вдоль) по+*dat*; *vt* повыша́ть *impf*, повы́сить; *vi*

U

(*leap up*) взять *pf*; *adj*: **~-to-date** совреме́нный; (*fashionable*) мо́дный; **~-and-coming** многообеща́ющий; *n*: **~s and downs** (*fig*) превра́тности *f pl* судьбы́.

upbringing /'ʌp͵brɪŋɪŋ/ *n* воспита́ние.

update /ʌp'deɪt/ *vt* модернизи́ровать *impf* & *pf*; (*a book etc.*) дополня́ть *impf*, допо́лнить *pf*.

upgrade /ʌp'greɪd/ *vt* повыша́ть *impf*, повы́сить *pf* (по слу́жбе).

upheaval /ʌp'hi:v(ə)l/ *n* потрясе́ние.

uphill /'ʌphɪl/ *adj* (*fig*) тяжёлый; *adv* в го́ру.

uphold /ʌp'həʊld/ *vt* подде́рживать *impf*, поддержа́ть *pf*.

upholster /ʌp'həʊlstə(r)/ *vt* обива́ть *impf*, оби́ть *pf*. **upholsterer** /-rə(r)/ *n* обо́йщик. **upholstery** /-rɪ/ *n* оби́вка.

upkeep /'ʌpki:p/ *n* содержа́ние.

upland /'ʌplənd/ *n* гори́стая часть страны́; *adj* наго́рный.

uplift /ʌp'lɪft/ *vt* поднима́ть *impf*, подня́ть *pf*.

up-market /ʌp'mɑ:kɪt/ *adj* дорого́й.

upon /ə'pɒn/ *prep* (*position*) на +*prep*, (*motion*) на+*acc*; *see* **on**

upper /'ʌpə(r)/ *adj* ве́рхний; (*socially, in rank*) вы́сший; **gain the ~ hand** оде́рживать *impf*, одержа́ть *pf* верх (**over** над+*instr*); *n* передо́к. **uppermost** *adj* са́мый ве́рхний, вы́сший; **be ~ in person's mind** бо́льше всего́ занима́ть *impf*, заня́ть *pf* мы́сли кого́-л.

upright /'ʌpraɪt/ *n* сто́йка; *adj* вертика́льный; (*honest*) че́стный; **~ piano** пиани́но *neut indecl*.

uprising /'ʌp͵raɪzɪŋ/ *n* восста́ние.

uproar /'ʌprɔ:(r)/ *n* шум, гам.

uproot /ʌp'ru:t/ *vt* вырыва́ть *impf*, вы́рвать *pf* с ко́рнем; (*people*) выселя́ть *impf*, вы́селить *pf*.

upset *n* /'ʌpset/ расстро́йство; *vt* /ʌp'set/ расстра́ивать *impf*, расстро́ить *pf*; (*overturn*) опроки́дывать *impf*, опроки́нуть *pf*; *adj* (*miserable*) расстро́енный; **~ stomach** расстро́йство желу́дка.

upshot /'ʌpʃɒt/ *n* развя́зка, результа́т.

upside-down /͵ʌpsaɪd'daʊn/ *adj* перевёрнутый вверх дном; *adv* вверх дном; (*in disorder*) в беспоря́дке.

upstairs /ʌp'steəz/ *adv* (*position*) наверху́; (*motion*) наве́рх; *n* ве́рхний эта́ж; *adj* находя́щийся в ве́рхнем этаже́.

upstart /'ʌpstɑ:t/ *n* вы́скочка *m* & *f*.

upstream /'ʌpstri:m/ *adv* про́тив тече́ния; (*situation*) вверх по тече́нию.

upsurge /'ʌpsɜ:dʒ/ *n* подъём, волна́.

uptake /'ʌpteɪk/ *n*: **be quick on the ~** бы́стро сообража́ть *impf*, сообрази́ть *pf*.

upturn /'ʌptɜ:n/ *n* (*fig*) улучше́ние. **upturned** /-tɜ:nd/ *adj* (*face etc.*) по́днятый кве́рху; (*inverted*) перевёрнутый.

upward /'ʌpwəd/ *adj* напра́вленный вверх. **upwards** /-wədz/ *adv* вверх; **~ of** свы́ше+*gen*.

uranium /jʊ'reɪnɪəm/ *n* ура́н.

urban /'ɜ:bən/ *adj* городско́й.

urbane /ɜ:'beɪn/ *adj* ве́жливый.

urchin /'ɜ:tʃɪn/ *n* мальчи́шка *m*.

urge /ɜ:dʒ/ *n* (*incitement*) побужде́ние; (*desire*) жела́ние; *vt* (*impel*, **~** *on*) подгоня́ть *impf*, подогна́ть *pf*; (*warn*) предупрежда́ть *impf*, предупреди́ть *pf*; (*try to persuade*) убежда́ть *impf*. **urgency** /'ɜ:dʒ(ə)nsɪ/ *n* сро́чность, ва́жность; **a matter of great ~** сро́чное де́ло. **urgent** /'ɜ:dʒ(ə)nt/ *adj* сро́чный; (*insistent*) настоя́тельный. **urgently** /'ɜ:dʒ(ə)ntlɪ/ *adv* сро́чно.

urinate /'jʊərɪ͵neɪt/ *vi* мочи́ться *impf*, по~ *pf*. **urine** /'jʊərɪn/ *n* моча́.

urn /ɜ:n/ *n* у́рна.

US(A) *abbr* (*of* **United States of America**) США, Соединённые Шта́ты Аме́рики.

usable /ˈjuːzəb(ə)l/ *adj* го́дный к употребле́нию. **usage** /ˈjuːsɪdʒ/ *n* употребле́ние; (*treatment*) обраще́ние. **use** *n* /juːs/ (*utilization*) употребле́ние, по́льзование; (*benefit*) по́льза; (*application*) примене́ние; **it is no ~ (-ing)** бесполе́зно (+*inf*); **make ~ of** испо́льзовать *impf* & *pf*; по́льзоваться *impf* +*instr*; *vt* /juːz/ употребля́ть *impf*, употреби́ть *pf*; по́льзоваться *impf* +*instr*; (*apply*) применя́ть *impf*, примени́ть *pf*; (*treat*) обраща́ться *impf* с+*instr*; **I ~d to see him often** я ча́сто его́ встреча́л; **be, get ~d to** привыка́ть *impf*, привы́кнуть *pf* (**to** к+*dat*); **~ up** расхо́довать *impf*, из~ *pf*. **used** /juːzd/ *adj* (*second-hand*) ста́рый. **useful** /ˈjuːsfʊl/ *adj* поле́зный; **come in ~, prove ~** пригоди́ться *pf* (**to** +*dat*). **useless** /ˈjuːslɪs/ *adj* бесполе́зный. **user** /ˈjuːzə(r)/ *n* потреби́тель *m*.

usher /ˈʌʃə(r)/ *n* (*theat*) билетёр; *vt* (*lead in*) вводи́ть *impf*, ввести́ *pf*; (*proclaim*, **~ in**) возвеща́ть *impf*, возвести́ть *pf*. **usherette** /ˌʌʃəˈret/ *n* билетёрша.

USSR *abbr* (*of* **Union of Soviet Socialist Republics**) СССР, Сою́з Сове́тских Социалисти́ческих Респу́блик.

usual /ˈjuːʒʊəl/ *adj* обыкнове́нный, обы́чный; **as ~** как обы́чно. **usually** /-lɪ/ *adv* обыкнове́нно, обы́чно.

usurp /jʊˈzɜːp/ *vt* узурпи́ровать *impf* & *pf*. **usurper** /-ˈzɜːpə(r)/ *n* узурпа́тор.

usury /ˈjuːʒərɪ/ *n* ростовщи́чество.

utensil /juːˈtens(ə)l/ *n* инструме́нт; *pl* у́тварь, посу́да.

uterus /ˈjuːtərəs/ *n* ма́тка.

utilitarian /ˌjʊtɪlɪˈteərɪən/ *adj* утилита́рный. **utilitarianism** /-ˌnɪz(ə)m/ *n* утилитари́зм. **utility** /juːˈtɪlɪtɪ/ *n* поле́зность; *pl*: **public utilities** коммуна́льные услу́ги *f pl*. **utilize** /ˈjuːtɪˌlaɪz/ *vt* испо́льзовать *impf* & *pf*.

utmost /ˈʌtməʊst/ *adj* (*extreme*) кра́йний; **this is of the ~ importance to me** э́то для меня́ кра́йне ва́жно; *n*: **do one's ~** де́лать *impf*, с~ *pf* всё возмо́жное.

Utopia /juːˈtəʊpɪə/ *n* уто́пия. **utopian** /-pɪən/ *adj* утопи́ческий.

utter /ˈʌtə(r)/ *attrib* по́лный, абсолю́тный; (*out-and-out*) отъя́вленный (*coll*); *vt* произноси́ть *impf*, произнести́ *pf*; (*let out*) издава́ть *impf*, изда́ть *pf*. **utterance** /ˈʌtərəns/ *n* (*uttering*) произнесе́ние; (*pronouncement*) выска́зывание. **utterly** /ˈʌtəlɪ/ *adv* соверше́нно.

Uzbek /ˈʌzbek/ *n* узбе́к, -е́чка. **Uzbekistan** /ˌʌzbekɪˈstɑːn/ *n* Узбекиста́н.

V

vacancy /ˈveɪkənsɪ/ *n* (*for job*) вака́нсия, свобо́дное ме́сто; (*at hotel*) свобо́дный но́мер. **vacant** /-kənt/ *adj* (*post*) вака́нтный; (*post*; *not engaged, free*) свобо́дный; (*empty*) пусто́й; (*look*) отсу́тствующий. **vacate** /vəˈkeɪt/ *vt* освобожда́ть *impf*, освободи́ть *pf*. **vacation** /vəˈkeɪʃ(ə)n/ *n* кани́кулы (-л) *pl*; (*leave*) о́тпуск.

vaccinate /ˈvæksɪˌneɪt/ *vt* вакцини́ровать *impf* & *pf*. **vaccination** /-ˈneɪʃ(ə)n/ *n* приви́вка (**against** от, про́тив +*gen*). **vaccine** /ˈvæksiːn/ *n* вакци́на.

vacillate /ˈvæsɪˌleɪt/ *vi* колеба́ться *impf*. **vacillation** /-ˈleɪʃ(ə)n/ *n* колеба́ние.

vacuous /ˈvækjʊəs/ *adj* пусто́й. **vacuum** /ˈvækjʊəm/ *n* ва́куум; (*fig*) пустота́; *vt* пылесо́сить *impf*, про~ *pf*; **~ cleaner** пылесо́с; **~ flask** те́рмос.

vagabond /ˈvægəˌbɒnd/ *n* бродя́га *m*.

vagary /ˈveɪgərɪ/ *n* капри́з.

vagina /vəˈdʒaɪnə/ *n* влага́лище.

vagrant /ˈveɪgrənt/ *n* бродя́га *m*.

vague /veɪg/ *adj* (*indeterminate, uncertain*) неопределённый; (*unclear*) неясный; (*dim*) смутный; (*absent-minded*) рассеянный. **vagueness** /-nɪs/ *n* неопределённость, неясность; (*absent-mindedness*) рассеянность.
vain /veɪn/ *adj* (*futile*) тщетный, напрасный; (*empty*) пустой; (*conceited*) тщеславный; **in ~** напрасно.
vale /veɪl/ *n* дол, долина.
valentine /'vælən,taɪn/ *n* (*card*) поздравительная карточка с днём святого Валентина.
valet /'væleɪ/ *n* камердинер.
valiant /'væljənt/ *adj* храбрый.
valid /'vælɪd/ *adj* действительный; (*weighty*) веский. **validate** /-,deɪt/ *vt* (*ratify*) утверждать *impf*, утвердить *pf*. **validity** /və'lɪdɪtɪ/ *n* действительность; (*weightiness*) вескость.
valley /'vælɪ/ *n* долина.
valour /'vælə(r)/ *n* доблесть.
valuable /'væljʊəb(ə)l/ *adj* ценный; *n pl* ценности *f pl*. **valuation** /,væljʊ'eɪʃ(ə)n/ *n* оценка. **value** /'vælju:/ *n* ценность; (*math*) величина; *pl* ценности *f pl*; **~-added tax** налог на добавленную стоимость; **~ judgement** субъективная оценка; *vt* (*estimate*) оценивать *impf*, оценить *pf*; (*hold dear*) ценить *impf*.
valve /vælv/ *n* (*tech, med, mus*) клапан; (*tech*) вентиль *m*; (*radio*) электронная лампа.
vampire /'væmpaɪə(r)/ *n* вампир.
van /væn/ *n* фургон.
vandal /'vænd(ə)l/ *n* вандал. **vandalism** /-də,lɪz(ə)m/ *n* вандализм. **vandalize** /-də,laɪz/ *vt* разрушать *impf*, разрушить *pf*.
vanguard /'væŋgɑ:d/ *n* авангард.
vanilla /və'nɪlə/ *n* ваниль.
vanish /'vænɪʃ/ *vi* исчезать *impf*, исчезнуть *pf*.
vanity /'vænɪtɪ/ *n* (*futility*) тщета; (*conceit*) тщеславие.
vanquish /'væŋkwɪʃ/ *vt* побеждать *impf*, победить *pf*.
vantage-point /'vɑ:ntɪdʒ,pɔɪnt/ *n* (*mil*) наблюдательный пункт; (*fig*) выгодная позиция.
vapour /'veɪpə(r)/ *n* пар.
variable /'veərɪəb(ə)l/ *adj* изменчивый; (*weather*) неустойчивый, переменный; *n* (*math*) переменная (величина). **variance** /'veərɪəns/ *n*: **be at ~ with** (*contradict*) противоречить *impf +dat*; (*disagree*) расходиться *impf*, разойтись *pf* во мнениях с+*instr*. **variant** /-rɪənt/ *n* вариант. **variation** /-rɪ'eɪʃ(ə)n/ *n* (*varying*) изменение; (*variant*) вариант; (*variety*) разновидность; (*mus*) вариация.
varicose /'værɪ,kəʊs/ *adj*: **~ veins** расширение вен.
varied /'veərɪd/ *adj* разнообразный. **variegated** /'veərɪ,geɪtɪd/ *adj* разноцветный. **variety** /və'raɪətɪ/ *n* разнообразие; (*sort*) разновидность; (*a number*) ряд; **~ show** варьете *neut indecl*. **various** /'veərɪəs/ *adj* разный.
varnish /'vɑ:nɪʃ/ *n* лак; *vt* лакировать *impf*, от~ *pf*.
vary /'veərɪ/ *vt* разнообразить *impf*, менять *impf*; *vi* (*change*) меняться *impf*; (*differ*) разниться *impf*.
vase /vɑ:z/ *n* ваза.
Vaseline /'væsɪ,li:n/ *n* (*propr*) вазелин.
vast /vɑ:st/ *adj* громадный. **vastly** /-lɪ/ *adv* значительно.
VAT *abbr* (*of* **value-added tax**) налог на добавленную стоимость.
vat /væt/ *n* чан, бак.
vaudeville /'vɔ:dəvɪl/ *n* водевиль *m*.
vault[1] /vɔ:lt/ *n* (*leap*) прыжок; *vt* перепрыгивать *impf*, перепрыгнуть *pf*; *vi* прыгать *impf*, прыгнуть *pf*.
vault[2] /vɔ:lt/ *n* (*arch, covering*) свод; (*cellar*) погреб; (*tomb*) склеп. **vaulted** /-tɪd/ *adj* сводчатый.

VDU *abbr* (*of* **visual display unit**) монитóр.

veal /viːl/ *n* телятина.

vector /ˈvektə(r)/ *n* (*math*) вéктор.

veer /vɪə(r)/ *vi* (*change direction*) изменя́ть *impf*, измени́ть *pf* направлéние; (*turn*) повора́чивать *impf*, повороти́ть *pf*.

vegetable /ˈvedʒɪtəb(ə)l/ *n* óвощ; *adj* овощнóй. **vegetarian** /ˌvedʒɪˈteərɪən/ *n* вегетариáнец, -нка; *attrib* вегетариáнский. **vegetate** /ˈvedʒɪˌteɪt/ *vi* (*fig*) прозябáть *impf*. **vegetation** /ˌvedʒɪˈteɪʃ(ə)n/ *n* расти́тельность.

vehemence /ˈviːəməns/ *n* (*force*) си́ла; (*passion*) стрáстность. **vehement** /-mənt/ *adj* (*forceful*) си́льный; (*passionate*) стрáстный.

vehicle /ˈviːɪk(ə)l/ *n* трáнспортное срéдство; (*motor* ~) автомоби́ль *m*; (*medium*) срéдство.

veil /veɪl/ *n* вуáль; (*fig*) завéса. **veiled** /veɪld/ *adj* скры́тый.

vein /veɪn/ *n* вéна; (*of leaf*; *streak*) жи́лка; **in the same** ~ в том же ду́хе.

velocity /vɪˈlɒsɪtɪ/ *n* скóрость.

velvet /ˈvelvɪt/ *n* бáрхат; *adj* бáрхатный. **velvety** /-tɪ/ *adj* бархати́стый.

vending-machine /ˈvendɪŋ/ *n* торгóвый автомáт. **vendor** /-də(r)/ *n* продавéц, -вщи́ца.

vendetta /venˈdetə/ *n* вендéтта.

veneer /vɪˈnɪə(r)/ *n* фанéра; (*fig*) лоск.

venerable /ˈvenərəb(ə)l/ *adj* почтéнный. **venerate** /-ˌreɪt/ *vt* благоговéть *impf* пéред+*instr*. **veneration** /ˌvenəˈreɪʃ(ə)n/ *n* благоговéние.

venereal /vɪˈnɪərɪəl/ *adj* венери́ческий.

venetian blind /vɪˈniːʃ(ə)n blaɪnd/ *n* жалюзи́ *neut indecl*.

vengeance /ˈvendʒ(ə)ns/ *n* месть; **take** ~ мстить *impf*, ото~ *pf* (**on** +*dat*; **for** за+*acc*); **with a** ~ вовсю́. **vengeful** /ˈvendʒfʊl/ *adj* мсти́тельный.

venison /ˈvenɪs(ə)n/ *n* олéни́на.

venom /ˈvenəm/ *n* яд. **venomous** /-məs/ *adj* ядови́тый.

vent[1] /vent/ *n* (*opening*) вы́ход (*also fig*), отвéрстие; *vt* (*feelings*) давáть *impf*, дать *pf* вы́ход+*dat*; изливáть *impf*, изли́ть *pf* (**on** на+*acc*).

vent[2] /vent/ *n* (*slit*) разрéз.

ventilate /ˈventɪˌleɪt/ *vt* провéтривать *impf*, провéтрить *pf*. **ventilation** /-ˈleɪʃ(ə)n/ *n* вентиля́ция. **ventilator** /ˈventɪˌleɪtə(r)/ *n* вентиля́тор.

ventriloquist /venˈtrɪləˌkwɪst/ *n* чревовещáтель *m*.

venture /ˈventʃə(r)/ *n* предприя́тие; *vi* (*dare*) осмéливаться *impf*, осмéлиться *pf*; *vt* (*risk*) рисковáть *impf* +*instr*.

venue /ˈvenjuː/ *n* мéсто.

veranda /vəˈrændə/ *n* верáнда.

verb /vɜːb/ *n* глагóл. **verbal** /ˈvɜːb(ə)l/ *adj* (*oral*) у́стный; (*relating to words*) словéсный; (*gram*) отглагóльный. **verbatim** /vɜːˈbeɪtɪm/ *adj* дослóвный; *adv* дослóвно. **verbose** /vɜːˈbəʊs/ *adj* многослóвный.

verdict /ˈvɜːdɪkt/ *n* приговóр.

verge /vɜːdʒ/ *n* (*also fig*) край; (*of road*) обóчина; (*fig*) грань; **on the** ~ **of** на грáни+*gen*; **he was on the** ~ **of telling all** он чуть не рассказáл всё; *vi*: ~ **on** грани́чить *impf* с+*instr*.

verification /ˌverɪfɪˈkeɪʃ(ə)n/ *n* провéрка; (*confirmation*) подтверждéние. **verify** /ˈverɪˌfaɪ/ *vt* проверя́ть *impf*, провéрить *pf*; (*confirm*) подтверждáть *impf*, подтверди́ть *pf*.

vermin /ˈvɜːmɪn/ *n* вреди́тели *m pl*.

vernacular /vəˈnækjʊlə(r)/ *n* роднóй язы́к; мéстный диалéкт; (*homely language*) разговóрный язы́к.

versatile /ˈvɜːsəˌtaɪl/ *adj* многосторóнний.

verse /vɜːs/ *n* (*also bibl*) стих;

(*stanza*) строфа́; (*poetry*) стихи́ *m pl*. **versed** /vɜːst/ *adj* о́пытный, све́дущий (**in** в+*prep*).
version /'vɜːʃ(ə)n/ *n* (*variant*) вариа́нт; (*interpretation*) ве́рсия; (*text*) текст.
versus /'vɜːsəs/ *prep* про́тив+*gen*.
vertebra /'vɜːtɪbrə/ *n* позвоно́к; *pl* позвоно́чник. **vertebrate** /-brət/ *n* позвоно́чное живо́тное *sb*.
vertical /'vɜːtɪk(ə)l/ *adj* вертика́льный; *n* вертика́ль.
vertigo /'vɜːtɪˌgəʊ/ *n* головокруже́ние.
verve /vɜːv/ *n* жи́вость, энтузиа́зм.
very /'verɪ/ *adj* (*that* ~ *same*) тот са́мый; (*this* ~ *same*) э́тот са́мый; **at that** ~ **moment** в тот са́мый моме́нт; (*precisely*) как раз; **you are the** ~ **person I was looking for** как раз вас я иска́л; **the** ~ (*even the*) да́же, оди́н; **the** ~ **thought frightens me** одна́, да́же, мысль об э́том меня́ пуга́ет; (*the extreme*) са́мый; **at the** ~ **end** в са́мом конце́; *adv* о́чень; ~ **much** о́чень; ~ **much** +*comp* гора́здо +*comp*; ~+*superl*, *superl*; ~ **first** са́мый пе́рвый; ~ **well** (*agreement*) хорошо́, ла́дно; **not** ~ не о́чень, дово́льно +*neg*.
vessel /'ves(ə)l/ *n* сосу́д; (*ship*) су́дно.
vest[1] /vest/ *n* ма́йка; (*waistcoat*) жиле́т.
vest[2] /vest/ *vt* (*with power*) облека́ть *impf*, обле́чь *pf* (**with** +*instr*). **vested** /-tɪd/ *adj*: ~ **interest** ли́чная заинтересо́ванность; ~ **interests** (*entrepreneurs*) кру́пные предпринима́тели *m pl*.
vestibule /'vestɪˌbjuːl/ *n* вестибю́ль *m*.
vestige /'vestɪdʒ/ *n* (*trace*) след; (*sign*) при́знак.
vestments /'vestmənts/ *n pl* (*eccl*) облаче́ние. **vestry** /'vestrɪ/ *n* ри́зница.
vet /vet/ *n* ветерина́р; *vt* (*fig*) проверя́ть *impf*, прове́рить *pf*.
veteran /'vetərən/ *n* ветера́н; *adj* ста́рый.
veterinary /'vetəˌrɪnərɪ/ *adj* ветерина́рный; *n* ветерина́р.
veto /'viːtəʊ/ *n* ве́то *neut indecl*; *vt* налага́ть *impf*, наложи́ть *pf* ве́то на+*acc*.
vex /veks/ *vt* досажда́ть *impf*, досади́ть *pf* +*dat*. **vexation** /vek'seɪʃ(ə)n/ *n* доса́да. **vexed** /vekst/ *adj* (*annoyed*) серди́тый; (*question*) спо́рный. **vexatious, vexing** /vek'seɪʃəs, 'veksɪŋ/ *adj* доса́дный.
via /'vaɪə/ *prep* че́рез+*acc*.
viable /'vaɪəb(ə)l/ *adj* (*able to survive*) жизнеспосо́бный; (*feasible*) осуществи́мый.
viaduct /'vaɪəˌdʌkt/ *n* виаду́к.
vibrant /'vaɪbrənt/ *adj* (*lively*) живо́й. **vibrate** /vaɪ'breɪt/ *vi* вибри́ровать *impf*; *vt* (*make* ~) заставля́ть *impf*, заста́вить *pf* вибри́ровать. **vibration** /vaɪ'breɪʃ(ə)n/ *n* вибра́ция. **vibrato** /vɪ'brɑːtəʊ/ *n* вибра́то *neut indecl*.
vicar /'vɪkə(r)/ *n* прихо́дский свяще́нник. **vicarage** /-rɪdʒ/ *n* дом свяще́нника.
vicarious /vɪ'keərɪəs/ *adj* чужо́й.
vice[1] /vaɪs/ *n* (*evil*) поро́к.
vice[2] /vaɪs/ *n* (*tech*) тиски́ (-ко́в) *pl*.
vice- *in comb* вице-, замести́тель *m*; ~**-chairman** замести́тель *m* председа́теля; ~**-chancellor** (*univ*) проре́ктор; ~**-president** вице-президе́нт. **viceroy** /'vaɪsrɔɪ/ *n* вице-коро́ль *m*.
vice versa /ˌvaɪsɪ 'vɜːsə/ *adv* наоборо́т.
vicinity /vɪ'sɪnɪtɪ/ *n* окре́стность; **in the** ~ побли́зости (**of** от+*gen*).
vicious /'vɪʃəs/ *adj* зло́бный; ~ **circle** поро́чный круг.
vicissitude /vɪ'sɪsɪˌtjuːd/ *n* превра́тность.
victim /'vɪktɪm/ *n* же́ртва; (*of accident*) пострада́вший *sb*. **victimization** /ˌvɪktɪmaɪ'zeɪʃ(ə)n/ *n* пресле́дование. **victimize**

/ˈvɪktɪˌmaɪz/ *vt* преслéдовать *impf.*

victor /ˈvɪktə(r)/ *n* победи́тель *m*, ~ница.

Victorian /vɪkˈtɔːrɪən/ *adj* викториа́нский.

victorious /vɪkˈtɔːrɪəs/ *adj* победоно́сный. **victory** /ˈvɪktərɪ/ *n* побе́да.

video /ˈvɪdɪəʊ/ *n* (~ *recorder*, ~ *cassette*, ~ *film*) ви́део *neut indecl*; **~ camera** видеока́мера; **~ cassette** видеокассе́та; **~ (cassette) recorder** видеомагнитофо́н; **~ game** видеоигра́; *vt* запи́сывать *impf*, записа́ть *pf* на ви́део.

vie /vaɪ/ *vi* сопе́рничать *impf* (**with** с+*instr*; **for** в+*prep*).

Vietnam /ˌvɪetˈnæm/ *n* Вьетна́м. **Vietnamese** /ˌvɪetnəˈmiːz/ *n* вьетна́мец, -мка; *adj* вьетна́мский.

view /vjuː/ *n* (*prospect*, *picture*) вид; (*opinion*) взгляд; (*viewing*) просмо́тр; (*inspection*) осмо́тр; **in ~ of** ввиду́+*gen*; **on ~** вы́ставленный для обозре́ния; **with a ~ to** с це́лью+*gen*, +*inf*; *vt* (*pictures etc.*) рассма́тривать *impf*; (*inspect*) осма́тривать *impf*, осмотре́ть *pf*; (*mentally*) смотре́ть *impf* на+*acc*. **viewer** /ˈvjuːə(r)/ *n* зри́тель *m*, ~ница. **viewfinder** /ˈvjuːˌfaɪndə(r)/ *n* видоиска́тель *m*. **viewpoint** *n* то́чка зре́ния.

vigil /ˈvɪdʒɪl/ *n* бде́ние; **keep ~** дежу́рить *impf*. **vigilance** /-ləns/ *n* бди́тельность. **vigilant** /-lənt/ *adj* бди́тельный. **vigilante** /ˌvɪdʒɪˈlæntɪ/ *n* дружи́нник.

vigorous /ˈvɪgərəs/ *adj* си́льный, энерги́чный. **vigour** /ˈvɪgə(r)/ *n* си́ла, эне́ргия.

vile /vaɪl/ *adj* гну́сный. **vilify** /ˈvɪlɪˌfaɪ/ *vt* черни́ть *impf*, о~ *pf*.

villa /ˈvɪlə/ *n* ви́лла.

village /ˈvɪlɪdʒ/ *n* дере́вня; *attrib* деревéнский. **villager** /-dʒə(r)/ *n* жи́тель *m* дере́вни.

villain /ˈvɪlən/ *n* злоде́й.

vinaigrette /ˌvɪnɪˈgret/ *n* припра́ва из у́ксуса и оли́вкового ма́сла.

vindicate /ˈvɪndɪˌkeɪt/ *vt* опра́вдывать *impf*, оправда́ть *pf*. **vindication** /-ˈkeɪʃ(ə)n/ *n* оправда́ние.

vindictive /vɪnˈdɪktɪv/ *adj* мсти́тельный.

vine /vaɪn/ *n* виногра́дная лоза́.

vinegar /ˈvɪnɪgə(r)/ *n* у́ксус.

vineyard /ˈvɪnjəd/ *n* виногра́дник.

vintage /ˈvɪntɪdʒ/ *n* (*year*) год; (*fig*) вы́пуск; *attrib* (*wine*) ма́рочный; (*car*) архаи́ческий.

viola /vɪˈəʊlə/ *n* (*mus*) альт.

violate /ˈvaɪəˌleɪt/ *vt* (*treaty*, *privacy*) наруша́ть *impf*, нару́шить *pf*; (*grave*) оскверня́ть *impf*, оскверни́ть *pf*. **violation** /-ˈleɪʃ(ə)n/ *n* наруше́ние; оскверне́ние.

violence /ˈvaɪələns/ *n* (*physical coercion*, *force*) наси́лие; (*strength*, *force*) си́ла. **violent** /-lənt/ *adj* (*person*, *storm*, *argument*) свире́пый; (*pain*) си́льный; (*death*) наси́льственный. **violently** /-ləntlɪ/ *adv* си́льно, о́чень.

violet /ˈvaɪələt/ *n* (*bot*) фиа́лка; (*colour*) фиоле́товый цвет; *adj* фиоле́товый.

violin /ˌvaɪəˈlɪn/ *n* скри́пка. **violinist** /-nɪst/ *n* скрипа́ч, ~ка.

VIP *abbr* (*of* **very important person**) о́чень ва́жное лицо́.

viper /ˈvaɪpə(r)/ *n* гадю́ка.

virgin /ˈvɜːdʒɪn/ *n* де́вственница, (*male*) де́вственник; **V~ Mary** де́ва Мари́я. **virginal** /-n(ə)l/ *adj* де́вственный. **virginity** /vəˈdʒɪnɪtɪ/ *n* де́вственность. **Virgo** /ˈvɜːgəʊ/ *n* Де́ва.

virile /ˈvɪraɪl/ *adj* му́жественный. **virility** /-ˈrɪlɪtɪ/ *n* му́жество.

virtual /ˈvɜːtjʊəl/ *adj* факти́ческий; (*comput*) виртуа́льный. **virtually** /-lɪ/ *adv* факти́чески. **virtue** /ˈvɜːtjuː/ *n* (*excellence*) доброде́тель; (*merit*) досто́инство; **by ~ of** на основа́нии+*gen*. **virtuosity** /ˌvɜːtjʊˈɒsɪtɪ/ *n* виртуо́зность. **virtuoso** /ˌvɜːtjʊˈəʊsəʊ/ *n* виртуо́з. **virtuous** /ˈvɜːtjʊəs/ *adj* доброде́тельный.

virulent /ˈvɪrʊlənt/ *adj* (*med*) вируле́нтный; (*fig*) зло́бный.

V

virus /ˈvaɪərəs/ *n* ви́рус.
visa /ˈviːzə/ *n* ви́за.
vis-à-vis /ˌviːzɑːˈviː/ *prep* (*with regard to*) по отноше́нию к+*dat.*
viscount /ˈvaɪkaʊnt/ *n* вико́нт. **viscountess** /-tɪs/ *n* виконте́сса.
viscous /ˈvɪskəs/ *adj* вя́зкий.
visibility /ˌvɪzɪˈbɪlɪtɪ/ *n* ви́димость. **visible** /ˈvɪzɪb(ə)l/ *adj* ви́димый. **visibly** /ˈvɪzɪblɪ/ *adv* я́вно, заме́тно.
vision /ˈvɪʒ(ə)n/ *n* (*sense*) зре́ние; (*apparition*) виде́ние; (*dream*) мечта́; (*insight*) проница́тельность. **visionary** /ˈvɪʒənərɪ/ *adj* (*unreal*) при́зрачный; (*impracticable*) неосуществи́мый; (*insightful*) проница́тельный; *n* (*dreamer*) мечта́тель *m.*
visit /ˈvɪzɪt/ *n* посеще́ние, визи́т; *vt* посеща́ть *impf*, посети́ть *pf*; (*call on*) заходи́ть *impf*, зайти́ *pf* к+*dat.* **visitation** /ˌvɪzɪˈteɪʃ(ə)n/ *n* официа́льное посеще́ние. **visitor** /ˈvɪzɪtə(r)/ *n* гость *m*, посети́тель *m.*
visor /ˈvaɪzə(r)/ *n* (*of cap*) козырёк; (*in car*) солнцезащи́тный щито́к; (*of helmet*) забра́ло.
vista /ˈvɪstə/ *n* перспекти́ва, вид.
visual /ˈvɪzjʊəl/ *adj* (*of vision*) зри́тельный; (*graphic*) нагля́дный; **~ aids** нагля́дные посо́бия *neut pl.* **visualize** /-ˌlaɪz/ *vt* представля́ть *impf*, предста́вить *pf* себе́.
vital /ˈvaɪt(ə)l/ *adj* абсолю́тно необходи́мый (**to, for** для+*gen*); (*essential to life*) жи́зненный; **of ~ importance** первостепе́нной ва́жности. **vitality** /vaɪˈtælɪtɪ/ *n* (*liveliness*) эне́ргия. **vitally** /ˈvaɪtəlɪ/ *adv* жи́зненно.
vitamin /ˈvɪtəmɪn/ *n* витами́н.
vitreous /ˈvɪtrɪəs/ *adj* стекля́нный.
vitriolic /ˌvɪtrɪˈɒlɪk/ *adj* (*fig*) е́дкий.
vivacious /vɪˈveɪʃəs/ *adj* живо́й. **vivacity** /vɪˈvæsɪtɪ/ *n* жи́вость.
viva (voce) /ˈvaɪvə (ˈvəʊtʃɪ) *n* у́стный экза́мен.
vivid /ˈvɪvɪd/ *adj* (*bright*) я́ркий; (*lively*) живо́й. **vividness** /-nɪs/ *n* я́ркость; жи́вость.
vivisection /ˌvɪvɪˈsekʃ(ə)n/ *n* вивисе́кция.
vixen /ˈvɪks(ə)n/ *n* лиси́ца-са́мка.
viz. /vɪz/ *adv* то есть, а и́менно.
vocabulary /vəˈkæbjʊlərɪ/ *n* (*range, list, of words*) слова́рь *m*; (*range of words*) запа́с слов; (*of a language*) слова́рный соста́в.
vocal /ˈvəʊk(ə)l/ *adj* голосово́й; (*mus*) вока́льный; (*noisy*) шу́мный; **~ chord** голосова́я свя́зка. **vocalist** /-lɪst/ *n* певе́ц, -ви́ца.
vocation /vəˈkeɪʃ(ə)n/ *n* призва́ние. **vocational** /-n(ə)l/ *adj* профессиона́льный.
vociferous /vəˈsɪfərəs/ *adj* шу́мный.
vodka /ˈvɒdkə/ *n* во́дка.
vogue /vəʊg/ *n* мо́да; **in ~** в мо́де.
voice /vɔɪs/ *n* го́лос; **~ mail** голосова́я по́чта; *vt* выража́ть *impf*, вы́разить *pf.*
void /vɔɪd/ *n* пустота́; *adj* пусто́й; (*invalid*) недействи́тельный; **~ of** лишённый +*gen.*
volatile /ˈvɒləˌtaɪl/ *adj* (*chem*) лету́чий; (*person*) непостоя́нный, неусто́йчивый.
volcanic /vɒlˈkænɪk/ *adj* вулкани́ческий. **volcano** /-ˈkeɪnəʊ/ *n* вулка́н.
vole /vəʊl/ *n* (*zool*) полёвка.
volition /vəˈlɪʃ(ə)n/ *n* во́ля; **by one's own ~** по свое́й во́ле.
volley /ˈvɒlɪ/ *n* (*missiles*) залп; (*fig*) град; (*sport*) уда́р с лёта; *vt* (*sport*) ударя́ть *impf*, уда́рить *pf* с лёта. **volleyball** *n* волейбо́л.
volt /vəʊlt/ *n* вольт. **voltage** /ˈvəʊltɪdʒ/ *n* напряже́ние.
voluble /ˈvɒljʊb(ə)l/ *adj* говорли́вый.
volume /ˈvɒljuːm/ *n* (*book*) том; (*capacity, size*) объём; (*loudness*) гро́мкость. **voluminous** /vəˈljuːmɪnəs/ *adj* обши́рный.
voluntary /ˈvɒləntərɪ/ *adj* доброво́льный. **volunteer** /ˌvɒlənˈtɪə(r)/ *n* доброво́лец; *vt* предлага́ть *impf*, предложи́ть *pf*; *vi* (*offer*) вызыва́ться *impf*, вы́зваться *pf* (*inf*, +*inf*; **for** в+*acc*); (*mil*) идти́

impf, пойти́ *pf* доброво́льцем.
voluptuous /vəˈlʌptjʊəs/ *adj* сластолюби́вый.
vomit /ˈvɒmɪt/ *n* рво́та; *vt* (& *i*) рвать *impf*, вы́рвать *pf impers* (+*instr*); **he was ~ing blood** его́ рва́ло кро́вью.
voracious /vəˈreɪʃəs/ *adj* прожо́рливый; (*fig*) ненасы́тный.
vortex /ˈvɔːteks/ *n* (*also fig*) водоворо́т, вихрь *m*.
vote /vəʊt/ *n* (*poll*) голосова́ние; (*individual* ~) го́лос; **the ~** (*suffrage*) пра́во го́лоса; (*resolution*) во́тум *no pl*; **~ of no confidence** во́тум недове́рия (**in** +*dat*); **~ of thanks** выраже́ние благода́рности; *vi* голосова́ть *impf*, про~ *pf* (**for** за+*acc*; **against** про́тив+*gen*); *vt* (*allocate by* ~) ассигнова́ть *impf* & *pf*; (*deem*) признава́ть *impf*, призна́ть *pf*; **the film was ~d a failure** фильм был при́знан неуда́чным; **~ in** избира́ть *impf*, избра́ть *pf* голосова́нием. **voter** /-tə(r)/ *n* избира́тель *m*.
vouch /vaʊtʃ/ *vi*: **~ for** руча́ться *impf*, поручи́ться *pf* за+*acc*. **voucher** /-tʃə(r)/ *n* тало́н.
vow /vaʊ/ *n* обе́т; *vt* кля́сться *impf*, по~ *pf* в+*prep*.
vowel /ˈvaʊəl/ *n* гла́сный *sb*.
voyage /ˈvɔɪɪdʒ/ *n* путеше́ствие.
vulgar /ˈvʌlgə(r)/ *adj* вульга́рный, гру́бый, по́шлый. **vulgarity** /-ˈgærɪtɪ/ *n* вульга́рность, по́шлость.
vulnerable /ˈvʌlnərəb(ə)l/ *adj* уязви́мый.
vulture /ˈvʌltʃə(r)/ *n* гриф; (*fig*) хи́щник.

W

wad /wɒd/ *n* комо́к; (*bundle*) па́чка. **wadding** /-dɪŋ/ ва́та; (*padding*) наби́вка.
waddle /ˈwɒd(ə)l/ *vi* ходи́ть *indet*, идти́ *det*, пойти́ *pf* вперева́лку (*coll*).
wade /weɪd/ *vt* & *i* (*river*) переходи́ть *impf*, перейти́ *pf* вброд; *vi*: **~ through** (*mud etc.*) пробира́ться *impf*, пробра́ться *pf* по+*dat*; (*sth boring etc.*) одолева́ть *impf*, одоле́ть *pf*.
wafer /ˈweɪfə(r)/ *n* ва́фля.
waffle[1] /ˈwɒf(ə)l/ *n* (*dish*) ва́фля.
waffle[2] /ˈwɒf(ə)l/ *vi* трепа́ться *impf*.
waft /wɒft/ *vt* & *i* нести́(сь) *impf*, по~ *pf*.
wag /wæg/ *vt* & *i* (*tail*) виля́ть *impf*, вильну́ть *pf* (+*instr*); *vt* (*finger*) грози́ть *impf*, по~ *pf* +*instr*.
wage[1] /weɪdʒ/ *n* (*pay*) *see* **wages**
wage[2] /weɪdʒ/ *vt*: **~ war** вести́ *impf*, про~ *pf* войну́.
wager /ˈweɪdʒə(r)/ *n* пари́ *neut indecl*; *vi* держа́ть *impf* пари́ (**that** что); *vt* ста́вить *impf* по~ *pf*.
wages /ˈweɪdʒɪz/ *n pl* за́работная пла́та.
waggle /ˈwæg(ə)l/ *vt* & *i* пома́хивать *impf*, помаха́ть *pf* (+*instr*).
wag(g)on /ˈwægən/ *n* (*carriage*) пово́зка; (*cart*) теле́га; (*rly*) ваго́н-платфо́рма.
wail /weɪl/ *n* вопль *m*; *vi* вопи́ть *impf*.
waist /weɪst/ *n* та́лия; (*level of* ~) по́яс; **~-deep, high** (*adv*) по по́яс. **waistband** *n* по́яс. **waistcoat** *n* жиле́т.**waistline** *n* та́лия.
wait /weɪt/ *n* ожида́ние; **lie in ~ (for)** подстерега́ть *impf*; подстере́чь *pf*; *vi* (& *t*) (*also* ~ *for*) ждать *impf* (+*gen*); *vi* (*be a waiter, waitress*) быть официа́нтом, -ткой; **~ on** обслу́живать *impf*, обслужи́ть *pf*. **waiter** /-tə(r)/ *n* официа́нт. **waiting** /-tɪŋ/ *n*: **~-list** спи́сок; **~-room** приёмная *sb*; (*rly*) зал ожида́ния. **waitress** /-trɪs/ *n* официа́нтка.
waive /weɪv/ *vt* отка́зываться *impf*, отказа́ться *pf* от+*gen*.
wake[1] /weɪk/ *n* (*at funeral*) поми́нки (-нок) *pl*.
wake[2] /weɪk/ *n* (*naut*) кильва́тер;

in the ~ of по слéду +*gen*, за +*instr*.
wake[3] /weɪk/ *vt* (*also* ~ *up*) будúть *impf*, раз~ *pf*; *vi* (*also* ~ *up*) просыпáться *impf*, проснýться *pf*.
Wales /weɪlz/ *n* Уэ́льс.
walk /wɔːk/ *n* (*walking*) ходьбá; (*gait*) похóдка; (*stroll*) прогýлка; (*path*) тропá; **~-out** (*strike*) забастóвка; (*as protest*) демонстратúвный ухóд; **~-over** лёгкая побéда; **ten minutes' ~ from here** дéсять минýт ходьбы́ отсю́да; **go for a ~** идтú *impf*, пойтú *pf* гуля́ть; **from all ~s of life** всех слоёв óбщества; *vi* ходúть *indet*, идтú *det*, пойтú *pf*; гуля́ть *impf*, по~ *pf*; **~ away, off** уходúть *impf*, уйтú *pf*; **~ in** входúть *impf*, войтú *pf*; **~ out** выходúть *impf*, вы́йти *pf*; **~ out on** бросáть *impf*, брóсить *pf*; *vt* (*traverse*) обходúть *impf*, обойтú *pf*; (*take for ~*) выводúть *impf*, вы́вести *pf* гуля́ть. **walker** /ˈwɔːkə(r)/ *n* ходóк. **walkie-talkie** /ˌwɔːkɪˈtɔːkɪ/ *n* рáция. **walking** /ˈwɔːkɪŋ/ *n* ходьбá; **~-stick** трость.
Walkman /ˈwɔːkmən/ *n* (*propr*) вóкмен.
wall /wɔːl/ *n* стенá; *vt* обносúть *impf*, обнестú *pf* стенóй; **~ up** (*door, window*) задéлывать *impf*, задéлать *pf*; (*brick up*) замурóвывать *impf*, замуровáть *pf*.
wallet /ˈwɒlɪt/ *n* бумáжник.
wallflower /ˈwɔːlˌflaʊə(r)/ *n* желтофиóль.
wallop /ˈwɒləp/ *n* сúльный удáр; *vt* сúльно ударя́ть *impf*, ударить *pf*.
wallow /ˈwɒləʊ/ *vi* валя́ться *impf*; **~ in** (*give o.s. up to*) погружáться *impf*, погрузúться *pf* в+*acc*.
wallpaper /ˈwɔːlˌpeɪpə(r)/ *n* обóи (обóев) *pl*.
walnut /ˈwɔːlnʌt/ *n* грéцкий орéх; (*wood, tree*) орéховое дéрево, орéх.
walrus /ˈwɔːlrəs/ *n* морж.
waltz /wɔːls/ *n* вальс; *vi* вальсúровать *impf*.
wan /wɒn/ *adj* блéдный.
wand /wɒnd/ *n* пáлочка.
wander /ˈwɒndə(r)/ *vi* бродúть *impf*; (*also of thoughts etc.*) блуждáть *impf*; **~ from the point** отклоня́ться *impf*, отклонúться *pf* от тéмы. **wanderer** /-rə(r)/ *n* стрáнник.
wane /weɪn/ *n*: **be on the ~** убывáть *impf*; *vi* убывáть *impf*, убы́ть *pf*; (*weaken*) ослабевáть *impf*, ослабéть *pf*.
wangle /ˈwæŋg(ə)l/ *vt* заполучáть *impf*, заполучúть *pf*.
want /wɒnt/ *n* (*lack*) недостáток; (*requirement*) потрéбность; (*desire*) желáние; **for ~ of** за недостáтком +*gen*; *vt* хотéть *impf*, за~ *pf* +*gen*, *acc*; (*need*) нуждáться *impf* в+*prep*; **I ~ you to come at six** я хочý, чтóбы ты пришёл в шесть. **wanting** /-tɪŋ/ *adj*: **be ~** недоставáть *impf* (*impers*+*gen*); **experience is ~** недостаёт óпыта.
wanton /ˈwɒnt(ə)n/ *adj* (*licentious*) распýтный; (*senseless*) бессмы́сленный.
war /wɔː(r)/ *n* войнá; (*attrib*) воéнный; **at ~** в состоя́нии войны́; **~ memorial** пáмятник пáвшим в войнé.
ward /wɔːd/ *n* (*hospital*) палáта; (*child etc.*) подопéчный *sb*; (*district*) рaйóн; *vt*: **~ off** отражáть *impf*, отразúть *pf*.
warden /ˈwɔːd(ə)n/ *n* (*prison*) начáльник; (*college*) рéктор; (*hostel*) комендáнт.
warder /ˈwɔːdə(r)/ *n* тюрéмщик.
wardrobe /ˈwɔːdrəʊb/ *n* платянóй шкаф.
warehouse /ˈweəhaʊs/ *n* склад.
wares /weəz/ *n pl* издéлия *neut pl*, товáры *m pl*.
warfare /ˈwɔːfeə(r)/ *n* войнá.
warhead /ˈwɔːhed/ *n* боевáя головка.
warily /ˈweərɪlɪ/ *adv* осторóжно.
warlike /ˈwɔːlaɪk/ *adj* воинственный.
warm /wɔːm/ *n* теплó; *adj* (*also fig*)

W

тёплый; **~-hearted** серде́чный; *vt* & *i* греть(ся) *impf*; согрева́ть(ся) *impf*, согре́ть(ся) *pf*; **~ up** (*food etc.*) подогрева́ть *impf*, подогре́ть *pf*; (*liven up*) оживля́ть(ся) *impf*, оживи́ть(ся) *pf*; (*sport*) разминáться *impf*, размя́ться *pf*; (*mus*) разы́грываться *impf*, разыгра́ться *pf*. **warmth** /wɔːmθ/ *n* тепло́; (*cordiality*) серде́чность.

warn /wɔːn/ *vt* предупрежда́ть *impf*, предупреди́ть *pf* (**about** о+*prep*). **warning** /-nɪŋ/ *n* предупрежде́ние.

warp /wɔːp/ *vt* & *i* (*wood*) коро́бить(ся) *impf*, по~, с~ *pf*; *vt* (*pervert*) извраща́ть *impf*, изврати́ть *pf*.

warrant /ˈwɒrənt/ *n* (*for arrest etc.*) о́рдер; *vt* (*justify*) опра́вдывать *impf*, оправда́ть *pf*; (*guarantee*) гаранти́ровать *impf* & *pf*. **warranty** /-tɪ/ *n* гара́нтия.

warrior /ˈwɒrɪə(r)/ *n* во́ин.

warship /ˈwɔːʃɪp/ *n* вое́нный кора́бль *m*.

wart /wɔːt/ *n* борода́вка.

wartime /ˈwɔːtaɪm/ *n*: **in ~** во вре́мя войны́.

wary /ˈweərɪ/ *adj* осторо́жный.

wash /wɒʃ/ *n* мытьё; (*thin layer*) то́нкий слой; (*lotion*) примо́чка; (*surf*) прибо́й; (*backwash*) попу́тная волна́; **at the ~** в сти́рке; **have a ~** мы́ться *impf*, по~ *pf*; **~-basin** умыва́льник; **~-out** (*fiasco*) прова́л; **~-room** умыва́льная *sb*; *vt* & *i* мы́ть(ся) *impf*, вы́~, по~ *pf*; *vt* (*clothes*) стира́ть *impf*, вы́~ *pf*; (*of sea*) омыва́ть *impf*; **~ away, off, out** смыва́ть(ся) *impf*, смы́ть(ся) *pf*; (*carry away*) сноси́ть *impf*, снести́ *pf*; **~ out** (*rinse*) спола́скивать *impf*, сполосну́ть *pf*; **~ up** (*dishes*) мыть *impf*, вы́~, по~ *pf* (посу́ду); **~ one's hands (of it)** умыва́ть *impf*, умы́ть *pf* ру́ки. **washed-out** /wɒʃtˈaʊt/ *adj* (*exhausted*) утомлённый. **washer** /ˈwɒʃə(r)/ *n* (*tech*) ша́йба. **washing** /ˈwɒʃɪŋ/ *n* (*of clothes*) сти́рка; (*clothes*) бельё; **~-machine** стира́льная маши́на; **~-powder** стира́льный порошо́к; **~-up** (*action*) мытьё посу́ды; (*dishes*) гря́зная посу́да; **~-up liquid** жи́дкое мы́ло для мытья́ посу́ды.

wasp /wɒsp/ *n* оса́.

wastage /ˈweɪstɪdʒ/ *n* уте́чка.

waste /weɪst/ *n* (*desert*) пусты́ня; (*refuse*) отбро́сы *m pl*; (*of time, money, etc.*) тра́та; **go to ~** пропада́ть *impf*, пропа́сть *pf* да́ром; *adj* (*desert*) пусты́нный; (*superfluous*) нену́жный; (*uncultivated*) невозде́ланный; **lay ~** опустоша́ть *impf*, опустоши́ть *pf*; **~land** пусты́рь *m*; **~ paper** нену́жные бума́ги *f pl*; (*for recycling*) макулату́ра; **~ products** отхо́ды (-дов) *pl*; **~-paper basket** корзи́на для бума́ги; *vt* тра́тить *impf*, по~, ис~ *pf*; (*time*) теря́ть *impf*, по~ *pf*; *vi*: **~ away** ча́хнуть *impf*, за~ *pf*. **wasteful** /-fʊl/ *adj* расточи́тельный.

watch /wɒtʃ/ *n* (*timepiece*) часы́ (-со́в) *pl*; (*duty*) дежу́рство; (*naut*) ва́хта; **keep ~ over** наблюда́ть *impf* за+*instr*; **~-dog** сторожево́й пёс; **~-tower** сторожева́я ба́шня; *vt* (*observe*) наблюда́ть *impf*; (*keep an eye on*) следи́ть *impf* за+*instr*; (*look after*) смотре́ть *impf*, по~ *pf* за+*instr*; **~ television, a film** смотре́ть *impf*, по~ *pf* телеви́зор, фильм; *vi* смотре́ть *impf*; **~ out** (*be careful*) бере́чься *impf* (**for** +*gen*); **~ out for** ждать *impf* +*gen*; **~ out!** осторо́жно! **watchful** /-fʊl/ *adj* бди́тельный. **watchman** *n* (ночно́й) сто́рож. **watchword** *n* ло́зунг.

water /ˈwɔːtə(r)/ *n* вода́; **~-colour** акваре́ль; **~-heater** кипяти́льник; **~-main** водопрово́дная магистра́ль; **~ melon** арбу́з; **~-pipe** водопрово́дная труба́; **~-ski** (*n*) во́дная лы́жа; **~-skiing** водолы́жный спорт; **~-supply** водоснабже́ние; **~-way** во́дный путь *m*; *vt* (*flowers etc.*) полива́ть *impf*, полить *pf*; (*animals*) поить *impf*, на~ *pf*; (*irrigate*) орошать *impf*, оросить *pf*; *vi* (*eyes*) слезиться *impf*; (*mouth*): **my mouth ~s** у меня слюнки текут; **~ down** разбавлять *impf*, разбавить *pf*. **watercourse** *n* русло. **watercress** /-kres/ *n* кресс водяной. **waterfall** *n* водопад. **waterfront** *n* часть города примыкающая к берегу. **watering-can** /ˈwɔːtərɪŋˌkæn/ *n* лейка. **waterlogged** /ˈwɔːtəˌlɒgd/ *adj* заболоченный. **watermark** *n* водяной знак. **waterproof** *adj* непромокаемый; *n* непромокаемый плащ. **watershed** *n* водораздел. **waterside** *n* берег. **watertight** *adj* водонепроницаемый; (*fig*) неопровержимый. **waterworks** *n pl* водопроводные сооружения *neut pl.* **watery** /ˈwɔːtərɪ/ *adj* водянистый.

watt /wɒt/ *n* ватт.

wave /weɪv/ *vt* (*hand etc.*) махать *impf*, махнуть *pf* +*instr*; (*flag*) размахивать *impf* +*instr*; *vi* (~ *hand*) махать *impf*, по~ *pf* (**at** +*dat*); (*flutter*) развеваться *impf*; **~ aside** отмахиваться *impf*, отмахнуться *pf* от+*gen*; **~ down** останавливать *impf*, остановить *pf*; *n* (*in various senses*) волна; (*of hand*) взмах; (*in hair*) завивка. **wavelength** *n* длина волны. **waver** /-və(r)/ *vi* колебаться *impf*. **wavy** /-vɪ/ *adj* волнистый.

wax /wæks/ *n* воск; (*in ear*) сера; *vt* вощить *impf*, на~ *pf*. **waxwork** *n* восковая фигура; *pl* музей восковых фигур.

way /weɪ/ *n* (*road, path, route*; *fig*) дорога, путь *m*; (*direction*) сторона; (*manner*) образ; (*method*) способ; (*respect*) отношение; (*habit*) привычка; **by the ~** (*fig*) кстати, между прочим; **on the ~** по дороге, по пути; **this ~** (*direction*) сюда; (*in this ~*) таким образом; **the other ~ round** наоборот; **under ~** на ходу; **be in the ~** мешать *impf*; **get out of the ~** уходить *impf*, уйти *pf* с дороги; **give ~** (*yield*) поддаваться *impf*, поддаться *pf* (**to** +*dat*); (*collapse*) обрушиваться *impf*, обрушиться *pf*; **go out of one's ~ to** стараться *impf*, по~ *pf* изо всех сил +*inf*; **get, have, one's own ~** добиваться *impf*, добиться *pf* своего; **make ~** уступать *impf*, уступить *pf* дорогу (**for** +*dat*). **waylay** *vt* (*lie in wait for*) подстерегать *impf*, подстеречь *pf*; (*stop*) перехватывать *impf*, перехватить *pf* по пути. **wayside** *adj* придорожный; *n*: **fall by the ~** выбывать *impf*, выбыть *pf* из строя.

wayward /ˈweɪwəd/ *adj* своенравный.

WC *abbr* (*of* **water-closet**) уборная *sb.*

we /wiː/ *pron* мы.

weak /wiːk/ *adj* слабый. **weaken** /-kən/ *vt* ослаблять *impf*, ослабить *pf*; *vi* слабеть *impf*, о~ *pf*. **weakling** /-lɪŋ/ *n* (*person*) слабый человек; (*plant*) слабое растение. **weakness** /-nɪs/ *n* слабость.

weal /wiːl/ *n* (*mark*) рубец.

wealth /welθ/ *n* богатство; (*abundance*) изобилие. **wealthy** /-θɪ/ *adj* богатый.

wean /wiːn/ *vt* отнимать *impf*, отнять *pf* от груди; (*fig*) отучать *impf*, отучить *pf* (**of, from** от+*gen*).

weapon /ˈwepən/ *n* оружие. **weaponry** /-rɪ/ *n* вооружение.

wear /weə(r)/ *n* (*wearing*) носка; (*clothing*) одежда; (~ *and tear*) износ; *vt* носить *impf*; быть в+*prep*; **what shall I ~?** что мне надеть?; *vi* носиться *impf*; **~ off** (*pain, novelty*) проходить *impf*, пройти *pf*; (*cease to have effect*) переставать *impf*, перестать *pf* действовать; **~ out** (*clothes*) изнашивать(ся) *impf*, износить(ся) *pf*; (*exhaust*) измучивать *impf*, измучить *pf*.

weariness /ˈwɪərɪnɪs/ *n* усталость. **wearing, wearisome** /ˈweərɪŋ,

W

ˈwɪərɪsəm/ *adj* утоми́тельный. **weary** /ˈwɪərɪ/ *adj* уста́лый; *vt & i* утомля́ть(ся) *impf*, утоми́ть(ся) *pf*.

weasel /ˈwiːz(ə)l/ *n* ла́ска.

weather /ˈweðə(r)/ *n* пого́да; **be under the ~** нева́жно себя́ чу́вствовать *impf*; **~-beaten** обве́тренный; **~ forecast** прогно́з пого́ды; *vt* (*storm etc.*) выде́рживать *impf*, вы́держать *pf*; (*wood*) подверга́ть *impf*, подве́ргнуть *pf* атмосфе́рным влия́ниям. **weather-cock, weathervane** /ˈweðəˌkɒk, ˈweðəˌveɪn/ *n* флю́гер. **weatherman** *n* метеоро́лог.

weave[1] /wiːv/ *vt & i* (*fabric*) ткать *impf*, со~ *pf*; *vt* (*fig*; *also wreath etc.*) плести́ *impf*, с~ *pf*. **weaver** /-və(r)/ *n* ткач, ~и́ха.

weave[2] /wiːv/ *vi* (*wind*) ви́ться *impf*.

web /web/ *n* (*cobweb*; *fig*) паути́на; (*fig*) сплете́ние; (*the Web*) (*comput*) Всеми́рная паути́на; **~ page** веб-страни́ца, страни́ца в Интерне́те. **webbed** /webd/ *adj* перепо́нчатый. **weblog** *n* сетево́й журна́л, блог. **weblogger** *n* бло́ггер. **website** *n* сайт, веб-са́йт.

wedded /-dɪd/ *adj* супру́жеский; **~ to** (*fig*) пре́данный +*dat*. **wedding** /-dɪŋ/ *n* сва́дьба, бракосочета́ние; **~-cake** сва́дебный торт; **~-day** день *m* сва́дьбы; **~-dress** подвене́чное пла́тье; **~-ring** обруча́льное кольцо́.

wedge /wedʒ/ *n* клин; *vt* (**~** *open*) закли́нивать *impf*, закли́нить *pf*; *vt & i*: **~ in(to)** вкли́нивать(ся) *impf*, вкли́нить(ся) *pf* (в+*acc*).

wedlock /ˈwedlɒk/ *n* брак; **born out of ~** рождённый вне бра́ка, внебра́чный.

Wednesday /ˈwenzdeɪ/ *n* среда́.

weed /wiːd/ *n* сорня́к; **~-killer** гербици́д; *vt* поло́ть *impf*, вы́~ *pf*; **~ out** удаля́ть *impf*, удали́ть *pf*. **weedy** /ˈwiːdɪ/ *adj* (*person*) то́щий.

week /wiːk/ *n* неде́ля; **~-end** суббо́та и воскресе́нье, выходны́е *sb pl*. **weekday** *n* бу́дний день *m*. **weekly** /ˈwiːklɪ/ *adj* еженеде́льный; (*wage*) неде́льный; *adv* еженеде́льно; *n* еженеде́льник.

weep /wiːp/ *vi* пла́кать *impf*. **weeping willow** /ˈwiːpɪŋ ˈwɪləʊ/ *n* плаку́чая и́ва.

weigh /weɪ/ *vt* (*also fig*) взве́шивать *impf*, взве́сить *pf*; (*consider*) обду́мывать *impf*, обду́мать *pf*; *vt & i* (*so much*) ве́сить *impf*; **~ down** отягоща́ть *impf*, отяготи́ть *pf*; **~ on** тяготи́ть *impf*; **~ out** отве́шивать *impf*, отве́сить *pf*; **~ up** (*appraise*) оце́нивать *impf*, оцени́ть *pf*. **weight** /weɪt/ *n* (*also authority*) вес; (*load, also fig*) тя́жесть; (*sport*) шта́нга; (*influence*) влия́ние; **lose ~** худе́ть *impf*, по~ *pf*; **put on ~** толсте́ть *impf*, по~ *pf*; **~-lifter** штанги́ст; **~-lifting** подня́тие тя́жестей; *vt* (*make heavier*) утяжеля́ть *impf*, утяжели́ть *pf*. **weightless** /ˈweɪtlɪs/ *adj* невесо́мый. **weighty** /ˈweɪtɪ/ *adj* ве́ский.

weir /wɪə(r)/ *n* плоти́на.

weird /wɪəd/ *adj* (*strange*) стра́нный.

welcome /ˈwelkəm/ *n* приём; *adj* жела́нный; (*pleasant*) прия́тный; **you are ~** (*don't mention it*) пожа́луйста; **you are ~ to use my bicycle** мой велосипе́д к ва́шим услу́гам; **you are ~ to stay the night** вы мо́жете переночева́ть у меня́/нас; *vt* приве́тствовать *impf* (& *pf in past tense*); *int* добро́ пожа́ловать!

weld /weld/ *vt* сва́ривать *impf*, свари́ть *pf*. **welder** /-də(r)/ *n* сва́рщик.

welfare /ˈwelfeə(r)/ *n* благосостоя́ние; **W~ State** госуда́рство всео́бщего благосостоя́ния.

well[1] /wel/ *n* коло́дец; (*for stairs*) ле́стничная кле́тка.

well[2] /wel/ *vi*: **~ up** (*anger etc.*) вскипа́ть *impf*, вскипе́ть *pf*; **tears**

~ed up глаза́ напо́лнились слеза́ми.

well[3] /wel/ *adj* (*healthy*) здоро́вый; **feel ~** чу́вствовать *impf*, по~ *pf* себя́ хорошо́, здоро́вым; **get ~** поправля́ться *impf*, попра́виться *pf*; **look ~** хорошо́ вы́глядеть *impf*; **all is ~** всё в поря́дке; *int* ну(!); *adv* хорошо́; (*very much*) о́чень; **as ~** то́же; **as ~ as** (*in addition to*) кро́ме+*gen*; **it may ~ be true** вполне́ возмо́жно, что э́то так; **very ~!** хорошо́!; **~ done!** молоде́ц!; **~-balanced** уравнове́шенный; **~-behaved** (благо)воспи́танный; **~-being** благополу́чие; **~-bred** благовоспи́танный; **~-built** кре́пкий; **~-defined** чёткий; **~-disposed** благосклóнный; **~ done** (*cooked*) (хорошо́) прожа́ренный; **~-fed** откóрмленный; **~-founded** обосно́ванный; **~-groomed** (*person*) хо́леный; **~-heeled** состоя́тельный; **~-informed** (хорошо́) осведомлённый (**about** в+*prep*); **~-known** изве́стный; **~-meaning** де́йствующий из лу́чших побужде́ний; **~-nigh** почти́; **~-off** состоя́тельный; **~-paid** хорошо́ опла́чиваемый; **~-preserved** хорошо́ сохрани́вшийся; **~-to-do** состоя́тельный; **~-wisher** доброжела́тель *m*.

wellington (boot) /'welɪŋt(ə)n (bu:t)/ *n* рези́новый сапо́г.

Welsh /welʃ/ *adj* уэ́льский. **Welshman** *n* валли́ец. **Welshwoman** *n* валли́йка.

welter /'weltə(r)/ *n* пу́таница.

wend /wend/ *vt*: **~ one's way** держа́ть *impf* путь.

west /west/ *n* за́пад; (*naut*) вест; *adj* за́падный; *adv* на за́пад, к за́паду. **westerly** /'westəlɪ/ *adj* за́падный. **western** /'west(ə)n/ *adj* за́падный; *n* (*film*) ве́стерн. **westward(s)** /'westwəd(z)/ *adv* на за́пад, к за́паду.

wet /wet/ *adj* мо́крый; (*paint*) непросо́хший; (*rainy*) дождли́вый; **~ through** промо́кший до ни́тки; *n* (*dampness*) вла́жность; (*rain*) дождь *m*; *vt* мочи́ть *impf*, на~ *pf*.

whack /wæk/ *n* (*blow*) уда́р; *vt* колоти́ть *impf*, по~ *pf*. **whacked** /wækt/ *adj* разби́тый.

whale /weɪl/ *n* кит.

wharf /wɔ:f/ *n* при́стань.

what /wɒt/ *pron* (*interrog*, *int*) что; (*how much*) ско́лько; (*rel*) (то,) что; **~ (...) for** заче́м; **~ if** а что е́сли; **~ is your name** как вас зову́т?; *adj* (*interrog*, *int*) како́й; **~ kind of** како́й. **whatever, whatsoever** /wɒt'evə(r), ˌwɒtsəʊ'evə(r)/ *pron* что бы ни+*past* (**~ you think** что бы вы ни ду́мали); всё, что (**take ~ you want** возьми́те всё, что хоти́те); *adj* како́й бы ни+*past* (**~ books he read(s)** каки́е бы кни́ги он ни прочита́л); (*at all*): **there is no chance ~** нет никако́й возмо́жности; **is there any chance ~?** есть ли хоть кака́я-нибу́дь возмо́жность?

wheat /wi:t/ *n* пшени́ца.

wheedle /'wi:d(ə)l/ *vt* (*coax into doing*) угова́ривать *impf*, уговори́ть *pf* с по́мощью ле́сти; **~ out of** выма́нивать *impf*, вы́манить *pf* у+*gen*.

wheel /wi:l/ *n* колесо́; (*steering ~*, *helm*) руль *m*; (*potter's*) гонча́рный круг; *vt* (*push*) ката́ть *indet*, кати́ть *det*, по~ *pf*; *vt* & *i* (*turn*) повёртывать(ся) *impf*, поверну́ть(ся) *pf*; *vi* (*circle*) кружи́ться *impf*. **wheelbarrow** *n* та́чка. **wheelchair** *n* инвали́дное кре́сло.

wheeze /wi:z/ *vi* сопе́ть *impf*.

when /wen/ *adv* когда́; *conj* когда́, в то вре́мя как; (*whereas*) тогда́ как; (*if*) е́сли; (*although*) хотя́. **whence** /wens/ *adv* отку́да. **whenever** /wen'evə(r)/ *adv* когда́ же; *conj* (*every time*) вся́кий раз когда́; (*at any time*) когда́; (*no matter when*) когда́ бы ни+*past*; **we shall have dinner ~ you arrive**

во ско́лько бы вы ни прие́хали, мы пообе́даем.

where /weə(r)/ *adv* & *conj* (*place*) где; (*whither*) куда́; **from ~** отку́да. **whereabouts** /ˈweərəˌbaʊts/ *adv* где; *n* местонахожде́ние. **whereas** /weərˈæz/ *conj* тогда́ как; хотя́. **whereby** /weəˈbaɪ/ *adv* & *conj* посре́дством чего́. **wherein** /weərˈɪn/ *adv* & *conj* в чём. **wherever** /weərˈevə(r)/ *adv* & *conj* (*place*) где бы ни+*past*; (*whither*) куда́ бы ни+*past*; **~ he goes** куда́ бы он ни пошёл; **~ you like** где/куда́ хоти́те. **wherewithal** /ˈweəwɪˌðɔːl/ *n* сре́дства *neut pl*.

whet /wet/ *vt* точи́ть *impf*, на~ *pf*; (*fig*) возбужда́ть *impf*, возбуди́ть *pf*.

whether /ˈweðə(r)/ *conj* ли; **I don't know ~ he will come** я не зна́ю, придёт ли он; **~ he comes or not** придёт (ли) он и́ли нет.

which /wɪtʃ/ *adj* (*interrog*, *rel*) како́й; *pron* (*interrog*) како́й; (*person*) кто; (*rel*) кото́рый; (*rel to whole statement*) что; **~ is ~?** (*persons*) кто из них кто?; (*things*) что-что? **whichever** /wɪtʃˈevə(r)/ *adj* & *pron* како́й бы ни+*past* (**~ book you choose** каку́ю бы кни́гу ты ни вы́брал); любо́й (**take ~ book you want** возьми́те любу́ю кни́гу).

whiff /wɪf/ *n* за́пах.

while /waɪl/ *n* вре́мя *neut*; **a little ~** недо́лго; **a long ~** до́лго; **for a long ~** (*up to now*) давно́; **for a ~** на вре́мя; **in a little ~** ско́ро; **it is worth ~** сто́ит э́то сде́лать; *vt*: **~ away** проводи́ть *impf*, провести́ *pf*; *conj* пока́; в то вре́мя как; (*although*) хотя́; (*contrast*) а; **we went to the cinema ~ they went to the theatre** мы ходи́ли в кино́, а они́ в теа́тр. **whilst** /waɪlst/ *see* **while**

whim /wɪm/ *n* при́хоть, капри́з.

whimper /ˈwɪmpə(r)/ *vi* хны́кать *impf*; (*dog*) скули́ть *impf*.

whimsical /ˈwɪmzɪk(ə)l/ *adj* капри́зный; (*odd*) причу́дливый.

whine /waɪn/ *n* (*wail*) вой; (*whimper*) хны́канье; *vi* (*dog*) скули́ть *impf*; (*wail*) выть; (*whimper*) хны́кать *impf*.

whinny /ˈwɪnɪ/ *vi* ти́хо ржать *impf*.

whip /wɪp/ *n* кнут, хлыст; *vt* (*lash*) хлеста́ть *impf*, хлестну́ть *pf*; (*cream*) сбива́ть *impf*, сбить *pf*; **~ off** ски́дывать *impf*, ски́нуть *pf*; **~ out** выхва́тывать *impf*, вы́хватить *pf*; **~ round** бы́стро повёртываться *impf*, поверну́ться *pf*; **~-round** сбор де́нег; **~ up** (*stir up*) разжига́ть *impf*, разже́чь *pf*.

whirl /wɜːl/ *n* круже́ние; (*of dust*, *fig*) вихрь *m*; (*turmoil*) сумато́ха; *vt* & *i* кружи́ть(ся) *impf*, за~ *pf*. **whirlpool** *n* водоворо́т. **whirlwind** *n* вихрь *m*.

whirr /wɜː(r)/ *vi* жужжа́ть *impf*.

whisk /wɪsk/ *n* (*of twigs etc.*) ве́ничек; (*utensil*) муто́вка; (*movement*) пома́хивание; *vt* (*cream etc.*) сбива́ть *impf*, сбить *pf*; **~ away, off** (*brush off*) сма́хивать *impf*, смахну́ть *pf*; (*take away*) бы́стро уноси́ть *impf*, унести́ *pf*.

whisker /ˈwɪskə(r)/ *n* (*human*) во́лос на лице́; (*animal*) ус; *pl* (*human*) бакенба́рды *f pl*.

whisky /ˈwɪskɪ/ *n* ви́ски *neut indecl*.

whisper /ˈwɪspə(r)/ *n* шёпот; *vt* & *i* шепта́ть *impf*, шепну́ть *pf*.

whistle /ˈwɪs(ə)l/ *n* (*sound*) свист; (*instrument*) свисто́к; *vi* свисте́ть *impf*, сви́стнуть *pf*; *vt* насви́стывать *impf*.

white /waɪt/ *adj* бе́лый; (*hair*) седо́й; (*pale*) бле́дный; (*with milk*) с молоко́м; **paint ~** кра́сить *impf*, по~ *pf* в бе́лый свет; **~-collar worker** слу́жащий *sb*; **~ lie** неви́нная ложь; *n* (*colour*) бе́лый цвет; (*egg*, *eye*) бело́к; (**~ person**) бе́лый *sb*. **whiten** /-t(ə)n/ *vt* бели́ть *impf*, на~, по~, вы́~ *pf*; *vi* беле́ть *impf*, по~ *pf*. **whiteness** /-nɪs/ *n* белизна́. **whitewash** *n* побе́лка; *vt* бели́ть *impf*,

W

по~ *pf*; (*fig*) обеля́ть *impf*, обели́ть *pf*.

whither /ˈwɪðə(r)/ *adv* & *conj* куда́.

Whitsun /ˈwɪts(ə)n/ *n* Тро́ица.

whittle /ˈwɪt(ə)l/ *vt*: **~ down** уменьша́ть *impf*, уме́ньшить *pf*.

whiz(z) /wɪz/ *vi*: **~ past** просвисте́ть *pf*.

who /huː/ *pron* (*interrog*) кто; (*rel*) кото́рый.

whoever /huːˈevə(r)/ *pron* кто бы ни+*past*; (*he who*) тот, кто.

whole /həʊl/ *adj* (*entire*) весь, це́лый; (*intact, of number*) це́лый; *n* (*thing complete*) це́лое *sb*; (*all there is*) весь *sb*; (*sum*) су́мма; **on the ~** в о́бщем. **wholehearted** /-ˈhɑːtɪd/ *adj* беззаве́тный. **whole-heartedly** /-ˈhɑːtɪdlɪ/ *adv* от всего́ се́рдца. **wholemeal** *adj* из непросе́янной муки́. **wholesale** *adj* опто́вый; (*fig*) ма́ссовый; *adv* о́птом. **wholesaler** *n* опто́вый торго́вец. **wholesome** *adj* здоро́вый. **wholly** /ˈhəʊllɪ/ *adv* по́лностью.

whom /huːm/ *pron* (*interrog*) кого́ *etc.*; (*rel*) кото́рого *etc.*

whoop /huːp/ *n* крик; *vi* крича́ть *impf*, кри́кнуть *pf*; **~ it up** бу́рно весели́ться *impf*; **~ing cough** коклю́ш.

whore /hɔː(r)/ *n* проститу́тка.

whose /huːz/ *pron* (*interrog, rel*) чей; (*rel*) кото́рого.

why /waɪ/ *adv* почему́; *int* да ведь!

wick /wɪk/ *n* фити́ль *m*.

wicked /ˈwɪkɪd/ *adj* ди́кий. **wickedness** /-nɪs/ *n* ди́кость.

wicker /ˈwɪkə(r)/ *attrib* плетёный.

wicket /ˈwɪkɪt/ *n* (*cricket*) воро́тца.

wide /waɪd/ *adj* широ́кий; (*extensive*) обши́рный; (*in measurements*) в+*acc* шириной; **~ awake** по́лный внима́ния; **~ open** широко́ откры́тый; *adv* (*off target*) ми́мо це́ли. **widely** /ˈwaɪdlɪ/ *adv* широко́. **widen** /-d(ə)n/ *vt* & *i* расширя́ть(ся) *impf*, расши́рить(ся) *pf*. **widespread** *adj* распространённый.

widow /ˈwɪdəʊ/ *n* вдова́. **widowed** /ˈwɪdəʊd/ *adj* овдове́вший. **widower** /ˈwɪdəʊwə(r)/ *n* вдове́ц.

width /wɪtθ/ *n* ширина́; (*fig*) широта́; (*of cloth*) поло́тнище.

wield /wiːld/ *vt* (*brandish*) разма́хивать *impf* +*instr*; (*power*) по́льзоваться *impf* +*instr*.

wife /waɪf/ *n* жена́.

wig /wɪg/ *n* пари́к.

wiggle /ˈwɪg(ə)l/ *vt* & *i* (*move*) шевели́ть(ся) *impf*, по~, шевельну́ть(ся) *pf* (+*instr*).

wigwam /ˈwɪgwæm/ *n* вигва́м.

wild /waɪld/ *adj* ди́кий; (*flower*) полево́й; (*uncultivated*) невозде́ланный; (*tempestuous*) бу́йный; (*furious*) неи́стовый; (*ill-considered*) необду́манный; **be ~ about** быть без ума́ от+*gen*; **~-goose chase** сумасбро́дная зате́я; *n*: *pl* де́бри (-рей) *pl*. **wildcat** *adj* (*unofficial*) неофициа́льный. **wilderness** /ˈwɪldənɪs/ *n* пусты́ня. **wildfire** *n*: **spread like ~** распространя́ться *impf*, распространи́ться *pf* с молниено́сной быстрото́й. **wildlife** *n* жива́я приро́да. **wildness** /ˈwaɪldnɪs/ *n* ди́кость.

wile /waɪl/ *n* хи́трость.

wilful /ˈwɪlfʊl/ *adj* (*obstinate*) упря́мый; (*deliberate*) преднаме́ренный.

will /wɪl/ *n* во́ля; (*~-power*) си́ла во́ли; (*at death*) завеща́ние; **against one's ~** про́тив во́ли; **of one's own free ~** доброво́льно; **with a ~** с энтузиа́змом; **good ~** до́брая во́ля; **make one's ~** писа́ть *impf*, на~ *pf* завеща́ние; *vt* (*want*) хоте́ть *impf*, за~ *pf* +*gen*, *acc*; *v aux*: **he ~ be president** он бу́дет президе́нтом; **he ~ return tomorrow** он вернётся за́втра; **~ you open the window?** откро́йте окно́, пожа́луйста. **willing** /ˈwɪlɪŋ/ *adj* гото́вый; (*eager*) стара́тельный. **willingly** /ˈwɪlɪŋlɪ/ *adv* охо́тно. **willingness** /ˈwɪlɪŋnɪs/ *n* гото́вность.

willow /ˈwɪləʊ/ *n* и́ва.

willy-nilly /ˌwɪlɪˈnɪlɪ/ *adv* во́лей-нево́лей.

wilt /wɪlt/ *vi* поника́ть *impf*, пони́кнуть *pf*.

wily /ˈwaɪlɪ/ *adj* хи́трый.

win /wɪn/ *n* побе́да; *vt & i* выи́грывать *impf*, вы́играть *pf*; *vt* (*obtain*) добива́ться *impf*, доби́ться *pf +gen*; **~ over** угова́ривать *impf*, уговори́ть *pf*; (*charm*) располага́ть *impf*, расположи́ть *pf* к себе́.

wince /wɪns/ *vi* вздра́гивать *impf*, вздро́гнуть *pf*.

winch /wɪntʃ/ *n* лебёдка; поднима́ть *impf*, подня́ть *pf* с по́мощью лебёдки.

wind[1] /wɪnd/ *n* (*air*) ве́тер; (*breath*) дыха́ние; (*flatulence*) ве́тры *m pl*; **~ instrument** духово́й инструме́нт; **~-swept** откры́тый ветра́м; **get ~ of** проню́хивать *impf*, проню́хать *pf*; *vt* (*make gasp*) заставля́ть *impf*, заста́вить *pf* задохну́ться.

wind[2] /waɪnd/ *vi* (*meander*) ви́ться *impf*; извива́ться *impf*; *vt* (*coil*) нама́тывать *impf*, намота́ть *pf*; (*watch*) заводи́ть *impf*, завести́ *pf*; (*wrap*) уку́тывать *impf*, уку́тать *pf*; **~ up** (*vt*) (*reel*) сма́тывать *impf*, смота́ть *pf*; (*watch*) *see* **wind**[2]; (*vt & i*) (*end*) конча́ть(ся) *impf*, ко́нчить(ся) *pf*. **winding** /ˈwaɪndɪŋ/ *adj* (*meandering*) изви́листый; (*staircase*) винтово́й.

windfall /ˈwɪndfɔːl/ *n* па́далица; (*fig*) золото́й дождь.

windmill /ˈwɪndmɪl/ *n* ветряна́я ме́льница.

window /ˈwɪndəʊ/ *n* окно́; (*of shop*) витри́на; **~-box** нару́жный я́щик для цвето́в; **~-cleaner** мо́йщик о́кон; **~-dressing** оформле́ние витри́н; (*fig*) показу́ха; **~-frame** око́нная ра́ма; **~-ledge** подоко́нник; **~-pane** око́нное стекло́; **~-shopping** рассма́тривание витри́н; **~-sill** подоко́нник.

windpipe /ˈwɪndpaɪp/ *n* дыха́тельное го́рло. **windscreen** *n* ветрово́е стекло́; **~ wiper** дво́рник. **windsurfer** /ˈwɪndˌsɜːfə(r)/ *n* виндсёрфинги́ст. **windsurfing** /ˈwɪndˌsɜːfɪŋ/ *n* виндсёрфинг. **windward** /ˈwɪndwəd/ *adj* наве́тренный. **windy** /ˈwɪndɪ/ *adj* ве́треный.

wine /waɪn/ *n* вино́; **~ bar** ви́нный погребо́к; **~ bottle** ви́нная буты́лка; **~ list** ка́рта вин; **~-tasting** дегуста́ция вин. **wineglass** *n* рю́мка. **winery** /ˈwaɪnərɪ/ *n* ви́нный заво́д. **winy** /ˈwaɪnɪ/ *adj* ви́нный.

wing /wɪŋ/ *n* (*also polit*) крыло́; (*archit*) фли́гель *m*; (*sport*) фланг; *pl* (*theat*) кули́сы *f pl*. **winged** /wɪŋd/ *adj* крыла́тый.

wink /wɪŋk/ *n* (*blink*) морга́ние; (*as sign*) подми́гивание; *vi* мига́ть *impf*, мигну́ть *pf*; **~ at** подми́гивать *impf*, подмигну́ть *pf +dat*; (*fig*) смотре́ть *impf*, по~ *pf* сквозь па́льцы на+*acc*.

winkle /ˈwɪŋk(ə)l/ *vt*: **~ out** выко́вы́ривать *impf*, вы́ковырять *pf*.

winner /ˈwɪnə(r)/ *n* победи́тель *m*, ~ница. **winning** /ˈwɪnɪŋ/ *adj* (*victorious*) вы́игравший; (*shot etc.*) реша́ющий; (*charming*) обая́тельный; *n*: *pl* вы́игрыш; **~-post** фи́нишный столб.

winter /ˈwɪntə(r)/ *n* зима́; *attrib* зи́мний. **wintry** /ˈwɪntrɪ/ *adj* зи́мний; (*cold*) холо́дный.

wipe /waɪp/ *vt* (*also* **~** *out inside of*) вытира́ть *impf*, вы́тереть *pf*; **~ away, off** стира́ть *impf*, стере́ть *pf*; **~ out** (*exterminate*) уничтожа́ть *impf*, уничто́жить *pf*; (*cancel*) смыва́ть *impf*, смыть *pf*.

wire /ˈwaɪə(r)/ *n* про́волока; (*carrying current*) про́вод; **~ netting** про́волочная се́тка. **wireless** /-lɪs/ *n* ра́дио *neut indecl*. **wiring** /-rɪŋ/ *n* электропрово́дка. **wiry** /-rɪ/ *adj* жи́листый.

wisdom /ˈwɪzdəm/ *n* му́дрость; **~ tooth** зуб му́дрости. **wise** /waɪz/ *adj* му́дрый; (*prudent*) благоразу́мный.

wish /wɪʃ/ *n* желáние; **with best ~es** всегó хорóшего, с наилу́чшими пожелáниями; *vt* хотéть *impf*, за~ *pf* (**I ~ I could see him** мне хотéлось бы егó ви́деть; **I ~ to go** я хочу́ пойти́; **I ~ you to come early** я хочу́, чтóбы вы рáно пришли́; **I ~ the day were over** хорошó бы день ужé кóнчился); желáть *impf* +*gen* (**I ~ you luck** желáю вам удáчи); (*congratulate on*) поздравля́ть *impf*, поздрáвить *pf* (**I ~ you a happy birthday** поздравля́ю тебя́ с днём рождéния); *vi*: **~ for** желáть *impf* +*gen*; мечтáть *impf* о+*prep*. **wishful** /-fʊl/ *adj*: **~ thinking** самообольщéние; приня́тие желáемого за действи́тельное.

wisp /wɪsp/ *n* (*of straw*) пучóк; (*hair*) клочóк; (*smoke*) стру́йка.

wisteria /wɪ'stɪərɪə/ *n* глици́ния.

wistful /'wɪstfʊl/ *adj* тоскли́вый.

wit /wɪt/ *n* (*mind*) ум; (*wittiness*) остроу́мие; (*person*) остря́к; **be at one's ~'s end** не знать *impf* что дéлать.

witch /wɪtʃ/ *n* вéдьма; **~-hunt** охóта за вéдьмами. **witchcraft** *n* колдовствó.

with /wɪð/ *prep* (*in company of*, *together ~*) (вмéсте) с+*instr*; (*as a result of*) от+*gen*; (*at house of*, *in keeping of*) у+*gen*; (*by means of*) +*instr*; (*in spite of*) несмотря́ на+*acc*; (*including*) включáя+*acc*; **~ each**/**one another** друг с дру́гом.

withdraw /wɪð'drɔː/ *vt* (*retract*) брать *impf*, взять *pf* назáд; (*hand*) отдёргивать *impf*, отдёрнуть *pf*; (*cancel*) снимáть *impf*, снять *pf*; (*mil*) выводи́ть *impf*, вы́вести *pf*; (*money from circulation*) изымáть *impf*, изъя́ть из обращéния; (*diplomat etc.*) отзывáть *impf*, отозвáть *pf*; (*from bank*) брать *impf*, взять *pf*; *vi* удаля́ться *impf*, удали́ться *pf*; (*drop out*) выбывáть *impf*, вы́быть *pf*; (*mil*) отходи́ть *impf*, отойти́ *pf*. **withdrawal** /-'drɔːəl/ *n* (*retraction*) взя́тие назáд; (*cancellation*) сня́тие; (*mil*) отхóд; (*money from circulation*) изъя́тие; (*departure*) ухóд. **withdrawn** /-'drɔːn/ *adj* зáмкнутый.

wither /'wɪðə(r)/ *vi* вя́нуть *impf*, за~ *pf*. **withering** /-rɪŋ/ *adj* (*fig*) уничтожáющий.

withhold /wɪð'həʊld/ *vt* (*refuse to grant*) не давáть *impf*, дать *pf* +*gen*; (*payment*) удéрживать *impf*, удержáть *pf*; (*information*) утáивать *impf*, утаи́ть *pf*.

within /wɪ'ðɪn/ *prep* (*inside*) внутри́+*gen*, в+*prep*; (*~ the limits of*) в предéлах +*gen*; (*time*) в течéние +*gen*; *adv* внутри́; **from ~** изнутри́.

without /wɪ'ðaʊt/ *prep* без+*gen*; **~ saying good-bye** не прощáясь; **do ~** обходи́ться *impf*, обойти́сь *pf* без+*gen*.

withstand /wɪð'stænd/ *vt* выдéрживать *impf*, вы́держать *pf*.

witness /'wɪtnɪs/ *n* (*person*) свидéтель *m*; (*eye-~*) очеви́дец; (*to signature etc.*) завери́тель *m*; **bear ~ to** свидéтельствовать *impf*, за~ *pf*; **~-box** мéсто для свидéтельских показáний; *vt* быть свидéтелем+*gen*; (*document etc.*) заверя́ть *impf*, завéрить *pf*.

witticism /'wɪtɪˌsɪz(ə)m/ *n* острóта. **witty** /'wɪtɪ/ *adj* остроу́мный.

wizard /'wɪzəd/ *n* волшéбник, колду́н.

wizened /'wɪz(ə)nd/ *adj* морщи́нистый.

wobble /'wɒb(ə)l/ *vt* & *i* шатáть(ся) *impf*, шатну́ть(ся) *pf*; *vi* (*voice*) дрожáть *impf*. **wobbly** /'wɒblɪ/ *adj* шáткий.

woe /wəʊ/ *n* гóре; **~ is me!** гóре мне! **woeful** /-fʊl/ *adj* жáлкий.

wolf /wʊlf/ *n* волк; *vt* пожирáть *impf*, пожрáть *pf*.

woman /'wʊmən/ *n* жéнщина. **womanizer** /-ˌnaɪzə(r)/ *n* волоки́та. **womanly** /'wʊmənlɪ/ *adj* жéнственный.

womb /wuːm/ *n* мáтка.

W

wonder /ˈwʌndə(r)/ *n* чýдо; (*amazement*) изумлéние; **(it's) no ~** неудиви́тельно; *vt* интересовáться *impf* (**I ~ who will come** интерéсно, кто придёт); *vi*: **I shouldn't ~ if** неудиви́тельно бýдет, éсли; **I ~ if you could help me** не могли́ бы вы мне помóчь?; **~ at** удивля́ться *impf*, удиви́ться *pf* +*dat*. **wonderful, wondrous** /ˈwʌndəˌfʊl, ˈwʌndrəs/ *adj* замечáтельный.

wont /wəʊnt/ *n*: **as is his ~** по своемý обыкновéнию; *predic*: **be ~ to** имéть привы́чку+*inf*.

woo /wuː/ *vt* ухáживать *impf* за +*instr*.

wood /wʊd/ *n* (*forest*) лес; (*material*) дéрево; (*firewood*) дровá *pl*. **woodcut** *n* гравю́ра на дéреве. **wooded** /ˈwʊdɪd/ *adj* леси́стый. **wooden** /ˈwʊd(ə)n/ *adj* (*also fig*) деревя́нный. **woodland** *n* леси́стая мéстность; *attrib* леснóй. **woodpecker** /ˈwʊdˌpekə(r)/ *n* дя́тел. **woodwind** *n* деревя́нные духовы́е инструмéнты *m pl*. **woodwork** *n* столя́рная рабóта; (*wooden parts*) деревя́нные чáсти (-тéй) *pl*. **woodworm** *n* жучóк. **woody** /ˈwʊdɪ/ *adj* (*plant etc.*) деревяни́стый; (*wooded*) леси́стый.

wool /wʊl/ *n* шерсть. **woollen** /ˈwʊlən/ *adj* шерстянóй. **woolly** /ˈwʊlɪ/ *adj* шерсти́стый; (*indistinct*) нея́сный.

word /wɜːd/ *n* слóво; (*news*) извéстие; **by ~ of mouth** ýстно; **have a ~ with** поговори́ть *pf* с+*instr*; **in a ~** одни́м слóвом; **in other ~s** други́ми словáми; **~ for ~** слóво в слóво; **~ processor** компью́тер(-издáтель) *m*; *vt* выражáть *impf*, вы́разить *pf*; формули́ровать *impf*, с~ *pf*. **wording** /ˈwɜːdɪŋ/ *n* формулирóвка.

work /wɜːk/ *n* рабóта; (*labour*; *toil*; *scholarly ~*) труд; (*occupation*) заня́тие; (*studies*) заня́тия *neut pl*; (*of art*) произведéние; (*book*) сочинéние; *pl* (*factory*) завóд; (*mechanism*) механи́зм; **at ~** (*doing~*) за рабóтой; (*at place of ~*) на рабóте; **out of ~** безрабóтный; **~-force** рабóчая си́ла; **~-load** нагрýзка; *vi* (*also function*) рабóтать *impf* (**at, on** над +*instr*); (*study*) занимáться *impf*, заня́ться *pf*; (*also toil, labour*) труди́ться *impf*; (*have effect, function*) дéйствовать *impf*; (*succeed*) удавáться *impf*, удáться *pf*; *vt* (*operate*) управля́ть *impf* +*instr*; обращáться *impf* с+*instr*; (*wonders*) твори́ть *impf*, со~ *pf*; (*soil*) обрабáтывать *impf*, обрабóтать *pf*; (*compel to ~*) заставля́ть *impf*, застáвить *pf* рабóтать; **~ in** вставля́ть *impf*, встáвить *pf*; **~ off** (*debt*) отрабáтывать *impf*, отрабóтать *pf*; (*weight*) сгоня́ть *impf*, согнáть *pf*; (*energy*) давáть *impf*, дать *pf* вы́ход +*dat*; **~ out** (*solve*) находи́ть *impf*, найти́ *pf* решéние +*gen*; (*plans etc.*) разрабáтывать *impf*, разрабóтать *pf*; (*sport*) тренировáться *impf*; **everything ~ed out well** всё кóнчилось хорошó; **~ out at** (*amount to*) составля́ть *impf*, состáвить *pf*; **~ up** (*perfect*) вырабáтывать *impf*, вы́работать *pf*; (*excite*) возбуждáть *impf*, возбуди́ть *pf*; (*appetite*) нагýливать *impf*, нагуля́ть *pf*. **workable** /ˈwɜːkəb(ə)l/ *adj* осуществи́мый, реáльный. **workaday** /ˈwɜːkəˌdeɪ/ *adj* бýдничный. **workaholic** /ˌwɜːkəˈhɒlɪk/ *n* трýженик. **worker** /ˈwɜːkə(r)/ *n* рабóтник; (*manual*) рабóчий *sb*. **working** /ˈwɜːkɪŋ/ *adj*: **~ class** рабóчий класс; **~ hours** рабóчее врéмя *neut*; **~ party** комиссия. **workman** *n* рабóтник. **workmanlike** /ˈwɜːkmənˌlaɪk/ *adj* искýсный. **workmanship** *n* искýсство, мастерствó. **workshop** *n* мастерскáя *sb*.

world /wɜːld/ *n* мир, свет; *attrib* мировóй; **~-famous** всеми́рно извéстный; **~ war** мировáя войнá; **~-wide** всеми́рный.

W

worldly /ˈwɜːldlɪ/ *adj* мирской; (*person*) опытный.
worm /wɜːm/ *n* червь *m*; (*intestinal*) глист; *vt*: **~ o.s. into** вкрадываться *impf*, вкрасться *pf* в+*acc*; **~ out** выведывать *impf*, выведать *pf* (**of** у+*gen*); **~ one's way** пробираться *impf*, пробраться *pf*.
worry /ˈwʌrɪ/ *n* (*anxiety*) беспокойство; (*care*) забота; *vt* беспокоить *impf*, о~ *pf*; *vi* беспокоиться *impf*, о~ *pf* (**about** о+*prep*).
worse /wɜːs/ *adj* худший; *adv* хуже; *n*: **from bad to ~** всё хуже и хуже. **worsen** /ˈwɜːs(ə)n/ *vt* & *i* ухудшать(ся) *impf*, ухудшить(ся) *pf*.
worship /ˈwɜːʃɪp/ *n* поклонение (**of** +*dat*); (*service*) богослужение; *vt* поклоняться *impf* +*dat*; (*adore*) обожать *impf*. **worshipper** /-pə(r)/ *n* поклонник, -ица.
worst /wɜːst/ *adj* наихудший, самый плохой; *adv* хуже всего; *n* самое плохое.
worth /wɜːθ/ *n* (*value*) цена, ценность; (*merit*) достоинство; **give me a pound's ~ of petrol** дайте мне бензина на фунт; *adj*: **be ~** (*of equal value to*) стоить *impf* (**what is it ~?** сколько это стоит?); (*deserve*) стоить *impf* +*gen* (**is this film ~ seeing?** стоит посмотреть этот фильм?). **worthless** /ˈwɜːθlɪs/ *adj* ничего не стоящий; (*useless*) бесполезный. **worthwhile** *adj* стоящий. **worthy** /ˈwɜːðɪ/ *adj* достойный.
would /wʊd/ *v aux* (*conditional*): **he ~ be angry if he found out** он бы рассердился, если бы узнал; (*expressing wish*) **she ~ like to know** она бы хотела знать; **I ~ rather** я бы предпочёл; (*expressing indirect speech*): **he said he ~ be late** он сказал, что придёт поздно.
would-be /ˈwʊdbiː/ *adj*: **~ actor** человек мечтающий стать актёром.
wound /wuːnd/ *n* рана; *vt* ранить *impf* & *pf*. **wounded** /-dɪd/ *adj* раненый.
wrangle /ˈræŋg(ə)l/ *n* пререкание; *vi* пререкаться *impf*.
wrap /ræp/ *n* (*shawl*) шаль; *vt* (*also* **~** *up*) завёртывать *impf*, завернуть *pf*; **~ up** (*in wraps*) закутывать(ся) *impf*, закутать(ся) *pf*; **~ped up in** (*fig*) поглощённый +*instr*. **wrapper** /-pə(r)/ *n* обёртка. **wrapping** /-pɪŋ/ *n* обёртка; **~ paper** обёрточная бумага.
wrath /rɒθ/ *n* гнев.
wreak /riːk/ *vt*: **~ havoc on** разорять *impf*, разорить *pf*.
wreath /riːθ/ *n* венок.
wreck /rek/ *n* (*ship*) останки (-ов) корабля; (*vehicle, person, building, etc.*) развалина; *vt* (*destroy, also fig*) разрушать *impf*, разрушить *pf*; **be ~ed** терпеть *impf*, по~ *pf* крушение; (*of plans etc.*) рухнуть *pf*. **wreckage** /ˈrekɪdʒ/ *n* обломки *m pl* крушения.
wren /ren/ *n* крапивник.
wrench /rentʃ/ *n* (*jerk*) дёрганье; (*tech*) гаечный ключ; (*fig*) боль; *vt* (*snatch, pull out*) вырывать *impf*, вырвать *pf* (**from** у+*gen*); **~ open** взламывать *impf*, взломать *pf*.
wrest /rest/ *vt* (*wrench*) вырывать *impf*, вырвать *pf* (**from** у+*gen*).
wrestle /ˈres(ə)l/ *vi* бороться *impf*. **wrestler** /ˈreslə(r)/ *n* борец. **wrestling** /ˈreslɪŋ/ *n* борьба.
wretch /retʃ/ *n* несчастный *sb*; (*scoundrel*) негодяй. **wretched** /ˈretʃɪd/ *adj* жалкий; (*unpleasant*) скверный.
wriggle /ˈrɪg(ə)l/ *vi* извиваться *impf*, извиться *pf*; (*fidget*) ёрзать *impf*; **~ out of** увиливать *impf*, увильнуть от+*gen*.
wring /rɪŋ/ *vt* (*also* **~** *out*) выжимать *impf*, выжать *pf*; (*extort*) исторгать *impf*, исторгнуть *pf* (**from** у+*gen*); (*neck*) свёртывать *impf*, свернуть *pf* (**of** +*dat*); **~**

one's hands ломáть *impf*, с~ *pf* рýки.

wrinkle /ˈrɪŋk(ə)l/ *n* морщи́на; *vt* & *i* мóрщить(ся) *impf*, с~ *pf*.

wrist /rɪst/ *n* запя́стье; **~-watch** нарýчные часы́ (-cóв) *pl*.

writ /rɪt/ *n* повéстка.

write /raɪt/ *vt* & *i* писáть *impf*, на~ *pf*; **~ down** запи́сывать *impf*, записáть *pf*; **~ off** (*cancel*) спи́сывать *impf*, списáть *pf*; **the car was a ~-off** маши́на былá совершéнно испóрчена; **~ out** выпи́сывать *impf*, вы́писать *pf* (**in full** пóлностью); **~ up** (*account of*) подрóбно опи́сывать *impf*, описáть *pf*; (*notes*) перепи́сывать *impf*, переписáть *pf*; **~-up** (*report*) отчёт. **writer** /ˈraɪtə(r)/ *n* писáтель *m*, ~ница.

writhe /raɪð/ *vi* кóрчиться *impf*, с~ *pf*.

writing /ˈraɪtɪŋ/ *n* (*handwriting*) пóчерк; (*work*) произведéние; **in ~** в пи́сьменной фóрме; **~-paper** почтóвая бумáга.

wrong /rɒŋ/ *adj* (*incorrect*) непрáвильный, невéрный; (*the wrong ...*) не тот (**I have bought the ~ book** я купи́л не ту кни́гу; **you've got the ~ number** (*tel*) вы не тудá попáли); (*mistaken*) непрáвый (**you are ~** ты непрáв); (*unjust*) несправедли́вый; (*sinful*) дурнóй; (*out of order*) нелáдный; (*side of cloth*) лéвый; **~ side out** наизнáнку; **~ way round** наоборóт; *n* зло; (*injustice*) несправедли́вость; **be in the ~** быть непрáвым; **do ~** греши́ть *impf*, со~ *pf*; *adv* непрáвильно, невéрно; **go ~** не получáться *impf*, получи́ться *pf*; *vt* обижáть *impf*, оби́деть *pf*; (*be unjust to*) быть несправедли́вым к+*dat*. **wrongdoer** /ˈrɒŋˌduːə(r)/ *n* престýпник, грéшник, -ица. **wrongful** /-fʊl/ *adj* несправедли́вый. **wrongly** /-lɪ/ *adv* непрáвильно; (*unjustly*) несправедли́во.

wrought /rɔːt/ *adj*: **~ iron** свáрочное желéзо.

wry /raɪ/ *adj* (*smile*) кривóй; (*humour*) сухóй, ирони́ческий.

X

xenophobia /ˌzenəˈfəʊbɪə/ *n* ксенофóбия.

X-ray /ˈeksreɪ/ *n* (*picture*) рентгéн(овский сни́мок); *pl* (*radiation*) рентгéновы лучи́ *m pl*; *vt* (*photograph*) дéлать *impf*, с~ *pf* рентгéн +*gen*.

Y

yacht /jɒt/ *n* я́хта. **yachting** /ˈjɒtɪŋ/ *n* пáрусный спорт. **yachtsman** *n* яхтсмéн.

yank /jæŋk/ *vt* рванýть *pf*.

yap /jæp/ *vi* тя́вкать *impf*, тя́вкнуть *pf*.

yard[1] /jɑːd/ *n* (*piece of ground*) двор.

yard[2] /jɑːd/ *n* (*measure*) ярд. **yardstick** *n* (*fig*) мери́ло.

yarn /jɑːn/ *n* пря́жа; (*story*) расскáз.

yawn /jɔːn/ *n* зевóк; *vi* зевáть *impf*, зевнýть *pf*; (*chasm etc.*) зия́ть *impf*.

year /jɪə(r)/ *n* год; **~ in, ~ out** из гóда в год. **yearbook** *n* ежегóдник. **yearly** /ˈjɪəlɪ/ *adj* ежегóдный, годовóй; *adv* ежегóдно.

yearn /jɜːn/ *vi* тоскoвáть *impf* (**for** по+*dat*). **yearning** /-nɪŋ/ *n* тоскá (**for** по+*dat*).

yeast /jiːst/ *n* дрóжжи (-жéй) *pl*.

yell /jel/ *n* крик; *vi* кричáть *impf*, кри́кнуть *pf*.

yellow /ˈjeləʊ/ *adj* жёлтый; *n* жёлтый цвет. **yellowish** /-ɪʃ/ *adj* желтовáтый.

yelp /jelp/ *n* визг; *vi* визжáть *impf*, ви́згнуть *pf*.

yes /jes/ *adv* да; *n* утверждéние, соглáсие; (*in vote*) гóлос «за».

yesterday /ˈjestəˌdeɪ/ *adv* вчерá; *n*

вчера́шний день *m*; **~ morning** вчера́ у́тром; **the day before ~** позавчера́; **~'s newspaper** вчера́шняя газе́та.

yet /jet/ *adv* (*still*) ещё; (*so far*) до сих пор; (*in questions*) уже́; (*nevertheless*) тем не ме́нее; **as ~** пока́, до сих пор; **not ~** ещё не; *conj* одна́ко, но.

yew /juː/ *n* тис.

Yiddish /ˈjɪdɪʃ/ *n* и́диш.

yield /jiːld/ *n* (*harvest*) урожа́й; (*econ*) дохо́д; *vt* (*fruit, revenue, etc.*) приноси́ть *impf*, принести́ *pf*; дава́ть *impf*, дать *pf*; (*give up*) сдава́ть *impf*, сдать *pf*; *vi* (*give in*) (*to enemy etc.*) уступа́ть *impf*, уступи́ть *pf* (**to** +*dat*); (*give way*) поддава́ться *impf*, подда́ться *pf* (**to** +*dat*).

yoga /ˈjəʊgə/ *n* йо́га.

yoghurt /ˈjɒgət/ *n* кефи́р.

yoke /jəʊk/ *n* (*also fig*) ярмо́; (*fig*) и́го; (*of dress*) коке́тка; *vt* впряга́ть *impf*, впрячь *pf* в ярмо́.

yolk /jəʊk/ *n* желто́к.

yonder /ˈjɒndə(r)/ *adv* вон там; *adj* вон тот.

you /juː/ *pron* (*familiar sg*) ты; (*familiar pl, polite sg & pl*) вы; (*one*) *not usu translated*; *v translated in 2nd pers sg or by impers construction*: **~ never know** никогда́ не зна́ешь.

young /jʌŋ/ *adj* молодо́й; **the ~** молодёжь; *n* (*collect*) детёныши *m pl*. **youngster** /ˈjʌŋstə(r)/ *n* ма́льчик, де́вочка.

your(s) /jɔː(z)/ *poss pron* (*familiar sg; also in letter*) твой; (*familiar pl, polite sg & pl; also in letter*) ваш; свой. **yourself** /jɔːˈself/ *pron* (*emph*) (*familiar sg*) (ты) сам (*m*), сама́ (*f*); (*familiar pl, polite sg & pl*) (вы) са́ми; (*refl*) себя́; -ся (*suffixed to vt*); **by ~** (*independently*) самостоя́тельно, сам; (*alone*) оди́н.

youth /juːθ/ *n* (*age*) мо́лодость; (*young man*) ю́ноша *m*; (*collect, as pl*) молодёжь; **~ club** молодёжный клуб; **~ hostel** молодёжная турба́за. **youthful** /-fʊl/ *adj* ю́ношеский.

Yugoslavia /juːgəˈslɑːvɪə/ *n* Югосла́вия.

Z

zany /ˈzeɪnɪ/ *adj* смешно́й.

zeal /ziːl/ *n* рве́ние, усе́рдие. **zealot** /ˈzelət/ *n* фана́тик. **zealous** /ˈzeləs/ *adj* ре́вностный, усе́рдный.

zebra /ˈzebrə/ *n* зе́бра.

zenith /ˈzenɪθ/ *n* зени́т.

zero /ˈzɪərəʊ/ *n* нуль *m*, ноль *m*.

zest /zest/ *n* (*piquancy*) пика́нтность; (*ardour*) энтузиа́зм; **~ for life** жизнера́достность.

zigzag /ˈzɪgzæg/ *n* зигза́г; *adj* зигзагообра́зный; *vi* де́лать *impf*, с~ *pf* зигза́ги; идти́ *det* зигза́гами.

zinc /zɪŋk/ *n* цинк.

Zionism /ˈzaɪəˌnɪz(ə)m/ *n* сиони́зм. **Zionist** /ˈzaɪənɪst/ *n* сиони́ст.

zip /zɪp/ *n* (**~** *fastener*) (застёжка-)мо́лния; *vt & i*: **~ up** застёгивать(ся) *impf*, застегну́ть(ся) *pf* на мо́лнию.

zodiac /ˈzəʊdɪˌæk/ *n* зодиа́к; **sign of the ~** знак зодиа́ка.

zombie /ˈzɒmbɪ/ *n* челове́к спя́щий на ходу́.

zone /zəʊn/ *n* зо́на; (*geog*) по́яс.

zoo /zuː/ *n* зоопа́рк. **zoological** /ˌzəʊəˈlɒdʒɪk(ə)l/ *adj* зоологи́ческий; **~ garden(s)** зоологи́ческий сад. **zoologist** /zəʊˈɒlədʒɪst/ *n* зоо́лог. **zoology** /zəʊˈɒlədʒɪ/ *n* зооло́гия.

zoom /zuːm/ *vi* (*rush*) мча́ться *impf*; **~ in** (*phot*) де́лать *impf*, с~ *pf* наплы́в; **~ lens** объекти́в с переме́нным фо́кусным расстоя́нием.

Zulu /ˈzuːluː/ *adj* зулу́сский; *n* зулу́с, ~ка.

y

z

Spelling Rules

It is assumed that the user is acquainted with the following spelling rules which affect Russian declension and conjugation.

1. **ы**, **ю**, and **я** do not follow **г**, **к**, **х**, **ж**, **ч**, **ш**, and **щ**; instead, **и**, **у**, and **а** are used, e.g. **ма́льчик*и***, **крич*у́***; **леж*а́*т**, **ноч*а́*ми**, similarly, **ю** and **я** do not follow **ц**; instead, **у** or **а** are used.

2. Unstressed **о** does not follow **ж**, **ц**, **ч**, **ш**, or **щ**; instead, **е** is used, e.g. **му́ж*е*м**, **ме́сяц*е*в**, **хоро́ш*е*е**.

Declension of Russian Adjectives

The following patterns are regarded as regular and are not shown in the dictionary entries.

Singular	nom	acc	gen	dat	instr	prep
Masculine	**тёпл|ый**	**~ый**	**~ого**	**~ому**	**~ым**	**~ом**
Feminine	**тёпл|ая**	**~ую**	**~ой**	**~ой**	**~ой**	**~ой**
Neuter	**тёпл|ое**	**~ое**	**~ого**	**~ому**	**~ым**	**~ом**

Plural	nom	acc	gen	dat	instr	prep
Masculine	**тёпл|ые**	**~ые**	**~ых**	**~ым**	**~ыми**	**~ых**
Feminine	**тёпл|ые**	**~ые**	**~ых**	**~ым**	**~ыми**	**~ых**
Neuter	**тёпл|ые**	**~ые**	**~ых**	**~ым**	**~ыми**	**~ых**

Declension of Russian Nouns

The following patterns are regarded as regular and are not shown in the dictionary entries. Forms marked * should be particularly noted.

1 *Masculine*

Singular	nom	acc	gen	dat	instr	prep
	обе́д	~	~а	~у	~ом	~е
	слу́ча|й	~й	~я	~ю	~ем	~е
	марш	~	~а	~у	~ем	~е
	каранда́ш	~	~а́	~у́	~о́м*	~е́
	сцена́ри|й	~й	~я	~ю	~ем	~и*
	портфе́л|ь	~ь	~я	~ю	~ем	~е

Plural	nom	acc	gen	dat	instr	prep
	обе́д|ы	~ы	~ов	~ам	~ами	~ах
	слу́ча|и	~и	~ев	~ям	~ями	~ях
	ма́рш|и	~и	~ей*	~ам	~ами	~ах
	карандаш|и́	~и́	~е́й*	~а́м	~а́ми	~а́х
	сцена́ри|и	~и	~ев*	~ям	~ями	~ях
	портфе́л|и	~и	~ей*	~ям	~ями	~ях

2 *Feminine*

Singular	nom	acc	gen	dat	instr	prep
	газе́т|а	~у	~ы	~е	~ой	~е
	ба́н|я	~ю	~и	~е	~ей	~е
	ли́ни|я	~ю	~и	~и*	~ей	~и*
	ста́ту|я	~ю	~и	~е*	~ей	~е*
	бол|ь	~ь	~и	~и*	~ью*	~и*

Plural	nom	acc	gen	dat	instr	prep
	газе́т|ы	~ы	~	~ам	~ами	~ах
	ба́н|и	~и	~ь*	~ям	~ями	~ях
	ли́ни|и	~и	~й*	~ям	~ями	~ях
	ста́ту|и	~и	~й*	~ям	~ями	~ях
	бо́л|и	~и	~ей*	~ям	~ями	~ях

3 *Neuter*

Singular	nom	acc	gen	dat	instr	prep
	чу́вств|о	~о	~а	~у	~ом	~е
	учи́лищ|е	~е	~а	~у	~ем	~е
	зда́ни|е	~е	~я	~ю	~ем	~и*
	уще́л|ье	~ье	~ья	~ью	~ьем	~ье

Plural	nom	acc	gen	dat	instr	prep
	чу́вств|а	~а	~	~ам	~ами	~ах
	учи́лищ|а	~а	~	~ам	~ами	~ах
	зда́ни|я	~я	~й*	~ям	~ями	~ях
	уще́л|ья	~ья	~ий*	~ьям	~ьями	~ьях

Conjugation of Russian Verbs

The following patterns are regarded as regular and are not shown in the dictionary entries.

1. **-е-** conjugation

(a)	**чита́|ть**	~ю	~ешь	~ет	~ем	~ете	~ют
(b)	**сия́|ть**	~ю	~ешь	~ет	~ем	~ете	~ют
(c)	**про́б|овать**	~ую	~уешь	~ует	~уем	~уете	~уют
(d)	**рис|ова́ть**	~у́ю	~у́ешь	~у́ет	~у́ем	~у́ете	~у́ют

2. **-и-** conjugation

(a)	**говор|и́ть**	~ю́	~и́шь	~и́т	~и́м	~и́те	~я́т
(b)	**стро́|ить**	~ю	~ишь	~ит	~им	~ите	~ят

Notes

1. Also belonging to the **-е-** conjugation are:

i) most other verbs in **-ать** (but see Note 2(v) below), e.g. **жа́ждать**; (жа́жду, -ждешь); **пря́тать** (пря́чу, -чешь), **колеба́ть** (коле́блю, -блешь).

ii) verbs in **-еть** for which the 1st pers sing **-ею** is given, e.g. **жале́ть**.

iii) verbs in **-нуть** for which the 1st pers sing **-ну** is given (e.g. **вя́нуть**), **ю** becoming **у** in the 1st pers sing and 3rd pers pl.

iv) verbs in **-ять** which drop the **я** in conjugation, e.g. **ла́ять** (ла́ю, ла́ешь); **се́ять** (се́ю, се́ешь).

2. Also belonging to the **-и-** conjugation are:

i) verbs in consonant + **-ить** which change the consonant in the first person singular, e.g. **досади́ть** (-ажу́, -ади́шь), or insert an **-л-**, e.g. **доба́вить** (доба́влю, -вишь).

ii) other verbs in vowel + **-ить**, e.g. **затайть, кле́ить** (as 2b above).

iii) verbs in **-еть** for which the 1st pers sing is given as consonant + **ю** or **у**, e.g. **звене́ть** (-ню́, -ни́шь), **ви́деть** (ви́жу, ви́дишь).

iv) two verbs in **-ять (стоя́ть, боя́ться)**.

v) verbs in **-ать** whose stem ends in **ч**, **ж**, **щ**, or **ш**, not changing between the infinitive and conjugation, e.g. **крича́ть** (-чу́, -чи́шь). Cf. Note 1(i).

Английские неправильные глаголы

Инфинитив	Простое прошедшее	Причастие прошедшего времени
be	was	been
bear	bore	borne
beat	beat	beaten
become	became	become
begin	began	begun
bend	bent	bent
bet	bet, betted	bet, betted
bid	bade, bid	bidden, bid
bind	bound	bound
bite	bit	bitten
bleed	bled	bled
blow	blew	blown
break	broke	broken
breed	bred	bred
bring	brought	brought
build	built	built
burn	burnt, burned	burnt, burned
burst	burst	burst
buy	bought	bought
catch	caught	caught
choose	chose	chosen
cling	clung	clung
come	came	come
cost	cost, costed (*vt*)	cost, costed
cut	cut	cut
deal	dealt	dealt
dig	dug	dug
do	did	done
draw	drew	drawn
dream	dreamt, dreamed	dreamt, dreamed

Инфинитив	Простое прошедшее	Причастие прошедшего времени
drink	drank	drunk
drive	drove	driven
eat	ate	eaten
fall	fell	fallen
feed	fed	fed
feel	felt	felt
fight	fought	fought
find	found	found
flee	fled	fled
fly	flew	flown
freeze	froze	frozen
get	got	got gotten *US*
give	gave	given
go	went	gone
grow	grew	grown
hang	hung, hanged (*vt*)	hung, hanged
have	had	had
hear	heard	heard
hide	hid	hidden
hit	hit	hit
hold	held	held
hurt	hurt	hurt
keep	kept	kept
kneel	knelt	knelt
know	knew	known
lay	laid	laid
lead	led	led
lean	leaned, leant	leaned, leant
learn	learnt, learned	learnt, learned
leave	left	left

Инфинитив	Простое прошедшее	Причастие прошедшего времени
lend	lent	lent
let	let	let
lie	lay	lain
lose	lost	lost
make	made	made
mean	meant	meant
meet	met	met
pay	paid	paid
put	put	put
read	read	read
ride	rode	ridden
ring	rang	rung
rise	rose	risen
run	ran	run
say	said	said
see	saw	seen
seek	sought	sought
sell	sold	sold
send	sent	sent
set	set	set
sew	sewed	sewn, sewed
shake	shook	shaken
shine	shone	shone
shoe	shod	shod
shoot	shot	shot
show	showed	shown
shut	shut	shut
sing	sang	sung
sink	sank	sunk
sit	sat	sat
sleep	slept	slept
sling	slung	slung
smell	smelt, smelled	smelt, smelled

Инфинитив	Простое прошедшее	Причастие прошедшего времени
speak	spoke	spoken
spell	spelled, spelt	spelled, spelt
spend	spent	spent
spit	spat	spat
spoilt	spoilt, spoiled	spoilt, spoiled
spread	spread	spread
spring	sprang	sprung
stand	stood	stood
steal	stole	stolen
stick	stuck	stuck
sting	stung	stung
stride	strode	stridden
strike	struck	struck
swear	swore	sworn
sweep	swept	swept
swell	swelled	swollen, swelled
swim	swam	swum
swing	swung	swung
take	took	taken
teach	taught	taught
tear	tore	torn
tell	told	told
think	thought	thought
throw	threw	thrown
thrust	thrust	thrust
tread	trod	trodden
understand	understood	understood
wake	woke	woken
wear	wore	worn
win	won	won
write	wrote	written

The Russian Alphabet

Capital Letters	Lower-case Letters	Letter names
А	а	а
Б	б	бэ
В	в	вэ
Г	г	гэ
Д	д	дэ
Е	е	е
Ё	ё	ё
Ж	ж	жэ
З	з	зэ
И	и	и
Й	й	и кра́ткое
К	к	ка
Л	л	эль
М	м	эм
Н	н	эн
О	о	о
П	п	пэ
Р	р	эр

Capital Letters	Lower-case Letters	Letter names
С	с	эс
Т	т	тэ
У	у	у
Ф	ф	эф
Х	х	ха
Ц	ц	цэ
Ч	ч	че
Ш	ш	ша
Щ	щ	ща
Ъ	ъ	твёрдый знак
Ы	ы	ы
Ь	ь	мя́гкий знак
Э	э	э
Ю	ю	ю
Я	я	я

Английский алфавит

Заглавные буквы	Строчные буквы	Названия букв	Заглавные буквы	Строчные буквы	Названия букв
A	a	/eɪ/	N	n	/en/
B	b	/bi:/	O	o	/əʊ/
C	c	/si:/	P	p	/pi:/
D	d	/di:/	Q	q	/kju:/
E	e	/i:/	R	r	/ɑ:(r)/
F	f	/ef/	S	s	/es/
G	g	/dʒi:/	T	t	/ti:/
H	h	/eɪtʃ/	U	u	/ju:/
I	i	/aɪ/	V	v	/vi:/
J	j	/dʒeɪ/	W	w	/ˈdʌb(ə)lju:/
K	k	/keɪ/	X	x	/eks/
L	l	/el/	Y	y	/waɪ/
M	m	/em/	Z	z	/zed/

Also available from Oxford University Press

Oxford Russian Dictionary 4e
An invaluable text for any serious student of Russian, or any Russian native speaker learning English.
978-0-19-861420-3

Compact Oxford Russian Dictionary
The ideal dictionary for higher examinations
978-0-19-957617-3

Oxford Beginner's Russian Dictionary
Designed for the adult language learner
978-0-19-929854-9

Oxford Russian Grammar & Verbs
Clear explanations of modern Russian usage
978-0-19-860380-1

Oxford Russian Mini Dictionary 3e
This small dictionary is ideal for travel and quick reference.
978-0-19-870235-1